Macroeconomics In The Global Economy

Macroeconomics In The Global Economy

Jeffrey D. Sachs

Harvard University

Felipe Larrain B.

Pontificia Universidad Catolica de Chile

Prentice Hall, Englewood Cliffs, New Jersey 07632

Library of Congress Cataloging-in-Publication Data

Sachs, Jeffrey.
  Macroeconomics in the global economy / Jeffrey D. Sachs,
Felipe B. Larrain.
      p.   cm.
  Includes index.
  ISBN 0-13-544206-0
  1. Macroeconomics.   I. Larrain, Felipe, B.,
  II. Title.
  HB172.5.S23   1992
  339—dc20   91–44277
                                           CIP

Acquisition Editor: Steven Dietrich
Production Editor: Joanne Palmer
Cover and Interior Design: Donna M. Wickes
Prepress Buyer: Trudy Pisciotti
Manufacturing Buyer: Robert Anderson
Editorial Assistant: Diane DeCastro

Cover Art—A Projection by Oi Sawa.
82″ × 89″; oil on tin.
Courtesy of Viridian Gallery, New York.

Printed in the United States of America
10 9 8 7 6 5 4 3 2 1

ISBN 0-13-544206-0

Prentice-Hall International (UK) Limited, *London*
Prentice-Hall of Australia PTY. Limited, *Sydney*
Prentice-Hall Canada Inc., *Toronto*
Prentice-Hall Hispanoamericana, S.A., *Mexico*
Prentice-Hall of India Private Limited, *New Delhi*
Prentice-Hall of Japan, Inc., *Tokyo*
Simon & Schuster Asia Pte. Ltd., *Singapore*
Editora Prentice-Hall do Brasil, Ltda., *Rio de Janeiro*

To Sonia and Francisca

Contents

Preface

Macroeconomics is one of the most exciting disciplines in the social sciences. It helps us to find answers to some of the great questions concerning the economic life of a nation and of the entire world: What determines the rate of growth of an economy? What are the factors that cause high or low unemployment? Why are there business cycles? What is the proper role of the government in spurring growth, limiting inflation, and reducing high unemployment? How do economic changes in one country affect the economies of the rest of the world?

These are questions that are important not only for the economic health of a nation, but also for every individual—in deciding how much to save or borrow or spend, or in developing a strategy for finding or changing a job. Macroeconomics can also help people to become better citizens by improving their abilities to evaluate the proposals of political leaders regarding taxes, interest rates, public spending, and other policies that may have a crucial effect on the national and world economy.

Macroeconomics itself keeps evolving over time, both in the nature of the questions that it addresses and in the kinds of answers that it offers. These changes in the field reflect two kinds of forces at work. First, as in any science, new theoretical advances are frequently being made while at the same time old theories are being discarded in light of conflicts with the evidence or in the face of the new theories. Second, the world economy is itself evolving in ways that spur new questions and demand new answers. The greatest change in recent years has been the increasing interlinkages of the economies of individual countries. No longer does it make sense, for example, to study the separate economies of United States, Europe, or Japan without recognizing their strong interdependence.

We have written this textbook out of the belief that a new approach to studying macroeconomics is needed to keep up with the theoretical advances in the field and the changes in the world economy. We can mention three major ways in which this textbook addresses these important changes:

- This is the first modern macroeconomics textbook that focuses throughout on the global economy and the international aspects of macroeconomics, rather than on the economy of a single country. From the beginning to the end, we recognize that all economies in the world are linked to the others through international markets for goods, services, and capital.

- In line with this international perspective, we examine carefully the ways that countries differ in their important macroeconomic institutions (such as in the patterns of wage setting), and relate those institutional differences to observed differences in macroeconomic performance.

- Our theoretical presentations incorporate recent advances in macroeconomic theory, particularly regarding the role of expectations; the intertemporal choices of households, firms, and the government; and the modern theory of economic policy, including the problems of time consistency and international policy coordination.

Naturally, our own professional experiences have contributed to the design of this textbook. We have had the good fortune to be active not only as researchers and teachers, but also as macroeconomic advisors to several governments in Latin America and Eastern Europe. In the course of that work, we have been impressed by the important contribution that macroeconomics can make to the formulation of proper policies in an economy. This experience has convinced us that macroeconomics is an important and vibrant discipline, closely linked to real events, and not merely a tool for theoretical study. We hope that we successfully convey some of that "real world" excitement to the discussions in the textbook.

At the same time, our experience as economic advisors has also highlighted several things to us concerning the field. We have been impressed constantly by the extent to which policymakers in one country must respond to the international economic environment—hence our consistent focus on the international dimension of the discipline. Also, we have been impressed by the importance of institutions (in the labor market, in the political organization of the government, and elsewhere) for the proper choice of macroeconomic policies, and for a proper understanding of economic trends. While certain basic macroeconomic principles apply to all countries, other specific aspects of an economy must also be kept in mind.

Finally, we have been forced to view macroeconomics in practical terms. What can it really teach about the choices that a government should make in its attempt to heal a "sick" economy? What is really known, and what is just an intellectual fad? Where does the historical experience support the theories, and where are the theories merely clever but essentially unrealistic? These are, of course, judgments that academic researchers must make when they choose between theories, but these issues become particularly relevant in the context of actual economic decisionmaking.

Of course, our judgments will not coincide precisely with those of other macroeconomists. The discipline of macroeconomics remains deeply divided in its consideration of certain important topics. (Happily, professional macroeconomists also agree on many important issues!) But in all areas, we have strived to set out the major debates and the evidence in a fair-minded way, though of course we have not shirked from indicating our own judgments on many of the points of conflict.

Some Tips on Using the Book

This book has two main parts. The *core topics* (chapters 1–18) set out the basic macroeconomic framework. The *special topics* (chapters 19–23) treat particular issues in more detail, using the analytic framework already established. The core of the book itself falls into four parts: an introductory section (chapters 1–3), a section on intertemporal economics (chapters 4–7), a section on monetary economics (chapters 8–11), and a section dealing with economic fluctuations, stabilization policy, and growth (chapters 12–18).

Because later chapters tend to build on earlier chapters, we recommend studying the core text, chapters 2–18, in order. The special topics, chapters 19–23, build on the core material, but not directly on each other, with one important exception: the discussion on developing country debt (Chapter 22) benefits from a knowledge of the traded–nontraded goods model (Chapter 21).

Our presentation of intermediate macroeconomics assumes a solid preparation in economics at the introductory level. In particular, you will need a basic knowledge of microeconomic concepts including basic price theory, indifference curves, profit-maximization by the firm, and utility-maximization by households. If these ideas are new to you, we suggest that you work through this text with an introductory economics textbook alongside it.

We have avoided advanced mathematics in this book. The level of mathematics required is basic algebra, especially the ability to manipulate linear equations. On very few ocasions, and then only in footnotes, we refer to introductory differential calculus, but the use of calculus is never essential. Appendixes to certain chapters require the use of somewhat more advanced mathematical ideas. The several numerical and analytical exercises at the end of each chapter should help you deal very comfortably with the models contained in the text.

There is also a Study Guide that may be used along with this textbook. It provides further help in understanding the presentation in the main text.

One final piece of advice: Enjoy the study of macroeconomics! It is a thrilling discipline that sheds light on some of the most important issues confronting modern society. We hope that you find this subject as rewarding, challenging, and thought-provoking as we have throughout our own careers as students, scholars, and teachers.

Acknowledgments

Our preparation of this textbook has depended on the generous support, insights, and assistance of many people and institutions, and it is a great pleasure to offer our thanks here for the help that we have received.

The World Institute for Development Research (WIDER) in Helsinki, and Fundacion Andes in Santiago provided financial support in the early stages of the work. Harvard University and Universidad Catolica de Chile provided leave time and logistical support. Readers of the early drafts, including students, colleagues, research assistants, and several anonymous reviewers, all contributed to our work.

We would like to thank especially Alberto Alesina, Alain De Crombrughe, Robert Eisner, Stefan Gerlach, Dominique Hachette, Nouriel Roubini, Marcelo Selowsky, Philippe Weil and Joseph Zeira for helpful comments and suggestions. We are grateful as well to Thomas M. Beveridge of North Carolina State University, Thomas Harrilesky of Duke University, F. Trenery Dolbear, Jr., of Brandeis University, Rendigs Fels of Vanderbilt University, Leonard Lardaro of the University of Rhode Island, Douglas A. Houston of the University of Kansas, Christine Amsler of Michigan State University, and R. Newby Schweitzer of San Francisco State University for their comments on the book. We also benefitted from the very efficient research assistance of Jose Manuel Campa, Toni Estevadordal, Pablo Garcia, Loreto Lira, and Carlos Sales. Special thanks go to Martha Synnott for her invaluable support throughout this entire project.

Finally, we thank the staff of Prentice Hall and Harvester Wheatsheaf, our publishers, for assistance throughout the preparation of this book. In particular, we would like to thank Bill Webber and Peter Johns for their enthusiastic support of this project, Cheryl Kupper for her help in the editing of the manuscript, and Stephen Dietrich and Joanne Palmer for their support in the final stages of the work.

chapter 1

Introduction

1-1 WHAT IS MACROECONOMICS?

*M*acroeconomics is the study of aggregate behavior in an economy. While the economic life of a country depends on millions of individual actions taken by business firms, consumers, workers, and government officials, macroeconomics focuses on the overall consequences of these individual actions. In any given month, for example, thousands of business firms might raise the prices of their products, while thousands of other business firms might lower their prices. In setting out to understand the *overall* change in prices, macroeconomists would look at an *average* of the thousands of individual changes. To do this, they would construct and analyze a special price index, that is, an average of the individual prices, in order to measure the overall amount of price changes in the economy.

The basic approach of macroeconomics, then, is to look at the overall trends in the economy rather than at the trends that affect particular business firms, workers, or regions in the economy. Special summary measures of economic activity—the gross national product, the saving rate, or the consumer price index—give the "big picture" of changes and trends. These overall macroeconomic measures provide the basic equipment that allows macroeconomists to focus on the dominant changes in the economy rather than the particular influences hitting individual parts of the economy.

Macroeconomics thrives on the vast array of data that are collected in most countries in order to understand the overall trends in the economy. Indeed, the modern field of macroeconomics emerged only in the 1930s, when economic statisticians began to collect and publish the great body of statistical data used to describe aggregate economic behavior. The most important of these data are the *national income accounts,* which record the levels of aggregate output, income, saving, consumption, and investment in the economy. A proper understanding of the national income accounts provides the backbone of modern macroeconomic analysis.

Macroeconomics seeks an Olympian view of the economy, one that is not bogged down in excessive details about particular sectors or individual businesses. By its nature, then, it focuses on the great questions of economic life. What makes a country grow richer or poorer in a given period of time? How much do the citizens of the country save for the future? Why did most prices tend to rise rapidly for most of the past decade in Argentina, but only slowly or not at all in Switzerland? What determines the value of the U.S. dollar versus the Japanese yen? Why does the United States import more goods than it exports? These are the kinds of questions that macroeconomists study, and for which they can often provide convincing answers.

One of the great and lasting themes of macroeconomics since its inception has been that the overall trends in the economy are importantly affected by government policies, and in particular by monetary and fiscal policies. Most macroeconomists believe that changes in the budgetary policies of the government and in the monetary policies of the central bank have pervasive and largely predictable effects on the overall trends in production, prices, international trade, and employment. Some macroeconomists believe strongly that the government should manage its budgetary and monetary policies so as to influence the overall trends in the economy, while others believe that the links between these policies and the economy are too unpredictable and unstable to provide a basis for "managing" the economy.

Modern macroeconomics builds on the foundations of *microeconomics,* the study of the individual decisions of business firms and households, as they interact in the marketplace. Macroeconomists take explicit note of the fact that the overall trends in the economy are the result of millions of individual decisions. While they cannot hope to study each of those decisions, they recognize that their theories must be consistent, at least, with the underlying behavior of the millions of households and firms that make up the economy.

For this purpose, modern macroeconomics proceeds in three basic steps. First, macroeconomists try to understand on a theoretical level the decision processes of individual firms and households. Macroeconomic models typically begin with the simplifying assumption that there is a *representative* firm or household, a kind of *average* firm or household in the economy. Using the tools of microeconomics, the macroeconomist then studies how this typical firm or household behaves and will behave in a variety of economic circumstances.

Second, macroeconomists try to explain the overall behavior of the economy by *aggregating,* or adding up, all the decisions of the individual households and firms in the economy. The behavior of the typical firm or household is "multiplied" in some appropriate way (and this is one of the trickiest points) in order to predict the aggregate behavior of the economy. Key variables in the economy, such as prices, output, consumption, and so on, are aggregated, and macroeconomists derive various relations between the aggregated data, from which they try to explain the linkages among key economic variables.

Third, macroeconomists give empirical content to theory by collecting and analyzing actual macroeconomic data. The data might be used to test whether a proposed theoretical relationship is valid, or to measure a relationship quantitatively, or to explain the past history of an economy, or to support some prediction about the future course of the economy. The special field of *macroeconometrics* studies the formal ways of linking macroeconomic theory and aggregate data for these various purposes.

1-2 SOME OF THE KEY QUESTIONS ADDRESSED BY MACROECONOMICS

Many of the key issues studied in macroeconomics involve the overall levels of production, unemployment, prices, and international trade in the economy. Analysis of these key variables, in turn, rests on the answers to several questions. What determines their current levels in an economy? What determines changes in these variables in the short term? And what determines how these variables will change in the long term? In essence, we examine each of the key variables from various time perspectives: the present, the short run, and the long run. Each time horizon requires that we use different models as we try to uncover the particular factors that determine these macroeconomic variables.

The most important single measure of production in the economy is the *gross domestic product* (GDP), a statistic that aims to measure the total value of goods and services produced in the geographic boundaries of an economy within a given period of time. The calculation of GDP, that is, the adding together of the market value of all the millions of kinds of outputs in an economy in an appropriate way, is obviously not easy. Economic statisticians also take care to distinguish between *nominal* GDP, which measures the value of goods and services according to their current market prices, and the *real* GDP, which attempts to measure the physical volume of production. If the price of all goods doubles but physical production remains the same, then the measure of nominal GDP doubles while real GDP remains unchanged (because the physical volume of production is not affected by the price changes). *Gross national product* (GNP), a closely related concept, is the sum of GDP and the net income received by domestic factors of production (labor and capital) from outside the economy, that is, from the rest of the world.

Figure 1-1 shows the time path of real GNP (together with the time path of unemployment) in the United States during the twentieth century. Notice first that real GNP has followed an upward trend throughout the century. The United States, together with much of the world, has enjoyed long-term economic growth. Macroeconomists focus much of their effort on explaining this growth. What are the sources of long-term growth? Why do some countries grow faster than others for long periods of time? Can government policies affect the long-term growth rate of the economy?

Notice that growth in GNP may be positive over long periods, but it is not smooth year to year. In fact, GNP has actually declined from one year to the next on several occasions during the century. The period of decline usually lasts for a year or two before the upward ascent of GNP starts again. These short-term fluctuations are known as *business cycles*. The shaded areas in the figure identify the phases of the business cycles. The moment of maximum output expansion during a cycle is called the *peak*; the lowest point of a cycle is known as the *trough*. These points are identified in the graph with a vertical line. A full business cycle extends from one business trough to the next.

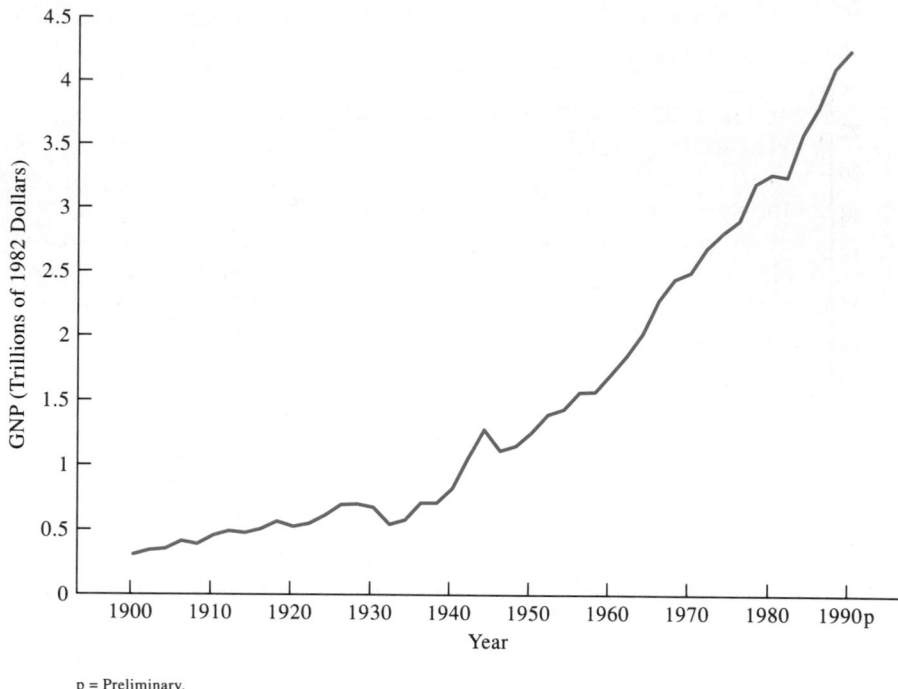

p = Preliminary.

Figure 1-1a

The Time Path of Real GNP in the United States, 1900–1990

(*Data from 1900 to 1970: U.S. Historical Statistics, Series D85–86 and F1–5; from 1970 to 1990:* Economic Report of the President, 1991, *Tables B-2 and B-32.*)

The United States has undergone 19 complete business cycles in this century. The Great Depression, starting in 1929 and ending only a decade later, is by far the longest and deepest cyclical downturn, a cataclysmic worldwide event to which we shall often return in subsequent chapters. The fall from peak to trough at the start of the Great Depression lasted 43 months, from August 1929 to March 1933, and the following expansion, from trough to peak, lasted 50 months, from March 1933 to May 1937. This level of output at this peak was still below the output of 1929. It was not until the next expansion, linked to the military buildup preceding World War II, that the 1929 level of production was reached. The longest peacetime cyclical upturn, measured by the period between a trough and the following peak, is the expansion of the 1980s, which lasted from November 1982 until the third quarter of 1990.

The understanding of business cycles is a major goal of macroeconomics. Why do business cycles occur? What determines the severity of a decline in output in any particular business cycle? What are the economic forces leading to a temporary decline in production, and what forces lead to a restoration of economic growth? Are business cycles caused by unexpected events, or "shocks," hitting the economy, or are they driven by the workings of predictable internal dynamic forces? What kinds of shocks to the economy are most significant? How regular are business cycles in their

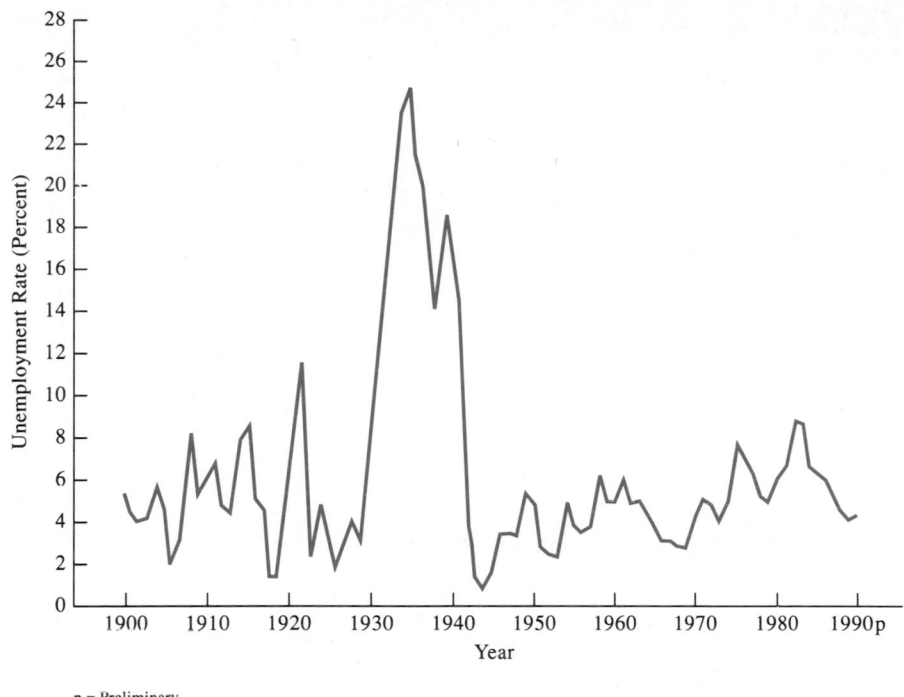

p = Preliminary.

Figure 1-1b

The Time Path of Unemployment in the United States, 1900–1990

(*Data from 1900 to 1970:* U.S. Historical Statistics, *Series D85–86 and F1–5; from 1970 to 1990:* Economic Report of the President, 1991, *Tables B-2 and B-32.*)

length, severity, and the intervals between them? Can government policies smooth out, or eliminate, the short-term fluctuations in the economy? These are some of the key questions that are raised, and at least partly answered, by modern macroeconomics.

   Unemployment is a second key variable that macroeconomics investigates. The unemployment rate, also shown in Figure 1-1, measures the number of people who are without a job and are actively searching for a job, as a proportion of the total labor force. Notice that there is no discernible long-term trend in the unemployment rate during the century. In each decade, the unemployment rate has tended to average around 6 percent of the labor force, with the notable exception of the Great Depression era of the 1930s, when unemployment reached unprecedented (and socially tragic) rates of over 25 percent or more. Short-term movements in the unemployment rate are related to business-cycle fluctuations, as the figure clearly shows. Downturns in output are associated with increases in unemployment; upturns are linked with declines in the unemployment rate. Thus, it is hardly surprising that the study of business-cycle fluctuations is intimately related to the study of unemployment fluctuations.

   A third key variable that interests macroeconomists is the *inflation rate,* which measures the percentage change in the average level of prices

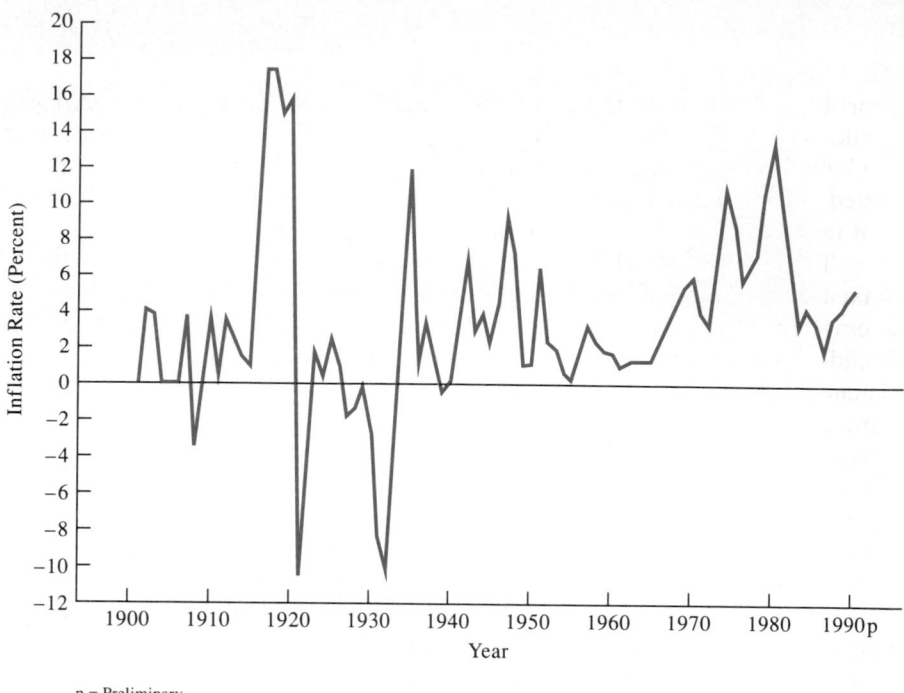

p = Preliminary.

Figure 1-2

Inflation Rates in the United States, 1900–1990

(*Data from 1900 to 1970:* U.S. Historical Statistics, *Series D85–86 and F1–5; from 1970 to 1990:* Economic Report of the President, 1991, *Tables B-2 and B-32.*)

in the economy. Figure 1-2 shows the inflation rate in the United States during the twentieth century, using as a measure of inflation the annual change in the consumer price index. This index, which we discuss in the next chapter, measures a weighted average of prices of consumer goods in the economy, where the weights in the average depend on the shares of consumer spending on each of the various types of goods.

Perhaps the most important thing to see in the diagram is the long-term change in the pattern of inflation during the century. Before World War II, inflation was both positive and negative; that is, prices both rose and fell from one year to the next. Aside from the burst of high inflation during 1914–1918 linked to World War I, inflation rates were generally low, and often negative, before World War II. The average price level in the United States actually fell sharply during the first four years of the Great Depression, from 1929 to 1933. After World War II, however, inflation has always been positive—that is, the price level has risen every year from the preceding year. Inflation tended to worsen at the end of the 1960s, and got relatively high in the 1970s, though nowhere nearly as high as it was in some developing countries that we study later. In the 1980s, the average inflation rate fell below that in the 1970s, but it was still high by the standards of the first half of the twentieth century.

These shifts in inflation over the course of the century raise several very important and perplexing issues. What determines the long-term average level of inflation in an economy? Why has inflation in the United States been higher in the second half of the twentieth century? What determines short-term fluctuations in the inflation rate? Why, for example, was inflation particularly high in the 1970s but less high in the 1980s? How are changes in the inflation rate related to the business cycle? Specifically, are booms associated with increased rates of inflation and recessions with declines in inflation rates?

These questions about inflation become even more intriguing when we make a comparison of international inflation rates. In Table 1-1, we show the average inflation rates for two different groups of countries during the past decade. The differences are, indeed, enormous. While annual inflation never reached 10 percent on average in the industrial countries, it was above 100 percent for 6 years out of 10 in Latin America (and in 1989 it went over 1,000 percent). Why are inflation rates in Latin America consistently far above the rates in other parts of the world? We shall see that inflation is intimately connected with the monetary system of an economy. Long-term patterns in inflation rates are related to the methods of issuing money in an economy. Short-term movements in inflation are often closely connected with changes in the money supply that result from budget deficits or changes in monetary policy of a country's central bank. In particular, Latin America's high inflation rates are linked to large budget deficits in the past decade.

The fourth major variable that macroeconomists look at is the *trade balance*, which measures a country's exports to the rest of the world minus

TABLE 1-1

INFLATION IN THE 1980s: LATIN AMERICA AND THE INDUSTRIAL COUNTRIES (PERCENT)

Year	Latin America	Industrial Countries
1980	56.1%	9.3%
1981	57.6	8.8
1982	84.6	7.4
1983	130.5	5.2
1984	184.7	4.4
1985	274.1	3.7
1986	64.5	3.4
1987	198.5	2.9
1988	778.8	3.2
1989	1,161.0	3.9
1990	1,491.5	3.9

Source: For Latin America, see Economic Commission for Latin America and the Caribbean, United Nations, Preliminary Overview of the Latin American Economy, *1990; for the industrial countries, see International Monetary Fund,* World Economic Outlook, *May 1990.*

its imports from the rest of the world. When a country is exporting more than it is importing, we say that the country has a *trade surplus,* while in the opposite case, when imports outrun exports, we say that a country has a *trade deficit.* For most of the twentieth century, for example, the United States had a trade surplus. After 1970, however, it more frequently had a trade deficit, and during the 1980s, the trade deficit reached several percent of GDP, and thus became quite significant.

The trade balances of the United States, Germany, and Japan during the past decade, measured as a fraction of each country's GDP, are depicted in Figure 1-3. Note that the U.S. deficits have been matched by surpluses in the trade balances of the other two countries. While the United States has been importing more goods than it has been exporting, the opposite is true in Germany and Japan.

What is the significance of the trade balance, and what determines its movements in the short run and long run? One key to understanding the trade balance is to understand that trade imbalances are closely linked to financial flows between countries. Generally speaking, when a country imports more goods from the rest of the world than it exports, it must pay for those imports by borrowing from the rest of the world, or by cashing in on loans that were made to the rest of the world in an earlier period. On the other hand, when exports exceed imports, then the country is generally lending to the rest of the world. Thus, our study of trade imbalances is closely linked to our study of why residents in one country borrow or lend

Figure 1-3

The Trade Balance as a Percentage of Gross Domestic Product in Germany, Japan, and the United States, 1980–1989

(*From International Monetary Fund, International Financial Statistics, selected issues.*)

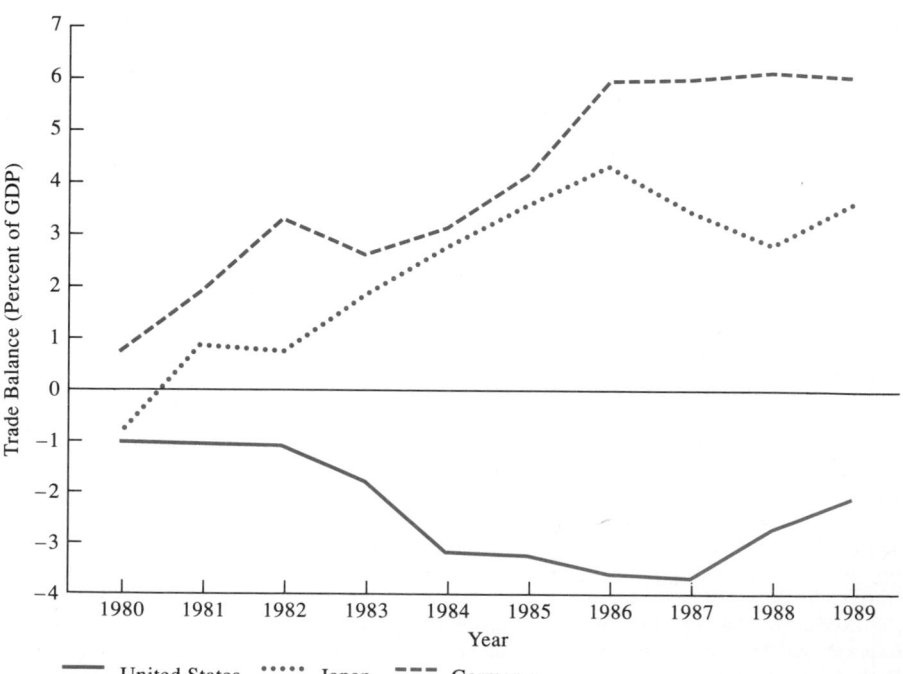

from residents in other parts of the world. The United States has become a major borrower from the rest of the world in the past decade, while German and Japan have become major lenders. Why? And what are the consequences for the United States in the short run, medium run, and long run of borrowing from the rest of the world? What are the consequences for Germany and Japan of lending to the rest of the world, including the United States?

1-3 MACROECONOMICS IN HISTORICAL PERSPECTIVE

If we view macroeconomics in its broadest terms as the study of aggregate trends in an economy, then we can say that the field has been a central concern of economists for centuries. David Hume made one of the earliest breakthroughs in macroeconomics in the eighteenth century when he studied the linkages between the money supply, trade balance, and price level in an economy.[1]

This great breakthrough, now known as the *monetary approach to the balance of payments,* still provides a starting point for theories linking monetary policy and international trade patterns. Similarly, studies of money in the eighteenth and nineteenth centuries uncovered the basic *quantity theory of money* which is still the foundation for modern monetary analysis.

Despite these vital contributions to our understanding of aggregate economics, the field of macroeconomics was not really recognized as a separate discipline until the twentieth century. Three events were of fundamental importance in the development of the field. First, economic statisticians began to *collect and systematize aggregate data* which provided the scientific basis for macroeconomic investigations. Much of this data collection was prompted by World War I, during which governments recognized that they needed better statistical information in order to be able to plan and carry out their war efforts. After the war, there was a major push to improve statistical collection and analysis.

The National Bureau of Economic Research (NBER), a private U.S. research institution, carried out some of the seminal work in data collection and analysis, beginning in the 1920s. This effort was led by Simon Kuznets, who would later win the Nobel Prize in Economics for his fundamental contributions in this area and in the study of modern economic growth. By the 1930s, using concepts developed by Kuznets and others, the United States had a consistent set of national income accounts data which could be used to study macroeconomic trends. In the following decades, the national accounts were systematized by other economists, including Richard Stone, another Nobel laureate, and now almost all countries in the world prepare the basic national accounts data that are vital for macroeconomic analysis.

A second major impetus of modern macroeconomics was the careful identification of the *business cycle* as a recurrent economic phenomenon. The advance in empirical knowledge of the business cycle was made possible by the very improvements in the macroeconomic data that we just described. Once again, from the 1920s on the NBER played a key role in

[1] Hume's classic work on this subject, "Of the Balance of Trade," was originally published in 1752. See his *Essays, Moral, Political and Literary,* Vol. 1 (London: Longmans Green, 1898).

improving the understanding of the business cycle. Through the studies of the economist Wesley Clair Mitchell, it became increasingly apparent that the U.S. economy was subject to recurrent and essentially similar business cycles. Mitchell showed that key economic variables such as inventories, production, and prices tended to change in a systematic way in the course of a typical business cycle.

The third great impetus toward the creation of modern macroeconomics was a cataclysmic historical event, the *Great Depression*. This disaster continues to horrify the world in the scale of human suffering that it provoked, and in the political consequences that followed that suffering. Democratic governments were toppled in the course of the economic crisis, to be followed by fascist governments in Germany, Italy, and Japan which went on to start World War II. The Great Depression started in 1929, when almost the entire world suffered an enormous decline in output and an unprecedented rise in unemployment. In the early 1930s, for example, around one-fourth of the entire labor force in the United States could not find a job. (Box 1-1 describes the dimensions of the Great Depression in more detail.)

The Great Depression defied the understanding of the classical economists, who predicted that normal market forces would prevent large-scale and sustained unemployment of the sort experienced worldwide in the 1930s. The event called into question the basic tenets of economics up to that time. The brilliant British economist John Maynard Keynes, who lived from 1883 to 1946, put macroeconomics on its modern course by proposing a new theoretical framework to explain the Great Depression (as well as lesser economic fluctuations) and by suggesting specific government policies to counteract the Depression.

Keynes's main ideas concerning economic fluctuations were contained in *The General Theory of Employment, Interest and Money*, which Keynes published in 1936. This is probably the most influential economic tract of the twentieth century, even though we now see important shortcomings in the analysis. Keynes himself made great contributions that went beyond the ideas in this book, such as his work on establishing the International Monetary Fund and the post–World War II international monetary system. His overall influence on economics was so extensive that macroeconomists have ever since classified themselves as "Keynesian" and "non-Keynesian," depending on how closely they wished to associate themselves with Keynes's views and policy recommendations. (We shall see, however, that half a century after the Great Depression, this distinction has become a bit threadbare.)

Keynes's central assertion was that market economies are not smoothly self-regulating; that is, they do not guarantee low levels of unemployment and high levels of production on a regular basis. Instead, he proposed, economies are subject to large fluctuations that are due, at least in part, to swings between optimism and pessimism that affect the overall levels of business investment. A swing to pessimism in the business community prompts a sharp drop in investment which, in turn, can provoke an overall fall in production and a rise in unemployment.

Once an economic downturn as deep as the Great Depression gets underway, Keynes argued, it is not eliminated rapidly by market forces alone. This is in part because certain key prices in the economy, particularly the average wage level, are not very flexible and do not move rapidly when

Box 1-1
The Great Depression

The Great Depression of the 1930s was the largest economic debacle of modern times. Between 1929 and 1932, industrial production plummeted worldwide, falling almost 50 percent in the United States, about 40 percent in Germany, close to 30 percent in France, and "only" 10 percent in the United Kingdom, where the economic downturn had started in the 1920s. Figure 1-4 shows the trend in industrial production during the period 1925–1938 for these four countries which then had the largest industrialized economies in the world.

The industrial countries also experienced an unparalleled *deflation,* with prices falling by almost 25 percent in the United Kingdom, slightly over 30 percent in Germany and the United States, and more than 40 percent in France. The greatest human costs, however, were reflected in unemployment, which soared to astounding, indeed tragic, levels. The U.S. unemployment rate rose to one-fourth of the entire labor force in 1933. Germany also experienced a catastrophic rise in unemployment during the 1930s.

The Great Depression was a global phenomenon, spreading outward from the developed countries to the developing countries. Throughout Latin America, Africa, and Asia, economies collapsed when the prices of raw materials exports fell in world markets following a sharp drop in demand from the industrial countries. Political instability followed in the wake of economic collapse. Dictatorships arose in many countries in Europe, Japan, and the developing world, as democracies were unable to cope with economic chaos. Hitler's rise to power can be linked directly to the profound economic crisis in Germany.

The leading industrialized countries responded to the crisis by imposing trade barriers on imports from other countries, with the aim of increasing demand for domestically produced goods and thereby putting people back to work. The policy, however, was seriously misguided, since it had the indirect effect of increasing unemployment abroad. When virtually all major countries pursued this disastrous course, international trade collapsed, efficient economic linkages among countries were ruptured, and in the end, unemployment was exacerbated everywhere. Charles Kindleberger has illustrated this startling collapse of world trade as the inward spiral shown in Figure 1-5.

What were the causes of this large and generalized economic downturn? Economists, historians, and social scientists in general have not lacked for hypotheses. Indeed, more than any other event, the Great Depression has spurred the field of macroeconomics. Keynes was the first to provide a lucid explanation of the phenomenon. He blamed the instability of investor confidence as a major factor in the onset of the Depression, and in the *General Theory* he provided a rich macroeconomic framework within which to account for the prolonged unemployment during the period, as well as to propose some roles that fiscal and monetary policies might play in counteracting the crisis.

A generation later, Milton Friedman, the Nobel laureate, and his coauthor Anna Schwartz, centered their explanation of the Great Depression on the overly contractionary monetary policy practiced in the United States during the years 1929–1933.[2] In their now classic text, Friedman and Schwartz stress that monetary policy failed completely to counteract a tidal wave of bank failures in the United States in the early 1930s, and thereby failed to prevent a normal downturn in the business cycle from turning into a calamitous depression.

The explanation of Friedman and Schwartz has been hotly contested by others. Charles Kindleberger of MIT, an acclaimed economic historian, has argued for a more international interpretation.[3] In his view, the major countries did not counteract the economic downturn that started in the late 1920s because there was no economic leadership at the world level. Thus, the downturn became a depression. Neither the United States nor the United Kingdom exercised the leadership that could have put a brake on the downward spiral of the world economy, by calling a halt to the tariff escalation that crippled world trade, for instance, or by providing credit to help finance an economic recovery. Not only did the United States not provide leadership in preventing the breakdown of world trade, but by adopting the highly protectionist Smoot–Hawley tariff in 1930, it was, in fact, one of the worst offenders.

In Kindleberger's view, this lack of leadership was an accident of history: the United Kingdom was fading as a world leader, but the United States had not yet taken up the responsibilities of leadership in the 1930s. Nor were there the international institutions like the International Monetary Fund and the World Bank that might have contributed to an amelioration of the crisis by providing loans to countries in distress.

Still another explanation has been offered by Peter Temin of MIT, who argues that the Great Depression was the delayed result of World War I and the continuing conflicts after the war.[4] In other words, the conflicts over the war were simply carried over to conflicts over the peace. The victors and the vanquished in the war argued bitterly over war reparations, international loans, and other financial issues. A fragile web of war debts and war reparations left most of the countries in Europe extremely weak financially. Moreover, it was difficult to solve these conflicts because they were in part a proxy for deeper fears and animosities among the conflicting European countries.

If the war and subsequent economic and political disputes in Europe were key shocks that led to the Great Depression, as Temin proposes, what were the mechanisms that propagated the depression from country to country, first among the industrial countries, and then to the rest of the world? Temin argues forcefully that the international monetary arrangement at the time, the gold standard, was the main force in propagating the economic collapse. As we shall see, the gold standard prevents countries from pursuing independent monetary policies, especially expansionary

[2] See Chapter 7, "The Great Contraction, 1929–33," in M. Friedman and A. Schwartz, *A Monetary History of the United States, 1867–1960* (Princeton, NJ: National Bureau of Economic Research, Princeton University Press, 1963).

[3] Kindleberger's views are presented in his book *The World in Depression 1929–1939* (Berkeley and Los Angeles: University of California Press, 1973).

[4] See his *Lessons from the Great Depression* (Cambridge, MA: The MIT Press, 1989).

policies that could have contributed to the reversal of the Depression. As Barry Eichengreen and Jeffrey Sachs have shown, countries that broke from the gold standard earliest were also the first to recover from the depths of the Depression.[5]

As with many issues in economics, there is no universally accepted view of the causes and propagation mechanisms of the Great Depression. Rather, there remain several different explanations, each focusing on a different aspect of the crisis, and each conveying a part of what is undeniably a complex macroeconomic phenomenon.

Figure 1-4

Industrial Production in France, Germany, the United Kingdom, and the United States, 1925–1938

(*From Peter Temin,* Lessons from the Great Depression, *Cambridge, MA: MIT Press, 1989, p. 2.*)

adverse shocks hit the economy. Keynes suggested that critical adjustments in macroeconomic policies, especially shifts in government spending and taxation and in monetary policy, are needed to counteract economic downturns and stabilize the economy. Keynes's argument that governments could implement *stabilization policies* to prevent or counteract economic downturns came to be so widely accepted that his ideas were collectively christened the "Keynesian Revolution."

Though his specific ideas about economic fluctuations have proven less "general" than the *General Theory* suggests, Keynes made a fundamental

---

[5] See their article "Exchange Rates and Economic Recovery in the 1930s," *Journal of Economic History,* December 1985."

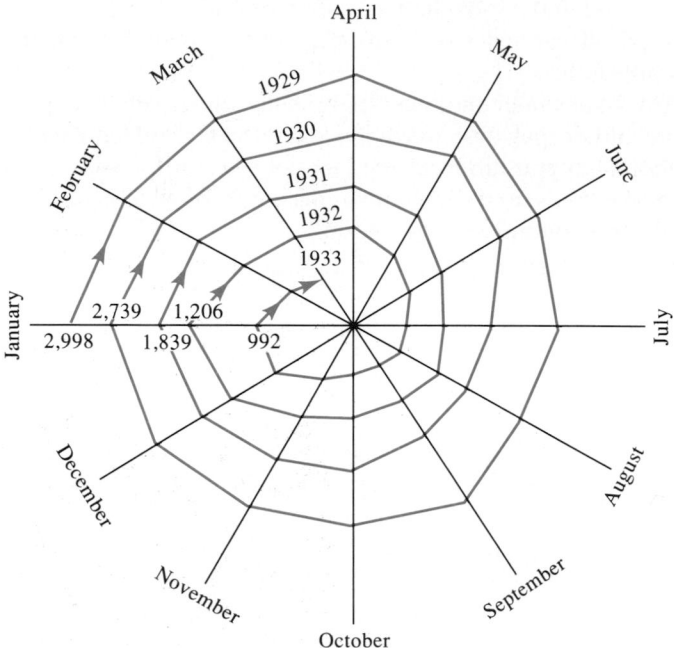

THE WORLD IN DEPRESSION

Figure 1-5

The Collapse of World Trade, January 1929—March 1933

(*From Charles Kindleberger,* The World in Depression 1929–1939, *Berkley and Los Angeles: University of California Press, 1973, p. 172. Copyright © 1986 by Charles P. Kindleberger*)

and permanent contribution to the scientific study of the macroeconomy. Many of his basic ideas, his aggregate demand and supply framework, for example, are still at the center of modern macroeconomics. Other key ideas, especially those involving policy recommendations about management of the budget and the money supply, are in dispute, however.

For the first 25 years after the end of World War II, Keynes's policy recommendations were in the ascendancy throughout the world. There was a growing confidence that governments could prevent economic downturns by actively manipulating budgetary and monetary policies. Most of the world's economies grew rapidly, without serious economic downturns and without high inflation. Events seemed to substantiate the arrival of a new era of macroeconomic stability. But then, in the 1970s, the economic picture darkened, and confidence in Keynesian economics began to wane. Much of the world experienced *stagflation*, a combination of economic *stag*nation (low or negative output growth and high unemployment) together with high in*flation*. This particular economic affliction seemed to be impervious to Keynesian policy recommendations. There seemed to be no way to use macroeconomic policies to keep the economy stable.

In fact, to many economists and noneconomists, it began to appear that stabilization policies were actually a major source of renewed instability. A ''counterrevolution'' began, in which people began to blame activist government policies themselves for the stagflation. This ''counterrevolution'' had its share of brilliant and influential thinkers, of which the most important has been Milton Friedman. A Nobel laureate, Friedman, together with his colleagues at the University of Chicago, put forward a doctrine that was antithetical to Keynesianism, the doctrine that became known as *monetarism*.

The monetarists argued first that market economies were self-regulating; that is, if left alone, economies would tend to return to full employment on their own. Second, they argued that activist macroeconomic policies were part of the problem, not part of the solution. Based on an extensive historical analysis of the United States, Friedman and his coauthor Anna Schwartz argued in *A Monetary History of the United States* that economic fluctuations are to an important extent the result of shifts in the money supply. Friedman and his followers suggest that a stable money supply, rather than a variable money supply (the presumable result of an activist macroeconomic policy), is the true key to a stable macroeconomy.

The monetarist counterattack on Keynesian ideas was pushed even farther during the 1970s and 1980s by the so-called school of *new classical macroeconomics* led by Robert Lucas of the University of Chicago, Robert Barro of Harvard University, and others. These economists argued even more strongly than Friedman that market economies were self-regulating and that government policies were ineffectual in systematically stabilizing an economy. The proponents of this theory invoked the concept of *rational expectations*, to which we shall return many times, to justify their position. Their idea is that if individuals and businesses form their expectations about future economic events in a ''rational'' way (as the theorists define that term), then changes in government policy will have much less effect than standard Keynesian models predict. These ideas of the new classical macroeconomists are challenging, but highly controversial.

Other schools of thought have recently joined the debate. Advocates of the *real business-cycle theory* argue that both Keynesians and monetarists are wrong when they identify the sources of shocks to the economy. They contend that it is technological shocks, rather than demand shocks or policy shocks, that explain the observed fluctuations in the economy. Other so-called ''neo-Keynesians'' are attempting to put Keynes's basic ideas (that market economies are not automatically self-regulating, that nominal wages and prices do not adjust rapidly to preserve full employment, and that government policies can help to stabilize the economy) on a sounder theoretical basis.

Forty-five years after Keynes's death, and after considerable debate and progress in economic thinking, one conclusion certainly can be drawn. Even though it was a path-breaking contribution, Keynes's ''general theory'' was not general enough. Keynes focused on shocks to the economy coming from shifts in investment; we now recognize that the economy is vulnerable to many other kinds of shocks as well. While Keynes stressed that an economy would not necessarily be able to adjust smoothly to an adverse shock—that is, it could not maintain high levels of output and low levels of unemployment—we now know that the ability of an economy to adjust depends importantly on its economic institutions, and these vary around the world. Thus, our analysis of economic fluctuations stresses the great variety of causes and outcomes possible rather than a single theory.

1-4 PROVIDING A BROADER FRAMEWORK FOR MACROECONOMIC ANALYSIS

Much of the agenda of modern macroeconomics has emerged from the debates that Keynes initiated over economic fluctuations. Are economies vulnerable to prolonged downturns? What kinds of shocks hitting the economy can account for such downturns? Can market forces by themselves reverse a deep economic downturn, or should government policies be used to reestablish a high level of production and low unemployment?

While short-term economic fluctuations and stabilization policies should certainly be important concerns of macroeconomics, they should not be the only concerns, or even the main concerns. Other issues, such as the determination of economic growth rates, or the international patterns of borrowing and lending, should be central concerns as well. An adequate theory of economic fluctuations must also reflect the fact that economic institutions and the structure of the economy differ across countries. What is a good theory of economic fluctuations for the United States might be a rather poor theory for Europe, or Japan, or Latin America.

This book, therefore, aims to provide an especially broad view of macroeconomics, and it does so in three ways. First, attention to the debate over short-term economic fluctuations and stabilization policy has been restricted in order that we may focus more attention on other central concerns of macroeconomics. Second, considerable attention has been given to the differences in economic institutions in different countries in order that we may discover a more general macroeconomic theory. An American student, for example, should care about more than U.S. institutions and U.S. macroeconomic theory. In the global economy of the 1990s, an understanding of global macroeconomic events is necessary even to an adequate understanding of developments within one's own economy.

Third, we recognize from the outset that economies are *open* to the world through trade flows and capital flows, and that the international linkages among economies play a critical role in their overall macroeconomic performance. This open-economy focus stands in contrast to the typical closed-economy focus of much of postwar macroeconomics in the United States. For a long time, American macroeconomists treated the United States as a closed economy under the assumption that it was simply too big to be heavily influenced by economic events in the rest of the world. This assumption was never true, and it has become more and more dangerous as the U.S. economy has become more open over time (as measured, for example, by the ratio of exports and imports to GDP). And if the assumption was false for the United States, it was preposterous for most other economies in which trade and capital flows are a dominant, if not *the* dominant influence on the national economy.

The closed-economy bias of U.S. macroeconomists permeated macroeconomic debates worldwide because of the predominance of the United States in the development of the field for much of the postwar period. That predominance is now fading, for the healthy reason that macroeconomic science is booming throughout the world. But at the same time, the legacy of the closed-economy thinking has been hard to shake even when macroeconomic models have been applied to countries that are far more open to world markets than is the United States. To rectify the mistaken attention to closed-economy thinking, we use open-economy models throughout the text. This change of emphasis is important if we are to understand the United States, and absolutely essential if we are to understand almost all other countries. It is also crucial if we are to understand properly that the macroeconomic fortunes of the various parts of the world are now closely bound together.

1-5 An Outline of the Book

This book is divided into two main parts, the *core topics* (Chapters 1–18) and the *special topics* (Chapters 19–23). The core of the book itself consists of four parts: an introduction to macroeconomics; a section on intertemporal topics; a section on monetary economics; and a section concerned with business fluctuations, stabilization policy, and growth.

The introductory chapters (2–3) introduce some of the basic concepts of macroeconomics, including the measurement of aggregate output and prices, the differences between stocks and flows, and the role of expectations in economic models. These are important building blocks for later theories. We also introduce the basic framework for studying economic fluctuations and the (possible) role of stabilization policies. Here we also describe for the first time the central ideas of aggregate supply, aggregate demand, and macroeconomic equilibrium.

The chapters (4–7) on *intertemporal economics* take up one of the most important questions in macroeconomics: what determines the share of current income that a society devotes to current consumption versus saving? Saving can (usually) be viewed as a choice to increase future consumption at the expense of current consumption. Thus, we ask here how households, firms, and governments decide between present and future needs and wants. In order to study these intertemporal issues, we ignore economic fluctuations and rely on a simplified model of the economy in which there is always full employment.

The section on *monetary economics* (Chapters 8–11) examines the role of money in the economy and the pervasive and deep effects that monetary policies have on the economy. Changes in the money supply play a fundamental role in determining inflation, and a crucial role in budgetary finance in many countries. The role of money in an economy is tightly connected with its exchange-rate regime, which determines how its money is exchanged for the money of other countries. In this section, as in the last, we neglect the interaction of money and economic fluctuations, holding off that issue until the following section.

In the fourth core section, on *output determination* (Chapters 12–18), we return to the issue of economic fluctuations and the role that government can play in stabilizing an economy. We describe the Keynesian theory of output determination, with special emphasis on the case of an open economy. We also talk about possible trade-offs between unemployment and inflation, the role of labor-market institutions in determining macroeconomic performance, and the role of different kinds of shocks in causing economic instability.

The final part of the book (Chapters 19–23) present some important special topics that are of central interest to policymakers and macroeconomists but are too advanced for inclusion in the main part of an intermediate macroeconomics course. These chapters are largely, though not completely, self-contained, so they can be taken in any order, although reading them in order produces the best results. They describe issues of economic policy, the role of traded and non-traded goods in an economy, the structure and role of financial markets, the developing country debt crisis, and the problem of ending high inflations.

Basic Concepts in Macroeconomics

Before we can analyze the many theories that attempt to explain macro-economic behavior and the empirical evidence that does (or does not) support them, we need to understand some of the basic concepts of macroeconomics. First, we look at different measures of aggregate income and output and their interrelationships. The process of aggregating across many different goods and services requires some common unit of measure, and this leads us to a second topic, the role of prices and price indexes. A third important subject that permeates much of the discussion in macroeconomics is the distinction between stocks and flows. Fourth, we describe two factors that influence the intertemporal decisions of economic agents: the interest rate and present value. And, finally, we look at the concept of expectations, another factor that is vital in understanding decision making across time periods.

2-1 GROSS DOMESTIC PRODUCT AND GROSS NATIONAL PRODUCT

If macroeconomics is the study of aggregate economic, its building blocks must be aggregate measures of economic activity. In this section, then, we describe the meaning of the two most important measures of overall economic activity in an economy, the gross domestic product and the gross national product.

Gross Domestic Product

Gross domestic product (GDP) is the total value of the current production of final goods and services within the national territory during a given period of time, normally a quarter or a year. An economy produces millions of different goods (cars, refrigerators, dishwashers, hamburgers, apples, and so on) and services (medical operations, legal advice, banking services, haircuts, and so on). The GDP sums all this up as a single statistical measure of the overall production of these goods and services. To add all these items together, it is necessary, however, to express them in a common unit of measure, typically a monetary unit. In the United States, for example, GDP is expressed as the dollar value of all production; in Britain, it is stated as the value of production in pounds sterling; and so forth. In 1990, U.S. GDP reached $5.4 trillion.

The GDP figure captures the *current production* of *final goods* valued at market prices. "Current production" means that we do not count the resale of items that were produced in an earlier period. A sale of an existing home from one investor to another does not contribute to GDP because it is a transfer of assets, not a form of current production. The same holds for sales of artworks, existing factories, and other forms of capital. "Final goods" means simply that we do not count the value of raw materials and intermediate (semifinished) goods that are used as inputs in the production of other goods.

Two methods can be used to calculate the GDP. Take the case of GDP produced by the petroleum sector (to get overall GDP, we add up the GDP in each sector). Suppose, for example, that one company produces crude oil and sells it to a refiner that produces gasoline. The crude oil sells for $20 per barrel to the refiner; the refiner then resells the finished product for $24 per barrel. The first and most direct way to calculate the GDP of this sector is to count only the final goods that are produced. Thus, the GDP would include the $24 of the refined output, but not the $20 of the crude oil production. This is the *output method* of calculating GDP.

A second way to calculate the GDP, which gets to the same result, is to sum up the value added produced at each stage of the production process. Roughly put, the value added is the market value of output at each stage *minus* the market value of inputs used in the production of that output. For example, the value added to the unrefined oil at the refinery is not the full $24 per barrel but only $4 (= $24 − $20). This is the *increase* of value per barrel due to the refining process, and it would be added to the value added to the oil at the wellhead, or $20, for a total value added of $24 from crude oil to final output. Thus, the *value-added method* of calculating GDP produces the same $24 that we found simply by valuing the output of final goods.

Because most kinds of output are sold in market transactions, the transactions prices are usually used to measure the market value of outputs and inputs. In some circumstances, however, transactions prices are not available—or do not exist. This is the case for many government services, including the "outputs" provided by the army, the judicial system, and the regulatory apparatus of the state. The solution here is to use the cost of producing these services, that is, what the government spent on these services, in the absence of a better indicator of value. Still other goods and services, however, are not counted at all in GDP because they do not go through the market and there is no clear information about what they cost. Examples include the services provided by housekeepers working in their own homes and the produce grown in home gardens and consumed directly by households.

The Circular Flow of Income   When a business sells some of its output to a customer, the value of the purchase by the customer equals the revenues received by the business. In turn, the revenue received by the business is distributed in one of four ways: to pay for inputs from other firms, to pay workers, to pay interest on loans, or to keep or spend as profits. The last two categories, payments of interest and profits, may be considered the income earned by the owners of the capital that the firm uses, that is, the creditors and the owners of the plant, the machinery, and the land. Thus, if we add up all the firms in the economy, we have the following sort of identity:

$$
\begin{aligned}
\text{Total purchases by domestic customers} &= \text{total revenue of firms} \\
&= \text{wages} + \text{capital income} \\
&\quad + \text{interfirm purchases}
\end{aligned}
$$

(2.1)

Strictly speaking, this identity holds only for a closed economy. In an open economy, as we shall later see, purchases by domestic consumers can differ from the revenues earned by domestic firms, because some of the things purchased are imports from foreign firms, and some of the things sold are exports to foreign purchasers. Furthermore, some of the income earned by domestic residents comes from capital or labor employed in foreign firms abroad and not in domestic firms. But for the moment, it is convenient to ignore these complications.

Note that the purchases in identity (2.1) are of two types, those made by final users of the product and those made by firms that use other firms' products to produce their own products. Let us now subtract the amount of interfirm purchases from each of the items in the identity (2.1). Total purchases minus interfirm purchases equals final demand. Total revenues minus purchases from other firms equal the *value added* of the firms in the economy. When we have done this, we find a new identity (which, again, is only exactly true in a closed economy):

$$
\text{Final demand} = \text{value added} = \text{wages} + \text{capital income} \quad \textbf{(2.2)}
$$

Thus, income flows in a circle. Spending by households equals the value added by firms, which in turn equals the income of households, who own the capital and labor used by the firms. This *circular flow of income* is depicted in Figure 2-1. Households make demands for the output of firms, and they also supply the inputs of labor and capital to the firms. In turn, the firms produce the output that is sold to the households, and those firms'

Figure 2-1
The Circular Flow of Income

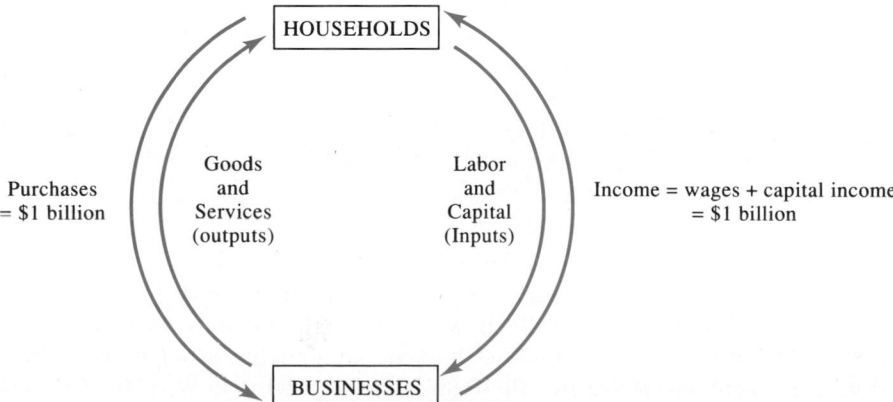

earnings are used to pay for the workers and the capital that they need. In the figure, final demand from households equals $1 billion, which is the value of total GDP. This $1 billion is also equal to the value added produced by the firms in the economy, which in turn is the sum of the income earned by labor (wages) and capital (profits and interest) employed in the economy.

Different Ways to Measure GDP   The basic identity in (2.2) allows us to view the gross domestic product in three ways, each amounting to the same thing: the GDP is the sum of all final purchases in the economy, it is the sum of the value added of all the enterprises in the economy, and it is the sum of all the incomes from factors of production (labor and capital) in the economy. Each of these descriptions of GDP suggests a different way of measuring GDP in practice that should each lead to the same total GDP for an economy. (Small differences in the three measures do typically occur because of data errors, however.)

The first way to calculate GDP is to use the *expenditure method*. By this process, the GDP is measured as the sum of all the final demands for output in the economy. There are several kinds of such final demands. The output produced in the economy can be used for consumption by households (C), consumption by the government (G), investment in new capital in the economy (I), or net sales to foreigners (that is, net exports). Next, let us say that consumption goods have the price P_C and that a quantity C is purchased; investment goods have the price P_I, with quantity I purchased; government purchases have the price P_G, with quantity G purchased; exports have the price P_X, with quantity X sold abroad; and imports have the price P_M, with quantity IM imported from abroad.

The market value of consumption is thus $P_C C$, the product of the consumer price and the quantity of consumption goods purchased. The market value of investment ($P_I I$), government spending ($P_G G$), exports ($P_X X$), and imports ($P_M IM$) can be found the same way. This being the case, then, GDP is calculated as follows:

$$\text{GDP} = P_C C + P_I I + P_G G + (P_X X - P_M IM) \qquad \textbf{(2.3)}$$

Thus, GDP is the sum of the market values of all the final demands in the economy, measured at current market prices. Note that the expenditures in parentheses, $P_X X - P_M IM$, are the *net* exports of the economy; that is, they are equal to the market value of exports minus the market value of imports.

Table 2-1 shows the decomposition of GDP among the different expenditure categories for the United States in 1990. Private consumption is, by far, the most important component of GDP, with more than two-thirds of the total. Government purchases of goods and services follow far behind, with some 20 percent of GDP, while investment takes up slightly less than 14 percent of total output. Net exports accounted for a *negative* 1.4 percent of GDP. Net exports were the difference of exports (10 percent of GDP) and imports (slightly over 11 percent of GDP).

The *value-added method* is a second way to calculate GDP. Here, the GDP is achieved by summing up the value added produced in each of the sectors of the economy. Thus, GDP is the sum of value added in agriculture, plus value added in mining, plus value added in manufacturing, and so forth. A division of the economy into nine sectors is shown in Table 2-2 for the year 1988. Note that manufacturing is the single largest sector (roughly 20 percent of the entire economy), while agriculture and mining are the smallest sectors (2.1 percent and 1.7 percent of the economy, respectively).

The third method of measuring GDP is to add up the *incomes* of all factors (labor and capital) that contribute to the production process. In par-

TABLE   2-1

GROSS DOMESTIC PRODUCT IN THE UNITED STATES BY TYPE OF EXPENDITURE, 1990*

	Gross Domestic Product ($ billions)	As a % of Total GDP
Gross domestic product	$5,424.4	100.0%
Private consumption (C)	3,658.1	67.4
Investment (I)	745.0	13.7
Government consumption (G)	1,098.0	20.2
Net exports (NX) of which	−76.6	−1.4
Exports	534.7	9.9
Imports	−611.3	−11.3

* Totals may not add due to rounding.
Source: Economic Report of the President, 1991, *Table B-1, and U.S. Department of Commerce, Bureau of Labor Statistics,* Survey of Current Business, *Washington, D.C.: U.S. Government Printing Office, January 1991).*

TABLE   2-2

GROSS DOMESTIC PRODUCT BY INDUSTRY, UNITED STATES, 1988*

	Gross Domestic Product ($ billions)	As a % of Total GDP
Agriculture, forestry, and fisheries	$ 99.8	2.1%
Mining	80.4	1.7
Construction	232.6	4.8
Manufacturing	948.6	19.6
Transportation and public utilities	441.4	9.1
Wholesale and retail trade	780.8	16.1
Finance insurance and real estate	830.3	17.1
Services	872.5	18.0
Government and government enterprises	570.6	11.8
Statistical discrepancy	−9.6	− 0.2
Total	$4,847.4	100.0%

* GDP decomposition by industry is unavailable beyond 1988.
Source: Economic Report of the President, 1991, *Table B-10 (Washington, D.C.: U.S. Government Printing Office, 1991).*

TABLE   2-3

LABOR AND CAPITAL PARTICIPATION IN U.S. DOMESTIC INCOME, 1990*

	Domestic Income ($ billions)	As a % of Total DI
Labor compensation	$3,244.2	73.9%
Capital remuneration	1,173.3	26.7
Proprietor's income	402.4	
Rental income of persons	6.7	
Corporate profits	297.1	
Net interest	467.1	
Less: Net factor payments	29.6	0.7
Domestic income	$4,387.9	100.0%

* Totals may not add due to rounding.
Source: Economic Report of the President, 1991, *Table B-24 (Washington, D.C.: U.S. Government Printing Office, 1991).*

ticular, the *domestic income* (DI) of the economy is the sum of labor income and capital income. The domestic income, in turn, is closely related to GDP. Table 2-3 shows the breakdown of U.S. domestic income into labor income and capital income for 1990. Interestingly, labor income accounts for almost three-fourths of domestic income, with capital income accounting for the rest. Labor income is simply the remuneration of salaried employees. Capital income has more varied sources, including the income of the self-employed as well as interest income, rental income, and corporate profits.

Note that domestic income is not exactly equal to GDP. The most important adjustments that have to be made in GDP to get to DI are subtractions for capital depreciation and indirect taxes. For one thing, buildings, equipment, and residential property naturally wear out through time, a process known as *depreciation of the capital stock*. A part of current output must be reinvested in any given period simply to make up for depreciation. Obviously, that part of output which is used to make up for depreciation should not be counted as part of income. When depreciation is subtracted from GDP, we get *net domestic product* (NDP). To get from NDP to DI, we must first note that GDP is measured at *market prices,* while domestic income is calculated using the *net-of-tax prices* actually received by producers. The difference between the two prices is the value of sale and excise taxes, also referred to as indirect taxes, which forms part of government revenue. We find DI by subtracting these indirect tax revenues from NDP.

Gross National Product

A concept closely related to GDP is *gross national product* (GNP), the total value of income that domestic residents receive in a given period of time. In a closed economy—one that is cut off from trade and capital flows to the rest of the world—the GDP and GNP are equal. In all actual economies, however, the two measures are different, if only by a small amount in some countries, because in practice there is always some part of domestic production owned by foreigners and some foreign production which is the income of domestic residents.

Let us look a little more closely at the difference between these two concepts. In all economies, some of the factors of production are owned by foreigners. Thus, part of the income received by labor and capital in the economy actually belongs to foreigners. This is easiest to see when foreign workers are employed in the home economy. It is also clearly the case when foreigners own some of the capital stock in the home economy. At the same time, domestic residents may receive some of their income from abroad. They may actually work abroad, or they may own shares of stock in foreign companies. The GDP measures the income of factors of production *within the nation's boundaries,* no matter who earns that income. The GNP measures the income of *residents of the economy,* no matter whether the income is earned in domestic production or in foreign production.

Suppose, for example, that a part of domestic production comes from an oil well that is actually owned by a foreign (nonresident) investor. The income earned on the oil well does not flow to domestic residents but to its foreign owner. Since the oil output is produced within the territory of the country, it is part of GDP. At the same time, however, the oil income is *not* counted in the country's GNP, but rather in the GNP of the country where the oil investor lives. The country's GDP would therefore be greater than its GNP.

This means that we must amend the circular flow of income, shown earlier in Figure 2-1, to make clear that part of domestic product may flow out to foreigners and part of the national income of domestic residents may flow in from abroad. The revised circular flow diagram in Figure 2-2 indicates the fact that part of houshold demand is satisfied by imports while part of business sales are exports. At the same time, part of the income of firms is paid out to foreign factors of production while domestic households receive some of their income from abroad.

Now, suppose that a resident of one country, say, a U.S. citizen, borrows from a resident of another country, say, a Japanese bank, in order to undertake an investment project. The project pays $2 million in annual income, but the loan from Japan requires an interest payment each year of $100,000. The U.S. income resulting from the investment is thus $1.9 million, while the Japanese income is $100,000. The investment project produces an increase in U.S. GDP of the full $2 million, but a GNP increase of only $1.9 million. Japanese GDP is, of course, unaffected, but its GNP increases by $100,000. Once again, then, we see the difference between GDP and GNP from a different angle.

There are in fact many ways that a country's income can differ from its output. Foreigners may own part of the production in the domestic country (as in the case of the oil well), or they may lend money to finance some domestic project (as in the case of the Japanese bank), or foreign workers can work in the domestic country and send their labor earnings home as worker remittances. In each case, part of the domestic output is income of a foreign resident. That portion of domestic production that becomes the net income earned by foreigners must be subtracted out of GDP to calculate GNP. Of course, if the country, on balance, is earning income from the rest

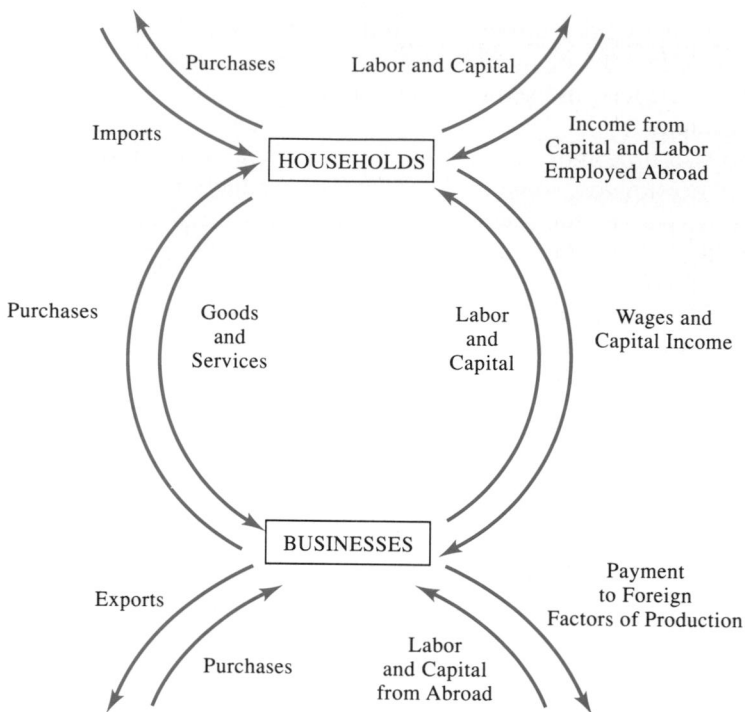

Figure 2-2
The Circular Flow of Income Considering Foreign-Owned
Factors of Production

of the world, rather than paying income to the rest of the world, the earnings coming from other countries must be added to domestic output to get gross national product.

Thus, we have another important macroeconomic identity. Let NFP equal the *net* factor income (payments) received from abroad (equal to the earnings of domestic residents on foreign profits, loans, and worker remittances, *minus* the earnings of foreigners in the domestic economy). Then,

$$GNP = GDP + NFP \qquad (2.4)$$

Notice especially that whenever domestic factors of production working abroad earn more than foreign factors of production working in the domestic economy (NFP > 0), GNP will be higher than GDP.

Table 2-4 shows the evolution of GDP and GNP in the United States between 1980 and 1990. Throughout this period, GNP has consistently been higher than GDP, because net factor payments to domestic residents have been positive. However, the difference between GDP and GNP has been declining. This reflects the fact that U.S. residents, including the U.S. government, borrowed heavily from the rest of the world during the 1980s. Therefore, the payments of interest to foreigners has been growing sharply, and this has caused a decline in NFP.

GNP Per Capita and Economic Well-Being   A country's level of GNP *per capita,* that is, per person, is the most commonly used yardstick of economic development. Countries with a high level of GNP per capita—the rich

GNP, GDP, AND NET FACTOR
PAYMENTS IN THE UNITED STATES,
1980–1990
(BILLIONS OF CURRENT DOLLARS)

Year	GNP	GDP	NFP
1980	$2,732.0	$2,684.4	$47.6
1981	3,052.6	3,000.5	52.1
1982	3,166.0	3,114.8	51.2
1983	3,405.7	3,355.9	49.9
1984	3,772.2	3,724.8	47.4
1985	4,014.9	3,974.1	40.7
1986	4,231.6	4,197.2	34.4
1987	4,515.6	4,486.7	29.0
1988	4,873.7	4,840.2	33.5
1989	5,200.8	5.163.2	37.6
1990	5,463.0	5,424.4	38.6

Source: Economic Report of the President, 1991,
*Table B-24 (Washington, D.C.: U.S. Government
Printing Office, 1991).*

countries—are typically presumed to have a higher level of economic well-being than countries with lower levels of GNP per capita. By the measure of per capita GNP, the richest country in the world in 1989 was Switzerland, with $29,880, followed by Japan ($23,810) and Norway ($22,290); the United States came in sixth with $19,840.[1] At the other extreme, the poorest countries were Mozambique, with a mere $80 in GNP per capita, and Ethiopia, with $120.

The measure of GNP per capita does indeed convey a lot of information about the economic well-being of countries. As we can see in Table 2-5, countries with high per capita incomes also have, on average, high levels of personal consumption, education, and life expectancy. But important caveats must be kept in mind when using GNP per capita as a yardstick of economic welfare.

First, GNP measures output at market prices, not necessarily at the *true social value of the output*. For example, certain kinds of output are simply not counted in the official GNP statistics because they do not have market prices. Transactions that take place outside of the monetary economy—such as work at home and barter exchanges—are typically not

[1] The dollar GDP is calculated by the World Bank and is found by converting the GDP in the local currency into dollars using the market exchange rate. (In fact, the World Bank uses a kind of average exchange rate for the years 1987, 1988, and 1989.) The data are from the World Bank, *World Development Report, 1991* (New York: Oxford University Press, 1991).

TABLE   2-5

GNP per Capita and Economic Well-being Across Countries, Selected Years, 1985–1989

Country	GNP per Capita in 1989	Daily Calorie Supply per Capita in 1988	Life Expectancy at Birth in 1989 (years)	Adult Illiteracy in 1985 (percent)
Switzerland	$29,880	3,547	78	*
Japan	23,810	2,848	79	*
United States	20,910	3,666	76	*
Singapore	10,450	2,892	74	18%
Mexico	2,010	3,135	69	11
Botswana	1,600	2,269	67	29
Philippines	710	2,255	64	14
India	340	2,104	59	57
Bangladesh	180	1,925	51	67
Mozambique	80	1,632	49	62

Less than 5%.
Source: *World Bank,* World Development Report, 1991 *(New York: Oxford University Press, 1991).*

counted in the GNP, so that the official GNP statistics *underestimate* the actual income of the economy. There are goods whose market value overstates the true social value. Consider, for example, a power plant that produces electricity (which has a market price) but also produces pollution. The GNP statistics reflect the market price of the electricity, but the social value of the electricity should be computed as the market value of the electricity *minus* the social costs of the pollution. In other words, a proper measure of GNP should subtract the social costs of the pollution in the production process.[2]

Second, the economic well-being that is achieved by a given value of GNP depends on the *market prices of the output.* Suppose, for example, that two economies each have a per capita GNP of $1,000 but that the prices of outputs in the first economy are lower than the prices of outputs in the second economy. Even though the GNPs are the same in the two countries, real economic welfare would be greater in the first country than in the second because each $1 of GNP would purchase more goods and services.

Of course, in making actual comparisons across countries, the situation is far more complicated. There are literally millions of individual prices in an economy, some higher in the first country than in the second, and some

[2] In some countries, taxes are levied on pollution-producing outputs to account for the social costs of production. In such a case, the net-of-tax market value of these outputs would more accurately reflect the social value of these outputs.

lower. To make a comparison between the countries requires us to take an "average" of prices, that is, to construct a price index, in order to make a valid comparison. And constructing such an index of prices that helps us compare income levels across countries is fraught with technical difficulties.

In Chapter 21 we shall examine one attempt to make such a comparison, an important project undertaken by the World Bank known as the Intercountry Comparison Project (ICP). What the researchers found is that, for reasons described in Chapter 21, the prices in poor countries tend to be lower than the prices in rich countries. For that reason, the gap in economic well-being between poor countries and rich countries tends to be somewhat overstated by the official GNP statistics.

Consider one example. According to official data, the per capita GNP in India in 1980 was $240, while in the United States it was $11,360. This suggests an income gap of 47.3 times (47.3 = $11,360/$240). In fact, however, the ICP found that prices in India are systematically lower than they are in the United States, so that each dollar in India purchases more goods and services than a dollar in the United States. According to the estimates of the ICP, India's income *adjusted for price differences* was $614 in 1980, 2.6 times greater than the official statistics. Of course, India was still much poorer than the United States—with a gap of 18.5 times—but not by the magnitude suggested by the simple GNP data.

A third important reason why per capita GNP can be an inaccurate measure of overall economic well-being in an economy is that the measure of per capita GNP does not take account of the *degree of income inequality* in an economy. Consider the man with his head in an oven and his feet in a block of ice, who would have to acknowledge that "on average, the temperature is comfortable." If the distribution of a country's GNP between the very rich and the very poor is extremely unequal, the social situation in the country is apt to be highly strained (and in the view of many people, highly immoral as well). Amartya Sen, an economic philosopher and development specialist at Harvard University, has pointed to many cases in which poor countries with relatively equal income distribution show *higher* indicators of social well-being than do richer countries with less equal distribution.

Compare, for example, Costa Rica, with a per capita income of $1,780 in 1989, and Brazil, with a per capita income of $2,540 on the same year. Costa Rica, however, has a more equitable income distribution than Brazil, partly as a result of a more extensive social welfare system. The result, as seen in Table 2-6, is that Costa Rica has higher levels of literacy, life expectancy, and caloric intake, than does Brazil, even though the former is the poorer country.

2-2 REAL VERSUS NOMINAL VARIABLES

Throughout the study of macroeconomics, we are concerned with comparisons of macroeconomic variables at different points of time, or in different economies at the same point of time. To make meaningful comparisons, it is usually vital to know whether differences in macroeconomic variables reflect differences in the prices of the goods or differences in the physical volumes of goods. Take, for example, a 10 percent rise in per capita GNP from one year to the next. This rise in GNP has a very different interpretation if it results from a rise in all prices and wages by 10 percent (in which case

TABLE 2-6

GNP per Capita and Welfare: A Comparison of Brazil and Costa Rica, Selected Years, 1985–1989

Country	GNP per Capita in 1989	Daily Calorie Supply per Capita in 1988	Life Expectancy at Birth in 1989 (years)	Adult Illiteracy in 1985 (percent)
Brazil	$2,540	2,709	66	22%
Costa Rica	1,780	2,782	75	6

Source: World Bank, World Development Report, 1991 *(New York: Oxford University Press, 1991).*

probably nothing much has changed in the real economic conditions of the population) than if it results from an increase in the physical output in the economy by 10 percent (in which case real living standards have likely increased).

The Construction of Price Indexes

The millions of prices and outputs in an economy make it difficult, however, to say whether changes in GNP result from price changes or quantity changes. What is needed is a way to summarize the vast number of prices and outputs into simple indexes.

Consider, for example, the aggregate value of consumption expenditures in the economy. The aggregate market value of consumption expenditures is equal to the sum of the market value of expenditures on all different types of consumption goods. Suppose that there are N types of consumption goods. For each type of good, there is a price and a physical volume of consumption. Thus, the nominal value of consumption, denoted $P_C C$, is equal to

$$P_C C = P_1 C_1 + P_2 C_2 + P_3 C_3 + \cdots + P_N C_N \qquad (2.5)$$

We then calculate the "average price" of consumption goods by constructing a *price index,* denoted P_C, which is a weighted average of all the prices of the individual types of consumption goods. The typical way to calculate this index for year t (P_{Ct}) is as follows:

$$P_{Ct} = w_1\left(\frac{P_{1t}}{P_{10}}\right) + w_2\left(\frac{P_{2t}}{P_{20}}\right) + w_3\left(\frac{P_{3t}}{P_{30}}\right) + \cdots + w_N\left(\frac{P_{Nt}}{P_{N0}}\right) \qquad (2.6)$$

Here, the weights $w_1, w_2, \ldots, w_N$ reflect the varying importance that is attributed to the various individual prices. Prices with a large weight have an important effect on the overall price index. The sum of the weights is equal to 1.[3] The prices P_{10}, P_{20}, P_{30}, and so on, are the prices of the goods in a "base year," denoted as time 0. The resulting price index is sometimes called the *consumer price index* (CPI) or the *consumption price deflator*.

Note how this price index works. At time 0, the "base year," the price index is exactly equal to 1.0 by construction, since all prices are equal to their base-year values. Suppose that in year t, all prices are twice their base year value. That is,

$$P_{1t}/P_{10} = P_{2t}/P_{20} = P_{3t}/P_{30} = \cdots = P_{Nt}/P_{N0} = 2.$$

Then, the consumer price index in year t would be $P_{Ct} = 2$. In calculating the index, the weights do not change from year to year. Thus, the price index in any given year is a weighted average of the prices in that year relative to the base year, using the constant set of weights.

The *real* value of consumption C_t is then equal to the *nominal* (market) value of consumption expenditure divided by the consumption price deflator of the corresponding year:

$$C_t = \frac{\text{nominal consumption expenditure}}{P_{Ct}} = \frac{P_{Ct}C_t}{P_{Ct}} \qquad \textbf{(2.7)}$$

Changes in the real value of consumption can be attributed to changes in the physical volumes of consumption of the various goods rather than to changes in the prices of the goods. The time series for the United States of nominal consumption expenditures, real consumption expenditures, and the price deflator between 1980 and 1990, are shown in Table 2-7. Notice that by construction the nominal consumption equals the real consumption in the base year, in this case, 1982.

Just as we have described the construction of a consumption deflator, it is possible to construct a deflator for investment spending (P_I), government spending (P_G), exports (P_X), and imports (P_M).

Real GDP

It is useful to have a measure of real production in the economy, so that when GDP changes, we know whether the change is due to prices or to real production. To calculate real production, we think of the GDP of the economy as equal to the product of the "average" price level in the economy, multiplied by the level of real production in the economy. That is, if we start with GDP at current market prices, then we can set GDP equal to the product of a price index P, called the *GDP price deflator*, and the *real GDP* (an index of physical production):

$$\text{GDP} = PQ \qquad \textbf{(2.8)}$$

---

[3] Typically, the weight given to commodity 1 is equal to the share of consumption of commodity 1 in the total consumption basket, as determined by a survey of consumption patterns in a given base year. Thus, $w_1 = P_1C_1/P_CC$ in the year of the survey upon which the consumption price index is based.

TABLE   2-7

NOMINAL CONSUMPTION AND REAL CONSUMPTION
IN THE UNITED STATES, 1980–1990

Year	Nominal Consumption (current US$ billions)	Real Consumption (1982 US$ billions)	Price Deflator of Consumption (1982 = 100)
1980	$1,732.6	$2,000.4	86.6
1981	1,915.1	2,024.2	94.6
1982	2,050.7	2,050.7	100.0
1983	2,234.5	2,146.0	104.1
1984	2,430.5	2,249.3	108.1
1985	2,629.0	2,354.8	111.6
1986	2,797.4	2,446.4	114.3
1987	3,009.4	2,515.8	119.6
1988	3,238.2	2,606.5	124.2
1989	3,450.1	2,656.8	129.9
1990	3,658.1	2,682.2	136.4

Source: Economic Report of the President, 1991 *(Washington, D.C.:
U.S. Government Printing Office, 1991), Tables B-1, B-2, B-3.*

The trick is to separate nominal GDP into P and Q in a sensible way. (Note that P is a deflator, or price index, for all of GDP, while P_C is a price deflator just for consumption expenditures).

The standard method of constructing Q is this. We start with the definition of nominal GDP in equation (2.2) as the sum of final expenditures throughout the economy. Then, we use the price indexes for consumption, investment, government spending, exports, and imports to calculate a time series of *real* expenditures for each of these categories. For example, nominal consumption expenditure is divided by the price index P_C in a given year, in order to find real consumption expenditure C. Real $I, G, X,$ and IM are found in the same way. Note that the price index for each component of GDP is equal to 1 in the base year, so that in that year, nominal and real expenditures are the same.

Once we have found these real expenditures, we can define real GDP (denoted as Q) as the sum of the real expenditures:

$$Q = C + I + G + (X - IM) \qquad (2.9)$$

Once we have used (2.9) to give us real gross domestic product, Q, then we can compute the GDP price deflator P using the formula (2.10), which is simply a rearrangement of equation (2.8). Specifically, our formula for P is

$$P = \frac{GDP}{Q} \qquad (2.10)$$

Note that we calculate the price index in an indirect, or "implicit," way. We first take nominal GDP and construct a measure of real GDP, or Q. Then, P is found implicitly as the ratio of GDP to Q. Thus, the resulting GDP price deflator is also sometimes called the *implicit GDP price deflator*.

By way of illustration, let us take a primitive economy that produces only two goods, apples and oranges. Now we know that it is impossible to add apples and oranges, as the old saying goes. To solve this problem, Table 2-8 shows how to construct the nominal GDP, real GDP, and the GDP price deflator. The information is for the years 1982 (the base year) and the current year 1991. Nominal GDP is calculated simply by multiplying price times quantities for apples and oranges and then adding up the two values. Real GDP is found by multiplying the quantities in the given year by the prices in 1982. The implicit price deflator is found by dividing nominal GDP by real GDP.

Now consider the actual GDP data for the United States. Table 2-9 shows the data for real GDP with a base year of 1982. Note that nominal and real GDP were equal in the base year. (This is, of course, a matter of definition.) Note too that while nominal GDP went up from 1981 to 1982, the real GDP actually declined. Thus, actual production fell in 1982—it was a year of recession—but inflation was sufficiently high that nominal GDP rose nonetheless. Note as well that real GDP rose every year from 1983 through 1990, an eight-year stretch that saw the longest peacetime economic expansion in U.S. history.

TABLE 2-8

CALCULATION OF GDP AND THE GDP DEFLATOR:
AN EXAMPLE

	1982	1991
(a) Physical outputs (pounds)		
Apples	30	36
Oranges	50	80
(b) Prices ($/pound)		
Apples	$1.50	$2.00
Oranges	1.00	1.40
(c) Nominal expenditures (a × b)		
Apples	$45	$ 72
Oranges	50	112
(d) Price indexes (1982 = 1.0)		
Apples	1.0	1.33
Oranges	1.0	1.40
(e) Real expenditures (c/e)		
Apples	$45	$54
Oranges	50	80
(f) Nominal GDP (current prices)	$95.00	$184.00
(g) Real GDP (1982 prices)	$95.00	$134.00
(h) GDP deflator (f/g)	1.00	1.37

TABLE   2-9

NOMINAL GDP, AND THE GDP DEFLATOR, 1980–1990

Year	Nominal GDP (billions of current dollars)	Real GDP (billions of constant 1982 dollars)	GDP Deflator (1982 = 100)
1980	$2,684.4	$3,131.7	85.7
1981	3,000.5	3,193.6	93.9
1982	3,114.8	3,114.8	100.0
1983	3,355.9	3,231.2	103.9
1984	3,724.8	3,457.5	107.8
1985	3,974.1	3,581.9	110.9
1986	4,197.2	3,687.4	113.8
1987	4,486.7	3,820.0	117.5
1988	4,840.2	3,988.6	121.4
1989	5,163.2	4,087.6	126.3
1990	5,424.4	4,126.2	131.5

Source: Economic Report of the President, 1991 *(Washington, D.C.: U.S. Government Printing Office, 1991), Tables B-8 and B-9.*

2-3 FLOWS AND STOCKS IN MACROECONOMICS

Now we must look at two more key concepts of macroeconomics, flows and stocks. A *flow* is an economic magnitude measured *as a rate per unit of time,* such as the production of Cadillacs per week, the consumption of French wine per year, and the total output of the economy per quarter. A *stock,* on the other hand, is a magnitude measured *at a point of time,* such as the total number of two-story houses in London in 1900, the number of known Rembrandt paintings as of today, or the total holdings of gold of the U.S. Treasury in December 31, 1990.

Most of the concepts that we have discussed so far are flows: GDP, GNP, domestic income, investment, government spending. A few concepts, such as the amount of capital in the economy, are stocks. In this section we want to focus on specific flow-stock relations that are especially important in macroeconomics.

Investment and the Capital Stock

The *capital of an economy* is its accumulated stock of residential structures, machinery, factories, and equipment that exist at a point in time and that add to the productive power of the economy. (Residential structures add to the productive power of the economy in the sense that they raise the capacity of the economy to provide housing services to the population.) *Investment spending* is the flow of output in any given period that is used to maintain or to increase the capital stock of an economy. Thus, we have the identity

$$K = K_{-1} + I \qquad (2.11)$$

where K refers to the stock of capital at the end of the current period. The equation holds that the stock of capital at the end of the current period is equal to the stock of capital at the end of the previous period (K_{-1}) plus the investment during the period just ended. Or, to put this another way, the change in the stock ($K - K_{-1}$) is equal to the flow (I).[4]

Actually, however, we must specify the relationship between the capital stock and investment a bit more carefully. The problem is that some of the capital stock wears out just from old age and use. The wearing-out process is known as *depreciation*, which we will denote DN. Because of depreciation, we must rewrite (2.11) as (2.11'):

$$K = K_{-1} + I - DN \qquad (2.11')$$

The investment flow I is called "gross," or total, investment, while I minus DN is called "net" investment. Thus, the change in the stock of capital ($K - K_{-1}$) is equal to the flow of net investment ($I - DN$). In the United States in 1990, gross investment was \$745 billion (Table 2-1), and depreciation was estimated at \$576 billion. Thus, *net* investment was \$169 billion.

Note that macroeconomists use the term "investment" somewhat differently from the colloquial usage. In the usage of macroeconomics, investment refers to the purchase of *new* capital in the economy, not the trading of existing capital from one person to another. Thus, when a new house is built, that is investment in the macroeconomic sense. On the other hand, when one person buys an existing house from another person, no investment has taken place in the macroeconomic sense, even though the buyer may consider that she has indeed made an investment.

Saving and Wealth

Wealth and saving also represent a stock-flow relationship like that between capital and investment. Saving, S, is the part of current income that is not consumed, but is instead used to accumulate financial wealth, which we denote as W. Suppose, for example, that the Smith family has a total income of \$30,000 in 1990, which includes all income from labor and capital services, for example, bank accounts and shares of stock owned by the family. If the family's consumption is \$24,000 for the year, and the rest of the income is used for saving, the stock of wealth at the end of 1990 will be \$6,000 higher than it was at the end of 1989. In formal notation,

$$W - W_{-1} = S \qquad (2.12)$$

Once again, we see that a change in a stock variable, W, is equal to a flow variable, S.

---

[4] Throughout the book, we adopt the convention that variables with no explicit time subscript refer to the current period unless otherwise indicated. Variables of previous or future periods are indicated by a subscript which subtracts or adds, respectively, the corresponding number of periods.

The Current Account and Net International Investment Position

A third crucial stock-flow relationship is that between a country's current account (CA) and its net international investment position (NIIP). As we shall see in later chapters, the *current account* of an economy is a flow variable measuring the rate at which the residents of a country are borrowing from or lending to the rest of the world. When the current account is positive in a given period, then the nation's residents are, on net balance, lending funds to the rest of the world (some residents may be borrowing, but this borrowing is less in total than the total lending that is also taking place). When the current account balance is negative, it means that domestic residents are, on net balance, borrowing from the rest of the world.

The *net international investment position* (NIIP) measures the net stock of outstanding loans between a country and the rest of the world as a result of past borrowing or lending. When the NIIP is positive, it means that domestic residents have a stock of net *claims* against the rest of the world; that is, the rest of the world, on net, owes money to the country. We say that the country is a net creditor vis-à-vis the rest of the world. When the NIIP is negative, it means that the domestic residents have a stock of net *debt,* or owe net funds, to the rest of the world. Such a country is a net debtor.

The formal stock-flow relationship is like the others we have looked at:

$$\text{NIIP} = \text{NIIP}_{-1} + \text{CA} \qquad \textbf{(2.13)}$$

The change in the stock, $\text{NIIP} - \text{NIIP}_{-1}$, is equal to the flow, CA.

At the beginning of the 1980s, the United States was a net creditor of the rest of the world (NIIP equaled \$140.9 billion in 1980). Since 1982, however, the United States has run large deficits in its current account, which succeeded in turning NIIP from a positive to a large negative number. As of the end of 1988, the NIIP of the United States had reached about −\$500 billion.[5] In later chapters, we shall see what the implications of this kind of net indebtedness are.

Deficits and The Stock of Public Debt

A fourth important stock-flow relationship that we will use repeatedly is that between a government's net stock of debt, $D^g,$ and its budget deficit, *DEF,* which is a flow. The government collects revenues mainly from taxes. It spends money to purchase goods and services and to make income transfers to the public. Very rarely do the figures for revenues and expenditures of the government coincide, however. When expenditures exceed revenue, we say that the government runs a *budget deficit*. When revenues exceed expenditures, by contrast, the government runs a *budget surplus*.

In general, the government "finances" its budget deficit; that is, it pays for its expenditures in excess of revenues, by borrowing. Through its treasury, the government issues bonds which it sells to the public, or to banks, or sometimes to the central bank. The stock of the government's debt (D^g) rises when there is a budget deficit ($DEF > 0$), and falls when there is a

---

[5] Recent revisions, based on new estimates of the value of U.S. investments abroad, have placed the NIIP at about −\$360 billion for 1990.

Table   2-10

The Relationship Between Stocks and Flows:
Some Examples

Stock	Flow	Relationship: Change in Stock = flow
Capital (K)	Net investment ($I - $ DN)	$K - K_{-1} = J$
Financial wealth (W)	Saving (S)	$W - W_{-1} = S$
International investment position (NIIP)	Current account (CA)	$\text{NIIP} - \text{NIIP}_{-1} = \text{CA}$
Government debt (D^g)	Budget deficit (DEF)	$D^g - D^g_{-1} = DEF$

budget surplus ($DEF < 0$). In formal terms, we write

$$D^g - D^g_{-1} = DEF \tag{2.14}$$

The change in the stock of debt is equal to the deficit, which is a flow.

In the United States, the government budget has been in deficit for 29 of the 31 years between 1960 and 1990. As a result, the stock of debt of the federal government held by the public has increased from less than $300 billion in 1960 to $3.2 trillion as of September 1990. Of this total, about $2.2 trillion is held by private investors, almost 20 percent of it by foreigners. (As we shall see later, an additional amount of government debt is also held by the U.S. central bank, the Federal Reserve System.)

Table 2-10 summarizes this introduction to the relationships between stocks and flows that we have discussed here.

2-4 Some Intertemporal Aspects of Macroeconomics: Interest Rates and Present Values

Many key macroeconomic issues involve choices that not only take place in time but that involve decisions about timing. A household's decision of how much to save in a given year is really a choice about *time:* whether to consume now or whether to consume later. By saving today, the household forgoes current consumption in order to increase its consumption in the future. When this happens, we say that the household is making an *intertemporal* choice, a choice involving the allocation of consumption at different points in time. A firm's choice of how much to invest in a given year is also intertemporal. Essentially, the firm must decide whether to forgo current dividends or to borrow more now in order to increase its future output capacity and create higher profits later.

We shall study optimal intertemporal choices at great length in the coming chapters. At this point, we need only introduce two crucial elements in the analysis of intertemporal decisions, interest rates, and net present values.

Interest rates are simply the terms at which money or goods today may be traded off for money or goods at a future date. Suppose, for instance, that the interest rate in the bank is 10 percent per year. This means that an additional $1 deposit today will yield $1.10 next year. To have $1 next year requires a deposit today of about $0.91 (= $1/1.1). We can say, then, that the *present value*—that is, the value today—of $1 next year is equal to $0.91.

Using interest rates, we can translate a given time path of money in the future into a present value today. Suppose, for example, that interest rates are 10 percent per year, and you want to find the present value of having $1 in *each* of the next two years. We have just seen that $1 in one year's time has a present value of $0.91. An extra $1 in two years time can be obtained by depositing about $0.83 today, since $0.83 × 1.10 × 1.10 is approximately equal to $1.0. Therefore, by depositing $1.74 (= $0.91 + $0.83) today, you can have $1 in each of the next two years. Briefly, then, the present value of an income stream of $1 next year and $1 the year after is $1.74.

More generally, suppose that the interest rate is i per year. Let us calculate the present value of a stream of future income denoted as $\$Y_1$ in year 1, $\$Y_2$ in year 2, $\$Y_3$ in year 3, and so on, up to $\$Y_N$ in year N. In order to achieve $\$Y_1$ in one year's time, we would need $\$Y_1/(1 + i)$ today. Similarly, in order to achieve $\$Y_2$ in two year's time, we would need $\$Y_2/(1 + i)^2$ today. When we carry out this operation for each of N years, we find the present value of the entire income stream to be equal to

$$\text{PV} = \frac{\$Y_1}{(1 + i)} + \frac{\$Y_2}{(1 + i)^2} + \frac{\$Y_3}{(1 + i)^3} + \cdots + \frac{\$Y_N}{(1 + i)^N} \qquad \textbf{(2.15)}$$

In many cases, a household, a firm, or a government must decide whether to invest $\$I_0$ today in order to receive an income stream of future $\$Y$'s. To see whether it is worthwhile to undertake the investment, one can either compare the present value of the income stream with the cost of the investment, or one can calculate the net present value (NPV) of the investment by subtracting $\$I_0$ and adding up the present value of its future income earnings:

$$\text{NPV} = -I_0 + \frac{\$Y_1}{(1 + i)} + \frac{\$Y_2}{(1 + i)^2} + \cdots + \frac{\$Y_N}{(1 + i)^N} \qquad \textbf{(2.16)}$$

If the NPV is positive, the investment is a good idea; if it is negative, it should be rejected. (We analyze investment decisions in far greater detail in later chapters.)

One special and very important case involves an investment that pays a given amount of income per period forever. Consider a bond that pays $\$Y$ per year forever (such a perpetual bond is known as a *consol*). Its present value PV today may be calculated as follows:

$$\text{PV} = \frac{\$Y}{(1 + i)} + \frac{\$Y}{(1 + i)^2} + \cdots + \frac{\$Y}{(1 + i)^N} + \cdots \qquad \textbf{(2.17)}$$

This formula is an infinite sum. The value of this infinite sum is easy to find inasmuch as the sum is a *geometric progression*. From simple algebra, we know that the following holds:

$$1 + a + a^2 + a^3 + \cdots + a^N + \cdots = \frac{1}{(1 - a)}$$

The sum in (2.17) can then be rewritten as

$$\frac{\$Y}{(1 + i)} [1 + a + a^2 + a^3 + \cdots + a^N + \cdots]$$

where $a = 1/(1 + i)$. Thus, we find that PV $= \$Y/(1 + i)[1/(1 - a)]$, with $a = 1/(1 + i)$. It is then straightforward to calculate that

$$\text{PV} = \frac{\$Y}{i} \qquad \textbf{(2.17a)}$$

2-5 THE ROLE OF EXPECTATIONS

At the time that economic agents—households, firms, the government—make intertemporal choices, they are generally uncertain about the future. A business firm contemplating an investment needs to know the future path of income that will result from the investment. But future earnings can be estimated only with considerable uncertainty. If there is a boom in the future, then the future earnings may be high; if there is a recession, then the earnings may be low. But the actual exact future state of the economy is virtually unknowable.

This is why households and firms have to formulate some *expectations* about the future in order to make most intertemporal choices. Indeed, they must often cope with complex assessments of the relative likelihoods of many different possible events—the educated guesses that households have to make about the future value of income, for example. We will denote these expectations about future income as Y^e, and Y_{+1}^e will signify the expectation of the value of Y next period that is formed in the current period (before Y_{+1} is actually known). Thus, if we say that $Y_{+1}^e = \$1,000$, it means that the economic agent expects that income next year will be $1,000. (Expectations are formed not just about income, of course, but about prices, GNP, and other variables of economic importance.)

A great debate has gone on among economists and psychologists in recent years over the ways that economic agents *actually* formulate their expectations about the future and the ways that macroeconomists should *assume* they do this in their theoretical models. Some economists believe that individuals rely on simple "rules of thumb" in forming expectations. Others believe that individuals use complicated decision-making processes to arrive at their expectations about the future.

Perhaps the simplest rule of thumb is to act as if next year is going to be like this year, a "rule" that is called *static expectations*. Formally, static expectations would be represented as the assumption that

$$Y_{+1}^e = Y \qquad \textbf{(2.18)}$$

Another simple rule of thumb that we will encounter later is that of *adaptive expectations*. In this view, individuals update their expectations about the future depending upon the extent to which their expectations about the present period turned out to be wrong. To describe this, let Y^e signify the expectation of Y in this period that *was held* as of the previous period. In that case, $(Y - Y^e)$ represents the *error* in the forecast that was made in the previous period; that is, the amount by which the forecast turned out to be wrong. Under adaptive expectations, Y_{+1}^e is formed this year by updating the expectations Y^e by a fraction Γ of the forecast error:

$$Y_{+1}^e = Y^e + \Gamma(Y - Y^e) \tag{2.19}$$

where $0 < \Gamma < 1$. By rewriting (2.19) we see that the forecast of next year's value of Y is in fact a weighted average of *last year's forecast* and *this year's actual value* of Y:

$$Y_{+1}^e = (1 - \Gamma)Y^e + \Gamma Y \tag{2.20}$$

Note that when $\Gamma = 0$, expectations are completely unchanging period to period: $Y_{+1}^e = Y^e$. When $\Gamma = 1$, expectations are "static," in that $Y_{+1}^e = Y$.

In recent years, many economists have argued, and argued persuasively, that these mechanical models of expectations are far too crude. Individuals should use more sophisticated means of forming expectations, they say, especially when high stakes are involved, as when, for example, a business must make an investment decision. These economists have argued that individuals and firms use all available information, together with what they understand about the economic model governing the economy, when they formulate their expectations of future economic variables. The general hypothesis that individuals make efficient use of all available information is known as the *rational expectations* (RE) *hypothesis.*

The assumption of RE does not, by itself, say much about the specific expectations held by economic agents. To specify actual Y_{+1}^e under the RE hypothesis, we would have to know what economic model the individual is using and just what economic information he or she has at hand. But the RE hypothesis does say several important things nonetheless. It implies, among other things, that people do incorporate readily available information into the formation of their expectations, that people do not make simple and repeated errors if the good information that will prevent such errors is publicly available, and that people's expectations should be consistent with the economic model they believe to be in effect. In later chapters, we have much more to say about the empirical content of the RE hypothesis.

2-6 SUMMARY

Macroeconomics is the study of aggregate economic behavior, and aggregate measures of economic activity are its building blocks. *Gross domestic product* is the total value of the current production of final goods and services within a national territory during a given period of time. To add up all the final goods and services, it is necessary to express them in a common unit of measure, typically in monetary units (dollars in the United States, pounds in the United Kingdom, and so on). In addition to adding up the final goods and services produced in the economy, GDP may also be found by summing up the *value added* (the market value of output minus the market value of inputs) produced in each sector of the economy. A third way to obtain GDP is to add up the *incomes* of all the factors of production used in producing domestic output.

Gross national product is the total value of income received by the domestic residents in a given period of time. The difference between GDP and GNP is the *net factor income received from abroad,* equal to the earnings of domestic residents on foreign profits, loans, and worker remittances *minus* the earnings of foreigners in the domestic economy. Whenever domestic factors of production abroad are paid more than foreign factors of production working in the domestic economy, GNP will be higher than GDP.

GNP per capita, that is, per person, is the most commonly used measure of economic development. Countries with high levels of GNP per capita are presumed to have a higher level of economic well-being than are countries with lower levels of GNP per capita. However, there is more to economic welfare than GNP per capita. First, GNP misses things. It measures output at market prices, not at the true social value of output. It also omits transactions that take place outside the money economy. Second, the economic well-being achieved by a given value of GNP depends on the purchasing power of, say, $1 in different economies. Third, GNP per capita does not take into account the degree of income inequality in an economy. In many cases, poor countries with relatively equal income distributions show higher indicators of social well-being than do richer countries with less equal incomes.

To make meaningful comparisons, it is crucial to know whether changes (or differences) in macroeconomic variables reflect changes (or differences) in the prices of goods or changes in their physical volumes. In other words, it is necessary to know whether changes are nominal or real. A 10 percent rise in GNP, for example, may result from all prices and wages increasing by 10 percent or from physical output rising by 10 percent. Since there are many goods and services in the economy, measuring aggregate price movements involves the calculation of an "average price," or *price index. Nominal GDP,* for example, is the value of production at current market prices. *Real GDP* is the value of production at the prices of a given year, known as the *base year*. The *implicit GDP price deflator* is the ratio of nominal GDP to real GDP.

A *flow* is an economic magnitude measured as a rate per unit of time. A *stock* is a magnitude measured at a point in time. The *capital stock* of the economy, for example, is the accumulated stock of residential structures, machinery, factories, and equipment that exist at a point in time. *Investment* is the flow of output in any given period that is used to maintain or to increase the capital stock. Other examples of stock-flow relationships like that between capital and investment are *saving* and *wealth,* the *current account* and the *net international investment position,* and *fiscal deficits* and the *stock of public debt*.

Many key macroeconomic issues involve choices about time. Saving, for example, involves a choice between consuming now and consuming later; it is, thus, an *intertemporal choice.* Two key building blocks in the study of intertemporal decisions are interest rates and present values. The *interest rate* is the terms at which money or goods today may be traded off for money or goods at a future date. Using interest rates, it is possible to translate a given time path of money in the future into a *present value* today.

Households, firms, and the government generally must make intertemporal choices in the face of uncertainty about the future. Thus, most intertemporal choices require economic agents to form *expectations* about the future. At the least, expectations must be formulated about future income and prices. How economic agents actually form their expectations has been a topic of much debate. Some economists argue that individuals rely on simple "rules of thumb"; others believe that they use complex decision-making processes to arrive at their expectations about the future.

The simplest rule of thumb is a belief that next year will be like this year, a rule called *static expectations*. Individuals may also update their expectations about the future based on their previous errors in forecasting, a process called *adaptive expectations*. A more sophisticated mechanism known as *rational expectations* specifies that agents make efficient use of all available information and their understanding of the economic model governing the economy in order to formulate their expectations. Empirical evidence on how people actually form their expectations is, however, not conclusive.

Key Concepts

gross domestic product
gross national product
current production
final goods
intermediate goods
value added
net factor income from abroad
circular flow of income
GNP per capita
price index
nominal GDP
real GDP
base year
implicit GDP price deflator
flows
stocks
investment

capital stock
saving
wealth
current account
net international investment
    position
fiscal deficit
public debt
intertemporal choices
interest rates
net present values
expectations formation
    mechanisms
static expectations
adaptive expectations
rational expectations

Problems and Questions

1. Should the value of the following transactions be included as part of GDP? Why?

   a. A consumer pays for a meal at a restaurant.

   b. A company buys an old building.

   c. A supplier sells computer chips to a firm that makes personal computers.

   d. A consumer buys a car from a dealer.

2. A factory that produced televisions closes this year. How would GDP be affected? How would this change be detected when using the expenditure method to calculate GDP? The value-added method? The domestic income method?

3. What would happen to the discrepancy between GDP and domestic income if the rate of depreciation of the stock of capital in the economy rose? Why?

4. During the late 1970s and early 1980s, many Latin American countries became highly indebted. How would this affect their net factor payments? Which was larger in those countries during that period, GDP or GNP?

5. Does a higher GNP per capita necessarily imply higher welfare? What other elements should be taken into account to evaluate economic well-being?

6. Consider a simple economy with only three goods. The market price of each good is $P_1 = 5$, $P_2 = 10$, and $P_3 = 15$. The production (and consumption) of each good during 1990 was $Q_1 = 20$, $Q_2 = 25$, and $Q_3 = 10$.

  a. What is the value of nominal GDP?

  b. Construct a consumer price index using as weights the share of each good in total consumption.

  c. Assume that in 1991 prices rise to $P_1 - 6$, $P_2 - 12$, and $P_3 - 17$ and quantities produced (and consumed) go to $Q_1 = 21$, $Q_2 = 27$, and $Q_3 = 11$. Calculate the value of nominal GDP and real GDP, using 1990 as the base year. What is inflation, as measured by the GDP deflator? What is the real rate of growth of the economy?

  d. What does your answer tell you about the importance of using price deflators?

7. Are the following economic variables stocks or flows?

  a. The income of a blue-collar worker.

  b. The wealth of that same worker.

  c. The net factor payments to the rest of the world.

  d. The value of all the houses in the economy.

8. Suppose that the stock of capital in the economy is the same as last year's. Assuming a positive rate of depreciation, was there any gross investment in the economy? Was there any net investment?

9. Consider an investment project that costs $100 to get started and yields $50 for the next three years and then stops being productive.

  a. If the interest rate is 10 percent, what is the present value of the project?

  b. How does your answer change if the interest rate rises to 15 percent? Why?

10. What is the importance of expectations for economic behavior?

11. "Static expectations is a special case of adaptive expectations." Discuss.

chapter 3

Output Determination: Introducing Aggregate Supply and Aggregate Demand

Every economy is subject to fluctuations in employment, unemployment, industrial production, and GNP. In some years, output falls sharply and unemployment soars; in other years, output booms and unemployment falls steeply. What causes these fluctuations? Can the government take actions to stabilize the economy and maintain high levels of employment? These are the issues that we introduce in this chapter and then examine more completely later, in Part IV.

Economic fluctuations have long been a central concern of macroeconomics. Indeed, one can say that macroeconomics as a distinct field grew up as the study of output and employment fluctuations in the wake of the Great Depression in the 1930s. The horrendous human cost of the Great Depression, during which unemployment rates reached more than 20 percent of the labor force throughout the industrial world, left economists deeply puzzled. Classical theory had promised that labor markets would adjust to preserve the full employment of labor. Why did this not happen? The greatest contribution to understanding the Great Depression, and the starting point of modern macroeconomics, came with the publication of *The General Theory of Employment, Interest and Money* by John Maynard Keynes.

Much of macroeconomics has been an extended debate over Keynes's theories. And if two general truths can be stated, they are that Keynes made fundamental contributions to our understanding of output and employment fluctuations, but that the "general theory" was not general enough. For example, any full account of output and employment fluctuations must involve a careful examination of the *institutional* features of the labor market in the economy involved. Keynes's theories were appropriate for the labor markets of the 1930s which they described. For different times and places, however, Keynes's basic theoretical findings require important modifications or even fundamental changes. Also, Keynes and his followers put great stress on certain kinds of shocks—shifts in investment demand by businesses, for example, and changes in government spending—as the key determinants of economic fluctuations. More recently, economists have recognized that other kinds of shocks, often coming from the supply side of the economy, can be important. One type of supply shock is a change in the relative price of a key input in the production process. The large swings in world oil prices since 1973 have been the most evident supply shocks in the world economy in the past two decades.

3-1 MACROECONOMICS AS THE STUDY OF ECONOMIC FLUCTUATIONS

To get started on the study of output and employment fluctuations, we must discuss several key concepts. The first is the unemployment rate itself. The "unemployment rate" is a measure of the total number of unemployed persons as a proportion of the labor force. The simplicity of this definition is deceptive, however. Who is "unemployed"? Someone who is actively looking for a job? A jobless person too discouraged to look for work? A person who works a few hours per week at odd jobs but would like to work on a more steady basis? We shall see that seemingly simple concepts can in fact become quite problematic.

When employment fluctuates, so too does output, since output is produced using labor inputs. Just as we measure the extent to which employment falls short of the full-employment level, we also can measure the extent to which output falls short of the level that would be produced if all labor were fully employed. We use the concept of *potential output* to represent the level of output that the economy can reach when all productive factors, especially labor, are at their fully employed levels. Because some unemployment of labor and other factors of production is normal, *current output* is generally lower than its potential. The *output gap* measures the difference between potential and actual output.

These concepts have a very significant practical implication. Economic performance is not only measured in terms of the general trend of output, but also in terms of whether the output gap is increasing or decreasing. Arthur M. Okun, chairman of the U.S. Council of Economic Advisors under President Lyndon Johnson, was a leading analyst of the output gap. In studying the relationship between unemployment and output, Okun found with great regularity that a reduction of unemployment of 1 percent of the labor force in the United States was associated with a rise in GNP and fall in the output gap of 3 percent. Known today as Okun's law, this relationship has proven to be quite robust in the United States and applicable in other countries as well, though with a different factor of proportionality between unemployment and output.

Within macroeconomic analysis, two types of economic fluctuations are of particular interest. Long and sustained deviations of unemployment from historical averages are certainly one type. Cases of a continuing period of intractable high unemployment include that of the Great Depression in the 1930s, that of Western Europe from 1975 to the late 1980s, and that of Latin America in the 1980s. These cases are illustrated in Figures 3-1a through 3-1c.

Of equal interest are synchronized shifts in important macroeconomic variables around a trend, a phenomenon known as the *business cycle*. Unlike periods of sustained unemployment, business cycles represent shorter-term fluctuations of output and employment, typically lasting three to four

Figure 3-1a
Unemployment in the United States, 1925–1945

(From U.S. Historical Statistics, *Series D-85–86.)*

Figure 3-1b
Unemployment Rate in Europe, 1965–1985

(From Organization of Economic Cooperation and Development, Economic Outlook.*)*

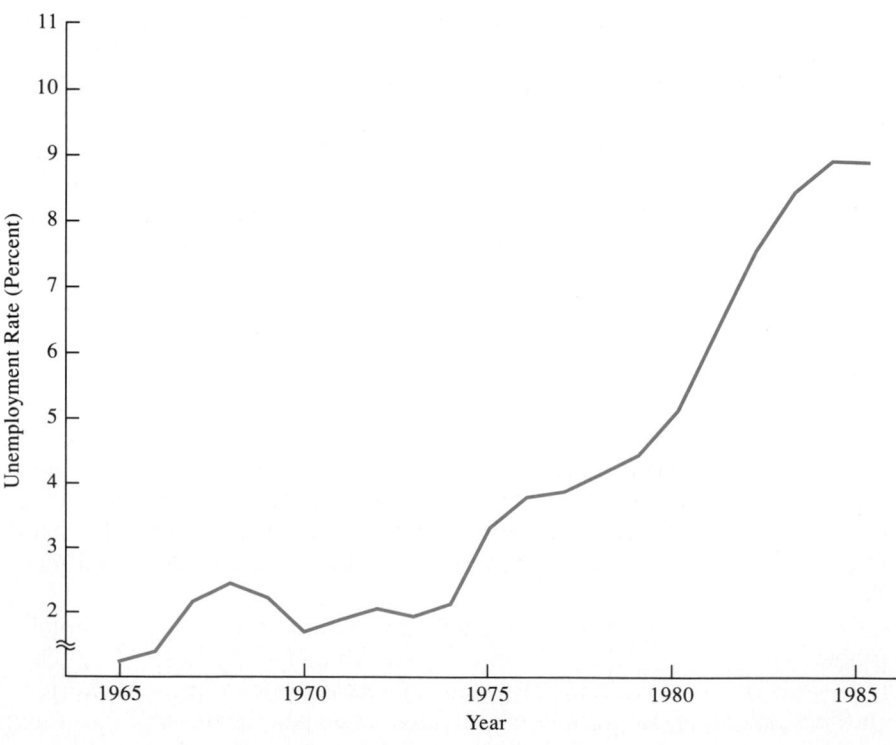

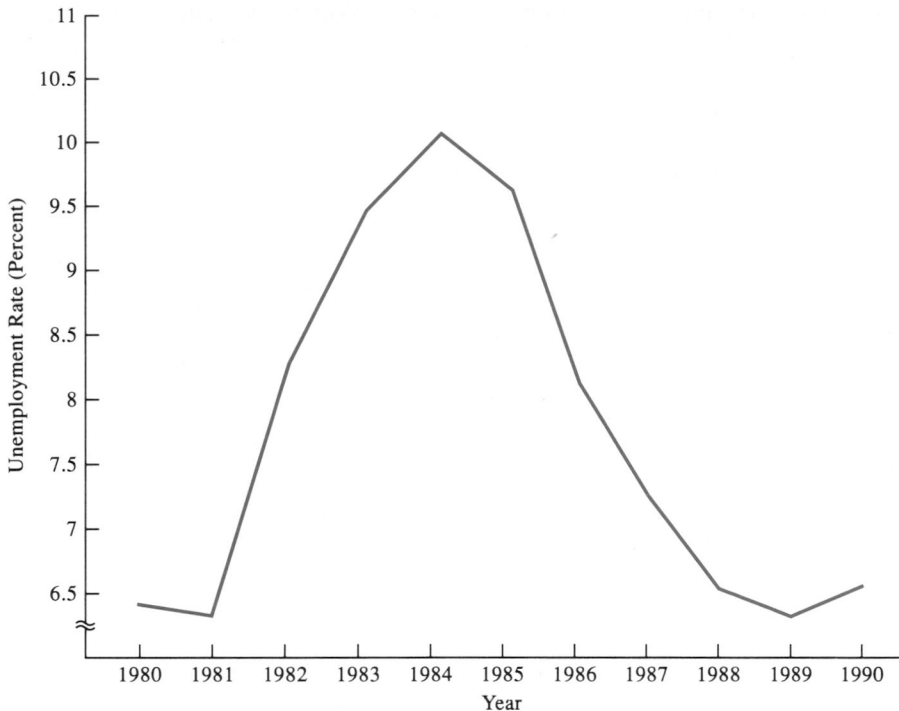

Figure 3-1c
Unemployment Rate in Latin America, 1980–1990

(From ECLA, Preliminary Overview of the Economy of Latin America and the Caribbean, *United Nations, New York, 1990.)*

years. A key feature of business cycles is that important macroeconomic variables—output, prices, investment, business profits, and various monetary variables—tend to move together in a systematic fashion. This basic characteristic of business cycles was carefully documented in path-breaking studies by Wesley Claire Mitchell, who undertook his work as an associate of the National Bureau of Economic Research (NBER), the institution that is still the official arbiter of business-cycle trends in the United States.[1]

Much of modern macroeconomic research is devoted to the study of business-cycle fluctuations. Business-cycle research is, in fact, an area of great controversy. Despite heated debates in recent years, there is no single shared paradigm for explaining these cycles, but rather several different ones: the Keynesian paradigm in its many variations, the new classical paradigm, and the monetarist paradigm, to name only the most important schools of thought. These labels can, however, hide more than they reveal, since important overlap exists among these different approaches.

In this chapter, we begin our discussion of macroeconomic fluctuations and consider the major theories about them. Then, in Parts II and III, we put the issue of output fluctuations aside in order to develop the building blocks

---

[1] Mitchell described his key findings in the book *What Happens During Business Cycles?* (New York: National Bureau of Economic Research, 1951). To this day, the National Bureau of Economic Research is the organization that judges whether the U.S. economy is in a recession or boom and decides on the specific dates of business cycle peaks and troughs.

of macroeconomics—consumption, saving, investment, and the monetary system. In fact, it is easier to discuss these subjects under the unrealistic assumption of full employment. In Part IV, we return to the topic of output fluctuations in much greater detail, using the building blocks that we have developed.

The major theories of macroeconomic fluctuations rely on ideas of aggregate supply and aggregate demand, to which we now turn.

3-2　THE DETERMINATION OF AGGREGATE SUPPLY

Aggregate supply is the total amount of output that firms and households choose to provide, given the pattern of wages and prices in the economy. Firms decide on how much output they want to supply in order to maximize profits, taking into account the price of output, the costs of inputs, the stock of capital, and the available production technology. Households also make a supply decision, how much labor to supply, based on the level of the real wage.

In practice, optimal supply decisions can be very complicated. For example, a firm might decide on how much to produce based not only on current prices, but also on expectations about future prices since some of today's production will be sold in the future. Similarly, households might make their labor-supply decisions on the basis of expected future wages as well as current wages. In the discussion that follows, we largely ignore these complications, focusing instead on the case in which supply decisions are based entirely on current wages and prices.

The concept of aggregate supply is also complicated by the fact that there are many kinds of goods in the economy, produced by a very large number of firms and households. Aggregating all these various producers to arrive at a concept of aggregate supply involves statistical issues that are quite complex. As we established in Chapter 2, our theoretical framework ignores these complications and assumes that the economy produces a single output. (Later, in Chapter 21, we add a bit of realism by distinguishing two types of domestically produced goods, tradable goods and nontradable goods.)

With these simplifying assumptions in mind, we now turn to the aggregate supply curve for the economy which describes the relationship between aggregate output and the price level. We start with a *production function* for an individual firm.

The Production Function

Economies are composed of a large number of firms that use capital (K) and labor (L) to produce output (Q). The capital of the firm is its factory, its equipment, and its inventories of goods. We summarize the total capital by a single variable, K. We also assume that the level of technology, denoted by τ, determines how much output is produced for a given level of K and L. A rise in τ, then, indicates some technological improvement in the production process that results in higher output. For simplicity, we also assume there is only one standard production function which applies to each firm in the economy,

$$Q = Q(K, L, \tau) \qquad \text{(3.1)}$$
$$+ \quad + \quad +$$

where the plus sign below each variable indicates that each has a positive influence on output (a minus sign would indicate a negative effect).

In equation (3.1), output is a function of the capital and labor used in production and of the state of technology. For example, the production of cars at General Motors depends on the machines, buildings, and inventories that the company has; the total number of employees and the number of hours that they work; and the technological knowledge built up inside the company.

Our time horizon is the short run (say, a period of two to three years), during which time we can suppose that the economy's capital stock is fixed at the level determined by past investments. During this short-run time frame, all output fluctuations must reflect changes in labor input because the level of the capital input is unchanging.

The production function has two important characteristics. First, an increase in the amount of any input will make output go up. The marginal productivity of labor ($MPL = \Delta Q/\Delta L$), that is, the rise in output resulting from an increase of labor by one unit, is positive. So is the marginal productivity of capital ($MPK = \Delta Q/\Delta K$). Second, we assume that the marginal productivity of each factor declines as more of that factor is used with a fixed amount of the other factor. Take, for example, an automobile stamping plant. If only five workers are available per machine, the hiring of another worker might add enormously to output. If the manager keeps adding labor without increasing the number of machines, however, she will discover that the increase in total output generated by each new worker becomes smaller in every round.

We can graph the level of output as a function of the amount of labor input (L) for a given amount of K, as shown in Figure 3-2. Notice how the two assumptions about the production function affect the shape of the curve. The slope of the curve at any point measures MPL, the marginal product of labor, because the slope, shown as $\Delta Q/\Delta L$, measures the increase of output that results from a small increase in labor input. The fact that the curve has a positive slope reflects that the marginal productivity of labor is positive; the fact that the slope gets less steep as more labor gets used reflects the declining marginal productivity of labor. Thus, ($\Delta Q/\Delta L$) at point B is less than ($\Delta Q/\Delta L$) at point A.

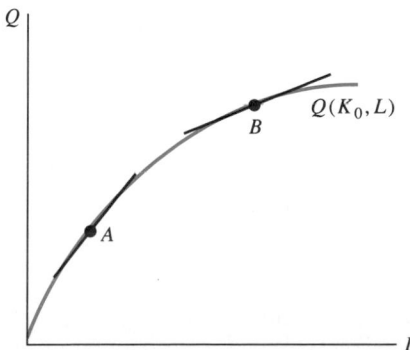

Figure 3-2
The Production Function with
Variable Labor Input

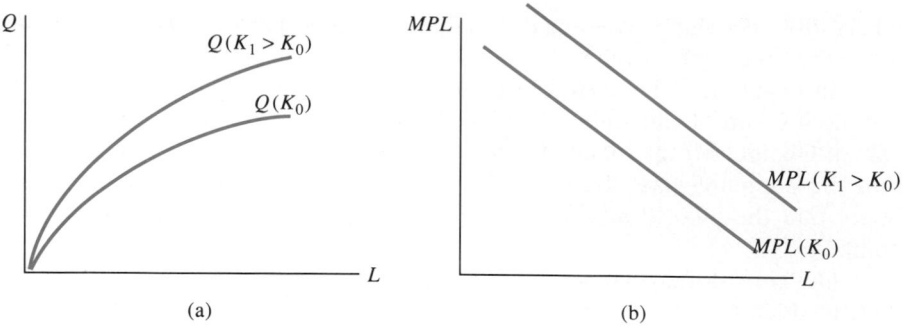

Figure 3-3
Effects of an Increase in the Capital Stock: (a) The Production Function, (b) the Marginal Productivity of Labor

In Figure 3-3b, the *MPL* is shown as a function of the amount of labor. This schedule is drawn for a given amount of capital and a given state of technology. What would happen if, suddenly, more capital became available to the production process? Because capital itself has a positive marginal product, an increase in K would shift the output curve upward, as in Figure 3-3a. For any given L, more output would be produced if the input of K were to rise. Moreover, we also expect that for any given level of L, higher K leads to an increase in the marginal productivity of L. Thus, the *MPL* schedule in Figure 3-3b also shifts upward when K shifts up.

So far, we have concluded that the amount of output produced may vary in the short run as firms use more or less labor in the production process. Next, we address the question of how much labor firms *will* use.

The Demand for Labor and the Output Supply Function

In Figure 3-4, we show the *MPL* as a function of L. This graph can be used to find the level of labor input that a profit-maximizing firm will wish to use. To see this, let us consider how a profit-maximizing firm decides how much labor to hire. We suppose that the firm sells its output for a price P in the output market, and that it hires labor at the wage w in the labor market. Each

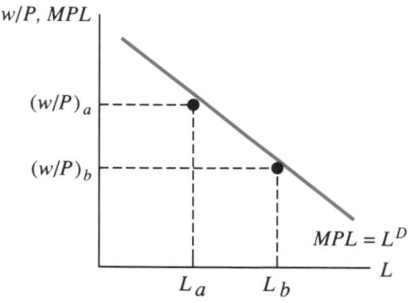

Figure 3-4
The Demand for Labor: The Marginal Productivity of Labor Schedule

additional increment of labor ΔL raises the labor costs of the firm by the amount $w\Delta L$, where w is the wage rate. The extra unit of labor generates ΔQ in additional output and, therefore, $P\Delta Q$ in additional revenue. Thus, it pays to hire the labor as long as the extra cost, $w\Delta L$, is less than or equal to the additional value of output, that is, as long as $w\Delta L < P\Delta Q$, or as long as $(w/P) < \Delta Q/\Delta L$. But, of course, $\Delta Q/\Delta L$ equals the *MPL* of labor. *The firm should, therefore, hire labor until the marginal product of labor input equals the real wage, w/P.*[2]

In this way, we can determine the amount of labor that the firm would choose to hire at each level of the real wage. Using Figure 3-4, if the real wage equals $(w/P)_a$, then the firm chooses L_a as the amount of labor input. If w/P equals $(w/P)_b$, then the firm chooses L_b as the amount of labor input. Thus, we see that the *MPL* schedule is, in fact, the demand schedule for labor. Note that since the *MPL* curve is downward sloping, so too is the demand for labor, in other words, the higher (w/P), the lower the level of labor that the firm will want to hire.

Figures 3-2, 3-3, and 3-4 are drawn for a given level of the capital stock and for a given technology. If capital increases, the level of output associated with any amount of labor also goes up, as illustrated in Figure 3-3a. The marginal product of labor also rises for any given level of L, as shown by the shift in the *MPL* schedule upward and to the right in Figure 3-3b. The same effect also occurs when some technological improvement raises the efficiency of the capital stock (which is like having more capital in place).

We can summarize these findings by writing the demand for labor as a function of the real wage (with a negative relationship) and the levels of capital and technology (with positive relationships):

$$L^D = L^D(w/P, K, \tau) \qquad \textbf{(3.2)}$$
$$ - \;\; + \;\; +$$

Using the labor-demand schedule, we can now derive an output supply schedule which shows the amount of output the profit-maximizing firm will supply at each level of w/P, K, and τ. We simply rewrite the production function (3.1) using (3.2), to find

$$Q^S = Q^S[L^D(w/P, K, \tau), K, \tau] \qquad \textbf{(3.3)}$$
$$ - \;\; + \;\; + \;\; + \;\; +$$

Note that Q^S is a negative function of w/P for an "indirect" reason: according to the production function, higher w/P means lower L^D, and lower L^D means lower output. Note also that Q^S is a positive function of K and τ, for direct and indirect reasons. Directly, higher K leads to higher output via the production function; indirectly, higher K leads to a higher demand for L^D and this also raises output. (A technological improvement works the same

---

[2] Notice that what matters here is the nominal wage in terms of the price of output, w/P. This ratio is sometimes called the *product wage*, since it measures the wage in units of output. Sometimes it is useful to measure the wage relative to the consumer price index P_C rather than the output price, resulting in the ratio w/P_C. This alternative ratio is sometimes called the *real consumption wage*. In our simple model, there is only one output good, so that P equals P_C. In practice, however, the price of output could readily differ from the price of consumption, especially if part of consumption is imported rather than produced by domestic firms. In such a case, the product wage and the real consumption wage will not be the same.

way.) Equation (3.3) can be written more simply, to show that output supply is a negative function of w/P and a positive function of K and τ:

$$Q^S = Q^S\,(w/P,\ K,\ \tau) \qquad\qquad \textbf{(3.4)}$$
$$-\ \ +\ \ +$$

Note that in (3.3) and (3.4) we write output as Q^S rather than as Q, to signify that this is a *supply* equation, meaning that it describes the output the firm wants to supply if it is to maximize profits. Because it refers to profit-maximizing behavior, it differs from (3.1), the production function, which expresses a merely technical relationship between inputs and output.

The Supply of Labor

The next step in determining aggregate supply is to derive the supply schedule for labor, L^S, as a function of the real wage that households receive for work.

We start with a simple labor-supply decision in which the household must choose between supplying labor and enjoying leisure, the so-called "labor-leisure decision." The day has only 24 hours, and every hour more that is devoted to work is one hour less that can be devoted to leisure; thus households must choose how to divide their time between the two. In real life, the labor-supply decision is far more complicated. A worker's time may be divided not only between work and leisure but also among many other activities—on-the-job training, education, and searching for another job, to mention only a few.

For this analysis, however, we suppose a very simple situation in which a worker must choose only between labor and leisure and in which he consumes all his wage earnings, which are his only source of income. We also suppose that he can choose to work any number of hours per day, not an entirely realistic assumption, but a convenient one. In practice, time is not so flexible. Workers might have to choose between a standard eight-hour day, a standard day plus some overtime, half days, or no work at all.

People receive utility from consuming both goods and leisure, so our utility function should show the utility level as positively related to the consumption level, C, and negatively related to the amount of time the worker devotes to work, L, remembering that higher labor time means less leisure time:

$$UL = UL(C,\ L) \qquad\qquad \textbf{(3.5)}$$
$$+\ \ -$$

Equation (3.5) indicates that people's utility increases when consumption rises and decreases when they spend more time at work.

An indifference curve will show all the combinations of C and L that produce a particular level of utility, and a map of these curves between consumption and labor appears in Figure 3-5a. In this case, the indifference curves have a positive slope because labor produces "disutility." Suppose that a worker is at point A in the indifference curve UL_0; if she increases her hours of work by ΔL, then consumption will have to go up by ΔC_0 in order for her to remain indifferent to the original position at A. Note also that higher indifference curves are associated with higher utility. Utility on the indifference curve UL_2 is higher than utility on the indifference curve UL_1.

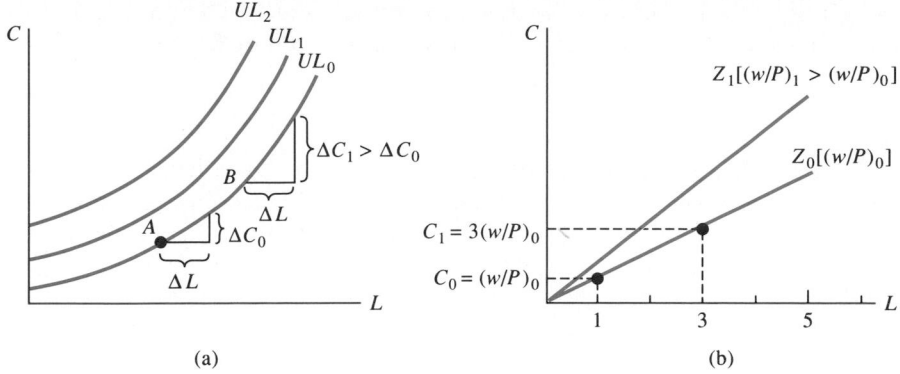

Figure 3-5
(a) The Indifference Map; (b) the Wage-Consumption Line

As we move in the northeast direction *along* the indifference curve U_0, a given increase in labor services ΔL must be matched by an ever-increasing amount of consumption ΔC in order to keep the worker at the same utility level. In Figures 3-5a and b, ΔC_1 is greater than ΔC_0, or, to put this another way, the slope at point B is steeper than the slope at point A.[3] Here is the reason. As L increases, there is less and less time left over for leisure. The worker is less and less eager to give up her increasingly scarce leisure time in return for more consumption. Therefore, at a given utility level, each incremental cutback in leisure must be balanced by an ever-greater increase in consumption.

How much labor and consumption workers actually choose depends both on the utility function (as summarized by the indifference map) and on the real wage level. We can specify the set of consumption-leisure possibilities available to the worker by recognizing that the level of consumption is simply given by the wage earnings, $C = (w/P)L$. Thus, in Figure 3-5b, the straight line Z, with slope w/P, shows the consumption and labor choices open to the worker. The Z line starts at the origin, since if a household works no hours, it has no income, and thus cannot consume. A rise in the real wage clearly causes a rotation of the Z line to a steeper slope.

The equilibrium amount of labor supply is found by superimposing the preferences, represented by the map of indifference curves, onto the wage-consumption line. For each real wage, workers will attempt to reach the highest possible indifference curve. The equilibrium is then the point of tangency between the corresponding Z line and an indifference curve. If the real wage is $(w/P)_0$, then workers will want to supply L_0 labor services, which will enable them to consume C_0, as shown in Figure 3-6a.

We can now derive a labor supply curve showing how labor supply varies with different levels of the real wage. Suppose that the real wage increases to $(w/P)_1$. With higher hourly pay, workers will be able to reach a higher indifference curve. The relevant Z line for $(w/P)_1$ is Z_1; thus, workers

---

[3] Technically, the *marginal rate of substitution* between consumption and leisure, which is measured by the slope of the indifference curve at a given point, increases as leisure decreases (and L increases).

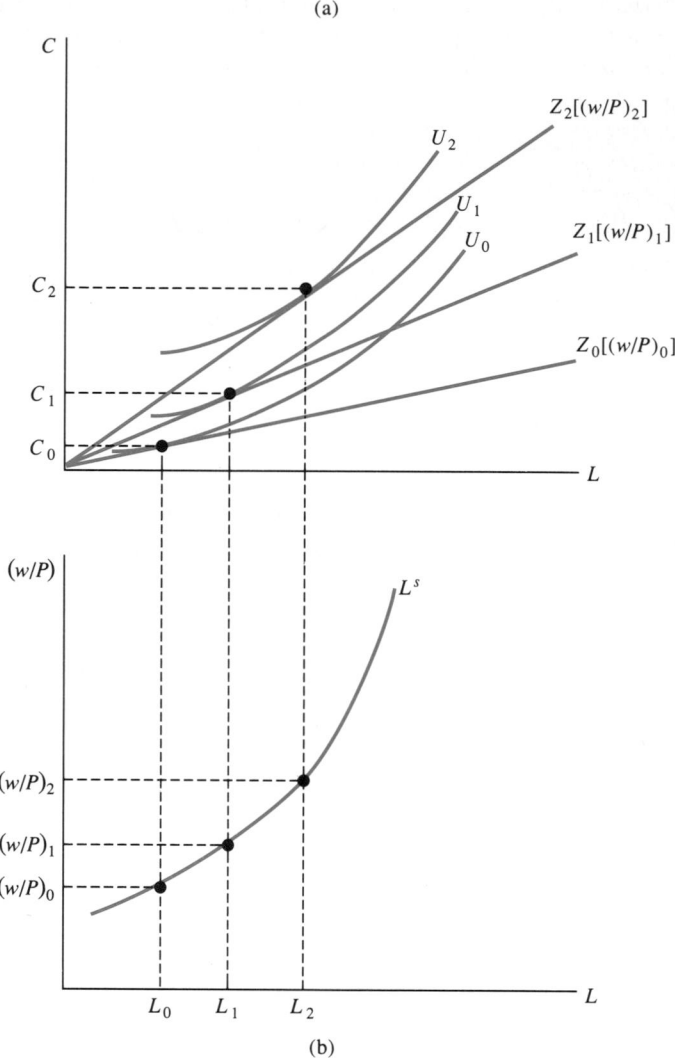

Figure 3-6
(a) Effects of Real Wage Changes in the Amount of
Labor Services Supplied; (b) the Labor-Supply Curve

can reach indifference curve UL_1, and the desired supply of labor services is L_1. Furthermore, if the real wage rises to $(w/P)_2$, then the Z line is Z_2 and the equilibrium L is L_2. Figure 3-6b plots the hours of labor supplied as the real wage increases, using the information provided by the analysis in Figure 3-6a. As described in this figure, labor supply is upward sloping: a higher real wage provokes an increase in the amount of labor that workers want to supply. This phenomenon may be expressed as follows:

$$L^S = L^S(w/P) \tag{3.6}$$
$$+$$

Somewhat surprisingly, perhaps, higher wages do not always lead to a higher labor supply. They may, in fact, result in a *smaller* supply of labor or have *no* effect on labor supply. This is because two forces are at work when real wages increase, a substitution effect and an income effect, and the latter works to reduce labor supply when real wages increase. A *substitution effect* occurs because higher wages make leisure time "more expensive"; that is, each hour of leisure represents a greater amount of forgone consumption of goods when the real wage goes up. With leisure more expensive, households "substitute" away from it and choose longer working hours.

On the other hand, an *income effect* occurs because when w/P goes up households are richer and can afford to choose more leisure, a desired good. For a given amount of L, higher w/P means that a larger amount of consumption is possible. By the same token, the original amount of consumption can now be achieved by a smaller number of working hours. If the household has a target level of consumption spending, for example, it can afford to *reduce* working hours when w/P goes up because it can reach the target with fewer hours of work.

Thus, the effect of a rise in wages on the supply of labor is theoretically ambiguous: the substitution effect tends to increase L, the income effect tends to decrease L. The relative influence of these two effects depends on household preferences. Empirical studies, however, tend to support the idea of an upward-sloping labor supply curve, like that shown in Figure 3-6b, thereby suggesting that the substitution effect dominates the income effect. Jerry Hausman of MIT has found a significant positive response of the labor supply to the real wage net of taxes for the United States.[4] A similar qualitative effect has been reported for Sweden, where increases in tax rates on labor income, that is, reductions in the net-of-tax wage for a given gross wage, have provoked a substantial negative response in the supply of labor.[5] In what follows, then, we shall assume that the labor supply is a positive function of the after-tax real wage.

3-3 THE CLASSICAL APPROACH TO AGGREGATE SUPPLY

We have already derived the aggregate supply *function*, shown in equation (3.4), the demand for labor (3.2), and the supply of labor (3.5). Now we take an important step, combining these equations and summarizing the results in an *aggregate supply curve* which describes the relationship between the supply of output and the price level. The shape of this curve remains a matter of much controversy, in large part because it depends heavily on what assumptions we make about the labor market, assumptions that are themselves hotly contested. We start first with the classical approach; then we turn to the Keynesian approach.

The simplest version of the classical approach assumes that, for any price level, the nominal wage is fully flexible and adjusts to keep the supply of labor and the demand for labor equilibrated. Thus, the real wage is determined so as to clear the labor market. Labor is always fully employed, in the

---

[4] See, for example, his article "Taxes and the Labor Supply," in Alan Auerbach and Martin Feldstein, eds., *Handbook of Public Economics* (New York: Elsevier Science, 1985). Hausman's work is discussed in more detail in Chapter 7.

[5] Charles E. Stuart, "Swedish Tax Rates, Labor Supply and Tax Revenues," *Journal of Political Economy*, October 1981.

precise sense that firms want to hire as much labor, L^D, as workers want to supply, L^S, at the real wage set in the marketplace.

This classical labor-market setting can be graphed quite simply. Figure 3-7b shows the labor market clearing at the point of intersection between labor demand and labor supply. This point of intersection determines the equilibrium level of labor, which we label as L_f to denote the "full-employment" level. The equilibrium real wage is $(w/P)_f$. Given L_f, the production function in Figure 3-7a determines the full-employment level of output, which we denote Q_f.

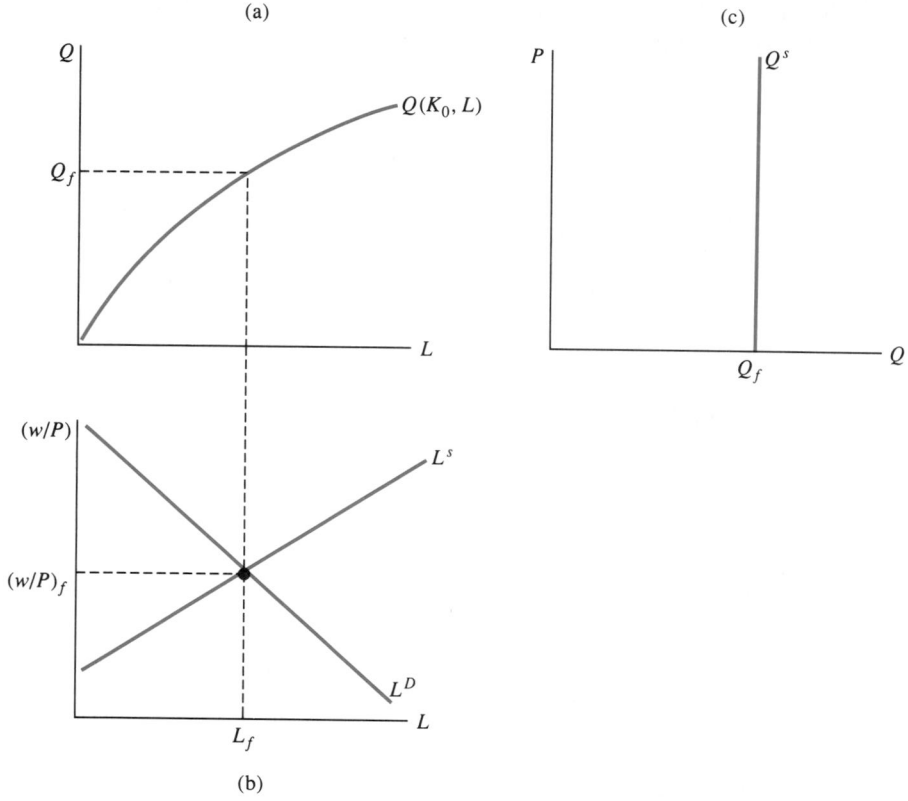

Figure 3-7

The Classical Case: (a) The Production Function, (b) the Labor Market Equilibrium, and (c) the Aggregate Supply Schedule

Deriving the Aggregate Supply Curve

Now we have enough information to draw the aggregate supply curve. The question is: How does the supply of aggregate output respond when the price level increases? To answer this question in a formal way, we use equations (3.2), (3.4), and (3.5), taking P as given and solving for Q. Then we vary P to see how Q changes.

As P rises, there tends to be excess demand in the labor market if the nominal wage remains unchanged (a lower real wage would result, causing a rise in L^D and a fall in L^S). But given that wages are perfectly flexible, the nominal wage will rise by the same amount as the price level in order to reestablish the market-clearing real wage, $(w/P)_f$. Thus, the real wage remains unchanged, as does the equilibrium level of employment, L_f. Clearly, the supply of output also remains unchanged. The fundamental result, then, is that in the classical model, the real wage is given by the equilibrium of the labor market, and if nothing disturbs the demand or the supply of labor, the level of output remains unchanged. For any given price level, the aggregate supply of the economy is the same, Q_f. Therefore, the aggregate supply curve is a straight line drawn at the full-employment level of output, as in Figure 3-7c.

Formally, the classical case can be reduced to just two equations—the aggregate supply function (3.4) and a wage equation:

$$Q^S = Q^S(w/P,\ K,\ \tau) \qquad\qquad\qquad \textbf{(3.4)}$$
$$- \ \ + \ \ +$$

$$w = P\bar{w}_f \qquad\qquad\qquad\qquad \textbf{(3.7)}$$

The wage equation (3.7), which describes the equilibrium in the labor market, guarantees that w/P is equal to $\bar{w}_f$. (The bar over w_f signifies that the wage is fixed at the market-clearing level.) According to the classical approach, the aggregate supply of the economy can change with any shifts in the labor-supply or labor-demand schedules. Consider the case in which the economy experiences an increase in its stock of capital. A higher amount of capital increases the marginal product of labor at any given level of L, and thus causes a rightward shift in the labor demand schedule, as shown in Figure 3-8b. In the new equilibrium, employment increases to L_{f1} and the real wage to $(w/P)_1$. Now, the higher amount of labor services and the increased capital stock shift the equilibrium amount of output to Q_{f1}, the new full-employment level of output. This provokes a shift in the aggregate supply curve to Q_1^S in Figure 3-8c.

Notice that in this exercise the increased demand for labor causes a rise in the real wage, which has a dampening effect on output. Now suppose for a moment that real wages did not increase, which would occur if the labor supply curve were perfectly elastic, that is, if workers were willing to supply any amount of labor at the wage $(w/P)_0$. In this case, employment would increase to L_{f2}, output would move to Q_{f2}, and the new aggregate supply curve would be Q_2^S.

Unemployment in the Classical Approach

One problem with the simple classical approach is that in theory the economy is always at full employment, despite the fact that unemployment is an obvious phenomenon in actual economies. How do classical economists explain this apparent contradiction?

They offer a variety of amendments to the basic model. One amendment allows for the fact that some people may choose voluntarily to be unemployed, at least for short periods of time, such as when a worker quits one job and is searching for another. A second amendment emphasizes that various forces in the labor market—laws, institutions, traditions—may prevent the real wage from moving to its full-employment level. If the real wage is stuck above the full-employment level, then unemployment results. Be-

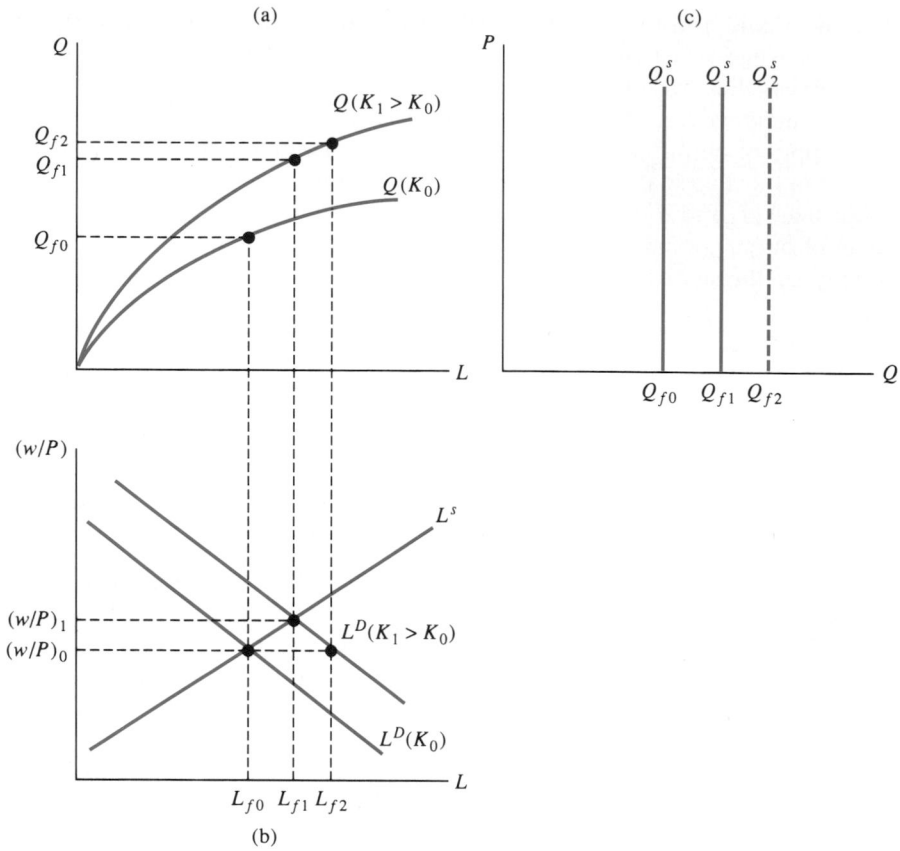

Figure 3-8
The Classical Case with an Increase in the Capital Stock: (a) The Production Function, (b) the Labor Market Equilibrium, and (c) the Aggregate Supply Schedule

cause this latter explanation has been a central argument of classical economists, this kind of unemployment is often called ''classical unemployment.''

Let us use our graphical apparatus to represent a case of classical unemployment. Suppose that the real wage is stuck at $(w/P)_u$, above the market-clearing level, as shown in Figure 3-9b. At that wage, the quantity of labor demanded by firms is L_u^D, while the supply of labor is L_u^S, so that there is an excess supply of labor in the amount of $(L_u^S - L_u^D)$. This gap between labor supply and demand constitutes unemployment in the classical framework. Firms will choose to hire L_u^D units of labor, which results in the level of output Q_u. If the real wage is stuck at $(w/P)_u$, so that increases in P lead to increases of w by the same proportion, then, as in the classical case with full employment, the aggregate supply schedule will be vertical. This will occur, however, only at a level of output Q_u which is below the full-employment level, as shown in Figure 3-9c. The *output gap* (which we mentioned at the beginning of the chapter) is the difference between the actual output, Q_u, and potential output, Q_f, and so is equal to $Q_f - Q_u$. Formally, the supply

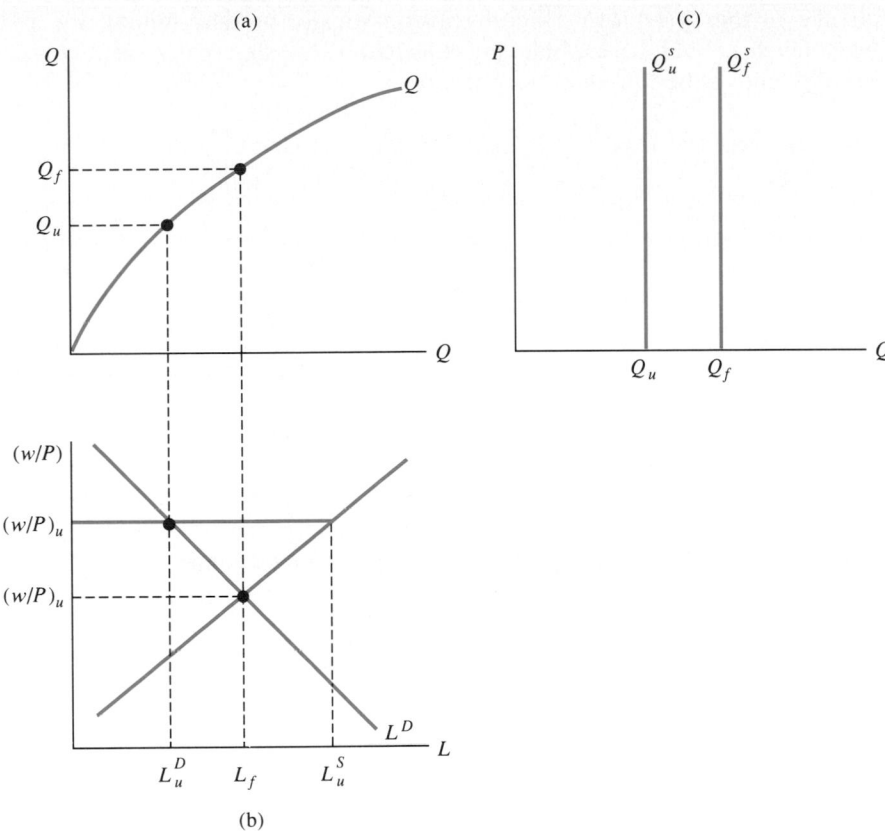

Figure 3-9
Unemployment in the Classical Case: (a) The Production Function, (b) the
Labor Market Equilibrium, and (c) the Aggregate Supply Schedule

curve is found as the solution to two equations:

$$Q^S = Q^S(w/P, K, \tau) \qquad\qquad \textbf{(3.4)}$$
$${-}\ \ {+}\ \ {+}$$

$$w = P\bar{w}_u \qquad\qquad \textbf{(3.8)}$$

This is the same system that is used to describe the full-employment case,
except that $\bar{w}_u$ replaces w_f.

Real wages might be stuck at excessively high, nonmarket-clearing
levels for many reasons. Legally established minimum wages (a feature of
most economies) may be set above the market-clearing wage. Unemployment insurance payments might be so generous that people refuse to accept
a wage below w_u. Powerful labor unions may force wages for their members
above levels at which unemployed people outside of the union would be
willing to work. In economies where wages are indexed to prices, the nominal wage is linked mechanically to the price level by a numerical rule. In
some important historical examples, the indexation clause for an entire
economy has provided that the nominal wage shall be adjusted fully for any

change in the price level, thereby automatically predetermining the real wage level. In such cases, indexing rules can result in a real wage level that is stuck above the full-employment rate.

3-4 THE KEYNESIAN APPROACH TO AGGREGATE SUPPLY

The Keynesian model of unemployment is built on the notion that nominal wages and prices do not adjust quickly to maintain labor-market equilibrium. This model differs from the classical unemployment model in its focus on nominal rigidities rather than real rigidities. The Keynesian model has many variants. Keynes himself put most stress on the rigidity of nominal wages. Others, also considered Keynesians, put the emphasis on nominal price rigidity. Such different assumptions have different consequences for the explanation of unemployment.

In the rest of the chapter, we will speak of "rigid" or "sticky" nominal wages and prices. Obviously, nominal wages and prices are not completely rigid in any economy. Keynes himself recognized that nominal wages would adjust to labor-market disequilibrium over time. But Keynes's point was that the adjustment would be slow, too slow, in fact, to guarantee that labor would always remain fully employed. In the static Keynesian model we are about to consider, we will simply assume that w or P is fixed. When we take up dynamic models in later chapters, we will explicitly model the dynamic adjustments of w and P to shocks hitting the economy.

Sticky Wages

Among the several features of actual labor markets that may contribute to nominal wage stickiness, one feature provides the most straightforward explanation: *long-term labor contracts*. Unions normally negotiate wage contracts with employers at regular intervals of time, in many countries once every year, and in some cases for longer periods. (U.S. unions typically bargain for three-year wage agreements.) These long-term contracts generally stipulate either a level of nominal wages that will remain in effect throughout the contract period or a preset formula for adjusting the nominal wage during the length of the contract. In countries with a history of very high inflation, the length of contracts tends to be shorter. For example, in Brazil, contract length declined in recent years, in a clear response to higher rates of inflation. Price increases had been accelerating since 1973, and by 1979 they reached almost 80 percent in the year. At that point, Congress approved a shortening of contract periods from one year to six months. The inflation rate continued escalating to new heights during the 1980s, and in late 1985, contracts started to be revised every three months.[6]

Suppose now that the nominal wage of a firm is fixed by a labor contract at the level $\bar{w}$. Suppose also that once the nominal wage is fixed, workers at the firm will supply all the labor demanded by the firm—even to the point, if necessary, of working in excess of the desired labor supply

---

[6] See Eliana Cardoso and Rudiger Dornbusch, "Brazil's Tropical Plan," *American Economic Review*, May 1987.

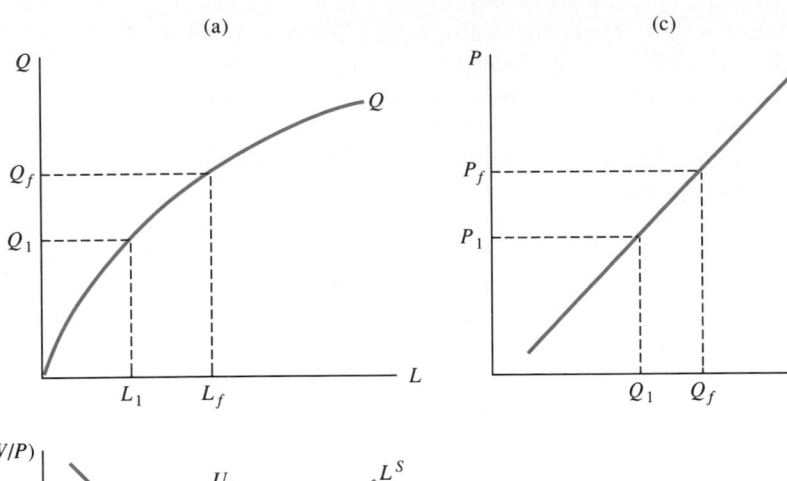

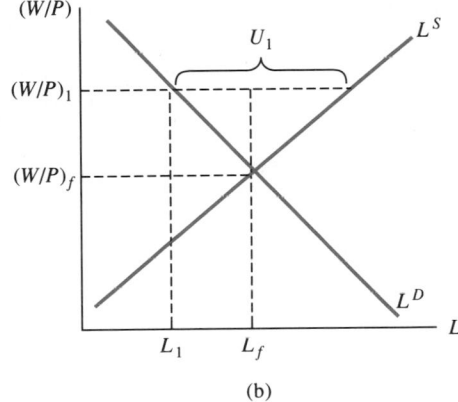

Figure 3-10
The Aggregate Supply Schedule and the Labor Market in the Basic Keynesian Case

based on the labor-leisure choice.[7] The basic idea of the simplest Keynesian model is that with w fixed, the level of the *real* wage w/P will vary inversely with the price level.

Under these conditions, the formal equations for the aggregate supply curve are simply

$$Q^S = Q^S(w/P, K, \tau) \tag{3.4}$$
$$- \;\; + \;\; +$$

$$w = \bar{w} \tag{3.9}$$

As the price level (P) rises, the real wage falls, and according to equation (3.2), the desired level of labor input goes up, while according to (3.4), the desired level of output supply also rises. As a result, the aggregate supply curve is upward sloping, as shown in Figure 3-10c. Suppose that when the price level is at P_f in the figure, the wage is at the full-employment

---

[7] This is a simplifying assumption that is not really needed for Keynesian analysis. It simply helps us to focus on the case in which the nominal wage is fixed and firms are able to hire all the labor they want at that fixed wage.

level ($w_f = w/P_f$). Then, the output corresponding to P_f would be Q_f. With $P_1 < P_f$, the real wage is higher than the market-clearing level ($w/P_1 > w_f$), and the output level Q_1 is less than Q_f. In the labor market, depicted in Figure 3-10b, labor supply would exceed labor demand at the real wage level equal to w/P_1. This excess supply of labor is the amount of unemployment, shown as U_1 in the figure.

The fact that the Keynesian aggregate supply curve is upward sloping has important consequences for economic policymaking. As we shall later see, in this situation the government may have a significant effect on the level of output and employment in the economy. By taking policy actions that affect the price level, the government also affects the real wage, and therefore the level of output supply. A currency devaluation, for example, will tend to raise prices, lower the real wage, and increase employment if nominal wages are rigid, while the same policy will simply raise the price level without any change in real wages or employment under the classical model.

One very important special case of the Keynesian model deserves mention here, when the marginal product of labor is a constant. Suppose, for example, that the production function is $Q = aL$, where a is a constant equal to the marginal product of labor. In this case, firms will demand no labor if $w/P > a$ and an unlimited amount of labor if $w/P < a$. If the nominal wage is fixed, the aggregate supply curve then has a particularly simple shape: it is flat, at the level $P = w/a$, as shown in Figure 3-11. As long as the nominal wage is fixed, the price level will also be fixed, and output will be determined entirely by conditions of aggregate demand, as we shall later see. We refer to this situation as the *extreme Keynesian case*.

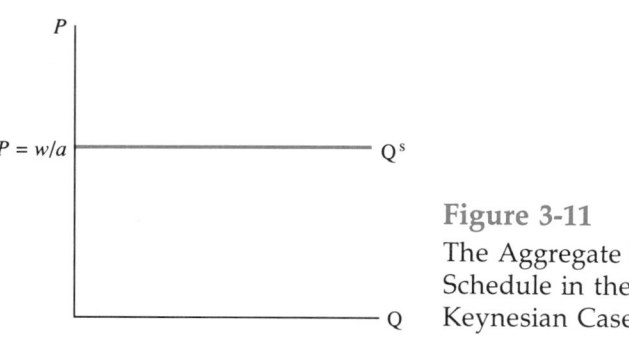

Figure 3-11
The Aggregate Supply
Schedule in the Extreme
Keynesian Case

Involuntary Unemployment

The notion of involuntary unemployment is that some people who are willing to work at the wage received by other workers of comparable ability cannot do so. Of course, such a person may be able to obtain a lower-paying job, or engage in some form of self-employment. But as long as these work opportunities do not provide earnings similar to those achieved by other workers with their same skill levels and the out-of-work person chooses to remain unemployed while he looks for an adequate job, he will be considered involuntarily unemployed.

The question is, then: Why does involuntary unemployment arise? Some market imperfection must prevent wages from clearing the labor market. This might occur either because of nominal wage rigidity, identified as the source of Keynesian unemployment, or because of real wage rigidity, as in the case of classical unemployment.

But why might wages be rigid? There are, in fact, several explanations, which we later describe in more detail. Labor unions may protect their members from nonmembers who would be willing to work at similar or lower wages. Government regulations, such as minimum wage laws, may also lead to rigidities in nominal wages. Labor contracts may lock workers into specific nominal wages that do not correspond to the equilibrium of supply and demand. Or firms may find it to their own advantage to keep wages above the market-clearing level if this helps them to reduce costly hiring and training or to attract more productive workers—the so-called "efficiency wage" approach to wage rigidity and unemployment. We investigate these different hypotheses in Chapters 16 and 17.

Aggregate Supply: A Summary

The different shapes of the aggregate supply curve tell the story of our analysis so far. Figure 3-12a shows the shape of classical aggregate supply, which is perfectly inelastic at the full-employment level of output. Changes in the price level have no effect on supply because with flexible wages and prices, labor-market equilibrium ensures a given level of the real wage, $(w/P)_f$, and a given level of labor, L_f, which, in turn, determines the level of output.

Figure 3-12b describes the Keynesian case, in which sticky wages make the aggregate supply curve slope upward. The crucial linkage between prices and output takes place through real wages. Increases in the price level, by reducing the real wage, make firms willing to hire more labor and thus to supply more output. Notice, however, that in this case the determination of the real wage does *not* establish equilibrium in the labor market, and there may be widespread unemployment. Finally, the aggregate supply curve is perfectly flat in the extreme Keynesian case of wage rigidity combined with a constant marginal product of labor, as shown in Figure 3-12c.

The aggregate supply curve can shift, of course, in response to a num-

Figure 3-12
A Summary of the Aggregate Supply Schedule: (a) Classical, (b) Basic Keynesian, and (c) Extreme Keynesian

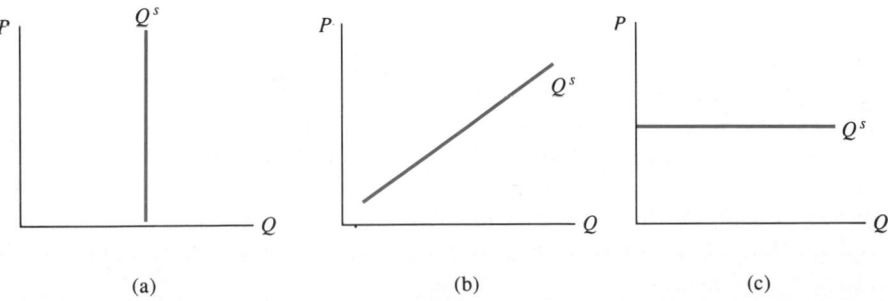

(a)   (b)   (c)

ber of different shocks. Using the basic Keynesian case in Figure 3-12b, we can see that an increase in labor productivity, for example, allows firms to produce the same amount of output at a lower cost, thereby shifting Q^S down and to the right. An exogenous increase in the capital stock, say, from past investment, has a similar effect. Or suppose that labor unions are able to push up wages in the economy and thus production costs go up. When this happens, the same amount of output will be offered at a higher price, and the aggregate supply curve will shift up and to the left. Each of these shocks will have consequences on output and employment once we allow for the interaction of aggregate supply and aggregate demand, and it is to the latter topic that we now turn.

3-5 THE DETERMINATION OF AGGREGATE DEMAND

The equilibrium level of output and the price level over an entire economy is determined by the interaction of aggregate supply and aggregate demand. The analogy with equilibrium in any given single market is clear: the amount of cars produced and their price, for example, is determined by the supply of and demand for cars. At the level of the whole economy, of course, the relationships are more complicated because they involve all goods and services. We have already briefly analyzed the determination of aggregate supply. Before we can say anything further about the equilibrium of the economy, however, we must next look at the characteristics of aggregate demand.

The simplest strategy is to start with a *closed economy* which, by definition, does not trade at all with the rest of the world. In such an economy, aggregate demand can be defined as the total amount of goods and services demanded by domestic residents at the given level of output prices. Thus, it is the sum of the demands for consumption, investment, and government spending, a relationship shown in equation (3.10) as

$$Q^D = C + I + G \qquad \textbf{(3.10)}$$

where the superscript D refers to aggregate demand.

The relationship in (3.10) always holds as an accounting identity (as we made clear in Chapter 2). It can also become the basis for calculating the level of aggregate demand once we specify the ways that C, I, and G are determined in the economy. In particular, we want to ask how much output will be demanded by consumers, investors, and the government for a given price level P. Once we establish this, we can draw an aggregate demand curve and find the equilibrium of aggregate supply and aggregate demand. (At this stage, we will be satisfied with this general approach to the determination of aggregate demand. Later chapters are more rigorous and detailed in their analysis.)

Perhaps the simplest way to establish the shape of the aggregate demand curve is to start from a point on the aggregate demand schedule, such as A in Figure 3-13. At the price P_0, the amount of output demanded is Q_0^D. Starting from A, consider the effect of a rise in the price level to P_1. What happens to aggregate demand? One immediate effect of a price increase is to reduce the real value of money held by the public. If people hold a given

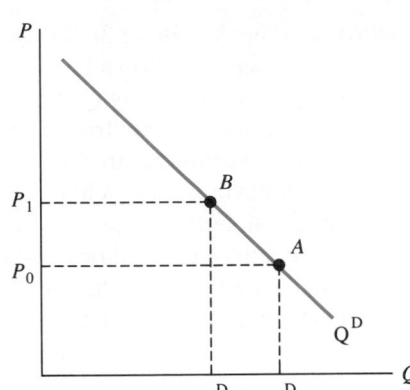

Figure 3-13
The Aggregate Demand
Schedule in a Closed Economy

amount of currency and bank balances and the price level rises, they will be able to buy fewer goods with their money.

One result is that households cut back on their desired level of purchases. This effect, in which falling real money balances reduce consumption spending, is known as the *real balance effect*. Thus, higher prices go together with a reduction in output demand. In Figure 3-13, the new quantity of output demanded is Q_1^D, which corresponds to point B. As the graph shows, then, the aggregate demand schedule in a closed economy is downward sloping. (We demonstrate this with more care in later chapters.)

In an *open economy,* aggregate demand is the total amount of domestic goods demanded at the given level of prices by both domestic and foreign purchasers. It is equivalent to the sum of the demands for consumption, investment, and government spending of domestic residents that fall on *domestic* goods (as opposed to imports), plus foreign demand for domestic goods, that is, export demand. The precise specification of aggregate demand in an open economy is fairly complicated because the nature of the aggregate demand curve depends on the type of exchange-rate regime (fixed versus floating), the type of goods in international trade (especially the substitutability in consumption of domestic and foreign goods), the openness of the economy to international capital flows, and several other considerations. (We make a detailed analysis of aggregate demand in the open economy in Chapters 13 and 14.)

Nonetheless, we can say that in the open economy, as in the closed economy, a rise in the price level tends to cause a fall in aggregate demand. And, once again (but for somewhat different reasons), the result is a downward-sloping aggregate demand schedule. In an open economy, a rise in the domestic price level is likely to push up domestic prices relative to foreign prices. (There is also a real balance effect, as we saw in the closed economy case.) This rise in domestic prices compared with foreign prices makes it more expensive to buy domestic goods and relatively less expensive to buy foreign goods. When this happens, households and businesses cut back on their purchases of domestic goods and start to import more, and foreigners cut back on their purchases of exports from the domestic economy. In simple terms, the rise in the price level means that the domestic economy loses competitiveness by pricing itself out of the world market.

3-6 EQUILIBRIUM OF AGGREGATE SUPPLY AND AGGREGATE DEMAND

The aggregate supply–aggregate demand framework is a useful apparatus for determining the equilibrium of output and the price level. In particular, we can use this framework to study the effects of specific economic policies as well as of external shocks on the equilibrium levels of Q and P.

We have seen that, in both closed and open economies, the aggregate demand curve is downward sloping, that is, as P rises, Q^D falls. The supply curve is either upward sloping under basic Keynesian conditions or vertical under classical conditions. *Output market equilibrium is given by the intersection of the aggregate demand curve and the aggregate supply schedule.* In other words, the economy will settle at the output and price level given by the equilibrium of aggregate demand and supply. This equilibrium will also determine the level of employment in the economy. It is worth noting here that this equilibrium does not signify the optimal ("best") level of output, or even a necessarily desirable one, however. Indeed, there might be a big output gap and widespread unemployment at the overall equilibrium in the economy. Equilibrium is simply a measure of what *will* happen in an economy under certain conditions, not what *should* happen.

We shall later see in more detail how changes in monetary, fiscal, and exchange-rate policies shift the position of the aggregate demand schedule. In general, however, expansionary monetary policy, that is, an increase in the money supply as a result of actions by the central bank, shifts the aggregate demand curve up and to the right. A similar effect (but with some important differences) is produced by a fiscal expansion, such as a rise in government spending, or by an exchange-rate devaluation. Such policy changes are normally referred to as "aggregate demand expansions," given their effect on the overall aggregate demand curve. The specific effects of these policies depend on the particular economic circumstances in which they are carried out. Monetary policies have different effects under fixed and flexible exchange rates, for example. Nonetheless, we can make some initial observations here.

In the classical case shown in Figure 3-14a, the aggregate demand shift provokes an excess demand at the original price P_0. As prices start to increase, the real wage is driven downward. This, in turn, creates an excess

Figure 3-14

A Demand Expansion in the Classical and Keynesian Cases: (a) Classical, (b) Basic Keynesian, and (c) Extreme Keynesian

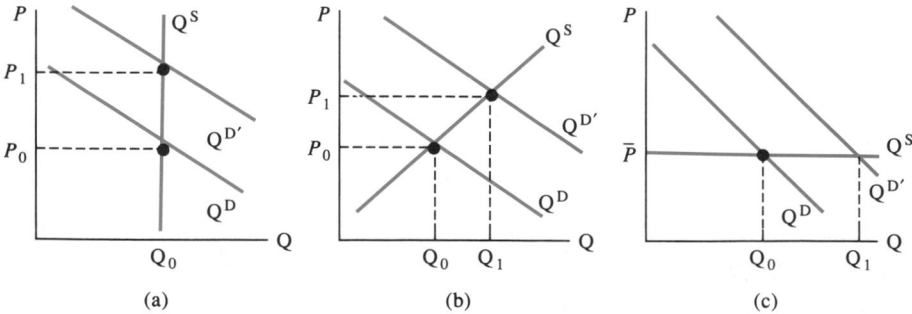

demand in the labor market that is rapidly met by an increase in the nominal wage. Prices continue to rise as long as there is unsatisfied demand in the goods market. Nominal wages increase along with prices so that the real wage is maintained. In the end, all that happens is that the price level and the nominal wage increase by the same amount. With unchanged real wages, both output and employment remain at their original levels. Thus, under classical conditions, *a rise in aggregate demand leads only to a rise in prices, with no effect on output.*

In the Keynesian case of sticky nominal wages, the aggregate demand expansion also leads to excess demand at the initial price level, and once again output prices rise. But in this case, with the nominal wage fixed, the rise of prices leads to a decline in the real wage. This, in turn, leads firms to increase their demand for labor and their supply of output. This result appears in Figure 3-14b. In the new equilibrium, output and prices are higher, and real wages (not shown in the graph) are lower. In the extreme case of a flat aggregate supply curve, the demand expansion raises output without actually increasing the price level, as shown in Figure 3-14c. Thus, in the Keynesian case, *an aggregate demand expansion raises output (and employment) as well as the price level. Since the nominal wage does not change, the rise in the price level also implies a fall in the real wage.*

Even this very general discussion has led us to the important conclusion that *policy changes can, in the Keynesian cases, at least, affect output.* To the extent that the Keynesian case holds, economic authorities can pursue output and employment stabilization policies, that is, policies that aim to set output and employment at particular levels.

Consider now how a supply shock affects the equilibrium of aggregate supply and aggregate demand. Suppose that the economy experiences a once-and-for-all technological improvement, that is, more output can now be produced out of each combination of inputs. Figure 3-15a shows the classical case, where the aggregate supply curve shifts to the right, from Q_0^S to Q_1^S. The new equilibrium is at the new, higher full-employment level of output Q_1. Given the aggregate demand schedule, there is excess supply of output at the price P_0, which forces the price level down to P_1.

In the basic Keynesian case, shown in Figure 3-15b, the aggregate supply curve shifts down and to the right, from Q_0^S to Q_1^S, because firms will want to supply a larger amount of output at any given price. In the new

Figure 3-15

A Technological Improvement in the Classical and Keynesian Cases: (a) Classical, (b) Basic Keynesian, and (c) Extreme Keynesian

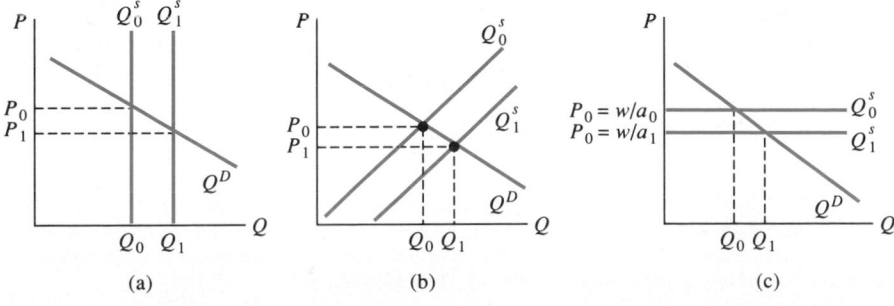

equilibrium, output increases to Q_1, and prices decline from P_0 to P_1. Finally, we can interpret the technological improvement in the extreme Keynesian case (where the marginal product of labor, *MPL*, is constant) as an upward shift in the *MPL* (which we represented as parameter a in Section 3-3). In this case, the aggregate supply curve is flat at the level $P = w/a$. Thus, an increase in a from a_0 to a_1 shifts the aggregate supply curve down from Q_0^S to Q_1^S, where Q_1^S is a flat curve at the level $P_1 = w/a_1$. In the new equilibrium, represented in Figure 3-15c, the price level declines to P_1 and output increases from Q_0 to Q_1.

Demand Contraction: A Historical Example

One historical case of demand management policy is of extreme interest for the development of macroeconomic theory. Before World War I, the industrialized countries were operating under the gold standard, a type of monetary policy that we discuss more fully in Chapters 9 and 10. During the war, however, many governments had to print money to pay the bills for wartime expenses, and this (as we shall explain later) forced many countries to leave the gold standard. In 1925, Great Britain decided to return to the gold standard. In order to do this, the British government had to run a very contractionary monetary policy, while at the same time revaluing the exchange rate of the pound sterling, thereby making it 10 percent more expensive in terms of dollars.[8]

Both the change in monetary policy and the exchange-rate change had the effect of causing a sharp contraction in aggregate demand in Great Britain. If a foreigner wanted to buy British goods using dollars, he now had to pay more in dollars because of the change in the exchange rate. The result of the aggregate demand contraction was a sharp fall in output and a rise in unemployment.

An impressive cast of characters figured in this episode. Britain's chancellor of the exchequer (the equivalent to a finance minister in most countries or secretary of the treasury in the United States) was none other than Winston Churchill. His leading critic was none other than the British economist John Maynard Keynes, who condemned the policy as highly contractionary. Keynes attacked Churchill's policy with unusual strength in an article destined to become a classic, entitled "The Economic Consequences of Mr. Churchill."[9] This short piece contained many of the key arguments that would later be formalized in Keynes's new theory of macroeconomic adjustments.

Keynes saw clearly that Britain's monetary policy was bound to reduce aggregate demand and cause prices to start to fall. He knew that if nominal wages fell far enough, the predictions of the classical model would be fulfilled: prices would fall, but wages would fall by the same amount, so that there would be no loss of output or rise in unemployment. But Keynes

---

[8] That is, the dollar price of 1 British pound went from \$4.42 to \$4.86.

[9] This work started originally as a sequence of three articles that appeared on the *Evening Standard* on July 22, 23, and 24 of 1925. Keynes expanded this into a pamphlet which was later condensed in his *Essays in Persuasion.* A rather recent edition of this work appears in *The Collected Writings of John Maynard Keynes* (London: Macmillan, 1972).

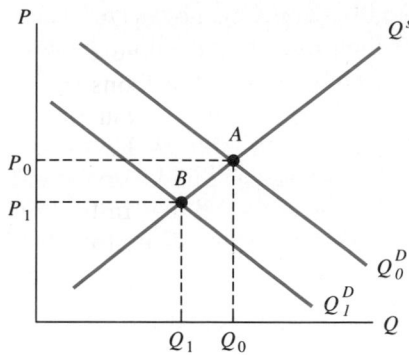

Figure 3-16

The Effects of a Revaluation Based on the 1925 British Experience

was concerned that nominal wages would not fall quickly by the necessary amount. In Keynes's words,

> The policy of improving the foreign-exchange value of sterling up to its pre-war value in gold from being about 10 percent below it, means that, whenever we sell anything abroad, either the foreign buyer has to pay 10 percent *more in his money* or we have to accept 10 percent *less in our money*. . . . Now, if these industries found that their expenses for wages and for transport and for rates and for everything else were falling by 10 percent at the same time, they could afford to cut their prices and would be no worse off than before. But, of course, this does not happen.[10]

Keynes argued strongly, and as it turned out correctly, that workers would resist the nominal wage cuts and would accept them only after unemployment had risen sharply enough to scare the workers into agreeing to wage reductions. He judged correctly that each group of workers would resist wage cuts until other workers had made similar concessions and that, in the end, the entire process of wage reduction would be long, arbitrary, and bitter. Keynes foresaw that the fall in aggregate demand would therefore depress prices more than wages and, as a result, would cause firms to cut back on their demand for labor. This, in turn, would produce an output contraction.

Now let us analyze Churchill's policy change within our simple framework of aggregate demand and aggregate supply. We suppose, as Keynes did, that nominal wages were sticky, so that the output supply curve in Britain was upward sloping. As shown in Figure 3-16, the initial equilibrium is at point A, with prices at P_0 and output at Q_0. The shift to tight money and the exchange-rate change shift the aggregate demand curve down. The price level falls to P_1, but output also declines from Q_0 to Q_1. Thus, the model predicts that the appreciation of the pound provokes a deflation in prices, accompanied by an output contraction and increased unemployment. And this is precisely what happened in 1925 Britain.

This is not what the chancellor of the exchequer intended, of course. Under classical assumptions that wages and prices are fully flexible, Mr.

---

[10] John M. Keynes, "The Economic Consequences of Mr. Churchill," in ibid., p. 208.

Churchill's policy would have resulted in a fall in domestic prices *and* wages of the same amount. The real wage would then have remained unchanged, and output and employment would have remained at the original levels. But this is not what happened.

When one sees a flawed economic policy like this one, based as it was on the mistaken idea that nominal wages would simply fall by the necessary proportion, and causing in the end so much harm to the economy, one naturally wonders why it was implemented. Keynes's judgment was quite harsh in this respect:

> . . . [Mr. Churchill] in doing what he did in the actual circumstances of last spring, was just asking for trouble. For he was committing himself to force down money wages and all money values, without any idea how it was to be done. Why did he do such a silly thing? Partly, perhaps, because he has no instinctive judgement to prevent him from making mistakes; partly because, lacking this instinctive judgement, he was deafened by the clamorous voices of conventional finance; and, most of all, because he was gravely misled by his experts.[11]

Sources of Economic Fluctuations

Macroeconomists tend to differ in their interpretation of economic events in two ways. First, they differ about the shape of the aggregate supply schedule, that is, whether it is vertical, upward sloping, or flat. Second, they differ about the relative importance of the different kinds of shocks that hit an economy. Are most shocks on the demand side, leading to shifts in the aggregate demand schedule, or are most shocks on the supply side, causing movements of the aggregate supply schedule? There is no agreement among macroeconomists on these issues, either within the United States or in other countries. It is also likely that countries themselves differ in the two critical dimensions, aggregate supply and shocks to the economy, so that what is true in one country might be false in another.

In a very general way, we can classify schools of macroeconomics according to their views on these two dimensions of the macroeconomy. Economists in the classical tradition believe in a vertical supply schedule. One group of such economists, the monetarists, led by Milton Friedman, have stressed that most shocks to the economy come from the demand side, and in particular from the unstable monetary policies of the central bank. The rational expectations theorists, led by Robert Lucas and Robert Barro, also put great stress on monetary instability as a major, if not *the* major, source of macroeconomic shock. Other economists in the classical tradition, particularly those associated with the so-called "real business-cycle" theory (which we take up in Chapter 17), believe that the predominant shocks are technological, and on the supply side of the economy.

Keynes and his postwar followers not only stressed the upward-sloping nature of the supply curve, but also the instability of aggregate demand. In their view, that instability arose from shocks in the private markets, mainly the result of swings in investor confidence that led to swings in investment

---

[11] Ibid., p. 212.

demand by businesses. Since so much stress was put on demand shocks, it was natural for Keynes and his followers to propose that active budget and monetary policies could be used to offset these private demand disturbances. More recently, economists in the Keynesian tradition but armed with new analytical techniques—the so-called "new-Keynesian economists"—have maintained Keynes's supply curve assumptions, but have taken a broader view of the sources of shocks to the economy, acknowledging that they might come from the supply side as well as the demand side. (Some of the new-Keynesian ideas are reviewed in Chapter 17.)

To summarize, then, two types of shocks are identified: demand disturbances, such as changes in fiscal and monetary policy and shifts in investment spending by private businesses, and supply shocks, which include technological changes and fluctuations in input prices, such as the oil price shocks that started in the 1970s. Some analyses assume market clearing, others do not. In Figure 3-17, the classical model appears in the northwest quadrant, where markets clear and demand is the source of economic fluctuations. The Keynesian school, which also assumes that shocks come from the demand side but that nominal wage rigidities prevent the labor market from clearing, is in the northeast quadrant. This may be a bit crude, but perhaps it helps to categorize the different viewpoints.

ASSUMPTION ABOUT AGGREGATE SUPPLY CURVE

	Vertical	Upward Sloping
Demand Side	Classical Monetarists	Keynes New-Keynesians
Supply Side	Real Business Cycles	Considered Also By New-Keynesians

SOURCE OF SHOCKS

Figure 3-17
Sources of Economic Fluctuations and Assumptions About Aggregate Supply

3-7 AGGREGATE SUPPLY AND DEMAND IN THE SHORT RUN AND THE LONG RUN

Keynes stressed that nominal wages do not necessarily adjust instantly to maintain full employment. Thus, the Keynesian aggregate supply curve is based on a fixed nominal wage. But Keynes himself, and later economists working in his tradition, recognized that nominal wages are not truly fixed; they simply adjust slowly to imbalances of aggregate demand. If we allow for gradual adjustment of nominal wages, rather than permanent stickiness, a synthesis of the Keynesian and the classical positions can emerge. In the short run, the wage adjustment is too slow to ensure full employment, but in the long run, wages eventually adjust by enough to reestablish full employment and the classical equilibrium.

To illustrate this, let us assume a very simple kind of wage adjustment. We know that whenever output is below the full-employment level, some workers are involuntarily unemployed. They would like to work, but because the overall wage level is too high, there is not enough demand for labor. In this case, we suppose that nominal wages will tend to decline as the unemployed workers offer their labor services at a discount relative to the prevailing wage. And when output is above the full-employment level, we suppose that the tight labor market leads to a rise in nominal wages.

We can formalize these ideas by writing a dynamic equation for wages, which describes how wages change over time in response to unemployment. Let us denote the wage in the current period as w (a period could be a month, a quarter, or a year; we need not be precise on this for the illustration). Also, let us use the notation $\hat{w}_{+1}$ to signify the percentage change in the wage between this period and the next one, $\hat{w}_{+1} = (w_{+1} - w)/w$. We will assume that the change in the wage is a function of the output gap. When output is below the full-employment level, there is involuntary unemployment, and the nominal wage tends to decline:

$$\hat{w}_{+1} = a(Q - Q_f) \tag{3.13}$$

(In Chapter 15, we refine this analysis of wage setting.)

Now, consider an economy that starts at full-employment equilibrium, shown as point E in Figure 3-18. Next, suppose that aggregate demand declines, perhaps because of a Churchillian monetary policy. The immediate result is to shift output from Q_f at point E down to Q_1 at point A. A rise in unemployment would be an immediate result. But it is no longer the end of the story.

With the reduction of output, nominal wages tend to fall. And as nominal wages fall, the aggregate supply curve shifts to the right, as shown in Figure 3-18. We see that the delayed reduction in the nominal wage leads to

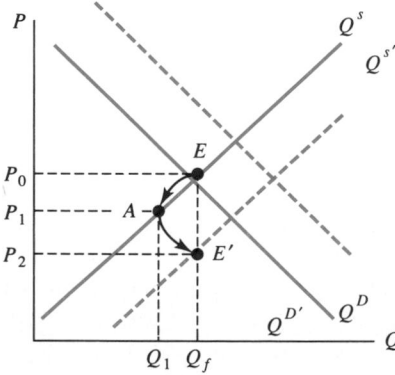

Figure 3-18
Short- and Long-Term Effects of an Aggregate Demand Contraction

a delayed recovery of output, from the low level of point A. As long as output remains below Q_f, the tendency for nominal wages to fall and for output to rise continues. According to equation (3.13), the fall in wages will stop only when output has returned to Q_f.

Notice, then, the long-run effect of the decline in aggregate demand. After the full adjustment of nominal wages, output is back to the full-employment level, and the full effect of the shock to aggregate demand appears as lower prices rather than lower output. Thus, we see the dynamic response to a fall in aggregate demand. Initially, prices decline by a moderate amount while output falls sharply. Over time, nominal wages are reduced in response to the output decline; then this gives way to a process in which prices fall by more while output begins to recover. Eventually, the full-employment level of output is completely restored. The long-run effect is exactly the one that would be predicted by the classical model: prices and wages decline by enough following the aggregate demand shock so that output (and employment) remain at the full-employment levels.

To summarize these results, we can say that *the economy shows Keynesian properties in the short run and classical properties in the long run*. In the short run, shifts in aggregate demand affect both output and prices, while in the long run, they affect only prices. In this sense, the debate between modern Keynesian and modern classical economists is mainly about timing. Both groups of economists recognize that the economy has tendencies to return to full-employment equilibrium following an aggregate demand shift. The question is, how fast does it happen? The Keynesian economist answers that the response of the economy will be gradual, perhaps so gradual that macroeconomic policy instruments—monetary policy, fiscal policy, the exchange rate—can be used to help speed the return to full employment. The classical economist, on the other hand, answers that the economy will quickly return to full employment, so quickly that there is no need for the help of macroeconomic policies and, indeed, no time for them.

With this brief introduction to output determination, we now shift gears. For the next eight chapters we will work within the assumptions of the classical case. We do this because our focus now turns to the building blocks of the macroeconomy—consumption, saving, investment, international capital flows, and money supply and demand—and these issues are complex enough, even with output regarded as fixed. They become even more complex in the Keynesian setting.

Therefore, we will do ourselves a favor and learn first about these various key aspects of the macroeconomy using a simple model. In Chapter 12, we return to the issues of output determination using a series of more descriptive and complicated models.

3-8 SUMMARY

Two types of economic fluctuations are of particular interest in macroeconomics, the long and sustained deviations of unemployment from historical averages and the synchronized shifts in important macroeconomic variables around a trend, a phenomenon known as the *business cycle*.

Potential output is the level of output that the economy can reach when all productive factors, especially labor, are fully employed. Normally, there is some unemployment of labor and other inputs, so that current output is less than potential output. The *output gap* is the difference between potential and actual output. *Okun's law,* an empirical regularity found for the United States, states that a reduction of unemployment in 1 percent is associated with a rise in GNP and fall in the output gap of 3 percent.

Aggregate supply is the total amount of output that firms and households will choose to supply as a function of the price level. Firms decide how much output to supply in order to *maximize profits,* taking into account the price of output, the costs of inputs, the stock of capital, and the production technology. Households also make a supply decision, how much labor to supply, based on the level of the real wage.

The *production function* is a technical relationship between the level of output (Q) and the level of inputs, capital (K) and labor (L). The *marginal productivity* of both factors is positive, but it declines as more of each factor is used with a given amount of the other input. A profit-maximizing firm hires labor until its marginal product equals the real wage. The demand for labor is, then, the marginal productivity of labor schedule.

Individuals decide on their labor supply based on their preferences for consumption and leisure. Their utility depends positively on their consumption level and negatively on the time they devote to work. The equilibrium amount of labor supplied depends both on people's preferences and on the real wage. An increase in the real wage has two possible effects, a *substitution effect* that makes leisure more expensive, and thus tends to increase the amount of labor supplied, and a positive *income effect* that makes workers want to consume more leisure (and consumption goods), which thereby tends to reduce the supply of labor. We assume that the substitution effect dominates the income effect, so that the labor supply is upward sloping.

The *aggregate supply* curve describes the relationship between the supply of output and the price level, and its shape depends heavily on the assumptions made about the labor market. In the *classical approach,* wages are fully flexible and adjust to keep the supply of labor and the demand for labor equilibrated. Labor is always fully employed, meaning that firms want to employ as much labor as workers want to supply. Thus, the aggregate supply is a straight line drawn at the full-employment level of output. In the classical case, unemployment can occur only if the real wage is kept above the market-clearing level.

The *Keynesian model* is based on the idea that nominal wages or prices do not adjust automatically to maintain labor market equilibrium. The stress here is on *nominal* rigidities, as opposed to *real* rigidities. Keynes himself put most emphasis on nominal wage stickiness, which arises from institutional features such as long-term labor contracts. Under these conditions the aggregate supply curve is upward sloping because a rise in the price level (P) depresses real wages, making it more attractive for firms to hire additional labor and thus to increase the supply of output. An important special case of the Keynesian model occurs when the marginal product of labor is constant, which happens, for example, if the production function is linear in labor input. In this case, the aggregate supply curve is flat when the nominal wage is rigid.

Involuntarily unemployed individuals are those who are willing to work at the wage received by other workers of comparable ability but who cannot find a job. This occurs when some market imperfection prevents wages from clearing the labor market, either because of nominal wage rigidity (the Keynesian case) or because of real wage rigidities (the classical case).

In a *closed* economy, *aggregate demand* is the total amount of goods and services demanded by domestic residents at the given level of output prices. It is the sum of the demands for consumption, investment, and government spending. The *aggregate demand curve* is downward sloping because a rise in prices reduces the value of *real money balances* (the real value of money held by the public) and thus decreases the amount of goods demanded.

In an *open* economy, *aggregate demand* is the total amount of domestic goods and services demanded by both local and foreign agents, at the given level of prices. It is the sum of the local demand for consumption, investment, and government spending, plus net exports (that is, exports net of imports). In this setting, the aggregate demand curve is downward sloping, both because of the real balance effect (as in the closed economy) and because a rise in the price level is likely to push up domestic prices relative to foreign prices. With domestic goods relatively more expensive (and thus with foreign goods relatively cheaper), net exports will decline as both domestic and foreign residents shift their demands from domestic goods to foreign goods.

Output market equilibrium is given by the intersection of a downward-sloping aggregate demand curve and the aggregate supply schedule. This equilibrium determines the level of output and prices. An expansion in *monetary policy* or in *fiscal policy* will increase aggregate demand. The specific implications on output and prices will depend on the type of economy. In the classical case, aggregate supply is vertical, and all the effect of a demand shift goes into prices, with no effect on output. In the Keynesian case of rigid nominal wages, the aggregate supply is upward sloping, and an expansion of demand results in both higher prices and increased output. In the extreme Keynesian case of a flat aggregate supply curve, a demand expansion raises output without affecting the price level.

A *supply shock,* such as a technological improvement or a change in input prices, causes a shift in the amount of output that is supplied at any given price. A favorable supply shock shifts the aggregate supply curve vertically to the right in the classical case, down and to the right in the basic Keynesian case, and horizontally downward in the extreme Keynesian case. In all three cases, the qualitative result is the same (output increases and the price level declines), although the magnitudes differ.

Allowing for gradual adjustment of nominal wages rather than having complete wage stickiness allows us to *synthesize Keynesian and classical views*. In the short run, the nominal wage adjustment is too slow to ensure full employment, but in the long run, wages adjust by enough to reestablish full employment and the classical equilibrium. Thus, in this synthesis, the economy presents Keynesian properties in the short run and classical properties in the long run. In this sense, the debate between modern classical and modern Keynesian economists is mainly about *timing*.

Key Concepts

potential output
output gap

Okun's law
business cycle

aggregate supply
profit maximization
labor supply
production function
marginal productivity of capital
marginal productivity of labor
real wage
demand for labor
labor-leisure decision
substitution effect
income effect
aggregate supply function
aggregate supply curve

classical equilibrium
Keynesian equilibrium
involuntary unemployment
aggregate demand
real money balances
monetary policy
fiscal policy
output market equilibrium
supply shock
short run
long run
Keynesian-classical synthesis

Problems and Questions

1. Assume that because of better training, workers become more productive.

   a. What would happen to the demand for labor?
   b. What would happen to the equilibrium real wage?
   c. What are the effects on total employment in this economy?
   d. Is involuntary unemployment changed? How does your answer depend on whether the real wage is flexible or not?

2. In the Republic of Atlantis, the real wage is fixed above its equilibrium level.

   a. Is there any involuntary unemployment?
   b. Assume that workers from a neighboring country migrate to Atlantis. What would happen to total employment, production, and involuntary unemployment in Atlantis?
   c. How would your answer to (b) change if real wages were flexible in Atlantis?

3. Discuss what happens to the aggregate supply curve under the classical, basic Keynesian, and extreme Keynesian cases when

   a. There is a technological improvement.
   b. An earthquake destroys half the capital stock of the country.
   c. Workers' preferences change, and they want to work more at any wage rate.
   d. New, more productive machines are invented, but only a third of the labor force knows how to operate them.

4. Find the aggregate supply curve when

   a. The production function is $Q = 3LK$, labor demand is $L^D = 10 - 2w/P$, labor supply is $L^S = 4w/P$, and capital stock in the economy is fixed at $K = 4$.
   b. Is the aggregate supply curve you derived in (a) representative of the classical, basic Keynesian, or extreme Keynesian cases?
   c. How would your answers to (a) and (b) change if the nominal wage were fixed at 3?

5. Is it possible that the amount of labor supplied is reduced when the real wage increases? Why? If so, use the apparatus in Figure 3-7 to derive a labor supply curve whose slope changes from positive to negative above a given real wage, say, $(w/P)_3$.

6. Derive the equilibrium price level and output for an economy with the following characteristics:

    a. Consumption is $C = 10 - 5P$, investment is $I = 20$, government spending is $G = 15$, aggregate supply is $Q^S = 5 + P$.

    b. What happens to production and prices if government spending raises to $G = 25$?

    c. How would your answers to (a) and (b) change if aggregate supply were $Q^S = 10$?

7. During the early 1980s, the United States experienced both increases in the price level and reductions in the levels of production and employment. How can the aggregate supply–aggregate demand model explain this situation? What would have happened if the government increased its spending to ameliorate the decline in production?

8. During the last decades, Argentina has undergone long periods of high inflation. People there are used to substantial variation in prices and wages. Contracts usually cover only short periods of time. Switzerland, on the other hand, has had a very stable price level for a long time. Contracts are often set to cover several years. In which of the two countries would an increase in government spending be more effective in raising the level of output? (*Hint:* Think of the shape of the aggregate supply curve in each country.)

9. During the Great Depression of the 1930s, the United States suffered a deflation as well as a significant increase in involuntary unemployment. Which of the aggregate supply cases do you think is most relevant in analyzing this situation?

Some people recommended that the government reduce its spending. Do you think that was a wise advice in the framework of the aggregate supply–aggregate demand model?

10. In the economy of Atlantis, a certain reduction in consumption is matched with an increase in investment of exactly the same amount. Which are the short-run effects on the equilibrium level of prices, output, and wages? How would your answer change in the long run?

chapter 4

Consumption and Saving

In this chapter, we take up another central issue in macroeconomics, that of how households divide their income between consumption and saving. This is one of the key economic decisions that people make. On the level of an individual household, this decision affects its economic welfare in the course of time. Clearly, households that choose to consume more today (and, therefore, save less) will be able to consume less in the future. On the level of the aggregate economy, the cumulative effect of the consumption and saving decisions of households helps to determine the rate of growth of the economy, the trade balance, and the level of output and employment.

Our analysis of this issue relies heavily on a *life-cycle* theory of consumption and saving. The household earns a stream of income throughout a lifetime that lasts for several "periods," or years, and it must choose a path of consumption over its lifetime that is consistent with its lifetime earnings. In any given period, the household may consume less or more than its income in that period. If it consumes less and saves more, that saving will eventually be used to pay for higher consumption in some future period. If it consumes more, it must dissave in the present period, and its future consumption will be reduced as a result of that dissaving.

Another component of this theory holds that households decide on their consumption today based on their expectations about their future income, as well as on the interest rate that they can earn by saving or the interest rate that they must pay if they borrow. This decision-making behavior is thus *intertemporal*; that is, we assume that households carefully take into account how their present decisions will affect their future consumption opportunities. Once we have developed this theory, we examine the empirical evidence on consumption and saving decisions and modify the basic theory to account for any important characteristics of actual consumption behavior that we have missed.

This emphasis on intertemporal choice stands in contrast to the early theories of consumption first propounded by Keynes and his successors. Keynes's consumption function was the first formal attempt to develop a model of current consumption based on household income, and that alone made his contribution an outstanding one. While Keynes's model has been superseded, the Keynesian consumption function played a vital role in the development of ideas in this area.

Keynes's approach started on this observation:

> The fundamental psychological law, upon which we are entitled to depend with great confidence both *a priori* from our knowledge of human nature and from the detailed facts of experience, is that men are disposed, as a rule and on the average, to increase their consumption as their income increases, but not by as much as the increase in their income.[1]

On this basis, Keynes posited a simple model of consumption linking current income and current consumption,

$$C = a + cY$$

where Y is current income. The coefficients a and c are constants that are meant to represent Keynes's psychological law. Keynes assumed that c would be less than 1. As we shall see, this equation has the problem that it neglects the role of interest rates and future income in the decision on current consumption.

As we construct our theory of household saving and consumption, we focus on the choice of consuming or saving out of *disposable personal income*. Some of the total income that is earned in the economy is not directly available to households for consumption or spending because it is taxed by the government, because it is used by firms to replace part of the capital stock that has worn away during the production period, or because it has been retained by firms for new investments in addition to the replacement of worn-out capital. Disposable income, then, is the income that households earn in a given period that is available for consumption or saving.

Once we look at household consumption and saving decisions, we add our analysis of the saving decisions of business firms. The sum of household saving and business saving gives us the total of *private saving* in the economy. The government sector also consumes and saves (we get to that in Chapter 7), and the sum of private saving plus government saving is equal to national saving. Thus, our strategy in understanding total saving in the economy is to start with the household, then add firm behavior, and finally add government saving behavior.

4-1 NATIONAL CONSUMPTION AND SAVING

Table 4-1 shows the pattern of saving and consumption by households in the United States in 1990. In the table, the top row shows the gross national product (GNP), which is then adjusted to arrive at disposable personal income (row 19). Disposable personal income is in turn divided between per-

---

[1] John Maynard Keynes, *The General Theory of Employment, Interest and Money*. In *The Collected Writings of John Maynard Keynes* (London: Macmillan, 1972), p. 92. This work, considered one of the fundamental economic pieces of all time, was originally published in England in February 1936.

TABLE   4-1

GNP, NATIONAL INCOME, CONSUMPTION, AND SAVING IN THE UNITED STATES, 1990
(BILLIONS OF CURRENT DOLLARS)

1. Gross National Product	$5,463.0
2. − Capital consumption	575.7
3. = Net national product	$4,887.4
4. − Indirect business tax	440.4
5. − Business transfers	35.0
6. − Statistical discrepancy	3.1
7. + Subsidies	2.5
8. = National income	$4,417.5
9. − Corporate profits with inventory valuation and capital consumption adjustments	297.1
10. − Net interests	467.1
11. − Contributions for social insurance	506.9
12. − Wage accruals less disbursements	0.0
13. + Government transfer payments	659.5
14. + Personal interest income	680.9
15. + Personal dividend income	123.8
16. + Business transfer payments	35.0
17. = Personal income	$4,645.0
18. − Personal tax and nontax payments	699.8
19. = Disposable personal income	$3,945.8
20. − Personal consumption expenditures	3,658.1
21. − Interest paid by consumers to business	107.8
22. − Net transfer payments to foreigners	0.9
23. = Personal saving	$ 179.1
24. + Gross business saving	604.8
25. = Total gross private saving	$ 783.9
26. + Government saving	126.0
27. + Total gross national saving	$ 657.9

Source: Economic Report of the President, 1991, *(Washington, D.C.: U.S. Government Printing Office, 1991), Tables B-22, B-23, B-26, and B-28.*

sonal consumption expenditures (row 20), other payments by consumers (rows 21 and 22), and personal saving (row 23). Note how we go from GNP to disposable personal income. The idea here is to subtract from GNP that part of income that never actually gets to the households. First, we subtract capital consumption (the wearing away of the capital stock) to arrive at net national product (NNP) in row 3. Then we subtract part of NNP to account for the fact that some of the net national product is paid directly to the government in the form of indirect taxes and to account for the items shown in rows 5, 6, and 7, to arrive at national income (NI) (row 8). Then, we subtract the parts of NI that are taxed away or kept by firms to arrive at disposable income.

To get from national income to disposable personal income, we must make three basic kinds of adjustments. First, some business profits stay in firms, without being distributed to households. This part of national income is subtracted in order to calculate the disposable income of households. Second, we subtract the part of income that is earned by households but is given to the government in the form of direct tax payments. Third, some households receive transfer payments from the government that augment the income they earn in the marketplace—social security payments, unemployment insurance, welfare payments, for example. These transfers are added to national income to arrive at disposable income. With all these adjustments made, we finally arrive at disposable personal income (row 19).[2]

Note that in 1990, disposable income was $3,946 billion out of a GNP of $5,463 billion, so that disposable income represented about 72 percent of GNP. Out of total disposable income, households saved only $179 billion, or about 3.3 percent of GNP, a very low personal saving rate by international comparison. To find the total national saving, we must add to this business saving and government saving, as we do in the last rows of Table 4-1. In 1990, gross business saving amounted to $605 billion. Therefore, total private saving equaled about $784 billion, or about 14.4 percent of GNP. To find total *net* private saving, we subtract the amount of capital consumption from gross saving, to find $208 billion. This is the amount of saving available after the capital that has depreciated during the year has been replaced.

The rate of gross private saving has been fairly stable in the United States in the postwar period, as we can see from Figure 4-1, which plots personal saving, business saving, and total private saving, all as a percentage of GDP. Note that the private saving rate has varied between 15 and 20 percent every year since 1948, with the exceptions of 1987 and 1990 when the ratio was 14.8 percent and 14.5 percent, respectively. The personal saving rate declined by a couple of percentage points in the mid-1980s, while business saving rose by about one percentage point compared with a decade earlier.[3]

During the period 1985–1989, the U.S. government sector (including federal, state, and local governments) was a net dissaver, meaning that the government's expenditure exceeded its income, and the government had to borrow to cover its spending. Overall, government saving was −$126 billion in 1990, down from −$105 billion the year before. When we add this dissav-

---

[2] While this paragraph describes the route from national income in row 8 to personal income in row 17, the items in rows 9 through 16 are a bit more complex. For example, to remove from national income the retained earnings of firms, the procedure is to subtract all corporate profits, in line 9, and then to add back the part of profits that are received as dividends by households, in line 15.

[3] Because of possible measurement errors and the shortness of the period over which the shifts in the saving rate have been observed, we should not overinterpret these recent changes. There are, indeed, reasons to be worried about the quality of the data, both in actual measurement and in conceptual design. The biggest conceptual problem is that the data understate the rate of saving by counting all expenditures on consumer durables (such as purchases of automobiles) as consumption, even though as we explain later in this chapter, such spending is partly a kind of investment spending as well.

Figure 4-1
Gross Private Savings in the United States, 1940–1990

(From Economic Report of the President, 1991, *Tables B-8 and B-28.)*

ing to the private saving of $784 billion, we find that total national saving in 1990 was equal to $658 billion, or about 12 percent of GNP.

The United States saves a relatively small share of its gross national product, as we can see by the international comparisons in Table 4-2. Among the nations listed, only Argentina saves a smaller share, just 10.3 percent of GNP during 1989. The East Asian economies of Korea and Japan are in a league of their own, saving more than 30 percent of GNP. We shall see later that these high saving rates help to account for the large trade surpluses in these countries, as well as their rapid growth rates.

We address two key questions in the remainder of the chapter. First is: What determines the household's choice between saving and consumption out of a given amount of disposable income? In particular, how do changes in income and in interest rates affect the desired levels of consumption and saving in a given period? Second is: What interaction between business saving and household saving determines the overall level of private saving? Once we introduce the government sector into the analysis in Chapter 7, we

TABLE   4-2

THE GROSS NATIONAL SAVING
RATIO ACROSS COUNTRIES IN 1989
(% GDP)

JAPAN	34.9[1]
GERMANY	25.8[2]
UNITED KINGDOM	16.6
FRANCE	21.1
ITALY	21.5[1]
INDONESIA	32.5
SOUTH KOREA	36.5
ARGENTINA	10.3
BRAZIL	21.5

[1] Refers to Gross Domestic Saving. (Gross National Saving unavailable.)
[2] Data for 1988. (1989 data unavailable.)

can examine the relationship between government saving and private saving. The relationships between consumption and saving and other macroeconomic variables such as growth, investment, anl output levels are taken up in subsequent chapters.

4-2 THE BASIC UNIT: THE HOUSEHOLD

Initially, we want to understand how a household, or family, makes consumption and saving decisions. The household is traditionally the basic unit of analysis, and much data are collected on that level, rather than on the level of the individuals that compose the family. Although a household may have one or several members, it is conventionally regarded as operating as a single unit, with a single well-defined set of objectives summarized by a household utility function.

Let us begin with a very simple model in which there is just one type of good, Q, which has a fixed price of 1. We say that this good is the *numeraire,* in that all measures of income, saving, and so forth will be in units of this good. Later, we will measure these variables in monetary units, such as dollars. But because we are beginning our study with a nonmonetary economy, we must measure the key variables in units of output Q instead. Of course, Q should be thought of as a "composite commodity," such as one unit of real GNP, that includes many different types of output.

We suppose that a given household produces a stream of output Q_1, $Q_2, \ldots, Q_T$, over T periods and consumes an amount $C_1, C_2, \ldots, C_T$. If the household lives in isolation, and if the output is not storable, then the household has no choice but to consume each period exactly what it produces or let some of its output go to waste. Assuming that more consumption is better than less consumption (that is, assuming that the household is not satiated with its consumption of Q), then the household will simply consume according to the rule $C_1 = Q_1$, $C_2 = Q_2$, and so on.

If the commodity is storable, the household might be able to improve on this consumption pattern by storing some of the output in some periods and then consuming out of this accumulated savings in other periods. For example, if the household consumed $C_1 < Q_1$ and saved the difference, then in the next period it would be possible to have $C_2 > Q_2$, because the household could consume not only what was produced in period 2, but also part of what was saved in the first period. The decision to save part of first-period output would represent saving (in the sense that output is greater than consumption) and investment in physical inventories. We will put aside this kind of physical investment for the rest of this chapter and take it up again in Chapter 5.

Even if the output Q is not storable, however, the household still can save if the household is linked to other households through a market for financial assets. For the moment, let us consider just one type of financial asset, a bond. Each bond acquired in the current period, at a price of 1, pays its owner an amount $(1 + r)$ in the next period. In other words, the owner of the bond earns a one-period interest rate r on the bond and gets back the principal invested in the bond as well.

With the existence of these financial assets, the household's consumption can differ from its income in a given period. If it earns more than it consumes, then it accumulates bonds, which can be cashed in later for higher future consumption. If the household spends more than it earns, then it must cash in its stock of bonds, or even have negative holdings of bonds (in which case it is a debtor to other households). The existence of opportunities to borrow and lend via bonds greatly enhances the possibilities open to households to adjust their profiles of consumption over time for any given time path of output. As we shall see later on, this possibility increases the welfare of the household.

Even in this simplified setting, we must be careful to distinguish between the income and output of the household. The output in the current period is simply Q; income, on the other hand, includes the interest earned on previously accumulated bonds. The stock of bonds held by households at the *end of the previous period* will be denoted B_{-1}. Note that these bond holdings are measured in units of output, so that bond holding of the amount B_{-1} signifies bonds that are worth, at the end of the previous period, B_{-1} units of the output Q. The total interest earned is rB_{-1}.

In any period, the household's income, denoted by the letter Y, is defined as the sum of output in the period, and the interest received on the stock of bonds that were held as of the end of the previous period, and therefore owned by the household at the beginning of the current period, when the interest is paid:

$$Y = Q + rB_{-1} \qquad \textbf{(4.1)}$$

Note, then, that the difference of output (Q) and income (Y) is the earnings on the financial assets of the household.

The household's stock of bonds evolves over time, depending on the balance between income and consumption. If the household consumes more than its current income, its bond holdings go down. If, on the contrary, it consumes less than its income, its bonds accumulate. This is summarized in equation (4.2):

$$B = B_{-1} + (Y - C) = B_{-1} + (Q + rB_{-1} - C) \qquad \textbf{(4.2)}$$

We see from (4.2) that B will be bigger than B_{-1} if the household earns more than it consumes and that B will be less than B_{-1} if the household consumes more than it earns. Since saving can be defined as the difference between income and consumption, $S = Y - C$, the accumulation of bonds in any period corresponds exactly to the saving in the period:

$$B - B_{-1} = S \qquad \textbf{(4.3)}$$

4-3 THE INTERTEMPORAL BUDGET CONSTRAINT

Let us continue our discussion using our formal model to describe a case in which households live for two periods. These periods are not necessarily equal in length. We can think of the first period as "the present" and the second period as "the future." (It is also convenient to think of period 0 as "the past.") At the abstract level of this discussion, we do not have to be precise about the number of years represented by each period. This simplified framework, known as the *two-period model*, has the advantage of capturing most of the interesting intertemporal aspects of economic decisions in a simple setting. (When we turn to empirical work, we will revert to a more realistic many-period setting.)

The Budget Constraint in the Two-Period Model

Initially, we suppose that households inherit no assets from the past ($B_0 = 0$) and finish their life with no assets either ($B_2 = 0$). For now, we rule out any motive to leave bequests to a future generation, and we assume that an individual is not allowed to die in debt (that is, it cannot happen that $B_2 < 0$). With these assumptions, first-period saving corresponds to the value of bonds at the end of period 1, since $B_1 - B_0 = B_1 = S_1$. Analogously, since $B_2 - B_1 = S_2$, and since $B_2 = 0$, we see that $-B_1 = S_2$. Thus, we see that saving in the first period, S_1 (equal to B_1), equals the opposite of saving in the second period, S_2 (equal to $-B_1$).

This shows us an important result, namely, that when households are born with no assets and die with no assets, their saving in the first period exactly matches their dissaving of the second period ($S_2 = -S_1$). Thus, the decision for households is not whether to save or whether to borrow, but rather *when* to save and *when* to borrow. If households save while "young" (in period 1), they will dissave when "old" (in period 2), and if they dissave when young, they will save when they are old.

By our definition of saving, we have that

$$S_1 = Y_1 - C_1 = Q_1 - C_1 = B_1 \qquad \textbf{(4.4)}$$

$$S_2 = Y_2 - C_2 = Q_2 + rB_1 - C_2 \qquad \textbf{(4.5)}$$

Because $S_2 = -S_1$, we can combine the equations (4.4) and (4.5) to obtain $C_1 - Q_1 = Q_2 + r(Q_1 - C_1) - C_2$, or upon rearranging,

$$C_1 + \frac{C_2}{(1 + r)} = Q_1 + \frac{Q_2}{(1 + r)} = W_1 \qquad \textbf{(4.6)}$$

where W stands for wealth.

Equation (4.6) is the *intertemporal budget constraint* of the household. It states that the present value of consumption must be equal to the present value of output. The present value of output can also be considered to be the household's wealth (W_1) at the beginning of the first period (before first-period consumption is chosen). The fundamental condition demonstrated by this equation also makes intuitive sense. Households can consume more than their income in a given period. But over their entire lifetimes, they obviously cannot consume more than their resources, and so far we assume that they do not consume less than their lifetime resources and leave bequests. The present-value condition indicates that a family can choose *any combination* of consumption through time (C_1 and C_2), as long as the present value of consumption equals the present value of income. Households must live within their means, not period to period, but over the course of their lifetimes.[4]

We can now add two important extensions to this relationship. If a households starts its life with assets, for example, if it receives an inheritance, then the household has more resources to spend during its lifetime. The budget constraint then changes to

$$C_1 + \frac{C_2}{(1 + r)} = (1 + r)B_0 + Q_1 + \frac{Q_2}{(1 + r)} \qquad \textbf{(4.7)}$$

where $(1 + r)B_0$ is the value of an inheritance B_0 as of the first period, including both principal B_0 and interest payments rB_0.

If, instead of two periods, families live many periods, the budget constraint is naturally extended to

$$C_1 + \frac{C_2}{(1 + r)} + \cdots + \frac{C_T}{(1 + r)^{T-1}}$$

$$= (1 + r)B_0 + Q_1 + \frac{Q_2}{(1 + r)} + \cdots + \frac{Q_T}{(1 + r)^{T-1}} = W_1 \quad \textbf{(4.8)}$$

This relationship may be found by repeatedly using equation (4.2), applied for t periods ($t = 1, 2, \ldots, T$).[5]

---

[4] There is a way to write the budget constraint that makes it look more like a budget constraint of standard consumer theory. Let us define P_2 as the price of second-period consumption in terms of first-period consumption. Note that in order to increase second-period consumption by one unit, it is necessary to decrease first-period consumption by $1/(1 + r)$ units (in other words, it is necessary to increase saving by that amount). Thus, $P_2 = 1/(1 + r)$. The price of the first-period consumption good in terms of the first-period consumption good is obviously 1. This gives us a system of prices (which can be called "intertemporal prices" since they express the price of second-period goods in terms of first-period goods). Using these prices, we can write the budget constraint as $P_1 C_1 + P_2 C_2 = P_1 Q_1 + P_2 Q_2$, which looks like a standard consumer budget constraint.

[5] Take the expression $B_1 = Q_1 + (1 + r)B_0 - C_1$, and substitute into $B_2 = Q_2 + (1 + r)B_1 - C_2$. This gives $B_2 = Q_2 + (1 + r)(Q_1 - C_1) + (1 + r)^2 B_0 - C_2$. Then, substitute this expression

If households want to leave bequests to the next generation, then they will not consume all their wealth during their lifetimes. Let BQ_T be the amount of the bequest at the end of period T. Then, the definition of wealth would remain the same as in equation (4.8), but the discounted value of consumption would be set equal to $W_1 - BQ_T/(1 + r)^{T-1}$.

Graphical Treatment of the Budget Constraint

The two-period model has the advantage that it can be easily represented in graphic form. Let the horizontal axis of Figure 4-2 represent variables in the first period, and the vertical axis represent variables in the second period. Point A is the endowment point, which reflects the particular combination of first and second period output of the household. In other words, point A is the ordered pair (Q_1, Q_2).

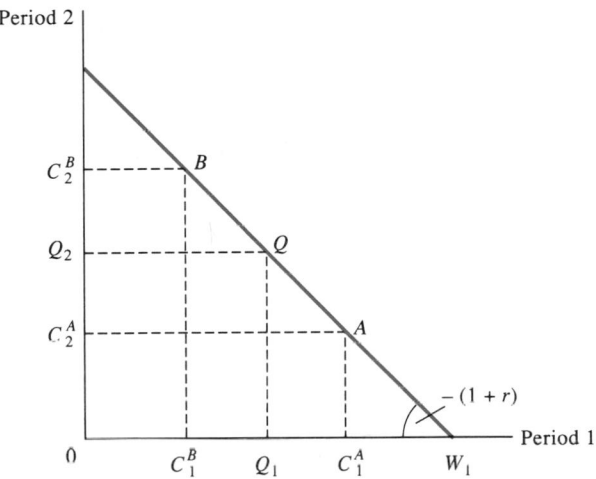

Figure 4-2

Graphical Representation of the Budget Constraint

The budget constraint in (4.6) can be easily graphed once we rewrite it as $C_2 = Q_2 - (1 + r)C_1 + (1 + r)Q_1$. Clearly, the budget constraint is a straight line with slope of $-(1 + r)$ that goes through point (Q_1, Q_2). This line represents all the possible consumption possibilities (C_1, C_2) consistent with the intertemporal budget constraint. The household can choose any consumption pair on this line. The household can shift future income to the present by borrowing at the rate r, or it can shift present output to the future by lending at the rate r. Therefore, r measures the market opportunities for converting present consumption into future consumption, or vice versa, through the holding of financial assets.

---

into $B_3 = Q_3 + (1 + r)B_2 - C_3$. If we continue this process until $B_T = Q_T + (1 + r)B_{T-1} - C_T$, for some $T > 3$ and set $B_T = 0$, we can rearrange the resulting expression to arrive at the formula given in (4.8).

If the household chooses to consume at point A in Figure 4-2, it would be borrowing in the first period since $C_1^A > Q_1$. Clearly, the household would be a net debtor at the end of the first period. As a result, C_2^A must be less than Q_2 (as is evident from the diagram), since the debt has to be repaid. Thus, the downward-sloping line reflects the fundamental intertemporal trade-off. Given a path of output, if a family decides to increase present consumption, it can only do so at the expense of future consumption. At a point like B, by contrast, the household is limiting first-period consumption ($C_1^B < Q_1$) in order to consume more in the future.

The discounted value of consumption is found by the intercept of the budget line with the horizontal axis, shown as W_1. Note that $W_1 = Q_1 + Q_2/(1 + r)$, and thus is the household's level of wealth.[6]

4-4 Household Decision Making

So far, we have specified the consumption possibilities that households face, but we have not explained how they make their consumption decisions from among these possibilities. We now turn to this decision-making process.

We assume that the household derives utility from consumption in each period. We also assume that the level of utility achieved by some combination of C_1 and C_2 is characterized by a utility function $UL = UL(C_1, C_2)$. At time 1, we assume that the household chooses the combination of C_1 and C_2 that yields the highest value of utility just as long as C_1 and C_2 lie on the budget constraint.

The intertemporal utility function $UL(C_1, C_2)$ behaves like any other utility function familiar from consumer theory. For example, $UL(C_1, C_2)$ is an increasing function of both C_1 and C_2: the household is better off with more rather than less C_1 or C_2. And as with any standard utility function, the simplest way to graph the properties of the function is to show the household's *indifference curves*.[7] Consider, as shown in Figure 4-3, the set of consumption points (C_1, C_2) that result in a given level of utility UL_0. What we have done here is to graph the set of points $UL_0 = U(C_1, C_2)$, with the result that the indifference curve for UL_0 is downward sloping and concave or bowl shaped.

It is important to understand this shape. Suppose that we are at point A, with $UL_0 = UL(C_1^A, C_2^A)$. Now, let us see what happens when some C_1 is taken away from the household, while enough C_2 is given to the household so that utility remains at UL_0. The result might be a move to point B, with less C_1 and more C_2 than at A. The indifference curve slopes down because the household must receive more C_2 if it is to remain equally well off after the loss of some C_1.

The bowl shape results from the fact that the amount by which C_2 must be *increased* for a given reduction in C_1 depends on the initial combination of C_1 and C_2 in a particular way. At a point like A, the slope of the indifference

---

[6] To see why the intercept with the X axis is equal to wealth, note that the line segment $0W_1$ is composed of two parts: $0W_1 = 0Q_1 + Q_1W_1$. The length of $0Q_1$ is simply Q_1. The length of Q_1W_1 is $Q_2/(1 + r)$.

[7] For a full discussion of indifference curves, and their use in consumer analysis, see Paul Samuelson and William Nordhaus, *Economics* (New York: McGraw-Hill, 1989).

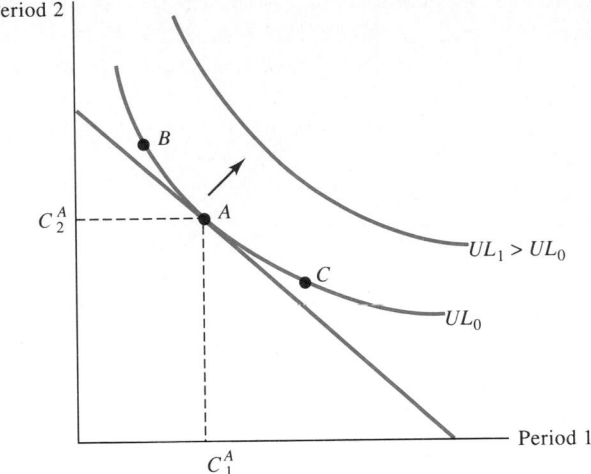

Figure 4-3
Household's Indifference Curves

curve measures the amount that C_2 must be increased in order to compensate the household for a small drop in C_1. This ratio, $-(\Delta C_2)/\Delta(C_1)$, is called the *marginal rate of substitution* (note that, with the minus sign in front, it is defined as a positive number). The key assumption is that the marginal rate of substitution declines; that is, the absolute value of the slope diminishes as one moves in the southeast direction along the indifference curve.

How, then, does the household behave? When it is planning to consume a little in the current period and a lot in the future, as at point B, it must receive a lot more future consumption in order to be compensated for even a little reduction in present consumption. Since present consumption C_1 is already relatively small, the household is loath to reduce it further. On the other hand, at a point like C, the household is already devoting most of its consumption to the present, and just a little to the future. In this case, it is more willing to give up a unit of current consumption for just a small increase in future consumption. The result of this declining marginal rate of substitution is the bowl-shaped indifference curve shown in the diagram.

In Figure 4-3, the budget constraint of the household is superimposed on a family of indifference curves. Note that as we move in the northeast direction among the indifference curves (as shown by the arrow), we are moving in the direction of increasing household utility. The household maximizes its utility by finding the indifference curve with highest utility that touches the budget constraint. As shown in Figure 4-3, the solution is given by the indifference curve that is *tangent* to the budget constraint at point A. Notice that any other curve which touches the budget line provides a lower level of utility. And any indifference curve which represents a higher level of utility than UL_1 is unattainable.

Consider the specific solution depicted in Figure 4-4a. At A, consumption in the first period exceeds output, so that the household is a net borrower. In the second period, the household must consume less than its income, so that it can repay the debt incurred in the first period. Figure 4-4b represents the case of a household that lends in the first period, and there-

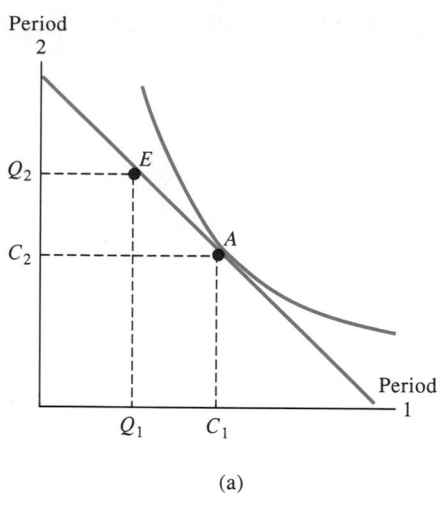

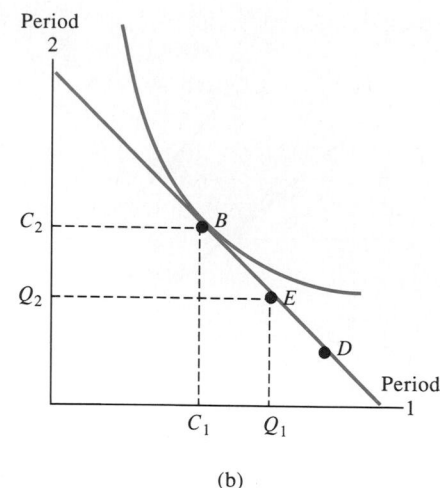

Figure 4-4
(a) Net Borrowers; (b) Net Lenders

fore is able to consume more than its income in the second period. It is apparent that a household that has its output heavily concentrated in the second period tends to be a net borrower, while a household with its output concentrated in the first period tends to be a net lender.

Thus, we see that for a given level of current income, Y_1, consumption C_1 depends not only on current income but also on *future* income. It also depends on the interest rate, which determines the slope of the budget constraint, and on the specific tastes of the household, which determine the shape of the indifference curves.

Also note that in both Figures 4-4a and 4-4b the household is better off if it borrows or lends in the bond market than if it remains in financial isolation (or financial "autarky"). Without the bond market (or some other financial market for borrowing and lending), the household must simply consume its output in each period. We can find the utility level an isolated household can reach by finding which indifference curve passes through the endowment point E. In both graphs, that indifference curve represents a lower level of utility than the one reached by using the bond market to borrow or lend. Thus, the use of financial assets raises household welfare by allowing an intertemporal redistribution of consumption. These are the basic ideas that we shall develop in the rest of the chapter.

4-5 THE PERMANENT-INCOME THEORY OF CONSUMPTION

One of the main implications of the two-period model is that household consumption should depend not only on current income but also on income expected in the future. More precisely, this year's consumption should depend on an "average" level of income expected this year and in future years. This basic idea was first developed in the 1950s by Nobel Prize–winning economist Milton Friedman, who used the term *permanent income* to signify the average income that the household should expect over a long time horizon. The permanent-income model was first presented in Friedman's classic 1957 study *A Theory of the Consumption Function*.[8]

The starting point of Friedman's model is that households tend to smooth consumption over time. Households prefer a stable consumption path to an unstable one. (Technically, this is because of the property of declining marginal rates of substitution between current and future income, which gives the indifference curves the bowl shape that we have seen.) In Figure 4-4b, for example, the utility level of consumption at B (where C_1 is similar to C_2) is clearly higher than at D (where C_1 is significantly higher than C_2). Because income is bound to fluctuate year to year, our results so far suggest that households will use capital markets to maintain fairly steady consumption against a backdrop of fluctuating income.

Consider, for example, the case of a farmer whose income is high at the time of harvest and very low during the rest of the year. It is unlikely that the farmer wants consumption to vary according to the season, high at harvest time and negligible the rest of the year. Rather, he tries to smooth consumption over the course of the year, saving during the harvest season in order to dissave, or consume more than income, the rest of the time. The farmer also experiences substantial income fluctuations from year to year, depending on weather conditions and crop prices. Once again, he tries to smooth consumption in the face of these fluctuations. During good years, he saves; during bad years, he dissaves, thus maintaining a stable living standard.

According to the permanent-income model, consumption responds to *permanent income* (Yp), which is defined as a kind of average of present and future incomes. Specifically, for a household with a fluctuating income stream, Yp is defined as the *constant* level of income that would give the household the same intertemporal budget constraint as it has with its fluctuating income stream. Mathematically, we can proceed as follows. The household's intertemporal budget constraint (in the two-period example) is $C_1 + C_2/(1 + r) = Q_1 + Q_2/(1 + r)$, with Q_1 and Q_2 usually being different. Now, let us find a value for Yp such that the household would have the same intertemporal consumption possibilities if output equals Yp in each period. Clearly, Yp must satisfy the equality in (4.9):

$$Yp + \frac{Yp}{(1 + r)} = Q_1 + \frac{Q_2}{(1 + r)} \qquad \textbf{(4.9)}$$

Equation (4.9) can be solved for Yp in terms of Q_1 and Q_2.

$$Yp = \frac{(1 + r)}{(2 + r)}\left[Q_1 + \frac{Q_2}{(1 + r)}\right] \qquad \textbf{(4.10)}$$

Notice that permanent income would be an exact average of present and future output in the particular case in which the interest rate is zero (and

---

[8] The book was published by Princeton University Press, Princeton, New Jersey.

in which the household inherits no stock of financial assets at time 1).[9] But in general the interest rate is not zero, and thus we say that permanent income is a "kind" of average of future output.

A graphical representation of permanent income is provided in Figure 4-5. To find Yp we draw a 45-degree line from the origin to the budget constraint. The value of Yp lies at the intersection of these two lines, point A, the only point with equal output in both periods that lies on the budget constraint. Notice that given the position of the endowment point, E, we see that in this case $Q_1 > Yp$ and $Q_2 < Yp$.

In an important special case of utility maximization, the household tries to maintain a perfectly stable consumption path so that it consumes the same every period. In that case, consumption is set exactly equal to permanent income ($C_1 = C_2 = Yp$). Thus, in this case, *saving is given by the gap between current and permanent income*:

$$S_1 = Q_1 - C_1 = Q_1 - Yp \tag{4.11}$$

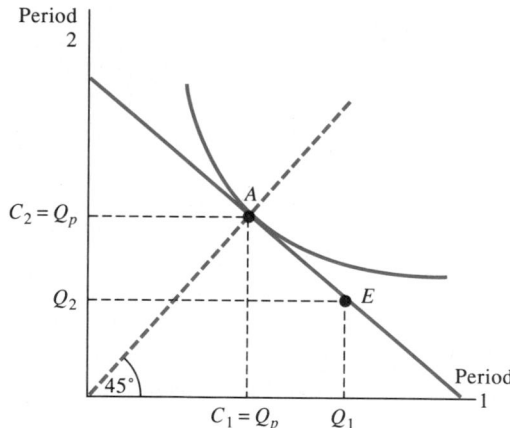

Figure 4-5
Household Consumption and Permanent Income

In Figure 4-5, the indifference curve is tangent to the budget line at the same point where the budget line intersects the 45-degree line. Consumption is the same in both periods, equal to permanent income Yp.

This special case of equal consumption each period holds only for particular kinds of utility functions, but nonetheless, the ideas behind this

---

[9] If there is an initial stock of financial assets, the budget constraint equation must be modified accordingly, as in equation (4.7). Then, permanent income would be found by equating

$$Yp + \frac{Yp}{(1 + r)} = (1 + r)B_0 + Q_1 + \frac{Q_2}{(1 + r)}$$

Therefore, the equation for Yp is

$$Yp = \left[\frac{(1 + r)}{(2 + r)}\right]\left[(1 + r)B_0 + Q_1 + \frac{Q_2}{(1 + r)}\right]$$

case have more general validity.[10] Households decide their consumption levels on the basis of their permanent incomes, not their current incomes. To the extent that current incomes are higher than average, they will tend to save the difference. To the extent that current incomes are lower than average, they will tend to dissave, borrowing against their higher future income.

It is useful to distinguish the effects on consumption of three prototypical kinds of shocks to income, *temporary current shocks, permanent shocks,* and *anticipated future shocks.* With a temporary shock (which we take to be a negative shock for purposes of discussion), Q_1 falls while Q_2 remains the same; with a permanent shock, Q_1 and Q_2 fall by the same amount; and with an anticipated shock, Q_1 remains unchanged but the household expects Q_2 to fall. It should be easy to see that households tend to dissave in response to a temporary shock, since C_1 falls by less than Q_1; they tend to adjust fully to a permanent shock, with C_1 falling by about the same amount as Q_1, with little change in saving; and they tend to raise current saving in response to an anticipated shock, with C_1 falling even though Q_1 remains unchanged.

These results can be restated in terms of permanent-income theory. With a temporary shock, permanent income doesn't change by very much, so that consumption doesn't change by much. Current saving therefore falls when Q_1 falls. With a permanent shock, permanent income changes (approximately) by the extent of the shock. Consumption falls a lot and saving changes little. With an anticipated shock, permanent income drops, even though current output does not, causing a rise in saving.

At an abstract level, the permanent-income theory is very appealing. But in general, households only know their current income with much confidence. When their income changes, how can they know whether the change is transitory or permanent? This brings us to a very central issue in economics that we introduced in Chapter 2: the role of *expectations*. Before people can make decisions about the future, they almost always have to form expectations about future economic variables. Economists have spent considerable effort studying ways in which people do that.

In his original work, Friedman assumed that expectations of future income are arrived at by means of a mechanism known as "adaptive" expectations. This simply means that people readjust ("adapt") their estimates of permanent income (Yp) each period, based on their previous estimates of Yp and actual changes in output. Specifically, this period's expectation of per-

---

[10] The utility function must be such that the indifference curve is tangent to the budget line along the 45-degree line from the origin. (In that case, optimal consumption will require that $C_1 = C_2$.) A mathematically important class of utility functions that can have this property is called the "isoelastic utility functions." An example is the logarithmic function

$$UL(C_1, C_2) = \log(C_1) + \left[\frac{1}{(1 + \delta)}\right] \log(C_2)$$

where δ is a parameter called the "intertemporal rate of discount." When the rate of time discount δ equals the market rate of interest r, then the logarithmic utility function will have the property of tangency to the budget line along a 45-degree line from the origin. As δ rises relative to r, households discount (or care less) about future consumption relative to current consumption. Therefore, when $\delta > r$, households raise their first-period consumption so that it is greater than permanent income. When $\delta < r$, households discount their second-period consumption by a smaller amount. They therefore tend to reduce their first-period consumption to be less than permanent income.

manent income, which we denote Y_p^e, is a weighted average of *last period's* expectations, Y_{p-1}^e, and actual income this period, Y, or

$$Y_p^e = \alpha Y_{p-1}^e + (1 - \alpha)Y \qquad (4.12)$$

Economists have grown increasingly dissatisfied with this approach, as we said in Chapter 2. For one thing, it is "too mechanical"; for another, people would take more care in estimating their future income than just using a recursive formula. This has prompted many economists to adopt the hypothesis of *rational* expectations, in which it is assumed that households use a more detailed conceptual model of the economy to form their expectations. For example, households might try to specify a numerical model of how their income will develop in future years, based on their specific understanding of the industry and region in which they work, as well as developments in the overall economy. Although economists have had problems applying the idea of "rational" expectations in their research, much of the current study of consumption behavior is based on it, and we return to the rational expectations approach many times in the book.

In some cases, of course, the distinction between transitory and permanent income changes is not that difficult. Think of an Argentine farmer who is growing wheat in Patagonia. As a result of an unusual drought in the United States in 1988, which destroyed much of the U.S. wheat harvest, prices of wheat almost doubled in the international markets. The harvest in Patagonia was quite good in 1988, and the Argentine farmer enjoyed a large rise in income when world prices increased. As the U.S. drought was unlikely to recur again soon (given the standard patterns of rainfall in the United States), the farmer would probably be correct to see a large part of his 1988 income as transitory. According to the permanent-income theory, such a farmer would be prone to *save* most of his extra income.

Empirical Evidence on the Permanent-Income Model

For several decades, even before the permanent-income model, economists have studied consumption and saving on an empirical level by observing both the consumption behavior of individual households in statistical samples and the consumption behavior of the household sector in aggregate data.

The basic research strategy has been to state the statistical relationship between consumption and income as

$$C = a + cY \qquad (4.13)$$

The standard statistical approach is regression analysis, in which the parameters a and c are estimated using a least-squares estimation procedure. The data used in the regression analysis of equation (4.13) might involve consumption and income levels for a given year for a large sample of households, or it might involve consumption and income over a period of years for a sample of households, or it might involve the aggregate consumption of the household sector of the economy and aggregate income, using national income accounts data of the sort shown in Table 4-1. A considerable interest has focused on the statistical estimate of the parameter c in the equation. This parameter is known as the *marginal propensity to consume* (MPC), and it evidently measures the increase in consumption when income goes up by one dollar. It is expected that $0 < c < 1$, so that consumption rises along with income, but by something less than income.

We should understand from the theoretical discussion that the value of c will depend on the measure of income that we use in the statistical estimation of (4.13). Consider the two-period model, for example. Suppose that the utility function is such that households simply consume their permanent income: $C_1 = Yp_1$. If we estimate an equation using household data in which we regress C_1 for each household on the *permanent* income of the household, then we should expect to find that $a = 0$ and $c = 1$. In other words, the intercept of the equation would be 0, and the slope would be 1.

If, on the other hand, we regress C_1 for each household on the current income of the household, then we should expect to find an estimate for c lower than 1. In particular, since

$$Yp = \left[\frac{(1 + r)}{(2 + r)}\right]\left[Q_1 + \frac{Q_2}{(1 + r)}\right]$$

and since $C_1 = Yp$, we see that

$$C_1 = \left[\frac{(1 + r)}{(2 + r)}\right] Q_1 + \left[\frac{1}{(2 + r)}\right] Q_2 \qquad \textbf{(4.14)}$$

Clearly, for a *given* level of Q_2, the marginal propensity to consume out of current income is $(1 + r)/(2 + r)$, which is less than 1. When economists estimate the relationship between C_1 and Q_1, they tend to find a marginal propensity to consume that is less than 1 and a positive intercept.

Before Friedman presented his permanent-income model, researchers were generally using current income as the variable in the regression analysis, and were indeed finding a marginal propensity to consume that was less than 1, along with an intercept coefficient a that was positive. But many economists drew a faulty inference from these findings. They reasoned that with a marginal propensity to consume less than 1, when households get richer, their saving rates would tend to rise.[11] However, Simon Kuznets, who later was awarded the Nobel Prize, discovered that in the United States over the period of a century, the saving rate had not risen. This seemed to contradict the idea of a marginal propensity to consume of less than 1.[12] Friedman's permanent-income theory, with its implication that saving rates rise when *temporary* income rises but not when *permanent* income rises, resolved the paradox.

The new theory gives rise to the crucial insight that the MPC out of current income is substantially smaller than is the MPC out of permanent income. Recent empirical work on consumption, using ever-more-sophisticated econometrics, has supported the theory. The MPC out of current

---

[11] Suppose that $C = a + bY$. Saving is $S = Y - C$, and the saving rate is $s = S/Y = (1 - b) - a/Y$. Note that as Y rises, the saving rate would rise to a maximum of $1 - b$.

[12] Simon Kuznets, *National Income, a Summary of Findings* (New York: National Bureau of Economic Research, 1946).

income has been estimated at between 0.2 and 0.3, while the MPC out of permanent income has been found to be close to 1, as expected.[13]

The permanent-income hypothesis has several other implications for empirical research. First, we should expect that the measured MPC out of current income is smaller for households with a highly variable income than for households with stable income. In the first case, a change in current income is likely to signal little about a change in permanent income, while in the latter case, a change in current income is likely to signal a change in permanent income as well. As Friedman himself pointed out in his original study, this explains why farmers (whose income varies greatly from year to year) tend to show lower MPCs than do urban wage earners (whose incomes are not subject to large fluctuations due to weather). Second, younger households tend to show lower MPCs than do older households for a similar reason: a given change in current income tends to have less effect on permanent income for the younger household than it does for the older one.

Another recent application of the permanent-income model shows up in the *random-walk consumption function* of Robert Hall at Stanford University.[14] Hall showed that under some conditions, a household's estimate of its permanent income as of this year should also be the best predictor of its permanent income as of next year. This means that the household's consumption this year (C) should also be the best predictor of the household's consumption next year. Or put another way, next year's consumption C_{+1} should equal C plus a random amount (e_{+1}) that results from the unexpected shocks next year that will affect the household's estimate of its permanent income. From this insight, Hall tested some of the implications of the permanent-income hypothesis, by examining whether $C_{+1} = C + e_{+1}$ is a good model of consumption.[15] He found some empirical support for the hypothesis in that next year's consumption is closely related to this year's consumption, but he also found that other current variables helped to predict future consumption, contrary to the theory. (One possible source of discrepancy is the presence of liquidity constraints on household borrowing, an issue we take up later.)

Durables and Nondurables

The permanent-income hypothesis applies to consumption, and consumption is not exactly the same thing as the expenditure on consumer goods. Households want to attain a stable flow of consumption *services*, and it is those services that are the source of utility to the households from a given kind of commodity. Some commodities give consumption services only in

---

[13] These results are contained in two papers: Marjorie Flavin, "The Adjustment of Consumption to Changing Expectations About Future Income," *Journal of Political Economy*, October 1981, and Robert Hall and Frederick Mishkin, "The Sensitivity of Consumption to Transitory Income: Estimates from Panel Data on Households," *Econometrica*, March 1982. Support for the permanent-income theory is also found in earlier empirical works such as Robert Eisner, "The Permanent Income Hypothesis: Comment," *American Economic Review*, December 1958.

[14] R. Hall, "Stochastic Implications of the Life Cycle—Permanent Income Hypothesis: Theory and Evidence," *Journal of Political Economy*, December 1978. This original and quite technical piece has inspired substantial subsequent research.

[15] Technically, an equation of the form $C_{+1} = C + e_{+1}$ is known as a random-walk model. Hence the name given to Hall's theory.

the course of using them up—a meal, a newspaper, a weekend vacation. Other commodities, by contrast, deliver services to the household over a long period of time. Automobiles, television sets, and refrigerators, for example, may be used for several years. Economists therefore distinguish between *nondurables*, which provide services over a short period of time, and *durables*, which last for many years.

Consumption is properly measured as the sum of expenditures on nondurables *plus* the flow of services rendered by the existing stock of consumer durables. That is, most of current expenditures on consumer durables are actually investment spending (an investment in future consumption services) rather than consumer spending. On the other hand, there is some consumption each year that takes place by enjoying the services of durables that were purchased in earlier years.

Consumption is commonly identified with consumer expenditures rather than with consumer services. That is, consumption is measured as the spending on nondurables plus durables, rather than the spending on nondurables plus the *services* of durables. The proper measure of consumption corrects measured expenditures by subtracting off the expenditures on durables and adding back in an estimate of the flow of consumption services of the existing stock of durables. (This estimate is found by assuming that the cost of the durable represents a flow of services that is distributed over a period of years.)

The permanent-income hypothesis performs best empirically when permanent income is related to the flow of consumer services rather than to consumer expenditures. It is easy to see why. Consider a household that buys a new car every five years. The data on its consumer expenditures would show an unstable pattern, with a large jump in expenditures every time it gets a new car. On the surface, then, it looks as if this household is not smoothing its consumption at all. But in reality it is consuming "automobile services" at a far more stable rate. While a new car may provide more "automobile services" than an older car, the household's consumption of automobile services is in fact much smoother than its observed five-year cycle of expenditures on automobiles suggests.

Consumption and Taxes

So far, we have not mentioned taxes, and in real life, taxes have a big influence on consumption and saving decisions. We give taxes a thorough treatment in Chapter 7 when we discuss the role of the government. For the moment, it will suffice to incorporate taxes into the determination of the household's disposable income.

In our discussion of Table 4-1, we noticed the links between disposable income (Yd), which determines the budget constraint of households, and total income, or GNP. While many factors determine the difference between Yd and GNP, here we will stress the role of taxes paid by households to the government. When we subtract taxes from the income received by households each period, the budget constraint of the household changes to

$$C_1 + \frac{C_2}{(1 + r)} = (Q_1 - T_1) + \frac{(Q_2 - T_2)}{(1 + r)}$$

$$= Qd_1 + \frac{Qd_2}{(1 + r)} \qquad\qquad \textbf{(4.15)}$$

where Qd_1 and Qd_2 stand for disposable output periods 1 and 2, respectively. Note that $Yd = Qd + rB_{-1}$ when B_{-1} does not equal 0.

Higher taxes tend to reduce consumption for a given path of output by reducing the present discounted value of disposable income available to the household.[16] The effect of higher taxes, T_1, on C_1 of course depends on whether the tax increase is expected to be transitory or permanent (in the two-period model, whether it lasts for one period or for two periods). A transitory increase in taxes reduces permanent income by $(1 + r)/(2 + r)$ times the rise in taxes. A permanent increase in taxes will reduce permanent income by the amount of the rise in taxes. To see this, simply go back to equation (4.10) and interpret Q_1 and Q_2 on the right-hand side as disposable output in periods 1 and 2.

These theoretical predictions have practical policy implications when governments attempt to change consumption spending through a change in taxes. In the United States in 1968, the Johnson administration attempted to raise taxes in order to reduce consumption and thereby free up national resources for higher military spending during the war in Vietnam. A *temporary* tax surcharge was imposed, but the measure failed to restrain demand. Households knew that the tax measure was temporary, and this being the case, it had very small impact on consumption. According to one estimate, the effect of the temporary tax surcharge on consumption was very close to zero, thereby confirming the theory.[17]

4-6 THE LIFE-CYCLE MODEL OF CONSUMPTION AND SAVING

The life-cycle model, like the permanent-income model, builds on the theory that consumption in a particular period depends on expectations about life-time income and not on the income of the current period. The distinctive contribution of the life-cycle hypothesis is its observation that income tends to fluctuate systematically over the course of a person's life and that personal saving behavior is therefore crucially determined by one's stage in the life cycle. Franco Modigliani, the 1986 Nobel laureate in Economics, developed the life-cycle model in a series of papers written in the 1950s and early 1960s in association with Richard Brumberg and Albert Ando.[18] Modigliani's Nobel lecture, "Life Cycle, Individual Thrift and the Wealth of Nations," offers a survey of this fundamental contribution to economics.[19]

When people are young, their incomes are low, and they often go into

---

[16] Taxes may have other important effects on income by changing the incentives for work versus leisure, or savings versus consumption, for a given level of disposable income. We will return to these incentive effects in Chapter 7.

[17] See Alan Blinder and Angus Deaton, "The Time Series Consumption Function Revisited," *Brookings Papers on Economic Activity,* 2:1985.

[18] The classical works are Franco Modigliani and Richard Brumberg, "Utility Analysis and the Consumption Function: An Interpretation of Cross-section Data," in K. Kurihara, ed., *Post-Keynesian Economics* (New Brunswick, NJ: Rutgers University Press, 1954), and Albert Ando and Franco Modigliani, "The Life-Cycle Hypothesis of Saving: Aggregate Implications and Tests," *American Economic Review,* March 1963.

[19] The Nobel lecture is an up-to-date exposition of the theory and the empirical evidence on the life-cycle hypothesis; see the *American Economic Review,* June 1986.

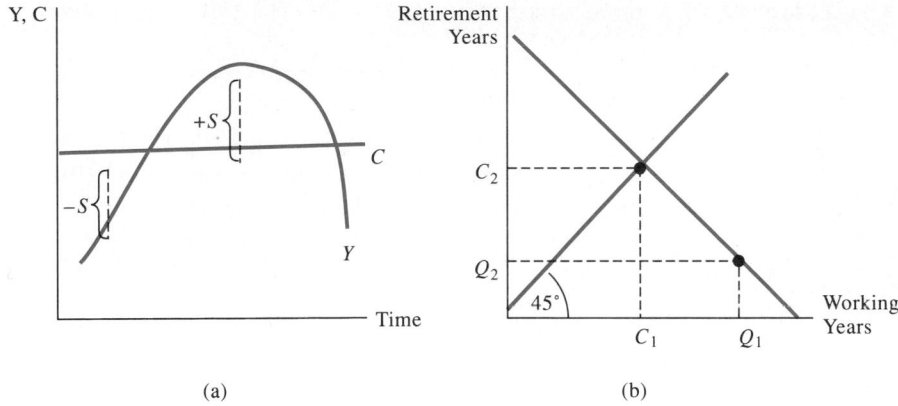

Figure 4-6
The Life-Cycle Hypothesis of Consumption and Saving

debt (dissave) because they know that they will be earning more money later in their lives. During their working years, income rises to reach a peak at around middle age, and they repay the debt incurred earlier and save for their retirement years. When retirement arrives, income from work goes to zero and people consume their accumulated resources. This pattern is depicted in Figure 4-6a.

Notice that there are two periods of dissaving in an individual's life: the early years and the later years. Figure 4-6b presents this same idea in the now-familiar representation of the two-period model. If we reinterpret period 1 as the working years and period 2 as the retirement years, the same type of conclusions emerge. (Unfortunately, a two-dimensional graph is not rich enough to capture a third, younger period of life.) People save during their working years to provide for retirement, and they do this because income in the first period is larger than income in the second. (To put this another way, first-period income is greater than permanent income.)

Consumption during retirement is financed both from savings accumulated during the working years and from transfers that older people receive from the government and from their children. While there is no organized system to transfer income from children to parents specifically, most countries have an indirect transfer system from the young to the old via the government. In the United States, young workers pay social security taxes which are then distributed to retired workers. Such a system has important consequences for saving decisions. The more generous a social security system, the less a household must save during its working period to provide for its consumption during its retirement period. The result may well be a drop in saving by the household, and perhaps in the aggregate saving in the economy. Box 4-1 discusses the implications of social security for saving, a research topic that has been important in the economic agenda.

Now let us explore some other implications of the life-cycle theory. In the case in which consumption is equalized in all periods, consumption is equal to permanent income. From equation (4.14), we can write C_1 as a multiple of wealth:

$$C_1 = \left[\frac{(1 + r)}{(2 + r)}\right]\left[Q_1 + \frac{Q_2}{(1 + r)}\right] = k(r)W_1 \qquad \textbf{(4.16)}$$

Box 4-1
Social Security and Saving

In social security programs, the government makes payments to retired workers, financed out of taxes on younger workers and (in some countries) the profits earned on a fund that has been accumulated out of past taxes. By reducing the needs of workers to save for their retirement, then, social security programs may reduce private saving. Martin Feldstein of Harvard University has been the leading scholarly advocate of just this position. In 1974, he published an influential article in which he claimed that the U.S. social security scheme reduced private saving by about 50 percent, thus reducing the aggregate capital stock and output.[20] In later studies, he has maintained that the effect is strong, though perhaps not as large as he originally thought.

Feldstein's view is not universally accepted. Some empirical researchers have claimed to find a weaker effect than Feldstein has indicated. Others, such as Robert Barro of Harvard University, have raised some theoretical objections as well. Barro has shown on theoretical grounds that if households recognize that their social security benefits will be paid by taxes levied on their children, they might increase their saving in order to leave a larger bequest to their heirs, in effect, leaving them part or all of the income that they will need to pay the social security contributions. In such a case, the negative effect on saving for one's own retirement is counteracted by a positive effect on saving in order to leave a bequest to one's offspring. This theoretical argument, known as Barro–Ricardian equivalence, is considered in Chapter 7.

The evidence on this issue outside the United States is far from conclusive. Two studies comparing savings in a number of countries found little empirical support for the depressing effect of social security on private saving. Feldstein, in his own international research, remained convinced of his original finding for the United States.[21] The controversy has, so far, not been settled.

Thus, consumption is a fraction of wealth, with the factor of proportionality (k), or the marginal propensity to consume out of wealth, depending on the interest rate. In practice, the factor of proportionality k will depend on other things as well, such as the rate of time preference and the ages of individuals in the household.

---

[20] See his article, "Social Security, Induced Retirement and Aggregate Capital Accumulation," *Journal of Political Economy*, September/October 1974.

[21] The two skeptical studies are R. Barro and G. MacDonald, "Social Security and Consumer Spending in an International Cross-section," *Journal of Public Economics*, June 1979, and F. Modigliani and A. Sterling, "Determinants of Private Saving with Special Reference to the Role of Social Security—Cross-country Tests," in F. Modigliani and R. Hemming, eds., *The Determinants of National Saving and Wealth* (London: Macmillan, 1983). Feldstein's article is "Social Security and Private Saving: International Evidence in an Extended Life-Cycle Model," in M. Feldstein and R. Inman, eds., *The Economics of Public Services* (London: Macmillan, 1977).

In the two-period model, $k = (1 + r)/(2 + r)$, which is between 1/2 and 1. With a larger number of periods, k would be smaller. Why? Because a one-unit increase in wealth would then have to be divided among many periods. Therefore, the marginal propensity to consume depends inversely on the age of the household, with older households consuming a *larger* fraction of wealth in any period than younger households. What counts for a particular household is the number of periods remaining in the planning horizon, with older households tending on average to have shorter horizons than younger households.

Evidence on the Life-Cycle Model

Modigliani and Ando provided one of the first empirical tests of the life-cycle model in their joint 1963 study.[22] They ran the following regression,

$$C = c_1 Yd + k_1 W$$

where Yd is disposable labor income and W is the financial wealth of the household sector. The equation was estimated using annual data. We would expect to find c_1 less than 1, since c_1 measures the MPC out of current income. We would also expect to obtain a coefficient k_1 a little greater than the annual rate of interest. Why? Because a person behaving according to the life-cycle theory would like to spend her assets over the entire lifetime. If she consumes only the interest income in each period, she would die with her assets intact; she must, therefore, consume a little more than the interest earnings. Ando and Modigliani estimated the value of c_1 at 0.7, and k_1 at 0.06, the latter slightly more than the annual real rate of interest.

The findings of Ando and Modigliani were encouraging for the life-cycle theory. Further tests of the life-cycle model have provided some substantiation, but they have also turned up some empirical inconsistencies. It seems that households indeed save more during the prime of working years than they do when they are young or old.[23] But at the same time, older people appear not to dissave very much.[24] In other words, they keep their assets intact, and eventually pass along these assets to their heirs rather than use their wealth for consumption during their own lifetimes. The failure of the old to run down their wealth remains one of the important puzzling counterexamples to the reasoning of the life-cycle model.

The Role of Bequests

When people die, they often leave wealth to their children. These transfers of wealth are called *bequests*. Two key questions have to be addressed before we can incorporate bequests into life-cycle theory. First, what motivates bequests? Second, and more generally, how can bequests be incorporated into a theory of saving?

---

[22] Ando and Modigliani, "The Life-Cycle Hypothesis of Saving."

[23] See, for example, Mervyn King and Louis Dicks-Mireaux, "Asset Holding and the Life Cycle," *The Economic Journal*, June 1982.

[24] For a discussion of the evidence on dissaving by the old, see the excellent survey article by Lawrence Kotlikoff, "Intergenerational Transfers and Savings," *Journal of Economic Perspectives*, Vol. 2, no. 2, Spring 1988, pp. 41–58.

Economists by no means agree on the motivation of bequests. There are (at least) four basic schools of thought, two of which ascribe to parents specific attributes toward their heirs. Robert Barro, among others, has suggested that people leave bequests for altruistic reasons—they care about their children, and try to raise their children's well-being by income transfers. Douglas Bernheim, Andrei Schleifer, and Lawrence Summers have argued that parents have less altruistic motives, planning their bequests in order to influence the behavior of their children *during* the parents' lifetime ("I'll leave you the money if you take good care of me while I'm alive").

A third school of thought holds that bequests are largely unintended. By and large, people do not know when they will die, and they want to have plenty of resources available in case that they live much longer than expected.[25] Thus, if the life expectancy of a 65-year-old is 80 years, this person would keep enough wealth to survive until, say, 95 years of age. Obviously, an elderly person does not want to starve, or even to suffer the discomforts of poverty, because of greater than expected longevity.

Finally, a fourth school of thought holds that much wealth accumulation is not for future consumption in any event, but rather simply for the power and prestige it brings. Thus, the wealthy derive utility directly from their holdings, irrespective of the consumption their wealth might finance. This opinion offers the most direct challenge to the life-cycle point of view, since it suggests a theory of saving that is not directly tied to consumption, either of the current generation or of succeeding generations. Keynes described nineteenth-century saving behavior of the upper classes along these lines in a famous section of his *Economic Consequences of the Peace*:[26]

> The duty of "saving" became nine-tenths of virtue and the growth of the cake [national wealth] the object of true religion. . . . And so the cake increased but to what end was not clearly contemplated. . . . Saving was for old age or for your children; but this was only in theory,—the virtue of the cake was that it was never to be consumed, neither by you nor by your children after you.

The idea that parents leave bequests to their children for altruistic reasons may significantly affect life-cycle theory. Barro has stressed one possible modification. He holds that current consumption can be affected by the expected income of the *future* generation. Suppose that a household which cares about its children receives news that makes the children's economic future appear more bleak than had previously been expected. In that case, the household might choose to leave larger bequests to compensate for their children's potential losses. Thus, Barro has shown, the appropriate budget constraint for the household could involve not just the current generation's lifetime income, but also the future generation's lifetime income.

---

[25] These views are presented, respectively, in the following articles: Robert Barro, "Are Government Bonds Net Wealth?" *Journal of Political Economy*, November 1974; Douglas Bernheim, Andrei Schleifer, and Lawrence Summers, "The Strategic Bequest Motive," *Journal of Political Economy*, December 1985; and Andrew Abel, "Precautionary Savings and Unintended Bequests," *American Economic Review*, September 1985.

[26] John Maynard Keynes, *The Economic Consequences of the Peace* (New York: Harcourt, Brace, and Howe, 1920), p. 20.

Barro's argument formalizes an old idea known as *Ricardian equivalence* after the work of the early British economist David Ricardo. The empirical relevance of this ingenious argument is subject to dispute—even Ricardo doubted its relevance—and recent studies suggest that it has only a small degree of practical importance. (We return to this issue in greater detail in Chapter 7.)

The biggest challenge to the life-cycle theory on empirical grounds has come from Lawrence Kotlikoff and Lawrence Summers. Based on measurements which showed that much of the wealth in the United States was the result of bequests rather than life-cycle savings, these authors have argued that the importance of life-cycle saving considerations has been exaggerated.[27] Defending the relevance of the life-cycle model (which he developed), Modigliani swiftly counterattacked in his Nobel lecture. In the United States, he claimed, many old people put together their assets with those of their children in trust funds. Thus, while the funds might be increasing, it is quite possible that parents still deplete their own personal wealth from the fund, or pass on no more than the bequests, plus interest, that they received. So far, the issue of the importance of bequests for lifetime consumption behavior has not been settled.

4-7 HOUSEHOLD LIQUIDITY CONSTRAINTS AND CONSUMPTION THEORY

Modern theory has gone out of its way to stress the weakness of so simple a link between current income and current consumption as that which Keynes first proposed. And yet, one set of important considerations does suggest that for *many* households, Keynes was right after all to stress the strong link between current income and current consumption. To the extent that households are denied access to borrowing, their consumption behavior might indeed be linked only to current income rather than to future income. Households that cannot borrow and that lack a stock of financial wealth are said to be "liquidity constrained," in that the most they can spend is the income that they earn in the current period.

Liquidity constraint can be defined generally as the inability of certain individuals to borrow against future income, perhaps because lenders believe they are unlikely to repay their loans. Intertemporal theories of consumption are explicitly based on the assumption that agents can freely borrow and lend within the limits of their lifetime budget constraint. To the extent that many households are liquidity constrained, therefore, these theories are called into serious question.

Imagine, for example, a college freshman who correctly thinks that she has good future income perspectives. If she applies for a loan, she might be lucky enough to obtain financing sufficient to pay for her studies (perhaps under a government-sponsored program), but almost assuredly she will not obtain sufficient loans to raise her living standards to the level of her expected permanent income. Financial markets normally lend against collateral, not just the promise of future earnings from labor. College freshmen

[27] Lawrence Kotlikoff and Lawrence Summers, "The Role of Intergenerational Transfers in Aggregate Capital Accumulation," *Journal of Political Economy*, August 1981.

don't generally have real assets with which to guarantee a loan, and thus they are not generally able to borrow enough to smooth their consumption stream.

Empirical research has shown that liquidity constraints are important for part of the U.S. population. According to a study by Fumio Hayashi, liquidity constraints affect about 20 percent of the U.S. population.[28] For this group, consumption is linked to current disposable income rather than to lifetime wealth. In other recent work, Hayashi has found that the proportion of liquidity-constrained households is higher among young households than older households. He also estimates that liquidity constraints reduce consumption below the level that would be desired on life-cycle grounds by about 5.5 percent.[29]

Going back to the example of the college freshman, suppose she expects that 5 years from now she will earn a high salary. Consider, for example, her reaction to a bequest from a distant relative. Clearly, her consumption spending will tend to go up significantly more than the amount that life-cycle theory would predict. Consider also the case of a tax cut that is expected to be reversed in the future so that the *present value* of taxes remains unchanged. This would not affect consumption for someone behaving along life-cycle lines. It will, however, increase the consumption expenditures of a liquidity-constrained household.

4-8 AGGREGATE CONSUMPTION AND NATIONAL SAVING RATES

Up to now, we have carefully confined our theory to individual behavior. Even though our final goal is understanding the functioning of the aggregate economy, it is, after all, the behavior of individual households that we will be aggregating. We now proceed to the problem of aggregating the behavior of millions of individual households in order to understand aggregate consumption behavior in the entire economy. Macroeconomists have a name for this kind of research strategy in which individual behavior is studied first and then aggregated to understand economywide behavior. It is called providing "microeconomic foundations" for macroeconomic variables.

What are some of the problems of aggregating from the individual household to the whole economy? Consider first the simplest case. If all individuals have the *same* MPC out of permanent income, then aggregate consumption is just that MPC times permanent global income. In equations, if $C_i = cYp_i$ for individual i, and c is the same for all i, then $C = cYp$, where C is the sum of consumption of all households and Yp is the sum of the incomes of all households.

If the MPC varies across households, however, and in general it *does*, the aggregation issue becomes considerably more complicated. As we have already seen, not only do households differ in their preferences for con-

[28] F. Hayashi, "The Permanent Income Hypothesis: Estimation and Testing by Instrumental Variables," *Journal of Political Economy*, October 1982.

[29] F. Hayashi, "The Effect of Liquidity Constraints on Consumption: A Cross-sectional Analysis," *Quarterly Journal of Economics*, February 1985. Other interesting work on the subject is Marjorie Flavin, "Excess Sensitivity of Consumption to Current Income: Liquidity Constraints or Myopia?" *Canadian Journal of Economics*, February 1985.

sumption today versus the future, they also differ in their stage in the life cycle. An economy includes young adults in their prime working years who have a low MPC and a large income and who are net savers as well as old people in retirement who have a high MPC and a low income level and who are net dissavers. Thus, young savers coexist with older dissavers. The aggregate saving in the economy is determined by the balance of saving and dissaving, averaged over the entire population. Economic models that stress the coexistence of young and old households in the economy are referred to as models with "overlapping generations."

In an economy with a stable distribution of young and old and in which there is no per capita economic growth (that is, no rise over time in income per person) and no overall population growth, the saving of the young tends to be offset by the dissaving of the old. In this case, even if the young generation is saving for retirement, the aggregate saving in the economy is zero, because the older generation are dissaving at the same rate.

More commonly, most economies are characterized by positive population growth and positive growth in output per person because of technological improvements in the production process (a topic we take up when we study economic growth in Chapter 21). Each generation is richer than the previous one, and also more numerous. Thus, young savers are generally more plentiful and richer than old dissavers. In the aggregate, saving exceeds dissaving, and such economies show an overall positive rate of saving. Faster-growing economies, all other things being equal, tend to show a higher aggregate saving rate because of their demographics, with younger savers being more numerous and richer than the older dissavers. Thus, even if all the individual households in two economies have the *same* saving profile over their life cycles, one economy may show a higher aggregate saving rate because it has faster population growth or faster technical change from generation to generation.

Nathaniel Leff has prompted an interesting empirical debate concerning the role of demographics in aggregate saving. In a provocative 1969 article, he first published the basic finding that the higher the dependency rate in a country (that is, the proportion of retired people plus the very young to the working population), the lower its aggregate saving.[30] He justified this finding on the grounds that, as we have just noted, an economy with a high proportion of retired and young people tends to be an economy with a high proportion of dissavers relative to savers. Leff tested this hypothesis by looking at the saving rates and demographic characteristics of 74 countries, including developing and developed economies, and argued that the data supported the basic hypothesis. Others who have joined the debate, using different data sets and other statistical tests, have questioned the strength of Leff's conclusions, and the issue—as are many issues in macroeconomics—remains open to debate.

Despite the rich modeling of consumption behavior and the findings based on the overlapping generations framework, one of the great unsolved puzzles in economics remains the question of why some countries save at a very high rate while others save so little. Many analysts have tried to ex-

---

[30] Nathaniel Leff, "Dependency Rates and Saving Rates," *American Economic Review*, September 1969.

plain, for example, why Japan's saving rate appears to be so large compared to that of the United States.[31] Indeed, while in 1987 the ratio of national saving to GDP was 34 percent in Japan, it was only 14 percent in the United States.

Part of the difference in saving rates is accounted for by differences in the measurement of saving in the two countries that artificially overstate Japan's saving rate and understate the U.S. saving rate. U.S. households spend a higher proportion of their income on consumer durables. This spending is conventionally classified as pure consumption rather than partly as investment. If consumption were properly redefined, then, the gap between the U.S. saving rate and the Japanese saving rate would narrow. But even after correcting for definitional and data problems and comparing the saving rates of comparable age groups in Japan and the United States, the differences in saving rates seem to remain largely unexplained.

Part of the gap in saving rates could result from the fact that because of Japan's rapid economic growth, the young savers are much richer than the old dissavers, thereby raising the national saving rate in Japan. Some researchers have stressed that Japan's tax system promotes saving more than the tax system in the United States does and that the smaller coverage of Japan's social security system provides an added incentive for thrift. Others have suggested that Japan's high saving reflects, in part, the need to accumulate large pools of financial assets in order to be able to purchase houses, something that is very difficult to do given the high land prices in Japan and the poor markets for housing finance.

In the final analysis, however, the relative importance of these various explanations for the difference in saving rates between the United States and Japan remains in dispute. More generally, there also remains a strong sense that additional explanations are needed to account for differences in saving behavior across countries.

4-9 CONSUMPTION, SAVING, AND THE INTEREST RATE

We now shift away from the effects of income and wealth fluctuations on consumption and saving and turn to the effects of interest-rate changes. There has been a long debate as to whether or not saving tends to rise as interest rates increase. It is often supposed, somewhat naively, that as interest rates rise, and thus, as the rate of return to saving increases, it must be the case that saving will also increase. Such a supposition, however, is incorrect. Even on a purely theoretical level, the relationship between the interest rate and the saving rate is more complex.

Consider a household with an endowment, E, facing an interest rate given by the slope of the budget constraint, as shown in Figure 4-7a. Initially, consumption is given by point A. When the interest rate rises, the budget constraint rotates through the point E in a clockwise direction (that is, the budget constraint becomes steeper). The new consumption equilib-

[31] See Fumio Hayashi, "Why Is Japan's Savings Rate So Apparently High?" in Stanley Fischer, ed., *Macroeconomics Annual* (New York: National Bureau of Economic Research, 1986).

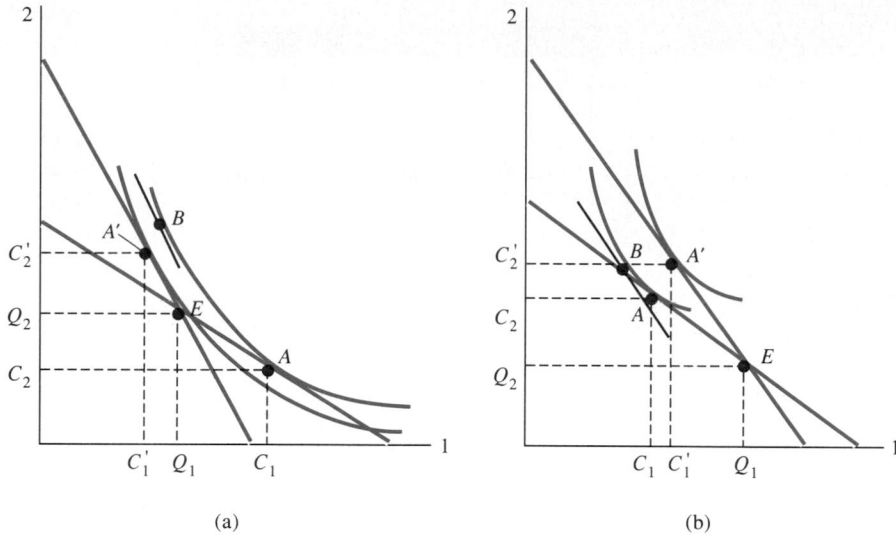

Figure 4-7
The Effect of Interest-Rate Changes on Consumption and Saving

rium is at point A', with C_1 falling and C_2 rising relative to the initial equilibrium. In the graph, then, we have a case in which higher interest rates reduce current consumption and thus raise current saving. In Figure 4-7b, by contrast, the same rise in interest rates produces an *increase* in consumption and thus a *fall* in saving. Evidently the effect of a rise in interest rates on household saving is ambiguous.

In order to account for this ambiguity, it is useful to divide the effect of the interest-rate increase into two parts: a "substitution effect," which always tends to *raise* saving, and an "income effect," which may raise or lower saving. Let us consider these two effects.

When the interest rate goes up, there is a rise in the amount of future consumption that can be gained by a given increase in current saving. Specifically, a fall in C_1 and an equivalent rise in saving of the amount $\Delta S_1 = -\Delta C_1$ leads to an increase in C_2 in the amount $(r\Delta S_1)$. In effect, future consumption becomes "cheaper" relative to current consumption, and households tend to substitute away from current consumption and to increase their desired purchases of future consumption. The pure substitution effect measures the change in the household's desired level of C_1 and C_2 when interest rates change, assuming that households remain on the initial indifference curve. Graphically, this "substitution effect" is represented in Figure 4-7a by a move along the original indifference curve from point A, where the slope equals the initial interest rate, to point B, where the slope equals the new higher interest rate. Note that the direction of this effect is unambiguous: higher interest rates always lead to a reduction of C_1 and a rise in C_2, and thus to a rise in S_1.

The income effect measures the fact that the household is made richer or poorer by the change in interest rates to the extent that it was initially a net lender or a net borrower. If the household was initially a net lender, the rise in interest rates makes the household richer by virtue of the fact that

TABLE   4-3

EFFECT OF AN INTEREST RATE INCREASE
ON SAVING

	Net Borrower	Net Lender
Substitution effect	+	+
Income effect	+	−
Total effect on saving	+	?

with *unchanged* C_1, the household will unambiguously be able to afford a higher level of C_2. On the other hand, if the household was initially a net borrower, then the rise in interest rates makes the household unambiguously poorer by virtue of the fact that with unchanged C_1, the household will no longer be able to afford the original level of C_2.

We can describe the income effect in the following way. If the income effect is positive, that is if the household is made richer, then the household will tend to raise its consumption levels of C_1 and C_2; if the income effect is negative, that is, if the household is made poorer, then the household will tend to reduce its consumption levels of C_1 and C_2. A positive income effect, therefore, reduces saving (because it increases C_1), while a negative income effect raises saving (because it decreases C_1). Thus, the income effect tends to raise the saving rate of a borrower and to lower the saving rate of a lender. The income effect may be understood graphically as the shift from point B to point A' in Figure 4-7. When the household is a net lender (Figure 4-4b), the income effect is positive and the shift from B to A' involves a rise in C_1 (and a fall in saving); when the household is a net borrower (Figure 4-4a), the income effect is negative and the shift from B to A' involves a fall in C_1 (and hence a rise in saving).

Finally, we can summarize the overall effects of a rise in interest rates as we do in Table 4-3. The substitution effect always tends to raise saving. The income effect tends to raise saving for net borrowers and to lower saving for net lenders. Thus, the total effect of a rise in interest rates is to raise saving unambiguously in the case of a borrowing household and to raise or lower saving in the case of a lending household (depending on whether the substitution or income effect dominates). Figure 4-7a shows unambiguously the rise in saving rates for a net borrower.[32] Figure 4-7b shows a case in which saving falls for a net lender.

What then should we expect about the effect of higher interest rates on *aggregate* saving? In general, the presumption is that the income effects of net borrowers and net lenders tend to cancel each other at the aggregate level so that the substitution effects (which work in the same direction for all households) tend to dominate. For this reason, we can usually suppose that a rise in interest rates will reduce current consumption and raise aggregate

[32] Note that, as shown in Figure 4-4a, the net borrower becomes a net lender after the interest rate increase. This is not necessarily the case. The graph could have been drawn so that the household remains a net borrower.

saving, even though we know that for some lending households, saving might fall.

Empirical evidence on the relationship between aggregate saving and interest rates is far from conclusive, however. Few studies have found a clear effect of interest rates on saving in developing countries.[33] For the United States, the best known study finding a positive effect of the interest rate on the saving rate is that of Michael Boskin.[34] But most other research has found a low or negligible effect. It may be the difficulty of measuring interest rates properly—in taking account of taxes that affect the costs of borrowing and the returns to lending, for example—that greatly complicate the research. This alone might help to explain why the research on this topic has been so inconclusive.

4-10 BUSINESS SAVING AND HOUSEHOLD SAVING: THEORY AND EVIDENCE

In our investigations of household saving behavior, we have not mentioned much about the behavior of firms. At one level, this is clearly problematic. In describing Table 4-1, we said that total private saving is equal to the sum of household saving (sometimes called personal saving) and business saving, and we noted that business saving in the United States is actually larger than household saving. Yet our comparative neglect of business saving has a certain subtle justification. Business firms are ultimately owned by households, and therefore the overall level of private saving is still basically determined by household behavior, and the division of saving between households and firms is somewhat arbitrary.

To investigate this problem, let us reuse the two-period framework. Suppose that in addition to the output of the household, Q_1 and Q_2, the household also receives a payment stream of dividends, DV_1 and DV_2, from a firm that it owns. The firm earns profits Pr_1 and Pr_2, and pays out part of the profits in dividends. The firm may choose to *retain some earnings* in the first period and invest in bonds, B_{f1}, according to the simple budget constraint $B_{f1} = Pr_1 - DV_1$. We define the firm's saving S_{f1} as its retained earnings, so that $S_{f1} = B_{f1} = Pr_1 - DV_1$. In the second period, the firm sees no point in retaining any earnings. Thus, it pays as dividends the total profit of period 2 plus the value of the bonds with their accumulated earnings: $DV_2 = Pr_2 + (1 + r)B_{f1}$.

It is easy to derive an intertemporal budget constraint for dividend payments using these new relationships:

$$DV_1 + \frac{DV_2}{(1 + r)} = Pr_1 + \frac{Pr_2}{(1 + r)} \tag{4.17}$$

Note that the budget constraint for the firm has the same form as the household's budget constraint: the discounted value of dividends must equal the

[33] See, for example, Alberto Giovannini, "Savings and the Interest Rate in LDCs," *World Development*, July 1983.

[34] Michael Boskin, "Taxation, Savings and the Interest Rate," *Journal of Monetary Economics*, March 1982.

discounted value of profits. Saving by the firm (S_{f1}), is defined as the retained earnings, as we just explained.

Let us see how a change in business saving affects overall saving of the private sector. The budget constraint for the household that owns the firm is amended as follows. Disposable income now includes the receipt of dividend payments of the firm, so that $Yd_1 = Q_1 + DV_1$ and $Yd_2 = Q_2 + rB_1 + DV_2$. The household's budget constraint, as usual, holds that the discounted value of consumption equals the discounted value of disposable income:

$$C_1 + \frac{C_2}{(1 + r)} = Q_1 + \frac{Q_2}{(1 + r)} + DV_1 + \frac{DV_2}{(1 + r)} \qquad \textbf{(4.18)}$$

Using (4.17) and (4.18) we can write the household's budget constraint as follows:

$$C_1 + \frac{C_2}{(1 + r)} = Q_1 + \frac{Q_2}{(1 + r)} + Pr_1 + \frac{Pr_2}{(1 + r)} \qquad \textbf{(4.19)}$$

Notice that the household's consumption choices depend on the overall profit stream of the firm, but not on when those profits are paid out in dividends. Thus, the firm's own saving policy—when it does or does not pay profits out in dividends—is *irrelevant* for the household's consumption choices C_1 and C_2.

Now let us consider what happens to the saving rate when the firm alters its saving policy. If the firm saves an additional dollar in the first period rather than paying it out in dividends, the household's disposable income drops by one dollar, since disposable income is the sum of the household's own output and its receipt of dividends. Saving by the business firm and by the household are now defined as follows:

$$S_{f1} = Pr_1 - DV_1 \qquad \text{(business saving)}$$
$$S_1 = Yd_1 - C_1 = Q_1 + DV_1 - C_1 \qquad \text{(household saving)} \qquad \textbf{(4.20)}$$

Since C_1 is not affected by the cutback in the dividend payment, it is clear to see that household saving falls by one unit when business saving rises by one unit. Overall private saving, which is the sum of S_1 and S_{f1}, remains unchanged.

We have reached a remarkable theoretical result. *If the firm chooses to save an additional dollar, overall private saving will be unchanged because households will respond by decreasing personal saving.* In other words, if firms save more, households will save less, because they will regard the firms as doing the saving for them. This conclusion has been given an illuminating name. When households make their own saving compensate for changes in the firm's saving, it is said that they "pierce the corporate veil." Since the firm is owned by the households, changes in the firm's policies do not affect the basic consumption decisions of the household.

The empirical evidence gives some support to the idea that households at least partly pierce the corporate veil. A look at Figure 4-1 suggests this point. While gross private saving (as a percentage of GDP) has been very stable in the United States since World War II, the variability of personal and business saving has been significantly higher, indicating that movements in personal saving have tended to compensate the shifts in business saving during the period. This casual evidence points in favor of the argument that households pierce the corporate veil.

More rigorous studies of the problem have tended to qualify this conclusion, however. In particular, it has been found that changes in corporate saving induce an offsetting effect on personal saving, but one that is only partial. For example, James Poterba of the Massachusetts Institute of Technology, has found for the United States that a $1 decline in corporate saving reduces total private saving by 25 to 50 cents.[35]

In conclusion, the idea that households pierce the corporate veil is no doubt an approximation. Liquidity constraints, tax policies, imperfect information to shareholders about the saving of firms, and other kinds of capital market imperfections can limit the extent to which households actually offset the saving behavior of firms. Nonetheless, as we start to close in on a theory of private saving, it is probably safe to leave business saving out of the picture and to focus our attention mainly on the household.

4-11 SUMMARY

The modern analysis of consumption and saving was initiated by John Maynard Keynes, who specified a *consumption function* linking current consumption to current income. This important step forward in economic analysis was subsequently superseded by the *intertemporal approach* to consumption and saving, a theory which stresses that households divide their income between consumption and saving in order to maximize utility. This choice is influenced not only by current income, as in the Keynesian model, but also by expected future income as well as the interest rate. In choosing a consumption path, households are bound by the *intertemporal budget constraint*, which requires that the present value of consumption be equal to the present value of the output produced by the household plus any initial financial assets owned by the household minus the present value of any bequests left by the household.

The *two-period model*, which assumes that households live for only two periods, the present and the future, simplifies the study of intertemporal choice. This model allows us to find consumer equilibrium by superimposing the household's indifference curves on the intertemporal budget constraint in a neat graphical way.

The *permanent-income model* provides us with one application of the intertemporal approach. It builds on the basic observation that households prefer a stable consumption path to an unstable one. Since income may experience fluctuations from period to period, it is not current income but permanent income which determines consumption, where permanent income is a kind of average of present and expected future incomes. In the case of a *temporary* decline of income, permanent income changes little, and consumption does not decline by much. Because consumption drops little in the face of a decline in current income, saving falls. In the case of a permanent decline in income—and one that is perceived to be permanent—consumption falls by approximately the amount of the decline, and saving does not change by much. Because future income cannot be known for sure, however, the formation of expectations is a crucial issue in applying the permanent-income model.

---

[35] See his article "Tax Policy and Corporate Saving," *Brookings Papers on Economic Activity*, 2: 1987.

Empirical estimates of the consumption function have been centered on attempts to measure the *marginal propensity to consume* (MPC), that is, the amount that consumption rises when income goes up by one dollar. In accord with the permanent-income model, the empirical evidence indicates that the MPC out of current income is substantially smaller than the MPC out of permanent income (which is close to 1). On the other hand, the evidence also suggests that for a portion of households, consumption is determined largely by current income rather than permanent income, presumably because those households face *liquidity constraints* which impose limitations on their ability to borrow against future income. For such households, the (old-fashioned) Keynesian link between consumption and current income would tend to be quite strong.

The *life-cycle model* is a specific application of the intertemporal model of consumption and saving. Its distinctive feature is its emphasis on the regular pattern of income over the lifetimes of most households. Since households want to maintain a smooth consumption path, they are led to dissave when young (when income is low or zero), save during the working years (to repay the debts incurred when young and to accumulate wealth for old age), and to dissave when old. Empirical evidence supports many of the crucial implications of the life-cycle model, such as the fact that the MPC should vary over the life cycle, but there are major empirical puzzles as well. Most strikingly, older households appear not to dissave by the amount predicted by the life-cycle model, but instead leave much of their wealth as a bequest to their heirs.

Taxes have an important effect on consumption. Higher taxes reduce the present value of *disposable income*, and thus reduce consumption. The response of consumption to a change of taxes depends in an important way on whether the tax change is believed to be temporary or permanent. As many historical episodes have shown, consumption reacts more to a tax change that is perceived to be permanent.

Consumption and saving theory is for the most part built around the individual household and then generalized to the economy. In moving from an analysis of the individual household to that of the overall economy, we must deal with the problem of *aggregation*. Of course, if everyone had the same MPC, aggregation would be no problem. But this is not the case. The MPC varies across households because people have different tastes and are at different stages of life. The aggregate saving rate should depend, therefore, on the age distribution of the population and on income growth, both of which help to determine the wealth of young savers compared to that of old dissavers. The higher the proportion of working-age individuals to very young and very old people, the higher the saving rate of a country should be. Similarly, the faster the country grows, the higher should be the saving rate.

The effect of the interest rate on saving and consumption is unclear both theoretically and empirically. A higher interest rate increases the present price of consumption relative to the future (the *substitution effect*), and thus provides an incentive to increase saving. However, if the household is a net lender, the interest rate rise also raises lifetime income, and thus tends to increase consumption and decrease saving (the *income effect*). The substitution effect is usually assumed to be stronger than the income effect, and therefore saving responds positively to a rise in the interest rate. Some empirical evidence has supported this, but the results are for the most part inconclusive.

Most of the analysis of private saving takes place at the level of the household, thereby neglecting *business saving*. In the United States and other countries, however, business saving tends to be an important part of total saving. Does this introduction of business saving require a fundamental reworking of our model? Fortunately, the answer is no. Since business firms are ultimately owned by households, total private saving (the sum of household and business saving) is still basically determined by household behavior. Under some conditions, the distinction between households saving and firm saving is somewhat arbitrary. If the firm retains more earnings, the household will save less by a corresponding amount. When this happens, the household is said to "pierce the *corporate veil*."

Key Concepts

disposable income
consumption function
intertemporal theory
two-period model
utility function
indifference curves
intertemporal budget constraint
marginal rate of substitution
life-cycle theory
permanent income
temporary shock

permanent shock
marginal propensity to consume
durables and nondurables
bequests
Keynesian consumption theory
liquidity constraints
overlapping generations
income effect
substitution effect
aggregation
"corporate veil"

Problems and Questions

1. For a given level of GNP, discuss what happens to personal income, disposable personal income, personal consumption expenditures, and personal saving if
   a. Personal taxes go up.
   b. Personal interest income rises.
   c. Personal consumption expenditures decline.
   d. Corporate profits go down.

2. The model analyzed in this chapter assumed that the relevant decision for households was when to save and when to borrow rather than whether to borrow or to save. Is this a sensible assumption?

3. a. Draw the budget constraint for a household that lives for two periods and earns $100 in the first period and $200 in the second period. The interest rate is 10 percent.
   b. What is this household's permanent income?
   c. If the household's preferences are such that it wants to consume exactly the same amount in both periods, what would be the value of its consumption in each period?
   d. How would the budget constraint change with respect to (a) if the household could lend but could not borrow? If its preferences stay the same, will the household be better off or worse off?

4. In the framework of the two-period model, consider two households which receive exactly the same income in each period. Because of differ-

ences in preferences, however, household 1 saves $100 whereas household 2 saves $1,000. Which household is more likely to increase its savings if the interest rate rises? Why?

5. What would the permanent-income hypothesis imply about the living standards of students attending business school compared to those studying archaeology if they both come from families with the same amount of economic resources?

6. In most developing countries, the share of young people in the total population is larger than in most developed countries. However, developed countries tend to have higher saving rates than do less developed ones. Discuss how this observation may be reconciled with the hypothesis that the young tend to save more than the old.

7. In the two-period model, what would happen to consumption and personal saving in periods 1 and 2 if

  a. Country A discovers huge oil reserves.
  b. Country B has an unusually good harvest this year.
  c. Country C develops a new production technique that would raise income in years 1 and 2 in the same proportion?

8. A household lives two periods, and it is a net lender in the first period. Could it become a net borrower if the interest rate goes up? Could a net borrower become a net lender if the interest rate increases?

9. If households really "pierce the corporate veil," then a temporary increase in business profits will have no effect on private savings. Discuss.

10. Some economists have argued that the U.S. private saving rate is too low and that the government should adopt some measures to increase it. What type of policies might achieve this end, how and why?

Investment

The production of output requires the inputs of labor, capital, and technology. As we use the term here, *capital* refers to the accumulated stocks of machinery, factories, and other *durable* factors of production. *Investment* is the flow of output in a given period that is used to maintain or increase the capital stock in the economy. By increasing the capital stock, investment spending augments the future productive power of the economy. Thus, like consumption theory, investment theory must necessarily be *intertemporal,* because the motivation for investment now is to increase production possibilities in the future.

The investment decisions of firms and households deserve study for several important reasons. First, adding the theory of investment described here to the theory of consumption outlined in the previous chapter enriches our understanding of how the output in a given period is allocated between current uses (consumption) and future uses (investments to raise future output). Second, fluctuations in firms' investments play a role in determining the level of output and unemployment in an economy, as we explain in later chapters. Third, as Chapter 18 shows, investment spending contributes in significant ways to long-term growth of the economy.

Our analysis of investment theory in this chapter rests on the assumptions that labor is always fully employed and that output is therefore at its full-employment level as well. Thus, fluctuations in output come solely from shifts in the capital stock, or from other supply-side shocks to the production function, but not from shifts in aggregate demand. Essentially, we have simplified the discussion of investment behavior by assuming full-employment, classical properties for the economy. And, indeed, we continue to assume these same simplified conditions until we reach Chapter 12, when we once again take up the Keynesian model.

5-1 TYPES OF CAPITAL AND INVESTMENT

Capital exists in many forms in an economy, and thus there are many forms of investment spending. The national accounts identify three major areas of investment spending. The first major category of investment spending is *fixed business investment,* which measures the spending by businesses on "plant" (the physical structure occupied by a factory or business office) and "equipment" (machinery and vehicles). The second major component of capital expenditures is *inventory investment.* Inventories are stocks of raw materials, unfinished goods in the production process, or finished goods held by firms. Inventory investment is the change in those stocks of goods in a given period, and a rise in inventories constitutes positive investment while a decline in inventories is a form of disinvestment. The third major category is *investment in residential structures,* which includes expenditures both on the maintenance of housing and on the production of new housing. Note that when one household purchases an existing house from another household, no investment occurs because in terms of the economy as a whole, there is no change in the capital stock, only in its ownership.

One key distinction that applies to all types of investment is the difference between *gross investment* and *net investment.* Most types of capital tend to wear out over time and are eventually scrapped. Economists term this process "capital depreciation" or "capital consumption." For a given amount of total investment in the economy, part serves to replace the capital that is depreciating, and the rest serves to increase the capital stock. The total level of investment is referred to as *gross investment.* The part of investment that raises the capital stock is referred to as *net investment.* We have, then, the simple relationship that gross investment equals net investment plus capital depreciation (or capital consumption). It is often assumed that a given fraction of capital depreciates each period, and thus we have the relationship:

$$I = J + dK \tag{5.1}$$

where I is gross investment, J is net investment, and d is the parameter of depreciation, say, 5 percent per year (so that dK represents the depreciation of capital in the current period).[1] The change in the capital stock is equal to the rate of net investment:

$$K_{+1} - K = J \tag{5.2}$$

Combining (5.1) and (5.2), we can write the basic capital accumulation equation:

$$K_{+1} = (1 - d)K + I \tag{5.3}$$

Some Facts About Investment

Investment spending is far more volatile than consumption spending, a fact that is seen vividly in Figure 5-1. The figure shows the year-to-year changes

---

[1] In fact, depreciation is more complex than suggested here. First, different kinds of investment goods have different lengths of life, so that the rate of depreciation differs. Second, some capital goods wear away gradually, losing some of their usefulness each year, while other goods—such as light bulbs—are good to the end and then stop working. Third, depreciation is an economic decision as well as a technological fact of life. When to scrap a factory or a piece of machinery depends as much on market conditions as on the life of the capital good. A machine used more intensively may wear out more quickly, leading to an economic trade-off between intensity of use and total length of life.

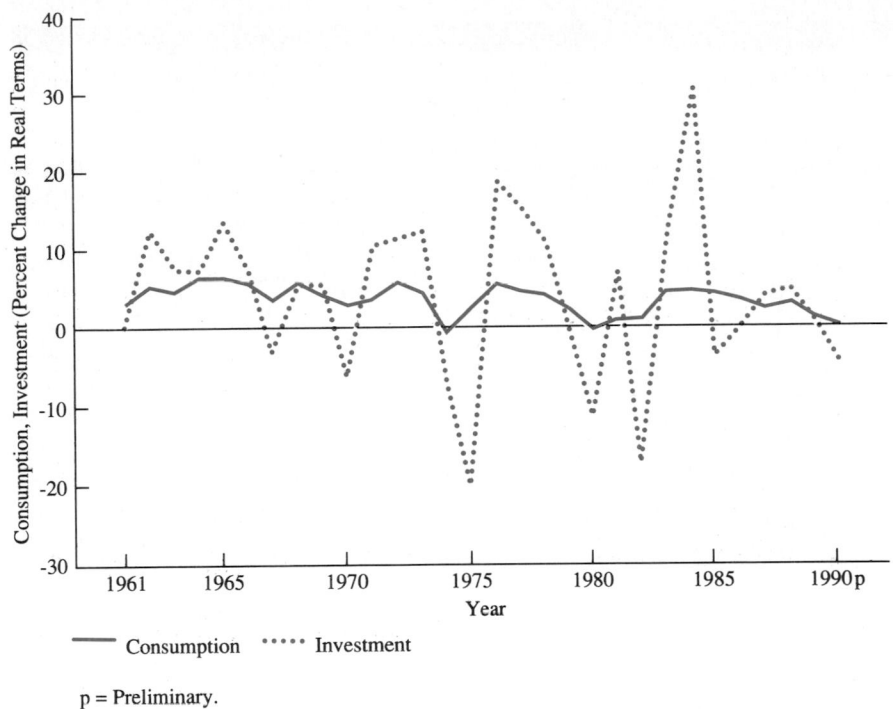

p = Preliminary.

Figure 5-1
The Volatility of Investment and Consumption in the United States, 1961–1990

(From Economic Report of the President, 1991, *Table B-2.)*

in investment spending and consumption spending as defined (imperfectly) in the national income accounts. This result is not entirely surprising. Optimizing consumers will want to *smooth* consumption levels over time, but, as we shall note, optimizing firms have much less reason to smooth their investment spending. The high volatility of investment spending has been noted for decades, and indeed Keynes argued in the *General Theory* that the large fluctuations in investment spending are a driving force of the business cycle. (We return in Chapter 17 to the possible role of investment fluctuations in provoking short-run fluctuations in GNP and unemployment.)

Table 5-1 gives an empirical overview of the importance of various types of private investment spending in the United States for the period 1988–1990. Total private investment has fluctuated between 13.7 and 15.4 percent of GDP.[2] Of this amount, about two-thirds to three-fourths in recent years is capital depreciation, and thus does not represent a net increase in the capital stock of the United States. Net investment in 1990 was only 3.7 percent of GDP, equal to only about 30 percent of overall investment spending. Since the fixed capital stock of the United States was about 180 percent of GDP at the end of 1989, the net investment of 3.7 percent of GDP repre-

[2] As we shall see later on, total investment has been between 15 and 20 percent of GDP in the United States since the early 1970s, or about one-third to one-fourth of consumption spending.

TABLE   5-1

DIFFERENT CATEGORIES OF INVESTMENT IN THE UNITED STATES,
1988–1990
(BILLIONS OF CURRENT DOLLARS)

	1988	1989	1990p
Gross private domestic investment	747.1	771.2	745.0
(% GDP)	(15.4)	(14.9)	(13.7)
− Capital depreciation	514.3	554.2	575.7
(% GDP)	(10.6)	(10.7)	(10.6)
= Net private domestic investment	232.7	216.8	169.3
(% GDP)	(4.8)	(4.2)	(3.1)
− Change in inventories	26.2	28.3	−2.2
= Net fixed investment	206.5	188.5	171.5
(% GDP)	(4.1)	(4.2)	(3.7)
Residential	118.0	104.5	—
Nonresidential (business investment)	88.6	84.0	—
Structures	18.1	16.8	—
Producers' durable equipment	70.4	67.2	—

p = preliminary.
Source: Economic Report of the President, 1991, *(Washington, D.C.: U.S. Government Printing Office, 1991), Table B-16.*

sents a growth in the capital stock of about 2.1 percent (= 3.7/1.8), almost double the growth rate of GDP in 1990.

Net investment in Table 5-1 is divided among business fixed investment in structures and equipment, residential investment, and inventory investment. Business fixed investment (nonresidential) has been between one-third and 40 percent of the total, with spending on equipment roughly three to four times the spending on structures. Residential housing is the most important component of net investment, equal to more than half of the total. Changes in inventories fluctuated around 13 percent of total net investment.

In a cross-country comparison of total gross fixed capital formation among industrialized economies measured as a percentage of GDP, the United States is at the low end of the list. Figure 5-2 shows how Japan has consistently invested close to one-third of its GDP in the period 1970–1989, although this ratio has tended to decline through the period. France's fixed capital formation has been between 20 and 25 percent of GDP during the same period. This ratio has fluctuated between 15 and 20 percent in the United States and the United Kingdom, among the lowest in the industrialized world.[3]

---

[3] As in all cross-country data, one must be a bit wary. The data for the United States, for example, undercount public investment spending (which is wrongly classified as consumption). This may be true to a lesser extent elsewhere, thus diminishing the gap between the United

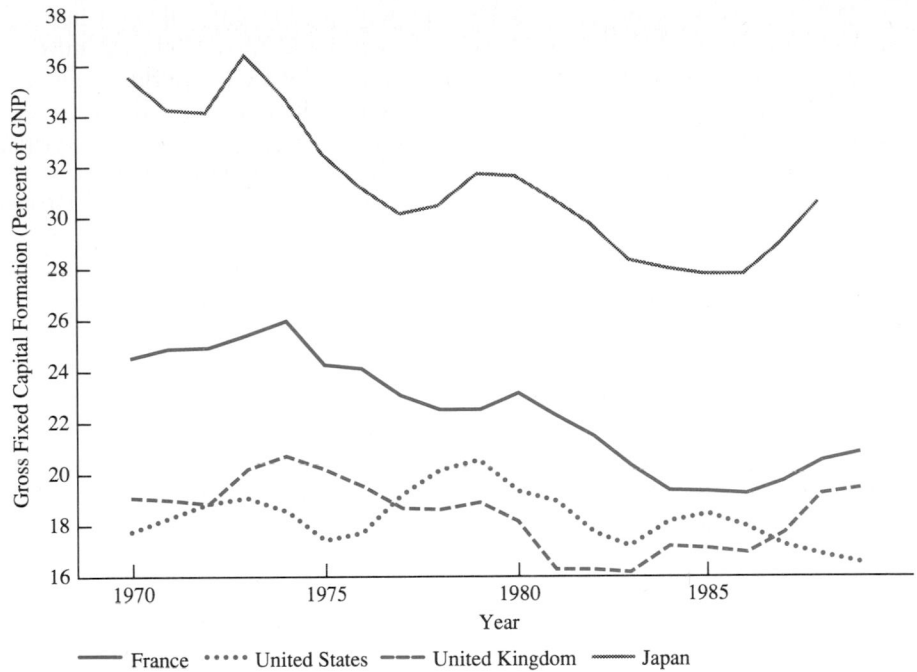

Figure 5-2

Gross Fixed Capital Formation in Selected Countries, 1970–1989

(From International Monetary Fund, International Financial Statistics, *selected issues.)*

Shortcomings in the Measurement of Investment Spending

While business fixed investment, inventories, and housing are the three main categories of investment that are measured in the national income accounts, they are not the only kinds of investment in the true economic sense of spending on durable goods that raise the future productive capacity of the economy. Consumer durables such as cars, refrigerators, and dishwashers provide consumption services for many periods in the future. Purchases of new consumer durables should therefore be considered a form of investment spending, and the total stock of consumer durables should be considered a part of the capital stock. Typically, however, spending on such goods is counted as consumption expenditure in the national income accounts rather than as investment spending. Government spending on highways and other infrastructure is also a form of investment spending, but this too is called consumption expenditure in the U.S. national income accounts.

The kinds of capital mentioned so far are called "reproducible" capital because the stock of such capital can be increased through new production

---

States and the other countries. Also, the data do not include spending on consumer durables investment, a form of investment spending that is misclassified as consumption in the national income accounts (a point we make in the next section). Since such spending is relatively high in the United States, the correction of the investment data for consumer durables spending would also tend to close some of the gap with the other countries.

—firms can invest in new plant and equipment, people can build new houses, and so forth. Another class of capital, which includes land and mineral deposits, is "nonreproducible" in that it cannot be augmented through production. Mineral deposits are not only nonreproducible, they are also "exhaustible"; that is, as they are used, they get used up. In economic terms, the pumping of oil from an oil well or the mining of a mineral vein represents a form of negative investment (or disinvestment) because the stock of the resource falls as the resource is extracted. The national income accounts do not typically count such activities as negative investment, however.

The official data also neglect many other kinds of nonphysical capital that should be counted in a country's capital stock. A well-trained labor force embodies a kind of *human capital*, since worker training raises the productive capacity of the labor force. Gary Becker of the University of Chicago has contributed brilliantly to our understanding of the economic returns to various kinds of investment in human capital (such as education and on-the-job training).[4] Yet, as with expenditures on consumer durables, spending on education and training is typically misclassified in the national accounts as consumption spending rather than investment spending. Research and development spending is still another form of investment in the nonphysical capital stock of the economy inasmuch as a more sophisticated level of technology can be regarded as part of an economy's overall capital stock.

For all these reasons, and as Robert Eisner of Northwestern University has persuasively shown, the amount of investment spending in the economy tends to be significantly understated, while the amount of consumption spending tends to be overstated. According to Eisner's calculations, investment spending in the United States was roughly 37 percent of his revised GNP figure for 1981, compared with the official estimate of 17 percent of GNP, once government investment is counted and once spending on items such as consumer durables, research and development, education and training, and health are taken into account.[5]

5-2 THE BASIC THEORY OF INVESTMENT

Most investment spending is undertaken by business firms, not households (though households do invest in consumer durables and in their own human capital). Nonetheless, it is useful, if a bit theoretical, to begin our inquiry with an understanding of how a household makes investment decisions. It turns out that the optimal investment rule for households simply carries over to the more realistic setting in which business firms make the investment decisions and households own the business firms.

Let us return to the household, which we met in Chapter 4, that is concerned with allocating its purchasing power between the present and the future. We noted in Chapter 4 that if the household produces Q_1, Q_2,

---

[4] One of his seminal contributions on the subject is *Human Capital, a Theoretical and Empirical Analysis with Special Reference to Education* (Chicago: University of Chicago Press, 1980).

[5] For a discussion of the undervaluation of investment in U.S. national income accounts, see Robert Eisner, "Extended Accounts for National Income and Product," *Journal of Economic Literature*, December 1988.

$Q_3, \ldots$, it can choose to allocate that production among consumption C_1, $C_2, C_3, \ldots$, subject to the constraint that the present value of consumption must equal the present value of production. In the previous chapter, we allowed for only one way to allocate some of today's production for future consumption: keeping consumption less than output and accumulating financial assets equal to current saving. The financial markets thus allowed the household to reallocate purchasing power over time.

The key to understanding the decision of whether or not to invest is to recognize that purchases of capital goods are *another* way to allocate consumption over time. Rather than buying bonds, the household (or the firm that the household owns) may purchase investment goods and thereby increase its future consumption possibilities. In effect, households have two ways to transfer purchasing power from the present to the future, via financial assets or via capital accumulation (that is, additions to the capital stock). The theory of investment that we are about to construct thus rests on one simple idea: investment spending should be increased whenever there is a higher rate of return in saving for the future via purchases of investment goods rather than through the purchase of financial assets.

In this chapter's model, households produce a certain amount of output (Q) in each period as they did in the last chapter's model. As they could not before, however, now they can alter the amount of future output that they produce by making investment choices in the current period. To establish the link between current investments and future output, we rely on the production function, which gives us a formal way to describe the connections between the amounts of inputs (such as capital) used in production and the levels of output that result.

Once again, for the moment we are putting aside all Keynesian ideas about links between fluctuations in aggregate demand and output. Instead, we use the *classical* model in which output is determined only by supply considerations and not by shifts in the aggregate demand curve. Moreover, to simplify the analysis even further, we are neglecting shifts in the price level. The price of output remains fixed at 1, and therefore we need not consider any effects of changes in the price level.

The Production Function

Let us begin with the production function introduced in Chapter 3:[6]

$$Q = Q(K, L) \qquad \textbf{(5.4)}$$
$$+ \quad +$$

The production function is by now a familiar concept. Note that in view of the diverse forms of capital, equation (5.4) represents an enormous (but useful) simplification in that all types of capital are summarized by the single variable K. We also assume that the rate of utilization of capital is constant, although this is not normally the case in real life. (This is described more fully in Box 5-1.)

Several characteristics of the production function are worth recalling. First, an increase in the capital input, or an increase in the labor input, leads to more output. This is indicated in equation (5.4) by the pluses (+) shown

---

[6] For simplicity here, we omit the term for technology (τ).

Box 5-1
Capacity Utilization in the United States

In the real world, the economy uses its installed capital stock capacity at rates that vary over time. The overall level of capacity utilization (KU) is a result of the decisions of many different firms. During booms, KU tends to increase significantly, while it goes down at times of recession. A constant rate of capacity utilization, which implies that the capital stock is used with a constant intensity, is nonetheless a useful simplifying assumption.

Figure 5-3 presents the data for capacity utilization in the United States for the period 1948–1990. As a proportion of total capacity, the average capacity utilization over the period is about 81 percent. It has fluctuated between a low of 70 percent in 1982 to a maximum of 91 percent in 1966. Figure 5-3 identifies the peaks (P) and troughs (T) of each business cycle between 1948 and 1990. Notice that the maximum levels of capacity utilization have been reached close to peaks, while the lowest levels have occurred in the vicinity of troughs. Every major expansion coincides with a sharp rise in KU: During the period of the first post–World War II expansion, KU went from 74 percent to 89 percent. Similarly, capacity utilization rose strongly during 1962 to 1969, 1974 to 1979, and 1982 to 1989. By contrast, KU fell sharply during recessions, as is evident from the recessions that followed the 1973–1974 and 1979–1980 oil price shocks.

Countries can experience recoveries from recessions with rapid GNP growth, even with low levels of investment, if they can call on existing unused capacity. However, as soon as utilization rates approach the available capacity, capital becomes a constraint on economic growth.

below K and L. In technical terms, we say that the marginal product of capital (MPK) and the marginal product of labor (MPL) are both positive. Second, the marginal product of each factor declines as more of that input is used, holding fixed the amount of the other factor. For example, each additional unit of capital input increases the level of output, but to a smaller and smaller extent as K gets larger. This property of the production function is known as the *declining marginal productivity* of capital. (This was described more fully in Section 3-2 of Chapter 3.)

Figure 5-4a shows the level of output as a function of the amount of capital, holding constant the amount of labor employed in the production process. The slope of the output curve, which measures the incremental change in output for an incremental change in capital, charts the MPK at all given levels of capital. Note that for low levels of K, the slope is very steep, while for large levels of K, the slope is very flat. If K is already large, adding more K adds little to output. This observation once again reflects the declining marginal productivity of capital.

Figure 5-4b shows the MPK as a function of the amount of capital. In the figure, the MPK schedule is drawn for a given amount of labor. But what

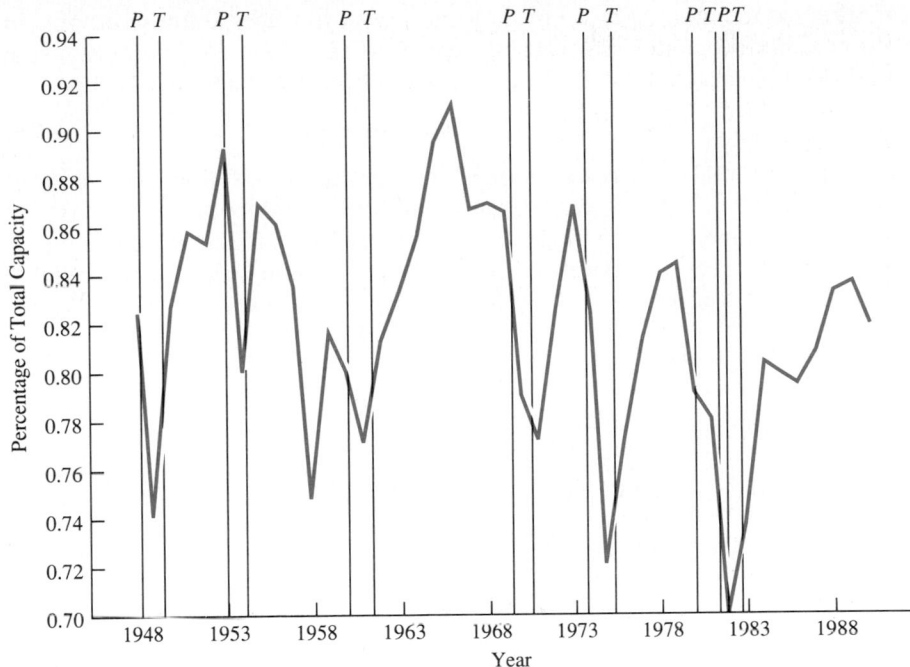

Figure 5-3

Capacity Utilization in the United States, 1948–1990

(From Economic Report of the President, 1991, *Table B-51.)*

would happen if, suddenly, more labor would become available to the production process? For any given level of K, we shall assume that higher L
leads to an increase in the marginal productivity of K. Thus, the MPK
schedule in Figure 5-4b would also shift upward when L shifts up.

The Household's Investment Decisions

Using the production function that we have described, let us now return to
the basic two-period model. Families now have two different ways to transfer purchasing power across time: they can either lend money in financial

Figure 5-4

The Production Function and the Marginal Productivity of Capital

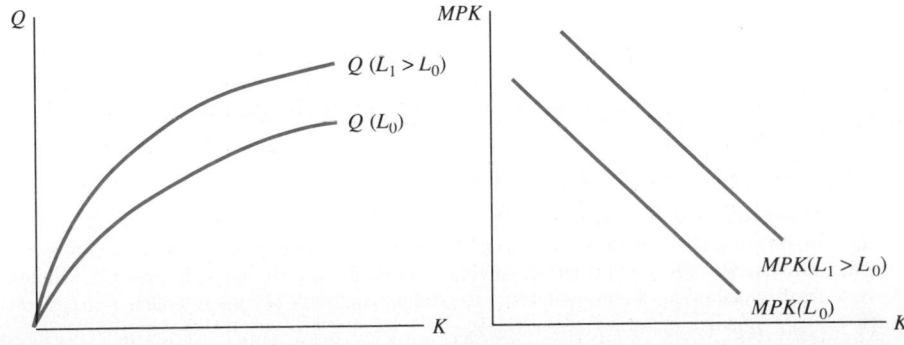

markets at the interest rate r or they can invest to increase future output. In the two-period model, this can be expressed as follows (assuming as usual that the household does not begin with any bond holdings, B):

$$Q_1 - C_1 = S_1 = B_1 + I_1 \tag{5.5}$$

Equation (5.5) tells us simply that saving, the difference between income and consumption, can be allocated to a combination of bonds and capital investment. When the household reaches period 2, it will consume all available resources so that it completes its life with no wealth. The available resources are output Q_2 and the income from the bonds $(1 + r)B_1$. Consequently,

$$C_2 = Q_2 + (1 + r)B_1 \tag{5.6}$$

Next we combine equations (5.5) and (5.6), rewriting (5.5) as $B_1 = Q_1 - C_1 - I_1$ and then substituting this expression for B_1 into (5.6). After this rearrangement, we can now obtain the intertemporal budget constraint of the household:

$$C_1 + \frac{C_2}{(1 + r)} = (Q_1 - I_1) + \frac{Q_2}{(1 + r)} = W_1 \tag{5.7}$$

Notice that this relationship is very similar to equation (4.6) in Chapter 4. The only difference is that now, in addition to saving in the form of bonds, households also invest in the first period to produce more output in the second period. Wealth, which is available for present and future consumption, is now defined as the present value of current and future output net of investment spending.

The intertemporal choice that the household must make is now a little more complicated. It must decide not only how much to consume and save $(B_1 + I_1)$ but also how to divide saving between investment and bonds. Fortunately, this problem can be tackled in two steps. First, the household chooses investment I_1 so as to maximize total wealth. Second, given the resulting value of wealth, the household then decides how much to consume today and how much to save.

If households can know with certainty what the marginal productivity of capital will be, and this is an assumption that we are going to make for now, then maximizing total wealth is straightforward in this two-period model.[7] The household should undertake all investments for which the marginal productivity of capital is greater than $(1 + r)$. To see this, let us write down the formula for the *change* in wealth when investment is raised by one unit:

$$\Delta W = -1 + \frac{MPK_2}{(1 + r)}$$

To derive this expression, we have made use of the definition of wealth in (5.7), that $W = (Q_1 - I_1) + Q_2/(1 + r)$. We have also used the fact that the

---

rise in Q_2 when investment increases by one unit is equal to MPK_2. Obviously, as long as MPK_2 is greater than $(1 + r)$, the increase in investment raises wealth, while if MPK_2 is less than $(1 + r)$, the increase in investment lowers wealth.

Thus, we arrive at an important conclusion. The wealth of the household is maximized by equating the marginal product of capital in period 2 with the market rate of interest:

$$MPK_2 = (1 + r) \tag{5.8}$$

In this expression, $(1 + r)$ is sometimes called the *cost of capital*. Equation (5.8), then, says that the wealth-maximizing level of investment is that level which equates the marginal product of capital with the cost of capital.

So far, we have analyzed how the household can maximize its wealth by choosing the optimal amount it will invest. The household still has to choose its optimal consumption path, however, given its wealth. This step is shown in Figure 5-5. The line W_1A represents the consumption possibility

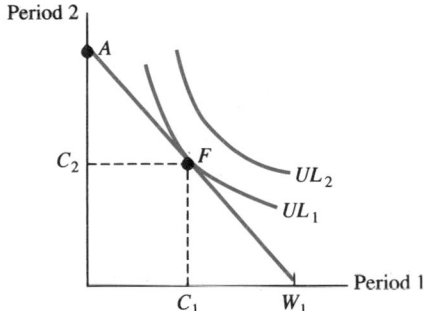

Figure 5-5
The Household's Consumption
Decision Given an Optimal
Investment Choice

frontier for the household with a level of wealth W_1 (which was achieved by an optimal investment choice). We can now superimpose a set of indifference curves, and select the optimal consumption at the tangency of the highest indifference curve, UL_1, with the W_1A line, or point F in the figure. First-period consumption, then, is C_1.

Remember that a household may decide how much to invest without any attention to its intertemporal preferences. The goal in the first stage of the decision-making process is simply to maximize wealth, and that decision has nothing to do with individual preferences. The fact that the investment decision can be taken separately from the consumption decision is a property sometimes called *the separation of optimal investment and consumption decisions*.

We have already seen that households maximize their wealth when the marginal productivity of capital is equal to the interest rate, and this is how they can determine their optimal level of investment. From here, it is relatively easy to establish that investment demand is a negative function of the interest rate. Let us go back to Figure 5-4b. Since the MPK schedule is a downward-sloping function of K, and since MPK_2 must be equal to $(1 + r)$, we can see that a rise in r must imply a *fall* in the optimal K_2. In turn, $I_1 =$

$K_2 - K_1$, so that if the wealth-maximizing level of K_2 declines, so too does the wealth-maximizing level of investment in the first period. In summary, we can derive an optimal (wealth-maximizing) investment schedule of the form

$$I_1 = I_1(r) \qquad \text{(5.9)}$$

This notation means that I_1 is a function of r. The minus sign under the interest rate r means that investment is a negative function of the interest rate.

At the household level, then, the declining marginal productivity of capital accounts for the negative response of investment demand to a change in the interest rate. For any given interest rate, we can add up the investment levels chosen by each household in order to find the aggregate level of investment in the economy. In fact, if we add up the investment functions of each household, we arrive at an aggregate investment function of the form in equation (5.9).[8] The result is a downward-sloping investment schedule as

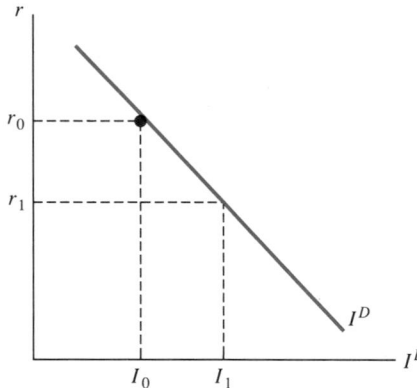

Figure 5-6
The Investment Demand
Schedule

shown in Figure 5-6. When interest rates are high, at r_0, investment is low, at I_0. When interest rates are low, at r_1, investment is high, at I_1.

The Case of Many Periods

The equilibrium condition described in (5.8) is actually a particular condition for the two-period model. In the two-period model, all K_2 is completely useless after period 2, simply because there are no future periods. In a more realistic many-period model, one in which K_2 is useful in period 3 and so on, we must change the expression. Instead of equating MPK with $(1 + r)$, we equate MPK with $(d + r)$, where d is the rate of depreciation (the two-period model supposes complete depreciation, $d = 1$, in the second period). Thus,

---

[8] Adding up investment demands across households presents none of the problems we had with adding up consumption demands. We saw that different households would have different marginal propensities to consume out of income, depending, for example, on the age of the household. Thus, we could not easily write aggregate consumption as a function of aggregate income, except with a bit of hand-waving. For investment, however, we can simply add the investment schedules of the individual households to derive the aggregate schedule.

the more general condition is

$$MPK_{+1} = (r + d) \qquad \textbf{(5.10)}$$

In this expression, $(r + d)$ is now the multiperiod expression for the cost of capital. Note that the cost of capital is the sum of the interest rate and the rate of depreciation.

We can derive (5.10) as follows. Suppose that the household is considering the purchase of some additional machine—a personal computer, say—in a given period, at the cost of ΔI,[9] which it plans to sell in the next period. (It may actually decide to keep the machine, but let us assume that it will sell the machine in the next period and then decide whether or not to repurchase it again.) Is the investment worthwhile? The ΔI investment will produce $\Delta I(MPK_{+1})$ in the next period and will then be sold at the original price, *minus* the depreciation (we assume that prices are stable over time). Suppose, then, that the computer depreciates at the rate d, so that the resale price is $\Delta I(1 - d)$.

The operation will raise household wealth as long as the net present value of the investment is positive. In this case, net present value is equal to the *sum of three items:* $-\Delta I$, the cost of the investment; $\Delta I(MPK_{+1})/(1 + r)$, the increase in production next period as a result of the investment, in present value; and $\Delta I(1 - d)/(1 + r)$, the resale price of the computer in present value. Thus, the NPV is equal to

$$
\begin{aligned}
\text{NPV} &= -\Delta I + \frac{\Delta I(MPK_{+1})}{(1 + r)} + \frac{\Delta I(1 - d)}{(1 + r)} \\
&= \Delta I \left[\frac{(-1 - r + MPK_{+1} + 1 - d)}{(1 + r)} \right] \\
&= \Delta I \left[\frac{(MPK_{+1} - (r + d))}{(1 + r)} \right] \qquad \textbf{(5.11)}
\end{aligned}
$$

Clearly, the net present value of this investment will be positive if and only if MPK_{+1} is greater than or equal to $(r + d)$, which is exactly the condition in (5.10).

To summarize, in order for households to choose the wealth-maximizing level of capital (denoted as K^*), they should set the capital stock at the level of K at which the MPK_{+1} is equal to the cost of capital $(r + d)$. This results in a choice of capital K^*_{+1}. To achieve this level of capital in the next period, it is necessary to choose the investment level I in this period so that

$$I = K^*_{+1} - K + dK \qquad \textbf{(5.12)}$$

The Role of Expectations

Investments depend on judgments about the future marginal productivity of capital, and so far we have treated that factor as a sure thing, something that can be known simply from a production function. In practice, investment decisions are fraught with uncertainty. There are millions of kinds of goods, and the marginal product of capital in producing any of them depends on the future demand for them (which determines the price at which they can be

[9] We use the notation ΔI to stress that the purchase of the computer is a *marginal* investment decision (which involves spending ΔI dollars).

sold in the future). It also depends on countless uncertain conditions, technological and otherwise, that affect the production process. These uncertainties are exacerbated by the fact that investments typically require judgments about business conditions for many years in the future, not just for one period.

Part of the volatility of investment, and thus of the uncertainty that surrounds it, stems from shifts in expectations about the future. These shifts in expectations may be firmly based on evidence about business conditions, including models of consumer demand, opinion surveys, observed shifts in technology and demand, and so forth, or they may result simply from waves of optimism or pessimism that can wash through an economy for no apparent reason. Economists have differed, and often sharply, on the extent to which swings in investor confidence reflect shifts in "fundamentals," on the one hand, or inexplicable shifts in mood, on the other.

John Maynard Keynes is certainly the most influential advocate of the view that many investment shifts reflect swings in confidence not grounded in fundamental shifts in the economy. In the *General Theory,* Keynes attributed investment decisions to "animal spirits" rather than to precise mathematical calculations:

> Most, probably, of our decisions to do something positive, the full consequences of which will be drawn out over many days to come, can only be taken as a result of animal spirits—of a spontaneous urge to action rather than inaction, and not as the outcome of a weighted average of quantitative benefits multiplied by quantitative probabilities.

We shall see in Chapter 17 that Keynes's view of investment behavior also played a fundamental role in his interpretation of business cycles, which he believed to be provoked, in large part, by swings in investment.

5-3 EXTENSIONS TO THE BASIC THEORY

We now return to the basic theory in order to extend our analysis in two ways. The first extension separates the household and the firm. The second brings taxes into the investment decision.

The Separation of Households and Firms

So far, the production process has been very simple. Households are self-employed, and they produce their own output. More realistically, however, the production process is carried out by firms, which hire workers (L) in the labor market and pay them a wage (w) for their services. The owners of the firm, that is, the owners of the capital, receive the profits after labor costs (wL) are paid. How does the investment decision change in this more realistic setting?

The answer to this question is striking and important. When households and firms are separated, firms need know nothing about the intertemporal preferences of their shareholders. Each firm must act solely to maximize its own market value, which in the simplest theoretical case is equal to the discounted value of future dividend payments to the shareholders. To do this, the firm should follow the *identical* investment decision rules that we have identified for households, in which the marginal product of capital is equated with the cost of capital. Following these rules, each firm will maximize the wealth of the households that own the firm.

The proof of this proposition in the two-period model appears in the appendix to this chapter, but the importance of the proposition can be summarized here. In modern societies, large firms are typically owned by thousands of individual investors who each own shares in the firm. How should the firm decide on how much to invest if each of its shareholders has different intertemporal preferences? The conclusion is that the firm should not be concerned about those preferences. Rather, the firm management should simply strive to maximize the market value of the firm, and this, in turn, will maximize the wealth of the shareholders. It is the shareholders, then, that undertake to divide that wealth into a path of consumption over time by their own individual borrowing and lending decisions.

Taxes and Subsidies

Now let us add one more bit of realism to our model. In practice, firms are subject to various taxes and subsidies that affect optimal investment decisions. The classical study of tax effects on investment decisions was made by Dale Jorgenson of Harvard University and Robert Hall of Stanford University.[10] More recent contributions include those of Lawrence Summers.[11]

Suppose that a firm is taxed at rate t on profits. Then the marginal benefit of a one dollar increase in investment is $MPK(1 - t)$. In addition, suppose that the firm is also entitled to various tax benefits, including tax credits on the investment, an accelerated depreciation schedule for tax purposes that is more rapid than the true economic depreciation,[12] and tax deductibility of interest costs. These tax-saving opportunities are represented as a proportion (s) of the purchase price of the investment good. The rate s includes the saving from the investment tax credit, and the tax reductions due to accelerated depreciation allowances and interest deductibility.

If the cost of borrowing is r, and the true rate of depreciation (different from the legal rate) is d, then the net-of-tax cost of a one dollar addition to the capital stock is $(r + d)(1 - s)$. In equilibrium, the firm will equate $MPK(1 - t)$ to the net cost of capital:

$$MPK(1 - t) = (r + d)(1 - s) \qquad \textbf{(5.13)}$$

or

$$MPK = \left[\frac{(1 - s)}{(1 - t)}\right](r + d)$$

---

[10] Their joint work on investment theory and taxes started with a paper published in the mid-1960s: "Tax Policy and Investment Behavior," *American Economic Review*, June 1967.

[11] Lawrence H. Summers, "Taxation and Corporate Investment: A q-Theory Approach," *Brookings Papers on Economic Activity*, 1: 1981.

[12] A company is allowed to subtract from its corporate tax a cost reflecting the depreciation of its capital. The depreciation schedule is not necessarily linked to the rate of economic depreciation, and it often allows a depreciation rate that is considerably higher than economic depreciation. The faster the depreciation according to the tax schedule, the greater the present value of tax savings from the depreciation allowance.

Notice that (5.13) is quite similar to equation (5.10) in which the marginal product of capital is equated with the cost of capital, though now the measure of the cost of capital includes the factor $[(1 - s)/(1 - t)]$. If $s = t$, the effect of the profits tax is exactly compensated by the incentives of the tax credit and the depreciation allowance, and we are back to the original conditions in which $MPK = (r + d)$. In that case, the level of investment is not affected by the tax code. This is not normally the case, however. If $s > t$, a net incentive results, and the adjusted cost of capital is lower. The firm will invest more than it would without taxes. Analogously, if $t > s$, a net disincentive arises from the existence of taxes, and the firm will invest less. The adjusted cost of capital is raised, and the firm will invest less.

Note, though, that taxes can spur private investment indirectly if they are used to finance public spending that raises the productivity of investment. More spending on roads increases the investment in transportation equipment. More spending on police and fire fighting units raises the returns on private investment. Do not think, then, that a smaller public sector, with lower taxes, necessarily stimulates more private investment. The important thing is how the taxes are being used.

Not surprisingly, various fiscal instruments, including both taxes and subsidies, have been used throughout the world to affect investment decisions. When capital formation has seemed insufficient or the economy sluggish, policymakers have at times resorted to a rise in the investment tax credit (equivalent to an increase of s in our discussion). In the United States, for example, this instrument was in place for most of the period between 1962 and 1986. Conversely, when the economy has shown signs of becoming overheated, such fiscal incentives have been reduced or withdrawn.

A crucial distinction with respect to fiscal incentives is whether or not the public anticipates them. A case in point is the U.S. tax reform of 1986. Because many of the bill's provisions were thoroughly discussed by Congress and by various analysts before its enactment, it offers a clear case of an anticipated policy. Firms rapidly discovered that the net effect of the proposed measures on investment incentives was going to be negative. Thus, they stepped up capital expenditures in the last quarter of 1985 in order to take advantage of the existing incentives while they lasted. When the law was finally passed by Congress in early 1986, investment fell.

The fact that the private sector reacts to anticipated policies can have important implications. Suppose that an economy is becoming truly overheated and the authorities suggest a reduction of the investment tax credit in order to check investment demand. During the period after the policy is proposed but before its enactment, investment is bound to go up, not down, as firms take advantage of the tax credit before they lose it. Thus, while the original intention of the policy was to cool down the economy, in practice, it causes the economy to become even more overheated.

Another essential distinction must be made between policy changes perceived to be temporary and those perceived to be permanent. A transitory increase in the investment tax credit, for example, will provoke a larger response in capital expenditures than a permanent increase, because agents will rush to make their investments while the incentives last rather than taking their time.

5-4 INVENTORY ACCUMULATION

Changes in inventory holdings represent an important and highly volatile type of investment spending. The motivations of firms for holding inventories and for undertaking inventory investment, that is, for increasing their stock of inventories, have been carefully investigated, and this research has led to important theories of optimal inventory management by business firms.

There are three basic kinds of inventory stocks: *primary inputs* to production, *semifinished goods* in the course of production, and *finished goods* ready for sale to final users. Table 5-2 presents some data on the relative sizes of these three kinds of inventory stocks during 1990 for manufacturing in the United States. Note that each type of inventory accounts for about one-third of the total inventory stock of the manufacturing sector. Inventories in total were around 60 percent greater in value than the total value of shipments (that is, sales) of manufacturing goods during the year.

Firms need inventories of primary materials to economize on the costs of producing final output. A car factory requires not only buildings and machines, but also steel, glass, tires, and engine parts. In general, it is not efficient to order these inputs on a daily basis, just as they are required. By holding inputs of inventories, firms save time as well as administrative, communications, and delivery costs. They also gain the assurance that inputs will be available when needed. Nonetheless, firms in different industries and even different countries differ in their strategies for managing inventories of primary goods. Many Japanese firms, for example, have introduced a system of inventory management known as *kanban,* or "just-in-time" management, in which actual inventories are held to a bare minimum and suppliers indeed deliver the inputs necessary for production just as they are needed.[13]

Most formal theories of inventory management focus on final goods inventories. The expenses involved in holding stocks of finished output include interest costs, insurance, storage, and depreciation, and they tend to run high. Why, then, do producers keep such stocks? Theories of finished goods inventories generally identify two motives: production smoothing and avoidance of stockouts, that is, situations in which a firm cannot meet an order because it has run out of finished output.

According to the first explanation, firms hold finished goods inventories so that they can maintain a smooth rate of production despite a variable rate of demand for their output. The idea is that because of rising marginal costs of production (each extra unit is more expensive to produce than the previous unit), it pays to keep a fairly stable level of production rather than to alternate between very low and very high production rates. Thus, firms believe they should maintain a rather stable production level, irrespective of demand conditions. During periods of low demand, they build their inventory stocks; during periods of high demand, they run them down. According to this theory, the flow of production should have smaller fluctuations (tech-

---

[13] For a detailed discussion of the *kanban* system, see James C. Abegglen and George Stalk, Jr., *Kaisha: The Japanese Corporation* (New York: Basic Books, 1985).

TABLE 5-2

INVENTORY STOCKS IN U.S. MANUFACTURING, 1990
(US$ BILLIONS AND PERCENT)

	Inventory Stocks (US$ billions)	As a % of Total Inventories	As a % of Annual Shipments
Primary materials	$114.2	30.8%	49.3%
Work-in-process	138.2	37.3	59.6
Finished goods	118.6	32.0	53.6
Total	$371.1	100.0%	160.1

Source: Economic Report of the President, 1991 *(Washington, D.C.: U.S. Government Printing Office, 1991), Table B-56.*

nically, a smaller variance) than the flow of demand, with the difference accounted for by inventory investment and disinvestment. The pioneering study of production smoothing and inventory holdings, done by Holt, Modigliani, Muth, and Simon, appeared in 1960.[14]

The second reason that firms hold finished inventory is that they want to avoid stockouts. Each period the firm must prepare its investment schedule before it observes the level of demand that it will face. If demand becomes greater than current production, it can satisfy that demand only by drawing upon stocks of inventories carried over from an earlier production period. If demand is greater than the *sum* of production and inventory holdings, then the firm runs out of stock before it can satisfy the current demand. The firm suffers various costs if it cannot meet demand. Most directly, it forgoes the profits that it might have earned on the unmet demand. Indirectly, it may acquire a reputation for unreliability, and its customers may go to other firms.

The firm must thus balance the costs of inventory holdings against the costs of involuntary stockouts. In some important special cases (using particular assumptions about costs of production and inventory holdings), it is possible to derive a precise mathematic rule for optimal inventory management. One famous special rule is the so-called *S-s rule,* where *S* and *s* denote levels of inventories at which key inventory investment decisions take place.

The *S-s* rule, when it is applicable, goes like this. The profit-maximizing firm sets production each period according to expected demand, plus a constant (which depends on various cost factors). Over time, inventories will fluctuate: if demand is higher than expected, inventories will fall; if demand is lower than expected, inventories will rise. The firm replenishes its inventories whenever these fall below a certain low level, *s.* When inventories fall below this point, the firm carries out an especially large production run in the following period. Specifically, the firm targets production so that it

---

[14] See C. Holt, F. Modigliani, J. Muth, and H. Simon, *Planning, Production, Inventories and the Work Force* (Englewood Cliffs, NJ: Prentice Hall, 1960).

will meet expected demand and also increase inventory holdings back up to a level, *S,* where *S* is greater than *s.*

Note that this theory predicts very different inventory responses to expected versus unexpected changes in demand. When the demand rises unexpectedly, inventories are drawn down. If they are drawn down enough, then there is a subsequent increase in inventories to get the inventory back to normal levels. On the other hand, if the firm experiences an *expected* increase in demand (if, say, the marketing department has been able to predict a surge in demand), then inventories will generally rise in response to the increase in demand because the firm will prefer to carry larger inventories on average when demand levels are high.

5-5 EMPIRICAL INVESTIGATIONS OF INVESTMENT EXPENDITURE

Even armed with these economic theories of investment, however, economists have found it quite difficult to explain—much less to predict—patterns of investment spending. Several econometric models have been developed to explain actual investment behavior, including the investment accelerator model, the adjustment-cost model, and models based on credit rationing. None of these models has decisively proved its superiority over the others; in fact, it is clear that each picks up only part of a complex reality. Still, these three kinds of models form the core of most empirical investigations of aggregate investment behavior, and thus they deserve some attention here.

The Accelerator Model of Investment

The empirical evidence shown in Figure 5-7 indicates a close relationship between the rate of investment spending and changes in aggregate output, although the movements in investment are more pronounced than those of output. Early investigators of investment spending noted the close association of output changes and investment spending, and this observation was very important to the development of the accelerator model, the oldest theory of investment still in empirical use.[15]

This model starts with the assumption that there is a stable relationship between the stock of capital that a firm desires and the firm's level of output. More precisely, it suggests that the desired amount of capital (K^*) is a constant fraction (h) of output (Q):

$$K^* = hQ \qquad (5.14)$$

This relationship is postulated rather than proved. But a relationship like that shown in (5.14) can be derived from the principles we have outlined earlier. For some production functions, the optimal condition $MPK = (r + d)$ implies that K^* is a multiple (or linear function) of Q as in (5.14).[16] However, the multiple h is itself likely to be a function of the cost of capital.

---

[15] A classical early work on the accelerator theory is that of J. M. Clark, "Business Acceleration and the Law of Demand: A Technical Factor in Economic Cycles," *Journal of Political Economy,* March 1917.

[16] We can mention a case in which K^* is a linear function of Q, by referring to a specific mathematical form of the production function. Suppose that the only inputs of production are

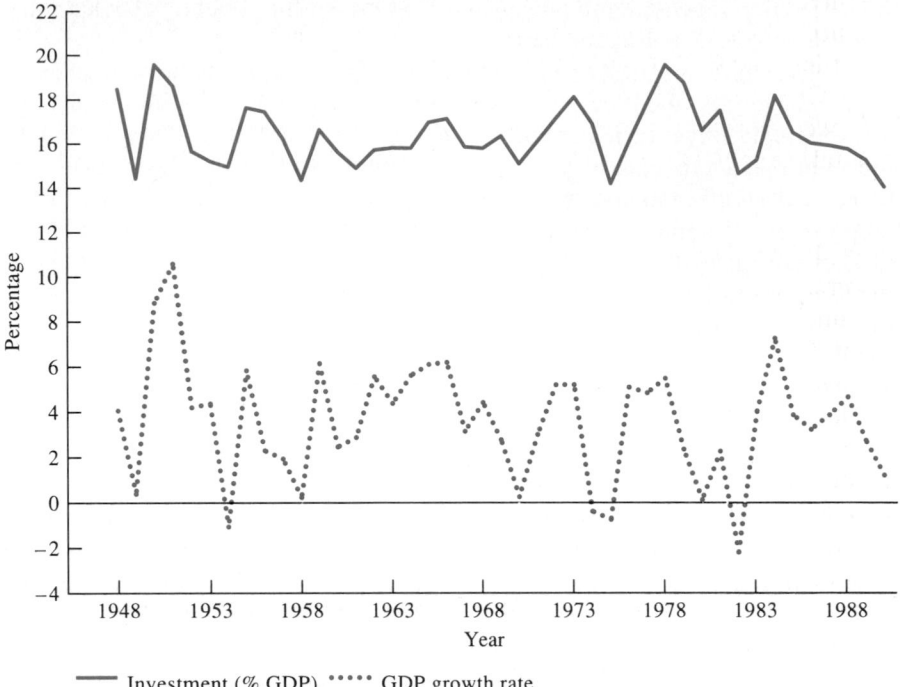

Figure 5-7

Investment and Output Growth in the United States, 1948–1990

(*From* Economic Report of the President, 1991, *Tables B-9 and B-28.*)

Thus, the linear relationship between the desired capital stock and the level of output will be stable only if the cost of capital ($r + d$) does not change very much.

If firms can invest without delay in order to keep the actual level of the capital stock equal to the desired level, K^* will always equal K. Net investment (J), then, would be

$$J = K^*_{+1} - K$$
$$= hY_{+1} - hY$$
$$= h(Y_{+1} - Y) \tag{5.15}$$

J is net investment, equal to the increase in the capital stock. This very simple equation for net investment tells us something quite important: that

---

capital (K) and labor (L). A particular class of production functions, known as Cobb–Douglas, have the following form:

$$Q = K^\alpha L^{1-\alpha}, \qquad \text{with } 0 < \alpha < 1$$

where α is a parameter of the production technology, with a value between 0 and 1. In this case, it is possible to use elementary differential calculus to show that the MPK is equal to $\alpha(Q/K)$. Specifically, $\Delta Q/\Delta K$ can be shown to equal $\alpha(Q/K)$. (Those of you unfamiliar with calculus need not be concerned here with the derivation.) If the *MPK* is then equated to ($r + d$), then we find, $Q/K = (r + d)/\alpha$. Thus, the ratio of desired capital to output is given by $\alpha/(r + d)$, a ratio that is constant as long as r and d are unchanging. Changes in Q, then, lead to equal proportionate changes in K^*.

net investment is proportional to the *change* in output rather than the level of output. We can now see why this is called an accelerator theory: investment increases when output accelerates.

Gross investment equals net investment plus depreciation. If, as earlier, we assume a constant depreciation rate for the capital stock (d) then the capital depreciation is equal to dK, and we can write gross investment as

$$I = h(Y_{+1} - Y) + dK \qquad\qquad \textbf{(5.16)}$$

The derivation of the investment model in equation (5.16) is weak in two respects. First, the ratio of desired capital to the level of output (h) is assumed to be constant. We have said already that h might indeed be constant if the cost of capital is fixed. On the other hand, if the cost of capital changes, either because of changes in the market interest rate or changes in tax laws regarding investment, then we would expect that h would change as well, at least in the medium term. Second, the model assumes that investment is always sufficient to keep the actual capital stock equal to the desired capital stock, period to period. This assumption is also unrealistic. Because of the costs of adjusting the capital stock and inevitable lags in the installation of capital, it is more likely that the capital stock will adjust only gradually to the desired level. Also, since next period's output will usually not be known with certainty, investment must be based on expectations of next period's desired level, and such expectations may turn out to be faulty.

In spite of these limitations, the accelerator model in its simple form accurately describes much about the movements of investment. Quite surprisingly to many economists, the accelerator theory generally outperforms many other more sophisticated theories in explaining and predicting actual investment patterns.[17]

The Adjustment-Cost Approach

Contrary to the assumption of the accelerator model, actual and desired levels of the capital stock are not always equal. In general, a firm might require a considerable amount of time to calculate and install the "desired" level of capital. For any given investment proposal, there must be feasibility studies, marketing analyses, and financial negotiations. Once an investment decision is made, it takes time to construct a new factory, to install the new machines, and to train the workers to operate the new facilities. Moreover, overall investment costs tend to rise if the company rushes to finish its investment project in a very short period of time. Thus, it is not only technical constraints but also profit maximization that leads a firm to make gradual changes in the levels of its capital stock. Some studies have concluded that no more than one-third of the gap between actual and desired capital is closed by investment within a given year.[18]

---

[17] See, for example, Peter Clark's survey and econometric investigation of alternative investment models, "Investment in the 1970s: Theory, Performance and Prediction," *Brookings Papers on Economic Activity*, 1: 1979. For a modern exposition of the multiplier accelerator theory, see Olivier J. Blanchard, "What Is Left of the Multiplier Accelerator?" *American Economic Review*, May 1981.

[18] Clark, "Investment in the 1970s."

Empirical models of investment spending based on adjustment costs and delivery lags are rather new, newer, at least, than the accelerator model.[19] The simplest amendment to the accelerator model was to specify a *partial adjustment mechanism,* which describes the gradual adjustment of K to the desired level K^*:

$$J = K_{+1} - K = g(K_{+1}^* - K) \tag{5.17}$$

Here, g is a parameter known as the coefficient of partial adjustment, with $0 < g < 1$. When $g = 1$, we have the accelerator model of equation (5.16), since $K_{+1} = K_{+1}^*$. When $g < 1$, then actual K adjusts only gradually through the gap between actual and desired capital; the lower the g, the slower the adjustment. Thus, g measures the speed at which the actual capital stock approaches the optimal desired capital stock.

Suppose that $g = 0.6$, for example. This means that net investment in period t will equal 60 percent of the difference between K^* and K. Assuming that the optimal amount of capital does not change, 60 percent of the current gap will be closed by next period's investment, 60 percent of the remaining gap will be closed by next period's investment, and so on. The gap closes gradually through time.

The partial adjustment mechanism lends itself to easy econometric implementation inasmuch as the parameter g can be estimated using time-series data. But the partial adjustment mechanism remains an incomplete theory until we can explain why firms would behave in the way shown in equation (5.17). What, for example, determines the rate at which K approaches K^*? Recent studies have tried to strengthen the theoretical understanding of the partial adjustment mechanism. All these theories use essentially the same line of reasoning, which goes like this.

Suppose that a firm realizes lower than expected profits whenever K_{+1} does not equal K_{+1}^*. The firm suffers this loss in the amount $c_1(K_{+1}^* - K_{+1})^2$, where c_1 is a constant. Obviously, there is no loss when K_{+1} equals the desired level K_{+1}^*, and the loss gets bigger as the gap widens. We assume that the loss is actually proportional to the *square* of the gap between K_{+1} and K_{+1}^* (this kind of loss function is called a *quadratic* loss function). For example, if the gap between K and K^* doubles in size, then the loss to the firm goes up four times.

Suppose also that the firm pays a cost whenever its net investment rate is high. Specifically, assume that the cost of investment is also quadratic; that is, it rises according to the square of the rate of investment, so that the cost of investment equals $c_2(K_{+1} - K)^2$, where c_2 is a constant. Remember that $K_{+1} - K$ equals the rate of net investment.

The total loss is given by

$$\text{Loss} = c_1(K_{+1}^* - K_{+1})^2 + c_2(K_{+1} - K)^2 \tag{5.18}$$

As the firm attempts to minimize the loss in potential profits arising from its investment decision, it must balance two kinds of costs: the quadratic cost of

[19] Early theoretical formulations were those of Robert Eisner and R. Strotz, "The Determinants of Business Investment," in Commission on Money and Credit, *Impacts of Monetary Policy* (Englewood Cliffs, NJ: Prentice Hall, 1963), and that of Robert Lucas, "Adjustment Costs and the Theory of Supply," *Journal of Political Economy,* August 1967.

having its capital stock deviate from the desired level and the quadratic cost of undertaking too rapid a rise in investment spending. The firm maximizes its profits by choosing the level of K_{+1} that minimizes the loss in equation (5.18).

It is easy to show (although we must use calculus to do so) that the optimal choice of K_{+1} is as follows:[20]

$$K_{+1} - K = \left[\frac{c_1}{(c_1 + c_2)}\right](K_{+1}^* - K) \qquad (5.19)$$

Note that (5.19) has the same form as (5.17), with $g = c_1/(c_1 + c_2)$. Thus, when c_1 is very large, so that the costs of deviating from K^* are very large, then g is close to 1, and we are back to the accelerator model. When c_2 is very large, on the other hand, so that the costs of rapid investment are very large, then g is close to 0. In that case, the capital stock adjusts very gradually to the target level.

The explanation for gradual adjustment here has relied on quadratic costs of changing the capital stock. There is another reason for gradual adjustment. When firms are uncertain about their production technology, that is, about how much output they will produce for given levels of capital, then it may make sense for firms to adjust their capital stock gradually if they want to maximize their expected profits, even when adjustment costs to investment are not quadratic.[21]

The q Theory

James Tobin of Yale University, who won the Nobel Prize in Economics in 1982, has pioneered another important model of investment behavior based on the idea of adjustment costs. Tobin's famous q theory of investment starts from the idea that the stock market value of a firm helps to measure the gap between K and K_{+1}^*.[22]

The variable q is defined as the stock market value of the firm divided by the replacement cost of the capital of the firm. The "replacement cost of capital" refers to the cost that one would have to pay to purchase the plant and equipment of the firm in the output market. If the firm sells for $150 million on the stock market, and the replacement cost of the capital of the firm is equal to $100 million, then q would be equal to 1.5. Thus, q is the ratio

---

[20] If you are familiar with elementary calculus, you will know that the loss is minimized when $\partial\,\text{loss}/\partial K_{+1} = 0$. This minimization condition leads to the equation

$$2c_2(K_{+1} - K) = 2c_1(K_{+1}^* - K_{+1})$$

Rearranging terms and subtracting c_1K on both sides of the equation leads to

$$(c_1 + c_2)(K_{+1} - K) = c_1(K_{+1}^* - K)$$

from which equation (5.19) follows immediately.

[21] This result was found in Joseph Zeira, "Investment as a Process of Search," *Journal of Political Economy*, February 1987.

[22] An early discussion of the q theory is found in J. Tobin, "A General Equilibrium Approach to Monetary Theory," *Journal of Money, Credit and Banking*, February 1969. Many other authors, especially Fumio Hayashi and Lawrence Summers, have elaborated on the q theory approach.

of the cost of acquiring the firm through the financial market versus the cost of purchasing the firm's capital in the output market.

Tobin and his followers have shown conditions under which q is a good indicator of the profitability of new investment spending. Specifically, when q is greater than 1, it tends to mean that K^*_{+1} is greater than K, so that investment should be high. Similarly, when q is less than 1, the market is indicating that K^*_{+1} is less than K, so that investment should be low. Let us see why this might be so.

In the simplest theoretical setting, the value of q for an enterprise equals the discounted value of future dividends paid by the firm per unit of capital of the firm.[23] Suppose that the capital stock is constant, that the MPK is constant, and that depreciation occurs at rate d. In this case, the dividend in each period per unit of capital equals $MPK - d$, and the value of q equals

$$q = \frac{(MPK - d)}{(1 + r)} + \frac{(MPK - d)}{(1 + r)^2} + \frac{(MPK - d)}{(1 + r)^3} + \cdots \qquad (5.20)$$

In this simple setting in which the MPK is the same in each future period, the expression for q can be rewritten as

$$q = \frac{(MPK - d)}{r} \qquad (5.21)$$

We can see that *q will tend to be greater than 1 if MPK is greater than $(r + d)$ in future periods, and q will tend to be less than 1 if MPK is less than $(r + d)$ in future periods.*[24]

Now, let us relate q and $(K^*_{+1} - K)$. When the capital stock is at its desired level, then $MPK = (r + d)$. This we found earlier in equation (5.10). If K is *less* than K^*, then MPK will be greater than $(r + d)$, while if K is greater than K^*, then MPK will be less than $(r + d)$.[25] Thus, if K^* is greater than K in future periods, q will be greater than 1; if K^* is less than K on average, in future periods, q will be less than 1.

In this sense, the stock market gives a sensitive and easily available indication of the investment incentives facing a firm. When the stock market price is high (relative to the cost of a unit of new capital), the market is signaling the fact that the capital stock should be raised gradually over time in order to raise K up to K^*. When the stock market price is low, the market is signaling the need for K to fall back to a lower level of K^*.

There is as well another, more intuitive way to understand Tobin's q theory approach. If q is greater than 1, it means that the price per share of

---

[23] Intuitively, the stock value of the firm V is equal to the discounted value of dividends paid by the firm. Thus the discounted value of dividends per unit of capital is equal to V/K. If the replacement cost of the capital of the firm is simply K (this is true when the price of capital equals 1, which is the price of output in the model), then V/K is—by definition—the q value of the firm. This is the basis for the expression for q in this text. For a general but highly mathematical discussion of the equation for q, see Fumio Hayashi, "Tobin's Marginal q and Average q: A Neoclassical Interpretation," *Econometrica*, January 1982.

[24] This follows directly from equation (5.25). $q > 1$ implies that $MPK - d > r$ or that $MPK > d + r$. Similarly, $q < 1$ implies that $MPK < d + r$.

[25] Note carefully that the MPK is a declining function of the capital stock, so that if $MPK = (r + d)$ when $K = K^*$, then $MPK < (r + d)$ when $K > K^*$, and $MPK > (r + d)$ when $K < K^*$.

capital on the stock exchange is greater than the physical cost of capital. A firm could then issue new shares, use the money to undertake the physical investment, and still have some extra earnings left over for the benefit of the shareholders. Thus, q greater than 1 can signal directly that by selling shares, the firm can profitably finance a new investment project.[26]

The q theory of investment is relatively easy to test because the value of q can be directly computed, and we can observe whether fluctuations in investment are closely linked to movements in q. Some research has shown that the q values of individual firms relates to the investments undertaken by those firms. Other evidence has tried to link the economywide average of q to the aggregate level of investment. Lawrence Summers of Harvard University, among others, has shown that the value of q in the U.S. economy is positively related to the value of aggregate investment, but that the relationship is quite weak.[27] Movements in q do not explain much of the observed fluctuation in investment. It is clear that other variables in addition to q, such as changes in output and the cash flow of the firm, also help to account for fluctuations in aggregate investment spending.[28]

Theories Based on Credit Rationing

So far, all our analysis has assumed that individuals and firms can freely borrow at the interest rate r to finance their investment projects. In that case, it is worthwhile to invest as long as the return on investment is higher than $(r + d)$. In practice, however, firms and households might be unable to obtain the credit necessary to carry out an investment project even when the project passes the test of profitability. If firms are credit rationed, the rate of investment will depend not only on the market interest rate and the profitability of investment, but also on the availability of investible funds, which, in turn, will depend on the cash flow of the enterprise considering the investment project.

The analogy with household consumption should be clear. We saw in Chapter 4 that current consumption might depend on current income rather than permanent income if a household is liquidity constrained. In the same way, for the firm that faces credit rationing, investment spending might depend on the firm's current cash flow rather than on the discounted marginal productivity of capital.

The phenomenon of credit rationing has two principal causes, disequilibrium interest rates and differential risks in the face of uncertainty. Disequilibrium interest rates arise when government authorities impose interest-rate ceilings on lending institutions, resulting in interest rates held below

---

[26] A hidden assumption here is that the new shares will sell for the same price q as the existing shares. If the new investment project to be undertaken is a poor one, however, then floating new shares to undertake the project will depress the share value per unit of capital, and therefore not necessarily pay for the investment.

[27] Summers, "Taxation and Corporate Investment." His finding is that a 10 percent rise in the stock market price index increases the ratio of investment to the capital stock (I/K) by 0.009. This estimate agrees with other studies.

[28] See, for example, Andrew Abel and Olivier Blanchard, "The Present Value of Profits and Cyclical Movements in Investment," *Econometrica*, March 1986.

the equilibrium level.[29] With interest rates kept artificially low, investment demand tends to exceed the supply of saving, and firms that want to borrow to make investments are rationed. The problem of credit rationing resulting from artificially low interest rates has been acute in many developing countries, particularly in situations of high inflation. Interest-rate ceilings are typically set in nominal terms, so that as inflation rates increase, the *real* interest-rate ceiling falls, often to negative rates. Ronald McKinnon of Stanford University has described the serious economic inefficiencies that can result from extensive credit rationing caused by administrative controls on interest rates.[30]

Credit rationing also arises when lenders are unable to assess the risks of lending to a particular borrower. In general, investment spending is risky: the returns to a particular project can be estimated, but not known with certainty. Therefore, before a loan is made to finance an investment project, the lender must evaluate the credit risk involved and decide how likely it is that the borrower will be able to repay the loan. Will the investment project generate an adequate stream of profits to assure repayment? Does the borrower have other sources of wealth that can be used as collateral to guarantee the repayment of a loan?

In practice, it is very hard for banks to assess the risks of particular borrowers. Many of the specific risks of an investment project are not easily observable. The bank might have to rely on a few observable characteristics of a borrower, even though observable signs do not address all the risks of the particular loan. The size of the business is one such characteristic, and small companies are much less likely to get loans than large companies. Lenders also tend to discriminate among borrowers on the basis of net worth. The higher the value of total equity of a given firm, the less likely that it would find its credit rationed.[31]

The crucial implication of credit rationing, regardless of its source, is that the internal resources of the firm acquire a fundamental importance in determining the overall level of investment. When firms cannot simply borrow at the market interest rate r, their ability to finance investment projects depends on their retained earnings and their future generation of cash flow. Under these circumstances, the capital stock will not adjust in every period to its optimal level as determined by the market interest rate and the marginal productivity of capital. Thus, credit rationing provides another reason, along with costs of adjustment, for the slow movement of the capital stock to the desired level.

---

[29] Interest-rate ceilings are sometimes imposed as a measure of purported "macroeconomic management" and sometimes for political purposes or to channel cheap credits to favored sectors of the economy. But, often, interest-rate ceilings are an expression of the old Christian and Islamic injunctions against *usury,* which hold that lending at "high" interest rates is contrary to religious precepts.

[30] McKinnon's classical work on this subject is his book *Money and Capital in Economic Development* (Washington, D.C.: The Brookings Institution, 1973).

[31] See Charles Calomiris and Glenn Hubbard, "Firm Heterogeneity, Internal Finance and Credit Rationing," National Bureau of Economic Research Working Paper No. 2497, January 1988.

5-6 Investment in Residential Structures (Optional)

Investment in residential structures is the expenditure on new houses and apartments, as well as the improvement and maintenance of existing units. As we noted at the beginning of the chapter, residential investment spending has generally constituted more than 40 percent of total net private investment spending in the United States. Thus, it is very important to have a good understanding of this form of investment. While the basic principles of investment theory apply to the housing sector (especially regarding the intertemporal dimensions of investment), one theoretical model has proved particularly useful in analyzing this kind of investment.

Our development of a theory of residential investment spending proceeds in two steps. First we derive the average price for existing homes and apartment buildings; second, we derive the level of new construction as a function of the price of existing homes and apartments. For simplicity, we will focus on the market for rental apartments, while pointing out that the market for owner-occupied homes behaves in a very similar manner.

At any given date, there is a supply of apartment units that results from the accumulated past investment in apartment buildings. Let the total stock of apartment buildings be denoted as K_h (where h denotes housing). Furthermore, at any moment there is a demand for rental units that depends on the rental rate, which we denote as RR. As in any usual market, the rental rate is determined by the equilibrium of supply and demand for apartment rentals, as shown in Figure 5-8a.

Consider the value of investing in an apartment building and then renting it to a tenant at the rental rate RR. Suppose that the apartment unit costs P_h to purchase, that it depreciates at the rate d, and that it has a resale value P_{h+1} in the next period. Then, the rate of return on buying the apartment, earning the rent RR, and then reselling the unit in the next period, is given as

$$\text{Rate of return} = \frac{RR + P_{h+1}(1 - d)}{P_h} \qquad \textbf{(5.22)}$$

Figure 5-8

Equilibrium in the Housing Market: (a) The Market for Rentals, (b) the Supply of New Housing

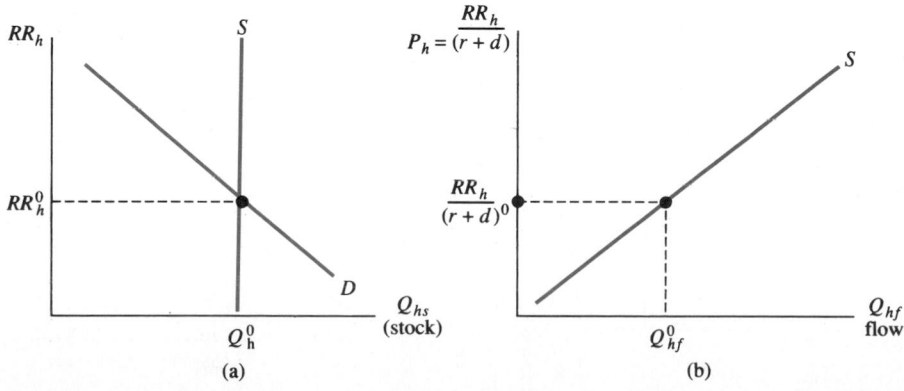

If allowed to, people will exploit unrealized profit opportunities, a conduct known as arbitrage. If there is arbitrage between the loan market and the market for apartment buildings, the rate of return in the apartment market must equal $(1 + r)$. The price of the apartment building, P_h, will adjust to guarantee that the rate of return on owning apartments equals $(1 + r)$. Thus,

$$(1 + r) = \frac{RR + P_{h_{+1}}(1 - d)}{P_h} \qquad (5.23)$$

In the simple case in which $P_{h_{+1}} = P_h$, which will be true if RR is forever fixed at a given rental rate, say, RR_0, then equation (5.23) reduces to a very simple expression:

$$P_h = \frac{RR_0}{(r + d)} \qquad (5.24)$$

In words, the price of the apartment building is simply equal to the rental rate divided by the cost of capital, $(r + d)$.

The demand for apartment rentals determines the rental rate, which in turn, together with the market interest rate, determines the sale price of an existing apartment building. In turn, fluctuations in P_h determine the new supply of apartment buildings, for the simple reason that the construction industry will supply more apartment buildings as the sale price for apartment buildings, P_h, rises. The supply of new apartment buildings is shown in Figure 5-8b, as the upward-sloping supply curve. Note, then, what happens when the demand for apartment rentals increases, as shown in Figure 5-9. There is an outward shift in the demand schedule, causing a rise in rental rates RR. This rise in RR is immediately capitalized into the sale price for apartment buildings, which in turn causes the supply of *new* apartment units to increase.

This theory has been developed for the case of rental apartments, but it can also be applied to the case of owner-occupied housing. In this case, RR refers not to a direct rental cost (since the owner does not, presumably, pay rent to himself), but to an imputed rent that can be viewed as equal to the rent that the owner would pay if the household were actually renting the unit from a different owner. In real life, the main distinction between the rental

Figure 5-9
Effects of an Increase in the Demand for Apartment Rentals: (a) The Market for Rentals, (b) the Supply of New Housing

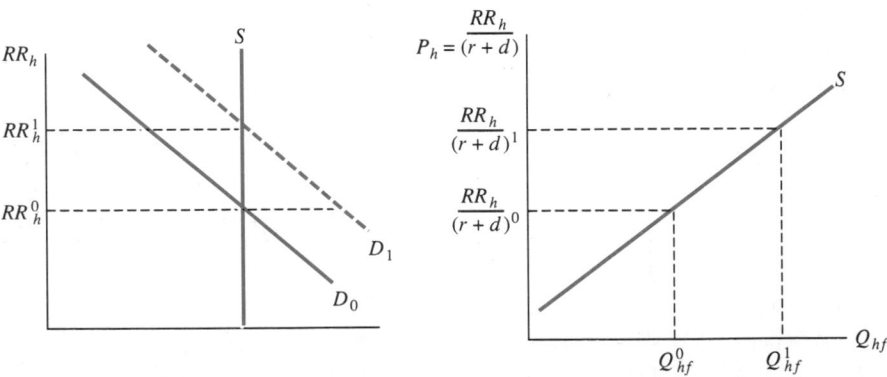

market and the owner-occupied housing market involves a number of tax regulations that are different for the two parts of the housing market.

Various studies have examined the factors that determine the demand for housing services, and thus for aggregate residential investment. One of the most important variables is the age structure of the population, since demand for housing services depends importantly on the age and composition of households. In a widely discussed study, Gregory Mankiw of Harvard University and David Weil of Brown University, showed that demographic trends in the United States are likely to result in a fall in housing demand in the 1990s, with several important economic effects, including a likely drop in the housing prices.[32]

5-7 SUMMARY

Investment is the flow of output used to maintain or increase the *capital stock* in the economy. Most discussions of investment refer to physical investment, though other kinds of investment, such as that in *human capital,* are of enormous importance. The national accounts, which focus on physical investment, measures three main kinds of investment: *investment in residential structures, fixed business investment,* and *inventory investment.*

Investment expenditures are far more volatile than consumption expenditures. While households attempt to smooth consumption over time, both firms and households have much less incentive to smooth investment spending. According to Keynes, and others in the same tradition, these large fluctuations of investment are a major force behind the business cycle.

During the 1980s, the United States has had lower rates of investment—as a share of gross domestic product—than most other industrialized countries. In particular, physical investment in Japan as a proportion of GDP was almost double that of the United States. If consumer durable expenditures are included in the measure of investment, the difference in investment rates between the two countries is reduced somewhat, but the gap still remains significant.

The basic theory of investment starts by recognizing that physical investment spending is an alternative to financial saving as a way to allocate consumption over time. This means that, for the marginal investment, the return to investment should equal the return to saving. The marginal productivity of capital (*MPK*) should therefore be equated to the real rate of interest, adjusted for depreciation. Investment and consumption decisions can be taken separately, in the sense that *MPK* can first be equated to $(r + d)$, no matter what the household utility function might be, after which the household optimally allocates its consumption spending over time.

The existence of taxes and subsidies modifies the investment decision. Taxes on profits reduce the net (private) benefit of investment, while tax credits and *accelerated depreciation* raise the private return on investment. The *investment tax credit* has been used, on and off, in the United States since the early 1960s as a way to stimulate business investment spending. The response of investment to an ITC depends crucially on whether the ITC

[32] Gregory Mankiw and David Weil, "The Baby Boom, the Baby Bust and the Housing Market," National Bureau of Economic Research Working Paper No. 2794, December 1988.

is expected to be *temporary* or *permanent*. A temporary ITC causes firms to speed up their investment spending in order to take advantage of the ITC during its short period of operation.

Inventory accumulation is the most volatile component of investment. There are three types of inventories: *primary inputs* to production, *semifinished goods* in the course of production, and *finished goods* ready to be sold. Firms need stocks of primary inputs to economize on the cost of producing final output, and they need finished goods inventories to smooth production and to avoid *stockouts*. In the United States, each type of inventory accounts for about one-third of the total inventory stock of the manufacturing sector.

Several empirical models have been used to describe investment, of which the *accelerator model* is one of the simplest and most popular. The accelerator model is based on the idea that there is a stable relationship between the desired stock of capital and the level of output. Under this assumption, investment is proportional to the *change* in output, and thus investment rises when output accelerates. This theory has two main weaknesses. First, the model assumes the ratio of desired capital to output to be constant, even though that ratio will vary as the cost of capital and technology vary. Second, it assumes that investment is always sufficient to keep the desired capital stock equal to the actual capital stock, even though that is not normally the case. In spite of its simplicity and obvious limitations, the accelerator theory has performed reasonably well in explaining actual investment patterns.

The *adjustment-cost approach* acknowledges that the actual and desired levels of the capital stock are not generally equal. Firms require time to plan an investment, construct a new factory, install new machines, and train new workers. Moreover, total investment costs tend to rise if the firm rushes to complete an investment project in a very short period of time. Thus, in addition to technical constraints, profit maximization also leads firms to a gradual reduction of the gap between actual and desired investment. Tobin's *q theory of investment,* which is also implicitly based on the idea of costs of adjustment, adds the central idea that the stock market value of a firm relative to the replacement cost of its capital helps to measure the gap between actual and desired capital.

In practice, not all households and firms can freely borrow at the market interest rate to finance an investment, even when the project is profitable. When a firm is credit rationed, investment depends not only on the rate of interest and the profitability of investment, but also on the cash flow of the firm. *Credit rationing* arises principally in two cases: first, when governments put *ceilings on interest rates* that keep them below market equilibrium, and second, when lenders cannot accurately assess the risks of lending to particular borrowers.

Investment in residential structures is the expenditure on new houses and apartments, as well as the improvement and maintenance of existing dwelling units. Such investment accounts for almost one-half of total physical investment spending in the United States. The development of a theory of residential investment proceeds in two steps. First, an equilibrium rental rate is determined in the market for housing rentals as it fluctuates to balance the supply and demand for existing rental units. Second, the rental rate (and expected future rental rates) determines the sale price of an apartment unit.

High sale prices of existing apartment units spur the construction of new apartment buildings and thereby leads to a rise in residential investment spending. This same basic approach can also be applied to the analysis of owner-occupied housing investment.

Key Concepts

physical capital
human capital
gross investment
net investment
capacity utilization
marginal product of capital
investment tax credit
cost of capital
inventory accumulation
primary inputs

semifinished goods
finished goods
fixed business investment
accelerator model
partial adjustment approach
Tobin's q theory
desired capital
credit rationing
residential investment

Problems and Questions

1. Should the following forms of expenditure be considered investment or consumption? Discuss your answers and note if they differ from the treatment in the national income accounts.

   a. A family buys a personal computer.
   b. A corporation buys a personal computer.
   c. A corporation pays for a computer course for its employees.
   d. A student pays for her tuition.
   e. A firm builds a new building.
   f. A firm buys an old factory.
   g. A Texas oil company extracts more oil from its wells.

2. In country A, the initial capital stock is worth $100 million. Gross investment is $8 million in year 1 and $15 million in year 2. If capital depreciates at 10 percent per year, what is the net investment in each of the two years?

3. In the two-period model of investment, assume the following: the production function is $Q = 2 K^{1/2}$, the initial stock capital is $K_1 = 81$, the interest rate is 11 percent.

   a. What is optimal amount of investment if capital does not depreciate?
   b. How would your answer to (a) change if capital depreciated by 10 percent per year?

4. The general manager of ACME Industries thinks that he is doing a very good job because the marginal productivity of capital (net of depreciation) in his firm is higher than the interest rate. Is he really doing a good job? Why?

5. Households A and B have exactly the same productive resources, and they face the same interest rate. The only difference between them is that household A has a stronger preference for future consumption than household B.

   a. Would intertemporal optimization imply that household A should invest more than household B?
   b. How would your answer to (a) change in the presence of credit rationing?

6. Which of the following policy measures would be more effective in raising next year's investment?

   a. A permanent subsidy on investment.

   b. A temporary subsidy effective only next year.

   What would be the effect of (b) on this year's investment?

7. Suppose that country A has a very stable demand for final products, while country B's demand varies significantly. According to the production-smoothing theory of inventories, which country is likely to have higher inventory investment?

8. Discuss the main differences between the accelerator model, the adjustment-costs approach, and the q theory of investment.

9. If firms are credit rationed, would one expect to see investment going up when corporate profits go down?

10. According to the residential housing model, what would happen to the price of apartment buildings, the rental rate, and the stock of apartment buildings if the interest rate declines?

APPENDIX: INVESTMENT RULES WHEN HOUSEHOLDS AND FIRMS ARE SEPARATE ENTITIES

In modern economies, most investment is carried out by firms rather than by households. The firms, however, are owned by households, and they should operate to maximize the utility of their owners. In this appendix, we explore how the separation of households and firms affects optimal investment decisions.

Let us examine a two-period model which assumes that households and firms are separate entities and that firms undertake the investment decisions. The firm produces output (Q), using labor and capital. The short-run profits of firms are equal to output *minus* labor costs. Let the wage be w and the amount of labor input in production be L. Profits (Pr) in periods 1 and 2 are given as follows:

$$Pr_1 = Q_1 - w_1 L_1; \qquad Pr_2 = Q_2 - w_2 L_2 \qquad \textbf{(A.1)}$$

In the first period, the firm earns profits, makes investments of I_1, and then distributes the rest of the earnings to the owners of the firm. Thus, in the first period, the owners receive $Pr_1 - I_1$. In the second period, the owners receive all the second-period profits, since, there being no subsequent periods, there is no investment. The market value of the firm (V_1) is simply the *discounted value of the cash flow of the firm:*

$$V_1 = (Pr_1 - I_1) + \frac{Pr_2}{(1 + r)} \qquad \textbf{(A.2)}$$

Households as a whole earn the wages, or income from labor, and own the firms. Thus, the total wealth of households in period 1 has to include both the present value of their labor income, and the value of the firms which they own:

$$W_1 = w_1 L_1 + \frac{w_2 L_2}{(1 + r)} + V_1 \qquad \textbf{(A.3)}$$

By substituting V_1 from (A.2), and Pr_1 and Pr_2 from (A.1), we find that aggregate wealth is

$$W_1 = (Q_1 - I_1) + \frac{Q_2}{(1 + r)} \qquad \textbf{(A.4)}$$

Not surprisingly, this expression for household wealth is exactly the same as the one presented in equation (5.7). The division of the economy into households and firms, in which the households supply labor and own the firms, does not affect the expression for the wealth of the households. Even though part of the wealth of the economy is generated by firms, the fact that these firms are owned by the households themselves means that the expression for wealth is unchanged.

What criterion should guide the investment decisions of firms? Their goal is to maximize the wealth of the households that own them. This can be accomplished if firms maximize the value of their shares. Thus, the I_1 selected must maximize V_1. Consider then the effect of an incremental investment ΔI_1 on V_1. When investment rises, the second-period capital stock also rises. This, in turn, raises second-period profits. We can indeed show that Pr_2 changes in the amount $\Delta I_1 MPK_2$.[1] The change in the value of the firm is then equal to the change in profits, discounted by $(1 + r)$, minus the cost of the investment:

$$\Delta V_1 = \frac{\Delta I_1 MPK_2}{(1 + r)} - \Delta I_1$$

This change is positive if and only if $MPK_2 > 1 + r$. Thus, just as in the case of the household investor, the firm should invest whenever MPK_2 is greater than or equal to $(1 + r)$.

In a multiperiod setting, the criterion for a profit-maximizing firm would be no different from that for households alone. In particular, in all cases MPK_{+1} should be greater than or equal to $(r + d)$, or the investment should not be undertaken.

---

[1] The proof of this is actually trickier than it looks. Since second-period profits are given by

$$Pr_2 = Q_2 - w_2 L_2$$

the change in profits is

$$\Delta Pr_2 = \Delta Q_2 - w_2 \Delta L_2$$

The change in Q_2 is given by $MPK_2\, \Delta K_2 + MPL_2\, \Delta L_2$, where ΔL_2 is the change in labor input that is induced by the incremental investment. Also, $\Delta K_2 = \Delta I_1$, since $K_2 = (1 - d)K_1 + I_1$. If the firm is profit maximizing, it is setting $MPL_2 = w_2$, so that we find the following:

$$\Delta Pr_2 = MPK_2\, \Delta K_2 + MPL_2\, \Delta L_2 - w_2\, \Delta L_2$$
$$= MPK_2\, \Delta K_2 + (MPL_2 - w_2)\, \Delta L_2$$
$$= MPK_2\, \Delta K_2$$

Thus, the change in second period profits is just equal to MPK_2 multiplied by the size of the investment.

chapter 6

Saving, Investment, and the Current Account

In a completely closed economy, one that is cut off from the rest of the world, aggregate saving would necessarily equal aggregate investment. The output in the economy is divided between current consumption uses and investment, so that $Q = C + I$. At the same time, the income received by households, which is also equal to Q, must be divided between consumption and saving, so that $Q = C + S$. We see immediately that $I = S$, that investment must always equal saving. Both saving and investment represent that part of national output which is not used for current consumption.

Of course, the saving and the investment in a national economy are not necessarily made by the same households (and firms).[1] Some households might want to save without having investment projects to undertake, while other households might have investment projects but no saving. Financial markets solve the problem of getting the saving to those who want to invest. Through them, the savers would accumulate financial assets while the investors accumulate financial liabilities. To take one simple example, the investors could issue bonds to finance their investments that could be purchased by the households that seek to save.

In an open economy, however, in which a nation's residents trade goods and financial assets with residents in other economies, it is no longer true that a nation's saving must always equal the investment that takes place within the country. A nation's households might want to save more than they want to invest at home, with the excess saving lent to investors in other countries. In this case, the country would accumulate net financial claims against residents abroad.

But what happens to the national output that is produced but neither consumed nor invested? It is exported to foreigners. As we shall see, there is an intimate relationship between the saving-investment balance of a country and the net exports of the country.

---

[1] For analytical purposes, it is not necessary to distinguish at this point between households and firms, so our discussion is in terms of households for simplicity.

In this chapter, we study the determinants of national lending and borrowing from the rest of the world. The *current account of the balance of payments* is the key concept at the center of our discussion. (In addition to the economic analysis of the current account given in the chapter, we also discuss the *accounting* of the current account balance in an appendix.) When residents in one country lend more to foreigners than they borrow, and thus accumulate a net financial claim against the rest of the world, we say that the country has a *current account surplus*. When the country is accumulating a net liability (or running down its net claims) against the rest of the world, the economy has a *current account deficit*. A current account surplus exists when national saving exceeds national investment (with the difference lent abroad), and a current account deficit exists when national investment exceeds national saving. We shall see that the current account balance is closely related to the net export balance.

The current account has a crucial intertemporal dimension. The economy as a whole, like the individual households (and firms) that compose the economy, has an intertemporal budget constraint. If the economy runs a current account deficit today, its residents are increasing their net debt to the rest of the world. Eventually, the country will have to cut back on domestic consumption in order to pay the interest on the accumulated debts. As domestic consumption is cut back, national output that was used for consumption is increasingly used for net exports. As we shall see, the country's net exports are, in essence, its method of paying the interest burden on the liabilities accumulated while running current account deficits.

6-1 A FORMAL ANALYSIS OF SAVING, INVESTMENT, AND THE CURRENT ACCOUNT

We now turn to a formal model of the current account. In order to simplify the theory, we continue (as in the past two chapters) to assume a classical, fully employed economy, with a stable price level for goods ($P = 1$). (Later on in the book, we will discuss the implications for the current account of aggregate demand–induced fluctuations in output within the framework of the Keynesian model.)

In a closed economy, saving must equal investment. Since both saving and investment are a function of the domestic interest rate, r, we can draw the saving and investment schedules, as we do in Figure 6-1, with saving an increasing function of r and investment a decreasing function of r.[2] Of course, saving and investment are also functions of many other things: current and future income, expected profitability, and so on. These other factors are held fixed in the background when we draw saving and investment schedules like those in the graph. The domestic interest rate adjusts to equilibrate saving and investment at the level given by the equilibrium point E.

We can see the effects of various kinds of shocks on domestic saving, investment, and interest rates quite clearly. Consider, for example, the ef-

---

[2] Remember from Chapter 4 that the effect of a rise in the interest rate on saving is ambiguous because the substitution effect tends to cause saving to rise while the income effect may cause saving to fall. As we said in Chapter 4, we take the normal case to be one in which a rise in interest rates is associated with a rise in saving.

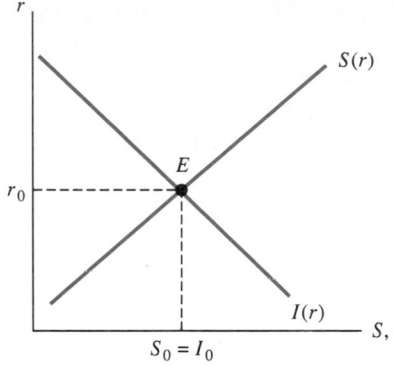

Figure 6-1
Saving, Investment, and the Interest Rate in a Closed Economy

fects of a temporary increase in output resulting from a favorable supply shock—a bountiful harvest, for example. Households will want to save more at any given interest rate, so that the saving schedule will shift to the right, as shown in Figure 6-2a. The investment schedule will not shift, however, if the output change is strictly temporary. As long as the future production function remains unchanged, the desired capital stock in the future also remains unchanged. Thus, the I schedule will not shift. The result of the temporary output increase, therefore, is a fall in interest rates and an increase in current saving and investment, as the equilibrium shifts from E to E' in Figure 6-2a.

Now let us consider the effects of an anticipated future increase in income, one that also shifts upward the marginal productivity of capital in the future. In this case, current saving will tend to fall, as households borrow against their higher future income; investment will tend to increase as well, to take advantage of the higher marginal productivity of capital. The result is shown in Figure 6-2b, as a leftward shift in the saving schedule and a rightward shift in the investment schedule. We can say with certainty that interest rates will rise, while overall saving and investment might rise or fall.

Figure 6-2
Effects of Economic Shocks on Saving and Investment in a Closed Economy

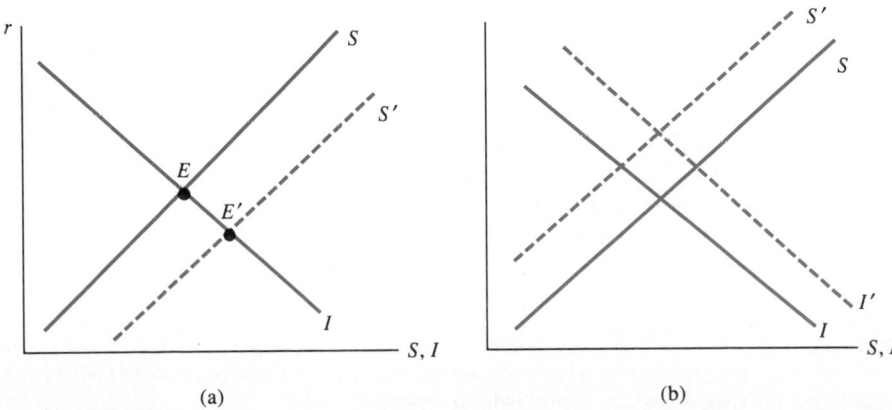

(a)   (b)

Most economies in the world are not closed, however, so the assumption that a country's saving and investment must always balance is not very useful. Residents in one country can generally lend or borrow from the rest of the world, and thereby build up claims or liabilities vis-à-vis residents in other countries. Thus, saving and investment analysis must be expanded to take into account the international flows of financial assets.

Let B^* be the net claims of a country's residents on residents in the rest of the world. (We use the asterisk in general to denote a "foreign variable." The asterisk here stresses that B^* is a claim on foreign output.) B^* is sometimes called the country's *net international investment position*, or the *net foreign asset position*. It may be thought of as an asset in the form of a bond (hence, the notation), though in fact claims against the rest of the world can be held in many forms: bonds, money, equities, and so on. B^* measures the assets of national residents vis-à-vis foreigners, *minus* the liabilities vis-à-vis foreigners. When B^* is positive, the country is a *net creditor* of the rest of the world, and when B^* is negative the country is a *net debtor* of the rest of the world.

We define the country's current account (CA) as the change in its net financial asset position with respect to the rest of the world:

$$CA = B^* - B^*_{-1} \qquad \textbf{(6.1)}$$

Note that current account surpluses imply an accumulation of foreign assets or a reduction in foreign liabilities. Deficits imply a decumulation of foreign assets or an increase in foreign liabilities.

Equation (6.1) tells us that the current account in this period (CA) is the change in net foreign assets, which we denote by B^*, between this period and the *previous* period (denoted by the subscript $_{-1}$). Notice that the level of B^* in a given period is a result of past current account surpluses and deficits. Starting from an initial year (arbitrarily denoted year 0), the net international investment position of a country in year t (B^*_t) is equal to B^*_0 plus the sum of current accounts in the years between 0 and t:

$$B^*_t = B^*_0 + CA_1 + CA_2 + \cdots + CA_t \qquad \textbf{(6.2)}$$

In many countries, especially in the developing world, B^* is a negative number, because the countries' current accounts have been negative for a long time. The situation of the heavily indebted developing countries has generated much attention and discussion during the past decade and has become known as the Third World debt crisis. We analyze this crisis in detail in Chapter 22.

Table 6-1 presents the evolution of the U.S. current account and its net foreign asset (NFA) position since 1970.[3] The NFA measures the creditor or debtor status of the United States vis-à-vis the rest of the world; that is, it measures the balance of total foreign assets *minus* total foreign liabilities.

Note that the current account deficits of the United States during the 1980s have transformed this country from the major international creditor country to the world's biggest net debtor. Indeed, by the end of 1988 the

---

[3] According to current usage, we will treat the terms "net international investment position" and "net foreign asset position" as synonyms.

TABLE 6-1

THE CURRENT ACCOUNT AND THE NET INTERNATIONAL INVESTMENT IN THE UNITED STATES, 1970–1989
(BILLIONS OF CURRENT DOLLARS)

Year	Current Account Balance	Net International Investment Position
1970	2.3	58.6
1971	−1.4	56.1
1972	−5.8	37.1
1973	7.1	61.9
1974	2.0	58.8
1975	18.1	74.6
1976	4.2	82.6
1977	−14.5	72.4
1978	−15.4	76.7
1979	−1.0	95.0
1980	1.1	106.3
1981	6.9	140.9
1982	−5.9	136.7
1983	−40.1	89.0
1984	−99.0	3.3
1985	−122.3	−111.4
1986	−145.4	−267.8
1987	−162.3	−378.3
1988	−128.9	−532.5
1989	−110.0	—

Source: Economic Report of the President, 1991, *(Washington, D.C.: U.S. Government Printing Office, 1991), Tables B-101 and B-102, various issues.*

United States had accumulated over $500 billion of net foreign liabilities.[4] This is more than three times the debt of Brazil or Mexico, the largest developing country debtors. In spite of its size, however, the U.S. problem

[4] We should acknowledge at this point that the data underlying Table 6-1 have many measurement problems. Some authors have argued that the United States did not really become a net debtor during the 1980s because the value of U.S. assets abroad is much higher than the official data indicates. For one thing, U.S. investments abroad have been measured traditionally at historic cost. Other kinds of errors in the data do tend to understate U.S. debts to foreigners, however. While we cannot be sure of the overall level of the net U.S. debt, it is surely the case that the U.S. net international investment position fell sharply in the 1980s, moving from a large surplus to a much smaller surplus or to a deficit. Indeed, a recent estimate based on the market value of investments revised the U.S. NIIP upward to −$268 billion in 1989, still a sizable number, but much less than the −$532 billion shown in the table.

is of a smaller magnitude relative to income; the net international liabilities of the United States represent only about 10 percent of its GDP, while Mexico's net debt is well over 50 percent of its GDP.

Note also that the current account is not exactly equal to the change in net foreign assets. A variety of factors account for this discrepancy: unrecorded capital flows,[5] which sometimes show up in the balance of payments under the category "errors and omissions," valuation changes on existing assets and liabilities which affect the net asset position but not the current account, expropriations of foreign assets, and defaults on international debt.

To show how the current account is related to saving and investment, we must first look back at the budget constraint of an individual household. Recall from equation (5.5) of the previous chapter that for a given household i, the change in financial assets is equal to the difference between the saving and investment of the household:

$$B^i - B^i_{-1} = Q^i + rB^i_{-1} - C^i - I^i \tag{6.3}$$

Now, write the household's income as $Y^i = Q^i + rB^i_{-1}$, and use the fact that saving S^i equals $Y^i - C^i$ to find

$$B^i - B^i_{-1} = S^i - I^i \tag{6.4}$$

An individual household can hold claims against other domestic households or against foreigners. If we add up all the net claims of households to get the net asset position of the entire economy, the claims that are owed by one household to another net out of the sum of all households, since claims between households are assets for some households but equal liabilities for others. What remains are the net claims of the economy against the rest of the world, which we have denoted B^*. Thus, in adding (6.4) over all households we find for the economy as a whole

$$B^* - B^*_{-1} = Q + rB^*_{-1} - C - I \tag{6.5}$$

Once again substituting $Y = Q + rB^*_{-1}$ (GNP = GDP + net income from abroad), and $S = Y - C$, we can now write

$$B^* - B^*_{-1} = S - I \tag{6.6}$$

Equation (6.6) can be interpreted quite simply. Since it can be rewritten as $S = I + (B^* - B^*_{-1})$, it tells us that domestic saving can be used for two things: domestic investment (I) or net foreign investment ($B^* - B^*_{-1}$).

Equations (6.1) and (6.6) make it clear that the current account can be expressed as the difference between national saving and investment:

$$CA = S - I \tag{6.7}$$

As long as domestic residents can borrow and lend from foreign residents, domestic saving and investment do not have to be equal. The difference between saving and investment is precisely measured by the current account balance. Clearly, in a closed economy, the current account concept is irrele-

---

[5] In industrialized countries, these unrecorded capital flows are known by the elegant technical term *portfolio reallocations*. In the developing world, these flows are called *capital flight*, a term that has a distinctly negative connotation. We analyze the issue of capital flight in Chapter 22.

TABLE   6-2

SAVING, INVESTMENT, AND THE CURRENT ACCOUNT IN THE UNITED STATES, 1950–1990
(AS PERCENTAGE OF GDP)

Year	Gross Saving	Gross Private Domestic Investment	Saving – Investment	Balance on Current Account	Statistical Discrepancy
1950–59	16.2%	16.3%	−0.1%	0.1%	0.2%
1960–69	16.4	15.6	0.8	0.5	−0.3
1970–79	16.9	16.7	0.2	0.0	−0.2
1980	16.6	16.3	0.3	0.1	−0.2
1981	17.4	17.2	0.2	0.3	0.1
1982	14.3	14.4	0.0	−0.2	−0.2
1983	13.8	15.0	−1.2	−1.3	−0.2
1984	15.3	17.8	−2.6	−2.8	−0.2
1985	13.4	16.2	−2.8	−2.8	−0.1
1986	12.5	15.7	−3.2	−3.2	0.0
1987	12.3	15.6	−3.3	−3.2	0.1
1988	13.3	15.5	−2.2	−2.6	−0.4
1989	13.5	14.9	−1.5	−2.1	−0.6
1990p	12.1	13.7	−1.6	—	—

p = preliminary.
Source: Economic Report of the President, 1991 *(Washington, D.C.: U.S. Government Printing Office, 1991), Tables B-28 and B-102.*

vant. In an economy completely isolated financially from the rest of the world (no net claims), the current account is always zero.

Table 6-2 presents the time series of saving, domestic investment, and the current account as a percentage of GDP for the United States in the period 1950–1990.[6] Notice that in the 1950s, 1960s, and 1970s the United States consistently experienced a current account surplus. This situation was sharply reversed in the 1980s. During 1981–1990, the average current account deficit was about 2 percent of GDP. Interestingly, the current account decline in the 1980s was due to a sharp fall in the national saving rate rather than to a rise in domestic investment. In fact, domestic investment

---

[6] We should point out one data distortion in Table 6-2. In the United States, gross saving is measured as the sum of private saving and the public surplus. The public surplus is government saving minus government investment. Thus, government investment is subtracted from gross saving rather than being included in total investment, which includes only private capital formation. Thus, for this reason, the data understate both saving and investment by misclassifying government investment. Nonetheless, even if government investment were properly classified, the direction of change in recent years (toward lower national saving and a lower current account balance) would remain.

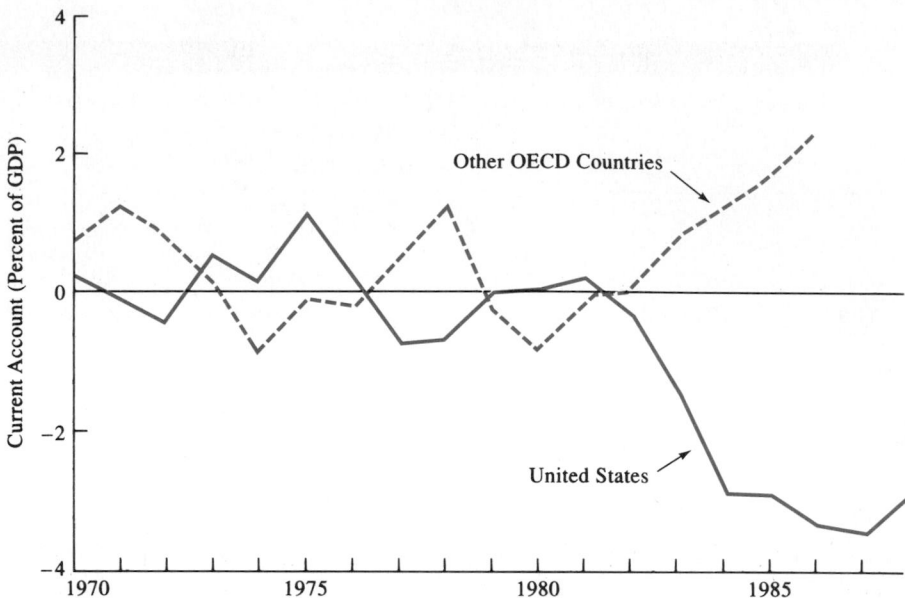

The six major OECD trading partners of the U.S. are Canada, France, Germany, Italy, Japan, and the United Kingdom. The figure shows the sum of their current accounts, measured in dollars, as a percentage of their combined GDP, also measured in dollars.

Figure 6-3
The Current Account in the United States vis-à-vis Other Industrialized Countries

(From International Monetary Fund, International Financial Statistics.*)*

also declined in this period, but the drop in saving was even more pronounced. (In turn, most of the fall in national saving is due to the behavior of the public sector, a point we study in greater detail in the next chapter, when we analyze formally the role of the government sector.)

As the current account balance of the United States declined during the 1980s, the rest of the world had to be running a current account surplus vis-à-vis the United States. After all, the world as a whole is a closed economy. Figure 6-3 depicts the behavior of the current account in the United States vis-à-vis the rest of the member countries in the Organization for Economic Cooperation and Development (OECD).[7] The graph clearly shows the negative relationship between the U.S. current account and that of the rest of the OECD countries. As the U.S. CA *deficit* increased to over 3 percent of GDP, the CA *surplus* among the other OECD members reached over 2 percent of their combined GDP.

Of course, the *average* for the other 23 OECD member countries hides important differences in individual behavior. Indeed, this average is strongly influenced by the vast current account surpluses in Japan and West Germany as well as the relative weight of their economies within the OECD. Table 6-3 shows a breakdown of the current account behavior for the United States

---

[7] The OECD is an association of 24 major industrialized countries. These are Australia, Austria, Belgium, Canada, Denmark, Finland, France, Germany, Greece, Iceland, Ireland, Italy, Japan, Luxembourg, the Netherlands, New Zealand, Norway, Portugal, Spain, Sweden, Switzerland, Turkey, the United Kingdom, and the United States.

TABLE 6-3

THE CURRENT ACCOUNT IN THE UNITED STATES AND ITS MAJOR TRADING PARTNERS, 1980–1989

Year	United States	Canada	France	Germany	Italy	Japan	United Kingdom
Billions of U.S. Dollars							
1980	1.8	−1.0	−4.2	−14.0	−10.0	−10.8	7.5
1981	6.9	−5.1	−4.8	−3.4	−9.7	4.8	14.5
1982	−7.0	2.2	−12.0	5.0	−6.4	6.9	8.0
1983	−44.3	2.5	−5.2	5.4	1.4	20.8	5.8
1984	−104.2	2.0	−0.9	9.7	−2.5	35.0	2.6
1985	−112.7	−1.4	0.0	17.0	−3.5	49.2	4.7
1986	−133.2	−7.6	2.4	40.1	2.9	85.8	0.1
1987	−143.7	−7.0	−4.4	46.1	−1.6	87.0	−7.4
1988	−126.6	−8.3	−3.5	50.5	−5.4	79.6	−26.7
1989	−105.9	−16.6	−4.3	55.7	—	56.8	−34.1
Percentage of GDP							
1980	0.1	−0.4	−0.6	−1.7	−2.2	−1.0	1.4
1981	0.2	−1.7	−0.8	−0.5	−2.4	0.4	2.8
1982	−0.2	0.7	−2.2	0.8	−1.6	0.6	1.7
1983	−1.3	0.8	−1.0	0.8	0.3	1.8	1.3
1984	−2.8	0.6	−0.2	1.6	−0.6	2.8	0.6
1985	−2.8	0.4	0.0	2.7	−0.8	3.7	1.0
1986	−3.2	−2.1	0.3	4.5	0.5	4.4	0.0
1987	−3.2	−1.7	−0.5	4.1	−0.2	3.6	−1.1
1988	−2.6	−1.7	−0.4	4.2	−0.7	2.8	−3.2
1989	−2.0	−3.0	−0.4	4.7	—	2.0	−4.1

Source: *International Monetary Fund,* International Financial Statistics, *selected issues.*

and its six major OECD trading partners, Canada, France, Germany, Italy, Japan, and the United Kingdom, for the 1980s.

There is yet another way to express the current account. Notice from equations (6.3) and (6.7) that

$$CA = Y - (C + I) \qquad (6.8)$$

We define "absorption," A, as the sum of consumption and investment, that is, total spending by the domestic residents,[8] or

$$A = C + I \qquad (6.9)$$

[8] Strictly speaking, consumption and investment should be interpreted here to include government consumption and investment. We explicitly introduce the government in our framework in the next chapter.

Therefore, the current account is also the difference between income and absorption:

$$CA = Y - A \qquad\qquad (6.10)$$

This was an important insight of Sidney Alexander of the Massachusetts Institute of Technology in the early 1950s.[9]

Equation (6.10) has a very intuitive appeal. Countries run current account deficits when they spend (or absorb) more than they earn. This requires them to run down their foreign assets or to increase their net liabilities to the rest of the world.

Thus, a current account deficit occurs when a country "spends beyond its means" (absorption is greater than income) or when it "invests in excess of its own saving." While these two ways of measuring the current account are equivalent, they certainly conjure up different value judgments about a current account deficit. When economists want to complain about a current account deficit, they tend to say that the country is living beyond its means; when they want to defend a current account deficit, on the other hand, they say that the country's investment climate is highly favorable (causing investment in excess of national saving). Of course, a current account deficit is—by itself—neither a good nor a bad thing. The appropriateness of the current account position must be evaluated in terms of the intertemporal prospects facing an economy.

Using the diagram in Figure 6-1, we can readily see how the current account is determined. There we depicted saving as an increasing function of the interest rate and investment as a decreasing function of the interest rate. In the closed economy, the interest rate adjusts to equilibrate saving and investment, as we saw earlier.

Now, let us assume that the economy is open and that in fact its residents can borrow and lend freely at a given world interest rate, which we call r. In effect, we are making the *small-country assumption*, that saving and investment decisions in the home country—whose saving and investment are depicted in Figure 6-4a—do not affect the world interest rate. For a given world r, saving and investment need not be equal in the country, with the gap reflecting the current account deficit or surplus of the country. If the world interest rate is relatively high, say, r_H in Figure 6-4a, saving in the domestic economy will be higher than investment and the country's current account will be in surplus. (The current account surplus is measured by the horizontal difference between the S and I schedules at the rate r_H.) Conversely, if the world interest rate is relatively low, say, r_L, investment will exceed saving in the domestic economy and the economy will be running a current account deficit.

Using this simple framework, we can represent the current account as an increasing function of the interest rate, as shown in Figure 6-4b. At every interest rate, the horizontal difference between the saving and investment schedules in Figure 6-4a measures the current account. By shifting the interest rate, we can draw the curve CA in Figure 6-4b. Notice that the CA schedule is always flatter than the S schedule, because a higher interest rate

[9] Sidney Alexander, "The Effects of Devaluation on a Trade Balance," *International Monetary Fund Staff Papers*, 1952, pp. 263–278.

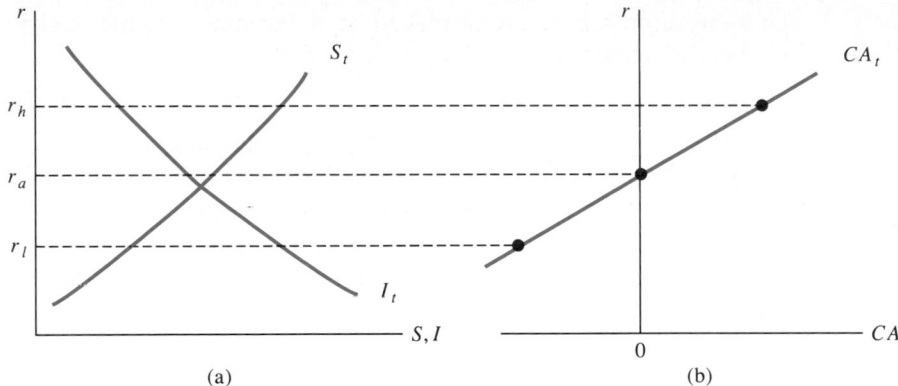

Figure 6-4
Saving, Investment, and the Current Account

not only increases saving but also reduces investment, and both of these effects improve the current account. In a later section, we examine more carefully those factors that are likely to affect a country's current account balance.

6-2 THE CURRENT ACCOUNT AND INTERNATIONAL TRADE

So far, we have described the current account without mentioning international trade. This may be surprising, since most of us typically think about the current account as a trade phenomenon, a matter of exports and imports. In truth, there is an intimate link between the saving-investment balance and the export-import balance, a link which leads us to a more subtle understanding of current account imbalances.

When a country absorbs more than it produces ($A > Q$), it is using more resources than are available to it from domestic production alone. A country can do that only by importing goods from the rest of the world. More precisely, the country must import more from the rest of the world than it exports to the rest of the world, so that *on balance* it is receiving real resources from abroad. For this reason, a current account deficit tends to be associated with an excess of imports over exports, and a current account surplus tends to be associated with an excess of exports over imports. Now let us look more closely at this relationship.

For a given amount of total domestic absorption A, the total spending is divided between absorption on domestic goods (denoted A_d) and absorption on imports (denoted IM):[10]

$$A = A_d + IM \qquad (6.11)$$

---

[10] Technically, all goods will be measured in units of the home goods. That is, IM signifies the nominal value of total imports divided by the price index of the domestic output.

At the same time, all goods produced at home must be either sold domestically (in the amount A_d) or exported, X. Thus,

$$Q = A_d + X \tag{6.12}$$

The country's trade balance is measured as the value of exports minus the value of imports ($TB = X - IM$). But since exports are equal to total output minus the portion of it that is consumed domestically ($X = Q - A_d$), we can conclude that

$$TB = X - IM = Q - A_d - IM = Q - A \tag{6.13}$$

Now, with the trade balance equal to output minus absorption, and with the current account equal to income minus absorption, the difference between the trade balance and the current account balance is the net factor payments from abroad (NF). In our model, NF is simply the interest payments on net foreign assets, equal to rB^*_{-1}.[11] Consequently, because CA $= Y - A$, we also can write CA $= Q + rB^*_{-1} - A$. Then, using (6.13), we have

$$CA = TB + rB^*_{-1} \tag{6.14}$$

Under ordinary circumstances, rB^*_{-1} is small relative to the trade balance, in which case the current account balance and the trade balance are nearly the same. Current account deficits often signal not just an excess of investment over saving, or absorption over income, but also an excess of imports over exports. It is possible, however, to have a current account deficit with a trade-balance surplus (or vice versa), if the earnings on the net foreign assets are relatively large. In Box 6-1, we examine the current account balances of several countries to see how the overall balances actually depend on trade, interest payments, and other items.

To summarize, there are four different ways to describe the current account: (1) as the change in net foreign assets (CA $= B^* - B^*_{-1}$), (2) as national saving net of investment (CA $= S - I$), (3) as income minus absorption (CA $= Y - A$), and (4) as the trade balance plus net factor payments from abroad (CA $= X - IM + NF$).

In past years, some economists have argued as if these different definitions hinted at different "theories" of the current account, including an intertemporal theory that stresses saving and investment; an "elasticity approach" that stresses factors determining imports and exports; an "absorption approach" that stresses the determinants of absorption relative to income; and so forth. This debate among the various schools of thought has been fruitless, however. All formulations of the current account are equally true, and all are linked together by simple accounting identities. There is no

---

[11] In real life, though not in our simplified model, there are some other items that cause the current account and the trade balance to differ. For example, the receipt of foreign aid from abroad raises the current account relative to the trade balance, though the foreign aid is a form of transfer payment and not a receipt of income on foreign assets. A complete breakdown of the difference in the two balances is shown in Table 6-4. Note that the difference between the trade balance and the current account balance includes two categories: "other goods, services, and income" and "unilateral transfers." The "other goods, services, and income" category includes income received on net foreign assets (the subcategory "interest and dividends"), as well as receipts on travel (tourism), workers' remittances, and some other items. The "unilateral transfer" category includes foreign aid as well as transfers from the private sector.

Box 6-1

What Is Hidden by a Summary Current Account Statistic?

Cross-country comparisons of current account behavior, like those shown in Table 6-3, often do not go beyond the most aggregated level: the ratio of the current account to GDP. But while this summary statistic conveys some important information, it also hides quite a bit. Is a given current account deficit due to high investment levels or to low saving? Is the explanation for the deficit found in a trade deficit or in high interest payments on foreign debt? The answers vary substantially across countries, a point that shows up clearly in Table 6-4. (For a discussion of balance-of-payments accounting, see also the appendix to this chapter.)

Consider the current account balances of various countries in 1989. Notice that in the United States the current account deficit is almost completely accounted for by the trade deficit, with the rest of the current account close to equilibrium. In Japan, a major trade surplus is the principal cause of the current account surplus. Behind these figures, the country runs an important deficit on services, as the Japanese have grown fond of traveling abroad. Of course, this situation is not static. The United States used to have a huge surplus in services due to high profit remittances and interest payments on U.S. loans abroad. Persistent current account deficits have deteriorated its net foreign asset position, however, as we saw in Table 6-1, and this has obviously reduced the net income from capital. Japan has persistently accumulated net foreign assets during the period, and thus it presents the opposite case.

For major debtors, such as Brazil in the table, the current account shows a relatively small surplus of $4.1 billion despite a massive trade surplus of $19.1 billion. Huge interest payments on foreign debt account for most of the discrepancy. Because of this factor, in 1988 Brazil had a current account deficit together with a huge trade surplus. Among service payments, workers' remittances are a very important source of foreign exchange on the current account for countries such as Turkey, and, to a lesser extent, the Philippines. Notice also that workers' remittances represent a substantial outflow of funds from the United States and Japan, as foreign workers attracted by high wages in the United States send money back to their families in their native countries. In other countries such as Spain and Thailand, tourism is a major foreign-exchange earner. Indeed, tourism is the most important source of foreign exchange in Spain, with a net contribution of over $13 billion in 1989, or about 30 percent of the country's exports.

A final group of countries get much of their foreign exchange on current account through unilateral transfers, that is, gifts from other nations. China, India, Indonesia, Bangladesh, Egypt, and Israel collect the most dollars through official development assistance, as shown in Table 6-5. However, if the ranking is made as a proportion of the recipient country's GDP, the top 11 earners of grants are in Africa.

TABLE 6-4

THE COMPOSITION OF THE CURRENT ACCOUNT BALANCE FOR SELECTED COUNTRIES, DECEMBER 1989
(MILLIONS OF U.S. DOLLARS)

	United States	Japan	Brazil*	Mexico	Turkey	Philippines	Spain	Thailand
Trade balance	−114,870	−76,890	−19,168	−645	−4,201	−2,598	−24,495	−2,948
Exports	360,460	269,550	33,773	22,765	11,771	7,821	43,301	19,824
Imports	−475,330	−192,660	−14,605	−23,410	−15,972	−10,419	−67,797	−22,772
Other goods, services, and income	18,680	−15,620	−15,118	−5,153	4,672	661	10,370	250
Travel	−550	−19,350	−588	−548	1,992	392	13,121	3,004
Interest and dividends	7,840	19,690	−12,122	−8,010	−1,792	−1,395	−3,418	−911
Workers' remittances	−910	—	−15	321	3,063	358	1,415	—
Other	12,300	−15,960	−2,393	3,085	1,408	1,306	−748	−1,843
Unilateral transfers	−13,850	−4,280	109	351	495	472	3,192	243
Official transfers	−13,430	−3,290	−13	156	423	357	1,444	197
Other	−420	−990	122	195	72	115	1,748	46
Current account balance	−110,040	56,990	4,159	−5,447	966	−1,465	−10,933	−2,455

* December 1988.
Source: *International Monetary Fund, Yearbook, Balance of Payments Statistics, 1990.*

TABLE   6-5

COUNTRIES THAT RECEIVE EXTENSIVE OFFICIAL DEVELOPMENT ASSISTANCE, 1989

Amount (millions of US$)		As a % of GDP	
China	$2,227	Mozambique	59.2%
India	1,874	Somalia	38.9
Indonesia	1,830	Tanzania	32.0
Bangladesh	1,791	Lesotho	26.0
Egypt	1,578	Malawi	24.9
Israel	1,192	Chad	23.5
Pakistan	1,119	Mali	22.6
Kenya	967	Lao PDR	22.5
Tanzania	918	Mauritania	19.4
Philippines	831	Burundi	18.6
Sudan	760	Central African Republic	17.1
Mozambique	759	Nepal	16.0

Source: World Bank, World Development Report 1991 *(New York: Oxford University Press, 1991), Table 20.*

separate "intertemporal theory" or "trade theory" of the current account. Each of the approaches, properly specified, must lead one back to the same more basic considerations.

6-3 THE DETERMINATION OF THE CURRENT ACCOUNT

In this section we study at greater length the factors that influence the current account balance in a small country facing a given world interest rate. We focus on the effects of different shocks that may hit the economy—changes in world interest rates, fluctuations in the terms of trade, and investment movements.

World Interest Rates

The first factor of importance is the world interest rate itself. Note in Figure 6-4 that as the world interest rate rises from r_a to r_h, domestic investment falls, saving rises, and the current account moves to a surplus. Thus, there is a positive relationship between the current account for the small open economy and the world interest rate at which its residents borrow and lend.

Remember that current account changes have effects on both financial and trade flows. Suppose for a moment that the economy starts from current account balance at point r_a in Figure 6-4. A rise in interest rates makes the current account go to a surplus, as consumers save more (consume less) and invest less out of the fixed amount of national income. The decline in domestic absorption means that imports fall and that a greater amount of domestic production is available for export. Thus, the shift to current account surplus also implies an increase in net exports, a *trade* phenomenon. The *financial* counterpart of the improvement in the trade balance is the accumulation of net foreign assets, B^*.

Investment Shocks

Suppose that investment prospects improve in a small economy that faces a given world interest rate. In Figure 6-5, this is represented as a shift to the right in the investment schedule. If the economy started from equilibrium at point A, the current account moves to a deficit of magnitude AB. In Figure 6-2, the effect of the investment shock on a closed economy, was mainly to raise interest rates. Here, in an open economy, the domestic interest rate is given by the world rate. Thus, an investment surge has a deteriorating effect on the current account, while interest rates remain unchanged.

A good example of such a phenomenon took place in Norway after the major world oil price increase in 1973. The oil shock made it highly profitable

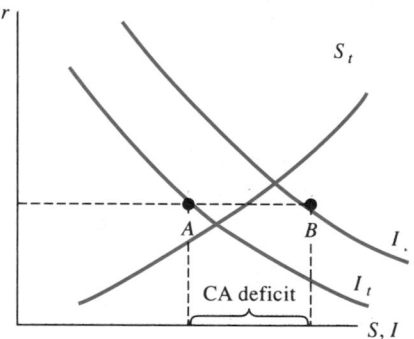

Figure 6-5
The Current Account and
Improved Investment
Opportunities

to invest in oil exploration and development in the North Sea. Norway's investment-to-GDP ratio, which had averaged 28 percent during 1965–1973, increased by a full 10 points to 38 percent during 1974–1978. Most of this surge in capital formation went to energy and energy-related ventures, including the oil and gas pipeline between Norway and West Germany. Because the country's saving rate changed little (and even fell a bit), however, the result of this investment surge was a massive current account deficit, which reached almost 15 percent of GDP in 1977.[12]

Output Shocks

In many countries, output occasionally drops temporarily because of unfavorable weather conditions or other exogenous shocks to a major sector of the economy. Take the case of an agricultural country hit by a severe

---

[12] For an analysis of current account behavior in both industrialized and developing economies, see Jeffrey Sachs, "The Current Account and Macroeconomic Adjustment in the 1970s," *Brookings Papers on Economic Activity*, 1: 1981.

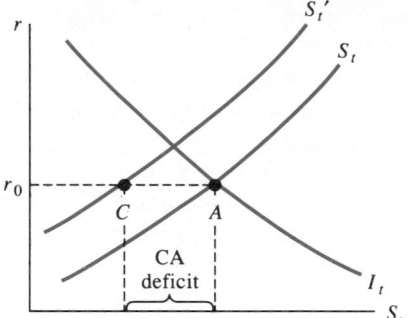

Figure 6-6

The Current Account and a
Transitory Output Decline

drought, or a Caribbean country hit by a hurricane. The life-cycle theory of saving predicts that people want to maintain a stable consumption level despite the temporary decline in output, and thus aggregate saving will decline in response to the shock. For a given amount of investment, the current account will deteriorate, as Figure 6-6 shows. If the country started from equilibrium at point A, the current account deficit after the temporary shock is AC in the graph. (Remember from Figure 6-2 that in response to a temporary adverse shock, the closed-economy response is a rise in interest rates, and some decline in domestic investment.)

If the shock is permanent, however, then saving should not fall significantly in response to the shock. Instead, it makes more sense to reduce consumption by the amount of the fall of output when the decline in output is permanent. Thus, with a permanent decline in output, the current account does not shift into deficit. (In fact, if investment demand falls in response to some long-term adversity, the current account might actually turn to surplus despite the decline in current output.)

Terms-of-Trade Shocks

The terms of trade, which will be denoted as TT, is the price of a country's exports relative to the price of its imports ($TT = P_X/P_M$). Because countries export more than a single good, P_X should be interpreted as a price index for all export goods. The same applies to P_M. A crucial aspect of terms-of-trade changes is that they cause income effects for the country, effects that are akin to shifts in national output. A rise in the terms of trade means that P_X has gone up relative to P_M. With the same physical quantity of exports, the country can now import more goods. The country's real income rises because of the greater availability of imports.[13]

A transitory rise in the terms of trade implies a transitory increase of income relative to permanent income. Consequently, aggregate saving in the country will tend to rise because of consumption-smoothing behavior. Start-

---

[13] A simple measure of the percentage rise in real income caused by the change in TT is found as follows: multiply the percentage change in the terms of trade by the share of imports in GNP. Thus, if the terms of trade improves by 10 percent, while the import-GNP ratio is 20 percent, the terms of trade improvement is akin to a 2 percent (20 percent times 0.10) improvement in real national income.

ing from equilibrium, the current account will tend to move to a surplus. Following a permanent rise in the terms of trade, however, households will adjust their real consumption upward by the amount of the terms-of-trade improvement. Saving rates do not necessarily rise in this case, and the current account does not necessarily move toward or into surplus.

Colombia, for example, has experienced sizable temporary income fluctuations when the price of its major export, coffee, has changed relative to other prices. In the late 1970s, a major rise in the relative price of coffee had significant effects throughout the economy. The macroeconomic result was true to the theory. Domestic saving went up as a proportion of GDP and the current account improved significantly.[14]

The theory of the current account, therefore, offers an important prescription for the "optimal" response to fluctuations in the terms of trade. If a change in the terms of trade is temporary, it should be absorbed by changes in the current account; that is, a terms-of-trade improvement should result in a surplus, while a terms-of-trade decline should lead to a deficit on the current account. If a change in the terms of trade is permanent, households adjust their consumption levels in response to the shocks so that saving rates do not fluctuate. Permanent shifts in the terms of trade should therefore have little effect on the current account (except as the *TT* shock might affect investment spending).

This basic wisdom is sometimes encapsulated in the phrase "finance a temporary shock; adjust to a permanent shock." The term "finance" here means to borrow or lend—to run current account surpluses or deficits—in response to transitory disturbances; the term "adjust" means to vary the consumption level up or down in response to permanent *TT* shocks. This general principle is a fundamental guidepost for the lending policies of the International Monetary Fund (IMF). The IMF was formed immediately after World War II to assist countries with external payments difficulties and to promote international stability in the monetary system. In 1962, the IMF created the Compensatory Financing Facility (CFF), a loan fund designed explicitly to make loans to countries suffering *temporary* shortfalls in export earnings. To qualify for a CFF loan, the country must demonstrate in precise detail both that it has suffered a decline in export earnings and that the shortfall is temporary. If the shortfall appears to be permanent, then the IMF does not make a CFF loan, and instead advises the country to cut back on spending levels to match the shortfall in its exports.

The idea of financing a temporary shock but adjusting to a permanent shock represents both a "normative" theory (what *should* happen) and a "positive" theory (what *will* happen) of the current account. But, as we shall see, positive theory sometimes falls short of predicting what actually happens to the current account. The positive theory of the current account depends on various assumptions: that economic agents are rational, intertemporal optimizers; that they are able to distinguish temporary from permanent shocks; and that they are able to borrow and lend freely in response to those shocks. We shall soon see that these assumptions may well be violated

---

[14] Sebastian Edwards has studied this interesting experience in his article "Commodity Export Prices and the Real Exchange Rate in Developing Countries: Coffee in Colombia," in S. Edwards and L. Ahamed, eds., *Economic Adjustment and Exchange Rates in Developing Countries* (Chicago: University of Chicago Press, 1986).

in real economies. In particular, when governments act as borrowers and lenders, they often fail to act as farsighted intertemporal maximizers.

Thus, when many developing countries enjoyed large terms-of-trade improvements at the end of the 1970s, they failed to run current account surpluses as theory predicted they would. Instead, the governments in these countries often acted as if the terms-of-trade improvements were permanent instead of transitory, and they raised spending by the full amount of the real income gain, even though the gain was likely to be short-lived. Mexico, for example, spent the huge windfall in oil export earnings that arose when oil prices shot up during 1979 and 1980. Once the terms of trade reversed in the early 1980s, Mexico and other such governments found themselves with unsustainably high spending levels and big political difficulties in cutting spending back down to manageable levels. Often it took a deep crisis— economic and political—before government spending levels were cut back to sustainable levels. (We will discuss some of these adjustment problems in the next chapter, and again in Chapter 22, when we analyze the developing country debt crisis.)

6-4 A COUNTRY'S INTERTEMPORAL BUDGET CONSTRAINT

We have seen that personal saving and investment decisions in a particular period influence someone's future path of consumption and income. A person who borrows today must consume less than his or her income in the future in order to repay the loan. Similarly, the levels of national saving, investment, and the current account influence the future path of consumption and income for the economy as a whole.

Suppose that a natural disaster makes output fall temporarily in the current year. A decline in the country's output translates into lower income for the average household. As individual households attempt to smooth their consumption by borrowing against higher future income, aggregate saving declines, and the national economy experiences a deterioration in the current account. The country then borrows from abroad, or at least runs down its existing stock of foreign assets. In the future, it will have to consume less than income in order to repay the debts incurred today.

An example of this phenomenon was Ecuador in 1987. When a major earthquake destroyed 35 kilometers of the country's oil pipeline, it left oil production interrupted for five months. Oil is Ecuador's principal export, and the earthquake produced a sharp but temporary decline in the country's income. Consequently, national saving collapsed and the current account reached a deficit of about 12 percent of GDP. Following that crisis and the foreign borrowing that it provoked, Ecuador will have to restrict consumption to service the debts incurred during that year.

The Intertemporal Budget Constraint in the Two-Period Model

We can also examine the country's intertemporal budget constraint formally using the two-period model. Suppose, as we did at the household level, that the country starts with no foreign assets ($B_0^* = 0$). In that case, the value of B^* in period 1 (B_1^*) is equal to the current account surplus in the first period:

$$B_1^* = Q_1 - C_1 - I_1 = CA_1 \qquad \textbf{(6.15)}$$

The change in net foreign assets from the first to the second period is the current account balance in the second period:

$$B_2^* - B_1^* = Q_2 + rB_1^* - C_2 - I_2$$

or

$$B_2^* = (1 + r)B_1^* + Q_2 - C_2 - I_2 \qquad \textbf{(6.16)}$$

But under the rules of a two-period model, the country must end with no net foreign assets ($B_2^* = 0$), and it undertakes no investment in the second period ($I_2 = 0$). Therefore, we can combine equations (6.15) and (6.16) to obtain

$$C_1 + \frac{C_2}{(1 + r)} = (Q_1 - I_1) + \frac{Q_2}{(1 + r)} \qquad \textbf{(6.17)}$$

Thus, we see that what was true for individual households is also true for the nation as a whole. Countries too are bound by a *national intertemporal budget constraint:* the discounted value of aggregate consumption must be equal to the discounted value of national production net of investment.

Take a simple case where there are no attractive investment opportunities. Under these conditions, the economy's only decision is how much to consume today and how much to save. In Figure 6-7, the country's budget constraint is shown by the line CC. For all the points on CC, $C_1 + C_2/(1 + r) = Q_1 + Q_2/(1 + r)$. To the southeast of point Q, the economy would be running a current account deficit in the first period, with $C_1 > Q_1$. To the northwest of point Q, the country would be running a current account surplus. The point where the economy will actually locate along the budget line depends on the preferences of the society.

Three fundamental conclusions emerge from this analysis:

1. If consumption is greater than output in the first period ($C_1 > Q_1$), then consumption has to be smaller than output in the second period ($C_2 < Q_2$). The reverse is also true: if $C_1 < Q_1$, then $C_2 > Q_2$.

2. Since, in the absence of investment, the trade-balance surplus is the difference between output and consumption ($TB_1 = Q_1 - C_1$), then the trade deficit in the first period must be matched by a trade surplus in the second period.

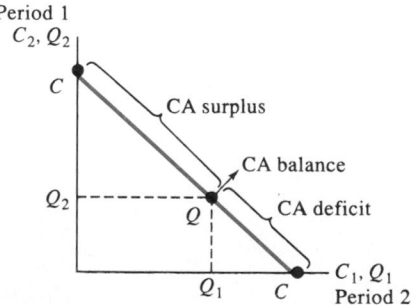

Figure 6-7
The Country's Budget
Constraint and the Current
Account

3. If the country runs a current account deficit in the first period, thereby incurring foreign debt, it must run a surplus in the future, in order to repay the debt. Similarly, if it runs a surplus in period 1, it must run a deficit in period 2.

Algebraically, we can state the country's intertemporal budget constraint in several analogous ways. First, we have seen that the discounted value of consumption must be equal to the discounted value of output net of investment. Second, we can rearrange terms in equation (6.17) to describe it in terms of the trade balance in the two periods. Since $TB_1 = Q_1 - C_1 - I_1$ and $TB_2 = Q_2 - C_2$, it is easy to verify that the discounted value of the trade balances has to be equal to zero:

$$TB_1 + \frac{TB_2}{(1 + r)} = 0 \qquad (6.18)$$

This means that a trade deficit in the first period must be balanced by a trade surplus in the second period of equal present value.

The third way of expressing the country's intertemporal budget constraint is in terms of the current account. Since an economy's current account is equal to the economy's accumulation of net foreign assets, we have $CA_1 = B_1^* - B_0^*$ and $CA_2 = B_2^* - B_1^*$. Assuming that the country starts with no net foreign assets ($B_1^* = 0$) and ends with no assets ($B_2^* = 0$), we must have

$$CA_1 + CA_2 = 0 \qquad (6.19)$$

Before moving on, we should stress one key qualification. This analysis assumes that a debtor always honors its debts, and the budget constraint is derived under that assumption. There are cases, of great importance, in which a debtor either cannot or chooses not to repay debts incurred in an earlier period. In a domestic economy, debtors sometimes go bankrupt and are unable to repay. In the international economy, where enforcement of contracts is more difficult, debtors sometimes choose not to repay. In these cases, the budget constraint may not be as stringent as most arguments suggest. (We return to this issue at the end of the chapter, and again in Chapter 22, when we discuss the developing country debt crisis.)

Let us consider a specific illustration of the intertemporal budget constraint to clarify concepts further. Suppose that the saving and consumption preferences of individual households lead to a particular choice of consumption in the CC schedule so that, say, $C_1 < Q_1$ for the economy as a whole. This situation is represented in Figure 6-8, and the appropriate balance-of-payments accounts are shown in Table 6-6. The horizontal distance between Q_1 and C_1 measures the current account surplus and the trade-balance surplus in period 1. Notice that there is no difference between the two measures in this case. Why? Because the country starts with no net foreign assets.

Domestic households will be lending, on aggregate, an amount $B_1^* = Q_1 - C_1$ to the rest of the world. This capital outflow exactly balances the current account surplus. In the second period, the country consumes $C_2 > Q_2$. The current account is in deficit while there is a capital inflow.

It is worthwhile to mention how these transactions would be recorded in the balance-of-payments accounts kept by the government. (A detailed description of balance-of-payments accounting is given in the appendix to

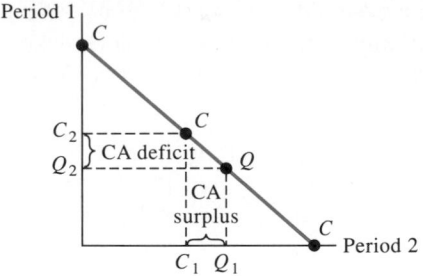

Figure 6-8
The Budget Constraint and a
Contemporary Current
Account Surplus

this chapter.) The accounting of the balance of payments for this hypothetical country will look like the schedule shown in Table 6-6. We need to introduce here just one new point in order to proceed. A capital outflow is termed, by accounting convention, to be a deficit in capital account of the balance of payments. (And a capital inflow is termed, by accounting convention, to be a surplus in the capital account of the balance of payments.) This means that the current account and the capital account automatically add to zero, as shown in the table.

The Intertemporal Budget Constraint with Many Periods

So far we have derived the intertemporal budget constraint in a two-period framework, but it is easy to extend the analysis to many periods. For T periods, with $T > 2$, we simply derive expressions that are analogous to equations (6.17), (6.18), and (6.19), showing that the discounted value of consumption must equal the discounted value of output net of investment, that the present discounted value of trade balances must equal zero, and that the current account balances between $t = 0$ and $t = T$ must sum to zero.

The extensions from a two-period model to a T-period model are rather straightforward. A new subtlety is added, however, in the (quite realistic!) case that there is no known final period T at which all loans must be paid off. If time just goes on without a final date, does this mean that a country can

TABLE   6-6

BALANCE-OF-PAYMENTS ACCOUNTING IN THE
TWO-PERIOD MODEL

	Period 1	Period 2
Current account	$Q_1 - C_1$	$-(Q_1 - C_1)$
Trade balance	$Q_1 - C_1$	$-(1 + r)(Q_1 - C_1)$
Service account	0	$r(Q_1 - C_1)$
Capital account	$-(Q_1 - C_1)$	$(Q_1 - C_1)$
Total (of current account and capital account)	0	0

borrow *any* amount from the rest of the world, without concern for repayments, knowing that it can always simply borrow more in the future to repay any past debt? The answer is no. The international capital markets will still require that the country live within its means, in that *no lender will lend so much to a country for which the only way to repay is to borrow the amount due each period.*

A scheme in which a borrower takes on too much debt (to increase current consumption, for example), and then plans to repay it by borrowing the money needed for debt servicing, is known as a *Ponzi scheme.*[15] Consider what happens in such a scheme. Suppose the borrower owes a debt D. When the debt D comes due, the borrower owes $(1 + r)D$. If it takes a new loan equal to $(1 + r)D$ to pay off the old lender, it now owes a larger amount to the new lender. In the next period, the borrower will have to pay $(1 + r)^2D$, and again, it plans to borrow this larger amount to make the repayment. In the following period, the borrower will owe $(1 + r)^3D$. In each period, then, the debt will grow at the geometric rate $(1 + r)$.

Credit markets prevent this behavior (or they do not support such behavior indefinitely): lenders require that a borrower's debt stay within bounds, and at least they do not allow it to grow at the geometric rate $(1 + r)$. It can be proven mathematically that when the debt is constrained—by the prudent behavior of lenders—to grow less rapidly than the geometric rate $(1 + r)$, the borrower is forced to live within its means in the sense that the present discounted value of all its future consumption must equal the initial wealth plus the present discounted value of all future output net of investment:

$$C_1 + \frac{C_2}{(1 + r)} + \cdots = (1 + r)B_0^* + (Q_1 - I_1) + \frac{(Q_2 - I_2)}{(1 + r)} + \cdots \quad \textbf{(6.20)}$$

Let us define the country's net debt as D^*, which is just equal to $-B^*$. In other words, when B^* is negative (so that the country is a net debtor), D^* is positive. Now we can derive a very interesting equation. By bringing the terms in $(Q - I)$ to the other side of the equation, and remembering that the trade balance is equal to output minus absorption ($TB = Q - C - I$), we can write (6.20) in the form

$$(1 + r)D_0^* = TB_1 + \frac{TB_2}{(1 + r)} + \cdots \quad \textbf{(6.21)}$$

This very important relationship says that if a country is a net debtor, and owes $(1 + r)D_0^*$ in the first period, then the economy must run trade surpluses in the future whose present discounted value (over the entire future) equals the initial net debt. The country services its debt into the future by a stream of trade-balance surpluses whose present value equals the net debt that is owed to the rest of the world.

Be careful to interpret the condition established in equation (6.21) correctly, however. It does not require that a debtor country have a trade surplus in every period, but only that the present value of all future trade balances must be in surplus, equal to the value of the net debt. For example,

---

[15] After Charles Ponzi, a Boston wheeler-dealer, who became rich with a scheme of chain letters in the 1920s.

the United States at the end of 1988 had net foreign liabilities in the order of $532 billion. This means that from 1989 onward, the United States will have to run trade surpluses in present-value terms of $532 billion. Of course, this does not imply that the United States will have to run trade surpluses in every period.

Notice, however, another subtle point. Even though a country cannot run a debt that grows forever at the rate of interest, it never has to pay off its debt fully either. What is required is that the country pay *interest* on its foreign debt (by running trade surpluses), not that the debt go to zero by some specific date. Thus, a country could maintain a given net debt D each year, and pay the interest due, rD, by running a trade surplus, without the principal D ever returning to zero.

The intertemporal budget constraint of the country is sometimes stated in terms of the *net resource transfer* (NRT) that a country must make. The NRT measures the cash flow between the country and its creditors, and it is measured as the net loans made to the country by its creditors, minus the interest that the country pays on its foreign liabilities (what creditors "take"). Thus the NRT in period t is given as

$$NRT = (D^* - D^*_{-1}) - rD^*_{-1} \qquad \text{(6.22)}$$

Notice that in a "Ponzi scheme," the net resource transfer is precisely zero, since the amount of new borrowing is just enough to pay the old debt: $D^* = (1 + r)D^*_{-1}$, so that NRT = 0.

Because the increase in net foreign debt $(D^* - D^*_{-1})$ corresponds to the current account deficit $(-CA)$, while the interest payments correspond to the deficit on the service account, equation (6.22) can readily be restated in terms of the trade balance:[16]

$$NRT = -TB \qquad \text{(6.23)}$$

Thus, when a country is running a trade-balance deficit, it is receiving a net resource transfer from its creditors, and when it is running a trade-balance surplus, it is making a net resource transfer to its creditors (in which case, we sometimes say that the NRT to the country is negative).

Now the budget constraint for a debtor can be stated as the condition that the negative of the discounted value of future net resource transfers must equal the size of debt:

$$(1 + r)D^*_0 = -NRT_1 - \frac{NRT_2}{(1 + r)} - \frac{NRT_3}{(1 + r)^2} - \cdots \qquad \text{(6.24)}$$

Obviously, this condition is the same as (6.21), since the NRT is equal to the trade-balance surplus. Note also that the NRT condition rules out a Ponzi scheme because in a Ponzi scheme, the NRT is always zero.

We should mention, once again, a limitation we pointed to earlier. The "no-Ponzi scheme" condition is a plausible condition for capital markets, but lenders do not always impose it successfully. Sometimes borrowers are—inadvertently—allowed to borrow so much that they simply cannot

---

[16] Actually, the NRT is equal to the trade balance plus nonfactor services (mostly tourism, freight, and insurance). For simplicity, we have not considered in our analysis nonfactor services. However, the equations can be easily extended to include this account, and nothing substantial would change.

repay their loans. We have so far assumed that defaults do not happen, but we shall return to that issue at the end of the chapter.

6-5 LIMITATIONS ON FOREIGN BORROWING AND LENDING

So far, when we have discussed the open economy, we have assumed that residents in one country can borrow from or lend to foreigners on a world capital market at a given interest rate r. This, of course, is a highly idealized view. We must now add in three major limitations to our basic framework: (1) administrative controls, which limit the access of domestic residents to foreign capital markets; (2) the effects of the country's own saving and investment decisions on the world interest rate; and (3) the risk and enforcement problems in foreign borrowing and lending, which limit the extent of international capital flows.

Administrative Controls

Many governments, especially those in developing countries, impose restrictions on the ability of domestic residents to borrow and lend abroad. Here we look at the basic consequences of these controls and some of the reasons that such controls are instituted. In later chapters we shall examine their effects in further detail.

With complete capital controls there could be no borrowing from or lending to the rest of the world. The country would live in financial isolation. Its current account would have to balance in every single period. Domestic interest rates would bear no relationship to world rates. They would simply adjust to equilibrate saving and investment as they did in the model of the closed economy described at the beginning of the chapter.

Let us return for a moment to Figure 6-4. Without capital controls, the current account is in surplus at the rate r_h. If the government decides to impose controls, excess domestic saving cannot be used to buy foreign bonds or to invest abroad. With saving higher than investment, r_h cannot be the equilibrium interest rate at home. Because the current account has to be balanced, the domestic rate will have to fall until saving equals investment. This occurs at the rate r_a. For a country that would have a current account surplus with *free* capital mobility, the net effect of controls is to reduce domestic interest rates, raise investment, and lower saving.

By forcing the economy into financial autarky (that is, isolation from the rest of the world), capital controls can have adverse effects on the level of economic well-being. We can use the two-period model to illustrate this quite simply. In Figure 6-9, let E be the endowment point, with the utility level UL_0. If world interest rates are at level r, then the country would like to borrow in the first period and consume at the point A. This would allow economic agents to reach the utility level UL_1. Instead, the economy must stay at E because of the capital controls. The same loss in welfare as the result of capital controls is readily found in the case in which the country would be in current account surplus in the first period in the absence of capital controls.

With capital controls in place, the kinds of shocks that we considered earlier will, in general, affect the domestic interest rate rather than the

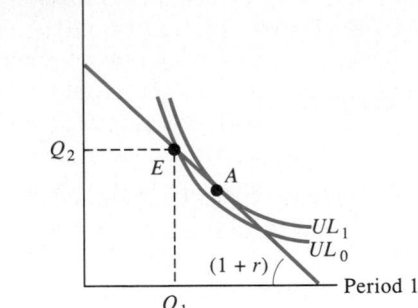

Figure 6-9
Capital Controls and the
Economic Well-being of the
Country

current account. For example, a temporary decline in output following a drought caused a current account deficit in Figure 6-6. Now, the effect is to raise interest rates, as Figure 6-10 shows.

To summarize, then, the shocks which shift the saving curve to the left tend to increase the domestic interest rate rather than to worsen the current account. The same applies for shocks that increase investment possibilities at home. With full capital controls, a rise in the world interest rate does not have a direct effect on the domestic interest rate, saving, or investment. By virtue of its restrictions on capital, the country becomes insulated from foreign interest-rate shocks.

One crucial policy implication of capital controls involves national saving policies. Many governments adopt policies to encourage saving (tax incentives, for example), with the aim of increasing investment. When capital markets are open, a policy that raises national saving tends to increase the current account surplus but not domestic investment. In this case, capital controls might be useful to translate a rise in domestic saving into a rise in domestic investment.

Large-Country Effects on World Interest Rates

The notion that domestic residents can borrow or lend freely at a given rate r is based on the assumption that their particular economy is a small part of the world capital market. This is a good approximation for most countries in

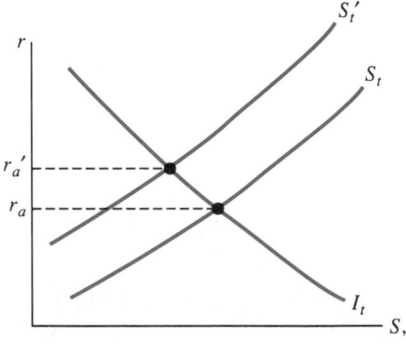

Figure 6-10
A Temporary Output Drop
Under Capital Controls

the world, other than a handful of the largest industrialized economies. Even a major industrial economy such as the Netherlands represents only 1.6 percent of the total output of the industrialized countries.[17] Therefore, even fairly sizable shifts in this country's saving or capital formation would not have much effect on world capital market equilibrium. In contrast, the United States contributes about 36 percent of the total output of the industrialized countries. Movements of desired saving and investment in the United States tend to have significant effects on world interest rates. The same is true of Japan and Germany, and to a lesser extent in the United Kingdom, France, Italy, and Canada.[18]

The key to understanding large-country effects is to examine the determination of the world interest rate (r_w). In an integrated global capital market, r_w is determined so that total world saving S_w (equal to the sum of saving in country 1, country 2, and so on, so that $S_w = S_1 + S_2 + \cdots$) is equal to total investment $(I_w = I_1 + I_2 + \cdots)$. The world as a whole is a closed economy. Therefore it must be the case that $S_w = I_w$.

Let us consider now the case of an economy, say, the United States, which is large relative to the overall world market. (Following our usual convention, an unstarred variable refers to the home country, while a starred variable refers to the rest of the world.) The global equilibrium occurs where

$$I(r) + I^*(r) = S(r) + S^*(r) \tag{6.25}$$

Condition (6.25) states that world investment equals world saving. By rearranging its terms, we see that this expression is equivalent to saying that the U.S. current account balance must equal the opposite of the current account balance of the rest of the world:[19]

$$S(r) - I(r) = -[S^*(r) - I^*(r)] \tag{6.26}$$

or

$$CA(r) = CA^*(r) \tag{6.26'}$$

Figure 6-11 shows the equilibrium world interest rate as that rate at which the U.S. current account deficit is equal in value to the foreign current account surplus. If the two regions start in financial autarky, either because the United States or the rest of the world has capital controls, the equilibrium interest rates would be set separately in the two markets. As drawn in the graph, the domestic rate in the United States (r_a) would be higher than the rate in the rest of the world (r_a^*). This is because the United States has been drawn (realistically!) as having a low saving rate.

---

[17] Figure for the year 1988, from The World Bank, *World Development Report 1990* (New York: Oxford University Press, 1990).

[18] These largest seven industrial countries are often called the Group of Seven, or G-7 for short.

[19] In theory, the sum of the current accounts of all the countries in the world should sum to zero. In practice, this is not the case. There is, in fact, a "world current account discrepancy," in which the total of the current accounts of all the countries in the world have summed to a large negative number in recent years, on the order of $-$67 billion in 1989 (International Monetary Fund, *International Financial Statistics*, 1989 Yearbook). This discrepancy is attributed to a variety of measurement problems, including unrecorded capital flows and under- and overinvoicing of exports and imports, often for the purposes of smuggling.

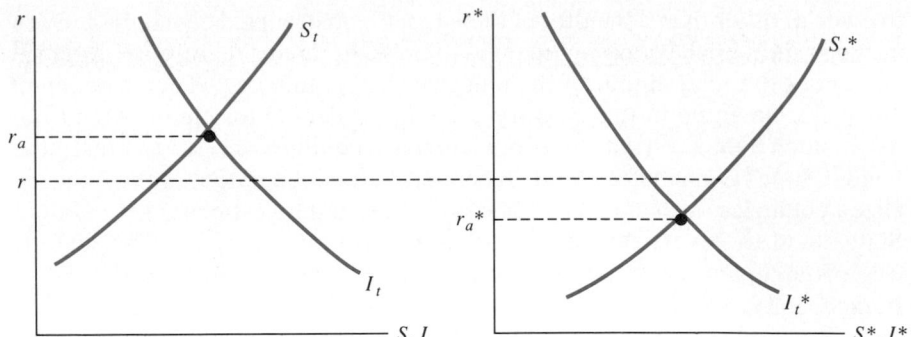

Figure 6-11
Global World Equilibrium of Saving and Investment

If complete capital mobility between the two regions were established, for example, via a capital market liberalization in the restricted region, a single world interest rate would result. The domestic interest rate in the U.S. economy would fall and the rate in the rest of the world would rise until both rates became the same. Investment would increase and saving would fall in the United States, and its current account would move into deficit. In the rest of the world, saving would rise and investment would fall: its current account in the rest of the world would move into surplus. In the final equilibrium, total world saving would equal total world investment, and the U.S. current account deficit would be exactly matched by the surplus in the rest of the world.

These two diagrams help us to discover another important point: for a large country, shifts in saving and investment provoke effects on world (and domestic) interest rates as well as in the current account. Consider, for example, a fall in the U.S. saving rate, as shown in Figure 6-12. (Such a decline in saving might arise because of a rise in expected future income in the United States). At the initial interest rate (r_0), the decline in saving leads to an excess of world investment over world saving. World interest rates therefore rise to r_1, where $(I - S)$ again equals $(S^* - I^*)$.

Figure 6-12
Global Effects of a Decline in United States Saving

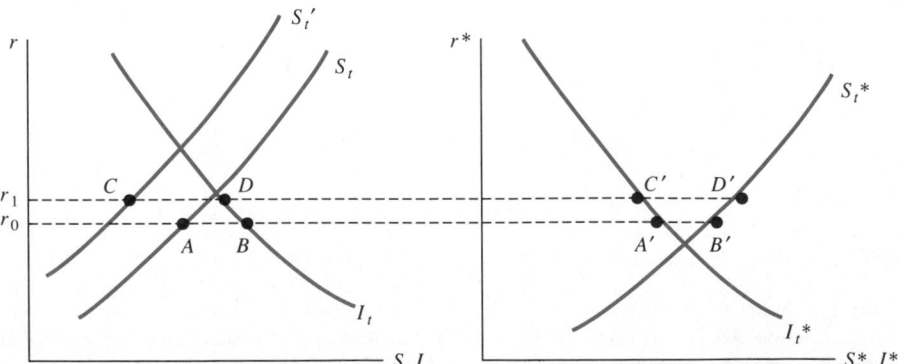

TABLE 6-7

THE EFFECTS OF SAVINGS AND INVESTMENT SHOCKS UNDER
DIFFERENTIAL CAPITAL MOBILITY AND SIZES OF COUNTRIES

Kind of Shock	Cases		
	Free Capital Mobility (small country)	Capital Controls	Free Capital Mobility (large country)
Rise in the S curve	Rise in CA; no effect on r	No effect on CA; fall in r	Rise in CA; fall in r
Rise in the I curve	Fall in CA; no effect on r	No effect on CA; rise in r	Fall in CA; rise in r
Rise in $(S^* - I^*)$	Fall in CA; fall in r	No effect on CA; no effect on r	Fall in CA; fall in r

The final effect is an increase in the world interest rate and a worsening of the current account in the United States (from AB to CD), coupled with an improvement in the current account in the rest of the world (from $A'B'$ to $C'D'$). The larger the United States is in world markets, the more adjustment will occur through a rise in the interest rate. The smaller the United States is, the more adjustment will come through a deterioration in the U.S. current account. Thus, the large-country case falls somewhere between the small-country model and the capital controls case in the effect of the shift in saving on the current account and on the interest rate.

Table 6-7 summarizes the various cases we have considered here. Each column in Table 6-7 corresponds to one of the three cases analyzed: a small country with free capital mobility, a small country with capital controls, and a large country with free capital mobility. Each row corresponds to a different type of shock: an increase in the desired saving in the home country, an increase in desired investment, and a rise in saving in the rest of the world. The rest of the table describes the effects for each combination.

Risk and Enforcement Problems

To simplify the analysis, we have assumed so far that all loans are repaid (or serviced in full in present-value terms). There are at least two reasons why, in reality, this might not be the case. First, the borrower might become insolvent, that is, unable to service the debts in full out of the stream of current and future income. Second, the borrower might choose not to repay the loans, believing that the costs of nonpayment are less than the burden of repayment.

Voluntary nonpayment can occur because international loans present a serious problem of enforcement. It is hard for lenders to collect their loans when a foreign debtor has a repayment problem, because the problems of legal enforcement of contracts is particularly difficult when the creditor and debtor are in different countries. This is especially true of loans to foreign governments, which are often called *sovereign loans*, since it is difficult to compel a foreign government to honor a debt. In this case, lenders will not provide all the funds that the foreign borrower wants at the prevailing interest rate. Rather, they will lend only as much as they think can be collected.

When a borrower government has a large external debt, it must grapple with the choice of repaying the loan versus suspending its debt-service payments. The government must calculate the benefits of suspending payments (the foreign exchange that it saves) versus the costs of such action. These include various penalties for nonpayment, plus the costs of a bad reputation, which can harm the country in its future dealings with foreign creditors. The direct penalties that can be imposed by disgruntled creditors include (1) a suspension of further lending, (2) a withdrawal of short-term lending to support exports and imports, (3) an attempt to disrupt the international trade of the country, and (4) an attempt to disrupt the foreign relations of the country. These penalties can impose burdens on defaulting countries, but they do not generally yield much in the way of direct financial benefits for the lenders.

These penalties help to define the limits of safe lending. If the penalties for nonpayment are very high, and are known to be high, then the debtor government attempts to repay as much as possible, lest the penalties be incurred. In this case, it is safe to lend to a foreign government, since it will make a strong attempt to repay its loans. If the penalties are small, foreign governments will not make much of an effort at repayment, so it is rather unsafe to lend even small amounts.

What is important for us here is that as long as enforcement problems exist, there will probably be a smaller flow of international lending than there would be if contracts were perfectly enforceable. At first, residents of a borrower country will find that they face a higher rate of interest the more their country borrows from the rest of world, the higher interest rate representing a risk premium to compensate the lenders for the growing risk of default. After a certain amount of debt has been incurred, the risks of lending to the country cannot be compensated by a higher risk premium, and the country is simply cut off from additional credits.

The full implications of this kind of credit rationing require a thorough and separate analysis. But in essence, the current account behaves somewhat like the case of a large country: shifts in saving and investment affect *both* the current account and the interest rate. (These points are discussed in more detail in later chapters.)

6-6 SUMMARY

In an economy with free capital mobility, national saving does not have to equal national investment. The excess of saving over investment is the *current account of the balance of payments*. The current account balance tends to be an increasing function of the interest rate because a higher interest rate tends to increase saving (though the effect is theoretically ambiguous) and to reduce investment.

A current account *surplus* also means that a country is accumulating net international assets; that is, its net claims on the rest of the world are increasing. A current account *deficit* means that a country is decumulating net international assets. Thus, the current account is also defined as the change in the *net international investment position* (NIIP) of a country.

When the NIIP is positive, the country is a net creditor of the rest of the world, and when it is negative the country is a net debtor. There are two additional ways to define the current account: first, as the difference between national income and absorption; and second, as the sum of the trade account and the service account of the balance of payments.

During the 1980s, the United States was transformed from the world's largest international creditor into the world's largest debtor as a result of large and sustained current account deficits. (Nonetheless, data problems prevent us from getting an exact measure of the net debt position.) Over the same period, Japan and West Germany ran vast current account surpluses and became the major international creditors.

Many factors influence the current account. A rise in world interest rates will tend to improve the CA balance of a small country by raising saving and reducing investment. Increased investment prospects (say, because of a natural resource discovery) tend to reduce the CA balance. A transitory fall in national income (say, because of a fall in the terms of trade or an unfavorable harvest), tends to lower the CA balance by reducing national saving. A permanent decline in national income, however, should have little or no effect on the current account, since consumption spending should fall by approximately the same amount as the decline in income. (Of course, if the permanent shock is widely but wrongly interpreted to be temporary, then the current account would nonetheless decline.) In general, the optimal response to supply shocks (either in output levels or the terms of trade) can be summarized in the phrase "finance a transitory shock; adjust to a permanent shock."[20]

Countries, like individuals, are bound by an intertemporal budget constraint: the discounted value of aggregate consumption must be equal to the discounted value of national production minus the discounted value of investment, *plus* the initial net international investment position. This can be put another way. If a country is a net debtor, then the economy must run trade surpluses in the future with a present discounted value equal to the initial net debt.

Several limitations must be added in to the basic model of borrowing and lending. First, some governments establish administrative restrictions (*capital controls*) to international borrowing or lending. With complete capital controls, there is no borrowing from or lending to the rest of the world, and the country must live in financial isolation. Domestic interest rates would differ from world rates and the current account would have to be zero every period. Domestic saving would always have to equal domestic investment.

Second, the basic model of borrowing and lending assumes that the country is sufficiently small that shifts in its domestic investment and saving do not affect the world interest rate. This assumption pretty well describes the case for most countries in the world except for a handful of industrialized economies. For these large economies, changes in domestic saving and investment will tend to have significant effects on world interest rates. In an

---

[20] "Finance," here, means to run a current account deficit; "adjust" means to lower consumption by enough to absorb the shock without borrowing.

integrated world capital market, the international interest rate is determined so that total world saving is equal to total investment.

Third, the basic model assumes that all loans are repaid (or at least serviced in full in present-value terms). However, some borrowers may become insolvent (unable to service their debts in full out of current and future income), while others who could pay may choose to default, knowing that it is hard for the creditor to force a repayment of the loans. The difficulty of enforcing loan payments is especially great for sovereign loans, that is, loans to foreign governments. When potential lenders understand that the borrower may have an incentive to default in the future, they will restrict the supply of loans to that borrower to the level that the lender believes will be repaid.

Key Concepts

balance of payments
current account
net international investment
   position
net creditor country
net debtor country
absorption
small-country assumption
trade balance
service balance
official development assistance
terms of trade

capital account
capital outflow
capital inflow
official foreign-exchange reserves
errors and omissions
national intertemporal budget
   constraint
net resource transfer
capital controls
capital mobility
large-country effects
sovereign loans

Problems and Questions

1. Country A is a small open economy. Would it be possible for this country to have an interest rate different from that of the rest of the world? Why?

2. Countries that run current account surpluses are likely to decrease their consumption in the future. True or false? Explain.

3. Discuss why the United States shifted during the 1980s from being a major creditor into being the world's largest debtor.

4. Discuss the relation between an increase in the net holdings of international assets, a surplus in the current account, and a positive trade balance.

5. Assume that country B is a net creditor. The value of national saving is fixed at a certain level, and initially, its current account is zero. What would happen to the following variables if the value of this country's international assets goes up because of changes in their valuation?
   a. Net international investment position.
   b. Current account.
   c. Investment.

6. How would Figures 6-4a and 6-4b change if the income effect for savers becomes larger than the substitution effect above a certain level of the international interest rate?

7. Describe the effects on the interest rate, domestic savings, and domestic investment of the following events (analyze the cases of a closed economy, a small open economy, a large open economy, and an economy with capital controls.

   a. Country C discovers large new reserves of oil. The reserves are highly profitable, but it will take five years of new physical investments to bring them into operation.

   b. Cold weather in country D forces extensive factory closings for three months. The lost production cannot be recouped, but production returns to normal by the spring.

   c. New synthetic fibers reduce the demand for copper, permanently lowering its price relative to other goods. Consider the effect on country E, a copper exporter.

8. Assume that investment and saving are determined by the following equations: $I = 50 - r$; and $S = 4r$.

   a. If the economy is closed, what are the equilibrium levels of the interest rate, savings, investment, and the current account?

   b. How would your answer to (a) change if the country is a small open economy and the international interest rate is 8 percent? What would happen if the interest rate rises to 12 percent?

   c. How would your answers to (a) and (b) change if the investment function becomes $I = 70 - r$?

9. Consider an economy with the following characteristics: production in period 1 (Q_1) is 100; production in period 2 (Q_2) is 150, consumption in period 1 (C_1) is 120, and the world interest rate is 10 percent. (Assume that there are no investment opportunities.) In the framework of the two-period model, calculate

   a. The value of consumption in the second period.

   b. The trade balance in both periods.

   c. The current account in both periods.

10. If there is no final period in which debts have to be repaid, debtor countries are not constrained by the intertemporal budget constraint. True or false? Explain.

11. Assume that Figure 6-11 represents the situation of two large countries in the first period of the two-period model. What would the diagrams look like in the second period? Which curves would have to shift so that the two countries maximize their welfare subject to their intertemporal budget constraint?

12. How would the following transactions be recorded in the balance of payments?

   a. A U.S. corporation exports $50 million of merchandise, using the proceeds to open up a foreign factory.

   b. U.S. residents receive dividends on holdings of Toyota stocks in the amount of $10 million.

   c. Sylvester Stallone receives $20 million in royalties from overseas box office sales of *Rambo*.

   d. U.S. holdings in Libya are nationalized without compensation.

APPENDIX: BALANCE-OF-PAYMENTS ACCOUNTING

In this section we will study how the balance-of-payments accounts of a country are actually measured. The current account is measured over a specified interval of time, usually a month, a quarter, or a year. For a typical country during one of these time intervals, there are millions of transactions of individual households, firms, and the government, which must be summed up to calculate the overall current account balance.

The basic idea of balance-of-payments accounting relies on the fact that there are two definitions of the current account: as the trade balance plus net factor payments from abroad and as the change in the country's net foreign investment position. Imbalances in trade have as their counterpart an accumulation or decumulation of net international assets. The basic method of balance-of-payments accounting takes advantage of the fact that trade flows and financial flows are two sides of each transaction.

In the balance-of-payments accounts, the transactions are divided between current flows (exports, imports, interest receipts, etc.) and capital flows (changes in ownership of financial assets), as shown in Table A-1. The top part of the table is sometimes called simply the current account items, while the bottom part of the table measures the so-called capital account. In principle, the current account and the capital account must be identical in value, when the change in international reserves is included in the capital account. In practice, because of errors and omissions in the actual recording of transactions, the items in the current account do not always sum to the same amount as the items in the capital account.

TABLE A-1

THE BALANCE-OF-PAYMENTS ACCOUNTS

1. Current Account ($CA = 1.1 + 1.2 + 1.3$)
   1.1 Trade balance
       Exports of goods
       Imports of goods
   1.2 Service balance
       Nonfactor services (freight, insurance, tourism, etc.)
       Capital services (interest receipts, profit remittances)
       Labor services (worker's remittances)
   1.3 Unilateral transfers
2. Capital Account ($CAP = 2.1 + 2.2 + 2.3$)
   2.1 Net foreign investment received
   2.2 Net foreign credits received
       Short term
       Long term
3. Errors and Omissions
4. Balance-of-payments result ($BP = 1 + 2$)
       (= change in net official international reserves)

In theory, all transactions that affect the current account require *two entries* in the table. For example, consider the accounting in the U.S. balance of payments when a West German firm sells $10 million of machinery to a U.S. importer, which the importer pays for by writing a $10 million check to the West German firm, which the firm deposits in its U.S. bank account. There are two parts to the transaction: the shipment of goods, recorded under "imports," and the payment of the check, which increases the U.S. bank balances of the West German firm, and thus is recorded under "change in liabilities to foreigners."

The accounting conventions for these two items are determined so that the pair of transactions sums to zero. In particular, imports are given a negative sign in the table (that is, the transaction would be entered as $-\$10$ million); the increase in liabilities to foreigners is recorded as a positive entry in the capital account (the transaction would be entered as $+\$10$ million). If this were the only transaction to be considered, the current account deficit would equal $-\$10$ million, while the capital account balance (the mirror image of the current account balance) would equal $+\$10$ million.

An increase in the country's net foreign assets B^*, which can mean a rise in claims against foreigners or a fall in liabilities owed to foreigners, is called a *capital outflow*. A decrease in net foreign assets is called a *capital inflow*. Thus, in the transaction we have been describing, we can say that there is a capital inflow that is financing the current account deficit in the United States. Alternatively, we can say that a surplus in the capital account is financing a deficit in the current account.

The following conventions apply to balance-of-payments accounting:

1. Export earnings and receipts of interest from abroad are entered as positive items in the current account.

2. Import payments and payments of interest on foreign liabilities are entered as negative items in the current account.

3. Increases in claims against foreigners and decreases in liabilities to foreigners (capital outflows) are entered as negative items in the capital account.

4. Decreases in claims against foreigners and increases in liabilities to foreigners (capital inflows) are entered as positive items in the capital account.

If all transactions in the balance of payments were actually recorded as they occur, according to the conventions just outlined, the balance of payments would sum to zero (adding up the current account and the capital account). As we will note, however, some transactions are recorded only in part, so that the statisticians that prepare the balance of payments are sometimes left without a complete record of transactions, with the result that the recorded items of the current and capital accounts do not add up to exactly zero.

Consider the following set of transactions. Study carefully how they are recorded in the accompanying Table A-2. (Each transaction is lettered, and the entries in the balance of payments are recorded with the transaction number shown in parentheses.)

(a) A U.S. exporter ships $5 million of grain to the Soviet Union on a 90-day credit (in other words, the Soviet importer owes the $5 million in 90 days).

TABLE A-2

BALANCE OF PAYMENTS ACCOUNTING BETWEEN THE UNITED STATES AND THE REST OF THE WORLD (US$ MILLIONS)

	(a)	(b)	(c)	(d)	(e)	(f)	Total
Current Account							−4
Trade balance							
Exports	+5		+15				+20
Imports					−10		−10
Services							
Interests							
Dividends		+1					+1
Other							
Unilateral transfers			−15				−15
Capital Account							+4
Net foreign investment		−1					−1
Net credits							
Short term	−5				+10		+5
Long term							
Balance of Payments							0

(b) A U.S. individual receives a dividend payment of $1 million from a factory that he owns abroad, and he uses the money to reinvest in the factory.

(c) Following an earthquake in Armenia, U.S. private relief agencies send $15 million worth of first aid equipment and clothing.

(d) A Japanese firm imports $20 million of oil from Saudi Arabia, paying for the oil by writing a check on its account at the New York branch of Chase Manhattan Bank. The check is deposited in the Saudi Arabian account at the same bank. (In this case, no entry is made, as the transaction does not affect the U.S. balance of payments.)

(e) A U.S. importer buys $10 million of merchandise from a Japanese electronics firm and pays for the transaction with a loan from a Japanese bank that finances the deal.

(f) The U.S. Treasury sells official reserve holdings of Deutsche marks to U.S. securities houses for $20 million in cash.

Note that for each capital transaction, care must be taken to record the transaction in the correct subcategory in the capital account. Distinctions are made between short-term and long-term capital, with bank balances, for example, constituting a form of short-term capital and long-term bonds and equities constituting a form of long-term capital.[1] Long-term capital is subdivided further into securities and foreign direct investment, with the latter signifying direct ownership and control over a firm operating in a foreign country (or foreign ownership and control over a firm operating in the United States).

Another crucial distinction is made between financial assets owned (or owed) by the government versus those owned (or owed) by the private sector. The central banks of most countries (and sometimes the treasuries as well) maintain holdings of short-term foreign assets, such as short-term Treasury bills issued by foreign governments. These holdings are called the *official foreign-exchange reserves* of the central bank. We shall see in later chapters how these reserves may be used by the central bank to help manage the exchange rate of the domestic currency, through a process in which the central bank buys and sells foreign reserves in return for domestic currency held by the public.

Because of the importance of foreign-exchange holdings for the ability of a government to manage the exchange rate, special care is given to accounting for changes in foreign-exchange reserves. The *official reserve transactions balance* measures the change in the net official foreign reserve balances of the government. The country is said to have a positive balance if the government is accumulating net international reserves and a negative balance if official reserves decline within the period. Note how this concept is related to the current account and the capital account. If we measure in the capital account all capital items *except* the official holdings of foreign exchange, then we have the following:

Official reserve transactions balance = change in net official foreign reserves

= current account + nonofficial capital account

By adding up the current account and all capital account items except the official reserves, we get the official reserve balance, with the sign convention that a positive value indicates an increase in net foreign reserves.

The official reserve balance is sometimes loosely called the "overall balance of payments." Countries are said to have an "overall" surplus if they are accumulating official reserves and an overall deficit if they are loosing reserves.

Note that from an economic point of view, it might be more accurate to say that the overall balance of payments is always zero. When we count changes in official reserves as *part* of the capital account and use the earlier convention that increases in net claims against the rest of the world are entered into the accounts with a negative sign (so that reserve increases are measured negatively), then it remains true that the current account and the capital account will always sum to zero. The "overall" balance can be

---

[1] In the U.S. balance of payments, long-term assets and liabilities are financial claims with an *original* maturity of 1 year or more. Thus, for example, a 20-year asset issued 19½ years ago and coming due in half a year is considered a long-term asset for purposes of the balance-of-payments accounts.

different from zero only when we separate the changes in official reserve balances from the capital account; then, the current and nonreserve capital account do not have to sum to zero. This is why we create a category "change in net official international reserves," item 3 in Table A-1.

There is one additional reason why the overall balance of payments might not sum to zero: statistical discrepancies. If each international transaction were separately recorded, the accounts would necessarily balance for the reasons shown. But in fact, the transactions are not recorded one-by-one as they occur. Statisticians that prepare the international accounts often observe the trade flows (exports and imports) and the capital flows (changes in net claims against the rest of the world) separately. They receive reports from customs about the international flows of goods, and separate reports from the financial markets about the changes in claims and liabilities vis-à-vis foreigners. But many transactions, both in trade and in financial assets go unreported, both because of the huge number and complexity of the transactions involved, and because of deliberate attempts to avoid detection (as in the case of money laundering or tax evasion).

For this reason, a separate item must appear on the balance-of-payments accounts, called "Errors and omissions," or "balancing item." It is given the value equal to the opposite of the sum of the current account plus the capital account (including official reserves), so that in fact the sum of all items in the accounts—including errors and omissions—equals zero. In the United States, the errors and omissions account was large and positive for many years in the 1980s. This suggested to many observers that foreigners were accumulating assets in the United States, but not reporting the increase in such assets to the authorities. Thus, the measured capital inflows were too small, and what would have been a larger positive entry in the capital account (measuring the accumulation of foreign claims on U.S. residents) became a positive entry in the errors and omissions line of the balance of payments.

Countries face quite diverse circumstances regarding capital account flows and their net foreign asset positions. For comparative purposes, we can briefly analyze the cases of Japan and the United States during the 1980s. As we have already seen, the United States shifted into substantial deficits in the current account, while Japan experienced surpluses during the period. As a counterpart to these current account developments, there has been a capital account surplus in the United States and a capital account deficit in Japan. In other words, foreigners have been accumulating claims of different forms on the United States (Treasury bonds, stocks, real estate, productive companies), which has implied a capital *inflow* (capital account surplus). By contrast, Japan has been a net investor in the rest of the world: its purchase of foreign assets represent a capital *outflow* (capital account deficit). Table A-3 shows the capital account (a flow) and the net foreign asset position (a stock) for the two countries.[2]

---

[2] We should stress once again that while the data in this table show an unmistakable trend, in which the U.S. net foreign investment position is falling and that of Japan is rising, the specific magnitudes in the table are subject to several measurement problems.

TABLE A-3

THE CAPITAL ACCOUNT AND THE NET FOREIGN ASSETS POSITION IN THE UNITED STATES AND JAPAN, 1980–1988 (BILLIONS OF CURRENT DOLLARS)

Year	Japan		United States	
	Net Foreign Assets Position	Capital Account	Net Foreign Assets Position	Capital Account
1980	11.5	−5.4	106.3	−28.0
1981	10.9	−7.4	140.9	−27.9
1982	24.7	−16.5	136.7	−30.8
1983	37.3	−17.7	89.0	28.7
1984	74.3	−54.0	3.3	71.5
1985	129.8	−65.4	−111.4	102.3
1986	180.4	−133.0	−267.8	129.6
1987	240.7	−112.6	−378.3	156.5
1988	291.7	−111.4	−532.5	137.2

Source: For Japan, Management and Coordination Agency, Japan Statistical Yearbook, *various issues; for the United States,* Economic Report of the President, 1990, *and Department of Commerce,* Survey of Current Business *(Washington, D.C.: U.S. Government Printing Office, June 1990).*

Appendix Summary

The balance-of-payments records all (known) transactions between a country's residents and the rest of the world. Balance-of-payments accounting relies on two different definitions for the current account: the trade balance plus net factor payments from abroad and the change in the country's net international investment position. Trade flows and financial flows are two sides of each transaction. Thus, trade imbalances have as their counterpart an accumulation or decumulation of net international assets. An increase in the country's net foreign assets is called a capital outflow; a decrease in net foreign assets is called a capital inflow. In principle, double-entry bookkeeping ensures that a current account surplus (deficit) is matched by an identical capital account deficit (surplus). In practice, the current account and capital account may differ because of errors and omissions in data collection.

chapter 7

The Government Sector

Our study of national saving, investment, and the current account has so far ignored one key part of the economy, the government sector, also called the "public sector." Saving and investment by the government have important and sometimes subtle effects on overall national saving and investment, and therefore on the current account balance as well. The government's saving and investment policy is part of its overall *fiscal* policy, that is, the pattern of spending, taxing, and borrowing decisions of the public sector. In this chapter, we take our first detailed look at the economic effects of fiscal policy.

The role of a government in the economy extends far beyond fiscal policy, of course. Government policy also includes monetary and exchange-rate policies, and we examine those in later chapters. The government also establishes and enforces the laws that govern private economic activity, including the commercial codes for private contracts, company laws for establishing new firms, regulations governing international capital mobility, regulatory codes for environmental protection and antitrust regulation, and so forth. In many countries, the government also produces goods via state-owned enterprises (sometimes called "parastatal" firms). Our present focus on fiscal policy allows us to touch only briefly on many of these other important aspects of government policy, however.

Many, though not all, aspects of fiscal policy are determined by the government budget which establishes the income and outlays of much of the public sector in a particular period (though some public spending is typically done outside of the formal budget). The difference between government outlays and government revenues is the *budget surplus*—or deficit—which determines the amount of lending or borrowing of the public sector. One of our principal concerns in this chapter is to explore in some detail the relationship between this government budget surplus (or deficit) and the overall level of national saving and investment.

As we do this, we continue with the same limits to our conceptual framework that we have used for the past three chapters. That is, we put aside Keynesian considerations and adopt the *classical* assumptions that output is determined by supply and that shifts in aggregate demand do not affect aggregate output. For the theoretical models in the chapter, we also maintain the assumption that the price level is constant and equal to one ($P = 1$). (In fact, we do not lift these conditions until Part III of the text, after our complete description of fiscal and monetary policy.)

7-1 GOVERNMENT REVENUES AND EXPENDITURES

The most important sources of public revenue are the different types of taxes levied on the economy. These taxes can be divided in three broad categories: *income taxes* on individuals and corporations, including the social security tax on wage earnings; *expenditure taxes,* including sales taxes, excise taxes and import tariffs; and *property taxes,* including a wide variety of levies on houses and buildings, agricultural and residential land, and inheritances.

Taxes are also classified as *direct* versus *indirect,* though these terms are somewhat imprecise. The classification "direct" generally refers to those taxes that are levied directly on individuals and business firms, while indirect taxes are those levied on commodities and services. Income and property taxes fall into the first category, while sales taxes and trade tariffs fall into the second.

Developed and developing countries tend to have very different tax structures. Developed economies generally derive a high proportion of government revenues from direct taxes. In the United States, for example, the biggest source of fiscal revenues by far—over 85 percent of the total—are direct taxes, the largest portion of which are paid by individuals. Developing countries, on the other hand, tend to raise most of their revenues via indirect taxes, including taxes on trade. In Argentina, for example, only about 40 percent of total government revenue comes from direct taxes. One reason why indirect taxes are so important as a source of revenue in developing countries is straightforward: they are generally simpler to collect than taxes on income. However, a tax system based on indirect taxes tends to be regressive, with the taxes paid by the poor representing a higher proportion of their own income than the taxes paid by the rich.

Another source of public sector revenue is the profits of those state enterprises and agencies that sell goods and services. Although public enterprises have little quantitative importance in the United States, they have greater significance in Western Europe, and often considerable significance in developing countries. In many resource-rich developing countries, the revenues of state-owned resource producers may account for a large proportion of public revenues. For example, in Venezuela the oil sector is owned by the state, and it provided an astonishing 77 percent of government revenues in the early 1980s.[1]

These general points are clearly shown by the data of Table 7-1, which describes the sources of government revenue for 104 countries divided into four categories of economic development: industrial, semi-industrial, middle-income, and least developed countries. There we see that the more developed the group of countries, the larger the share of revenue coming

[1] See Miguel Rodriguez, "Public Sector Behavior in Venezuela: 1970–85", in Felipe Larrain and Marcelo Selowsky, eds., *The Public Sector and the Latin American Crisis* (San Francisco: ICS Press, 1991).

TABLE 7-1

COMPOSITION OF GOVERNMENT REVENUES, COUNTRIES GROUPED BY DEGREE OF ECONOMIC DEVELOPMENT
(PERCENTAGE OF TOTAL REVENUES, AROUND 1980)

Country Group (number of countries)	Tax Revenues				Nontax Revenue
	Direct Taxes		Indirect Taxes		
	Income and Profits	Social Security	Domestic Goods and Services	International Trade	
Industralized (20)	33.3%	25.0%	26.0%	3.7%	9.0%
Semi-industrialized (15)	25.3	13.0	30.6	14.5	11.1
Middle income (55)	23.7	4.1	23.1	28.9	14.9
Least developed (14)	17.0	1.6	21.7	41.6	13.0

Source: Richard Goode, Government Finance in Developing Countries *(Washington, DC: The Brookings Institution, 1984).*

from direct taxes; the poorer the group, the heavier the reliance on indirect taxes, especially taxes on international trade.

Public outlays can also be divided into four categories. (1) *Consumption* by the government, which we denote as G, includes the wages government pays to public sector workers as well as its payments for goods purchased for current consumption. (2) Government *investment* (I^g) includes a variety of forms of capital expenditure, such as the construction of roads and ports. (In practice, some items counted as government consumption in the national income accounts of most countries should actually be included in I^g).[2] (3) *Transfers* to the private sector (Tr) include retirement pensions, unemployment insurance, veterans' benefits, and other welfare payments. (4) *Interest on the public debt* (rD^g) is the final type of government outlay. Sometimes, the fiscal spending is divided only in two groups: *current expenditures,* which comprise wage payments and purchases of goods and services (G), interest outlays (rD^g), and transfers (Tr); and *capital expenditures,* or investment (I^g). For macroeconomic analysis, as we shall see, it is important to distinguish among these categories.

Table 7-2 presents the structure of government outlays for several developed and developing countries. Note that the overwhelming portion goes for current expenditure items, while investment gets a very low fraction of spending, generally below 10 percent. (Remember, however, that some categories of investment spending are probably misclassified as consumption

---

[2] As an example, public spending on education can be viewed as a form of government investment in human capital. Nonetheless, most education spending, except possibly that for direct expenditures on school buildings, are counted as a kind of consumption spending. Another example of misclassification is counting government expenditure on research and development as current spending rather than investment spending. Thus, I^g is understated in the official accounts, while G is overstated.

TABLE 7-2

STRUCTURE OF CENTRAL GOVERNMENT EXPENDITURES, SELECTED COUNTRIES, 1988–1990
(AS PERCENTAGE OF TOTAL EXPENDITURE)

			Current Expenditure				
			Consumption				
Country	Year*	Total Expenditure	Wages and Salaries	Goods and Services	Interest Payments	Subsidies and Transfers	Capital Expenditure
United States	1989A	100%	11.67%	18.99%	15.20%	49.46%	5.16%
France†	1982D	100	17.04	9.92	4.55	64.38	4.56
Germany†	1989A	100	8.38	24.91	4.97	56.82	4.91
United Kingdom	1988C	100	13.23	17.40	10.57	53.86	4.93
Rep. of Korea†	1990C	100	14.41	24.50	4.14	41.68	15.26
Malaysia†	1990C	100	32.27	18.50	22.11	12.13	18.12
Thailand	1989D	100	33.63	26.64	16.55	9.00	14.58
Argentina	1988C	100	23.77	8.73	7.43	49.49	10.56
Brazil	1988B	100	9.09	8.29	51.88	34.26	3.74
Mexico†	1990C	100	20.59	5.28	44.20	15.76	14.14

* Letters A–D following year indicate percent of general government tax revenue accounted for by central government as follows: A, 60–69.9 percent; B, 70–79.9 percent; C, 80–89.9 percent; and D, 90–95 percent. Owing to adjustment items and unallocated transactions, components may not add up to totals.
† Data are in whole or in part provisional, preliminary, or projected.
Source: *International Monetary Fund, Government Finance Statistics Yearbook, 1990.*

TABLE   7-3

PUBLIC EXPENDITURE IN SELECTED COUNTRIES AND SELECTED YEARS, 1938–1988
(AS A % OF GDP)

Year	France	Germany	Japan	Nether-lands	United States	Italy	United Kingdom
1938	21.8	42.4	30.3	21.7	18.5	29.2	28.8
1950	27.6	30.4	19.8	26.8	22.5	30.3	34.2
1965	38.4	36.6	19.0	38.7	27.4	34.3	36.1
1973	38.5	41.5	22.4	45.8	30.6	37.8	40.6
1982	50.4	49.4	33.7	61.6	36.5	47.4	47.1
1988	50.3	46.6	32.9	57.9	36.3	50.8	43.2*

1987.

Source: *N. Roubini and J. Sachs, "Government Spending and Budget Deficits in the Industrial Economies,"* Economic Policy, *no. 8 (Cambridge, Mass.: Cambridge University Press, April 1989), Table 1, and Organization for Economic Cooperation and Development,* Historical Statistics 1960–1989, *various issues.*

spending.) It is particularly interesting that the four developed countries in the table (France, Germany, the United Kingdom, and the United States) all dedicate 5 percent or less of government spending to investment. By contrast, the Southeast Asian governments (Korea, Malaysia, and Thailand) devote more than 10 percent of their outlays to capital expenditures. Note also that the big Latin American debtors in the sample (Brazil and Mexico) devote a staggering proportion of their budgets to the payment of interest on domestic and foreign debt. Although the table does not show changes during the 1980s, it has been widely documented that the international debt crisis was a major factor in the collapse of public investment and other budget outlays in the Latin American debtor countries. (We explore this problem at greater length in Chapter 22.)

Throughout the world, total government spending has been increasing relative to GDP since the beginning of the twentieth century. As we see in Table 7-3, many industrialized countries have experienced a doubling—or more—in the ratio of government spending to GDP compared with 1938. In the Netherlands, for example, the proportion of public expenditure to GDP almost tripled in 50 years. In France it has more than doubled, and in the United States it has doubled. The only countries that have defied this trend are Germany and Japan, where the size of government, measured as in Table 7-3, was similar in 1988 to what it was in 1938.

The nineteenth-century German economist Adolph Heinrich Wagner predicted this increasing share of government spending in GDP, and his formulation has since become known as Wagner's law.[3] The most common explanation of the phenomenon is that government services are a "superior good"; that is, the income elasticity of demand for government spending by

---

[3] A. H. Wagner, *Finanzwissenschaft,* Vols. I and II (Leipzig: C. F. Winter, 1877 and 1890).

households is greater than 1. In other words, each 1 percent increase in household income leads to a *greater* than 1 percent rise in the household's demand for G. Therefore, as *per capita* income rises, the share of G in Y tends to rise as well.

Before we move on to study government saving and investment, we should add a warning on the macroeconomic meaning of the terms "government sector" or "public sector." The term "government" can mean quite different things in different contexts. For most countries, it is important to distinguish between the *central* government, the *general* government, the *nonfinancial public-enterprise* sector, and the *financial* public sector. The "central government" refers to the public governance and administrative agencies at the national level. The "general government" includes the central government and the various regional governments and decentralized institutions such as a national pension fund or public universities. The consolidation of the general government and the nonfinancial public-enterprise sector is called the "nonfinancial public sector." Finally, when we add in the accounts of the central bank and publicly owned financial institutions, we arrive at the "consolidated public sector."

7-2 GOVERNMENT SAVING, INVESTMENT, AND BORROWING

While households derive most of their income from the output they produce (Q), the government gets most of its income from taxes. Assume for the moment that taxes (T) are raised as lump-sum payments. In other words, each household pays a set amount irrespective of its income or spending. Thus, these taxes do not directly affect the decisions of households as to how much labor to supply, how much to invest, or how much to produce, except insofar as the taxes affect the overall income of the households. Because most taxes have direct effects on household decisions (by taxing saving relative to consumption, or work relative to leisure), we consider more realistic forms of taxation later on.

When its spending and income differ, the government borrows or lends, just as the private sector does. In fact, we can derive a budget constraint for the government that is analogous to the budget constraint for households. It is important to do this, since it will allow us to see some subtle links between household wealth and fiscal policies.

Let B^g be the government's stock of net financial assets, whose evolution in time is given by

$$B^g = B^g_{-1} + rB^g_{-1} + T - (G + I^g) \qquad (7.1)$$

The variable G here refers to consumption spending of the government, while I^g refers to investment expenditures, and T represents taxes net of transfers. The equation says that the government's assets at the end of the current period o is equal to the government assets at the end of the previous period, plus the interest earned on these assets, plus the taxes collected by the government, minus government spending on consumption and investment.

Governments do indeed hold *gross* financial assets, like foreign exchange reserves and gold, but normally *net* financial assets are negative because liabilities are higher than assets. It is convenient to write (7.1) in terms of the government's net debt D^g, where $D^g = -B^g$. Thus,

$$D^g = D^g_{-1} + rD^g_{-1} + G + I^g - T,$$

or

$$D^g - D^g_{-1} = G + rD^g_{-1} + I^g - T, \tag{7.2}$$

The right-hand side of equation (7.2) is the budget deficit, which is equal to total expenditures minus revenues. As the equation shows, the change in the government's net debt is equal to the budget deficit.

At this point, we are assuming that D^g is held entirely by the private sector; that is, the government finances its deficits solely by borrowing from the private sector. In reality, part of D^g can also be held by a nation's central bank. We shall see later, when the central bank increases its holdings of government debt, the deficit is in effect financed by an expansion of the money supply.

The change in debt can also be written in terms of government saving and investment. As usual, government saving (S^g) is the difference between income ($T - rD^g_{-1}$) and consumption G, so that

$$S^g = (T - rD^g_{-1}) - G \tag{7.3}$$

From equations (7.2) and (7.3), we can write the government's budget deficit (*DEF*) as the difference between investment and saving of the public sector:

$$DEF = D^g - D^g_{-1} = I^g - S^g \tag{7.4}$$

A budget surplus, obviously, is the opposite of a deficit and is therefore equal to saving minus investment.

7-3 THE GOVERNMENT BUDGET AND THE CURRENT ACCOUNT

At last, we are ready to integrate the public sector into our analysis of the current account. In the last chapter, the current account was the difference between total saving and investment of the economy ($CA = S - I$). But now total saving is the sum of government saving (S^g) and private saving (S^p). Investment also has a public and a private component. Therefore,

$$\begin{aligned} CA &= (S^p + S^g) - (I^p + I^g) \\ &= (S^p - I^p) + (S^g - I^g) \\ &= (S^p - I^p) - DEF \end{aligned} \tag{7.5}$$

Thus, the current account is equal to the private financial surplus ($S^p - I^p$) minus the budget deficit.

Note that (7.5) suggests a link between the size of the government budget deficit and the current account balance. If the private surplus remains constant, a rise in the budget deficit is associated with a fall in the current account. Thus, the International Monetary Fund typically recommends that the best way to overcome a current account deficit is through a reduction in the public-sector deficit. Of course, equation (7.5) states only an identity and not a theory of the current account. We certainly cannot assume, for example, that the private surplus is invariant to changes in the budget deficit. However, as we shall later see, changes in the budget deficit generally do have an important effect on the current account balance.

TABLE   7-4

CHANGES IN GENERAL GOVERNMENT FINANCIAL BALANCES AND CURRENT ACCOUNT IMBALANCES, INDUSTRIAL COUNTRIES, 1978–1986*

Country	Change in Government Financial Balance	Change in Current Account
United States	−3.65%	−2.75%
Japan	4.15	3.65
Germany	1.32	3.05
France	−1.60	−0.97
United Kingdom	0.95	0.30
Italy	−1.90	−2.00
Canada	−3.70	0.85

* *The change in the government financial balance measures the change in the ratio of the general government financial balance as a percentage of GNP or GDP. The change is calculated as the average of the ratio for the years 1985–1986, minus the average value for 1978–1979. The change in the current account is measured similarly.*
Source: *J. Sachs, "Global Adjustments to a Shrinking U.S. Trade Deficit." Brookings Papers on Economic Activity, 1988: (Washington, DC: Brookings Institution.)*

The experiences of several industrialized countries during the period 1978–1986 illustrate this effect quite clearly. Table 7-4 shows the *change* in the government financial balance (an approximate measure of the budget deficit or surplus) and the change in the current account, as a proportion of total output, between 1978–1979 and 1985–1986. The negative numbers indicate that the fiscal budget or the current account has deteriorated. In the United States, the deterioration in the fiscal budget closely mirrors the fall-off in the current account, and a similar phenomenon can be seen in France and Italy. In Japan and Germany the situation is quite the opposite: the improvement in government finances has gone hand-in-hand with a strengthening in the current account. The only exception to the rule is Canada, where the fiscal balance declined in the period and yet the current account balance increased. Even aside from Canada, of course, the changes in fiscal and current account balances do not exactly coincide because private saving-investment balances did not remain unchanged during this period.

Equation (7.5) enables us to incorporate the public sector into many of the formulas that we derived earlier. Before we do this, however, we need to expand our definition of private saving (S^p). S^p is equal to the difference between private income and consumption. *Private income,* usually called *disposable income,* is output plus interest earnings *minus* taxes:

$$Yd = Q + rB^p_{-1} - T \tag{7.6}$$

The private sector earns interest on its stock of financial wealth, B^p, which is the sum of private holdings of government bonds, D^g, and of foreign assets, B^*. Thus, we can write $B^p = D^g + B^*$, where an asterisk "*," as usual, denotes a foreign variable.

Private saving is disposable income minus consumption:

$$S^p = Yd - C = (Q + rB^p_{-1} - T) - C \qquad (7.7)$$

Combining equations (7.7) and (7.3), then we can write *total national saving* as

$$
\begin{aligned}
S &= S^p + S^g \\
&= [(Q + rB^p_{-1} - T) - C] + [(T - rD^g_{-1}) - G] \\
&= Q + rB^*_{-1} - C - G \\
&= Y - (C + G) \qquad (7.8)
\end{aligned}
$$

Note that we have made use of the fact that $B^p_{-1} - D^g_{-1} = B^*_{-1}$ and the fact that $Y = Q + rB^*_{-1}$.

Once we have added public and private saving, we arrive at an intuitive definition of total national saving, as GNP (Y) minus public plus private consumption ($C + G$). Now, we can describe the current account by the familiar-looking statement that

$$CA = S - I = Y - (C + G + I) \qquad (7.9)$$

Expression (7.9) once again says that the current account is the difference of income and absorption, but now absorption is defined to include government consumption and investment. And because the current account is simply the trade balance (TB) plus net factor payments from abroad (rB^*_{-1}) and $Y = Q + rB^*_{-1}$, we can also say that

$$TB = Q - (C + I + G) \qquad (7.10)$$

Thus, we have arrived once again at the expressions for the current account that are found in Chapter 6. This time, however, they include spending and revenues of the public sector.

We can also integrate the government into the graphical apparatus of Chapter 6. In Figure 7-1, S^p represents the saving schedule of the private sector. In order to obtain total saving, we simply add public saving to private saving. In the graph, public saving is given by the horizontal distance between the S (total saving) and S^p schedules. Notice that S and S^p are *parallel*,

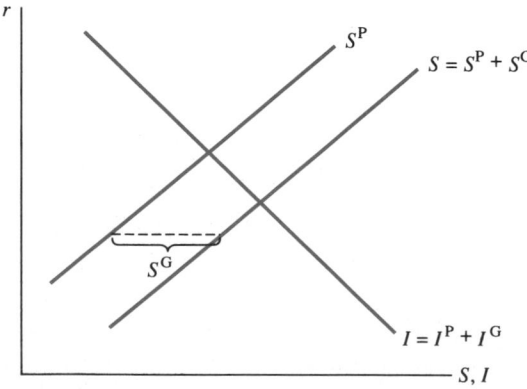

Figure 7-1
The Government and the Saving-Investment
Process

on the assumption—for simplicity—that government saving is exogenous and independent of the interest rate (therefore, a change in the interest rate does not affect the horizontal distance between the S and S^p schedules). Similarly, we can obtain the total investment schedule by adding the private investment demand and a given level of government investment. In Figure 7-1, we simply draw the I schedule, which includes both public and private investment. This figure will allow us to study the effects of fiscal policies on the current account balance.

7-4 THE INTERACTION OF THE PRIVATE AND PUBLIC SECTORS

Government fiscal policy decisions affect household actions most directly through the effects of taxes on the household's intertemporal budget constraint. The two-period household budget constraint is written in terms of income net of taxes, so changes in taxes have a direct effect on it. To reestablish how this works, recall equation (4.15), reproduced here as

$$C_1 + \frac{C_2}{(1 + r)} = (Q_1 - T_1) + \left[\frac{(Q_2 - T_2)}{(1 + r)}\right] = W_1 \qquad \textbf{(7.11)}$$

Clearly, fiscal policy can affect the time path of consumption through changes in T_1 and T_2.

We can also use (7.11) to compare the effects of *temporary, permanent,* and *anticipated* changes in taxes. As we do this, assume initially that the government runs a balanced budget, so that changes in taxes always correspond to equal changes in government spending. We relax this assumption later when we need to examine the more realistic setting of deficit financing.[4]

A Temporary Tax-Financed Increase in Government Spending

Consider now the effect of a temporary, tax-financed increase in G, say, a rise in government spending in order to pay for a war. Let us assume that G_1 and T_1 rise by an equal amount, while S_1^g, as well as G_2 and T_2 remain unchanged. Our consumption model tells us that C_1 will fall, but not by as much as T_1 rises. Recall that consumption was shown to be a linear function of private wealth ($C_1 = kW_1$),[5] with the marginal propensity to consume out of wealth (k) being less than one. Thus, as W_1 falls because of higher taxes, consumption falls by less than the wealth decline. Our intuition tells us that because a *temporary* rise in taxes represents a temporary fall in disposable income, households trying to maintain a smooth consumption path will borrow against the future during the period of temporarily high taxes. Thus, private saving will fall with a temporary rise in taxes.

---

[4] The analysis that follows has one important limitation. As in Chapters 4 and 5, we are making the classical assumption that demand fluctuations do not affect output. Remember that we do not take up the Keynesian model until Part IV, after we have analyzed the building blocks more fully. Thus, we rule out—by assumption—any effects that changes in G and T might have on output as a result of changes in aggregate demand, even though such output consequences are another channel through which public-sector and private-sector spending might interact.

[5] See equation (4.16) in Chapter 4.

Because government saving remains unchanged when G_1 and T_1 rise by the same amount while private saving falls, the overall level of national saving declines. What is the effect of this on the current account?

For a small country facing a given world interest rate, the decline in saving for a given investment reduces its current account balance. In Figure 7-2a, which represents this case, note that total saving is shown as the sum of private saving and (unchanged) public saving. Starting from equilibrium at point A, the current account moves to a deficit of the magnitude AB. Thus, a temporary tax-financed increase in government spending causes the current account to worsen. In the case of capital controls, however, presented in Figure 7-2b, the decline in national saving provokes a rise in the domestic interest rate rather than a deterioration in the current account (which must always be balanced).

If the transitory increase in spending and taxes occurs in a large country like the United States, however, this analysis has to be modified. The

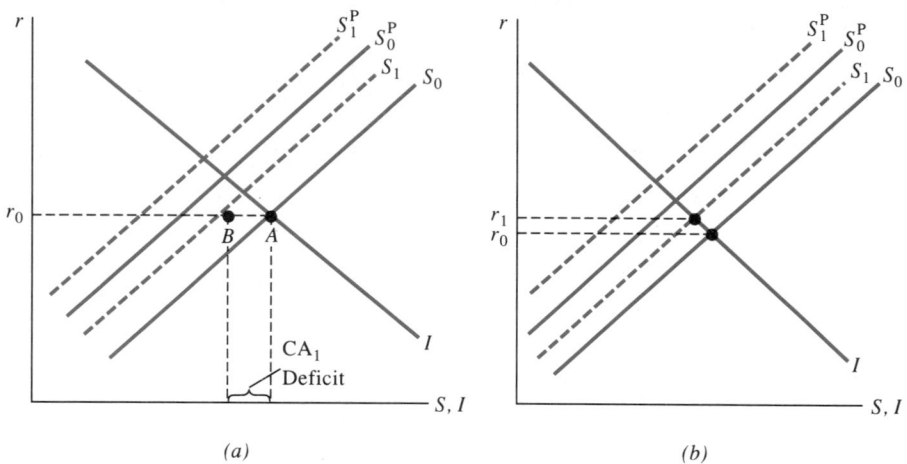

Figure 7-2

Effects of a Temporary Tax-Financed Increase in Government Spending: (a) The Small Country Case; (b) Capital Controls

decline in U.S. saving affects the world interest rate, causing it to edge upward. At the same time, however, the fall in saving deteriorates the U.S. current account, as shown in Figure 7-3. The rest of the world also feels the effects of the tax increase. The consequently higher interest rates increase saving and drive down investment in the rest of the world, improving the foreign current account. In summary, a temporary tax-financed expansion in government spending in the United States drives up the world interest rate, increases the current account deficit in the United States, and augments the current account surplus abroad.

A Permanent Increase in Government Spending

Let us now consider a *permanent* rise in government spending financed by higher taxes. In this case, G_1 and G_2 increase by the same amount ΔG, and T_1 and T_2 rise by an equal amount ΔT. Government saving is unchanged, as was

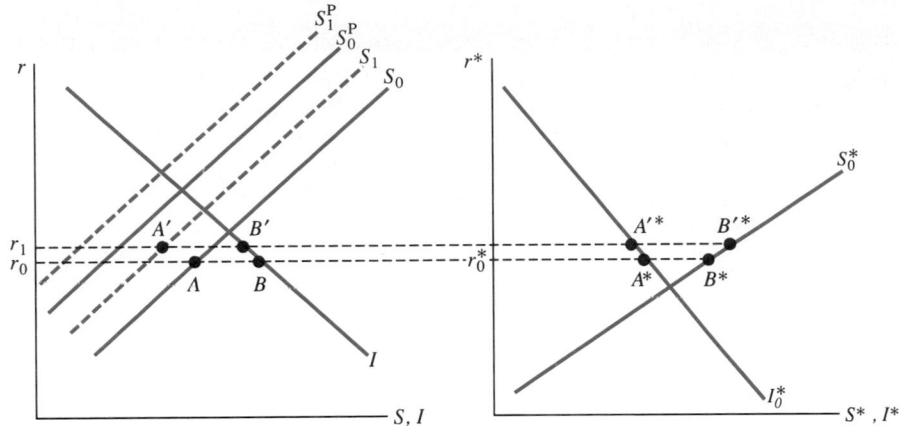

Figure 7-3
Effects of a Temporary Tax-Financed Increase in Government Spending: (a)
The Large Country Case; (b) Capital Controls

the case with the temporary spending and tax increases. But now private
saving is affected less. The permanent tax rise amounts to a drop in permanent disposable income. Households have to adjust by revising their consumption downward more than they did with a transitory tax increase. Thus,
private saving will not fall as much—and perhaps not at all.

When we apply this scenario to our benchmark case from Chapter 4
where consumption was exactly equal to permanent income, we see that the
permanent rise in spending and taxes will have *no* effect on the current
account. Remember that there we saw that consumption was proportional to
wealth, $C_1 = kW$, with k equal to $(1 + r)/(2 + r)$. When T_1 and T_2 increase by
the same amount ΔT, wealth falls by the amount $\Delta W = -\Delta T + -\Delta T/$
$(1 + r) - -\Delta T [(2 + r)/(1 + r)]$. Thus, the change in first-period consumption, ΔC_1, is equal to $k\Delta W = -\Delta T$. Private consumption falls by the same
amount that taxes increase, and no change occurs in private saving.

Table 7-5 summarizes these effects of permanent and transitory increases in government expenditure.

Fiscal "Crowding Out"

Crowding out is a general term for any fall in private spending that accompanies a rise in public spending. Most frequently, "crowding out" refers to a
decline in private investment that is brought about by an expansion in government spending. In an open economy, however, other forms of spending—such as net exports, for example—might also get crowded out when G
rises.

Let us examine the crowding-out phenomenon in the two cases we
have just posed. We take first the *temporary* tax-financed increase of government spending. In a small country with free capital mobility, this fiscal
action has no effect on interest rates, and private investment is therefore not
affected. The deterioration in the current account suggests a different form
of crowding out: a decline in the country's net exports. Without additional
information, however, we cannot tell how the decline in net exports is di-

TABLE   7-5

EFFECTS OF PERMANENT AND TRANSITORY INCREASES IN GOVERNMENT EXPENDITURE (BALANCED BUDGET)

Kind of Shock	Cases		
	Free Capital Mobility (small country)	Capital Controls	Free Capital Mobility (large country)
Temporary increase in G (general case)	Fall in S; fall in CA; no effect on r	Fall in S; no effect on CA; rise in r	Fall in S; fall in CA; rise in r
Permanent increase in G (general case)	Fall in S (smaller); Fall in CA (smaller); No effect on r	Fall in S (smaller); No effect on CA; Rise in r (smaller)	Fall in S (smaller); Fall in CA; Rise in r (smaller)
Permanent increase in G (benchmark case)	No effect on S; CA; or r	No effect on S; CA; or r	No effect on S; CA; or r

vided between higher imports (resulting from higher G) and lower exports. Where a small country does have capital controls, on the other hand, we find that higher government spending crowds out investment rather than net exports (net exports must always equal zero due to the controls). The decline in saving increases domestic interest rates, thereby depressing domestic investment. (Note that private consumption may also be crowded out, if consumption is a decreasing function of the interest rate.) In a large country with open capital mobility, the transitory rise in fiscal expenditure crowds out *both* domestic private spending and net exports, as well as investment and consumption abroad.

When a government pursues a *permanent* expansion in spending (assuming a balanced budget), however, the crowding out of investment or net exports is necessarily smaller, or even eliminated (as in our benchmark case, when the drop in consumption equals the rise in permanent government spending).

All this analysis holds only under the assumption of classical full employment, of course. If Keynesian demand effects are also present when G and T change, then the analysis has to be modified. It is those modifications we take up when we turn to Keynesian analysis in Part IV.

7-5 RICARDIAN EQUIVALENCE

Ricardian equivalence is an interesting theoretical proposition which shows that under certain circumstances a change in the path of taxes over time—lower taxes in the present, higher taxes in the future, say—does not affect private expenditures and therefore does not affect national saving, investment, or the current account. This notion leads to some striking theoretical findings, for example, cases in which a tax cut that raises the budget deficit has no effect whatsoever on the current account despite the seemingly strong link that we noted in equation (7.5). Ricardian equivalence was first introduced (and largely dismissed on practical grounds) by the great British economist David Ricardo in the nineteenth century.[6] More recently, it has been both formally treated and popularized by Robert Barro of Harvard University.[7] Let us now see how this theory works.

A Statement of the Ricardian Equivalence Theorem

Consider the budget constraint of the private sector in equation (7.11). With some minor manipulation, we can write it in the following way:

$$C_1 + \frac{C_2}{(1 + r)} = Q_1 + \frac{Q_2}{(1 + r)} - \left[T_1 + \frac{T_2}{(1 + r)} \right] \qquad \textbf{(7.12)}$$

Here we see that lifetime consumption equals the present value of output minus the present value of taxes. The time path of taxes does not matter for the households' budget constraint as long as the present value of taxes is not changed.

Consider now what happens when current taxes (T_1) are cut in the amount ΔT, while future taxes (T_2) are raised by $(1 + r)\Delta T$ (by design, the present value of taxes is left unchanged):

$$\Delta T_1 + \frac{\Delta T_2}{(1 + r)} = -\Delta T + \frac{(1 + r)\Delta T}{(1 + r)} = 0 \qquad \textbf{(7.13)}$$

Despite the cut in current taxes and the rise in current disposable income, forward-looking households will not change their present level of consumption C_1. The reason is simple. The tax cut does not affect their lifetime wealth because future taxes will go up to compensate for the current tax decrease. In accounting terms, we say that current private saving (S_1^p) rises when T_1 falls: *households save the income that they receive from the tax cut in order to pay for the future tax increase.*

Of course, this greatly simplifies what is likely to occur. A number of studies have shown empirically that under certain conditions, current consumption does in fact rise when T_1 is cut. The existence in real life of liquidity constraints, uncertainty, the marginal incentive effects of taxes, and differing time horizons of governments and households, all may cause simple Ricardian equivalence to break down. Furthermore, the expansionary effects of a cut in taxes, as envisioned by Keynes, can also cause a change in consumption spending.

The theoretical importance of considering a current tax cut that leaves unchanged the present value of taxes becomes apparent when we consider the government's intertemporal budget constraint. Governments, like households, must balance their spending and income over time, though not necessarily on a period-by-period basis. To see this, we can derive a two-

[6] This idea is stated in David Ricardo, "Funding System," in Piero Sraffa, ed., *The Works and Correspondence of David Ricardo,* Vol. 4 (Cambridge: Cambridge University Press, 1951).

[7] The first formal treatment of Ricardian equivalence is Barro's "Are Government Bonds Net Wealth?" *Journal of Political Economy,* November/December 1979.

period budget constraint for the government using equation (7.2). As we did for private agents, we shall once again suppose that the government begins with no net debt ($D_0^g = 0$). Therefore,

$$D_1^g = G_1 + I_1^g - T_1$$
$$D_2^g = D_1^g + rD_1^g + (G_2 + I_2^g - T_2)$$

We can combine these two equations (as we have already done for households) to obtain the government's intertemporal budget constraint:

$$G_1 + I_1^g + \frac{G_2 + I_2^g}{(1 + r)} = T_1 + \frac{T_2}{(1 + r)} + \frac{D_2^g}{(1 + r)} \qquad \textbf{(7.14)}$$

According to (7.14), the present value of government spending (the left-hand side of the equation) must equal the present value of taxes plus any debt left over at the end of the second period (the right-hand side of the equation).[8]

What has this to do with Ricardian equivalence? The proposition states that for a *given time profile* of government consumption (G_1 and G_2), investment (I_1^g and I_2^g) and second-period debt (D_2^g), the time path of consumption (C_1 and C_2) does not depend on the time path of taxes (T_1 and T_2). This is easily proved, at least in theory, from equations (7.12) and (7.14). From the government's budget constraint in (7.14), we see that for given G_1, G_2, I_1^g, I_2^g, and D_2^g, the present value of taxes is also given. From (7.12) we see that the household budget constraint depends not on the time path of taxes but on the present value of taxes. Thus, changes in T_1 and T_2 that preserve $T_1 + T_2/(1 + r)$ have no effect on the household intertemporal budget constraint.

We have already hinted at the powerful theoretical implications of this proposition. Suppose, for example, that a government begins with its budget balanced period to period, with $G_1 + I_1^g = T_1$ and $G_2 + I_2^g = T_2$. Now assume that the government cuts T_1 by ΔT without any change in its spending. In this case, public debt will rise by the amount of the tax cut. Next period, taxes (T_2) will have to be raised by $(1 + r)\Delta T$ in order to keep D_2^g from rising. Note that future taxes have to go up by more than the tax cut because the government must pay the interest, as well as the principal, on its period 1 borrowing. According to Ricardian equivalence, then, C_1 and C_2 will be unaffected by the change in T_1 and T_2.

Look, too, at the effect on saving of this change in the timing of taxes. When T_1 is cut, government saving goes down by the amount of the tax cut ($S_1^g = T_1 - G_1$). Private saving increases by the amount of the tax decrease [$S_1^p = (Q_1 - T_1) - C_1$]. Therefore, national saving remains unaffected by the tax cut, since the fall in government saving is exactly offset by the rise in private saving. Thus, Ricardian equivalence implies that one form of expansionary fiscal policy, in this case a tax cut with no change in government expenditures, has no effect on national saving and, therefore, on the current account or on interest rates. These results hold for the three kinds of economies we have described: those of small countries with free capital mobility,

---

[8] In the two-period model of the household, we ruled out any debt or assets at the end of period 2. But for now, we will leave open the possibility that the public sector may "live" beyond the two-period lifetime of the households that are now alive, and therefore we allow for the possibility of government debt at the end of period 2. (Thus we capture the idea that governments generally have longer lives than individuals, an idea we will use later on.)

those with capital controls, and those of large countries with no restrictions in capital flows.

This finding indicates some of the limitations of the ceteris paribus assumption we used when discussing equation (7.5). There, we casually noted that higher budget deficits would tend to lead to a worsening of the current account, assuming that higher budget deficits do not affect private saving. Now we see conditions in which higher budget deficits indeed affect private saving, and indeed exactly offset them.

Limitations of Ricardian Equivalence

Loosely stated, Ricardian equivalence says that the time path of taxes does not affect consumption, provided that government spending remains constant. This is quite a provocative idea, and we need to examine it closely for limitations.

One key limitation lies in the fact that public sectors may have a longer borrowing horizon than households. If the U.S. government cuts taxes this year, it can continue accumulating debt for several decades before it raises taxes in the distant future. In that case, the future tax increase would not be paid by households alive today, but by yet-unborn future generations.[9] Thus, today's households would regard the current tax cut as a real windfall, one that will not be taken away by future tax increases that *they* will pay. The implications, then, are clear. Such a tax cut would produce a rise in consumption and a fall in national saving inasmuch as private saving would not rise fully to compensate for the fall in government saving. As a result, the current account balance would tend to decrease.

Our theoretical framework gives us the means to describe this situation with some precision. With the help of equation (7.14), consider a tax cut ΔT in period 1 that is not balanced by a rise in T_2, but is rather financed by a rise in D_2^g, the debt at the end of the second period. Specifically, the increase in second-period debt is $-(1 + r)\Delta T$. In equation (7.12), we can see that from the household's point of view the tax cut is a pure rise in lifetime wealth, where $\Delta W = -\Delta T$. In other words, households alive today care about the taxes that *they* pay, but not about the increase in future government debt (D_2^g) that will require taxes on *future* generations. The increased wealth in turn leads to a rise in consumption. C_1 will rise by $k\Delta T$, where k is the factor of proportionality between wealth and consumption. Since $k < 1$, private saving rises, but by less than the fall in taxes. Disposable income rises by the

---

[9] If the government leaves debt in the second period, it must be paid for in later periods. Specifically, any government debt left at the end of period 2 will have to be paid for by an excess of taxes (T) over government spending on consumption and investment ($G + I^g$) in periods 3 and beyond. More precisely, the discounted value of future surpluses defined as ($T - G - I^g$) must equal the value of the debt left at the end of period 2:

$$D_2^g = \frac{(T_3 - G_3 - I_3^g)}{(1 + r)} + \frac{(T_4 - G_4 - I_4^g)}{(1 + r)^2} + \cdots$$

$T - G - I^g$ is sometimes called the *primary* budget surplus. (It is not the overall budget surplus since it does not include interest payments on public debt.) Thus, debt must be "paid for" by future primary surpluses. The equation does not, of course, say that the public sector has to achieve a primary surplus in every period after period 2, but only a primary surplus in present value.

amount of the tax cut, ΔT, while consumption goes up by $k\Delta T$, so that private saving changes as follows:

$$\begin{aligned} \Delta S_1^p &= \Delta Y_1^p - \Delta C_1 \\ &= \Delta T - k\Delta T \\ &= (1 - k)\Delta T \end{aligned}$$

At the same time, public saving falls by the full amount ΔT, so that national saving, equal to $S_1^p + S_1^g$, falls:

$$\begin{aligned} \Delta S_1 &= \Delta S_1^p + \Delta S_1^g \\ &= (1 - k)\Delta T - \Delta T \\ &= -k\Delta T \end{aligned}$$

Robert Barro has constructed a theoretical case in which Ricardian equivalence holds even when tax increases are postponed to the distant future. (We touched on this situation in Chapter 4.) Barro argues that households today may care about the taxes their children (or their children's children!) will have to pay in the distant future. To ensure their offsprings' economic well-being, the saving of current households may rise to offset a current tax cut fully even though tax increases are not expected until they are long gone. The current generation would want to leave private savings for their children to help them pay the government debt in the future. In some extreme cases of intergenerational affection, households might adjust to a decline in current taxes ΔT *as if they themselves would have to pay for the tax increase in the future*. This extension of Ricardian equivalence is sometimes termed Barro-Ricardian equivalence.

There are many other reasons as well to doubt the relevance of Ricardian equivalence. Consider, for example, the household that would like to spend more now based on future wealth, but is unable to borrow against future income because of imperfections in the financial markets (for example, the bank cannot tell whether the individual will really have high earnings in the future, and thus does not find it safe to lend). For this liquidity-constrained household, any increase in current disposable income will allow it to spend more. Under these circumstances, Ricardian equivalence breaks down. Liquidity-constrained agents will choose to increase their spending when they experience a tax cut rather than saving the windfall income to compensate their children for future tax increases. James Tobin and Willem Buiter of Yale University have noted this point, as have Glenn Hubbard of Columbia University and Kenneth Judd of the Hoover Institution.[10]

Uncertainty is another powerful factor that undermines the case for Ricardian equivalence. Martin Feldstein of Harvard University has shown that when households are unsure of their future income levels, a current tax cut tends to increase private consumption even when households do care about the taxes their children may have to pay later. Furthermore, the Ricardian equivalence proposition might be undermined if taxation is not lump sum. For example, a current tax cut in labor income might imply a future

---

[10] See Willem Buiter and James Tobin, "Debt Neutrality: A Brief Review of Doctrine and Evidence," in George von Furstenberg, *Social Security versus Private Saving* (Cambridge, Mass.: Ballinger, 1979), and Glenn Hubbard and Kenneth Judd, "Liquidity Constraints, Fiscal Policy and Consumption." *Brookings Papers on Economic Activity*, 1:1986.

increase in taxes on capital income. Such a tax cut might induce a fall, rather than rise, in private saving.[11] Finally, progressive taxes on bequests have also been shown to disrupt Ricardian equivalence.[12]

Empirical studies have also called the Ricardian equivalence proposition into question. Martin Feldstein tested the effects of U.S. tax policy on consumption during the period 1930–1977. His estimates indicate that a tax cut, holding fixed government spending, tends to raise private consumption.[13] Lawrence Summers of Harvard University and James Poterba of MIT have studied the relevance of Ricardian equivalence to the U.S. economy in the 1980s.[14] The United States ran large budget deficits in the 1980s, which were caused by a cut in taxes. According to Ricardian equivalence, this should have led to a rise in private saving, to the extent that households anticipated a rise in future taxes. Instead, Summers and Poterba find that private saving rates stayed the same or even fell after the tax cuts. This evidence is consistent with the existence of a significant number of liquidity constrained households. (It is, however, also consistent with the possibility that households expected the tax cuts to be balanced in the future by cuts in government spending rather than by rises in taxes.) As our model for a large country like the United States predicts, the decline in national saving in the United States was also accompanied by a deterioration of the U.S. current account balance and in a rise of interest rates.

In a thorough survey of the evidence on the Ricardian equivalence proposition, Douglas Bernheim has concluded that

> A succession of studies have [sic] established the existence of a robust short-run relationship between deficits and aggregate consumption. While there are many potential explanations for this pattern, it is at least consistent with the traditional Keynesian view [of no Ricardian equivalence]. . . . Thus, while time-series evidence weighs against Ricardian equivalence, it does not by itself tip the scale. However, in the context of theoretical reasoning and behavioral analyses, a coherent picture emerges in which the Ricardian outcome appears relatively unlikely.[15]

7-6 Some Reasons Why Governments Overspend

So far, we have treated fiscal policy largely as if it were exogenous. We have taken levels of G and T simply as given and have not attempted to explain them within the terms of our models. We can, however, use various politi-

---

[11] See Alan Auerbach and Lawrence Kotlikoff, *Dynamic Fiscal Policy* (Cambridge: Cambridge University Press, 1987).

[12] See Andrew Abel, "The Failure of Ricardian Equivalence Under Progressive Wealth Taxation," National Bureau of Economic Research Working Paper No. 1983, July 1986.

[13] See Martin Feldstein, "Government Deficits and Aggregate Demand," *Journal of Monetary Economics,* January 1982.

[14] See James Poterba and Lawrence Summers, "Recent U.S. Evidence on Budget Deficits and National Savings," National Bureau of Economic Research Working Paper No. 2144, February 1987.

[15] See B. Douglas Bernheim, "Ricardian Equivalence: An Evaluation of Theory and Evidence," *NBER Macroeconomics Annual,* Vol. 2 (New York: National Bureau of Economic Research, 1987), p. 291.

cal-economic models of government behavior to explain policy with regard to G and T. Economists have become increasingly interested in seeing how the political environment a government faces relates to the budgetary decisions it actually makes. It is by now widely recognized, for example, that incumbent administrations are likely to stimulate their economies on the eve of political elections. In the United States, a positive correlation has been found between disposable income and preelection periods during which the incumbent government attempts to help its party at the polls by enlarging transfer payments, by cutting taxes, and/or by increasing government spending.[16]

Normally, when tax increases or spending cuts are necessary to balance the budget, the incumbent administration waits until after an election. A case in point is Israel in 1973. When a commission recommended introducing a value-added tax (VAT) together with a reduction in the income tax, the latter was promptly implemented, but the VAT tax was introduced only after the next election.

Seeing a windfall gain in income, however temporary, many governments find it hard to resist the political pressures to spend it. And if conditions allow them access to easy credit, many governments will borrow even if future repayment terms might be arduous. Take the case of Mexico. In 1979–1980, this oil-exporting country benefited from the surge in world oil prices, which provoked a major increase in public revenues. The government of President Lopez Portillo went ahead and spent all the extra income, and even borrowed heavily on world markets in anticipation of future oil earnings. The result was an enormous and painful debt crisis (which we study in detail in Chapter 22).

Theoretical investigation suggests that in countries where political power changes frequently between rival political parties, each administration is likely to spend a lot when it is in power, and thus to leave a high public debt to its successor, which most often is the opposition party.[17] This high level of debt constrains the expenditures of later governments, but the current administration does not care much about this.

A recent empirical study of budget deficits in the industrial countries has shown that governments that are divided between many political parties—as are the multiparty coalition governments in Italy, for example— tend to have the largest deficits. Presumably, with many parties in the governing coalition, it is very difficult to form a consensus on politically painful austerity measures.[18] One-party governments, such as those in the United Kingdom and Japan, or two-party governments as in Germany, have proven to be much more effective in keeping budget deficits under control than do multiparty governments in other countries in Europe, such as Italy.

Table 7-6 shows the evolution of government debt, as a proportion of

---

[16] The classical work in this subject is Edward Tufte, *Political Control of the Economy* (Princeton, NJ: Princeton University Press, 1978). See also William Nordhaus, "The Political Business Cycle," *Review of Economic Studies,* April 1975.

[17] See Alberto Alesina and Guido Tabellini, "A Positive Theory of Fiscal Deficits and Government Debt in a Democracy," National Bureau of Economic Research Working Paper No. 2308, July 1987.

[18] See Nouriel Roubini and Jeffrey Sachs, "Political and Economic Determinants of Budget Deficits in the Industrial Democracies," *European Economic Review,* May 1989.

TABLE   7-6

GENERAL GOVERNMENT NET DEBT-TO-GDP RATIO, 1960–1990

Year	United States	Germany	Italy*	Belgium	United Kingdom
1960	45.00	−13.20	NA	82.30	123.20
1961	44.70	−15.40	NA	80.00	120.90
1962	42.50	−15.50	NA	76.80	116.10
1963	40.40	−13.30	NA	74.50	109.20
1964	38.30	−14.80	23.16	68.90	102.60
1965	35.30	−12.80	26.19	66.60	96.70
1966	32.50	−11.90	29.66	65.10	92.50
1967	32.40	−10.10	29.58	63.30	92.40
1968	30.70	−8.80	32.00	62.20	86.80
1969	28.30	−8.90	31.83	59.20	82.10
1970	27.80	−8.10	33.91	55.50	74.80
1971	27.90	−7.10	38.08	54.60	70.10
1972	25.80	−5.70	43.28	52.60	65.30
1973	23.00	−6.70	45.10	50.90	57.90
1974	22.20	−4.70	42.67	47.50	54.90
1975	24.60	1.00	51.87	49.80	57.20
1976	24.40	4.60	52.73	50.10	56.00
1977	23.30	7.00	52.65	53.70	55.70
1978	21.30	9.40	55.33	57.50	53.40
1979	19.80	11.50	55.25	61.70	48.70
1980	19.70	14.30	53.60	68.90	47.50
1981	19.30	17.40	57.30	81.30	46.70
1982	21.60	19.80	63.50	92.60	45.40
1983	24.10	21.40	68.80	103.70	45.70
1984	25.30	21.70	74.40	108.70	47.40
1985	27.40	22.00	81.30	112.30	46.20
1986	29.90	21.70	86.20	116.30	45.20
1987	31.10	23.10	90.90	121.20	42.60
1988	31.40	23.70	93.70	123.10	36.00
1989	30.70	22.30	95.90	121.30	30.70
1990	31.20	22.60	98.20	120.60	28.90

NA = Not available.
* For Italy, Roubini and Sachs's series has been linked to the OECD series.
Source: *For the period 1960–1979, see N. Roubini and J. Sachs, "Political and Economic Determinants of Budget Deficits in the Industrial Democracies," National Bureau of Economic Research Working Paper, No. 2682, 1988; for the period 1980–1990, see Organization for Economic Cooperation and Development,* Economic Outlook, *various issues.*

GDP, for several industrial democracies over the period 1960–1990. In all countries except Italy, the ratio of public debt to GNP either fell, or rose slowly, in the years 1960–1973. These were high-growth years for the world economy. Tax revenues increased rapidly because of the high growth, and it was fairly easy for most governments to maintain deficits under control. When economic growth in the world economy slowed down after 1973, budget deficits tended to increase, and public debt as a percentage of GDP rose in most countries. The increases tended to be greatest in countries such as Italy and Belgium, where there are multiparty coalition governments. The increases were moderate in Germany and the United States, and the public debt actually fell as a percentage of GDP in the United Kingdom, which always had a single government in power during the period.

A more general point also emerges here. Governments are not, in general, run by a single person, or even a single political party. What is called fiscal "policy" is not generally one policy after all, but the sum of the effects of decisions made by myriad separate decision makers. Finance ministers of many debtor countries in the 1980s attempted to reduce budget deficits, only to find themselves politically hamstrung by parliaments, regional governments, or powerful state enterprises that were able to block an effective overall measure of fiscal discipline. Unfortunately, models which emphasize the "rationality" of fiscal policymaking may neglect the key fact that fiscal policy is the outcome of a complex political bargaining process, and not the result of some optimizing decision taken by a single agent.

The implications of excessive government deficits are clear to see in the simple framework of our model. If a rise in deficits causes an increase in D_2^g (and if Barro-Ricardian equivalence does not apply), the excessive deficits will contribute to a low level of national saving, a crowding out of private investment, and large current account deficits. Heavy borrowing from abroad to finance the deficits can set the stage for a severe debt crisis, a case that we examine in Chapter 22.

7-7 OTHER INTERACTIONS BETWEEN THE PUBLIC AND PRIVATE SECTORS

Our framework for regarding government expenditures and taxes is still very simple. In particular, we have assumed that government spending influences the private sector mainly through the intertemporal budget constraint and through the effects that taxes and spending induce on interest rates. There are, of course, other important channels through which fiscal policy and private spending decisions can interact.

One possibility is that the utility of private consumption is affected in important ways by the level of public spending. For example, if the public sector builds a road to a new recreational area, the result could be an increase in private consumption spending on recreation. On the other hand, if the government builds a new park, the private sector might reduce its spending on private park areas. Because of the links between public goods and services and private spending, the time path of government spending could have direct effects on the time path of private spending. There is, however, relatively little known about the substitutability of public and private consumption, though some recent studies have started to fill in the picture.[19]

Another type of interaction involves the effects of public spending on private aggregate supply. Government spending on goods and services can decrease the marginal production costs of the private sector, thereby increasing aggregate supply. For example, if police services increase, firms will be able to spend less on security (private guards, sophisticated alarm systems, and so on) and more on the production of final goods for consumption. Once again, however, there are few reliable estimates concerning the direct effects of public spending on private aggregate supply.

Another important vehicle for interaction between the public and the private sectors is taxation. So far, we have confined ourselves to the effects of lump-sum taxes, which affect private consumption decisions directly through the budget constraint. But most taxes in reality are not lump sum. They are levied on income, expenditure, and property, and thereby affect the decisions of the household sector to work, to save, and to invest in financial and physical assets.

Deadweight Losses of Taxes

By distorting our choices between work and leisure, or between consumption and investment, taxes impose costs on the economy. In essence, the taxes cause a misallocation of resources by distorting the relative prices that households and firms face in their economic decisions. As a result of the taxes on certain goods and activities, people may work too little, or save too little, or purchase too little of commodities that are heavily taxed and too much of commodities that are lightly taxed. These actions that result from the distorting effects of taxes on the relative prices in the economy, cause economic welfare to decline. These costs of taxes, often called the *deadweight losses* of taxes, are unavoidable to some extent, because taxes are necessary to pay for desired government spending. But an optimal tax system will *minimize* the deadweight losses for any given level of revenues that are to be collected by the government.

Now we need to look, at least briefly, at the workings of a tax system based on income taxes rather than lump-sum taxes. With a personal income tax, each additional dollar of earnings results in a rise of *MTR* dollars in taxes (where *MTR* stands for the marginal tax rate of the income tax). Consider the effect of an increase in the personal income tax rate on work effort. For every extra dollar earned, individuals receive a smaller income net of taxes, and one of two types of effects follows. On the one hand, because the returns to an additional hour of work are reduced, households may tend to work less and take more leisure time. This is known as the *substitution effect*. On the other hand, the rise in taxes has simultaneously reduced take-home pay, and individuals might work harder to maintain the

[19] See, for example, David Aschauer's estimates of the productivity of government investment spending, in "Is Public Expenditure Productive?" *Journal of Monetary Economics,* 1989, and Robert Barro's demonstration that government investment spending seems to be positively associated with economic growth in a large sample of countries, in "Economic Growth in a Cross Section of Countries," mimeo, Harvard University, 1989.

income levels they enjoyed before the tax increase. This *income effect* holds that households will take *less* leisure when they are made poorer by an increase in income taxes.

Evidently, the substitution effect and income effect work in opposite directions, with the first effect, after a rise in the income tax rate, tending to reduce work effort and the second tending to raise work effort. Theoretically, then an income tax increase has an indeterminate effect on work effort. Empirically, however, it has generally been found to reduce the work effort; that is, the substitution effect is stronger than the income effect. A general reduction in work effort, in turn, has a negative impact in the aggregate supply of the economy. Jerry Hausman of the Massachusetts Institute of Technology found that the tax system in the United States of the mid-1970s reduced desired labor supply by about 8 percent, with an even stronger effect for high-wage people, as compared to a no-tax situation.[20] In Sweden, the negative effect appears to be much larger: compared to a no-tax situation, the tax system was found to reduce labor supply by around 13 percent. This is not surprising, given Sweden's substantially higher tax rates.[21]

Since the income taxes distort the choice of households between work and leisure, they impose a deadweight loss on the economy. It can be shown that this loss is an increasing function of the marginal rate of taxation, and that indeed, a doubling of the marginal tax rate leads to more than a doubling of the distortionary costs of the taxes. As a first approximation, a 20 percent marginal tax rate is four times as distorting as a 10 percent marginal tax rate (the distortion is a function of the square of the marginal tax rate).[22]

Income tax changes also affect the return on saving. The interest received by individuals is generally considered to be part of taxable income.[23] An increase in the income tax, then, lowers the net interest rate that savers receive. The effect on saving is again indeterminate: the lower after-tax return on saving tends to lower saving due to the substitution effect, but it may also raise saving due to the income effect. Michael Boskin of Stanford University has found a positive effect of the after-tax interest rate on saving in the United States, but other researchers have not confirmed such strong effects.[24]

Corporate taxes also affect investment decisions. A rise in profit taxes, or a fall in the investment tax credit or in depreciation allowances, is likely to reduce investment spending. In turn, a fall in investment raises the current

---

[20] Jerry Hausman, "Taxes and Labor Supply," in Alan Auerbach and Martin Feldstein, eds., *Handbook of Public Economics* (New York: Elsevier Science, 1985).

[21] See S. Blomquist, "The Effect of Income Taxation on Male Labor Supply in Sweden," *Journal of Public Economics,* 1983.

[22] A discussion on the deadweight loss, or the "excess burden," of taxation is found in Lecture 12 of A. Atkinson and J. Stiglitz, *Lectures on Public Economics* (New York: McGraw-Hill, 1980).

[23] There are some exceptions, though. In some countries, like Japan, most interest income is not taxed in order to provide an incentive for saving. In other places, some types of interest income, for example, that from long-term bonds and pension savings, are not taxed, while other forms of interest income are taxed.

[24] Michael Boskin, "Taxation, Savings, and the Interest Rate," *Journal of Monetary Economics,* March 1982.

account balance, and, at least in the case of a large country, reduces interest rates.

The Case for Tax Smoothing

Deadweight losses from distortionary taxes can be kept to a minimum by the careful choice of taxes and their timing. In particular, the fact that distortionary costs of a tax increase by *more* than in proportion to the tax rate, has important implications for the tax system. These implications have been emphasized by Robert Barro.[25] In order to avoid the *very* high distortionary costs of high marginal tax rates, it is better to have a tax system in which marginal tax rates are constant over time, rather than a tax system in which marginal tax rates are erratic, sometimes low and sometimes high.

In other words, governments should seek to *smooth* the marginal tax rate over time. For example, it is less costly to have a tax system with marginal tax rates always at 30 percent year after year, rather than a tax system where marginal tax rates vary between 20 and 40 percent.

Suppose that a government suddenly faces a sharp but temporary increase in expenditures. Perhaps it has to raise expenditures to fight a war or to pay the temporary costs of a natural disaster. Using our two-period model, we could think of this as a case in which first-period spending G_1 must be much greater than second-period spending, G_2. But now suppose that the taxes used to pay for these expenditures are distortionary—an income tax, say, in which tax revenues are a multiple of income, or $T_1 = t_1 Y_1$ and $T_2 = t_2 Y_2$, where t_1 and t_2 are the income tax rates.

How should t_1 and t_2 be chosen? We know that the government must obey an intertemporal budget constraint, such that the discounted value of tax revenues equals the discounted value of government expenditures, but we also know that the budget does not have to be balanced each period. If the government tries to balance the budget *each period,* and if G_1 is much larger than G_2, it is likely that t_1 would have to be much larger than t_2 (unless, of course, Y_1 is also much larger than Y_2, in which case the tax base is also greater in the first period). Barro argues, however, that such a policy would result in unnecessarily high distortionary costs.

It would be better, Barro suggests, to set t_1 and t_2 at the *same* level. This would result in a budget deficit during the first period and a rise in public debt, but it would also bring about a budget surplus in the second period during which time the debt would be repaid. The budget is balanced intertemporally, but not in every period. In this way, the government covers its expenditures out of taxes, but it avoids the distortionary costs of very high tax rates in the first period. Thus, tax rates should be calibrated according to the average level of spending, rather than to the spending of the particular period in question. Just as private consumption is based on permanent income, so government tax rates should be based on a concept of "permanent" government spending.

Barro suggests that this idea of tax smoothing is not only a normative concept; that is, it describes how governments *should* behave, but also, to some extent, an explanation of how governments actually behave. Using

---

[25] Barro's theory, known today as the tax-smoothing proposition, was first presented in the paper "On the Determination of Public Debt," *Journal of Political Economy,* October 1979.

data for the past two centuries in the United States and the United Kingdom, he demonstrates that the biggest temporary increases in government spending occur during wartime. Barro also observes that governments tend to run deficits, and thereby increase public debt, during wartime and to reduce the debts through budget surpluses during peacetime. This seems to confirm that governments *do* levy taxes according to *average* levels of government expenditures.[26]

Tax Rates and Tax Revenues

When governments raise their revenues out of income taxes, the authorities can change the *rate* of the tax, but they cannot directly control the resultant *revenue*. If the tax distorts the choice between work and leisure, the level of income itself is likely to be a function of the tax rate, so that the tax base changes along with tax revenue. Two extreme cases should make this point quite clear. If the tax rate t is zero, then total revenue ($T = tY$) is also zero. If the tax rate is 100 percent—that is, if all income must be paid in taxes—nobody will have an incentive to generate income, Y will be zero, and total revenues T will be zero. The general conclusion we can draw from all this is that governments may very well collect *less* in tax revenue at high tax rates than at low tax rates if the high tax rates create a severe disincentive to generate income.

More formally, we can suppose that income Y is a function of the tax rate t. We write this functional relationship as $Y = Y(t)$. We have already noted that a rise in t has both an income effect and a substitution effect on work effort, so that income might rise or fall as t increases. However, for very high tax rates, near 100 percent, Y will surely be a negative function of t. Total revenue, in turn, can be written as $T = tY(t)$. Thus, as the tax rate is increased, the effect on total revenues is ambiguous. Higher t certainly leads to higher tax collections for any given level of Y, but because Y itself may decline as t is increased, the overall effect on revenues may be positive or negative. Revenues might actually *fall* with very high tax rates, not only because of a real decline in work effort but also because taxpayers have a greater incentive to *evade* their taxes illegally, and to *avoid* their taxes legally by diverting their efforts to activities with lower tax rates.

Thus, starting from a zero tax rate, increases in t necessarily lead to increases in revenue. But after some point, subsequent increases in the tax rate stop producing more revenue because of negative incentive effects. When we graph the relationship between tax rates and tax revenues, we find an inverted U-shaped curve of the sort shown in Figure 7-4. For tax rates below t_A, higher tax rates produce higher tax revenues; for tax rates in excess of t_A, higher rates produce lower revenues.

This curve is frequently referred to as the Laffer curve, after the economist Arthur B. Laffer who popularized it in the United States during the early 1980s (and who claimed to have drawn it for the first time on a napkin in a Washington, D.C., restaurant). The Laffer curve became particularly popular with a group of economists, known as "supply-siders," who were

---

[26] See, for example, his article "Government Spending, Interest Rates, Prices and Budget Deficits in the United Kingdom, 1701–1918," *Journal of Monetary Economics,* September 1987.

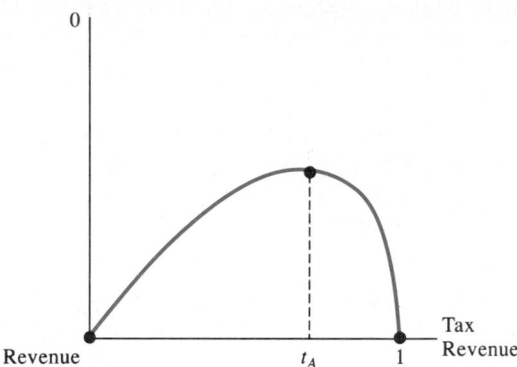

Figure 7-4

The Relationship Between Tax Rates and
Total Revenues: the Laffer Curve

highly influential in the Reagan administration. Asserting, in effect, that
U.S. tax rates were so high that they were greater than the rate t_A in Figure
7-4, they claimed that a tax cut in the United States would increase overall
revenue.

The arguments of the supply-siders were at least partially responsible
for the sharp cut in U.S. income tax rates in the early 1980s. The increase in
income resulting from better work incentives, they said, would more than
pay for the revenues lost from a lower tax rate. But things did not turn out
that way: total tax revenues declined, and the U.S. budget deficit widened
substantially. The failure of tax revenues to rise more strongly after the tax
cut did not invalidate the concept of the Laffer curve, however. Rather, the
error lay in the prediction that the U.S. economy was operating to the right
of t_A before the tax cuts of the early 1980s.

In general, it is difficult to derive a precise estimate for the rate t_A at
which revenues begin to fall when tax rates are increased. It has been estimated that in Sweden, for example, t_A is at a marginal tax rate of around 70
percent.[27] The marginal tax rate in Sweden in the mid-1980s was close to 80
percent, and under those conditions, a tax cut might have produced a rise in
overall revenues. (Marginal tax rates declined to 51 percent in early 1991,
thus giving an opportunity to test this prediction in the near future). In the
United States during the early 1980s, however, the marginal tax rate facing
the average taxpayer was on the order of 32 percent, and it is unlikely that
the point t_A had been reached.[28]

The Cyclical Pattern of Budget Deficits

Another factor that determines the size of budget deficits, at least in the
short run, is the fluctuation in national output. Such fluctuations, or business
cycles, are endemic in free economies. In periods of recession, when Q is

---

[27] See Charles Stuart, "Swedish Tax Rates, Labor Supply and Tax Revenues," *Journal
of Political Economy,* October 1981.

[28] See Robert Barro and Chaipat Sahasakul, "Measuring the Average Marginal Tax Rate
from the Individual Income Tax," *The Journal of Business,* October 1983.

low, budgets tend to be in deficit, while in booms, budgets tend to be in surplus. This pattern is shown clearly in Figure 7-5, which graphs the U.S. federal budget deficit as a percentage of GNP during troughs, or recessions, and peaks, or booms, in the business cycle.

Several phenomena, some on the revenue side of the budget and some on the expenditure side, account for this pattern of deficit and surplus. During business cycle downturns, tax collections from income taxes and other direct taxes fall sharply as the tax base shrinks. At the same time, certain categories of government spending are *countercyclical*, meaning that they rise during downturns and fall during upturns. The largest countercyclical category is, of course, transfer payments to households that are hard hit by the recession, including items such as unemployment insurance (which

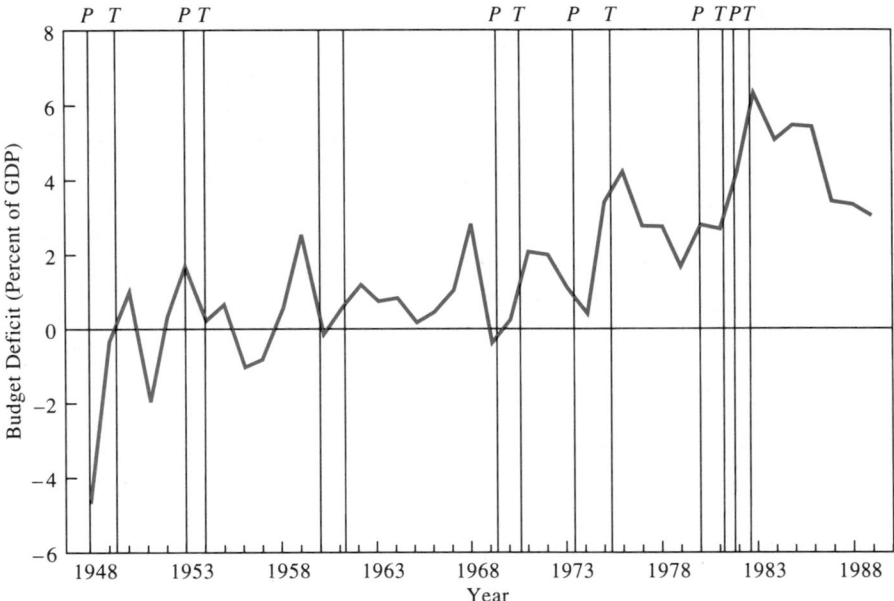

Figure 7-5

The U.S. Budget Deficit and the Business Cycle, 1948–1990

(From Economic Report of the President, 1991, *Table B-76.)*

obviously rises as the unemployment rate increases) and social welfare spending (on food stamps and so on).

Because tax revenues fall and transfers increase during economic downturns, it is easy to see that the disposable income of the household sector tends to fluctuate by less than GDP during the business cycle. (Later we shall also see that this relative stability of disposable income also helps to moderate cyclical fluctuations of output and employment.)

7-8 SUMMARY

The government budget describes the revenues and outlays of the public sector. The difference between outlays and revenues is the budget surplus (or deficit), which determines the amount of lending or borrowing that the public sector must do. More precisely, the budget deficit is equal to the increase in the government debt (when, as we have assumed, no money financing is available).

Taxes are the most important source of government revenue, and these fall into three broad categories: *income taxes* and *property taxes* paid by individuals and firms and *expenditure taxes* linked to the purchase of commodities. The first two are also called *direct taxes;* the last is referred to as *indirect taxes.* Developed economies tend to derive a high proportion of government revenues from direct taxes, while developing countries rely more strongly on indirect taxes. The profits earned by state enterprises and agencies are another (less significant, in general) source of government revenue.

Public outlays fall into four categories: *consumption* by the government, *investment* by the government, *transfers* to other sectors, and *interest* on the public debt. Government spending may also be described another way: as *current expenditures* and *capital expenditures.* Throughout the world, total government spending has increased significantly as a proportion of GDP during this century.

The government sector can readily be integrated into our ongoing analysis of the current account. We have already defined the current account as saving minus investment. Therefore, we can also say that it is equal to the private financial surplus (private saving minus private investment) plus the public financial surplus (public saving minus public investment). The public financial surplus is also equal to the budget surplus. Thus, holding the private surplus fixed, a fall in the budget surplus—or a rise in the budget deficit—leads to a decline in the current account balance. Of course, one of the key questions is whether the private surplus does or does not respond to shifts in the public surplus. The data show that for most of the large industrialized countries, the evolution of the budget in the 1980s closely mirrors the path of the current account.

Government fiscal actions affect private behavior most directly through their effects on the household's intertemporal budget constraint. A *temporary* rise in taxes translates into a temporary reduction in disposable income, which in turn leads to a fall in private saving. A *permanent* tax increase amounts to a drop in permanent disposable income. This makes private consumption go down by an approximately equal amount, and therefore a permanent tax increase has little effect on private saving.

Crowding out is a term that refers to the fall in private spending that accompanies a rise in public spending. Generally, "crowding out" refers to a decline in private investment brought about by an expansion of government spending. In an open economy, however, the rise in public expenditure may induce a reduction in other forms of spending, particularly a reduction of net exports.

The *Ricardian equivalence proposition* states that under certain circumstances (and holding fixed the path of government spending), a change in the path of taxes over time—lower taxes in the present, higher taxes in the future, for example—will not affect private consumption expenditures as long as the present value of taxes remains unchanged. Thus, neither national saving, nor investment, nor the current account will be affected. A tax cut today compensated for by a tax hike tomorrow, for example, will raise current disposable income, but the entire increase will be saved rather than consumed in order to pay for the future tax increase, and consumption will not be affected.

Although an interesting theory, the Ricardian equivalence proposition is doubtful as an empirical description of actual behavior. The theory is limited for several reasons. First, the public sector may have a longer borrowing horizon than households. If the government cuts taxes this year but raises them again in the very distant future, the future tax increase may not have to be paid by the current generation. In this case, households will probably not save their windfall to pay the future tax increase and will instead raise their consumption. Robert Barro has argued that even in this case the proposition might hold if the current generation cares about the taxes paid by its children, but the empirical evidence stands against Barro's theory.

Ricardian equivalence also fails to hold when households are operating under liquidity constraints. A liquidity-constrained household tends to spend an increase in disposable income, even if it expects future higher taxes for itself or its descendants. Finally, the Ricardian equivalence proposition is undermined by uncertainty about future income levels.

Budgetary actions are, of course, linked to the political and institutional environments in which governments make their decisions. For example, it is widely recognized that incumbent administrations may increase certain kinds of government spending on the eve of elections. Contractionary measures are normally taken after elections. And, in general, most governments that see windfall revenue gains, however temporary, find it hard to resist the pressures to spend them.

Governments are not usually run by a single person, or even a single political party. Fiscal policy is, in general, the sum of actions taken by many decision makers and entities, such as the central government, decentralized government institutions, regional governments, and large-scale public enterprises. Therefore, theories that emphasize the rationality of fiscal policy-making may neglect the key fact that fiscal policy is the outcome of a complex political bargaining process.

Public spending not only influences the private sector through the intertemporal budget constraint and through induced effects on interest rates, but also through a variety of other channels. For example, most taxes are levied on income, expenditure, or property (and are therefore not lump sum). As a result, tax levels affect private decisions to work, to save, and to invest. Income taxes are likely to have an effect on work effort. Although the direction of the effect is theoretically ambiguous (substitution and income effects operate in opposite directions), income tax increases have generally been found to reduce work effort. Individual income taxes may also affect the decision to save, while taxes on corporate income influence decisions to invest.

The distortionary costs, or "deadweight losses," of taxes increase more than proportionately to the increase in the marginal tax rate. In order to avoid the very high distortionary costs of high marginal tax rates, it is best to have a tax policy in which the marginal tax rates are fairly constant over time, rather than a policy in which tax rates are unpredictable, sometimes low and sometimes high. The general desirability of stable marginal tax rates is known as the *tax-smoothing proposition*. A corollary of tax smoothing is that the budget should be in deficit during periods of temporarily high public spending, and should be in surplus during periods of temporarily low public spending.

The relationship between tax rates and tax revenues, drawn as an inverted U, has become known as the *Laffer curve*. Starting from a zero tax rate, a rise in the rate will lead to an increase in tax revenues, but only up to a point. After that point, subsequent increases in the tax rate will produce negative incentive effects, and thus lower rather than higher revenues.

The business cycle also plays an important role in determining the size of the budget deficit. In periods of recession budget deficits tend to go up, while in booms budgets tend to improve. Two factors contribute to this pattern: first, tax collections tend to increase sharply during booms, and they tend to fall during recessions, and second, some categories of government spending, such as transfers to the unemployed, are countercyclical. That is, spending in these categories tends to rise in downturns and fall in upturns.

Key Concepts

fiscal policy	permanent tax change
government budget	crowding out
government revenues	Ricardian equivalence
government expenditures	Barro-Ricardian equivalence
direct taxes	incentive effects of taxes
indirect taxes	differing time horizons
current expenditures	budget deficit
capital expenditures	government overspending
state enterprises	tax smoothing
government debt	Laffer curve
temporary tax change	political economy models

Problems and Questions

1. Describe the different types of government expenditures. What are the different ways in which the government can finance those expenditures?

2. Due to the coming elections, the private sector in country A expects that the government will cut taxes next year. What will happen to country A's current account this year?

3. Would a temporary increase in government spending financed by taxes reduce private investment? Would this depend on whether the country is small or large?

4. Suppose that a small country, with access to international borrowing and lending, decides that for national security reasons the government should double the level of military expenditures. Discuss the likely effect of such an action on the current account, paying attention to the expected duration of the military buildup (temporary or permanent) and the method of financing the buildup (through taxation or borrowing). How would your answer change if the country were large?

5. Ricardian equivalence implies that a reduction in this year's government expenditure will have no impact on either national savings or the current account. (Assume that the pattern of future government expenditures remains unchanged.) True or false? Explain.

6. In the two-period model, suppose that people's preferences are such that they want complete smoothing of consumption (that is, $C_1 = C_2$). The government has a larger horizon than households, so it has a certain amount of debt by the end of the second period (that is, its intertemporal budget constraint is $G_1 + G_2/1 + r = T_1 + T_2/(1 + r) + D_2^g/(1 + r)$. The structure of this economy is the following: household production is $Q_1 = 200$, $Q_2 = 110$; government spending is $G_1 = 50$, $G_2 = 110$; taxes are $T_1 = 40$, $T_2 = 55$; interest rate is $r = 10\%$.

a. What is the present value of the government spending? What is the present value of taxes? What is the value of the government's debt at the end of the second period (assume that initially the government had no debt)? How much would households consume in each period?

b. What are total national saving, private saving, and government saving in periods 1 and 2?

c. Assume that the government modifies taxes so that $T_1 = 50$ and $T_2 = 44$ but leaves expenditures unchanged. Did the present value of taxes change? What is the value of the government debt at the end of the second period? What is total national saving, private saving, and government saving in periods 1 and 2? What does your answer tell you about Ricardian equivalence?

d. How would your answer to (c) change if the new taxes were $T_1 = 30$ and $T_2 = 44$.

7. Discuss why one-party governments are more likely to be successful in achieving budget austerity than multiparty coalition governments.

8. Analyze the advantages and disadvantages of income taxes with respect to lump-sum taxes. Which one do you think is preferable on efficiency grounds? Which one is more equitable?

9. How does the cyclical pattern of budget deficits affect the current account? How does your answer depend on the behavior of the private sector during the business cycle?

10. The Allies face a combined expense of over $100 billion from the Gulf War. Would it make more sense for governments to finance it out of taxes or to borrow the money?

chapter 8

Money Demand

8-1 What Is Money?

Money plays a fundamental role in all modern economies. Yet because money seems like such a natural feature of economic life, we do not generally think about what would life be without it. But without money, economic life would be exceedingly burdensome. At the very least, simple operations of buying and selling would be almost too complex and cumbersome to manage.

Up to this point, we have ignored the fundamental role of money in our analysis. We have considered an economy with output (Q) and a financial asset (B), but it had no money. As we start to integrate money into our analytical framework, perhaps our first important task is to define money. This is, surprisingly, rather complicated. Money is a *set* of financial assets (including currency, checking accounts, traveler's checks, and other instruments) with very special characteristics which differentiate it from other kinds of financial claims.

Like all financial assets, money gives command over resources. Unlike those assets, though, it has one special property: it can be used for *transactions*. One component of what we will call money is currency (''greenbacks'' in the United States). When someone goes to the movies, buys groceries, or purchases a car, she never attempts to pay with bonds or stocks. She uses some form of money to perform the transaction. It is this characteristic, being a readily acceptable *medium of exchange,* that is the quintessential function of money.

One important reason why money is so useful as a medium of exchange deserves special mention. In general, a national currency is *legal tender*. If you take a U.S. dollar bill of any denomination, you will notice in the upper left a legend that says: ''This note is legal tender for all debts, public and private.'' What this means is that all obligations can *by law* be settled with money. Under the law, nobody can refuse to be paid for an obligation with money. And typically, governments insist that taxes be paid in the national currency.

Suppose for a moment that money did not exist. People would then have to conduct their transactions through barter. If, for example, a farmer wants to learn some economics, he will have to find an economist willing to accept his wheat or poultry in exchange for a lesson. If a painter becomes sick and has to go to the hospital, he will have to convince the administrators to accept some of his paintings in exchange for medical services. Under these circumstances, transactions would be very hard to make. A barter economy requires a *mutual coincidence of wants* for transactions to take place.

And even if agents are able to find others who want what they have to offer, the problem of determining the price for the transactions still remains. In a very simple economy where only two goods exist, say, lunches and cloth, it would be necessary to determine only one relative price: that of a lunch in terms of a unit of cloth. However, in modern economies there are hundreds of thousands of goods and services, let us say some large number denoted "n." If there is no single commodity or asset in which all goods are priced, then an exchange ratio (how much food for how much cloth) would have to be determined for *each pair* of goods, specifically for $n(n-1)/2$ pairs of commodities.[1] With money, just n prices in terms of money are needed.[2] Thus, money also acts as *a unit of account,* and having a unit of account greatly simplifies the setting of relative prices in the economy.

Even this brief description of a barter economy casts some light on the importance of money. In fact, money plays three fundamental roles in this story. First, it is a medium of exchange. People are ready to accept money in return for goods and services, and therefore a mutual coincidence of wants is not required for a transaction to take place. Second, money serves as the unit of account. As such, prices are quoted in money units rather than in terms of other goods and services. In both these roles, money eases the process of exchange.

Finally, money is also a *store of value.* In this role, it is like other financial assets. When people receive money in exchange for goods or services, they do not need to spend it immediately because it can maintain its value (except in periods of high inflation, in which case money ceases to be used as a store of value). Ice would certainly not make a good money: if it were not immediately frozen, it would soon start losing value, and people would have to rush to a freezer after each transaction. Thus, two necessary characteristics of money is that it maintain its value physically and that it be inexpensive to store. For this reason, the most popular forms of money in history have been precious metals, coins, and paper currency.

Gresham's law captures one interesting regularity in the use of money. This law states that bad money drives good money out of the market. For

---

[1] If there are n goods and services, each of them will have to have a price in terms of the other $n-1$. (It is not necessary to determine the price of a good with respect to itself, which is 1.) This will make $n(n-1)$ prices. But, for example, the price of pears in terms of apples provides the same information as the price of apples in terms of pears. This happens for every pair of goods you take. It is necessary, then, to determine only $n(n-1)/2$ prices.

[2] Think of the savings. With 100,000 goods, there are 5,000,050,000 distinct pairs of commodities, which would each require a separate exchange ratio. This compares with 100,000 prices in terms of money.

example, in Tanzania, cattle were used for a while as money. Soon, people started to realize that only thin and sick cattle were used to pay in transactions. The reason was simple: the values of goods and services were quoted simply in number of cattle, but prices did not differentiate between good and bad cattle. Because cattle have an intrinsic value for their meat, milk, skin, and the transportation services that they provide, it was more convenient to pay with bad cattle and keep the good ones.

Something like this has also occurred in countries that have had "bimetallic" currency systems. In China, for example, gold and silver coins circulated together at the end of the last century. The prices of goods and services were quoted in both metals, and the rate of conversion between them was held fixed. But gold and silver were independently traded as commodities. Whenever the relative price of these metals in commodity markets differed from their rates of conversion as money, the "good" money disappeared from circulation. For example, if 1 gold coin was worth 3 silver coins but 1 oz of nonmonetary gold (that is, gold not in the form of money) could buy 4 oz of nonmonetary silver, gold coins would disappear as money and only silver coins would circulate.

While most kinds of money in earlier centuries were commodities used for purposes of exchange (whether cattle or gold coins), paper money was increasingly introduced by governments in the past century (see Box 8-1 on the history of money). In most cases, however, these paper notes were convertible into precious metals, in the sense that the government stood ready to exchange each note for a definite number of ounces of gold or silver. Money that is backed by a precious metal or other commodity is known as *fiduciary money*. These days, most people identify money with *fiat money*. Fiat money is unbacked money: paper notes printed by the government that the government does not stand ready to exchange for another commodity. Fiat money has been widely used only in the twentieth century. Nowadays, all countries use fiat money.

The definition of money is a tricky matter. Coins and currency are obviously money, but what about checking accounts, traveler's checks, savings accounts, and so on? Where should the line be drawn between money and other kinds of financial assets? For practical purposes, economists have come up with a classification of different kinds of money and "near" monies according to the extent to which these various assets fulfill the main functions of money—as a medium of exchange, as a unit of account, and as a store of value. Table 8-1 shows the definitions of different categories of money and their value in the United States. (See page 224.)

The main criterion for defining "money" is the ease with which an asset can be used for transactions, and in particular the *liquidity* of the asset. Liquidity is the ability to convert an asset quickly into cash without any loss in its value. Currency (coins and central bank paper money) itself is the most liquid asset, against which other assets are judged. Currency in circulation, together with cash reserves that banks keep at the central bank, are termed "high-powered" money (Mh). This is a key variable, we shall see, since Mh is the category of money that can be directly controlled by the central bank. Demand deposits at the bank are the next most liquid asset compared with currency, inasmuch as currency can be withdrawn from such accounts "on demand," without any wait or penalties. Checks written on demand deposits

Box 8-1
A Brief History of Money

Since very early in the history of humanity, societies have recognized the many inconveniences of barter and turned to the use of money. It is unclear, however, when some form of money was used for the first time. What is known with more precision is that metallic money came into use around the year 2000 B.C. Although metals have many advantages over other forms of nonpaper money, they have by no means been used exclusively. Up until relatively recent times, people have used all sorts of things as money, ranging from colored shells in India, to cigarettes in concentration camps during World War II, whale's teeth in Fiji, and large stone disks in the island of Yap.

Metallic forms of money were in the beginning neither standardized nor certified, and this made it necessary to weigh the metals and to certify their authenticity in general before most transactions. (Remember, all that glitters is not gold!) Coinage, which appeared around the seventh century B.C. in Greece, was a useful way to ameliorate this problem, and it soon became widely used. Coins substantially reduced the need for weighing and certification, thereby facilitating transactions.[3] For nearly 400 years, up until the third century B.C., the Athenian *drachma* maintained its silver content virtually unchanged and became by far the dominant coin in use in the Old World.

In the days of the empire, the Romans introduced a bimetal scheme based on the silver *denarius,* which coexisted with the gold *aureus.* During the first century A.D., at the time of the infamous Emperor Nero, the precious metal content of these coins began to shrink as both the gold and the silver were combined with increasing quantities of alloy. It should come as no surprise, then, that prices expressed in these units of account went up at unprecedented rates. Behind this inflationary process lay increasing government deficits that the Roman government failed to check by controlling spending or raising taxes. Some historians have, in fact, attributed an important role in the decline of the Roman Empire to inflation.

Gold and silver were for a long time the most popular metals for money, although other metals were occasionally used. For example, Sweden adopted copper coinage in the early seventeenth century, strongly influenced by the fact that the largest copper mine in the world was located there. In the battle between silver and gold, silver took a decisive lead during the second half of the sixteenth century. The recently discovered New World proved to be much richer in silver than in gold, especially after the rich silver mines in Mexico and Peru were discovered and subsequently exploited.

Paper money only gained strength in the late eighteenth century. Initially, it took a *fiduciary* form, that is, it consisted of paper certificates

---

[3] Coinage by no means eliminated these problems, however. As late as in 1529, King Francis I of France had to pay a ransom of 12 million *escudos* to rescue his two sons who were held hostage by Spain. The Spanish needed four months to count and test the payment, and they rejected 40,000 coins for failing to reach adequate standards.

that promised to pay a given amount of gold or silver. These obligations were issued at the beginning by private agents (companies and banks), but later on the government assumed an increasing role. At the same time, another form of paper money appeared, *fiat* money. These notes had an established value in units of domestic currency (dollars, marks, francs, and so on), but they were not obligations to pay any amount of gold, silver, or other commodity. Their value rested simply on their acceptability by other agents as means of payment.

Fiat money was used early on, for example, by the French government at the time of the Revolution in the late eighteenth century, and by the American colonies. Large-scale transitions to fiat money occurred when governments suspended the convertibility of notes drawn against gold or silver that had been issued under an originally fiduciary scheme. Such was the case of the United States during the Civil War. Generally, suspensions of convertibility occurred when governments needed to undertake a major increase in spending, such as during a war or revolution. The government printed part of the money it needed for the increased purchases, a process of inflationary finance that we discuss at considerable length, especially in Chapter 11.

In the second half of the nineteenth century, the world saw a massive shift to a gold standard. Under such a scheme, currencies in the form of coins and fiduciary notes were convertible into gold at an established parity. By the end of the nineteenth century, the use of silver for monetary arrangements had been all but discontinued. Of the major countries, only China continued with a bimetallic scheme, using both gold and silver. Some economies adopted the gold-exchange standard—a slight modification of the gold standard—in which the local currency was convertible into a foreign currency at a given rate, and that currency, in turn, was convertible into gold.

With the advent of World War I, most countries suspended convertibility of their currencies into gold, and the gold standard collapsed. Attempts to restore it after the war were half-hearted, and the Great Depression and World War II delivered the fatal blows. Toward the end of World War II, in 1944, monetary arrangements were once again reorganized. The Bretton Woods accord led to the general acceptance of a gold-exchange standard based on the U.S. dollar, in which all major currencies were pegged to the dollar and the dollar was convertible into gold. The Bretton Woods arrangement collapsed in 1971 when U.S. President Richard Nixon suspended the convertibility of the dollar into gold. Since then, the world has lived in a system of national fiat monies, with flexible exchange rates between the major currencies.

are also a generally accepted means of payment in most economies. Adding up currency, demand deposits, traveler's checks, and other deposits against which checks can be drawn, we obtain a monetary aggregate known as M1.

Money market accounts and savings accounts, which allow a limited number of withdrawals per month, are considered less liquid. When these assets are added to M1, they constitute a monetary aggregate called M2. Certificates of deposit (CDs) are fixed-term financial assets that are also a form of money, though one that is less liquid than the items in M2. Thus,

TABLE   8-1

THE DIFFERENT MONETARY AGGREGATES IN THE UNITED STATES,
1960 AND 1990
(BILLIONS OF DOLLARS)

	1960	1990*
1. Currency	28.7	244.7
2. Traveler's checks	0.4	8.4
3. Demand deposits	111.6	277.2
4. Other checkable deposits (including NOW accounts)	0.0	292.3
5. M1 (1 + 2 + 3 + 4)	140.7	822.6
6. Overnight repurchase agreements and overnight Eurodollars	0.0	77.6
7. Money market mutual funds (general-purpose and broker/dealer)	0.0	340.3
8. Money market deposits account	0.0	507.0
9. Savings deposits	159.1	413.8
10. Small-denomination time deposits	12.5	1,156.0
11. M2 (5 + 6 + 7 + 8 + 9 + 10)	312.4	3,317.3
12. Money market mutual fund (institutions only)	0.0	120.1
13. Large-denomination time deposits	2.0	506.6
14. Term repurchase agreements	0.0	91.4
15. Term Eurodollars	0.8	72.6
16. M3 (11 + 12 + 13 + 14 + 15)	315.3	4,108.0
17. Savings bonds	45.7	125.2
18. Short-term Treasury securities	36.7	347.9
19. Banker's acceptances	0.9	34.0
20. Commercial paper	5.1	357.7
21. M3 plus other liquid assets (16 + 17 + 18 + 19)	403.7	4,972.8

* *November 1990.*
Source: Economic Report of the President, 1991, *U.S. Government Printing Office, Tables B-67 and B-68.*

CDs are included in M3, along with M2. In summary, the monetary aggregates M1, M2, M3, and so on are ordered according to degree of liquidity, with M1 being the most liquid. Furthermore, each M of a higher, more inclusive order contains all items in the lower-numbered levels. Thus, M3 includes M2, which in turn includes M1.

The definitions of the various monetary aggregates—that is, the particular instruments that each category includes—have changed through time as various financial innovations have led to changes in the ways that transactions are carried out. Notice from Table 8-1 that NOW accounts and money market accounts do not appear in any monetary aggregate in 1960, but they do show up in 1990. These assets, of course, did not exist in the 1960s; in fact, they only started appearing in the mid-1970s. What is considered "money," then, varies over time for technological and regulatory reasons. This is a theme that recurs when we proceed with our analysis of financial markets in Chapter 20.

The money supply in any given economy exists within a particular historical and political context, and that context has two special features. (These will become critical in later chapters.) One is that the right to print high-powered money is almost always a legal monopoly of the government. This monopoly gives the government an important source of revenues, and it is one area that is always open to potential abuse. Governments have not always monopolized the issuance of money, however. In earlier periods, when certain goods were used as money, anybody who could produce those goods was able to create money. When paper money started coming into use in many countries, some private banks, as well as the central bank, could issue currency. This created problems, since the different moneys that circulated inside a country could have different values, according to the solvency of the issuing institution. As time passed, then, the central banks around the world progressively acquired the monopoly over the printing of money.

The second interesting observation about the supply of money is that as a general rule, each country has one, and only one, "official" money that serves as the legal tender. Why does each small country in Latin America, for example, have its own currency, whereas all the states of the United States share a common currency? Would it be better for all the countries in the European Community to share a single currency? The latter question is now being hotly debated. (We will take up the issue of European Monetary Union in Chapter 14.)

There are a few noteworthy exceptions to the rule of one unique national currency per country. Some countries, like Liberia and Panama, do not have their own currency, and the U.S. dollar is legal tender there. In other countries, more than one money circulates during certain periods. This is typically the case of unstable nations, where a foreign currency becomes more trusted than the domestic one. For example, during experiences of very high inflation in different countries during this century, the U.S. dollar has been used alongside the local currency, not only as a store of wealth, but also as the medium of exchange.

So far, we have introduced only the special role of money. Once we look more deeply into the role of money, we can begin to explain many other important features of the economy. Prices, for example, are nothing more than the value of goods in terms of money, so changes in money supply and demand play a fundamental role in determining what the price level will be. The exchange rate, too, is simply the price at which one national money trades for another money, so a theory of money demand and money supply is also crucial to understanding how that rate is determined.

8-2 TOWARD A THEORY OF MONEY DEMAND

Most theories of money demand start with the special function of money as a means of payment. Money provides "liquidity services" that other assets do not provide. The usefulness of money as a transactions medium explains why individuals hold money even though money tends to be *dominated* by other financial assets (money is said to be a "dominated asset"). This term simply means that other assets, Treasury bills, for example, are equally safe as money as a financial investment and yet pay a higher interest rate than money. High-powered money pays no interest and demand deposits and other forms of money generally pay interest rates lower than those paid by other safe securities.

In order to construct a theory of money demand, it is important first to introduce some basic ideas about prices and the interest rate. In particular, we have to introduce the concept of inflation and the difference between nominal and real interest rates. To do this we are going to change part of the framework we have used in Chapters 4–7 where we set $P = 1$ and then ignored the price level. Now, as the money supply changes, prices change, and these changes in the price level indeed become one of our central concerns. We do, however, maintain the earlier *classical model,* ignoring the effects of aggregate demand on output and assuming instead that aggregate demand shocks affect prices while output is determined by supply factors.

Interest Rates and Prices in a Monetary Economy

Once we start to consider money, we cannot escape the need to address the role of prices and the price level. *Prices* are simply the rate at which money can be traded for goods. If a good has a price P (P dollars, for example, in the United States), it means that P units of money must be exchanged for one unit of the good. For our purposes here, each unit of output Q has a price P in the current period. Real GDP is Q and nominal GDP is PQ ("real" refers to the volume of output and "nominal" to its value in terms of money). In the same way, nominal consumption is PC and nominal investment is PI.[4]

Inflation measures the percentage change in the general price level in a given period. If P is the price level at the end of period t, and P_{-1} the corresponding value at the end of period $t - 1$, then inflation ($\hat{P}$) is defined as

$$\hat{P} = \frac{(P - P_{-1})}{P_{-1}} \tag{8.1}$$

so that $P/P_{-1} = 1 + \hat{P}$.

Once we introduce money we must also distinguish between *real* and *nominal* interest rates. The real interest rate measures the returns to savings in terms of the volume of goods that can be purchased in the future for a given amount of saving today. The nominal interest rate refers to the returns to savings in terms of the amount of money that is obtained in the future for a

---

[4] A technical point has to be made, at least for those interested in formal details. In reality, consumption goods may be different from domestic output, so that sometimes we may need to distinguish Pc from P (where Pc is the price of consumption goods in the current period). (A similar distinction arises with investment goods.) For example, if consumption includes both imports (Cm) and domestic goods (Cd), then the price of consumption goods (Pc) would be a weighted average of the price of imports expressed in local currency (Pm) and the price of domestic goods (P). Thus, in this case $Pc = aP + (1 - a)Pm$, where a is a number between 0 and 1; technically, Pc is referred to as a weighted average of P and Pm. We will be assuming in the first part of the book that the relative price between imports and the domestic good, Pm/P, is fixed and exogenous. In fact, by appropriate choice of units we can set $Pm = P$, so that $Pc = aP + (1 - a)P = P$.

given amount of saving today. To be more precise, let us consider two questions:

1. If an individual consumes one less unit of *output* today and uses the saving to buy a financial asset, how many more units of output can he consume in the next period?[5]
2. If an individual consumes one less unit of *money* (i.e., $1) today and uses the saving to buy a financial asset, how many more units of money will he have in the next period?

The *real* interest rate is the answer to question 1, while the *nominal* interest rate is the answer to 2. Notice that in the models we have analyzed so far in the book, we have been using the real rate as the interest rate *r*, since it corresponds to the amount of real commodities that can be purchased in the future for a given real savings in the present.

The returns on most financial assets are stated as nominal rates. For example, an 8 percent annual interest rate on a one-year Treasury bill means that each $1 invested in the T-bill today yields $1.08 next year. To find the implicit *real* interest rate from the nominal rate, we can think through the following exercise. Suppose that output currently has a price P and that next year's price is P_{+1}. If you save one unit of output today, this P units of money are made available to buy a financial asset. If you then invest $\$P$ at the nominal yield i, you will have $\$P(1 + i)$ next year. Because one unit of output will then cost P_{+1}, each unit of output put away from consumption today can buy $P(1 + i)/P_{+1}$ units of output next year. Up to this point, we can then define the real interest rate as

$$(1 + r) = \frac{P(1 + i)}{P_{+1}} \tag{8.2}$$

We know from equation (8.1) that $P/P_{+1} = 1/(1 + \hat{P}_{+1})$, so we can also say that

$$(1 + r) = \frac{(1 + i)}{(1 + \hat{P}_{+1})} \tag{8.3}$$

Thus, $(1 + r)(1 + \hat{P}_{+1}) = (1 + i)$, or $1 + r + \hat{P}_{+1} + r\hat{P}_{+1} = 1 + i$. Because $r\hat{P}_{+1}$ normally tends to be a very small term, we can conclude, as an approximation, that

$$r = i - \hat{P}_{+1} \tag{8.4}$$

The current real interest rate is, then, (approximately) equal to the current nominal interest rate minus the rate of inflation between this period and the next. Note from the definition in equation (8.4) that when the inflation rate is zero, there is no difference between the nominal and the real interest rates. Figure 8-1 shows the behavior of the nominal and real interest rates in the United States, a country that experiences moderate inflation.

---

[5] Note that in our model, in which there is just one generalized kind of output in the economy, there is no difference between the output good Q and the consumption good C. If this is the case, we can indeed talk of a single real interest rate, either in terms of output or of the consumption good. If Q and C are different goods, with the relative price of C in terms of Q changing over time, then we would have to distinguish between a real interest rate in terms of consumption goods and a real interest rate in terms of output.

There is no such a thing as *the* interest rate, of course, but the interest rate on U.S. Treasury bills for the period 1970–1989 illustrates this point. Note that while the nominal interest rate has fluctuated between 3 percent and 15 percent per year, the expost *real* interest rate has varied in the much wider range of −12 to +13 percent.

How well does equation (8.4) approximate the exact definition of *r* in equation (8.3)? Suppose, for example, that you buy a certificate of deposit which pays 8 percent in the next period. If the inflation rate is 5 percent, then the real interest rate according to equation (8.4) is 3 percent. The exact rate is, however, 2.86 percent.[6] At these figures, then, the approximation has an error of 0.14 percent. Keep in mind, though, that as the inflation rate increases, the error grows accordingly. Therefore, equation (8.4) is a good approximation for countries that characteristically have low to very moderate inflation, like Japan, West Germany, Switzerland, and, in some periods, the United States. However, it would lead to important errors in economies like Argentina or Brazil that have very high inflation rates.

It might seem strange that the inflation rate we need to calculate *this* period's real interest rate is *next* period's. The reason for this is simple. The nominal yield on the savings invested this period will be paid next period. Therefore, the inflation rate that matters is the one between the end of this period and the end of next period; this is, by definition, $\hat{P}_{+1}$. In many cases, P_{+1} is not known in the current period. This means that, in practice, the real yield on a bond that pays a nominal rate of return can only be "guessed." We can then distinguish between the ex ante real interest rate, based on what people estimate that the inflation will be, versus the ex post real interest rate, based on what inflation actually turns out to be between periods *t* and *t* + 1. (The real interest rate measured in Figure 8-1 is the ex post real interest rate.) Later on, we analyze how people are likely to go about making their guesses or, to put it more formally, "expectations" about the future.

In some particular cases it is possible to know the ex post real interest rate on saving in advance. Some financial assets specify their payment schedules in real terms, by linking repayments in the future to the actual inflation that will occur. Such assets are known as *indexed assets*. In many developing countries, where inflation rates have been quite high and variable, the only way to write financial contracts acceptable to both borrowers and lenders is to remove the inflation risk through indexation. An indexed bond has a yield of inflation (whatever that is) plus a specified real rate. In countries with a history of high inflation, financial assets with terms of over one year (and sometimes with terms of six months or less) typically do not have their return specified in nominal terms.

Money and the Household Budget Constraint

Let us now use the two-period model to see how money affects the household budget constraint. In previous chapters, household savings could be used for investment (*I*) or for the accumulation of bonds (*B*). Now, households also have the opportunity to accumulate money (*M*). This enhances their portfolio opportunities. At the same time, however, it modifies the analysis. In particular, we should be careful to distinguish between nominal

---

[6] The real rate is given by $(1 + r) = (1.08/1.05) = 1.0286$, so that $r = 2.86$ percent.

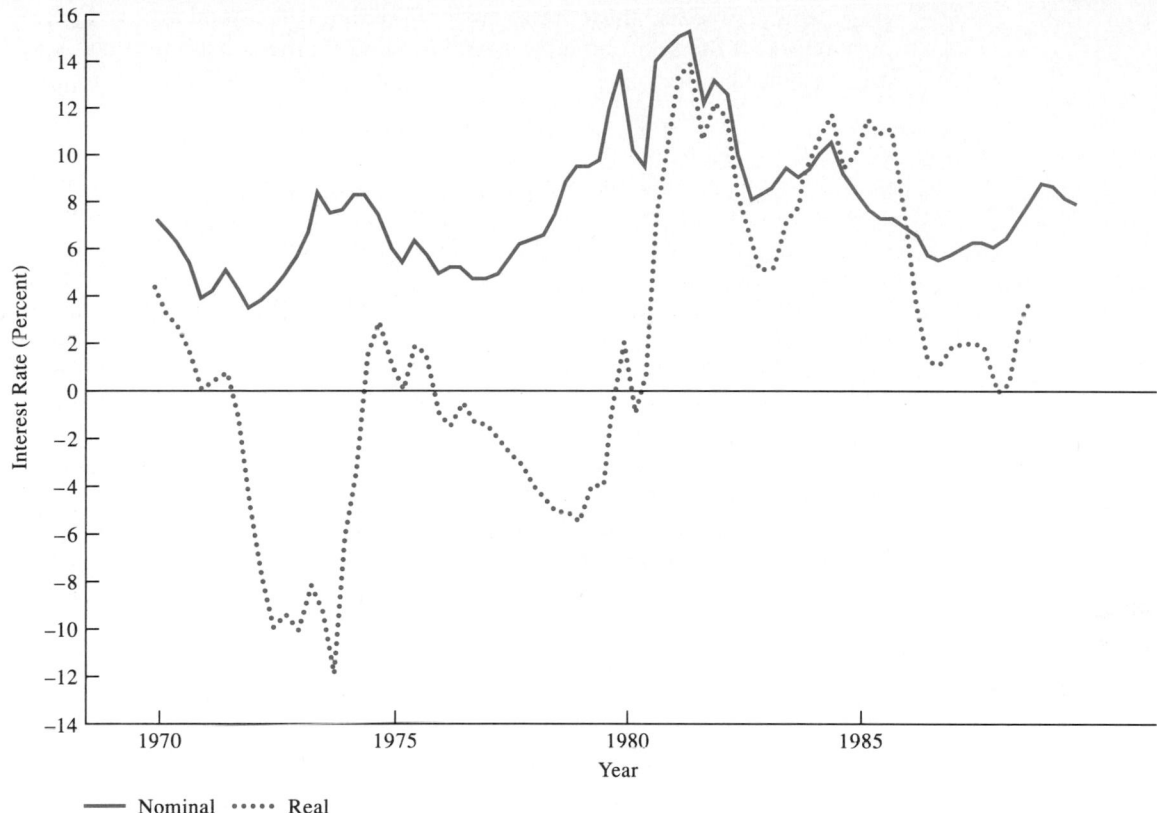

Figure 8-1

Nominal and Real Interest Rates on U.S. Treasury Bills (Annual Rate over Same Quarter of the Following Year), 1970–1989

(From International Monetary Fund, International Financial Statistics, *quarterly data.)*

and real values of variables and to distinguish between the returns on holding bonds and the returns on holding money. A key assumption here will be that money pays zero interest, an assumption that is exactly true for currency (although less true for other components of M1 or M2 which pay interest but usually at a rate lower than bonds).

Nominal disposable income (PYd) is now defined as

$$PYd = PQ + i_{-1}B_{-1} - PT \qquad (8.5)$$

where Yd, Q, and T are measured in real terms, and the bonds (B) are measured in nominal terms, that is, in dollars. Nominal saving of the private sector is then given by

$$PS^p = PYd - PC \qquad (8.6)$$

where S^p is real savings.

We also know that savings (PS^p) can be used for investment (PI), the accumulation of bonds ($B - B_{-1}$), or the accumulation of money ($M - M_{-1}$). Therefore,

$$PS^p = PI + (B - B_{-1}) + (M - M_{-1}) \qquad (8.7)$$

Now consider these relationships within the standard two-period framework. If the household has saved B_1 and M_1, the consumption possibilities in period 2 are

$$P_2C_2 = P_2(Q_2 - T_2) + (1 + i)B_1 + M_1 \tag{8.8}$$

or

$$P_2C_2 = P_2(Q_2 - T_2) + (1 + i)(B_1 + M_1) - iM_1$$

Note that if someone decides to place one more unit of her saving in bonds rather than money, she increases her consumption possibilities in the future in the amount i/P_2. The reason is clear. Because bonds pay interest while money does not, higher holdings of B balanced by smaller holdings of M lead to higher income in period 2.

Next we should derive the two-period budget constraint for a household that starts and ends with no assets, or, put another way, one for which $M_0 = M_2 = 0 = B_0 = B_2$. In the first period, the consumption for such a household will be given by

$$P_1C_1 = P_1(Q_1 - T_1) - P_1I_1 - (B_1 + M_1) \tag{8.9}$$

(This is a direct application of (8.6) and (8.7) for the two-period model.) In the second period, the household can consume all its income plus its accumulated assets, as shown in equation (8.8). Combining (8.8) and (8.9), and after some minor manipulation, we obtain the two-period budget constraint of the household:[7]

$$C_1 + \frac{C_2}{1 + r} = (Q_1 - T_1 - I_1) + \frac{(Q_2 - T_2)}{1 + r} - i\frac{(M_1/P_2)}{(1 + r)} \tag{8.10}$$

Notice that equation (8.10) is basically the same budget constraint that we found in Chapter 7 (see equation (7.11)), with one significant difference: the appearance of the term $i(M_1/P_2)/(1 + r)$. The reason for this is easy to explain. Holding money, as compared to holding bonds, has an opportunity cost in the amount of forgone interest. The exact measure of this cost is the rate of interest (i) that is not paid on the real money balances (M/P). Since this interest is lost in period 2, the real money balances are measured by dividing M1 by the second-period price level P_2, and are then discounted by the real interest rate to get the loss in present-value terms. Note that the money term in the right-hand side of (8.10) can also be written as $i(M_1/P_1)/(1 + i)$, in which case the loss is measured in terms of M_1/P_1. This latter way of writing the money term is somewhat more conventional.

Thus, holding money has a cost in terms of consumption possibilities, and this cost increases as the nominal interest rate (i) increases. In fact, because i rises with high inflation (later we shall see why), the cost of holding money increases with inflation. If keeping money has such costs in terms of forgone consumption possibilities, why then do people hold it?

---

[7] The derivation to get equation (8.10) is presented in Appendix 8-1 of this chapter.

8-3 THE DEMAND FOR MONEY

The Baumol–Tobin Model

The most popular theory of money demand, called the *inventory approach,* is based on the separate contributions made by William Baumol and James Tobin during the mid-1950s.[8] Today it is widely known as the *Baumol–Tobin model.* Both Baumol and Tobin pointed out that individuals maintain inventories of money in the same way that firms maintain inventories of goods. At any given time, a household holds some of its wealth in the form of money in order to make purchases in the future. If it keeps a lot of its wealth in the form of money, the household always has money available for transactions. If it keeps little of its wealth in the form of money, it will have to convert other wealth into money, by selling bonds, for example, whenever it wants to make a purchase. In general, the household must bear a cost, such as a brokerage fee, each time it sells an interest-bearing asset to get the money needed to make a purchase.

The household therefore faces a trade-off. By holding a lot of wealth in the form of money, the household loses the interest that it would have earned by holding interest-bearing assets instead. But at the same time, the household lowers the transactions costs of converting bonds into money each time it wants to make a purchase. Thus, the household must balance the opportunity cost of holding money (the forgone interest) against the transactions costs of frequently converting other assets into money. Such a problem is like the problem of a firm that must decide what level of inventories to keep. With a large stock of inventories, the firm always has inputs readily available for production or for sales. But at the same time, inventories are costly, since they do not earn interest and they require payments for storage and insurance. Thus, the firm must balance the convenience of having large inventories against the costs (both opportunity costs and direct carrying costs) of holding them.

Here is how Baumol and Tobin formalized this idea. Suppose that a household earns an income, the nominal value of which is PQ per period—per month, let us say.[9] We assume that these earnings are automatically deposited at the beginning of each period in an interest-bearing savings account at the bank. Further, we assume that the household's consumption expenditures represent a constant flow during the month, a sum that adds up to PQ for the entire month. The household can only use noninterest-bearing money to make its purchases. In particular, it cannot use the savings account to pay for expenditures. Therefore, in advance of purchases, the household must withdraw money from the savings account. There is also a *fixed cost* (Pb) each time money is withdrawn from the savings account (b is

---

[8] See W. Baumol, "The Transactions Demand for Cash: An Inventory Approach," *Quarterly Journal of Economics,* November 1952, and J. Tobin, "The Interest-Elasticity of the Transactions Demand for Cash," *Review of Economics and Statistics,* August 1956.

[9] For later convenience, we use here Q rather than Y as income. As we know, Q is output, which is very closely related to income. The question here is, what does money demand depend on? In their model, Baumol and Tobin make money demand dependent on consumption (as all income is consumed there).

the real cost; *Pb* is the nominal cost). This cost represents the time and expense of actually going to the bank and waiting in line to make a withdrawal from a savings account. (If the household held other interest-bearing assets, this cost would represent the brokerage fees that must be paid for selling those assets and having the money from the sale deposited in a checking account.)

The household must decide, then, how many times it will go to the bank each month and how much money it will withdraw on each visit to the bank. Because its rate of spending on goods is constant throughout the month, it will visit the bank at regular intervals and withdraw the same amount of money, let us say M^*, on each visit. This situation is depicted in Figure 8-2. The vertical axis measures the amount of money that households hold at every moment during the month; the horizontal axis measures time (one unit of time may be interpreted as one month). Notice that at the time of a cash withdrawal, the household has M^* in cash. This level of cash balances then gradually falls as the household spends the money. When the household

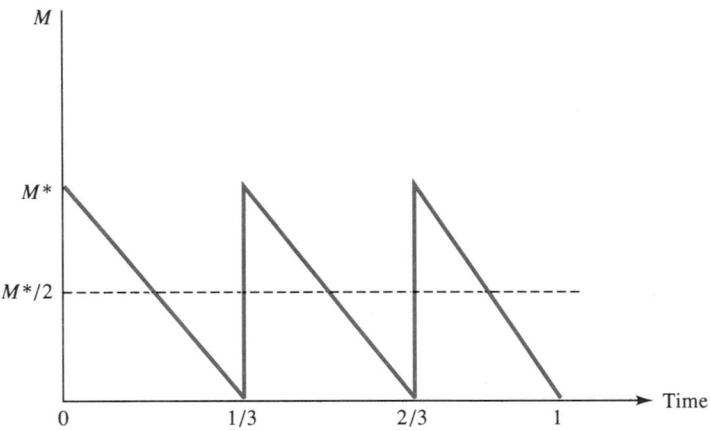

Figure 8-2
Household Money Balances through Time

is left with no money in its pocket, it goes to the bank again and withdraws M^*, and the cycle is repeated.

This pattern of demand for money is shown visually in Figure 8-2. If the household starts each month holding M^* and reduces this balance gradually to zero, the *average* money holdings over the month are $M^*/2$.[10] We will define money demand to be this *average* amount of money held during the month. The question now is how the household should determine the amount M^* that it withdraws on each visit to the bank, and therefore, what is the level of money demand.

The optimal level of money demand will depend on various costs. First, there is the cost of each trip to the bank, *Pb,* and the number of trips

---

[10] Technically, the demand for money is the total area of the three triangles in Figure 8-2. As intervals are equally spaced, the base of each triangle is 1/3 (approximately 10 days if the interval is 1 month); the height is M^*. Then the total area is $(1/2)[(1/3) + (1/3) + (1/3)](M^*) = M^*/2$. Notice that the expression $M^*/2$ will not vary for any number of triangles.

during the month is PQ/M^*.[11] Thus, the total cost during the month for trips to the bank is $Pb(PQ/M^*)$. Also, there is the opportunity cost of holding money, the interest rate forgone on the average money holdings, which we term $i(M^*/2)$.

The household therefore observes the following trade-off. The higher M^* is, the fewer the household's trips to the bank, but also the greater its loss of interest during the month. The household can minimize the costs of going to the bank by making one large withdrawal at the beginning of the month ($M^* = PQ$) that will give the household all the money that it needs for the entire month's expenditures. But such a large M^* also maximizes the interest the household loses during the month. Indeed, with no wealth kept in its savings account, the household will earn no interest at all.

Therefore, the household must balance the costs of frequent trips to the banks (if M^* is low) against the forgone interest (if M^* is high). The optimal choice of M^* is found by minimizing the total cost of holding money

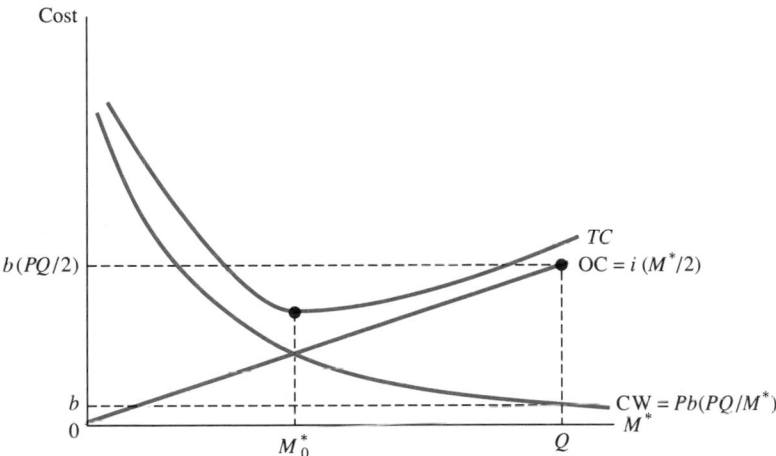

Figure 8-3
The Costs of Holding Money and the Optimal Money
Holdings

(TC), and we can find this as the sum of the transactions costs and the opportunity cost of lost interest earnings:

$$TC = Pb\left(\frac{PQ}{M^*}\right) + i\left(\frac{M^*}{2}\right) \tag{8.11}$$

The optimal M^* is found in Figure 8-3, where the vertical axis measures TC as a function of M^* on the horizontal axis. The curve CW measures the cost of withdrawals, $Pb(PQ/M^*)$. (The CW curve is a rectangular hyperbola, since the costs are inversely proportional to M^*). The straight line from the origin is the opportunity cost, $OC = i(M^*/2)$. By adding up both costs vertically we obtain the total cost schedule (TC), which is U-shaped. The

---

[11] To see this, take a simple example of a household that earns \$1,000 per month and withdraws \$250 each time. It is clear that the number of visits to the bank is 4.

minimum of the total cost curve is reached at point A, which determines M_0^* as the optimum amount of money to withdraw each time. Money demand (*average* money holdings during the month) is then $M^D = (M_0^*/2)$.

We can also obtain an algebraic expression for money demand in the Baumol–Tobin model. This exercise is interesting, because it allows us to express money demand as a function of three key variables: income, the interest rate, and the fixed cost. It can be shown that[12]

$$\frac{M^D}{P} = \frac{M_0^*}{2P} = \left(\frac{1}{2}\right)\left(\frac{2bQ}{i}\right)^{1/2}$$

(8.12)

One fundamental inference we can draw from the Baumol–Tobin framework is that the demand for money is a demand for *real* balances. In other words, people are concerned only with the purchasing power of the currency they hold, not with its nominal value. This characteristic of money demand is generally known as the absence of "money illusion." We can see from (8.12) that if the price level doubles, while all other variables (i, Q, b) remain the same, then the demand for M will also double. More generally, we can conclude that a change in the price level affects desired nominal money holdings by the same proportion, but it leaves real money demand unchanged.

The model also captures important effects of income, the interest rate, and the fixed cost, b, on the demand for money. As is clear from equation (8.12), an increase in real income, Q, raises desired money holdings. In other words, a higher level of income causes a household to increase its expenditures, and in order to support the higher volume of its transactions, the household increases its average holdings of money. But the Baumol–Tobin model allows us to go further. We can even indicate the *exact quantitative effect* of an increase in income.

Consider, for example, a lucky household that experiences a real income rise of 10 percent. Its level of Q, then, becomes $1.10Q$. Using expression (8.12), we can see that money demand goes up by approximately 5 percent.[13] In technical terms, we say that the *real-income elasticity* of money demand is 1/2; that is, an increase of α percent in real income Q will bring about a rise in desired money holdings of $\alpha/2$ percent. An important consequence flows from this. Because the percentage increase in money is less than the percentage increase in income, a rise in real income leads to a fall in the proportion of money to income. In other words, households economize

---

[12] For those who feel comfortable with calculus, the money demand expression can be obtained by minimizing the total cost equation with respect to M^*. We take the derivative of TC with respect to M^*, and set the expression equal to zero:

$$\frac{\partial(TC)}{\partial M^*} = -Pb\left(\frac{PQ}{M^{*2}}\right) + \frac{i}{2} = 0$$

Now, solving for M^*, we have $M^{*2} = (2Pb)(PQ)/i$. Therefore,

$$M^* = P\left(\frac{2bQ}{i}\right)^{1/2}$$

Since the average holding of money is given by $M^*/2P$, equation (8.12) immediately follows.

[13] More precisely, it increases by 4.88 percent. This can be verified by performing the calculation in equation (8.12).

on their money holdings as their real income goes up. To use a familiar concept in economics, there are *economies of scale* in the holding of money.

A rise in the interest rate precipitates a decline in the demand for money. This result is easy to explain intuitively: a higher interest rate raises the opportunity cost of holding money, and this causes households to cut down on their money holdings. We can also use Figure 8-4 to see how this works. The higher interest rate moves the straight line $i(M^*/2)$ upward, without affecting the curve CW (the rectangular hyperbola). The total cost curve also moves upward. It is now easy to see that the minimum total cost occurs at a lower level of withdrawals. Thus, the optimal level of M^* declines. Once again, equation (8.12) can give us an exact relationship between M^D/P and i. A rise in the interest rate of 10 percent produces a decline in money demand of about 5 percent. Thus, the *interest elasticity* of money demand is $-(1/2)$.

Finally, we can consider the effect on money demand of an increase in the fixed cost of withdrawing money from the savings account. It is easy to see that a rise in this cost provides an incentive to go less frequently to the bank. Accordingly, the amount of each withdrawal will be larger, and thus the average amount of money held in any given period will go up. Expression (8.12) indicates that the elasticity of money demand with respect to the fixed cost b is $-(1/2)$.

So far, we have worked under the assumption that money pays no interest ($i_m = 0$). This is clearly true for cash. It was also true for funds held in checking accounts for a long time in the United States, where a famous piece of legislation, known as Regulation Q, banned the payment of interest on demand deposits. But this banking legislation was liberalized in 1980, and since then, checking accounts have paid interest at the discretion of the bank. Many other countries, however, still have laws forbidding such interest payments.

The Baumol–Tobin theory easily expands to cover the case in which money pays some interest, denoted as i_m. We have only to reinterpret the opportunity cost of holding money as, now, the difference between the

Figure 8-4

Interest-Rate Increases and the Optimal Withdrawal

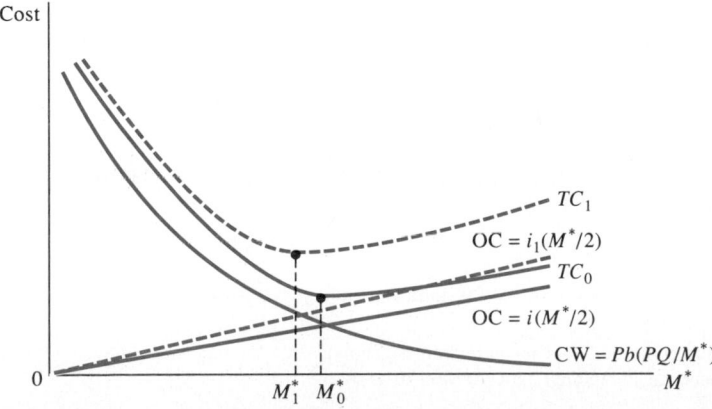

interest rate on bonds (the other "opportunity") and the interest rate on money, i_m. Because monetary assets pay a lower interest rate than bonds, some opportunity cost of holding money still exists, and is given by $(i - i_m)$. In calculating i_m, one must be careful to include the charges on checking accounts when these apply. If, for example, someone holds $1,000 in his checking account at 5 percent interest but there is a service charge of $20 per year, the net interest received is only 3 percent. This is the corrected figure for the opportunity cost of holding money.

The Baumol–Tobin model provides an interesting explanation of the demand for money of households. However, in many economies, business firms also account for a significant share of total money holdings. How well does the theory apply to firms? About one decade after the Baumol–Tobin model appeared, Merton Miller and Daniel Orr tackled this issue.[14] According to Miller and Orr, the fundamental difference between firms and households is that firms face greater fluctuations in their incomes. Private agents often have labor contracts that stipulate given salaries; firms have no such security about their revenues. Thus, firms accumulate money when their receipts from sales exceed their expenditures, and they draw down their money holdings when their expenditures exceed their receipts.

Once again, we have a question of optimal cash management, but this time under conditions of uncertainty. Firms want to avoid accumulating too much currency, because when they do they lose substantial interest payments. On the other hand, if they keep too little cash, they must sell other assets (and thereby incur brokerage fees) in order to get the cash that they need. It turns out that the optimal policy for firms is very similar to that revealed by the Baumol–Tobin rule. Money demand of firms is a demand for real balances; thus, if the price level doubles, the desired holdings of currency also double. As with households, the firm's money demand responds negatively to a rise in the interest rate and positively to an increase in transactions costs.

The exact magnitudes of these responses are not the same as in Baumol–Tobin, but qualitatively they are similar. An interesting additional feature of Miller and Orr is the effect of uncertainty on money demand. If the variability of the firm's net cash flow increases with the vicissitudes of business, the company's best response is to increase its average holdings of money balances. This enables it to face unexpected variations in net receipts more successfully.[15]

In summary, we can finally say that real money demand is simply a function "f" of the nominal interest rate and the real level of income, as shown in equation (8.13):

$$\frac{M^D}{P} = f(i, Q) \qquad \textbf{(8.13)}$$

Take particular note of this expression because it will be useful for our analysis later on.

---

[14] See their paper "A Model of the Demand for Money by Firms," *Quarterly Journal of Economics,* August 1966.

[15] Using modern methods of cash management, however, U.S. businesses have cut down sharply on their demand for money as a fraction of GDP.

Demand for Money as a Store of Wealth

Our theory of money demand so far acknowledges the usefulness of money for transactions. This covers money's functions as a medium of exchange and as a unit of account. Now we need to accommodate the other purposes that money serves.

In the first section of this chapter we said that money has a function as a store of wealth. But in that other assets that are as safe as money (like Treasury bills) pay higher interest, money is also a "dominated asset." For this reason, money is held mainly for its special characteristics as a medium of exchange and a unit of account—that is, for transactions purposes—and not as a general store of wealth. Nonetheless, there are still some reasons why money may be attractive as a store of wealth.

For one thing, money protects the anonymity of its holder, as compared, for example, to a checking account in a bank. This attribute of money is highly valued by people and firms engaged in illegal activities—such as tax evasion, drug trafficking, and smuggling, to mention only a few. It is much harder for the tax authorities, for example, to track down payments when transactions are made in currency rather than in bank checks. Similarly, the authorities are much less likely to uncover illegal wealth (say, drug money) when it is held in cash rather than in bank balances or securities. As expected, the magnitude of illegal activities in the so-called underground economy is very hard to measure, but it is no doubt very large in several countries (see Box 8-2).

Second, while for U.S. residents currency might be dominated by other assets such as Treasury bonds, the situation can be different abroad. In some foreign countries which have experienced periods of high instability and high inflation, the expected yield on holding U.S. dollars may well be higher than the yield on domestic financial assets. At the same time, people in these countries might have access to U.S. currency (via a black market), but not to interest-bearing dollar-denominated assets. Or they might have access to interest-bearing assets, but only at very high transactions costs. In this case, U.S. dollar currency might dominate the other assets available to the local population. In fact, there is good evidence that a significant proportion of U.S. dollars in circulation are actually held "under the mattress" in Latin America, Eastern Europe, and Asia.

Economists use the term *currency substitution* for the case in which local residents hold part of their wealth in foreign money. We have just seen why residents of a given country might hold part of their wealth in a foreign currency. In times of extreme instability residents may actually start to use the foreign money not just as a store of value, but also as a medium of exchange. Thus, in countries with very high inflation, where its rapid loss of value makes domestic currency very costly to hold, the U.S. dollar is often used as a second medium of exchange, especially for large transactions.

Another reason that households sometimes hold part of their wealth as money is that they may distrust financial institutions. In periods of financial insecurity, people run to the banks to withdraw their deposits. An important run on American banks occurred in 1930 during the Great Depression, when the demand for currency increased spectacularly as people worried that the banks would fail and that they would not get their balances out. Charles Kindleberger, of the Massachusetts Institute of Technology, has provided a

Box 8-2
The Underground Economy

The underground economy is variously referred to as the "black," "parallel," or "informal" economy. Although no consensus has been reached on a definition of this phenomenon, we can safely use the one provided by Vito Tanzi, an economist at the IMF who has been at the forefront of research on this topic: "[the underground economy] is gross national product that, because of unreporting and/or underreporting, is not measured by official statistics."[16]

There are two sets of reasons that explain this phenomenon. First, economic agents who want to avoid paying taxes tend to underreport (or simply not report) their income, or to evade the payment of indirect taxes, such as sales taxes, in transactions. Second, government prohibitions on established economic activities rarely eliminate them entirely; rather, they push them into the underground, or informal, economy. Examples are plentiful—drug trafficking, illegal gambling, prostitution. What is common to most illegal activities, aside from their illegality, of course, is their heavy, or even exclusive, use of currency as the means of payment. In this way, the "traders" attempt to hide the incriminating traces of their booty that checks and other financial instruments would leave.

If it were possible to measure accurately the size of the underground economy, it would no longer be underground. Nevertheless, researchers have not surrendered to this difficulty, and they have come up with estimates using several different methods. One of the most popular methods works with the monetary data itself, on the assumption that the use of currency—and especially currency in large denominations—is closely related to illegal activities. Unfortunately, estimates of the size of the underground economy range widely, and, in general, no one number is accepted for any given country. For the United States, the estimates range from about 5 percent of GNP to 25 percent. Figure 8-5 shows ranges of estimates of the underground economy for 19 countries, most of them industrialized.[17]

Although these data must be interpreted cautiously, there appears to be at least two groups of countries. In one group, including France, Germany, Japan, Norway, Switzerland, and the United Kingdom, the informal economy is apparently between 0 and 10 percent of GDP. In the other group of countries, including Belgium, Canada, Italy, and the United States, there is reason to believe that the underground economy may be between 10 and 20 percent of GDP. India is in a league of its own: it has the broadest range of estimates in the sample, from less than 10 percent of GNP to almost 50 percent!

The underground economy has reached a remarkable size in some developing countries. A case in point is Peru, where a group of research-

---

[16] Vito Tanzi, "Underground Economy and Tax Evasion in the United States: Estimates and Implications," p. 70, in Vito Tanzi, ed., *The Underground Economy in the United States and Abroad* (Lexington, Mass.: Lexington Books, 1982).

[17] The figure is taken from Vito Tanzi, "The Underground Economy," *Finance and Development,* December 1983.

ers led by Hernando de Soto have provided a wealth of detail on this subject.[18] According to their estimates, the underground—or informal—economy in Peru is equal in magnitude to almost 40 percent of measured GDP and employs around 48 percent of the economically active population. What is there about Peru that accounts for this huge size of its underground economy? De Soto attributes it to the deficiency of legal institutions in the country, which render it excessively expensive for many individuals and firms to operate in the formal sector. This conclusion is supported by field experience. A team of college-educated researchers attempted to register legally a small clothing factory, without paying bribes unless it proved absolutely necessary to further the task of registration. It took them 289 days (and a few bribes) to obtain the 9 different prerequisite approvals to establish the firm, at a total cost of 32 times the minimum wage. Thus, it is not hard to understand why many would-be entrepreneurs avoid the legal path.

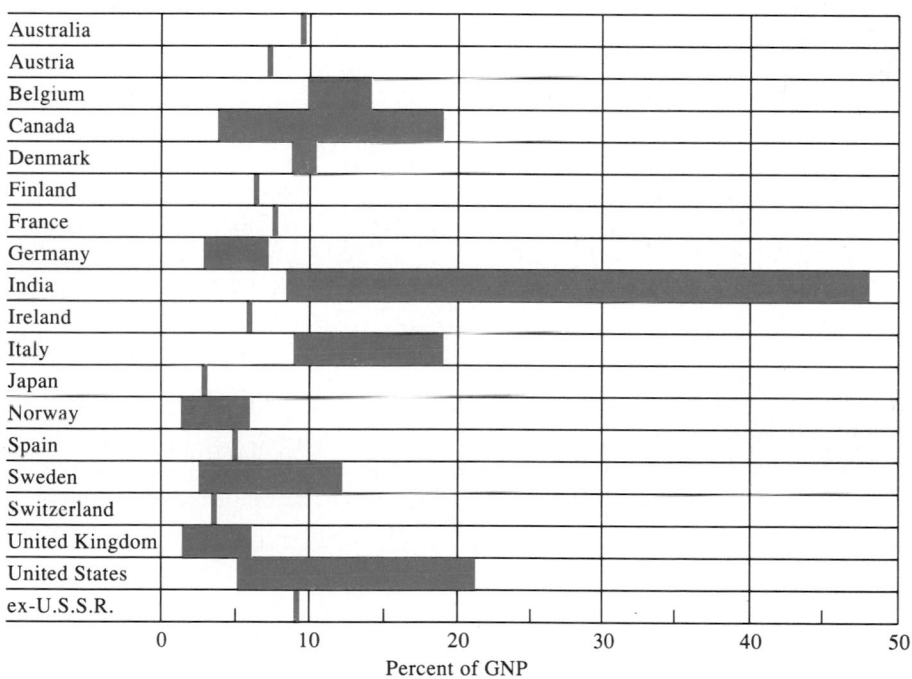

[1]These data show the range of estimates made for each country at different times; they are suggestive and should not be taken to be precise.

Figure 8-5

How Big Is the Underground Economy? (estimates, as a percentage of GNP)

[18] An interesting account of their results was published in a book by Hernando de Soto: *The Other Path: The Invisible Revolution in the Third World* (New York: Harper & Row, 1989).

vivid account of the events that followed the 1929 depression in the United States, among them the run on the banks.[19]

A final theory of money demand is sometimes called the *speculative demand for money*. This theory, discussed by Keynes in the *General Theory*, and then by Tobin and others, holds that the demand for money is positive because interest-bearing assets are risky, and can actually result in capital losses.[20] Suppose, for example, that a household can choose between holding money at zero interest and a long-term bond at a positive interest rate but fluctuating price. Even though the average return on the bond is positive, it is possible that the household will suffer a capital loss on the bond. If these are the only assets available, then a risk-averse household (one that tries to reduce risk) will choose to hold some of its wealth in the safe money, even though on average the alternative asset provides a safer rate of return. (A more complete discussion of portfolio selection under risk appears in Chapter 20.)

The speculative demand for money may be important only when no safe, liquid asset other than money is available. In most advanced economies, however, the theory no longer applies because of the availability of safe, short-term assets that pay a positive interest rate, but pose no risk of capital losses. The best example of such an asset is a short-term Treasury bill, which is nearly riskless and which pays a positive return. Assets like these maintain their dominance over money in that they have the same low risk but a higher return.

The Velocity of Money

The *income velocity of money* (*V*) is the ratio of national income (usually GNP) to money, a ratio that follows from the *quantity equation (MV = PQ)*:

$$V_j = \frac{P \, Q}{M_j} \tag{8.14}$$

This ratio is called a "velocity" since it may be thought of as the number of times during a given period (normally a year) that each unit of money circulates in the economy. With the U.S. GNP equal to $5,201 billion in 1989 and U.S. money supply (M1) equal to $795 billion, each dollar had to support 6.5 dollars of final demand, so that M1 had to circulate 6.5 times on average during the year.

Notice that we have put a subscript on *M* and *V*. This is because there are different definitions of money (*Mh*, M1, M2, and so on), and each of them has a corresponding velocity associated with it. Thus, we will also have *Vh*, V1, V2, and so on. While V1 (corresponding to M1) was 6.5 in 1989, V2 (corresponding to M2, equal to $3,222 billion in 1989) was 1.6.

Another concept of velocity is known as the *transactions velocity of money*. This is defined as the number of times that money circulates in a given period to support the total value of transactions in the economy. It is

---

[19] Kindleberger has written a nontechnical and fascinating historical analysis of financial crises. See his *Maniacs, Panics and Crashes: A History of Financial Crises* (New York: Basic Books, 1978).

[20] See James Tobin, "Liquidity Preference as Behavior Towards Risk," *Review of Economic Studies*, February 1958.

easy to see why the value of transactions in a given year is much higher than the value of income: each time a given commodity is resold from one agent to another, a transaction takes place without any income being generated. Thus, the transactions velocity of money is always higher than the corresponding income velocity of money.

Figure 8-6 illustrates the income velocity of money, for *Mh,* M1, and M2 in the United States during the period 1960–1990. Notice the underlying upward trend in velocity for *Mh* and M1, and the long-term stability for M2. The long-term upward trend in V_h and V_1 are almost surely related to the technological changes, such as electronic teller machines and the widespread use of credit cards, which allow households and firms to economize on money balances. The long-term rise in average inflation rates and nominal interest rates since the 1960s provides another incentive for economizing on money balances. The velocity of M2, on the other hand, has not increased, presumably because *M*2 pays interest, and because many of the technological changes have actually led to a shift out of *Mh* and into interest-bearing *M*2.

The Baumol–Tobin model can also be used as a theory of money velocity. In that model, we derived an expression for M^D—equation (8.12)—that can be converted into an expression for *V:*

$$V = \frac{PQ}{M^D} = \left(\frac{2iQ}{b}\right)^{1/2} \qquad \textbf{(8.15)}$$

This equation makes several predictions about the effects of economic factors on velocity. First, the price level itself has no effect on velocity. A

Figure 8-6
The Income Velocity of Money in the United States, 1960–1990

(From Economic Report of the President, 1991. *Tables B-1 and B-69.)*

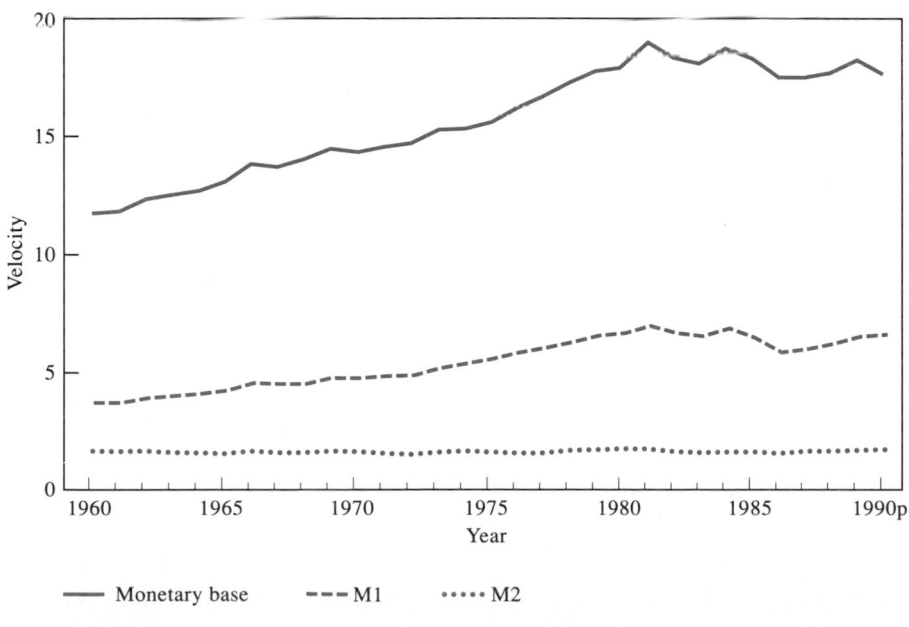

p = Preliminary.

doubling of the price level, for the same levels of real income, real transactions costs, and the nominal interest rate, should have no effect on V.

Second, interest rates certainly do have an important effect on velocity. As i rises, we know that households economize on their money holdings by going more frequently to the bank. Thus, for given Q, there is a fall in M^D/P. The result is that higher interest rates should lead to a higher velocity of money. This important relationship has been empirically verified, and it plays a key role in our discussions in later chapters.

Third, there is the effect of an increase in real income on velocity. We have already noted that the real income elasticity of money demand is 1/2 in the Baumol–Tobin model. As real income rises, so too does real money demand, but at a slower rate. Thus, the ratio of income to money tends to rise, showing that velocity should be an increasing function of real income. This, of course, restates—and supports—our earlier statement that there appear to be economies of scale to money holding.

Finally, we can note that velocity is an increasing function of b, the real transactions cost of converting interest-bearing assets into money. In practice, b is heavily influenced by both technological change and financial regulations. Changes in banking technology, such as the introduction of credit cards, electronic transfers of deposits, or cash machines, make it easier to make transactions without requiring trips to the bank. Insofar as banking regulations determine the conditions under which interest-bearing accounts can be converted into checking accounts or into currency, they also affect the ease—and the costs—of converting interest-bearing assets into money.

Equation (8.15) showed the specific form of V in the Baumol–Tobin model. A general form for the income velocity of money can be specified more simply as a (positive) function of the interest rate and real income:

$$V = V(i, Q) \qquad \textbf{(8.16)}$$
$$+ \ +$$

Later on, in Chapter 10, we take an even simpler position. There, we assume that V is a function of the interest rate only:

$$V = V(i) \qquad \textbf{(8.16')}$$

Equation (8.16') corresponds to a special case in which the income elasticity of money demand is 1. In that case, M/P can be written as $Q/V(i)$.

8-4 Empirical Studies of Money Demand

So far, we have analyzed theoretical arguments about money demand. Now we must see how the theory squares with the facts. In particular, how do the predictions of the Baumol–Tobin model fare when confronted with the empirical evidence?

Evidence on Baumol–Tobin and the Transactions Demand for Money

In an influential work, Stephen Goldfeld of Princeton University undertook a thorough study of the demand for money in the United States for the period 1952–1972.[21] Using the basic framework of the Baumol–Tobin model, Goldfeld estimated an econometric equation of the following form:

$$\log(M/P) = a_0 + a_1 \log(M/P)_{-1} + a_2 \log(Q) + a_3 i \qquad \textbf{(8.17)}$$

where a_0 is a constant; a_1, a_2, and a_3 are the coefficients of lagged real money balances, income, and the interest rate, respectively. Note that the equation was estimated in logarithmic form: the logarithm of real money balances was regressed on the logarithms of real money balances of the previous quarter, of real GNP, and on the interest rate.[22]

The big difference between the basic Baumol–Tobin model and the Goldfeld equation is that Goldfeld writes the demand for money as a function of lagged money demand—that is, money holdings in the previous quarter. This suggests that there is a delay in the adjustment of actual money balances to their ideal level as determined by Q and b.

Using quarterly data, Goldfeld found some interesting results. His first important finding was that money demand is a demand for real balances, just as the Baumol–Tobin model predicts. A rise in the price level leads to an equiproportional increase in the demand for money that keeps real money holdings unchanged. Many other studies have confirmed this result, and it is generally accepted these days as empirically established.

The effect of income on money demand (in this case, demand for M1) turned out to be positive. The *short-run* income elasticity of money demand was about 0.2. That is, a 10 percent rise in income leads to an estimated 2 percent increase in desired money holdings in the same quarter. This is only a short-run effect, however. If the rise in income is sustained for one year, money demand rises by 0.5 percent. In the long run, the income elasticity is calculated to be 0.7. Thus, about five-sevenths, or 70 percent, of the adjustment of money demand to a rise in income is completed by the end of the first year; about 90 percent is completed by the end of the second year according to Goldfeld's estimates.

Analyzing the influence of interest-rate changes on money demand is slightly more complicated because in the real world, there is no such a thing as *the* interest rate. Researchers have to identify the interest rate (or rates) that they think is most relevant for their model. Goldfeld estimated demand-for-money equations using both the interest rate on commercial paper and the interest rate on time deposits. As expected, the effect of these two interest rates on money demand was negative. A 10 percent increase in the commercial paper rate produced a 0.2 percent decline in the demand for money in the first quarter and a cumulative drop of 0.5 percent in money demand by the end of the first year. The same proportional change in the time deposits rate had a bigger impact on desired money holdings. After such a stimulus, they dropped by 0.5 percent in the first quarter, and by an accumulated 1.2 percent in one year. The long-run interest elasticities of money demand were −0.1 for the commercial paper rate and −0.2 for the

---

[21] See Stephen Goldfeld, "The Demand for Money Revisited," *Brookings Papers on Economic Activity*, No. 3: 1973.

[22] An important technical point about this equation is discussed in Appendix 8-2 of this chapter.

time deposit rate. As before, over 90 percent of the total adjustment was completed by the end of the second year.

It does appear, therefore, that the data bear out the basic predictions of the Baumol–Tobin model. The fact that nominal money balances rise in proportion to prices was strongly supported by the data. Furthermore, the income elasticity of money demand, although not exactly 0.5, was not too far from this figure. Thus, the evidence points to the existence of economies of scale in the holdings of money balances. The effects of interest-rate changes, on the other hand, although smaller than those suggested by the theory, are in the predicted direction. Notice also that Goldfeld made his estimations using aggregate data. While the Baumol–Tobin model was designed for a single household, Goldfeld's work (and that of other researchers) seems to establish it as an adequate representation of the aggregate economy.

Not all is rosy with econometric estimates of money demand equations, however. Just a few years after Goldfeld's important work, the equation started to go awry. It significantly overpredicted the demand for money in the United States after the mid-1970s. And in retrospect, there seems to have been a structural change in the aggregate demand for money in the mid-1970s that has persisted ever since. Among the first to warn about this problem was Stephen Goldfeld himself. In 1976 he published an article suggestively titled "The Case of the Missing Money."[23] In this paper, Goldfeld puzzled over the poor results of his new attempt at estimating the money demand. Subsequent analyses on this subject confirmed a clear shift in money demand after 1973.[24] This kind of instability in the money demand equation has also been verified in developing countries.[25]

The most popular explanation for the overprediction problem points to the substantial financial innovations and also the deregulation of banking that occurred during the 1970s. Traditional money demand equations had been able to capture the influence of interest rates and income, but they could not accommodate the separate effects of the innovations. Among the new devices that appeared were automatic teller machines, and computerized and telephone transfers of funds, both of which lowered the costs of converting interest-bearing assets into cash. More extensive use of credit cards provided a good substitute for money in transactions. Moreover, the granting of overdraft privileges and the creation of financial management accounts also allowed wealthholders to economize on their money balances.

All these changes led to a decline in the amount of money necessary to perform a given volume of transactions. Some reduced the transaction costs of converting assets into money; others provided a good substitute for

---

[23] The paper appeared in *Brookings Papers on Economic Activity*, No. 3: 1976.

[24] V. Vance Roley showed this shift in the demand for money working with two different sample periods: 1959–1973 and 1974–1983. The structural change has implied a significant variation in the values of the estimated coefficients in these two subsamples. See his "Money Demand Predictability," *Journal of Money, Credit and Banking*, November 1985.

[25] In Chile, for example, Felipe Larrain and Anibal Larrain have found strong and persistent overprediction by the traditional money demand equations. Their results are reported in "El Caso del Dinero Desaparecido: Chile, 1980–1985," *Cuadernos de Economia*, August 1988.

money. All of them meant that for given income and interest rates, the desired level of money holdings would decline. Therefore, it is not at all strange that the equations estimated by Goldfeld and others substantially and consistently overpredicted actual money demand.

Theoretically, the Baumol–Tobin model is able to handle some financial innovations. Most of them amount to a reduction in the transactions cost of converting less liquid assets into money. This means a decline in the parameter b of the model, and such a decline would lead to a drop in the demand for money. The difficulty lies in measuring the effects of the different innovations in b. Some researchers have had encouraging results in this demanding task. For example, Michael Dotsey was able to show that money demand declined after the introduction of electronic transfers of funds.[26]

The important point to remember here is simply this: despite all the problems encountered in estimating money demand after the mid-1970s, the basic qualitative conclusions of the Baumol–Tobin model still apply. Money demand is negatively influenced by a rise in interest rates and positively affected by an increase in income.

The Evidence on Other Motives for Holding Money

We have this far concentrated on the traditional transactions motive for holding money. What about the other sources of money demand that we discussed in the previous section? Some casual evidence supports the existence of substantial money holdings that are unexplained by simple transactions purposes. Most important, average money holdings amounted to no less than $855 per person in the United States in 1988, an amount that seems far higher than normal transactions needs would seem to warrant. Moreover, we know that a large proportion of high-denomination U.S. notes, $100 bills, for example, circulates outside the United States.

It is likely that a substantial part of the U.S. money stock is being used to support illegal activities both in the United States and abroad. Another large portion is used legally as a store of value in foreign countries that are buffeted by high inflation. As we said before, in some countries the U.S. dollar has quite evidently taken over some of the traditional functions of the local money, finding use both as a store of wealth and as a unit of account. This process, known as currency substitution, is most conspicuous in economies where there is political and economic instability. Some recent studies have documented the importance of this phenomenon in various developing countries of Latin America and Africa.[27]

---

[26] See his paper "The Use of Electronic Funds Transfers to Capture the Effect of Cash Management Practices on the Demand for Demand Deposits," *Journal of Finance,* December 1985.

[27] For Latin America, two interesting studies are Guillermo Ortiz, "Currency Substitution in Mexico: The Dollarization Problem," *Journal of Money, Credit and Banking,* May 1983, and C. L. Ramirez-Rojas, "Currency Substitution in Argentina, Mexico and Uruguay," *International Monetary Fund Staff Papers,* March 1988. For Africa, see Mohamed El-Erian, "Currency Substitution in Egypt and the Yemen Arab Republic," *International Monetary Fund Staff Papers,* March 1988.

8-5 THE DOCTRINE OF MONETARISM

One major school of thought about money demand is that of *monetarism*. Many heated, well-publicized debates have occurred, and still do, over all kinds of ''monetarist'' issues. Yet in spite of the wide and familiar use of this term, there are still many conflicting definitions of monetarism, and much of the public argument has rendered it a loose concept. Nonetheless, we should look at the term here and describe some of the basic issues in the debate.[28] (We shall have occasion to discuss monetarist ideas in later chapters as well.)

At one level, monetarists distinguish themselves from other economists by stressing the existence of a *stable* money-demand function. In other words, they say that $(M/P)^D$ is a function of a few identifiable variables. One implication of the stability of money demand, monetarists suggest, is that the best way to stabilize the economy is to stabilize the rate of growth of the money supply at a low level.

The belief in the stability of the money demand relationship is applied, roughly speaking, in the following way. Assuming that output is determined exogenously (by the microeconomic supply decisions of households and firms) so that Q can be taken as given, then the definition of velocity implies

$$P = \frac{M\,V}{Q} \tag{8.18}$$

If V is fairly stable, and Q is exogenous, the equation implies that changes in M translate into changes in the price level. Thus, monetarists stress that changes in M are the key to controlling the price level, at least when price changes are considered over a period of a few years. They hold that money should be allowed to rise at a constant rate per year (the so-called X-percent rule, which allows money to grow at a given X percent per year), in order to produce a constant rate of price increase each year. Thus, controlling inflation becomes merely a problem of controlling M.

Nonmonetarists challenge this point of view on several grounds. They hold first that V is not a constant, so that a constant growth of M will not necessarily lead to a constant growth of P, even in the medium term. Not only is V a function of i and Q, but it is also susceptible to shocks because of technological and regulatory changes. Second, changes in M are likely to affect Q as well as P in the short term (a point acknowledged by most monetarists). For nonmonetarists, the likely effects of shifts in M on Q have two implications. First, an attempt to implement the monetarist policy prescription of a stable money growth might involve a big shift in policy (from the previous monetary rules) and, therefore, might provoke an undesirable swing in Q. Second, a fixed money growth rule also precludes using monetary policy in an activist way, in order to help to stabilize Q in the short run.

Most monetarists reject the notion that monetary policy should be used for short-run stabilization purposes. While monetarists often acknowledge that money affects real output in the short term, they assert that the linkages

---

[28] For an excellent summary discussion of monetarist doctrines, see also the entry on monetarism by Phillip Cagan in *The New Palgrave: A Dictionary of Economics* (New York: Stockton Press, 1988).

between money and output are "long and variable," and in fact too unreliable for short-run stabilization purposes. Therefore, they argue that monetary policy should be geared to the medium run, in which case they suggest that a stable and low money growth will produce a stable and low rate of inflation.

We shall revisit this interesting debate at several points later on.

8-6 SUMMARY

Money is a fundamental financial asset in all modern economies. Without it, people would have to use barter to make any transactions. That would be highly inefficient, not only in requiring a mutual coincidence of wants but also in the need to have the price of each good or service in terms of all others. The existence of money eliminates the need for barter, by acting as a medium of exchange and a unit of account. It also serves, under some circumstances, as a store of wealth.

Defining money is somewhat tricky, largely because there are many kinds of assets that can qualify as money (coins, currency, checking accounts, savings accounts, and so on). Thus, economists have classified the different kinds of money and "near" money in several aggregates according to their liquidity. Coins, currency, and cash reserves at the central bank are the most liquid kind of asset, and these are termed "high-powered money" (Mh). Adding coins and currency, demand deposits, traveler's checks, and other checkable deposits results in the monetary aggregate M1. The next category, M2, includes money market accounts and savings accounts. The different monetary assets, as well as the definitions of M1, M2, and so on, have evolved over time.

The context within which the money supply is determined has special features. First, the right to print high-powered money is almost always a legal monopoly of the government. Second, as a general rule each country has one, and only one, official money. There are only a handful of exceptions to this rule, the economies of Liberia and Panama, for example, both of which use the U.S. dollar as legal tender.

Bringing money into our model allows us to address the role of prices and inflation in the economy. Prices, after all, are simply the rate at which money can be traded for goods. Inflation is a measure of the percentage change in the general price level in a given period. In the presence of inflation, it is necessary to distinguish between two concepts of the interest rate. The *nominal interest rate* measures the *additional units of money* that an individual may obtain by using $1 to buy a financial asset. The *real rate* measures the *additional units of output* that can be obtained by doing the same operation. The real interest rate is (approximately) equal to the nominal interest rate minus the inflation rate.

The existence of money affects the household intertemporal budget constraint because money is an alternative asset in which households can hold their savings. Holding money, as compared to bonds, has an opportunity cost equal to the interest that is forgone. This opportunity cost is an increasing function of the nominal interest rate and the level of real money balances.

Most theories of money demand are based on the special role money plays as a medium of exchange. This is the case of the inventory approach (also known as the Baumol–Tobin model), the most popular model of money demand. The essential idea behind this theory goes like this. Households need money to make transactions, and they face a trade-off in balancing the opportunity cost of holding money (the forgone interest) against the transactions costs of frequently converting other assets into money. This problem is much like that facing a firm which must decide on its optimum level of inventories.

The fundamental inferences we can draw from the Baumol–Tobin model are that the demand for money is a demand for real balances (that is, there is no *money illusion*) and that money demand depends positively on real income and negatively on the interest rate. Moreover, the Baumol–Tobin model provides specific quantitative estimates of the elasticity of money demand with respect to real income (1/2) and to the interest rate (−1/2).

Money may also be attractive as a store of wealth, even though other available assets, such as Treasury bills, are as safe as money and pay higher interest. First, money protects the anonymity of its holder, a highly valued attribute for agents involved in illegal activities such as tax evasion, drug trafficking, and smuggling. The magnitude of illegal activities in the *underground economy* is very hard to measure, but it is very large in several countries. Second, money is a safe and readily available store of wealth in countries that have experienced periods of high instability and high inflation. Distrust of financial institutions is another reason to hold money in its most liquid form. A shift toward money when people have lost confidence in banks has occurred in particular periods in history, such as the bank runs of 1930 in the United States. Finally, money might be held for speculative purposes if no alternative safe asset (such as a short-term Treasury bill) that pays a positive rate of interest is available.

The *income velocity of money* is an important monetary concept. It is defined as the ratio of national income to money. In other words, income velocity is the average number of times that money circulates in the economy during a given period (normally a year) to support the total value of nominal income.

Empirical studies of money demand have, on the whole, supported the Baumol–Tobin model. Demand for real balances is unaffected by changes in the price level, but it responds positively to a rise in real income and negatively to an increase in nominal interest rates. Estimates of the quantitative impact of these variables on money demand do not vary too much from the results of the theoretical model. Since the mid-1970s, however, traditional money-demand equations have tended consistently to overpredict the true demand for money in the United States. This inaccuracy has also been observed in other countries. The most popular explanation for the overprediction problem is the role of financial innovations and banking deregulation, which had the effect of lowering the cost of converting interest-bearing assets into cash and of providing substitutes for money.

The doctrine of monetarism stresses the existence of a stable money demand function, in which real balances are a function of a few identifiable variables. If this is the case, as the monetarists say it is, stabilizing the money supply can be a useful policy for stabilizing the economy. Monetarists also hold that the income velocity of money is very stable, and thus they believe that controlling the money supply is an effective way to stabilize nominal GNP.

Key Concepts

barter economy
monetarism
legal tender
mutual coincidence of wants
unit of account
medium of exchange
Gresham's law
store of value
high-powered money (Mh)
liquidity
M2
M1
dominated asset
M3

nominal interest rate
real interest rate
indexed assets
inflation
inventory approach to money
  demand
money illusion
income velocity of money
real balances
underground economy
opportunity cost
quantity equation
currency substitution
financial innovation

Problems and Questions

1. Discuss the role of money as a medium of exchange, unit of account, and store of value. Do you think that some reproducible commodity, for example, cocoa seeds, would make a good money? Why?

2. Assume that the financial system undergoes substantial changes and that people become able to draw checks on their saving deposits. What would happen to money demand? Would there be a case for redefining the monetary aggregates?

3. Consider an economy in which there are two types of bonds. Bonds A pay a 10 percent nominal interest rate. Bonds B are indexed bonds and their real interest rate is 5 percent. Which one yields a higher return if people expect inflation to be 2 percent? What if expected inflation is 8 percent? In which bonds would you prefer to have $1,000 if you lived in Switzerland? If you lived in Brazil?

4. In the two-period model, a household decides to hold $100 in currency, while bonds pay a 10 percent nominal interest rate.

  a. Calculate the present value of the opportunity cost for the household of holding such amount of cash.

  b. If holding money is costly, why do people hold it?

5. The absence of ''money illusion'' implies that an increase in the price level will raise the nominal monetary holdings of households. True or false? Explain.

6. An individual earns $1,000 each month. The cost of going to the bank and making a withdrawal is $2 per trip. The nominal interest rate on bonds is 10 percent.

  a. Use the Baumol–Tobin model to calculate the optimal average money holdings during the month.

  b. How many trips to the bank will the person make each month?

  c. How would your answers to (a) and (b) change if the cost per trip to bank increases to $3.125? Why?

  d. Now consider the case in which the cost per trip to the bank stays at $2 but the interest rate rises to 14.4 percent. What are your answers to (a) and (b) under these conditions?

7. In the Baumol–Tobin model, consider the effects of the following events on the desired real money balances of households:

    a. Real income rises by 5 percent.

    b. Interest rates go down by 10 percent.

    c. The interest rate and real income rise by 10 percent. Analyze also what happens to the proportion of monetary balances to real income.

8. What would happen to desired real monetary holdings of households if the real interest rate rises but the nominal interest rate does not change?

9. Would you expect the velocity of money to be higher in a country with a stable price level or in a country with high inflation? Why?

10. Which explanation can you give to the "case of the missing money" reported by Goldfeld? Do Goldfeld's findings bear any implication for the doctrine of monetarism?

APPENDIX: 8-1

Combining equations (8.8) and (8.9) leads to

$$P_1C_1 + \frac{P_2C_2}{(1 + i)} = P_1(Q_1 - T_1 - I_1) + \frac{P_2(Q_2 - T_2)}{(1 + i)}$$
$$- \frac{iM1}{(1 + i)}$$

Now, we divide both sides by P_1:

$$C_1 + \frac{P_2C_2}{(1 + i)P_1} = (Q_1 - T_1 - I_1) + \frac{P_2(Q_2 - T_2)}{(1 + i)P_1}$$
$$- \frac{iM1}{(1 + i)P_1}$$

Let us examine this expression closely. The term $P_2C_2/[P_1(1 + i)]$ can be rewritten as $C_2/(1 + r)$, since the real interest rate is given by $(1 + r) = P_1(1 + i)/P_2$. Similarly, the term $P_2(Q_2 - T_2)/(1 + i)P_1$ can be written as $(Q_2 - T_2)/(1 + r)$. Finally, the term $iM1/(1 + i)P_1$ can be rewritten as $i(M1/P_2)/(1 + r)$. With this, equation (8.10) immediately follows.

APPENDIX: 8-2

An important technical point can be made about equation (8.17). If the logarithm of real money balances is regressed on the *logarithms* of the other variables, the coefficients a_1, a_2, and a_3 can be directly interpreted as the elasticities of money demand with respect to the different right-hand-side variables, and these elasticities are constrained to be constant throughout the sample period. If the level of M/P is regressed on the *levels* of the other variables, the coefficients do not directly represent the elasticities, and the implied elasticities would not be the same throughout the estimation period.

In fact, when an equation is specified in *levels,* the elasticity varies systematically with the value of the variables. Suppose for example that the money demand equation is specified as follows:

$$\left(\frac{M}{P}\right) = b_0 + b_1 Q$$

Then, the income elasticity of the demand for money can be calculated as follows:

$$\frac{[\Delta(M/P)/(M/P)]}{[\Delta Q/Q]} = \frac{[\Delta(M/P)/\Delta Q]}{[(M/P)/Q]} = \frac{b_1}{[(b_0 + b_1 Q)/Q]} = \frac{b_1 Q}{b_0 + b_1 Q}$$

We see that the implied elasticity of money demand with respect to income would not be constant but, instead, would be a function of the level of income. The equation implies that when income is very low (Q is near zero), the elasticity of money demand would be near zero. When Q is very large, the income elasticity would be close to 1.0, since $(b_1 Q)/(b_0 + b_1 Q_1)$ would approximately equal $b_1 Q_1/b_1 Q_1$ (when Q is large we can ignore the effect of b_0). This variability of the elasticity of money demand does not seem to be very accurate empirically, which suggests that the money demand equation should not be specified in linear form.

chapter 9

The Money Supply Process

The way that the money supply is determined in most economies has fundamentally changed during this century. Until recent decades, fiat money was not widely used. Rather, commodities, usually precious metals like gold and silver, were used as money, and paper currency, when it existed, was typically convertible into the designated precious metal at a fixed price. Under such monetary systems, changes in the supply of money were importantly determined, or even mainly determined, by the production of the precious metals. By contrast, under a fiat system, the supply of money is determined mainly by government policy. This is a crucial distinction, as we are about to see.

Until recent decades, then, most important increases in the supply of money had little to do with a preconceived government policy. For example, the discovery of vast reserves of gold and silver in the New World brought about a substantial increase in the amount of these precious metals circulating in Europe. Much of this gold and silver was minted into coins, and the infusion of these new coins into the money supply, in turn, provoked a significant increase in prices in the second half of the sixteenth century. A similar phenomenon occurred in connection with the gold discoveries in California and Australia during the late 1840s, and again during the late 1890s with the increased production of gold in Alaska, Canada, and South Africa, partly due to new discoveries and partly due to better extraction techniques.[1]

9-1 THE MONEY SUPPLY AND THE CENTRAL BANK: AN OVERVIEW

Under a fiat regime, government policy is the basic, but not the only, determinant of the money supply. Most countries have an official institution, typically the *central bank*, that has the legal authority to issue

---

[1] Richard Cooper of Harvard University has presented an interesting survey of the gold standard in "The Gold Standard: Historical Facts and Future Perspectives," *Brookings Papers on Economic Activity*, No. 1: 1982.

money. In the United States, the central bank is the Federal Reserve Board; in the United Kingdom, the Bank of England; in West Germany, the Deutsche Bundesbank; and in Japan, the Bank of Japan. In modern times, the central bank generally has authority and sole power to issue currency. There are, however, several countries that do not have central banks, or if they do, these banks lack the authority to issue a national currency. The central banks in Liberia and Panama, for example, have lacked the authority to issue money. In those two countries, the U.S. dollar circulates as the legal tender and medium of exchange. In many countries in French-speaking West Africa,[2] the local currency is linked to the French franc, and the national authorities have little control over the domestic money supply.

As a general rule, the central bank of each country can determine the supply of *high-powered money (Mh)*, that is, the currency that circulates in the economy, together with the reserves held by banks at the central bank. Take, for example, a U.S. dollar. You will notice that it is a "Federal Reserve Note," as it says in the top center of the bill (it is also, as we noted in the last chapter, "legal tender for all debts, public and private"). Because the central bank is the only authority that can issue a Federal Reserve note, it determines the supply of such notes in the economy (which are either held as currency by the public or as bank reserves). Remember, though, that high-powered money is only one category of money and is not even one that measures the nonbank public's money holdings (since *Mh* includes bank reserves). There are several broader categories—M1, M2, M3, and so on. In general, the amounts of these higher Ms in circulation are determined by a combination of how much high-powered money the central bank issues, regulations governing the banking system (usually determined by the central bank), and the financial instruments people choose for their investment portfolios. The way this interaction works is one focus of this chapter.

The fundamental way in which the central bank changes the amount of high-powered money in the economy is through its purchases of assets—Treasury bills, for example—from the public and its sales of assets to the public. Say that the public has previously purchased short-term bills directly from the Treasury. At a later date, the central bank makes a purchase of these bills, paying the private sector with high-powered money, receiving the Treasury bills formerly held by the public. This change is reflected on the balance sheet of the central bank, as a rise in central bank holdings of assets and a rise in high-powered money issued by the central bank, which is counted as a central bank liability. To understand this better, let us examine the balance sheet of the U.S. Federal Reserve, that is, its assets and liabilities, as of December 1990 (Table 9-1).

By far the most important kind of asset that the Fed holds is *securities of the U.S. Treasury*. We shall describe how the Fed acquires these bonds through so-called "open market" operations in which the Fed purchases the bonds from the public rather than directly from the Treasury (the term "open market" is used to signify that the central bank purchase takes place in the public market for bonds, rather than in a private trade). Another major class of Fed assets is its *foreign-exchange reserves*, which are generally

---

[2] Including Cameroon, the Ivory Coast, Madagascar, Mali, Mauritania, and Senegal.

TABLE   9-1

THE BALANCE SHEET OF THE U.S. FEDERAL RESERVE, DECEMBER 1990
(US$ MILLIONS)

Assets		Liabilities	
Gold reserves (GR)	$ 11,058	Federal Reserve notes	$267,000
Foreign exchange (FE)	32,633	Deposits of financial institutions (DF)	38,658
Loans to financial institutions (LF)	190	Deposits of the U.S. Treasury (DT)	8,960
U.S. Treasury securities (TS)	252,103	Other liabilities (OL)	7,504
Other assets (OA)	31,589	Total liabilities (TL)	322,727
Total assets (TA)	$327,573	Net worth (NW)	4,846
		Total liabilities and net worth (TL + NW)	$327,573

Source: Federal Reserve Bulletin, *March 1991.*

short-term liabilities of foreign governments. These foreign-exchange reserves are held not only as a store of value for the Fed but also as a means to intervene in the foreign-exchange markets in order to stabilize the value of the dollar.

The Fed also makes loans to private financial institutions (banks, savings and loan associations) through what is known as its discount window, a process that we analyze later on in greater detail. These *loans to financial companies* constitute an asset for the Fed. Notice that the Fed does not make direct loans to private nonfinancial institutions like General Motors or IBM. This limitation does not exist in every country, however. The central banks in many developing economies grant loans directly to private firms in priority sectors, often agriculture. In these situations, the central bank plays not only the role of monetary authority, but also the role of commercial bank.

Among the assets of the Fed we also find *gold reserves,* which are not valued at their market price, but rather at $42 per ounce, the price of gold in 1973 when the United States severed the last links of the money supply to gold. Occasionally, the Fed buys and sells gold in the open market, but the ups and downs of the Fed's holdings in gold now have little to do with changes in the money supply. This was not the case when the United States was under the gold standard.

On the other side of the balance sheet, the *outstanding stock of federal reserve notes* held by the public is the most important liability of the Fed. But in what sense is this a liability, that is, something that the Fed owes? Under the gold standard, agents had the legal right to convert money into gold at the Fed at a fixed price. This made the *monetary base* (another term for high-powered money) a clear liability of the Fed, in the sense that the Fed had to supply gold in return for high-powered money to anybody that demanded gold. Under the current setup, there is no automatic right to convert high-powered money into anything else, so that the money is a liability of the Fed mainly in an accounting sense.[3] We shall see later that under a fiat money system with fixed exchange rates the central bank does commit itself to convert domestic money into foreign currency at a fixed price. Under these conditions, high-powered money becomes a liability on the Fed's foreign-exchange holdings. However, under flexible exchange rates, like in the United States during the 1980s, this liability does not exist.

Other liabilities of the Fed include the *deposits it holds from private financial institutions*. By law, a proportion of commercial bank deposits have to be held as reserves at the Fed. This institution also keeps a special account for *deposits of the U.S. Treasury*, and this is another of its obligations. As usual, the total value of assets has to coincide with the value of liabilities, honoring the accounting principle of double-entry bookkeeping.

With this overview complete, we now turn to an expanded look at the operations of the central bank and their links with the private banking sector, the general public, the government budget, and the overall economy.

9-2 CENTRAL BANK OPERATIONS AND THE MONETARY BASE

Many theoretical studies in economics talk about a "helicopter" drop of money as the way to increase the money supply.[4] Yet, oddly enough, the central bank has never used this method to inject money into the economy. The three types of operations more commonly used by the monetary authority to change the stock of high-powered money are these: open market operations, rediscount operations, and foreign-exchange operations.

Open Market Operations

The transactions of central banks when they purchase and sell bonds in the open market are known, not surprisingly, as *open market operations*. A *purchase* of financial instruments by the central bank, in its role as monetary authority, results in an *increase* in the supply of high-powered money held by the public. The reason this happens should be clear: the bank buys the assets with money, which is then put into circulation. Conversely, a *sale* of securities by the bank brings about a *decline* in the monetary base.

Let us see how the Fed accounts for an open market purchase of $500 million in Treasury bills, as shown in Table 9-2 (remember that the Treasury bills were probably sold at some time in the past directly by the Treasury to the general public). We suppose that the private sector, more specifically households, originally holds these assets. After the transaction takes place,

---

[3] A famous anecdote tells that in 1961 Senator Paul Douglas (of the Cobb—Douglas function), then chairman of the Joint Economic Committee, met with Douglas Dillon, the U.S. secretary of the treasury. Senator Douglas then handed Secretary Dillon a $20 bill, urging him to honor his liability. To the surprise of many in the room, Douglas Dillon did not hesitate to take the $20 bill and exchanged it for two $10 bills!

[4] The origin of the "helicopter drop" is attributed to Milton Friedman. Since then, it has become one of the most popular phrases economics professors use to describe an infusion of money into the economy.

TABLE 9-2

AN OPEN MARKET SECURITY PURCHASE OF $500 MILLION BY THE FED

Federal Reserve Bank

Assets		Liabilities	
Gold reserves + foreign exchange		Federal reserve notes	+500
Loans to financial institutions		Deposits of financial institutions	
U.S. Treasury securities	+500	Deposits of the U.S. Treasury	
Other assets		Other liabilities	
		Net worth	
Total assets	+500	Total liabilities + net worth	+500

Households

Assets		Liabilities	
Deposits in banking systems		Loans from banking systems	
Currency	+500		
U.S. Treasury securities	−500		
Other assets		Other liabilities	
Total assets		Total liabilities	

the Fed has $500 million more in assets in the form of T-bills, and at the same time, $500 million more in liabilities of high-powered money that the public now holds. The private sector sees the mirror-image change in its balance sheet: a decrease in household claims on the Treasury and an increase in claims on the central bank in the form of $500 million of high-powered money. Note well, however, that neither the Fed nor the private sector experiences any *direct* change in net wealth (assets minus liabilities) as a result of this transaction (although there may be some indirect effects due to a change in the price level or in long-term bond prices).

In reality, the Fed pays for its purchases with a check rather than with cash. This means that the accounting will be slightly different, because we now have to bring in the banking system. When households receive a check from the Fed, they deposit that check in their banks, and that changes the asset side for households in Table 9-2. Their deposits go up by $500 million and their currency remains unchanged. The banking system, after cashing the Fed's check, finds itself with $500 million more in reserves. (As we will see later, the banks normally choose to lend out a substantial part of the additional deposits received.)

Open market operations are the most important tool used by the Fed to affect the stock of high-powered money in the economy. One reason for this is that the Fed can predict exactly what effect these operations have on the monetary base. If the Fed wants to increase high-powered money by, say, $200 million, it only needs to instruct its brokers to purchase Treasury bonds for that amount, not more or less. With other types of Fed operations, such as a cut in the discount rate of interest (which we take up in the next section), it is not so easy to predict the exact effect of a policy change on the monetary base.

In some countries, there is insufficient private trading in government securities to make open market operations possible. The market for government debt tends to be thin in many developing countries, as it is in economies with high and unpredictable inflation and in countries where people do not trust in the government's ability to repay its debts. In the last case, the public may simply be unwilling to hold public-sector debt, or it may require a very high interest-rate premium to compensate for the risk.

In the United States and most other developed countries, by contrast, government bonds offer a lower return than private-sector bonds because government obligations are considered to be the safer assets. The market for government debt securities is thus very active, with enormous daily turnover. The governments of many industrialized countries are considered such safe credit risks, and their economies so stable, that public bonds are attractive not only to domestic residents but to foreign residents as well. Table 9-4 shows the composition of ownership of U.S. public bonds for the period 1976–1990.

It is noteworthy that foreigners hold a significant amount of U.S. public debt. Indeed, as of September 1990, external agents held $405 billion worth of U.S. public bonds. This represents almost 20 percent of the total outstanding government debt of $2.2 trillion. The rest is held by domestic U.S. agents: commercial banks, insurance companies, corporations, money market funds, state and local governments, and—most significantly—individual households.

Box 9-1
Open Market Operations, Bond Prices, and Interest Rates

A *bond* is a financial instrument that promises to pay a given amount per period (let us say per year), for a specified amount of time. Take the case of a very-long-term instrument that pays one dollar per year indefinitely, starting next period. Bonds of these type are called *perpetuities*, or *consols*. What is the price (P_b) of this bond? The answer is the *present value* of the future interest payments, a concept that we studied in Chapter 2:

$$P_b = \frac{1}{(1 + i)} + \frac{1}{(1 + i)^2} + \frac{1}{(1 + i)^3} + \cdots$$

The infinite sum of the foregoing terms is a *geometric progression*,[5] a long mathematical expression that is simply equal to

$$P_b = \left(\frac{1}{i}\right)$$

This leads us to a very important conclusion: the price of the bond is *inversely* related to the interest rate i. Think for a moment about what this means. Suppose that the Treasury or finance ministry of a country is trying to sell a perpetuity that pays $10 per year. If the market interest rate is 10 percent, the value of the bond will be $100. Why? Because $100 deposited forever at 10 percent interest will provide the same stream of payments as the bond. But what happens if the market interest rate doubles to 20 percent? The same bond paying a fixed coupon of $10 per year will fall in value by half to $50, just as $50 deposited at 20 percent will earn $10 per year. (Using the same reasoning, you can determine the effect of an interest-rate drop to 5 percent on the bond's price.)

Consider now a *short-term* bond that pays $110 next year ($10 in interest and $100 in principal), and then is extinguished. What is the price, $P_{b'}$, of this financial instrument? It is simply

$$P_{b'} = \frac{\$110}{(1 + i)}$$

If the interest rate is 10 percent, $P_{b'}$ is $100. Now, if the market interest rate doubles to 20 percent, $P_{b'}$ falls to $91.70; conversely, if the interest rate halves to 5 percent, $P_{b'}$ rises to $104.80.

The fundamental conclusion of this analysis is that short- and long-term bond prices are inversely related to the market interest rate. Long-term bonds are much more sensitive to interest-rate changes than short-term bonds, however. The examples we have just looked at clearly made this point. When the interest rate was 10 percent, both bonds were worth

---

[5] A simple form of geometric progression is $X(1 + g + g^2 + g^3 + \cdots)$. If one knows the ratio between each two consecutive terms, g in this case, there is a formula to calculate the exact value of the sum. For this example, $X(1 + g + g^2 + g^3 + \cdots) = X[1/(1 - g)]$. In the case in the text, $X = \$1/(1 + i)$ and $g = \$1/(1 + i)$, so that the sum is simply ($\$1/i$).

$100. But when *i* doubled to 20 percent, the price of the perpetuity halved, while that of the short-term bond dropped by only 8 percent. By the same token, when *i* was cut in half, the price of the long-term bond doubled while the price of the short-term bond increased by less than 5 percent.

Table 9-3 presents the prices for bonds of different maturities (1 year, 10 years, and a perpetuity—that is, a note with no finite maturity) for three different interest rates (5 percent, 10 percent, and 20 percent). The perpetuity pays $10 per period indefinitely; the other bonds pay $10 per period and $110 at maturity. Note how the 10-year bond is less sensitive to interest-rate fluctuations than the perpetuity but considerably more sensitive than the 1-year bond.

When the Fed makes an open market purchase of government debt, this amounts to an increase in demand for public bonds, and increased demand puts pressure on the price of these instruments. This will tend to increase the price of local bonds. As we have seen, an increase in price is the same as a reduction of the interest rate. Conversely, if the Treasury sells public bonds, the increased supply of these bonds will put downward pressure on their price, thereby provoking an increase in domestic interest rates. It may well happen, however, that after this initial change in prices, other forces in the economy—such as an inflow or outflow of internationally mobile capital—reverses part or all of the price change.

TABLE   9-3

PRICES FOR BONDS OF VARYING
MATURITIES AT DIFFERENT
INTEREST RATES (US$)

Maturity	Interest Rate		
	5	10	20
1 year	104.8	100.0	91.7
10 years	135.5	100.0	59.7
Perpetuity	200.0	100.0	50.0

The Discount Window

Another way that the central bank can affect the money supply is by lending money to the private sector. In some countries, the central bank makes loans directly to nonfinancial enterprises as well as to private banks. In the United States, the Fed does not make loans to nonfinancial firms, but it does lend to private banks through the so-called *discount window*. The interest rate at which the Fed is willing to lend money to commercial banks is known as the *discount rate*.

Private banks make use of this credit option for two different purposes: (1) to adjust the cash reserves they hold in case their reserves fall short of their desired level, or of the level required by Fed regulations (we say more about reserve requirements later), and (2) to obtain funds that the bank can

TABLE 9-4

THE COMPOSITION OF OWNERSHIP OF U.S. PUBLIC DEBT SECURITIES, 1976–1990*
(PAR VALUES, BILLIONS OF CURRENT DOLLARS)

	Total	Commercial Banks	Indi- viduals	Insurance Companies	Money Market Funds	Corpo- rations	State and Local Government	Foreign Investors	Other Investors
1976	409.5	103.5	101.6	16.2	1.1	23.5	40.9	78.1	44.6
1977	461.3	98.9	107.8	19.9	0.9	18.2	58.1	109.6	47.9
1978	508.6	95.0	114.0	20.0	1.5	17.3	76.1	133.1	51.6
1979	540.5	88.1	118.0	21.4	5.6	17.0	81.7	119.0	89.7
1980	616.4	112.1	117.1	24.0	3.5	19.3	87.9	129.7	122.8
1981	694.5	111.4	110.8	29.0	21.5	17.9	96.8	136.6	170.5
1982	848.4	131.4	116.5	44.1	42.6	24.5	115.0	149.5	224.8
1983	1,022.6	188.8	133.4	65.3	22.8	39.7	149.0	166.3	257.3
1984	1,212.5	186.0	143.8	64.5	25.9	50.1	173.0	192.9	376.3
1985	1,417.2	198.2	154.8	78.5	25.1	59.0	226.7	224.8	450.1
1986	1,602.0	203.5	162.7	105.6	28.6	68.8	262.8	263.4	506.6
1987	1,731.4	201.5	172.4	104.9	14.6	84.6	284.6	299.7	569.1
1988	1,858.5	193.8	190.4	107.3	11.8	86.0	313.6	362.2	593.4
1989	2,015.8	174.8	216.5	130.1	14.9	93.4	338.7	392.9	654.5
1990†	2,207.3	188.0	233.5	138.9	33.6	99.1	344.0	404.8	760.4

* Data as of December of each year.
† Refers to September of that year.
Source: Economic Report of the President, 1991, *Table B-86.*

loan to customers if market conditions make it attractive to do so. In either case, the banks compare the conditions of the loan from the discount window with the conditions for obtaining funds from alternative sources. A crucial element, but not the only element, in the bank's decision is the value of the discount rate relative to other market rates. For example, if a bank is borrowing to increase its cash reserves, it will compare the discount rate with the *federal funds rate* (the rate that other banks charge for short-term, interbank loans), and it will take the loan from the least expensive source.

A different situation exists when a commercial bank sees an opportunity to expand its loan portfolio by obtaining funds from the discount window. For a project like this to be profitable, the discount rate must be smaller than the interest rate commercial banks charge their customers. This is normally the case, but even so, the bank may still not use the discount window. Why not? Because there are transactions costs that must be covered by the spread between the borrowing and lending rate, and because the lending rate must be high enough to compensate for the risk of default. Another important consideration is that the Fed, and central banks in general, do not grant all the loans that are requested at the going discount rate. Normally, the Fed imposes formal and informal quantitative restrictions on bank borrowing; that is, it limits the amount of funds that a private bank can borrow at the discount window.

Discount operations lead to changes in the supply of high-powered money. A loan through the discount window produces an increase in the money base by the amount of the loan. Suppose, for example, that the private banking system borrows $150 million from the Fed through the discount window. In Table 9-5, we show the balance sheets of the Federal Reserve and the private banking system after this operation. The commercial banks borrowed from the Fed because they saw profitable loan opportunities. Thus, the assets of the Fed increased by $150 million, on account of the higher value of loans to the financial sector. The supply of high-powered money, a liability of the Fed, is increased by the same amount as the funds enter the commercial banks.

The situation of the private banking system appears on the right side of Table 9-5. Its assets have gone up by $150 million because it has increased its loans to the public with the credit obtained from the Fed. At the same time, its liabilities have increased by a similar amount, reflecting its increased obligation to the Fed.[6]

Central banks have a powerful tool that they can use to influence the supply of high-powered money and the amount of credit available for the private sector: they can raise and lower the discount rate. A lowering of this rate makes it more attractive for the banks to borrow at the discount window, and when they borrow more, this increases the monetary base and the availability of credit in the economy. A relaxation of quantitative constraints on central bank lending to commercial banks, if such restrictions matter, also expands the money base and credit availability. Conversely, an increase in the discount rate makes it less attractive for the private financial sector to

---

[6] In fact, the table is oversimplified, because it ignores the "multiplication" of money through the banking system, a topic we take up in detail in Section 9-3.

TABLE 9-5

COMMERCIAL BANK BORROWING THROUGH THE DISCOUNT WINDOW

Federal Reserve Bank

Assets		Liabilities	
Gold reserves + foreign exchange		Federal reserve notes	+150
Loans to financial institutions	+150	Deposits of financial institutions	
U.S. Treasury securities:		Deposits of the U.S. Treasury	
Other assets		Other liabilities	
		Net worth	
Total assets	+150	Total liabilities + net worth	+150

Private Banking System

Assets		Liabilities	
Gold + foreign exchange		Deposits from the public	
Currency		Loans from the Fed	+150
Loans to the public		Other liabilities	
Deposits at the Fed	+150		
Other assets			
Total assets	+150	Total liabilities	+150

borrow from the central bank. A higher discount rate might even encourage a prepayment of old debts.

Some analysts have argued that the discount window should be used to implement a very contractionary policy. If the discount rate were placed above the market rate, they say, this would automatically penalize banks that need to borrow because their cash reserves have fallen below the required level, and thus a higher discount rate would encourage bank discipline. So far, most countries, the United States among them, have not taken this suggestion. The discount rate is normally kept below the market rate, and it adjusts with a lag to fluctuations in that rate.

The central bank can tell what direction the effects of discount rate changes will take, and it may even obtain an estimate of its magnitude. However, it usually cannot know in advance what the exact effect of its discount rate policy will be on the supply of high-powered money. To enhance its control over the monetary base, the central bank sometimes uses open market policy to offset the monetary effects of its operations through the discount window. Suppose, for example, that banks suddenly increase their borrowing at the discount window by $600 million. The monetary authority—the central bank—might not want to raise the discount rate or to place drastic limits on bank borrowing. At the same time, the Fed might be worried by the increase in high-powered money brought about by the larger volume of discount operations. The Fed can undo, or *sterilize,* the effects of the discount lending by selling $600 million in bonds to the public (and thus calling in $600 million in high-powered money). The use of an open market operation to offset the monetary effects of other policies is a standard maneuver known as a *sterilization* operation.

Rediscounting the Paper of Nonfinancial Firms

In some countries, but not in the United States, the central bank purchases commercial paper (short-term debt) or bonds of private firms. This operation is usually referred to as *rediscounting,* and its monetary effects are similar to those of an open market operation.

Foreign-Exchange Operations

The central bank also influences the money supply when it buys or sells assets denominated in foreign currencies. In the simplest case, the central bank buys or sells foreign money in exchange for domestic money. In other cases, the central bank buys or sells an interest-bearing asset in a foreign currency, typically a Treasury bill of a foreign government. As with open market operations, these transactions have direct effects on the amount of high-powered money held by the public.[7]

In the next chapter, we analyze the workings of a fixed versus floating exchange-rate system. Suffice it here to note that the essence of a fixed exchange-rate system is the commitment of the central bank to buying and selling foreign money, or foreign exchange, at a given price in terms of the domestic money. Take, for example, a Latin American country that maintains a fixed exchange rate of 10 *pesos* per dollar. Under the fixed-rate

---

[7] Foreign-exchange operations do not affect the monetary base abroad, however.

system, the central bank would be obligated to sell dollars to the public at a price of 10 pesos per dollar or to purchase dollars from the public using pesos at the same 10:1 ratio.

A standard kind of foreign-exchange transaction in this same Latin American country might go like this. An exporter earns $1 million, which it remits to the central bank in order to get local currency. With the exchange rate at 10 pesos per dollar, the supply of high-powered money increases by 10 million pesos. On the other hand, an importer has to buy foreign exchange from the central bank to make its purchases abroad. If the value of the transaction is again U.S. $1 million, this operation will lead to a decline in the local monetary base of 10 million pesos. If over a given year the central bank is a net purchaser of foreign exchange, then these operations will lead to a net increase in high-powered money. Conversely, if the monetary authority ends up as a net seller of foreign exchange, the monetary base will decline as a result of these operations.[8]

The situation is very different in countries that have a floating exchange-rate regime. Under a *clean float,* the central bank does not intervene at all in the foreign-exchange market. An exporter who earns $1 million may sell those dollars directly to an importer (usually through the banking system) or keep them in order to invest in dollar-denominated assets. Similarly, an importer that wants to purchase foreign exchange must bid for the foreign exchange in the open market. Thus, foreign-exchange transactions have no effects on high-powered money because the monetary authority is simply a bystander in the market. Note that inasmuch as the central bank does not stabilize the price of foreign exchange by buying and selling pesos for dollars at a fixed price, the *exchange rate fluctuates over time.*

In the real world, even with floating currencies, central banks often do become actively engaged in foreign-exchange operations to smooth fluctuations in the exchange rate. When this happens, the exchange-rate system is then called a *dirty float,* to distinguish it from a clean float in which the central bank completely abstains from foreign-exchange operations. Take the case of the United States in 1988. After the dollar depreciated for almost three years—that is, the price of yen, Deutsche marks, francs, and other currencies rose in terms of dollars—it started to climb again. When this happened, the Fed repeatedly intervened in the market by buying foreign currency and selling dollars because it did not want the dollar to appreciate too much.

The accounting of a Fed purchase of $100 million worth of Japanese yen appears in Table 9-6. On the asset side, foreign exchange held by the Fed increases by $100 million, while high-powered money goes up by the same $100 million on the liabilities side. Thus, foreign-exchange operations of the central bank have the same effect on the monetary base under fixed and floating rates. The main difference is that in a clean float the monetary authority simply does not engage in these transactions. In practice, however, almost all floating exchange-rate regimes are dirty floats, with the central banks participating actively in the market.

---

[8] The net final change in the monetary base during a given period reflects the impact of other central bank operations (open market operations and loans at the discount window) as well.

TABLE   9-6

A PURCHASE OF FOREIGN EXCHANGE BY THE U.S. FEDERAL RESERVE

Assets		Liabilities	
Gold reserves		Federal reserve notes	+100
Foreign exchange	+100	Deposits of financial institutions	
Loans to financial institutions		Deposits of the U.S. Treasury	
U.S. Treasury securities		Other liabilities	
Other assets		Net worth	
Total assets	+100	Total liabilities + net worth	+100

A Fundamental Equation for Changes in the Money Stock

Now we can pull together all of our analysis in this section and derive an equation for changes in the stock of high-powered money (or, in the alternative phrase, the monetary base). Let D_c^g be the stock of government bonds held by the central bank; B_c^*, the stock of foreign reserves; and L_c, the stock of loans made to the banks through the discount window. In addition, E is the exchange rate, measured in units of domestic currency per unit of foreign currency, so that $E(B_c^*)$ equals the domestic currency value of the foreign reserves. Then, we can write the change in the monetary base as

$$(Mh - Mh_{-1}) = (D_c^g - D_{c-1}^g) + E(B_c^* - B_{c-1}^*)$$
$$+ (L_c - L_{c-1}) \qquad \textbf{(9.1)}$$

In words, any change in the stock of high-powered money is an effect of one or more causes: an increase (or decline) of government debt held by the central bank, a rise (or drop) in the stock of international reserves, and a change in the amount of net credit granted to the commercial banks through the discount window. Each of these events, in turn, arises out of one of the central bank's operations that we have analyzed in this section.

Notice, however, one important detail. Equation (9.1) includes a change in international reserves in the right-hand side. With free capital mobility, the change in reserves corresponds to the net result of the balance of payments, including both the current and private capital accounts. But if capital controls block the international movement of private funds (as we discussed in Chapter 6), the private capital account is closed and the change in reserves will equal the trade balance. In this case, equation (9.1) can be rewritten as

$$Mh - Mh_{-1} = (D_c^g - D_{c-1}^g) + E(TB) + (L_c - L_{c-1}) \qquad \textbf{(9.1')}$$

Thus, the accumulation (or decumulation) of foreign reserves under capital controls corresponds to the trade balance surplus (or deficit). A trade surplus increases high-powered money, while a trade deficit reduces it. The mechanics of this are simple enough. When exporters remit their foreign-exchange earnings to the central bank and sell them for domestic currency, the money supply goes up. When importers use domestic currency to buy foreign exchange from the central bank in order to purchase their imports, however, the domestic money supply goes down. If exports exceed imports, the net effect on the money supply is positive. If exports fall short of imports, then the net effect on the money supply is negative.

9-3 THE MONEY MULTIPLIER AND THE MONEY SUPPLY

So far, we have studied the ways in which central bank policy affects the stock of high-powered money. Now, given the level of Mh, we need to see how M1 is determined. This leads us into the roles of the banking sector and of private agents as determiners of the money supply.

High-powered money is the value of all currency (bills and coins) in circulation (CU) in the economy, as well as bank reserves (R). This relationship is expressed in equation (9.2):

$$Mh = CU + R \qquad\qquad (9.2)$$

In addition to deposits held at the central bank (D_c) the private banks keep some vault cash (VC), which is also counted as part of reserves. Total bank reserves (R), therefore, are given by $R = D_c + VC$.

Now, let us consider a simple balance sheet of a private commercial bank. The bank takes in deposits and gives out loans to the public. Some fraction of the deposits are kept as reserves (R), and that fraction, the reserve-to-deposit ratio, we designate as $r_d = (R/D)$, so that $R = r_d D$. This ratio between reserves and deposits is determined mainly by central bank regulations which stipulate the *required reserves* that banks must maintain as a fraction of their deposit base. In addition to these required reserves, banks might opt to keep additional reserves on hand at the central bank to maintain high liquidity and to avoid falling below the required reserve ratio if there were unexpected fluctuations in their deposit base.

The money supply, now expanded as M1, is the sum of currency in circulation (CU) and demand deposits held in the banking system (D). By this definition, we can describe the money supply as

$$M1 = CU + D \qquad\qquad (9.3)$$

The difference between "high-powered money" and the "money supply" is apparent from equations (9.2) and (9.3). Both include currency, but Mh adds reserves held by banks, while M1 adds the bank deposits of the public.

What, then, is the relationship between the money supply (M1) and the high-powered money (Mh)? And in particular, how can a given stock of high-powered money support a much higher value of M1? In the United States, for example, high-powered money was $309.5 billion in December 1990, while M1 was $825.5 billion. This differential is not just some peculiarity of the U.S. economy. In almost all economies, the stock of M1 exceeds the stock of high-powered money. The explanation for this phenomenon lies in the process of money creation within the banking system, and the public's choices among financial instruments also play an important role. In fact, it is said that commercial banks "multiply" the monetary base, a process that we analyze in detail when we study the money "multiplier" shortly.

To simplify the analysis, we narrow down the ways that private firms and individuals can choose to hold money to two: they can hold currency, or they can hold demand deposits. We indicate the ratio of currency to deposits by c_d ($c_d = CU/D$) and note that this ratio will depend on the preferences expressed by the private sector in choosing between CU and D. At the same time, banks hold a certain fraction of their deposits as reserves, both because of legal requirements and because they want enough liquidity to satisfy their customers' needs. We call this fraction r_d ($r_d = R/D$), the reserves-to-deposit ratio.

In order to obtain an expression for the money multiplier we perform a simple exercise. Let us divide equation (9.3) by (9.2) and then divide the numerator and denominator of the resulting expression by the value of deposits, D, as shown:

$$\frac{M1}{Mh} = \frac{(CU + D)}{(CU + R)} = \frac{(CU/D + D/D)}{(CU/D + R/D)}$$

$$= \frac{(c_d + 1)}{(c_d + r_d)} \tag{9.4}$$

In a slightly different form we can write

$$M1 = \left[\frac{(c_d + 1)}{(c_d + r_d)}\right] Mh = \phi Mh \tag{9.5}$$

where $\phi = (c_d + 1)/(c_d + r_d)$.

Equation (9.5) says that the money supply is some multiple of the stock of high-powered money, with the factor of proportionality given by ϕ, the *money multiplier*. Therefore, to understand the process for determining M1, we have to examine the two components of that process: the determination of high-powered money (Mh) and the determination of the money multiplier (ϕ). We have seen how Mh is determined. Now we need to know about the money multiplier.

The money multiplier depends on two variables: the currency/deposit ratio (c_d) and the reserve/deposit ratio (r_d). Before we go on to analyze each of these variables, it is important to note that ϕ is greater than 1. Since the banks maintain only a fraction of their deposits as reserves, r_d is smaller than 1, so that the numerator in (9.5) is bigger than the denominator.

To see why M1 is larger than high-powered money, let us take a case in which the central bank undertakes a $100 million purchase of bonds in the open market. Suppose that the reserve/deposit ratio of the banking system is equal to 10 percent and that the currency/deposit ratio of the public is equal to 25 percent. Of its proceeds from the initial open market operation, then, the public will keep $20 million in cash, and it will deposit $80 million in the banking system ($c_d = CU/D = 20/80 = 0.25$). In turn, the banks that receive the $80 million will want to keep 10 percent, or $8 million, in bank reserves, and they will lend the remaining $72 million out to borrowers. (They might have to cut the interest rate on loans in order to attract new borrowers for the $72 million, but, after all, it is better to accept lower interest rates on the $72 million than it is to keep it at zero interest rates in reserves.)

Part of the loaned-out $72 million will, in turn, be kept as cash ($14.4 million), and part will return to the banking system as new deposits ($57.6 million). Of these new deposits, the banks will keep 10 percent as reserves, $5.76 million, and re-lend the rest, $51.84 million. This process will continue, apparently indefinitely. In each round, part of the bank's loans are held by the public in cash, and part are redeposited. In turn, the bank holds part of the resulting deposits in reserves, and part is re-lent to the public.

TABLE 9-7

AN OPEN MARKET PURCHASE OF BONDS AND THE OPERATION OF THE MONEY MULTIPLIER

	$\Delta(Mh)$	$\Delta(CU)$	$\Delta(D)$	$\Delta(R)$	$\Delta(Loan)$*	$\Delta(M1)$†
First round	100.0	20.0	80.0	8.0	72.0	100.0
Second round	—	14.4	57.6	5.8	51.8	72.0
Third round	—	10.4	41.4	4.1	37.3	51.8
Fourth round	—	7.5	29.8	3.0	26.8	37.3
Fifth round	—	5.4	21.4	2.1	19.3	26.8
Sixth round	—	3.9	15.4	1.5	13.9	19.3
Seventh round	—	2.8	11.1	1.1	10.0	13.9
Eighth round	—	2.0	8.0	0.8	7.2	10.0
Ninth round	—	1.4	5.8	0.6	5.2	7.2
Tenth round	—	1.0	4.2	0.4	3.6	5.2
Accumulated at tenth round		68.8	274.7			343.5

* $\Delta(Loan) = \Delta(D) - \Delta(R)$
† $\Delta(M1) = \Delta(CU) + \Delta(D)$

In Table 9-7, we show several rounds of this process, which continue until the changes in M1, CU, and D are very small. Although in principle, the process continues as an infinite series of steps, in practice, after a few periods the changes become negligible and the process stops. (Note that in the table, as in the calculations that follow, we are assuming that the money multipliers are constant, that the average propensities to hold CU and D are equal to the marginal propensities, and that the ratio of reserves to deposits is also constant.)

But now we want to find the *total* increase in the money stock M1 brought about by the $100 million increase in high-powered money. Consider the currency, for example. In the first round, the public held $20 million of the payment it received in the original open market operation. Then, after a round of bank lending, it held another $14.4 billion as cash, and so on. Thus, the increase in cash holdings (ΔCU), as shown in the second column of Table 9-7, is given by

$$\Delta CU = \$20 + \$14.4 + \cdots$$

The sum of terms in the right side of ΔCU, which become smaller in every subsequent round, is technically known as a *geometric progression* (the same type of expression as that used to describe the price of a perpetuity, P_b, in Box 9-1). When we calculate the sum of this geometric progression, we find $71.4 million.[9] The increase in demand deposits (ΔD) also yields a

---

[9] Applying the same technique we used in the footnote in Box 9-1 for obtaining the price of the bond, we simply need to express this sum as $X(1 + g + g^2 + g^3 + \cdots) = X[1/(1 - g)]$. The only difficulty is to identify X and g. In the case at hand, $X = \$20$ million, and $g = (1 - r_d)/(1 + c_d) = 0.9/1.25 = 0.72$, so that the sum is 20 million$[1/(1 - 0.72)] = \$71.4286$ million.

geometric progression, which is shown in the third column of Table 9-7:

$$\Delta D = \$80 + \$57.6 + \cdots$$

The sum of these numbers is \$285.7 million.[10] If the total change in M1 (money) is the sum of the changes in CU and D, then, that figure is \$357.1 million.

The money multiplier gives the same answer to this problem, but more quickly. The total increase in the money supply brought about by the \$100 million rise in the monetary base is

$$\Delta\text{M1} = \phi\,\Delta Mh$$
$$= \left[\frac{(0.25 + 1)}{(0.25 + 0.1)}\right] 100$$
$$= \left(\frac{1.25}{0.35}\right) 100 = (3.571)\,100 = \$357.1 \text{ million}$$

Once we find that the money multiplier is 3.571, we see that the rise in the supply of money (M1) out of the \$100 million increase in the stock of high-powered money equals \$357.1 million.

We must look more deeply into the two key factors that determine the money multiplier, the ratio of reserves to deposits (r_d) and the ratio of currency to deposits (c_d).

The Ratio of Reserves to Deposits (r_d)

The reserve/deposit ratio has a crucial influence on the money multiplier, and through the money multiplier, on the money supply. An increase in r_d lowers the multiplier. This can be checked using equation (9.5), but it can also be demonstrated using only intuition. The higher is r_d, the lower is the amount of new loans that the banking system will grant out of an initial deposit. This being the case, the lower is the value of subsequent new deposits that will be created. Think of an extreme case in which 100 percent of deposits are kept as reserves. In this situation, there will be no financial intermediation through the banking system. The money multiplier will be equal to 1, as can be verified from equation (9.5). Thus, the monetary base and the supply of money will be the same. Of course, this is an extreme example. In almost all countries, banks maintain only a fraction of deposits as reserves.

The total amount of reserves that a bank holds has two components. There is a minimum amount of funds that the institution is legally required to hold: we call these funds *required reserves*. In addition, the bank maintains some extra funds known as *excess reserves*. The money multiplier is determined by the *total* amount of reserves. Thus, the reserve/deposit ratio is determined both by the behavior of the banking system and by the legal reserve requirements established by the central bank.

---

[10] In this case, $X = \$80$ million, and g is again equal to 0.9/1.25. Thus, we have the sum equal to \$80 million/0.28 = \$285.7 million.

The central bank sets the amount of required reserves as an instrument of monetary control. As a matter of prudence, required reserves are also established to guarantee that the banks have enough cash on hand to meet the needs of their depositors. In some countries, however, the reserve requirements are targeted mainly to help finance a large government budget deficit. For example, the central bank increases the reserve requirements and allows commercial banks to hold part of their reserves in Treasury bonds. Those reserves would then earn some interest, but generally less than the free-market interest rate. Reserve requirements also vary depending on the type of deposit taken in by the bank; normally, demand deposits have a higher required reserve ratio than do time or savings deposits.[11]

The commercial banks control their own excess reserves. Notice that this is the part of reserves that the bank can readily use to satisfy its customers' needs in case of emergency—a large unexpected withdrawal by the depositors, for instance. When banks consider how much they want to hold in excess reserves, they perform a cost-benefit analysis. On the one hand, holding reserves has an opportunity cost in the interest rate forgone. On the other hand, if excess reserves are kept very low and an unexpected withdrawal of funds occurs, a bank may have to borrow money to cover its cash needs. There are two principal sources for such loans: the discount window, at a cost equal to the discount rate (i_d); and short-term loans from other banks, whose cost in the United States is the federal funds rate (i_f).

The reserve/deposit ratio of the banking system is therefore a function of four main variables: the required reserve ratio (rr_d); the market interest rate (i), which represents the opportunity cost of holding reserves; the discount rate (i_d); and the federal funds rate (i_f). This relationship is expressed in equation form as follows:

$$r_d = f(rr_d, i, i_d, i_f) \tag{9.6}$$

A rise in the market interest rate (i) tends to decrease the overall reserve/deposit ratio by raising the opportunity cost of holding excess reserves. An increase in the discount rate or in the federal funds rate has the opposite effect. Higher i_d and i_f tend to raise the reserve/deposit ratio by making it more costly to borrow in case of insufficient reserves. Finally, a rise in the required reserve ratio will normally produce an upward movement in r_d.

The level of required reserves has varied over time. In the United States, for example, the trend has been toward lower requirements. As of mid 1991, the required level was 12 percent for checking deposits, 3 percent for time deposits of original maturity of less than $1\frac{1}{2}$ years, and 0 for time deposits of higher maturity. Excess reserves have also fallen sharply over time. In the early 1930s, they were around 50 percent of total reserves, while in 1989 they were only 1.6 percent of total reserves. At the beginning of the 1930s, banks had to hold reserves to fend off panic withdrawals by their depositors. With the advent of deposit insurance, the risk of a panic with-

---

[11] In the United States since 1980, reserve requirements apply for all institutions that receive deposits from the public, except money market funds. Before 1980, only commercial banks were legally required to maintain reserves.

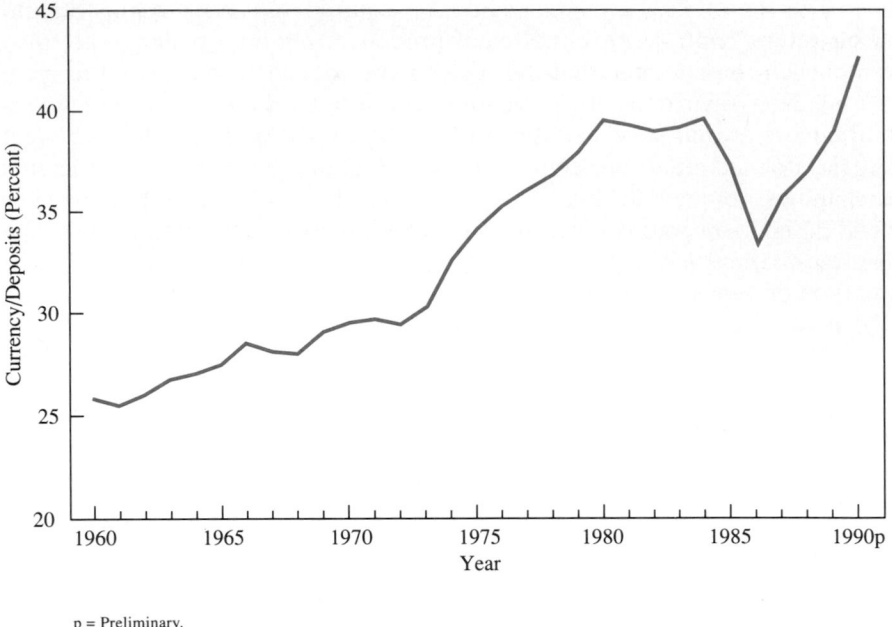

p = Preliminary.

Figure 9-1
The Currency/Deposit Ratio in the United States, 1960–1990

(From Economic Report of the President, 1991, *Tables B-68 and B-69.)*

drawal of funds has subsided.[12] Also, more advanced methods of money management have allowed banks to economize on their excess reserve.

The Ratio of Currency to Deposits

An increase in the currency/deposit ratio (c_d) makes the money multiplier fall, and thus decreases the money supply. This result, which is apparent from equation (9.5), can also be explained intuitively. If c_d rises, the loans granted by commercial banks will produce a lower value of deposits because agents are holding more of their money as currency. And lower deposits diminish the ability of the banking system to create money.

The currency/deposit ratio is influenced by several factors. A rise in the market interest rate will precipitate a decline in the c_d ratio as agents switch out of noninterest-bearing currency and into bank deposits that pay interest. The c_d ratio also responds to banking panics. If people lose confidence in the solvency of the banking system, as they did in the United States in the early 1930s, they will try to switch out of deposits and into cash, with the effect of raising the c_d ratio and ultimately reducing the overall money stock. The possibility of a banking panic has fallen in the United States, partly because of deposit insurance, but bank panics still do occur occasion-

---

[12] In the United States, all deposits of $100,000 or less are insured by the Federal Deposit Insurance Corporation (FDIC). In practice, even deposits of more than $100,000 have also been insured, as was the case in the failures of the Continental Illinois Bank, the Bank of New England, and many others.

ally in the developing countries. The c_d ratio also shows a strong seasonality. During the Christmas period, for example, people normally hold more currency in order to do their Christmas shopping.

Figure 9-1 shows the evolution of the currency/deposit ratio in the United States for the period 1960–1990. Notice that from the early 1960s to the late 1970s, and since 1986, it moved consistently upward, a trend that perhaps suggests a rise in underground activities or an increasing use of the U.S. dollar as a store of value and medium of exchange in foreign countries that have unstable local currencies.

The Central Bank's Control Over the Money Supply

The central bank can influence the money supply in important ways, but it cannot fully control it. As we have seen, the central bank has reasonably effective control over the stock of high-powered money through its use of open market operations. Using these, it can sterilize changes in Mh that come from other sources, such as borrowing from the discount window or foreign-exchange operations.[13] The monetary authority has less control of the multiplier than it does of the monetary base. The central bank does determine reserve requirements and the discount rate, both of which influence the level of reserves that banks actually hold.[14] It cannot directly determine the reserve/deposit ratio, however, and it has even less control over the ratio of currency to deposits that the public holds.

In the United States there has been a long debate over which monetary variable the Federal Reserve should attempt to control. For a long time, the Fed centered its attention on influencing the market interest rate and directed monetary policy to that purpose. Its primary tool was its open market operations. If the Fed thought the interest rate was too high, it would purchase bonds in the market and thereby increase the money supply until the interest rate came down within the target range. If it thought the interest rate too low, the Fed would sell bonds. This targeting policy came under heavy attack from monetarist economists, led by Milton Friedman. The monetarists argued that the Fed tried normally to push interest rates too low, leading to inflationary increases in the money supply. Thus, they said, the Fed should set clear targets in terms of the monetary aggregates (such as the growth of M1), which they thought were more likely to be targeted in a noninflationary manner.

In 1979, when inflation had reached very high levels by U.S. standards, the Fed changed its policy and switched its target from interest rates to the rate of monetary growth. (This change coincided with the appointment of Paul Volcker as the chairman of the Federal Reserve Board.) At the beginning of each year, the Board sets a maximum rate of increase in the monetary aggregates. The fact that these maximum rates have been increased during the year on several occasions since 1979, however, indicates that this policy has proved to be rather flexible.

---

[13] We should note, however, that sterilization of the monetary effects of foreign-exchange operations has its limits. We shall see in later chapters that monetary control becomes very difficult, if not impossible, under fixed exchange rates and open capital markets.

[14] Notice that the discount rate is the only variable directly controlled by the central bank that affects *both* the monetary base and the money multiplier.

Different countries take different approaches to monetary control. In the United Kingdom, for example, the Bank of England aims to control a variant of M3, but it does so by targeting interest rates rather than high-powered money. Thus, if sterling M3 is growing too fast, the Bank of England raises the interest rate by undertaking an open market sale of bonds; if M3 is growing too slowly, it lowers interest rates through an open market purchase. It might seem strange that the government would target the money supply, but then rely on interest rates rather than its controls over the monetary base. The reason is that the Bank of England believes that the money multiplier linking high-powered money to sterling M3 is too volatile and unpredictable to serve as a reliable basis for control.

The question of which targets the monetary authority should aim to control is a difficult one. The ultimate interest of policy is to promote economic stability and growth under low inflation. To this end, interest rates and monetary aggregates are only intermediate targets, which policymakers seek to control in order to influence their final targets, variables such as output, employment, and inflation. Although some have urged the monetary authority to concentrate on controlling these final targets, that is a formidable task. While output, employment, and inflation are what ultimately matter, the central bank has a good chance of controlling only intermediate targets. For example, it has been suggested that the monetary authority concentrate on achieving a desired growth rate of nominal GDP. Even if this mission is already very difficult, what matters is real GNP rather than nominal GDP, and real GNP is much harder to manage.

We return to the specific question of appropriate monetary policy instruments, and to the issue of targets and instruments later, especially in Chapter 19.

9-4 THE MONEY SUPPLY AND THE GOVERNMENT BUDGET CONSTRAINT

When the government budget is in deficit, the Treasury raises money to pay the government's bills by issuing bonds. Who are the potential buyers of the Treasury's bonds? In essence, bond buyers fall into four categories: foreigners (either public or private sector), domestic households and firms, the national private banking system, and the country's central bank.[15] In many economies, the central bank is the most important purchaser of Treasury bonds and is also the most *automatic* lender. Sometimes the central bank has no choice and is forced by the government (the executive) to buy Treasury bonds directly from the Treasury. Other times, the central bank has discretion over its purchases of Treasury notes and may buy the bonds not directly from the Treasury but in the course of open market operations. The purchase of public debt by the central bank is generally termed the *monetization of the budget deficit*.

As we shall see, the central bank purchase of Treasury bonds essentially allows the government to buy goods and services *simply by printing money*. The debt that the Treasury owes to the central bank does not really

---

[15] Notice that this classification corresponds very closely to the situation of the United States presented in Table 9-4.

have to be repaid: it represents only a *claim* by one part of the government on another part. Thus, the final effect when the central bank purchases debt is that the government gets to run a budget deficit that it pays for by increasing the money supply held by the public. Since it is inexpensive to print money, the government can get goods and services at little direct cost. There is a catch, however. A monetization of the budget deficit generally leads to inflation, a point we stress in great detail in Chapter 11. In essence, then, the government finances its purchases of goods and services by an inflation tax.

Let us now analyze this idea of the monetization of the deficit more formally. The budget constraint of the government can be expressed as follows:

$$D^g - D^g_{-1} = P(G + I^g - T) + iD^g_{-1} \qquad \textbf{(9.7)}$$

The first term of the left-hand side $(D^g - D^g_{-1})$ is the change in government debt between the current and the previous period. This is also the amount of Treasury bonds that must be sold to cover the excess of expenditures over revenues in the right-hand side of the equation. Equation (9.7) is almost the same as equation (7.2), with some small changes.[16] For one thing, we now include the price level and distinguish between variables defined in nominal terms (D) and real terms (G, I, T). For another, we apply the nominal interest rate rather than the real rate to the government debt. (In the model in Chapter 7, we did not have money so a distinction between the real and the nominal interest rates was unnecessary.)

Remember that Treasury bonds can be held by the public, both domestic and foreign, and by the central bank. Thus, a rise in government debt has two components: an increase in the Treasury's debt to the public $(D^g_p - D^g_{p-1})$ and a rise in the stock of debt owed to the central bank $(D^g_c - D^g_{c-1})$. Thus, the change in the debt held by the central bank is equal to the overall change in debt minus the change in debt held by the public:

$$D^g_c - D^g_{c-1} = (D^g - D^g_{-1}) - (D^g_p - D^g_{p-1}) \qquad \textbf{(9.8)}$$

We can now combine equation (9.8) with equation (9.1), which describes the change in high-powered money. Ignoring the discount window for simplicity, we know from (9.1) that

$$Mh - Mh_{-1} = (D^g_c - D^g_{c-1}) + E(B^*_c - B^*_{c-1}) \qquad \textbf{(9.9)}$$

Then, substituting the expression for $(D^g_c - D^g_{c-1})$ from equation (9.8) into (9.9), and rearranging the resulting expression, we find

$$D^g - D^g_{-1} = (Mh - Mh_{-1}) + (D^g_p - D^g_{p-1}) \qquad \textbf{(9.10)}$$
$$- E(B^*_c - B^*_{c-1})$$

Equation (9.10) is very important. It says that there are essentially three ways to finance a budget deficit, $D^g - D^g_{-1}$: (1) by an increase in high-powered money, $Mh - Mh_{-1}$; (2) by an increase in the public's holdings of Treasury bonds, $D^g_p - D^g_{p-1}$; or (3) by a loss of foreign-exchange reserves at the central bank, $E(B^*_c - B^*_{c-1})$. In short, the government can "print money," borrow, or run down its foreign reserves.

---

[16] Equation (7.2) is $D^g - D^g_{-1} = G + I^g - T + rD^g_{-1}$.

We should note, however briefly, some of the things this conclusion means. The Treasury starts out to finance its deficit *only* by borrowing. But to the extent that the central bank buys Treasury bonds, then, in fact, the government is financing its own deficit by increasing the money supply. If the central bank subsequently sells foreign exchange to offset the increase in the money supply, then, in fact, the government is financing its own deficit by decreasing its foreign-exchange holdings. In essence, it is not enough to examine how the Treasury finances the deficit—it always does this through bonds. We must also ask who buys the bonds, and what monetary policies are brought into play.

Now we shall combine equations (9.7) and (9.8) to get an equation for deficit finance that is related to the underlying expenditures and taxes of the government:

$$(D_p^g - D_{p-1}^g) + (Mh - Mh_{-1}) - E(B_c^* - B_{c-1}^*)$$
$$= P(G + I^g - T) + iD_{-1}^g \quad \textbf{(9.11)}$$

One last technical wrinkle remains, though. In the United States, the Treasury pays interest to the Fed on the debt that the Fed holds, but then the Fed gives the interest right back to the Treasury in a budgetary transfer! Thus, the Treasury really pays interest only on the debt held by the public, not on debt held by the Fed. Instead of iD_{-1}^g in equation (9.8), we should have iD_{p-1}^g. In addition, the Fed transfers to the Treasury the interest that it earns on the foreign-exchange reserves, thereby adding to Treasury revenues an amount $E(i^*B_{-1}^*)$. Thus, we now have

$$(D_p^g - D_{p-1}^g) + (Mh - Mh_{-1}) - E(B_c^* - B_{c-1}^*)$$
$$= P(G + I^g - T) + iD_{p-1}^g - E(i^*B_{c-1}^*), \quad \textbf{(9.12)}$$

an equation sometimes called the budget constraint of the *consolidated public sector* because it puts together the budgets of the central bank and the Treasury.

It is typical in countries with very high inflation that the public does not buy new government debt and the central bank has run out of reserves. The government, then, has no other option but to finance the deficit on the right-hand side of (9.12) mainly by printing money, $Mh - Mh_{-1}$. The theory of hyperinflation is largely a theory of the monetization of fiscal deficits, as we shall see in detail in Chapters 11 and 23.[17]

Table 9-8 presents an index of the degree of independence between central banks and executive branches for 17 industrialized countries, along with the average inflation rates in those countries. The classification is based on several institutional characteristics such as who appoints the top management of the bank, whether government officials sit on the Board of the central bank, what types of contacts exist between the executive and the central bank, and whether or not there are rules regulating government borrowing from the bank. Based on these elements, central banks are ranked from least independent (1) to most independent (4). Only the central banks of

---

[17] Thomas Sargent of the University of Minnesota has forcefully stressed this aspect of hyperinflations. See his paper, "The End of Four Big Inflations," in Robert Hall, ed., *Inflation: Causes and Effects* (Chicago: National Bureau of Economic Research, University of Chicago Press, 1982).

Box 9-2
The Central Bank and Politics

Rapid increases in the money supply can produce high inflations that destabilize an economy. Controlling the money supply is the crucial job of the central bank, yet. The bank faces many powerful political forces that put continued pressure on it to extend cheap credits, or to help finance a large budget deficit. Experience has shown that the central bank may have a hard time indeed resisting these political pressures unless it has some institutional independence from the government's executive and legislative branches.

In practice, the degree of independence the central bank has varies widely across countries. In the United States, for example, the Federal Reserve is independent from the rest of the public sector. The Fed chairman is appointed by the president and, having passed muster for his or her technical capacity and his or her future independence from the executive branch, confirmed by the Senate. The chairman heads a Board of Governors of the Federal Reserve System, and each member has an appointment that lasts 14 years, though few serve for that long. The chairman is appointed for four years, after which he or she may become a regular member of the Board.

In Germany, the president of the Bundesbank exercises even greater independence than in the United States. But in many developing countries, the central bank enjoys little independence. Often, the central bank is part of the treasury, or the central bank president sits at the pleasure of the country's president and is subject to removal at any time. Under these circumstances, the central bank will find it extremely hard to resist political pressures coming from the executive branch to increase lending to the government or to favored interests in the private sector. Many analysts believe that this situation should be changed, and a number of developing countries have taken steps in recent years to give greater independence to their central banks.[18]

West Germany and Switzerland have achieved the highest degree of independence (4), followed by those of Japan and the United States (3). At the lower end of the scale lie the banks of Italy (1/2) and Spain, New Zealand, and Australia (1).

The table shows a clear relationship between the degree of independence and inflation: the higher the central bank's independence in a given country, the lower that country's inflation rate. Thus, Germany and Switzer-

---

[18] The counterargument to this has been presented, for example, by William Greider, in *Secrets of the Temple: How the Federal Reserve Runs the Country* (New York: Simon & Schuster, 1987). Greider and others have worried that those who control central bank policy will be too conservative and that insulation of the central bank from the political process may very well lead to an overly contractionary monetary policy. Greider argues that the Federal Reserve Board should be brought under much tighter, not looser, control, of the U.S. Congress.

TABLE 9-8

A CROSS-COUNTRY COMPARISON OF
CENTRAL BANK INDEPENDENCE AND
INFLATION RATES, 1973–1986

Country	Average Inflation	Index of Central Bank Independence
Italy	13.7	$\frac{1}{2}$
Spain	13.6	1
New Zealand	12.0	1
United Kingdom	10.7	2
Finland	9.8	2
Australia	9.7	1
France	9.2	2
Denmark	8.8	2
Sweden	8.7	2
Norway	8.4	2
Canada	7.8	2
Belgium	6.9	2
United States	6.9	3
Japan	6.4	3
Netherlands	5.5	2
Switzerland	4.1	4
Germany	4.1	4

Source: Alberto Alesina, *"Politics and Business Cycles in the Industrial Democracies,"* Economic Policy, *April 1989.*

land have the lowest inflation rates in the group, while Italy, Spain, and New Zealand have the highest.

9-5 EQUILIBRIUM IN THE MONEY MARKET

In the previous chapter, we concluded that money demand is a function of the interest rate and the level of income. In this chapter, we have examined the money supply as it is determined by a specified multiple of high-powered money. In equilibrium, the supply of money has to be equal to the demand for money. We can put together equations (8.14) and (9.5) to express this equilibrium as

$$M^D = Pf(i, Y) = \phi Mh = M^S \qquad \textbf{(9.13)}$$

Recall that the demand for money is a demand for *real* balances. Thus, it is proportional to the price level, or, in other words, a rise in P produces a

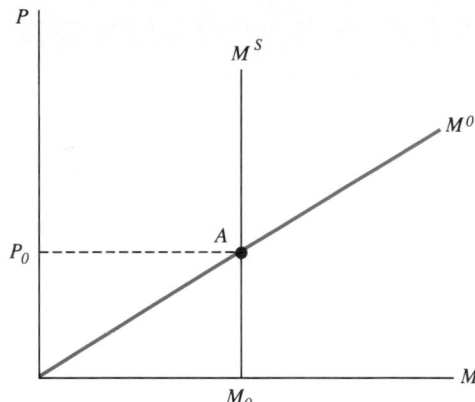

Figure 9-2
A Representation of Equilibrium in the Money Market

rise of the same proportions in M^D. On the other hand, the money supply that we have derived is a supply of *nominal* high-powered money. It is convenient to represent the equilibrium of the money market in a graph (with nominal money in the Y axis), as shown in Figure 9-2.

In our simple framework, the money supply is represented as a vertical line because it is independent of the price level. The demand for money, in turn, is shown as a straight line rising from the origin. The straight line means that the real value of desired money balances is unchanged when the price level changes.[19] It may seem strange that a demand curve is upward sloping. But remember that we are describing *money* demand, and higher prices of goods mean a higher demand for nominal money balances. Of course, in drawing the demand for money, we are assuming that the interest rate and the level of income are constant. Changes in i and Y would shift the money demand curve. The equilibrium is in point A, the intersection of the two lines. At A, the demand for money is equal to the supply of money. Notice that point A also determines the equilibrium price level.

Suppose now that the central bank makes an open market purchase of bonds, which, in turn, increases the monetary base. At the initial level of prices, interest rates, and income, there would be an excess supply of money. How would the money market reequilibrate? The answer is, in fact, very complex because the new equilibrium could be reached by at least *four* different means: (1) a rise in prices, which would raise money demand to equal the higher money supply; (2) a fall in interest rates, which would also raise money demand by decreasing the velocity of money; (3) a rise in income, which would raise the demand for money; or (4) an endogenous fall in the money supply, which would bring the money supply back down in line with money demand. Finally, some combination of these events could occur, with mixed effects, partly raising money demand and partly lowering money supply back toward its initial level.

Let us see how these four cases would appear in the graphical analysis. Case 1 appears in Figure 9-3a. The money supply shifts to the right, and the

---

[19] Technically, the slope of the M^D line is P/M, the inverse of the real money demand.

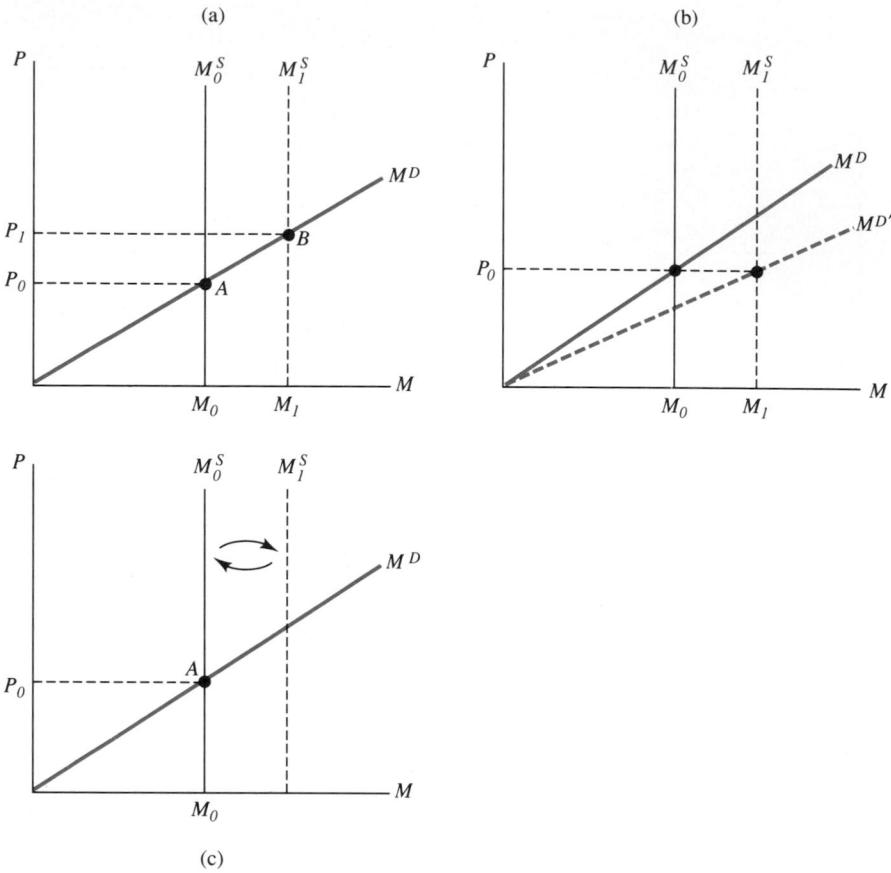

Figure 9-3
The Different Ways to Equilibrate the Money Market After an Increase in
the Money Supply

new equilibrium is along the original demand schedule at the higher price
level. Figure 9-3b shows case 2. The higher money supply lowers interest
rates, thereby reducing the velocity of money. Since the slope of the money
demand schedule is simply V/Y, the fall in V leads to a downward shift in
M^D. At the new equilibrium, the price level is unchanged, with higher M,
lower i, and therefore lower V. Figure 9-3b depicts case 3 as well. The
increase in M leads to a rise in Y. Once again, the slope of the money
demand (V/Y) schedule falls, and equilibrium occurs at the same price level,
with higher M, unchanged i, and higher Y. Case 4 is shown in Figure 9-3c.
The increase in M is reversed by an endogenous reduction of M, and the
initial equilibrium is thereby restored.

In the next few chapters we explore models that illustrate these different results. Case 1 is what happens in a small open economy with no capital
controls and floating exchange rates, a small open economy with fixed exchange rates and capital controls is the setting for case 2, case 3 is the
outcome for an economy with sticky nominal wages, and case 4 occurs when
a small open economy has free capital mobility and a fixed exchange rate.
You need not know all about these cases just yet. The important point here is

that monetary equilibrium can be reached by a variety of means, depending on whether the economy has fixed or floating exchange rates, flexible or sticky nominal wages, capital controls or free capital mobility.

Case 1 constitutes the benchmark case of the competitive, classical model. If velocity is constant, and if there is full employment in the economy, then an increase in M will lead to a proportionate increase in the price level. Changes in M tend to be associated with changes in P, and higher rates of monetary growth tend to be associated with higher inflation rates. How does this basic prediction fare with empirical evidence? Figure 9-4 presents cross-country evidence on the average inflation rate and the rate of growth in the money supply for the period 1965–1985. When it comes to distinguishing countries that have very high inflation rates from those with very low inflation rates, at least, the growth of the money supply is closely correlated with the rate of price increase. As the figure shows, however, for countries with relatively low inflation rates, the links between money growth and price inflation are not so tight.

It is clear that countries with low rates of money growth also tend to have low inflation rates, while countries with high money growth rates tend to have rapid inflation. This correlation suggests, but does not prove, causality. Nonetheless, this relationship has been an important motivation behind many analyses of inflation. (We study this important phenomenon at greater length later on in the book, especially in Chapters 11 and 23.)

Notice that normally we must consider the general equilibrium of the

Figure 9-4
Inflation and the Growth of the Money Supply: Cross-country Evidence, 1965–1985

(From International Monetary Fund, International Financial Statistics, various issues.)

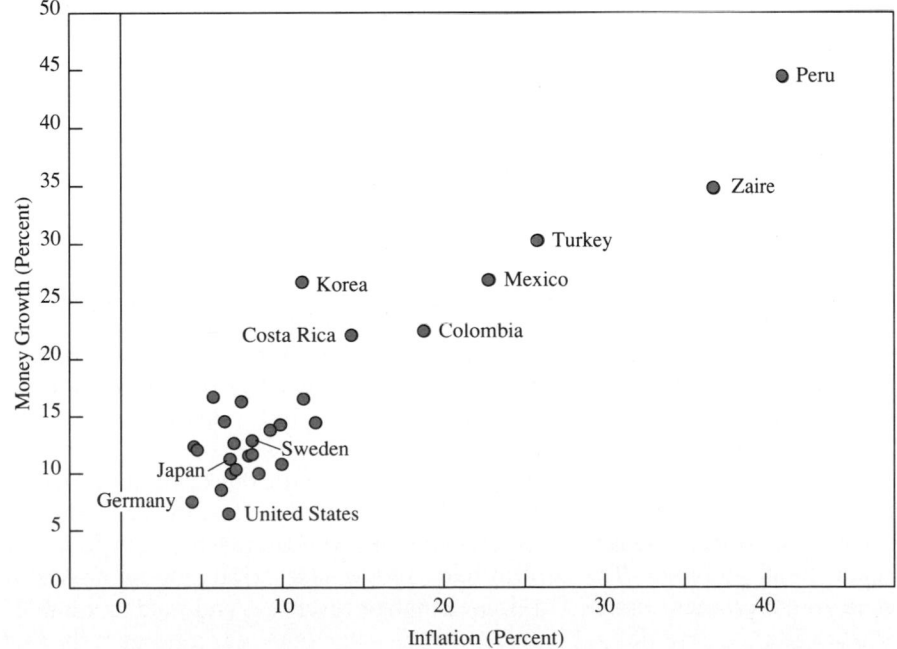

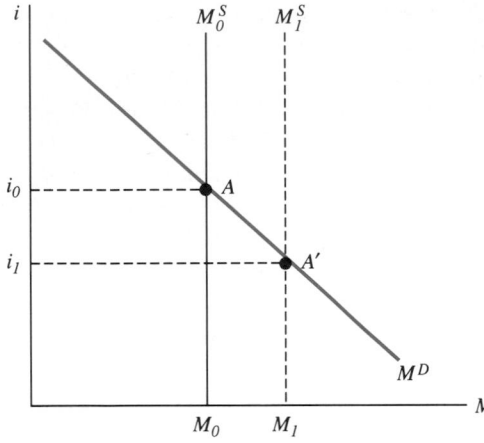

Figure 9-5
A Monetary Expansion and the Money Market in Partial Equilibrium

economy when analyzing the effects of an increase in the money supply. That is, we must take into account what happens in all important markets in order to assess the effects of such a policy. But as a building block for later analysis, it is useful to stress one *partial equilibrium* result, the effect of a money supply increase on interest rates, where the level of M is exogenous and the levels of income Y and prices P are given. When the interest rate is the only variable that can establish money market equilibrium, we can depict money market equilibrium with the interest rate in the vertical axis, as we do in Figure 9-5.

In Figure 9-5, M^D has a negative slope because an increase in the interest rate reduces money demand. For simplicity, the money supply schedule can be drawn as a vertical line, showing that M^S is exogenously given. Equilibrium is then at A. When an increase in the money supply shifts the M^S curve to the right, for given output and price levels, the interest rate will have to fall in order to clear the money market. The new equilibrium is at A'. This basic result, that a money supply increase causes a fall in the interest rate (with given levels of output, price, and the money supply itself), will be useful later in the book, especially in Part IV.

9-6 SUMMARY

Until recent decades, in most countries the money supply was mainly determined by the supply of commodities such as gold or silver. When paper currency was used, it was typically convertible into some designated precious metal at a fixed price (a *fiduciary* regime), at least under normal circumstances. (During wartimes, the linkage generally broke down.) Under a *fiat* regime, however, where money is backed only by trust in the issuer, government policy is the basic, although not the only, determinant of the money supply.

Most countries have an official institution with the legal authority to issue money, typically a *central bank*. In the United States, the central bank is the Federal Reserve Board; in Germany, it is the Bundesbank; in Japan, it is the Bank of Japan. The central bank possesses various kinds of assets, such as government bonds, foreign-exchange reserves, and gold. Its liabilities include high-powered money, deposits of financial institutions, and deposits of the government.

The supply of money in the economy varies as the central bank purchases and sells assets in return for domestic currency. Central banks often purchase or sell bonds in the open market, a transaction known as an *open market operation*. A purchase of bonds by the monetary authority leads to an increase in the stock of *high-powered money* held by the public, while a sale of bonds results in a decline in the *monetary base*. Open market operations are generally the most important tool of monetary control that central banks have. In some countries, however, open market operations are not possible because there is not sufficient private trading in government securities. This is typically the case in developing countries.

Another way in which the central bank can affect the money supply is by lending money to the private sector. These loans are typically made through the *discount window*. In the United States, the Fed establishes an interest rate, known as the *discount rate,* at which it is willing to lend money to commercial banks. The commercial banks use this credit to adjust their cash reserves or to obtain funds that they can loan out. *Discount operations* lead to changes in the supply of high-powered money. A lower discount rate makes it more attractive for banks to borrow at the discount window, and thereby increases the monetary base. Thus, the discount rate serves as another tool of monetary control. The central bank can undo the effects of an increase in the money supply brought about by its policy at the discount window by selling bonds to the public, an operation known as *sterilization*. Central banks also restrict the access to the discount window as another form of control.

Foreign-exchange operations are transactions in which the central bank buys or sells assets denominated in foreign currencies. In the simplest case, this operation involves an exchange of foreign money for domestic money. In other cases, the central bank buys or sells an interest-bearing asset denominated in a foreign currency. These transactions have direct effects on the amount of high-powered money Mh in the economy. A purchase of foreign assets increases Mh, while a sale reduces Mh. Foreign-exchange operations occur under a fixed exchange rate or a managed floating rate, but not under a clean float, wherein the central bank does not intervene at all in the foreign-exchange market.

The monetary aggregate M1 (the sum of currency and demand deposits) depends both on the stock of high-powered money and on two additional elements: the *reserve/deposit ratio* of commercial banks (r_d) and the *currency/deposit ratio* held by the public (c_d). A given stock of Mh gives rise to a much higher value of M1 because of the way the commercial banks create money. The link between Mh and M1 is given by the *money multiplier* (ϕ) and described by the formula M1 $= \phi\, Mh$, where ϕ depends on both r_d and c_d.

An increase in the reserve/deposit ratio lowers the money multiplier because it reduces the amount of new loans that the banking system can grant out of an initial deposit. This, in turn, lowers the value of subsequent new deposits that the public will make. A rise in the currency/deposit ratio also lowers the money multiplier, but for a different reason. In this case, loans granted by commercial banks produce a lower value of deposits, because agents hold more of their money in currency rather than in bank deposits.

The central bank can have an important influence on the money supply, but it cannot fully control it. The central bank has reasonably effective control over the stock of high-powered money via open market operations, but even here it can lose its control if there are fixed exchange rates and open capital mobility (as we show in the next chapter). The central bank has much less control over the money multiplier. It does determine reserve requirements and the discount rate, both of which influence the level of reserves that banks hold, but it cannot directly control the reserve/deposit ratio. It has even less control over the currency/deposit ratio of the public.

There has been a long debate in the United States over which monetary variable the Fed should attempt to control. For a long time the Fed focused on influencing the market interest rate and directed monetary policy toward that goal. The monetarists attacked this policy, arguing that the Fed normally attempted to push interest rates too low, leading to inflationary increases in the money supply. In 1979, when inflation had reached very high levels by U.S. standards, the Fed changed its policy and started to target the rate of money growth. In the United Kingdom, by contrast, the Bank of England attempts to target M3, not through high-powered money, but rather through interest rates.

The government can finance a budget deficit by borrowing from the public or by borrowing from the central bank. When the central bank buys up public debt, this is known as the *monetization of the budget deficit*. Although the Treasury incurs a debt with the central bank, in practice the government really finances the deficit by printing money. The ability of the Treasury to rely on money financing depends on the degree of independence of the central bank from the executive branch of the government. Empirical evidence across industrialized countries shows that the greater the central bank independence from the political establishment, the lower the rate of inflation tends to be.

Equilibrium in the money market occurs when the supply of money is equal to the demand for money. If this equilibrium is perturbed by, say, an open market purchase of bonds, there is initially an excess supply of money. Equilibrium in the money market can be restored when one of four possible reactions (or some combination of the four) occurs: a rise in prices, which reduces the supply of real balances; a fall in interest rates or a rise in income, which raise money demand; or an endogenous fall in the amount of nominal money. In later chapters, we shall see that just what happens depends on overall monetary policy, including the exchange-rate regime, whether or not there are capital controls, and whether the economy has classical or Keynesian features.

Key Concepts

fiat money	currency/deposit ratio
clean float	discount rate
Federal Reserve Board (Fed)	excess reserves
money multiplier	discount operations
Fed's balance sheet	monetization of the budget
reserve/deposit ratio	deficit
perpetuities	sterilization

federal funds rate

banking system

central bank

required reserves

foreign-exchange operations

consols

open market operations

central bank independence

dirty float

discount window

Problems and Questions

1. Which are the most important assets and liabilities in the central bank's balance sheet? How would the balance sheet of the central bank look like if money were convertible into gold?

2. What is the price of a bond that pays $15 next year and then $10 per year indefinitely if the interest rate is 10 percent? What would it be if the interest rate rises to 15 percent? Why?

3. The Federal Reserve sells $100 million in Treasury bills to households. To buy them, households use $20 million from their local currency holdings and sell $80 million worth of their foreign currency holdings to the Federal Reserve.

  a. Describe the transactions using the balance sheets for the Federal Reserve and the households.

  b. What is the net change in high-powered money?

4. Country A has capital controls and is running a surplus in its trade balance of $800 million a year.

  a. What is the effect of the trade surplus on the money supply?

  b. How can the central bank sterilize the monetary impact of the trade surplus?

5. Assume that the ratio of reserves to deposits is 0.2 and the ratio of currency to deposits is 0.25.

  a. What is the money multiplier?

  b. The central bank decides to increase the money supply (M1) by $200 million through an open market operation. How much should it buy in bonds?

  c. How would your answer to (a) and (b) change if the ratio of reserves to deposits were 0.1? Why?

6. The effect of an increase in the discount rate on the money supply is ambiguous because it reduces the amount of high-powered money in the economy but increases the value of the money multiplier. True or false? Explain.

7. Discuss the conditions under which a central bank has more effective control over the money supply.

8. Assume that the government of country A will run a budget deficit next year. Government officials do not want the budget deficit to affect the money supply.

  a. How might a budget deficit alter the money supply?

  b. How can government officials in country A finance the deficit without affecting the money supply?

9. Assume a money demand function of the form $Md = \frac{1}{2}(Y/i)P$. Real income (Y) is $500, and the nominal interest rate (i) is 20 percent. The money supply is fixed at $2,500.

  a. If the money market is in equilibrium, what is the price level?

    b. Depict the money supply and money demand functions in diagrams that have money in the horizontal axis and

        i. the price level in the vertical axis (hold fixed $Y = 500$ and $i = 0.2$).

        ii. the interest rate in the vertical axis (hold fixed $Y = 500$ and $P = 2$).

        iii. the real income in the vertical axis (hold fixed $P = 2$ and $i = 0.2$).

        Be sure to identify the equilibrium points in all the diagrams.

    c. Assume that the money supply doubles to $5,000.

        i. If the adjustment is through the price level, what is the new *P?*

        ii. If the adjustment is through the interest rate, what is new *i?*

        iii. If the adjustment is through real income, what is the new *Y?*

10. How does an increase in the interest rate affect the ratio of reserves to deposits? Taking this effect into account, how would the money supply function look like in a diagram with the interest rate in the vertical axis and the quantity of money in the horizontal axis?

Money,
Exchange Rates, and Prices

In the last chapter, we began to analyze equilibrium in the money market. We found, however, that we really could not say anything very specific about supply and demand without knowing more about the determination of prices, the exchange rate, and other features of the economy outside the money market. In viewing the money market in isolation from the rest of the economy, we have so far been able to talk only about *partial* equilibrium, without considering the effects of the money market on other parts of the economy. Our task is more ambitious in this chapter. In order to examine the repercussions of monetary policy throughout the economy, we need to do some *general* equilibrium analysis.

We continue here with a very simple *classical* model of the economy, in which output is always at its full-employment level. In general, we also assume that capital is perfectly mobile between the domestic and international markets, so that domestic and foreign interest rates are equal. We also assume that only one type of good is produced and consumed in the economy and that it can be imported or exported at a fixed international price P^*. This type of theoretical structure most closely resembles that of a small open economy.

In this chapter we examine monetary equilibrium and price determination under the two main exchange-rate regimes, fixed and floating. Our previous analysis of money demand and money supply plus some general equilibrium theory will lead us to a more adequate understanding of how the exchange rate, the price level, and the money supply are determined when all markets are considered together. Before we proceed, however, we should look more closely at the two main exchange-rate regimes.

10-1 EXCHANGE-RATE ARRANGEMENTS

The predominant exchange-rate arrangements during the nineteenth century were fixed-rate systems. The gold standard, in its many versions, is a fixed exchange-rate system in that it commits the monetary authority to a fixed price relationship between the domestic money and gold. In the United States between 1879 and 1933, for example, 1 ounce of gold could

TABLE 10-1

EXCHANGE-RATE ARRANGEMENTS IN THE WORLD

		Currency Pegged to			Flexibility Limited in Terms of a Single Currency or Group of Currencies	
U.S. Dollar	French Franc	Other Currency	SDR	Other Composite[2]	Single Currency[3]	Cooperative Arrangements[4]
Afghanistan	Benin	Bhutan	Burundi	Algeria	Bahrain	Belgium
Angola	Burkina Faso	(Indian	Iran, I. R. of	Austria	Qatar	Denmark
Antigua and Barbuda	Cameroon	rupee)	Libya	Bangladesh	Saudi Arabia	France
Bahamas, The	C. African Rep.	Kiribati	Myanmar	Botswana	United Arab	Germany
Barbados	Chad	(Australian	Rwanda	Bulgaria	Emirates	Ireland
Belize	Comoros	dollar)	Seychelles	Cape Verde		Italy
Djibouti	Congo	Lesotho		Cyprus		Luxembourg
Dominica	Côte d'Ivoire	(South		Czechoslovakia		Netherlands
Dominican Rep.	Equatorial	African		Fiji		Spain
Ethiopia	Guinea	rand)		Finland		United Kingdom
Grenada	Gabon	Swaziland		Hungary		
Guyana	Mali	(South		Iceland		
Haiti	Niger	African		Israel		
Iraq	Senegal	rand)		Jordan		
Liberia	Togo	Tonga		Kenya		
Oman		(Australian		Kuwait		
Panama		dollar)		Malawi		
St. Kitts and Nevis		Yugoslavia		Malaysia		
St. Lucia		(Deutsche		Malta		
St. Vincent and the		mark)		Mauritius		
Grenadines				Morocco		
Sudan				Nepal		
Suriname				Norway		
Syrian Arab Rep.				Papua New		
Trinidad and Tobago				Guinea		
Yemen, Republic of				Poland		
				Romania		
				Sao Tome and		
				Principe		
				Solomon		
				Islands		
				Sweden		
				Tanzania		
				Thailand		
				Uganda		
				Vanuatu		
				Western Samoa		
				Zimbabwe		

[1] *Excluding the currency of Democratic Kampuchea, for which no current information is available. For members with dual or multiple exchange markets, the arrangement shown is that in the major market.*

[2] *Comprises currencies which are pegged to various "baskets" of currencies of the members' own choice, as distinct from the SDR basket.*

[3] *Exchange rates of all currencies have shown limited flexibility in terms of the U.S. dollar.*

Source: IMF, *International Financial Statistics, April 1991.*

AS OF DECEMBER 31, 1990[1]

Adjusted According to a Set of Indicators[5]	More Flexible	
	Other Managed Floating	Independently Floating
Chile	China, P.R.	Argentina
Colombia	Costa Rica	Australia
Madagascar	Ecuador	Bolivia
Mozambique	Egypt	Brazil
Zambia	Greece	Canada
	Guinea	El Salvador
	Guinea-Bissau	Gambia, The
	Honduras	Ghan
	India	Guatemala
	Indonesia	Jamaica
	Korea	Japan
	Lao P.D. Rep	Lebanon
	Mauritania	Maldives
	Mexico	Namibia
	Nicaragua	New Zealand
	Pakistan	Nigeria
	Portugal	Paraguay
	Singapore	Peru
	Somalia	Philippines
	Sri Lanka	Sierra Leone
	Tunisia	South Africa
	Turkey	United States
	Viet Nam	Uruguay
		Venezuela
		Zaire

[4] *Refers to the cooperative arrangement maintained under the European Monetary System.*
[5] *Includes exchange arrangements under which the exchange rate is adjusted at relatively frequent intervals, on the basis of indicators determined by the respective member countries.*

be purchased from the government for $18.85. Because many currencies, including the dollar, the British pound sterling and the French franc, were simultaneously tied to gold for extended periods, these currencies could also be exchanged among themselves at a fixed rate.[1] The gold standard prevailed during the "Golden Age," from 1870 to 1914, and sporadically in the 1920s and early 1930s, until its collapse during the Great Depression.

After World War II, the Bretton Woods agreement established a fixed exchange-rate system among the member nations of the International Monetary Fund (IMF), which included most of the market economies in the world. Under this agreement, these countries were to set a value of their currency in terms of the U.S. dollar, and the dollar in turn was to be convertible into gold at a fixed price of $35 per ounce. The link to gold was only partial, however. U.S. citizens were not allowed to own monetary gold, and the Federal Reserve Board was not obliged to convert dollars into gold for private citizens. The Bretton Woods arrangement collapsed in 1971 when President Richard Nixon suspended the convertibility of dollars into gold (in particular, the United States would no longer automatically sell gold to foreign governments in return for dollars) and unilaterally changed the *parity* (that is, the exchange rate) of the dollar vis-à-vis the other international currencies.

Since 1973, the major currencies of the industrialized world have been operating under a scheme of managed floating exchange rates (the fact that it is managed makes it a "dirty" float). The main currencies—the U.S. dollar, the German Deutsche mark (DM), and the Japanese yen—have floated against each other since 1973. Since the second half of the 1980s, however, the major governments have often intervened in the foreign-exchange markets to maintain their currencies at informal target levels. Within Europe, since 1979 the currencies have been linked together in a system of stable but adjustable rates, known as the European Monetary System (EMS).

For most developing nations, however, the fixed exchange-rate regime, in one of its many variations, is still the most predominant arrangement. Most countries in Latin America, Asia, and Africa peg their monies to a foreign currency or to a basket of currencies. The most common choice is to fix the rate to the U.S. dollar, but there are many other kinds of arrangements. For example, many French-speaking countries in West Africa peg their currencies to the French franc, in the so-called French franc zone (member countries include Cameroon, Ivory Coast, Madagascar, Mali, Mauritania, and Senegal).[2]

Table 10-1 provides a complete list of the exchange-rate arrangements of the member countries of the IMF, and Table 10-2 shows the frequency of the various exchange-rate arrangements from 1984 to 1990. Note that a large majority of countries were in some sort of pegged arrangement at the end of

---

[1] Each ounce of gold was fixed at 3.87 British pounds and also at $18.85. Therefore, each British pound was implicitly fixed at $4.87. That is, the *exchange rate* was 4.87, in dollars per pound.

[2] An analysis of the African Franc Zone is provided in Jorge Braga de Macedo, "Collective Pegging to a Single Currency: The West African Monetary Union," in Sebastian Edwards and Liaquat Ahamed, eds., *Economic Adjustment and Exchange Rates in Developing Countries* (Chicago: University of Chicago Press, 1986).

TABLE 10-2

THE FREQUENCY OF EXCHANGE-RATE ARRANGEMENTS, 1984–1990

Classification Status[1]	1984	1985	1986	1987	1988			1989				1990			
					QII	QIII	QIV	QI	QII	QIII	QIV	QI	QII	QIII	QIV
Currency pegged to															
U.S. dollar	34	31	32	38	38	38	36	31	32	32	32	30	28	25	25
French franc	14	14	14	14	14	14	14	14	14	14	14	14	14	14	14
Other currency of which:	5	5	5	5	5	5	5	5	5	5	5	5	5	5	6
Pound sterling	(1)	(1)	(—)	(—)	(—)	(—)	(—)	(—)	(—)	(—)	(—)	(—)	(—)	(—)	(—)
SDR	11	12	10	8	7	7	8	8	7	7	7	7	7	7	6
Other currency composite	31	32	30	27	31	31	31	31	32	32	34	34	35	37	35
Flexibility limited vis-à-vis a single currency	7	5	5	4	4	4	4	4	4	4	4	4	4	4	4
Cooperative arrangements	8	8	8	8	8	8	8	8	9	9	9	9	9	9	10
Adjusted according to a set of indicators	6	5	6	5	5	5	5	5	5	5	5	4	4	3	5
Managed floating	20	21	21	23	20	21	22	25	24	25	21	23	21	23	23
Independently floating	12	15	19	18	18	17	17	19	18	18	20	21	23	26	25
Total[2]	148	149	151	151	151	151	151	151	151	152	152	152	151	154	154

[1] Excluding the currency of Democratic Kampuchea, for which no current information is available. For members with dual or multiple exchange markets, the arrangement shown is that in the major market.

[2] Including the currency of Democratic Kampuchea. Effective May 22, 1990, the Yemen Arab Republic and the People's Democratic Republic of Yemen merged as the Republic of Yemen.

Source: IMF, International Financial Statistics, April 1991.

1990, with only 48 of the 154 countries classified as either "managed float-ing" or "independently floating." Of those with currencies pegged to an-other currency, as of 1990, 25 countries were tied to the dollar, 14 were tied to the French franc, and 35 were tied to a composite of currencies (a weighted average of several currencies). In addition, 10 countries belong to the cooperative arrangement of the European Monetary System, in which the European currencies are linked together by stable but adjustable ex-change rates.

The Operations of a Fixed Exchange-Rate Regime

In a fixed exchange-rate system, the central bank (or whatever the national monetary authority is) fixes the relative price between the domestic currency and a foreign currency. This fixed price is sometimes called the *par value* of the currency. In some cases, however, the par value of a currency has little economic meaning, because even though the currency has a stated exchange rate, it is not possible to buy and sell it at the official price. The central bank, say, might be unwilling or unable to change dollars for the local currency at the posted price. In this case, we say that the currency is *inconvertible*. Most of our analysis here, however, is confined to the case of a *convertible* cur-rency, in which the fixed exchange rate is in fact the price at which the national money can be converted to the foreign currency. Box 10-1 discusses the issue of convertibility in greater detail.

Suppose, for example, that the Bank of France decides to fix the franc at the rate of 3 francs per Deutsche mark, and to maintain convertibility. This means that the bank commits itself to sell 3 French francs for each Deutsche mark or to sell 1 DM for each 3 French francs delivered to the bank. This commitment does not mean that the Bank of France intervenes every time that anyone chooses to convert francs to Deutsche marks (or vice versa), but only that it stands ready to intervene if the private market price were to move away from 3 FF/DM. As long as the private sector has confi-dence that the Bank of France will honor its commitment, private banks and other financial firms will be willing to trade francs for Deutsche marks at the official price, plus a small commission, knowing that they can always re-verse the transaction in a direct operation with the Bank of France (if the private bank buys Deutsche marks from the public, it can subsequently sell the Deutsche marks to the Bank of France). In reality, note that with a fixed exchange rate, the central bank generally establishes a band of allowable prices within which the price of foreign currency is allowed to fluctuate. With a ±2 percent band, for instance, the exchange rate in our example can move between 2.94 FF/DM and 3.06 FM/DM.

Before we proceed, we should mention a problem in terminology. In technical discussions, the term *fixed* exchange rate is often used to mean an irrevocably set price between currencies, without possibility of change. A pegged exchange rate, then, indicates that the price is set by the central bank but can be changed if circumstances change. Indeed, central banks are sometimes quite explicit about the possibility of future realignments of cur-rency, stressing that the currency system is an *adjustable peg*. As others do in general discussions of this issue, we shall talk about "fixed" and "pegged" exchange rates as if they meant the same thing. When we mean *irrevocably* fixed rates, we will say so explicitly.

Box 10-1
Currency Convertibility

A currency is judged to be convertible if people are able to exchange domestic currency for foreign currency at the official exchange rate without many restrictions. If there are a lot of restrictions, the currency is considered *inconvertible*. This is clearly a loose definition, and that very looseness underscores the point that convertibility is generally a matter of extent rather than an all-or-nothing proposition.

A variety of restrictions can be imposed on convertibility. In some countries, for example, the importation of luxury cars is banned: the central bank will not make foreign exchange available for an import of a Mercedes Benz or a Lamborghini. If that is the only restriction on the purchase of foreign exchange, it might be considered a part of trade policy rather than of monetary policy, and the exchange rate would still be considered convertible. But if the restrictions apply to a vast array of consumer goods, then the currency might be considered to be inconvertible.

Commonly, capital account transactions are subject to restrictions. Domestic residents are often barred from purchasing foreign assets like bonds, stocks, and real estate or from holding money in foreign bank accounts. This does not mean that everybody inside the country plays by the rules. Restrictions on capital account transactions are often easier to evade than those that apply to current account operations. It is easier to hold a foreign bank account than to smuggle a Rolls Royce into a country that bans this type of import.

It is IMF policy to oppose restrictions on current account transactions. Article VIII of the IMF Articles of Agreement says that "no member shall, without the approval of the Fund, impose restrictions on the making of payments for current international transactions." In practice, many countries—and even members of the IMF—maintain restrictions on current account convertibility, some of which are sanctioned by the Fund and some of which are tolerated but certainly not endorsed. The IMF Articles of Agreement do not require convertibility on capital account transactions, and from the point of view of the IMF, countries are free to impose capital controls without approval of other countries or the IMF itself.

A common indication of inconvertibility is the spread between the official exchange rate and the black market exchange rate, sometimes referred to as the *exchange-rate gap*. To the extent that individuals are not allowed to buy foreign exchange legally for certain purposes, or to the extent that the legal foreign exchange is rationed by the central bank, an informal market will tend to arise in which foreign exchange can be purchased. If the black market exchange rate is greatly depreciated relative to the official exchange rate—meaning that a unit of foreign exchange is much more expensive on the unofficial market than on the official one—the central bank is probably not making foreign exchange widely available at the official price. This, in turn, is a strong sign that the currency is not effectively convertible.

Table 10-3, from the *World Currency Yearbook,* shows the average spread between the official and the black market exchange rate for several inconvertible currencies at the end of 1988. Note the high spreads in Angola, Cuba, and the Soviet Union, which reached more than 1,000 percent. Although not so spectacular, the spreads in Argentina, Brazil, Bangladesh, and Poland were still very high.

In general, exchange rates are defined as the number of units of *domestic* currency which are necessary to buy 1 unit of *foreign* currency. Thus, in France the exchange rate is stated as 3 FF/DM, while in Germany, the same exchange rate is stated as 0.33 DM/FF. The United States and the United Kingdom are the two major exceptions to this rule. Exchange rates vis-à-vis the dollar are almost always stated as units of the foreign currency per U.S. dollar; similarly, exchange rates versus the British pound are typically stated as units of foreign currency per pound. These conventions reflect the centrality of the dollar in the monetary system since World War II and the former importance of the pound in the world monetary system before World War II.

When a government intervenes to support a given exchange rate, it employs almost the same techniques that it uses to support the price of wheat or some other commodity. Suppose that the government fixes a price of $100 per ton of wheat and that the private supply and demand are given as

TABLE   10-3

SPREADS BETWEEN OFFICIAL AND BLACK MARKET EXCHANGE RATES IN SELECTED COUNTRIES DECEMBER 1988

Country	Official Exchange Rate*	Black Market Exchange Rate*	Black Market Gap†
Italy	6.059	6.18	1
France	1,305.8	1,318.8	2
South Korea	684.1	752.5	10
Mexico	2,281	2,623.15	15
Israel	1.685	1.988	18
Argentina	13.37	20.055	50
Brazil	0.765	1.201	57
Bangladesh	32.27	134.888	318
Poland	502.55	3,201.24	537
Soviet Union	0.606	7.2417	1,095
Cuba	0.829	37.346	4,405
Angola	25.5	1,576.6	6,083

* *Domestic currency units per U.S. dollar.*
† *Percentage of the black market rate over the official rate.*
Source: *International Currency Analysis, Inc., Brooklyn, NY.* WORLD CURRENCY YEARBOOK, 1988–1989.

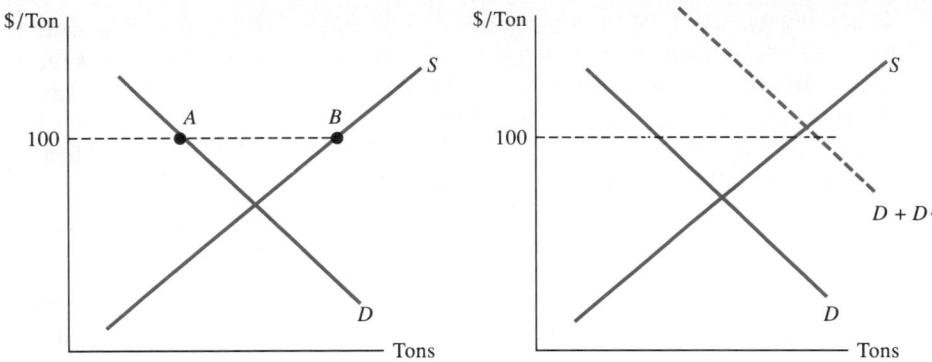

Figure 10-1
Government Price Support in the Wheat Market

in Figure 10-1a. Here, there is an excess supply of *AB* units of wheat at the fixed price. The authorities must buy wheat in exchange for dollars so as to stabilize the dollar price of wheat at the appropriate level. This is shown in Figure 10-1b, where the demand curve has shifted horizontally by the amount $D^g = AB$ of government demand.[3] The private sector ends up with dollars and the government ends up with wheat, and supply and demand equilibrate at the desired price. If the free market equilibrium goes above $100 per ton, of course, the authorities would sell wheat for dollars and reduce their wheat reserve.

   In foreign-exchange operations under a fixed exchange rate, the central bank converts home money in exchange for foreign money (or vice versa) in order to stabilize the exchange rate. Instead of increasing or reducing its holdings of wheat, it increases or decreases its holdings of foreign assets, as it exchanges domestic money for foreign money in order to keep the exchange rate constant. As we saw in the previous chapter, purchases of foreign reserves by the central bank lead to variations in the supply of domestic high-powered money. In other words, the domestic money supply will generally change up and down as the central bank trades the domestic money for foreign money in order to keep the exchange rate constant.

   How is a particular exchange rate established in a fixed exchange-rate system? A given country (which we by convention call the domestic country) can fix an exchange rate by unilaterally pegging its currency to that of other nation, and then being ready to buy and sell the foreign money in return for domestic money at the selected exchange rate. Or there may be a joint arrangement among the countries whose currencies are to be pegged. A *unilateral* peg (sometimes called a one-sided peg) is typical of developing economies that fix their currency to that of an industrialized country. Here, the domestic country undertakes the full responsibility of holding the exchange rate at the level it has committed itself to. Consider the case of Argentina, a fairly large developing country which has at various times pegged its currency, the austral, to the U.S. dollar. The Central Bank of

---

[3] The same operation could be viewed as a supply curve shift, where supply is viewed as a "supply net of government purchases."

Argentina assumes the full responsibility for supporting the exchange rate it has chosen, and the U.S. Federal Reserve generally does not intervene to assist the Argentine government in keeping the exchange rate stable. If Argentina decides to end the pegged-rate arrangement, or to change the price at which the exchange rate is stabilized, that too would be a unilateral decision, without the need for approval from the United States.[4]

In other cases, a fixed rate of exchange is maintained as a shared responsibility among the countries affected. We call such a system a *cooperative exchange-rate arrangement* (and we examine such cooperative systems in more detail later in this chapter). Agreements of this type are characteristic of medium to large economies, such as the 10 Western European countries that participated in the exchange-rate mechanism of the European Monetary System at the end of 1990. For example, both the central banks in France and Germany share in the responsibility of maintaining the exchange-rate peg that is set within the European Monetary System. Even in this case, however, experts disagree as to whether the responsibilities are really shared. Some analysts have claimed that the Bundesbank does not really share in the process of pegging the European exchange rates and that the other central banks in the EMS shoulder most of the burden of maintaining their exchange rates vis-à-vis the Deutsche mark.[5]

The Operations of a Flexible Exchange-Rate Regime

Under a regime of flexible, or floating, exchange rates, the monetary authority has no commitment whatsoever to support a given rate. (Note that we use the terms *flexible* exchange rate and *floating* exchange rate interchangeably.) Instead, all fluctuations in the demand for and supply of a foreign currency are accommodated by changes in the price of that foreign money relative to the domestic currency. The central bank sets the money supply without committing itself to any particular exchange rate, then lets the exchange rate fluctuate in response to economic disturbances. If the central bank does not intervene at all in the foreign-exchange markets by buying or selling foreign currency, we say that the domestic currency is in a *clean float*. Things are rarely so clean, however. Countries that operate under flexible rates often attempt to influence the value of their currency by undertaking foreign-exchange operations. This is what we call a *dirty* float.

For many decades, policymakers and academic economists have debated the benefits of having a fixed or a flexible exchange-rate regime. Moreover, the debate goes on within each of these arrangements over the specifics of fixed and flexible systems.[6] No consensus is yet in sight. Some analysts argue for a return to a fixed exchange-rate system among the industrialized countries. Many supporters of this idea look back favorably upon

---

[4] There would be a formal obligation of the Argentine authorities (or any other member of the IMF) to notify the IMF of the exchange-rate change, and a formal obligation to avoid exchange-rate changes that would "prevent effective balance-of-payments adjustment" or lead to "an unfair competitive advantage over other members" of the IMF. This commitment is described in Article IV of the IMF Articles of Agreement.

[5] Unlike the case of Argentina, however, individual members of the EMS are not supposed to change their exchange rates without the approval of the other EMS members.

[6] One example of such debate is Michael Connolly's piece, "The Choice of an Optimal Currency Peg for a Small, Open Country," *Journal of International Money and Finance,* 1982.

the experience of the Bretton Woods system, at least during the period from the late 1950s to the late 1960s. They suggest that the system broke down because of specific policy errors, such as the overinflationary policies of the U.S. government while it was financing the Vietnam war at the end of the 1960s. Others argue that the system broke down precisely *because* a fixed exchange-rate arrangement among the major economies is untenable. These arguments are discussed in detail later on in the book.

At this point, we need to set up a terminology that will help us analyze the exchange rate. Thus, E is the price of foreign exchange, measured as the number of units of domestic currency per unit of foreign currency. A rise in E is called a *devaluation* of the currency if it takes place under a pegged exchange-rate system, and a *depreciation* if it happens under a floating-rate system. Similarly, a fall in E is called a *revaluation* of the currency if it occurs under a pegged exchange-rate system, and an *appreciation* if it takes place under a floating-rate system.

Note that a rise in E is actually a fall in the purchasing power of the domestic currency, in that higher E means that it costs more to buy a unit of foreign exchange. Thus, when E goes up, the domestic currency is actually weakening. This can lead to endless confusion, since a rise in the exchange rate seems to suggest (incorrectly) a strengthening of the currency. Generally, then, we will use the terms "devaluation," "depreciation," "revaluation," and "appreciation" rather than "rise" and "fall" when we talk about the exchange rate.

10-2 THE BUILDING BLOCKS OF A GENERAL EQUILIBRIUM MODEL

Once we have a theoretical model of the economy that determines the equilibrium values of the price level (P), the exchange rate (E), and the quantity of money (M), we will use it to assess the effects of specific policies on these variables. As usual, our assumptions in the model will be highly simplified: output and income are always exogenous, and at full-employment level, only a single good exists, and so on. These are not, of course, very realistic. Still, to explain the behavior of certain variables, P, E, and M, in this case, we are almost forced to abstract only certain features from the overwhelmingly complex economic environment. Then, too, it is also useful to start with simple models and introduce more and more realistic assumptions only as we need them.

We start by introducing two building blocks of the general equilibrium model, purchasing power parity and interest parity. These concepts allow us to link domestic prices and interest rates to world prices and world interest rates.

Purchasing Power Parity

Purchasing power parity, or PPP, is an old concept. Its origins date back as far as the Salamanca school in sixteenth-century Spain and the work of Gerrard de Malynes in early seventeenth-century England.[7] It was not until

---

[7] For a lucid exposition of the history of PPP, see Rudiger Dornbusch's "Purchasing Power Parity," in *The New Palgrave: A Dictionary of Economics* (New York: Stockton Press, 1988).

the second decade of this century, however, that the Swedish economist Gustav Cassel provided the christening for the concept and popularized its use.[8] Since then, Cassel's name has been associated with PPP.

The basic idea behind PPP is the *law of one price*, that is, that any commodity in a unified market has a single price. If we assume that a domestic market and a foreign market are closely integrated for a set of commodities (in that the commodities can easily be traded between the two markets), then the law of one price states that the prices of those commodities should be the same in the two countries. The complication arises because the same good will be priced in the domestic currency in the home market and in the foreign currency abroad. The law of one price requires that the two prices be the same *when expressed in a common currency*. Thus, to apply the law of one price, we need an exchange rate to convert foreign into domestic prices (and vice versa).

Suppose that the foreign-currency price of the commodity in the external market is P^*. When this price is expressed in the domestic currency, the price is simply P^* multiplied by the exchange rate. The law of one price holds that the domestic price P should also be equal to EP^*:

$$P = EP^* \tag{10.1}$$

Thus, if gold in Germany costs 700 DM per ounce, and there are 3 French francs per Deutsche mark, then the French franc price of gold in Germany is evidently 2,100 francs per ounce:

$$2{,}100 \text{ FF/ounce} = 700 \text{ DM/ounce} \times 3 \text{ FF/DM}$$

The assumption of the law of one price is that if trade in gold is free between Germany and France, the price in France should also be 2,100 FF/ounce.

Arbitrage is the process that ensures that the law of one price actually holds. Suppose that the price of gold in France were 2,500 FF. There would then be a profit opportunity in importing gold from Germany to sell it in France. Competition among importers would drive down the price to 2,100 FF. Or, to put it another way, the French would not purchase gold in France if they could get it more cheaply abroad. (This also explains why a price of, say, 1,800 FF per ounce of gold cannot be an equilibrium price in this example.)

The doctrine of *purchasing power parity* attempts to extend the law of one price from individual commodities to the basket of commodities that determines the average price level in an economy. The reasoning goes like this. Because the law of one price should apply for each commodity in international trade, it should apply generally for the home price index (P), which is a weighted average of the individual commodity prices. The latter should be equal to the world price index (P^*) times the exchange rate (E). This relationship, expressed in equation (10.1) (if we take P and P^* as prices of baskets of goods), is the simplest form of purchasing power parity (PPP).

PPP is a very convenient assumption, and we will use it in much of our subsequent analysis. However, like many assumptions, it oversimplifies re-

---

[8] In his article entitled "Abnormal Deviations from International Exchanges," *Economic Journal,* December 1918.

ality. The relationship that it states holds true only under several unrealistic conditions: (1) that there are no natural barriers to trade, such as transport and insurance costs; (2) that there are no artificial barriers, such as tariffs or quotas; (3) that all goods are internationally traded; and (4) that domestic and foreign price indexes have the same commodities, with the same weighting. In practice, we know that these conditions never hold exactly. A slightly less restrictive version of purchasing power parity allows the domestic price index to deviate from the foreign price index (multiplied by the exchange rate) because of natural and artificial barriers (transport costs, tariffs) but argues that if these barriers are stable over time, percentage changes in P should approximately equal percentage changes in EP^*. Technically, this version of PPP appears in equation (10.2), which is simply relationship (10.1) expressed as *changes* over time:

$$\frac{(P - P_{-1})}{P_{-1}} = \frac{(EP^* - E_{-1}P^*_{-1})}{E_{-1}P^*_{-1}} \qquad (10.2)$$

Note that the percentage change in EP^* can be approximated as the *sum* of the percentage changes in E and P^*:

$$\frac{(P - P_{-1})}{P_{-1}} = \frac{(E - E_{-1})}{E_{-1}} + \frac{(P^* - P^*_{-1})}{P^*_{-1}} \qquad (10.2')$$

In other words, equation (10.2') states that under PPP, domestic inflation is equal to the rate of currency depreciation (or devaluation) plus the rate of foreign inflation.

Yet even this less restrictive version of PPP is unlikely to hold precisely. Many goods are not traded, or not easily traded, and the baskets of goods in the price indexes of different countries are likely to differ in at least some respects. Thus, it is by no means certain that full price parity will take place between two price indexes.

To see the kind of price discrepancies that can arise for goods that are not easily traded across national borders, consider the wide variation in dollar prices for haircuts, as shown in Table 10-4. Prices range from a low of $6.50 in Mexico City to a high of $34.47 in Zurich, a variation of almost 500 percent.

Notice that countries are ranked in the table in decreasing order according to per capita income. In Chapter 21, we shall see why the poorer countries in the table tend to have lower-priced haircuts and, in general, have lower average price levels (for a common basket of goods) than do the richer countries.

Why does the law of one price break down in this case? Very simply, transport costs are too high for arbitrage to operate. There is about a $15 gap between the price of a haircut in New York and in Mexico City. But nobody is likely to take a plane from New York to Mexico City in order to economize on a haircut. The round-trip air ticket between the two cities is upward of $400, not to mention the time involved.

One measure of a country's overall competitiveness in international markets—for example, how attractive its exports are relative to those of other countries—is the price of that country's goods relative to the price of the goods of the competitor countries. The term "real exchange rate" is sometimes applied to the ratio $e = E\,P^*/P$. When e rises, foreign goods

TABLE 10-4

AN INTERNATIONAL COMPARISON OF HAIRCUTS PRICES, 1989
(US$)

City	Man's Haircut	Woman's Cut and Blow Dry	Country's per Capita Income 1988
Zurich	34.47	36.83	27,500
Tokyo	27.68	46.40	21,020
New York City	21.66	27.00	19,840
Frankfurt	13.64	20.20	18,480
Paris	23.87	36.81	16,090
London	17.32	28.60	12,810
Sydney	18.05	25.99	12,340
Hong Kong	14.06	18.75	9,220
Sao Paulo	7.33	15.95	2,160
Mexico City	6.50	9.94	1,760
Moscow	6.78	9.57	NA

Sources: The New York Times, *November 5, 1989; World Bank,* World Development Report 1990, *(New York: Oxford University Press)*
NA = Not available.

become more expensive than domestic goods, and we speak of a *real exchange-rate depreciation;* conversely, when e falls, we speak of a *real exchange-rate appreciation.* Obviously, the assumption behind PPP is that e is constant, or at least nearly constant, over time.

To test this, let us look at the real exchange rate for Canada vis-à-vis the United States during the period 1960–1989, as shown in Figure 10-2. Because these economies are closely integrated, we might expect that PPP would apply well for this pair of countries. Let P be the Canadian price level and $E P^*$ be the U.S. price level expressed in Canadian dollars (so that E is the exchange rate in Canadian dollars per U.S. dollar). Note that e fluctuates significantly year to year, with large depreciations between 1976–1978 and 1983–1985, and a large appreciation during 1985–1988. But note as well that over the 20-year period, the real exchange rate from the beginning to the end only changed by about 4 percent. Over the long run, there is no discernible trend in the real exchange rate, suggesting that PPP might be a good description over a period of several years for these two countries. More generally, Paul Krugman of MIT has recently found that PPP works well in the long run for a group of major industrialized economies.[9]

---

[9] P. Krugman, ''Differences in Income Elasticities and Trends in Real Exchange Rates,'' *European Economic Review,* May 1989.

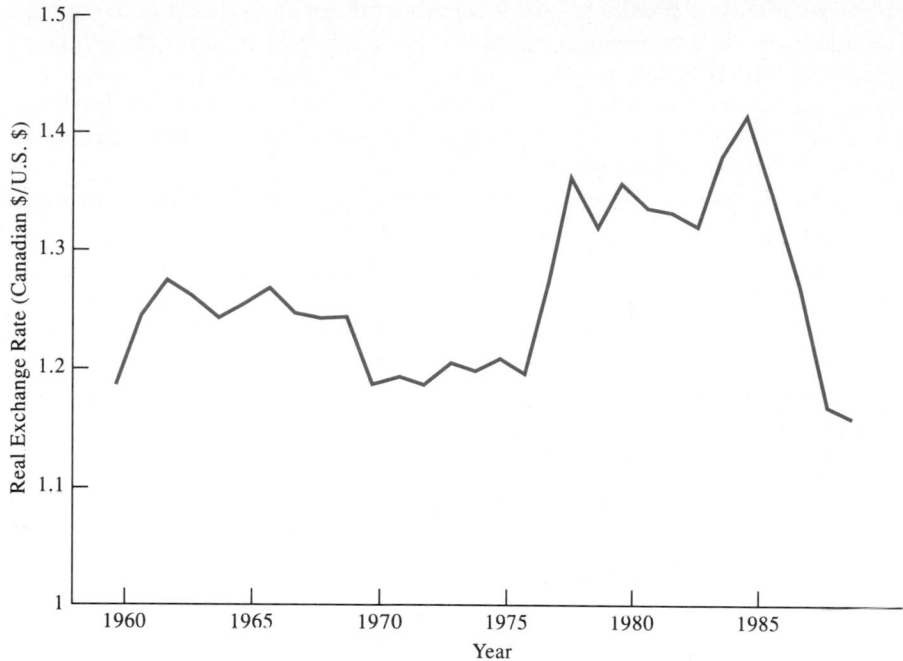

Figure 10-2

The Real Exchange Rate and Purchasing Power Parity: United States and Canada, 1960–1989

(From International Monetary Fund, International Financial Statistics.*)*

International Interest Arbitrage

At a given moment in time, households and firms in the domestic economy have a certain level of wealth that has been accumulated by past savings. This wealth is allocated among a portfolio of financial assets according to the characteristics of those assets, principally their risk and return, and the preferences of agents. (The way that agents select their portfolio of assets is taken up in detail in Chapter 20.)

A fraction of total wealth is held in the form of monetary assets. What that fraction is, of course, depends on the value of transactions expected in a given period, and the opportunity cost of holding money. And, as we saw in the previous chapter, households must choose between an array of monetary assets—currency, demand deposits, NOW accounts, and money market funds, to mention only a few. Households and firms will also choose to keep part of their wealth in domestic nonmonetary assets—Treasury bills, municipal bonds, and equity ownership of private corporations, for instance. In our analysis here, we shall assume that there is a single type of domestic money, M, and a single type of domestic interest-bearing asset, a default-free bond, B.

If there are no exchange-rate restrictions on purchasing foreign assets, domestic residents may also want to hold assets denominated in foreign currencies. Notice, however, that while local residents want to hold domestic money, they generally want to hold little, if any, foreign money, M^*.

Foreign money is usually not an acceptable means of payment in the domestic economy, and as a way to hold wealth it tends to be inferior to holding foreign interest-bearing assets.[10] For simplicity's sake, then, we assume that domestic agents do not hold any foreign money, M^*, and that they hold only one type of interest-bearing asset denominated in the foreign currency, a bond, which we denote by B^*.

Under these assumptions, the nominal value of households' financial wealth (W) is

$$W = M + B + E B^* \qquad (10.3)$$

Notice that while M and B are measured in local currency, B^* is the value of foreign bonds denominated in foreign currency. In order to express the value of B^* in domestic currency, we need to multiply B^* by the exchange rate. The real value of wealth is then

$$\frac{W}{P} = \frac{M}{P} + \frac{B}{P} + \frac{E}{P} B^* \qquad (10.4)$$

Using the PPP rule from equation (10.1), we can express (10.4) as

$$\frac{W}{P} = \frac{M}{P} + \frac{B}{P} + \frac{B^*}{P^*} \qquad (10.4')$$

Once M/P is chosen based on the considerations described in Chapter 8, the household must then divide the rest of its financial wealth between B and B^*. It makes this choice based on an assessment of the risk and returns of the different assets. In a world of no uncertainty, the household would simply check whether B or B^* has the higher rate of return and invest the whole portfolio in the asset with the higher rate of return. But if capital moves freely between the home and foreign capital markets, and we assume that it does, arbitrage will operate to equate the returns on the two assets. Let us see how this happens.

The first step is to express the returns on B^* in the domestic currency, so that they can be compared with the returns on holding B. For the domestic asset, the interest rate is simply i. If we take the United States as the home country, one dollar invested on Treasury bonds will be transformed into $(1 + i)$ dollars in the next period. The calculation of the dollar-denominated interest rate on B^* is a little more complicated. The question we want to answer is this: If we take $1 today and invest it in B^*, how many dollars will there be in the next period?

To calculate this return, we need to take several steps. First, the investor takes the dollar and converts it into foreign currency. Say that the bonds are French. One dollar will buy $1/E$ French francs in the current period, where E is the exchange rate measured as dollars per French franc (recall that E is normally quoted the other way around, as French francs per dollar). If the French interest rate is i^*, then investing the $1/E$ French francs in the

---

[10] Remember, however, some exceptions to this from Chapter 8. In some countries, foreign currencies are perfectly acceptable as a means of payment (a good example is the U.S. dollar in high-inflation Latin American economies). And in some cases, residents can buy foreign money on the black market, but they face high transaction costs in actually buying foreign interest-bearing assets.

foreign bond will yield $(1/E)(1 + i^*)$ French francs in the next period. To convert this back to dollars, the owner will have to sell the French francs for dollars, at next period's exchange rate E_{+1}. Therefore, the return of one dollar invested in the French bonds *expressed in U.S. currency* is (E_{+1}/E) $(1 + i^*)$.

Arbitrage should ensure that the dollar interest rate on U.S. bonds and on French bonds should be equalized, assuming no barriers to international trade in financial assets. If the French assets offered a higher rate of return, for example, all investors would try to buy the French assets, thereby bidding down the French interest rate and bidding up the U.S. interest rate. Therefore, in a kind of law of one price for financial assets, we can assert

$$(1 + i) = \left(\frac{E_{+1}}{E}\right)(1 + i^*) \qquad (10.5)$$

This expression can be rewritten as the following approximation:[11]

$$i = i^* + \frac{(E_{+1} - E)}{E} \qquad (10.6)$$

Equation (10.5) [or equation (10.6)] states an extremely important relationship called *interest arbitrage*. As equation (10.6) puts it, it says that the domestic interest rate must equal the foreign interest rate *plus* the rate of exchange-rate depreciation. We explore this proposition in greater detail in Chapter 20 where we examine the qualifications that arise from uncertainty. Of course, even without uncertainty, capital controls can undermine the relationship in (10.5).

10-3 GENERAL EQUILIBRIUM OF PRICE, THE EXCHANGE RATE, AND MONEY

Now we are ready to put together the three basic relationships that we have just analyzed to see how equilibrium in this economy is achieved. Remember from Chapter 8 that we wrote the equilibrium condition in the money market as equation (8.16)[12]; with minor manipulation we can write this as

$$M^D = \frac{PQ}{V(i)} = M \qquad (10.7)$$

Here, M is the supply of money. Money demand M^D is given as $PQ/V(i)$,

---

[11] Note that $(E_{+1}/E)(1 + i^*)$ is equal to

$$1 + i^* + \frac{(E_{+1} - E)}{E} + i^*\left[\frac{(E_{+1} - E)}{E}\right]$$

Since i^* and $(E_{+1} - E)/E$ are both usually small numbers, their product is very small, and can be ignored. Then, we have that

$$1 + i = 1 + i^* + \frac{(E_{+1} - E)}{E}$$

as shown in equation (10.6).

[12] Equation (8.16) is $V = PQ/M^D$.

where $V(i)$ is the velocity of money and is assumed to be an increasing function of the interest rate.

To arrive at a full characterization of equilibrium, we now need to add in two other relationships. One is purchasing power parity, in equation (10.1) $(P = E P^*)$. The other is interest arbitrage, which we just derived in equation (10.5). For the moment, we will restrict ourselves to an equilibrium condition with prices, the exchange rate, and other variables held constant, so that $E = E_{+1}$. With $E = E_{+1}$, the relationship in (10.5) boils down to the simpler statement that domestic and foreign interest rates are equal:

$$i = i^* \tag{10.8}$$

Because the domestic interest rate is equal to the world rate i^* (which we take to be fixed), the velocity of money, which depends on the interest rate, is also fixed.

We now put together all these pieces to find a simple relationship between the money supply and the exchange rate. Using the money market equilibrium in equation (10.7), purchasing power parity in equation (10.1), and the simplified expression for interest arbitrage in (10.6), we find the following key relationship:

$$M \, V(i^*) = E \, P^* \, Q \tag{10.9}$$

The relationship between M and E is shown in Figure 10-3. Notice that as E rises, money demand M also goes up. A depreciation (that is, a rise) of E leads to higher domestic prices and therefore to a greater demand for money balances.

Equation (10.9) can be used to describe M as a function of E or, conversely, E as a function of M. In the first case, we have $M = (E \, P^* \, Q)/V(i^*)$. In the latter case, we write $E = [M \, V(i^*)]/(P^* \, Q)$. Whether we want to think of the relationship in equation (10.9) as M as a function of E, or as E as a function of M depends on the kind of exchange-rate system being managed by the central bank.

If the exchange rate is *fixed* by the central bank, then equation (10.9) should be rewritten in the form showing M as a function of the level of E

Figure 10-3

The Equilibrium Relationship Between
M and E

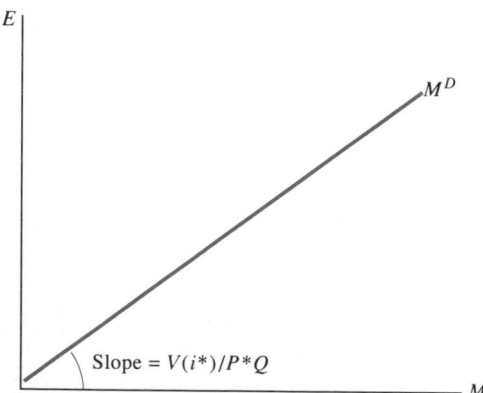

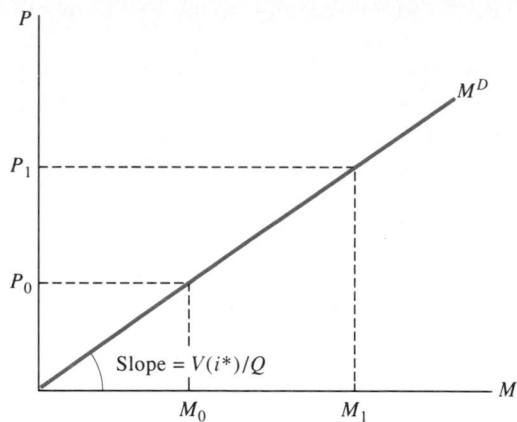

Figure 10-4

The Equilibrium Relationship Between M and P

chosen by the central bank:

$$M = \frac{(E\ P^*\ Q)}{V(i^*)} \qquad \textbf{(10.10)}$$

Under fixed exchange rates, the stock of money in the economy adjusts automatically, or *endogenously,* so that (10.10) holds for the value of E selected by the central bank. We shall see precisely how this happens in the next section. On the other hand, if the exchange rate is *flexible,* then equation (10.9) should be rewritten in the form showing the level of E that is consistent with the level of M that the central bank has chosen:

$$E = \frac{[M\ V(i^*)]}{P^*\ Q} \qquad \textbf{(10.11)}$$

In technical terms, if the exchange rate is fixed by the central bank, then E becomes an *exogenous* variable in equation (10.10); that is, E is determined by forces outside of the model (in this case, by the policy preferences of the central bank). $M,$ on the other hand, is an endogenous variable, that is determined by the equilibrium conditions of the economy. If the exchange rate floats, then E is an endogenous variable in equation (10.11) and M becomes an exogenous variable.

Notice that for given output and the external interest rate, there is a positive linear relationship between money and prices, just as there is between money and the exchange rate. As Figure 10-4 shows, a higher amount of money accompanies a higher level of prices in the economy. When the money supply is at the level M_0, prices are at the level P_0; when the money supply is at the higher level M_1, prices are also at a higher level P_1.

10-4 MONETARY POLICY UNDER FIXED AND FLOATING EXCHANGE RATES

In Chapter 9, we defined open market operations. As we now analyze some of the effects of such operations on the economy, we shall see how the results differ depending on whether the economy is operating under fixed or flexible exchange rates.

When the central bank makes a purchase of bonds in the open market, we know from equation (9.1) that initially the stock of high-powered money rises, with

$$Mh - Mh_{-1} = D^g_C - D^g_{C-1}$$

The right-hand side of this expression, the increase in the central bank's holding of government debt, measures the size of the open market operation. High-powered money initially rises by the amount of the purchase of bonds. But domestic households find that they have more money than they desire to hold at the given interest rates, prices, and income levels. Money holders will therefore try to convert part of their excess money balances into the other forms of wealth, B and B^*. But demand for B cannot absorb the excess domestic money because purchases of B by some households with excess cash simply produce excess money holdings for the households that sold the bonds. Nor can changes in interest rates absorb the excess supply of money because international arbitrage keeps i equal to i^*.

Thus, the excess supply of money leads, at least in part, to an increase in demand for B^*, the foreign asset.[13] Households try to buy foreign currency with their domestic money holdings so that they can convert the foreign currency into foreign bonds. In this way, the excess supply of money starts to raise the price of foreign exchange, or, put another way, higher M leads to an incipient depreciation of the exchange rate. Now let us see what happens, first under fixed exchange rates, and then under floating exchange rates.

Fixed Exchange Rates

Because E cannot move under a fixed-rate regime, the central bank will stand ready to intervene in the market to prevent E from depreciating. In particular, the central bank will sell foreign-exchange reserves in order to prevent the price of foreign exchange from rising (that is, to prevent E from depreciating). The central bank's sale of foreign-exchange reserves to the public causes the stock of high-powered money to fall, and the increase in the money supply caused by the original open market operation is reabsorbed. But as long as M remains higher than it was before the open market operation, the excess supply of money will continue. The central bank will have to keep selling reserves until M returns all the way down to the level that it started. Thus, if the central bank had undertaken the open market purchase with the goal of increasing the money supply, it will be frustrated in achieving that goal.[14]

---

[13] In the very short run, domestic interest rates might fall relative to foreign rates, but this would quickly lead to a shift in demand toward the foreign asset, driving down the price of the domestic bond (and therefore increasing the domestic interest rate) until $i = i^*$ is restored.

[14] The idea that a monetary expansion translates into a loss of foreign exchange reserves is a basic result of the monetary approach to the balance of payments, a framework that dates back to David Hume's work in the eighteenth century.

In the end, the central bank loses in reserves exactly the amount of the original increase in the money supply. In particular, we find

$$E(B_c^* - B_{c-1}^*) = -(D_c^g - D_{c-1}^g) \qquad \textbf{(10.12)}$$

When the dust has settled, the central bank's balance sheet will show fewer foreign-exchange reserves exactly matched by more domestic bonds, with the total value of assets unchanged. The quantity of money, on the other hand, remains unchanged:

$$Mh - Mh_{-1} = (D_c^g - D_{c-1}^g) + E(B_c^* - B_{c-1}^*) = 0 \qquad \textbf{(10.13)}$$

The balance sheet for households now shows fewer domestic bonds, exactly matched by a higher level of foreign bonds. But money holdings are unchanged. This observation leads us to the truly remarkable result that *in a fixed exchange-rate regime, with free capital mobility, the central bank cannot affect the quantity of money.* Any attempt to do so, say, through an open market operation, just produces a loss of international reserves. Thus, the money stock is endogenous, and not controllable by the central bank. And, as we will see later, in Chapter 13, this remarkable conclusion extends even to the Keynesian case in which output may fluctuate with aggregate demand.

The *offset coefficient* (*OC*) of an open market operation is defined as the ratio of the loss of foreign reserves to the increase in the central bank's bond holdings. Technically, *OC* is defined as

$$OC = -\frac{[E(B_c^* - B_{c-1}^*)]}{[D_c^g - D_{c-1}^g]} \qquad \textbf{(10.14)}$$

In the simple model we are considering, the offset coefficient is −1 because the government exactly loses in reserves the value of the bonds that it acquires. In more complex models (for example, with less than full international capital mobility), *OC* tends to be between −1 and 0.

Some interesting empirical work has been done on this subject. In a well-known article, Pentti Kouri and Michael Porter[15] studied the magnitude of the offset coefficient for Germany, Australia, the Netherlands, and Italy. The analysis was confined to the period 1960–1970, when these economies were operating under fixed exchange rates. Kouri and Porter's estimates show that the *OC* fluctuates between −0.8 for Germany and −0.43 for Italy. In other words, expansionary monetary policy provokes an offsetting loss of reserves that ranges from 80 percent of the initial expansion in Germany to 43 percent in Italy.

How can the value of the offset coefficient be different from the value −1 that is predicted by our model? As usual, the model outlined in this chapter simplifies reality in that, among other things, it assumes perfect capital mobility, a condition that overstates the degree of global capital market integration. Nonetheless, the theory outlined in this chapter does a good job of predicting the qualitative effect of an open market operation on official reserves and the money supply for a small, open economy operating under fixed exchange rates.

---

[15] Their paper, "International Capital Flows and Portfolio Equilibrium," was published in the *Journal of Political Economy*, May/June 1974.

Flexible Exchange Rates

As we have seen, the excess supply of money following an open market operation translates into increased demand for foreign currency. When the exchange rate then starts to depreciate, under a flexible exchange-rate regime the central bank does not intervene. As the exchange rate continues to depreciate, domestic prices increase in equal proportion, according to purchasing power parity—that is, depreciation raises the domestic currency price of the foreign goods, which raises the domestic price of domestically produced goods as well. In turn, the price rise acts to correct the excess supply of money by reducing the *real* quantity of money. Notice that as long as M/P remains higher following the open market purchase (OMP), an excess supply of money remains, and this continues to push the exchange rate and prices upward. Eventually, prices will rise in proportion to the increase in the money stock, so that M/P falls back to its initial level. Thus, the excess supply of money is resolved by a rise in domestic prices, and real money balances fall back to their levels before the open market purchase. Money and prices rise by the same proportion in this case.

We can sum up our discussion so far with the following basic statements. Under fixed exchange rates, the money stock is endogenous and the exchange rate is exogenous. Under flexible rates, the reverse is true; that is, the exchange rate is the endogenous variable, while the stock of money is exogenous. These results, however, must be amended when the economy has capital controls, and we shall look at that case later in this chapter.

10-5 GLOBAL FIXED EXCHANGE-RATE ARRANGEMENTS

In this section, we discuss the alternative global arrangements which are possible under a fixed exchange-rate system. The basic idea is that when two or more countries have a fixed exchange-rate arrangement, the responsibility for maintaining the fixed exchange rates can be allocated among the central banks in a variety of ways.

If there are two countries, for example, then there are three basic ways in which the responsibility can be shared. First, both central banks can peg their respective currencies to gold or to a common third currency. Second, one of the central banks can undertake the *full* responsibility to maintain the fixed exchange rate, while the other central bank operates without attention to the exchange rate. Such an arrangement is known as a unilateral peg. Third, the two central banks can share the responsibility for maintaining the fixed rate, but without reference to a third currency or to gold. This kind of arrangement is called a *cooperative peg*. Let us consider each of these three exchange rate arrangements in greater detail.

The Gold Standard

The origins of the gold standard date to the early eighteenth century in Britain. It was not, however, until the second half of the nineteenth century that the gold standard became widely accepted throughout the world. Analysts have singled the 1870s as the start of the classical gold standard period, and have dated the demise of the system to the early 1930s (with a significant interruption during World War I and its aftermath).[16]

Under the gold standard, the central bank fixes the domestic currency price of gold, so that 1 ounce of gold is assigned a fixed nominal price in terms of the local currency. The central bank then uses a stock of gold reserves to stabilize the price of gold, by buying or selling gold at the fixed price. In the United States during 1914–1933, the price of 1 ounce of gold was fixed at 20.67 dollars, or one dollar was equivalent to about 0.05 ounces of gold. When two or more currencies are tied to gold in this way, they are also fixed in value to each other.

The gold standard imparts a crucial economic relationship on the world economy. The money supply and the price level in each country depend on the global supply of gold. When there is a gold discovery, as in California in 1849, money supplies and prices tend to rise in all countries on the gold standard. When there is a long period with few new gold discoveries, as in the period 1873–1896, then world prices tend to be stable or to fall.

These crucial properties can be shown in a simple two-country model. Suppose that 1 ounce of gold has a price of Pg units of home currency, while 1 ounce of gold has a price of Pg^* units of foreign currency. Thus, there are Pg units of home currency per Pg^* units of foreign currency, so that the exchange rate (in units of home currency per unit of foreign currency) is

$$E = \frac{Pg}{Pg^*} \qquad (10.15)$$

Consider a numerical example. If 1 ounce of gold has a price of 20.67 dollars and 1 ounce of gold has a price of 4.25 pounds sterling, the exchange rate is dollars per pound ($E = \$4.86/£$). (This was the case in 1925.)

In the purest form of a gold standard, the central bank holds gold reserves that are equal in value to the amount of paper currency that it issues. The stock of paper currency changes only when the central bank buys or sells gold reserves. Gold may also circulate directly as money, in the form of gold coins. Thus, the money stock in the home country (M) is equal to monetary gold in the country, where the monetary gold is defined as the sum of the central bank gold reserves plus the gold circulating as gold coins. Let GS be the stock of monetary gold in the home country and GS^* be the stock in the foreign country. Then, since the money supply equals the value of the monetary gold in each country, we have

$$M = PgGS \qquad (10.16a)$$

$$M^* = Pg^*GS^* \qquad (10.16b)$$

For illustrative purposes, assume that the "world" supply of monetary gold in this two-country model is fixed in the amount GS_w, and is divided between the two countries:

$$GS + GS^* = GS_w \qquad (10.17)$$

---

[16] An excellent and accessible analysis of the gold standard—and of modern proposals to reinstitute it—is Richard Cooper, "The Gold Standard: Historical Facts and Future Prospects," *Brookings Papers on Economic Activity*, No. 1: 1982.

GS_w is determined exogenously, by the total amount of gold that has been discovered and mined, minus the gold that is used for jewelry, industry, or other nonmonetary purposes.

The money demand in each country may be specified in the usual way:

$$MV = PQ \qquad \text{(10.17a)}$$

$$M^*V^* = P^*Q^* \qquad \text{(10.17b)}$$

From these equations (10.15, 10.16a, 10.16b, 10.17, 10.7a, 10.7b) and the purchasing power parity condition ($P = EP^*$), it is straightforward to derive the following relationships. The stock of world monetary gold determines the stock of money in each country. Both M and M^* are simply a linear function of the world gold stock:

$$M = \left[\frac{V^*Q}{(V^*Q + Q^*V)}\right]GS_w \qquad \text{(10.18a)}$$

$$M^* = (1/E)\left[\frac{Q^*V}{(V^*Q + Q^*V)}\right]GS_w \qquad \text{(10.18b)}$$

Once M and M^* are known, it is easy to find the price level in each country, since $P = MV/Q$ and $P^* = M^*V^*/Q^*$. Thus, we find:

$$P = kGS_w \qquad \text{(10.19a)}$$

$$P^* = \left(\frac{1}{E}\right)kGS_w \qquad \text{(10.19b)}$$

where k is a parameter between 0 and 1 [$k = VV^*/(VQ^* + V^*Q)$].[17] Thus, the money stocks and price levels in the two economies are determined by the *world* gold stock. A given proportionate rise in GS_w—say, because of a gold discovery—raises prices by the same proportion.

Notice also from (10.18a) and (10.18b) that the price levels tend to decline if GS_w remains unchanged while output rises. If Q and Q^* increase, but there are no gold discoveries, there would be a *fall* in the price level. The reason is straightforward. Higher Q and Q^* lead to an increase in the demand for real money balances. But if the supply of money is unchanged because GS_w is unchanged, then the higher demand for real money balances must be satisfied by a fall in the price level rather than a rise in the money supply.

How do these predictions square with the actual experience under the gold standard? As it turns out, the predictions work remarkably well. Figure 10-5 shows the evolution of the price index in the United States from 1810 to 1914. There are four key phases.

During 1816–1849, world output was rising while little new gold was discovered. Consequently, prices tended to fall in the United States (and in other countries linked to gold). From 1849 to about 1870, following the major discoveries of gold in California and Australia, prices rose significantly. During 1870 to the late 1890s, once again output tended to expand, but little new gold was discovered, leading to a period of falling prices. Finally, during

[17] The algebraic derivation to obtain equations (10.18a), (10.18b), (10.19a), and (10.19b) is shown in the appendix to this chapter.

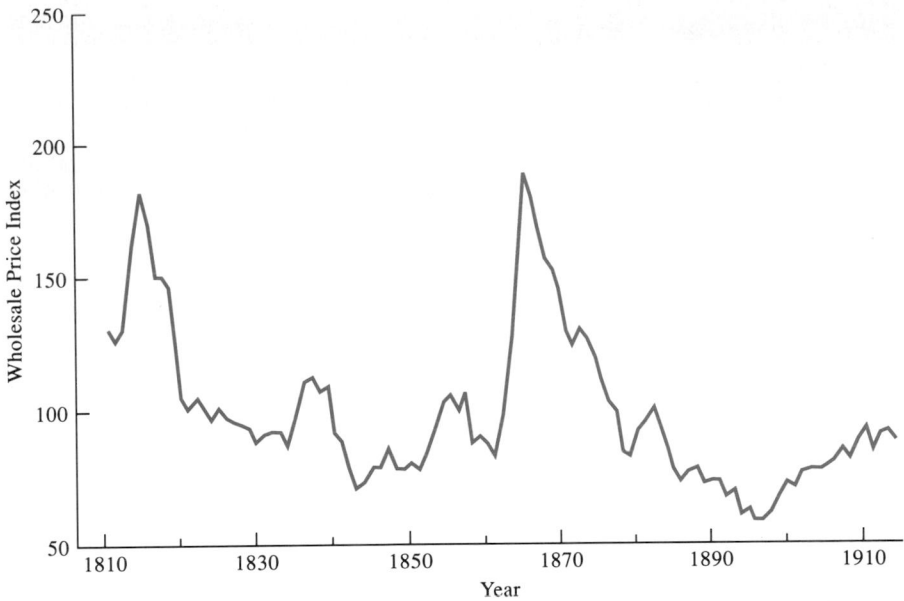

Figure 10-5

The Wholesale Price Level in the United States, 1810–1914 (1910–1914=100)

(From G. F. Warren and F. A. Pearson, Prices, *John Wiley, New York, 1933, pp. 12–13.)*

1896–1913, there were once again significant increases in the world stock of gold, accompanied by increases in the price level.

Despite obvious differences in national circumstances, price movements throughout the period 1820–1913 were very closely related across the major industrial countries (France, Germany, the United States, and the United Kingdom), as shown in Table 10-5. This supports the assumption of purchasing power parity that was made in the simple model discussed earlier. All of the countries reflect the four phases just described: falling prices during 1816–1849; rising prices during 1849–1873, falling prices once again during 1873–1896; and rising prices during 1896–1913.

A Unilateral Peg

Another way to fix the exchange rate between two countries is for one country to bear the full responsibility for keeping the exchange rate fixed. This is called a unilateral peg. The pegging country adjusts its monetary policy in order to preserve exchange-rate stability. The central bank stands ready to buy or sell foreign exchange at the fixed exchange rate. The foreign central bank, by contrast, does not undertake any actions to support the exchange rate and is thus free to vary its monetary policy.

A typical example of a one-sided peg is that of a developing country which sets its rate vis-à-vis the U.S. dollar (still the most popular currency for peggers, as was shown in Table 10-1). When Brazil, for instance, pegs its currency to the U.S. dollar, it is the responsibility of the Central Bank of Brazil, not the U.S. Federal Reserve Board, to sustain the rate. And if the Brazilian monetary authority faces a balance-of-payments problem and de-

Table   10-5

Price Levels in France, Germany, the United States, and the United Kingdom, Selected Years, 1816–1913

Year and Period	France	Germany	United States	United Kingdom
Indexes (1913 = 100)				
1816	143	94	150	147
1849	94	67	82	86
1873	122	114	137	130
1896	69	69	64	72
1913	100	100	100	100
Changes (percent)				
1816–1849	−33	−29	−45	−41
1849–1873	30	70	67	51
1873–1896	−45	−40	−53	−45
1896–1913	45	45	56	39

Source: R. Cooper, "The Gold Standard: Historical Facts and Future Prospects," Brookings Papers on Economic Activity, *No. 1, 1982, p. 9*

cides to devalue the *cruzado* vis-à-vis the dollar, the Fed has little or no say on the decision.

Under the Bretton Woods par value system, which governed international monetary relations among the industrialized countries from 1944 to 1971, all countries except the United States operated on a unilateral peg to the U.S. dollar.[18] Individual countries pegged their currencies to the dollar and bore the responsibility to sustain the exchange rate. The U.S. monetary authority almost never intervened to maintain a stable exchange rate vis-à-vis another currency. International reserves of member countries were held in gold or dollars, which could be used to stabilize the domestic currency vis-à-vis the dollar.

The United States had no direct responsibility in maintaining the exchange rate of the dollar. It could vary the money supply without regard to the exchange rate, since all the *other* countries in the world had to adjust their monetary policies in line with the U.S. monetary policies. The United States did, however, have one important obligation that put a constraint on its monetary policy. The United States was required to stand ready to convert dollars into gold at a fixed price. The price of gold was established at $35

---

[18] The Bretton Woods system gets its name from the city of Bretton Woods, New Hampshire, where the International Monetary Conference of the United and Associated Nations was held in July 1944. This agreement bears the imprint of the two most influential economists that participated in the meeting and its preparation—John Maynard Keynes of Great Britain and Harry Dexter White of the United States. It was signed by 44 countries and laid the foundations of the International Monetary Fund (IMF), and the par value system of exchange rates. A detailed analysis of the Bretton Woods system is provided by Robert Solomon, *The International Monetary System 1945–1976* (New York: Harper & Row, 1977).

per ounce, which remained valid throughout the period 1944–1971. (In practice, as U.S. gold reserves fell in the 1960s, the United States often discouraged foreign governments from converting their monetary gold into dollars). In short, the Bretton Woods system instituted a kind of gold-exchange standard: the currencies of participating countries were convertible into dollars, and dollar reserves of countries outside the United States were convertible into gold by the United States at a fixed price (though with some considerable discouragement from the United States).

Let us now analyze a one-sided peg in a formal model. We assume that the home country bears the responsibility for pegging the exchange rate, while the foreign country chooses monetary policy (M^*) without regard to the exchange rate. (Thus, in the Bretton Woods system, the United States plays the role of the "foreign" country in this model, since it was free to choose monetary policy without regard to the exchange rate.) The key to the one-sided peg is that all relevant nominal magnitudes—such as the money supplies in the two countries and the price levels—are determined by the foreign country's choice of M^*. In other words, the foreign country (the one that does *not* intervene to stabilize the exchange rate) determines the monetary variables in the same way that the world gold stock did under the gold standard. This is obviously quite a privilege for the foreign country!

To show this formally, we start by writing the foreign price level as a function of M^*. It is immediate from equation (10.17b) that

$$P^* = \frac{M^*V^*}{Q^*} \tag{10.20a}$$

Since purchasing power parity holds ($P = EP^*$), then

$$P = E\left(\frac{M^*V^*}{Q^*}\right) \tag{10.20b}$$

Now, from equation (10.17a) and (10.20b), we can determine the equilibrium value of the money supply in the home country as

$$M = EM^*\left(\frac{V^*}{V}\right)\left(\frac{Q}{Q^*}\right) \tag{10.19c}$$

Thus, a change in the money supply in the foreign country is transmitted to foreign prices (P^*), domestic money (M), and domestic prices. A given percentage increase in M^* leads to the same percentage increase in P^*, P, and M. The foreign country therefore determines the world inflation rate. The home country, which must select M in order to maintain the fixed exchange rate, has absolutely no effect on the nominal magnitudes in the economy!

When there are N countries (with $N > 2$) in a fixed exchange-rate system, it is possible to have the first $N - 1$ countries each undertake the burden of pegging to the Nth country. The Nth country then is free to set the monetary policy as it sees fit, and all the other countries adjust their money supplies in order to keep the exchange rates stable. Once again, the Nth country sets the basic nominal parameters (money supplies and price levels) in all the countries in the fixed exchange-rate system. The United States was the Nth country in the Bretton Woods system, though the freedom of maneuver of the United States was limited to some extent by the obligation of the United States to maintain gold convertibility at $35 per ounce.

A Cooperative Peg

Fixed exchange rates are sometimes maintained as a shared responsibility between countries. These types of agreements have been adopted by closely linked groups of economies, such as the members of the European Monetary System (EMS).[19] The EMS was created in 1979 with the intention of limiting exchange-rate fluctuations among the countries in the European Community. The EMS brought with it a new monetary unit of account, the European Currency Unit (ECU), which is a basket of currencies of all the countries in the European Community.

The exchange-rate mechanism (ERM) of the EMS is, basically, a scheme of adjustable pegs among member countries, with a narrow band for fluctuation. The currencies inside the EMS, however, float with respect to the currencies outside of the EMS. The EMS establishes a pegged *central rate* for each EC country, as the price of one ECU in units of the country's currency. Central rates are fixed, but are subject to sporadic revisions at times of realignment. EC countries that have joined the ERM have been able to opt for one of its two variants: a narrow band, which allows currencies to fluctuate up to 2.25 percent on each side of the central rate, and a broader band, which permits fluctuations of up to 6 percent on each side of the central rate.[20]

Every two currencies in the EMS have a *bilateral central rate* determined by the ratio of their ECU central rates. Central banks of any two countries are forced to intervene when their bilateral exchange rate reaches the limits of the band (2.25 percent above or below the central rate in the generality of the cases). Since the EMS was conceived as a cooperative arrangement, countries are supposed to share the burden of adjustment. Thus, intervention is to be made *jointly* by the two monetary authorities involved. When a particular currency is tending to depreciate vis-à-vis another currency, both central banks must intervene in order to buy the weak currency by selling the strong currency.

A cooperative peg system does not permit any country to carry out a completely independent monetary policy. At least in principle, there is no *N*th country that plays the role played by the United States during the Bretton Woods period. The ability to pursue monetary policy is formally symmetric for all countries in this scheme. Some analysts have argued, however, that the EMS is not in practice a cooperative peg, but is in fact a system of one-sided pegs in which Germany is the Nth country. In essence, Germany is at the center of a "greater Deutsche mark area," in the same way that the dollar was at the center of the Bretton Woods system.[21] Arguments in support of this view are that countries which have been unable or unwilling to follow Germany's monetary policy have had to adjust their exchange rates vis-à-vis the Deutsch mark.

---

[19] A good analysis of the EMS is found in Francesco Giavazzi and Alberto Giovannini, *Limiting Exchange Rate Flexibility: The European Monetary System*, MIT Press, Cambridge, MA, 1989.

[20] All EC nations are members of the EMS. As of late 1990, 10 of the 12 countries had also joined the ERM.

[21] Giavazzi and Giovannini, *Limiting Exchange Rate Flexibility*.

Why have countries accepted this situation? Presumably, because they value sharing the anti-inflationary reputation of Germany, which is an important asset at the time of pursuing disinflation. Analysts have gone as far as describing the EMS as "an arrangement for France and Italy to purchase a commitment to low inflation by accepting German monetary policy."[22] Recent proposals to move from the EMS to European Monetary Union are discussed in Chapter 14.

10-6 THE EFFECTS OF DEVALUATION

Consider the effects of a change in E_t in an economy where the central bank pegs the exchange rate. Suppose the economy starts in equilibrium, with $M = EP^*Q/V(i^*)$, and the central bank unexpectedly and permanently increases E. What are the effects in our model on prices, money, and the balance sheets of the private sector and the central bank?

Immediately, the increase in E leads to a proportionate increase in prices, according to the PPP relationship. All of a sudden, there is an excess demand for money, since with P^*, Q, and $V(i^*)$ all unchanged, and with E increased, the demand for M has risen but its supply has so far remained unchanged. Households will try to sell B and B^* in order to shift more of their wealth into M. But sales of B are to no effect: the interest rate on B is fixed at $i = i^*$ by international arbitrage, and sales of B from one household to another simply shift the excess demand for M from one household to the next. On the other hand, the attempt of the public to sell B^* (or equivalently, to borrow from abroad in order to increase money holdings) tends to cause the domestic currency to appreciate because the sales of B^* lead to an accumulation of foreign money, which is then used to purchase domestic currency.

Since the central bank is attempting to fix the exchange rate at the new, more devalued level, it must intervene in the foreign-exchange market to prevent the domestic currency from appreciating. It does this by selling domestic currency to buy up the foreign assets the public now holds in order to stabilize the exchange rate at its depreciated level. As a result, the central bank gains foreign-exchange reserves, while the public's shortage of money is alleviated by the bank's sales of domestic currency. This process of foreign-exchange intervention must continue until the excess demand for the domestic currency is met. This will occur when the money supply has risen in the same proportion as the currency depreciation and the resulting increase in domestic prices.

What is the end result of the devaluation? The central bank has *gained reserves,* or in technical terms, run a surplus on the official balances account. In selling B^* in order to replenish its money balances, the private sector has reduced its holding of foreign assets. In the end, *the central bank is made wealthier and the private sector is made poorer by the devaluation.* The central bank has gained real reserves without increasing the real value of its liabilities, M/P. Households, on the other hand, have sold B^* merely to return M/P back to its initial level.

---

[22] Stanley Fischer, "British Monetary Policy," in R. Dornbusch and R. Layard, eds., *The Performance of the British Economy* (Oxford: Oxford University Press, 1987).

How has this happened? The devaluation acts like a tax. The sudden rise in P sharply reduces the household's real money balances, a capital loss that results in a decline in household wealth as well as a drop in liquidity. The government is the recipient of the capital loss of households. Ultimately, the central bank gets to accumulate new foreign-exchange reserves as households sell B^* in order to replenish their money balances.

So far, we have been working under the dictates of the purchasing power parity relationship that exchange-rate changes provoke proportionate increases in the price level. How does the empirical evidence square with this theory? When analyzing the real exchange rate between the United States and Canada in Figure 10-2, we argued that PPP holds better over the long run than in the short run. Accordingly, we now measure annual exchange-rate changes and inflation over the 20-year period 1965–1985 for a wide group of countries. When we have computed the average annual rates of inflation and of devaluation (or depreciation) for each country, we can plot the results, as shown in Figure 10-6.

We see here a striking correlation between these two variables. (The correlation would be present, but much less striking for a time horizon of one or two years.) Countries with high rates of devaluation such as Peru, Zaire, and Turkey also experienced high rates of inflation of the same order of magnitude. By contrast, the countries with low rates of devaluation also had low rates of inflation. Notice that, in general, inflation is higher than the rate of devaluation for each country. This is as expected. According to the modified version of PPP in equation (10.2′), the rate of domestic inflation is

Figure 10-6
Exchange-Rate Changes and Inflation in Selected Countries (Annual Averages), 1965–1985

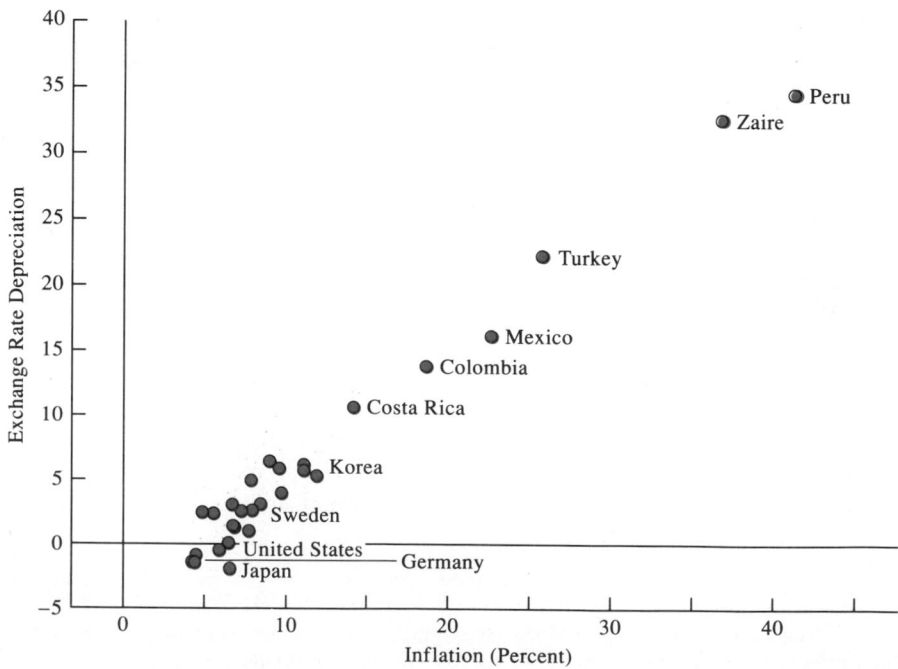

approximately equal to the depreciation of the local currency plus the international rate of inflation (in this case, the inflation rate in U.S. dollars).

10-7 THE CASE OF CAPITAL CONTROLS

We have based our analysis up to this point on the working assumption of free capital mobility. But international capital flows are often constrained by the monetary authorities, or by other factors such as default risk or imperfect information. Capital controls have the effect of breaking the condition of interest arbitrage. That is, the domestic interest rate becomes divorced from the international interest rate because asset holders are not allowed to make an arbitrage operation if there is a gap between i and i^*. In terms of the model we have been using, equations (10.5) and (10.8) no longer hold.

Let us now look at the effect of an open market purchase of bonds under conditions of constrained capital flows. As usual, we shall assume that PPP holds. Once again, we start first with the case of fixed exchange rates, and then turn to that of floating exchange rates.

Fixed Exchange Rates with No Capital Mobility

The excess supply of money resulting from the OMP leads to an excess demand for domestic bonds. (Remember that now demand is not allowed to increase for B^*.) This tends to push up the price of domestic bonds, and thus to drive down domestic interest rates. With free capital mobility, we could assume that any fall in i would be quickly eliminated by international arbitrage, as wealthholders sold domestic bonds and purchased foreign bonds. But with capital controls, households cannot reverse the fall in i by purchasing foreign bonds because they are not allowed to purchase foreign bonds. This being the case, interest rates decline after the OMP, and the fall in i is enough to restore money market equilibrium. Thus, if the money supply has gone up by ΔM, domestic interest rates go from the initial i to a new level i' that satisfies

$$M + \Delta M = [V(i')](E \, P^*Q)$$

But this is not the end of the story. Under our normal assumptions, a lower i (which is also a lower real interest rate)[23] reduces saving and increase investment, and the current accounts goes into deficit. And the current account deficit has monetary repercussions. With imports of goods and services exceeding exports, the central bank sells more foreign exchange to the public than it buys. The net result is a fall in international reserves, and a decline in high-powered money:

$$\begin{aligned} Mh - Mh_{-1} &= E \, (B_c^* - B_{c-1}^*) \\ &= S(r) - I(r) = CA \end{aligned} \tag{10.21}$$

Over time, the money supply falls as a result of the current account deficit. As the money supply falls, interest rates start to rise back to their

---

[23] Because PPP is assumed to hold, and because the exchange rate is constant, the price level is also constant. Therefore, the real interest rate r will be equal to the nominal interest rate i. Changes in i are thus tantamount to changes in the real interest rate.

level before the open market operation. The current account deficits eventually are sufficient to eliminate the excess supply of money, thereby driving interest rates back up to their initial level, and driving the current account back into balance.

Notice this very interesting result. Now that the capital account is closed, people get rid of their excess cash balances by running current account deficits through time (as a result of spending in excess of income). This process continues until the excess supply of money disappears. Then, interest rates go back to their original level. In the end, the central bank loses foreign-exchange reserves equal to the initial open market operation.

Compare this process with the case of capital mobility. There, the excess supply of money is eliminated by a one-time, instantaneous capital outflow of the private sector, in which the private sector exchanges its excess money for foreign reserves sold by the central bank. Yet the end result is the same: the money supply increase is eliminated, and the central bank loses reserves equal to the open market operation, but the timing and channels through which this takes effect are quite different.

Flexible Exchange Rates With No Capital Mobility

As with fixed exchange rates, under flexible exchange rates, the excess supply of money after the open market operations tends to drive down interest rates. A drop in interest rates ordinarily produces a current account deficit. But this is not possible now. If there is no private capital mobility because of the capital controls, and if the central bank does not sell foreign-exchange reserves (because it does not intervene in the foreign-exchange market under the flexible exchange-rate system), the economy as a whole cannot borrow from the rest of the world. Thus, the combination of capital controls and flexible exchange rates means that the current account must be in balance at all times.

The current account stays balanced following the open market operation because the exchange rate depreciates. This depreciation leads, through PPP, to an increase in the domestic price level. The price level increase, in turn, eliminates the excess supply of money. In the end, P is higher, but M/P is unchanged. The result for the flexible exchange case is therefore the same with and without capital mobility: the exchange rate depreciates enough to raise prices by the same proportion as the increase in the nominal money stock. M/P returns to its initial level, and interest rates and the current account are unchanged by the OMP.

Devaluation With No Capital Mobility

As a final exercise, consider the effects of a devaluation of the currency in the case of no capital mobility. Let us start from an equilibrium and suppose that the central bank devalues the exchange rate, in a regime of pegged exchange rates. Recall that in the case of perfect capital mobility, the devaluation leads to a jump in prices, a loss of household wealth as M/P falls, a sale of B^* by the private sector in order to replenish M/P, and an instantaneous increase in central bank reserves, as the central bank buys foreign exchange and sells the domestic currency in order to peg the exchange rate.

When capital cannot move, the devaluation leads to a jump in prices and a decline in M/P, just as before. But now, households cannot sell their foreign bond holdings in order to replenish M/P because of the capital controls. Rather, the decline in M/P leads to an immediate jump in the domestic interest rate. With the rise in the nominal interest rate, the *real* interest rate r also rises (Because this is a one-time devaluation, the price level subsequently stabilizes so that there is no continuing inflation.) But a higher r leads to a current account surplus, as $S(r) - I(r)$ increases. The surplus, in turn, leads to a rise in the domestic money stock and a corresponding increase in the foreign-exchange reserves of the central bank, as equation (10.20) tells us. Eventually, this process returns the level of real money balances back to their level before the devaluation, and the current account returns to balance.

10-8 OTHER KINDS OF EXCHANGE-RATE REGIMES

So far, we have contemplated exchange rates at the two extremes: purely fixed (or pegged) and perfectly flexible (or floating). In practice, exchange-rate arrangements are often more complicated. For example, when exchange controls exist, the official rate of exchange does not apply for certain transactions, and they must be carried out at an alternative exchange rate (perhaps the rate given in an illegal foreign-exchange market). Exchange controls almost always give rise to a system of dual or multiple exchange rates. Many developing countries have extensively used multiple exchange-rate mechanisms despite the fact that such arrangements are strongly resisted by the International Monetary Fund.

In a typical case of dual exchange markets, one rate exists for commercial transactions and a more depreciated rate (often a black market floating rate) exists for capital account operations. There are two basic ideas behind this policy. One is to isolate the goods market from shocks that might occur in domestic and international assets markets. The second is to limit the holdings of foreign assets by the private sector in the hope of preventing a loss of foreign-exchange reserves at the central bank. As we shall see in Chapter 11, the central bank may well lose its ability to peg the exchange rate if it runs out of foreign-exchange reserves when households attempt to convert their domestic money holdings into foreign currency. A dual exchange rate, in which the capital account rate floats, is often aimed at avoiding a mass conversion of domestic currency into foreign financial assets.

One problem with a dual exchange rate arises when the gap widens between the official rate and the parallel floating rate. Suppose that the capital market rate is 50 percent higher than the official one. By law, exporters are usually required to remit their foreign-exchange earnings at the (low) official exchange rate. But exporters also have an incentive to underinvoice, that is, declare lower earnings than they have actually made, in order to leave some of their revenue abroad and subsequently convert these earnings at the higher parallel rate. On the other hand, importers are tempted to overinvoice their sales abroad. By declaring more imports than they will actually purchase, the importers get foreign exchange from the central bank at the low official exchange rate that they can sell in the black market at a much higher price. Overinvoicing and underinvoicing are classical forms of *capital flight*, that is, capital flows out of the country that are not registered in the balance of payments.

Some countries have not been satisfied to have only two exchange rates. Rather, they have put in place differentiated exchange rates even for various types of commercial transactions. The objective of these arrangements is to discourage the import of some goods and services and to maintain low domestic prices for other "sensitive" imports. Often, lower exchange rates are established for basic foodstuffs, pharmaceuticals, and capital goods, and higher (that is, more depreciated) exchange rates are set for manufactured imports and "luxury goods." At the same time, these exchange-rate systems normally include low exchange rates for traditional exports like agricultural goods and primary materials. The goal of this policy is twofold: to keep the cost of living under control and to provide a source of revenue for the government. In fact, such policies are highly distorting of trade flows and rarely serve any valid purpose.

A simple example illustrates the motivation of such a policy, however misguided such policies are in practice. Suppose that the import rate is set at 100 *pesos* per dollar, while the export rate is 50; then, for every dollar that the government purchases from exporters and sells to importers, it obtains a profit of 50 *pesos*. This works exactly as a tax on exports, which obviously discourages their production. Clearly, a multiple exchange-rate system for imports and exports leads to a breakdown of purchasing power parity.

A striking example of multiple exchange rates occurred in Chile in 1973. At the time, the country had 15 different exchange rates, with the highest one being about *80 times* the lowest. Normal trade flows were thoroughly disrupted by the system. Copper, the principal export, received the lowest rate. A more recent, although less extreme, case of multiple rates is Venezuela, as shown in Table 10-6.

Multiple exchange rates on current account transactions can lead to serious economic distortions. They tend to cause severe resource allocation problems, as purely artificial advantages render some activities more profitable than others. Typically, multiple exchange rates heavily discourage the

TABLE 10-6

VENEZUELA'S MULTIPLE EXCHANGE RATE REGIME

Date	Exchange Rate (bolivars/US$)	Transaction Category
February 1983	4.3	Petroleum exports, debt service, basic food
	6.0	Most imports
	Unregulated	All other transactions
February 1984	4.3	Basic food
	6.0	Petroleum exports
	7.5	Services, most imports, debt service
	Unregulated	Nontraditional exports, nonessential imports, capital account transactions

Source: R. Dornbusch, "Special Exchange Rates for Capital Account Transactions," The World Bank Economic Review (Washington, DC: World Bank, September 1986.)

domestic production of primary exports and import substitutes, and this leads to an unhealthy dependence on imports of such commodities in the medium term.

Finally, we should not overlook a special arrangement that is currently used in several developing countries, particularly in Latin America, the *crawling peg* system. This scheme establishes an initial, pegged exchange rate that is adjusted periodically according to a predetermined schedule or formula. Thus, the crawling peg is a system of frequent, preannounced small devaluations, sometimes even on a daily basis. One rule that has been used devalues the nominal exchange rate at a rate that is equal to the difference between the target rate of domestic inflation and the anticipated rate of international inflation. Such a policy aims to maintain a given value of the real exchange rate, $e = EP^*/P$.

Suppose, for example, that the Colombian central bank is aiming for an inflation rate of 15 percent per year, while the U.S. inflation rate is expected to be 5 percent for the year. One policy might be to devalue the Colombian peso at a very gradual rate so that over the course of the year, the peso would be devalued by 10 percent, the gap in the two inflation rates.[24] John Williamson, of the Institute for International Economics, has been a leading analyst of crawling peg systems.[25]

10-9 SUMMARY

In a *fixed-exchange regime,* the predominant form of exchange-rate arrangement during the past century, the monetary authority fixes the relative price between the domestic currency and a foreign currency. To sustain the parity exchange rate, the central bank commits itself to buy or sell foreign exchange at the given rate. In the *gold standard,* a special kind of fixed exchange-rate system, each monetary authority committed itself to fixing the price of an ounce of gold in its domestic currency. Inasmuch as each currency was pegged in value to gold, the various national currencies were in fact pegged to each other.

A fixed exchange rate can also be set by one country when it pegs its currency *unilaterally* to that of other nation. In this case, the country undertakes the full responsibility of holding the exchange rate at the level it has committed to. Or the exchange rate can be maintained as a shared responsibility ("cooperatively") between the countries that are party to it, such as in the European Monetary System. Or each currency can be pegged to a common third currency or commodity (such as gold), and therefore, de facto, each is pegged to the other.

A currency is *convertible* if the public is able to exchange domestic currency for foreign currency at the official exchange rate without important restrictions. If there are significant restrictions on currency exchange, the currency is considered to be *inconvertible.* Convertibility is generally a mat-

---

[24] If the exchange rate is devalued each week, the weekly rate of devaluation would be 0.183 percent, as this would yield a 10 percent depreciation in 52 weeks $[(1.00183)^{52} = 1.10]$.

[25] See, for example, his edited volume *The Crawling Peg: Past Performance and Future Prospects* (New York: Macmillan, 1982).

ter of extent rather than an all-or-nothing proposition. Some restrictions on convertibility apply to capital account transactions, others to certain imports. A common indicator of inconvertibility is the spread between the official exchange rate and the black market or parallel market rate, the so-called *exchange-rate gap*.

Under a *floating exchange-rate regime,* the monetary authority makes no commitment to support a given exchange rate. Fluctuations in the demand and supply of money are accommodated by changes in the exchange rate. If the central bank does not buy or sell foreign currency at all, the exchange-rate regime is called a "clean float." If the monetary authority undertakes foreign-exchange operations, we speak of a "dirty float."

Movements in the exchange rate receive different names according to the exchange-rate regime in which they occur. We define the exchange rate E as the number of units of domestic currency per unit of foreign currency. A rise in E is called a *devaluation* if it takes place under a pegged exchange rate and a *depreciation* if it occurs under a floating-rate system. Similarly, a fall in E is called a *revaluation* if it occurs under a pegged exchange-rate system, and an *appreciation* if it takes place under floating rates.

The *law of one price* states that if the domestic market and a foreign market are unified, then the prices of commodities should be the same in the two countries, when expressed in a common currency. *Arbitrage* is the force ensuring that the law of one price actually holds. The doctrine of *purchasing power parity* extends the law of one price from individual commodities to the basket of goods and services that determines the average price level in an economy. Under a less restrictive version of PPP, domestic inflation is equal to the rate of currency depreciation (or devaluation) plus the rate of foreign inflation.

Agents hold their wealth in a combination of domestic assets and foreign assets. When there is no uncertainty, agents simply try to hold their entire portfolio in the asset with the higher return. Under free capital mobility between the home and foreign capital markets, arbitrage equates the rates of return on home and foreign bonds when those are expressed in a common currency. This condition is known as *interest arbitrage,* which states that the domestic interest rate (in domestic currency) is equal to the foreign interest rate plus the percentage rate of currency depreciation.

The effects of monetary policy depend crucially on what type of exchange-rate regime the policy works within. Under *fixed* exchange rates and free capital mobility, the central bank cannot influence the quantity of money (at least not beyond the very short run). Any attempt to increase high-powered money, say, through an open market purchase of bonds, produces only a loss of international reserves. Thus, the money stock is endogenous, and not controllable by the central bank. The *offset coefficient* of an open market operation is defined as the ratio of the loss of foreign reserves to the increase in the central bank's bond holdings after an open market operation. With high capital mobility, the offset coefficient is close to -1. Under *flexible* exchange rates, however, the role of the money supply and the exchange rate is the opposite of the role under fixed exchange rates. The exchange rate becomes the endogenous variable, which adjusts to a change in the quantity of money. The stock of money is exogenous and is controlled by the central bank.

The results concerning fixed exchange rates depend on the exact nature of the exchange-rate system. The text assumes that the country in question is undertaking a *unilateral peg*. In this case, the domestic monetary policy is largely ineffective, and key nominal variables will be decided by the foreign central bank. If there is a *cooperative peg* instead, then both the domestic and foreign central banks are constrained in their behavior to observe certain shared rules. In the case of a gold standard, the fixed exchange rate between two currencies arises indirectly from the fact that each of the currencies is independently pegged to gold. In this case, the vagaries of discoveries of world gold will have a central effect on global monetary conditions.

In our simple classical model, which assumes fixed output and perfectly flexible prices, a devaluation leads to a proportional increase in the price level. This, in turn, provokes an excess demand for money. In order to satisfy this demand, local agents sell their foreign asset holdings to the central bank in exchange for local currency. In the process, the central bank gains international reserves, and the private sector reduces its holdings of foreign assets.

When *capital controls* exist, interest arbitrage does not hold and interest rates are not equalized internationally. Under *fixed* exchange rates and no capital mobility, an open market purchase leads to a reduction in the domestic interest rate, which tends to raise investment and lower saving, and thereby pushes the current account to a deficit. This deficit reduces international reserves and thus the stock of high-powered money. As the money supply falls over time, interest rates rise back to their initial levels. In the end, the central bank loses foreign-exchange reserves equal to the open market operation. Under *flexible* exchange rates, the excess supply of money brought about by the open market operation reduces interest rates and tends to produce a current account deficit. Since there cannot be a current account deficit in this case, as there is no way to finance such a deficit, equilibrium is achieved through an exchange-rate depreciation and a corresponding increase in the domestic price level, which raises prices and reduces real money balances to their initial level.

In practice, exchange-rate arrangements are often more complicated than the extreme cases of purely fixed and purely flexible exchange rates. A typical case occurs when one exchange rate is set for current account transactions and a more depreciated rate exists for capital account operations. In some cases, different exchange rates apply for different types of commercial transactions as well. A special arrangement used in several developing countries is the *crawling peg* system. This scheme establishes an initial, pegged exchange rate that is adjusted periodically according to a predetermined schedule or formula. Thus, the crawling peg is a system of minidevaluations.

Key Concepts

partial equilibrium
appreciation
exchange-rate regime
law of one price
Bretton Woods agreement
international interest arbitrage
pegged exchange rate
endogenous variables

currency convertibility
multiple exchange rates
cooperative exchange-rate
   arrangement
crawling peg regime
depreciation
general equilibrium
fixed exchange rate

gold standard
flexible exchange rate
purchasing power parity (PPP)
exchange-rate gap
real exchange rate
devaluation

exogenous variables
revaluation
offset coefficient
unilateral peg
exchange controls

Problems and Questions

1. Describe the main differences between a floating and a fixed exchange-rate regime. Can a floating currency be nonconvertible?

2. In a unilateral peg only the central bank of the country which decided to peg the currency has the responsibility of holding the exchange rate at the committed level. True or false? Explain.

3. For which of the following goods is it more likely that purchasing power parity would hold? Why?

  a. Personal computers.
  b. Laundry services.
  c. Oil.
  d. Telephones.
  e. Telephone calls.

4. Assume that domestic prices are rising faster than foreign prices.

  a. If purchasing power parity holds, what would happen to the exchange rate?
  b. If the exchange rate is fixed, what would happen to the real exchange rate?

5. Suppose that the U.S. domestic interest rate is 5 percent and that the interest rate in a Latin American country is 10 percent. The current market exchange rate is 250 pesos per dollar.

  a. If the exchange rate in one year goes from 250 to 255 pesos per dollar, is it more profitable to invest in U.S. bonds or in bonds from the Latin American country?
  b. If interest-rate parity holds, what would the exchange rate be one year from now?

6. Assume that the central bank pegs the exchange rate. Describe the effects on the price level and on the official reserve holdings of the central bank of the following events, once the money market equilibrium is reestablished.

  a. A devaluation of the currency.
  b. A purchase of domestic assets by the central bank.
  c. A rise in foreign prices.
  d. A rise in the foreign interest rate.
  e. An anticipation of a future devaluation.

7. Assume now that the central bank allows a clean float of the exchange rate. Analyze the effects on the exchange rate and on the price level of the following events:

  a. A selling of domestic assets by the central bank.
  b. A rise in foreign prices.
  c. An increase in the foreign interest rate.

8. Suppose that a small open economy begins to use credit cards for the first time, starting from monetary equilibrium. The credit card allows households to economize on their money balances and thus to hold more of their wealth in interest-bearing assets. Discuss the effects of the introduction of credit cards on the nominal money supply, the real money supply, official foreign-exchange reserves of the central bank and the exchange rate assuming

a. Fixed exchange rates.

b. Flexible exchange rates.

9. Consider a small open economy with a fixed-exchange-rate system and complete capital controls. Analyze the effects of a rise in foreign prices on the domestic interest rate, the current account, the money supply, and the foreign-exchange reserves of the central bank.

10. Assume that a small open economy has a multiple exchange-rate system. If purchasing power parity holds, how will the domestic relative prices of goods in this economy compare with the relative prices of goods in international markets?

APPENDIX

From equations (10.17a) and (10.17b), we can solve for P and P^* to obtain:

$$P = \frac{MV}{Q} \tag{A.1a}$$

$$P^* = \frac{M^*V^*}{Q^*} \tag{A.1b}$$

We know from equations (A.1a) and (A.1b) that $P = EP^*$, and thus

$$\frac{MV}{Q} = E\left(\frac{M^*V^*}{Q^*}\right) \tag{A.2}$$

Solving for M^* in equation (A.2):

$$M^* = \left(\frac{1}{E}\right)\left(\frac{MQ^*V}{V^*Q}\right) \tag{A.3}$$

From equations (10.15) and (10.16), $M + EM^* = GS_w$; replacing new M^* from (A.3) leads to

$$M + \frac{MQ^*V}{V^*Q} = GS_w \tag{A.4}$$

and solving for M in equation (A.4) one gets to

$$M = \left[\frac{V^*Q}{(V^*Q + Q^*V)}\right]GS_w \tag{A.5}$$

Replacing (A.5) back in (A.3), we obtain a solution for M^*:

$$M^* = \left(\frac{1}{E}\right)\left[\frac{Q^*V}{(V^*Q + Q^*V)}\right]GS_w \tag{A.6}$$

(A.5) and (A.6) corespond to equations (10.18a) and (10.18b), respectively. Equations (10.19a) and (10.19b) are obtained directly by replacing expressions (A.5) and (A.6) into (A.1a) and (A.1b).

chapter 11

Inflation: Fiscal and Monetary Aspects

Continuing with our simple framework of fixed output, purchasing power parity, and free capital mobility, we now turn for the first time to the study of inflation. Although this simplified framework lacks realism, it helps us focus on important particular monetary and fiscal aspects of inflation. Later in the book we shall consider many more realistic complications, as they come up in the discussion.[1]

Inflation is defined as the percentage change in the price level. Therefore, we should take pains to identify the price level properly from the start. In the model we have developed so far, the price level P applies to the single output in the economy. Later on, when we start to deal with differentiated goods produced at home and abroad, the price level will be an average of the prices of domestic and foreign goods. In practice, inflation is normally measured by the change in the consumer price index (CPI), the average price of the basket of goods and services consumed by a representative household.

We need to distinguish early on between *once-and-for-all* price increases and *persistent* price rises. The former result from particular shocks, such as one-time increases in world oil prices, while the latter usually result from some chronic economic problem, such as a large and persistent budget deficit. It is also useful to distinguish inflations by their severity. In some countries, such as West Germany and Switzerland, inflation has been below 10 percent per year for decades. In others, price rises have exceeded 20 percent per year for long periods of time. In a third group of countries, including Argentina, Brazil, and Peru, inflation has exceeded 100 percent per year for most of the 1980s.

---

[1] In later chapters, we discuss the implications of a breakdown in purchasing power parity. We also analyze the effects of different forms of wage-setting behavior on the dynamics of inflation. In fact, one of the most interesting aspects of inflation, the so-called Phillips curve, is importantly affected by the nature of wage bargaining. These and other issues are the main focus of Chapters 15 and 16.

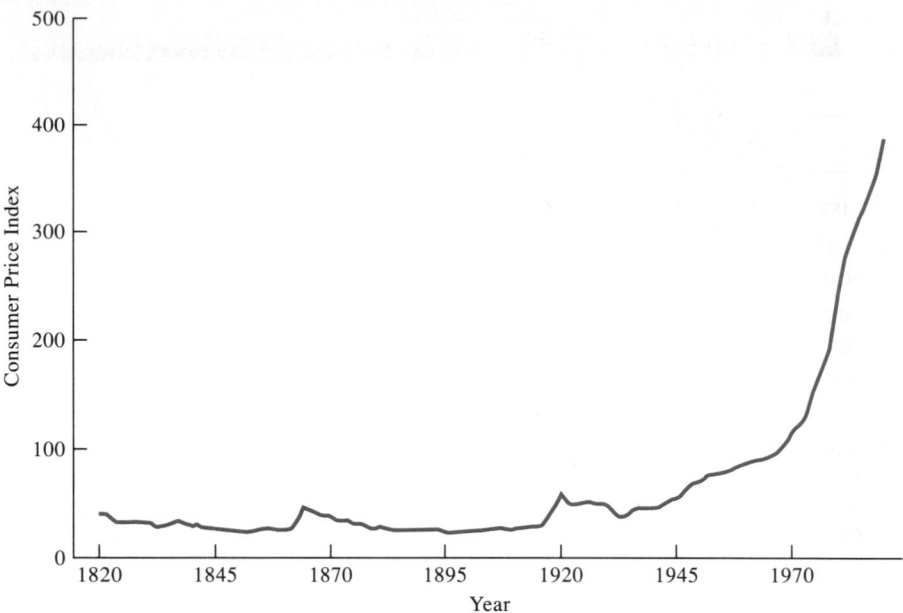

Figure 11-1

Evolution of the Price Level in the United States, 1820–1990 (CPI, 1967=100)

(Data from 1820–1970: U.S. Historical Statistics; *data from 1970–1990:* Economic Report of the President, 1991.*)*

In some extreme episodes, inflation has reached an excess of 50 percent per month (an annual rate of about 13,000 percent per year), in which case the high inflation is termed a *hyperinflation.*[2] Hyperinflations are very rare, and also fascinating—except perhaps for the residents of the afflicted country! Recent hyperinflations include those in Bolivia during 1984–1985 and those in Peru, Argentina, Brazil, Nicaragua, Poland, and Yugoslavia during 1989. (The problem of ending very high inflations is treated in Chapter 23.)

Throughout history, the United States has generally had a low rate of inflation. The highest sustained inflation during the post–World War II period came in the late 1970s, when inflation reached about 10 percent per year. Inflation was brought down in the early 1980s, partly through a sharp rise in unemployment, and partly through a fall in the international price of oil. Figure 11-1 shows the long-term path of the *price level* in the United States. Note that during the long period from 1820 to 1933, the United States was on the gold standard, with the result that money supply growth and therefore inflation were linked to variations in the amount of gold available. Prices rose relatively rapidly after new gold discoveries in 1849 and 1896, but they declined during long stretches between these discoveries, such as the

---

[2] Philip Cagan introduced the formal criterion for hyperinflation as a case of inflation in excess of 50 percent per month. Cagan's great contribution to the subject is ''The Monetary Dynamics of Hyperinflation,'' in Milton Friedman, ed., *Studies in the Quantity Theory of Money* (Chicago and London: University of Chicago Press, 1956).

TABLE   11-1

INFLATION IN SELECTED AREAS, 1981–1990

Area	1981	1982	1983	1984	1985	1986	1987	1988	1989	1990
Industrial countries*	8.8	7.4	5.2	4.4	3.7	3.4	3.0	3.3	4.0	4.1
Asia developing countries†	10.7	6.4	6.6	6.1	6.0	8.7	9.5	14.4	11.7	7.9
Western hemisphere developing countries†	59.7	67.1	108.7	133.5	145.1	87.8	130.9	286.4	533.1	768.0

* *Average of percentage changes in GNP deflators for individual countries weighted by the average U.S. dollar value of their respective GNPs over the preceding three years.*
† *Percentage changes of geometric averages of indices of consumer prices for individual countries weighted by the average U.S. dollar value of their respective GNPs over the preceding three years.*
Source: *International Monetary Fund,* World Economic Outlook, *May 1991.*

period between 1873 and 1896. This pattern of rising and falling prices kept inflation low during an entire century: indeed, the price level in 1913 was below the price level in 1820! After World War II, the progressive delinking of the currency from gold gave the Fed more freedom to increase the money supply. This allowed more room for inflation, and the price level has risen in every year since 1945.

Table 11-1 presents the inflation rates of different regions of the world for the period 1981–1990. The remarkably high levels of inflation in the developing countries of the Western hemisphere, mainly Latin America, during the 1980s is particularly striking. Probably no other region in economic history, with the possible exception of Central Europe in the 1920s, has experienced such high rates of inflation for such a prolonged period of time. In the Latin American countries, this high inflation can be traced to large and persistent budget deficits which are monetized by the central bank—that is, they are paid for by printing money. The heavy foreign debt burden of the Latin governments has played a fundamental role in the process, both by enlarging the budget deficits and by limiting the government's ability to finance these deficits by borrowing rather than by monetization. The process of money financing of budget deficits is a subject of much interest in this chapter.

11-1 GOVERNMENT DEFICITS AND INFLATION

Suppose that the public sector spends more than it takes in. We saw in Chapter 9 that it can pay for the deficit in three ways: it can borrow from the public, it can run down foreign-exchange reserves, or it can print money. A government that has borrowed a lot in the past has already accumulated a heavy debt, and it will have difficulties borrowing further, either domestically or from abroad, because of doubts about its capacity to service its debts. Typically, such a government has also exhausted its stock of foreign-exchange reserves after a prolonged period of large budget deficits. For these reasons, a government with chronically large budget deficits is likely to find itself eventually compelled to pay for those deficits by printing money.

Now, one can ask why the government continues to run a deficit in the face of very high inflation. In principle, it can avoid a deficit through a combination of spending cuts and tax increases. The problem is that these kinds of policies are hard to implement, and they often require mustering a majority in the legislature that may be very difficult to assemble. Powerful organized forces—lobbying groups, trade unions, political parties in a coalition government—find it possible to exercise a veto over measures that hit the particular groups they represent. Nouriel Roubini and Jeffrey Sachs have shown that coalition governments have a harder time closing budget deficits than do governments in which a majority party rules by itself.[3]

Budget Deficits Under Fixed Exchange Rates

Let us now consider an economy with an ongoing budget deficit. In this case, we assume that it is operating under fixed exchange rates. Further, let us say that the government does not have access to direct borrowing from the public, either at home or abroad, and that it has exhausted its foreign-exchange reserves. Thus, its only option is to borrow from the central bank.

To put this in a formal framework, we start from the consolidated government budget constraint. We already analyzed this in Chapter 9, more specifically in equation (9.12), which we rewrite as

$$(D_p^g - D_{p-1}^g) + (Mh - Mh_{-1}) - E(B_c^* - B_{c-1}^*) = P(G + I^g - T) + iD_{p-1}^g - E(i^*B_{c-1}^*)$$

where a "*," as usual, denotes a foreign variable (B_c^* is the stock of net foreign assets held by the central bank).

The right side of the equation is the fiscal deficit: the excess of government spending (current spending, investment, and interest payments on domestic debt) over government income (taxes plus interest receipts on foreign-exchange reserves). The left side of the equation shows the sources of deficit finance. Now, if the government cannot borrow from the public, then $(D_p^g - D_{p-1}^g) = 0$. For the sake of simplicity, let us say that high-powered money (Mh) is equal to the money supply (M). Finally, let us define DEF as equal to the nominal budget deficit, deflated by the price level: $DEF = (G + I^g - T) + (iD_{p-1}^g - Ei^*B_{c-1}^*)/P$.

Under these conditions, equation (9.12) becomes

$$(M - M_{-1}) - E(B_c^* - B_{c-1}^*) = P(DEF) \tag{11.1}$$

With fixed exchange rates, the stock of money is determined solely by money demand, as we saw in the previous chapter. Recall that in such an exchange regime the equilibrium quantity of money is determined from equation (10.9) as

$$M = \frac{EP^*Q}{V(i^*)}$$

---

[3] See their article "Government Spending and Budget Deficits in the Industrial Economies," *Economic Policy*, Spring 1989.

Similarly,

$$M_{-1} = \frac{E_{-1}P^*_{-1}Q_{-1}}{V(i^*_{-1})}$$

But if the exchange rate is fixed, then $E = E_{-1}$; with full employment (and no growth), $Q = Q_{-1}$; and since world variables are given and constant in our analysis, $P^* = P^*_{-1}$ and $i^* = i^*_{-1}$. With all these assumptions, M will simply equal M_{-1}. Using this result in (11.1), we get

$$-E(B^*_c - B^*_{c-1}) = P(DEF) \qquad \textbf{(11.2)}$$

This statement tells us something quite fundamental: if money demand is constant, and if the government can borrow only abroad or from the central bank, then, in effect, all borrowing is from abroad, even if the government actually *tries* to borrow from the central bank! Any attempt to borrow from the central bank simply leads to an increase of high-powered money that, in turn, causes a loss of reserves and a subsequent reversal of the money supply increase. Thus, a finance minister who decides to cover a deficit by borrowing from the central bank will indirectly be financing the deficit out of international reserve losses.

This outcome has important implications for real-world events. Governments, especially in the developing world, often find themselves with few available sources of financing. When they are virtually unable to borrow from domestic residents, and when their international creditworthiness is severely impaired abroad, their only option to finance a deficit is to borrow from the central bank. But as we have seen, according to our benchmark result, direct borrowing from the central bank, under fixed exchange rates and perfect capital mobility, leads indirectly to losses in foreign reserves. It is as if the budget deficit were being paid for directly by running down foreign reserves.

Take, for example, the case of Chile in 1970–1973, shown in Figure 11-2a. During this period, the public-sector deficit swelled from slightly over 6 percent of GDP to about 30 percent of GDP, mostly financed by monetary emission of the central bank. Not surprisingly the level of international reserves dropped from 41 percent of annual imports to a mere 9 percent of imports. Thus, the average level of reserves in 1973 covered about one month of imports, which is extremely low by any prudent standard. In effect, a large part of the fiscal deficit was financed by spending international reserves. A similar picture of Peru emerges for the period 1985–1988, as shown in Figure 11-2b.

What does all this tell us about inflation? As long as foreign reserves continue to be available, the country can avoid inflation. The exchange rate remains fixed at its pegged level, and the external price level is given. With purchasing power parity, domestic prices also remain stable. If the fiscal deficits persist, however, the government eventually runs out of reserves. At that point, when domestic residents attempt to exchange their home money for foreign currency, the government cannot continue to intervene in the market. The central bank has no option but to allow the exchange rate to depreciate, either as the result of devaluation of the local currency or because it allows the domestic money to start floating. The collapse of a pegged exchange-rate system when the central bank runs out of reserves is called a *balance-of-payments crisis*.

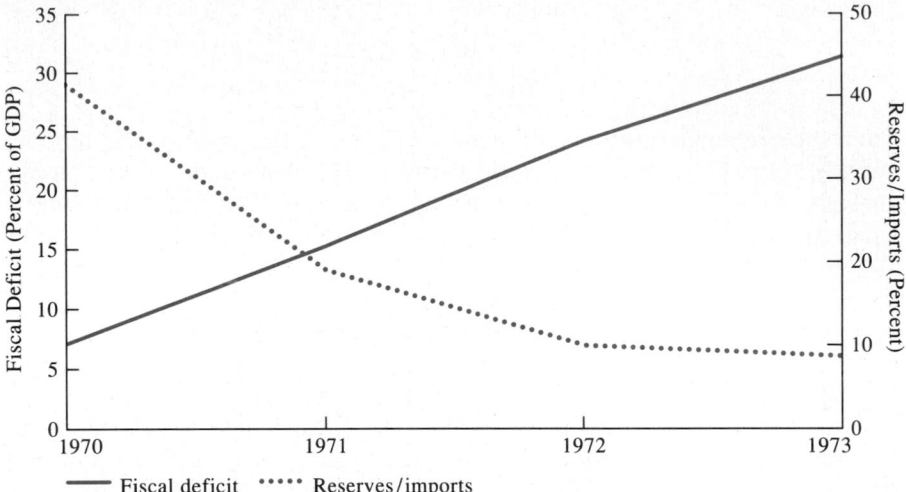

Figure 11-2a
Public Sector Deficits and International Reserves in Chile, 1970–1973

(From F. Larrain, "Public Sector Behavior in a Highly Indebted Country: The Contrasting Chilean Experience," in F. Larrain and M. Selowsky, eds., The Public Sector and the Latin American Crisis, *San Francisco: ICS Press, 1991.)*

Figure 11-2b
Public Sector Deficits and International Reserves in Peru, 1985–1988

(From C. Paredes, "The Behavior of the Public Sector of Peru—A Macroeconomic Approach—and Central Bank of Peru," in F. Larrain and M. Selowsky, eds., The Public Sector and the Latin American Crisis, *San Francisco: ICS Press, 1991.)*

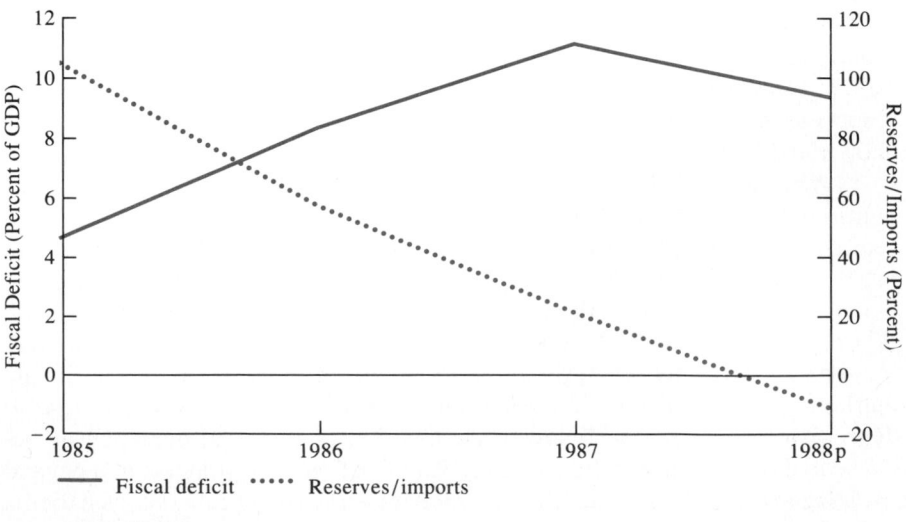

p = Preliminary.

The breakdown of a fixed exchange-rate regime is often accompanied by great political drama and a sense of crisis. In one of several studies of this issue, Richard Cooper analyzed 24 devaluations in developing countries over the years between 1953 and 1966.[4] In about 30 percent of the cases, Cooper found, the government in power fell within a year of the devaluation. Of course, this does not say that the government fell *because* of the devaluation. But it is interesting that only 14 percent of governments that did not devalue their currencies fell within a year. For finance ministers, the evidence is even stronger: 60 percent of those who presided over a devaluation lost their job in the following year, as compared to only 18 percent in the group that did not move their exchange rates. Thus, we can sympathize with the reluctance of finance ministers to devalue.

Budget Deficits Under Floating Exchange Rates

Let us continue with the hapless finance minister who presides over continuing fiscal deficits after the central bank has run out of reserves. This time, however, the exchange-rate system changes from fixed to floating. Under these circumstances, the government cannot borrow and it no longer has foreign-exchange reserves, so the only way to finance the deficit is through money creation. With $B_c^* - B_{c-1}^* = 0$, equation (11.1) becomes

$$\frac{(M - M_{-1})}{P} = DEF \tag{11.3}$$

The real value of the deficit is now equal to the real value of the change in the money supply.

This change in the money supply is going to cause inflation. By manipulating equation (11.3) we can draw a link between the budget deficit and the inflation rate. We first rewrite equation (11.3) as

$$DEF = \left[\frac{(M - M_{-1})}{M}\right]\left(\frac{M}{P}\right) \tag{11.3'}$$

Next, from equation (10.9), we borrow the fact that $M = (PQ/V)$. If we assume that DEF is constant period to period and that Q also does not change, these assumptions, in turn, guarantee that velocity (V) is also constant. Thus, $M_{-1} = (P_{-1}Q/V)$. Replacing M and M_{-1} in the first term of the right side of equation (11.3'), and canceling the common terms, we obtain

$$DEF = \left[\frac{(P - P_{-1})}{P}\right]\left(\frac{M}{P}\right) \tag{11.4}$$

By multiplying the right-hand side by P_{-1}/P_{-1}, we can write

$$DEF = \left[\frac{(P - P_{-1})}{P_{-1}}\right]\left(\frac{P_{-1}}{P}\right)\left(\frac{M}{P}\right) \tag{11.4'}$$

---

[4] This important study by Richard Cooper is "Currency Devaluation in Developing Countries," *Essays in International Finance*, No. 86 (Princeton, N.J.: Princeton University Press, June 1971).

Finally, we can use the definition of inflation, $\hat{P} = (P - P_{-1})/P_{-1}$, and the fact that $P/P_{-1} = 1 + \hat{P}$, to rewrite (11.4') in the form that we want to use here:

$$DEF = \left[\frac{\hat{P}}{(1 + \hat{P})}\right]\left(\frac{M}{P}\right) \tag{11.5}$$

Expression (11.5) has very powerful implications. Under floating rates, the deficit results in inflation, and there is a definite link between the size of the deficit and the rate of inflation. Each deficit leads to a given rate of inflation. Subject to the qualifications that follow, higher deficits are accompanied by higher inflation rates.

One way to describe (11.5) is to say that the budget deficit is being financed through an *inflation tax* on real money balances. The tax rate is $\hat{P}/(1 + \hat{P})$, where $\hat{P}$ is the inflation rate. The tax base is the level of real money balances, M/P. The product of the *tax rate* and the *tax base* is the total tax revenue, which is used to finance the budget deficit.

Why do we characterize the right-hand side of equation (11.5) as an "inflation tax"? In what sense does the government receive the tax revenues from this tax? In essence, the government is paying for its expenditures by printing money. The real goods and services that the government purchases with the money that it prints each period is the measure of the "tax" revenue collected by the government as the result of this inflationary policy. The increase in the money supply each period is causing inflation. That is, the money printing is the precise way that the government collects the inflation tax.

The inflation tax is, of course, a special kind of tax; for example, its collection requires neither the approval of any law nor the administration of any tax collection agency. The tax is paid automatically as households suffer the loss in value of their money holdings each period as the price level rises. (We shall see later on how to measure the precise burden on households of the inflation tax.)

Remember the key elements in the chain of causation that links the budget deficit to inflation. The deficit leads to an increase in the nominal supply of money, as the central bank buys the treasury bonds issued by the deficit-ridden government. At given prices and interest rates, there is an excess supply of money, which, as households attempt to convert part of their excess money into foreign assets, causes the exchange rate to depreciate. With no reserves at its command, the central bank cannot intervene to stop the depreciation. And given the presence of purchasing power parity, the depreciation in the exchange rate leads to price inflation at the same rate.

Consider now a numerical example based on equation (11.5), where we express magnitudes as a proportion of GDP. (To get this, we simply divide both sides of the equation by GDP.) Suppose that a country with money balances at 30 percent of GDP is running a fiscal deficit of 5 percent of GDP. What inflation rate will be needed to finance such a deficit? The answer is 20 percent. You can verify this by performing the computations in equation (11.5). Note that with the same deficit, but real money balances of only 15 percent of GDP, the inflation rate required is 50 percent. What has happened? The base of the inflation tax has declined, meaning that collecting the same revenue collection (the 5 percent of GDP needed to finance the deficit) now requires a higher tax rate.

TABLE   11-2

DEFICIT FINANCING AND THE EXCHANGE-RATE REGIME

	Exchange Rate Regime	
Deficit Financing	**Fixed**	**Flexible**
Direct mechanism	Money creation	Money creation
Ultimate mechanism	International reserves	Inflation tax

We now have an important insight into the inflationary process. Under fixed exchange rates, the government can run a fiscal deficit without generating inflation, even when the financing is done through central bank purchases of government debt. This can happen because under fixed exchange rates, agents get rid of their excess money through purchases of foreign assets, and the deficit ends up being financed through a loss of central bank reserves. But reserves eventually dry up. At that point, the central bank can no longer defend the parity of its currency, and the exchange rate is left to depreciate. From that point on, continuing deficits are translated into a floating exchange rate, with a persistent depreciation of the domestic currency. With purchasing power parity at work, the inflation rate will equal the rate of currency depreciation. In effect, then, the financing for the deficit comes from the inflation tax. Table 11-2 summarizes the major steps in the process of financing a fiscal deficit under fixed and flexible exchange rates.

There is, then, an important link between budget deficits and the choice of an exchange-rate system. Countries with chronic and large budget deficits will find it hard to maintain a fixed exchange rate, and either they will have to go to a floating rate or at least they will frequently have to adjust the currency parity. Several countries in Latin America have had large and persistent fiscal deficits which have made it impossible for them to maintain a stable currency. But the issue is also relevant for those countries in the European Monetary System that have high fiscal deficits. For example, Italy has generally had larger budget imbalances than her EMS partners. At the same time, within the EMS the Italian lira has been pegged to the French franc, the Deutsche mark, the Dutch guilder, and so on. On several occasions, the lira has had to be devalued vis-à-vis the other currencies.

Balance-of-Payments Crises: The Transition from Fixed to Floating Rates

We can now take a closer look at the precise period of a *balance-of-payments crisis,* that is, when the central bank runs out of reserves and is forced to abandon the fixed exchange-rate parity. As before, the starting point is an underlying fiscal deficit, under fixed exchange rates, which slowly reduces the amount of reserves held by the central bank. With a finite amount of reserves, it is clear that the authorities will not be able to peg the exchange rate indefinitely. In addition, the public may well see the collapse coming and take actions which, in fact, help to trigger the sudden exhaustion of foreign-exchange reserves, as people rush *en masse* to convert their domestic currency into foreign currency just on the eve of the exchange-rate crisis.

Let us look closely at what happens to the demand for real money balances during the transition from low inflation under fixed exchange rates to high inflation under floating rates. Once the exchange-rate depreciation starts, the domestic interest rate rises. To see this, remember that perfect capital mobility requires that

$$(1 + i) = \left(\frac{E_{+1}}{E}\right)(1 + i^*)$$

Thus, as soon as the depreciation is underway (so that $E_{+1} > E$), the domestic interest rate (i) rises. Velocity, an increasing function of i, rises and this causes the demand for real money balances to decline, since $M/P = Q/V(i)$.

During the transition between the fixed rate and the floating rate, the demand for real money balances declines. Meanwhile, the public may understand the way the economy works well enough to know that the exchange rate is about to collapse. (This is a good assumption in a country like Argentina, which has suffered a collapse of a fixed exchange-rate system many times in recent years.) People will also understand that at the moment of the exchange crisis they do not want to be holding large real money balances because inflation is about to increase. They will therefore convert their excess money into foreign assets on the eve of the collapse of the exchange rate. If they wait until after the collapse, and then suddenly try to convert their domestic currency into foreign assets, the central bank will no longer be willing or even able to buy the domestic currency. In addition, the exchange rate will depreciate sharply as people flee out of domestic money, and households that still hold excess balances will suffer capital losses that they can avoid if they convert their money in time.

During this whole process, we can see an interesting pattern of reserve losses emerging over time. If the central bank starts with a large stock of foreign-exchange reserves, then reserves fall gradually, with the loss of reserves equaling the budget deficit, as described in equation (11.2). Then, just as reserve levels are getting so low that the public suspects an imminent collapse of the exchange-rate system, households suddenly move to convert massive amounts of domestic money into foreign assets because they anticipate a sharp rise in inflation.

As the public rushes in to reduce its holdings of domestic currency, the reserve loss becomes an avalanche. In fact, the stampede of households to change money into foreign assets, in what is called a *speculative attack* against the central bank's reserves depletes the bank's remaining reserves and pushes the economy off of fixed exchange rates and into floating exchange rates and high inflation. The overall process of the collapse of the fixed exchange rate is termed a *balance-of-payments crisis*. (See Box 11-1.) This process has been analyzed with great clarity by Paul Krugman of the Massachusetts Institute of Technology.[5]

The dynamics of a balance-of-payments crisis are depicted in Figure 11-3. Under fixed exchange rates, the central bank starts at time 0 with a level of reserves B_0^*. As time goes by, the fiscal deficit causes a decline in the

---

[5] One of the first rigorous analysis of the problem is his article "A Model of Balance-of-Payments Crises," *Journal of Money, Credit and Banking,* August 1979.

Box 11-1
A Case of Balance-of-Payments Collapse: Argentina in 1989

A clear example of a balance-of-payments collapse occurred in Argentina in the spring of 1989. The level of reserves at the central bank had been fairly stable at around $3 billion in the last quarter of 1988. By early 1989, however, the budget deficit proved uncontrollable, confidence in the economic program dwindled, and the central bank started to lose reserves. With foreign financing unavailable and domestic borrowing prohibitively expensive, the authorities initially dealt with the growing demand for foreign currency by drawing down their external assets. Thus, in the two months from December 1988 to February 1989, the central bank lost $1.1 billion of reserves, roughly one-third of its foreign-exchange holdings. The pegging of the exchange rate was held; that is, it was defended with official reserves, and it remained stable during this period.

When the central bank was still holding about $1.6 billion of reserves in March 1989, the speculative attack occurred. When foreign reserves at the bank had declined by another $600 million in March, the authorities realized that they could not maintain the exchange rate pegged for much longer. To defend the few remaining reserves, the central bank devalued by almost 200 percent between March and April. But that was not enough. In just two months, the exchange rate went from 20 australs per dollar in March to 200 in late May, a depreciation of 900 percent! Central bank reserves dwindled to a mere $930 million in June. Uncertainty exacerbated by a presidential election prevented calm from returning to the economy, however. During a respite achieved in August 1989 (which proved to be short-lived), the exchange rate stood at 655 australs per dollar, over 40 times its level at the end of 1988.

Figure 11-3
The Collapse of a Fixed Exchange-Rate Regime

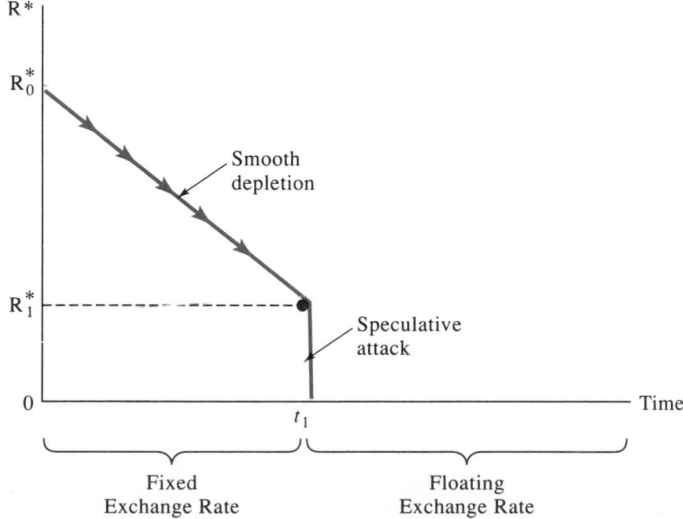

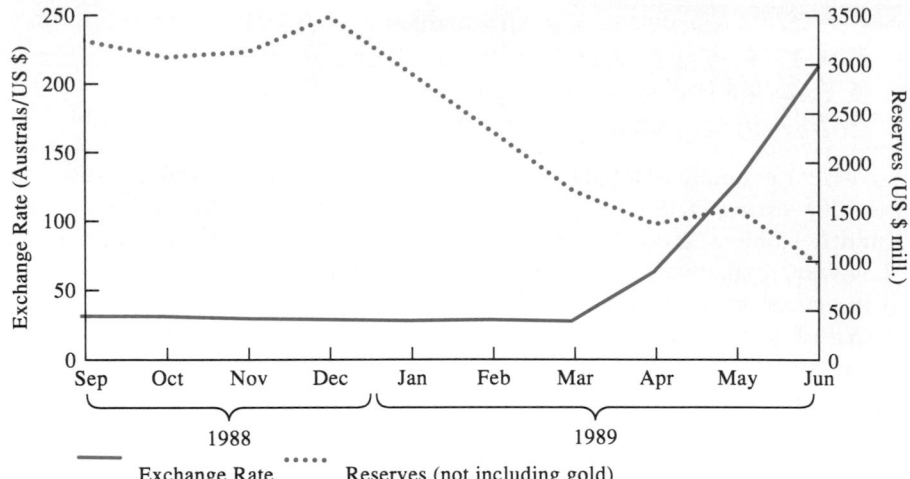

Figure 11-4

The Exchange Rate and International Reserves in Argentina, 1988–1989

(From ECLA, Economic Panorama of Latin America, 1989, *and International Monetary Fund,* International Financial Statistics, *various issues.)*

holdings of official foreign exchange. When the level of reserves reaches R_1, at time 1, a speculative attack against the currency depletes the reserves.[6] From then on, the central bank cannot any longer intervene in the foreign-exchange market, and the economy enters a regime of floating rates.

Can Domestic Borrowing Be Used To Avoid Inflation?

So far, we have looked at cases where a fiscal deficit is financed either by drawing down international reserves or by an open inflation. There are other ways to finance a deficit, of course, at least in the short run. The most important of them is the possibility of financing the deficit by borrowing from domestic residents. In this case, the treasury issues bonds which are purchased not by the central bank but by private agents. Borrowing of this sort allows the government to sustain a deficit without reserve losses or increases in the money supply.

Financing the fiscal deficit with higher domestic debt often postpones the day when the inflation tax comes into effect. The problem with domestic borrowing is that, although it provides resources today, it itself is a debt that has to be serviced tomorrow. Interest payments on government debt add to fiscal expenditures, and thereby increase the deficit over time. This may lead to higher inflation in the future, a problem that does not occur when money financing is used right from the beginning. In other words, borrowing today might postpone inflation, but at the risk of even higher inflation in the future. Now let us examine this proposition in further detail.

---

[6] Reserves need not actually fall to zero. Instead, they fall to a level below which the central bank refuses to intervene in the foreign-exchange market. This level can still be positive, but the central bank feels that its "last reserves" should be kept to protect the country in case of a natural disaster, war, or some other dire eventuality, rather than used up defending the exchange rate.

Suppose a government starts with no debt and a balanced budget. Then it decides to cut taxes or increase expenditures, and it starts running a deficit. If this deficit is financed with money (under floating exchange rates), people will cover the deficit by paying an inflation tax today and the government will not accumulate obligations for the future. If instead the deficit is covered by selling domestic debt to the public, then the government will increase its liabilities. If the *primary deficit,* that is, the deficit excluding interest payments, remains unchanged as the domestic debt accumulates, the overall deficit will grow because of the rising interest burden on the debt. If the government tries to pay for that rising interest bill through still more domestic borrowing, the debt-to-GNP ratio will tend to grow over time.[7]

At some point, buyers of bonds will be unwilling to hold more public debt in their portfolios, because they doubt that the government will be able to service any additional debt. Then the government has no option but to use money financing. But by now, increases in the money supply each period will also have to cover the higher interest payments on the domestic debt. Clearly, inflation cannot be postponed forever through domestic borrowing, as Thomas Sargent and Neil Wallace have pointed out in an article suggestively entitled "Some Unpleasant Monetarist Arithmetic."[8]

Notice, however, that a future increase in inflation is not the inevitable consequence of bond-financed deficits. Debt financing may truly give the government time to implement the expenditure cuts or tax increases that will eventually close the deficit. Thus, a government may well have a rational, noninflationary reason to run a budget deficit. All we are saying is that although debt financing *by itself* does not allow a government to escape from inflation, it may buy time to carry out other strategies that will.

11-2 THE INFLATION TAX AND SEIGNIORAGE

At this point we need to differentiate between two closely related concepts: the *inflation tax* and *seigniorage.* The former term refers to the capital losses suffered by money holders as a result of inflation. As we saw earlier, the inflation tax (*IT*) can be measured as

$$IT = \left[\frac{(P - P_{-1})}{P} \right]\left(\frac{M}{P}\right) \qquad \textbf{(11.6)}$$

Seigniorage (*SE*), is the revenue collected by the government as a result of its monopoly power to print money. Printing money is virtually without cost,

---

[7] For this to happen, the real interest rate on the government debt must be higher than the real growth rate of the economy. This condition gives rise to a Ponzi scheme in which the government's attempt to service the old debt by issuing new debt results in a debt-GNP ratio that would rise without bound. In this discussion, we assume that the condition holds in which the real interest rate is higher than the growth rate.

[8] Published in the *Federal Reserve Bank of Minneapolis Quarterly Review,* Fall 1981, this article gave rise to an interesting controversy on the subject. It was followed three years later by Michael Darby with "Some Pleasant Monetarist Arithmetic," *Federal Reserve Bank of Minneapolis Quarterly Review,* Spring 1984. Another contributor to the debate was Bennett McCallum in his "Are Bond Financed Deficits Inflationary?" *Journal of Political Economy,* February 1984.

and the bills and coins can be exchanged for goods and services. Thus, seigniorage may be measured as the purchasing power of the money put into circulation in a given period:

$$SE = \frac{(M - M_{-1})}{P} = \left[\frac{(M - M_{-1})}{M}\right]\left(\frac{M}{P}\right) \qquad \textbf{(11.7)}$$

Under certain conditions, in particular when households want to maintain a constant value of real money balances, the inflation tax and seigniorage are equal. Suppose that $M/P = M_{-1}/P_{-1}$. Since M_{-1}/M is then equal to P_{-1}/P, we can write $(M - M_{-1})/M$ as $(P - P_{-1})/P$. Thus, $SE = IT$ when M/P does not change over time.

Although SE and IT may on occasion be equal, however, they are not the same thing. One simple illustration should clarify the difference between the two. Suppose that inflation is zero and that the exchange rate is fixed. The inflation tax is evidently zero as well. Now suppose that a decline in world interest rates leads to a decline in domestic interest rates. The velocity of money falls, and the demand for real money balances, M/P, increases. In fact, households will then increase their money balances by selling foreign assets to the central bank in return for domestic currency. The central bank gains international reserves at the tiny cost of printing up the increased nominal money that the public wants to hold, and the government can use those foreign-exchange reserves to finance a larger budget deficit. In essence, this rise in money demand has given the government some "free" resources. This gain in purchasing power is precisely what is meant by seigniorage and measured in equation (11.7).

To what extent do governments use seigniorage as a source of revenue in the real world? All the countries shown in Table 11-3 used seigniorage, but in very different magnitudes, during the period 1975–1985. Notice that seigniorage in Germany was only 3.8 percent of government revenues; in Canada and the United States it was in the order of 6 percent. By contrast, Peru used seigniorage to collect about one-third of government revenue from other sources. But the highest proportion of seigniorage to total revenue during 1975–1985 was posted by Bolivia, where seigniorage provided significantly more resources for the public sector than all other sources of revenue. It is not surprising, then, that Bolivia experienced one of the worst hyperinflations in world history at the end of the period.

We now turn to some specific topics concerning the inflation tax and seigniorage.

The Inflation Tax and the Household Budget Constraint

Inflation has important effects on the household budget constraint. To see how this works, we start with the standard budget constraint which shows that disposable income net of consumption must equal the accumulation of money or bonds:[9]

$$P(Q - T) + iB_{-1} - PC = (B - B_{-1}) + (M - M_{-1}) \qquad \textbf{(11.8)}$$

---

[9] We ignore investment and accumulation of foreign bonds, without affecting the point of this section.

TABLE 11-3

SEIGNIORAGE IN SELECTED COUNTRIES, 1975–1985*

Country	As a % of Nonseigniorage Government Revenue	As a % of GDP
United States	6.02	1.17%
Canada	6.61	1.26
United Kingdom	5.31	1.91
Italy	28.00	6.60
France	7.19	2.73
Germany	3.85	1.08
Bolivia†	139.50	5.00
Brazil	18.36	4.13
Chile	7.48	2.39
India	14.30	1.81
Korea	10.70	1.84
Mexico	18.70	2.71
Philippines	7.79	0.99
Thailand	7.06	0.94
Turkey‡	24.40	5.09
Venezuela	10.76	3.05
Peru	29.71	4.92
Israel	24.55	2.99

* Average for the period of annual data.
† Refers to the period 1977–1985.
‡ Does not include 1982.
Source: *International Monetary Fund*, International Financial Statistics,
various issues, 1975–1985.

From equation (11.8) we can solve for consumption (C) as

$$C = (Q - T) - \frac{B}{P} + \frac{(1 + i)B_{-1}}{P} - \frac{(M - M_{-1})}{P}$$

With some minor manipulation,[10] we can express this as

$$C = \left[Q + r\left(\frac{B_{-1}}{P_{-1}}\right) - T \right] - \left[\left(\frac{B}{P}\right) - \left(\frac{B_{-1}}{P_{-1}}\right) \right] - \left[\frac{(M - M_{-1})}{P} \right] \quad \textbf{(11.9)}$$

---

[10] Before we proceed, we need to decompose the nominal interest rate into the real rate and the inflationary component. The manipulation, then, is

$$\frac{(1 + i)B_{-1}}{P} = (1 + r)\frac{[1 + (P/P_{-1}) - 1]B_{-1}}{P} = \frac{(1 + r)B_{-1}}{P_{-1}}$$

From here, equation (11.9) directly follows.

Notice that the first term on the right-hand side of equation (11.9) is the disposable income of households using the *real* rather than the nominal interest rate. The second term is the change in the real value of bonds from the previous period to the current one. The third term is the change in the nominal stock of money evaluated at current prices, $(M - M_{-1})/P$, which corresponds to the definition of seigniorage.

Remember that if $M/P = M_{-1}/P_{-1}$, then seigniorage is also equal to the inflation tax as defined in (11.6). Therefore, under the assumption that real money balances are not changing period to period, we can rewrite (11.9) as (11.9'):

$$C = \left[Q + r\left(\frac{B_{-1}}{P_{-1}}\right) - T \right] - \left[\left(\frac{B}{P}\right) - \left(\frac{B_{-1}}{P_{-1}}\right) \right] - IT \qquad \textbf{(11.9')}$$

This leads us to a straightforward, but very important point. If people want to maintain their real stock of money in an inflationary environment, they will have to make a sacrifice and reduce their consumption by the amount IT. Each period, inflation reduces the real value of money balances. Thus, each period, households have to save merely to replenish their real money balances to desired levels. The exact amount of saving required to keep real money balances constant is equal to the inflation tax.

To put this another way, the conventional measure of household disposable income is $Q + r(B_{-1}/P_{-1}) - T$. But this overstates true disposable income because the household must devote some of its income to accumulating the nominal money balances needed just to keep the real money balances from falling. A corrected measure of disposable income that takes inflation into account would be $Q + r(B_{-1}/P_{-1}) - T - IT$.

The Laffer Curve for the Inflation Tax

In Chapter 7 we looked at the Laffer curve for taxes, which has the shape of an inverted U (see Figure 7-5). The idea there was that, starting from a low tax rate, fiscal revenues increase as the tax rate goes up, but only up to a point. There is some tax rate at which the maximum revenue collection is reached. Beyond that point, further increases in the tax rate bring about a *decline* in revenues.

The reason explained there was as follows. Tax revenues are equal to the tax rate times the tax base, where the tax base is the thing being taxed. The revenues from an income tax, for example, equals the rate of the income tax times the amount of household income. As the tax rate rises, however, households may cut back on their labor effort. Even though the tax rate goes up, the tax base goes down, and the overall revenues may fall.

The same reasoning applies to the inflation tax. There is some inflation rate that maximizes the inflation tax of the government but beyond which the government loses revenues rather than gains revenues. In other words, there is a "Laffer curve" for the inflation tax, as shown in Figure 11-5. As drawn, curve $0ML$ represents the value of the inflation tax for different rates of inflation, assuming that the economy is in equilibrium with an *unchanging rate of inflation* period to period.

When the inflation rate is zero, revenue is also zero. As inflation increases, the tax base—in this case, the demand for real money balances—goes down. There is a maximum inflation tax shown as $IT_{\max}$, at the inflation

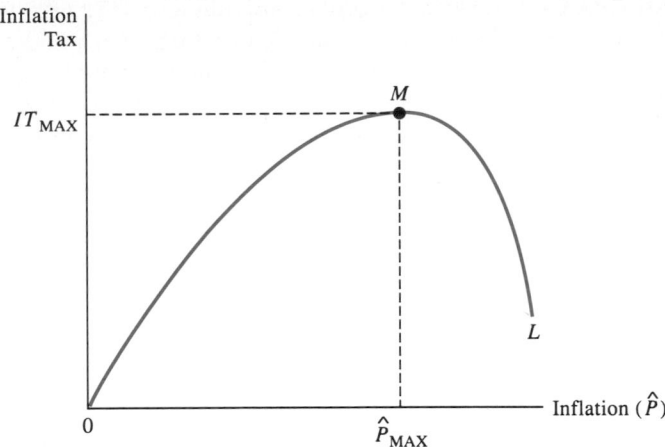

Figure 11-5
The Laffer Curve for Inflation

rate $\hat{P}_{max}$. Further increases in inflation bring about a drop in revenue, because the higher inflation is more than offset by the fall in the real money balances that are being taxed. This occurs along the segment ML.

This leads to an important point. Assuming a steady rate of inflation, there is a maximum deficit, equal to IT_{max}, that can be financed by printing money. It may be possible for the government to temporarily finance a deficit higher than IT_{max}, but at the cost of *accelerating* inflation rather than a steady rate of inflation.[11] If a government tries persistently to finance a deficit higher than IT_{max}, hyperinflation is the likely result. (We return to an analysis of this point in Chapter 23.)

Can a Government Earn Seigniorage under Fixed Exchange Rates?

As we have seen, under fixed exchange rates a fiscal deficit is ultimately financed out of reserves. Does this mean that such a regime makes it impossible for the government to collect seigniorage? In two important cases, the public sector can indeed collect seigniorage, while simultaneously maintaining the currency parity and its international reserves.

First is the case in which the rest of the world is also experiencing inflation. As the external price level (P^*) rises, purchasing power parity dictates that domestic prices will also increase. When this happens, the real value of money balances declines and an excess demand for money develops. This provides the central bank with an opportunity to increase the money supply just enough to offset the price increase, leaving real money balances unchanged. Notice that in this case the government collects seigniorage along with a rising price level, and does not lose any reserves.

---

[11] During an accelerating inflation, it may be the case that the public is persistently underestimating the inflation that will occur each period, and is therefore holding higher money balances than it would were it to know precisely what the inflation is going to be. The government may be able to take advantage of these mistaken perceptions, at least for a while, in the sense of collecting seigniorage revenue in excess of IT_{max}.

A second possibility for seigniorage occurs when there is a growth in demand for real money balances in the economy, perhaps because of underlying GDP growth. If the central bank increases the money supply just enough to satisfy the increase in money demand, there will be no excess supply of money and no inflation (assuming, as usual, that P^* is constant). In these circumstances, the government collects seigniorage, but there is no inflation tax and no loss of reserves.

Who Gets the Seigniorage?

So far, we have assumed that the domestic country's government collects the seigniorage. But this is not always the case. In at least three interesting situations, some entity other than the domestic government receives these revenues.

If a country uses the currency of another country, it is the *issuing* country's government that gains the seigniorage. For example, both Liberia and Panama use the U.S. dollar as official currency. The absence of a local currency means that the governments of Panama and Liberia surrender the possibility of collecting seigniorage to the U.S. government. If the citizens of Liberia and Panama want to increase their money holdings, the country as a whole needs to run a balance-of-payments surplus, either borrowing the dollars or running a trade surplus to accumulate the dollars. But if the choice is to borrow, the debt in any event has to be serviced, so in either case the country has to give real goods or services in exchange for accumulating the foreign money. On the other hand, the United States gains real resources by the privilege of printing up the paper notes that the two countries will use.

This same sort of thing also happens when currency substitution exists in an economy. Currency substitution, as you saw in Chapter 8, occurs when the domestic central bank has the monopoly over creating domestic currency, but, perhaps because of a history of monetary instability, the country's residents also use a foreign currency for domestic transactions. Thus, two monies function as a medium of exchange. The seigniorage is then collected partly by the domestic government and partly by the foreign government.

There are also historical cases in which the private sector had the right to print paper money, and thereby the right to collect part or all the seigniorage. Before the creation of modern central banks, currency was often issued by private banks. Some have advocated the extreme free market position that this system of private money creation should be reimplemented.[12]

11-3 THE COSTS OF INFLATION

Inflation is widely considered a social evil. Governments usually enter office with pledges to bring it down; opposition politicians watch it closely and attack the authorities when it rears its head. The general public is highly concerned about inflation, and vigilant in tracking monthly changes in the consumer price index, the most important measure of inflation. Yet for all the preoccupation and the charged rhetoric about price increases, too little is

---

[12] See Friedrich Von Hayek, *Denationalization of Money* (London: Institute of Economic Affairs, 1976).

said about its real costs. It is fair to ask, then, why do people so much want to keep inflation low?[13]

Some negative effects of inflation are evident: money loses its purchasing power, and the nominal cost of goods and services increases. But if all wages and prices were adjusted upward at the same rate, would inflation still be costly? Yes it would. In contrast to the costs of unemployment, which are more evident in terms of output forgone (and which we analyze in detail in Chapters 15 and 16), many of the effects of price changes are subtle, but nonetheless important.

Before we study the main problem, however, we need to distinguish between two different kinds of inflation. *Anticipated* inflation is inflation that is built into the expectations and the behavior of the public before it occurs— in other words, it is inflation for which people are more or less prepared. *Unanticipated* inflation, on the other hand, is inflation that comes as a surprise to the public, or at least comes before people have had time to adjust fully to its presence.

Anticipated Inflation

Suppose that everybody in the economy knows that inflation will be 10 percent this year, up from zero inflation last year. In such a case, everyone will incorporate this expected higher level of inflation into their plans. Both borrowers and lenders will be interested in the *real* interest rate that they will pay and receive, and nominal interest rates on loan contracts will be adjusted upward by about 10 percent.[14] House and apartment rentals will also be adjusted upward by 10 percent. Negotiated labor contracts will stipulate wage increases to reflect the higher inflation (if workers do not have money illusion). In general, all economic decisions will incorporate expected price changes.

Inflation still imposes costs, of course, even when it is totally anticipated. First, and most obviously, the inflation is a tax, and one that has not been voted by the public. The uproar that accompanies inflation may reflect nothing more than opposition to a newly imposed tax that has not been justified by legislative action. In fact, inflation may be occurring precisely because the government cannot muster the political support to raise taxes directly.

In addition to the burden of the inflation tax (which, after all, might be recouped in part or in whole from increased public services or government transfers financed by the tax), there are pure efficiency losses associated with anticipated inflation. Recall, for example, that money is the most efficient means of payment in a modern economy. An expected higher inflation rate translates into higher interest rates, and this increases the opportunity cost of holding money. Thus, as the Baumol–Tobin framework specifies,

---

[13] For an analysis of the costs of inflation, see Stanley Fischer and Franco Modigliani, "Towards an Understanding of the Real Effects and Costs of Inflation," *Weltwirtschaftliches Archiv.,* 1978, pp. 810–833.

[14] The statement that the nominal interest rate increases by the same percent as inflation is an approximation. The nominal interest rate (i) that maintains the real rate (r) when inflation goes to 10 percent is given by the following equation: $(1 + r)(1 + \hat{P}) = (1 + i)$. As you have seen before, the lower the level of inflation, the more accurate the approximation.

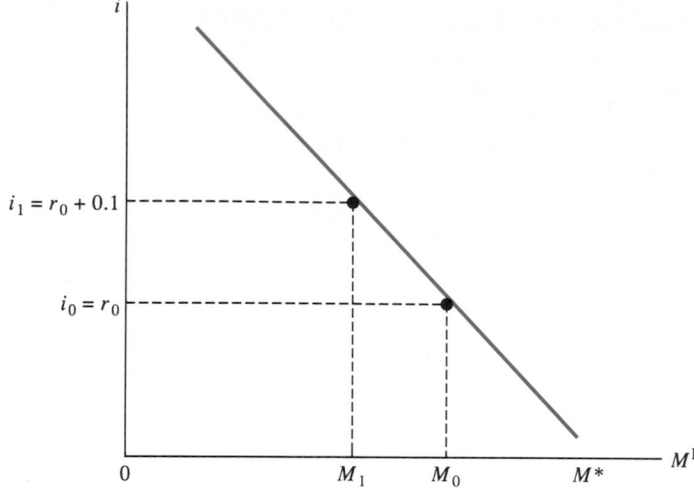

Figure 11-6
The Optimal Quantity of Money in a Partial Equilibrium Framework

people reduce their average money balances, make more trips to the bank, and they rush to make purchases to stay ahead of price hikes. Economic agents make more complicated financial transactions in order to reduce their holdings of real money balances. They may also allocate more of their wealth to consumer durables as a protection against the inflation tax. All these efforts involve real costs. The higher the inflation, the greater the costs.

In view of the fact that inflation imposes a cost on monetary transactions, economists have been led to speculate about the "optimal" rate of inflation for an economy. Is price stability, that is, zero inflation, best? The issue is considered in Box 11-2.

Another effect of anticipated inflation is what is known as *menu costs,* a general term that describes the inconvenience of having to adjust certain prices to keep them in line with inflation. The concept borrows its name from the fact that restaurants often need to write in higher prices of the dishes on their menus, and maybe print new menus, as the prices of their inputs increase. Real costs are also incurred changing over vending machines and public phones when the nominal price level changes. Owners have to spend real resources—technical personnel, transportation services, and so on—in order to alter prices. Companies that sell by mail order also have to revise, reprint, and reissue their catalogs more frequently when inflation rises.[15]

Anticipated inflation can also lead to resource misallocation through the effects of inflation on the tax system.[16] The effects of inflation on income tax brackets are one example. Suppose that marginal tax brackets are stated in nominal terms. As time goes by and nominal income rises, people are

---

[15] For a survey of the menu cost literature, see Julio Rotemberg, "The New Keynesian Microfoundations," *NBER Macroeconomics Annual 1987* (Cambridge, Mass.: MIT Press for the National Bureau of Economic Research, 1987).

[16] Martin Feldstein of Harvard University has been a prominent analyst of the effect of inflation via the tax structure. See, for example, "Inflation, Income Taxes and the Rate of Interest: A Theoretical Analysis," *American Economic Review*, December 1976, and "Inflation, Tax Rules and the Stock Market," *Journal of Monetary Economics*, July 1980. See also his joint piece with Lawrence Summers, "Inflation, Tax Rules and the Long-Term Interest Rate," *Brookings Papers on Economic Activity,* No. 1, 1978.

Box 11-2
The Optimal Rate of Inflation

If anticipated inflation imposes costs, by forcing households to economize on money balance, what is the *optimal* rate of inflation? Is it zero, negative, or positive? According to Milton Friedman, the optimal inflation rate is negative, specifically, the negative value of the real interest rate.[17] If the real interest rate is 5 percent per year, Friedman recommends an annual inflation rate of −5 percent per year. He reaches that conclusion through the following reasoning.

Since money is costless to produce (the government can just print the bills), the opportunity cost of holding money should be as low as possible, to encourage the public to make use of the conveniences of money as much as possible. The demand for real money balances by the public should be maximized. The government should then aim for a nominal interest rate equal to zero, so that there is no opportunity cost to holding money. Since the nominal interest rate is equal to the real interest rate plus the inflation rate, Friedman's recipe is for the government to aim for an inflation rate which is the negative value of the real interest rate, thereby producing a nominal interest rate equal to zero.

This idea can be shown graphically, as in Figure 11-6. We can represent the demand for real money balances as the demand curve MM. It is a negative function of the nominal interest rate. The demand for money is maximized at the level $(M/P)^*$, which occurs at a zero nominal interest rate.

When the nominal interest rate is positive, the optimal quantity of money is not achieved. Notice that even with zero inflation, there is an opportunity cost of holding money, equal to the real interest rate. Increased inflation above zero only makes things worse, as people further economize on their money holdings. Suppose the real interest rate is r_0; with stable prices, households will demand $(M/P)_0$ of money. If inflation goes to 10 percent, the nominal interest rate will increase to $i_1 = r_0 + 0.1$; at that level, money demand will be $(M/P)_1$.

Friedman's conclusion has been modified by Edmond Phelps of Columbia University, who argued that while inflation was indeed distortionary, so too are taxes. Because all taxes produce some distortions, it may make sense for the government to rely on the inflation tax—at least to a small extent—in order to reduce the heavy reliance on other distortionary taxes. Generally speaking, the optimum rate of inflation has to be determined as that which minimizes the distortions from the *overall* tax system, including the inflation tax, which arise when the government must raise a given amount of fiscal revenue.[18]

---

[17] See Friedman's article "The Optimum Quantity of Money," Chapter 1 in his book, *The Optimum Quantity of Money and Other Essays* (Chicago: Aldine, 1969).

[18] See Edmond Phelps, "Inflation in the Theory of Public Finance," *Swedish Journal of Economics*, January/March 1973.

pushed into higher tax brackets, increasing their marginal tax rates. A person whose pretax real income is constant thereby suffers a gradual increase in her tax liabilities, and a consequent loss of disposable income, simply because of inflation. Until the tax reform of 1986, the United States was a case in point. Tax brackets were fixed in nominal terms, and inflation inadvertently pushed individuals into higher brackets. Successive tax cuts voted by the Congress prior to 1986 undid some of the effect of the bracket creep, but such relief came unpredictably, and at irregular intervals. Since 1986, income tax brackets have been indexed to inflation.

In most countries, corporations—and sometimes individuals—are allowed to deduct interest payments as expenses from their taxable income. In the presence of inflation, nominal interest rates rise, and the tax deduction increases even while the real interest rate remains the same. In some countries, such as Chile, the tax laws have been reformed so that only the *real* interest portion of the payment can be deducted from the tax bill.

Further, consider the effects of inflation on the system of historic cost depreciation allowed by the tax code. Often, companies are permitted to subtract from their taxable income some specified amount of depreciation on their buildings and equipment. If the depreciation allowance is based on the historical costs of the investment, that is, its original costs, rather than on the replacement costs, the real value of the depreciation allowance can be substantially wiped out by inflation. This increases the tax burden on companies, and this, in turn, can act as a disincentive for productive investment. A similar problem occurs with capital gains. The tax on capital gains is calculated on the difference between the sale price and the purchase price of an asset. If the purchase price is taken at its historic value, then people will be taxed on capital gains even if the asset value has done nothing more than just keep up with inflation.

Finally, inflation also affects the real value of the tax burden when there are significant lags in tax collection. The problem is that tax obligations are accrued at a certain point, but the payment is made at a later date. In many countries, no mechanism exists to maintain the real value of the tax liability during this lag. Thus, any increase in the rate of inflation during this period reduces the tax burden. This phenomenon is known as the *Olivera–Tanzi effect,*[19] and it can lead to a vicious circle. An increase in the fiscal deficit pushes up inflation, which, in turn, reduces tax revenues; lower tax revenues, in turn, further increase the fiscal deficit, and so on. This process can be very destabilizing, and it has contributed in important ways to many of the high inflations in the developing world in the 1980s.

A dramatic illustration of the Olivera–Tanzi effect is provided by the experience of Bolivia in the first half of the 1980s, as shown in Figure 11-7. Government revenues were close to 10 percent of GDP in 1980–1981, and inflation was around 25 percent per year. In 1982, inflation soared to almost 300 percent, and revenues halved as a percentage of GDP. This downward trend continued, and the worst came in 1985, when Bolivia entered into a full-blown hyperinflation. At that time, tax revenues declined to a mere 1.3

---

[19] This effect takes its name from Julio Olivera and Vito Tanzi. See Olivera's "Money, Prices, and Fiscal Lags: A Note on the Dynamics of Inflation," *Quarterly Review,* Banca Nazionale del Lavoro, September 1967, pp. 258–267, and Tanzi's "Inflation, Lags in Collection and the Real Value of Tax Revenue," *International Monetary Fund Staff Papers,* March 1977.

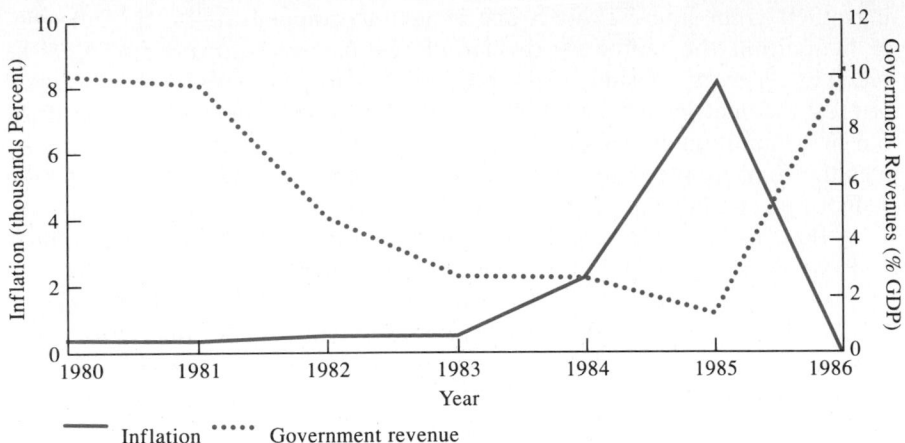

Figure 11-7
An Illustration of the Olivera-Tanzi Effect: Bolivia, 1980–1986

(Data for inflation from CEPAL, Economic Survey for Latin America, *1988; data for government revenues from J. Sachs, "The Bolivian Hyperinflation and Stabilization," National Bureau of Economic Research Working Paper No. 2073, May 1986.)*

percent of GDP, which could well have been the lowest tax burden in the world. Note, however, the sharp reversal in 1986. As a successful stabilization program was implemented, and inflation dropped to 66 percent for the year, government revenues increased to over 10 percent of GDP.[20]

Unanticipated Inflation

Countries with higher rates of inflation also tend to show more variability in inflation. When changes in inflation are frequent and marked, this instability makes it difficult to guess correctly about price level changes, even in the very near future. This problem is not confined to developing countries. Since the 1970s, most industrialized economies have experienced an increase in both the level and the variability of inflation. When variability increases, inflation tends to have a larger unanticipated component.

The main effects of unanticipated inflation are redistributional. Surprises in inflation rates lead to shifts of income and wealth between various groups in the population. To see this, let us discuss first the case of *wealth redistribution.* Consider a loan contract between a creditor and debtor that specifies a nominal interest rate of 10 percent, based on an expected real rate of interest of 5 percent and an expected inflation rate of 5 percent. Now suppose that inflation ends up being abnormally high, say, at a rate of 10 percent. Who wins and who loses?

Clearly, the debtor wins, since he was supposed to pay a real rate of 5 percent and ends up paying a zero real interest rate. Essentially, he gets the loan for free! The creditor gets back only the original real value of the loan,

---

[20] Of course, other things were changing in the economy as well: in 1986, the government put through an important tax reform which helped to increase revenues.

inasmuch as the interest rate is just enough to compensate for the inflation. If, in addition, the debtor can deduct interest payments for tax purposes, he receives an extra subsidy; if the creditor has to pay taxes on her nominal interest income, she loses part of the principal of the loan. Thus we can draw our first important conclusion: unexpected increases in inflation redistribute wealth from creditors to debtors, and unexpected reductions in inflation redistribute wealth the opposite way.

But this principle applies to more than loan contracts. In general, any-body holding a financial asset, the returns of which are all or in part fixed in nominal terms, will tend to suffer a loss from unanticipated price increases. Assets of this sort are called *nominal* assets, and they include money and fixed interest-rate bonds. By contrast, *real* assets have their value adjusted in line with inflation. To protect the assets held by economic agents from unexpected changes in the price level, some economies have developed indexed financial instruments. A bond that is protected in this way promises only to pay a certain *real* interest rate. In other words, people do not know in advance what nominal interest will be paid; that rate is determined only after the inflation rate of the period is known. Indexed assets are more likely to be found in countries that have experienced long inflationary histories. For example, while Brazil and Chile make widespread use of indexed assets, the United States does not.

In general, economic agents hold both nominal assets and liabilities. Thus, the full effect of unexpectedly high inflation for individual agents depends on their *net* asset positions. If one is a net creditor in nominal assets, one will lose. If, in contrast, one is a net debtor, one will become better off. The evidence for the United States indicates that the household sector is a net nominal creditor, while businesses and the government are net debtors. Thus, an unanticipated increase in inflation benefits firms and the government at the expense of households. Of course, households own the firms and pay taxes to the government, so the overall nature of the redistrib-ution is not quite this simple.

Within the household sector there are also strong differences. Home-owners with mortgages on their homes, for example, benefit from unex-pected inflation (assuming, of course, that their holdings of other nominal assets do not offset this effect). The net asset position for households also varies with age. Older people tend to hold more net nominal assets than younger people. Thus, unexpected rises in the general price level tend to redistribute wealth away from the old.[21]

Unanticipated inflation also provokes *income redistributions* among the different sectors of the population. For people locked into labor con-tracts, an increase in inflation that exceeds expectations means a deteriora-tion of their real wages. This happens not only to those who have contracts without cost-of-living adjustment clauses (COLAs) but also to those with indexing clauses that operate with a lag, or that compensate for only a fraction of the inflation. In general, because wages are reset only sporadi-cally, higher inflation leads to increased variability of a worker's wages over time. Just after a wage increase, the real wage tends to be high. Then, as

---

[21] This has been documented by G. Bach and J. Stephenson, "Inflation and the Distribu-tion of Wealth," *Review of Economics and Statistics,* February 1974.

inflation continues while the wage remains unchanged, the real wage declines, until the time of the next wage hike. Even if inflation does not affect
the average real wage of the worker, it certainly affects the variability of the
real wage. A dramatic illustration of that variability is shown in Figure 11-8,
which graphs the behavior of the real minimum wages in Peru during the high
inflation period 1985–1989. The sawtooth pattern shows the extreme variations over time.

One final distributional issue concerns the inflation tax on money holdings that we have talked about earlier. Because the income elasticity of
money demand is likely to be less than one, the inflation tax itself is likely to
be regressive—that is, poorer people pay a higher proportion of their income
as inflation tax than richer people do.

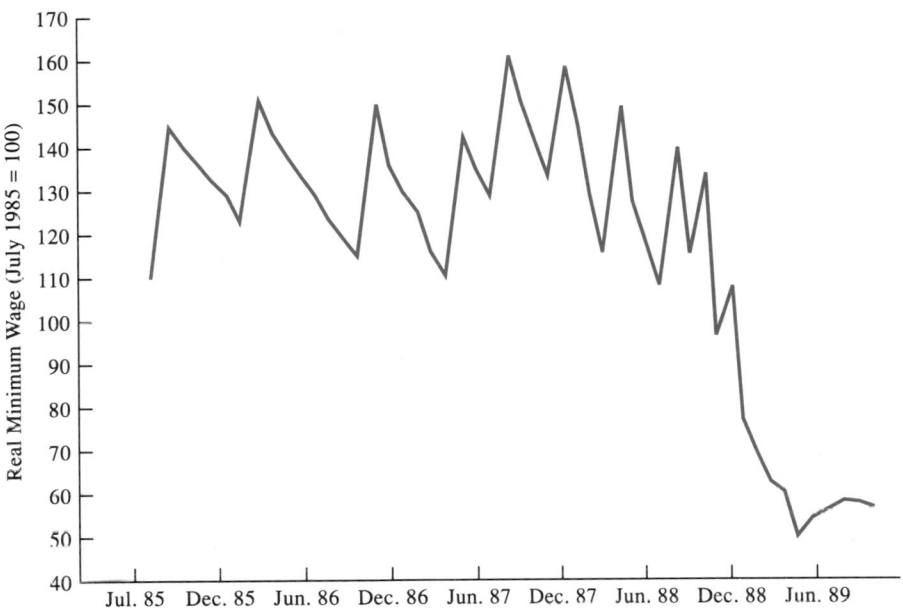

Figure 11-8
Inflation and the Real Minimum Wage in Peru, 1985–1989

(From INE, Ministerio de Trabajo, Peru.)

In addition to the distributional effects of unanticipated inflation,
shocks to inflation can also cause households and enterprises to make erroneous supply and demand decisions. Suppose, for example, that a firm expects
inflation to be low, but that in fact inflation throughout the economy turns
out to be high. Prices rise for the output of the particular firm as well as the
outputs of all other firms in the economy. When the enterprise notices that
the price of its own product is rising faster than it expected, the firm might
suspect that there has been a particular increase in demand for its product,
rather than a rise in prices of all products in the economy. In essence, the
firm confuses a general inflation for a particular increase in demand. As a
result, the firm might erroneously choose to increase output in the mistaken

belief that there is a boom in demand for its particular product. If this behavior is repeated by many firms throughout the economy, there can be a mistaken shift in aggregate supply that leads to a distorted level of output in the economy.[22]

Should Countries Learn to Live with Inflation?

Economists are divided from time to time between two strategies for confronting inflation. Some say we should learn to live with it, coping with its effects by indexing the tax system, wage bargains, contracts, and so on. Others want to confront it head on, embracing whatever macroeconomic measures are necessary, even a recession perhaps (for reasons described in Chapters 15 and 23), in order to eliminate it from the system.

At first blush, improving the economy's resilience to inflation through widespread indexation might appear to be costless. If inflation does not occur, nothing is lost; if it does, its distortionary effects will be less. But as Stanley Fischer and Lawrence Summers have recently argued, reducing the costs of inflation also increases the incentives for policymakers to pursue overinflationary policies.[23] Therefore, while "inflationproofing" the economy may lower the costs of inflation for any given level of inflation, it may also raise the inflation rate that policymakers will target. Whether the economy is then better off or worse off is hard to say. Fischer and Summers cite examples in which inflationproofing leads to such a large increase in inflation that the overall losses to the economy from inflation actually rise.

In general, we can say that inflationproofing is desirable if most inflationary episodes are likely to result from shocks that are beyond the control of policymakers. In that case, the measures to index the economy will simply reduce the efficiency losses that result from the shocks. If most inflation is likely to arise from deliberate or merely careless overinflationary policies of the monetary and fiscal authorities, however, then inflationproofing might just increase the policymaker's "addiction" to a costly and hidden form of taxation.

11-4 SUMMARY

Inflation is the percentage change in the price level, normally measured as the increase in the consumer price index. It is important to distinguish between *once-and-for-all* price increases and *persistent* price rises. It also is useful to distinguish inflations by their severity, whether an inflation is simply high or whether it is a hyperinflation. Industrialized countries have tended to show much lower levels of inflation than developing economies. The highest chronic inflations are generally found in Latin America.

Public-sector deficits can be covered in three ways: borrowing from the public, using foreign reserves, or printing money. Governments which have

---

[22] Clearly, if inflation turns out to be *less* than expected, then all firms might *reduce* output, leading to a recession. The general idea that firms might confuse overall inflationary shocks with shifts in demand for their particular products was first elaborated by Robert Lucas. See his article "Some International Evidence on Output-Inflation Tradeoffs," *American Economic Review*, June 1973.

[23] See their joint article "Should Governments Learn to Live with Inflation?" *American Economic Review*, May 1989.

run persistent deficits in the past are likely to have low international reserves, and they also have difficulties borrowing further. Thus, eventually,
such governments turn to monetary financing.

Under fixed exchange rates, deficits financed by printing money are
ultimately financed by a loss of international reserves. As long as reserves
are available, the exchange rate may remain fixed and the country can avoid
inflation. If the deficit persists and reserves are depleted, however, the central bank will have no option but to devalue (or float the exchange rate).
Then, inflation cannot be avoided. The collapse of a fixed exchange-rate
system is known as a *balance-of-payments* crisis. The anticipation of this
collapse by the public leads to a speculative attack that cleans out the foreign
reserves of the central bank. Under floating exchange rates, persistent deficits cause the exchange rate to depreciate continuously, and the deficit is
ultimately financed through an inflation tax on real money balances.

Domestic borrowing cannot be used to postpone inflation indefinitely.
For a given *primary deficit,* that is, the deficit excluding interest payments,
the overall fiscal deficit grows due to the rising interest burden of the debt.
Continued debt financing makes the debt-to-GDP ratio grow over time. At
some point, people will be unwilling to hold more public debt because they
doubt the government's ability to service the additional debt. The government will then be forced to use money financing.

The *inflation tax* is the capital loss suffered as a result of inflation by
those who hold money. *Seigniorage* is the revenue that the government
collects by virtue of its monopoly power to print money; it is equal to the
purchasing power of the money that it puts into circulation in a given period.
Seigniorage is normally collected by the domestic country's government, but
when nationals hold some of their money balances in foreign currencies,
those foreign governments whose currencies are held collect part of the
seigniorage. In general, the inflation tax and seigniorage are not exactly
equal. They are the same when real money balances are unchanging. In an
inflationary environment, agents who want to maintain their real stock of
money will have to sacrifice consumption by an amount equal to the inflation
tax.

Inflation has a number of costs. Price increases, even if fully anticipated, impose a tax on the public. In addition, inflation produces pure efficiency losses. Expected increases in inflation reduce average money balances held by the public. Attempts to economize on money, the most
efficient means of payment, involve real costs (more frequent trips to the
bank, more complicated financial transactions, and so on). *Menu costs* are
another effect of *anticipated inflation.* Real resources are spent in making
the adjustments required by higher prices as costs of production increase.
Anticipated inflation also leads to resource misallocation through its effects
on the tax system, if the tax system is not indexed. Finally, inflation also
affects the real value of tax revenues when there are significant lags in tax
collection.

Higher than expected inflation causes important wealth redistributions
from creditors to borrowers when financial assets are not *indexed* to inflation. *Unanticipated inflation* also leads to income redistributions among the
different sectors of the population. This depends, for example, on how real
wages and profits respond to the price increases. The distributional consequences of the inflation tax are likely to be *regressive.* The income elasticity

of money demand is likely to be less than one, and thus poorer people tend to pay a higher proportion of their income as inflation tax than richer people do. Unanticipated inflation can also impose costs by inducing firms and households to make erroneous supply and demand decisions, for example, by making firms confuse an overall increase in prices with a specific increase in prices for the firms own product.

Key Concepts

inflation
price level
hyperinflation
balance-of-payments crisis
inflation tax
speculative attack
primary deficit
seigniorage
anticipated inflation
unanticipated inflation

income redistribution
wealth redistribution
menu costs
bracket creep
Olivera–Tanzi effect
nominal assets
real assets
indexed assets
regressive tax

Problems and Questions

1. Discuss the effects on the exchange rate (under purchasing power parity) of three different phenomena: a once-and-for-all change in the price level, inflation, and hyperinflation.

2. The government of country A is running a budget deficit of 500 million pesos per year. To finance it, the government sells treasury bills to the central bank. The exchange rate is fixed at 20 pesos per dollar. Assume that the international price level is fixed and that the central bank has a large amount of foreign reserves.

a. Calculate the yearly change in the foreign reserves of the central bank. Would you expect this process to be smooth over time? Why?

b. Describe the evolution of the price level, the exchange rate, and nominal and real monetary balances before and after the exhaustion of the foreign reserves of the central bank.

3. Explain why a government running a large budget deficit may choose to devalue the currency before the central bank runs out of foreign reserves.

4. The government of country B has a budget deficit of 2 percent of GDP. Real money demand is also growing at 2 percent of GDP per year. The government monetizes the deficit.

a. Under fixed exchange rates, describe the evolution of the foreign reserves of the central bank.

b. Under floating exchange rates, what would the rate of inflation be in country B?

5. Assume that the government of country C is running a budget deficit equal to 6 percent of GDP, financed entirely by money creation. Assume that the exchange rate is allowed to float, international inflation is 3 percent per year, and the velocity of money is fixed at 4.

a. What is the rate of inflation consistent with this deficit?

b. What is the rate of depreciation of the currency?

6. Consider a government that is running a constant and persistent budget deficit, financed by selling bonds to the central bank. There is a floating exchange-rate regime. When would you expect inflation in this country to be higher, when the velocity of money is constant or when it is a positive function of the nominal interest rate? Why?

7. Assume that inflation is greater than the rate of growth of nominal monetary balances.

   a. What happens to real monetary balances?

   b. Which is greater, the inflationary tax or seigniorage? Why?

8. Suppose that the government needs to raise 1/5 percent of GDP using seigniorage. The demand for money is given by $3M = PQ$, where $Q = 12$. Calculate the inflation rate that will accompany this level of seigniorage finance.

9. Some economists have argued that in order to prevent inflationary finance of budget deficits certain countries should not have a national currency. Instead, they should use the currency of a country with a long history of price stability. What are the pros and cons of this proposal?

10. Explain why companies tend to finance a higher proportion of their investment projects using loans rather than their own resources when inflation increases.

11. Do you think the costs of a sudden increase in inflation would be higher in a country that has usually had a stable price level or in one that has endured through many inflationary episodes?

Macroeconomic Policies and Output Determination in a Closed Economy

In Chapter 3, we began our study of output determination. There we saw that the level of output in the economy is determined by the interaction of aggregate supply and aggregate demand. Shifts in aggregate demand lead to shifts in output, and hence in employment as well, when the aggregate supply schedule is upward sloping—that is, when nominal wages do not adjust immediately to ensure full employment. Under the classical assumptions of fully flexible wages and prices, shifts in aggregate demand affect only prices, and the level of aggregate output is determined by the full-employment equilibrium in the labor market.

With this chapter, we introduce the crucial idea that macroeconomic policies—both fiscal policy involving government spending and taxes and monetary policy—can have important and systematic effects on aggregate demand. Thus, the government itself, through its effects on the total level of demand, can be one of the most important determiners of the level of output in the economy. On the optimistic side, economists in the Keynesian tradition assert that the government may therefore use macroeconomic policies to *stabilize* the economy at the full-employment level, adjusting monetary and fiscal policies to counteract other kinds of demand shocks.

On the pessimistic side, other economists sustain that the macroeconomic authorities at the Treasury and the central bank may well become key sources of output instability as they manipulate their policy instruments erratically. Still others, mainly the "supply-side" economists in the United States, argue that macroeconomic policies affect aggregate supply, in the main, and not aggregate demand. If the economy adjusts classically, as they assume it does, pure demand shocks affect prices rather than output. But, the supply-siders say, changes in government spending and particularly taxes can have important effects on the desired level of supply and the efficiency of production.

Before we can assess these arguments, we must first know how macroeconomic policies affect aggregate demand, and thereby, output and employment. The links between macroeconomic policies and aggregate demand are both profound and subtle, and we need some new models, especially the *IS-LM* framework, in order to study the interaction between the output market and the money market. This relationship is made more complicated by the existence of many different kinds of exchange-rate regimes: fixed or floating rates, with free or restricted international capital mobility. And, it turns out, the nature of the exchange-rate regime has a fundamental effect on the determination of aggregate demand.

From here, we shall proceed in two steps. In this chapter, we pretend—since it is never strictly true—that the economy is *closed,* so that we can study the effects of monetary and fiscal policies without having to cope with the complications raised by international trade, exchange rates, and capital mobility. Our tool for doing this is basic *IS-LM* analysis. In the next chapter, we proceed to the more accurate open-economy model.

12-1 AGGREGATE DEMAND AND THE KEYNESIAN MULTIPLIER

In order to see how fiscal and monetary policies affect aggregate demand, we first derive an aggregate demand schedule. Then we combine it with the aggregate supply schedule that we derived in Chapter 3 to find the overall effects on output.

Defining Aggregate Demand

Remember that we defined aggregate demand in Chapter 3 as the level of total demand in the economy for a given level of prices, adding up consumption, investment, and government spending (and net exports in an open economy). (To do this, we also assumed equilibrium in the money market.) Thus, we calculate aggregate demand for a particular price level P, and then show how that level of aggregate demand depends on variables such as current government spending (G), current taxes (T), future disposable income $[Q - T]^F$, the expected future marginal productivity of capital (MPK^E), and the money supply (M). After some analysis, we will be able to find a relationship of the form

$$Q^D = Q^D (G, T, [Q - T]^F, MPK^E, M, P) \qquad \textbf{(12.1)}$$

From this equation we see that, for given values of $G, T, [Q - T]^F, MPK^E$, and M, aggregate demand Q^D is a negative function of the price level P, as we saw in Chapter 3 (Figure 3-14).

To derive (12.1), let us start with the basic identity that the level of total demand is the sum of consumption, investment, and government spending. (Remember, we are dealing with a *closed* economy; demand in an open economy does not come up until the next chapter.) Or, as we said in equation (3.10):

$$Q^D = C + I + G \qquad \textbf{(12.2)}$$

We have already looked at the individual components of spending in some detail, when we discussed theories of consumption in Chapter 4, investment in Chapter 5, and government spending in Chapter 7. In general, we found that consumption and investment spending are functions of several interacting variables, including the interest rate, the level of taxation, expectations about future income and other variables, and so on. In particular, we can summarize our findings for each of these factors fairly simply.

Consumption is a decreasing function of the interest rate (assuming the "normal" case that higher interest rates lead to more saving), an increasing function of current disposable income, and an increasing function of expected future disposable income:

$$C = C(i, Q - T, [Q - T]^F) \tag{12.3}$$

Note that we have simplified the notation for future disposable income, $[Q - T]^F$ (where T is taxes and F is future), even though this term is really an expectation of the discounted value of disposable income over several future periods. We have also simplified the definition of disposable income merely as output minus taxes, neglecting interest earnings on foreign assets because of our closed-economy assumption for this chapter.

Investment demand is a negative function of interest rates and a positive function of the expected future marginal productivity of capital, MPK^E:

$$I = I(i, MPK^E) \tag{12.4}$$

Once again, we have simplified the concept of MPK^E, which is really a complicated expression that covers many periods in the future. We have also neglected any considerations of the accelerator and other complications of investment theory.

Note also that in both (12.3) and (12.4) we have used the nominal interest rate rather than the real interest rate as the determinant of spending. We should use real interest, but we are ignoring inflation in this chapter and we can make things easier by not using it.

Total demand is found by adding consumption, investment, and government spending on goods and services, G, to get

$$Q^D = C(i, Q - T, [Q - T]^F) + I(i, MPK^E) + G \tag{12.5}$$

In this equation, however, output appears both on the left-hand side, as the measure of total demand, and the right-hand side, as one of the determinants of consumption spending. Because in equilibrium Q^D will have to equal Q, we still have to "solve out" for Q, so that output appears only on the left-hand side of the equation.

We can best do this by assuming that the consumption equation (12.3) and the investment equation (12.4) are in linear form (this is not strictly necessary for the mathematics, only for the convenience). For example, let us write

$$C = c(Q - T) - ai + c^F[Q - T]^F \tag{12.6a}$$
$$I = -bi + dMPK^E \tag{12.6b}$$

In these expressions, the variables c, a, c^F, b, and d are positive numerical constants (for example, perhaps $c = 0.6$), but we don't need any actual numerical values here. We use the variable c to denote the marginal propensity to consume out of current income, measured by the coefficient on $Q - T$. Similarly, c^F stands for the marginal propensity to consume out of future income.

When we substitute the linear expressions for C and I into (12.5), let $Q^D = Q$ (which will be true in equilibrium), and then solve, we find

$$Q^D = \left[\frac{1}{(1-c)}\right] G - \left[\frac{c}{(1-c)}\right] T + \left[\frac{c^F}{(1-c)}\right] [Q - T]^F \quad \textbf{(12.7)}$$

$$+ \left[\frac{d}{1-c}\right] MPK^E - \left[\frac{(a+b)}{(1-c)}\right] i$$

What, then, do we conclude from (12.7)? Aggregate demand is a positive function of government spending, a negative function of taxes, a positive function of expected *future* income, a positive function of the expected future marginal productivity of capital, and a negative function of the interest rate.

Unfortunately, equation (12.7) is not yet a theory of aggregate demand because it does not explain enough. For one thing, the equation shows that Q^D is a negative function of the interest rate, i, but it does not yet tell us how the interest rate gets determined. And, of course, an aggregate demand equation is even less a theory of output determination. For that we need to combine the aggregate demand schedule with the aggregate supply schedule.

The Keynesian Multiplier

In the early days of Keynesian analysis, Keynes and his followers put great stress on an important special case, that of fixed output prices and a fixed nominal interest rate. With fixed prices, the level of aggregate demand determines the level of output, and with a fixed nominal interest rate, an equation like (12.7) can be used to determine the level of aggregate demand.

Keynes also emphasized one interesting implication of an equation like (12.7). According to the equation, a rise in government spending G leads to a rise in aggregate demand that is *even larger than the initial rise in government spending*. As Keynes described this phenomenon, then, government spending has a multiplier effect. In particular, we see from (12.7) that each one dollar increase in government spending increases aggregate demand by $1/(1-c)$ dollars.[1] Since the marginal propensity to consume, c, is less than one (except in the extreme case of absolutely permanent changes in disposable income), the effect of a one dollar rise in government spending is greater than one dollar.

Let us see how this multiplier effect works. When G goes up by one dollar, total aggregate demand initially rises by one dollar, assuming that private consumption and investment at first stay unchanged (a big—and generally incorrect—assumption, that we will soon take into account). But then, if output is determined by aggregate demand, disposable income rises by one dollar, and this, in turn, raises consumption. In particular, the rise in disposable income induces an increase in consumption of $c(\$1)$. This rise in private consumption, in turn, induces a further increase in total output, and a *further* increase in disposable income, leading to a *further* increase of consumption.

In the first round of output increase, consumption rises by $c(\$1)$. In the next round of output increase, consumption rises by c times the first round

---

[1] This is the multiplier for a rise in G that is not matched by a rise in taxes T. That is, the multiplier is for a bond-financed, not a tax-financed, increase in government spending.

increase, or by $c[c(\$1)]$. This cycle of higher consumption leading to higher income leading to higher consumption, and so on, is damped over time: each round leads to a smaller and smaller increase. In particular, the overall effect is equal to a geometric sum:[2]

$$\text{Change in } Q = \$1 + c(\$1) + c^2(\$1) + c^3(\$1) + \cdots$$

$$= \$1 \left[\frac{1}{(1 - c)} \right]$$

The multiplier is a rather artificial construct in the following sense. When G goes up without a corresponding increase in T, the increased spending must be financed by bonds. Two things are likely to happen. First, interest rates will tend to rise, and this has an additional dampening effect on the output increase. Second, *future* taxes will rise or *future* government spending will fall in order to satisfy the government's intertemporal budget constraint. If future taxes rise, and if those increases are anticipated by households, that will also dampen the multiplier effect. (Basic Keynesian analysis does not usually accommodate these anticipation effects.)

If both G and T are increased by an equal amount, another multiplier, the *balanced-budget multiplier* comes into play. According to (12.7), in the case of a *balanced-budget* increase in government spending, a $1 rise in G by itself raises output by $\$1/(1 - c)$, while a $1 rise in T lowers output by $\$c/(1 - c)$. The combined effect of a balanced-budget increase is therefore $[\$1/(1 - c)] - [\$c/(1 - c)]$, which is equal to $[\$(1 - c)/(1 - c)] = \$1$. Thus, we find that a tax-financed increase in government spending has a multiplier effect of 1. In other words, output goes up by exactly the same amount as the rise in tax-financed spending.

The balanced-budget multiplier formula is subject to the same limitations as the formula for the government-spending multiplier, however. It neglects the effects of changes in G and T on interest rates, and it neglects the effects of current G and T on future G and T, which also affect household consumption through the intertemporal budget constraint.

12-2 THE *IS-LM* FRAMEWORK

A useful and very popular way to derive the aggregate demand schedule, and to see the effects of macroeconomic policies, is the *IS-LM model*, a graphical framework developed in 1937 by the Nobel Prize–winning British economist Sir John Hicks.[3]

The IS Curve

The *IS* (investment-saving) curve relates the level of aggregate demand Q^D to the level of interest rates, i, holding fixed all other variables such as G and T. As equation (12.7) makes clear, a rise in the interest rate depresses aggregate demand through its effects on both consumption and investment. When

---

[2] See the discussion of the geometric sum in the last section of Chapter 2 and the geometric sum related to the money multiplier in Chapter 9.

[3] See John Hicks, "Mr. Keynes and the Classics: A Suggested Interpretation," *Econometrica*, April 1937.

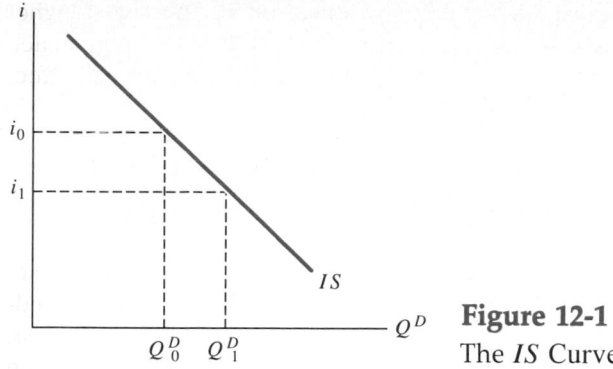

Figure 12-1

The *IS* Curve

we represent this relationship graphically, we will find a downward-sloping schedule, known as the *IS* schedule, such as the one shown in Figure 12-1 (the *IS* schedule is drawn as a straight line, but it need not be).

For every interest rate i, there is a corresponding equilibrium level of aggregate demand Q^D, holding fixed the values of the other variables. If we take, for example, the rate i_0, aggregate demand is Q_0^D. If the interest rate declines to i_1, aggregate demand increases to Q_1^D. The other variables that we have here held constant determine the position of the *IS* curve. An increase in government spending raises aggregate demand for any given level of the interest rate. This means that the *IS* curve shifts to the right. A rise in expected future disposable income also causes a rise in aggregate demand for a given level of the interest rate, and therefore shifts the *IS* curve to the right. Conversely, a rise in taxes or a fall in expected future disposable income causes a decline in aggregate demand for a given level of the interest rate, causing the *IS* curve to shift to the left. These movements are indicated by the arrows in Figure 12-2.

The **LM** *Schedule*

As we have said, equation (12.7) shows the level of aggregate demand for a given level of interest rates. To determine the level of interest rates, we must now turn to the money market. We can express money market equilibrium

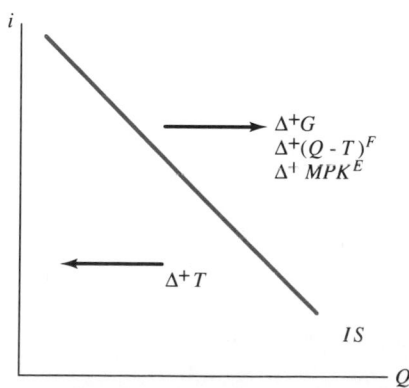

Figure 12-2

Variables That Shift the *IS* Curve

according to a conventional money-demand equation of the sort that we used in earlier chapters:

$$\frac{M}{P} = L(\underset{-}{i}, \underset{+}{Q^D})$$ (12.8)

In words, the supply of real balances (M/P) is equal to the demand for real money balances, given by $L(i, Q^D)$. We can rewrite this equation in a linear fashion as

$$\frac{M}{P} = -fi + vQ^D$$ (12.9)

Here, the characters f and v are simply positive numerical constants.

The *LM* schedule, presented in Figure 12-3, shows the combinations of aggregate demand and interest rates consistent with money market equilibrium *for a given level of real money balances, M/P.* The *LM* schedule is upward sloping. For example, the linear equation for the graph in Figure 12-3 would be

$$i = \left(\frac{v}{f}\right) Q^D - \left(\frac{1}{f}\right)\left(\frac{M}{P}\right)$$

The slope, in this case v/f, is therefore positive, as you can see.

Why does the *LM* curve slope upward? A higher interest rate reduces the demand for money, while a higher Q^D raises the demand for money. Thus, *for a given level of M/P,* money demand can be equal to the given money supply only if any increase in interest rates, which tends to lower money demand, is matched by a rise in aggregate demand—which tends to raise money demand.

By way of illustration, consider an initial point of money market equilibrium, say, point *A* in Figure 12-3, with interest rate i_0 and output level Q_0^D. If the interest rate rises from i_0 to i_1, and M/P remains unchanged, there would be a drop in demand for money. The only way that the money market can be in equilibrium at the higher interest rate is if Q^D is also higher than Q_0^D when the interest rate is at i_1. With a higher Q^D, the negative interest-rate effect on money demand is compensated for by a positive output effect on money demand. Thus, both points *A* and *B* are points of monetary equilibrium for a given stock of money, M/P.

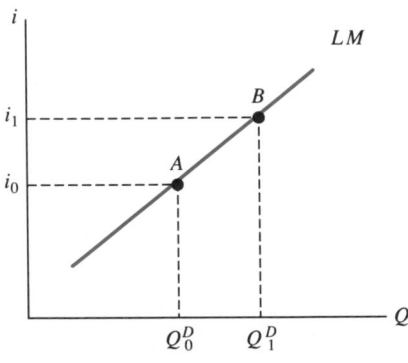

Figure 12-3
Money Market Equilibrium
and the *LM* Schedule

The position of the *LM* curve depends on the value of *M/P* in the economy. A rise in *M/P*, which may be caused either by an increase in the money supply or a decrease in the price level, shifts the whole *LM* curve down and to the right. Now an excess supply of money exists at the initial combinations of interest rates and output demand represented by the original *LM* curve. To restore equilibrium, the interest rate must fall, the level of Q^D must rise, or some combination of the two must occur so that money demand rises enough to equal the higher money supply.

Determining the Level of Aggregate Demand with the IS-LM Model

We can find the level of aggregate demand at the intersection of the *IS* and the *LM* curves. The intersection of the *IS* and *LM* curves shows the values of Q^D and *i* so that equations (12.7) and (12.8) both hold. That is, we are finding the values of Q^D and *i* for which output demand is consistent with the underlying behavioral relations for consumption and investment, and it

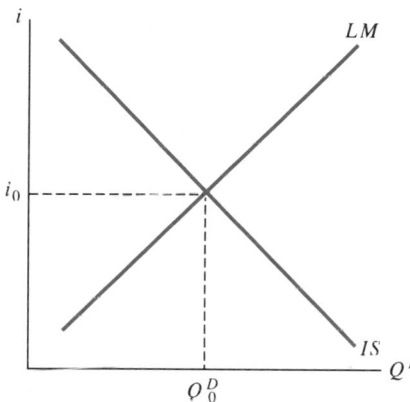

Figure 12-4
Equilibrium in the *IS-LM* Framework

means that the money market is in equilibrium. But remember that the *IS-LM* equilibrium only determines the nature of the aggregate demand curve, not the overall equilibrium of the economy. The *IS-LM* curves are drawn *for a given price level*. In order to determine the price level and the level of output in the economy, we must combine the aggregate demand curve with the aggregate supply curve.

The *IS-LM* equilibrium appears in Figure 12-4. Note carefully that the curves are drawn not only for a given price level *P*, but also for given levels of the policy instruments *G*, *T*, and *M*. Holding these variables constant, there is one single level of the interest rate (i_0) and of output demanded (Q_0^D) at which the output market and money market are simultaneously in equilibrium.

In Figure 12-5a we can see what happens to this equilibrium if we keep the level of *G*, *T*, and *M* unchanged, but increase the price level *P*. The *IS* curve remains unchanged because the basic factors that determine it, government spending, taxation, and future expected income, are also unchanged. The *LM* curve, however, shifts up and to the left because the real

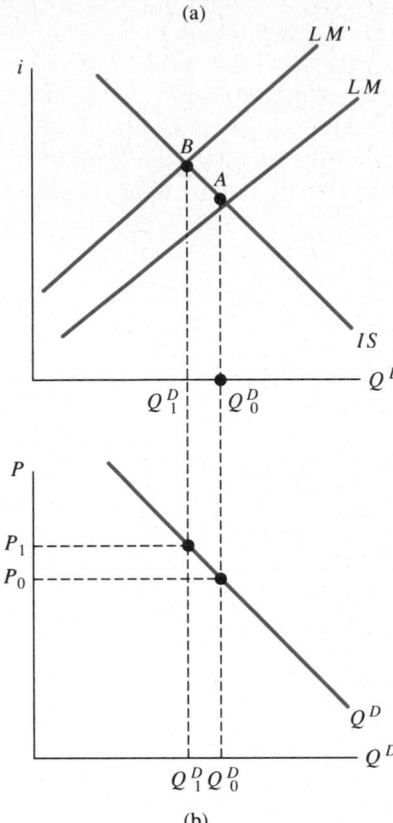

Figure 12-5

Effects of a Price Increase—the Shape of the Aggregate Demand Schedule: (a) The *IS-LM* Framework; (b) the Aggregate Demand Schedule

money supply M/P is now lower. Money market equilibrium therefore requires some combination of higher interest rates and lower output than it did on the original *LM* curve. Thus, equilibrium moves from point A to point B. Aggregate demand falls, and the interest rate rises.

Suppose next that for given G, T, and M, we make a graph relating the equilibrium value of Q^D to all possible levels of the price level. As P increases, Q^D decreases. The result, shown in Figure 12-5b, is a curve relating the level of aggregate demand to the level of prices, in other words, the result is the *aggregate demand schedule*. We have determined that the aggregate demand schedule is downward sloping, because a higher price level means a lower level of real money balances.

The *IS-LM* model has allowed us to derive the aggregate demand schedule based on a graphical analysis of the *IS* and *LM* curves. If instead we proceed algebraically, we solve Q^D and i using the equations (12.7) and (12.9). This is done formally in the appendix. But we can establish here the basic result, that aggregate demand is a function of the following form:

$$Q^D = Q^D(\underset{+}{G}, \underset{-}{T}, [\underset{+}{Q - T}]^F, \underset{+}{MPK^E}, \underset{+}{M}, \underset{-}{P})$$

This is the equation that we first introduced in (12.1).

12-3 THE EFFECTS OF MACROECONOMIC POLICIES
   ON AGGREGATE DEMAND

We are now ready to consider the effects of various policies on aggregate demand, using the *IS-LM* graphical apparatus. In all these inquiries, we take the price level as given. What we want to see is how each projected policy change affects the equilibrium level of Q^D.

Effects of a Rise in Government Spending

Suppose that the government starts a public works program that requires a significant increase in expenditures. At a given interest rate, demand increases in the goods market, and this shifts the *IS* curve to the right, as shown in Figure 12-6a. In fact, we have already determined the size of this rightward shift: it is the fiscal multiplier, $1/(1 - c)$, times the size of the initial increase in fiscal spending.

If the multiplier were the end of the story, the new equilibrium would be at the point *B*, with aggregate demand raised by the change in government spending (which we denote ΔG) times $1/(1 - c)$. But as the diagram clearly shows, point *B* is not a new equilibrium because at that point there is an

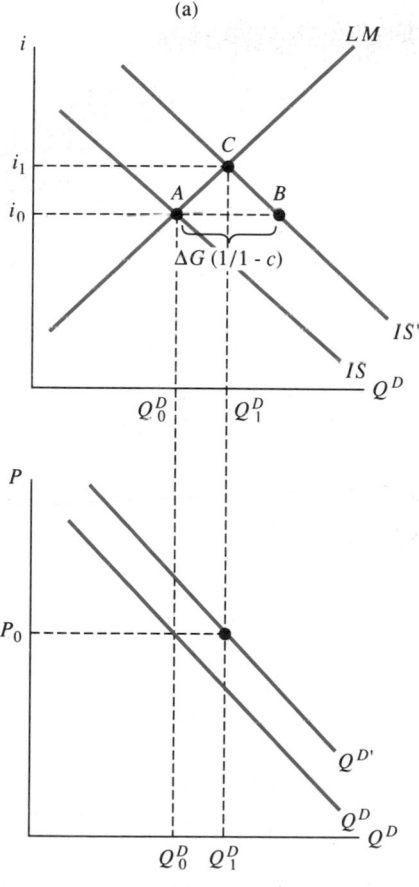

Figure 12-6

Effects of a Rise in Government Spending: (a) The *IS-LM* Framework; (b) the Aggregate Demand Schedule

excess demand for real money balances. In other words, with M/P unchanged, a rise in output must be accompanied by a rise in interest rates. If it is not, households will find that they have insufficient money balances.

In particular, facing higher output at point B, households will try to shift their portfolios from bonds into real money balances because they want money to support a higher level of transactions. However, as they try to sell bonds and increase their money holdings, bond prices fall—and interest rates rise. The interest-rate increase helps to eliminate the excess demand for M/P in two ways. It reduces household demand for money—that is, it makes them less eager to hold their wealth as money—and it also reduces aggregate demand from the high level reached at point B. In fact, the rise of interest rates continues until the excess demand for money is choked off. That occurs in the diagram at point C, at the intersection of the IS and LM curves.

What may we conclude? *The rise in G has led to a rise in overall aggregate demand, but by a smaller amount than the simple Keynesian multiplier predicted.* One effect of the increase in fiscal spending is a rise in interest rates, which tends to reduce investment and private consumption. The dampening effect of higher interest rates on consumption and investment brought about by an increase in government expenditure is referred to as *crowding out*, because higher G ultimately "crowds out" private spending. The crowding-out effect is only partial, however, in that aggregate demand increases in spite of the discouraging effect of higher interest rates on private spending. For any given level of prices, then, Q^D tends to be higher after the fiscal expansion. Thus, the impact of a higher level of government spending may be represented as a rightward shift of the aggregate demand schedule. This effect is illustrated in Figure 12-6b.

But what happens to the equilibrium level of output and prices after a rise in government spending? We can answer this question with the help of our discussion in Chapter 3. The *ultimate* effect of the fiscal expansion in the economy depends on the shape of the aggregate supply curve. In the classical case, with a vertical supply curve as shown in Figure 12-7a, the entire rise in aggregate demand ends up as a price level increase, while the level of output remains unchanged. In the basic Keynesian case, with an upward-sloping supply curve as shown in Figure 12-7b, the rise in aggregate demand

Figure 12-7
Fiscal Expansion and Equilibrium Output and Prices: (a) The Classical Case; (b) the Normal Keynesian Case; (c) the Extreme Keynesian Case

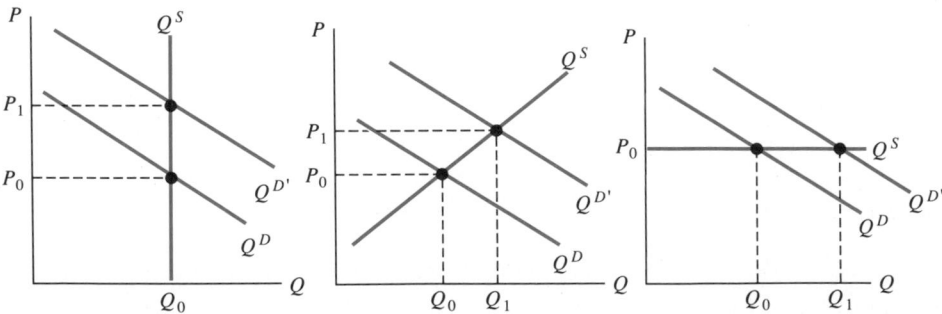

is split between output, which increases from Q_0 to Q_1, and prices, which rise from P_0 to P_1. In the extreme Keynesian case, with a horizontal supply curve as shown in Figure 12-7c, the entire effect shows up as an output increase, with prices fixed at the level P_0.

In case (c), sometimes taken to be the "standard" case in Keynesian analysis, we do not need to draw the aggregate demand–aggregate supply picture to know the result. Because the price level is fixed, the *IS-LM* framework is enough. The increase in aggregate demand from Q_0^D to Q_1^D in Figure 12-6a exactly corresponds to the rise in output from Q_0 to Q_1 in Figure 12-7c. With a flat aggregate supply curve, everything that is demanded is supplied at the given price. More generally, the initial increase in demand gets distributed between output and prices depending on the slope of the aggregate supply curve, which, in turn, represents different assumptions about the way in which the economy works.

Effects of a Cut in Taxes

The effects of a cut in taxes are the same as those of a rise in government spending. The *IS* curve shifts to the right. At the initial price level, interest rates and aggregate demand rise. This leads to a rightward shift of the aggregate demand schedule. The division of the demand expansion between a rise in output and a rise in prices depends on the slope of the aggregate supply schedule.

Effects of a Money Supply Increase

An increase in the money supply can also affect aggregate demand. The *IS-LM* model shows us that a rise in M leads to a rightward shift of the *LM* curve. At the interest-rate and output levels in effect before the policy change, there is an excess supply of money. In response, households convert their money to bonds, which drives up the price of bonds, and drives down the interest rate. The fall in the interest rate, in turn, stimulates consumption and investment spending, causing aggregate demand to increase. If the price level does not change, the new equilibrium involves a fall in interest rates and a rise in output, as shown by the shift from point A to point B in Figure 12-8.

Once again, the *IS-LM* analysis is not the end of the story. We have determined that aggregate demand increases, but we have not determined how that increase in aggregate demand gets divided between higher output and higher prices. That will depend on the shape of the aggregate supply schedule. The effects on output and prices will be the same as they were in Figure 12-7. In the classical case, price increases will absorb the entire increase in aggregate demand; in the basic Keynesian case, both output and prices will rise; and in the extreme Keynesian case of a flat aggregate supply curve, the entire increase in demand will show up as a rise in output.

Because the *IS-LM* curve is drawn for a given price level, there is actually a two-way feedback between the *IS-LM* curves and the aggregate supply–aggregate demand curves. Consider the effects of a money supply increase in the case of classical output supply. Initially the *LM* curve shifts to the right, and aggregate demand expands. With a vertical aggregate sup-

(a)

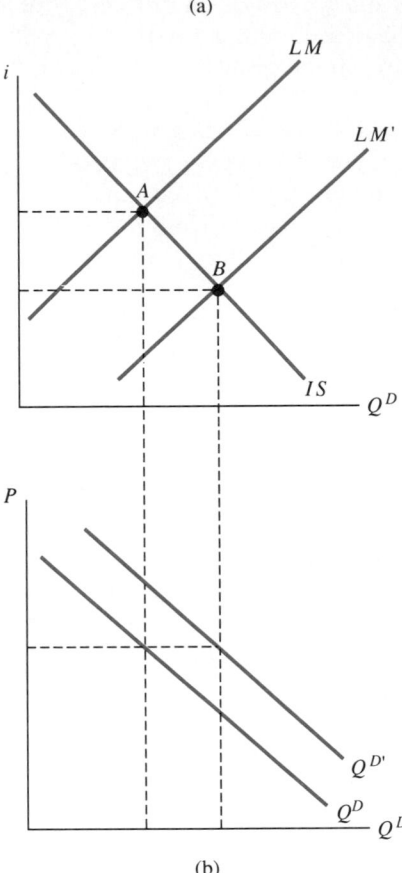

Figure 12-8
Effects of an Increase in the
Money Supply: (a) The *IS-LM*
Framework; (b) the Aggregate
Demand Schedule

(b)

ply curve (the classical case), prices tend to rise. But as the price P rises, and real money balances M/P fall, the LM curve starts to shift back to the left. As shown in Figure 12-9, the initial shift in the LM curve is eventually reversed by a rise in the price level.

In the final equilibrium, the level of output has not changed and prices have risen in proportion to the increase in M. *Thus, M/P is unchanged, and interest rates return to their initial level.* We are back to the classical case in which a rise in money simply leads to an equiproportional rise in prices.

Some Important Special Cases

Three famous special cases of *IS-LM* analysis have had an important influence on doctrinal debate in macroeconomics. In the first instance, shown in Figure 12-10, the case is considered in which the LM curve is perfectly vertical. This is the situation when money demand is not sensitive to the interest rate, that is, when velocity is a constant. The money demand equation is then simply $M/P = L(Q^D)$. In this case, as we see from the diagram, *a fiscal expansion has no effect on aggregate demand.* Rather, a rightward shift of the IS curve only results in a rise of the interest rate, without any

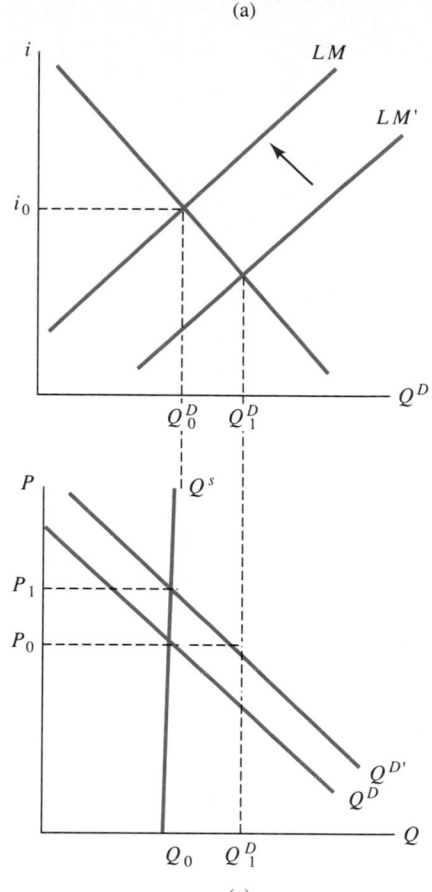

Figure 12-9

Equilibrium Effects of a Money Supply Increase in the Classical Case: (a) The *IS-LM* Framework; (b) the Aggregate Demand–Aggregate Supply Framework

effect on output demand.[4] That is, there is only one level of aggregate demand consistent with money market equilibrium.

Notice that a fiscal expansion in the face of a vertical *LM* curve produces *full* crowding out, as opposed to only partial crowding out when the *LM* curve has the "normal" upward-sloping shape. While the total level of aggregate demand remains unchanged in this case, the composition of aggregate demand has changed fundamentally. The increase in government spending is now equal in magnitude to the combined reduction in private consumption and investment.

The belief in a vertical *LM* curve is sometimes associated with a crude form of *monetarism,* which stresses the overriding importance of the nominal money supply in determining the level of nominal aggregate demand. Indeed, the extreme version of monetarism represented by a vertical *LM* curve holds that shifts in fiscal policy have no effect on aggregate demand. In the complicated world of ideological labels, however, many so-called

---

[4] Formally, the result is easy to prove. Since $M/P = L(Q^D)$, the L function can be inverted to write $Q^D = f(M/P)$, where the function f is the inverse of the function L. Thus, we see that there is a single level of Q^D consistent with the level of real money balances M/P.

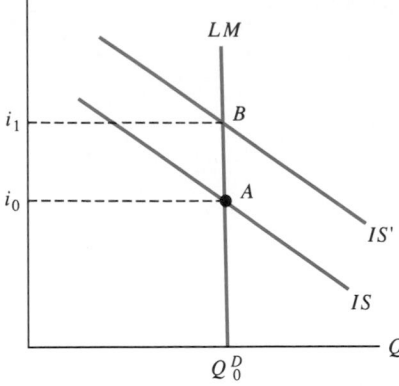

Figure 12-10
A Vertical *LM* Curve and Full
Crowding Out of Private
Spending

"monetarists" do not insist on the idea that money demand is unresponsive
to the interest rate, or interest inelastic. Notice also that when the *LM* curve
is vertical, monetary policy is very effective in shifting aggregate demand. A
money supply increase, represented by a rightward shift of the vertical *LM*
curve, has a strong effect on lowering interest rates and increasing Q^D.

A second extreme case that was suggested by Keynes as having applicability during the Great Depression (but which is now viewed mainly as a
theoretical curiosity) is that of a horizontal *LM* curve. In this situation,
money demand is infinitely elastic with respect to the interest rate. There is,
in this case, only one interest rate consistent with money market equilibrium. In such a case, fiscal policy has a powerful effect on aggregate demand. Monetary policy, on the other hand, has no effect because the interest
rate is fixed and cannot be reduced by a monetary expansion.

A flat *LM* was thought to occur only at very low interest rates. In these
circumstances, people may feel that the opportunity cost of holding money
is very low, and may decide to hold any increase in the money supply that
comes through as money—that is, to stay "liquid." This is why economists
refer to the situation in which there is a horizontal *LM* curve as a *liquidity
trap*, a case shown in Figure 12-11.

A third important special case occurs when consumption and investment demand are interest inelastic, that is, when *C* and *I* are not responsive
to the interest rate. In such a case, the *IS* is vertical. Now, as Figure 12-12

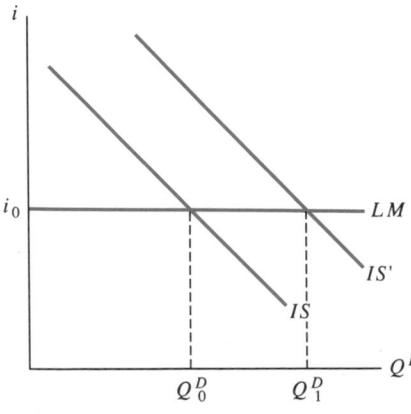

Figure 12-11
Fiscal Expansion Under a
Horizontal *LM* (the "Liquidity
Trap" Case)

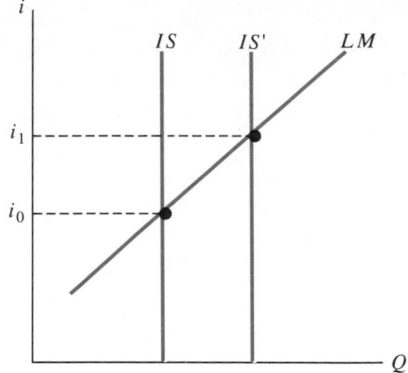

Figure 12-12
Fiscal Expansion When the *IS*
Is Vertical

shows, *fiscal* policy has a powerful effect on aggregate demand—indeed, the full fiscal multiplier $1/(1 - c)$ applies—but now *monetary* policy has no effect on aggregate demand.

   Note that fiscal policy is fully effective; that is, there is no crowding out, *both* when the *IS* is vertical and when the *LM* is horizontal. The reasons, however, are very different in each case. When there is a liquidity trap (a flat *LM* curve), the interest rate remains unchanged because there is only one interest rate consistent with money market equilibrium. Thus, a fiscal expansion does not cause a rise in the interest rate, and no crowding out occurs. By contrast, when the *IS* is vertical, interest rates do go up (provided the *LM* has the regular shape), but private spending—consumption and investment—does not fall in response to the higher interest rate.

TABLE   12-1

SUMMARY OF THE RESULTS OF *IS-LM* ANALYSIS IN A CLOSED ECONOMY

For given P	Monetary Expansion	Government Spending Increase	Tax Increase
(effect on)			
Aggregate demand	+	+	−
Interest rates	−	+	−

General Equilibrium	Monetary Expansion			Government Spending Increase			Tax Increase		
	Classic	Basic Keynes	Extreme Keynes	Classic	Basic Keynes	Extreme Keynes	Classic	Basic Keynes	Extreme Keynes
(effect on)									
Output	0	+	+	0	+	+	0	−	−
Price level	+	+	0	+	+	0	−	−	0
Interest rates	0	−	−	0	+	+	0	−	−

The Effects of Fiscal and Monetary Policies

The standard results of *IS-LM* analysis are summarized in Table 12-1. This summary ignores the extreme cases and focuses on the intermediate cases in which the *IS* curve is downward sloping and the *LM* curve is upward sloping. We show the results of changes in G, T, and M on aggregate demand and interest rates *for a given price level*, and then show the ultimate effects on output and prices and interest rates for the three cases of classical supply, Keynesian supply, and extreme Keynesian supply.

We see that in all cases, a rise in G, fall in T, or rise in M, results in an expansion of aggregate demand. This demand expansion raises output in all cases except the case of classical supply, and it raises the price level in all cases except the case of extreme Keynesian supply. A rise in G and a fall in T raise the interest rate, while a rise in M lowers the interest rate.

12-4 Implications of the *IS-LM* Analysis for Stabilization Policy

Because *IS-LM* analysis reveals the conditions under which changes in fiscal and monetary policy might affect the overall level of output in the economy, it can be used to suggest the kinds of policies a government should use to hit target levels of output or employment, for example. Believers in *activist demand management policies* say that the government should use the *IS-LM* framework—in some numerically refined form contained in a large-scale econometric model of the economy—to choose macroeconomic policies that will enable the government to hit particular output targets.[5]

The basic idea behind this approach is that "shocks" to the economy from the private sector, such as shocks to investment demand or to money demand, show up as fluctuations in output and prices. If macroeconomic policies remain unchanged when such shocks occur, then the ensuing fluctuations in overall aggregate demand will translate into fluctuations in output and employment—assuming a Keynesian aggregate supply curve for the economy. Activists believe that the government should counteract these shocks. A drop in private investment demand, for example, could be met by a rise in G, a cut in T, or a rise in M. Similarly, a rise in the demand for money, which would show up as a contractionary leftward shift in the *LM* curve, can also be met by a rise in G, a cut in T, or a rise in M.

For example, Keynes argued that investment spending had collapsed during the Great Depression because of an exogenous decline in entrepreneurs' expectations about future profitability. In our notation, we would say that MPK^E had declined, though for no apparent reason. The *IS* curve had shifted down and to the left as a result, leading to falls in output and in interest rates. The aggregate demand schedule had therefore moved down and to the left, and output and employment had declined as a result. To counteract this, Keynes strenuously argued for an increase in government spending G as a way to restore full employment.

---

[5] We analyze the case for and against policy activism in further detail in Chapter 19. Evidence on the large-scale econometric models is provided later on in this chapter.

The Debate Over Activist Demand Management

During the 1950s and 1960s, most economists had confidence that activist monetary and fiscal policies could be effective in offsetting shocks that emanated from the private sector of the economy. They advocated that policy authorities at the Treasury and the central bank should maintain a flexible control over G, T, and M, always vigilant to any adjustment needed in these variables in the quest for full employment. But when inflation in the United States and other industrial countries began to rise at the end of the 1960s, confidence in using so-called "stabilization policies" began to wane. Many economists began to feel that the government, rather than the private sector, had become a major source of economic instability.

The doubts over activist macroeconomic policy management were expressed in several different ways. Skeptics of macroeconomic stabilization policies adopted some or all of the following positions:

- The aggregate supply curve is vertical, so expansionary demand policies have little effect on raising output and employment, only on raising prices.

- Private shocks to the economy are hard to identify, especially in a timely way, so it is difficult if not impossible to offset these shocks with monetary and fiscal policies.

- Activist monetary policies are likely to be overinflationary because politicians routinely try to expand the economy, even beyond the full-employment level.

- Economists do not know enough empirically about the shape of the IS, LM, and aggregate supply curves, to choose the quantitative measures that could stabilize the economy.

- Activist policymakers are subject to political pressures that cause them to follow shortsighted policies that help them get reelected.

At this point, we can only highlight some of the objections to the activist policy position. In the following chapters, particularly in Chapters 15 and 19, we will have occasion to assess many of these assertions.

Adding Intertemporal Considerations into IS-LM Analysis

In addition to other criticisms, *IS-LM* analysis has been accused of being an inaccurate guide to stabilization policy by failing to capture many of the intertemporal considerations that we focussed on in Chapters 4 through 7. Indeed, the *IS-LM* model is static, and it does downplay the effects of current policy actions on the future state of the economy. Households make current decisions in part based on their expectations of the future, and thus the model fails to capture some important aspects of private sector behavior.

In a formal sense, this shortcoming can be corrected. We have included the expected level of future disposable income, $[Q - T]^F$, in the consumption function, and the expected future marginal productivity of capital, MPK^E, in the investment equation. We have not said much about these variables in considering various policies in the *IS-LM* framework, however.

Let us, then, reconsider fiscal policy with more care. A rise in fiscal spending, G, must be paid for out of current taxes, future taxes, or future cuts in government spending. To the extent that future taxes will be increased, we should pay attention to that fact in considering the consequences for aggregate demand of a fiscal expansion. If G rises permanently, for example, and it is announced (or merely expected) that future taxes will be raised to pay for the increase in G, households may cut back on their consumption in anticipation of higher future taxes. In an extreme case which we studied in Chapter 7, consumption will fall one-for-one with the permanent increase in G. If this happens, the *IS* curve will not even shift at all after G goes up.

In general, the extent of the *IS* shift following a rise in G will depend on how permanent the increase in G is expected to be. If the increase in G is permanent, households will expect a larger future increase in taxes than if the rise in G is temporary. The larger future increases in taxes are expected to be, then, the more consumption spending will fall.

We can thus incorporate the intertemporal dimension back into the *IS-LM* model. The standard treatment of the *IS-LM* model usually neglects these kinds of intertemporal considerations, but there is no fundamental contradiction in the *IS-LM* approach with the intertemporal analysis.

12-5 *IS-LM* IN THE SHORT RUN AND THE LONG RUN

Another dynamic aspect of the economy that the simple *IS-LM* framework usually neglects is the adjustment of wages and prices in response to unemployment. We saw in Chapter 3 that an economy may display Keynesian features in the short run and classical features in the long run if nominal wages adjust to the gap between actual output and potential output (where potential output refers to the level of Q at full employment of the labor force).

Now let us try to embed these adjustments into the context of the *IS-LM* model. To do so, one must reconsider the case, examined in Chapter 3, in which aggregate supply is Keynesian in the short term, with nominal wages predetermined within a period, but later adjusting as follows:

$$\hat{w}_{+1} = a(Q - Q^f) \qquad \textbf{(12.10)}$$

Now, as in Figure 12-13a, suppose there is an increase of the money supply. The *LM* curve shifts to the right in the graph, and at the initial price level, the new equilibrium would be at point B, with lower interest rates and higher aggregate demand.

The effects of the expansion in demand are divided between higher prices and higher output. The rise in prices is shown by the aggregate supply–aggregate demand equilibrium in Figure 12-13b. Because of the price increase, the *LM* curve immediately shifts part of the way back to its initial position (to *LM''*). Thus, the new equilibrium is given by point C in Figure 12-13a, and by point C' in Figure 12-13b.

But in this new situation, there is more than full employment, with output Q greater than Q^f. Nominal wages now start to rise, pushing the Q^S curve up and to the left, with the result that prices rise and output falls, as seen in Figure 12-13b. The shift in the Q^S curve leads to a shift in the northwest direction along the Q^D curve, and the level of aggregate demand falls as prices rise. To see why demand falls, note that the rise in output prices means that the *LM* curve is shifting to the left (remember that the

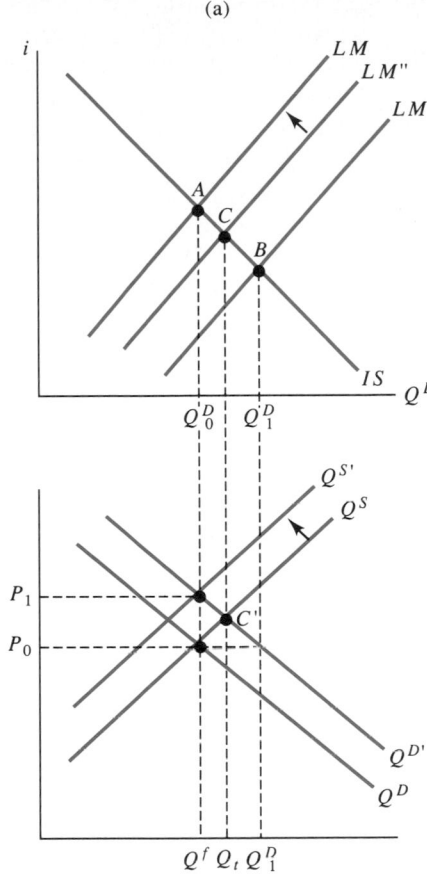

(a)

(b)

Figure 12-13

Dynamic Effects of a Money
Supply Increase in the Basic
Keynesian Case: (a) The *IS-LM*
Framework; (b) the Aggregate
Demand–Aggregate Supply
Framework

position of the *LM* curve depends on the level of output prices). Interest
rates rise over time as real money balances fall, and the rise in interest rates
causes a cutback in consumption and investment demand.

We can plot the time path of all the key variables following a rise in M.
Output, prices, and the real money supply initially jump, while the interest
rate and the real wage initially fall. Because output is greater than Q^f, nominal wages begin to rise, with the result that output starts to diminish while
prices, interest rates, and the real wage all increase. Eventually, wage increases are sufficient that real money balances are restored to their initial
level. All the key variables—output, interest rates, the real wage, and real
money balances—return to their initial levels, while the price level and the
nominal wage rise in the same proportion as the initial increase in the money
supply. The time path of these variables is shown in Figure 12-14.

As we noted in Chapter 3, the economy has Keynesian properties in
the short term but classical properties in the longer term. In the short run,
higher nominal money balances raise output; in the long run, higher money
balances only raise prices.

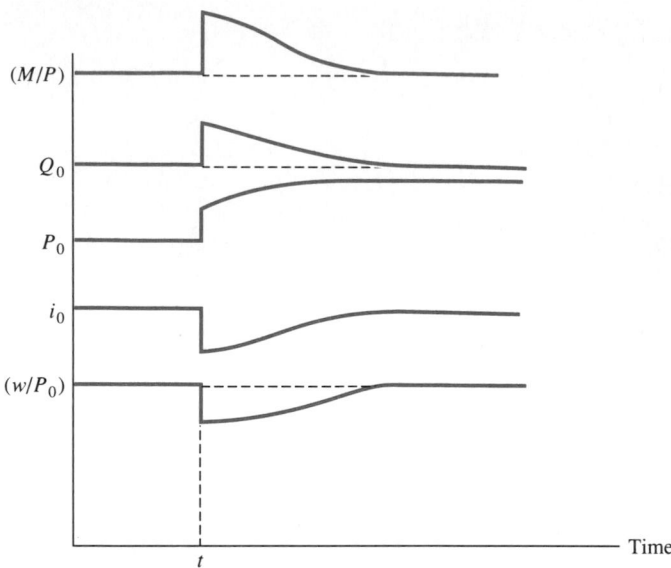

Figure 12-14
The Time Path of Key Macroeconomic Variables After a
Monetary Expansion

12-6 THE EMPIRICAL EVIDENCE

So far, we have studied the theoretical model and have suggested how the model helps to account for some actual historical cases. We have looked only at "signs" of the effects of macroeconomic policy, however. Now we will see how the effects of different policies have been quantitatively assessed.

As it turns out, all the econometric models of the United States and the world economy include the realistic complication that the United States is an open economy. The effect of macroeconomic policies in an open economy is the subject of the next two chapters. At this stage, then, we introduce the econometric models and some quantitative estimates of the effects that fiscal and monetary policies have on output and the price level, leaving until later the discussion of the exchange rate, the trade balance, and international repercussions.

Lawrence Klein, of the University of Pennsylvania, is considered the pioneer and most important contributor to the building of large-scale econometric models (LSEMs). For this work, the Swedish Academy of Sciences awarded him the Nobel Prize in Economics in 1982. Box 12-1 introduces some of the work by Klein and others on LSEMs.

Recently, Ralph Bryant, John Helliwell, and Peter Hooper performed simulations of various economic policies in the United States using many of

Box 12-1
Large-Scale Econometric Models

An LSEM is a complex system of econometric equations that attempts to describe the world economy or a particular region of it. The number of equations in these models can run in the hundreds, and even the thousands. Of course, no human being is able to solve such models analytically, so a computer must be used to perform the numerical computations. Nonetheless, the basic structure of the models is quite similar to the framework we have been exploring. The complications come from the refinement of the breakdown of the relationships among consumption, investment, money demand, and so on. LSEMs are generally used to perform *simulations*. These exercises attempt to answer the question: What will be the quantitative effect on the endogenous variables (output, prices, and so forth) of a change in some exogenous variable (in the area, say, of fiscal policy, monetary policy, or the exchange rate)?

The first version of a worldwide LSEM was *Project LINK,* pioneered at the end of the 1960s at the University of Pennsylvania by Lawrence R. Klein and his associates.[6] LINK consists of 79 submodels, each representing a country or a particular geographic region, so as to cover the whole world. Every one of the submodels, in turn, is a large-scale model on its own.

Project LINK is perhaps the best known, but it is only one of several large-scale econometric models. Several others have been developed by official agencies around the world, including (1) EPA, the world econometric model of the Japanese Economic Planning Agency,[7] which contains nine country models for Australia, Canada, France, Italy, Japan, United Kingdom, United States, and West Germany, as well as six regional models that cover the rest of the world; (2) EEC, the model of the European Economic Commission,[8] with four submodels for the United States, Japan, Europe, and the rest of the world; (3) MINIMOD, the rather small model used by the International Monetary Fund, which contains only two submodels, one for the United States and the other for the rest of the Organization of Economic Cooperation and Development (OECD), and which was developed through the joint efforts of Richard Haas and Paul Masson.[9]

---

[6] A useful reference about LINK is the volume edited by R. J. Ball, *The International Linkage of National Economic Models* (Amsterdam: North Holland, 1973). In particular see the article in this book by Lawrence Klein and A. Van Peetersson, "Forecasting World Trade with Project LINK."

[7] This model is presented in many different places. A well-known descriptive piece is Masaru Yoshitomi and others, "EPA World Econometric Model," EPA World Econometric Model Discussion Paper No. 16, Economic Planning Agency, Tokyo, July 1984.

[8] This is described in Andre Dramais, "COMPACT: Prototype of a Macro Model of the European Community in the World Economy," Discussion Paper No. 27, Commission of the European Communities, Directorate General for Economic and Financial Affairs, March 1986.

[9] The standard reference is Richard Haas and Paul Masson, "MINIMOD: Specification and Simulation Results," *International Monetary Fund Staff Papers,* December 1986.

Large-scale models have also been developed by private firms of economic consultants and forecasters, among them (4) DRI, the model of Data Resources Incorporated, with 3 country submodels for Canada, Japan, and the United States and a regional model for Europe,[10] and (5) WHARTON, the model of Wharton Econometrics Forecasting Associates, which contains 23 submodels for each OECD country, 1 for South Africa, and 6 regional models for the rest of the world.[11] Finally, other academicians have also tried their own models. Among them we find MSG, the McKibbin-Sachs global model, developed by Warwick McKibbin and Jeffrey Sachs at Harvard University. It includes 5 submodels representing Japan, the United States, other OECD countries as a block, OPEC countries, and other developing countries.[12]

the better known LSEMs, including those described in the box.[13] They report the *average* results of the models, in order to get a balanced picture that avoids the quirks of any particular model.

First, let us consider the effects of a sustained reduction in government spending in the United States. Based on the *IS-LM* model, we would predict a decline in output, prices, and the interest rate. Bryant, Helliwell, and Hooper simulate an annual reduction of government spending in the United States by 1 percent of GDP that lasts for a period of six years. They find that, under these conditions, U.S. output declines by a little over 1 percent in the first year.[14] During the second year, output recovers somewhat, but without yet going back to its original level. Prices decline by very little (less than one-tenth of 1 percent) in the first year, and the short-term interest rate declines by 1.09 basis points (109 hundredths of a percentage point).

A second policy these authors considered was an expansion in the U.S. money supply of 1 percent that lasts for six years. Our theoretical model leads us to expect a decline in interest rates, a rise in output, and a rise in the price level. In the simulation models, U.S. interest rates indeed fall sharply in the first year and then recover somewhat. U.S. output increases by

---

[10] See Roger Brinner, "The 1985 DRI Model: An Overview," in *Data Resources Review of the US Economy* (Lexington, Mass.: Data Resources/McGraw-Hill, September 1985).

[11] See John Green and Howard Howe, "Results from the WEFA World Model," Brookings Discussion Paper No. 59-B, March 1987.

[12] Sources for the MSG model are Warwick McKibbin and Jeffrey Sachs, "Comparing the Global Performance of Alternative Exchange Rate Arrangements," National Bureau of Economic Research Working Paper, September 1986, and Warwick McKibbin and Jeffrey Sachs, "Coordination of Monetary and Fiscal Policies in the OECD," in Jacob Frenkel, ed., *International Aspects of Fiscal Policies*. Unlike the other models, the equations are based on "guesses" for the key parameters, using estimates by others, rather than new econometric estimates.

[13] See their joint work, "Domestic and Cross-Border Consequences of U.S. Macroeconomic Policies," in R. Bryant et al., eds., *Macroeconomic Policies in an Interdependent World* (Washington, D.C.: International Monetary Fund, 1989).

[14] All results are expressed as deviations from a trend. Thus, when we say that output declines by 1 percent, we mean that it is 1 percent lower than what it would have been had the fiscal action not been taken.

$\frac{1}{4}$ percent in the first year and a further amount in the second year and then begins to fall back toward its original level.

Thus, the qualitative results obtained in our basic theoretical model are the same as those found by highly complex large-scale econometric models. Of course, the real world presents many complications that our simple framework cannot handle and that LSEMs can. For example, we cannot consider appropriately the effects of phased-in policies and the effects of lags. But the crucial test for a simple model is to capture the most important aspects of reality and to be able to make sensible predictions. In terms of these goals, at least, it appears that the *IS-LM* framework, combined with the Q^S/Q^D model, can do the job for many kinds of short-run policy changes.

12-7 SUMMARY

In a closed economy, aggregate demand is the sum of the demands for consumption, investment, and government spending. Using our earlier findings, consumption can be expressed as a positive function of both current and future disposable income and a negative function of the interest rate. Investment responds positively to the expected future marginal productivity of capital and negatively to the interest rate. Government spending is taken, for simplicity, as exogenous. When combining the underlying equations for *C, I,* and *G,* we find a reduced-form expression for aggregate demand as a positive function of expected future income, the expected future marginal productivity of capital and government spending, and a negative function of the interest rate and taxes.

A rise in government spending leads to a rise in aggregate demand that is even larger than the initial rise in government spending. The reason for this *multiplier effect* is the following. When *G* rises by one dollar, total aggregate demand initially rises by one dollar, for given *C* and *I*. But if output is determined by aggregate demand, disposable income will tend to rise by one dollar, which in turn will raise consumption. The rise in consumption will in turn induce a further increase in total output, and a further increase in disposable income, leading to a further increase in consumption. In the special case of a balanced-budget increase in government spending, the multiplier is 1: output goes up by exactly the same amount as the rise in tax-financed spending.

The *IS-LM framework* is a useful and popular way to assess the effects of macroeconomic policies on aggregate demand. The *IS schedule* relates the level of aggregate demand to the interest rate, holding fixed all other variables such as government spending and taxes. It is downward sloping because a rise in the interest rate depresses aggregate demand through its effects on both consumption and investment. The *LM schedule* represents the combination of interest rates and aggregate demand consistent with money market equilibrium for a given level of real money balances. It is upward sloping because a rise in interest rates reduces the demand for money and requires aggregate demand to rise in order to restore monetary equilibrium.

The intersection of the *IS* and *LM* schedules determines the level of aggregate demand but not the equilibrium of the economy, because *IS* and *LM* are drawn for a given price level. In order to determine the equilibrium level of output and the price level, one must combine aggregate demand and aggregate supply. Graphically, the aggregate demand curve can be derived from the *IS-LM* apparatus by considering an increase in the price level. Since the *LM* curve shifts back and to the left, while the *IS* remains unchanged, a rise in *P* lowers aggregate demand; thus, the aggregate demand schedule is downward sloping. The *IS-LM* analysis can easily incorporate intertemporal considerations through the effect of expected future variables on consumption and investment.

A rise in government spending (or a cut in taxes, or an increase in expected future income) shifts the *IS* curve to the right, and thus increases aggregate demand. The rise in aggregate demand, however, is less than predicted by the Keynesian multiplier because interest rates increase due to the fiscal expansion, reducing private consumption and investment. The dampening effect of fiscal policy on private spending is known as crowding out. Although aggregate demand unambiguously rises following the increase in government spending, the final effect on output and prices depends on the shape of the aggregate supply curve. In the classical case all the effect goes to prices, and equilibrium output remains unchanged. In the extreme Keynesian case, all the effect goes to output, while prices remain fixed. In the general Keynesian case, the effect is distributed between increased output and higher prices.

An increase in the money supply shifts the *LM* curve downward. The consequent reduction of the interest rate increases private consumption and investment, causing aggregate demand to rise. Once again, the final effect on output and prices will depend on the shape of the aggregate supply curve, just as in the previous case. The main difference between this policy and the fiscal expansion lies on the final composition of output between the public and the private sector.

There are three important special cases in *IS-LM* analysis. When money demand is not sensitive to the interest rate, the *LM* schedule is vertical, and thus a fiscal expansion has no effect on aggregate demand. A horizontal *LM* curve—widely discussed at the time of the Great Depression—occurs when the money demand is infinitely elastic with respect to the interest rate. In this case, known as the *liquidity trap,* monetary policy has no effect on output because a money expansion cannot reduce interest rates, while fiscal policy powerfully affects aggregate demand. Finally, when consumption and investment demand are interest inelastic, the *IS* curve is vertical; here fiscal policy strongly affects aggregate demand, while monetary policy has no effect on it.

Believers in policy activism argue that the government should use fiscal and monetary policies to stabilize output and prices. On their view, the government should counteract the effect of private shocks. A drop in private investment demand, for example, could be offset by a rise in *G*, a cut in *T*, or an increase in *M*. Others argue against policy activism based on some of the following arguments: the aggregate supply curve may be vertical, shocks are hard to identify with precision, activist policies tend to be overinflationary, and political pressures may lead to shortsighted policies.

A dynamic aspect usually neglected in the simple *IS-LM* framework is the adjustment of wages and prices in response to unemployment. It is not complicated, however, to incorporate dynamic aspects into *IS-LM* analysis. The crucial difference is then between short-term and long-term equilibrium. An expansionary fiscal or monetary policy that pushes output initially beyond the full-employment level will eventually be reversed as nominal wages and prices rise through time. In this dynamic extension, the economy shows Keynesian properties in the short run, but classical features in the long term.

Theoretical models such as the *IS-LM* provide the direction of effects of policy actions, but can also give quantitative answers. Econometric models have been built to estimate the precise impacts of policy actions on relevant macroeconomic variables. In the United States and abroad there exists a rich tradition of *large-scale econometric models* which have been developed since the 1960s. These models have hundreds and even thousands of equations which are solved with the use of powerful computers. The qualitative results obtained in the basic theoretical model are verified by the highly complex econometric models.

Key Concepts

reduced form
Keynesian multiplier
balanced-budget multiplier
IS schedule
LM schedule
the *IS-LM* framework
fiscal expansion
crowding out

liquidity trap
interest inelastic
stabilization policy
policy activism
economic shocks
dynamic *IS-LM* framework
large-scale econometric models
(LSEMs)

Problems and Questions

1. Under which assumptions can macroeconomic policies have effects on aggregate demand? When will they also affect the level of output in the economy?

2. Describe what happens to the Keynesian multiplier in the following cases:
  a. The marginal propensity to consume increases.
  b. Consumption and investment become more sensitive to changes in the interest rate.
  c. People expect future changes in government expenditures to offset any current change in taxes or government expenditures.

3. What happens to the *IS* curve if
  a. Consumption becomes more responsive to changes in the interest rate?
  b. The marginal propensity to consume rises?
  c. Investment becomes less sensitive to the interest rate?

4. Analyze the effects on the *LM* curve of the following events:
  a. The demand for money becomes more sensitive to the interest rate.
  b. The demand for money becomes more responsive to the level of output.

5. Using the *IS-LM* model, study the effects on the interest rate and aggregate demand of
  a. An increase in government expenditures together with an increase in the money supply.
  b. A decrease in government expenditures coupled with an increase in the money supply.
  c. A decrease in taxes and a decrease in the money supply.
  d. An equal increase in the money supply and the price level.

6. What are the effects of the following economic policies on aggregate demand, the level of output, and prices? Analyze the classical case and the basic and extreme Keynesian cases.

  a. A reduction in government expenditures.
  b. A decline in government expenditures together with a decrease in the money supply.
  c. An increase in taxes and an increase in the money supply.
  d. An increase in taxes and an increase in government expenditures by the same amount.

7. Consider the following structure of an economy:

Consumption: $C = 0.8(Q - T)$

Investment: $I = 20 - 0.4i$

Government spending: $G = 10$

Taxes: $T = 20$

Money supply: $M^S = 50$

Money demand: $M^D = (0.5Q - i)P$

  a. Find the *IS* curve and the Keynesian multiplier.
  b. Find the *LM* curve, assuming that the price level is 2.
  c. Find the equilibrium interest rate and aggregate demand (continue to assume $P = 2$).
  d. Find the aggregate demand curve.
  e. Find the effects on output, the interest rate and the price level if government expenditures increase to $G = 12$. Analyze the extreme Keynesian case (assume $P = 2$) and the classical case (assume $Q = 60$).

8. Suppose that the government wants to increase output as well as private investment. Which type of policy would you recommend?

9. Discuss under which circumstances an economy would be closer to the monetarist case than to the liquidity trap case.

10. The government thinks that it can use monetary and fiscal policies to achieve a certain level of output. Which policies would you recommend it to implement if the following events occur:

  a. A technological improvement raises the marginal productivity of capital.
  b. People expect an increase in their future income.
  c. The introduction of credit cards increases the velocity of money.
  d. People expect a rise in taxes in the future.

11. Is expansionary fiscal policy more likely to increase output in an economy with widespread long-term contracts or in one in which contracts are fixed for very short periods of time?

APPENDIX

In this appendix, we use a linear macroeconomic model to solve for output (Q) and the price level (P) in a closed economy. Because we use a linear model, we are able to derive explicit algebraic equations for the key economic variables. For example, we are able to show explicitly how output is a function of monetary and fiscal policy. We accomplish with algebra what we accomplished with the graphical *IS-LM* analysis in the text.

We begin with linear equations for consumption and for investment. (A.1a) is similar to equation (12.6a) in the chapter, and (A.1b) is similar to equation (12.6b).

$$C = c(Q - T) - ai + c^F[Q - T]^F \qquad \textbf{(A.1a)}$$

$$I = \bar{I} - bi + dMPK^E \qquad \textbf{(A.1b)}$$

In these expressions, the variables c, a, c^F, b, d, and $\bar{I}$ are positive numerical constants (for example, perhaps c equals 0.6). Since we are studying a general linear model, we don't need to specify actual numerical values here. Note that the coefficient c stands for the marginal propensity to consume. Similarly, c^F stands for the marginal propensity to consume out of future income. Next, we use the identity $Q^D = C + I + G$. When we substitute the expressions for C and I into this identity and let $Q^D = Q$, we may solve the resulting equation to find

$$Q^D = \left[\frac{1}{(1 - c)} \right] [c^F(Q - T)^F - cT + \bar{I} + dMPK^E \qquad \textbf{(A.2)}$$

$$- (a + b)i + G]$$

This is the *IS* schedule, whose slope, $\Delta i / \Delta Q^D$, is $-(1 - c)/(a + b) < 0$.

As we pointed out in the chapter, this equation is not really the final expression for aggregate demand, since we have not yet specified how the interest rate is formed. To do this, we need to use the *LM* equation. We write the *LM* schedule as equation (A.3). Note that to make things simpler, we approximate (M/P) by $(M - P)$.[1]

$$(M - P) = vQ^D - fi \qquad \textbf{(A.3)}$$

From (A.3), we can also write

$$i = \left(\frac{v}{f} \right) Q^D - \left(\frac{1}{f} \right) (M - P) \qquad \textbf{(A.4)}$$

We now replace the interest rate in (A.2) by using the expression in (A.4), and then solve the equation for Q^D to obtain a relationship between output demand and several other macroeconomic variables, including the

---

[1] (M/P) is approximately equal to $(1 + M - P)$ when M and P are close to one; we leave out the 1 because, as a constant, it will not have an important influence in the results. The usefulness of this approximation is that the solution for P will be linear.

price level

$$Q^D = \phi \left\{ c^F(Q - T)^F - cT + \bar{I} + dMPK^E \right.$$

$$\left. + \left[\frac{(a + b)}{f}\right] M - \left[\frac{(a + b)}{f}\right] P + G \right\} \tag{A.5}$$

where $\phi = f/[(1 - c)f + (a + b)v]$. In general functional form, equation (A.5) looks like

$$Q^D = Q^D[(Q - T)^F, T, \bar{I}, MPK^E, M, P, G] \tag{A.6}$$

What do we see from (A.5) and (A.6)? Q^D is a positive function of expected *future* income, expected future marginal productivity of capital, and government spending; Q^D is a negative function of taxes and the price level.

Finding the Aggregate Supply–Aggregate Demand Equilibrium

Now, the overall equilibrium of the economy is reached when output equals aggregate supply equals aggregate demand ($Q = Q^S = Q^D$). Recall from Chapter 3 that there exist three possible forms for the aggregate supply curve: classic, basic Keynesian, and extreme Keynesian. The easiest cases are the two extremes, which we treat first.

Classical

In this case, aggregate supply is vertical at the full-employment level of output, ($Q^S = Q$). The equilibrium level of output is clearly given by

$$Q = \bar{Q} \tag{A.7}$$

Substituting $Q = \bar{Q} = Q^D$ into equation (A.5), we can obtain the solution for the price level P

$$P = M + a_0(Q - T)^F - a_1T + a_2\bar{I} + a_3MPK^E + a_4G - a_5\bar{Q} \tag{A.8}$$

where the values of the coefficients (all positive) are

$$a_0 = \frac{fc^F}{(a + b)}; \quad a_1 = \frac{fc}{(a + b)}; \quad a_2 = a_4 = \frac{f}{(a + b)};$$

$$a_3 = \frac{fd}{(a + b)}; \quad \text{and} \quad a_5 = \frac{f}{\phi^2(a + b)}$$

In this case, anything that increases aggregate demand also increases the price level. Anything that decreases aggregate demand also decreases the price level. But shifts in aggregate demand have no effect on output. Note that changes in the money supply (M) are transmitted *one-to-one* into prices. The economic meaning of this is that a proportionate change in the money supply leads to an equal proportionate change in the price level, so that M/P remains unchanged.

Extreme Keynesian

Now, the aggregate supply schedule is horizontal at the exogenous price level $\bar{P}$:

$$P = \bar{P} \tag{A.9}$$

Aggregate demand uniquely determines the equilibrium level of output:

$$Q = \phi \left\{ c^F (Q - T)^F - cT + \bar{I} + dMPK^E + \left[\frac{(a + b)}{f} \right] M \right. \quad \textbf{(A.10)}$$

$$\left. - \left[\frac{(a + b)}{f} \right] \bar{P} + G \right\}$$

Note that expression (A.10) is the same as (A.5), with Q in place of Q^D. This is because in the extreme Keynesian case, aggregate demand is the sole determinant of output.

Basic Keynesian

This is the most complicated case, because the aggregate supply curve is upward sloping, and thus a change in aggregate demand will affect both output and prices. The aggregate supply function can be written in linear form as[2]

$$Q^S = g - z(w - P) \qquad \textbf{(A.11)}$$

In equilibrium, $Q = Q^D = Q^S$. Using equations (A.5) and (A.11), this leads to the following solution for the price level (P)

$$P = b_0 M + b_1 w - b_2 g + b_3 [c^F (Q - T)^F - cT + \bar{I} + dMPK^E + G] \quad \textbf{(A.12)}$$

where the coefficients are

$$b_0 = \frac{\phi(a + b)/f}{z + \phi(a + b)/f}; \quad b_1 = \frac{z}{z + \phi(a + b)/f}; \quad b_2 = \frac{1}{z + \phi(a + b)/f};$$

$$b_3 = \frac{\phi}{z + \phi(a + b)/f}$$

To find the equilibrium level of output, it is necessary to replace the solution for P in equation (A.12) back in the aggregate supply equation (A.11).[3]

$$Q = c_0 M - c_0 w + c_2 g + c_3 [c^F (Q - T)^F - cT + \bar{I} + dMPK^F + G] \quad \textbf{(A.13)}$$

and the coefficients are

$$c_0 = \frac{z\phi(a + b)/f}{z + \phi(a + b)/f}; \quad c_2 = \frac{\phi(a + b)/f}{z + \phi(a + b)/f}; \quad c_3 = \frac{z\phi}{z + \phi(a + b)/f}$$

Note that an increase in the money stock causes a rise in prices but less than one-for-one (the coefficient of M in the price equation, b_0, is less than 1). As a general statement, we can say that all variables that shift upward the aggregate demand curve—M, $[Q - T]^F$, MPK^E, G—cause both output and prices to increase. Variables which shift the aggregate demand curve down, such as taxes, T, cause both output and prices to decrease.

The nominal wage w shifts the aggregate supply curve; specifically, a rise in the nominal wage causes output supply to fall, as we see in (A.11). From (A.12) and (A.13), we see that a rise in w causes output to fall and prices to rise.

---

[2] Note that we use again an approximation. This time we write (w/P) as $(w - P)$. See the previous footnote.

[3] The same solution for Q would be obtained if the equilibrium price level were replaced in the aggregate demand equation, but the algebra would be more cumbersome.

Macroeconomic Policies in the Open Economy: The Case of Fixed Exchange Rates

We have just seen some of the effects of macroeconomic policies in a closed economy. Now we take an important step toward realism by adapting our approach for an open economy. This adds many complexities, indeed so many complexities that macroeconomics textbooks often skip over most open-economy analysis. But given that all economies in the world are open to at least some international trade, and in view of the fact that openness has a big effect on how macroeconomic policies work, it simply makes no sense to neglect the open economy.

To make things as straightforward as possible, two chapters are devoted to the open-economy analysis of macroeconomic policies, one focusing on the case of a fixed exchange-rate system, and the other focusing on a floating-rate system. For the vast majority of countries, the fixed-rate system is the relevant one. For a few large regions, however, including the United States, Japan, and the European Community viewed as one economic region, the floating-rate case is important. As we shall see, monetary and fiscal policies have very different effects under these different exchange-rate arrangements.

Even within the fixed-rate category, however, there are still many cases to consider. Some countries have open capital markets; others have capital controls that limit the movements of capital across national borders. Most countries in the world are too small to have much effect on macroeconomic conditions in the rest of the world (the small-country case). A few countries, including the United States, have such extensive economies that changes in them have important effects on the rest of the world (the large-country case). Once again, the effects of fiscal and monetary policy differ in small-country and large-country cases.

Throughout this chapter and the next, we use a well-known conceptual framework of open-economy macroeconomics, one that allows for both differentiated goods and capital mobility. The *Mundell–Fleming model* is named after Robert Mundell and J. Marcus Fleming, whose path-breaking work was done at the beginning of the 1960s.[1] These two econo-

---

[1] Mundell published his work in many different journal articles and books. Perhaps the best known are his paper "Capital Mobility and Stabilization Under Fixed and Flexible

mists recognized the major changes that were taking place in the world economy. During the 1950s, the exchange rates of the major industrial countries had been fixed by the Bretton Woods agreement. International trade flows had also been more important than international capital flows. As time went by, however, technological improvements in communications and the dismantling of capital controls increased the volume of capital flows on the international scene until they started to overcome trade flows in their importance.

Mundell and Fleming spotted one particularly interesting fact, that the speed of capital flows was much higher than that of trade flows. International investors were increasingly able to arbitrage differences in interest rates across countries as they sought to take advantage of unrealized profit opportunities. Thus, differences in interest rates between two countries generated massive flows of capital that tended to reduce or eliminate the differences. In contrast, trade flows responded much more slowly to changes in underlying economic conditions. This simple observation gave a powerful insight to Mundell and Fleming, and it captures the spirit of the model that we analyze in this and the next chapter. We will assume that interest rate in the home economy must be equal to the interest rate in the world economy, except in cases where capital controls exist. Interest rates are in reality not equal throughout the world, and to treat them as if they are, for example, we must assume away expectations of exchange-rate movements.[2] However, the simple assumption that home and foreign interest rates are equal gives us a powerful apparatus with which to examine the effects of different policies in the economy when there is international capital mobility.

We begin with a standard case, *a small country without capital controls*. Then, we shift to a small country *with capital controls*. Finally, we see how our conclusions differ when we consider a large country. Throughout this chapter, we assume fixed exchange rates; in the next chapter, we cover the same ground assuming floating exchange rates.

13-1 A MODEL OF INTERNATIONALLY DIFFERENTIATED PRODUCTS

In this chapter and the next, we shall assume that the home country produces a single output, but one that is differentiated from the output produced by the rest of the world. Thus, the United States makes Ford automobiles, while Japan makes Toyotas. These goods are substitutes, but not perfect substitutes. If the price of Toyotas rises relative to the price of Fords, we would expect consumers to shift from Toyotas to Fords, but we would not expect *all* consumers to shift. Thus, the relative price of Toyotas to Fords is not fixed, but as it changes consumers will revise the proportions of the two kinds of goods that they buy.

Exchange Rates," *Canadian Journal of Economics and Political Science,* November 1963, and his book *International Economics* (New York: Macmillan, 1968). Fleming's classic piece is "Domestic Financial Policies Under Fixed and Under Floating Exchange Rates," *International Monetary Fund Staff Papers,* November 1962.

[2] Recall our discussion of this in Chapter 10. In the process of going from equation (10.5) to equation (10.8), we assumed that the exchange rate was expected to remain stable.

Let us now put this more technically. We have the domestic economy producing a single good that is consumed both by domestic and foreign agents.[3] Total production of that good is Q, with a price P. Whatever is produced but not purchased domestically is exported. There is also a foreign good which is not produced at home and which is imported. The local currency price of the imported good is P_M. Contrary to the assumption of purchasing power parity, we will allow P_M/P, the relative price of the foreign good to the home good, to vary.

The law of one price applies to both goods. That is to say, the local price of the imported good (P_M) is determined by its foreign currency price (P^*), multiplied by the nominal exchange rate (E):

$$P_M = EP^* \tag{13.1}$$

At the same time, the foreign currency price of the domestic good is equal to the domestic price, P, divided by the exchange rate, or $P_x^* = P/E$, where P_x^* is the foreign currency price paid for exports of the domestic good. P_x^* is not fixed. When P_x^* rises (say, because the domestic price P rises), fewer goods are exported abroad; when P_x^* falls, more goods may be exported abroad.

With this model of differentiated goods in mind, we can now derive an aggregate demand schedule. Most of the time we shall proceed graphically, using an adapted *IS-LM* model for the open economy. We also use a linear model to provide algebraic derivations. The model is set out in full in the appendix to this chapter.

13-2 THE DETERMINATION OF AGGREGATE DEMAND

We have already established that households consume both the domestic and the foreign good. The total nominal value of consumption, then, is given by:

$$PC_d + P_M C_M = P_C C \tag{13.2}$$

where C_d and C_m are the quantities of the domestic and foreign good consumed, respectively. To convert these quantities into values in local currency, we multiply the quantities purchased by the domestic prices P and P_M. The total value of consumption can be expressed as $P_C C$, where P_C is the consumer price index (also known as the CPI) and C is a measure of real consumption.

The consumer price index, which was introduced in Chapter 2, is, in fact, an extremely important concept. It reflects the cost of a "representative" consumption basket that includes the goods and services consumed by a typical household. It is, of course, one of the most closely watched economic statistics in any country. Given this importance, we should look at some of its technical aspects in somewhat more detail here.

The CPI is constructed as a *weighted average* of the prices of different consumption goods and services. In our simple economy, we have only two goods. Therefore, the CPI can be generally constructed as

$$P_C = \lambda P + (1 - \lambda)P_M \tag{13.3}$$

---

[3] In Chapter 21 we will allow for a different structure of domestic production in which the domestic economy produces two goods, one tradable good and one nontradable good that is sold entirely on the home market.

where λ and $(1 - \lambda)$ are the weights attached to domestic goods and foreign goods, respectively, in the consumption basket. These weights are given by the proportion of consumption expenditures that a typical household devotes to each of the goods, as determined by a special survey of household consumption.[4] In the United States, for example, consumption expenditure is heavily concentrated on domestic goods, which account for about 90 percent of the total expenditure, while imported goods account for only about 10 percent of consumption spending. Thus, λ would take a value of about 0.9 and $(1 - \lambda)$ would equal approximately 0.1.

Once we have constructed the consumer price index, we can divide the *nominal* value of consumption expenditure $PC_d + P_M C_M$ by the consumer price index, in order to calculate the *real* value of consumption:

$$C = \frac{(PC_d + P_M C_M)}{P_C} \tag{13.4}$$

We can arrive at a price index for investment spending (P_i), and then calculate the *real* value of investment spending, in a similar way. We define the total nominal value of investment expenditures as the sum of spending on domestic goods and spending on imports:

$$P_I I = P I_d + P_M I_M \tag{13.5}$$

Then, we define the price index for investment spending as a weighted average of domestic and import prices:

$$P_I = P \left(\frac{I_d}{I}\right) + P_M \left(\frac{I_M}{I}\right) \tag{13.6}$$

While P_C and P_I are both weighted averages of P and P_M, the consumer price index and the investment price index tend to be different because of different weights on the domestic good and foreign good. (And in reality, since the kinds of domestic and foreign goods used for consumption and investment tend to differ, even the domestic component and foreign component of the two price indexes also tend to be different.)

We will assume for simplicity that all government spending falls on the domestic good. In fact, a large proportion of government spending in most

---

[4] A technical point must be made here. The CPI is always some kind of average of the prices of consumption goods. The average need not be weighted as it is in equation (13.3), however. Sometimes, a geometric average is used, which renders the formula for the CPI as

$$P_C = P^\lambda P_M^{(1-\lambda)}$$

There is an extensive economic literature about the most appropriate form of the price index. The idea, basically, is to create an index so that when nominal consumption is divided by the CPI, the resulting measure of real consumption is a measure of the level of utility of the household. It turns out, therefore, that the mathematical form of the utility function determines the appropriate mathematical form of the consumer price index. For example, if the utility function is of the Cobb–Douglas type, so that

$$U = C^\lambda C_M^{(1-\lambda)}$$

then, the geometric average should be used. If the utility function is of the so-called "fixed-proportions" type, in which consumption of C_M is always a fixed proportion of the consumption of C, then the arithmetic weighted average should be used.

For further theoretical discussion of the construction of the CPI, see Hal Varian, *Intermediate Microeconomics: A Modern Approach* (New York: W. W. Norton, 1987).

countries is for the wages and salaries of public sector workers, so this simplifying assumption is not off the mark. We can write this relationship as

$$P_G G = PG_d \tag{13.7}$$

We now proceed to rewrite *aggregate demand as the sum of domestic absorption plus the trade balance*. This derivation, which closely follows our earlier discussion in Chapter 6, helps us to formulate an equation of aggregate demand for later use.

The total nominal demand for domestic goods is given by

$$PQ^D = PC_d + PI_d + PG_d + PX \tag{13.8}$$

Note that PQ^D corresponds exactly to the demand-based measure of nominal value of gross domestic product (GDP).[5] To see this, we can rewrite equation (13.8) in the following form:

$$PQ^D = (PC_d + P_M C_M) + (PI_d + P_M I_M) + PG_d + PX$$
$$- (P_M C_M + P_M I_M) \tag{13.9}$$

By using equations (13.4), (13.5), and (13.7), and by using the fact that the nominal value of imports $P_M IM$ is equal to $P_M C_M + P_M I_M$, we arrive at

$$PQ^D = (P_C C + P_I I + P_G G) + (PX - P_M IM) \tag{13.10}$$

But look at what we have here. The first expression on the right-hand side of (13.10) is nominal absorption, the sum of nominal consumption, investment, and government spending. The second expression is the nominal trade balance, exports minus imports. Thus, (13.10) can be written succinctly as

$$PQ^D = A + PTB \tag{13.11}$$

where PTB is the nominal trade balance, defined as

$$PTB = PX - P_M IM \tag{13.12}$$

Now, we divide both sides of (13.11) and (13.12) by the price level P:

$$Q^D = \left(\frac{A}{P}\right) + TB \tag{13.13}$$

$$TB = X - \left(\frac{P_M}{P}\right) IM \tag{13.14}$$

Equation (13.13) says that aggregate demand is the sum of real absorption plus the real trade balance. Equation (13.14) defines the real trade balance as the nominal trade balance divided by the price level.

We have spent a lot of time deriving (13.13) and (13.14) since they will be very useful in specifying the model of aggregate demand for the open economy. Before getting to that model, note one important difference in the closed and open economy. In a closed economy, absorption and aggregate demand are the same thing: $C + I + G$. In the open economy, however, they are different. Absorption measures total spending by domestic residents;

---

[5] Remember from Chapter 2 that GDP can be measured from the demand side or from the production side.

aggregate demand measures total spending by domestic residents *and foreigners* on domestic goods. Thus, aggregate demand is equal to absorption *plus* the trade balance, as is shown in (13.13).

The expression for aggregate demand Q^D in (13.13) is an identity so far since the sales of the domestic good *must* equal real absorption plus the trade surplus, measured in units of the domestic good, as $X - (P_M/P)IM$. To see what real-life behavior this equation represents, we must first see what factors determine absorption, exports, and imports. By specifying the equations which determine absorption and the trade balance, we will be constructing the *IS* curve for the open economy.

We write down a *reduced-form* equation for absorption, based on the fact that absorption is the sum of consumption, investment, and government spending. Since we know the variables that affect consumption and investment, we can write down an equation for absorption:

$$A/P = a(\underset{+}{G}, \underset{-}{T}, \underset{+}{[Q - T]^F}, \underset{+}{MPK^E}, \underset{-}{i}) \qquad \textbf{(13.15)}$$

According to (13.15), overall absorption is an increasing function of government spending, a decreasing function of taxes, an increasing function of expected future disposable income $[Q - T]^F$, an increasing function of expected future marginal productivity of capital and a decreasing function of the interest rate.

Next, we need a similar reduced-form equation for the trade balance. First, when absorption increases, the trade balance tends to worsen, because part of higher absorption is spent on imports. Thus, we expect *TB* to be a negative function of A/P. At the same time, *TB* is a positive function of A^*/P^* (foreign absorption), because when foreign absorption increases, part of the increase in foreign purchases is spent on domestic goods, so that exports rise.

Finally, we assume that *TB* is a positive function of EP_M^*/P, the relative price of the foreign good to the domestic good.[6] (EP_M^* is the domestic currency price of the foreign good.) We define the ratio of this price to the domestic price as the *real exchange rate* and denote it by e:

$$e = \frac{EP_M^*}{P} \qquad \textbf{(13.16)}$$

When e rises, foreign goods become more expensive compared with home goods. Thus, the volume of exports goes up and the volume of imports comes down. Both foreigners and domestic residents shift part of their consumption to the relatively less expensive home good. We call a rise in the value of e a *real depreciation*; a fall in e is a *real appreciation*.[7] Therefore,

---

[6] When EP_M^*/P rises, it becomes more costly—in units of domestic goods—to buy any given level of imports IM. For this reason, even if a real depreciation of the domestic currency lowers the *volume* of imports, the overall real expenditure on imports, equal to $(EP_M^*/P)IM$, can still go up. Technically, therefore, the trade balance could actually worsen when EP_M^*/P rises, even if the volume of exports goes up and the volume of imports goes down. In other words, the total spending on imports could still rise enough to reduce the trade balance. We assume, however, that conditions (known as Marshall–Lerner conditions) are such that the trade balance always improves when the real exchange rate depreciates.

[7] Note that since e depends on the nominal exchange rate and the price levels at home and abroad, a change in e can result from a change in the exchange rate, or a movement in the price levels, or some combination.

the trade balance would seem to improve with a real depreciation of the home currency. To summarize,

$$TB = TB(A/P, A^*/P_M^*, e) \qquad (13.17)$$
$${\scriptstyle-}{\scriptstyle+}{\scriptstyle+}$$

How good is the theory that export volume depends on the real exchange rate? It does, at least, describe the case of the United States in the 1980s quite well. Figure 13-1 shows a time series of the real exchange rate and the real value of exports for the United States in the period 1980–1988. The graph shows that U.S. exports were hurt when the real exchange rate appreciated relative to its historical average (that is, when e was unusually low). The real exchange rate reached its most appreciated, or lowest, value in February of 1985, and afterward depreciated. The depreciation of the U.S. currency clearly helped U.S. exports recover some of the lost ground.

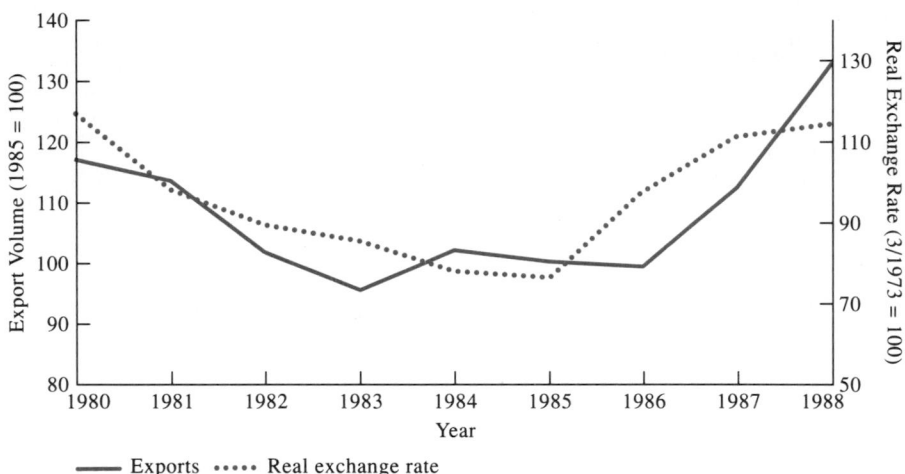

Figure 13-1

The Real Exchange Rate and Exports in the United States, 1980–1988

(From Economic Report of the President, 1990, *and International Monetary Fund,* International Financial Statistics.*)*

We are now ready to combine our equations for absorption and the trade balance to come up with a single equation for aggregate demand:

$$Q^D = a(i, G, T, [Q - T]^F, MPK^E) + TB(A^*/P^*, A/P, EP_M^*/P) \qquad (13.18)$$

Note that in the trade balance part of the equation, TB is written as a function of A/P. We can substitute equation (13.15) for A/P in the trade balance equation, and then write a single equation for Q^D of the following form:[8]

$$Q^D = Q^D(i, G, T, [Q - T]^F, MPK^E, A^*/P^*, EP^*/P) \qquad (13.19)$$

---

[8] The details of moving from (13.18) to (13.19) are shown in the appendix to this chapter.

With equation (13.19) we have arrived at the aggregate demand function in the open economy that we shall use from this point on.

13-3 THE *IS-LM* MODEL FOR THE OPEN ECONOMY

In order to derive the *IS-LM* model for the open economy in the case of fixed exchange rates, we need to make at least two basic assumptions. First, the exchange rate E is fixed by the monetary authorities. Second, we will take the levels of G, T, $[Q - T]^F$, MPK^E, A^*/P^*, and P as given. On this basis, we can draw a negative relationship between the interest rate i and the level of domestic demand, Q^D. This, then, becomes the *IS* curve for the open-economy model that is shown in Figure 13-2.

Properties of the IS Curve

As in the closed economy described in Chapter 12, the *IS* curve shifts to the right—that is, demand expands—for any of the following reasons: a rise in G, a cut in T, a rise in $[Q - T]^F$, and a rise in MPK^E. In addition, the *IS* curve

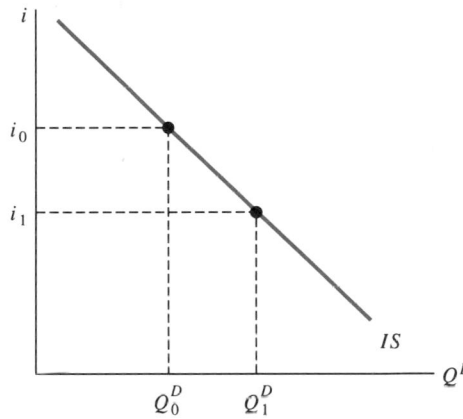

Figure 13-2
The *IS* Curve in the Open Economy

shifts to the right when A^*/P^* rises because this means that foreigners will then raise their demand for domestic goods and exports will rise. Finally, the *IS* curve shifts to the right when EP_M^*/P rises, that is, when the real exchange rate depreciates, because this means that demand shifts from foreign goods to domestic goods. These conclusions are summarized in Figure 13-3.

Let us now look more closely at the effect of a change in EP_M^*/P. Suppose that the economy operates under fixed exchange rates and the monetary authority decides to devalue.[9] Holding domestic prices fixed—a key assumption underlying the *IS* curve—the real exchange rate depreciates. Exports of the home country become more competitive in world markets while imports become more expensive. As a result, the trade balance

---

[9] Remember that the term "devaluation" refers to a rise in E only for an economy operating under a fixed exchange-rate regime. *Devaluation* is a policy option. In countries that have flexible exchange rates, an increase in E is termed a *depreciation*. If E rises under a floating exchange rate, the depreciation should not be considered an exogenous policy change engineered by the authorities.

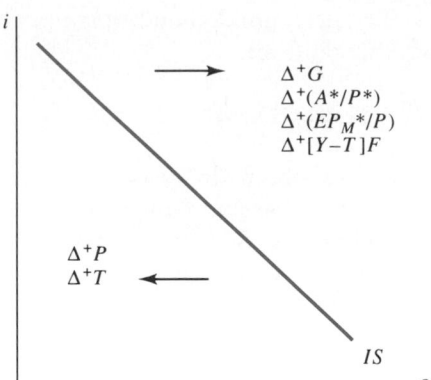

Figure 13-3
Variables that Shift the
Open-Economy *IS* Curve

improves, and, in turn, aggregate demand increases at every level of the interest rate. Thus, the *IS* curve shifts to the right.

The **LM** *Curve and Capital Mobility*

The *LM* curve is based on the money demand equation $M/P = L(i, Q^D)$, (as it was in the last chapter). Thus, the *LM* schedule is an upward-sloping line in Figure 13-4. To complete the open-economy equilibrium, however, we need one extra piece. If capital flows freely across borders, the domestic interest rate (i) will be equal to the foreign rate (i^*), and therefore we have the additional relationship[10]

$$i = i^* \qquad (13.20)$$

We can call equation (13.20) the *capital mobility* (*CM*) line. Now, under free capital mobility, the full equilibrium of the economy must lie at the intersection of *IS*, *LM*, and *CM*, as shown in point *A* of Figure 13-4.

In the closed economy, the level of *M* is a policy choice. The monetary authorities set *M*, and that determines the position of the *LM* curve. In a regime of *fixed exchange rates and capital mobility*, however, the monetary authorities are not able to choose both the money supply and the exchange rate. When the monetary authorities fix *E*, households may convert their domestic money into foreign assets as they see fit. With high capital mobility and fixed exchange rates, the domestic interest rate must always equal the world interest rate, so that $i = i^*$ (the economy must lie on the *CM* line). The money demand by households is then given by $M/P = L(i^*, Q^D)$, and the money supply will adjust endogenously (as households buy or sell domestic money in return for foreign assets), so that the money supply is equal to the money demand. This is, in fact, the same issue that we discussed in the simpler framework of Chapter 10 (where output was fixed at the full-employment level): with fixed exchange rates and free capital mobility, the money supply is endogenous.

---

[10] For the moment, we assume that there are no expectations of changes in the exchange rate. Otherwise equation (13.20) would not hold. Also, we are assuming that there are no reasons—such as riskiness of the assets, or tax considerations—that could drive a wedge between the domestic and foreign assets. Technically, we are assuming that the domestic assets are *perfect substitutes*.

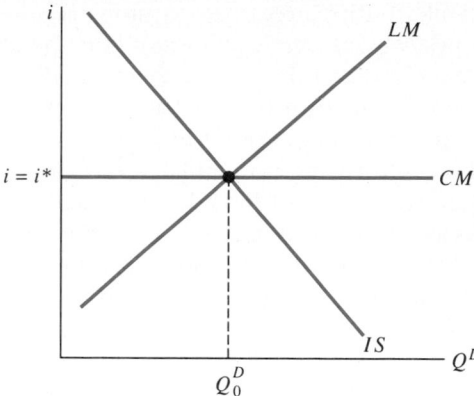

Figure 13-4

IS, LM, CM, and Aggregate Demand Equilibrium in the Open Economy

Equilibrium in the IS-LM-CM Framework

Let us see how this works. Suppose that the *IS, LM,* and *CM* curves initially intersect at point *A* in Figure 13-5. Now suppose that the monetary authorities undertake an open-market purchase of bonds, thus temporarily increasing the money supply. The *LM* curve would shift down and to the right, as shown in the figure. In the closed economy, point *B* would mark the new equilibrium, and we would conclude that aggregate demand had risen. But notice that *i* would be less than *i**. Clearly, we are not at the end of the story for the open economy.

At point *B*, domestic residents would try to sell their domestic bonds to buy foreign bonds. The domestic interest rate would quickly rise back to *i** through arbitrage with the international capital market. The economy would remain on the *IS* curve at point *A*, with demand in the goods market consistent with the interest rate *i**. At the same time, there would be an excess supply of money. Therefore, households would convert some of their money into foreign bonds, and the central bank would sell reserves and reabsorb the increase in *M*. In the process, the increase in the money supply would be reversed and the *LM* curve would shift back to the original position. This endogenous shift is shown by the arrows in the figure. Note that in the process of *LM* shifting left, the central bank is suffering a decline in its international reserves.

In essence, under fixed exchange rates and capital mobility, the position of the *LM* curve is endogenous. It adjusts as households buy and sell

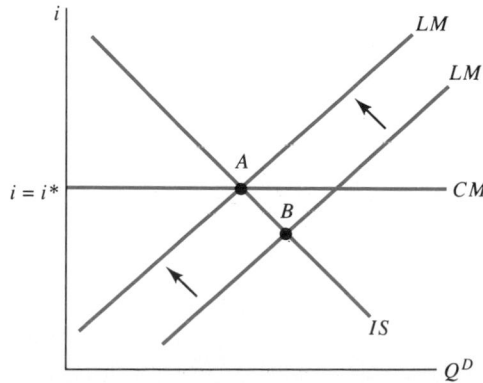

Figure 13-5

Adjustment to a Monetary Expansion Under Capital Mobility

foreign exchange from the central bank. With perfect capital mobility, the economy must operate at the world interest rate, so equilibrium must be at some point along the CM line (where $i = i^*$), and the *LM* curve must adjust to be consistent with this. An endogenous rightward shift of the *LM* curve signifies that households are selling foreign assets in order to increase their holdings of domestic money, and the central bank accumulates foreign reserves in the process. A leftward endogenous shift of the *LM* curve signifies that households are buying foreign assets in order to decrease their holdings of domestic money, and the central bank loses foreign reserves in the process. (For comparison, remember that in the closed economy, shifts in the *LM* curve were *exogenous* policy changes, not endogenous responses to capital flows.)

Now let us take another example. Suppose, for whatever reason, that the *IS* curve shifts to the right. This could result from a rise in *G*, a cut in *T*, a rise in future expected income, or some other shock to the economy that expands domestic demand. The interest rate must remain at i^*. *The new equilibrium is therefore at point* C, *at the intersection of the new* IS *curve and the* CM *line.* (In the closed economy, the new equilibrium would be at point *B*, with a rise in interest rates.)

As we can see from Figure 13-6, there is an excess demand for money at the initial level of *M*. With high capital mobility and fixed exchange rates, the excess demand for money is eliminated as households convert some of their wealth into domestic money. The central bank would sell *M* and buy foreign exchange. The result would be an endogenous increase in the money supply, and the *LM* curve would therefore shift to *LM'*, so that the new equilibrium would be at point *C*. Note that the money supply expands enough so that the interest rate remains at $i = i^*$.

To summarize these findings, under *fixed exchange rates and perfect capital mobility, the equilibrium point occurs at the intersection of the* IS *curve and the* CM *line ($i = i^*$). The* LM *curve adjusts endogenously to intersect the* IS *curve at that point.* The adjustment of the *LM* curve reflects the actions of individual households, as they readjust their portfolios between domestic money and foreign assets.

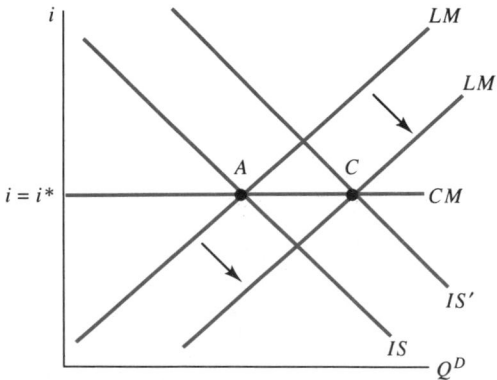

Figure 13-6
Adjustment to a Fiscal Expansion Under Capital Mobility

13-4 THE DETERMINATION OF OUTPUT
AND THE PRICE LEVEL

Let us now use our modified *IS-LM* analysis to study the effects of fiscal and monetary policy on output and prices. (We already know that, when there is high capital mobility, these policies cannot affect interest rates.)

The first step is to derive the aggregate demand schedule for a given level of G, T, and other variables that affect the position of the *IS* curve. We start from the equilibrium shown in Figure 13-7, with a given price level P_0.

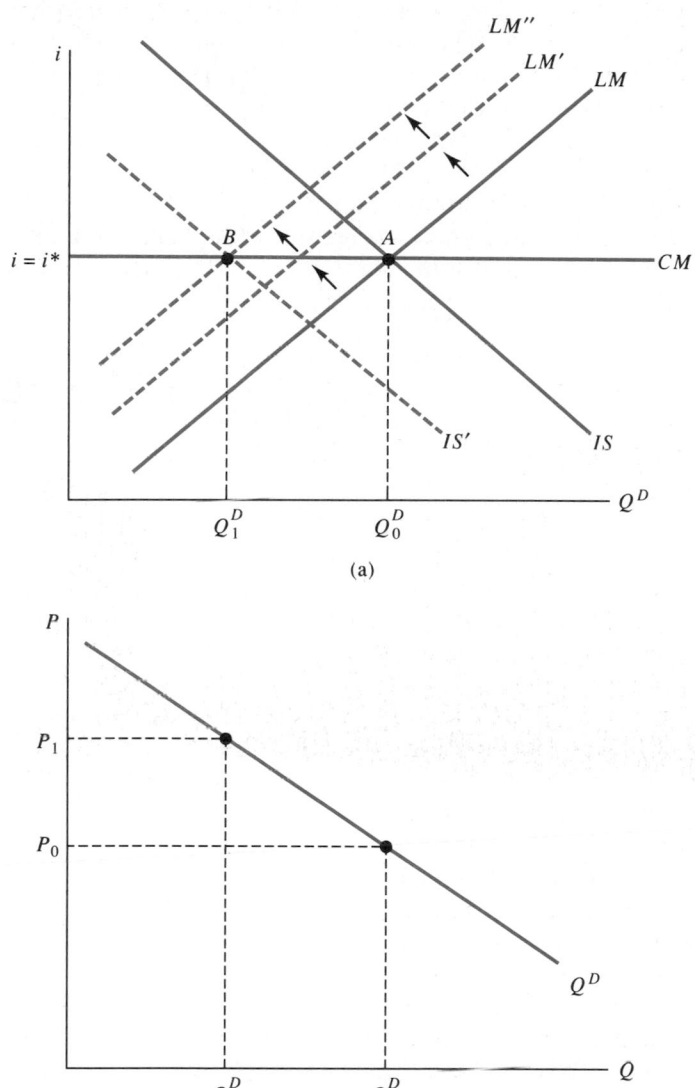

(a)

(b)

Figure 13-7
Effects of a Price Increase Under Fixed Exchange Rates—
The Shape of the Aggregate Demand Schedule: (a) The
IS-LM Framework; (b) the Aggregate Demand Schedule

Suppose now that the price level rises to P_1. How does that affect the level of aggregate demand? We know that the new equilibrium will be at the point of intersection of the new *IS* schedule and the line $i = i^*$, so the first thing to do is to see how the *IS* curve shifts when the price level rises.

A higher domestic price causes the real exchange rate to appreciate (that is, EP_M^*/P falls), hurting the country's exports and increasing its imports, and thereby deteriorating the trade balance. At every interest rate, then, aggregate demand will decline, shifting the *IS* curve down and to the left. The new equilibrium is then at point *B*, at the intersection of the new *IS* curve and the *CM* line. The *LM* curve now has to adjust endogenously to intersect with the *IS* curve at point *B*, as shown in Figure 13-7 by the arrows.

Thus, we see that a rise in prices causes a fall in aggregate demand. This is the same finding we came to in Chapter 12, and has the same implication, that *the aggregate demand schedule is downward sloping*. But there is a subtle difference here. The reason why Q^D is downward sloping is not the same in the closed economy as it is in the open economy. In the closed economy, the downward slope reflects the fact that higher P means lower M/P. In the open economy with fixed exchange rates, the higher P means lower EP_M^*/P, and thus a lower trade balance.

With this understanding, we are now ready to consider the effect of various policies on aggregate demand and the equilibrium level of output and prices.

Effects of a Fiscal Expansion

Suppose that the government starts a public works program that involves a significant increase in expenditures. At a given interest rate, demand will increase in the goods market. This shifts the *IS* curve to the right, as shown in Figure 13-8a. In a closed economy, the fiscal expansion would lead to a new equilibrium at point *B*, as the intersection of the new *IS* curve and the original *LM* schedule. In an open economy with fixed exchange rates and high capital mobility, the equilibrium must be at point *C*, along the *CM* line (where $i = i^*$). The money supply will rise endogenously as households convert foreign assets into domestic money in order to satisfy their demand for money at the new equilibrium. The central bank will intervene by buying foreign exchange and selling domestic currency. Therefore, the *LM* curve shifts to intersect the *IS* curve and the *CM* line at point *C*.

Notice that the fiscal expansion is highly effective in raising aggregate demand, because there is no rise in interest rates to crowd out investment or consumption when G rises. As a result of the fiscal expansion, aggregate demand increases from Q_0^D to Q_1^D, the shift in the aggregate demand schedule up and to the right shown in Figure 13-8b. At a given price, the level of output demanded increases. What happens to the equilibrium level of output and prices depends on the nature of the aggregate supply schedule, exactly as in the closed economy described in the previous chapter. With a classical supply schedule, the entire demand expansion is reflected in higher prices. With a basic Keynesian supply schedule, both output and prices rise. With an extreme Keynesian supply schedule, only output rises while prices remain unchanged. The three possibilities are shown in Figure 13-9.

The same diagram would of course describe the effects of several other shocks to the economy. A devaluation of the domestic currency, a tax cut,

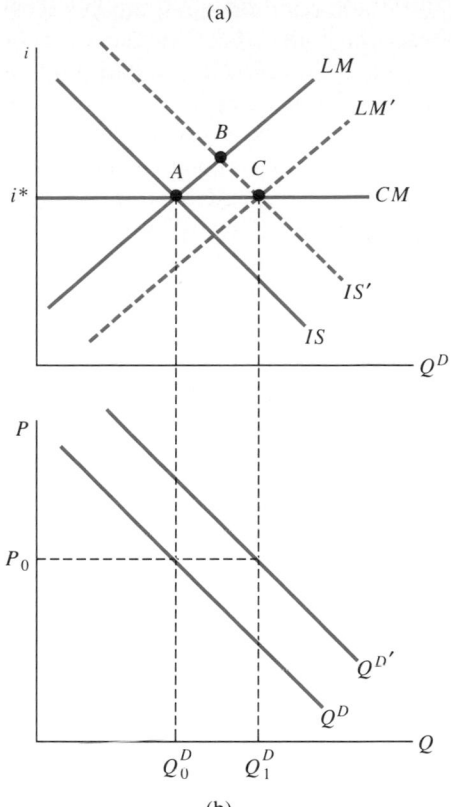

Figure 13-8
Effects of a Fiscal Expansion
Under Fixed Exchange Rates:
(a) The *IS-LM* Framework;
(b) the Aggregate Demand
Schedule

an increase in foreign absorption, or a rise in expected future income would
all have a similar representation in the diagram. The *IS* curve would shift up
and have a similar representation in the diagram. The *IS* curve would shift
up and to the right, prompting a subsequent rightward shift in the *LM* schedule. As a result, the aggregate demand shifts to the right, and the final effect
depends on the shape of the aggregate supply curve. Of course, the specific
magnitude of the effect will vary in each case, depending on the magnitude
of the original shift in the *IS* curve. But the nature of the effect remains the
same in all the cases.

Figure 13-9
A Fiscal Expansion and Equilibrium Output and Prices: (a) The Classical
Case; (b) the Normal Keynesian Case; (c) the Extreme Keynesian Case

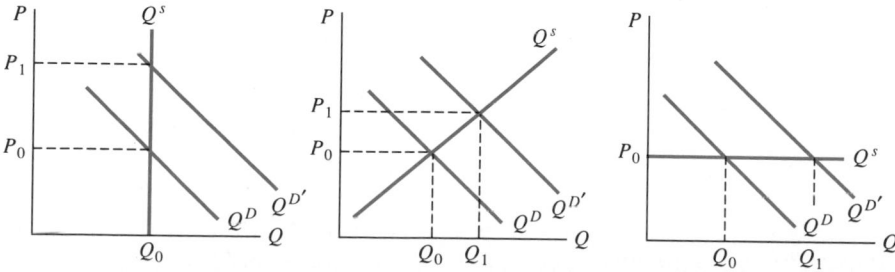

Before leaving this section, we should add one important amendment. Changes in the fiscal policy of a large economy, like the United States, or Japan, or the European Community, do have an effect on world interest rates. The "small-country" assumption that i^* may be taken as given does not hold when a very large economy undertakes a fiscal policy change. In particular, a U.S. fiscal expansion will cause both i and i^* to rise, thus leading to a *smaller* multiplier than the one shown in the *IS-LM* diagram. (Remember that we investigated the effects of fiscal policy in one country on the world interest rate in Chapter 7.) The large economies have exchange rates that float against each other, however, and so we leave further investigation of this issue to the next chapter.

Effects of a Monetary Expansion

Suppose now that the central bank undertakes an open-market purchase of domestic bonds, an operation that increases the quantity of money in circulation. Economic agents now find their portfolios thrown out of equilibrium; that is, at the initial interest rate, they have too much money and too few bonds. This excess supply of money implies that the *LM* curve shifts downward to *LM'*, as shown in Figure 13-10a. But with neither the *IS* curve nor the world interest rate changing, equilibrium remains at its initial point.

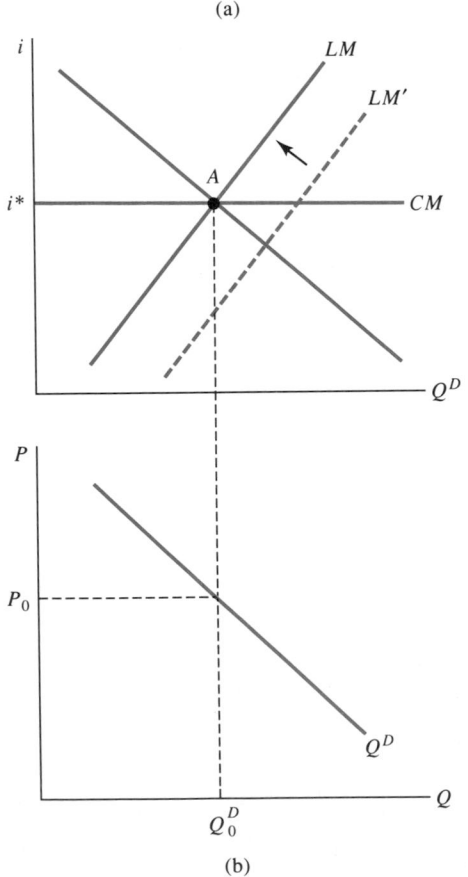

Figure 13-10
Effects of a Monetary Expansion Under Free Capital Mobility: (a) The *IS-LM* Framework; (b) the Aggregate Demand Schedule

Therefore, households with excess supplies of money try to purchase foreign assets with the excess M. As households try to buy foreign assets to reduce their money holdings, the exchange rate would tend to depreciate. The central bank therefore intervenes, by selling foreign exchange and absorbing the domestic currency. This means that the LM curve shifts back to the left as M falls, and the central bank loses reserves. In other words, the monetary expansion provokes a capital outflow, which in turn reverses the money expansion.

This process does not end until the LM curve shifts all the way back to the initial equilibrium. That is, ultimately the money supply is unchanged, and aggregate demand does not change either. Thus, we have a result that we first saw in Chapter 10: under fixed exchange rates and high capital mobility, the monetary authority is unable to change the quantity of money in circulation. Has the open-market operation, then, had no effect? Almost, but not quite. Output, prices, the interest rate, and the quantity of money are unchanged. But the central bank has lost international reserves, and households have gained foreign assets.

This is a truly remarkable result. *Even under Keynesian conditions regarding aggregate supply, a monetary expansion has no effect on output under fixed exchange rates and perfect capital mobility.* This contrasts sharply with the effects of a monetary expansion in a closed economy, and, as we shall see in Chapter 14, with the effects of a monetary expansion under floating exchange rates.

In conclusion, then, under fixed exchange rates and perfect capital mobility, fiscal policy is highly effective in shifting aggregate demand, but monetary policy is completely ineffective. Regardless of the shape of the aggregate supply schedule, a monetary expansion affects neither output nor prices.

Effects of a Devaluation

Under a fixed exchange-rate regime, the exchange rate itself is a policy variable determined by the authorities. Suppose now that the authorities decide to devalue the domestic currency.

Consider the effects in the *IS-LM* framework. Because domestic prices do not respond to the devaluation, the real exchange rate depreciates together with the nominal rate. Exports of the home country become more competitive in world markets while imports become relatively more expensive at home. As a result, the trade balance improves and therefore aggregate demand increases at every level of the interest rate. Thus, the IS shifts up and to the right as in Figure 13-11a. Because the interest rate is given at the world level ($i = i^*$), the incipient increase in the domestic interest rate prompts a capital inflow. The central bank purchases foreign exchange, which increases the domestic money supply; thus, the LM shifts down and to the right.

The new equilibrium is reached at point B in the graph, where the IS, LM, and CM schedules intersect. Aggregate demand increases from Q^D to $Q^{D'}$ in Figure 13-11b. Note that in this framework a devaluation has an effect similar to that of an increase in government spending. Thus, it is highly effective in increasing aggregate demand.

(a)

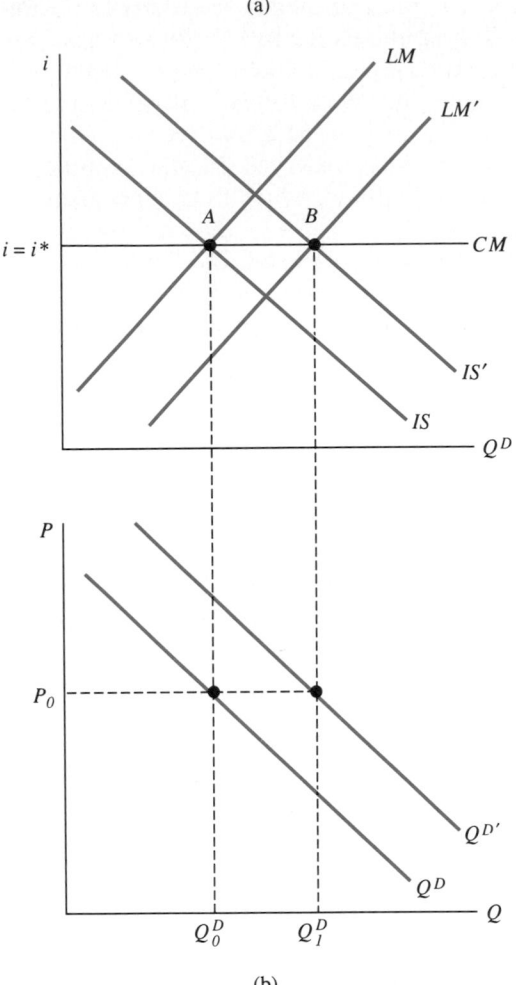

(b)

Figure 13-11
Effects of a Devaluation Under Perfect Capital Mobility: (a) The *IS-LM* Framework; (b) the Aggregate Demand Schedule

The United States as a Special Case

The previous discussion has so far concealed one subtle point about fixed exchange rates. If there are two countries, there is only one exchange rate between them, a point that we stressed in Chapter 10. Thus, only one central bank has the obligation to intervene in order to peg the exchange rate. The other central bank can be free to set monetary policy as it wants, with the former central bank doing all the intervention needed to keep the exchange rate stable.

So far, we have always assumed that the "home" country is the one with the responsibility to peg the rate. Historically, this assumption applies to virtually all countries in the world except the United States. As we described in Chapter 10, during the fixed exchange-rate period under the Bretton Woods system, all countries in the world that were members of the International Monetary Fund took on the obligation to peg their currencies to the U.S. dollar. The United States, on the other hand, was not obligated to intervene in the foreign-exchange market to keep its currency pegged to any other currency.[11]

In this case, the U.S. monetary authorities were not subjected to an endogenously shifting *LM* curve. Rather, their policies set the position of the U.S. *LM* curve, but other countries had to adjust their own money supplies to be consistent with changes in U.S. monetary policy. In this important sense, U.S. monetary policy behaved more like that in the closed-economy case we considered in the previous chapter, than like that in the open-economy case we have studied here. In particular, even during the fixed exchange-rate period, U.S. monetary policy had an important effect on U.S. aggregate demand which was not quickly undone by capital inflows and outflows as it was in other countries.

13-5 CAPITAL CONTROLS

High capital mobility is characteristic of most of the developed world. In the advanced industrial countries, most capital controls were eliminated in the 1980s, and investors can now freely convert domestic assets into foreign assets without significant administrative barriers. Thus, the model that we have just explored provides an appropriate framework for understanding the effects of monetary and fiscal policy in these countries.

In much of the developing world, however, capital controls remain in place. For those countries, we have to modify some of our results. In particular, with capital controls in place, i need no longer equal i^*. Nor can households convert foreign assets to domestic money rapidly. The central bank simply will not sell or buy foreign exchange reserves for this purpose. Circumstances like this in developing economies mean that monetary and fiscal policies operate somewhat differently than they do in fully developed ones.

In a world of capital controls, a fixed exchange-rate regime works slightly differently than it does under full capital mobility. The central bank of an economy with capital controls stands ready to buy and sell foreign exchange at a given exchange rate, but only for *current account transactions*. That is, exporters receive the official exchange rate when they sell their foreign exchange earnings for domestic currency, and importers buy foreign exchange at the official exchange rate. If a household wants to obtain dollars to buy foreign bonds or to invest in a stock market abroad, however, the central bank will not provide the necessary foreign exchange. Similarly, domestic residents are often barred from taking loans from abroad.[12]

---

[11] Remember from Chapter 10, however, that the United States was obligated to exchange dollars held by other central banks for gold at $35 per ounce. While the United States maintained this commitment until 1971 (when it unilaterally suspended gold convertibility), it discouraged other central banks from exercising their option to receive gold. For the small gold conversions that took place, the United States was able to offset the monetary effects through open-market operations and other monetary policy actions.

[12] It may help here to refer to the discussion of exchange controls for capital account transactions in Chapter 10.

In these circumstances, the domestic interest rate can differ from the world interest rate, and the monetary authorities can determine the position of the LM curve, at least in the short run. When the central bank increases M, households cannot simply convert the excess M into foreign assets. Thus, the central bank can raise the money supply without the effect of the increase being instantly undone.

Even in the case of capital controls, however, *the position of the LM curve is still endogenous, but now the LM curve shifts more gradually than with free capital mobility*. With capital controls, the monetary expansion is not immediately reversed. Rather, the money expansion causes the trade balance to change. In turn, the shift in the trade balance causes the money supply to change, and the *LM* curve shifts endogenously.

In Chapter 10, we saw that under capital controls, the *change* in the money supply in any period is related to the trade balance in that period. Briefly, here is why. When exporters earn foreign exchange and sell those earnings to the central bank in return for domestic money, the money supply increases by the amount of the export sales. Similarly, when importers buy foreign exchange from the central bank in order to make imports, the money supply falls by the amount of the imports. Thus, the net change in the money supply is equal to the trade balance, assuming that there are no other direct actions by the central bank affecting the money supply (such as an open-market operation).

The counterpart of the change in the money supply caused by a trade surplus or deficit is, of course, a change in central bank reserves. When net exports are positive, both money and foreign reserves will rise; when net exports are negative, both money and foreign reserves will fall.

In any given period, the position of the *LM* curve is determined by the past history of trade imbalances and the open-market operations of the central bank. From period to period, however, assuming no open-market operations, the *LM* curve adjusts as the result of trade imbalances, moving to the right when there are trade surpluses and moving to the left when there are trade deficits. This endogenous adjustment has important effects on aggregate demand.

The Case of a Monetary Expansion

Now let us examine a monetary expansion under fixed exchange rates and capital controls. We start from an equilibrium, shown in Figure 13-12, which is characterized by balanced trade and a stationary *LM* curve. Note that the interest rate at point A need not equal i^*. Suppose that the monetary authorities expand the money supply, shifting the *LM* curve to the right. The immediate result is a fall in interest rates and a rise in aggregate demand.

No *immediate* force will shift the *LM* curve back to the initial position, because capital controls block interest arbitrage with the world capital markets. So far, the result looks very much like the closed-economy case. The effects of the aggregate demand expansion on overall output and prices depend, of course, on the shape of the aggregate supply schedule. Assuming a normal Keynesian supply schedule, like that shown in Figure 13-9(b), output rises.

But there is more to the story. With interest rates lower and the exchange rate stable, the economy will move into a trade deficit. After all, A/P

(a)

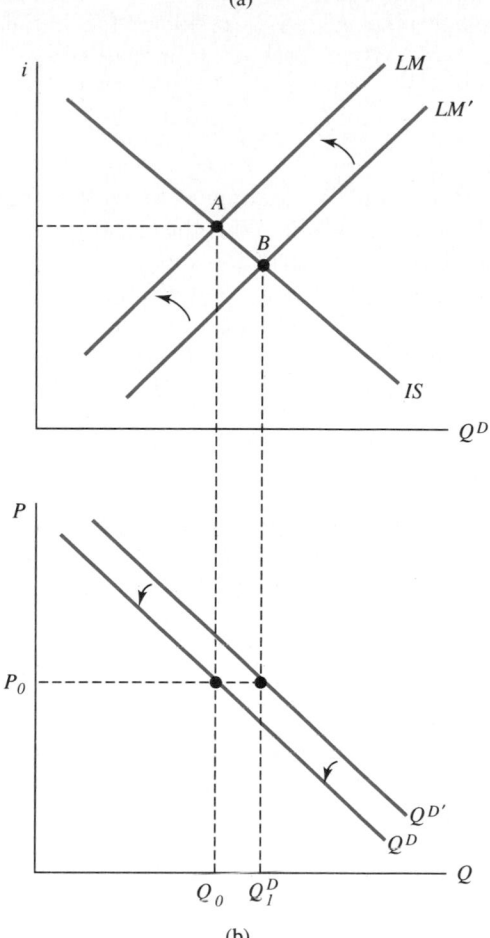

Figure 13-12

Effects of a Monetary
Expansion Under Capital
Controls: (a) The *IS-LM*
Framework; (b) the Aggregate
Demand Schedule

has risen, thereby causing total imports to rise. At the same time, EP_M^*/P has
either stayed the same (if the price level is constant) or has fallen (if the price
level has increased). Thus, imports will rise while exports will remain unchanged or will actually fall. At point *B*, the economy is seeing a trade
deficit.

Now comes the interesting part, a phenomenon not seen in the closed-
economy case or the case of fixed exchange rates with high capital mobility.
The trade deficit implies a drop in the money supply. Each period, the *LM*
curve therefore shifts back to the left, causing a progressive tightening of
monetary policy and a progressive reduction of aggregate demand. The monetary expansion is therefore *gradually* reduced. Eventually, the accumulated trade deficits match the initial increase in the money supply, and at that
point, the entire increase in *M* will have been offset. The *LM* curve is back at
its initial level, and the trade account is back in balance.

Thus, monetary policy has a short-run effect that is extinguished over
time. Interest rates initially fall, and the economy expands, with the trade
balance moving into deficit. But the deficit causes a gradual reversal of the
process. Interest rates start to rise back to their initial level, the money
supply falls, and output is restored to its premoney supply increase level.

One change, however, is permanent. In the course of the trade deficits, the central bank has lost foreign exchange reserves. As a result of the initial money expansion, there is a permanent loss of foreign exchange reserves equal to the sum of the trade deficits.

The Case of a Fiscal Expansion

Consider also the effects of a fiscal expansion. We assume as usual that the economy starts in equilibrium, with balanced trade. With the fiscal expansion, say, a rise in G, the IS curve shifts to the right, as shown in Figure 13-13a, increasing aggregate demand. Absorption rises, and as a result, the trade balance goes into deficit. Over time, however, the trade deficit provokes a decline in the money supply. As M declines, the LM schedule shifts upward and to the left, a shift that continues until the trade deficit is elimi-

Figure 13-13
Effects of a Fiscal Expansion Under Capital Controls: (a) The IS-LM Framework; (b) the Aggregate Demand Schedule

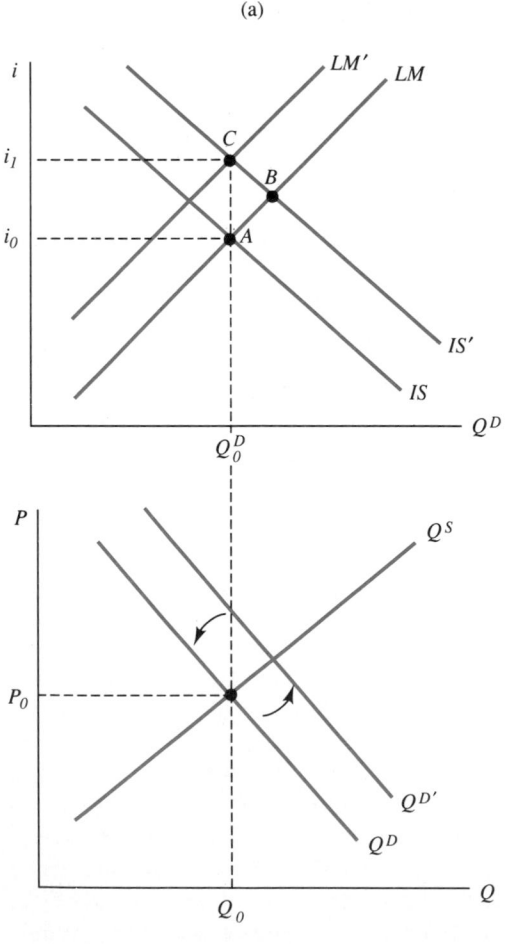

(a)

(b)

nated. This occurs when aggregate demand returns to its initial level, shown in the figure at point C. Notice that the interest rate rises sharply in the long-run as a result of the fiscal expansion.

Several points about this adjustment process are important. First, fiscal policy is effective only in the short run. Over time, when the money supply adjusts to the fiscal shock, aggregate demand goes back to its original position. Second, the increase in government spending crowds out private spending partially in the short run, and this crowding out is distributed between reduced private consumption and reduced investment in response to higher interest rates. Over the long term, however, the crowding out is total: the increase in interest rates (provoked both by the original increase in government spending and by the reduction in the money supply that comes from the accumulated trade deficits) fully crowds out private consumption and investment. In the end, aggregate demand has returned to its former level, but its composition has changed: government spending has increased at the expense of private investment and consumption.

13-6 SUMMARY

In this and the next chapter, the open-economy analysis of macroeconomic policies is carried out within the framework of the *Mundell–Fleming model*. In this chapter, the exchange rate is fixed, while in the next chapter, the exchange rate is floating.

We assume that the home country produces a single output which is distinct from the single output produced by the rest of the world. The home and the foreign good are imperfect substitutes in consumption, and thus the relative price of the home good to the foreign good influences the amount of consumption of each type of good.

Aggregate demand is the sum of domestic *absorption* plus the *trade balance*. In a closed economy, absorption and aggregate demand are the same thing, namely, $C + I + G$. In the open economy, however, absorption measures total spending by domestic residents, while aggregate demand measures total spending on domestic goods, whether by domestic and foreign residents. Consumption of foreign goods by domestic residents is part of absorption, but not aggregate demand; exports of domestic goods to foreign buyers is not part of absorption, but is part of aggregate demand.

The trade balance decreases when domestic absorption increases, because part of the extra spending falls on imports. The trade balance is a positive function of foreign absorption, because part of increased spending abroad is directed to the domestically produced good, thereby increasing exports. And it is a positive function of the relative price of foreign to domestic goods, the *real exchange rate*, $e = EP^*/P$. An increase in e—a real depreciation—makes foreign goods more expensive relative to home goods, which tends to increase exports and reduce imports.

The *IS* curve in the open economy has, as in the previous chapter, a negative slope. It shifts to the right (that is, demand expands) with a rise in government spending, a cut in taxes, a rise in expected future income, or an increase in the expected marginal product of capital. In addition, it shifts to the right with an increase in foreign absorption or a rise in the real exchange rate. A devaluation moves the *IS* to the right by making domestic exports more competitive in world markets, while imports become more expensive.

The *LM* schedule is upward sloping, as in the previous chapter. To complete the open-economy equilibrium, an assumption is needed about capital flows. If capital moves freely across borders, the domestic interest rate will be equal to the foreign interest rate. Graphically, this implies adding the capital mobility line. Finally, the aggregate demand schedule is downward sloping in the open economy, because an increase in the price level reduces both real monetary balances and the real exchange rate; the latter effect hurts exports and encourages imports.

Under fixed exchange rates and capital mobility, the monetary authorities are not able to choose both the money supply and the exchange rate since households may convert their domestic money into foreign assets as they see fit. A monetary expansion in this framework shifts the *LM* curve downward, but as the domestic interest rate tends to fall, capital flows out of the country. In this process, agents are converting their local money into foreign exchange, and the *LM* shifts back upward. The final equilibrium is at the initial position, with unchanged output and prices, and the interest rate given at the world level.

A fiscal expansion shifts the *IS* upward, and tends to increase interest rates. But it is not possible for interest rates to rise in equilibrium, because capital flows from abroad guarantee that the local interest rate will remain at world levels. The capital inflow is converted into local money at the fixed exchange rate; thus the money supply increases, and the *LM* curve shifts to the right. In the final equilibrium the interest rate is unchanged and aggregate demand goes up by the full amount predicted by the Keynesian multiplier. A devaluation also shifts the *IS* to the right by improving the trade balance, with a similar qualitative effect as the fiscal expansion.

Thus, under fixed exchange rates and capital mobility, fiscal policy is highly effective in shifting aggregate demand, while monetary policy is completely ineffective. Independently of the shape of the aggregate supply function, a monetary expansion will neither affect output nor prices. For large economies, however, the results are not so extreme. In economies like the United States, Japan, or the European Community, both fiscal and monetary policy will affect the world interest rate. A fiscal expansion in the United States, for example, will increase both U.S. and foreign interest rates, thus leading to a smaller multiplier than in the case of a small country (which can take the world interest rate as given).

The assumption of free capital mobility is not met in many countries of the developing world, where important restrictions to capital flows are in place. When capital controls exist, the domestic interest rate is no longer equal to the foreign rate, and the central bank does not sell foreign exchange for many (or all) capital account transactions. A monetary expansion is able to affect aggregate demand now, but only transitorily. The money supply increase shifts the *LM* down, lowers interest rates and increases aggregate demand. But with lower interest rates and a fixed exchange rate, the economy moves to a trade deficit. This lowers the money supply and moves the *LM* back up. Eventually, the accumulated trade deficits will equal the initial increase in the money supply, and the *LM* goes back to its initial position. Thus, monetary policy has a short-run effect that is extinguished over time.

A fiscal expansion shifts the *IS* to the right. Starting from trade balance under capital controls, the economy moves to a trade deficit. Over time, the trade deficit reduces the money supply and moves the *LM* schedule upward until the trade deficit is eliminated. In the end, aggregate demand goes back to its initial level, but the interest rate has risen sharply (both because of the initial fiscal expansion and the subsequent monetary tightening). In the long term, the crowding out of fiscal policy over private investment and consumption is total.

Key Concepts

Mundell–Fleming model	appreciation
differentiated goods	devaluation
home good	capital mobility line
foreign good	money supply endogeneity
domestic absorption	effectiveness of fiscal policy
real exchange rate	ineffectiveness of monetary
depreciation	policy

Problems and Questions

1. Why do capital flows respond more rapidly to changes in economic conditions than trade flows do? What is the importance of this phenomenon for economic policies?

2. Discuss the relation between the law of one price and the real exchange rate. Can the law of one price hold if the real exchange rate changes?

3. Consider a country with only two goods: imports and a domestic good. The price of the domestic good is 20. The price of the foreign good in terms of foreign currency is 2. The exchange rate is 3 (in units of domestic currency per unit of foreign currency). The domestic good represents 80 percent of total consumption.

   a. Calculate the consumer price index for this economy.
   b. What happens to the consumer price index if the price of the domestic good doubles?
   c. What happens to the consumer price index if the price of the imported good doubles?
   d. What happens to the consumer price index if the exchange rate depreciates to 4?

4. Describe what happens to absorption and aggregate demand under the following circumstances:

   a. Foreigners buy more domestic goods.
   b. Domestic residents buy more imported goods, but their total consumption is unchanged.
   c. Private investors buy more domestic goods and leave their total imports unchanged.
   d. The government raises taxes.

5. Use the *IS-LM* model to analyze the effects of a decrease of government expenditures on aggregate demand, the interest rate, and foreign reserves of the central bank in a small economy with no capital controls. How would your answer change if the central bank had matched the decrease in spending by selling bonds in an amount enough to shift the *LM* curve to its new equilibrium position?

6. Consider again a small economy with full capital mobility. What is the effect on aggregate demand and on the foreign reserves of the central bank of an increase of the same proportion in domestic and foreign prices? Why?

7. Analyze the effects of the following events on aggregate demand, foreign reserves of the central bank, money balances, prices, and output for a small economy with complete capital mobility. Consider the classical case, and the normal and extreme Keynesian cases.

   a. An increase in the world interest rate.

   b. An increase in foreign output (which raises the demand for exports of the domestic country).

   c. An increase in the money supply and a decrease in taxes.

8. Consider two small economies with full capital mobility. The two countries are exactly the same except that country A's total exports and total imports represent a larger percentage of GDP than country B's. In which of the two countries would a devaluation be more effective in raising aggregate demand? Why?

9. For the case of a small economy, describe the effects on the domestic interest rate, monetary balances, foreign reserves of the central bank, and aggregate demand of the following policies. Analyze the cases of full capital mobility and complete capital controls to identify the different effects in the short and long runs.

   a. The government reduces taxes.

   b. The central bank buys treasury bills from the public.

APPENDIX

In this appendix, we solve analytically the small-country, open-economy model under fixed exchange rates. The aim is to obtain equilibrium values for prices, output, and money as a function of the exogenous variables. Why do we need to solve for money too? Because under fixed exchange rates, as we analyzed in Chapter 10, money is endogenous; thus, its equilibrium value is not determined by the government, but by the workings of the economy. The exchange rate, by definition, is determined by the authorities; thus, it is an exogenous variable. As in Chapter 12, we solve the simplest case of a fully linear model.

In the open economy, the trade balance (or net exports) is part of aggregate demand. A linear version of equation (13.17) is

$$TB = h_0 \left(\frac{A^*}{P_M^*} \right) - h_1 \left(\frac{A}{P} \right) + h_2 \left(\frac{EP_M^*}{P} \right) \qquad \textbf{(A.1)}$$

From equation (13.13), we know that $Q^D = (A/P) + TB$. Using the linear expressions for the components of absorption (consumption, investment, and government spending) introduced in the appendix to Chapter 12, and equation (A.1), we can solve for Q^D in expression (13.13) to obtain

$$
\begin{aligned}
Q^D = {} & \phi_0[c^F[Q - T]^F - cT + \bar{I} + dMPK^E - (a + b)i + G] \\
& + \phi_1[h_0 A^* + (h_2 - h_0)P_M^* + h_2(E - P)]
\end{aligned} \qquad \textbf{(A.2)}
$$

where

$$\phi_0 = \frac{1 - h_1}{1 - c(1 - h_1)}; \qquad \phi_1 = \frac{1}{1 - c(1 - h_1)}$$

Once again, as in the appendix to Chapter 12, we have used the approximation of expressing the real exchange rate, $e = EP^*/P$, as $E + P_M^* - P$, and real foreign absorption (A^*/P^*) we have expressed as $A^* - P_M^*$.[1] This is a very helpful simplifying device.

Equation (A.2) is the *IS* schedule for the open economy. Note that the open-economy Keynesian multiplier $\{\phi_0 = (1 - h_1)/[1 - c(1 - h_1)]\}$ is smaller than in the closed-economy case. The reason is that out of every increase in income, a part of the induced rise in spending is diverted abroad in the form of additional imports.

As in the closed economy, aggregate demand depends positively on expected *future* income, autonomous investment, expected future marginal productivity of capital, and government spending, and it is a negative function of taxes and the interest rate. Now, however, two additional factors exert a positive influence on aggregate demand—foreign absorption and the real exchange rate—as explained in the text.

Once again, equation (A.2) is not yet a final expression for aggregate demand, since we have not yet specified how the interest rate is formed. The

---

[1] EP_M^*/P is approximately equal to $1 + E + P_M^* - P$ when E, P_M^*, and P are close to 1; A^*/P_M^* is approximately equal to $1 + A^* - P_M^*$ when A^* and P_M^* are close to 1. See footnote 1 of the appendix to Chapter 12.

LM curve, representing equilibrium in the money market, is the same as in the previous chapter.

$$M - P = vQ^D - fi \tag{A.3}$$

But now, the interest rate is not determined domestically. Because of full capital mobility, i is simply equal to the world interest rate (i^*). Thus,

$$i = i^* \tag{A.4}$$

Replacing i from (A.4) back on the *IS* equation, we obtain the aggregate demand function. This is simply equal to expression (A.2), with i^* in the place of i.

$$Q^D = \phi_0[c^F[Q - T]^F - cT + \bar{I} + dMPK^E - (a + b)i^* + G] \tag{A.5}$$
$$+ \phi_1[h_0 A^* + (h_2 - h_0)P_M^* + h_2(E - P)]$$

Note one important result in (A.5), which we obtained graphically in the text. In this simple model, aggregate demand is not affected by monetary policy because the interest rate is given by the world rate.

Global equilibrium of the economy is reached when aggregate supply is equal to aggregate demand ($Q^S = Q^D$). This opens up three possible cases, depending on the form of the aggregate supply curve.

Classical

Here, aggregate supply is vertical at the full-employment level of output, $Q^S = \bar{Q}$. Thus, output is simply

$$Q = \bar{Q} = Q^D \tag{A.6a}$$

To obtain the equilibrium price level, we simply replace $\bar{Q} = Q^D$ in equation (A.5) and solve for P.

$$P = E + \left[\frac{(h_2 - h_0)}{h_2}\right] P_M^* + \left(\frac{h_0}{h_2}\right) A^* - \left(\frac{1}{\phi_1 h_2}\right) \bar{Q} \tag{A.6b}$$

$$+ \left(\frac{\phi_0}{\phi_1 h_2}\right) [c^F[Q - T]^F - cT + \bar{I} + dMPK^E - (a + b)i^* + G]$$

where ϕ_0 is the open-economy Keynesian multiplier.

Note that changes in the exchange rate result in a one-to-one response in P. Why? Since output is fixed, changes in E do not affect the *real* exchange rate; only the nominal exchange rate moves to compensate, and thus the trade balance is unaffected. As for the rest of the variables in equation (A.6b), all those that increase aggregate demand have a positive effect in the price level, and vice versa. The particular feature of the classical model is that aggregate demand movements affect only prices.

What happens to money? We note from equations (A.3) and (A.6a) that $M = P + v\bar{Q} - fi^*$. Thus, the equilibrium M can be obtained by simply replacing the solution for P (from A.6b) in the right-hand side of this expression. (We do not do it here, though.) What is important to note is that $\Delta M = \Delta P$. Thus, price changes lead to equivalent movements in money, so that real balances ($M - P$ in our model) are unaffected.

Extreme Keynesian

Now, aggregate demand by itself determines the level of output, since the aggregate supply schedule is horizontal at the exogenous price level $\bar{P}$. The equations showing the equilibrium are

$$P = \bar{P} \tag{A.8a}$$

$$Q = \phi_0[c^F[Q - T]^F - cT + \bar{I} + dMPK^E - (a + b)i^* + G] \tag{A.8b}$$
$$+ \phi_1[h_0 A^* + (h_2 - h_0)P_M^* + h_2(E - \bar{P})]$$

Aggregate demand changes have full effect on output and do not affect the price level.

The equilibrium value of money can be found by replacing equation (A.8b) for Q in the expression $M = \bar{P} + vQ - fi^*$. Thus, changes in money are given by $\Delta M = v\Delta Q$. Now, it is output changes that motivate movements in M, and real money balances are affected by these changes.

Basic Keynesian

Since now the aggregate supply curve is upward sloping, a change in aggregate demand will affect both output and prices. The linear form of the aggregate supply curve is the same as in the appendix to Chapter 12:[2]

$$Q^S = g - z(w - P) \tag{A.9}$$

Using equations (A.5) and (A.9) to determine equilibrium ($Q^S = Q^D$), allows us to solve for the price level (P):

$$P = a_0 w + a_1[c^F[Q - T]^F - cT + \bar{I} + dMPK^E - (a + b)i^* + G] \tag{A.10a}$$
$$- a_2 g + a_3[h_0 A^* + (h_2 - h_0)P_M^* + h_2 E)]$$

where

$$a_0 = \frac{z}{z + \phi_1 h_2}; \quad a_1 = \frac{\phi_0}{z + \phi_1 h_2}; \quad a_2 = \frac{1}{z + \phi_1 h_2}; \quad a_3 = \frac{\phi_1}{z + \phi_1 h_2}$$

To find the equilibrium level of output, we replace the solution for the price level (equation A.10a) in the aggregate supply equation (A.9).[3]

$$Q = b_0 g + b_1[c^F[Q - T]^F - cT + \bar{I} + dMPK^E - (a + b)i^* + G] \tag{A.10b}$$
$$- b_2 w + b_3[h_0 A^* + (h_2 - h_0)P_M^* + h_2 E)]$$

where

$$b_0 = \frac{\phi_1 h_2}{z + \phi_1 h_2}; \quad b_1 = \frac{z\phi_0}{z + \phi_1 h_2}; \quad b_2 = \frac{z\phi_1 h_2}{z + \phi_1 h_2}; \quad b_3 = \frac{z\phi_1}{z + \phi_1 h_2}$$

Note that positive supply shocks (increases in g) raise output and reduce prices, while an increase in the nominal wage (which is assumed rigid in this model) would increase prices and lower output. The qualitative effect of all the other variables on P and Q is the same as their effect on aggregate demand. A devaluation, for example, increases aggregate demand through its effect on the trade balance; it raises both P and Q.

Finally, money balances respond here to both Q and P. In this model, $M = P + vQ - fi^*$. Thus, $\Delta M = \Delta P + v\Delta Q$.

---

[2] Note that we use again the approximation of (w/P) as $(w - P)$.

[3] The solution for output is the same if the equilibrium price level is replaced in the aggregate demand equation. Only the algebra would be more unpleasant.

chapter 14 ===================

Macroeconomic Policies in the Open Economy: The Case of Flexible Exchange Rates

In Chapter 13 we studied the effects of macroeconomic policies on output in an open economy operating with a fixed exchange rate. This case applies to much of the world, including almost all developing countries and many developed countries, such as the individual members of the European Monetary System (EMS). But, as we have noted, the large industrialized regions—the United States, Japan, and the European Community taken as a whole—are linked by flexible exchange rates. In this chapter, then, we shall see how macroeconomic policies and their effects might differ when exchange rates are flexible.

As before, we take a small country without capital controls as our basic case. Later, we look at the effects of capital controls, as well as what happens in a large country which affects world variables, particularly the world interest rate. Finally, we review the empirical evidence on the effects of fiscal and monetary policies under flexible exchange rates and report the results of several large-scale econometric models.

14-1 THE *IS-LM* FRAMEWORK WITH FLEXIBLE EXCHANGE RATES

We need not repeat the derivation of the *IS* curve for the open economy here. To set the scene, however, we should say again that with all other variables (G, T, $[Q - T]^F$, MPK^E, A^*/P^*, P, and E, for instance) held constant, the *IS* curve reflects the relationship between the interest rate and the level of aggregate demand. It has the same downward slope when exchange rates are flexible as when they are fixed. Again, the *LM* curve, which represents the combinations of interest rates and aggregate demand levels that clear the money market, slopes upward.[1] And as before, *high capital mobility ensures that equilibrium must take place along the CM*

---

[1] If you have come directly to this chapter, we recommend that you review Sections 13-2 and 13-3 in the previous chapter which discuss the determination of aggregate demand and the *IS-LM* framework in the open economy.

(capital mobility) line, on which i = i*, in the manner that we shall soon describe.[2]

Under flexible exchange rates, of course, the exchange rate is no longer a policy variable. *E* moves endogenously according to the forces of supply and demand. And because the position of the *IS* curve depends on *E* through its effects on trade flows, the *IS* curve also moves endogenously. In particular, it moves to the right when the exchange rate depreciates and moves to the left when the exchange rate appreciates. We can say, then, that *just as the LM curve moves endogenously in the case of fixed exchange rates, the IS curve moves endogenously in the case of floating exchange rates.* When exchange rates float, the monetary authorities lose control over the exchange rate, but they regain control over the money supply. The central bank can determine the level of the money supply, and thus the position of the *LM* curve (just as in the closed economy). Clearly, then, the *LM* curve no longer adjusts endogenously as it did in the case of fixed exchange rates.

Let us take an example of an endogenous shift in the *IS* curve. Consider an initial *IS-LM* equilibrium, say, the one at point *E* where the *IS, LM,* and *CM* lines intersect in Figure 14-1. If the monetary authority decreases the money supply by selling bonds to the public, the *LM* curve will shift up and will intersect the *IS* schedule at point *B*. This would be the new equilibrium in a closed economy. But in an open economy with high capital mobility, the domestic interest rate cannot remain higher than *i**. At point *B*, therefore, domestic and foreign wealthholders would shift out of foreign bonds into domestic bonds, prompting a capital inflow.

The key difference between fixed and floating exchange rates lies in the adjustment to this capital inflow. The capital inflow leads to an incipient appreciation (that is, the beginning of an appreciation) in the exchange rate. Under fixed exchange rates, the inflow would prompt an increase in the money supply as the central bank purchased foreign exchange with domestic money in order to prevent the appreciation, and the *LM* curve would shift endogenously to the right by enough to restore the capital mobility condition *i = i**. But under flexible exchange rates, the monetary authority does not intervene, and the money supply remains unchanged (the *LM* curve remains at *LM'*). Now it is the exchange rate that adjusts.

The capital inflow prompts an appreciation of the domestic currency, which, in turn, reduces net exports. When this happens, the *IS* curve shifts to the left. Note that as long as *i* remains above *i**, foreign capital keeps flowing in, the exchange rate keeps appreciating, and the *IS* keeps shifting to the left. The final equilibrium is reached at point *C*, on the *CM* line, *where the interest rate has gone back to the world level* and aggregate demand has declined from Q^D to $Q^{D'}$. Therefore, a monetary squeeze has a highly con-

---

[2] The condition *i = i** is actually the result of three assumptions: high capital mobility, perfect substitutability between home and foreign assets, and expectations of an unchanging exchange rate. When the exchange rate is expected to change, then the interest rates at home and abroad will differ according to the expected rate of currency change. Since we study a static model most of the time, we examine the case in which the exchange rate is not changing. When we explicitly consider dynamics later on, we will need a more complicated expression for capital market equilibrium.

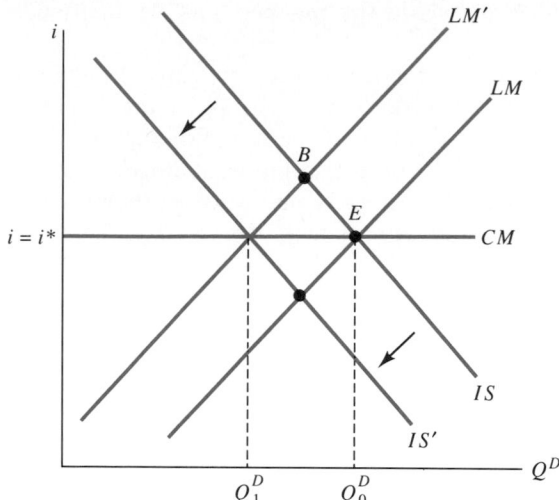

Figure 14-1
An Open-Market Sale of Bonds by the Central
Bank and the Endogenous *IS* Shift

tractionary effect on aggregate demand, and thus on output if we assume Keynesian supply conditions.

The lesson of the analysis is this. Under flexible exchange rates and high capital mobility, equilibrium must be at a point where $i = i^*$ (this condition also assumes no expected change in the exchange rate). The position of the *LM* curve is fixed by monetary policy, and the *LM* curve does not move endogenously. Therefore, the equilibrium level of aggregate demand is found where the *CM* line intersects the *LM* curve, and *the IS curve must adjust endogenously to intersect the LM curve at the same point.* It is movements in the exchange rate that cause this endogenous adjustment. A move of the *IS* curve to the right is due to an exchange-rate depreciation; a movement of the *IS* curve to the left is due to an exchange-rate appreciation.

Let us now find the shape of the aggregate demand schedule under flexible exchange rates. To do this, we start with an *IS-LM* equilibrium and consider the effects of an increase in the domestic price level. A higher price level reduces real money balances, and this causes the *LM* curve to shift to the left, say, to *LM'*, as shown in Figure 14-2. The new equilibrium will be at point *B*, the intersection of the *LM'* curve and the *CM* curve. The *IS* curve must move endogenously to this new intersection. It is clear that the new equilibrium is at a lower level of Q^D. Aggregate demand falls when the price level rises, and thus, the aggregate demand schedule is downward sloping.

The shift in the *IS* curve deserves careful attention. Inasmuch as a higher domestic price means less competitiveness in international trade, the *IS* curve must shift to the left. But there is no guarantee that the leftward shift of the *IS* curve is as great as the leftward shift of the *LM* curve. The price effect on the *IS* curve might be smaller, as shown in Figure 14-2, where the *IS"* line represents the shift in *IS* caused by the price level effect alone. The flexible exchange rate must also appreciate in order to push the *IS* curve

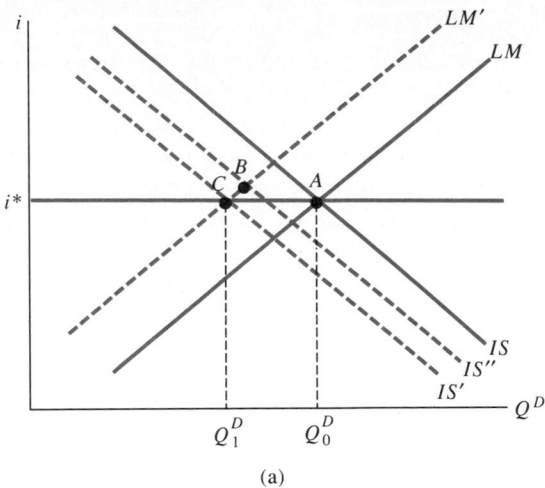

(a)

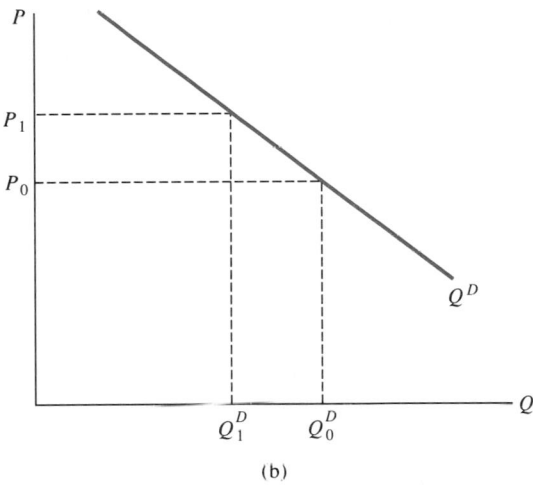

(b)

Figure 14-2

Effects of a Price Increase Under Flexible Exchange Rates—The Shape of the Aggregate Demand Schedule: (a) The *IS-LM* Framework; (b) the Aggregate Demand Schedule

all the way to point *B*. In this case, then, a rise in *P* causes aggregate demand to fall and also causes the exchange rate to appreciate. (And note that an exchange-rate depreciation could also be possible.)

14-2 MACROECONOMIC POLICIES IN A SMALL COUNTRY UNDER FREE CAPITAL MOBILITY

Now that we have seen how the *IS-LM* model works under flexible exchange rates and high capital mobility, we may see how a small economy with these features responds to fiscal and monetary policy.

Effects of a Fiscal Expansion

Let us now consider the effects of expansionary fiscal policy. An increase in government expenditure shifts the *IS* curve to the right. At the intersection of the new *IS* curve and the *LM* curve, domestic interest rates are higher than world interest rates, prompting a capital inflow and an appreciation of the currency. The appreciation of the exchange rate causes a deterioration of the trade balance, and the *IS* starts to shift back to the left. As long as the interest rate remains above the international level, capital inflows will continue to appreciate the exchange rate. The *IS* curve will continue to shift to the left. The final equilibrium is reached at point *A* of Figure 14-3a when the *IS* returns to its original position. Aggregate demand remains unchanged. (And, indeed, the aggregate demand schedule does not move from Q^D in Figure 14-3b.)

Under fixed exchange rates, the fiscal expansion provoked an endogenous increase in the money supply. Here, by contrast, the fiscal expansion prompts an appreciation of the home currency, which exactly offsets the expansionary demand effect of the higher government spending. Aggregate demand therefore stays right where it started. This is a remarkable result: fiscal policy is totally *crowded out* by a decline in net exports. In other words, since $Q^D = C + I + G + TB$, the rise in *G* is matched by the fall in *TB*.

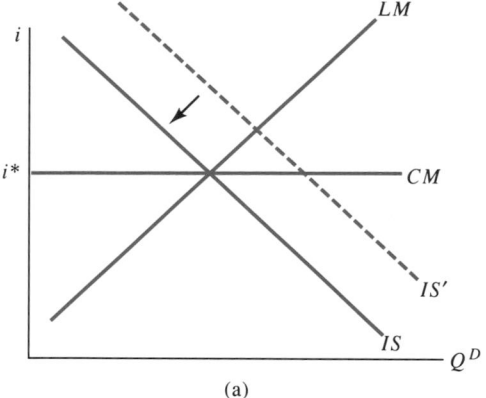

(a)

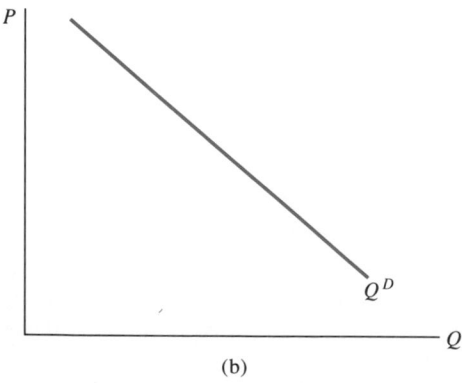

(b)

Figure 14-3

Effects of a Fiscal Expansion Under Flexible Exchange Rates: (a) The *IS-LM* Framework; (b) the Aggregate Demand Schedule

The trade balance worsens by exactly the amount that the government spending increases.

In the closed economy, we are used to thinking of crowding out in terms of investment spending. With a vertical LM curve, for example, a fiscal expansion raises interest rates and crowds out interest-sensitive consumption and investment spending by the same amount as the fiscal expansion. With $Q^D = C + I + G$, the rise in G is matched by a fall in $C + I$. But in the open economy with flexible exchange rates and capital mobility, the interest rate cannot rise; the crowding out occurs with net exports rather than with investment.

An interesting recent case of a fiscal expansion under flexible exchange rates is that of the United States in the early 1980s, during the first term of the Reagan presidency. Under the combination of an increase in military spending and a cut in income tax rates, there was a sharp rise in the fiscal deficit. The rise in the deficit in turn increased local interest rates, attracted capital from abroad, and appreciated the dollar. This hurt exports and caused a deterioration in the trade balance, all as expected. However, the U.S. case must be analyzed in more detail in a large-country setting, since unlike the model we are now considering, the U.S. fiscal actions had important effects on world interest rates. We therefore leave the U.S. experience now and return to it later in the chapter.

Expansionary Monetary Policy

Now we should see what happens when the central bank increases the money supply through an open-market purchase of domestic bonds. This action shifts the LM schedule downward in Figure 14-4a. The incipient decline in the interest rate provokes a capital outflow from the country, as investors respond to the gap between low domestic interest rates and higher world interest rates. This capital outflow causes the exchange rate to depreciate and improves the trade balance, thereby inducing an endogenous rightward shift of the IS curve. As long as local interest rates remain below world levels, pressure on the exchange rate continues, and this shifts the IS curve farther to the right. The new equilibrium is at point C, at the intersection of the CM line (where $i = i^*$) and the LM curve. The IS curve has moved endogenously to this intersection from the original intersection, via currency depreciation.

Interest rates are unchanged in the new equilibrium. Aggregate demand has increased from Q_0^D to Q_1^D in Figure 14-4a, however. This increase in demand comes from a rise in net exports which occurred because of the currency depreciation. *Thus, for a small open economy with high capital mobility and flexible exchange rates, monetary policy works through its effect on the exchange rate rather than through its effect on interest rates as it would in a closed economy.* With $Q^D = C + I + G + TB$, monetary policy under floating exchange rates (in a small open economy with high capital mobility) works through its effects on TB, not $C + I$. Since the IS and LM schedules are drawn for a given price level, this implies that the aggregate demand schedule shifts to the right in Figure 14-4b. The effects on equilibrium output and prices will depend on the shape of the aggregate supply schedule, as usual.

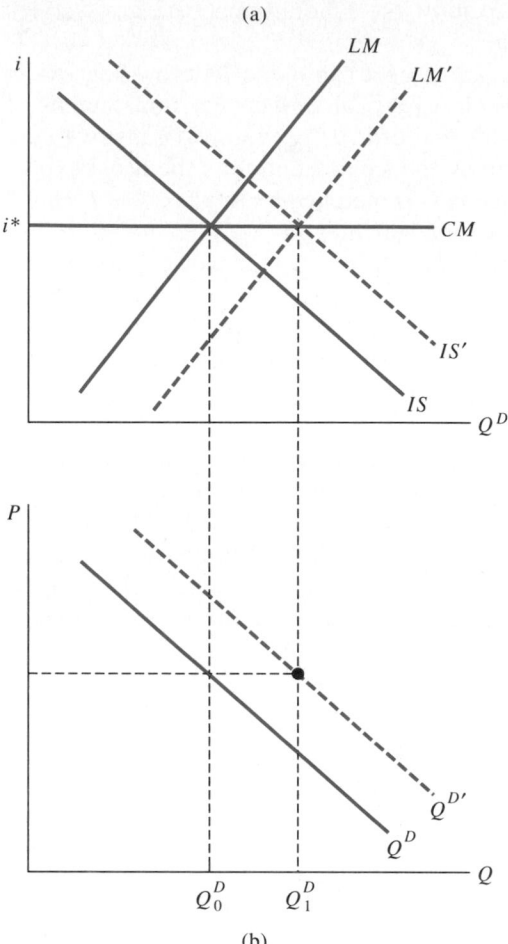

Figure 14-4
Effects of a Monetary Expansion Under
Flexible Exchange Rates: (a) The *IS-LM*
Framework; (b) the Aggregate Demand
Schedule

A Comparison of Macroeconomic Policy Under Fixed and Flexible Exchange Rates

Let us reflect on the main lessons of this section for a moment. Table 14-1 summarizes the outcome of a monetary expansion, a fiscal expansion, and a devaluation on the equilibrium levels of output, the price level, international reserves, and the exchange rate. Notice that in each case it is necessary to be precise about the exchange-rate regime under which the economy operates. To arrive at meaningful conclusions, it is also crucial to specify the shape of the aggregate supply schedule. For the purposes of this exercise, we assume that the economy is characterized in the short run by normal Keynesian conditions, so that the aggregate supply curve is upward sloping.

Perhaps the most intriguing finding in this and the last chapter is that the effects of a given economic policy vary dramatically depending on what kind of exchange-rate regime is in place. Fiscal policy has maximum effec-

TABLE 14-1

EFFECTS OF MONETARY, FISCAL AND EXCHANGE-RATE POLICY IN A
SMALL COUNTRY WITH PERFECT CAPITAL MOBILITY

| Effect on: | Monetary Expansion | | Fiscal Expansion | | Devaluation |
	Fixed E	Flexible E	Fixed E	Flexible E	Fixed E
Output (Q)	0	+	+	0	+
Price level (P)	0	+	+	0	+
International reserves (R^*)	−	0	+	0	+
Exchange Rate (E)	0	+	0	−	+

tiveness on aggregate demand under fixed exchange rates and no effect whatsoever under flexible rates. Monetary policy works exactly the other way around. These results, of course, apply only for a small country that operates under perfect capital mobility and faces given world interest rates.

14-3 EXCHANGE-RATE DYNAMICS

So far we have neglected dynamic adjustment issues. One source of dynamics in many economies is the gradual adjustment of nominal wages over time in response to the gap between actual employment and full employment. As we saw in Chapter 3 and again in Chapter 12, a process of slow wage adjustment leads to an economy with Keynesian properties in the short run and classical properties in the long run. It also turns out that slow adjustment in wages, and hence in prices, has important implications for the flexible exchange-rate system.

Exchange-Rate Overshooting

Let us see what happens when the central bank raises the money supply. Immediately, aggregate demand rises. Then, in the short run, assuming that nominal wages do not jump instantly, output expands. In the long run, after nominal wages adjust fully to the money supply increase, wages and prices go up by the same proportion as money, and output returns to its initial level. (Chapter 12 describes this in detail). Thus, in the period when M rises, P goes up by less than M (and even remains completely unchanged in the extreme Keynesian case), while in the long run, P goes up by the same proportion as M. The short-run and long-run equilibria are shown in the Q^S–Q^D framework in Figure 14-5b (where an intermediate value of P is shown as P'', for later reference).

With an increase in the money supply, the exchange rate depreciates in the same proportion as the rise in money, wages, and prices in the long run. That is, if the money supply increase is 10 percent, then the long-run depreciation of the exchange rate is also 10 percent, and wages and prices also rise by 10 percent in the long run. In this way, M/P is unchanged in the new long-run equilibrium, as is EP_m^*/P (because E and P rise by the same amount).

The exchange rate also depreciates in the short run, as is clear from the *IS-LM* model. Consider the short-run equilibrium in Figure 14-5a. We start

(a)

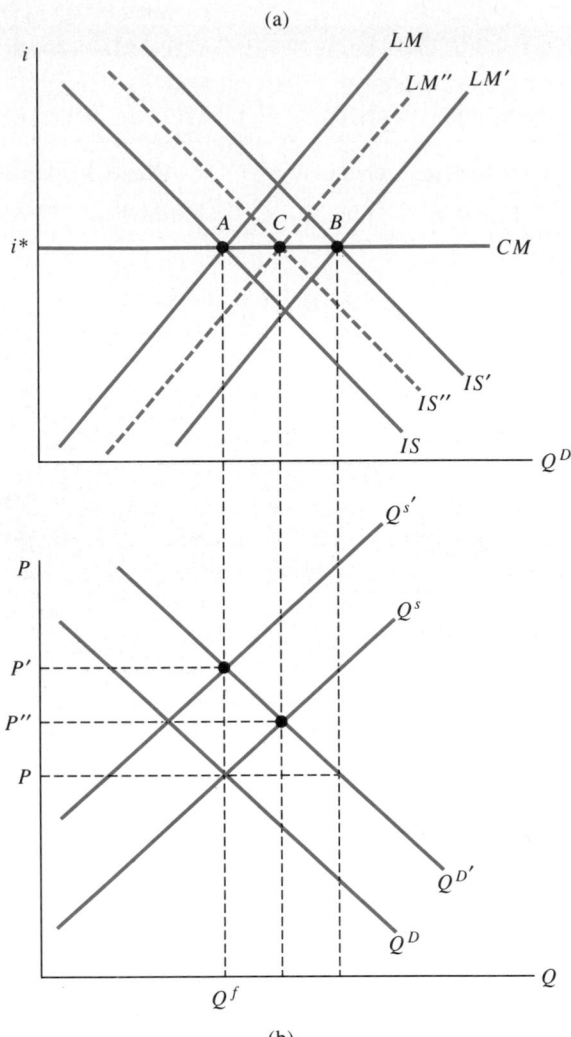

(b)

Figure 14-5
Exchange Rate Overshooting After a Monetary
Expansion: (a) The *IS-LM* Framework; (b) the
Aggregate Demand Schedule

out at point *A* in the figure. When the money supply rises, the *LM* curve
shifts to *LM'*. Assuming $i = i^*$ because of capital mobility (we return to this
assumption in a minute), the new short-run equilibrium is at point *B*. The *IS*
curve adjusts to point *B* endogenously, through a depreciation of the exchange rate. So far, all this is familiar.

How big is the depreciation in the exchange rate needed to shift the *IS*
curve so that it goes through point *B?* The answer is that the short-run
change can be larger or smaller than the long-run change, depending on how
responsive output is to a change in the real exchange rate. If aggregate
demand is not very responsive to a real exchange-rate depreciation, the
initial depreciation of the exchange rate might have to be very large indeed.
A 1 percent rise in *M* can provoke a *greater than 1 percent* rise in *E* in the

same period. In that case, the depreciation of E in the short run is greater than the depreciation of E in the long run. In technical terms, the depreciation of E can *overshoot* its long-run value.

When "exchange-rate overshooting" occurs, the time path of the exchange rate is as shown in Figure 14-6. At the time of the monetary expansion, shown as t_0 in the figure, the exchange rate depreciates sharply, by more than in proportion to the monetary change. Over time, as the economy is adjusting to long-run equilibrium—especially as wages and prices are increasing in response to the high level of output and employment—the exchange rate gradually appreciates to its long-run value. In the long run, the depreciation is just equal in percentage terms to the increase in the money supply.[3] The time paths of prices and output are also shown in Figure 14-6. Note that prices rise gradually to their new long-run equilibrium, while output initially rises and then falls back to the original equilibrium level.

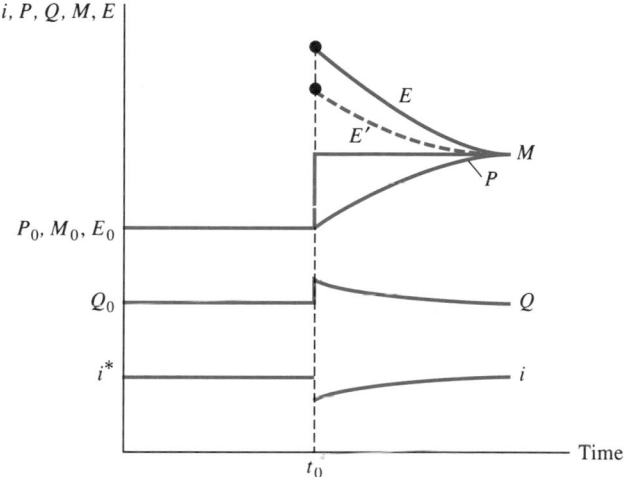

Figure 14-6
The Path of the Exchange Rate Following a
Monetary Expansion

Rudiger Dornbusch of MIT has amended this basic model of overshooting by noting an interesting aspect of asset-market behavior.[4] Dornbusch points out that the story must be modified to take into account that households and firms come to expect the appreciation later on down the adjustment path. With interest rates equalized across countries, and with an expectation that the domestic exchange rate will be appreciating, they know it is worthwhile to sell foreign assets and buy domestic assets.

---

[3] Figure 14-6 shows just one possible path for the exchange rate. It is possible that the initial depreciation of the exchange rate is less than the long-run value, in which case the exchange rate would depreciate over time to its long-run value, though it is generally felt that the overshooting case is the more realistic one. Remember, an important issue here is whether aggregate demand is highly responsive to changes in the real exchange rate. The *less* responsive is aggregate demand to changes in EP^*/P, the *more* likely is exchange rate overshooting.

[4] His classic article on the overshooting hypothesis is "Expectations and Exchange Rate Dynamics," *Journal of Political Economy*, December 1976.

The attempt to sell foreign assets and buy domestic assets will lead to a fall in the domestic interest rate relative to the foreign interest rate. The gap between the home and foreign interest rates must be exactly enough to equalize returns on the home and foreign assets, taking into account that the exchange rate is going to appreciate over time. In particular, in order to equalize rates of return on home and foreign assets when the exchange rate is expected to change, it must be the case that the home interest rate is less than the foreign interest rate by the amount of expected rate of exchange-rate depreciation.

This necessary condition for capital market equilibrium is nothing more than the interest arbitrage condition that we studied in Chapter 10, which we repeat here:

$$i = i^* + \frac{(E_{+1} - E)}{E} \tag{14.1}$$

During a period of currency appreciation (in which the last term on the right-hand side is negative, since E is *falling* each period on the path to long-run equilibrium), the domestic interest rate should be less than the world interest rate in order for the rates of return on home and foreign assets to be the same.

Here is what must occur in the asset markets. After the initial monetary expansion the asset markets are not quite in short-run equilibrium. Because a future appreciation is expected, capital flows in. The domestic interest rate moves below the foreign interest rate, by the amount of the expected appreciation in the next period. Over time, as the economy moves to its long-term equilibrium (with prices and wages rising, and the exchange rate appreciating), the interest rate will increase gradually back to the long-run value i^*. The time path for the interest rate is shown in Figure 14-6.

What is the importance of the overshooting phenomenon? It can help us to account for an empirical puzzle. After the breakdown of the Bretton Woods system of pegged exchange rates in the early 1970s, the currencies of the major industrial countries began to float against each other. It was widely believed that exchange-rate movements were due, in large part, to shifts in monetary policy, but it was also observed that the swings in exchange rates were greater than the accompanying swings in money supplies. The overshooting phenomenon helps to account for this fact, by showing that indeed, money supply changes can cause jumps in the exchange rate that are of larger proportion in the short run.

Expectations and Floating Exchange Rates

There is another reason for exchange-rate volatility in a floating-rate regime. Shifts in expectations about *future* economic variables can affect the *current* level of the exchange rate. Even if the only thing that changes in an economy are the expectations about the future, the shifts in expectations can have a very important effect on the current value of the exchange rate. Thus, fluctuations in expectations can provoke fluctuations in the exchange rate.

Let us see how that can occur. Suppose that it becomes widely expected that the money supply will be expanded in the next period, but not in the current period. We can surmise that in the future, the exchange rate will

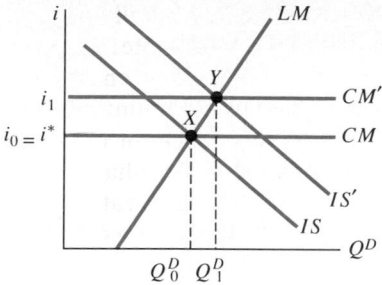

Figure 14-7
Macroeconomic Equilibrium Following
an Anticipated Monetary Expansion

depreciate, for the reasons we have just explored. Investors will come to expect a depreciation of the exchange rate between now and the time that the money supply is increased. Because of that expectation, investors will begin to sell domestic assets and buy foreign assets *until the difference in interest rates is equal to the expected change in the exchange rate.* Specifically, if there is an expectation that the exchange rate will depreciate between now and the next period, the domestic interest rate must exceed the foreign interest rate by the amount of the anticipated depreciation, as shown by equation (14.1).

This rise in the equilibrium interest rate affects the entire macroeconomic equilibrium. As shown in Figure 14-7, the *CM* curve shifts up in the *IS-LM* model, moving the aggregate demand equilibrium from point *X* to point *Y*. Note that the *IS* curve now moves endogenously to this new equilibrium. Since a rightward shift in the *IS* curve is required, we see that the exchange rate must depreciate. The result is striking: the expectation of future depreciation causes an initial depreciation, even *before* the money supply actually increases.

It is important to understand the subtle timing of events that is assumed in the case depicted Figure 14-7. Before time t_0, the economy is in a stationary equilibrium. At time t_0, it becomes widely expected (perhaps because of an announcement) that the money supply will increase at some future date, say time t_1. Even before the actual money supply increase, the economy starts to react. The exchange rate depreciates, though not by as much as it will in period t_1, when the money supply actually rises. Also, the interest rate jumps at time t_0 to equalize the returns on home and foreign assets, taking into account the expected depreciation of the exchange rate between time t_0 and t_1. Output expands in period t_0 as well, as a result of the real exchange-rate depreciation.

There is an important lesson here that bears repeating. Expectations concerning future events—not only monetary policy, but also fiscal policy, foreign demand, technology, and so on—affect the current exchange rate and interest rate, and thereby the entire macroeconomy. Fluctuations in the exchange rate might be traceable not to contemporaneous shocks in observable variables, but rather to shifts in expectations among the public about the future course of the economy.

14-4 MACROECONOMIC POLICIES UNDER FREE CAPITAL MOBILITY: THE LARGE-COUNTRY CASE

Up to now, our analysis has described the case of a country that is too small to influence the world's financial markets. In particular, i^* is taken as given in all the models. This assumption is relevant for most of the countries in the world, though not for the United States, Japan, Germany, or the European Community acting as a common regional economy. In those few cases (and to a smaller extent for smaller economies), domestic policy changes do affect world interest rates, which in turn affect the way those policies operate. Thus, we have to understand how global effects work to see properly how U.S. policies affect the U.S. economy, not to mention how U.S. policies affect the rest of the world.

Let us now consider how the effects of macroeconomic policy differ for a large versus a small country. The intuitive result is that the large country behaves somewhere between a small, open economy, and a closed economy. It is large enough to affect world variables, such as i^*. The direction of the effect is the same as in the closed-economy IS-LM model: a fiscal expansion tends to raise interest rates (both at home and abroad), and a monetary expansion tends to reduce interest rates.

A Fiscal Expansion

When a large country undertakes a fiscal expansion, the overall saving-investment balance in the world economy shifts, causing the world interest rate i^* and the domestic interest rate to rise. This effect is similar to that found in the closed-economy IS-LM model.[5] The effect on domestic and world interest rates leads to important differences in the effects of fiscal policies with those found for the small country. As before, the IS curve shifts to the right, but now the CM line also shifts up, as shown in Figure 14-8a. As in the small-country case, the equilibrium will be at the intersection of the LM and the CM curve. The IS curve shifts to the equilibrium via a currency appreciation, but note that it does not shift back fully to the original position, as it does in the small-country case. Instead, a new equilibrium is reached at point C, an equilibrium characterized by *higher aggregate demand, Q^D, a higher interest rate (both at home and abroad), and an appreciated currency*.

Why does aggregate demand increase in this case, when it does not in the small-country case? In the small-country case, the expansionary effect of the fiscal expansion is fully offset by the contractionary effect of the currency appreciation. In the large-country case, the fiscal expansion is not fully offset. The foreign interest rate rises, and the flow of capital into the home country is somewhat less, so that the exchange-rate appreciation is smaller. In the small-country case, the trade balance deteriorates by more than in the large-country case, because the exchange-rate appreciation is greater. In essence, there is less crowding out of net exports in the large-country case.

----

[5] The effect is also similar to that of the two-country full-employment model of Chapter 7. In both the small-country IS-LM model and the two-country full-employment model, a fiscal expansion tends to raise the interest rate.

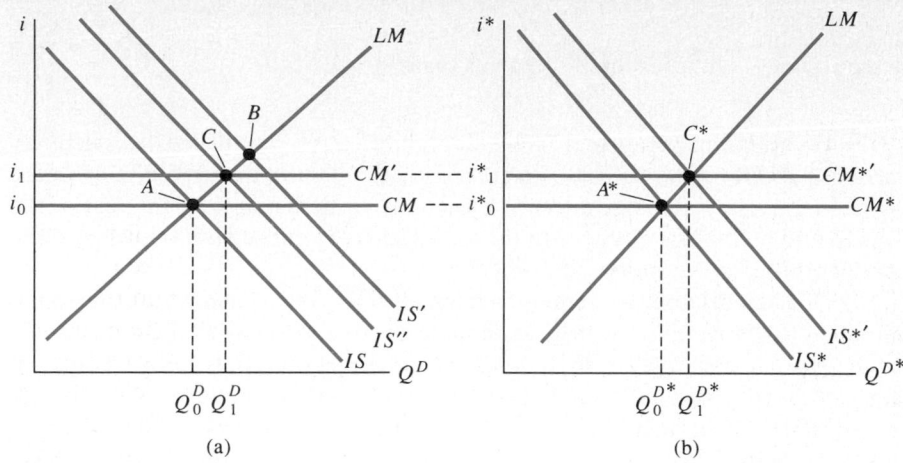

(a)   (b)

Figure 14-8

A Fiscal Expansion under Flexible Exchange Rates and Free Capital Mobility: The Case of Interdependence (a) The Home Country; (b) The Rest of the World

What happens *abroad* when the home country expands? The interest rate i^* rises and the foreign CM curve shifts up, as shown in Figure 14-8b. The new foreign equilibrium will be at the intersection of the $CM^{*\prime}$ curve and the LM^* curve. Aggregate demand abroad rises, from point A^* to point C^*. The foreign currency depreciates—this depreciation is the mirror image of the home currency appreciation—thus improving trade competitiveness abroad. Thus, the foreign IS^* curve moves endogenously to the right.

An Increase in the Money Supply

A money expansion reduces the domestic interest rate, as in the closed-economy *IS-LM* model. Thus, the LM curve shifts to the right and reduces the home interest rate, as shown in Figure 14-9a. In response, capital begins to fly abroad. Under floating rates, the exchange rate will depreciate, thereby improving the trade balance. Once that happens, the IS will shift to the right. At the same time, in the large-country case, the domestic monetary expansion reduces the world interest rate slightly, as shown in Figure 14-9a.

Figure 14-9

A Monetary Expansion Under Flexible Exchange Rates and Free Capital Mobility—The Case of Interdependence: (a) The Home Country; (b) the Rest of the World

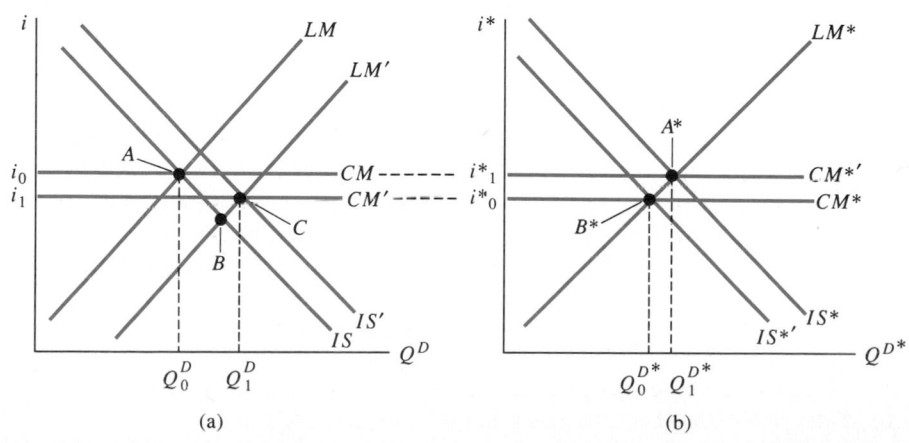

(a)   (b)

What happens abroad? The depreciation of the domestic currency brought about by the outflow of capital is equivalent to an appreciation of the foreign currency. This negatively affects the trade balance of the rest of the world and shifts its IS^* curve to the left. The CM^* curve shifts down and the new equilibrium is shown at point B^*.

One remarkable fact emerges from all this. The monetary expansion at home actually *reduces* aggregate demand abroad. We say that the *transmission effect* is negative, in that a policy that raises output at home reduces it abroad (sometimes called a "beggar-thy-neighbor" policy, because the expansionary effect at home comes at the expense of a contractionary effect abroad). With fiscal policy, by distinction, the transmission effect was positive: the home country fiscal expansion raised output both at home and abroad.

One final word of warning. The direction of transmission effects (positive for fiscal policies, negative for monetary policies) can be altered by minor changes in the assumptions about the two-country model.[6] If the economies have extensive wage indexation, for example, a monetary expansion in the home country is likely to provoke a rise in foreign output, while a fiscal expansion can provoke a fall in foreign output. We examine the empirical evidence on this at the end of the chapter.

14-5 CAPITAL CONTROLS AND FLOATING EXCHANGE RATES

When capital controls and floating exchange rates are in place, the current account must always be in balance. There is simply no way to finance a deficit or surplus. Private capital flows are ruled out, and the central bank does not buy or sell foreign-exchange reserves. Thus, the floating exchange rate always adjusts to be consistent with current account balance. But there are relatively few cases in the world of capital controls and floating exchange rates. Most developing countries have capital controls, but also pegged exchange rates. Most developed countries had removed their capital controls by the end of the 1980s.

Nonetheless, we should briefly summarize the implications of this atypical policy regime. For fiscal policy, an expansion in G raises output (as before), but this time the fiscal expansion provokes a currency depreciation rather than appreciation. (There is no capital inflow to cause the exchange rate to appreciate.) A money supply increase also raises output (as before) and causes a currency depreciation, as was true in the case of capital mobility. In the case of a fiscal expansion, interest rates rise, as they do in a closed economy; with a monetary expansion, interest rates decline.

It is important to note that the distribution of the demand expansion among C, I, G, and TB differs markedly in the case of capital mobility and the case of capital controls. With capital mobility, for example, the rise in G prompts a fall in TB; it is net exports that are crowded out. Because the interest rate remains unchanged at the level $i = i^*$, there is no crowding out of interest-sensitive investment and consumption. With capital controls, by contrast, domestic interest rates rise when G is raised, and it is interest-

---

[6] See Chapter 6 of Michael Bruno and Jeffrey Sachs, *The Economics of Worldwide Stagflation* (Cambridge, Mass.: Harvard University Press, 1985).

sensitive consumption and investment that are (partially) crowded out rather than the trade balance.

The effects of a monetary expansion also differ. Under capital mobility, the money supply increase expands demand through a higher trade balance. The money expansion causes a real exchange-rate depreciation, and hence a rise in TB. But because the interest rate remains at $i = i^*$, there is no effect on C and I. Under capital controls, the trade balance does not change, but the interest rate declines. The money expansion therefore works through a rise in C and I, just as it does in a closed economy.

14-6 THE POLICY MIX

Up to now we have considered the effects of one policy at a time, be it fiscal, monetary, or exchange-rate changes. In practice, policymakers often aim to achieve many targets, in which case they may want to change many policy variables at the same time. Indeed, to achieve a number (n) of targets—output, inflation, the current account, and so on—policymakers generally need n independent instruments—monetary policy, fiscal policy, and so forth. Often, there are more targets than independent instruments. In that case, not all goals can be achieved, and various trade-offs must be made. The theory of targets and instruments was developed by the Dutch economist Jan Tinbergen, who later went on to win the Nobel Prize in Economics[7] and whose work we study in detail in Chapter 19.

Here, let us take a simple case in which a government has two policy instruments and two targets. For example, suppose that a government wants to keep output unchanged while at the same time reducing the current account deficit and that it has monetary and fiscal policy at its disposal. This problem is more than hypothetical. The United States faced just these policy goals at the end of the 1980s. To keep the circumstances relevant to the United States, then, let us further suppose that the country is a large one, operating under flexible exchange rates.

This is how the thinking goes. A *fiscal contraction* by itself would improve the trade balance (by depreciating the currency, as described earlier), but would reduce output. A *monetary expansion* by itself would improve the trade balance (by depreciating the currency) but would raise output. Therefore, a combination—a ''policy mix''—of fiscal contraction and monetary expansion would improve the trade balance (since both policies point in the same direction) while having little effect on output (since the output effects of the two policies tend to cancel each other).

Another interesting policy mix was undertaken in the United States during the early 1980s. At the time, the big concern of policymakers was to reduce inflation. Under a floating exchange-rate regime, like that in the United States since 1971, disinflation can be attempted through a fiscal expansion together with an offsetting monetary contraction. Both policies push interest rates upward, and high interest rates provoke a massive capital inflow which appreciates the exchange rate. The decline in aggregate demand can be avoided, or at least mitigated, because the increase in government spending offsets the decline in net exports (prompted by the appreci-

---

[7] Many of Tinbergen's ideas are contained in his book *On the Theory of Economic Policy* (Amsterdam: North Holland, 1952).

ated exchange rate) and in investment (prompted by the higher interest rate). The effect on consumption is ambiguous: higher interest rates push it downward, but the reduced cost of imported goods pushes it upward.

These theoretical effects bear a remarkable similarity to the experience of the United States in the early 1980s.[8] The U.S. Federal Reserve, under the direction of Paul Volcker, pursued a contractionary monetary policy to reduce inflation. Soon after the monetary contraction was launched, the Reagan administration presided over a major fiscal expansion, induced both by tax cuts and by spending increases, especially on the defense buildup. As a result, inflation was quickly reduced; costs in terms of forgone output existed, but were smaller than they would have been without the fiscal expansion.

However, the massive deterioration in the trade balance and the current account that this policy brought about had as a counterpart an increase in foreign borrowing. The country sharply increased its debt, that will eventually have to be repaid. The actions required to remedy this amount to a reversal of policies. In particular, any remedy requires a fiscal tightening that is neither easy nor costless to accomplish. As the U.S. economy is now finding, many of the original gains made during the successful disinflation eventually have to be given up, and the process is not painless.

14-7 EMPIRICAL EVIDENCE

In this section, we investigate the quantitative effects of different macroeconomic policies using the large-scale models we discussed in Chapter 12. In particular, we review the open-economy results obtained by Ralph Bryant, John Helliwell, and Peter Hooper of the U.S. Federal Reserve System.[9] Their simulations of various U.S. economic policies used many well-known large-scale econometric models (LSEMs), including those described in Box 12-1. Because their results are averaged across models, what emerges is a balanced picture that avoids the specific features of particular models.

Consider first a cut in government spending. From our theoretical model, we expect a decline in U.S. output, a depreciation of the dollar, and a fall in output abroad (remember that in the basic model, fiscal policy is positively transmitted: its effects have the same direction in the United States and abroad). The trade balance of the United States improves as well, both because the dollar depreciates and because overall U.S. absorption declines. Let us see if these results are borne out by the large-scale model.

According to Bryant, Helliwell, and Hooper, an annual reduction of government spending in the United States by 1 percent of GDP during a period of six years reduces output by slightly over 1 percent in the first

---

[8] This experience has been analyzed by Jeffrey Sachs in his article "The Policy Mix and the Dollar," *Brookings Papers on Economic Activity,* no. 1, 1985.

[9] See their joint work, "Domestic and Cross-border Consequences of U.S. Macroeconomic Policies," in R. Bryant et al., eds., *Macroeconomic Policies in an Interdependent World* (Washington, D.C.: International Monetary Fund, 1989).

year.[10] Output recovers in the second year, but without going back to its original level. The exchange rate depreciates by 2 percent during the first year. Both the output decline and the depreciation of the dollar work to raise the current account in the United States. It is estimated that a $100 billion reduction in government spending improves the current account by about $20 billion in the first year of the spending cut and some $32 billion as of the third year.

Repercussion effects work mainly through trade flows. As expected, foreign GDP declines, although the magnitude of the effect on foreign output is not as great as in the United States. By the third year of the U.S. fiscal action, output in the rest of the Organization for Economic Cooperation and Development (OECD) countries declines by 0.4 percent. The transmission to Japan is greater than this, probably reflecting the large dependence of Japanese exports on the U.S. market.

Consider now an expansion in the U.S. money supply by 1 percent for six years. According to the theoretical model, a money supply expansion should raise output, cut interest rates, and provoke a depreciation of the dollar. In the simulation models, we find that the money supply increase indeed reduces interest rates sharply in the first year, but that interest rates rebound in subsequent years. Output goes up by $\frac{1}{4}$ percent in the first year, further increases in the second, and then declines toward its original level. The exchange rate depreciates initially by 1.5 percent and then climbs back to a level 1 percent over the starting point.

What about the effect on the U.S. current account balance? There are two conflicting effects: the fall in interest rates causes a rise in absorption, tending to worsen the current account balance, while the depreciation tends to improve the current account balance. Empirically, the net effect of a money supply increase on the current account is quite small—indeed, it is almost negligible. Regarding cross-country transmission, output tends to decline abroad, although the effect is not big. Thus, the large-scale simulation models tend to corroborate the theory that a monetary expansion under flexible exchange rates is negatively transmitted.

Finally, let us briefly review the results of a particularly interesting case, a U.S. policy mix aimed at improving the current account balance while stabilizing output. Consider a step-by-step reduction in government spending of 0.5 percent of GNP in each of four years, which culminates in a cumulative cut of G by 2 percent of GNP as of the fourth year. At the same time, suppose that the money supply increases during the first three years by 2 percent, 3 percent, and 4 percent, respectively, and gradually comes back to 2 percent above the original level in year 6.

As a result of this policy mix, the current account balance improves (by almost 0.5 percent of GNP as of the third year), the dollar depreciates, and output declines slightly (0.2 percent in the first year and 0.5 percent in the second). If the fiscal contraction were undertaken *without the money expansion,* the current account effect would be about the same but the loss of output would be higher (about 0.7 percent of output in the first year). Therefore, the use of expansionary monetary policy to offset contractionary fiscal policy helps to stabilize output.

---

[10] Results are expressed in deviations from trend. See footnote 14 in Chapter 12.

Once again, the qualitative results obtained in our basic Mundell–Fleming model are verified by the more complex LSEMs. Clearly, there are real-world complications that our simple framework cannot handle that LSEMs can. The basic theoretical models cannot consider appropriately the effects of phased-in policies, the effects of lags, and the spillover effects in many countries and regions. But the simple Mundell–Fleming model can still make sensible qualitative predictions.

14-8 THE CASE FOR POLICY COORDINATION

We have seen in Section 14-4 that macroeconomic policies undertaken in one country can have an impact on other economies. The *interdependence* effects are most important when policies are undertaken by large countries (or regions) such as the United States, Japan, Germany, and the European Community taken as a whole. When economies are interdependent, there may be a case for coordinating their policies. Policy coordination may be beneficial because decentralized decision making—that is, each country acting on its own—can lead to undesirable macroeconomic outcomes. The concern to improve global macroeconomic performance led in the 1980s to calls for increased macroeconomic policy coordination among the large economies. Within Europe, macroeconomic policy coordination is now carried to a very extensive degree, especially in the realm of monetary policy. What is the case for macroeconomic policy coordination among interdependent economies?

Game theory provides the analytical tools to study the case for cooperation. The game theoretic arguments can best be introduced with an example.[11] Consider two countries, the United States and Japan, linked by floating exchange rates. Suppose that both countries are trying to reduce a stubbornly high rate of inflation (a realistic case from the early 1980s). The economic authorities of each country must decide on the degree of monetary austerity to pursue. In a closed economy, policymakers would presumably consider the short-run trade-off between inflation and unemployment (an issue that we discuss at length in Chapter 15) in deciding how tight the monetary policy should be.

In an open economy, however, there is another dimension to the problem. Each country knows that by having a tighter monetary policy than abroad, the exchange rate will appreciate, thereby reducing import prices and domestic inflation. Thus, each country will be tempted to aim its monetary policy to produce a currency appreciation, in order to benefit from the anti-inflationary effect. The problem is, however, that an exchange-rate appreciation in one economy is a currency depreciation for the other. Both countries cannot simultaneously achieve a currency appreciation vis-à-vis the other country—that is an obvious impossibility—but both countries can be hurt if they try!

If policymakers in the two countries act in a decentralized way, *without* policy coordination, then each will try to tighten monetary policy enough

---

[11] The example is based on Jeffrey Sachs, "Is There a Case for More Managed Exchange Rates?" in *The U.S. Dollar—Recent Developments, Outlook and Policy Options*, Federal Reserve Bank of Kansas City, August 1985.

Loose Money   Tight Money

	Loose Money	Tight Money
Loose Money	$SL_1 = 11$ $SL_2 = 11$	$SL_1 = 14$ $SL_2 = 6$
Tight Money	$SL_1 = 6$ $SL_2 = 14$	$SL_1 = 12$ $SL_2 = 12$

COUNTRY 1

Figure 14-10
Policy Coordination and the Payoff Matrix

to appreciate the exchange rate in the attempt to reduce inflation. Both countries will pursue highly contractionary monetary policies. The net effect will be no change in the exchange rate (since the monetary polices in the two countries end up canceling each other out), but both countries suffer the recessionary impact of very restrictive monetary policies.

This problem can be illustrated numerically. Suppose that each country has the option of tight money or loose money. Inflation starts at 6 percent in each country, with a 5 percent unemployment rate. If both countries pursue tight money, then a deep recession occurs in each country, with unemployment at 10 percent and inflation reduced to 2 percent. If both pursue loose money, there is no recession. Unemployment remains at 5 percent, but inflation stays high at 6 percent. If one country pursues tight money while the other pursues loose money, the tight-money country enjoys the anti-inflation benefits of a currency appreciation, while the loose-money country experiences a sharp currency depreciation and a jump in inflation. Assume, for illustrative purposes, that the tight-money country ends up with zero inflation and 6 percent unemployment in this case, while the loose-money country ends up with 10 percent inflation and 4 percent unemployment.

Suppose as well that the policymakers in each country have a "loss" function which represents the costs to society of different combinations of inflation and unemployment. Suppose that the loss function of each economy is the so-called *Okun misery index*, equal to the sum of unemployment and inflation.[12] Under our assumptions, the social losses if both pursue tight money are 12 in each country (= 10 + 2), the social losses if both pursue loose money are 11 (= 5 + 6), the social loss from loose money if the other pursues tight money is 14 (= 4 + 10), and the social loss from tight money if the other pursues loose money is 6 (= 6 + 0). These magnitudes are shown in the so-called "payoff matrix" in Figure 14-10.

---

[12] This index was coined by Arthur Okun, a leading economic policy advisor in the Kennedy and Johnson administrations, as an intuitive "thermometer" of macroeconomic pain.

Consider now the strategic interaction of the two central banks. Suppose, first, that the central banks can observe each others' actions but that they do not directly coordinate their policies. From the point of view of each individual country, it is always better to pursue tight money, no matter what the other country does, since this strategy minimizes the social loss *taking as given the action of the other country*. If the other central bank pursues tight money, then the loss from a tight-money policy at home is 12, while the loss from a loose-money policy would be 14. Similarly, if the other central bank pursues a loose-money policy, then the loss from tight money at home is 6, while the loss from loose money would be 11. In either case, it makes sense to pursue tight money.

Thus, both countries are led to pursue a tight-money policy, and both end up with a loss of 12. This outcome is known technically as a *Nash equilibrium,* in which each player in the "game" chooses the strategy that minimizes its own loss (or maximizes its gain) taking as given the action of the other player.

The problem is, however, that the combination of tight-money policies is inefficient, in that both countries can be made better off by a different choice of policies. Specifically, if both countries simply loosened up their monetary policy, they would both end up with smaller losses of 11. But in the absence of policy coordination, or adequate rules of the game that guide each country to the efficient policy, each country is induced to be overly restrictive in its monetary policy.

There is, however, a better option. First, the two countries could simply meet (say, at a summit of their political leaders) and agree to a coordinated loosening of monetary policy. Alternatively, the countries could choose policy rules which would reduce the problems of lack of coordination. Suppose, for example, that the countries were linked by a fixed exchange rate with a common monetary policy set by agreement. Then it would be easy for both countries to assent to the loose monetary policy, because each country would be confident that its currency would not depreciate relative to its partner's. The cooperative equilibrium would then be the efficient one.

It is not unusual when interdependent countries interact with each other in a noncooperative way, that the resulting equilibrium is inefficient. In many situations, it is likely that all countries could be made better off by a cooperative—or coordinated—choice of policies, though the size of those gains from coordination is not easy to pin down.[13] But achieving coordination is by no means easy. Not only is it necessary to identify the specific areas where gains can be attained, but it is also crucial to surmount the political obstacles to policy coordination. Empirical research, however, has strongly supported the view that coordination can lead to gains for the countries involved, though the size of those potential gains remains in dispute.

The industrialized world has actually experienced increased macroeconomic policy coordination since the mid-1980s. In February 1985, the U.S.

---

[13] For an attempt to measure empirically the gains from coordinations, see, for example, Warwick McKibbin and Jeffrey Sachs, *Global Linkages: Macroeconomic Interdependence and Cooperation in the World Economy* (Washington, D.C.: Brookings Institution, 1991).

dollar had reached an historically appreciated level of about 260 yen and 3.3 marks. At that point, central banks of the major industrialized countries started to intervene in the foreign-exchange markets in a coordinated way so as to drive down the value of the dollar. Finance ministers of the Group of Five (G-5) then met at the Plaza Hotel in New York in September 1985.[14] The so-called Plaza agreement stated that the dollar was overvalued and that central banks would coordinate their policies to drive down its value. After substantial decline in the value of the dollar over the next year and a half, finance ministers met again at the Louvre in February 1987 and agreed that the dollar had fallen enough and that exchange rates were roughly correct.

Beyond the actual extent of policy coordination, there have been various proposals for increased coordination. Ronald McKinnon of Stanford University has been a leading critic of the flexible exchange-rate regime that ties the United States, Europe, and Japan. He has argued for a return to fixed exchange rates among these regions (perhaps with very narrow bands), based on a system of close monetary coordination.[15] John Williamson, of the Institute for International Economics, has argued for relatively wide target zones for exchange rates, again supported by cooperative monetary arrangements.[16] Richard Cooper of Harvard University advanced a radical proposal in the mid-1980s for a long-term reconstruction of the world monetary system that would aim for a single currency and single central bank by the year 2010 for all the industrial democracies.[17] This would of course be the ultimate step in monetary coordination among countries. In light of recent developments in the European Community, which we analyze in the next section, his proposal for a single currency no longer looked radical by the end of the 1980s.

14-9 POLICY COORDINATION WITHIN EUROPE

The 12 countries that now form the European Community (EC)[18] took a bold step in 1985, when they decided to pursue the idea of creating a fully unified economic market without internal barriers—called the "single market"—with major steps to be completed by 1992 (hence the catchphrase Europe 1992). This objective has captured the imagination of Europeans and potential foreign investors, who visualize the prospects of a market of 320 million people without internal barriers. Successful fulfillment of this goal

---

[14]At the time, the G-5 included France, Japan, the United Kingdom, the United States, and West Germany.

[15] McKinnon first outlined his proposal shortly after the collapse of Bretton Woods in "A New Tripartite Monetary Arrangement or a Limping Dollar Standard?" *Essays in International Finance,* No. 176 (Princeton, N.J.: Princeton University Press, October 1974). A more recent and refined version of his proposal is "Monetary and Exchange Rate Policies for International Financial Stability: A Proposal," *Journal of Economic Perspectives,* Winter 1988.

[16] J. Williamson and M. Miller, "Targets and Indicators: A Blueprint for the International Coordination of Economic Policy," *Policy Analyses in International Economics,* Institute for International Economics, Washington, D.C. No. 22, September 1987.

[17] R. Cooper, "A Monetary System for the Future," *Foreign Affairs,* Fall 1984.

[18] The 12 are Belgium, Denmark, France, Germany, Greece, Ireland, Italy, Luxembourg, the Netherlands, Portugal, Spain, and the United Kingdom.

would require an extraordinary degree of coordination in economic policies among member countries.

At a broad level, there are two parts to Project 1992: economic integration, or the completion of the single market, and monetary integration, or the creation of a single currency. This process is planned to be completed in stages. The first stage began on July 1990 and encompasses the completion of the borderless internal market, participation of all member countries in a tighter European Monetary System of pegged exchange rates, and closer policy coordination. The next steps will be toward monetary union, with the aim of creating a single currency and single European central bank, though the exact timing of this step has not been specified yet. This monumental reform is likely to have major effects on the growth perspectives of the European Community, as analyzed in detail in Chapter 18.

Our focus here is on monetary coordination. Most members of the EC participate in the European Monetary System, an arrangement that regulates the currency parities between member countries of the European Community. It establishes a pegged central exchange rate for currencies, which can fluctuate vis-à-vis each other within a narrow band around that central rate. Member nations have been able to opt for a narrow band (which allows currencies to fluctuate only within 2.5 percent of the central rate) or a broader band (which permits fluctuations of up to 6 percent from the central rate). By late 1990, 8 of the 12 member countries of the EC were in the narrow band variant. Spain and the United Kingdom adopted the broad band of the ERM in June 1989 and October 1990, respectively. Greece and Portugal had not yet joined the ERM.

The experience of the ERM has been quite successful in stabilizing exchange rates. Exchange-rate variability among participants of the ERM was reduced by around three quarters compared to what they had before joining. As a result of coordination on exchange rates, inflation rates within the Community have converged substantially since the creation of the EMS in 1979. More importantly, convergence has been toward lower inflation. This is a result of Germany being at the center of the EMS, while the other countries must adjust to German monetary policy.[19] Thus, the system has facilitated the transmission of financial discipline from Germany to the other member countries.

The decision to move toward monetary union—either in the form of immutably fixed currency parities or in the form of a single currency for Europe—was adopted in 1990. The decision was also taken to create a European Central Bank. A single currency would obviously imply that member states lose the possibility of conducting independent monetary and exchange-rate policy. For that reason, the proposal for complete monetary integration remains controversial, and the specific mechanisms and timetable for proceeding are still hotly debated within Europe.

Whether it is beneficial for the EC to have a single currency is equivalent to asking whether the Community is an *optimum currency area* (OCA). Three decades ago, Robert Mundell explored this issue for the first time and proposed a criterion to define the optimum geographic area which should

---

[19] See the earlier discussion on this point in Chapter 10.

share a common currency (an OCA).[20] Suppose, following Mundell, that there exist two regions—East and West—and that there is a sudden rise in demand for Western goods and away from Eastern goods. This tends to create a boom in the West and a recession in the East.

Could these fluctuations be avoided? If the two regions have separate exchange rates, a depreciation of the East's currency (an appreciation of the West's) would stabilize demand. Alternatively, if labor and capital can move freely between regions, there would be no need for exchange-rate adjustments. Resources would move from the depressed East to the booming West. Factor mobility would be a substitute for exchange-rate changes. Mundell held that the East and West should have different currencies if there is no factor mobility between the regions, while they should have a common currency if factor mobility is high, since with high factor mobility there is less need for exchange-rate changes to stabilize the regions after a shift in demand. Interestingly, the United States is a fertile area to study the effects of monetary integration, since the 49 states form a full monetary union. A recent study concludes that capital mobility is the principal way that the U.S. economy absorbs state-specific shocks.[21]

The completion of the single market in 1992, with free movement of factors of production across members' borders would seem to fulfill Mundell's requirement for an optimum currency area. There are, however, many other arguments to be weighed in assessing the benefits and costs of a monetary union for Europe.[22] On the plus side is the elimination of transactions costs between member countries' currencies, estimated at no less than 0.5 percent of the Community's GDP. Another advantage of monetary union is the elimination of exchange-rate variability and uncertainty. Local and foreign investment are likely to respond positively to a reduction of uncertainty. Another argument in support of the single currency is that price stability is more likely to be achieved by a fully independent European Central Bank than by the individual central banks of each of the member countries. Individual central banks are more vulnerable to pressure from their own governments, which is especially strong at times of elections.

On the cost side, one finds the loss of independent exchange-rate policies or monetary policies for the member countries. Countries would no longer be able to devalue their currencies or to increase the money supply (under a floating-rate arrangement) in order to spur output and employment. Of course, the ability to achieve a higher level of output through monetary policy depends on there being an upward-sloping aggregate supply schedule. If the aggregate supply schedule is vertical, then the loss of monetary independence won't make any difference in terms of stabilization policy. Also, countries would no longer be able to pursue independent inflationary policies in order to collect seigniorage to cover government deficits.

---

[20] R. Mundell, "A Theory of Optimum Currency Areas," *American Economic Review*, September 1961.

[21] See Barry Eichengreen, "One Money for Europe? Lessons from the U.S. Currency Union," *Economic Policy*, April 1990.

[22] A recent report of the European Commission evaluates in detail the costs and benefits of the monetary union. See "One Market, One Money," *European Economy*, No. 44, October 1990.

14-10 SUMMARY

In this chapter we analyze macroeconomic policies under flexible exchange rates, the arrangement that exists among the large industrialized regions—the United States, Japan, and the European Community taken as a whole. With a flexible exchange-rate regime, the exchange rate is no longer a policy variable, but rather moves endogenously in response to other changes in the economy.

From a formal point of view, the case of floating exchange rates alters the use of the *IS-LM* apparatus. Since the position of the *IS* curve depends on the exchange rate (through its effects on trade flows), the *IS* now moves endogenously. The *LM* schedule, however, is exogenous under floating rates because the central bank determines the level of the money supply and thus the position of the *LM*.

Our base case is that of a small country with free capital mobility. In this framework, a fiscal expansion shifts the *IS* curve to the right and tends to increase the interest rate. Higher interest rates prompt a capital inflow and an appreciation of the currency, which in turn moves the *IS* back to the left. As long as the local interest rate is above the world rate, capital inflows will continue to appreciate the exchange rate and the *IS* will continue shifting to the left. In the final equilibrium, the *IS* returns to its original position and aggregate demand remains unchanged. In essence, the expansionary effects of the fiscal policy are offset by the contractionary effects of the currency appreciation.

We also consider a monetary expansion. An open-market purchase of bonds shifts the *LM* schedule downward. The interest rate tends to decline and begins to flow out of the country. As a result, the exchange rate depreciates. This depreciation increases the demand for exports, and thereby shifts the *IS* curve to the right. The new equilibrium is reached at the same initial interest rate and at a higher level of aggregate demand. Thus, for a small open economy with high capital mobility and flexible exchange rates, monetary policy expands aggregate demand through its effect on the exchange rate, rather than its effect on the interest rate as in the closed economy.

When dynamic adjustment is considered, a monetary expansion gives rise to the possibility of *exchange-rate overshooting*, in which the exchange rate initially depreciates by more than the proportionate increase in the money supply. It is also possible that the exchange rate moves as a result of anticipated future events even before any changes actually take place in the economy. For example, an anticipated future expansion of the money supply causes an immediate exchange-rate depreciation.

For a large country, the world interest rate cannot be taken as given. When a large economy undertakes a fiscal expansion, the world interest rate rises. In this case, the expansionary effect of fiscal policy is not completely offset by a currency appreciation. A monetary expansion by a large country reduces domestic and world interest rates.

When capital controls exist under a floating exchange rate, the current account must always balance. A fiscal expansion in this case raises aggregate demand and provokes a currency depreciation rather than an appreciation (there is no capital inflow to cause the exchange to appreciate). Interest rates, now divorced from world rates, increase. A money supply increase also raises output and depreciates the currency, while interest rates go down.

Policymakers often move several policy variables at the same time, rather than shifting one variable at a time as we have considered. If, for example, a large country such as the United States wants to improve its trade balance without reducing output, it can pursue a combination—"*policy mix*"—of fiscal contraction and monetary expansion. While both policies tend to improve the trade balance, their effects on output offset each other.

Policy coordination among *interdependent* economies may be beneficial because decentralized decision making—that is, each country acting on its own—can lead to undesirable macroeconomic outcomes. A case in point is anti-inflationary policy in an open economy. Each country acting on its own would produce a very contractionary monetary policy, because monetary restraint will tend to appreciate the exchange rate. Since both currencies cannot appreciate at the same time (one's appreciation is the other's depreciation), the incentive is for a bigger monetary contraction. A better option is to coordinate policies.

An interesting, and far-reaching case of policy coordination is Europe's quest for a single market in 1992. Monetary coordination occurs now in the framework of the European Monetary System, which regulates the currency parities of member countries of the European Community. The goal, however, is to reach *monetary union,* that is, a single currency. This can be justified on the grounds that Europe would be an "*optimum currency area*" in 1992 because factors of production would then move freely across member countries' borders.

Key Concepts

dynamic adjustment   interest arbitrage
policy coordination   monetary union
exchange-rate overshooting   policy mix
interdependent economies   optimum currency area

Problems and Questions

1. Analyze the mechanisms that make endogenous the *LM* curve in the case of fixed exchange rates and the *IS* curve in the case of flexible exchange rates. How does this relate to whether the money supply or the exchange rate is endogenously determined in the economy?

2. Consider a monetary expansion in a small economy.
  a. What happens to the nominal exchange rate?
  b. Would the exchange rate vary more when exports and imports are very sensitive to changes in the exchange rate or when they are not?

3. Use the *IS-LM* model to analyze what happens to the nominal exchange rate when the price level rises. What happens to the real exchange rate? Can the nominal and real exchange rate move in opposite directions? Why?

4. Assume that the governments of countries A, B, C, and D have decided to use either monetary or fiscal policy to increase aggregate demand and output. Which policy will achieve this objective for each country? Describe also the effects of the policies on the price level.
  a. Country A has a fixed exchange rate and the aggregate supply is represented by the normal Keynesian case.

  b. Country B has a flexible exchange rate and the aggregate supply is represented by the extreme Keynesian case.

  c. Country C has a fixed exchange rate and the aggregate supply is represented by the classic case.

  d. Country D has a flexible exchange rate and the aggregate supply is represented by the classic case.

5. Analyze the effect of a monetary contraction on the exchange rate in a small economy. In which sense is there an ''undershooting'' of the exchange rate? How does your answer change when you consider that the interest-rate arbitrage condition must hold in the short and long runs?

6. What happens to aggregate demand and its components (consumption, investment, government expenditures, and the trade balance) when government spending increases? Consider the following cases:

  a. A small open economy.

  b. A large country. (Analyze the effects in the country and in the rest of the world.)

7. Describe the effects of a monetary expansion on the interest rate, the exchange rate, and output in a large open economy. What happens to the rest of the world?

8. Suppose a special case in which the trade balance depends only on the exchange rate. If there are complete capital controls, what would happen to the exchange rate if government expenditures increase?

9. Consider a large open economy in which the government desires to increase output without changing the interest rate. Why would the government want to do this? What type of policy mix would you recommend? What are the effects of this policy on the exchange rate and the trade balance?

10. Discuss why coordination of anti-inflation policies between two may be beneficial for both. How does this analysis apply under fixed exchange rates?

11. Analyze the potential gains from monetary union in Europe 1992. Can Europe be considered an optimum currency area? Why?

APPENDIX

Now we solve the small-country, open-economy model under flexible exchange rates. The linear model is the same as that used in the appendix to Chapter 13. The difference lies in the strategy to solve it. Now the exchange rate is no longer fixed, but moves freely in response to market forces—that is, the exchange rate is endogenous. The money stock, on the other hand, is determined by the economic authorities.

The aim is to obtain equilibrium values for prices, output, and the exchange rate as a function of the exogenous variables. We repeat here the *IS* and *LM* equations of Chapter 13 (expressions A.2 and A.3 in the appendix to that chapter) and make use of the interest parity condition ($i = i^*$):

$$Q^D = \phi_0[c^F[(Q - T)]^F - cT + \bar{I} + dMPK^E - (a + b)i^* + G]$$
$$+ \phi_1[h_0 A^* + (h_2 - h_0)P_m^* + h_2(E - P)] \tag{A.1}$$

where

$$\phi_0 = \frac{1 - h_1}{1 - c(1 - h_1)}; \quad \phi_1 = \frac{1}{1 - c(1 - h_1)}$$

$$(M - P) = vQ^D - fi^* \tag{A.2}$$

Equations A.1 and A.2 (*IS* and *LM*, respectively) are sufficient to determine aggregate demand. To solve for the global equilibrium of the economy, we also need aggregate supply. This opens up the usual three possibilities.

Classical

Aggregate supply is fixed at the full-employment level of output ($Q^S = \bar{Q}$). Thus,

$$Q = \bar{Q} = Q^D \tag{A.3a}$$

To obtain the equilibrium price level, we cannot just replace $\bar{Q} = Q^D$ in equation (A.1) and solve for P, because the solution for P would depend on the exchange rate (E), another endogenous variable. Using $Q^D = \bar{Q}$, P can be solved directly from the equilibrium condition of the money market, because all the other variables on that equation (M, $\bar{Q}$, i^*) are exogenous.

$$P = M - v\bar{Q} + fi^* \tag{A.3b}$$

Now we can substitute the equilibrium values of Q and P into the aggregate demand equation, to obtain the solution for E as a function of exogenous variables only.

$$E = M - a_1 P_M^* + a_2\bar{Q} - a_3(c^F[Q - T]^F$$
$$- cT + \bar{I} + dMPK^E - G) + a_4 i^* - a_5 A^* \tag{A.4}$$

where

$$a_1 = \frac{h_2 - h_0}{h_2}; \quad a_2 = \frac{1 - \phi h_2 v}{\phi_1 h_2}; \quad a_3 = \frac{\phi_0}{\phi_1 h_2}; \quad a_4 = \frac{\phi_1 h_2 f + \phi_0 (a + b)}{\phi_1 h_2};$$

$$a_5 = \frac{h_0}{h_2}; \quad \phi_1 = \frac{h_0}{[1 - c(1 - h_1)]}$$

and

$$\phi_0 = \frac{(1 - h_1)}{[1 - c(1 - h_1)]}$$

(the open-economy Keynesian multiplier).

Changes in the money stock result in a one-for-one response in both P and E in the classical case. Thus, the *real* exchange rate is not affected, and the trade balance remains unchanged. Note that an increase in absorption has the effect of reducing E, because an increase in absorption must be completely offset by a reduction in the trade balance for output to remain unchanged.

Extreme Keynesian

The aggregate supply schedule is horizontal at the exogenous price level $\bar{P}$, as shown here:

$$P = \bar{P} \tag{A.5a}$$

In this case, the equilibrium level of output cannot be determined directly, making $Q = Q^D$ in equation (A.1). Why? Because the solution would have Q depending on the exchange rate, which is an endogenous variable (another way of saying that such a "solution" is not a solution). Once again, the equation describing the *LM* curve comes to our rescue. The equilibrium level of output can be determined directly from equation (A.2), which leaves output as a function of exogenous variables only:

$$Q = \left(\frac{1}{v}\right)(M + fi^* - \bar{P}) \tag{A.5b}$$

We now substitute the equilibrium values of P and Q just obtained into the *IS* equation and solve for the exchange rate.

$$E = b_0 M + b_1 i^* + b_2 \bar{P} - b_3 P_m^* - b_4 A^*$$
$$- b_5 (c^F [Q - T]^F - cT + \bar{I} + dMPK^E + G) \tag{A.6}$$

where

$$b_0 = \frac{1}{\phi_1 h_2 v}; \quad b_1 = \frac{f + (a + b)\phi_0 v}{\phi_1 h_2 v}; \quad b_2 = \frac{(\phi_1 h_2 v - 1)}{\phi_1 h_2 v}; \quad b_3 = \frac{(h_2 - h_0)}{h_2};$$

$$b_4 = \frac{h_0}{h_2}; \quad b_5 = \frac{\phi_0}{\phi_1 h_2}$$

We can see from equations (A.6) and (A.5b) that a monetary expansion depreciates the exchange rate ($\Delta E = b_0 \, \Delta M$, from A.6) and increases output ($\Delta Q = \Delta M / v$ from A.5b). Fiscal policy has no effect on output in this model, and thus no fiscal variable appears in equation (A.5b), for the reasons noted in the chapter: the fiscal expansion is offset by the currency appreciation.

The fact that the fiscal expansion appreciates the exchange rate is seen in equation (A.6): $\Delta E = -b_5 \Delta G$.

Basic Keynesian

Algebraically, this is the most difficult case to solve. For a given price level, we can solve for output (Q) and the exchange rate (E) as a function of P, which leads exactly to equations (A.5b) and (A.6). But this is not a final solution, since now the price level is not given. Equation (A.5b) does not tell us the equilibrium level of output, but only aggregate demand. To close the model we need to incorporate aggregate supply, whose linear form is the same as in the appendix to Chapter 13.[1]

$$Q^S = g - z(w - P) \tag{A.7}$$

The equilibrium of aggregate supply and aggregate demand determines the solution for the price level (P) and output (Q) from equations (A.5b) and (A.7).

$$P = \frac{1}{1 + zv}(M + fi^*) + \frac{v}{1 + zv}(zw - g) \tag{A.8a}$$

$$Q = \frac{1}{1 + zv}(g) - \frac{z}{1 + zv}(w) + \frac{z}{1 + zv}(M + fi^*) \tag{A.8b}$$

Finally, the equilibrium exchange rate may be obtained by replacing the solution for P back into equation (A.6), which leads to

$$E = c_0 M + c_1 i^* + c_2(zw - g) - c_3 P_m^* - c_5[c^F[Q - T]^F$$
$$- (c - h_1)T + \bar{I} + dMPK^E + G + h_0 Q^{D*}] \tag{A.9}$$

where

$$c_0 = \frac{\phi_1 h_2 + z}{\phi_1 h_2(1 + zv)}; \quad c_1 = \frac{f(z + \phi_1 h_2) + (a + b)\phi_0(1 + zv)}{\phi_1 h_2(1 + zv)};$$

$$c_2 = \frac{(\phi_1 h_2 v - 1)}{\phi_1 h_2(1 + zv)}; \quad c_3 = \frac{(h_2 - h_0)}{h_2}; \quad c_4 = \frac{h_0}{h_2}; \quad c_5 = \frac{\phi_0}{\phi_1 h_2}$$

The results corroborate the graphical analysis performed in this chapter. Expansionary monetary policy raises both output and the price level, as shown in equations (A.8a) and (A.8b), and causes the exchange rate to depreciate. Fiscal expansion has no effect on output and the price level and causes the exchange rate to appreciate.

---

[1] Once again, we approximate (w/P) as $(w - P)$.

chapter 15 ═══════════════════════════════

Inflation and Unemployment

One of the most daunting problems of macroeconomic policy is the simultaneous management of inflation and unemployment. As we saw in Chapter 11, inflation can result when the government covers its expenditures by using seigniorage, that is, by printing money. Inflation is better controlled by keeping a firm grip on the budget and avoiding the need for seigniorage finance. In practice, however, controlling the budget deficit is rarely enough to end an inflation. Even when a fiscal imbalance is brought under control, inflation often persists, at least for a while. Very often, it seems, the economy must experience a period of high unemployment before the inflation returns to lower levels. This chapter focuses on the link between unemployment and anti-inflation policies and the challenge of policy to reduce the inflation rate at the least possible cost in terms of higher unemployment and lost output.

15-1 Supply Shocks and Inflation

Chapter 11 gave us largely a demand-side explanation of inflation: prices rise because aggregate demand increases following a rise in the money supply. Here we shall see that price increases can also result from shifts in aggregate supply, even when the position of the aggregate demand curve is constant. Consider the two different cases depicted in Figure 15-1. In Figure 15-1a, we see an increase in the price level caused by a rise in aggregate demand, due, perhaps, to an expansionary fiscal policy, the case analyzed at length in Chapter 11. In Figure 15-1b, we see an increase in the price level caused by a *contractionary* shift in aggregate supply (contractionary in the sense that desired supply is reduced at any given level of prices).

Types of Supply Shocks

Supply shocks can take many different forms. In agricultural economies, adverse weather conditions or crop pests can reduce a harvest and lead to a rise in prices together with a fall in output. Alternatively, an increase in

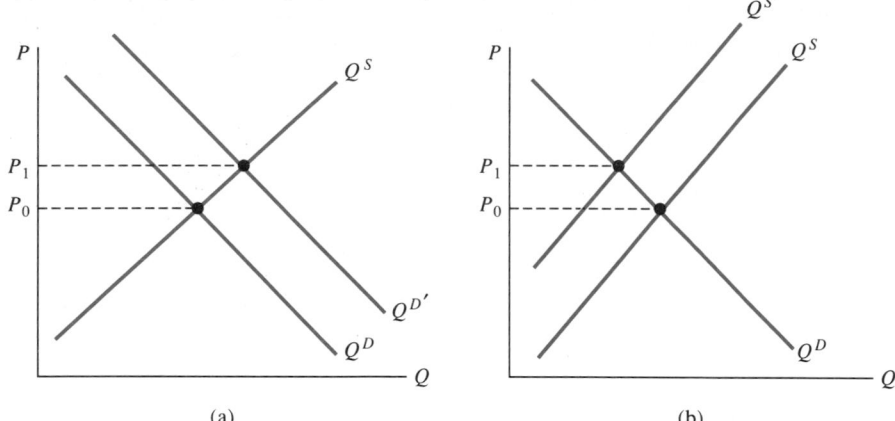

Figure 15-1
Demand and Supply Changes as the Source of a Rise in the Price Level:
(a) A Demand Increase; (b) a Supply Contraction

wages negotiated in a union contract can be interpreted as a supply shock because the rise in the nominal wage induces a leftward shift in the aggregate supply schedule. Or take the case of the worldwide oil price increases of 1973–1974 and 1979–1980 (we shall study this event in detail in the next chapter). As oil, an input in the production of virtually countless goods and services, became more expensive, firms found that the marginal cost of producing an additional unit of output had gone up. Therefore, the aggregate supply shifted to the left. At the new equilibrium after the supply shock, the price level is higher and the level of output lower.

A different—and somewhat more gruesome—adverse supply shock was the black plague that ravaged the population of Europe in the Middle Ages. During the second half of the fourteenth century, millions of people throughout Europe died as a consequence of this tragic epidemic. England was hit particularly hard by the plague. The economic effects of the black plague can be roughly represented as a major adverse supply shock affecting labor input. At any given price, then, the amount of output supplied went down. As a result, output declined and the price level increased, the situation depicted in Figure 15-2b. Recent research by economic historians shows that the price level increased by about 50 percent during the period in England, after having fallen for most of the early part of the century.[1] Figure 15-2a shows how the price level spiked in England at the time of the plague.

In actual experience, long and persistent inflations, in which prices continue to rise over a period of several years, are usually hard to explain by supply shocks alone. A stubborn inflation requires a persistent shift in aggregate demand or aggregate supply. It is easy to see how the aggregate demand curve can continue to rise over time. The government can continually issue new money in order to finance an ongoing budget deficit, for example. It is

---

[1] See Douglas C. North and Robert P. Thomas, *The Rise of the Western World: A New Economic History* (Cambridge: Cambridge University Press, 1973).

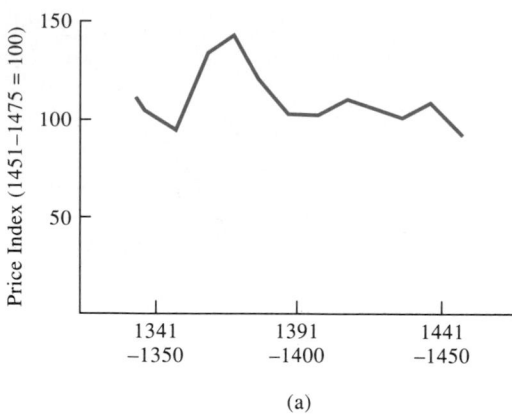

(a)

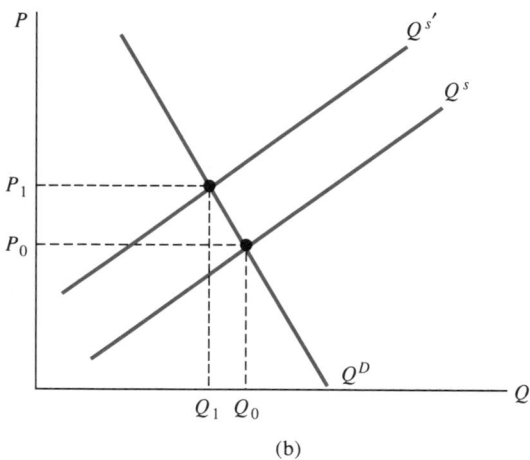

(b)

Figure 15-2

The Black Plague and the Price Level in England

(From Douglas C. North and Robert P. Thomas, The Rise of the Western World: A New Economic History, *Cambridge University Press, Cambridge, 1973, Figure 7.1.)*

harder to envision an ongoing shift in the aggregate supply schedule. Many kinds of supply shocks, the rise in oil prices being a prime example, tend to be one-time events. And we shall see that the other major kind of supply shock, a rise in nominal wages, usually will not continue for several years without accompanying increases in aggregate demand.

Wages and Aggregate Supply Shifts

When the wage is predetermined each period, any shift in that wage can be seen as a kind of supply shock, in the narrow sense that the supply curve shifts up and to the left when the nominal wage increases. Some economists might protest this interpretation, especially because "shocks" are usually thought of as exogenous (they come from sources outside the economy) and the nominal wage is an endogenous variable. Over these objections, we shall continue to view these wage shifts as shocks. Keep in mind, however, that a "wage shock" is often an endogenous response to other events within the macroeconomy.

The presence of long-term wage contracts makes it likely that nominal wage changes in the current period are determined by decisions taken in the past. A union wage contract signed this year, for example, often specifies the rate at which the union wage is to increase in the next three years. Consider, for example, the wage contract between United Parcel Service and 115,000 workers represented by the International Brotherhood of Teamsters, Chauffeurs, Warehousemen and Helpers of America. After several rounds of negotiations, in 1987 the parties signed a three-year labor contract calling for wage increases of 2.4 percent in August of 1987, 1988, and 1989. The agreement also included lump-sum payments of $1,000 for full-time employees and $500 for part-time workers in each of the three years.[2] In each year, a predetermined wage increase was set by terms of the contract, not by the contemporaneous conditions in the labor market. U.S. union contracts typically specify a path for wages over a three-year period, while union contracts in most other countries are shorter, usually only for one year.

We have noted before that wages in high-inflation countries are often linked by contract or by law to the inflation rate of the previous period, through the use of a wage indexation clause. In Chile during the period from 1979 to 1982, national labor codes mandated the use of wage indexation clauses. Workers participating in collective bargaining had a guaranteed nominal wage increase equal to 100 percent of the previous year's inflation. This labor legislation made it very difficult to slow inflation in the economy, and was one of the factors behind the deep depression in 1982, which, in turn, led to the elimination of the indexation law.

The existence of long-term union contracts means that nominal wage increases for different groups of workers are renegotiated at different times. Some unions are negotiating new contracts while other unions are living out contracts signed in earlier years. In any given period, only a fraction of contractual wages change according to new negotiations, while the rest are governed by earlier agreements. This situation is known as a case of *overlapping* contracts. When all wage agreements are renegotiated at the same time, the situation is called a case of *synchronized* contracts.

The "preprogramming" of wage increases in long-term, overlapping wage contracts raises a profound problem for the control of inflation. If an aggregate supply schedule is shifting to the left because of *predetermined* wage increases, policymakers will be unable to maintain both price stability and full employment. In such a case, tight controls on aggregate demand may be able to hold prices constant, but at the cost of rising unemployment. This poses a painful dilemma for those who manage macroeconomic policy. In short, they must choose how much to control inflation *versus* unemployment in the short run. This dilemma is at the heart of our discussion in this chapter.

---

[2] See William Davis et al., "Collective Bargaining in 1990," *Monthly Labor Review*, January 1990.

15-2 WAGE-PRICE DYNAMICS AND THE PROBLEMS OF STABILIZATION

Let us look first at a situation in which wages are set by one-year labor contracts negotiated between unions and employers. We will assume that in the current period, the wage is negotiated for next year, *before* the price level P_{+1} is known—that is, before we know the rate of inflation $\hat{P}_{+1} = (P_{+1} - P)/P$. (The "^" over a variable indicates a percentage change.) Now we need to know some of the factors that influence the wage level set by the contract. According to typical models of wage setting, two factors are crucial in determining the wage bargain, the rate of unemployment at the time of negotiations and the expected rate of inflation between the current year and the next year.

Our analysis starts with the simple idea that wages are influenced significantly by the conditions prevailing in the labor market. We used this assumption earlier when we said that nominal wages adjust to any gap between actual output and potential output. Here, we will elaborate on that basic idea with one more accurate specification that now the level of output affects the change in *real* wages, not just nominal wages.

When unemployment is low, employers find it hard to attract new workers, and they try to prevent their own employees from accepting jobs elsewhere. Under these conditions, the bargaining power of unions and workers is strong. In "tight" labor markets like this, real wages tend to increase. When unemployment prevails, on the other hand, workers and unions find themselves in a weak position because the firm can easily attract new workers. They have a hard time obtaining pay increases, and workers may even have to accept cuts in their real wages.

Figure 15-3 presents this idea graphically. The usual downward-sloping demand schedule, together with an upward-sloping labor supply curve (which we take to be the normal case[3]), represent the labor market. Full equilibrium occurs at the wage $(w/P)^f$ and the level of employment L^f. But let us say that real wages are not so flexible as to guarantee full equilibrium in any given year. Because of time lags in wage adjustments, wages generally differ from $(w/P)^f$, and they will adjust to $(w/P)^f$ only gradually over time. Among other things, this lack of rapid adjustment to equilibrium may reflect the fact that with overlapping contracts, only some wages adjust at any given time, while other wages are locked in place by previously negotiated contracts.

Consider the wage $(w/P)_1$, which is above equilibrium. At that wage level, more people would like to work than firms are prepared to hire. With a high level of unemployment, there is pressure on real wages to fall. At wage $(w/P)_2$, however, firms would be searching for very scarce workers. In such a tight labor market, unemployment will be low and real wages are bound to rise. We can formalize this idea that the *change* in real wages depends on the

---

[3] Recall that there are both substitution and income effects at work when the real wage increases. The labor supply is upward sloping if the substitution effect dominates the income effect, as we saw in Section 3-2, Chapter 3.

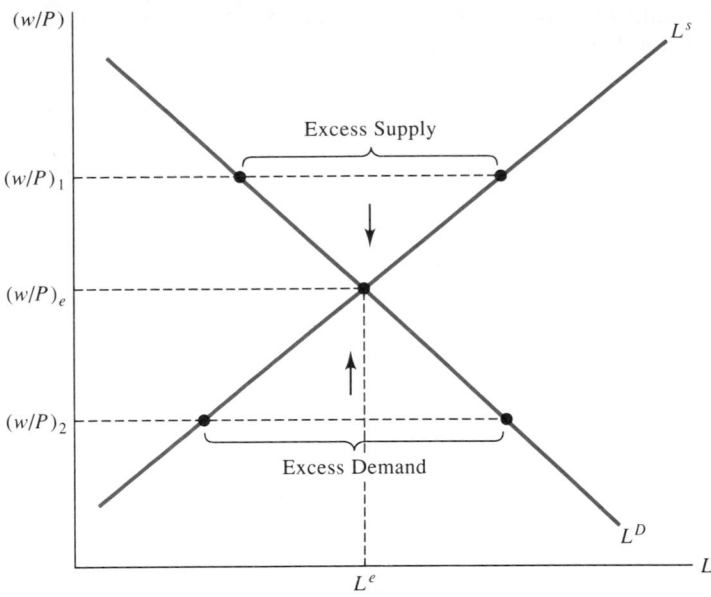

Figure 15-3

Real Wages and the Conditions of the Labor Market

level of unemployment by writing

$$(w/\hat{P})_{+1} = -b(U - U_n) \tag{15.1}$$

where U represents the rate of unemployment in the current period, U_n is the "natural rate of unemployment," and b is the coefficient determining the response of real wages to a given amount of unemployment. Also, $(w/\hat{P})_{+1} = [(w/P)_{+1} - (w/P)]/(w/P)$.

The *natural rate of unemployment U_n* will play an important role in the analysis that follows. As we shall see, this rate is essentially the long-term equilibrium rate of unemployment, in the sense that the economy will tend to move in the long term to the unemployment rate U_n. It is sometimes called the seemingly contradictory name of "full-employment rate of unemployment."[4]

Note that even in long-term equilibrium, an economy will not have zero unemployment. There will be some workers who are without jobs and are looking for work. Some workers will have quit their old jobs and will be searching for new jobs, some will have recently joined the labor force (such

---

[4] Milton Friedman gave the name "natural rate" to the unemployment rate in long-term equilibrium. In his paper "The Role of Monetary Policy," *American Economic Review*, March 1968, p. 8, he said: "The 'natural rate of unemployment' . . . is the level [of unemployment] that would be ground out by the Walrasian system of general equilibrium equations, provided there is embedded in them the actual structural characteristics of the labor and commodity markets, including market imperfections, stochastic variability in demands and supplies, the cost of gathering information about job vacancies and labor availabilities, the costs of mobility, and so on."

as recent school graduates) and will be hunting for their first jobs, and some will have lost their old jobs but will lack the skills to earn even the minimum wage at other jobs. Thus, even though we may speak of "full employment" when the economy is in long-term macroeconomic equilibrium, there may still be a sizable part of the labor force without jobs.

While the concept is of fundamental macroeconomic importance, the term "natural" is surely a misnomer. As we shall note in Chapter 16, the natural rate of unemployment will be affected by many particular characteristics of the labor force, such as the demographic composition between young and old workers, the degree of unionization, the nature of technological shocks hitting the economy, and the skills of the work force. Governments may even be able to affect the natural rate of unemployment through special labor market programs such as job retraining and programs to match job seekers with job vacancies.

Equation (15.1) says that the percentage change in the real wage between the current year and the next one responds to the rate of unemployment in the current period. If unemployment is above the natural rate, the real wage will fall; if it is below U_n, the real wage will rise. Notice that the effect is not instantaneous. Labor market conditions in this period affect the wage rate in the following period. Currently, the wage level is determined by decisions made in the previous period. Thus, we can say that wage adjustment is sluggish, or that wages are "sticky." This assumption of lagged adjustment is consistent with the empirical evidence and with the institutional characteristics of the labor market.

The percentage change of a fraction (X/Y) is equal to the percentage change of X minus the percentage change of Y. That is, $(X/Y) = \hat{X} - \hat{Y}$. Therefore, we can rewrite equation (15.1) as

$$\hat{w}_{+1} - \hat{P}_{+1} = -b(U - U_n) \tag{15.2}$$

And because a wage contract normally specifies the nominal wage level rather than the real wage level (except in the case of complete indexation), the nominal wage selected this period for the coming year will be

$$\hat{w}_{+1} = \hat{P}_{+1} - b(U - U_n) \tag{15.3}$$

When wage contracts are set for next period, employers and workers agree on the wage that will prevail, but they cannot observe in advance the rate of inflation that will occur. Therefore, they must use their best guess, that is, their *expectation*, to forecast inflation in the next period. Let us denote the expected inflation between this period and the next as $\hat{P}^e_{+1} = (P^e_{+1} - P)/P$. Note that we assume that both parties know the contemporaneous price level P when negotiations are taking place; the real problem is to make a prediction about the price level next year, P_{+1}. We should therefore amend (15.3) to accommodate the fact that the nominal wage is set according to *expected* inflation, not actual inflation:

$$\hat{w}_{+1} = \hat{P}^e_{+1} - b(U - U_n) \tag{15.4}$$

Equation (15.4) is sometimes called the *Phillips curve* equation, following the empirical investigations of A. W. Phillips who was professor at the London School of Economics (and whose work we discuss shortly). In general, a "Phillips curve equation" is a relationship that links inflation (either in prices or wages) to the level of unemployment. The use of the

Phillips curve relationship is widespread, though as we shall see, the precise specification of the Phillips curve depends heavily on the theory of wages and prices being put forward by the researcher.

Dynamic Links of Aggregate Supply and Aggregate Demand

We have now developed a dynamic Keynesian model. Within a given period, nominal wages are based on past agreements; that is, they are *predetermined*. Between periods, wages move according to inflationary expectations and the unemployment rate (relative to the natural rate). The dynamic properties of this model, that is, how the variables change from period to period, are extremely interesting. For example, today's level of aggregate demand not only has an effect on the current level of output and the price level, but also on future output and prices through the effects on wage negotiations.

In Figure 15-4, we see a graphic representation of this behavior. Consider a case in which nominal wages are rising in the current period, perhaps because unemployment was low in the previous period, or because back then inflationary expectations were high. The increase in nominal wages raises the cost of production, thereby shifting the aggregate supply curve, from Q^S_{-1} to Q^S in Figure 15-4. At this point, policymakers have several demand management options at their disposal, none of them very pleasant.

If the authorities do nothing, that is, if they keep aggregate demand constant ($Q^D = Q^D_{-1}$), the economy will experience a drop in output (from Q_0 to Q_1) and an increase in the price level, that is, inflation, between P_0 and P_1. This situation is represented by point A in the graph. Suppose instead that the authorities have taken a staunch anti-inflation stand. They will not tolerate the inflationary consequences of increasing wages, and they tighten fiscal and monetary policies to avoid the price level increase. The aggregate demand curve shifts back to Q^D_1, and equilibrium occurs at point B. Inflation has been avoided (since $P = P_{-1} = P_0$), but the cost in terms of falling output is significant (the distance BE in the graph).

Figure 15-4
Wage Adjustment and the Aggregate Demand-Aggregate Supply Framework

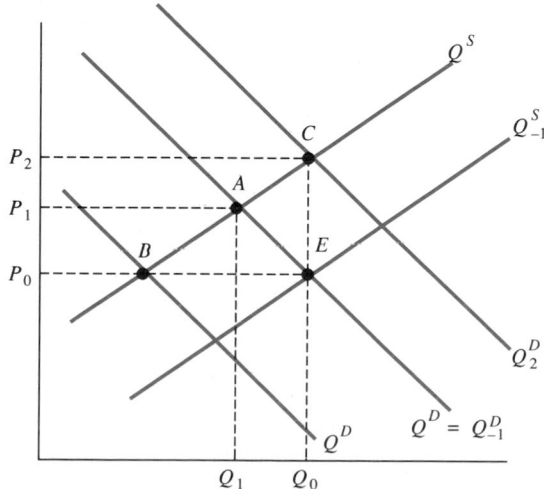

Or perhaps policymakers are extremely concerned about adverse effects on output and employment. If they expand aggregate demand to Q_2^D, output will not be affected by the rise in nominal wages, but the price level will increase significantly, as shown at point C. The policy of preserving full employment by allowing aggregate demand to expand as much as necessary is called a policy of *accommodation:* expansionary policies are used to increase aggregate demand and offset the negative effects of the wage increase on aggregate supply. In other words, aggregate demand policy accommodates the supply shock.

This brings us to an important point. In general, starting from a situation in which inflation expectations—which have been factored into nominal wage contracts—are positive, there is a *trade-off between price stability and employment*. An accommodation policy attempts to protect employment and output, but at the cost of higher inflation rates. Staunch anti-inflation policies can achieve price stability, or at least low inflation rates, but at the cost of increasing unemployment.

A Brief History of the Phillips Curve

Although the Phillips curve bears the name of A. W. Phillips, after his empirical work on unemployment and money wages for the United Kingdom, it was not Phillips but Irving Fisher who was the first to study the relationship between inflation and unemployment.[5]

Phillips's study of this phenomenon was not as refined as current work on the subject. He focused only on nominal wages and the actual rate of unemployment, disregarding inflationary expectations and the natural rate of unemployment, concepts that were elaborated in the decade following Phillips's original study. Thus, Phillips's original equation was specified as

$$\hat{w} = \text{constant} - bU$$

where b is the coefficient determining the response of the nominal wage to the current unemployment rate.

In this form, the Phillips curve may be graphed as shown in Figure 15-5. This relationship proved remarkably stable for some countries and some periods of time until the end of the 1960s. Over time, however, the use of inflation rather than wage changes became the standard feature of Phillips curve analysis (we say more about this in the next section). Figure 15-5b shows the curve plotted for inflation and unemployment in the United States during the period 1961–1969, one of the best known examples of a stable Phillips curve. As Figure 15-5b shows, the relationship between inflation and unemployment during this period is exactly that predicted by Phillips's original analysis.

---

[5] Phillips's work is presented in his article "The Relation Between Unemployment and the Rate of Change of Money Wages in the United Kingdom, 1861–1957," *Economica,* November 1958. Irving Fisher's piece is titled "A Statistical Relation Between Unemployment and Price Changes," *International Labor Review,* June 1926. This was reprinted in the *Journal of Political Economy,* under a section called "Lost and Found," in the issue of March/April 1973. In an attempt to do posthumous justice to Fisher, the article was retitled "I Discovered the Phillips Curve."

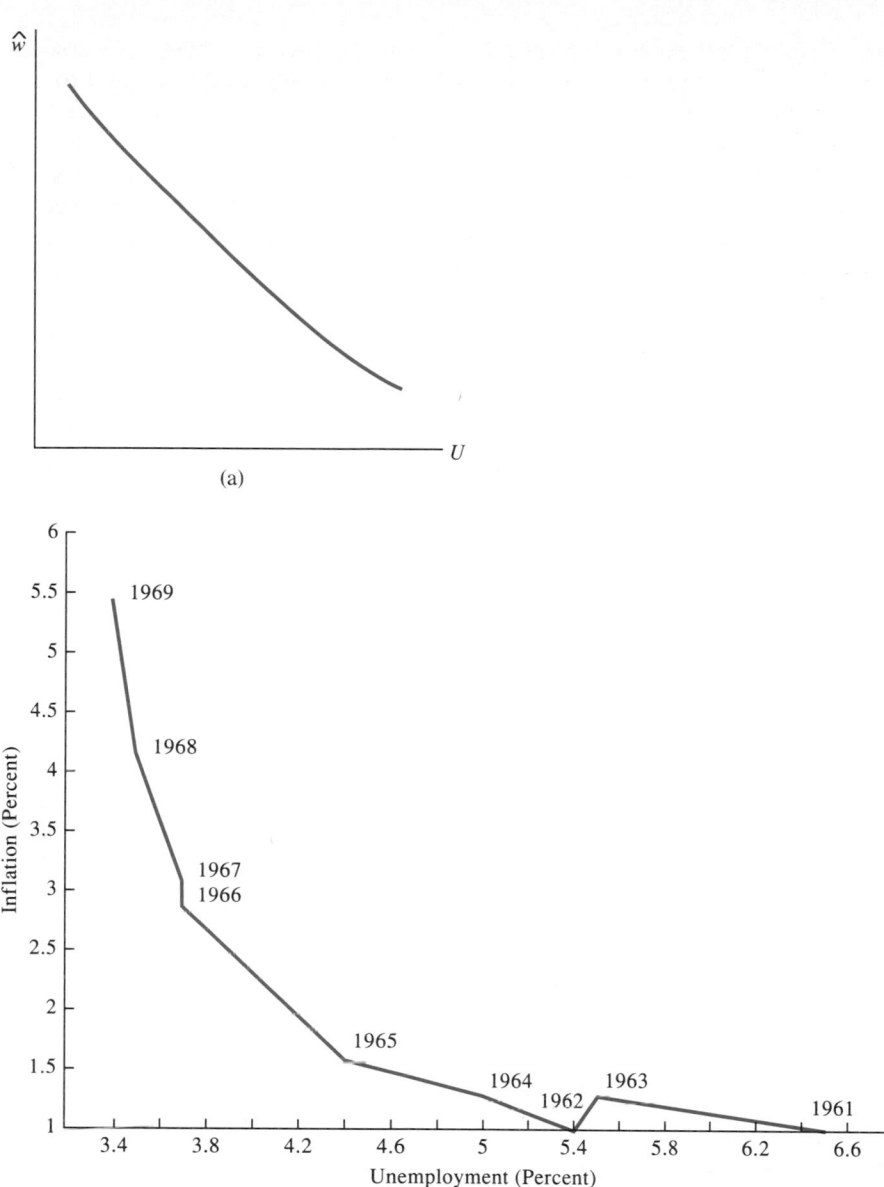

Figure 15-5
(a) The Original Phillips Curve (b) Inflation and Unemployment in the United States, 1961–1969

(From Organization of Petroleum Exporting Countries, Main Economic Indicators, *various issues.)*

However, Phillips's representation fails to account for the fact that the *real* wage is what matters, both to workers and employers. Workers are not concerned with the money wage *per se* but with the purchasing power of the wage. Employers are not concerned with the nominal wage *per se* but with the cost of labor relative to the price of output. This observation has led some prominent economists to question the validity of the Phillips curve as it was originally formulated. Milton Friedman and Edmund Phelps argued that since the real wage was what mattered, the change in nominal wages had to be corrected by inflationary expectations.[6] This led to a formulation such as the one in equation (15.2).

As inflation increased in the 1970s, it turned out that Friedman and Phelps were not only right in theory but correct in practice. Attempts made during the 1970s to predict inflation using the original Phillips curve were notoriously unsuccessful. The simple, observable regularity between the rate of increase in nominal wages and unemployment had disappeared. For any given level of unemployment, nominal wage inflation was higher in the early 1970s than it had been in the 1960s. Thus, the Phillips curve began to *shift up*. The best explanation was that inflationary expectations were also rising, meaning that $\hat{w}_{+1}$ was increasing at any given level of U.

Nonetheless, we still have a puzzle. If the Friedman-Phelps version of the Phillips curve is the correct one, how was it possible that the original representation by Phillips worked so well for so long, both for the pre–World War II British data and for the United States in the 1950s and 1960s? The answer seems to be rooted in the characteristics of the world economy at different periods. Before World War II, and in the 1950s and 1960s, there was remarkable long-run stability in prices in the United Kingdom and the United States. Inflation rates were generally low, and expectations of inflation must also have been low and stable. Therefore, for this period of time, it mattered little in the statistical analysis of wage inflation if $\hat{P}^e_{+1}$ were accurately measured, or if it were treated as a constant term in the wage equation. In the 1970s, there was a large expansion of the money supply in many countries, and the worldwide fixed exchange-rate system broke down. Inflation began to rise, and inflationary expectations also began to shift upward and become more variable. At that point, measures of $\hat{P}^e_{+1}$ became very important to statistical estimates of the wage and price equations.

Price Inflation and the Phillips Curve

Having seen how the Phillips curve links nominal wage changes, expected inflation, and unemployment, we can add an equation linking prices and wages so that we can study price dynamics as well. Let us reconsider the special case we examined in Chapter 3, in which output is a linear function of labor input.

Suppose that each unit of labor produces $(1/\alpha)$ units of output. Then the production function at the current period is given by

$$Q = \frac{L}{\alpha} \tag{15.5}$$

[6] The original articles where they presented their views are Milton Friedman, "The Role of Monetary Policy," *American Economic Review*, March 1968, and Edmund Phelps, "Money Wage Dynamics and Labor Market Equilibrium," *Journal of Political Economy*, Part 2, July/August 1968.

Since α units of labor are needed to produce one unit of output, labor costs are αw for each unit of output. The price of output can then be determined as[7]

$$P = \alpha w \tag{15.6}$$

With this set of assumptions, the aggregate supply curve is flat in any period (that is, we have the "extreme Keynesian" case). Since wages will change between periods, however, the flat aggregate supply curve shifts up and down between periods depending on the level of unemployment and the nature of inflationary expectations.

Under these conditions, the percentage rate of wage change will also be equal to the rate of price inflation:

$$\hat{P} = \hat{w}$$

$$\tag{15.7}$$

Now, we can substitute equation (15.7) back into expression (15.2) to obtain a price inflation version of the expectations-augmented Phillips curve:

$$\hat{P}_{+1} = \hat{P}^e_{+1} - b(U - U_n) \tag{15.8}$$

15-3 EXPECTATIONS FORMATION MECHANISMS AND THE PHILLIPS CURVE

So far, we have discussed the issue of expectations without formal details. We now address the question of how expectations are formed. This is a crucial question, because the trade-off between inflation and unemployment depends on the specific mechanisms used by economic agents to forecast future inflation. Economists have proposed many different mechanisms to account for the formation of inflationary expectations, though none of them has proven to be completely satisfactory in practice. We start with the case of *adaptive expectations*; then we take up *rational expectations* in the next section.

Under adaptive expectations agents make their forecast of future inflation based only on past inflation. Formally, this mechanism is often described as follows:

$$\hat{P}^e_{+1} = \hat{P}^e + v(\hat{P} - \hat{P}^e) \tag{15.9}$$

In interpreting this equation, it is important to remember that the term $\hat{P}^e_{+1}$ refers to expectations held *as of this period,* about inflation between this period and next period.

We can interpret expression (15.9) quite readily. The expectations for next period's inflation, $\hat{P}^e_{+1}$, are equal to the expectations that were held for this period's inflation, $\hat{P}^e$, adjusted for any error of prediction that was revealed during this period, $(\hat{P} - \hat{P}^e)$. In other words, if inflation this period turned out to be higher than the forecast, next period's expected inflation is

---

[7] An alternative way to think about this equation is that the marginal product of labor is $(1/\alpha)$. Therefore, $w/P = (1/\alpha)$, or $P = \alpha w$.

revised upward; if actual inflation turned out to be lower than forecast, next period's expected inflation is revised downward.

The factor of correction, v, measures the speed with which expectations are revised. When v is low, inflationary expectations change slowly, and the actual pattern of inflation has little effect on them. When v is close to 1, inflationary expectations adjust quickly in response to actual inflation. When the correction factor is equal to one ($v = 1$), we can simplify (15.9) significantly and write

$$\hat{P}^e_{+1} = \hat{P} \qquad \textbf{(15.10)}$$

In this case, forecasts of future inflation are exactly equal to current inflation. This simple assumption, which we used to describe the inflation-unemployment trade-off in the previous section, is a particular kind of adaptive mechanism, sometimes called *static* expectations.

Using the static expectations mechanism proposed in (15.10), the Phillips curve equation (15.6) is transformed to

$$\hat{P}_{+1} = \hat{P} - b(U - U_n) \qquad \textbf{(15.11)}$$

According to equation (15.11), then, inflation is unchanging only when the current unemployment rate U equals the natural unemployment rate U_n. When U is less than U_n, $\hat{P}_{+1}$ is greater than $\hat{P}$. And when U is greater than U_n, $\hat{P}_{+1}$ is less than $\hat{P}$. Thus, unemployment can be kept below its natural rate only by resorting to expansionary policies that bring about *increasing* rates of inflation.

This result, known as the *accelerationist* principle, means that in order to keep U below U_n, the authorities have to accept ever-increasing levels of inflation. The costs of such a policy grow through time, and eventually they become very high as inflation accelerates without bound. More specifically, equation (15.11) says that each percentage point of reduction in unemployment below the natural rate will cost the country an increase of b points in inflation in the next period. The accelerationist principle has given rise to another name for the natural rate of unemployment, the *nonaccelerating inflation rate of unemployment* (NAIRU). That is, the NAIRU is the level of unemployment U_n below which inflation tends to accelerate and above which inflation tends to decelerate.

The Short-Run and Long-Run Phillips Curve Trade-Off

The accelerationist principle leads us to an important conclusion. When Phillips first suggested his famous inflation-unemployment trade-off, many economists interpreted it to mean that policymakers could choose a permanently lower unemployment rate for the economy at the cost of a shift to a higher, but stable, inflation rate. Looking at the short-run Phillips curve in Figure 15-6 (PC_{SR}), they believed that it would be possible to move permanently from point A to point B, that is, to suffer high inflation for the sake of permanently lower unemployment. Perhaps, for example, an economy could choose a 5 percent unemployment with 1 percent inflation, or a 4 percent unemployment with 2 percent inflation, or a 3 percent unemployment with 3 percent inflation, and so forth.

But, the accelerationist principle teaches us, such trade-off is impossible in the long run. When unemployment is held below the natural rate,

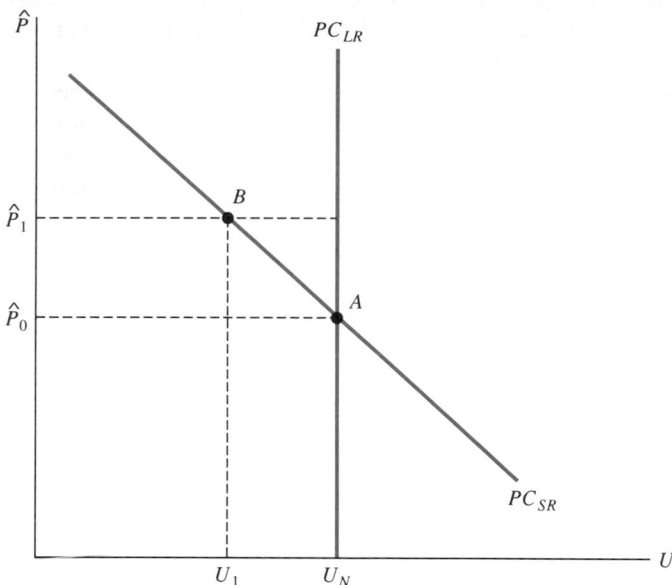

Figure 15-6

The Phillips Curve in the Short Run and the Long Run

inflation will not only be high, but will also be rising. When unemployment is held above the natural rate, inflation will be steadily falling. *In the long-run, there is no trade-off between inflation and unemployment.* Only the natural rate of unemployment is consistent with a stable inflation rate. Furthermore, the natural rate can be consistent with *any* stable inflation rate. The long-run Phillips curve (PC_{LR}) is therefore vertical, as shown in Figure 15-6. In other words, no matter what the inflation rate is, the unemployment rate must always return to its natural rate.

A Detailed Example

Consider an economy, with stable prices, which is at equilibrium at the natural rate of unemployment U_n. The equilibrium of aggregate supply and aggregate demand is shown in Figure 15-7a at point A, and the short-run Phillips curve—at zero inflation and unemployment U_n—goes through point A' in Figure 15-7b. The aggregate supply curve is perfectly flat in the short run, at the price level P_0. Why? Because with wages given within a period, the price level is also given, as shown in equation (15.6). The short-run Phillips curve is downward sloping, showing the relationship between current unemployment, U, and next period's inflation, $\hat{P}_{+1}$, assuming that inflation expectations are for zero inflation in period 2.

Suppose now that the government expands aggregate demand in period 1, in an attempt to pull unemployment below its natural rate U_n. The demand curve shifts out as shown in Figure 15-7a. Output is increased, and by Okun's law, unemployment is reduced, say, to a level U_1. According to the Phillips curve relationship, as seen in Figure 15-7b, next period's actual inflation will increase, to $\hat{P}_2$, though inflationary expectations are still zero.

Policymakers might now think that they have achieved a permanent inflation-unemployment trade-off—after all, unemployment has fallen below

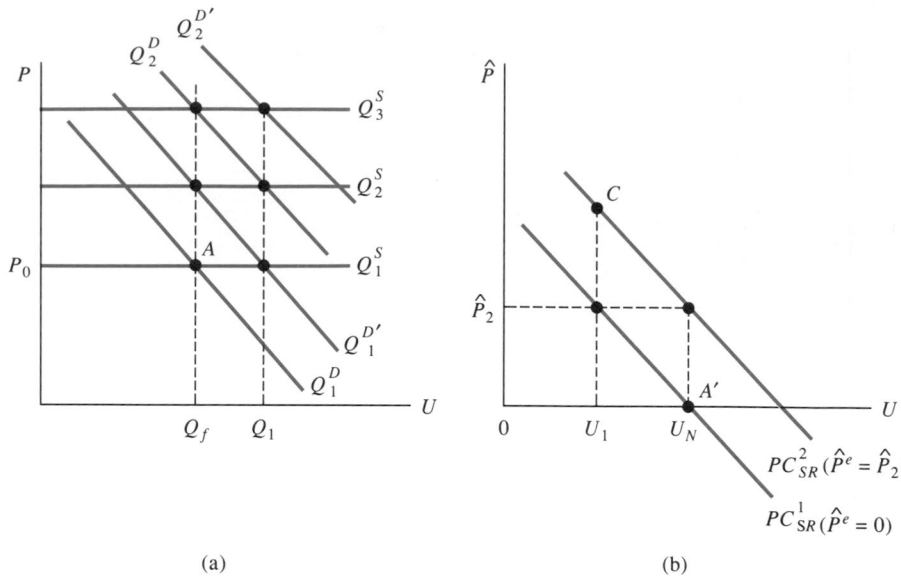

Figure 15-7

Demand Expansion and Equilibrium Economy (a) The Aggregate Supply-Aggregate Demand Framework (b) The Phillips Curve

U_n, while inflation has increased. But the trade-off cannot be sustained. Consider the same problem from the point of view of period 2. Because wages have increased between period 1 and period 2, the new aggregate supply schedule has shifted up, as shown in Figure 15-7a. Aggregate demand in period 2 thus must be raised simply to keep output at the same level it was at in period 1.

But, as a result of the inflation in period 2, inflationary expectations will also rise. Suppose, in fact, that inflationary expectations for period 3 rise all the way to the inflation rate actually experienced in period 2; that is, $\hat{P}_3^e = \hat{P}_2$. Thus, in period 2, workers and firms will build a positive expected inflation into their wage settlement for period 3. The short-run Phillips curve will now shift upward as shown in Figure 15-7b, and the inflation rate $\hat{P}_2$ will now prevail in period 3—even if unemployment rises again to U_n.

Now policymakers face a dilemma. If they want to keep unemployment at U_1 (below rate U_n) as they did in the first period, they may do so by once again expanding aggregate demand sufficiently in period 2. To do this, they would have to shift aggregate demand all the way to $Q_2^{D'}$ in Figure 15-7a. But once this is done, then inflation in period 3 will be even *higher* than $\hat{P}_2$ (at point C), as we can see by the Phillips curve in Figure 15-7b. In other words, *the unemployment rate can be kept below U_n only by an ever-increasing inflation rate.*

If, instead, the policymakers want to keep the inflation rate at $\hat{P}_2$, rather than letting it go higher, then they must allow unemployment to go back to the natural rate. In the end, the higher inflation produces a *temporary* reduction of unemployment, but not a permanent one. The higher inflation remains, but the unemployment rate returns to U_n. If it did not, inflation would continue to increase each period. Thus, the result of the inflationary

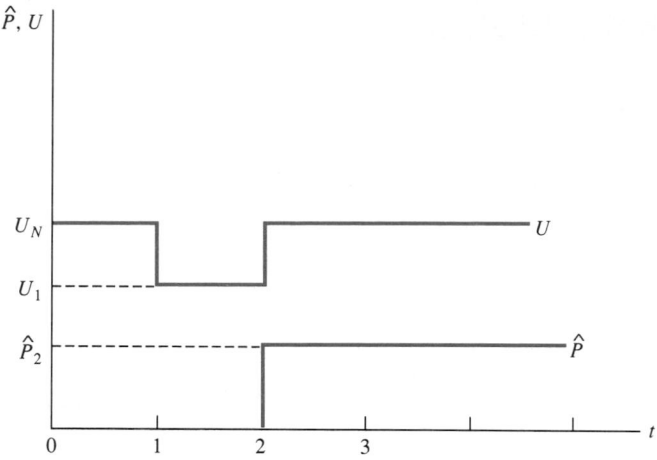

Figure 15-8
The Time Paths of Inflation and Unemployment

policy is not very attractive: a one-period reduction in unemployment, at the cost of a permanent increase in inflation!

The time paths of inflation and unemployment in this illustration are shown in Figure 15-8.

The Sacrifice Ratio

When inflation dynamics are determined by a Phillips curve mechanism as in equation (15.11), any attempt to reduce inflation will necessarily require a transitory increase in unemployment above the natural rate. The "cost" of disinflation, then, is the amount of transitory unemployment that must be endured to bring inflation down by a given amount. We can obtain a quantitative assessment of this cost by a minor transformation of equation (15.11), or

$$U - U_n = -\left(\frac{1}{b}\right)(\hat{P}_{+1} - \hat{P}) \tag{15.12}$$

To restate this in words, each percentage point reduction in inflation requires an increase in unemployment above the natural rate of $(1/b)$ points. The *sacrifice ratio* (SR) is a very useful concept with which to assess the unemployment costs of a disinflation. It measures the *cumulative unemployment gap*—that is, the excess unemployment over the natural rate—in a particular period, divided by the reduction in inflation over the same period. In simple terms, SR measures how many extra points of unemployment are necessary to bring about a given reduction in inflation. The lower the sacrifice ratio, the less costly the disinflation. Box 15-1, where we measure the sacrifice ratio for the U.S. disinflation during 1980–1984, provides a look at this concept in practice.

Formally, we write the SR between period 0 and period T as

$$SR = \frac{[(U_0 - U_n) + (U_1 - U_n) + \cdots + (U_T - U_n)]}{(\hat{P}_0 - \hat{P}_T)} \tag{15.13}$$

Box 15-1
The Sacrifice Ratio and the Reagan Disinflation

Between 1978 and 1980, inflation in the United States was persistently in double digits, a phenomenon not observed in more than half a century.[8] During his 1980 presidential campaign, Ronald Reagan had made a forceful pledge to reduce inflation. Toward this end, the new administration pursued an interesting policy mix after it came into office: monetary restraint, under the guidance of Fed Chairman Paul Volcker (who, incidentally, had been appointed by President Carter), combined with the fiscal expansion of President Reagan's tax cuts and military expenditure increases.

As the models we laid out in Chapters 12–14 would predict, the tight-money policy provoked a sharp recession, while the expansionary effects of the fiscal policy were blunted by a currency appreciation that led to a reduction of net exports. Both the high unemployment caused by the monetary squeeze and the appreciation of the dollar were key factors in the reduction of inflation, which declined from 10.4 percent in 1980 to 3.2 percent in 1982.

What was the cost of the disinflation in terms of higher unemployment? The sacrifice ratio between 1980 and 1984 has been calculated using 6 percent as the natural rate of unemployment in the United States.[9] For each year, we calculate the amount by which the unemployment rate exceeded 6 percent. When this excess is added up between the last quarter of 1980 and the last quarter of 1984, the cumulative excess unemployment over the 6 percent natural rate was 10.8 percent. From the beginning to end of the period, the drop in inflation was 7.2 percent. Thus, the SR was 1.5 (10.8 divided by 7.2), meaning that an increase in the unemployment rate of 1.5 percentage points (say, from 6.0 to 7.5) was associated with a reduction in annual inflation of 1 percentage point.

The sacrifice ratio can also be measured using the output gap (the difference between potential and actual output), whose cumulative value for the period has been estimated as 21.5 percent, using a time-series estimate of potential GNP. By this output-based measure, SR was equal to 3 (21.5 divided by 7.2), meaning that each reduction in annual inflation of 1 percentage point was associated with a loss of 3 percent of GNP, relative to potential, for one year.

These calculations do not say whether the Reagan disinflation was "worth it" or not, but only what the trade-offs involved were. There were

---

[8] An earlier period of very high inflation (in the double-digit range) occurred between 1916 and 1919. It was immediately followed by a big deflation.

[9] See Jeffrey Sachs, "The Dollar and the Policy Mix: 1985," *Brookings Papers on Economic Activity*, No. 1, 1985. The title of this article was borrowed from the seminal contribution of Robert Mundell, "The Dollar and the Policy Mix: 1971," *Essays in International Finance*, No. 85 (Princeton, N.J.: Princeton University Press, May 1971). There, Mundell argued that the appropriate policy package for the United States. at the time was tight money and easy fiscal policy. This was exactly the line followed by the Reagan administration on its early days.

several years of high unemployment and GNP below potential, but with the result of a sustained period of lower inflation. The sacrifice ratio gives a more precise quantitative measure of the trade-off.

The numerator is the cumulative unemployment gap between periods 0 and T; the denominator is the reduction of inflation in percentage points. Sometimes SR is measured in units of output (percentage losses of GNP) rather than unemployment. In that case the question, then, becomes what is the cumulative output gap (the percentage difference between actual and potential output) that accompanies a given reduction in inflation?

Note that with the static expectations mechanism it is easy to calculate the SR. Using (15.12), we have

$$U_0 - U_n = - \left(\frac{1}{b}\right) (\hat{P}_1 - \hat{P}_0)$$

$$U_1 - U_n = - \left(\frac{1}{b}\right) (\hat{P}_2 - \hat{P}_1)$$

$$U_2 - U_n = - \left(\frac{1}{b}\right) (\hat{P}_3 - \hat{P}_2)$$

$$\cdot$$
$$\cdot$$
$$\cdot$$

$$U_T - U_n = - \left(\frac{1}{b}\right) (\hat{P}_T - \hat{P}_{T-1})$$

Adding up these columns, we find

$$[(U_0 - U_n) + (U_1 - U_n) + \cdots + (U_T - U_n)]$$

$$= - \left(\frac{1}{b}\right) [(\hat{P}_1 - \hat{P}_0) + (\hat{P}_2 - \hat{P}_1) + \cdots + \cdots + (\hat{P}_T - \hat{P}_{T-1})]$$

$$= - \left(\frac{1}{b}\right) [- \hat{P}_0 + (\hat{P}_1 - \hat{P}_1) + (\hat{P}_2 - \hat{P}_2) + \cdots + \cdots + \hat{P}_T]$$

$$= - \left(\frac{1}{b}\right) [-\hat{P}_0 - \hat{P}_T]$$

And using equation (15.13) we obtain

$$SR = \frac{1}{b}$$

In words, the sacrifice ratio equals ($1/b$) in the case of static expectations.

Expectations and Wage Contracts in Inertial Inflation

The basic idea so far is that past inflation is likely to manifest itself in larger wage increases in the present, which in turn causes future inflation. Inflation, in turn, poses a difficult dilemma for macroeconomic policy authorities. They must either accommodate the inflation by expanding aggregate demand enough to maintain unemployment near the natural rate, or if they try to reduce inflation below the rate inherited from the past, they must accept a rise of U above U_n. Facing such a choice, policymakers generally choose to accommodate at least some of the inherited inflation.

To borrow an idea from physics, we can say that inflation displays *inertia*. After all, past inflation tends to result in future inflation. And, again as in physics, inertial inflation can only be ended if force is applied, in this case, the force of a temporary recession (in which U exceeds U_n and GNP is below potential). We have used the term "expectations" to characterize the mechanism that transmits past inflation into future inflation via wage contracts. But we should not be too literal in applying this term. The fact that past inflation tends to signal large current increases in nominal wages is the result not only of (psychological) expectations per se, but also of other institutional features of wage setting.

For one thing, since wage agreements often cover more than one year, next year's wage growth will result in part from decisions built into wage contracts settled two or three years before, not just from the current "expectations" about inflation. Another portion of current wage increases is likely to come from certain contractual arrangements, such as wage indexation, which specify formulas for nominal wage increases that are only loosely connected with expectations.

The point here is simply that it can be more helpful, and more accurate, to use the term "inertial inflation" rather than "expected inflation" for the variable $\hat{P}^e_{+1}$ in equation (15.8).

15-4 The Rational Expectations Approach

In the early 1970s, a group of influential economists led by Robert Lucas of the University of Chicago and Thomas Sargent of the Hoover Institute initiated a major critique of the inflation-unemployment analysis we have just studied. Their criticism had two parts. First, they doubted the relevance of a wage-adjustment mechanism like that in equation (15.4) on the grounds that the slow adjustment to equilibrium in the equation had no firm foundation. In their view, wages are set at the level which, barring unexpected developments, would always keep the labor market in equilibrium. Basically, then, they assumed that the labor market clears.

Second, they criticized the assumption of adaptive expectations as being arbitrary. Instead, they said, workers and firms find it in their self-interest to seek the most accurate means for forecasting future inflation. Errors in expectations of inflation, after all, lead to high costs, such as high unemployment and profit squeezes on firms. Specifically, Lucas and Sargent proposed that workers and firms behave as if they understand the "true" model of the economy and base their forecasts of inflation on that model, rather than on adaptive expectations or any other mechanical process. This approach was christened *rational expectations*, on the grounds that it would be rational for economic agents to form their expectations based upon their "model"—or general understanding—of the economy.

One important aspect of rational expectations theory is that workers and firms should form their expectations of future prices based on expectations about future government policies. Under adaptive expectations, by contrast, the inflation forecasts are based on past history. For this reason, rational expectations are sometimes called "forward-looking expectations," while adaptive mechanisms are termed "backward-looking" expectations.

This theory of rational expectations has generated an enormous controversy within the field of macroeconomics. As we shall see when we review the evidence, the approach has failed to deliver empirical results that live up to the early hopes of its advocates. Nonetheless, the rational expectations approach has significantly changed the way that economists think about the process of expectation formation as well as the process of macroeconomic policymaking. Thus, the rational expectations approach, in the context of anti-inflation policy, deserves a detailed examination.

According to the market-clearing assumption of the rational expectations approach, wages are set in each period in order to keep the labor market in equilibrium in the following period, based on expectations of future economic conditions.[10] To see how this might work, let us suppose that the nominal wage for the next period is selected so that next period's *expected real wage* will equal the full-employment wage, wp^f. Firms and workers do not know next period's price level, so they must form an expectation, specifically, $\hat{P}^e_{+1}$. The nominal wage for the next period is set according to the rule that the expected real wage equals the market-clearing wage, or $(w_{+1}/P_{+1})^e = wp^f$. As a first approximation, then, we can say that the nominal wage is set as follows:[11]

$$w_{+1} = (P^e_{+1})(wp^f) \tag{15.14}$$

Equation (15.14) tells us something quite significant. Assuming that workers and firms are correct about their forecast of next period's price level, the real wage will then be at the market-clearing level. Therefore, in the absence of forecast errors, the economy will exhibit full employment. And since the rational expectations approach assumes that workers and firms make price forecasts that are correct *on average*, the prediction is that the unemployment rate—on average—is at the natural rate. The unemployment rate can differ from the natural rate only because of mistakes that are likely to be random and temporary.[12]

We can be even more precise about this. Using (15.14), we see that the actual real wage for next period is given as follows:

$$\left(\frac{w_{+1}}{P_{+1}}\right) = \left(\frac{P^e_{+1}}{P_{+1}}\right)(wp^f) \tag{15.15}$$

---

[10] Actually, the rational expectations approach can be applied to many different formulations about the timing of wage setting and the nature of labor market equilibrium. Here, we assume that next period wages are set this period, based on rational expectations of economic conditions in the next period. This is in line with our approach in the first part of the chapter. Some rational expectations models work like this while others reject the importance of wage contracts altogether, claiming that nominal wages can be regarded as flexible *within* each period, so that nominal wages adjust as economic shocks, such as changes in macroeconomic policy, occur.

[11] We are using the approximation that the expected real wage is equal to the nominal wage divided by the expected price level, that is, $(w_{+1}/P_{+1})^e = w_{+1}/P^e_{+1}$. Technically, this is only an approximation, given the mathematical properties of "expected values."

[12] In more sophisticated applications of rational expectations theory, a mistake in price forecasts can set off a prolonged deviation of employment from the long-run equilibrium level. Nonetheless, the spirit of the rational expectations approach is that markets will return rapidly to full employment, based on the flexible wage and price setting of well-informed workers and firms.

After some further mathematical manipulations (described in the appendix to this chapter), we can approximate (15.15) as follows:

$$\left(\frac{w_{+1}}{P_{+1}}\right) = wp^f - wp^f(\hat{P}_{+1} - \hat{P}^e_{+1}) \tag{15.16}$$

This equation also tells us something important. When there is unexpected inflation, so that $\hat{P}_{+1}$ turns out to be greater than $\hat{P}^e_{+1}$, the actual real wage turns out to be less than the market-clearing real wage. By the same token, when $\hat{P}_{+1}$ turns out to be smaller than $\hat{P}^e_{+1}$, the actual wage turns out to be above wp^f. In simple terms: *unexpected inflation reduces the real wage below the market-clearing level, while less than expected inflation causes the real wage to exceed the market-clearing level.*

Before going further, however, beware of an assumption hidden in equation (15.16). This reasoning takes wp^f as a constant. Therefore, inflation surprises must be the result only of unexpected demand shifts, and not of unexpected supply shifts (which would also affect wp^f). Implicitly, then, the rational expectations theory of the inflation-unemployment relationship is based on unexpected demand shocks.

The Inflation-Unemployment Trade-Off Under Rational Expectations

Into this picture we now introduce rational expectations. The idea is that *on average* firms and households are correct about their inflation forecasts, and that mistakes in one period tend to be statistically independent of mistakes in another period. If our forecast error is denoted as $z = \hat{P} - \hat{P}^e$, the assumption is that, on average, z is zero, and that errors in one period (such as $z > 0$) are not connected to errors in another period. Each forecast error is like a coin flip: the outcome of one flip does not help to predict the outcome of the next coin flip.

Our next step is to note that the level of employment is a negative function of the real wage. When wp_{+1} is low, employment is high, and *unemployment* is low. When wp_{+1} is high, employment is low, and unemployment is high. These simple facts are evident from the labor supply and demand curves shown in Figure 15-3. The following equation summarizes the relationship between the real wage level and unemployment:

$$U_{+1} = U_n + g(wp_{+1} - wp^f) \tag{15.17}$$

This equation states that U_{+1} equals the natural rate of unemployment U_n when the real wage wp_{t+1} is equal to wp^f. When the real wage is higher than this level, so too is the unemployment rate, and when the real wage is lower, so too is unemployment.

By substituting equation (15.16) into (15.17), we arrive at the key equation for rational expectations theorists,

$$U_{+1} = U_n - h(\hat{P}_{+1} - \hat{P}^e_{+1}) \tag{15.18}$$

where h is a variable equal to $g(wp^f)$. Using a Phillips curve of this sort, rational expectations theorists find that unemployment in the next period is a function of the inflation forecast error in the same period. When inflation is higher than expected (so that z_{+1} is positive), unemployment is low (because the real wage is also low). When inflation turns out to be lower than expected, unemployment is high (because the real wage is too high).

Let us now use Okun's law to link the unemployment rate to the level of output. Recall that Okun's law established a simple relationship between the unemployment rate and the level of output.[13] Accordingly, we can rewrite (15.18) as

$$Q_{+1} = Q_{+1}^f + j(\hat{P}_{+1} - \hat{P}_{+1}^e) \qquad \textbf{(15.19)}$$

where j is a constant. Thus, when inflation is greater than expected, output is higher than the full-employment level (remember that Q_{+1}^f corresponds to an unemployment level U_n). When inflation is less than expected, output is lower than Q_{+1}^f.

We can now make use of the aggregate supply–aggregate demand framework. We have seen that the starting point for wage setting is the rational expectation of the future price level, P_{+1}^e. Workers and firms form this expectation of P_{+1} by forming *an expectation of the position of the aggregate demand schedule in the next period*. We denote this expected position as $Q_{+1}^{D^e}$, and it appears in Figure 15-9. P_{+1}^e is the point on this curve that corresponds to the full-employment level of output Q_{+1}^f. Then, nominal wages are set so that the aggregate supply schedule goes through the point P_{+1}^e at the full-employment level of output. Thus, the aggregate supply schedule, as shown in Figure 15-9, intersects the *expected* aggregate demand schedule $Q_{+1}^{D^e}$ at point E, with Q^f as the level of output and P_{+1}^e as the price level.

Now, let us suppose that actual aggregate demand turns out to be more contractionary than expected, so that the demand schedule in the next period is at $Q_{+1}^{D'}$. It is obvious from Figure 15-9 that in this case actual P_{+1} turns out to be less than P_{+1}^e—and also that $\hat{P}_{+1}$ is less than $\hat{P}_{+1}^e$. At the same time, output turns out to be $Q_{+1} < Q_{+1}^f$. Thus we get the expectations effect that we noted in equation (15.17): less than expected inflation leads to output below the full-employment level. When aggregate demand turns out to be more expansionary than expected, at the aggregate demand schedule $Q_{+1}^{D''}$ in Figure 15-9, for example, the results are the opposite: inflation results higher than expected and output turns out to be above its full-employment level.

---

[13] Okun's law says that a reduction in the unemployment rate of 1 percent makes output increase by 3 percent. Mathematically, we can express this relationship as

$$3(U - U_{+1}) = Q_{+1} - Q$$

If we start from full employment (Q^f), and thus from unemployment at its natural rate (U_n), this equation can be expressed as

$$3(U_n - U_{+1}) = Q_{+1} - Q^f$$

or

$$U_{+1} - U_n = \left(\frac{1}{3}\right)(Q^f - Q_{+1})$$

Substituting this into equation (15.18) leads immediately to (15.19), with $j = 3h$.

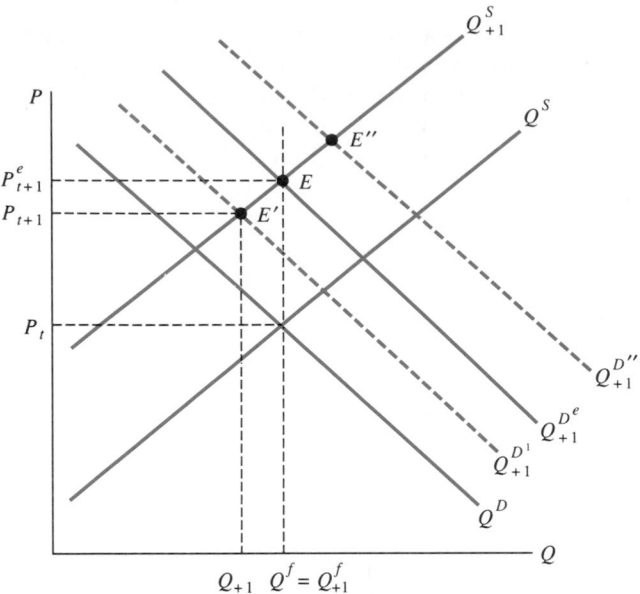

Figure 15-9
Equilibrium Under Rational Expectations

Credibility and the Costs of Disinflation

Under the rational expectations assumptions, there is no output-inflation trade-off. Policymakers, it is said, can achieve *zero* inflation in the next period without any loss of output or excessive unemployment! Suppose that policymakers tell the public that they intend to pursue a tight aggregate demand policy so that P^e_{+1} is set equal to P. In other words, they announce that there will be *zero inflation* in the next period, and they pursue aggregate demand policies that are sufficiently restrictive so that $P^e_{+1} = P$ (and, therefore, $\hat{P}^e_{+1} = 0$). Under these conditions, it is obvious from Figure 15-9 that output will be at the full-employment level, with $\hat{P}_{+1} = 0$.

The reasoning goes like this. With rational expectations, wages are set on the basis of forward-looking expectations. Past inflation *per se* does not matter, and thus there is no inertia. Inflation forecasts are based on what policymakers will do in the future, not what inflation happened to have been in the past. Therefore, the trick for policymakers is to announce a set of aggregate demand policies so that $\hat{P}^e_{+1}$ is zero. If this is done, and if the policies are carried out, then the wage is set automatically at the appropriate nominal level to ensure full employment and zero inflation.

Now compare this story with events under adaptive expectations. Suppose that inflation in the current period is positive. With adaptive expectations, expected inflation for next period will also probably be positive. Now, as we saw at the beginning of the chapter, comes the dilemma. Given that $\hat{P}^e_{+1} > 0$ (as the result of past inflation), policymakers face a choice. They can accommodate the inflation in order to preserve full-employment output, or they can tighten aggregate demand and keep inflation at zero, but only at the cost of output falling short of Q^f_{+1} and unemployment exceeding U_n.

With rational expectations, on the other hand, policymakers can achieve price stability and full employment as long as they are able to convince workers and firms that aggregate demand will in fact be tight enough to keep inflation at zero. Specifically, they must convince the public that the aggregate demand curve will go through the point Q^f_{+1} when P_{+1} equals P, as it does in Figure 15-9. In other words, the public must believe that aggregate demand will be tight enough to keep inflation at zero.

And this is the crucial point. Economic agents need to be convinced that the government will truly carry out the policy of zero inflation. It is not sufficient for policymakers to announce the policy. People first have to understand budgetary and monetary policies and then believe that the actual aggregate demand policies announced will be consistent with the goal of zero inflation so that they will base their wage-setting behavior on those policies. In other words, the policy must have *credibility*. If it does, people will adjust their expectations accordingly. Thomas Sargent has made a forceful case concerning the role of credibility in ending four hyperinflations in Central Europe in the 1920s.[14]

As you can guess, however, governments cannot easily establish the credibility of their declared policies. Suppose, for example, that a government announces that inflation will be reduced to zero in the next period, but households and firms know that the inflation up until now has resulted from the government's resort to seigniorage to finance an existing fiscal deficit. If economic agents doubt that the government can actually eliminate the budget deficit—perhaps because the administration lacks a majority in the legislature—they will also doubt that it can end the inflation rapidly. In fact, the government may have announced the same policy in the past and failed to deliver on its promise.

Some political uncertainty might also exist about who will actually govern in the future, thereby creating doubts about the continuity of demand management policies. For example, the government might declare its intention to reduce aggregate demand next year, but there might be an intervening election during this year. Households and firms may thus find it hard to believe that the party controlling the government will actually remain in power long enough to carry out its policies.

Further, the government might find some reason to promise a tough policy and then to *cheat* by carrying out a very expansionary policy. Why? Because if people believe the announcement and set their wages based on the expected low inflation, the government might then deliberately expand aggregate demand in order to reduce the unemployment rate below U_n and raise output above Q^f. Remember that "surprise" inflation, in which $\hat{P}_{+1} > \hat{P}^e_{+1}$, can cause a fall in unemployment, as shown in equation (15.19). Thus, the government might deliberately try to surprise the private sector by announcing one thing and then doing something else.

Note that when the government announces its low-inflation policies, it may truly *intend* to carry them out. But once wages are set and the opportunity to reduce U_n is at hand in the next period, the temptation to reduce the unemployment rate just a little bit may prove irresistible. The problem is one

---

[14] His work on this subject is today a classic. See "The Ends of Four Big Inflations," in Robert Hall, ed., *Inflation: Causes and Effects* (Chicago: National Bureau of Economic Research, University of Chicago Press, 1982).

of *dynamic inconsistency*.[15] Of course, if the government goes back on its word often enough, it will surely lose credibility. (We elaborate further on the problem of dynamic inconsistency in Chapter 19.)

We know that government credibility is not a sufficient condition to attain a costless disinflation. Even though the rational expectations theorists have downplayed the role of long-term wage contracts, it is true that employers and workers may be locked into contracts for several future periods. Predetermined wage increases—which we have called inertial inflation—can raise the costs of disinflation even if the government has great credibility. And individuals may certainly base their expectations not on what the government says, but on observations of past inflation, as the theory of adaptive expectations holds.

In sum, the theory of costless disinflation requires three things: rapid labor-market clearing (no long-term wage contracts), forward-looking expectations (and not adaptive expectations), and credibility of the announced policy. This combination is very rare, if it ever truly exists. In the end, the rational expectations theory of costless disinflation is itself not credible.

The empirical evidence on the Reagan disinflation that we analyzed in Box 15-1 clearly shows that the U.S. disinflation in the early 1980s was not costless. The Federal Reserve Board tried to explain and vigorously defend its tight credit policies. It did, in other words, try to establish its credibility. Nonetheless, it took more than two years for the tight money to translate into low inflation, and that occurred only as the United States fell into a deep recession in 1981–1982. Perhaps the monetary authorities established their credibility only slowly, and thus the lack of credibility deserves part of the blame for the costs of disinflation. But certainly existing long-term contracts also made it more difficult and costly to obtain the desired slowdown in inflation.

15-5 THE USE OF THE EXCHANGE RATE TO STABILIZE PRICES

So far, we have largely neglected the international aspects of the inflation—unemployment problem. It is not that the international aspects have been entirely absent. Some have only been submerged. For example, the shifts in aggregate demand that come from expansionary monetary policy are likely to involve movements in the exchange rate. Thus, each time that the aggregate demand curve has been shifted, say, to accommodate an increase in nominal wages, the exchange rate has also been shifting.

But the exchange rate affects the inflation—unemployment trade-off in more direct ways as well. First, imported goods are likely to rise in price in proportion to exchange-rate changes, and many imported *final* goods (not primary goods) are part of the consumer price index. With P the price of

---

[15] The importance of the incentives governments have to revise their plans after an initial announcement was described in an influential paper by Finn Kydland and Edward Prescott, "Rules Rather than Discretion: the Inconsistency of Optimal Plans," *Journal of Political Economy*, June 1977.

domestically produced goods, P_m the price of imports, and P_c the overall consumer price index, we have two key relationships:

$$P_m = EP_m^* \tag{15.20}$$
$$P_c = \delta P + (1 - \delta)P_m \tag{15.21}$$

where E is the nominal exchange rate, P_m^* the price of the imported good abroad, and δ a parameter between 0 and 1 that indicates the weight of domestic goods in the consumer price index (with $1 - \delta$ being the weight of the imported good). Thus, even if domestic prices P are not subject to purchasing power parity, that part of the overall consumer price index P_c made up of imported final goods is *directly* affected by the exchange rate.

Moreover, even though we have rejected PPP as the basis for domestic goods prices as a whole, for at least some domestic goods, PPP does in fact hold. For highly tradable commodities in an economy (such as raw materials), exchange-rate changes are likely to feed *directly* into domestic prices, irrespective of aggregate demand and supply conditions. (Later on, in Chapter 19, we will divide production in the economy into two kinds: tradable production and nontradable production.) *Tradable* production (denoted by T) has prices determined according to PPP: $P_T = EP_T^*$. *Nontradable* goods prices P_N are determined by the equilibrium of aggregate supply and aggregate demand. The overall domestic price level P is a weighted average of these two kinds of prices:

$$P = \phi P_T + (1 - \phi)P_N \tag{15.22}$$
$$= \phi(EP_T^*) + (1 - \phi)P_N$$

where ϕ is a parameter between 0 and 1 signifying the weight of the traded good in the overall domestic price level (and $1 - \phi$ is the weight of the nontraded good).

A third channel by which the exchange rate directly influences prices is through imported *intermediate* goods—oil, feed grains for animals, and primary metals, for example—which are used in domestic production. An exchange-rate depreciation raises the price of imported intermediate goods, and this, in turn, raises the price of final output. Equation (15.4), which described a particularly simple form for the aggregate supply curve, can be rewritten to take into account the costs of imported intermediate goods. To do this, we denote the price of the intermediate goods as P_n, which we can assume to be equal to EP_n^*, where P_n^* is the world price. Nontradables prices, for example, can then be written as a function of wages and P_n:

$$P_N = \alpha w + \beta P_n \tag{15.23}$$
$$= \alpha w + \beta EP_n^*$$

Combining equations (15.20) through (15.23), we capture three different channels by which the exchange rate directly affects the price level: (1) through prices of imported final goods, (2) through prices of domestic tradable goods, and (3) through imported intermediate goods that affect domestic production costs. The final overall equation for the consumer price index, then, looks like this:

$$P_c = [\alpha\delta(1 - \phi)]w + [\beta\delta(1 - \phi)P_n^* + \delta\phi P_T^* + (1 - \delta)P_m^*]E \tag{15.24}$$

As equation (15.24) shows, then, P_c is determined indirectly or directly by wages (w) and by the exchange rate (E).

The strong influence of the exchange rate on prices suggests that exchange-rate policy can play a direct role in anti-inflation policy above and beyond the indirect role of the exchange rate on aggregate demand and the overall level of unemployment. Some countries have attempted, through central bank intervention, to peg the exchange rate as a crucial, or even *the* crucial, feature of an anti-inflation program. In Bolivia in 1985, for example, the government successfully ended a 40,000 percent per year hyperinflation by stabilizing the exchange rate (which had previously been depreciating sharply). After a sharp cut in the budget deficit, the central bank could then stop the exchange rate from depreciating. Most prices in the economy were linked closely to the exchange rate, and as soon as the exchange rate was stabilized, the hyperinflation ended.

When PPP does not hold, however, fixing the exchange rate can be dangerous—unless some additional policies, such as a suspension of existing wage-indexation clauses, are followed at the same time. The trouble is that the fixed exchange rate can hold down some prices, such as tradables (P_T), imported inputs (P_n), and imported final goods (P_m), while other prices continue to rise. Suppose, for example, that the nominal wage continues rising after the exchange rate has been fixed. Exporters will be unable to raise their prices because they must remain competitive internationally. Meanwhile, the higher wages squeeze their profit margins, perhaps even to the point of forcing them out of business. In general, domestic prices will continue to rise because wage costs continue to increase, so that on average P will rise relative to EP^*. Domestic goods thus lose their international competitiveness, and firms that export goods or that produce goods that compete with imports may find themselves facing bankruptcy.

At the end of the 1970s, several Latin American countries—Argentina, Chile, and Uruguay are the main examples—attempted to end high inflations mainly by fixing their exchange rates, without taking adequate precautions to reduce their rates of nominal wage increases. Domestic prices continued to rise sharply, and export industries were hard hit. In the end, each of the governments had to reverse its policy and accept a large devaluation of the currency.

The experience in Argentina is instructive. In 1979, a policy was introduced to keep exchange-rate devaluations far below the prevailing rate of inflation on the grounds that this would quickly slow down overall inflation and bring it into line with the exchange rate. While this policy did succeed in ending inflation for some tradable goods, nominal wages continued their rapid rise, and overall inflation remained much higher than the rate of devaluation, as shown in Table 15-1. With the large gap between inflation on one hand and exchange-rate devaluation on the other, the export sector was hard hit, and speculation mounted that the exchange rate would have to be devalued sharply. Argentines converted their pesos into dollars, and the international reserves of the Central Bank of Argentina declined substantially. Eventually, the central bank lacked the reserves necessary to maintain the policy, and the exchange-rate policy had to be abandoned completely.

Neighboring Chile was even more radical in its use of the exchange rate to try to reduce inflation. After experimenting briefly with a series of mini-devaluations, the Chilean exchange rate was fixed firmly to the dollar in June

TABLE 15-1

ARGENTINA: THE CRAWLING PEG
AND THE RATE OF INFLATION,
1979–1980 (RATE OF CHANGE
PER QUARTER)

Quarter	Inflation	Devaluation
1979 : 1	32.1	15.8
1979 : 2	24.3	14.4
1979 : 3	28.1	12.8
1979 : 4	18.4	10.8
1980 : 1	18.5	8.8
1980 : 2	18.6	7.0
1980 : 3	14.7	5.2
1980 : 4	17.0	3.5

Source: Guillermo Calvo, "Fractured Liberalism: Argentina Under Martinez de Hoz," Economic Development and Cultural Change, April 1986 (Chicago: University of Chicago Press).

1979. At that time, there was still substantial inertial inflation, partly the legacy of a 1979 labor law which guaranteed that nominal wages must rise by at least the rate of the previous year's inflation. As a result of this wage indexation, inflation remained high despite the fixed exchange rate, the ratio P/EP^* rose sharply, and the country lost international competitiveness. The currency therefore had to be devalued in mid-1982, at the cost of increased inflation.

Even in the United States, however, the exchange rate can have an important direct effect on inflation. In the early 1980s, the United States pursued a policy of fiscal expansion combined with monetary contraction, which brought about a substantial appreciation of the exchange rate (by more than 50 percent between 1980 and 1984). Although the exchange rate was not being used as a policy instrument (and was, in fact, floating freely vis-à-vis its major competitors), the appreciation contributed notably to a sharp slowdown in price inflation. Perhaps 1.5 to 2 percentage points of the inflation slowdown between 1980 and 1984 could be attributed directly to the currency appreciation. But, as in the Latin American countries, the sharp appreciation was not sustainable. U.S. exporters were squeezed very hard both by the rise in wage costs and the appreciation in E, and as a result, after 1984 the United States reversed its official policy and supported a sharp depreciation of the dollar.

15-6 SUMMARY

Inflation can occur because of a sustained rise in the money supply, as we saw in Chapter 11. It can also result, however, from *supply shocks*, which cause upward shifts in the aggregate supply schedule, as we study in this chapter. Nonetheless, long and persistent inflations are hard to explain by supply shocks alone, unless those shocks are accommodated by increases in the money supply.

Wages are a crucial factor affecting aggregate supply. Wages are typically set in labor contracts, and are influenced by the rate of unemployment and the future inflation rate that is expected at the time of negotiation. In particular, the change in wages is inversely related to the rate of unemployment. If unemployment is above its *natural rate*, nominal wages will tend to rise by less than the expected inflation; if unemployment is below the natural rate, nominal wages will tend to rise by more than the expected inflation. The *Phillips curve* is the relationship linking the rate of nominal wage change to the expected rate of inflation and to the rate of unemployment relative to the natural rate.

We develop a *dynamic Keynesian model*, in which nominal wages are predetermined by labor contracts within a period, but in which nominal wages change between periods according to the unemployment rate and *inflationary expectations*. Today's aggregate demand not only influences current output and prices, but also future output and prices through the effects on wage changes. In a case where nominal wages are rising due to contract clauses, an attempt to stabilize prices is likely to impose a cost in terms of lost output and high unemployment. Alternatively, in view of the predetermined wage increases, the authorities may expand aggregate demand by as much as necessary to preserve full employment. Such a policy of maintaining full employment by expansionary monetary policy is known as *monetary accommodation*.

In its original version, the Phillips curve was simply an inverse relationship between nominal wage changes and unemployment. The original version of the Phillips curve worked relatively well for U.S. data in the stable economic environment of the 1960s, but fell apart when inflation began to rise significantly at the end of the 1960s. As a result of the empirical breakdown of the original Phillips curve, and as a result of new theoretical insights, the Phillips curve was amended to relate nominal wage changes not only to unemployment but also to inflationary expectations.

The trade-off between inflation and unemployment depends on the specific mechanisms used by agents to form inflation expectations. Under *adaptive expectations* individuals form their expectations of future inflation according to past rates of inflation. An important implication of adaptive expectations is the *accelerationist principle*. If the policy authorities attempt to maintain unemployment below the natural rate, the economy will suffer ever-increasing rates of inflation. In the long term, only the natural rate of unemployment is consistent with a stable inflation rate.

The *sacrifice ratio* measures how many extra points of unemployment are necessary to bring about a given reduction in inflation. Specifically, the SR is calculated as the cumulative *unemployment gap* (the excess unemployment over the natural rate) in a particular period divided by the reduction in inflation over the same period. In the U.S. disinflation of 1980–1984, for example, the sacrifice ratio was 1.5, meaning that on average, an excess of unemployment above the natural rate of 1.5 percentage points for one year, led to a reduction of inflation of one percentage point.

A major critique of the inflation-unemployment analysis was led by the *rational expectations* school. The rational expectations theorists doubted that inflationary expectations are set by arbitrary, backward-looking mechanisms such as adaptive expectations. They argued that agents form their inflation expectations using all the information available, and judgment about future economic policies. When inflation expectations are based on rational expectations, or *forward-looking expectations*, then the inflation-unemployment trade-off may disappear, even in the short run. Policymakers can achieve zero inflation without any loss of output or excessive unemployment, as long as they are able to convince agents that aggregate demand will be tight enough to maintain price stability. That is, as long as the anti-inflation policy is credible.

Governments cannot easily establish *credibility*. A commitment to end inflation by the authorities will be doubted by the public if, for example, there is an underlying fiscal deficit. There may exist political uncertainty about who will actually govern in the future. Additionally, the government may have the incentive to promise a tough policy and then "cheat" by actually carrying out a very expansionary policy. This latter problem is known as *dynamic inconsistency*.

In an open economy, the exchange rate has a very strong direct influence on prices. Exchange-rate policy can play a direct role in anti-inflation programs. Some countries have tried to peg the exchange rate as a crucial feature of an anti-inflation program, such as Argentina and Chile in the late 1970s and early 1980s. Such a policy can be dangerous, however, unless it is accompanied by other policies, such as a suspension of wage-indexation arrangements. Otherwise, a fixed exchange rate can hold down some prices in the economy (such as those of exportable and importable goods) while other prices and wages continue to rise. If the nominal wage keeps going up after the exchange rate has been stopped, the result can be a costly deterioration of the international competitiveness of domestic producers. The balance-of-payments situation eventually becomes unsustainable, and the exchange rate has to be devalued, eventually leading to renewed inflation.

Key Concepts

supply shocks
wage shock
wage indexation
overlapping contracts
tight labor market
natural rate of unemployment
Phillips curve
predetermined wages
accommodation

expectations formation
   mechanisms
adaptive expectations
rational expectations
accelerationist principle
sacrifice ratio
inflation inertia
dynamic inconsistency

Problems and Questions

1. Describe what happens to the price level in the following cases. Identify whether it is an aggregate demand or an aggregate supply shock that caused the movement, and whether it is temporary or permanent.

a. Due to bad weather, crops will be reduced significantly this year.

b. The country goes to war.

c. The government increases spending to build new public housing.

d. Unions get a 20 percent wage increase.

2. Discuss the reasons why nominal wages are sticky. How is wage stickiness related to the duration of labor contracts?

3. Assume that this year many unions are negotiating new contracts.

a. How does the current unemployment rate affect their negotiating power?

b. What is the importance of current wage negotiations for future inflation?

c. If unions are able to obtain high raises in future nominal wages, what policies can the government implement to keep full employment? At what cost?

4. Consider an economy in which unemployment is at its natural rate, unions expect next year's inflation rate to be 5 percent, and they are able to obtain a 5 percent nominal wage increase for next year. What happens to real wages, employment, and output if actual inflation next year is 5 percent? What if it is lower or higher than 5 percent?

5. Assume that people expect next year's inflation rate to be equal to this year's actual inflation. The government wants to lower unemployment below its natural rate permanently.

a. What type of policy would the government have to implement to achieve this objective? What would the future path of inflation look like?

b. What type of inflationary expectations must the public have in order to avoid accelerating inflation? Do you find it reasonable to assume that people would behave in such a way? Why?

6. Discuss how the following circumstances affect the value of the sacrifice ratio and the amount of inertial inflation in the economy:

a. Long-term contracts are pervasive in the economy.

b. People adjust their inflationary expectations very fast.

c. The government has a reputation of not being able to reduce its expenditures.

d. People have rational rather than adaptive expectations.

7. Discuss the main differences between rational and adaptive expectations. What does each imply about the effectiveness of macroeconomic policy?

8. Countries A and B are identical in all respects except one: in country A nominal wages are indexed to past inflation, while in country B they are not. In which country will disinflation be more costly? Does your answer depend on how people form their inflationary expectations?

9. Analyze the conditions under which fixing the exchange rate would be an effective way to control inflation.

10. Can the exchange rate be used as the only instrument to control inflation? What are the risks of fixing the exchange rate to control inflation while at the same time increasing government spending?

APPENDIX

The technical derivation to get from equation (15.15) to equation (15.16) is as follows. (P^e_{+1}/P_{+1}) is equal to

$$\frac{(P^e_{+1} - P_{+1})}{(P_{+1})} + 1$$

This expression in turn can be written as

$$\left[\frac{(P^e_{+1} - P_{+1})}{P}\right](P/P_{+1}) + 1$$

Notice that (P/P_{+1}) is simply $1/(1 + \hat{P}_{+1})$, where $\hat{P}_{+1}$ is the inflation rate between this period and next period. Also, note that the expression

$$\frac{(P^e_{+1} - P_{+1})}{P}$$

can be rewritten as

$$\frac{(P^e_{+1} - P)}{P} - \frac{(P_{+1} - P)}{P}$$

which in turn is equal to

$$\hat{P}^e_{+1} - \hat{P}_{+1}$$

If we put these pieces together, the original expression P^e_{+1}/P_{+1} can be rewritten as

$$\frac{(\hat{P}^e_{+1} - \hat{P}_{+1})}{(1 + \hat{P}_{+1})} + 1$$

Now, we use a trick. When $\hat{P}_{+1}$ and $\hat{P}^e_{+1}$ are small numbers (say, 10 percent per year), then $1 + \hat{P}_{+1}$ is close to 1.0, and dividing by $(1 + \hat{P}_{+1})$ is very close to dividing by 1.0. Therefore, the entire expression that we started with can be approximated as

$$\hat{P}^e_{+1} - \hat{P}_{+1} + 1$$

This means that equation (15.15) in the text can be written as equation (15.16).

Institutional Determinants of Wages and Unemployment

As the arguments in the previous four chapters have shown, the nature of wage setting is crucial for overall macroeconomic equilibrium. If *nominal* wages are fixed (or predetermined within a period), then monetary policy can be used to change both the level of output and the level of employment. If *real* wages are fixed (through wage indexing, for example), then monetary policy tends to affect prices and the exchange rate but *not* the level of output. Furthermore, if wage inflation exhibits *inertia*, because wage increases are set by long-term and overlapping contracts, then the process of stabilizing inflation may require a period of unemployment above the natural rate. On the other hand, if wage setting is flexible and governed by forward-looking expectations, then inflation can be controlled without excessive unemployment.

These options depend a great deal on the nature of the *labor-market institutions* in the country. Countries vary enormously in the extent of unionization, the duration of wage agreements, the use of indexation clauses, the extent to which wage contracts are synchronized or overlapping, and the involvement of the government in wage negotiations. These differences can sometimes be explained on economic grounds—countries that have experienced a high average rate of inflation tend to adopt wage indexation arrangements, for example—but often noneconomic factors, including the history of the country and its political evolution, account for the organizational features of the labor market.

In this chapter, we investigate the main institutions of the labor market and examine their effects on the inflation-unemployment trade-off and the patterns of unemployment more generally. As a benchmark illustration, we show how labor-market institutions cast light on why the industrial countries responded very differently to one of the key economic shocks of the 1970s, the rise of oil prices. Some countries experienced high unemployment as the result of the shocks; others did not. The patterns of wage setting in the different countries help us to understand these differences. After examining wage-setting patterns and the oil shock, we turn to a more detailed analysis of unemployment, and once again examine some of the important differences across countries.

16-1 LABOR-MARKET INSTITUTIONS AND AGGREGATE SUPPLY BEHAVIOR

Labor-market institutions differ markedly across countries in several major dimensions: (1) the extent to which wages are set in formal or informal contracts; (2) the extent to which wage contracts are negotiated collectively by unions and enterprises; (3) the degree to which negotiations are centralized, that is, whether wage agreements are concluded at the level of the nation, the industry, the region, or the firm; (4) the timing of wage contracts, including contract duration and the extent of synchronization among different wage contracts; (5) the role of the government in the wage bargain, both directly as an employer and indirectly as an influence on contracts reached between private firms and workers; and (6) the use of indexation in wage agreements.

Let us turn to each of these categories and describe briefly the patterns across countries and their macroeconomic significance.

Formal Versus Informal Wage Contracts

We have repeatedly noted that one of the sources of macroeconomic rigidity is a nominal wage predetermined by a long-term wage contract. From the outset, we should recognize that the use of any sort of formal wage contract is much greater in the advanced countries than in the developing countries. In countries with lower levels of per capita income, a large proportion of the work force is in agriculture working either as self-employed farmers or as hired laborers without formal contracts. For example, in the United States only 3 percent of the labor force is in the agricultural sector, whereas in Peru the number is more than 12 times that, at around 38 percent. Moreover, as stressed by Hernando de Soto and others in recent years, a large proportion of urban labor as well tends to be in the so-called informal sector, where workers are self-employed or working on a day-wage basis with no formal contract.[1]

Unionization

The nature of unionization is probably the most important source of differences in labor-market institutions among the industrial countries. Most long-term wage agreements are set between unions and employers, so that the coverage of long-term contracts depends directly on the extent to which wages are determined in collective bargaining settlements between unions and employers. Moreover, the existence of unions increases the bargaining power of workers employed within a firm in two ways, vis-à-vis their employers and also vis-à-vis workers *outside* the firm who would like to be hired by the firm.[2] In recent work, economists have described the latter

---

[1] For an influential discussion of the informal sector, see Hernando de Soto, *The Other Path: The Invisible Revolution in the Third World* (New York: Harper & Row, 1989).

[2] One important measure of the bargaining power of unions is the extent to which unionized wages exceed the wages of comparable nonunion workers. The so-called "union wage effect" in the United States is positive, and typically measured to be in the range of 20 to 30 percent. See Richard Freeman and James Medoff, *What Do Unions Do?* (New York: Basic Books, 1984), for a discussion of the U.S. case. A more recent estimate places the union wage

effect as strengthening insiders (workers already holding jobs) versus outsiders (workers seeing jobs).[3] As a result of this enhanced bargaining power, unions allow workers to bid up wages over the market-clearing wage and to prevent the real wage from falling in the face of adverse shocks.

The extent of unionization, that is, the proportion of the work force in unions, varies significantly across countries. The highest rates of union membership in the world are observed in the Scandinavian economies. In the mid-1980s, Denmark and Sweden had the highest rate of unionization, with 98 percent and 95 percent of nonagricultural employment, respectively; Finland's rate was 85 percent. High rates of unionization were also observed in Austria and Norway (over 60 percent) and the United Kingdom (around 50 percent), although union membership declined during the administration of Margaret Thatcher. By comparison, unionization rates in Japan were much lower in the mid-1980s, at around 29 percent. Among industrialized countries, the United States had one of the lowest unionization rates at the time (18 percent).[4] More recent estimates for the United States point toward a further drop in this rate, which has reached about 14 percent in 1988.[5]

The extent of unionization gives a rough idea of the influence of unions on overall wage setting, but unions often have greater influence than the membership numbers suggest. For example, non-unionized workers within firms with unions may obtain similar wage arrangements as their unionized counterparts. Second, union wage settlements often have a significant effect on government wages. Third, in some countries in Western Europe, the union wage agreements may be extended by the minister of labor to cover nonunion workers in the economy. Speaking generally, then, the agreements reached by organized labor receive considerable public attention and serve as a broad pattern for wage setting in the whole economy.

Centralization of Wage Negotiations

Another important dimension of wage setting concerns the level of wage bargaining, which can occur at the national, industry, regional, or plant level. In the Scandinavian countries, especially Norway and Sweden, negotiations are highly centralized, though there has been some movement toward decentralization in recent years. The first round of wage setting occurs at the national level, between national union federations and national employers' federations. The national agreement is then applied, in the course of further negotiations, at the regional and plant levels. Austria and Germany also have fairly centralized structures, with bargaining at the industry level. Canada, Japan, the United Kingdom, and the United States are at the other

---

effect at 28 percent for the United States in 1987–1988; see Michael Wachter and William Carter, "Norm Shifts in Union Wages: Will 1989 Be a Replay of 1969?" *Brookings Papers on Economic Activity*, No. 2, 1989.

[3] For a path-breaking treatment of the bargaining power that comes from being an insider within the firm, see Assar Lindbeck and Dennis Snower, *The Insider-Outsider Theory of Employment and Unemployment* (Cambridge, Mass.: MIT Press, 1988).

[4] See Richard Freeman, "Labour Market Institutions and Economic Performance," *Economic Policy*, April 1988.

[5] Daniel Mitchell, "Wage Pressures and Labor Shortages: The 1960s and the 1980s," *Brookings Papers on Economic Activity*, No. 2, 1989.

extreme; that is, they are decentralized, with most wage negotiations taking place at the plant level.

Highly centralized labor institutions have been termed "corporatist" systems by political scientists and economists. *Corporatism* refers to a mode of political organization in which so-called "peak associations" (national representatives of employers and workers) are given enormous power to bargain on behalf of their constituencies. In the 1970s, some industrialized corporatist economies managed relatively well in the face of the rise of world oil prices, as we shall see. Wage bargaining at the national level allowed them to adapt quickly and relatively efficiently to the changing international situation. A similar pattern of relatively successful adjustment was observed in some highly decentralized economies such as Japan and the United States. In these economies, greater flexibility of labor markets was an advantage. Perhaps, surprisingly, countries with intermediate levels of centralization, where bargaining takes place mostly at the industry level, tended to experience the biggest difficulties in adjusting to the oil shocks. (This issue is analyzed in greater detail in the next section.)

Timing of Wage Contracts

Two further institutional patterns that affect wage setting involve timing. Both the *duration* of wage contracts and the extent of *synchronization* in wage negotiations have implications for the extent of inertia in wage inflation. The simplest aspect of timing is contract duration. In the industrial countries, this tends to vary from one to three years, with contracts of one year being the most common. In the United States, however, most union wage agreements have been made for a three-year period.

Full synchronization means that all contracts are signed at the same time for the whole economy. At the other end of the spectrum, negotiations that are scattered evenly throughout the year are said to be *asynchronized*. The extent of synchronization is generally related to the level at which negotiations take place. As a general rule, the more centralized the negotiation process, the higher the degree of synchronization.

The Nordic countries, for example, have highly centralized and highly synchronized negotiations. Japan is an exception to the rule in that wage negotiations are highly synchronized even though the agreements are negotiated at the plant level. This stems from a peculiar Japanese practice whereby the national confederations of workers and entrepreneurs (SOYHO, DOMEI, and so forth) help to coordinate the plant bargaining during the spring wage offensive, or *shunto*. At the other extreme are Canada, the United Kingdom, and the United States, where negotiations happen mostly at the plant level and are staggered throughout the year.

When wage contracting is staggered, nominal wages tend to show more inertia. That is because the average wage in the economy at any time is a weighted average of wages that were set at very different times. If new information comes along, such as news that the central bank is tightening monetary policy, it will take wage setters several months—or years—before all the existing contracts can be renegotiated to accommodate the new facts. With synchronized wage negotiations, the wage level can move more quickly to reflect the new economic circumstances as soon as the wage agreement is renewed.

Thus, anti-inflation policies tend to have larger output costs in economies with staggered wage negotiations. Tight monetary policy has little direct effect on the nominal wage at the outset because wage increases have been preordained by existing contracts. In an economy where wages are all negotiated at one time of the year, on the other hand, credible anti-inflation policies announced just before this date could put a sudden halt to wage and price inflation, or at least slow it down.

Incomes Policy and the Role of Government in Wage Negotiations

The extent to which governments intervene in the bargaining process also varies, and it tends to change markedly over time within a country. Government participation has been prevalent in the Scandinavian economies, where the government is often involved informally in discussions preceding the national negotiations, and less frequently, intervenes directly in the wage-setting process. Interestingly, at certain times fiscal policies have even been linked to wage agreements in Sweden, where the authorities have used tax incentives as a means to keep wage increases under control.

In other cases and other countries, the authorities have tried moral suasion, political pressure, and even legislation to push unions into moderating their wage demands. This type of action, generally known as an *incomes policy,* was used in the United Kingdom during the Labor governments of the 1970s. The Labor party witnessed an escalation of wage inflation when it came to power in March 1974. Starting in the second half of 1975, the government introduced an incomes policy that included a low ceiling for wage adjustments throughout the economy. For their part, employers were by law prevented from passing through into prices any wage increases that were beyond the policy. At the beginning, unions enthusiastically supported the policy, which worked extremely well in reducing inflation. The ceilings were increasingly violated as time passed, however, and the policy collapsed around 1978.[6] Incomes policies have also been tried—with mixed results, we shall see in Chapter 23—in some Latin American anti-inflation programs during the 1980s.

As a general rule, the Canadian, the Japanese, and the United States governments have played little active role in labor negotiations. In the United States, there have been brief flirtations with incomes policies, including wage-price guidelines that were set up by the Kennedy administration in the early 1960s, by the Nixon administration in the early 1970s, and by the Carter administration in the mid-1970s. The experience during the Nixon years, for example, was similar to that in the United Kingdom. In 1971–1972, controls seemed to achieve a small reduction in the inflation rate and in wage increases. Inflation, however, escalated to unprecedented levels in 1973, and the program was suspended.[7] The U.S. government has some-

---

[6] For an analysis of the U.K. experience with incomes policy, see Richard Layard, *How to Beat Unemployment* (Oxford: Oxford University Press, 1986), especially Chapter 10.

[7] Robert Gordon has written a number of papers analyzing the experience of the United States with incomes policy in the early 1970s. See, for example, his article "The Response of Wages and Prices to the First Two Years of Controls," *Brookings Papers on Economic Activity,* No. 3, 1973.

times used its own negotiations with public employees as a rallying point for more general small wage increases. This was the strategy when President Reagan fired striking air traffic controllers in 1981 during a pay dispute. But as a general rule, the U.S. government has not intervened heavily in wage negotiations between private parties.

Wage Indexation

Workers and employers can either choose to establish predetermined nominal levels for future wages, or they can agree to adjust nominal wages in the future according to observed developments in some other variable. This practice is known as *wage indexation*. In principle, wages could be indexed to the GNP, the volume of sales, or some other variable. In practice, wage changes are almost always linked to (lagged) changes in the overall consumer price level, using a mechanism something like this:

$$\hat{w}_{+1} = v\hat{P} + \text{other factors} \tag{16.1}$$

Equation (16.1) is a general formula for backward-looking wage indexation. Wages are adjusted according to some proportion (v) of lagged inflation, where v is a number between zero and one. If $v = 1$, we say that indexation is total; that is, wages increase by the rate of inflation of the preceding period. But more commonly, v is less than 1, so that indexation is partial.

In many countries, the existence of backward-looking wage indexation can account to a large extent for the presence of $\hat{P}$ in the Phillips curve equation: $\hat{P}_{+1} = \hat{P} - b(U - U_n)$. In other words, $\hat{P}$ affects $\hat{P}_{+1}$ not only because of inflationary expectations, but also because of formal indexation provisions in wage agreements. This is one way wage indexation increases the persistence of inflation: prices feed into wages, which in turn affect prices, and so on. Indexation also introduces a significant degree of inflexibility in real wages, since, indeed, that is precisely what indexation is for, to insulate real wages from price fluctuations. The higher the degree of indexation, that is, the larger the coefficient v, the larger these two effects are.

This suggests that wage indexation is particularly problematic in two circumstances. First, when the macroeconomic authorities are trying to slow down an inherited inflation, backward-looking wage indexation can add inertia to inflation, and thereby raise the output costs of disinflation. Second, when adverse supply shocks which require that the real wage be reduced hit the economy, indexation can prevent or slow down the adjustment of the real wage to the new equilibrium level. Thus, economies with extensive wage indexing in the 1970s fared particularly poorly in the face of rising world oil prices, a point that we shall expand on shortly.

In fact, backward-looking wage indexation makes sense only in one situation. When inflation is high (because of the need for an inflation tax, for example) and expected to remain high, and the policymakers for one reason or another are loath to introduce an anti-inflation program, then wage indexation can provide an efficient way to adjust wages to the inflationary environment. However, once the government decides to curb inflation, it should generally encourage the suspension of indexation arrangements as one part of the overall anti-inflation program.

Countries with long histories of inflation have tended to incorporate cost-of-living adjustment clauses, or COLAS—another name for indexation—into labor contracts. In the developing world, Brazil and Chile, to take two prime examples, have had extensive wage indexation for long periods of time. With the large supply shocks of the last two decades, these practices have tended to do more harm than good, as they have helped to perpetuate inflation or have contributed to its acceleration.

COLAS are found in the industrialized world as well. In Italy, the famous *scala mobile* during the 1970s and early 1980s established approximately 100 percent wage indexation. The practice of wage indexation was also widespread in France until the mid-1980s. Most other European countries made less use of indexation clauses, and such arrangements are banned outright in West Germany. In the United States, cost-of-living adjustment clauses made increasingly frequent appearances in union contracts during the 1970s and early 1980s, as workers attempted to cope with higher rates of inflation. Thus, while in the late 1960s workers covered by COLA agreements were about one quarter of all employees involved in collective bargaining, in 1976–1979 that proportion surpassed 60 percent. With the slowdown of inflation in the 1980s, however, the use of indexation arrangements has definitely subsided. This pattern is shown in Figure 16-1.

By way of review, Table 16-1 summarizes some of the key institutional characteristics of labor markets for a large number of industrialized countries in the 1980s.

Figure 16-1

U.S. Workers Covered by Indexation Clauses in Collective Agreements, 1968–1987

(From Wayne Vroman and John Abowd, "Disaggregated Wage Developments," Brooking Papers on Economic Activity, *No. 1, 1988, Table 7.)*

TABLE 16-1

INSTITUTIONAL ASPECTS OF THE LABOR MARKET IN INDUSTRIALIZED COUNTRIES

Countries	Bargaining Level	Union Coverage (percent)	Synchronization	Duration of Contracts	Government Role
Austria	Industry level	61	High	12–15 months	Extensive
Canada	Plant level	37	Low	1–3 years (65% are 1 year)	Not active
Finland	Economy-wide agreement sets basis	85	High	1–2 years	Active
France	Industry and plant level	28	Low	Indefinite with annual changes	Active
Germany	Industry level	42	Low	1 year	Some
Italy	National guidelines and plant level	45	High	3 years	As mediator
Japan	Plant level	29	High	1 year	Little
New Zealand	All levels	46	Moderate-high	1 year	Has varied over time
Norway	National, centralized	61	High	2 years	Active
Sweden	National, centralized	95	High	1–2 years	Influential, not formal
United Kingdom	Plant level	52	Low	1 year	Little
United States	Mostly plant level	18	Very low	Mostly 3 years	Not active

Source: Union coverage, Richard Freeman, "Labour Market Institutions and Economic Performance," Economic Policy, April 1988, Table 2. For all other variables, see Michael Bruno and Jeffrey Sachs, The Economics of Worldwide Stagflation *(Cambridge, MA: Harvard University Press, 1985).*

16-2 LABOR-MARKET INSTITUTIONS AND THE SUPPLY SHOCKS OF THE 1970S

One of the most striking economic developments of the past 20 years has involved the enormous fluctuations in the price of oil. In the 1970s, oil prices skyrocketed, while in the mid-1980s they plummeted. These changes had enormous effects on the world macroeconomy, and they are of special interest here because they help to illuminate how different labor-market institutions caused various industrial economies to respond differently to the same global shock.

The path of the nominal price of oil (in dollars per barrel) and the real price (deflated by the U.S. consumer price index) are shown in Figure 16-2. Note the two main adverse supply shocks, in 1973–1974 and 1979–1980, and the positive supply shocks in the 1980s. (Note also that the shocks are "adverse" from the point of view of oil users, not oil producers.)[8] The oil

---

[8] The major increases in oil prices were prompted by developments on the supply side of the oil market. The worldwide production of crude oil dropped from an annual growth rate of 10 percent in 1955–1973 to zero growth between 1973 and 1979. This decrease was partly the result

Nominal   Real (nominal price deflated by U.S. consumer price index)

Figure 16-2

The Evolution of Nominal and Real Oil Prices, 1970– 1988

(From International Monetary Fund, International Financial Statistics, *various issues.)*

price increases in the 1970s were traumatic for the industrialized world, and they ushered in a decade of *stagflation*—that is, economic stagnation combined with high inflation—bringing to an end two decades of high growth with low inflation during the 1950s and 1960s.

A Framework to Analyze Oil Price Shocks

To analyze the consequences of the oil price shocks, we shall focus on the effects on aggregate supply.[9] To integrate the impact of an input price shock, such as higher oil prices, into our earlier aggregate supply analysis, we start

---

of the policies within the Organization of Petroleum Exporting Countries (OPEC), which attempted to keep world prices of oil high by restraining production, but also resulted from a slowdown in production in the United States and some other oil-importing countries. Subsequently, after a sharp drop in oil use in the industrial countries and the development of new energy sources, oil prices began to fall in the early 1980s, and collapsed in 1986.

[9] We should mention, however, that aggregate demand is also affected by higher oil prices (oil importers tend to suffer a decline in aggregate demand, while oil exporters experience a rise in aggregate demand). A more complete analysis of the macroeconomic effects of the rise in oil prices, on the demand side as well as the supply side, can be found in M. Bruno and J. Sachs, *The Economics of Worldwide Stagflation* (Cambridge, Mass.: Harvard University Press, 1985).

with the production function. The first thing we need to do is to make room for a third factor of production:

$$Q = Q(K, L, IN) \tag{16.2}$$
$$+ \; + \; +$$

Equation (16.2) is an expanded version of expression (3.1), leaving aside the effect of technological improvements. As usual, the level of output is a function of capital (which, as before, is fixed in the short run) and labor. But now we include an intermediate input (IN), in this case oil, which is a complement to capital and labor in the production process. Specifically, the marginal product of labor is a positive function of the amount of IN used in production. For a given level of L and K, higher IN means a higher MPL, and therefore a higher demand for labor and a higher overall supply of output.

The supply shock that the oil-importing countries experienced in the 1970s was the increase in the relative price of imported oil in terms of output (P_n/P). The demand for oil, as for other factors of production, depends negatively on its real price. Thus, the first effect of the rise in oil prices is that firms began to use less oil in their operations in order to economize. As companies reduce the amount of oil being used, the volume of production for a given amount of labor input goes down. This is shown as a downward shift in the production function in Figure 16-3a.

The less there is of the intermediate input (with a fixed amount of capital), the more the marginal productivity of labor declines. Thus, the demand for labor also goes down, as shown graphically in Figure 16-3b. And when demand goes down, the equilibrium level of the real wage surely declines. With an upward-sloping supply of labor, the lower real wage causes a reduction in household labor supply. The level of employment therefore declines, even if there is instantaneous wage adjustments and full labor-market clearing (which are not very likely). Output also drops, and the equilibrium goes down and to the left from point A to B in the graph.

Figure 16-3
Effects of An Oil Price Increase: (a) The Production Function; (b) the Demand for Labor

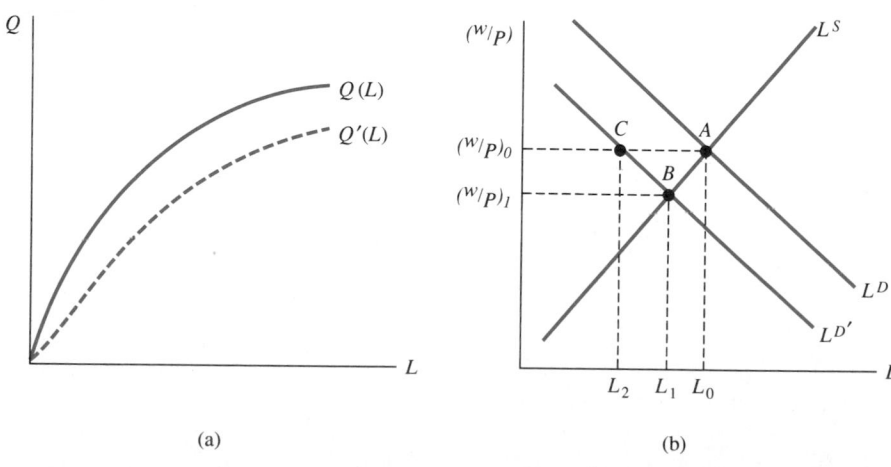

(a)   (b)

There is an even worse scenario possible. Suppose that real wages are *rigid* because of some institutional feature such as union wage setting, long-term contracts, or indexation, for example. In this case, the new equilibrium is at point *C,* indicating a still lower level of employment and output. Whatever the particular details of the story, the rise in oil prices shifts the aggregate supply curve to the left. If wages are flexible, as they are in classical labor-market analysis, the vertical aggregate supply curve shifts to the left. If real wages are rigid and protected, say, by indexation, the aggregate supply curve is still vertical, but now it shifts even farther to the left. And if nominal wages are rigid (or at least predetermined within the period), as they are in the Keynesian model, the aggregate supply curve is upward sloping, but it still shifts to the left.

The oil price increase is thus a quintessential stagflationary shock. As we see in Figure 16-4, it lowers output at the same time that it increases prices. This creates a terrible problem for the macroeconomic authorities. If they do nothing, they will have to suffer the combination of a contraction in economic activity and an increase in prices. Stagnation can be deepened for an oil importer because the higher oil prices are also likely to cause a decline in aggregate demand (since purchasing power is shifted toward oil purchases, and away from final goods purchases). As aggregate demand declines (the shift is not shown in the graph) along with the adverse shift in aggregate supply, stagnation for the oil-importing country intensifies.

If the authorities decide to accommodate the shock through expansionary government policies, the economy could reach a point like *C* in the graph if the policy succeeds. But the cost of keeping output and employment unchanged after the shock will be an even greater increase in the price level. Policymakers must understand, however, that Q_0 may no longer be obtainable at steady state because of a permanent reduction in the equilibrium level of employment.

The Response to the Oil Shock of the 1970s: Europe Versus the United States

A remarkable fact of the 1970s was the generalized nature of the stagflationary experience throughout the industrialized world. All 24 OECD mem-

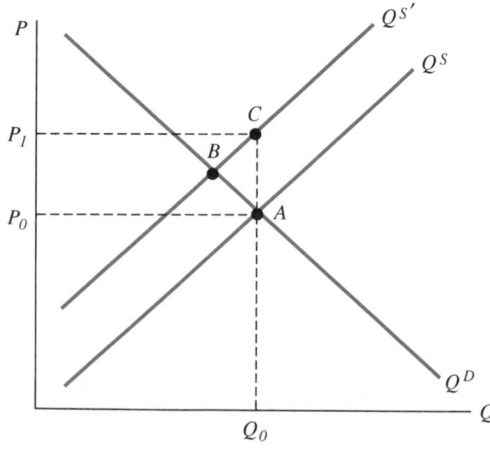

Figure 16-4
An Oil Price Increase in the Aggregate Supply—Aggregate Demand Setting

ber countries experienced a slowdown of economic growth after 1973.[10] And 23 out of 24, Switzerland excepted, suffered an increase in their inflation rate at the same time. Figure 16-5 shows the average rates of inflation and unemployment for the OECD as a whole over the period 1970–1985. Note how *both* magnitudes increase significantly after 1973, thereby reversing the original shape of the Phillips curve.

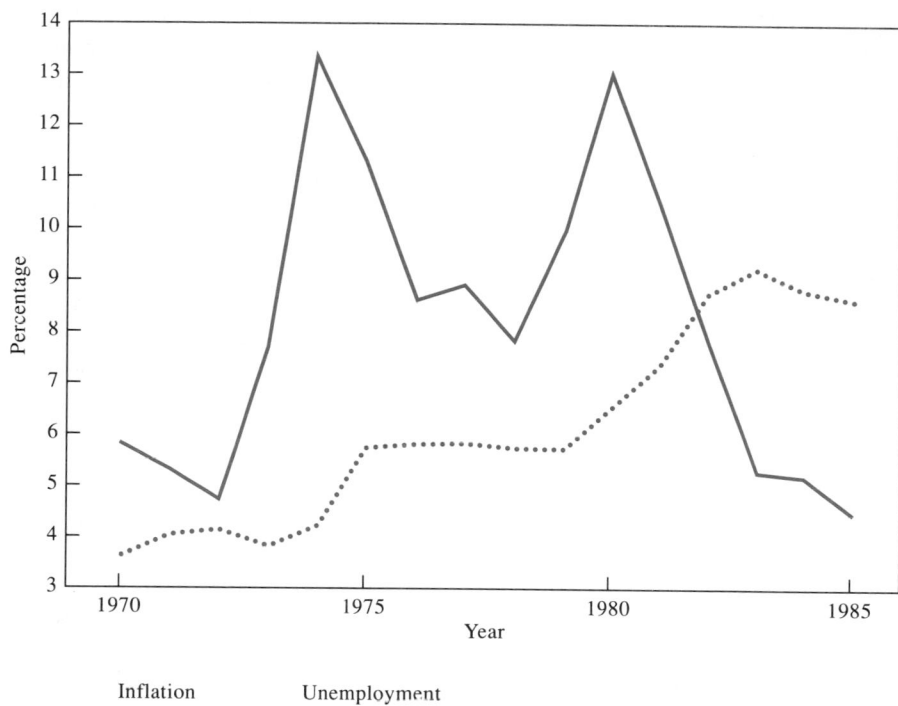

Inflation   Unemployment

Figure 16-5

Average Inflation and Unemployment in the OECD, 1970–1985

(From Organization for Economic Cooperation and Development, Economic Outlook, *December 1989, Tables R11 and R18.)*

The synchronization of these events across the different industrialized economies was striking at the time. The years 1973 to 1975, when the first wave of higher oil prices hit, witnessed a steep economic contraction and a brusque acceleration of inflation. From 1975 to 1979 the pattern was a generalized recovery and receding inflation. Then recession came back, accompanied by increasing inflation, at the time of the second oil price increase in 1979–1981.

Employment was a casualty of the adjustment to the oil shock. In most cases, unemployment rates increased to levels only matched in the immediate years after World War II. It is interesting, however, to notice a differ-

---

[10] The Organization for Economic Cooperation and Development (OECD) is an organization of the advanced industrialized countries.

ence between Europe and the United States in this respect. In Europe, unemployment increased steadily from 1973 to 1981; in the United States it rose during 1974–1975, but then came down in the following four years. Similarly, after the second oil shock, unemployment rose sharply for a prolonged period in Europe, while unemployment again rose and then fell in the United States. These differences are shown in Figure 16-6, for the years 1970–1985.

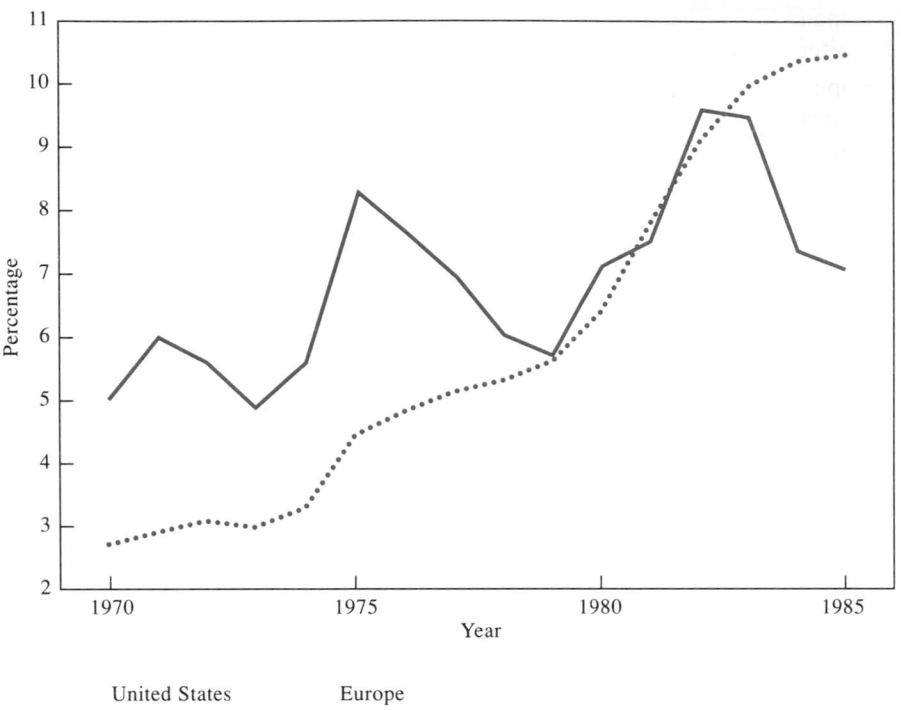

United States   Europe

Figure 16-6
Evolution of Unemployment: Europe Versus the United States, 1970–1985

(From Organization for Economic Cooperation and Development, Economic Outlook, *December 1989, Table R18.)*

The key element in the difference between the course of unemployment in the United States and that in Europe seems to be the greater downward flexibility of real wages in the United States (and Canada) as compared to Europe.[11] In terms of Figure 16-3b, the increase in oil prices moved the United States to a point like *B,* while Europe ended up around point *C.* It seems that differences in wage-setting institutions in the two regions hold the key to the explanation. In the United States, low rates of unionization and long-term wage contracts permitted a fairly rapid downward adjustment of the real wage. In Europe, by contrast, a high degree of unionization, as well as highly indexed short-term wage contracts, led to much greater rigidity in real wages.

---

[11] This hypothesis is presented and extensively analyzed in Michael Bruno and Jeffrey Sachs, *The Economics of Worldwide Stagflation* (Cambridge, Mass.: Harvard University Press, 1985).

TABLE 16-2

THE REAL WAGE GAP IN EUROPE VERSUS THE UNITED STATES AND CANADA, 1969–1981 (PERCENTAGE)

	1969	1973	1975	1979	1981
North America					
Canada	2.0	−1.4	−0.8	−1.4	NA
United States	0.6	5.1	1.3	6.3	7.4
Europe					
France	−5.5	−0.6	2.9	3.1	4.1
Germany	0.0	8.6	13.8	15.1	17.7
United Kingdom	1.8	4.9	10.4	17.3	25.3

NA = Not available.
Source: Michael Bruno and Jeffrey Sachs, The Economics of Worldwide Stagflation, *(Cambridge, MA: Harvard University Press, 1985).*

These differences in the real wage behavior can be measured by the *real wage gap*, which is the percentage difference between the real wage and the full-employment real wage, or $[(w/P) - wp^f]/wp^f$. When the wage gap is positive, the real wage is above the market-clearing level so that unemployment should be expected. As shown in Table 16-2, the evidence suggests that many European countries had large positive wage gaps in the late 1970s and early 1980s, while the United States and Canada showed a much smaller wage gap (it was even negative in the case of Canada), suggesting that in Europe, real wages failed to adjust downward when the economy was hit by the adverse supply shocks.

16-3 A DETAILED LOOK AT UNEMPLOYMENT

With good reason, unemployment is an overwhelming concern of policymakers and the general public. Unemployment often implies a waste of human resources that could otherwise be producing goods and services to satisfy the needs of society. At the same time, it can mean extreme personal hardship for the unemployed, and therefore it is an important social concern.

The unemployment rate fluctuates widely over time within a given country, in line with the business cycle. Unemployment increases during recessions and declines during booms. Recall Figure 3-2, which shows the history of the unemployment rate for the United States during the present century. Significant increases in unemployment occurred during the Great Depression (1929–1931), the first and second oil shocks (1973–1975 and 1979–1980), and the Reagan disinflation (1982–1983). The booms during World War II (1942–1945), the Korean conflict (1950–1953), and the 1960s (1961–1968) show large declines in the unemployment rate.

The average unemployment rate also varies widely across countries, as shown in Table 16-3. In the year 1985, for example, the jobless rate within our sample of countries ranges from almost 20 percent in Spain to a low of 2.6 percent in Japan. Simple differences in definitions of unemployment

TABLE 16-3

UNEMPLOYMENT RATE:
SELECTED COUNTRIES, 1989

Country	Unemployment*
Chile	5.3
France	9.5
Germany	7.9
Italy	12.0
Japan	2.3
Philippines	8.4
Republic of Korea	2.6
Spain	17.2
Switzerland	0.6
United Kingdom	6.3
United States	5.2

* Percentage of total employed.
Source: *International Labour Office,* Year-book of Labor Statistics, *1989–90.*

across countries account for some of these international variations. Structural differences in labor markets as well as institutional differences in wage setting also help to account for other differences in unemployment patterns across countries.

Now we take a detailed look at the phenomenon of unemployment and how it differs in various countries. We explore its many forms and their widely different implications for policy. Finally, we examine its costs, both long-term and cyclical.

Defining and Interpreting Unemployment

According to the International Labour Office (ILO), *unemployment* is defined as the pool of people above a specified age who are *without work,* are *currently available for work* and are *seeking work* during a period of reference.[12] All three conditions must be present for a person to be considered as unemployed. To be considered as seeking work, a person must take clear actions in pursuit of a job. Such actions include registration at an employment exchange, applications to employers, checking at worksites (farms, factory gates, market, and so on), and placing or responding to newspaper advertisements, to mention a few.

---

[12] See International Labour Office, *Yearbook of Labour Statistics,* Geneva, 1988. This definition comes from the Resolution of the Thirteenth International Conference of Labour Statisticians that took place in Geneva, 1982.

The *unemployment rate,* in turn, is defined as the number of unemployed people as a proportion of the *labor force*. The labor force is defined as all those with work or all those seeking work, that is, the sum of the employed plus the unemployed. Individuals that are neither employed nor seeking work are considered to be out of the labor force.

A broad common definition like this is no guarantee that unemployment is measured in the same way across countries, however. Measurements differ on the age limits used to define the labor force, on reference periods for job search (how frequently the person searches for work), on criteria for seeking work, on the statistical treatment of people temporarily laid off from work and expecting to be recalled, and on people looking for a job for the first time. The sources of information underlying the unemployment data also vary in different countries. Some countries use household surveys, others rely on social insurance data (such as the list of those receiving unemployment insurance benefits), while still others use employment office statistics.

In the United States, as in most countries, the unemployment rate is calculated from survey data, based on a representative sample of the population. It would be far too expensive, if not logistically impossible, to interview all working-age people in the country every month to calculate the unemployment rate. (Such a total survey of the population is carried out only once every ten years when the Census of Population is made.) Being unemployed in the United States, then, means not having a paid job and looking for a job within the last *four* weeks, or waiting to begin a job during the next four weeks, or having been laid off from a job but expecting to go back to the same job.

The interpretation of "being employed" or "actively looking for a job" is different in developing countries.[13] There, it is more likely that people work part-time or in low-productivity jobs such as street vendors. Although these people are underutilized, they are still considered to be employed. Other important phenomena in developing countries that affect the unemployment rate are the low participation of women in the labor force (most do their own domestic work at home, by no means less demanding than a formal job, but not counted as part of the labor force); the existence of a significant group of "discouraged workers," those who stop seeking a job because they believe that there are no jobs available for them; and the presence of a sizable informal sector (those working with no registration, permit, or other working papers) that is in all likelihood not counted in the official statistics.

Differences in interpreting unemployment data also appear among the developed economies. For example, Japan, Sweden, and Switzerland have had extremely low unemployment rates during the past 20 years, much below the levels of other industrial economies. Moreover, the unemployment rates in these countries did not rise sharply after the oil price shocks, as those in the United States and the rest of Europe did. A closer look at the data reveals that this was not because the economies of those countries were totally insulated from the oil shock, however.

---

[13] For a good introduction to labor markets in developing countries, see Malcolm Gillis, Dwight Perkins, Michael Romer, and Donald Snodgrass, *Economics of Development* (New York: W. W. Norton, 1983).

In Japan, for example, the criteria for being counted as "looking for work" are more stringent than in the United States, so many people who would be considered unemployed in the United States are simply counted as out of the labor force in Japan. Moreover, many women workers in Japan ceased to look for work after losing their jobs following the 1973 oil price increase. Sweden's low unemployment rate is partly explained by the fact that the government has traditionally undertaken major public retraining programs for laid-off workers, thereby keeping those who have lost their jobs out of the unemployment numbers. In Switzerland, the authorities have coped with recessions in part by "inviting" foreign workers to leave the country, or by not renewing work permits or not issuing new permits to foreign workers. Thus, even as employment has declined in Switzerland during recessionary periods, so too has the labor force, and thus the unemployment rate has remained low.

Despite difficulties in measurement and interpretation, the unemployment rate is still the best available index for comparing the degree of labor underutilization across countries. As our discussion suggests, however, a careful observer should not take the unemployment rate at face value.

Unemployment in the United States

So far, we have seen how the measurement and interpretation of unemployment differs across countries. During this process, we have implicitly treated the unemployed within a country as a homogeneous group. In reality, this is not the case. Some groups of people suffer unemployment more than others, and unemployment within all groups occurs for a wide variety of particular reasons. The importance of these distinctions is not purely academic. The welfare and policy implications of each of the various types of unemployment are fundamentally different. To give empirical content to this issue, we will focus principally on the experience of the United States.

Who Is Unemployed in the United States?   Unemployment is never distributed evenly among the population of a given country. Thus, one aspect of primary importance in diagnosing and, perhaps more important, treating unemployment is to understand well which groups of the population are hit especially hard by unemployment. Let us first consider the differences in unemployment rates for groups classified by age and gender, as described in Table 16-4.

The data show that unemployment is, on average, slightly higher among women than men. This difference is, however, overshadowed by the contrast between age groups. One of the striking findings in the table is the very high rate of teenage unemployment, which is about three times higher than the corresponding rate for adults. This pattern is often explained by the fact that teenagers generally spend time searching for the "right" job and are counted as unemployed during this search process. It should be noted, however, that many industrial countries, such as West Germany, show very low levels of teenage unemployment. The difference, it seems, is that West Germany has an elaborate system of job apprenticeships, vocational schools, and job placement services for teenagers, which cuts down sharply

TABLE 16-4

UNEMPLOYMENT RATES (PERCENT) IN
THE UNITED STATES BY AGE,
GENDER, AND ETHNIC ORIGIN

	1982	1990
Total*	9.7%	5.5%
Males	9.9	5.6
16–19 years	24.4	16.3
White	21.7	14.2
Black	48.9	32.1
20 years and over	8.8	4.9
White	7.8	4.3
Black	17.8	10.4
Females	9.4	5.4
16–19 years	21.9	14.7
White	19.0	12.6
Black	47.1	30.0
20 years and over	8.3	4.8
White	7.3	4.1
Black	15.4	9.6
White	8.6	4.7
Black	18.9	11.3

* Refers to the civilian unemployment rate.
Source: Economic Report of the President, *1991,*
Tables B-39 and B-4.

on the unemployment period at the beginning of a person's work life. Table 16-5 shows that Germany has strikingly low levels of teenage unemployment, not only in comparison to the United States, but also in relation to older age groups within that country (although the latter difference is less marked). The United Kingdom, in contrast, has a pattern that resembles the United States, with very high unemployment among teenagers.

A specific aspect of U.S. unemployment is its divergence by ethnic origin and race, typical of countries where the population is not entirely homogeneous. As Table 16-4 shows, the unemployment rate among blacks is several times higher than the corresponding figure for whites. Combining the effect of race with age, we can see that black teenagers are the most hard hit group of the population, with an almost 50 percent unemployment rate in 1982.

Normal Turnover Versus Hard-Core Unemployment   The group of unemployed in the economy is often thought of as an unchanging group of people who are unable to find work. This characterization applies to some part of the unemployed in any country, but not to others. People are constantly flowing into and out of unemployment, so that the category of "the unemployed" is much more dynamic than is often recognized. At any point in

TABLE 16-5

UNEMPLOYMENT RATE* BY AGE AND SEX, 1986

	Germany	United Kingdom
Males	5.88	14.27
15–19	5.75	21.56
20–24	7.70	21.32
25–44	5.69	12.36
45–54	4.74	11.37
55–59	8.31	18.64
60 and over	5.79	9.85
Females	8.71	9.09
15–19	9.13	17.03
20–24	9.87	15.40
25–44	8.88	7.33
45–54	6.94	5.80
55–59	11.78	9.33
60 and over	7.16	0.37

* Unemployed divided by economically active population.
Source: International Labour Office, Yearbook of Labor Statistics, 1988, *Table 9-B.*

time, the group of those who are unemployed is being augmented by those who are seeking a job for the first time, or "new entrants," those returning to the labor force after a period outside of it, or "reentrants," those leaving a job, either voluntarily or involuntarily, and starting to look for work at some other place, and those being temporarily laid off their jobs and expecting to be recalled.

At the same time, people are leaving the pool of unemployed by finding a job, ending their job search, or being called back to their previous employment after a layoff. The flow into and out of employment caused by temporary layoffs and recalls (when the laid-off worker returns to the same firm) is an important characteristic of the U.S. labor market. It has been estimated that between 60 and 65 percent of laid-off workers go back to their same job as their employer's economic situation improves.[14]

It is very important to know whether unemployment represents a lot of people being out of work for a short time, or fewer people being jobless for a long time. Each case has radically different implications. In the former, the burden of unemployment is distributed among many people, each of whom suffers relatively little, as many people go into and out of the unemployment pool without staying unemployed for long. This flow explanation of unemployment is sometimes called *normal turnover* unemployment. In the latter

---

[14] See Kim Clark and Lawrence Summers, "Labor Market Dynamics and Unemployment: A Reconsideration," *Brookings Papers on Economic Activity,* No. 1, 1979.

case, the burden of unemployment is borne largely by a small proportion of the whole. This alternative model of unemployment, which presumably carries higher social costs, we call *hard-core* unemployment.

The composition of unemployment in the United States was examined by Kim Clark and Lawrence Summers. As they wrote,

> most unemployment, even in tight labor markets, is characterized by relatively few persons who are out of work a large part of the time. We find that "normal turnover," broadly defined, can account for only a small part of measured unemployment. Much of observed joblessness is due to prolonged periods of inability or unwillingness to locate employment. These conclusions appear to hold at all points in the business cycle for almost all demographic groups.[15]

Their findings challenged an influential body of opinion which had held that unemployment was mainly of the normal turnover variety. The problem with the traditional view was that it had misinterpreted the data. Many researchers had noted the prevalence of very short spells of unemployment for most people (measuring the time between which they flowed into unemployment and then out of unemployment), and this suggested the accuracy of the normal turnover view. Clark and Summers observed that in many cases two periods of unemployment were divided by a brief period *outside* the labor force, rather than at a job. They argued persuasively that this period out of the labor force should most likely be considered simply a continuation of unemployment, so that the person really has experienced one long unemployment spell rather than two short spells.

If unemployment were mostly due to normal turnover, it could be argued that people were voluntarily deciding to be unemployed for short periods of time in order to search for appropriate work. Search theories of unemployment emphasize that people choose to invest time in finding a job, rather than going along with the first job opportunity that appears.[16] This search could be beneficial both in private and social terms because it helps to match people's abilities with society's needs; that is, it directs workers to where their skills are most productive. However, Clark and Summers found that more than 50 percent of unemployment is attributable to people who have been out of work for an average of over 6 months per year. Such a long duration of unemployment is almost surely not related to search per se, but to the fact that someone has lost his previous job and cannot find another one with an income level commesnurate with his earlier pay. This is more appropriately interpreted as involuntary unemployment, a concept that we discussed in Chapter 3.

---

[15] Ibid., p. 14.

[16] The idea of search as an explanation of unemployment was originally suggested by George Stigler, "The Economics of Information," *Journal of Political Economy,* June 1961. However, the modern theory of search was heavily influenced by Edmund Phelps, *Microeconomic Foundations of Employment and Inflation* (New York: W. W. Norton, 1970). A recent theoretical analysis is found in Peter Howitt, "Business Cycles with Costly Search and Recruiting," *Quarterly Journal of Economics,* February 1988. Empirical applications of the job search model are discussed in Section 2.3 of Dale Mortensen, "Job Search and Labor Market Analysis," in O. Ashenfelter and R. Layard, eds., *Handbook of Labor Economics* (Amsterdam: North Holland, 1986).

16-4 DETERMINANTS OF THE NATURAL RATE OF UNEMPLOYMENT

We have already spoken of the "natural" rate of unemployment as that rate which corresponds to macroeconomic equilibrium, in which expected inflation is equal to its actual level. We have used the term to mean the rate of unemployment to which the economy will return after a cyclical recession or boom. This concept was first suggested by Milton Friedman in 1968 and was developed independently by Edmund Phelps of Columbia University.[17]

The natural rate of unemployment is sometimes called the "full-employment" rate of unemployment to convey the sense that unemployment is excessive only when actual unemployment exceeds the natural level. But how can there be unemployment at full employment? As we shall see, there is no contradiction here.[18] The point is that the unemployment rate is never zero, since, for "normal" reasons, people are always flowing into and out of unemployment. After all, new workers are constantly entering the labor force, and existing workers frequently leave one job and look for another. During these transitions, they spend time on their job searches. And at the same time, even during boom periods, there may be mismatches between some people looking for work and the skills needed by, or the geographical location of, companies looking for workers.

The natural rate of unemployment is also called the nonaccelerating inflation rate of unemployment (NAIRU). In Phillips curve models with static expectations (equation 15.9 in the previous chapter), inflation tends to increase when U is less than U_n and to decrease when U is greater than U_n. Thus, U_n is the threshold below which there is an acceleration of inflation, hence the name abbreviated as NAIRU. We generally refer to the gap between actual unemployment and the natural rate as *cyclical unemployment*. In other words, cyclical unemployment is the amount of unemployment that can be reduced by expansionary macroeconomic policies without setting off an endless rise in the rate of inflation. Governments may try to reduce the natural rate of unemployment as well, but not through conventional macroeconomic policies. Instead, structural policies—job retraining, incentives to improve mobility, or tax incentives to accept jobs and stay out of unemployment, for example—are all possible measures to reduce U_n.

Now we turn to some of the factors that determine the natural rate of unemployment.

Migration and Demographics

As we have seen, the composition of the population is an important element in the determination of unemployment. In the United States, black teenagers have the highest rates of joblessness, up to about 50 percent. An economy's

---

[17] Friedman originally stated the argument in his presidential address to the American Economic Association in December 1967. It was subsequently published as "The Role of Monetary Policy," *American Economic Review*, March 1968. See also Edmund Phelps, "Money, Wage Dynamics and Labor Market Equilibrium," *Journal of Political Economy*, August 1968.

[18] This apparent contradiction was underscored in the title of an influential paper by Robert Hall of Stanford University: "Why Is the Unemployment Rate So High at Full Employment?" *Brookings Papers on Economic Activity*, No. 3, 1970.

natural rate of unemployment may be thought of as the weighted average of the natural rates of unemployment found for its different demographic groups, some of which are higher than others. As a consequence, a change in the proportions of these groups in the labor market affects the economywide natural rate.

During the 1950s and on into the early 1980s, women, blacks and Hispanics, and young workers in general increased their participation in the U.S. labor force. Because all these groups have higher than average natural unemployment rates, this phenomenon raised the overall natural rate in the U.S. economy. George Perry of The Brookings Institution introduced a weighted unemployment rate in the United States that takes the shifting proportions of major demographic groups into account. Robert Gordon of Northwestern University applied this methodology to study the evolution of the natural unemployment rate in the United States. According to his estimates, the natural rate rose by almost one full percentage point between 1956 and 1978 as a result of these demographic shifts alone.[19] During the 1980s, however, demographic changes, and especially the aging of the labor force, have worked to lower the natural rate of unemployment. Indeed, while in the mid-1960s the baby boomers were beginning to enter the labor force, by the late 1980s they were almost completely gone from the entry-age category.[20]

Minimum Wages

Minimum wage legislation aims to guarantee a decent floor of remuneration to all working people, and most countries of the world has it. The practice was introduced in the United States in 1938, when the minimum wage was set at $0.25 an hour. This minimum has been gradually raised through time, up to $3.35 in 1981. After a long battle between the Congress and the Executive in November 1989, President Bush signed a new law that raised the minimum wage in two steps, to $3.80 an hour in April 1990, then to $4.25 an hour in April 1991. A special provision established a subminimum wage for teenagers, one that could be in effect for up to 180 days if the young workers receive on-the-job training.

The existence of minimum wages, together with certain demographic characteristics of the labor force, have been identified by some economists as affecting the natural rate. Martin Feldstein of Harvard University argued in an influential study that the minimum wage increases the unemployment rate among teenagers because it sets a wage level above the market-clearing rate.[21] Feldstein stressed that the minimum wage reduces not only the incentive to hire the less qualified workers, but also the incentive to offer them on-the-job training. The issue is extremely important because, as we have seen, teenagers, and especially black teenagers, are the group most affected by the

---

[19] Perry's original study is "Changing Labor Markets and Inflation," *Brookings Papers on Economic Activity,* No. 3, 1970; Gordon's analysis is presented in "Inflation, Flexible Exchange Rates, and the Natural Rate of Unemployment," in Martin Baily, ed., *Workers, Jobs and Inflation* (Washington, D.C.: The Brookings Institution, 1982).

[20] See Daniel Mitchell, "Wage Pressures and Labor Shortages: The 1960s and the 1980s," *Brookings Papers on Economic Activity,* No. 2, 1989.

[21] See his "The Economics of the New Unemployment," *Public Interest,* No. 33, Fall 1973.

unemployment problem in the United States. The empirical evidence is, however, not conclusive. Between 1981 and 1989, the real level of the minimum wage fell year after year in the United States (because its nominal level was fixed) without an apparent significant effect on teenage unemployment.

A recent study has surveyed the evidence on this topic for the United States.[22] Its results suggest that an increase in the minimum wage would have some negative effect on the job opportunities of teenagers, but little or no effect for the other groups in the labor force. However, this survey suggests, the effect on teenagers is rather small. A 10 percent increase in the minimum wage is found to raise the unemployment rate of teenagers in a range from zero to 3 percentage points. The more recent studies analyzed in the survey show very small effects of less than 0.75 percentage points.

Sectoral Variability

David Lillien has suggested that the natural rate of unemployment depends on the growth characteristics of different sectors of the economy.[23] Even if the whole economy is growing at a constant rate, the rates of growth of its different sectors will always vary. Those that are expanding will absorb more labor, while those that are contracting will reduce their work forces. However, no quick match between availabilities and needs is possible because labor cannot be shifted instantaneously and costlessly from one sector to the other. As a consequence, the greater the variations in growth across sectors, the higher the overall unemployment rate. Lillien concluded that this structural factor accounts for most of the changes in unemployment in the United States during the 1970s—but not during the 1960s.

Some recent research has supported these findings. A 1987 study that analyzed the pattern of aggregate unemployment in the United States from the mid-1920s to the mid-1980s found that the dispersion of employment growth across sectors helps to explain the economywide rate of unemployment (which is attributed to the lags of intersectoral labor reallocation).[24] Other researchers, however, have questioned that the causality runs from sectoral variability to unemployment. In their view, changes in the aggregate unemployment rate are mainly related to global shocks that hit the economy, which, in turn, provoke different responses across sectors. Thus, according to this argument, the unemployment rate and sectoral dispersion move together because aggregate shocks hit them both.[25]

Unemployment Insurance

Another central piece of social legislation in most countries is some policy of income protection for workers who lose their jobs, a system generally known as unemployment insurance. Such a program has existed in the

---

[22] See Charles Brown, "Minimum Wage Laws: Are They Overrated?" *Journal of Economic Perspectives,* Summer 1988.

[23] See his "Sectoral Shifts and Cyclical Unemployment," *Journal of Political Economy,* August 1982.

[24] Steve Davis, "Allocative Disturbances and Specific Capital in Real Business Cycles," *American Economic Review,* May 1987.

[25] Katharine Abraham and Lawrence Katz, "Cyclical Unemployment: Sectoral Shifts or Aggregate Disturbances?" *Journal of Political Economy,* June 1986, Part 1.

United States since 1936. While not all workers are eligible to obtain unemployment benefits, the coverage of the program has gradually increased over time. Nowadays, about 85 percent of U.S. workers are covered by some form of unemployment insurance.[26] The proportion of the unemployed that can actually claim their benefits is substantially smaller, at about one-third of the labor force. This discrepancy arises in part because some covered workers are not immediately eligible for benefits. They may, for example, have insufficient work experience (one of the conditions for eligibility), or they may have quit their last job rather than being laid off. Then too, unemployment insurance cannot be used indefinitely. When people are unemployed beyond a certain period of time, normally between 26 and 39 weeks in the case of the United States, they lose their eligibility for benefits.

Unemployment insurance (UI) programs affect the natural rate of unemployment because they make it less burdensome for people to become and stay unemployed. Workers pay close attention to the ratio of their disposable income when unemployed to their disposable income while working, a measure known as the *replacement ratio*. The higher the replacement ratio, the lower the cost of being unemployed (for someone eligible for UI), and thus the more time a person tends to spend in unemployment while looking for another job.[27] The replacement ratio is affected both by the value of the jobless benefits as compared to the working salary and by the taxes levied on UI versus those on wages. For example, if unemployment benefits are not taxed, the difference between one's disposable incomes at work and out of work will be smaller than it is pretax. Until 1978, the United States had no tax on unemployment benefits. Since 1979, benefits have been taxed at one-half the worker's normal tax rate, but only if gross income exceeds a certain minimum. Below that minimum, UI is still exempt from taxes. A similar scheme of taxation applies in Canada too.[28]

Some prominent analysts have argued in favor of lowering unemployment benefits as a way of motivating jobless people to seek a job. Among them are Milton and Rose Friedman, who made their case in a 1980 bestseller.[29] This issue is not confined to the United States, of course. The same line of argument has been put forward in Europe, where replacement ratios are higher than they are in the United States, especially in the Scandinavian countries.[30]

Cross-country studies have tried to determine whether or not differences in unemployment insurance systems help to explain differences in the

---

[26] This figure is for 1988 (*Economic Report of the President, 1990,* Tables C-32 and C-42).

[27] Some studies have shown that a rise in the replacement ratio increases the duration of unemployment. See, for example, Martin Feldstein, "The Importance of Temporary Layoffs: An Empirical Analysis," *Brookings Papers on Economic Activity,* No. 3, 1975. For the argument that a higher ratio raises the wage at which a jobless individual is willing to accept a job offer (the *reservation wage*), see Martin Feldstein and James Poterba, "Unemployment Insurance and Reservation Wages," *Journal of Public Economics,* February/March 1984.

[28] See Orley Ashenfelter and David Card, "Why Have Unemployment Rates in Canada and the United States Diverged?" in C. Bean, R. Layard and S. Nickell eds., *The Rise in Unemployment* (Oxford: Basil Blackwell, 1987).

[29] Milton and Rose Friedman, *Free to Choose: A Personal Statement* (New York: Harcourt Brace Jovanovich, 1980).

[30] See, for example, Patrick Minford, *Unemployment, Causes and Cures* (Oxford: Basil Blackwell, 1985).

natural rate of unemployment across countries. The results have not been very clear, except in one important respect. A key feature of any unemployment insurance system seems to be the length of the period during which an unemployed person may draw benefits. In some countries, such as the United States, the period is strictly limited. In other countries, such as the Netherlands, the system is virtually open ended. There, someone can continue to draw unemployment insurance for about two and a half years.

The duration of these benefits seems to be a key variable in explaining the amount of long-term unemployment in an economy. Indeed, while replacement ratios by themselves provided a weak explanation for unemployment, the inclusion of the duration variable changes the picture a lot. A recent study has built an index of unemployment benefits that combines in one measure the monetary value of insurance per period with the duration of the benefits. The results were striking. Countries with more generous schemes (generous especially with regard to long duration of benefits) had significantly higher proportions of long-term unemployment within their unemployment pool. This pattern is especially clear in Belgium and the Netherlands, which have the most generous schemes among the 15 industrialized countries analyzed. At the other extreme were the United States, Japan, and Switzerland, with the least generous unemployment benefits schemes and the lowest proportion of long-term unemployment.[31] This pattern is shown in Figure 16-7.

Independent evidence for the United States has suggested that a one-week increase in the potential duration of benefits increases the average length of unemployment spells for those receiving unemployment insurance by 0.16 to 0.20 weeks. It is interesting that policies that extend the potential duration of benefits appear to have a significantly higher effect on long-term unemployment than do those that increase the value of benefits without affecting their duration (for a similar budgetary cost of the two measures).[32] In the United States, there is also direct evidence of the importance of UI duration. There it seems that many unemployed workers remain so just until the UI runs out, and then immediately accept a job.[33]

Union Power

The importance of labor unions in the industrial countries differs sharply, as we have noted. Unions have also experienced fluctuations in bargaining power through time in particular economies. In many Western European economies, for example, unions considerably increased their strength from the mid-1960s until the mid- to late 1970s, as measured by the share of workers in unions. In the first half of the 1980s the pattern has been more mixed, with union strength continuing to grow in a small group of countries (mostly Scandinavian), but declining in most European economies. Evi-

---

[31] The study is Michael Burda's "Wait Unemployment in Europe," *Economic Policy*, October 1988. The long-term unemployed were defined as those whose current out-of-work spell had lasted six months or more.

[32] Lawrence Katz and Bruce Meyer, "The Impact of the Potential Duration of Unemployment Benefits on the Duration of Unemployment," NBER Working Paper No. 2741, October 1988.

[33] Lawrence Katz and Bruce Meyer, "Unemployment Insurance, Recall Expectations, and Unemployment Outcomes," NBER Working Paper No. 2594, May 1988.

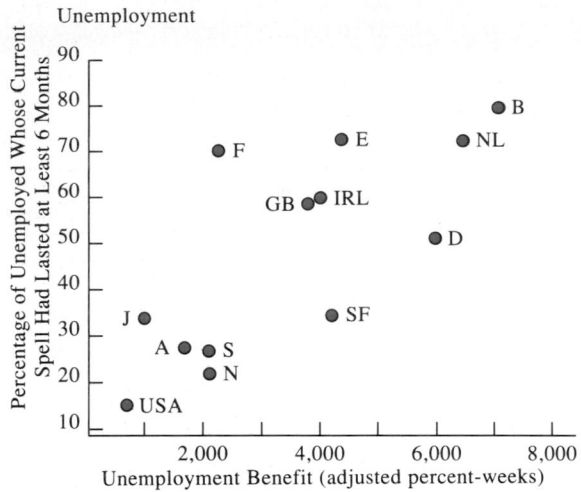

A = Austria, B = Belgium, D = West Germany, E = Spain, F = France, GB = Great Britain, IRL = Ireland, J = Japan, N = Norway, NL = Netherlands, S = Sweden, SF = Finland, US = United States

Figure 16-7
Index of Unemployment Benefits

(From Michael Burda, "Wait Unemployment in Europe," Economic Policy, *October 1988, Figure 3.)*

dence on the evolution of unionization across industrial countries since 1970 is shown in Table 16-6.

The United States has been a conspicuous exception to the overall trend. As Figure 16-8 shows, unions have declined markedly in their coverage of the labor force since the mid-1950s, when unionization reached its peak at almost 40 percent of the labor force in 1954. By 1989, unions could claim less than 13 percent of U.S. private workers outside of agriculture.

An extensive body of research has been accumulated focusing on the role of labor unions in affecting real wages and unemployment. Almost all studies agree that unions tend to raise the real wages of their membership and to lower the levels of employment in unionized sectors. The presence of unions also affects the way an economy responds to shocks. Many researchers have shown that unions tend to insulate the wages of "insiders" (their members) from the effects of economic disturbances at the cost of greater fluctuations in employment rates for "outsiders" (workers outside of the union). When an adverse supply shock hits, for example, a competitive labor market would lead to a reduction in real wage levels. In a unionized sector, however, the result might be a constant real wage for insiders, and a drop in employment and wage levels for outsiders. This insider-outsider distinction has been elaborated on in an important theoretical study by Assar Lindbeck and Dennis Snower.[34]

Some writers have stressed that the consequences of unions for unemployment depend heavily on the nature of union organization and wage

---

[34] Lawrence Katz and Bruce Meyer, "Unemployment Insurance, Recall Expectations, and Unemployment Outcomes," NBER Working Paper No. 2594, May 1988.

TABLE 16-6

THE EVOLUTION OF UNIONIZATION IN SELECTED
INDUSTRIAL COUNTRIES, 1970–1985
(PERCENT OF NONAGRICULTURAL EMPLOYEES)

| | Level | | | Change |
Countries with	1970	1979	1984–85	1970–85
Sharp increase in unionization				
Denmark	66	86	98	+32
Finland	56	84	85	+29
Sweden	79	89	95	+16
Moderate to no rise in unionization				
Italy	39	51	45	+6
Germany	37	42	42	+5
France	22	28	28	+6
Switzerland	31	36	35	+4
Canada	32	36	37	+5
Australia	52	58	57	+5
New Zealand	43	46	—	+3
Ireland	44	49	51	+7
Stable to declining unionization				
Norway	59	60	61	+2
United Kingdom	51	58	52	+1
Austria	64	59	61	−3
Japan	35	32	29	−6
Netherlands	39	43	37	−2
United States	31	25	18	−13
Average (all countries)	47	53	54	+7

Source: Richard Freeman, "Labour Market Institutions and Economic Performance," Economic Policy, *April 1988, Table 2.*

bargaining. When unions cover nearly all the labor force and bargain at the national level, as they do in Sweden, virtually all workers become insiders. The "national" union will tend to bargain for wage levels that are compatible with low rates of national unemployment. In other words, highly centralized unions tend to internalize the macroeconomic effects of their actions. In economies with strong unions organized at the industry level, by contrast, unions are more likely to choose wage levels that are good for their own members but too high to promote a low level of unemployment. Finally, in economies with highly decentralized unions (mostly operating at the plant level), real wages will tend to adjust fairly flexibly to preserve full employment.

Whether union organization is centralized, decentralized, or somewhere in between, has been shown empirically to affect the degree of real-

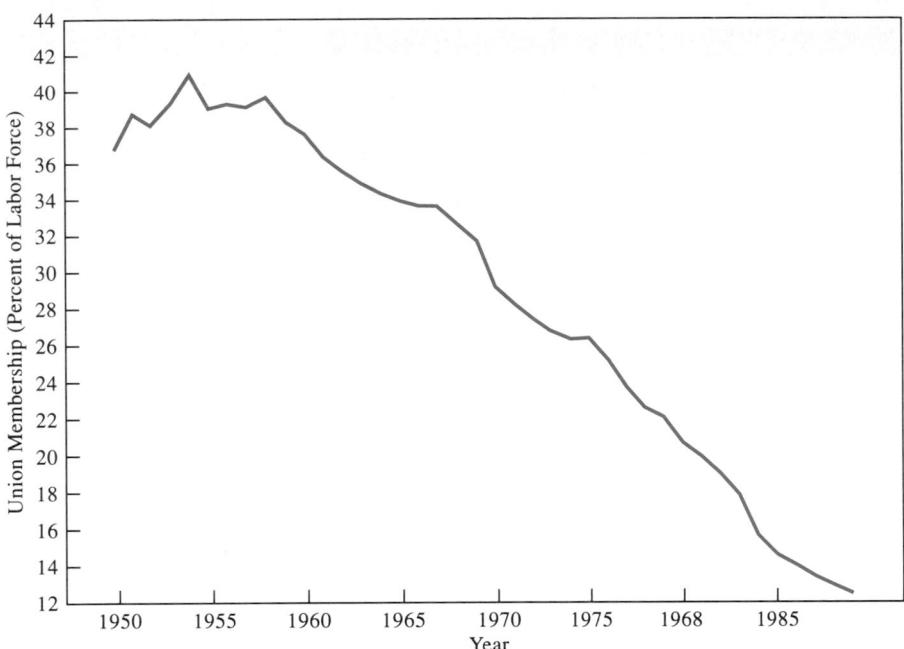

Figure 16-8

Unionization in the United States as a Percentage of the Labor Force, 1950–1989

(From U.S. Bureau of Labor Statistics: for 1950–1969, Handbook of Labor Statistics, *computed as all union members multiplied by the percentage of union members in nongovernment and divided by all nonagricultural employees minus government nonagricultural employees; for 1970–1989,* Employment and Earnings, *various issues.)*

wage rigidity (measured as the extent of unemployment needed to reduce the real wage by a given percent), and thus to affect unemployment itself. Table 16-7, taken from a recent study,[35] divides 17 industrialized countries into three groups according to the degree of centralization of their labor movements (centralized, intermediate, and decentralized), and then compares their performance with respect to unemployment over the last two decades.

As the figures show, both countries with centralized and decentralized union organizations had an average level of unemployment over the period 1974–1985 that was lower than that in the intermediate case. Moreover, the increase in unemployment from 1963–1973 to 1974–1985 is lower in the two extreme cases, suggesting a better pattern of adjustment to the oil shocks. Other recent research has found supporting evidence for the hypothesis that macroeconomic performance (measured by rates of inflation and unemployment) tends to be better in highly centralized or decentralized economies.[36]

---

[35] Lars Calmfors and John Driffill, "Bargaining Structure, Corporatism and Economic Performance," *Economic Policy,* April 1988.

[36] Freeman, "Labour Market Institutions and Economic Performance."

TABLE 16-7

CENTRALIZATION AND UNEMPLOYMENT PERFORMANCE IN SELECTED COUNTRIES (PERCENT)

| | Unemployment | |
	Level*	Change†
Centralized economies		
Austria	2.5	0.8
Norway	2.2	0.6
Sweden	2.4	0.4
Denmark	7.9	6.9
Finland	5.0	3.8
Average	4.0	2.3
Intermediate economies		
Germany	4.8	4.0
Netherlands	8.0	6.8
Belgium	9.3	7.1
New Zealand	2.2	2.0
Australia	6.3	4.4
Average	6.1	4.8
Decentralized economies		
France	6.4	4.3
United Kingdom	8.1	5.4
Italy	7.9	2.8
Japan	2.2	1.0
Switzerland	0.5	0.3
United States	7.3	2.8
Canada	8.5	3.7
Average	5.8	2.9

* Levels correspond to 1974–1985 averages.
† Changes are 1974–1985 averages less 1963–1973 average.
Source: *Lars Calmfors and John Driffill, "Bargaining Structure, Corporatism and Macroeconomic Performance,"* Economic Policy 6, *April 1988, Table 2.*

Labor Taxes

Notice that what matters for the determination of labor demand is the gross wage that employers pay, not the take-home pay that workers receive. The difference between the two is taxes on labor income, which have increased significantly as a percentage of the total wage bill in most industrial countries during the past three decades. This so-called "tax wedge" should be expected to have an effect on desired labor supply, and perhaps on the measured unemployment rate. For example, supply-siders in the United States have claimed, though with little direct evidence, that reductions in labor tax rates would have important positive effects on the labor supply.

Assar Lindbeck of the Institute for International Economic Studies in Stockholm has argued that the expanded size of public sectors has had a significant influence in European unemployment. For Western Europe as a whole, the ratio of public spending to GNP has increased from 30 percent in 1973 to 51 percent in 1984 (compared to an increase from 31 to 36 percent in the United States during the same period). Lindbeck argues that governments have increasingly relied on distortionary labor taxes, that is, on an increasing tax wedge, to finance the government expansion. This tax wedge raises real wage costs relative to labor productivity and increases the inflexibility of labor markets.[37]

Other analysts have suggested that high tax rates create a disincentive to entrepreneurship, and this may shed light on the modest growth of private employment and the disappointing performance of Europe in high-technology industry. High tax rates may also give a boost to the underground economy (as workers and enterprises hide their incomes to evade taxes), thereby leading to a rate of *measured* European unemployment that is higher than the real rate.[38]

Hysteresis in Unemployment

Recent research has suggested that the natural rate of unemployment might be affected by movements in the *actual* rate of unemployment, a phenomenon known as *hysteresis*.[39] Olivier Blanchard of MIT and Lawrence Summers of Harvard, among others, have argued that prolonged periods of high unemployment tend to increase the natural rate of unemployment.[40] Their argument is based on the insider-outsider model of wage setting. Unions normally bargain to promote the good of their own members. For example, unions tend to bargain for wage levels above the market-clearing rate, at a point where their own members remain fully employed while outsiders are stuck in unemployment. Blanchard and Summers point out that the boundary between insiders and outsiders tends to change according to the path of actual unemployment. Insiders that get fired become outsiders; unions stop caring about their employment prospects. Thus, if unemployment rises for a sustained period, former insiders become outsiders, and the unions begin to set wages only with a view to their (now fewer) members still at work. In this way, at least part of the rise in unemployment may become permanent. Another argument used to explain hysteresis is that unemployed workers

---

[37] A. Lindbeck, ''What Is Wrong with the West European Economies?'' *World Economy,* June 1985.

[38] Robert Gordon has stated these views in his article ''Back to the Future: European Unemployment Today Viewed from America in 1939,'' *Brookings Papers on Economic Activity,* No. 1, 1988.

[39] Hysteresis is a term from physics. Hysteresis occurs if, when a variable has been subjected to a temporary external force, the variable does not return to its original value even after the external force is removed. In the context of unemployment, hysteresis means that if a temporary shock causes the unemployment rate to rise, the unemployment rate might not return to its original level even after the shock is over. Put differently, the natural rate of unemployment might change as the result of a temporary rise in unemployment.

[40] See their joint work, ''Hysteresis and the European Unemployment Problem,'' *National Bureau of Economic Research Macroeconomics Annual 1986* (Cambridge, Mass.: MIT Press, 1986).

suffer a deterioration of human capital, so that they become unemployable even after the original shock that caused the unemployment is over.

The importance of this effect for actual movements in the natural rate of unemployment is open to debate. Some researchers have rejected the argument empirically, while others have claimed to find corroboration. A recent study, for example, reports evidence in support of the hysteresis hypothesis for major European countries in the postwar period.[41] Other analysts, among them Charles Schultze of The Brookings Institution, remain skeptical.[42] At any rate, the hysteresis argument has been mainly used to explain recent unemployment trends in Europe. So far it has shed no light on the evolution of the natural rate of unemployment in the United States during the postwar period.

Measures of the Natural Rate of Unemployment

Thus far we have defined the natural rate of unemployment and examined its determinants. Now we turn to empirical measurements of its magnitude, focusing especially on the widely researched case of the United States.

There is, in fact, no standard accepted procedure to estimate the natural unemployment rate, and this leads to disagreements about methods and magnitudes. A simple way to proceed is to calculate the average of the actual unemployment rate over a long period of time. The idea here is that a long-term average smoothes out cyclical deviations of unemployment above and below the natural rate. The average unemployment rate in the United States was 5.6 percent between 1948 and 1985. This rate of unemployment is indeed fairly close to the estimates of the natural rate used by many American macroeconomists. Another simple method is to pick a particular year when the economy was believed to be at full employment and expected inflation was approximately equal to its actual level. If we use the year 1989, which is one such a candidate, then the natural rate of unemployment in the United States is around 5.3 percent.

A more systematic method is to estimate an expectations-augmented Phillips curve and determine arithmetically the rate of unemployment corresponding with a nonaccelerating inflation rate. Robert Gordon has followed this strategy in several studies over the course of two decades and has found a fairly consistent estimate of the natural rate, around 6 percent of the labor force from the mid-1970s to the mid-1980s.[43]

Of course the natural rate might change over time, either as a result of demographics or because other shocks have hit the economy. We have already noted that demographic changes in the United States seem to have affected the natural rate of unemployment. The natural rate in the United States was believed to be around 4 percent in the 1950s and 1960s, increasing to the neighborhood of 5 percent in the early 1970s. Estimates for the 1980s range between 5.5 and 6.5 percent. A typical value used in recent years has

---

[41] See Robert Gordon, "Back to the Future: European Unemployment Today Viewed from America in 1939," *Brookings Papers on Economic Activity*, No. 1, 1988.

[42] See Schultze's "Real Wages, Real Wage Aspirations, and Unemployment in Europe," in Robert Lawrence and Charles Schultze, eds., *Barriers to European Growth: A Transatlantic View* (Washington, D.C.: The Brookings Institution, 1987).

[43] Robert Gordon, "Understanding Inflation in the 1980s," *Brookings Papers on Economic Activity*, No. 1, 1985.

been 6 percent. A 1989 study, however, has suggested that the natural rate may have fallen to the 5–5.5 percent range.[44]

The true value of the natural rate, although hard to know, is extremely relevant for policy. In 1991–1992, the U.S. unemployment rate has been above 6 percent. If the natural rate is between 5.5 and 6.0 percent, the economy is likely to experience a modest decline in inflation at the prevailing unemployment rates. There would be little chance of inflationary "overheating," that is, a rise in inflation because of excess demand, under the prevailing labor-market conditions.

It is clear that the adverse supply shocks of the 1970s substantially raised the natural rate of unemployment in many advanced industrial countries, particularly in Western Europe.[45] Fairly recent studies have placed the natural unemployment rate in many European countries at or above the 10 percent level, a substantial increase over past levels. These studies have estimated rates for the United Kingdom around 10 percent, for Belgium, 10.8 percent, and for Spain, 11.3 percent, for example. Germany with a natural rate reported at around 4 percent, is an exception, but this is a major rise over rates of 2 percent or so estimated for the country in the early 1970s.[46] Here, hysteresis effects may be partly to blame.

16-5 THE COSTS OF UNEMPLOYMENT

We have seen that a fundamental theme of economic analysis over the last three decades has been the trade-off between inflation and unemployment. Both inflation and unemployment involve significant costs to society, but it is crucial to understand these costs with some precision in order for policymakers to make the right short-run adjustments. In Chapter 11, we studied in some detail the costs of inflation. Now we undertake a similar task with respect to unemployment.

One important characteristic of unemployment is its very uneven distribution across society. So too are its costs unevenly distributed. In the United States, unemployment hits teenagers and minorities with special force, and it is concentrated among the poorest sectors of the population. The costs of inflation, by contrast, tend to be distributed less unevenly.

At the personal level, unemployment takes a heavy toll. The involuntarily unemployed not only suffer a loss of income and thus, generally, a deterioration in their standards of living, they also suffer psychological effects. Self-confidence is an early casualty. People who are unemployed

---

[44] Daniel Mitchell, "Wage Pressures and Labor Shortages: the 1960s and the 1980s," *Brookings Papers on Economic Activity,* No. 2, 1989.

[45] The effects of supply shocks on the natural unemployment rate are discussed in detail in Bruno and Sachs, *The Economics of Worldwide Stagflation.*

[46] Most of these studies have appeared in the volume edited by C. Bean, R. Layard and S. Nickell, *The Rise in Unemployment* (Oxford: Basil Blackwell, 1987). The individual studies are Henri Sneesens and Jacques Dreze, "A Discussion of Belgian Unemployment, Combining Traditional Concepts and Disequilibrium Econometrics"; J. J. Dolado et al., "Spanish Industrial Unemployment: Some Explanatory Factors"; and Wolfgang Franz and Heinz Konig, "The Nature and Causes of Unemployment in the Federal Republic of Germany Since the 1970s: An Empirical Investigation." For the United Kingdom, the source is Richard Layard, *How to Beat Unemployment* (Oxford: Oxford University Press, 1986).

against their will often feel a profound sense of uselessness. In the aftermath of the Great Depression, this feeling was expressed in remarks like "my time has no value" or "my time isn't worth anything when I don't have a job."[47] If joblessness persists, working skills start to deteriorate. The costs are borne not only by the unemployed themselves but also by their families. Family relations become more strained when breadwinners are involuntarily unemployed. Moreover, the unemployed many times lose their medical insurance when that is employer provided, and must bear their own health risks and medical costs.

It is difficult to measure these human costs with any precision. Economists have attempted to measure a different cost of unemployment, the lost output associated with the reduced utilization of labor in the economy. Here, it becomes crucial to distinguish between structural unemployment, which corresponds to the natural rate of unemployment, U_n, and cyclical unemployment, which corresponds to the gap between U and U_n.

Structural Unemployment

Structural unemployment is the unemployment that exists when the economy is operating at the natural rate U_n.[48] In turn, the natural rate of unemployment reflects many different phenomena and forces: union power, which raises real wages above wp^f; frictional unemployment, which results when people search for jobs; mismatch unemployment, which occurs when sectoral shifts lead to increased demand for some types of workers and decreased demand for other types (and thus a mismatch between job seekers and job vacancies); and geographical pockets of hard-core unemployment, such as the inner cities and poorer regions in the United States. Whatever the sources of U_n, the critical point here is that *macroeconomic policies alone cannot sustain an economywide unemployment rate below U_n without a continuing rise in the rate of inflation.*

Clearly, not all types of structural unemployment are simply a waste of resources. To the extent that unemployment is "frictional," that is, related to job search and job reallocation across sectors, unemployment facilitates an effective match between job seekers and job vacancies. It is a good thing that people do not take the first job they are offered, and search helps to locate the job where each person is most productive. The unemployed also gain increased leisure time which must however be balanced against the psychic costs of involuntary job loss and the costs of job search.

But only part of natural unemployment is of this type. Some workers have been jobless for a long time, with no real opportunity of employment. It is important to understand whether or not the impediments to employment that these people encounter represent forms of market failure, and whether

---

[47] As reported in E. Wight Bakke, *The Unemployed Worker: A Study of the Task of Making a Living Without a Job* (New Haven, Conn.: Yale University Press, 1940). Quoted in Robert Gordon, "The Welfare Cost of Higher Unemployment," *Brookings Papers on Economic Activity,* No. 1, 1973.

[48] Economists use the term "structural unemployment" in various ways. Some mean only job-mismatch unemployment, when some sectors are expanding and others are contracting; others use the term to mean geographical or demographic pockets of hard-core unemployment. Thus, while our use of the term to correspond to U_n is clear cut, it is not universally used in that way.

or not those market failures can be corrected by policy changes. For example, aggressive union wage setting can result in structural unemployment, but there may be no easy policy solution.

Some countries, notably Sweden, have long rejected the idea that unemployment beyond a very low rate must be a "natural" feature of a market economy. While unemployment rates in most of Western Europe are routinely between 5 and 10 percent of the labor force, in Sweden they are routinely below 3 percent. The Swedish government's labor-market policy has long included an aggressive program of state expenditures for job retraining, job matching, and job relocation. As a set of policies that can reduce the extent and costs of structural unemployment, the Swedish case deserves further study, though in recent years even many Swedish economists are having second thoughts about the fiscal costs and sustainability of the Swedish labor-market policies.

Cyclical Unemployment

A different story occurs with *cyclical unemployment,* that is, unemployment above the natural rate. In this case, output can be increased without a higher rate of investment because there are unutilized resources to use. The link between unemployment and lost output is given now by Okun's law, which for the United States holds that each 1 percentage point increase in cyclical unemployment is associated with a 2.5 to 3 percent reduction in GNP below potential. In the United States, potential output in 1989 was estimated at around $5.1 trillion.[49] Thus, if we use the lower range of Okun's law, 1 point of excess unemployment above the natural rate would cost $127 billion (1 × 2.5 × 5,100 billion) per year. This staggering amount gives an idea of what society loses when there is too much joblessness.

When output is below potential, losses are widely felt. The unemployed lose their salaries and obtain unemployment benefits, the government loses tax proceeds and has to pay for the extra benefits, and businesses lose profits. Should these losses be added to the output costs that we just calculated? No, that would amount to double counting. As we saw in Chapter 2, GDP can be determined from the market value of all final goods and services *or* from the income of all factors of production, including taxes.

There is, however, a benefit in cyclical unemployment which, strictly speaking, should be counted as a factor that somewhat offsets these costs. Someone who loses a job gains leisure time, which has some value, even if much of this leisure is involuntary and thus has substantially less value than the income loss due to unemployment. Some studies have attempted to refine the relationship between unemployment and output by considering the value of this leisure time, which Okun's original calculation did not cover. When this element is added, however, Okun's law is not significantly altered. A 1 percent decrease in cyclical unemployment was found to increase output by 2.3 percent (as opposed to the original 2.5 percent).[50]

In the last analysis, society as a whole loses more output than individuals lose income. Why? Because an employed worker pays taxes, while a

---

[49] See Raymond Torres and John Martin, "Potential Output in the Seven Major OECD Countries," Working Paper No. 66, OECD Department of Economics and Statistics, May 1989.

[50] See Gordon, "The Response of Wages and Prices to the First Two Years of Controls."

jobless person receives unemployment benefits. The output costs to society of one more unemployed worker above the natural rate can be summarized as the sum of three components: the income loss of the individual who loses her job, net of joblessness benefits; the value of unemployment benefits paid by the government; and the fiscal loss from less tax revenues.

Throughout our analysis of the costs of unemployment, we have concentrated on aggregate output costs. Thus, we have counted all dollars of output as similar, without considering the effects of a reduction in unemployment on the distribution of income. To the extent that the benefits of less unemployment are more heavily concentrated in the poorest sectors of society, and this seems to be the case, there is an additional gain in an improved income distribution.

16-6 SUMMARY

Labor-market institutions differ markedly across countries in several major dimensions: the importance of formal versus informal labor contracts; the extent to which wage contracts are negotiated collectively by unions and firms; the degree of centralization of negotiations; the timing of wage contracts, including their duration and degree of synchronization; the role of the government in negotiations; and the use of indexation in wage agreements.

Formal labor contracts are more widely used in industrialized countries than in developing economies, since the latter have a large informal sector. The extent of long-term contracts in an economy depends directly on the rate of *unionization*, that is, the proportion of total workers that belongs to unions. Among developed economies, unionization is highest in the Scandinavian countries and lowest in Japan and the United States. Another important aspect of wage negotiations is the *level of wage bargaining*, which can be at the national, industry, regional or plant level. Negotiations are *centralized* in the Scandinavian countries, and *decentralized* in Canada, Japan, the United Kingdom, and the United States, where they mostly take place at the firm level.

Full *synchronization* of negotiations means that all contracts are signed at the same time, while *staggering* means that negotiations are scattered throughout the year. Highly centralized negotiation processes tend to go together with high degrees of synchronization. *Contract duration*, on the other hand, tends to vary from one to three years, with one-year contracts being the most popular. Government intervention in private labor negotiations has been ample in the Scandinavian economies and probably lowest in Japan and the United States. Finally, *wage indexation* is the agreement to adjust future wages according to the observed evolution of some other variable, most commonly the consumer price level. Indexation is widespread in economies with a long history of high inflation.

The oil price shocks of the 1970s led to a decade of *stagflation*, that is, the combination of economic stagnation and high inflation. Since oil is an important input to the production process, higher oil prices lead to a decline in the productivity of labor. Even under fully flexible wages, employment and output will drop. But if real wages are rigid, the drop in employment and output will be larger than under conditions of full wage and price flexibility. After the first oil shock, unemployment increased steadily in Europe from

1973 to 1981. In the United States unemployment rose during 1974–1975 and then fell in the following four years. The key difference between the two regions seems to be that the United States had greater downward real wage flexibility than Europe. In turn, this was the result of different labor-market institutions in the two regions.

Although definitions vary across countries, *unemployment* is generally defined as the pool of individuals above a specified age who are without work, are currently available for work, and are seeking work during a reference period. The interpretation of unemployment has important special features in developing countries because many individuals work part-time or in low-productivity jobs (and are still considered to be employed), women generally have a low participation in the labor force, and there is a sizable informal sector not covered in the official statistics. On the other hand, unemployment rates are quite unevenly distributed among the population of a given country. In the United States, for example, the unemployment rate among teenagers is considerably higher than the average for the economy. Significant differences also exist according to ethnic origin. Teenage unemployment is also very high in other countries, such as the United Kingdom.

The *natural rate of unemployment* is the rate which corresponds to macroeconomic equilibrium, in which expected inflation is equal to its actual level. The natural rate of unemployment is also referred to as the *non-accelerating inflation rate of unemployment*. There is no standard accepted procedure to measure the natural rate. Estimates for the United States have placed it in the range of 5.5 to 6 percent. The natural rate, however, seems to be considerably higher in Europe, where fairly recent studies have placed it at or above 10 percent in several countries such as the United Kingdom, Belgium, and Spain. West Germany, on the other hand, seems to have a much lower natural rate.

Several elements help to determine the natural rate of unemployment: *demographics,* since the natural rate can be thought of as a weighted average of the natural rates of the different demographic groups in a population; the existence of *minimum wages*, which may set a wage level above the market-clearing rate; variability in the growth rates of the different sectors in the economy; *unemployment insurance,* which makes less burdensome for individuals to become or stay unemployed; the *power of unions,* which tend to raise the real wages of their membership and to lower the levels of employment in unionized sectors; the level of *centralization of wage bargaining,* with very decentralized and highly centralized bargaining seeming to lead to lower unemployment rates than the intermediate case; the level of *labor taxes,* which drive a wedge between the firm's cost of labor and the workers' take-home pay; *hysteresis,* or the effect by which prolonged periods of high actual unemployment rates seem to raise the natural rate.

The *costs of unemployment* are unevenly distributed across society. Although the human costs of unemployment may be staggering for those affected and their families, it is difficult to measure them with any precision. Thus, economists have attempted to measure a different cost: the lost output associated with the aggregate of unemployed labor. For this purpose, one should distinguish two types of unemployment. *Structural unemployment* is the unemployment that exists when the economy is operating at the natural rate. *Cyclical unemployment* is that above the natural rate. The costs of each are different. Clearly, not all forms of joblessness are simply a waste of resources. The part of structural unemployment related to job search, for example, facilitates an effective match between job seekers and job vacancies.

Referring to cyclical unemployment, the estimate for the United States, according to the famous Okun's law relationship, is that each one percentage point increase in cyclical unemployment, is associated with a 2.5 to 3 percent reduction in GNP below potential.

Key Concepts

labor-market institutions	real wage gap
formal contracts	labor force
informal contracts	normal turnover unemployment
unionization	hard core unemployment
insider-outsider model	search theories of unemployment
collective bargaining	natural rate of unemployment
centralization of negotiations	NAIRU
synchronized contracts	minimum wages
overlapping contracts	unemployment insurance
indexation	replacement ratio
backward-looking indexation	reservation wage
forward-looking indexation	hysteresis
stagflation	tax wedge

Problems and Questions

1. Analyze how the following institutional characteristics of the labor market affect the unemployment cost of disinflationary policies:

  a. Most of the labor force works in the formal sector.
  b. All wage contracts are negotiated and signed during the same month.
  c. The government plays an active role in the wage negotiation process.
  d. Wages are fully indexed to past inflation.

2. Most Latin American countries were affected by the debt crisis of the 1980s. They experienced an important contraction in employment in the formal sector while employment in the informal sector increased. How can the institutional arrangements of the labor market in each sector be used to explain this phenomenon?

3. Consider two countries at similar stages of economic development. The main difference between them is that one has a long history of price stability while the other has undergone high rates of inflation for several years. Discuss how labor-market institutions are likely to differ between the two countries.

4. The oil shocks of the 1970s helped oil-producing countries. They were able to use the additional revenues from oil sales to buy more final goods and intermediate inputs needed in the production process. Analyze the effects of the oil shocks on the labor market and on the aggregate supply curves for these countries. How does your answer depend on the institutional settings of the labor markets in each country?

5. What data, besides the unemployment rate, would you use to evaluate the level of employment and the utilization of the labor force in a developing country?

6. Discuss the different implications for economic policy depending on whether a high unemployment rate is caused mostly by hard-core unemployment or by normal turnover unemployment.

7. Some economists have suggested that unemployment benefits should be reduced over time; that is, as a person stays unemployed longer, she becomes eligible to get a smaller amount of benefits. Discuss the advantages and disadvantages of this proposal. Do you think it would have a stronger impact in normal turnover or hard-core unemployment?

8. Under which institutional arrangements of the labor markets would hysteresis be a more important source of unemployment? In the presence of hysteresis, do you think that unemployment would be higher in an economy with large and frequent fluctuations in output or in one with a mostly stable output level?

9. What would happen if the government tries to lower the natural rate of unemployment through macroeconomic policies? What types of measures would you recommend to reduce effectively the natural rate of unemployment?

10. Would it be desirable for an economy to have a zero rate of unemployment? Why might a positive rate of unemployment be beneficial for an economy?

Explaining Business Cycles

In the past few chapters, we have investigated the basic mechanisms that can cause changes in aggregate output and unemployment in an economy. We have seen that output and employment can vary for a number of reasons: shifts in macroeconomic policies, supply shocks, and changes emanating from the international economy, such as a change in world interest rates or foreign GDP. We have also noted that the effects of these shocks depend crucially on the underlying structure of the economy, including the nature of wage contracting, the exchange-rate regime, the degree of capital mobility, and so on.

In this chapter, we ask two related questions. First, given all the *possible* reasons for fluctuations in output and employment, which reasons *in practice* best account for the observed fluctuations in economic activity? Second, how should we account for the fact that in many countries, and certainly in the United States, output, employment, and other macroeconomic variables seem to move in *cycles*, with all the main variables going through periods of boom followed by periods of bust?

We can make some headway on these important issues, but we must start with two clear cautions. First, we are traveling through an area populated by very diverse macroeconomic views. As you will see, different schools of thought ascribe wholly different reasons to the observed business-cycle activity in the United States. To date, neither theoretical nor empirical work within the profession has succeeded in arriving at definitive judgments on the most important issues.

Second, any answers are likely to differ substantially across countries. While it would be satisfying indeed to have one theory of *the* business cycle for all countries, in practice such a goal cannot be achieved. Economic fluctuations differ substantially across countries, in their regularity, in their magnitude, and in their causes. Small countries, heavily exposed to international trade, show characteristics different from large countries, less dependent on trade. Countries dependent on raw material exports are subject to different kinds of shocks than are manufacturing exporters. No one explanation of economic fluctuations can adequately account for this diversity.

17-1 SOME GENERAL CHARACTERISTICS OF BUSINESS CYCLES

If different business cycles had no important common features, each one would have to be treated as a unique phenomenon, and any attempt at generalization (which is crucial for a theory) would be doomed to failure. Fortunately, although cyclical episodes are not all alike, they share important general characteristics that make them subject to systematic study.

The first major effort to understand the patterns of business cycles in the U.S. economy was made by Arthur Burns and Wesley Claire Mitchell. Their work, part of a large research project undertaken over several decades at the National Bureau of Economic Research, is summarized in the important study *Measuring Business Cycles*.[1] The classical definition of the business cycle was due to these contributors:

> Business cycles are a type of fluctuation found in the aggregate economic activity of nations that organize their work mainly in business enterprises: a cycle consists of expansions occurring at the same time in many economic activities, followed by similarly general recessions, contractions and revivals which merge into the expansion phase of the next cycle; this sequence of changes is recurrent but not periodic; in duration, business cycles vary from more than one year to ten or twelve years; they are not divisible into shorter cycles of similar character with amplitudes approximating their own.[2]

Variables can be classified according to whether they move *procyclically*, *countercyclically*, or *acyclically*. *Procyclical variables* are those which tend to rise during business expansions and fall during business contractions. *Countercyclical variables* tend to increase during downturns, and fall during expansions. *Acyclical variables* do not move in conjunction with the business cycle. A classification of key macroeconomic variables according to their business-cycle properties is shown in Table 17-1.

Burns and Mitchell studied the economic cycles in the United States between the midnineteenth century and midtwentieth century in great detail. Each episode that they observed started at a *trough*, or a low point of economic activity, from which a period of expansion began. Eventually, the economy reached a *peak*, the highest point of the cycle, and then underwent a period of contraction. After some time, the economy bottomed out in another trough, from which point another expansionary phase started. Thus, a complete business cycle goes from trough to trough, passing through a peak. And all cycles are connected in that the end of one coincides with the beginning of another. Figure 17-1 represents graphically this pattern of a business cycle, identifying its most important points and characteristics, the peak, the trough, and the underlying output trend.

---

[1] This book was published by the National Bureau of Economic Research, New York, 1946.

[2] Ibid., p. 3.

TABLE 17-1

SELECTED MACROECONOMIC VARIABLES AND THEIR BUSINESS CYCLE PROPERTIES

Procyclical		Countercyclical	Acyclical
High conformity with cycle	**Low conformity with cycle**		
Aggregate output	Production of non-durables	Inventories of finished goods	Exports (U.S.)
Sectoral outputs (in general)	Production of agricultural goods and natural resources	Inventories of production inputs	
Business profits			
Monetary aggregates	Prices of agricultural goods and natural resources	Unemployment rate	
Velocity of money		Bankruptcies	
Short-term interest rates	Long-term interest rates		
Price level			

Source: Based on Arthur Burns and Wesley Mitchell, Measuring Business Cycles *(New York: National Bureau of Economic Research, 1946), and Robert Lucas, ''Understanding Business Cycles,'' Carnegie-Rochester Conference Series on Public Policy, Vol. 5, 1977.*

Business Cycles in the United States

Beginning with the work of Burns and Mitchell, the NBER has had the recognized role in the United States of dating the different aspects of a cycle—the expansion phase, the contraction phase, the trough, and the

Figure 17-1
A Hypothetical Pattern of Business Cycles

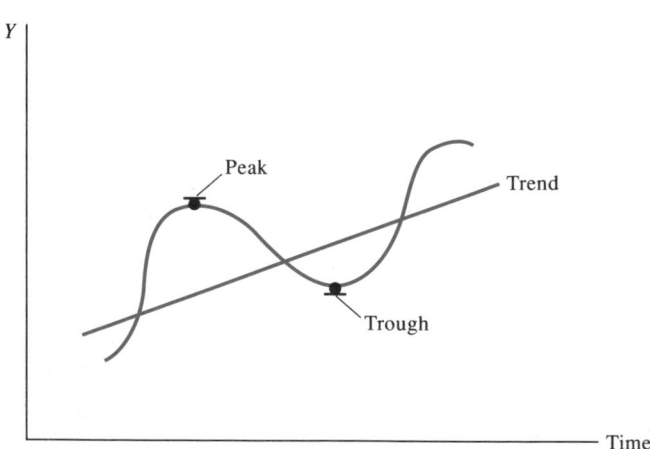

peak. All this information is recorded using one month as the basic time unit. Table 17-2 presents a summary of the timing of the 30 business cycles that the United States has experienced since the midnineteenth century. The table provides specific information for each cycle: month and year of trough and peak, the duration of the expansion and contraction phases (in months), and data that relate each cycle with the previous one, that is, the time to trough from previous trough and to peak from previous peak. Figure 17-2 provides a graphical representation of the U.S. business-cycle experience.

The contraction phase of the economy, between a business peak and trough, is also called a *recession*. (When it is extraordinarily deep, as during 1929–1933, it is called a *depression*.) In informal usage, the U.S. economy is often judged to be in recession when there are two consecutive quarters of decline in GNP. The NBER avoids this kind of mechanical rule, however, and judges whether or not the economy is in recession based on a wide range of indicators. According to the NBER, a recession is "a recurring period of decline in total output, income, employment, and trade, usually lasting from

Figure 17-2

Real GNP Growth Around Trend in the United States, 1875–1990: (a) 1875–1918; (b) 1919–1945; (c) 1946–1990

(Data for 1975–1983 are from R. J. Gordon, American Business Cycles, Continuity and Change, *Chicago: University of Chicago Press, 1986; data for 1984–1990 are from U.S. Department of Commerce,* Survey of Current Business, *U.S. Government Printing Office, Washington, D.C., various issues.)*

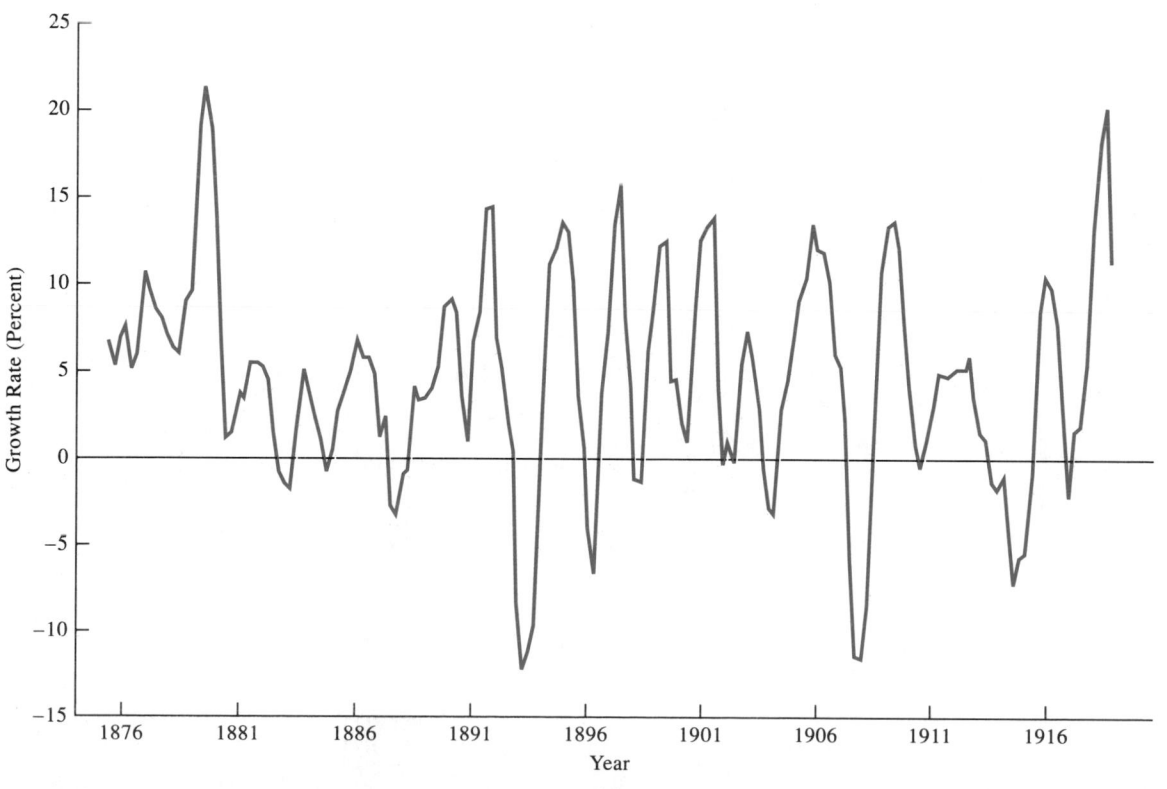

(a)

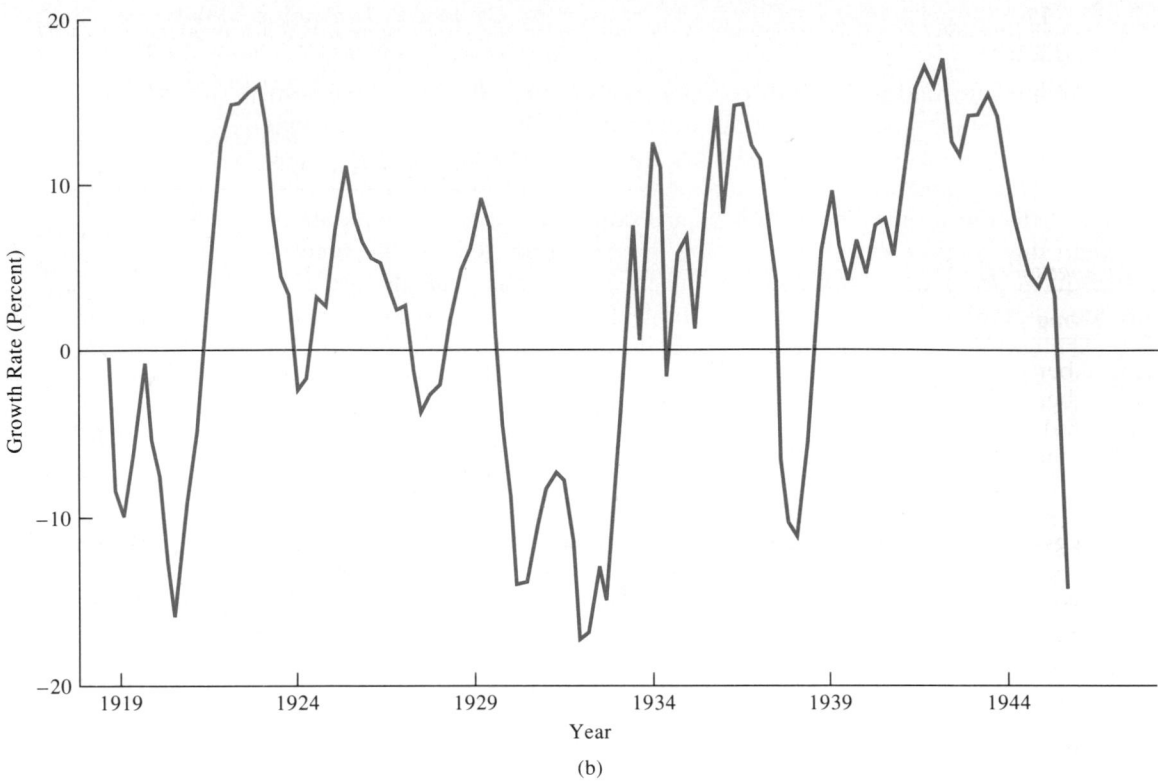

(b)

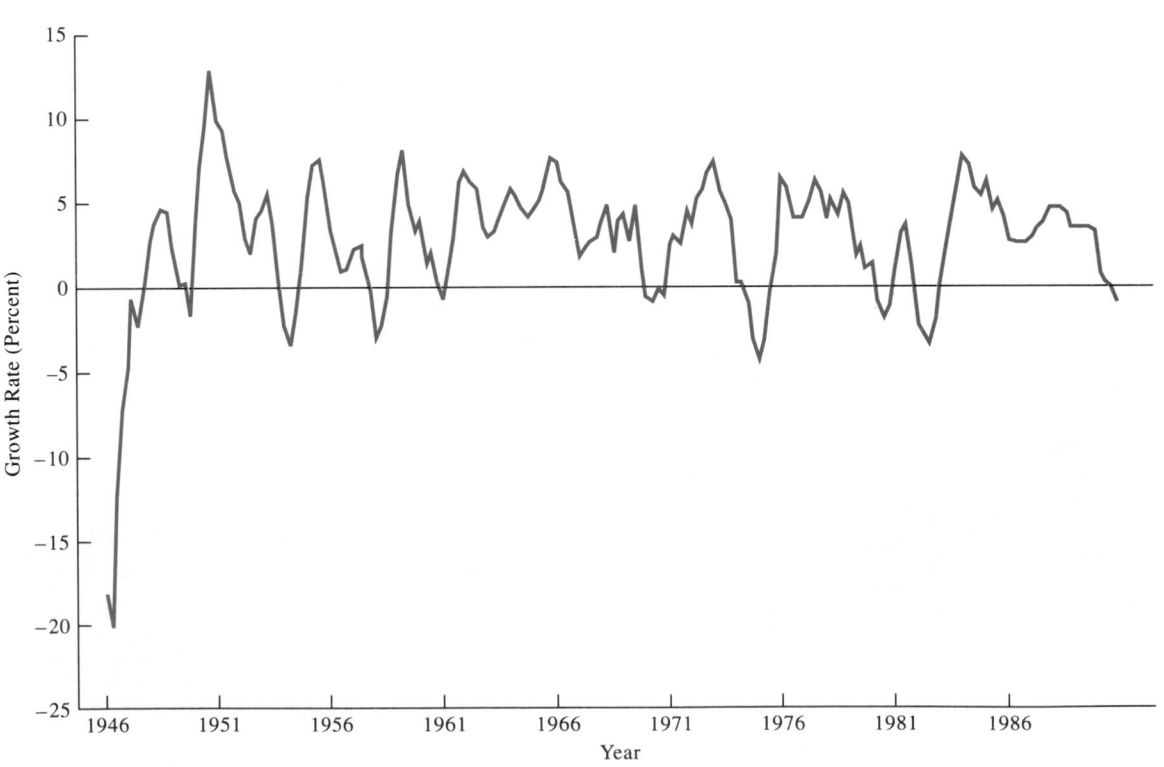

(c)

TABLE 17-2

BUSINESS-CYCLE EXPANSIONS AND CONTRACTIONS IN THE UNITED STATES, 1854–1990

Business-Cycle Reference Dates		Duration (months)*			
		Contraction (trough from previous peak)	Expansion (trough to peak)	Cycle	
				Trough from previous trough	Peak from previous peak
Trough	Peak				
December 1854	June 1857		30		
December 1858	October 1860	18	22	48	40
June 1861	April 1865	8	46	30	54
December 1867	June 1869	32	18	78	50
December 1870	October 1873	18	34	36	52
March 1879	March 1882	65	36	99	101
May 1885	March 1887	38	22	74	60
April 1888	July 1890	13	27	35	40
May 1891	January 1893	10	20	37	30
June 1894	December 1895	17	18	37	35
June 1897	June 1899	18	24	36	42
December 1900	September 1902	18	21	42	39
August 1904	May 1907	23	33	44	56
June 1908	January 1910	13	19	46	32
January 1912	January 1913	24	12	43	36
December 1914	August 1918	23	44	35	67
March 1919	January 1920	7	10	51	17
July 1921	May 1923	18	22	28	40
July 1924	October 1926	14	27	36	41
November 1927	August 1929	13	21	40	34
March 1933	May 1937	43	50	64	93
June 1938	February 1945	13	80	63	93
October 1945	November 1948	8	37	88	45
October 1949	July 1953	11	45	48	56
May 1954	August 1957	10	39	55	49
April 1958	April 1960	8	24	47	32
February 1961	December 1969	10	106	34	116
November 1970	November 1973	11	36	117	47
March 1975	January 1980	16	58	52	74
July 1980	July 1981	6	12	64	18
November 1982	July 1990	.16	.92	28	. . .
Average, all cycles:					
1854–1982 (30 cycles)		18	33	51	51†
1854–1919 (16 cycles)		22	27	48	49‡
1919–1945 (6 cycles)		18	35	53	53
1945–1982 (8 cycles)		11	45	56	55
Average, peacetime cycles:					
1854–1982 (25 cycles)		19	27	46	46§
1854–1919 (14 cycles)		22	24	46	47‖
1919–1945 (5 cycles)		20	26	46	45
1945–1982 (6 cycles)		11	34	46	44

* Underscored figures are the wartime expansions (Civil War, World Wars I and II, Korean war, and Vietnam war), the postwar contractions, and the full cycles that include the wartime expansions.
† 29 cycles.   ‡ 15 cycles.   § 24 cycles.   ‖ 13 cycles.
Source: National Bureau of Economic Research, Inc.

six months to a year, and marked by widespread contractions in many sectors of the economy.''

Two important conclusions emerge from the data in Table 17-2. First, full cycles, measured as the period from trough to trough, vary significantly in their duration, from 28 months for the shortest to 117 months for the longest. Thus, business cycles are not fixed waves of economic activity, as regular as the ocean tides or the cycles of sunspots. In fact, as we shall see, the cycles are best thought of as the result of random shocks hitting an economy. Second, since World War II, the contraction (or recession) phases have tended to become shorter, while expansions have become longer. During the period 1854–1938, the U.S. economy was in the contraction phase 45 percent of the time; by contrast, the time in contraction during 1945–1989 was only 26 percent. Moreover, the volatility of economic fluctuations has also declined, a pattern seen clearly in Figure 17-2.

The figure shows the quarterly growth rate of GNP for more than a century (1875–1990). The years that are covered here are divided into three periods—1875–1918, 1919–1945, and 1946–1990—with the turning points marked at the end of the two world wars.[3] A striking feature of the graphs is the reduced variability of GNP growth after 1945, as noted by Victor Zarnowitz of the University of Chicago. Indeed, by one measure of variability,[4] GNP growth after World War II is less than one-third that from 1919 to 1945 and about 60 percent that from 1875 to 1918. Two observations readily emerge from the data: first, the variability in GNP growth has moderated significantly in recent years; second, the variability in GNP growth was highest between 1919 and 1945.

Showing a similar pattern, the *amplitude* of fluctuations, that is, the extent of change in economic activity between peaks and troughs, has also tended to decline. For example, the average expansion of real GNP along the cycle (measured from trough to peak) has declined from 30.1 percent in 1919–1938 to 20.9 percent in 1948–1982. The decline in the amplitude of GNP contractions (measured from peak to trough) has been even more notable, going from −14.1 percent to only −2.5 percent in the two periods. The evidence clearly indicates that both contractions and expansions have become much milder.

Separating Trends and Cycles

One central hypothesis of the Burns–Mitchell approach to the business cycle is that output and employment have an underlying growth path, known as the trend growth, and that the business cycle represents fluctuations around this underlying trend. In fact, Burns and Mitchell devoted much effort to the separation of trend from cycle.[5] The trend path is the result of factors that determine long-term growth in the economy—the rate of saving, labor force growth, technical change, and so on. (We study these determinants of long-

---

[3] For an outstanding analysis of the business cycle experience in the United States, see Chapter 3 in Victor Zarnowitz, *Business Cycles: Theory, History, Indicators and Forecasting* (Chicago: University of Chicago Press for the National Bureau of Economic Research, 1991).

[4] We refer to the coefficient of variation of GNP growth, which is defined as the ratio of the standard deviation of GNP growth to the mean of GNP growth.

[5] See Burns and Mitchell, *Measuring Business Cycles*, especially Chapter 7.

term growth in Chapter 18.) It is generally assumed that those factors which determine the business cycle have little effect on the long-term trend path of the economy. In other words, the business cycle represents transitory deviations around a given path.

Some recent research has blurred the distinction between trend and cycle.[6] This research has presented evidence suggesting that a significant portion of output fluctuations result from permanent shocks, not temporary deviations around an unchanging trend. Put another way, the effect of random shocks to output are apt to be very persistent over time. If output jumps unexpectedly in a given year, the whole trend in output is likely to be higher for several years in the future. These results apply not only to the United States but also to other major industrialized countries.[7]

The difference between the traditional view and the new view is shown in Figure 17-3. At time t, an unexpected jump occurs in output, q. In the traditional view, output tends to return (perhaps after a business cycle) to the earlier trend line. In the alternative view, the entire path of output is raised in the future, perhaps by a fraction of the jump at time t. That is, a

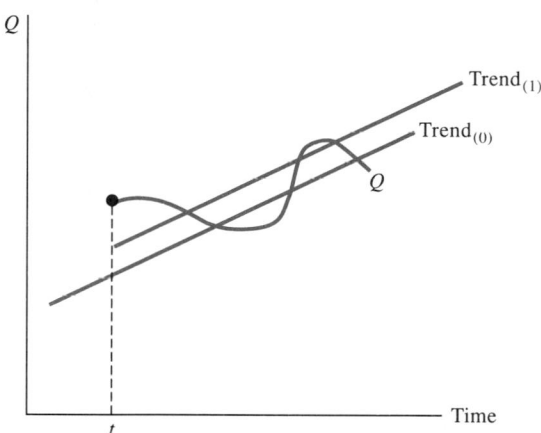

Figure 17-3
Business Cycles: Deviations Around a Trend
Versus Movements in the Trend.

given unexpected movement in output tends to be more persistent in the new view. The empirical evidence is not conclusive as to whether the traditional approach to cycles as deviations around a fixed trend or the alternative view, in which the trend itself is subject to important random fluctuations, is correct. In the words of Olivier Blanchard and Stanley Fischer of MIT,

---

[6] The earliest challenge came from Charles Nelson and Charles Plosser in their "Trends and Random Walks in Macroeconomic Time Series," *Journal of Monetary Economics*, September 1982. See also the work of Edward Prescott, "Theory Ahead of Business Cycle Measurement," *Federal Reserve Bank of Minneapolis Quarterly Review*, Fall 1986, and John Campbell and Gregory Mankiw, "Are Output Fluctuations Transitory?" *Quarterly Journal of Economics*, November 1987.

[7] The international evidence is reported in John Campbell and Gregory Mankiw, "International Evidence on the Persistence of Economic Fluctuations," mimeo, Harvard University, Cambridge, Mass., 1987.

the picture that emerges is . . . that of an economy in which both types of shocks play an important role. Transitory shocks matter and have a hump-shaped effect on output before their effects die out. But the path of output would be far from smooth even in the absence of those transitory shocks. What emerges is a more complex image of fluctuations, with temporary shocks moving output around a stochastic trend that itself contributes significantly to the movements in real GNP.[8]

17-2 THE IMPULSE-PROPAGATION APPROACH TO BUSINESS CYCLES

Some of the early studies of business fluctuations focused on *deterministic* theories, which predict that business cycles arrive with the regularity of ocean tides and with uniform features. This idea was superficially attractive, but it foundered on the fact that business cycles do not show the regularity that all deterministic models require.

Once this became clear, research shifted to an approach which sees cycles as caused by random disturbances, often termed "impulses," which hit the economic system and set off a cyclical pattern of responses in the economy. The cyclical nature of any particular response tends to diminish over time (if we take the traditional view of fluctuations around an unchanging trend). Business cycles recur, however, because new impulses arrive which again disturb the economy's equilibrium. Thus, the cyclical pattern observed in an economy is the result of a series of independent impulses hitting that economy over the course of time. Each of these impulses, or shocks, is then propagated through the economy in a manner that depends on the economy's underlying structure.

The Soviet economist Eugen Slutsky in 1927 laid the first foundations for analyzing business cycles as responses to random shocks. The ideas in his original work, "The Summation of Random Causes as the Source of Cyclic Processes," took a while to become disseminated, because, not surprisingly, Slutsky wrote in Russian.[9] Only a decade later was a revised version of his paper published in English.[10] A similar work was developed along parallel lines by the great Norwegian economist Ragnar Frisch of the University of Oslo. In fact, the impulse-propagation approach borrows its name from the title of Frisch's seminal contribution, "Propagation Problems and Impulse Problems in Economics."[11]

Some time elapsed before this theoretical framework was applied to the empirical study of economic fluctuations. But in the late 1950s, Irma and

---

[8] Olivier Blanchard and Stanley Fischer, *Lectures on Macroeconomics*, (Cambridge, Mass.: MIT Press, 1989), p. 14.

[9] This original piece was published in the book *Problems of Economic Conditions*, edited by The Conjuncture Institute, Moscow, 1927.

[10] Both papers shared the same title, but the newer version incorporated results obtained by Eugen Slutsky in the meantime. The English version was published in *Econometrica*, April 1937.

[11] Published in *Economic Essays in Honour of Gustav Cassel* (London: Allen and Unwin, 1933).

Frank Adelman performed a very interesting experiment using the Klein–Goldberger model for the U.S. economy. (As you recall from Chapter 12, especially Box 12-1, the Klein–Goldberger model was the first in a rich tradition of large-scale econometric models.) What made this model particularly attractive for the study of cycles was its rich dynamic structure and detailed description of the U.S. economy. When the Adelmans analyzed the effects of random shocks in the Klein–Goldberger model, they discovered that the amplitudes and the lengths of the cycles that were generated by shocks were strikingly similar to those in fact observed.[12] When the model was bombarded with random shocks of reasonable magnitude, the resulting business fluctuations appeared extremely similar to those that the National Bureau of Economic Research studies had described for the United States.

What are the main impulses—or shocks—that cause economic fluctuations? In the past several chapters, we have noted at least three types of economic disturbances. *Supply shocks* directly affect the production side of the economy. Such shocks include advances in technological knowledge, climatic changes, natural disasters, resource discoveries, or (from the point of view of a single country) changes in the world prices of raw material inputs. In some circumstances, shifts in nominal wages can also be considered a supply shock. *Policy shocks* follow from decisions made by the macroeconomic authorities, and mostly affect the demand side.[13] These include changes in the money supply, the exchange rate, and fiscal policy. Finally, we have *private demand shocks*, such as shifts in investment or consumption spending by the private sector, that may be provoked by changes in expectations about the future course of the economy. In all cases, the shocks might originate within the country in question, or might be transmitted from abroad, via a country's international trade and financial linkages.

The mechanisms that propagate the cyclical fluctuations after an initial shock occurs are the subject of disagreement. One important question is whether or not it is even possible for cycles to occur within an economic framework of perfectly competitive markets, flexible prices, and optimizing agents, or whether cycles require some important deviation of the economy from the conditions of perfect competition. Keynesian economists have generally answered that some kind of noncompetitiveness of the economy, that leads to nominal price or wage rigidities, are central to the propagation of cycles. More recently, advocates of the rational expectations school, including advocates of the more specific "real-business-cycle" approach, have shown in theoretical models that competitive economies *can* generate cycles following certain kinds of random shocks. Other researchers have recently explored other ways that random disturbances might be propagated, through the independent role played by financial markets, for example. We will first analyze one of the first Keynesian approaches to the propagation of business cycles, and then consider some of the alternative and more recent theories.

---

[12] See the article by Irma and Frank Adelman: "The Dynamic Properties of the Klein-Goldberger Model," *Econometrica*, October 1959.

[13] Of course, some policy changes also have supply-side effects. Consider, for example, the effects of a reduction in the personal income tax rate on work effort, as analyzed in Chapter 7.

17-3 INVESTMENT IMPULSES AND THE KEYNESIAN BUSINESS-CYCLE THEORY

We begin with the Keynesian approach, and in particular, with Keynes's own focus on *investment spending* as the main source of impulses that set off economic fluctuations. Keynes stressed (as we did in Chapter 5) that investment decisions depend on expectations about future profitability, but he also saw that such expectations are likely to be unstable. Keynes described this volatility of expectations by saying that investment decisions depend on the *"animal spirits"* of entrepreneurs, that is, their optimism or pessimism about the future:

> Most, probably, of our decisions to do something positive, the full consequences of which will be drawn out over many days to come, can only be taken as a result of animal spirits—of a spontaneous urge to action rather than inaction, and not as the outcome of a weighted average of quantitative benefits multiplied by quantitative probabilities. Enterprise only pretends to itself to be mainly actuated by the statements in its own prospectus, however candid and sincere. Only a little more than an expedition to the South Pole, is it based on an exact calculation of benefits to come. Thus if the animal spirits are dimmed and the spontaneous optimism falters, leaving us to depend on nothing but a mathematical expectation, enterprise will fade and die;—though fears of loss may have a basis no more reasonable than hopes of profit had before.[14]

Thus, Keynes underscored the fundamental instability of investment and made it his prime candidate to explain the business cycle. He assumed that fluctuations in investment, caused by shifts in animal spirits, led to shifts in aggregate demand, and thereby to aggregate output. Underlying Keynes's approach is the hypothesis of nominal wage rigidity, so that fluctuations in aggregate demand show up as fluctuations in output, not merely as changes in the price level. In order to get to the bare bones of this idea, we shall focus here only on aggregate demand, by using the simple case in which both nominal wages and prices are fixed, so that output is determined only by movements in the aggregate demand schedule.

The Pure Inventory Cycle

Let us enter Keynes's line of thought at the point where a business cycle is started by an autonomous increase in investment. A rise in autonomous investment by itself, however, is not enough to generate cycles. The Keynesian multiplier, which we examined in Chapter 12, explains the process by which output increases following the rise of investment. But the multiplier process is smooth and does not generate cycles. Some additional propagation mechanism must account for cyclical fluctuations following the shift in investment. In an important economic insight, the late Harvard economist Lloyd Metzler showed that swings in inventory investment could

---

[14] John M. Keynes, *The General Theory of Employment, Interest and Money* (London: Macmillan, St. Martin's Press, 1973), pp. 161–162.

provide the missing link between shifts in fixed investment and the business cycle.[15]

As we saw in Chapter 5, business firms maintain inventories as part of their production and sales strategies. An unexpected increase in demand is met by an (unexpected) increase in production and an (unexpected) reduction of inventories. Conversely, a contraction in demand is met by a fall in production and an increase of inventory stocks. Since firms normally want to maintain a given level of inventories relative to output, the firm will adjust its production following an unexpected shock in response to the unintended increases or decreases in inventory stocks. When a recession starts unexpectedly, for example, firms tend to accumulate inventories. Thereafter, the firm will cut back on production both because of reduced demand for output *and* to offset the unintended accumulation of inventories that occurred at the start of the recession.

This behavior with regard to inventories has the potential to generate cycles, as Metzler's model shows. Consider a very simple case in which there is no government sector. Output (Q) is used for sales to consumers, for inventory, and for noninventory investment:

$$Q = Q_u + Q_s + I_0 \qquad \textbf{(17.1)}$$

where Q_u is production for sales to consumers, Q_s is production for stocks, or inventory, and I_0 is noninventory investment determined by "animal spirits." Production for sales to consumers Q_u is based on expected sales in the current period. We make the most simple assumption, that this period's expected sales are equal to sales in the preceding period (or, in other words, that static expectations prevail). Sales, in turn, are equal to the consumption of the previous period. If consumption is a given proportion, b, of income—and income is equal to output in this simple model—then sales in the previous period are $C_{-1} = bQ_{-1}$. Therefore, since Q_u is equal to expected sales, which, in turn, is equal to actual sales in the previous period, we have

$$Q_u = bQ_{-1} \qquad \textbf{(17.2)}$$

Firms want to maintain a given level of inventories. When sales are unexpectedly high, however, inventories fall as firms sell out of stocks rather than out of current production; when sales are unexpectedly low, inventories rise. In period $t - 1$, the unexpected inventory change is equal to actual sales, bQ_{-1}, minus expected sales, bQ_{-2}. In the current period, the firm produces for inventory enough output to replace the *unexpected* drop in inventories that occurred in the previous period. Thus,

$$Q_s = bQ_{-1} - bQ_{-2} \qquad \textbf{(17.3)}$$

Replacing Q_u and Q_s in equation (17.1) by using (17.2) and (17.3), we arrive at an algebraic expression showing that this period's output is as a function of the lagged levels of output and of autonomous investment.

$$Q = 2bQ_{-1} - bQ_{-2} + I_0 \qquad \textbf{(17.4)}$$

[15] See his article "The Nature and Stability of Inventory Cycles," *Review of Economics and Statistics*, August 1941.

TABLE   17-3

AN INCREASE IN AUTONOMOUS INVESTMENT AND BUSINESS FLUCTUATIONS
(UNITS OF OUTPUT)

Period	Production for Sale	Production for Stocks	Autonomous Investment	Output	Sales	Inventories at End of Period
1	600	0	400	1,000	600	500
2	600	0	500	1,100	660	440
3	660	60	500	1,220	732	428
4	732	72	500	1,304	782	450
5	782	50	500	1,332	799	483
6	799	17	500	1,316	790	509
7	790	−9	500	1,281	769	521
8	769	−21	500	1,248	749	520
9	749	−20	500	1,229	737	512
10	737	−12	500	1,225	735	502
11	735	−2	500	1,233	740	495
12	740	5	500	1,245	747	493
13	747	7	500	1,254	752	495
14	752	5	500	1,257	754	498
15	754	2	500	1,256	754	500
16	754	0	500	1,254	752	502
17	752	−2	500	1,250	750	502

Source: Lloyd Metzler, "The Nature and Stability of Inventory Cycles," Review of Economics and Statistics, *August 1941, Table 2. Copyright by the President and Fellows of Harvard College.*

Following Metzler, we are now ready to investigate the effects of a given increase in noninventory investment I_0, using a numerical illustration. To do this, we start from an equilibrium, as presented in the first line of Table 17-3, where the different variables are assigned initial values (period 1). Since firms hold the exact amount of stocks that they want (500), production for stocks is 0 (column 2). Production of consumer goods for sale is set at 600 (column 1) and autonomous investment is 400 (column 3). Thus, the total value of output is 1000 (column 4), which is consistent with a marginal propensity to consume of 0.6.

In period 2 this equilibrium is upset, say, by an unexpected increase in noninventory investment from 400 to 500. As a result of this shock, output increases to 1100 and sales turn out to be unexpectedly strong at 660 (0.6 of 1100). But because production for sale is still 600, based on last period's sales, inventories drop unexpectedly by 60, and firms end up with less stocks than they want. In the next period (line 3) production for sale goes up to 660, and production for stocks also increases, from 0 to 60, to make up for the unexpected drop in inventories that occurred in the second period. Total sales are still higher than production, however, and inventories keep going down.

Only in period 6 do stocks reach the desired level and slightly exceed it. This point marks the start of inventory decumulation. As inventory investment starts to fall, total income also starts to drop. In turn, this begins a phase in which sales continually are less than expected (the opposite of the initial periods) and in which undesired inventories repeatedly accumulate. In each period, then, production for inventories is negative, and output therefore falls for several periods. Note from Table 17-3 that output reaches its peak in period 5 and then starts to decline until period 10 when it arrives at the trough. Then another cycle begins all over again, though the cycle is "damped"; that is, it has a smaller amplitude. Eventually, output reaches a new equilibrium in this example at the level 1250, as determined by the original increase in autonomous investment and the action of the Keynesian multiplier. This behavior of inventories, sales and output is presented graphically in Figure 17-4. Notice how quickly the cycle damps out in the figure.

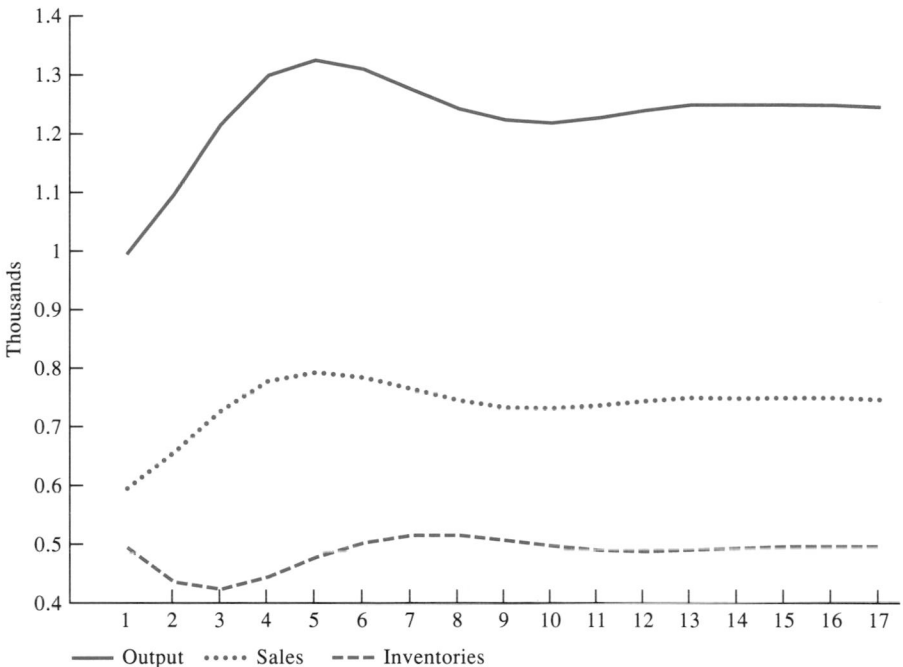

Figure 17-4
A Graphical Representation of the Pure Inventory Cycle

(From Lloyd Metzler, "The Nature and Stability of Inventory Cycles," Review of Economics and Statistics, *August 1941, Table 2.)*

The Multiplier-Accelerator Model

Inventory behavior is not the only way that investment may generate cycles. There is by now a long tradition of distinguished economists who have used the *multiplier-accelerator theory of investment* (which we analyzed in Chapter 5) as a way to explain cyclical fluctuations. Remember that according to the multiplier-accelerator model, investment is assumed to evolve according to the accelerator theory; that is, investment responds not to the level of output but rather to the *change* in output, for reasons that were discussed in

Chapter 5.[16] This assumption can lead to a business-cycle theory that is similar to the inventory model. One of the original contributions to the multiplier-accelerator theory of the business cycle was made by Nobel laureate Paul Samuelson of MIT in the late 1930s.[17]

Consider a very simple model where output is demand determined, as follows:

$$Q = C + I \tag{17.5}$$

Consumption is a function of income alone, but with a one-period lag; thus, $C = aQ_{-1}$. Investment is a function of the change in income, also with a one-period lag, and an exogenous level I_0, determined by "animal spirits":

$$I = b(Q_{-1} - Q_{-2}) + I_0 \tag{17.6}$$

Combining (17.5) and (17.6) we have

$$Q = (a + b)Q_{-1} - bQ_{-2} + I_0 \tag{17.7}$$

Notice the similarity in form of equation (17.7), which comes from the multiplier-accelerator model, and equation (17.3), which arises from the inventory model. In both, output is a function of its lagged levels in the two periods. Therefore, both models produce a similar kind of cyclical behavior following a rise in I_0.

The investment accelerator idea was for a long time the leading theory behind the explanation of cycles. In a now classic piece, the British economist Sir John Hicks, another Nobel laureate, wrote: "the main cause of fluctuations is to be found in the effect of changes in output (or income) on investment. There is nothing new in this contention; it is . . . nothing else but the familiar 'Acceleration Principle' which already has a long history."[18] Although several important developments have occurred in the theory of business fluctuations during the last three decades, many economists would agree with the distinguished macroeconomist Olivier Blanchard who has recently said that the accelerator principle of investment is still alive as an important explanation of the business cycle.[19]

17-4 POLICY SHOCKS AS A SOURCE OF BUSINESS-CYCLE IMPULSES

The Keynesian emphasis on "animal spirits" has proved to be an unsatisfying explanation for the source of business cycles in the United States since World War II. There has been a growing sense that many recessions have been "made in Washington" through macroeconomic policy actions, mainly those involving shifts in monetary policy. In fact, many recessions are widely judged to have been deliberately caused when the Federal Reserve

---

[16] The derivation of the key relationship linking investment to the change in output was shown in equations (5.14) and (5.15) of Chapter 5.

[17] See his paper "Interactions Between the Multiplier Analysis and the Principle of Acceleration," *Review of Economics and Statistics*, May 1939.

[18] John R. Hicks, *A Contribution to the Theory of the Trade Cycle*, 3rd ed. (Oxford: Oxford University Press, 1956), p. 37.

[19] See the paper by Olivier Blanchard, "What Is Left of the Multiplier Accelerator?" *American Economic Review*, May 1981.

knowingly tightened monetary policy to the point where it created a recession in order to reduce the prevailing level of inflation. In one of the most influential studies in modern economics, Nobel laureate Milton Friedman and coauthor Anna Schwartz documented in *A Monetary History of the United States* that major cycles in output in the United States were frequently preceded by major changes in the stock of money.[20]

Figure 17-5 tracks the apparent influence of monetary policy on movements in GNP in the United States from 1967 to 1985. The solid line shows year-to-year changes in the percentage growth rate of money; a positive number indicates that money growth was higher this year than the previous

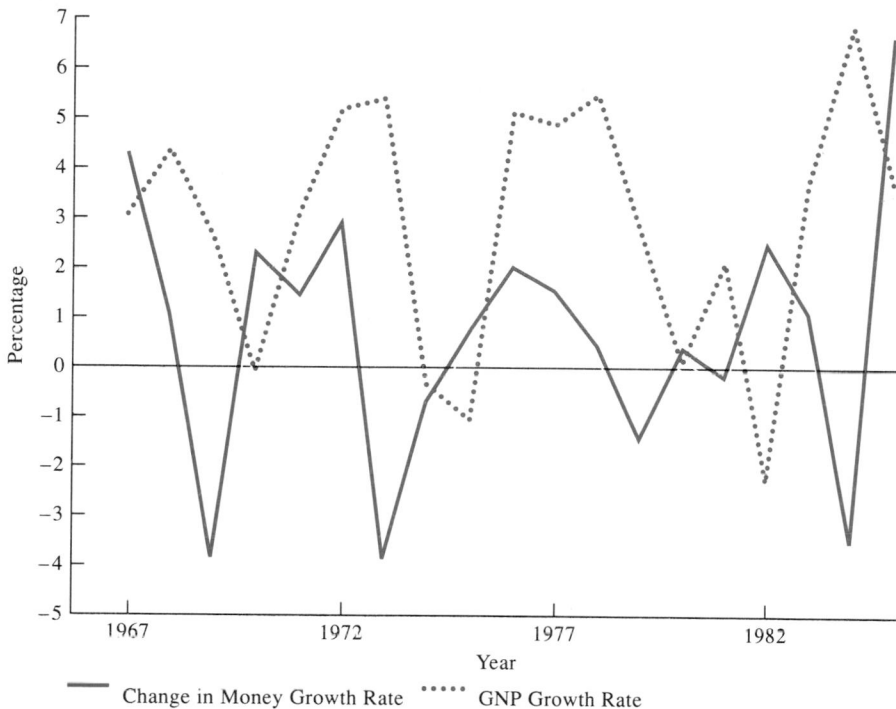

Change in Money Growth Rate ⋯⋯⋯ GNP Growth Rate

Figure 17-5

The Influence of Money Growth in GNP in the United States, 1967–1985

(From International Monetary Fund, International Financial Statistics, *various issues.)*

one. The dashed line shows the growth rate of GNP. Notice the close association between the two variables. GNP growth tends to decline when the rate of money expansion decelerates, usually with a one-year lag. And the more negative is the change in money expansion, the more negative tends to be the effect on output growth.

Thus, it is important to focus on monetary policy as a possible source of cyclical fluctuations. In some cases, monetary tightness has itself been the

[20] M. Friedman and A. Schwartz, *A Monetary History of the United States*, 1867–1960 (Princeton, N.J.: Princeton University Press, 1963).

endogenous response to other shocks. For example, in 1974–1975 and 1980–1982, the Fed tightened its monetary policy after large increases in world oil prices, in order to reduce their inflationary consequences. In these cases, we should judge the oil shocks, rather than the monetary policy itself, as being the cause of the recessions.[21] In other cases, monetary policy has seemed to shift for reasons not related to other economic shocks and may appropriately be considered as a source of observed fluctuations.

One very important source of fluctuation in monetary policy is the change in the political control of the White House. In general, the Democratic party favors more expansionary monetary policy, even at the cost of somewhat higher inflation; the Republican party favors tighter monetary policy. Even though monetary policy is made at the Fed and not at the White House, the president can affect monetary policy through appointments of members of the Board of Governors, and perhaps more importantly in the aftermath of a presidential election, through moral suasion. Thus, when Democrats are elected president, monetary policy is generally eased, while when Republican presidents are elected, monetary policy is generally tightened. As a result, Democratic presidents tend to have booms early in their tenure, while Republican presidents tend to preside over recessions in the first half of a new term.

These patterns were established in a recent study that covered nine U.S. administrations from 1949 to 1984, from Harry Truman to the first term of Ronald Reagan.[22] The GNP growth data, presented in Table 17-4, confirm the striking contrast in GNP growth during Democratic and Republican administrations. GNP growth rates have invariably been low in the second year of Republican administrations and have been very high in the second year of Democratic administrations. Evidently, Democratic administrations tend to begin with a monetary expansion (which shows up in the second year), while Republican administrations begin with a monetary contraction. All Republican administrations between 1953 and 1984 experienced a *fall* in GNP in the second year of the four year term, while by contrast, the second year has been on average the year of fastest growth for Democratic administrations.

17-5 NEW CLASSICAL THEORIES OF THE BUSINESS CYCLE

For the period of the 1940s to the 1970s, business-cycle analysis was dominated by Keynesian models. It was widely believed that the assumptions of classical economics—perfect competition and flexible wages and prices—were inconsistent with observed cyclical fluctuations. Under classical conditions, demand fluctuations affect prices but not output, since the aggregate supply curve is vertical. Thus, most economists assumed that business cycles resulted from the combination of aggregate demand fluctuations and Keynesian aggregate supply conditions.

---

[21] But even in these cases, it can be argued, with some justification, that the oil price increases themselves were the result of even earlier periods of excessively expansionary monetary policies in the United States.

[22] Alberto Alesina and Jeffrey Sachs, ''Political Parties and the Business Cycle in the United States, 1948–1984,'' *Journal of Money, Credit and Banking*, November 1987.

TABLE 17-4

U.S. GNP GROWTH RATES IN DEMOCRATIC AND REPUBLICAN ADMINISTRATIONS, 1948–1984

Administration	Year			
	First	Second	Third	Fourth
Democratic				
Truman	0.5	8.7	8.3	3.7
Kennedy	2.6	5.8	4.0	5.3
Johnson	6.0	6.0	2.7	4.6
Carter	5.5	5.0	2.8	−0.3*
Average	3.7	6.4	4.5	3.3
Average first/second halves	5.0		3.9	
Republican				
Eisenhower I	3.8	−1.2	6.7	2.1
Eisenhower II	1.8	−0.4	6.0	2.2
Nixon I	2.8	−0.2	3.4	5.7
Nixon II	5.8	−0.6	−1.2*	5.4
Reagan	2.5	−2.1	3.7	6.8
Average	3.3	−0.9	3.7	4.4
Average first/second halves	1.2		4.0	

* years of oil shocks
Source: *Alberto Alesina and Jeffrey Sachs, "Political Parties and the Business Cycle in the United States, 1948–1984,"* Journal of Money, Credit and Banking, *February 1988 (Vol. 20, Nov. 1).*

In recent years, however, economists have developed models with fully flexible wages and prices in which shocks do lead to cyclical fluctuations in output and employment. In these models, aggregate supply fluctuates in response to shocks, though different models have varying explanations for the supply fluctuations. In one group of these models, economic agents have incomplete information about the economy and so make errors in their supply decisions when certain shocks hit the economy. In another group of models, the economy is buffeted directly by technological shocks, and individuals make voluntary shifts in labor supply in response to these supply disturbances. The first approach is known as the imperfect information theory; the second approach as the real business-cycle theory. We now describe these two alternatives.

Imperfect Information

The idea that imperfect information can give rise to economic fluctuations, even in a perfectly competitive economy, has its roots in Milton Friedman's very important, and controversial, presidential address to the American

Economic Association, delivered in December 1967.[23] In evaluating the effects of expansionary monetary policy, Friedman argued that

> . . . most of the rise in (nominal) income will take the form of an increase in output and employment rather than in prices. People have been expecting prices to be stable, and prices and wages have been set for some time in the future on that basis. It takes time for people to adjust to a new state of demand. Producers will tend to react to the initial expansion in aggregate demand by increasing output, employees by working longer hours, and the unemployed, by taking jobs offered at former nominal wages. This is pretty standard doctrine. But it describes only the initial effects. Because selling prices respond to an unanticipated rise in nominal demand faster than prices of factors of production, real wages received have gone down—though real wages anticipated by employees went up, since employees implicitly evaluated the wages offered at the earlier price level.[24]

Friedman's argument explains why there is a short run trade-off between inflation and unemployment. The basis for this result is that economic agents are fooled by the monetary expansion because they lack complete information. Producers think that the price increase applies only to their product, thus believing it to be a change in *relative* prices, not in the overall price level. Workers are willing to supply more labor because they mistakenly consider the increase in the nominal wage to be a rise in the *real* wage. If these agents had complete information, they would understand that the nominal demand shocks had simply raised nominal wages and prices, without a change in relative prices or real wages. With complete information, workers would not supply more labor, and firms would not raise production.

A few years later, Robert Lucas formalized this idea in an influential paper.[25] According to Lucas, the market for each good is like an island. The participants in that market, like the inhabitants of an island, have all the information about it, but are isolated from the other markets (or islands) and learn about what is going on elsewhere only with a lag. Lucas pointed out that in such circumstances, producers face a particularly challenging problem. When the market price for their output increases, they are not sure whether the price of their output has gone up relative to the prices for other goods, in which case they would like to increase supply, or whether all prices have gone up, in which case they would not like to increase supply. In other words, the producer has a problem of how to interpret a given rise in price in an individual market.

A person or a firm acting on rational expectations, Lucas says, will see a given price increase in a local market *partly* as a general price increase and *partly* as a relative price increase. Thus, when a truly *economywide aggregate demand shock* hits the economy, each producer thinks that, to some

---

[23] This work was published under the title "The Role of Monetary Policy," *American Economic Review*, March 1968.

[24] Ibid., p. 10.

[25] See his article "Some International Evidence on Output-Inflation Trade-offs," *American Economic Review*, June 1973. This paper draws on a more rigorous treatment by the same author, "Expectations and the Neutrality of Money," *Journal of Economic Theory*, April 1972.

extent, the relative price of her output has gone up. This is a mistake in perception; in fact, relative prices are not changing, and only the aggregate price level is going up. Nonetheless, the result is that the aggregate-demand shock leads to a voluntary increase in aggregate supply.

One of the best-known outcomes of this theory is known as the Lucas supply function:

$$Q = Q_n + b(P - P^e) \qquad \textbf{(17.8)}$$

Equation (17.8) states that output in any given period is determined by two elements, the "natural" level of output, Q_n (the one consistent with the natural rate of unemployment, as discussed in Chapter 15), and a cyclical component equal to the difference between the actual price level (P) and the expected price (P^e). This so-called "price surprise" term grows directly out of the thinking just described; that is, when P is greater than P^e, each individual producer thinks that his own relative price has risen, even though it is only the economywide price level that has changed.

One of the striking implications of the Lucas model is that *anticipated* changes in the money supply should have no effect on output, but only on prices, assuming that all agents understand the functioning of the economy and have rational expectations. Only *unanticipated* monetary policy changes can have an effect on output in this theory. If all economic agents understand that a given money supply increase is going to take place, they should then know that prices will rise in equal proportion (as the aggregate demand curve shifts up along a vertical aggregate supply curve). When prices rise by the anticipated amount, then, the producers will not be fooled into believing that a relative price change has occurred, and aggregate supply will not change.

The story of imperfect information with rational expectations in a competitive economy produced much excitement during the 1970s. The models developed by Lucas and others were internally consistent and mathematically elegant. They seemed to dispense with the Keynesian notion of nominal rigidities while retaining the ability to explain observed output fluctuations. Moreover, empirical research by Robert Barro in the second half of the 1970s seemed to provide some support for the Lucas hypothesis.[26] Barro reported that, for the postwar period in the United States, only *unanticipated* increases in the money supply affected output. In the early 1980s, however, further research carried out by Frederic Mishkin, among others, found substantial evidence that anticipated monetary policy *did* affect output.[27] Moreover, Robert Barro himself presented additional evidence that cast further doubt on his earlier results.[28]

The imperfect-information approach also lost support when economists took a closer look at its underlying assumptions. The central assumption that agents do not know the general price level and therefore confuse

---

[26] See his article "Unanticipated Money, Output and the Price Level in the United States," *Journal of Political Economy*, August 1978.

[27] Mishkin's best-known work, a technically demanding piece, is his paper "Does Anticipated Monetary Policy Matter? An Econometric Investigation," *Journal of Political Economy*, February 1982.

[28] See Robert Barro and Zvi Hercowitz, "Money Stock Revisions and Unanticipated Money Growth," *Journal of Monetary Economics*, April 1980.

relative and general price changes, is rather implausible. Every month, and with great publicity, the economywide cost-of-living index and economy-wide producer price index are published. It is hard to believe that people remain unaware of this or that so short a lag in information can account for movements in output and employment that are as large as are observed. Moreover, individuals and firms frequently buy goods and services during any given month. Thus, they are aware of general price movements even before a price index is announced. Both empirical research and simple intuition seem to suggest, then, that the imperfect-information theory can explain only a small portion, if any, of the cyclical fluctuations in an economy.

Real Business Cycles

A second recent attempt to construct a classical model of the business cycle starts with the idea that technical change is the most important kind of economic disturbance behind business fluctuations. This approach, known as the "real-business-cycle" model, builds on the ideas of Joseph Schumpeter, the great economist of the midtwentieth century, who held that capitalism is characterized by waves of "creative destruction" in which the continuous introduction of new technologies constantly drives existing firms out of business. The real-business-cycle approach views cyclical fluctuations as arising from random shocks to technology. Influential advocates of the approach include John Long, Charles Plosser, and Edward Prescott.[29]

The two main assumptions of real-business-cycle models are that technical change is the all-important source of economic shocks and that these technical shocks are propagated in perfectly competitive markets. The latter assumption is, of course, shared with Lucas's imperfect-information approach, but the former assumption is not. Real-business-cycle theorists clearly reject the idea that the main source of business fluctuations is to be found either in demand shocks or in policy shocks such as changes in the money supply.

To see how real-business-cycle theory works, consider a positive technological shock. Once such a shock hits the economy, the productivity of labor goes up and firms increase their demand for labor. Output will go up even if employment does not, simply because output per worker increases as a result of the technological shock. In order for employment to expand, however, workers must be willing to supply more labor; that is, the labor supply schedule must be upward sloping. In Chapter 3, we saw that a wage increase produces two distinct outcomes, a positive income effect, which leads workers to consume more leisure (and thus supply less labor), and a substitution effect, which makes leisure now relatively more expensive and thus provides an incentive to increase the supply of labor. An upward-sloping labor supply exists when the substitution effect dominates the income effect, a circumstance which empirical evidence tends to support.[30]

---

[29] See J. Long and C. Plosser, "Real Business Cycles," *Journal of Political Economy*, February 1983, and E. Prescott, "Theory Ahead of Business Cycle Measurement," *Carnegie Rochester Conference Series on Public Policy*, Autumn 1986.

[30] Empirical evidence in support of an upward-sloping labor supply was discussed in Chapter 3.

A major problem confronting the theory, however, is that during business cycles, *small* changes in the real wage go together with *large* fluctuations in output and employment. For this to happen, not only must the labor supply schedule be upward sloping, but the response of labor supply to a rise in wages must also be substantial. Can such a large response occur? The advocates of the real business cycle argue that the answer is yes, if the labor supply response *is properly understood*. In their view, the sharp response of labor to small changes in the real wage results from the *intertemporal substitution of labor*.[31]

Specifically, the theory holds that households shift their labor supply over time, working many hours when the real wage is temporarily high, and working fewer hours when the real wage is temporarily low. In this case, households are not trading labor for leisure during a particular period of time (as they did in our static analysis of Chapter 3). Rather, they are trading work in one period for work in another period. For the labor supply to be very responsive to a small rise in the real wage, however, two conditions must hold: first, people must be highly flexible in their ability to substitute labor across time (technically, the intertemporal elasticity of substitution for leisure must be large), and second, workers must perceive a wage increase during the business cycle as transitory, so that they are willing to shift their labor supply sharply in order to take advantage of the temporarily high real wage.

Another important aspect of cycles is that output exceeds its usual trend not just for one period but for several periods following a shock,[32] and a sound theory of economic fluctuations has to have an explanation for this. Real-business-cycle theories give the following account of the persistence of output fluctuations. Consider a positive productivity shock that raises output. Since the marginal productivity of capital also rises, firms increase their investments. The higher investment raises the capital stock, and that, in turn, leads to the persistent rise in output above its previous trend, via the effects of a higher capital stock on the production function.

While all real-business cycle models focus on technological shocks as the main source of fluctuations, some also allow for certain other shocks, such as shifts in government spending, to provoke business fluctuations. But the mechanisms that propagate such shocks throughout the economy are very different from those of the Keynesian models. The output effect of a fiscal expansion, for example, now depends on intertemporal shifts in labor supply rather than on changes in aggregate demand as in Keynesian models. In some versions of real-business-cycle models, a temporary fiscal expansion increases interest rates, and thereby causes households to work more today, and less in the future. In effect, because of the higher interest rates, households choose to consume more leisure in the future and less leisure today—a form of saving response to the higher interest rates. In this way, current output rises when fiscal spending is temporarily increased.

---

[31] The first economists to develop a formal model in which transitory changes in the real wage lead to variations in employment due to intertemporal labor substitution were Robert Lucas and Leonard Rapping, "Real Wages, Employment and Inflation," *Journal of Political Economy*, September/October 1969.

[32] In technical words, we say that the series of output has positive serial correlation.

A crucial assumption of the real-business-cycle approach is that productivity shocks can be either positive or negative; that is, technology can progress or retrogress. It is the negative shocks, after all, that produce recessions according to this theory. This assumption raises some major doubts, however. An advance in technical knowledge usually remains in use until it is replaced by a still-more-advanced technique. This makes the notion of a retrogression in the level of technology seem rather odd, to say the least. Yet without negative technology shocks, the theory could explain only cyclical expansions but not recessions.[33] We have, of course, pointed out in recent chapters some cases of negative supply shocks—bad weather, natural disasters, and terms of trade declines. But shocks like these are easy to identify, and do not seem credible as causes that set off most U.S. business cycles.

The real-business-cycle approach also seems to founder on the evidence for intertemporal labor substitution. There is some indication that a rise in the real wage induces intertemporal substitution; that is, people consume less leisure today and more in the future, or to put it the other way around, they work more today and less tomorrow. But the evidence suggests that such a response is very weak, if it is present at all, and is unlikely to support the big responses in the labor supply across time that would be required to make the real-business-cycle theory conform with actual business cycles.[34]

Another criticism is that this theory downplays the direct evidence, cited in Figure 17-5, that changes in the nominal money stock seem to have played an important role in the onset of many U.S. recessions in the postwar period. Real-business-cycle theorists tend to attribute the correlation between monetary policy and output as a case of reverse causation: output fluctuations, they claim, have induced the money changes, not *vice versa*. While this may be a logically tenable position, it certainly runs contrary to the observations of policymakers themselves, who have frequently attributed business-cycle developments in the United States to the policy decisions of the Federal Reserve Board.[35]

---

[33] It is sometimes the case, however, that *measured* labor productivity declines during a cyclical recession. This cyclical fall in productivity seems to result not from a true negative shock to technical knowledge, but rather from the phenomenon of "labor hoarding." When firms face a temporary reduction in demand for their output, they may choose to maintain (or "hoard") their labor force in expectation of the coming upturn, since hiring and firing of workers has costs for the firm. Output therefore falls by more than labor input, so that output per unit of labor goes down.

[34] Two recent studies have reported a weak intertemporal substitution effect: Joseph Altonji, "Intertemporal Substitution in Labor Supply," *Journal of Political Economy*, June 1986 (Part 2), and John Pencavel, "Labor Supply of Men: A Survey," in Orley Ashenfelter and Richard Layard, eds., *Handbook of Labor Economics*, Vol. 1 (Amsterdam: North Holland, 1986).

[35] For a critical assessment of real-business-cycle theory, see Gregory Mankiw, "Real Business Cycles: A New Keynesian Perspective," *Journal of Economic Perspectives*, Summer 1989.

17-6 NEW KEYNESIAN THEORIES OF WAGE AND PRICE RIGIDITIES

The Keynesian tradition has long been based on the assumption that nominal wages and prices tend to be sticky. This assumption can explain both why an increase in aggregate demand has effects on real output and employment (as we saw in Chapters 12 to 14) and why disinflation generally involves a temporary drop in output and employment. It can also account for the observation that during business cycles, wages and prices tend to move less than employment and output. When combined with inventory cycles or multiplier-accelerator models of investment, it can explain how demand shocks can produce cyclical fluctuations.

Nonetheless, the basic Keynesian model has drawn increasing criticism because the assumption of nominal wage and price rigidity lacks adequate microeconomic foundations. The so-called "new Keynesian theories" have attempted to find richer theoretical explanations of nominal wage and price rigidities. Several considerations are under active study, including labor contracting, union wage setting, implicit contracts, menu costs (real costs of changing nominal prices), and efficiency wages. Although we have already described some of the work earlier, the following summary offers a general survey of recent ideas.

Labor Contracts

Throughout the last two chapters, we have referred to long-term contracts as a prominent feature of labor markets. A crucial aspect of long-term contracting is that wages are not determined in a spot market, that is, repeatedly on a daily or monthly basis, but are predetermined in contracts. Of course, this does not mean that supply and demand considerations have no effect on wages; in fact, all the empirical evidence points to the contrary. What it means is that wages do not move quickly to clear the labor market. Recall that traditional Keynesians do not assume fixed wages, but only *sticky* wages that adjust gradually to shifts in labor demand. This gradual adjustment of nominal wages is enough to account for the upward-sloping nature of the aggregate supply curve, and for the fact that aggregate demand fluctuations cause changes in output and employment.

In most advanced industrial countries with explicit wage contracting, wages are normally set for a period of one to three years. Labor contracts may establish several features of wage setting: a given nominal wage, or path of nominal wages, for the contract period; an indexation rule, which links changes in wages to past inflation; and, often, a reopening clause which establishes that a contract should be renegotiated in case inflation or some other macroeconomic variable exceeds a certain level. (Several features of wage contracting were analyzed at greater length in Chapter 16.)

One of the first formal treatments of wage contracting within a general-equilibrium macroeconomic model was given by Stanley Fischer of MIT.[36]

---

[36] This very important work is entitled "Long Term Contracts, Rational Expectations and the Optimal Money Supply Rule," *Journal of Political Economy*, February 1977.

Fischer considered the effects of expansionary monetary policy in an economy in which economic agents had rational expectations but also set long-term contracts. His results showed that even under rational expectations, monetary policy has an effect on output as long as wages are predetermined. In Chapter 16 we also noted that in many countries, wage contracts are not all signed at the same time. This staggering of wage contracts helps to explain why the effects of monetary policy may persist for several periods. John Taylor of Stanford University showed in a series of papers that when workers care about their nominal wages *relative to other workers*, and when contracts are staggered, the effects of monetary policy on output may persist far beyond the length of the wage contracts themselves.[37]

Union Wage Setting

Wage contracts typically arise in a particular institutional way, that is, through collective bargaining between unions and management. We described the effects of unions on wages and unemployment in Chapter 16, where we noted that unions generally bargain on behalf of their members (the "insiders," who hold unionized jobs), rather than on behalf of the labor force in general, which includes nonaffiliated workers ("outsiders") who might be interested in undercutting union wages. By strengthening the hand of insiders versus outsiders, unions help to account for the fact that unemployed workers cannot simply bid down nominal wages whenever involuntary unemployment develops. As we have noted in earlier chapters, the differing nature of union-wage bargaining in the advanced industrial countries might help to account for the differing responses of these countries to the global shocks during the 1970s and 1980s. An extensive analysis of the role of insiders versus outsiders in wage bargaining, and the implications for macroeconomic equilibrium, may be found in a recent volume by Assar Lindbeck and Dennis Snower.[38]

Implicit Contracts

Implicit contract theory attempts to explain wage rigidities from still another point of view.[39] The theory postulates that a basic asymmetry exists between workers and the companies that employ them. The assumption is that while firms are neutral to risk, workers are risk averse. Under these circumstances, the wage rate may not only set a standard of compensation for labor services, it also serves as a kind of insurance against the risk of income changes, especially when workers do not have access to financial markets

---

[37] One of Taylor's important contributions is "Staggered Wage Setting in a Macro Model," *American Economic Review*, May 1979.

[38] These researchers describe the conditions under which insiders are likely to have extensive bargaining power (such as when unions are powerful, or when the costs to the enterprise of hiring and firing are large), and various ways in which the insiders can mobilize their power (such as through strikes) in order to defend wage levels above market-clearing rates. See *The Insider-Outsider Theory of Employment and Unemployment* (Cambridge, Mass.: MIT Press, 1989).

[39] The classic references are Costas Azariadis, "Implicit Contracts and Underemployment Equilibria," *Journal of Political Economy*, December 1975, and Martin Baily, "Wages and Employment Under Uncertain Demand," *Review of Economic Studies*, January 1974.

where they can reduce their risks in other ways. In particular, firms may agree to keep real wages constant, even in the face of shocks, in order to protect risk-averse workers from fluctuations in income. This agreement might be formally embedded in labor contracts, or it might be *implicitly* reflected in the firm's wage-setting behavior, even in the absence of formally negotiated wage agreements.

Consider, for example, an economy subject to supply shocks, such as fluctuating prices for imported oil. Normally, equilibrium real wages would fluctuate along with the relative price of oil. When oil prices rise, real wages should generally fall. But if the firm is acting as an insurer as well as an employer, it might agree with workers (explicitly or implicitly) to hold their wages constant in the face of the oil price fluctuations.

While such a theory might help to account for real wage rigidities, its ability to account for employment fluctuations is open to debate. As Robert Barro has pointed out, if the firm is insuring the worker against income fluctuations, it would generally contract with the workers to keep employment levels as well as wage levels constant in the face of adverse shocks.[40] Up to this point, the theoretical and empirical investigation of implicit contract theory has still not established the actual importance of the role of risk sharing as an explanation of wage rigidities.

Efficiency Wages

So far we have treated "a unit of labor input" as a straightforward and well-defined concept. In practice, however, we know that this is not realistic. On the one hand, people differ widely in their abilities, as a result of training or innate skills. At the same time, a specific worker can vary the *effort* that he or she devotes to a given job. Obviously, firms have an intense interest in the worker's ability and in the amount of effort that the worker puts into the job. But it is neither easy nor costless for a firm to monitor these variables. These observations are the point of departure of *efficiency-wage theory*, which attempts to explain real wage rigidities as the result of the costs of evaluating the effort and productivity of individual workers.[41]

Suppose that workers have a tendency to "shirk" on their jobs, in other words, to put in little effort because they know that it is costly for the firm to find out how hard they are working. Nonetheless, the firm occasionally monitors work effort, and when workers are caught shirking, they are fired. The opportunity cost of being fired is the wage rate that the worker was receiving at the job, minus the wage rate that he can get at the next job. With this in mind, a firm may find it profitable to pay wages above the market-clearing level on the theory that if the worker at the firm receives a wage above the market level, he will find it riskier to shirk on the job: the costs of

---

[40] Robert Barro, "Long-Term Contracting, Sticky Prices and Monetary Policy," *Journal of Monetary Economics*, July 1977.

[41] The first formal models linking productivity (or effort) to the wage rate are Joseph Stiglitz, "The Efficiency Wage Hypothesis, Surplus Labor and the Distribution of Income in L.D.C.s," *Oxford Economic Papers*, July 1976, and Robert Solow, "Another Possible Source of Wage Stickyness," *Journal of Macroeconomics*, Winter 1979. For a good (and short) discussion of efficiency wage theory, see Janet Yellen, "Efficiency Wage Models of Unemployment," *American Economic Review*, May 1984.

getting fired will simply be too high. In effect, by paying above-market wages, the firm induces workers to cease shirking and apply their maximum effort.

Thus, the theory establishes a relationship between the level of the real wage paid by the firm and the level of productivity that results. Higher wages lead to higher productivity since they induce a reduction of shirking. Since productivity is positively related to wages, firms will bear a cost in cutting wages in the form of reduced productivity. The result is that the firm may keep the real wage rigid in the face of shocks, in order not to disturb worker productivity. The resulting wage rigidity may increase the extent to which employment fluctuations rather than wage fluctuations bear the brunt of shocks to the economy.

There are many other possible linkages between the real wage level paid by an enterprise and productivity of the workers. Higher wages can reduce labor turnover by providing a disincentive for workers to quit. If quits are costly to the firm in reduced productivity (or in the form of direct hiring and firing costs), the firm might choose to pay above-market wages in order to forestall quits. Furthermore, if workers have different abilities, a firm that offers higher wages will tend to attract more able workers, while by contrast, a cut in wages may induce a disproportionate number of high-productivity workers to quit.

"Menu Costs"

There are small direct costs to firms that change their prices. Vending machines need to be recalibrated, merchandise catalogs have to be revised and reprinted, restaurants must redo their menus, and so on. Economists give the blanket name "menu costs" to all the expenses involved in changing nominal prices. Gregory Mankiw of Harvard University and George Akerloff and Janet Yellen of Berkeley have shown that even very small menu costs may have large effects on the economy.[42]

If the costs of adjusting prices were large, it is clear that producers would think twice before moving prices, and price stickiness will result. The striking insight of Mankiw, and of Akerloff and Yellen, is that small costs can also generate significant rigidities in nominal prices, and therefore account for large fluctuations in output and employment. Here is the basic argument. When firms are imperfect competitors, oligopolists or perhaps monopolists, they exercise their market power by setting prices at an optimal level, P_o, in order to maximize profits. If prices are set not exactly at P_o, but at a price close to it, the firm will still come *very* close to maximizing profits.[43] In the vicinity of the optimum price, there is little incentive for the firm to adjust prices constantly to be exactly at the profit-maximizing price because being close to P_o is good enough.

The point is this. Suppose that a firm starts at the optimum price P_o,

---

[42] Mankiw's contribution is entitled "Small Menu Costs and Large Business Cycles: A Macroeconomic Model of Monopoly," *Quarterly Journal of Economics*, May 1985; Akerloff and Yellen's article is "A Near-Rational Model of the Business Cycle with Wage and Price Inertia," *Quarterly Journal of Economics*, Supplement 1985.

[43] Technically, a first-order deviation from the optimal price tends to lead to a second-order, that is, *very small*, deviation from the maximum profitability.

and that a demand shock, say, a rise in the money supply, hits the economy. The new optimum price might be slightly higher than P_o. If there are menu costs, however, the firm may well find it profitable to keep its prices at the old level, rather than adjusting them to meet the new demand condition. Demand will rise, but nominal prices will remain unchanged, and as a result, aggregate output will increase in the standard Keynesian way.

The menu cost approach has received support from some empirical studies of price setting. For example, it has been observed that prices of newspapers remain fixed for varying intervals and then are moved by a discrete increase.[44] Apparently, it makes sense for the newspaper company to maintain a given price as long as demand or supply shocks are small and to change the price only when the cumulation of shocks affecting the newspaper become large enough. A similar pattern of prices being held completely constant in between significant price changes has also been found for prices set in contracts among manufacturing firms in the United States.[45]

The menu cost approach seems to find empirical support, but it also raises some unanswered questions. One important question is why adjustment costs should exert so much influence over price changes and not over changes in output. If it is costly to adjust output as well as prices, then demand shocks might be met by price changes rather than output changes, in spite of menu costs.

Some Conclusions on New Classical and New Keynesian Models

The empirical evidence on alternative models of business cycles remains incomplete, but several observations can be made. First, it is clear that various kinds of shocks affect any economy. Some cycles are caused by demand disturbances while others are caused by supply disturbances. In the United States, it seems rather clear that swings in the money supply, sometimes induced by political changes and sometimes induced by external shocks to the economy (such as the rise in world oil prices during 1973–1974 and 1979–1980), have been the proximate factor in several recent recessions.

Second, while the new classical models have shown, ingeniously, that cyclical behavior can arise in perfectly competitive markets, the new Keynesian approach of stressing market imperfections seems to have the stronger empirical claim. Under the new classical theories, the swings in labor input during the business cycle are voluntary responses of workers to perceived changes in intertemporal work opportunities. But this theory simply does not jibe well with actual worker behavior. There is little evidence that business-cycle recessions really reflect a *voluntary* cutback in work effort by households who believe that their work opportunities are simply better in the future than in the present. Moreover, the real-business-cycle models that stress shocks to technology as being the source of fluctuations have to rely on the unconvincing idea of "negative" shocks to technology, that is, technological regress rather than technological progress.

---

[44] See Steven Cechetti, "The Frequency of Price Adjustment: A Study of the Newsstand Prices of Magazines, 1953 to 1979," *Journal of Econometrics*, April 1986.

[45] See Dennis Carlton, "The Rigidity of Prices," *American Economic Review*, September 1986.

As for Keynesian models of the business cycle, the continuing quest to account for market imperfections that lead to wage and price rigidities has certainly advanced, but not yet to a satisfactory conclusion. The new models stressing contracting and menu costs seem promising and are supported by bits and pieces of direct evidence, but it is clear that more empirical research into wage and price setting remains to be undertaken to test the new approaches.

17-7 SOME INTERNATIONAL ASPECTS OF BUSINESS CYCLES

Whether shocks are to aggregate demand or supply, and whether the propagation mechanisms are classical or Keynesian, we should note that the origins of economic shocks may be domestic or foreign. All economies are affected by economic events in other parts of the world, through trade and financial linkages. In Chapter 14 we examined the ways in which macroeconomic policies in one country are transmitted to another country. We could similarly have studied the transmission of other kinds of economic shocks.

Several researchers have analyzed the importance of an "international" component to the business cycle by examining the extent to which business cycles in one country are related to business cycles in other countries.[46] The evidence suggests a strong interrelationship of business cycles. Simply put, growth rates of GNP, and hence business cycles, are correlated across countries. By using sophisticated econometric techniques, it is possible to separate a "domestic" and an "international" component to the dynamics of GNP growth in a number of countries, and the international component appears to play an important role in the overall business cycle of many countries.

The correlation of GNP growth across countries lends itself to two possible interpretations. First, a set of common shocks may simultaneously affect many countries. Second, a set of shocks might originate in individual countries but then be transmitted internationally to other countries via trade and financial markets. The empirical evidence does not allow us to distinguish clearly between these alternatives, though there are clearly cases of each kind of occurrence being important. In 1973–1974 and again in 1979–1980, the price of oil in world markets rose sharply, leading to a simultaneous stagflationary supply shock throughout the industrial world. Almost all the advanced industrial countries simultaneously fell into a recession in each episode, clearly as a result of the common shock.

As for a shock that begins in one country and then spreads to others, we might cite the high interest rates in world markets in the early 1980s. These were related to the policy mix of tight money and expansionary fiscal policies pursued by the United States in the first years of the Reagan administration. The high interest rates appear to have contributed significantly to business-cycle developments in several countries. A similar occurrence has followed German Unification in 1989. As a result of the heavy financial costs

---

[46] For an up-to-date review, see Stefan Gerlach, "International Business Cycles: A Survey of Recent Empirical Research," *Finanzmarkt und Portfolio Management*, 4, no. 4, Jahrgang 1990.

of German Unification, the German government ran very large budget deficits in 1990 and 1991 which were combined with restrictive monetary policies of the Bundesbank, the German central bank. The result was high interest rates in Germany, which were transmitted to other European financial markets through free capital mobility in Europe. These high interest rates appeared to contribute to a slowdown of European growth during 1991.

17-8 SUMMARY

Business cycles are synchronized deviations of important macroeconomic variables from their trend. A cycle is an expansion occurring at the same time in several economic activities, followed by similarly general contraction of these variables. Cycles are recurrent, but not of a fixed period. Although cycles are not all alike across countries and over time, they share important general characteristics that make them the subject of systematic study.

Variables are classified according to whether they move *procyclically*, *countercyclically*, or *acyclically*, that is, whether they move with the cycle, against the cycle, or without reference to the cycle. Every cycle starts at a *trough* (a low point of economic activity) and goes into the expansion phase until the economy reaches a *peak* (the highest point of the cycle). A period of contraction then begins, until the economy reaches another trough. A complete cycle goes from trough to trough. Recent work for the United States has shown that after World War II, contraction phases have become shorter and expansions longer than during the pre–World War II cycles.

Early theoretical approaches to business cycles focused on deterministic models, in which cycles arrive with the regularity of ocean tides. Business cycles, however, are not like that. They are better accounted for by random shocks (''impulses'') that hit the economic system and set off a cyclical pattern of economic response. This is the so-called *impulse-propagation approach*, the basis of most theories of the cycle.

There are three main types of shocks which generate cycles: *supply shocks*, such as advances in technical knowledge, climatic changes or natural disasters; *policy shocks*, originating in decisions of the macroeconomic authorities; and *demand shocks*, originating in the private sector, such as shifts in investment or consumption spending. *Propagation* mechanisms spread the cycle after the initial shock occurs.

One important question is whether cycles can occur under the classical conditions of competitive markets and flexible prices. The Keynesian approach has suggested that explanations of the business cycle should be based on imperfections in markets that lead to some form of price or wage rigidities. Following Keynes himself, Keynesians focused initially on autonomous changes in investment spending as the main source of impulses setting off economic fluctuations. A rise in investment, however, is not enough to generate cycles. Some additional propagation mechanism must be introduced to account for the cyclical fluctuations following the shift in investment. One such mechanism is the swing in inventory investment following the initial shock, the so-called *pure inventory cycle*. Another mechanism is the *multiplier-accelerator model*, based on the accelerator theory of investment (studied in Chapter 5), which states that investment responds not to the level of output but to the change in output.

Policy shocks can also be a source of business-cycle impulses. Changes in monetary policy, for example, appear to have had an important role in business cycles in the United States. In some cases, monetary policy was tightened in response to other shocks, as after the large increases in world oil prices in 1974–1975 and 1980–1982. In other cases, monetary policy shifted for reasons unrelated to other economic shocks. One source of fluctuation in monetary policy in the United States may be the change of the political party in the White House. In general, Democratic administrations favor more expansionary monetary policy, while the Republican party favors tighter monetary policy.

For a long time, most macroeconomists held that business fluctuations could not be explained within a framework of perfectly competitive markets and price flexibility. More recently, however, *new classical* economists have developed models where prices and wages are fully flexible, and yet where shocks lead to cyclical fluctuations in output and employment. In one class of models, cycles occur when economic agents have *incomplete information*, and so make errors in supply decisions when certain shocks hit the economy. The implication of this approach is that only unanticipated changes in macroeconomic policy variables, such as the money supply, should affect real variables such as output and employment. Empirical evidence leans against this view, however.

In another group of models—known as *real-business-cycle theory*—the economy is buffeted by supply shocks and individuals make voluntary shifts in labor supply in response to these disturbances. In this theory, small changes in real wages result in large fluctuation in output and employment, a result that requires a strong intertemporal substitution of labor. Again, the evidence is not strongly supportive of the importance of intertemporal labor substitution which is at the core of the model.

New Keynesian theories of business cycles attempt to give a richer explanation of nominal wage and price rigidities than was offered by the original Keynesian models. Several possible causes of rigidities are now under active investigation. *Labor contracts* may imply that wages are predetermined for a significant period of time. *Unions* may bargain on behalf of their members (the "insiders") rather than on behalf of the labor force in general ("outsiders"), and thus prevent wages from adjusting to clear the labor market. Wages may be set in *implicit contracts* between firms and workers in order for firms to partially insure their workers against income fluctuations. This kind of risk sharing could result in wages that are rigid in response to external shocks.

According to *efficiency wage theory*, firms may have an incentive to pay wages above the market-clearing level to induce workers to apply their maximum work effort (and thus avoid the risk of being fired because of shirking). Thus, the firm may keep its wages rigid in response to demand or supply shocks, in order not to upset the productivity of the work force. Finally, small costs of changing nominal prices, called *menu costs*, can generate significant rigidities in nominal prices, and therefore account for large fluctuations in output and employment. If there are costs in changing prices, firms will find it unprofitable to constantly adjust prices when demand conditions change.

In open economies, the various kinds of shocks that we have described may originate in the home country or abroad. There is empirical evidence to suggest that business cycles in the major industrial countries are linked (as judged, for example, by a correlation of GNP growth rates across these countries). The evidence is not clear, however, on whether the linkages result mainly from common shocks simultaneously impacting on a group of countries, or rather from shocks that originate in individual countries that are then transmitted to other countries via output and financial markets. In fact, cases of both kinds of shocks have played a role in the world economy in recent years.

Key Concepts

business cycle	autonomous investment
procyclical	pure inventory cycle
countercyclical	accelerator theory of investment
acyclical	political business cycles
peak	imperfect information
trough	real business cycles
output trend	labor contracts
deterministic cycles	union wage setting
impulse-propagation approach	implicit contracts
supply shocks	efficiency wages
private demand shocks	menu costs
policy shocks	

Problems and Question

1. Classify the following variables according to their business-cycle properties (procyclical, countercyclical, acyclical). Consumption, investment, output, employment, real wage, real money balances, money stock, nominal interest rate, deposit turnover. Explain.

2. Explain the response to the business cycle of an industry
 a. that produces durable goods.
 b. that produces storable goods.
 c. with a three-year union wage contract.
 d. with monopoly power in the market.

3. Many economists have noted the existence of "building cycles" of roughly 20 years' duration based on series for expenditures on residential construction. Can you suggest an acceleratorlike explanation for these long cycles?

4. What is the mechanism through which changes in the level of government expenditures accounts for economic fluctuations according to the Keynesian view of business cycles? to the real-business-cycles approach?

5. The political business-cycle theory invokes the image of a cyclical government who manipulates employment and aggregate output solely because it wants to stay in office. Do you agree with this statement?

6. Explain the policy neutrality result of the Lucas model. What are the major implications for the effectiveness and conduct of countercyclical stabilization policy? Can the Lucas model based on imperfect information account for the "persistence" of the business cycle?

7. Explain why new classical theories of the business cycle are associated with the term "equilibrium" approach while the Keynesian tradition is associated with "disequilibrium" models of economic fluctuations.

8. According to the efficiency wage model labor productivity depends on the real wage paid by firms. Using the insight provided by this model explain the existence of wage differentials among workers of identical characteristics.

9. An observed stylized fact of business cycles is the procyclical behavior of labor productivity. How is this empirical observation explained by different views of the business cycle?

Long-Term Growth

In Part IV of this book we have analyzed various aspects of output movements. First, in Chapters 12 to 14 we studied the determination of output in the short term and the role of monetary, fiscal, and exchange-rate policies in affecting its behavior. Then, in Chapter 17 we analyzed the issue of business cycles, that is, the movement of output, employment, and other economic variables around a trend. Thus far, we have neglected the trend itself. For most countries over periods of a decade or more, the trend is positive. That is, most countries are experiencing *long-term economic growth*. While they may suffer from temporary downward movements in output, and even sharp and sustained recessions during a business cycle, the general trend in most economies is for output and employment to increase through time.

The issue of economic growth has been a central concern for a couple of centuries. Growth is required to provide a rising standard of living for a growing population. In the late eighteenth century, an argument was developed that the growth of population would be severely limited by the capacities of the earth to provide the basic needs for an increasing number of people. If population ran ahead of economic capacity, then population growth would be checked, if not by wars, then by various natural disasters, such as famines or epidemics. The British thinker Thomas Malthus was an eloquent proponent of this pessimistic point of view:

> The power of population is so superior to the power in the earth to produce subsistence for man that premature death must in some shape or other visit the human race. The vices of mankind are active and able ministers of depopulation. They are the precursors in the great army of destruction, and often finish the dreadful work themselves. But should they fail in this war of extermination, sickly seasons, epidemics, pestilence and plague advance in terrific array, and sweep off their thousands and ten thousands. Should success still be incomplete,

gigantic inevitable famine stalks in the rear, and with one mighty blow levels the population with the food of the world.[1]

Fortunately, Malthus's predictions have been far off track, and the world economy has experienced sustained positive economic growth during the past two centuries. Population growth has increased markedly, but so too has the aggregate output produced by the world's economies. Economic growth is generally measured by two indicators: total GNP and GNP per capita. By both standards, the world economy and most individual economies have shown significant sustained trends of economic growth. For the industrialized world as a whole, per capita output has grown at an annual average rate of about 1.6 percent between 1820 and 1980. Population has grown at almost 1 percent per year, on average, during the same period.

Economic growth rates diverge significantly across countries, as shown in Table 18-1. For the countries shown in the table, the average annual growth rate in GNP per capita for the period 1965–1989 ranged from −1.3 percent for Jamaica, to 7 percent for Singapore. Note that seemingly minor differences in annual growth rates can have major impacts on the level of income per capita over time. With a growth rate of 1 percent per year, it takes 70 years to double income per person, but if growth is 3 percent per year, a country would have to wait only 24 years to double its per capita income. This striking difference is due to the effect of compound rates of growth.[2]

Table 18-1 also shows countries ranked in order of increasing per capita GNP. While per capita GNP measured in dollars is not an accurate measure of purchasing power in the different countries, it is still the most widely used measure. But even correcting these figures to reflect more precisely the purchasing power of income in each country, the gaps between the rich and poor nations are still immense, as we analyze in Chapter 21.[3]

To appreciate the importance of differential economic growth across countries and the changes in growth rates for a given country through time, consider the case of Argentina. In 1895, Argentina's income per capita was similar to those of Belgium, the Netherlands, and West Germany and higher than those of Austria, Italy, Norway, Spain, Sweden, and Switzerland.[4] During the next three decades, Argentina's economic growth was among the highest in the world. This bright performance led to an enormous immigration into Argentina from Europe, especially from Italy, and it also attracted the interest of numerous analysts. But the situation changed dramatically after 1930. Argentina's growth faltered, and by 1989 its per capita income

---

[1] Thomas Malthus, *First Essay on Population 1798* (London: Macmillan, 1966), p. 139, quoted in Angus Maddison, *Phases of Capitalist Development* (Oxford and New York: Oxford University Press, 1982), p. 9.

[2] Compound growth is like the compound interest that we discussed in Chapter 9. The total growth rate over a period of 20 years for a country that grows steadily at 5 percent per year, is 165 percent ($1.05^{20} - 1$). Similarly, the total yield of a financial instrument that pays 5 percent per year over 20 years is 165 percent.

[3] See, in particular, Table 21-4.

[4] From Michael G. Mulhall, *Industries and Wealth of Nations* (London, New York, and Bombay: Longmans, Green and Co., 1896), quoted in Carlos F. Diaz Alejandro, *Essays in the Economic History of the Argentine Republic* (New Haven, Conn., and London: Yale University Press, 1970).

TABLE 18-1

PER CAPITA GNP IN LEVELS AND RATES OF GROWTH ACROSS THE WORLD

	Income per Capita, 1989 (US$)	Average Annual Growth, 1965–1989
Low income		
Ethiopia	120	−0.1
Tanzania	130	−0.1
Bangladesh	180	0.4
Nigeria	250	0.2
India	340	1.8
China	350	5.7
Pakistan	370	2.5
Indonesia	500	4.4
Lower middle income		
Bolivia	620	−0.8
Egypt	640	4.2
Philippines	710	1.6
Peru	1,010	−0.2
Ecuador	1,020	3.0
El Salvador	1,070	−0.4
Colombia	1,200	2.3
Thailand	1,220	4.2
Jamaica	1,260	−1.3
Turkey	1,370	2.6
Chile	1,770	0.3
Poland	1,790	—
Mexico	2,010	3.0
Malaysia	2,160	4.0
Argentina	2,160	−0.1
Upper middle income		
Venezuela	2,450	−0.1
Brazil	2,540	3.5
Hungary	2,590	—
Yugoslavia	2,920	3.2
Korea	4,400	7.0
Greece	5,350	2.9
High income		
Saudi Arabia	6,020	2.6
Spain	9,330	2.4
Israel	9,790	2.7
Singapore	10,450	7.0
Australia	14,360	1.7
United Kingdom	14,610	2.0
Italy	15,120	3.0
Netherlands	15,920	1.8

Table   **18-1** *continued*

PER CAPITA GNP IN LEVELS AND RATES
OF GROWTH ACROSS THE WORLD

	Income per Capita, 1989 (US$)	Average Annual Growth, 1965–1989
Belgium	16,220	—
Austria	17,300	2.9
France	17,820	2.3
Canada	19,030	4.0
West Germany	20,440	2.4
United States	20,910	1.6
Sweden	21,570	1.8
Norway	22,290	3.4
Japan	23,810	4.3
Switzerland	29,880	4.6

Source: World Bank, World Development Report 1991 *(Oxford: Oxford University Press, 1991).*

level was surpassed by a wide margin in all the countries to which it had earlier compared so favorably. By 1989, per capita income in Spain was more than four times that of Argentina, while per capita income in Switzerland was over 14 times greater.

18-1 PATTERNS OF GROWTH

For the past century, most of the world economy has experienced a sustained rise in total GNP and in per capita GNP. Economic growth has been such a widespread phenomenon that despite setbacks (such as those which occurred in much of the developing world in the 1980s), we take it for granted that the long-term trend of an economy will be upward. It is therefore important to reflect on the fact that sustained economic growth, especially sustained per capita growth, is a modern phenomenon, a characteristic of large parts of the world economy only for the past two centuries.

The Emergence of Modern Economic Growth

Table 18-2 shows an attempt to judge the evolution of world population and output per capita since the year 500 A.D. The economic historian and growth theorist Angus Maddison has divided this period of almost 15 centuries into four epochs: agrarianism (500–1500), advanced agrarianism (1500–1700), merchant capitalism (1700–1820), and capitalism (1820–1980). It is noteworthy that output per person does not seem to have grown at all during the extended initial period of ten centuries and that population grew at an annual average rate of a mere 0.1 percent. Some progress was experienced on both fronts over the next three centuries, but growth remained very low. The real jump began in the modern capitalist phase, when the rate of growth

TABLE   18-2

GROWTH OF POPULATION AND PER CAPITA OUTPUT OVER THE
LAST 15 CENTURIES (AVERAGE ANNUAL RATES)

	Population	Per Capita Output
Agrarianism (500–1500)	0.1	0.0
Advancing agrarianism (1500–1700)	0.2	0.1
Merchant capitalism (1700–1820)	0.4	0.2
Capitalism (1820–1980)	0.9	1.6

Source: Angus Maddison, Phases of Capitalist Development *(Oxford and New York: Oxford University Press, 1982), Table 1.2. By permission of Oxford University Press.*

of per capita output rose to an estimated 1.6 percent per year, and population growth more than doubled.

According to Simon Kuznets, the father of the quantitative study of economic growth, the origins of modern economic growth can be traced to the time of the Industrial Revolution, in Great Britain between 1780 and 1820, in the United States between 1810 and 1860, and in Germany between 1820 and 1870. In all these countries, the rise of modern economic growth coincided with the emergence of capitalism as the dominant economic system. In the early phases of economic growth in these countries, one observes an acceleration in the growth rate of total income as well as higher rates of growth in population, all intertwined with technological improvements. Kuznets points out that the birth of modern economic growth was a dramatic event, full of political and social consequences:

> . . . This early phase of transition to the modern industrial economy is characterized by great internal strains and conflicts, consequences of the shifts in relative economic position and power of various groups affected differently by the increases in numbers and by the opportunities of the new technology. These [phenomena] appear, when viewed statistically, as rather placid movements of steadily climbing lines. But under the surface there are major shifts among social groups, . . . which may involve serious strains on the pre-existing framework of society geared to a much slower rate of growth.[5]

Why did growth increase first in these countries and not others? This question has provoked extensive research and debate for generations, not only among economists but also among other social scientists. One of the most popular theories about this phenomenon was advanced by the German thinker Max Weber, who suggested a decisive relationship between religion and economics. According to Weber, capitalism is especially suited to flourish in countries that share Protestant values. Weber argued that Protestant-

[5] Simon Kuznets, *Toward a Theory of Economic Growth* (New York: W.W. Norton, 1968), pp. 21–22. A significant portion of Kuznets's classical contributions to the analysis of economic growth are contained on ten papers in the journal *Economic Development and Cultural Change,* published between October 1956 and January 1967.

ism encourages profit making as an honorable activity, while at the same time it stresses the virtues of thrift and self-restraint necessary for capital accumulation.[6]

Other theorists have stressed other factors, such as the role of technology[7] and the emergence of the institutions of private property. The economic historian Douglass C. North, in a series of path-breaking analyses, has stressed that the legal and institutional definition of property rights was central to the emergence of modern economic growth in Europe. In North's words,

> Efficient economic organization is the key to growth; the development of an efficient economic organization in Western Europe accounts for the rise of the West. Efficient organization entails the establishment of institutional arrangements and property rights that create an incentive to channel individual economic effort into activities that bring the private rate of return close to the social rate of return.[8]

Characteristics of Modern Economic Growth

As an economy enters the phase of modern economic growth, the growth process triggers an important evolutionary change in the structure of the economy. At least, a common "pattern of development" has been widely observed in growing economies.

The first characteristic of growing economies is that the agricultural sector tends to diminish in importance within the overall economy, in its share of output and of employment. In the United States, for example, 70 percent of the labor force was in agriculture in 1820; that share fell to less than 20 percent in 1940 and to only three percent in 1987. In Japan, the share of the labor force in agriculture fell from 72 percent in 1870 to less than 30 percent in the 1930s, and to 8 percent in the late 1980s. This phenomenon is evident in a given country over time, and in a cross section of countries ranked by stage of development. In poor countries, such as Indonesia and Pakistan, agriculture employs over 50 percent of all workers; among upper-middle-income developing countries, such as Brazil and Korea, the share is between 20 and 25 percent; and among the industrialized economies, the share is around five percent.

Why does the agricultural sector shrink so much in relative terms when income increases? The reasons have to do both with supply and with demand. On the supply side, agricultural productivity tends to rise very strongly in the course of development; thus a given amount of agricultural output can be produced with a shrinking agricultural labor force. On the demand side, the share of consumer demand that goes to food and other agricultural commodities tends to fall sharply as per capita income in-

---

[6] Max Weber, *The Protestant Ethic and the Spirit of Capitalism,* translation by Talcott Parsons (New York: Scribners, 1958).

[7] David Landes, *The Unbound Prometheus: Technological Change and Industrial Development in Western Europe from 1750 to the Present* (London: Cambridge University Press, 1969).

[8] Douglass C. North and Robert Paul Thomas, *The Rise of the Western World,* Cambridge: Cambridge University Press, 1973, p.1

creases. Technically, food is a *necessity* rather than a luxury in that the income elasticity of demand for food is less than one. The declining proportion of the budget devoted to food as per capita income rises is known as Engel's law, and it is one of the most reliable empirical generalizations in all of economics.[9]

The British economist Colin Clark noted that the counterpart of the decline in agriculture is, first, a rise in the industrial sector, and then later, a rise in the service sector.[10] In the early stages of rapid growth, the industrial sector grows sharply, then reaches a peak and begins to decline as a share of the total economy. The service sector, on the other hand, grows steadily and

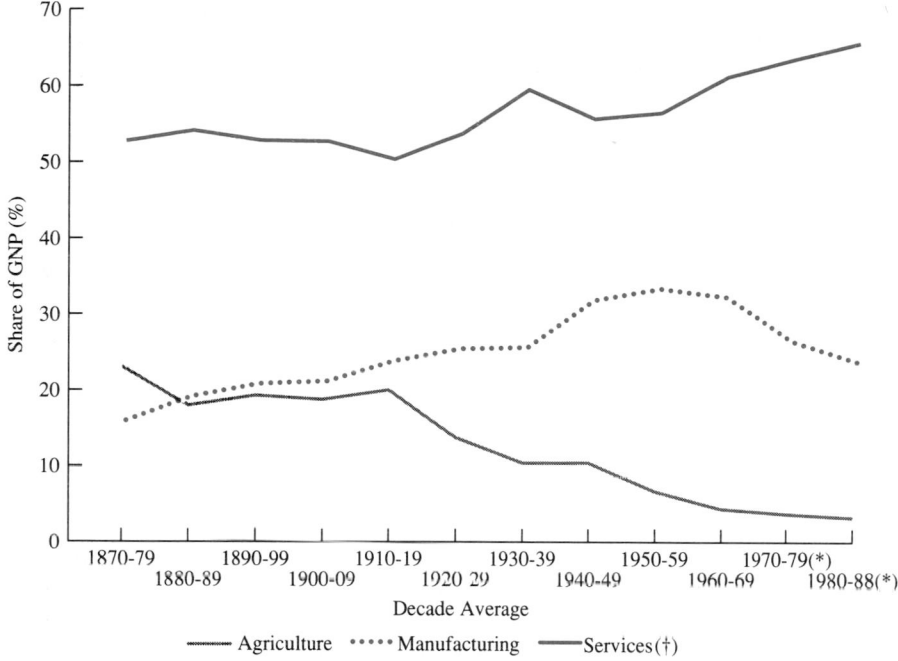

† Services plus wholesale trade plus government plus finance and miscellaneous.
*Agriculture, manufacturing and services over GNP; otherwise,national income.

Figure 18-1

Shares of Agriculture, Industry, and Services in GNP: United States, 1820–1980

(From Historical Statistics of the United States, Colonial Times to 1970, *and* Economic Report of the President, 1991.*)*

rises in its share of the economy as both industry and agriculture diminish. These trends within the different sectors are shown for the United States in Figure 18-1.

Another characteristic of development is the shift toward urbanization, defined by Kuznets as "the concentration of population in densely settled,

---

[9] The statistical relationship was specified by Ernst Engel in the late nineteenth century, in *Die Lebenkosten Belgischer Arbeiter-Familien: Fruher und Jetz* (Dresden: C. Heinrich, 1895).

[10] C. Clark, *National Income and Outlay* (London: Macmillan, 1937).

relatively large aggregates.'' This is a consequence of the decline in agriculture and the flourishing of industry. Industrial production occurs within large firms which can take advantage of *economies of scale* in production. These industrial firms find it advantageous to locate relatively close to each other in order to share a common infrastructure network—communications, transport facilities, energy supplies, and so forth. In addition, firms producing final consumption goods generally find it to their advantage to be close to the main consumption centers where their markets are. The cost savings that come from proximity to other firms are known as *economies of agglomeration*.

A broad study of development patterns carried out in the early 1970s by Hollis Chenery of Harvard University and Moshe Syrquin of Bar-Ilan University confirmed many of Kuznets's and Clark's earlier findings and enriched the analysis of modern economic growth.[11] The study included over 100 countries for the period 1950–1970. One of its important conclusions was that the notion of a dichotomy between developed and developing nations should be abandoned in favor of a concept of transitional stages between these two levels of development. This finding thus acknowledges the fact that developing countries show many characteristics of the earlier stages of developed economies and that the broad patterns of development across countries of quite diverse natures show a general consistency: a shift away from agriculture, an increased share of industry, and a trend toward urbanization.

Development studies have generally found that the abundance (or lack) of natural resources has not been an important factor in economic growth. There are many examples of resource-poor countries that have been quite successful in their growth performance. These countries typically export manufactured goods and import the needed raw materials. Japan and the so-called ''East Asian Dragons,'' Hong Kong, Korea, Taiwan, and Singapore, are prime examples of this pattern. The relative unimportance of raw materials to growth underscores the importance of the human factor in economic development, a subject that we discuss later when we analyze the role of human capital.

18-2 The Sources of Economic Growth

There is a large ongoing debate about the sources of growth. A look at recent growth experience, some of it contained in Table 18-1, calls to mind a number of issues. For example, why have Japan and some East Asian countries (principally Hong Kong, Korea, Singapore, and Taiwan) grown so much faster than the rest of the world? Clearly, economists do not have all the answers to the complex question of what determines growth. They have made some progress in identifying some key factors, however.

---

[11] Hollis B. Chenery and Moshe Syrquin, *Patterns of Development, 1950–70* (London: Oxford University Press, 1975). A more recent analysis of development patterns by these and other authors is found in a collection of essays titled *Industrialization and Growth. A Comparative Study*, edited by Hollis Chenery, Sherman Robinson, and Moshe Syrquin (London: Oxford University Press, 1986).

An Accounting Framework For Growth

The Nobel laureate Robert Solow of MIT developed an accounting frame-work for measuring the main factors in economic growth.[12] His starting point is the production function, which we introduced and analyzed in Chapters 3 and 5. For convenience, we rewrite equation (3.1), showing output (Q) as a function of the capital stock (K), of labor input (L), and of the state of technology (T).

$$Q = Q(K, L, T) \qquad (18.1)$$

Solow showed how the growth in output Q could be apportioned among the underlying factors, that is, growth in K, in L, and in T. To make this apportionment, Solow assumed a particular form of technological change, in which changes in T cause an equal increase in the marginal products of K and L. That is true when (18.1) is written in the special form:

$$Q = TF(K, L) \qquad (18.2)$$

where $F(K, L)$ is a normal neoclassical production function of capital and labor.

Starting from (18.2), we can write the change in output ΔQ as follows:

$$\Delta Q = \Delta TF(K, L) + TF_K \Delta K + TF_L \Delta L \qquad (18.3)$$

In equation (18.3), TF_K is the marginal product of capital, and TF_L is the marginal product of labor. This expression apportions the change in output ΔQ among ΔT, ΔK, and ΔL. (Note, for example, that the contribution of a change in L is equal to ΔL multiplied by the marginal product of labor, TF_L.)

The expression can be made more intuitive using a bit of algebra. With a constant-returns-to-scale production function, and perfect competition, TF_L is equal to w/P, the product wage.[13] Therefore, $(TF_L L)/Q$ is equal to the share of labor costs in total output, which we denote s_L. Similarly, $(TF_K K)/Q$ is equal to the share of capital costs in total output, which we denote s_K. The share of labor and capital add to one, that is, $s_L + s_K = 1$.

With this done, we can rewrite (18.3) as follows:[14]

$$\frac{\Delta Q}{Q} = \frac{\Delta T}{T} + \frac{s_L \Delta L}{L} + \frac{s_K \Delta K}{K} \qquad (18.4)$$

To put the same thing into words, the rate of growth in output ($\Delta Q/Q$) is equal to the sum of three terms: (1) the rate of technical progress ($\Delta T/T$); (2)

---

[12] Robert M. Solow, "Technical Change and the Aggregate Production Function," *Review of Economics and Statistics*, August 1957.

[13] Remember the definition of the product wage, as the nominal wage divided by the price of output. With perfect competition, the product wage is equal to the marginal product of labor.

[14] To get from (18.3) to (18.4), we divide both sides of equation (18.3) by Q, to get

$$\frac{\Delta Q}{Q} = \frac{\Delta TF}{Q} + \frac{TF_L \Delta L}{Q} + \frac{TF_K \Delta K}{Q}$$

Note that $\Delta TF/Q$ is equal to $\Delta T/T$, since $Q = TF$. Note also that $TF_L \Delta L/Q$ is equal to $[(TF_L L)/Q](\Delta L/L)$, which in turn may be written as $s_L \Delta L/L$. Similarly, $TF_K \Delta K/Q$ may be written as $s_K \Delta K/K$.

the rate of increase in labor input ($\Delta L/L$), weighted by the share of labor in output (s_L); and (3) the rate of growth of capital ($\Delta K/K$), weighted by the share of capital in output (s_K).

The shares of labor and capital are measured as part of the national income accounts. In the United States, for example, the share of labor now fluctuates between 0.7 and 0.75, while the share of capital is between 0.25 and 0.3. According to these figures, an expansion of about 1.3 percent in the labor force is necessary to produce a 1.0 percentage point increase in output (that is, with $s_L = 0.75$, $\Delta L/L$ must be about 1.3 percent for $s_L \Delta L/L$ to equal 1 percent). At the same time, because capital has a smaller share in total output, about 4 percent growth in the capital stock is necessary to achieve one extra point of expansion in GDP.

Using equation (18.4), we can obtain the growth of output per unit of labor input, that is, the growth of (Q/L). Recalling that the percentage change in a fraction is the rate of change in the numerator minus the percentage change in the denominator, the percentage growth of (Q/L) is equal to $\Delta Q/Q - \Delta L/L$. Then, by subtracting $\Delta L/L$ from both sides of equation (18.4) we obtain

$$\frac{\Delta(Q/L)}{(Q/L)} = \frac{\Delta Q}{Q} - \frac{\Delta L}{L} = \frac{\Delta T}{T} + s_K \left(\frac{\Delta K}{K} - \frac{\Delta L}{L} \right) \qquad \textbf{(18.5)}$$

If we assume for simplicity that the rate of population growth is equal to the rate of growth in the labor force, then expression (18.5) shows the two factors that contribute to the growth of output per capita: the rate of technical progress, $\Delta T/T$, and the growth in capital per worker ($\Delta K/K - \Delta L/L$) weighed by the income share of capital, s_K. [Note that $\Delta K/K - \Delta L/L$ is also equal to $\Delta(K/L)/(K/L)$.]

In general, technical progress cannot be observed directly. Thus, the framework in (18.5) is not usually tested but, rather, assumed. It is used, instead, to calculate $\Delta T/T$ as the residual element of the equation, after the observable causes of growth are measured, and subtracted off from $\Delta(Q/L)/(Q/L)$. In particular, (18.5) is rearranged in the following fashion:

$$\frac{\Delta T}{T} = \frac{\Delta(Q/L)}{(Q/L)} - s_K \left(\frac{\Delta K}{K} - \frac{\Delta L}{L} \right) \qquad \textbf{(18.6)}$$

$\Delta T/T$ is then calculated as the difference between the observed growth rate in output per worker, minus the change in capital per worker multiplied by the share of capital in output. This is the so-called *Solow residual,* which has been at the center of growth and productivity analysis for the last three decades.

Economists interpret the Solow residual as the part of economic growth due to technical progress. But in fact, it is really a measure of our ignorance, since it is calculated as the part of growth that is not readily explained by observable factors.

The Empirical Evidence

Solow was the first to use the production function framework to measure the sources of growth for the United States. Using equation (18.6), he applied the framework to the 40-year period between 1909 and 1949.[15] The starting

---

[15] Robert Solow, "Technical Change and the Aggregate Production Function."

point was to obtain the series of GNP per man hour, of capital per man hour, and of the income share of capital for the whole period. From there, he calculated the rates of growth in the first two variables and obtained the rate of technical progress as the residual.

The results of Solow's experiment were extremely interesting. Output per man hour had doubled in the United States between 1909 and 1949. What was striking were the *sources* of this growth. Only 12 percent was explained by the expansion of capital per worker, while the remaining 88 percent was accounted for by the residual, in this case, technical progress. Because technical progress is measured as a residual rather than directly observed, the estimate of $\Delta T/T$ actually stands for all the factors other than the capital-labor ratio that may have been omitted from the simple production function.

An early application of this framework to developing countries produced some results that were quite different from those found by Solow and others for the United States. A study of the seven largest Latin American countries for the period 1940–1974 found that capital accumulation accounted for a much bigger part than did technical progress (that is, the Solow residual) in the growth of per capita output.[16]

Much of the subsequent empirical work on growth has been based on refinements and extensions of the general framework presented in equations (18.5) and (18.6). Basically, the work has attempted to improve the quality of the data and has disaggregated the series of capital and labor by type. In the case of labor, for example, total labor input has been subdivided into labor categories classified by age, education, and gender. The weights for each subtype of capital and labor are, as usual, the shares of each of the groups in total national output. This is the approach pioneered by Edward Denison of the Brookings Institution[17] and by Zvi Griliches and Dale Jorgenson of Harvard University.[18]

Denison has authored the most detailed studies of the United States using the Solow framework. It is interesting that in spite of his highly refined accounting in which he carefully controls for the quality of capital and labor, Denison's conclusions on the sources of growth are broadly similar to those of Solow's early study. Denison recently analyzed the sources of U.S. growth for the period 1929–1982, and his main conclusions are summarized in Table 18-3.[19] During this long period of 53 years, the average annual growth rate of potential national income (thus smoothing away the business cycle) was 3.2 percent, and the rate for per capita income was 1.6 percent. As in Solow's original study, Denison found that capital deepening, that is, the increase of capital per unit of labor, played only a small role in overall growth. It accounted for about 15 percent of per capita output growth, almost exactly the same proportion as in Solow's original work. Even after a

---

[16] See Victor Elias, "Sources of Economic Growth in Latin American Countries," *Review of Economics and Statistics,* August 1977.

[17] Denison's first work on the subject was written in the early 1960s: "Sources of Economic Growth in the United States and the Alternatives Before Us," Supplementary Paper No. 13 (New York: Committee for Economic Development, 1962).

[18] See their paper "The Explanation of Productivity Change," *Review of Economic Studies,* July 1967.

[19] Edward Denison, *Trends in American Economic Growth, 1929–82* (Washington, D.C.: The Brookings Institution, 1985).

careful attempt to measure improvements in the quality of capital and labor, the unexplained "Solow residual" still accounts for a large proportion of the total growth.

Denison does show convincingly that education plays a major quantitative role as a factor in the rise of output per worker. This points to the importance of investment in human capital as a source of growth, a point to which we shall return later in the chapter. Denison also identifies certain factors that are detrimental to measured output growth, such as crime. Regulations on pollution and worker safety also reduce the *measured* output per unit of labor. But they may very well raise economic welfare nonetheless, once we consider that an improved environment and safer working conditions are distinct benefits even if they do not contribute to the statistical measure of output.

The average growth in output per worker between 1929 and 1982 hides important differences through time. Denison divides the entire period into three subperiods: 1929–1948, dominated by the Great Depression and World War II; 1948–1973, years of high growth; and 1973–1982, the period of the two oil shocks. Table 18-3 presents a decomposition of growth in output per worker for each of these subperiods.

The first thing to notice is the significant increase in the annual growth rate between 1929–1948 and 1948–1973, from 1.24 percent to 2.26 percent. This seemingly small difference—about one percentage point per year—accounts for a total additional growth of almost 40 percent in per capita income during the period 1948–1973. What explains this improvement? Al-

TABLE   18-3

THE GROWTH OF POTENTIAL OUTPUT PER PERSON IN THE UNITED STATES, 1929–1982 (GROWTH RATES, ANNUAL AVERAGES PER PERIOD)

	1929–1948	1948–1973	1973–1982	Total 1929–1982
National Income per person	1.24	2.26	0.23	1.55
Total factor input	0.23	0.61	0.15	0.38
Labor	0.40	0.18	−0.04	0.20
Education	0.38	0.40	0.44	0.40
Hours	−0.21	−0.24	−0.33	0.25
Age-sex composition	0.00	−0.15	−0.24	−0.11
Other	0.23	0.17	0.09	0.16
Capital	−0.12	0.48	0.26	0.23
Land	−0.05	−0.05	−0.07	−0.05
Output per unit of input	1.01	1.65	0.08	1.17
Advances in knowledge (residual)	0.49	1.08	−0.05	0.68
Economies of scale	0.22	0.32	0.21	0.27
Improved resource allocation	0.29	0.30	0.07	0.25
Legal and human environment	0.00	−0.04	−0.17	−0.04
Other	0.01	−0.01	0.02	0.01

Source: Edward Denison, Trends in American Economic Growth, 1929–82 *(Washington, D.C.: The Brookings Institution, 1985), Table 8-4.*

though capital per worker grew at a significantly higher rate in the latter period, the major increase came in the category "advances in knowledge," that is, the unexplained Solow residual!

The most striking feature in Table 18-3 is the decline in growth following 1973. The per capita growth rate averaged a dismal 0.23 percent per year, a startling decline in growth that has been the subject of much attention. This post-1973 decline in per capita growth has also been a worldwide phenomenon, affecting Europe and Japan as well. Table 18-4 shows an international comparison of growth for 16 industrialized countries, excluding the United States, that spans more than a century (1870–1979). Although the main subperiods differ slightly from those presented by Denison, the evidence is clear. All countries present a major expansion in growth from 1913–1950 to 1950–1973 and then a sharp deceleration after 1973.

What does Denison's analysis tell us about the sources of the growth slowdown in the United States? According to Table 18-3, there is a significant decline in the contribution of capital per worker, but this accounts for only a small portion of the reduction in growth. Once more, the most important change lies with technological progress, that is, with the residual, whose contribution to output growth was actually negative during 1973–1982. Because the residual is, by definition, the part that is not readily explained by observable data, explaining why the residual has declined is a big problem. Nonetheless, many hypotheses have been advanced—though none has been proved. The post-1973 productivity slowdown is the subject of Box 18-1.

TABLE 18-4

GROWTH IN OUTPUT PER MAN HOUR IN INDUSTRIALIZED COUNTRIES, 1870–1979 (GROWTH RATES, ANNUAL AVERAGES PER PERIOD)

	1870–1913	1913–1950	1950–1973	1973–1979
Australia	0.6	1.6	2.6	2.6
Austria	1.7	0.9	5.9	3.8
Belgium	1.2	1.4	4.4	4.2
Canada	2.0	2.3	3.0	1.0
Denmark	1.9	1.6	4.3	1.6
Finland	2.1	2.0	5.2	1.7
France	1.8	2.0	5.1	3.5
Germany	1.9	1.1	6.0	4.2
Italy	1.2	1.8	5.8	2.5
Japan	1.8	1.3	8.0	3.9
Netherlands	1.2	1.7	4.4	3.3
Norway	1.7	2.5	4.2	3.9
Sweden	2.3	2.8	4.2	1.9
Switzerland	1.4	2.1	3.4	1.3
United Kingdom	1.2	1.6	3.1	2.1

Source: Angus Maddison, Phases of Capitalist Development (Oxford and New York: Oxford University Press, 1982), Table 5.1. By permission of Oxford University Press.

Box 18-1
Possible Explanations of the U.S. Productivity Slowdown

The decline in productivity growth in the United States after 1973 has been both deep and puzzling. Many analysts have offered explanations for the phenomenon, but so far no consensus has emerged. It appears that there is no one single reason that can account for the phenomenon. Rather, there are probably a number of interacting factors.

Perhaps the most popular explanation of the slowdown relates it to the oil shocks of 1973–1974 and 1979–1980, which are nearly synchronous with the slowdown. The productivity slowdown was first detected between 1973 and 1974, and it worsened again in 1979. Moreover, the oil shock was common to all industrialized nations, and thus could help to explain why the productivity slowdown was common throughout the developed economies.

Martin Baily of The Brookings Institution has suggested that the oil price increase brought on early obsolescence in a significant part of the capital stock, thus accounting for the link between higher energy prices and slower productivity growth.[20] Michael Bruno and Jeffrey Sachs also suggested the importance of the oil price increases and the contractionary macroeconomic policies that followed these shocks.[21] This explanation lost some of its attraction after 1986, when oil prices fell but productivity growth did not increase significantly. Of course, it is possible that the effect only operated mainly in one direction: higher oil prices led to obsolescence of capital, but lower prices did not lead to a restored use of old capital.

Blame for the slowdown has also been put on the costs of increased regulation, such as antipollution and work-safety rules. Edward Denison has calculated that the costs of fighting pollution, of worker safety and health regulations, and of crime and dishonesty (what he calls the "legal and human environment") have reduced per capita growth in the United States by almost 0.2 percent in the period 1973–1982. This represents a sharp rise from the negative contribution of these factors to growth between 1948 and 1973, which was estimated only at 0.04 percent. Nonetheless, this explanation can still account for only a small fraction of the post-1973 productivity slowdown.[22] The negative effect of government regulations is also documented in international studies of the productivity slowdown among industrialized countries. While there is no reason per se why regulation would hamper growth, the estimates show a consistent negative contribution to economic expansion in the countries analyzed.[23]

---

[20] See Baily's "Productivity and the Services of Capital and Labor," *Brookings Papers on Economic Activity*, No. 1, 1981.

[21] See Chapter 12 in Michael Bruno and Jeffrey Sachs, *The Economics of Worldwide Stagflation* (Cambridge, Mass.: Harvard University Press, 1985).

[22] Denison, Trends in American Economic Growth, 1929–82.

[23] See, for example, John Kendrick, "International Comparisons of Recent Productivity Trends," in William Fellner, ed., *Contemporary Economic Problems* (Washington, D.C.: American Enterprise Institute, 1981).

There is no compelling evidence, however, that increased regulation could explain more than a small part of the worldwide phenomenon.

The slowdown of R&D expenditures has also been mentioned as another possible solution to the productivity puzzle. Indeed, the timing of this phenomenon is about right. R&D growth (measured in constant dollars) declined significantly in the late 1960s and did not recover till the beginning of the 1980s. Zvi Griliches of Harvard University has argued, however, that although R&D has an important role in productivity growth, the orders of magnitude involved preclude the assignment of anything more than a modest role to R&D in the productivity slowdown.[24]

Finally, there is always a suspicion that we may not be measuring things correctly, that part of the productivity slowdown is really due to measurement errors. Note, though, that for measurement problems to explain the slowdown, they must cause output growth to be understated by more in the post-1973 period than it was before. A recent study by Martin Baily of The Brookings Institution and Robert Gordon of Northwestern University found that there are indeed measurement errors, especially in two areas. First, the productivity improvement associated with the use of computers across several economic sectors has been underestimated, and they have carefully documented this in finance, insurance, and real estate. Second, they note that labor hours (the traditional measure of labor input) must be corrected for a decline in the quality of the work force. These two elements taken together might account for up to a third of the productivity slowdown.[25]

18-3 THE SOLOW GROWTH MODEL

Robert Solow's accounting framework attributes economic growth to capital accumulation, labor force growth, and technological change. We now introduce another model, also developed by Solow, to show the relationship of saving, capital accumulation, and growth. Solow first presented this model in 1956, and it continues to be the main theoretical framework for analyzing the relationship of saving, capital accumulation, and economic growth.[26]

Presentation of the Model

The starting point is, once again, the production function of equation (18.2). This time, however, we will express all variables in per capita terms. And again, we also assume that the population and the labor force are the same,

---

[24] See Z. Griliches, "Productivity Puzzles and R&D: Another Explanation," *Journal of Economic Perspectives*, Fall 1988.

[25] See M. Baily and R. Gordon, "The Productivity Slowdown, Measurement Issues, and the Explosion of Computer Power," *Brookings Papers on Economic Activity*, No. 2, 1988.

[26] "A Contribution to the Theory of Economic Growth," *Quarterly Journal of Economics*, February 1956. For a broader presentation of growth theory derived from a set of lectures presented at the University of Warwick, see Solow's *Growth Theory: An Exposition* (New York and Oxford: Oxford University Press, 1988).

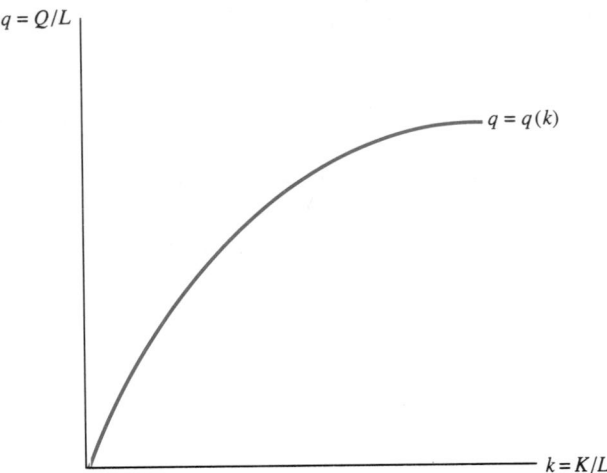

Figure 18-2
The Production Function in per Capita Terms

so that output per capita and output per worker are equal. We denote output per unit labor, Q/L, as q, and capital per unit labor, K/L, as k. From the production function in equation (18.2), we can write

$$q = T\,f(k) \qquad\qquad\qquad \textbf{(18.7)}$$
$$+$$

Equation (18.7) shows that output per capita is an increasing function of the capital-labor ratio. This version of the production function, in per capita units, is shown graphically in Figure 18-2. The vertical axis measures output per capita (q) and the horizontal axis measures capital per worker (k). As the figure shows, higher values of k lead to higher values of q, but at a decreasing rate.[27]

The simplified economy that we are dealing with will be initially closed to trade with the rest of the world, as in the original Solow presentation. Thus, domestic investment (I) is equal to national saving (S):

$$I = S \qquad\qquad\qquad \textbf{(18.8)}$$

The change in the capital stock is equal to investment net of depreciation. With a capital stock K, we assume (as in Chapter 5) that depreciation is a fixed proportion of K equal to dK. Then, the change in the capital stock is equal to investment minus depreciation:

$$\Delta K = I - dK \qquad\qquad\qquad \textbf{(18.9)}$$

We also assume that saving is simply a fixed proportion of national output. Thus, $I = S = sQ$. Therefore,

$$\Delta K = sQ - dK \qquad\qquad\qquad \textbf{(18.10)}$$

---

[27] The slope of the function $q = T\,f(k)$ is equal to the marginal productivity of capital. The fact that the slope declines in Figure 18-2 is nothing more than the familiar property that there is a *declining marginal productivity of capital.*

If we divide both sides of this expression by the size of the labor force, we have

$$\frac{\Delta K}{L} = sq - dk \qquad \textbf{(18.11)}$$

The population is assumed to grow at a constant proportional rate n, which is determined by biological and other factors outside the realm of the model. It is also assumed that the population growth rate is the same as the labor force growth rate. Thus, $\Delta L/L = n$. To complete the set of assumptions, we will take technological progress to be zero initially.

Now, since $k = K/L$, the proportional growth rate of k is given by

$$\frac{\Delta k}{k} = \frac{\Delta K}{K} - \frac{\Delta L}{L} = \frac{\Delta K}{K} - n \qquad \textbf{(18.12)}$$

Thus, $\Delta K = (\Delta k/k)K + nK$. Now, dividing both sides of this equation by L, we have

$$\frac{\Delta K}{L} = \Delta k + nk$$

If we replace this expression for $\Delta K/L$ in equation (18.11), we arrive at *the fundamental equation of capital accumulation:*

$$\Delta k = sq - (n + d)k \qquad \textbf{(18.13)}$$

This key equation states that the growth in capital per worker (Δk) is equal to the rate of saving per capita sq minus the term $(n + d)k$. Now let us look more closely at this last term. The labor force is growing at the rate n. A certain amount of per capita saving must thus be used merely to equip the new entrants in the labor force with k capital per worker. An amount of saving nk must be used for this purpose. At the same time, a certain amount of per capita saving must be used to replace depreciating capital. For this purpose, an amount of saving dk must be used. Thus, in total, $(n + d)k$ in per capita saving must be used just to keep the capital-labor ratio constant at the level k. Any saving *above* the amount $(n + d)k$ leads to a rise in the capital-labor ratio (that is, $\Delta k > 0$).

Saving used to equip new workers entering the labor force is called *capital widening* ("widening" refers to the expansion of the work force). Saving used to raise the capital output ratio is called *capital deepening* ("deepening" refers to the increase in capital per worker). Thus, the fundamental capital accumulation equation (18.13) states that

Capital deepening = per capita saving *minus* capital widening

Now we introduce the concept of the *steady state*, the position of long-term equilibrium. In the steady state, the capital per worker reaches an equilibrium value and remains unchanged at that level. As a result, output per worker also reaches a steady state (remember, that for the moment we are neglecting technical change). Thus, in the steady state, both k and q reach a permanent level. *For the steady state to be reached, per capita saving must exactly equal capital widening*, so that $\Delta k = 0$. Mathematically, we must have

$$sq = (n + d)k \qquad \textbf{(18.14)}$$

Even though the steady state means a constant value of q and k, it does not mean that growth is also zero. In fact, in the steady state, there is positive growth of output at the rate n. To see this, remember that the labor force is growing (as always) at the rate n. Therefore, since the capital-labor ratio is constant, it means that $\Delta K/K = \Delta L/L = n$. Thus, the capital stock is also growing at the rate n. Since both L and K are growing at the rate n, output is also growing at the rate n. (Another way to see this is that per capita output Q/L is constant, so that Q is growing at the same rate as L. That is, $\Delta Q/Q = \Delta L/L = n$.)

A Graphical Representation

The equilibrium of this economy can be represented with the help of Figure 18-3. We begin with the production function, as in Figure 18-2. Now, we define a new curve sq, which shows the saving per capita. Since saving is a constant fraction s of output (with $0 < s < 1$), this new curve has the same shape as the production function, but with a value on the vertical axis which is s times the value of the production function. Since $s < 1$, the new curve lies below the production function. We can also draw the line $(n + d)k$. This is a line that starts from the origin, with slope $(n + d)$.

In the steady state, the $(n + d)k$ line and the sq curve must intersect because $sq = (n + d)k$. This intersection is at point A in the figure. When the capital-labor ratio is k_A and output per capita is at q_A, saving is exactly sufficient for capital widening. That is, $sq_A = (n + d)k_A$. The saving per person is just enough to provide capital for the growing population and to replace the depreciating capital, without causing a change in the overall capital-labor ratio. (It is important to remember here that the steady state is "steady" only for per capita values of variables. At the steady state, the

Figure 18-3
Steady State Equilibrium of the Economy

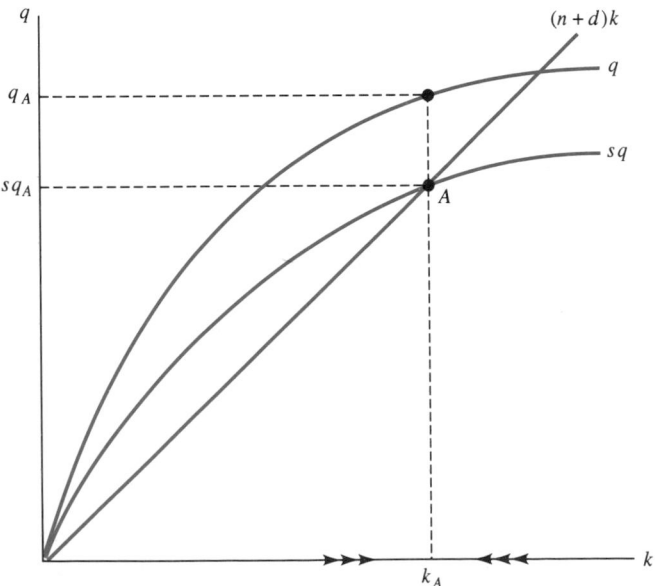

aggregate variables in the economy—output, labor, and capital—are all growing at the rate n.)

To the left of point A, the sq curve is higher than the $(n + d)k$ line. This means that saving is *greater* than necessary for capital widening. As a result, there is capital deepening when the economy is operating to the left of point A. Capital deepening means that the capital stock per worker will be rising, $\Delta k > 0$. Thus, to the left of point A, k will have a tendency to rise, as shown by the arrows drawn on the X axis. To the right of point A, just the opposite occurs. In this case, saving is not sufficient to provide for capital widening. We have $sq < (n + d)k$ to the right of point A. Thus, we would find $\Delta k < 0$. Therefore, to the right of point A, k will have a tendency to fall, as shown by the arrows on the horizontal axis.

Let us now see what happens to an economy when it begins at a point that is far away from the steady state. Suppose that the country is in the early stages of economic development, with a very low capital-labor ratio, say, k_A in Figure 18-4. The initial output per capita is also very low, at q_A. Because of the low capital stock, there is little need to use saving for capital widening, that is, $(n + d)k_A$ is small. Therefore, national saving, which is equal to sq_A, is greater than the capital-widening requirement, and the capital stock tends to expand. As the capital stock expands, the economy moves along the production function, to the right of point A. Over time, there is capital deepening, with k approaching k_B. As the capital stock deepens, eventually the amount of capital needed just for capital-widening increases to the point where all of saving is used merely to keep k constant. At this point, the economy arrives at the steady state.

What is the growth rate of the economy during the transition period to the steady state? Note that when the economy is in a phase of capital

Figure 18-4
Economic Development of a Hypothetical Country Through Time

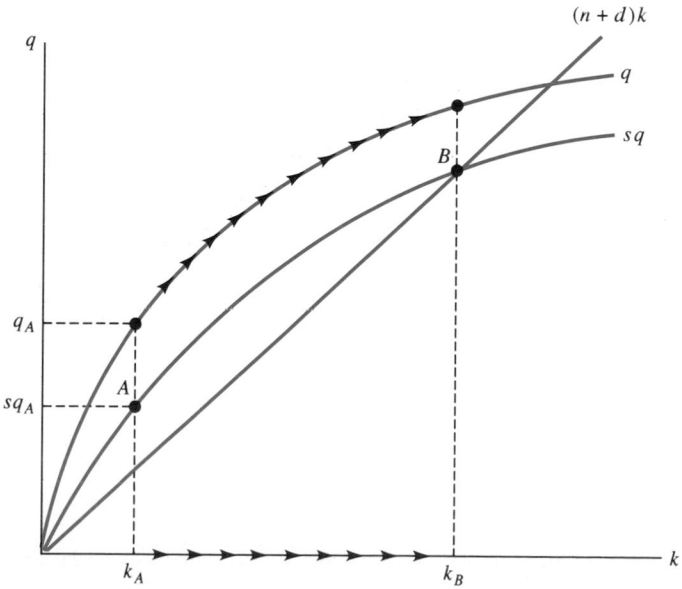

deepening, both q and k tend to rise over time. That is, Q/L and K/L rise toward their steady-state values. If Q/L is increasing, then Q is growing faster than L. Thus, $\Delta Q/Q > \Delta L/L = n$. This means that during a period of capital deepening, output growth is above its steady-state rate. Or, to put this more simply, we would expect (all other things being equal) that capital-poor countries would grow more rapidly than capital-rich countries. And as the capital stock deepens (as k approaches k_B), the growth rate should then slow down.

You can readily verify that when k is above k_B, capital per worker tends to decline to the steady-state level. (This is evident from the arrows in Figure 18-3.) National saving is insufficient merely to keep the capital-labor ratio constant. Note that if a capital-rich country has a declining capital-labor ratio, then output growth is below n.

We have thus determined that whenever the economy is away from a steady state, with either too much or too little capital per worker, there are forces that push it back to the long-term steady-state equilibrium. This feature of the Solow model is extremely important. It shows not only that the steady-state is a point at which all q and k are unchanging, but that the economy naturally tends to develop toward the steady state point. A dynamic system in which the variables tend naturally to move to a steady-state equilibrium is known as a *stable* system. Thus, the Solow growth model depicts a stable dynamic growth process.

Effects of the Saving Rate on Income and Growth

One of the popular recommendations for increasing economic growth is to raise the saving rate. Is it true that a higher rate of saving leads to faster economic growth? The answer is "yes and no." Perhaps surprisingly, the saving rate has *no effect* on the steady-state rate of growth in the Solow model. No matter what the value of s is, the economy grows at the rate n in the long run. The saving rate can, however, affect the growth rate in the short run, as well as the level of per capita income in the long-run steady state.

To examine this issue, let us once again use a graph. Consider two countries, one with a saving rate s_A and the other with a saving rate s_B which is greater than s_A. Both countries have the same rate of population growth and the same rate of capital depreciation. The difference in the two countries shows up as a difference in the point where the saving curve intersects the capital-widening line. Specifically, we can see from Figure 18-5 that *the country with the higher saving rate has a higher level of per capita income at the steady state and a higher steady-state capital-labor ratio.* In both cases, however, the growth rate in the steady state is the same, equal to the labor force growth rate n.

Consider now what happens when the saving rate in a country rises. Suppose, for example, that the country is in steady-state equilibrium with the low saving rate shown in Figure 18-6. A government policy is instituted to raise the private saving rate from s to s'. (Such a policy might involve a rise in the public saving rate, or a tax incentive to increase the private saving rate.) When the saving rate goes up, national saving now exceeds the requirements for capital deepening, and the capital-labor ratio starts to increase. Thus the economy moves from point q_0^* to q_1^* in the figure. *During*

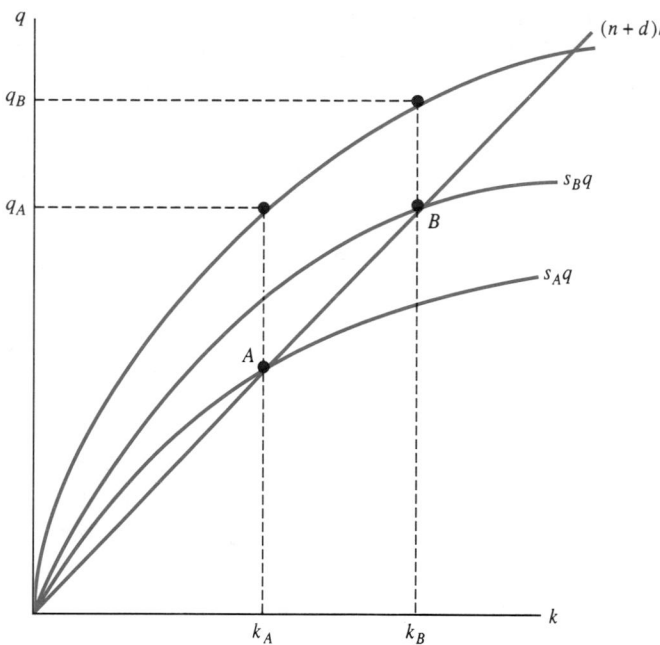

Figure 18-5
Different Saving Rates Across Countries: Effects on the
Capital Labor Ratio and per Capita GDP

Figure 18-6
Effects of an Increase in the Saving Rate

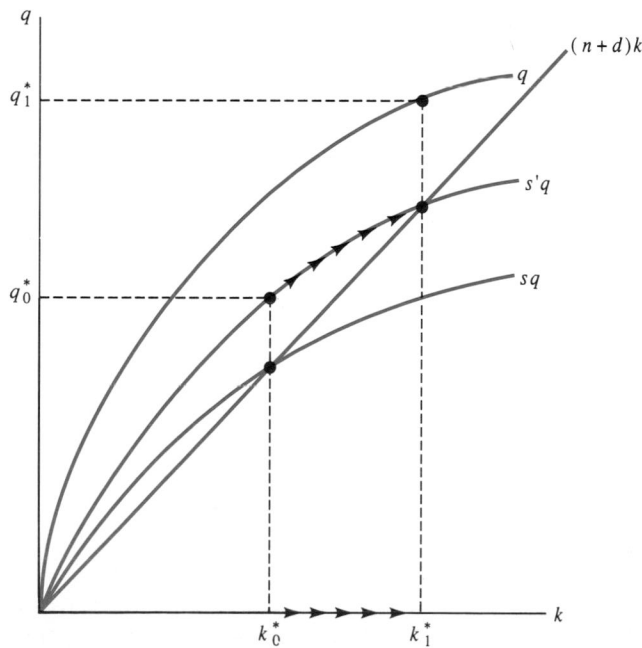

this transition, the growth rate of the economy increases above n, since $\Delta Q/Q > \Delta L/L = n$. As the new steady-state equilibrium is approached, the growth rate slows once again until it reaches the steady-state rate n.

To conclude the analysis, we can say that in the Solow model a rise in national saving results in a *temporary* increase in the growth rate and a permanent increase in the level of per capita income and in the capital-labor ratio. The steady-state growth rate is not affected, however, by the rise in saving because steady-state growth must equal the rate of labor force growth.

Effects of a Higher Rate of Population Growth

Another critical determinant of economic growth and per capita income is the rate of population growth (which, in our framework, is equal to the rate of labor force growth). When the economy is in the steady state, the population growth rate has two fundamental effects.

First, a higher population growth rate leads to a higher steady-state growth rate because, in the long-run equilibrium, all aggregate variables (Q, K, and L) increase at the rate of population growth. Second, the population growth rate determines how much of saving must be used for capital widening. Remember that because of the growth of the labor force, a certain amount of saving must be used just to equip the new workers with the same amount of capital that other workers already have. This capital widening is equal to nk. When the population growth rate increases, more saving must be used just to accomplish it, and this leads to a fall in the steady-state level of per capita income. That is, a higher population growth rate, all other things being equal, results in a decline in steady-state per capita income.

Once again, we can use a graph to illustrate these points. In Figure 18-7, we draw the equilibrium of an economy with two different population

Figure 18-7
An Economy with Two Alternative Rates of Population Growth

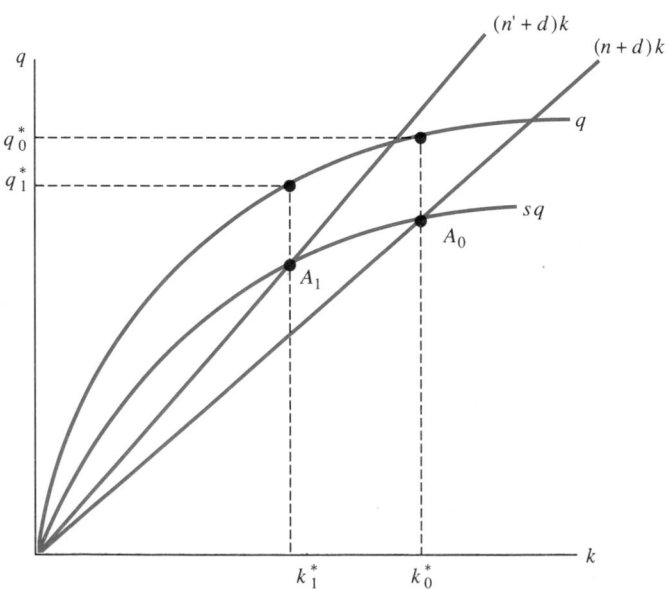

growth rates, n and $n' > n$. The only difference between these two cases is that the capital widening line, $(n + d)k$, is *steeper* in the case of more rapid population growth. Clearly, then, the steeper line leads to a steady-state equilibrium with a lower level of per capita income.

Consider now the effects on an economy of a slowing down of the population growth rate, shown in Figure 18-8, a situation we have seen, for example, in the developed countries in recent decades. The fall in population growth shifts the $(n + d)k$ line down and to the right. With the fall in population growth, the capital-widening requirements are reduced at the initial steady state. Thus, starting at k_0, there begins a process of capital deepening, with $\Delta k > 0$. The economy therefore begins to move along the production function as shown by the arrows, until the new steady state is reached. At the new steady state, the growth rate of the economy will be lower, while the level of steady state per capita income will be higher.

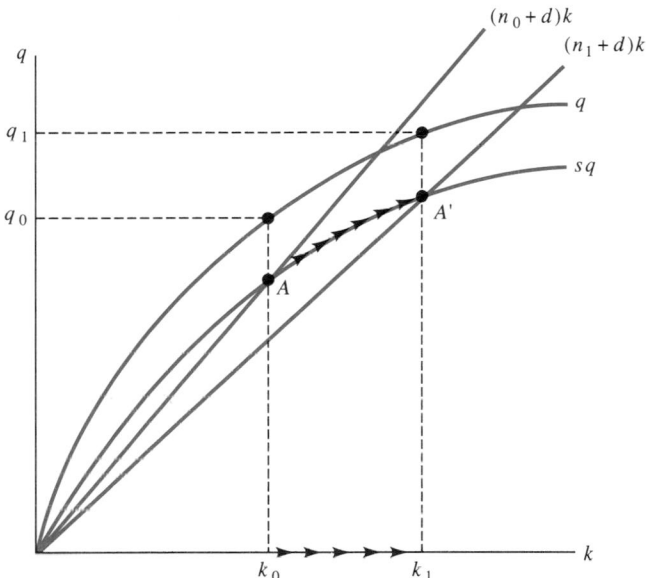

Figure 18-8
Fall in the Rate of Population Growth

What happens to growth along the transition path? Interestingly, the slowdown in population growth immediately *lowers* the aggregate growth rate of the economy, but it also *raises* the per capita growth rate. That is, at the time of the population growth slowdown, $\Delta Q/Q$ goes down while $\Delta q/q$ goes up. In the steady state, of course, $\Delta Q/Q$ is permanently lower (and equal to n'), while $\Delta q/q$ is equal to zero.

Technological Change in the Solow Model

So far, our model has included only two of the three sources of growth, labor and capital, but not technological progress. Fortunately, this is relatively straightforward to integrate into the Solow growth model. When this is done, we have a remarkably flexible and powerful analytical framework within which to account for economic growth. While we will not derive the mathematical results here, we can state the main conclusions concerning growth with technological progress.

The trick to integrating technological change into the model is to introduce it in a convenient analytical way. Specifically, we assume that technological change is "labor augmenting," meaning that the amount of labor input provided by a worker tends to increase over time, presumably because of rising knowledge of the job, better education, and so on. This can be specified in the production function as follows: $Q = F(K, TL)$. The technological change parameter T directly multiplies the amount of labor input.[28] A higher level of technological progress, signified by a greater value of T, means that the inputs provided by L are increased. Each worker produces more labor services for each hour of work time. The total amount of labor input, given by TL, is sometimes called the "effective labor input," or just effective labor, which we denote as L_e (where e stands for effective).

Let us suppose that technological change proceeds at a constant rate θ. That is, $\Delta T/T = \theta$. In that case, the growth rate of *effective* labor is equal to $n + \theta$. That is, effective labor grows for two reasons, population growth and higher productivity per worker. The growth rate of effective labor is the sum of these two growth rates.[29] Thus, technological change increases the steady-state growth rate of the economy, because it raises the growth rate of the labor force in effective units.

With this extended framework, it is possible to derive the effects of technological change on economic growth. The main conclusions are as follows. When there is a positive rate of labor-augmenting technological change, output in the steady-state equilibrium grows at the rate $n + \theta$, the sum of labor force growth plus the rate of technological change. At the steady state, output per *effective* worker and capital per *effective* worker are unchanging. Output per *actual* worker and capital per *actual* worker, however, grow at the rate θ, the rate of technological change. Thus, *the rate of technological change determines the steady-state rate of growth of per capita income, that is, the growth of output per person.*

18-4 NEW APPROACHES TO EXPLAIN GROWTH

Recent studies of economic growth have suggested that the role of capital, including human capital (investment in worker skills), is larger than measured by the Solow growth framework. The basic idea of this new research is that capital investment, whether in machines or in people, creates *positive externalities*. That is, investments improve not only the productive capacity of the investing firm or worker, but also the productive capacity of other related firms and workers. This can happen, for example, if there are spillovers in knowledge among firms or workers that are using new technologies. One firm gains some new experience, and the other firms in the vicinity could benefit from that knowledge. Such learning spillovers may help to

---

[28] In the original Solow model, the technological parameter multiplies the entire production function. Now it multiplies just the labor input. In fact, these alternative assumptions were made simply for their analytical convenience. There is no deeper theory of technical change that favors one formulation over the other.

[29] Formally, $L_e = TL$. Therefore, the growth rate of L_e is given by $\Delta L_e/L_e = \Delta T/T + \Delta L/L = \theta + n$.

explain why high-technology companies tend to cluster in specific areas, like Silicon Valley near San Francisco or Route 128 near Boston.

If these positive externalities are large, the implications for economic growth could be important. Among other things, the measured share of capital income in total income would underestimate the true contribution of capital to output growth. Paul Romer, of the University of Rochester, has suggested that the true total contribution to output growth of a one-percentage-point increase in capital is closer to 1 than to 0.25.[30] The positive externalities of capital in this case would be so important as to multiply its traditional weight (0.25) by a factor in the order of 4. If true, this conclusion would go a long way toward explaining the Solow residual, which appears to be too large because the weight attached to capital in the traditional models is too small. The theory, however, remains controversial.[31] Robert Lucas has also recently stressed the quantitative importance of human capital investment to growth.[32]

One of the most notable implications of theories that assume increasing returns to scale (or that assume important investment externalities) is that economies with increasing returns to scale do not necessarily reach a steady-state growth rate equal to the rate of population growth plus labor-augmenting technical change. Rather, growth at a higher level than this can be self-sustaining (or "endogenous," to use the new jargon). In the normal Solow growth model, capital accumulation at rates higher than the rate of growth of effective labor leads to diminishing returns to capital and a slowing down of growth. When the externalities of investment are sufficiently great, however, diminishing returns to capital do not set in. One result is that a rise in the saving rate may result in a *permanent* increase in the growth. (Remember that in the Solow model, a rise in the savings rate has no effect on the steady-state growth rate, only on the steady-state level of output per effective worker.)

In another recent area of research, economists have used a quantitative framework to examine some of the political and institutional factors that affect growth. For example, Gerald Scully has compared the growth rates of 115 market economies over the period 1960–1980 in order to examine the possible correlations of growth with measures of political, civil, and economic liberty. He found that economic growth is importantly affected by political institutions and specifically that growth has been highest in countries that are politically open and that protect the rights of private property:[33]

> The institutional framework has significant and large effects on
> the efficiency and growth rates of economies. Politically open

---

[30] This theory is presented and analyzed in two articles by Romer: "Increasing Returns and Long-Run Growth," *Journal of Political Economy*, October 1986, and "Crazy Explanations for the Productivity Slowdown," *Macroeconomics Annual 1987* (Cambridge, Mass.: National Bureau of Economic Research, 1987).

[31] See the comments to Romer's 1987 paper in the same volume.

[32] His set of Marshall Lectures, given at Cambridge University in 1985, were published under the title "On the Mechanics of Economic Development," *Journal of Monetary Economics*, July 1988.

[33] See G. W. Scully, "The Institutional Framework and Economic Development," *Journal of Political Economy*, June 1988. The quotation is from page 652.

societies, which subscribe to the rule of law, to private property, and to the market allocation of resources, grow at three times the rate and are two and one-half times as efficient as societies in which these freedoms are abridged.

18-5 ECONOMIC GROWTH IN THE OPEN ECONOMY

The Solow growth model was presented in a closed-economy framework in which domestic investment equals domestic saving and in which there is no international trade. In fact, of course, growth in an individual economy takes place in an international context which can greatly affect the growth process. For one thing, a country can borrow or lend funds as part of its growth process, and this will change the linkages of domestic savings, domestic investment, and growth. For a second thing, growth will be related to the international trade patterns of a country, and the extent to which it can import technological changes that occur in other parts of the world. Let us consider, then, the financial, trade, and technological aspects of growth in an open economy.

Growth and International Capital Flows

We know that in an open economy, domestic investment can be financed by world saving rather than by domestic saving alone. Let us therefore see how the Solow model can be extended to the open-economy setting. Suppose that the world is divided into two regions which are growing in isolation. Both countries have the same growth rates and are in steady-state equilibrium. We assume that country B has a higher saving rate than country A. We know from our earlier analysis that in steady-state growth, output per worker will be higher in B than in A and the capital-labor ratio will be higher as well. Because country B is using more capital per worker than country A, the marginal productivity of capital will be lower in B than in A, and the interest rate in B consequently will be lower as well.

Now suppose that the two economies open up to international capital flows. Seeking the highest possible return, capital will flow from country B to country A. Country B will run a current account surplus and country A will run a current account deficit, as the excess saving in B begins to finance investment spending in country A. Eventually, the capital-labor ratios in the two countries will be equalized, as will output per person, despite the fact that the saving rates are different. The country with the low initial level of k, and thus high returns to investment, receives a capital inflow. During the transition to the new steady state, the country that was initially capital scarce (country A) will have output growth above the steady-state rate, while the other country will experience output growth below the steady-state rate. A simple diagram of both countries before and after the opening of their economies is shown in Figure 18-9, using the saving-investment framework that we introduced in Chapter 6.

Thus, opening up the economy acts as an impetus toward reducing in the gaps between countries in per capita output and capital-labor ratios. This gives us no reason to think that growth rates will change permanently, however. After the reallocation of world saving, steady-state growth in both countries will equal the rate of population growth plus labor-augmenting

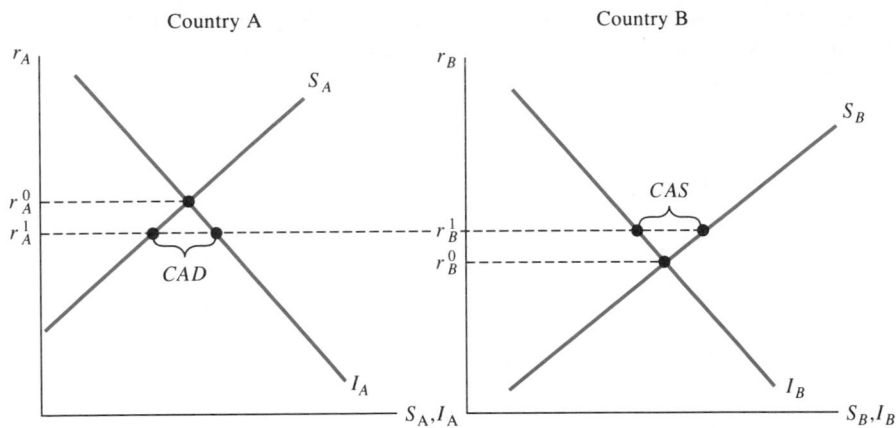

Figure 18-9
Investment, Saving, the Interest Rate, and Current Account Flows: The Case of Opening to Financial Flows

technological change. Since capital tends to flow from capital-rich to capital-poor countries, there are reasons to believe that countries will be capital importers early in the development process and capital exporters later on. This thought is the basis of the so-called *theory of the stages of the balance of payments*, which is discussed in Box 18-2.

Box 18-2
Stages in the Balance of Payments

The movements of capital across international boundaries have played an important role in the economic growth of many countries. For a country starting with a low capital-labor ratio and many highly productive investments, it may be desirable to borrow from the rest of the world in order to increase domestic investment above the level of domestic saving. In this case, the country will borrow from abroad in order to run a trade deficit and increase the rate of domestic investment. Over time, as the capital stock rises, the investment rate tends to diminish and the country shifts back to a trade surplus. Remember from Chapter 6 that the trade surplus can be thought of as the servicing of the debt accumulated during the borrowing phase. Eventually, if investment declines enough as the economy matures, and if the saving rate increases enough, the country may shift from current account deficit to current account surplus in its "mature" phase of development.

The logic of borrowing during the phase of rapid growth and repaying the debt during the period of mature growth (when the capital-labor ratio is near to it steady-state level) has produced a general theory of a "life cycle" of borrowing and repayment. This theory, known as the "stages of the balance of payments," was first introduced in the 1870s by John Cairnes, and it has been debated and elaborated on ever since that time. One popular formulation has countries going through six stages, depending on the position of their current account (CA) balance, trade balance (TB), service account (SA), and net foreign investment position (NFI). The stages are as shown in Table 18-5.[34]

In the first stage, the country borrows and begins to accumulate debt. In stage II, the country shifts to a trade surplus, but is still a net debtor, and the current account remains negative (that is, interest payments exceed the trade surplus). In stage III, the country shifts to a current account surplus, though it is still a net debtor. In stage IV, the current account surpluses have finally produced a positive net international investment position. The country has become a creditor. In stage V, the trade surplus has turned to deficit, as the country consumes from the income earned on its positive net foreign assets, and the current account is still in surplus. In stage VI the country is still a creditor, but the trade deficit is larger than the services surplus, and the current account goes into a deficit.

The United States has in fact roughly traversed these steps, though not in their pure form (year-to-year fluctuations have produced deviations from the prescribed path). Starting in the early nineteenth century, the United States began to borrow from the rest of the world to build the infrastructure that supported rapid growth (for example, canals in the first half of the century and railroads in the second half of the century). The investment rate as a fraction of GDP increased significantly, and the massive investment surge led to a persistent current-account deficit throughout most of the 1800s, especially in the second half of the century, as Table 18-6 shows. The United States was a net debtor vis-à-vis the rest of the world until the second decade of the twentieth century.

Starting in the 1870s, the United States began to run trade surpluses. The United States traversed stage II by 1896 and began to run current account surpluses. It reached stage IV in 1919, when the United States became a net creditor. From the 1920s to the early 1970s, the United States ran current account surpluses and trade surpluses in almost every year and became the world's most important net creditor. The country reached its "mature" phase in the early 1970s, when trade deficits were financed by service account surpluses. The sixth stage was reached in the late 1970s, when the current account went to a persistent overall deficit for the first time in decades, in spite of a positive service income. However, because of consistently large fiscal deficits throughout the decade, the United States seems to have added a seventh stage, that of being a large net debtor once again.

While the stages-of-the-balance-of-payments theory works rather well for the United States, its *general* applicability is open to some doubt. There are many cases of countries—Australia and Canada, for example— that borrowed heavily in the early stages of development and that remained major debtor countries all the way through to economic maturity. As we saw in Chapter 6, there is no reason why a net debt position has to

---

[34] This classification of stages is based on G. Crowther, *Balances and Imbalances of Payments* as quoted in N. Halevi. Other economists have found the six-stage division insufficient to account for intercountry differences. Nadav Halevi, for example, distinguishes 12 stages in his article "An Empirical Test of the 'Balance of Payments Stages' Hypothesis," *Journal of International Economics*, February 1971. In the end, he finds that the data do not support the theory, when studied in a cross section of countries.

TABLE   18-5

STAGES IN THE BALANCE OF PAYMENTS

	Current Account	Trade Balance	Service Account	Net Foreign Investment Position
I. Immature debtor-borrower	Deficit	Deficit	Deficit	Negative
II. Mature debtor-borrower	Deficit	Surplus	Deficit	Negative
III. Debtor-Lender and debtor-repayer	Surplus	Surplus	Deficit	Negative
IV. Immature creditor-lender	Surplus	Surplus	Surplus	Positive
V. Mature creditor	Surplus	Deficit	Surplus	Positive
VI. Creditor-drawers and borrowers	Deficit	Deficit	Surplus	Positive

TABLE   18-6

THE U.S. CURRENT ACCOUNT, TRADE BALANCE, AND NET INTERNATIONAL INVESTMENT POSITION 1800–1988 (MILLIONS OF DOLLARS)

Decade Average	Trade Balance	Current Account	Net International Investment Position
1800–1809	−19.3	8.5	−82.0
1810–1819	−22.8	2.5	−82.7
1820–1829	−3.7	−0.6	−84.6
1830–1839	−25.0	−25.1	−165.1
1840–1849	0.7	0.3	−217.2
1850–1859	−9.2	−31.3	−315.0
1860–1869	−18.6	−78.5	−688.6
1870–1879	92.7	−24.7	−1,681.4
1880–1889	103.3	−49.0	−1,952.5
1890–1899	262.5	63.1	−3,110.7
1900–1909	557.7	308.7	−3,200.5*
1910–1919	1,951.7	1,665.8	2,100.0†
1920–1929	1,117.1	1,434.6	11,250.0‡
1930–1939	448.8	1,083.5	15,533.3§
1940–1949	6,657.9	5,724.0	29,433.3‖
1950–1959	2,934.4	601.5	39,970.0
1960–1969	4,081.9	3,332.5	57,540.0
1970–1979	−10,383.1	−440.1	69,916.7#
1980–1988	−91,491.7	−45,428.4	−90,455.6

* Average for 1900 and 1908 only.
† Average for 1914 and 1919 only.
‡ Average for 1924 and 1927 only.
§ Average for 1930, 1931, and 1935 only.
‖ Average for 1940, 1945, 1946, 1947, 1948, and 1949 only.
Average for 1970, 1972, 1974, 1976, 1978, and 1979 only.

Source: Historical Statistics of the U.S. Colonial Times to 1970, *and* Economic Report of the President.

be converted to a net credit position in the long term. The only requirement is that the debt be serviced, and this can be done by trade balance
surpluses. The debt need not be extinguished. Thus, the transition after
stage III is neither theoretically necessary nor empirically confirmed for
many countries.

Moreover, there are apparently many capital-poor countries that
nonetheless have low marginal productivities of capital, and therefore do
not attract capital inflows. A country may be poor, for example, because
it does not protect private property rights very effectively. Thus, even
though the *social* returns of investment might be high, the private returns
to investment might be very low because of the unpredictability of getting
repaid on one's investments. Alternatively, the human capital of the work
force might be so low that workers could not make effective use of capital
inflows. In either case, the country would be poor but also be without
capital inflows, contrary to the theory of the stages in the balance of
payments.

Trade and Growth: The Developing Country Debate

Financial flows are just one way that the international economy affects a
country's growth. Another is through trade linkages. In the debate since the
1950s and 1960s over development strategies for poor and middle-income
countries, analysts have identified two contrasting patterns of development:
outward orientation, in which a country opens its markets to the rest of the
world and promotes its exports, and *inward orientation,* where a country
imposes significant barriers to international trade and focuses in the development of local industry to satisfy the domestic market. This strategy is also
known as the *import substitution* model of development.

Almost all studies in the past 25 years have documented the superior
growth performance of outward-oriented countries. Bela Balassa of Johns
Hopkins University studied economic growth during the period 1963–1984
in a large group of developing countries, which he divided between outward-
oriented countries (OOCs) and inward-oriented countries (IOCs). Among
the most prominent in the group of OOCs were the East Asian Dragons,
Korea, Singapore, and Taiwan, while the IOCs included Argentina, Egypt,
India, Jamaica, and the Philippines. As shown in Table 18-7, the OOCs
consistently outperformed the IOCs, and especially since the mid-1970s.
The only exception was the years 1979–1982, when the OOCs took drastic
adjustment actions to face the second oil shock. These policies soon paid
off, and the OOCs resumed their lead.

Consistent with this evidence on the success of outward orientation,
empirical studies have found a high correlation between overall GDP growth
and growth in export earnings. Countries which successfully developed markets for their exports also succeeded in achieving faster aggregate growth.
Anne Krueger of Duke University documented this pattern in her now classic work on trade liberalization in developing economies. Pooling the experience across the group of countries covered in the study, she found that a

Table   18-7

Outward Orientation and GNP Growth Rates in Developing Countries, 1963–1984 (percent, period averages)

	Outward-Oriented Countries	Inward-Oriented Countries
1963–1973	6.6	5.8
1973–1976	5.5	5.3
1976–1979	8.1	4.6
1979–1982	2.4	2.6
1982–1984	5.3	1.7

Source: Bela Balassa, *"Policy Responses to Exogenous Shocks in Developing Countries,"* American Economic Review, *May 1986, p. 77.*

one-percentage-point rise in the growth rate of export earnings increases the rate of growth of GNP by about 0.11 percent.[35]

A wealth of empirical evidence has by now shown that outward orientation leads to higher GNP growth. But what is behind this relationship? One possibility is the effect of trade on economies of scale. In developing countries, the size of the domestic market is quite small. A country such as Argentina, for example, has a dollar value of GNP smaller than that of Philadelphia, and the economy of Ecuador is about the size of Rochester, New York. Under the import-substitution strategy, domestic firms are encouraged to produce for the domestic market. This reduces the scope of their operations, and they lose the chance to benefit from economies of scale. The opening of trade enlarges the market, and local firms can expand through sales in the rest of the world. In addition, new companies with an eye on both the domestic and external markets will start up. When economies of scale are important, opening to the world market can provide the opportunity for industrialization and fast growth.

An open trade policy leads to increased competition from abroad, and the effects of that competition are another source of increased growth. Firms that are protected by artificial restrictions from the rest of the world can charge high prices and provide low-quality goods. Furthermore, in a highly protected economy businesses spend much of their time and energy lobbying for protection rather than improving their business performance.[36] When

---

[35] Anne Krueger, *Foreign Trade Regimes and Economic Development: Liberalization Attempts and Consequences* (New York: National Bureau of Economic Research, Ballinger, 1978). The estimates are presented in Chapter 11 of the book.

[36] This argument was pioneered by Anne Krueger, "The Political Economy of the Rent-Seeking Society," *American Economic Review*, June 1974.

barriers are eased, firms have to produce better goods—or lower their prices—in order to survive. Competition can then bring about productivity improvements at a faster pace. To the extent that it increases the rate of change of productivity, and not merely its level, competition from the world market can be a source of higher growth.

Empirical evidence tends to show a positive association between productivity improvements and export orientation. This pattern has been documented, for example, in a study of several industries in Korea, Turkey, and Yugoslavia.[37] In a study of 20 developing economies after World War II, Hollis Chenery has found that total input productivity has grown at yearly rates of over 3 percent in countries that followed outward-oriented, export-led strategies, while it grew at only about 1 percent in heavily import-substituting economies.[38]

Krueger provided yet another reason to explain the better performance of outward-oriented economies. According to her, outward orientation promotes better macroeconomic policies by the government. For example, when a country follows an export-oriented strategy, its policymakers must keep the exchange rate at a realistic level so that the country's exports can compete abroad. If this is ignored, subsidies may be required to improve the profitability of exports, and those are expensive for the fiscal budget. In a case like this, policymakers will be careful to avoid undue currency overvaluations.

A final and important reason for the link between outward orientation and economic growth is that the outward-oriented economies are in closer contact with foreign firms and are thus better able to absorb technological improvements that come from abroad. Developing countries generally lag far behind developed countries in the utilization of new technologies, and contacts that increase the rate of technology transfer can be a major source of productivity increases. Economies closed to trade also tend to be economies closed to new ideas and new technologies being used elsewhere.

Open Economies and Economic Convergence

One of the key questions in growth economics is whether the poorer countries tend to grow faster than the richer countries and thereby converge, or catch up, in living standards. For countries open to world trade and financial flows, there would seem to be strong reasons to expect convergence. First, to the extent that differences in levels of output per capita are the result of differences in capital-labor ratios, we expect capital to flow from capital-rich to capital-poor countries, thereby closing the gap.

Second, to the extent that income differentials result from differences in technology, we would expect that technological know-how would flow

---

[37] Mieko Nishimuzu and Sherman Robinson, "Trade Policies and Productivity Change in Semi-Industrialized Countries," *Journal of Development Economics,* September/October 1984.

[38] Chenery, "Structural Change," in Chenery, Robinson, and Syrquin, eds., *Industrialization and Growth, A Comparative Study.*

from technologically advanced countries to technologically lagging countries. These technical flows could occur through several means, including the transfer of knowledge through formal training, direct investments by high-tech firms in the lagging region, the purchase of sophisticated capital machinery by the lagging region, and the licensing of technologies by firms in the lagging region.

In fact, the international evidence on convergence is mixed. Within Western Europe, there is evidence of a strong tendency toward convergence in the post–World War II period. The poorer countries, such as Greece, Italy, Portugal, and Spain, tended to grow more rapidly than the wealthier core, which includes France, Germany, the Netherlands, and the United Kingdom, and thereby to close part or all of the gap in per capita income. For a wider sample of developing and developed countries, however, the evidence shows that the tendency toward convergence between rich and poor countries is present, but is relatively weak.[39]

Two kinds of explanations have been offered to explain the lack of strong convergence between the poor and rich countries. The first is that the forces of convergence only work well when the political, social, and economic institutions in the poorer countries are supportive of inward flows of foreign capital and technology.[40] If a poorer country is politically unstable, or fails to protect foreign investments and private property rights, or fails to provide for the education of the labor force, then the forces of convergence will be greatly weakened. This approach is consistent with the fact that the West European countries have tended to converge—since they share a basic framework of property rights and political and social institutions—while many of the poorer countries outside of Europe have not been able to grow more rapidly than the richer countries. It would also account for the fact that *some* of the poorer countries, particularly in East Asia, have been able to grow at very rapid rates for more than two decades, by fostering the conditions conducive to high investment rates and inflows of capital and technology from abroad.

A second approach to explain the weakness of convergence relies on the new growth theories of Romer and Lucas mentioned earlier. Under some theoretical conditions explored by these authors, an initial advantage of one country over another in the level of human capital per person will result in permanent difference in income levels between the countries. When the externalities related to human capital are strong, the richer country achieves sufficiently higher output as a result of its higher human capital endowment

---

[39] For a recent survey of the theoretical issues related to economic convergence, and empirical evidence for various groups of economies, see Robert J. Barro and Xavier Sala-i-Martin, "Convergence Across States and Regions," *Brookings Papers on Economic Activity,* No. 1, 1991. Barro and Sala-i-Martin find strong evidence of convergence among the U.S. states and within Europe but much weaker evidence in a broad sample of developing and developed countries.

[40] For a discussion of this point of view, see Moses Abramovitz, "Catching Up, Forging Ahead, and Falling Behind," *The Journal of Economic History,* Vol. 46, no. 2, June 1986, pp. 385–406.

that is able to maintain its lead indefinitely by generating enough new savings and investment compared with the other country.

The new growth models, if correct, would offer a bleak prognosis for the poorer countries, that they will tend to lag continually behind the richer countries. While the evidence on growth and convergence is far from conclusive, the weight of the empirical evidence—supported by the cases of East Asia and the poorer countries of Europe—seems to lean toward the conclusion that poorer countries have the *opportunity* to converge if they develop the appropriate legal, political, and economic institutions.

European Growth After 1992

Some of the arguments in favor of outward orientation and economic integration have played an important role in encouraging the development of Project 1992 in Europe, in which the European Community (EC) is establishing a "single" unified market by removing existing trade barriers. Economists expect that Europe will experience a rise in output, and perhaps even a sustained rise in growth as a result of Project 1992, through its effects of encouraging more efficient resource use in Europe.

The Cecchini Report, prepared by the economic staff of the European Community, attempted to quantify these gains. The report estimated that Europe will receive a cumulative efficiency gain of between 2.5 and 6.5 percent of the combined Community's GDP spread out over the next few years, as a result of increased competition and more integrated markets in the European Community.[41] This total benefit, however, will not be achieved instantly, but rather it will be distributed over several years after 1992. The efficiency gains identified by the report may be depicted as an upward shift of the production function (from q to q') in the standard Solow model, as shown in Figure 18-10. At the initial capital stock k_A^*, output rises from q_A^* to q_A'.

Some recent studies have found that the Cecchini Report calculations understate Europe's prospective gains. Richard Baldwin of Columbia University identifies two ways in which the gains are underestimated.[42] He points out that the Cecchini Report fails to consider the medium-term effects arising from the initial efficiency gain and also fails to account for the possibility that economies of scale in production following the unification of markets will increase the growth rate in Europe. Let us analyze these arguments separately.

The medium-term effect arises from a simple application of the Solow growth model, using Figure 18-10. After the initial rise from q_A^* to q_A', which is the static efficiency gain measured in the Cecchini Report, the higher output level will lead people to save and invest more. Both output and capital will start to grow, and a new steady state will be reached at B, with a per capita output of q_B^* and a capital-labor ratio of k_B^*. Thus, the medium-term growth "bonus" not considered in the Cecchini calculation would be the distance between q_A' and q_B^* in the figure.

---

[41] Paolo Cecchini, *The European Challenge, 1992: The Benefits of a Single Market.* Brookfield, VT: Gower, 1988.

[42] Richard Baldwin, "The Growth Effects of 1992," *Economic Policy*, October 1989.

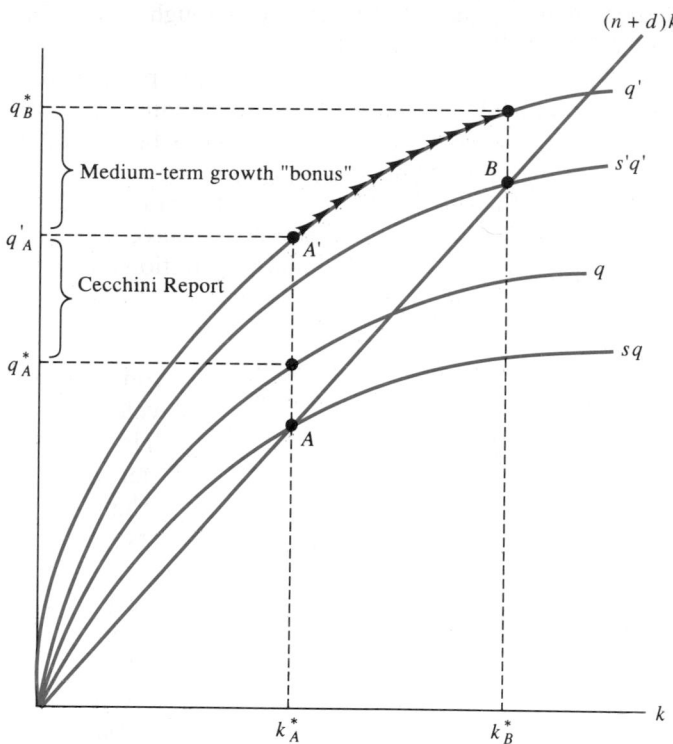

Figure 18-10
The Effects of Europe 1992 in the Solow Framework

There is a further possibility. According to the new growth models of Romer and Lucas discussed earlier in Section 18-4, the efficiency gains can lead to a permanent rise not only in per capita income but also in the growth rate. If there are important externalities in investment, and if market integration in Europe raises the investment rate (which would tend to occur if profitability is higher as a result of a larger unified market in which European firms can sell their output), then the result could be a sustained rise in the European growth rate.[43]

For these reasons, the benefits of European integration may be substantially higher than those suggested by the Cecchini Report. As a consequence of economies of scale, Baldwin has calculated that the long-term annual growth rate in Europe may increase by between 0.2 and 0.9 percentage points. Considering all the effects together, and measuring the present discounted value of future income gains, Baldwin calculates that the total benefits of 1992 could range between 11 and 35 percent of current GDP of the European Community.

---

[43] For a theoretical model showing how economic integration can raise the long-run growth rate, see Luis A. Rivera-Batiz and Paul Romer, "Economic Integration and Endogenous Growth," *National Bureau of Economic Research Working Paper,* No. 3528, December 1990.

18-6 MACROECONOMIC POLICIES TO PROMOTE GROWTH

What, then, determines output growth? The Solow model specifies that only higher population growth and faster technological change can promote a permanent increase in the growth rate. Higher saving and investment, on the other hand, may produce a temporary increase in growth and a permanent increase in output per capita. In the new theories that assume externalities in investment, a higher saving rate in fact produces a permanent increase in the growth rate. We can at least say in general, then, that a faster pace of economic growth requires some combination of increased growth in the capital stock, in labor inputs, or in technological progress. Now we ask whether government policies can promote growth by raising saving and investment rates, labor force growth, or faster technological progress.

No doubt among the most important measures are microeconomic measures, including protection of private property rights, maintenance of a stable policy environment, and promotion of international integration through a free-trade policy. In keeping with our main topic, however, let us turn our attention to possible macroeconomic measures.

Saving and Investment

In a closed economy, or in an economy without access to international loans, the only way to invest more is to save more. In this case, there is an evident trade-off: additional growth via faster capital accumulation means less present consumption. Of course, a government should not seek to maximize the saving rate at all costs because that would unduly punish current consumers. There is an optimum rate of saving, admittedly hard to measure, determined by a society's rate of time preference, that is, the value it places on future relative to present consumption. If investment projects generate a return that makes it worthwhile to forgo consumption now, then they should be carried out. According to the theory of the optimal saving rate, this balancing of the present and the future is best achieved when the marginal productivity of capital (*MPK*) is equal to the rate of time preference plus the rate of population growth, a famous relationship known as the "modified golden rule policy."[44]

In an open economy with free capital mobility, investment and saving need not be the same because the country can borrow or lend on world markets at the world interest rate and thus run current account deficits. All that should matter for domestic investments is that the investment project generates enough returns to pay the world interest rate on loans. In this case, the world interest rate determines domestic investment, while domestic saving determines the growth of national income (GNP) though not necessarily national output (GDP). Higher domestic saving would not necessar-

---

[44] This rule is derived in a mathematically sophisticated model of economic growth. For an advanced discussion of the "modified golden rule" policy, see Olivier Blanchard and Stanley Fischer, *Lectures on Macroeconomics* (Cambridge, Mass.: MIT Press, 1989), p. 45. This formula applies to the case in which there is no long-term technological change. When there is long-term technological change, the modified golden rule changes slightly to incorporate that technological progress.

ily result in higher domestic investment, but could simply result in less net borrowing from abroad.

If the country is cut off from the world capital markets, however, higher domestic saving will result in higher domestic investment. In this case, the government might be able to encourage capital formation by stimulating private saving, say, through a reduction in the tax rate on interest income. It has been claimed, for example, that Japan's high private saving rate is in part the result of the favorable tax treatment of interest income. Nonetheless, the empirical evidence on the effectiveness of tax policy in raising saving is far from conclusive.

This discussion has concerned private saving only. National saving may also be raised, however, through an increase in government saving or a reduction in dissaving if the government is running a budget deficit.[45] For example, the U.S. fiscal deficit increased tremendously in the 1980s. After peaking at over $220 billion in 1986, it declined to $150 billion in 1987. Since then it has been rising, and reached about $220 billion in 1990. This is still a sizable 4.1 percent of GDP in government dissaving, which reduces the overall saving rate of the country, assuming (as seems to be the case) that an increase in private saving does not compensate for the low level of public saving. Reducing the deficit would tend to increase the national saving rate.

As an alternative policy to spur capital formation, the government may decide to act directly on investment. In Chapter 5, we analyzed the effects of an increase in the investment tax credit, which acts as a subsidy on investment. The introduction of an investment tax credit could raise the overall level of investment, assuming that the policy does not merely cause a rise of investment in some categories and a fall of investment in others.[46] The government could also directly increase its own investment spending, especially on infrastructure. There is increasing evidence that government investment in infrastructure can have a marked effect on the aggregate growth rate. That is, infrastructure investment seems to have a high social return.[47]

Labor Services

What instruments does the government have to increase the amount of labor services offered? One possibility would be to reduce the tax rate on labor income. Lowering this rate will increase the after-tax real wage, which in

---

[45] In most countries, the deficit of the public sector cannot directly be interpreted as government dissaving, because government expenditures include public investment. Thus, the correct relationship is $DEF_{pu} = I_{pu} - S_{pu}$. In the United States, the national accounts treat all investment as made by the private sector, and thus the measurement of the deficit and government dissaving coincide.

[46] Lawrence Summers calculated that as of 1981, an increase of the investment tax credit (ITC) from 5.6 percent to 11.2 percent would raise investment in the United States by 9.4 percent over a decade. He showed that an increase in the ITC provides more stimulus to investment per dollar of forgone revenue than tax changes which affect new *and* old capital. See his article, "Taxation and Corporate Investment: A q Theory Approach," *Brookings Papers on Economic Activity,* No. 1, 1981.

[47] See, for example, David Aschauer, "Is Public Expenditure Productive?" *Journal of Monetary Economics,* March 1989, and Robert Barro, "A Cross-country Study of Growth, Savings, and Government," National Bureau of Economic Research Working Paper, No. 2855, February 1989.

turn will tend to increase the labor supply.[48] Nonetheless, in the case of tax cuts on labor income, as well as tax cuts on saving or subsidies to investment, an overriding question is how the lost revenue is to be made up. Taxes are almost always distortionary, but that does not mean that they should be eliminated. After all, the government services that they help to fund also have value. Thus, the goal is to make the tax system as efficient as possible for any given level of government revenues, and at the same time to equate on the margin the distortionary costs of tax collection with the benefits of increased public spending.

Another way to increase labor services is to increase the labor productivity of workers through increases in human capital, as discussed next.

Productivity

Designing effective policies to raise productivity is a tricky matter. However, if the new theories of growth are right that technological improvements are associated with capital formation and that significant positive externalities accrue from investment, there would be powerful arguments to encourage investment. By doing that, the government would be promoting technological change, and thus improving growth potential.

In the new growth theories developed by Robert Lucas, productivity growth has a closer association with investment in human rather than in physical capital.[49] Lucas has also argued that one person's investment in human capital raises not only her own productivity, but the productivity of others as well. In other words, there are positive externalities arising from investments in human capital. In his own estimation, this effect is quite substantial. Indeed, he finds, the elasticity of U.S. output with respect to the external effects of human capital on production is 0.4. Thus, a 10 percent increase in the positive externality of human capital gets translated into a 4 percent increase in output. The conclusion is, then, that education, on-the-job training and other activities that increase human capital should be *subsidized* by the government, perhaps at higher rates than they are now.

Finally, there is the effect of research and development on productivity. To estimate the effects of R&D on output, analysts generally consider R&D to be another type of capital which is included as an additional variable in the production function. Using this procedure, empirical work for the United States has estimated that the elasticity of output with respect to R&D capital ranges between 0.06 and 0.1. Thus, a 10 percent increase in the stock of R&D capital promotes a 0.6 to 1 percent increase in output.[50] Once again, tax benefits may be the prime way to increase R&D spending. The usual trade-offs between tax cuts and the benefits from government services must be carefully weighed, however.

---

[48] Remember though from Chapter 4 that a rise in the after-tax wage has an ambiguous effect on labor supply. The substitution effect tends to raise labor supply while the income effect tends to lower it. The empirical evidence suggests that the substitution effect will dominate in the event of a cut in the labor income tax.

[49] See R. Lucas, "On the Mechanics of Economic Development," *Journal of Monetary Economics,* July 1988.

[50] These results have been obtained by Zvi Grilliches and others in a number of papers. For a recent survey, see Z. Grilliches, "Productivity Puzzles and R&D: Another Nonexplanation," *Journal of Economic Perspectives,* Fall 1988.

18-7 Summary

Although economies may suffer temporary downward movements during business cycles, they tend to experience long-term growth characterized by sustained increases in total GNP and GNP per capita. Long-term economic growth, especially sustained growth in per capita income, is a characteristic of the world economy only for the past two centuries, however. The origins of modern growth can be traced to the time of the Industrial Revolution.

Growth provokes changes in the structure of an economy. A common *pattern of development* has been widely observed in growing economies. First, the share of agriculture in overall output and employment tends to fall. The counterpart of this decline in share of the economy is, first, a rise in the industrial sector, and then later, a rise in the service sector. *Urbanization*, the concentration of population in densely settled areas, also comes with growth.

To study the sources of economic growth, the *growth accounting* framework starts with an aggregate production function for the economy. The rate of growth of aggregate output, then, is the sum of three terms: (1) the rate of technological progress; (2) the rate of increase in labor input, weighted by the share of labor in output; and (3) the rate of growth of capital, weighted by the share of capital in output.

To apply this framework empirically, there exists information on the growth rates of both labor and capital, on their shares in output, and on output growth. Technological progress, however, is not directly observable and is typically calculated as the *Solow residual*, the difference between the observed growth rate of output and the part of that growth explained by labor and capital. Early applications of this accounting framework for the United States revealed that most output growth during this century is accounted for by the Solow residual. This result has been taken to mean that technological change has played a crucial role in overall growth.

Productivity growth declined significantly in the advanced countries after 1973. Many explanations have been advanced for this phenomenon, especially as it pertains to the United States, though none has been shown to be decisive. Some economists point to the oil shocks of the 1970s for causing early obsolescence in the capital stock, and for triggering a contractionary response in macroeconomic policies to fight inflation. Other factors mentioned are the costs of increased regulation and of crime, the reduction of R&D expenditures, and potential measurement problems.

Robert Solow of MIT, who developed the growth accounting framework, also developed a growth model that remains the main theoretical framework for analyzing the relationship of saving, capital accumulation, and growth. In the simplest version of the Solow model, output per capita is an increasing function of the capital-labor ratio and the state of technology, saving equals investment (a closed-economy feature), and the rate of population growth is assumed to be constant and exogenous. In *steady-state* equilibrium, capital, labor, and output, all grow at the same rate, given by the exogenous rate of population growth.

The *Solow growth model* produces several interesting results. A rise in the saving rate leads to a permanent increase in both the level of per capita output and the capital-labor ratio, but not in the steady-state growth rate of the economy. A higher rate of population growth leads to a permanent increase in the growth rate, but to a fall in the steady-state levels of per capita output. Technological progress allows for faster permanent growth.

Recent models of growth due to Romer and Lucas, suggest that the contribution of capital to growth is underestimated by the traditional Solow model, because there exist externalities in the use of capital. In these new models, and in contrast to the Solow growth model, higher rates of saving lead to higher steady-state rates of growth.

The Solow model can be readily extended to an open-economy framework. One implication of an open economy is that saving and investment rates need not be equal within a country. If interest rates tend to be equalized across countries, saving will flow from capital-rich to capital-scarce countries. Capital-labor ratios and output per capita will tend to converge. In fact, international capital flows have played an important role in financing the process of economic growth in many countries, and the pattern of capital flows between rich and poor countries has led to a theory of *stages in the balance of payments.*

Another aspect of growth in the open economy is the relationship of trade policies to growth. The debate on development strategies for poor and middle-income countries has focused on two contrasting trade strategies: *outward orientation,* in which a country opens its markets to the rest of the world and promotes its exports, and *inward orientation* (or *import substitution*), where a country imposes significant barriers to international trade and focuses on the development of local industry to satisfy the domestic market. Almost all studies in the past 25 years have documented the superior growth performance of outward-oriented countries.

What can government policies do to promote growth? A faster pace of economic growth requires some combination of increased growth in the capital stock, in labor inputs, or in technological progress. On a microeconomic level, governments can take measures to foster greater domestic saving and investment through a liberal trade policy, stability of policy measures, and protection of private property rights. On a macroeconomic level, governments may use fiscal policies to encourage saving, investment, and expenditures on research and development. Governments may also reduce budget deficits to raise the national saving rate.

Key Concepts

long-term economic growth	industrialization
economies of scale	Solow residual
U.S. productivity slowdown	capital-labor ratio
capital deepening	stability
labor-augmenting technological progress	positive externalities
	import substitution
outward orientation	urbanization
pattern of development	technological progress
economies of agglomeration	capital widening
output per capita	convergence theory
steady state	stages in the balance of payments
increasing returns to scale	
inward orientation	modified golden rule

Problems and Questions

1. Suppose the production function for country A is

$$Q = Q(K,L,T) = TK^{3/4} L^{1/4}$$

a. Does this production function exhibit constant or increasing returns to scale?

b. Write the production function in per capita terms.

c. Suppose there is no technological progress, and both capital and labor grow at the constant rate *n*. What is the growth rate of output? What are the contributions of labor and capital to that growth? Use mathematics.

2. Explain the following statement from the *1991 Economic Report of the President:* "To sustain robust economic growth, the United States must maintain a high rate of investment in new capital and new technology. That, in turn, requires an adequate flow of national saving. The substantial Federal budget deficits of recent years have decreased the national saving rate. Sound, growth-oriented fiscal policy thus requires that the Federal budget deficit be reduced."

3. "An increase in the after-tax wage rate raises the level of output." Discuss.

4. How can a country increase its level of investment without reducing current consumption? What are the limits to this option, if any?

5. Suppose that the saving rate of a country declines. Starting from steady state in the Solow model, what will be the effect on the capital labor ratio, output per capita, and output growth? Be careful to distinguish between the transition period and the new steady state.

6. Comment on the following statement: "International trade can promote long-term growth by encouraging technological innovation."

7. In the context of the Solow model, what will be the impact on the rate of economic growth for a country which has been destroyed by war? Is your answer consistent with the cases of Germany and Japan after World War II?

8. What do you think could be the impact of the U.S. Immigration Act of 1990, which promotes skilled labor immigration, on the long-term economic growth of U.S. economy?

9. Which is the main assumption that differentiates the new growth theories from the Solow model? What is the implication of this assumption for the sources of growth?

10. Discuss at least three different channels through which outward orientation can benefit growth.

The Theory and Practice of Economic Policy

Since the earliest days of economic analysis, the role of economic policymakers has been at the center of an ongoing debate, not only among economic scholars, but also among commentators in the press and the general public. The decisions of economic policymakers affect the lives and well-being of everyone in an economy. In many cases the effects of policymakers spill well beyond national borders into the economies of other countries. It is not surprising, therefore, that many of the greatest advances in economic science have arisen within the context of heated debates about specific public policy issues.

One branch of economic theory explores the important issue of how policymakers *should* act. This is the *normative theory of economic policy*. The questions asked by normative theorists center on a few main issues. Should the authorities actively intervene in the economy, or should they keep their intervention to a minimum and let markets act freely? If policymakers do decide to intervene, what are the most effective means for attaining their goals? And what are the best ways to calculate the optimal policies to apply?

Another branch of economic theory, which intersects with political science, studies how policymakers *do* act. This is the *positive theory of economic policymaking*. Positive theorists attempt to explain why economic authorities do what they do. Their actions are subject to many influences: political pressures, institutional constraints, economic theories, and changing practical goals. Positive theorists study economic policymaking, both within a country and in comparisons across countries, from these and other perspectives.

In this chapter, we focus mainly on normative theory of macroeconomic policymaking. We start with the so-called "Tinbergen framework," which is the starting point of most normative theories of policymaking. We go on to study the limitations of this basic theory, introducing issues of uncertainty; the instability of econometric models used for policy analysis (the focus of the so-called "Lucas critique"); and the problem of rules, discretion, and time consistency. At the end of the chapter, we turn to some of the models used in the *positive* analysis of macroeconomic policymaking.

19-1 THE BASIC THEORY OF ECONOMIC POLICY

The basic theory of economic policy was first analyzed systematically in the early 1950s by the Dutch economist Jan Tinbergen, the first recipient of the Nobel Prize in Economics, in 1969.[1] Inasmuch as Tinbergen's theory attempts to conceptualize how policymakers should behave, it is normative in character. Tinbergen carefully delineated the crucial steps of optimal policymaking. First, the policymaker must specify the *goals* of economic policy, usually in terms of the *social welfare function* that the policymaker is attempting to maximize. Based on the social welfare function, the policymaker identifies the *targets* that he or she wants to attain. Second, the policymaker must specify the policy *instruments* that are available to reach the targets. Third, the policymaker must have a model of the economy linking the instruments to the targets, in order to be able to choose the optimal value of the policy instruments.

Let us now consider each of these three components of policy, targets, instruments, and the model of the economy.

Instruments and Targets of Economic Policy

To study the normative theory of macroeconomic policymaking, we must first specify the objectives of policy in general, and then in particular. At the broadest level, macroeconomic policy should aim to maximize "social welfare," but this term is obviously too vague. A widely accepted set of targets—which we will adopt—is full employment and zero inflation. Even these targets are subject to debate, however. What, after all, is "full employment"? Is it average unemployment in the United States, around 5.5 percent of the labor force? Is it the 4 percent target specified in U.S. legislation (the so-called Humphrey-Hawkins law, which directs policymakers to aim for full employment)?

There is also a debate over whether zero inflation is really optimal. In some theories, such as those of Milton Friedman, the optimal inflation rate is negative.[2] In other theories, the optimal inflation rate may be positive because the inflation tax should be used to a small extent in an optimal tax system (recall our discussion of this issue in Chapter 11).[3] Nonetheless, the goals of full employment and zero inflation are *relatively* uncontroversial. Other, more controversial targets are sometimes suggested, including those that specify income distributional goals, the composition of output between the public and the private sector, and a balanced current account.

---

[1] Tinbergen's most important contribution is the book *On the Theory of Economic Policy* (Amsterdam: North Holland, 1952).

[2] M. Friedman, *The Optimum Quantity of Money and Other Essays* (Chicago: Aldine, 1969).

[3] E. Phelps, "Inflation in the Theory of Public Finance," *Swedish Journal of Economics,* January-March 1973. For a discussion of the views of Friedman and Phelps, see Section 11-3 in Chapter 11.

Once macroeconomic targets are set, the policymaker should specify the *instruments* that are available to help the economy hit these targets. In general, there are two kinds of policy instruments: those of fiscal policy and those of monetary policy.[4] The specific instruments available for macroeconomic policymaking depend, however, on the institutional setting. With pegged exchange rates and free capital mobility, for example, monetary policy is limited to a choice of level of the exchange rate. Once that is set, monetary policy—a change in the domestic money supply, for example—is largely exhausted as a means of working toward macroeconomic targets. On the other hand, under floating exchange rates, the level of the domestic money supply is an effective policy instrument, but the exchange rate is not.

In the same way, the particular content of fiscal policy also depends on the institutional environment. And the selection of instruments in this sphere may actually be more complicated because fiscal policy includes a number of separate instruments. For example, the government might use either an expenditure cut or a tax increase to cut a budget deficit. And, of course, there are different types of taxes and expenditures that have different effects on the economy. On the other hand, fiscal policy may offer no instrument at all. It may be that the economic policymaker in question, say, the Treasury, has little control over the budget because it is controlled, or at least strongly influenced, by the Congress. Theorists of policymaking must always be careful to identify which policymakers really control which instruments.

With both targets and instruments specified, the policy problem can be described like this. Some social welfare function, however it is defined, specifies both the optimal levels of the target variables and the costs to society of deviations from those levels. The economy, however, deviates from the optimum because of some exogenous shock—a change in tastes, a change in the terms of trade, a movement in the international interest rate, and so on. Now, policymakers have to choose their instruments and calibrate them so as to move the economy back to the optimum. For this, the authorities use their knowledge about the structure of the economy, and specifically about the relationship between targets and instruments. The formal framework for linking targets and instruments was first set forth by Tinbergen.

The Tinbergen Framework

Tinbergen used a simple linear framework to analyze the theory of economic policy, and we start with a linear model. To explore this setting, we start with the basic case in which there are only two targets and two instruments. The targets we denote generically as T_1 and T_2 and the instruments as I_1 and I_2. (Later, we shall examine a special case where we give both targets and instruments a specific macroeconomic content.) We shall also assume that

---

[4] Tinbergen stressed that instruments should be qualitative as well as quantitative. We talk here mainly about instruments of the quantitative type (fiscal and monetary policy). But many qualitative policy changes also have significant effects on the macroeconomy, for example, the deregulation of an industry (the deregulation of air traffic in the United States during the Carter administration), the opening of the economy (or a part of it) to trade with the rest of the world, and so on. Some of these instruments are not easily described in quantitative terms. However, most of Tinbergen's analysis centered on quantitative instruments, and that is the approach we follow here.

the desired levels of T_1 and T_2 are given by the specific values T_1^* and T_2^*. When an economy is operating at the desired levels, we say that it is at its *bliss point,* that is, its point of maximum happiness.

In this simple case, our targets are described as a linear function of the instruments:

$$T_1 = a_1 I_1 + a_2 I_2 \qquad \textbf{(19.1a)}$$
$$T_2 = b_1 I_1 + b_2 I_2 \qquad \textbf{(19.1b)}$$

Notice that each target is affected by *both* instruments. Given this situation, it is easy to show the fundamental result that policymakers can achieve the desired levels of both targets, as long as both instruments are available to the policymakers, and as long as the effects of the instruments on the targets are *linearly independent* of each other. Technically, for the effects of the instruments to be linearly independent, a_1/b_1 must not be equal to a_2/b_2. If in fact a_1/b_1 does equal a_2/b_2, then it is possible, in general, to hit only one of the two targets.

Mathematically, it is simple to solve for the optimal policies. Simply substitute T_1^* and T_2^* into equations (19.1a) and (19.1b), to get the 2×2 system of equations (that is, two equations and two unknowns):

$$T_1^* = a_1 I_1 + a_2 I_2$$
$$T_2^* = b_1 I_1 + b_2 I_2$$

Now we solve this equation for I_1 and I_2 in terms of T_1^* and T_2^*, which can be done as long as $(a_1 b_2 - b_1 a_2)$ does not equal zero, or as long as a_1/b_1 does not equal a_2/b_2. We find

$$I_1 = \frac{(b_2 T_1^* - a_2 T_2^*)}{(a_1 b_2 - b_1 a_2)} \qquad \textbf{(19.2a)}$$

$$I_2 = \frac{(a_1 T_2^* - b_1 T_1^*)}{(a_1 b_2 - b_1 a_2)} \qquad \textbf{(19.2b)}$$

Thus, if the conditions of linear independence are met, then an economy can reach its bliss point ($T_1 = T_1^*$ and $T_2 = T_2^*$) through an appropriate choice of the instrument values.

What happens if $a_1/b_1 = a_2/b_2$? Then, the two instruments have the same proportionate effects on the two targets. In effect, the policymaker just has *one independent instrument with which to try to hit two targets.* Usually this cannot be accomplished. The policymaker will be able to set $T_1 = T_1^*$ or $T_2 = T_2^*$, but not both simultaneously. It is not enough therefore to have two instruments to hit two targets; the instruments must have linearly independent effects on the targets in order to be truly separate instruments.

This result, that two independent instruments are enough to hit two targets, may be stated more generally. If, in an economy with a linear structure, the policymaker has N targets, these targets may be reached as long as there are at least N linearly independent policy instruments. Or, put another way, it is possible to hit as many targets as there are linearly independent instruments.

Now let us take a simple example. Suppose that the targets are output and inflation. At the bliss point, the output level will be at its potential ($Q = Q^*$), and inflation will be at zero ($\hat{P} = 0$). We assume that there are two instruments: monetary policy, M, and fiscal policy, G. The economy is described by two simple relationships analogous to equations (19.1a) and (19.1b):

$$Q = a_1 G + a_2 M \tag{19.3a}$$
$$\hat{P} = b_1 G + b_2 M \tag{19.3b}$$

The coefficients a_1, a_2, b_1, and b_2 measure the quantitative effect of G and M on Q and $\hat{P}$; they could be taken from a macroeconometric model of the sort described in Chapters 12 to 14.

Suppose that the economy starts at its output potential ($Q = Q^*$), but that inflation is at 2 percent per year. The goal is to reduce inflation to zero without reducing output. Can it be done? In this framework, the answer is yes, as long as the effects of G and M are linearly independent.

First, however, we need to restate the problem in terms of deviations from a baseline rather than in the levels of G and M. If ΔX denotes the deviation of variable X from its initial level in the baseline (the "baseline" is the starting values of the variables), then the equations in (19.3) can be rewritten as

$$\Delta Q = a_1 \Delta G + a_2 \Delta M \tag{19.3a'}$$
$$\Delta \hat{P} = b_1 \Delta G + b_2 \Delta M \tag{19.3b'}$$

One goal is to keep output at its baseline level, so the target for ΔQ is zero. Using our earlier notation, we set $\Delta Q^* = 0$. The other goal is to reduce inflation by two percentage points. Thus, we set $\Delta \hat{P}^* = -2$. Replacing these values in (19.3'), we have the following equations:

$$0 = a_1 \Delta G + a_2 \Delta M \tag{19.4a}$$
$$-2 = b_1 \Delta G + b_2 \Delta M \tag{19.4b}$$

The particular solution to this system of equations, then, as we saw generally in (19.2), is

$$\Delta G = \frac{2a_2}{(a_1 b_2 - a_2 b_1)} \tag{19.5a}$$

$$\Delta M = \frac{-2a_1}{(a_1 b_2 - a_2 b_1)} \tag{19.5b}$$

You can see that these results are correct by substituting ΔM and ΔG directly back into the two equations in (19.4).

Within this basic framework, price stabilization can be accomplished painlessly, with no loss of output. Is this result of painless price stabilization realistic? It might not be, for two related reasons. First, the result depends heavily on a_1/b_1 not being equal to a_2/b_2; that is, on monetary and fiscal policy having linearly independent effects on output and prices. What is the actual relationship between a_1/b_1 and a_2/b_2? In fact, they are indeed likely to be close in value, if not exactly equal.

Suppose, for example, that inflation is determined by a Phillips curve mechanism, in which monetary policy (M) and fiscal policy (G) affect output (Q), and output (Q) affects inflation ($\hat{P}$). In that case, the underlying model of the economy might be

$$Q = a_1 G + a_2 M$$
$$\hat{P} = gQ$$

Note that g is the coefficient on the short-run Phillips curve. If this is the economic model, then when we write the model as two linear equations linking the targets to the instruments, *we indeed find that the instruments are linearly related*. Specifically, when the model is written as in (19.3), we find

$$Q = a_1 G + a_2 M$$
$$\hat{P} = b_1 G + b_2 M$$

with $b_1 = ga_1$ and $b_2 = ga_2$ (you should check this point). Then, it is easy to see that both a_1/b_1 and a_2/b_2 would equal $1/g$, and the requirement of linear independence would *not* be satisfied.

The intuitive meaning of this should be clear. If the only way that monetary and fiscal policies can affect inflation is through their effect on the output level, then targeting *both* the output level and the inflation rate will generally be impossible. Once the output target is hit, the inflation target cannot be reached independently because inflation is determined only by output.

This example is probably too pessimistic, however. We can, in fact, think of reasons why a_1/b_1 would not exactly equal a_2/b_2. For example, we should expect that monetary policy would have a greater *direct* effect on inflation than would fiscal policy, per unit of effect on output. In that case, b_2/a_2 would be greater than b_1/a_1.[5] This is because expansionary monetary policy causes the exchange rate to depreciate (under a regime of flexible rates) while expansionary fiscal policy causes the exchange rate to appreciate. Thus, even when the effects of the two policies on output are the same, the effects of monetary policy on the price level should be larger.

Econometric evidence of the type presented in Chapter 14 (based on the large-scale econometric models, LSEMs) does indeed confirm that monetary policy has a stronger direct effect on inflation. According to one recent empirical investigation,[6] we find the following coefficients for our model of equations (19.3'):

$$a_1 = 1.33; \qquad b_1 = 0.14; \qquad a_2 = 0.28; \qquad b_2 = 0.13$$

As expected, then, b_2/a_2 (= 0.46) is greater than b_1/a_1 (= 0.11). Thus, monetary and fiscal policy are linearly independent, as the Tinbergen framework requires.

In a case like this, both output and inflation could be targeted using both monetary and fiscal policy. A monetary contraction would be combined with a fiscal expansion, in order to keep output unchanged, while at the same

---

[5] Note that b_2/a_2 measures the increase of inflation due to a monetary expansion that raises output by one unit. b_1/a_1 measures the increase of inflation due to a fiscal expansion that raises output by one unit.

[6] Ralph Bryant, John Helliwell and Peter Hooper, "Domestic and Cross-Border Consequences of U.S. Macroeconomic Policies," in R. Bryant et al., eds., *Macroeconomic Policies in an Interdependent World* (Washington, D.C.: International Monetary Fund, 1989). The results shown in the text correspond to the first-year effects of monetary and fiscal policy, in deviations from a baseline scenario (Tables A-5 and A-6). The units are as follows. One unit of monetary expansion is a one percentage-point increase in M. One unit of fiscal expansion is a rise in government spending equal to 1 percent of GNP. The output effect is measured as a percentage change relative to the baseline, and the inflation effect is measured as a change in inflation in percentage points per year.

time causing the exchange rate to appreciate enough to drive down the inflation rate by the desired amount. (In fact, we noted the possibility of using such a policy mix for anti-inflationary purposes in Chapter 14.)

There is a second problem with the proposed solution in (19.5), however, even when linear independence is present. If a_1/b_1 is close to but not equal to a_2/b_2, it might be possible, strictly speaking, to hit both targets, but only if M and/or G take very unusual values, far from their normal levels.[7] The solutions found by the Tinbergen approach might require an enormous budget deficit, for example, of a magnitude that would be intolerable.

We can check this out using the numerical values just described. In order to reduce inflation by two percentage points—the case shown in equations (19.5)—monetary policy would have to contract by 19.9 percent relative to baseline, and fiscal policy would have to expand by 4.2 percent of GNP. Clearly, such a policy mix is rather unrealistic to contemplate!

In this sense, then, linear independence is not enough in practice to achieve the desired results. The policy instruments must be effective enough, and independent enough, so that plausible movements in their values can achieve the desired targets.

Effective Market Classification

Robert Mundell posed the policy problem in a different way from Tinbergen. Mundell supposed that in many cases, the various instruments would actually be under the control of distinct policymakers. Monetary policy, for example, might be under the purview of the central bank and fiscal policy under the purview of the executive branch. Suppose that these policymakers do not coordinate their policies as Tinbergen supposed and, instead, for political or institutional reasons, choose their policies separately. Is there a way to solve the policy problem when policy is *decentralized*, in that each instrument is under the control of a distinct policymaker, and the various policymakers do not directly coordinate their actions?

Mundell proposed an ingenious solution to this problem.[8] He discovered the conditions under which each instrument can be *assigned* to one of the targets, together with a rule for how the instrument should be adjusted when the target has deviated from its optimal level. Mundell showed that, indeed, if targets are correctly assigned to instruments, it is possible to arrive at the optimal policy mix in a decentralized manner. Mundell based his solution on the concept of *effective market classification*. In essence, this means that each target should be assigned to the instrument that has the relatively strongest effect on that particular target, and thus has a comparative advantage in moving that target.

To see how this works, let us return to our example of inflation control. We have already argued that monetary policy has a relatively stronger effect on inflation than does fiscal policy. Given a change in M or G that causes a one-unit change in output, M is likely to have the greatest effect on inflation.

---

[7] Notice that the denominator in (19.5) is equal to $(a_1b_2 - a_2b_1)$. This will be close to zero when a_1/b_1 is close to a_2/b_2. In that case, the required movements in G and M might have to be very large.

[8] See Robert Mundell, "The Monetary Dynamics of International Adjustment under Fixed and Flexible Exchange Rates," *Quarterly Journal of Economics*, May 1960.

Mathematically, b_2/a_2 is likely to be greater than b_1/a_1.[9] In this case, the monetary authority should have the task of adjusting to inflation, while the fiscal authority should have the task of adjusting to fluctuations in output. According to Mundell's assignment rule, then, the monetary authority should reduce M whenever inflation is above the target and increase M whenever inflation is below the target; the fiscal authority should raise G whenever the output level is below the target and reduce G whenever the output level is above the target.

It can be proven mathematically that this policy rule will result in a gradual convergence of the levels of M and G to the optimal levels. It can also be shown that if the *fiscal* authority were told to stabilize inflation and the monetary *authority* were assigned the task of stabilizing output, the process would *not* converge. In this case, instead, the values of M and G would oscillate in ever-greater swings around the optimal values.

Fewer Instruments than Targets

Our inflation-output model gives us two instruments with which to hit two targets, and under favorable circumstances, this is enough. But what happens in the more likely case that, in fact, there are more targets than instruments? Continuing with the same model, let us see what choices the policy-maker has in this circumstance.

Suppose that the country is in a political stalemate over fiscal policy, a stalemate that has rendered it impossible to use government spending as a tool of macroeconomic policy. Fiscal policy is thus fixed at $\Delta G = 0$, even if that is not the optimal choice, and monetary policy alone is available to influence output and inflation. The government wants to reduce inflation with the minimum possible cost in terms of output, but is it now possible to eliminate inflation and leave output unchanged at its potential level? Clearly, the answer is no.

If fiscal policy cannot be used ($\Delta G = 0$), equations (19.3') become

$$\Delta Q = a_2 \Delta M \qquad \text{(19.6a)}$$
$$\Delta \hat{P} = b_2 \Delta M \qquad \text{(19.6b)}$$

But then $(\Delta Q/a_2) = \Delta M = (\Delta \hat{P}/b_2)$, and therefore

$$\Delta \hat{P} = \left(\frac{b_2}{a_2}\right) \Delta Q \qquad \text{(19.7)}$$

Now a costless disinflation cannot be achieved, even in theory. The government has only one instrument, and it cannot possibly hit two targets with it. As equation (19.7) says, inflation and output will have to move in the same direction. If the government runs a contractionary monetary policy to stop the inflation, then output will be hurt as well. And under our new assumptions, government spending can no longer expand to offset the recessionary effects of the monetary contraction. The policy constraint repre-

---

[9] The ratio b_2/a_2 measures the increase in inflation per unit increase in output, when the output expansion is caused by monetary policy. Similarly, the ratio b_1/a_1 measures the increase in inflation per unit increase in output when the output expansion is caused by fiscal policy. Because of the differing effects of M and G on the exchange rate, and thus on prices, we expect that b_2/a_2 is greater than b_1/a_1.

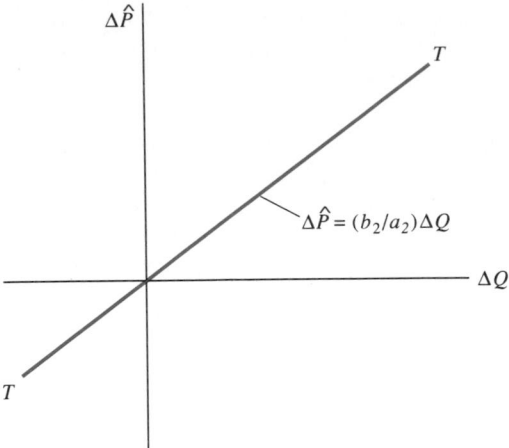

Figure 19-1
The Policy Constraint under Fewer Instruments than Targets

sented by equation (19.7) is shown graphically in Figure 19-1 as the line TT that links the two targets, $\Delta\hat{P}$ and ΔQ. As you can see there, any change toward a higher output, ΔQ, must be associated with a greater increase in the inflation rate, $\Delta\hat{P}$.

When instruments are so scarce, policymakers cannot achieve all the social goals desired, and they face the familiar problem of a *trade-off* between the different targets. In our case, lower inflation can only be obtained at a cost in terms of output. But even though the targets cannot be met, policymakers need not stand idle. What exactly should they do? Their first step should be to define a *social loss function*, a relationship that represents the cost to society of the deviations of the targets from their optimal values. A social loss function is like a utility function at the level of the society, but now we want to *minimize* a loss rather than maximize utility.

Consider a specific but standard example of a social loss function. Society, of course, loses whenever inflation and output targets are not hit, and we can suppose that big deviations are far more costly than small deviations. How much more costly? Specifically, we assume that the losses are in proportion to the *squared deviation* of the target from its optimal value. Double the size of the deviation, and get *four* times the loss! Thus, if ΔQ turns out to be different from ΔQ^*, the losses are measured as $(\Delta Q - \Delta Q^*)^2$. If $\Delta\hat{P}$ turns out to be different from $\Delta\hat{P}^*$, then the losses are assumed to be $(\Delta\hat{P} - \Delta\hat{P}^*)^2$. The total loss from missing both targets is the *sum* of the squared deviations from each target:

$$L = (\Delta Q - \Delta Q^*)^2 + (\Delta\hat{P} - \Delta\hat{P}^*)^2 \qquad \textbf{(19.8)}$$

More generally, the losses from missing the two targets may be given a differential weight by adding a weight α_0 in front of one of the terms, as follows:

$$L = (\Delta Q - \Delta Q^*)^2 + \alpha_0(\Delta\hat{P} - \Delta\hat{P}^*)^2 \qquad \textbf{(19.8a)}$$

In this case, the importance of missing the inflation target is given added weight when $\alpha_0 > 1$ and reduced weight when $\alpha_0 < 1$. In the example we

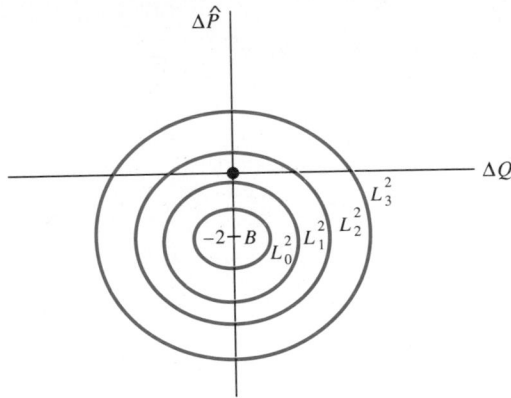

Figure 19-2
The Social Loss Function

have been working with, our goals are $\Delta \hat{P}^* = -2$ and $\Delta Q^* = 0$. Thus, the loss function (setting $\alpha_0 = 1$) is given as

$$L = (\Delta Q)^2 + (\Delta \hat{P} + 2)^2 \tag{19.9}$$

As usual whenever there is a utility function (or in this case, its opposite, a loss function), we can draw indifference curves, as shown in Figure 19-2. At the point $\Delta Q = 0$, $\Delta \hat{P} = -2$, the loss is zero. This is shown as the bull's-eye (point B) in the figure. As usual, we call the point of zero loss the bliss point. Consider the indifference curve for a loss of level L_0^2. We want to find all the points of ΔQ and $\Delta \hat{P}$ such that

$$L_0^2 = (\Delta Q)^2 + (\Delta \hat{P} + 2)^2$$

This turns out to be a circle, *centered on the bliss point,* with the radius L_0. If the loss is still greater, say $L_1^2 > L_0^2$, then the indifference curve is a larger circle, which is also centered on the bliss point.

Thus, the family of indifference curves is a set of concentric circles. The smallest loss is at the center, where the policymaker hits the targets exactly. The larger the miss, the greater the loss, so that the circles with a larger radius are associated with larger losses. Thus the graphic states the policymaker's goal quite simply: get to the indifference circle that is as close to the bliss point as possible.

To find the optimal policy using the indifference curves, we superimpose the policy constraint represented by equation (19.7) on the family of indifference curves, as shown in Figure 19-3. The policy constraint, remember, shows that changes in inflation and output must lie upon a particular line, TT. The equilibrium is reached at the point of tangency between the target constraint TT and the indifference curve closest to the bliss point. This is point E. Tangency assures that we are reaching the smallest possible circle, that is, the smallest loss within the feasible set of points that can be reached. Note that at the equilibrium (point E) there is some drop in output ($\Delta Q < 0$) and a *partial* disinflation, but not enough to eliminate inflation entirely. The policy compromises both goals, accepting some undesired output loss to reduce the high inherited inflation rate.

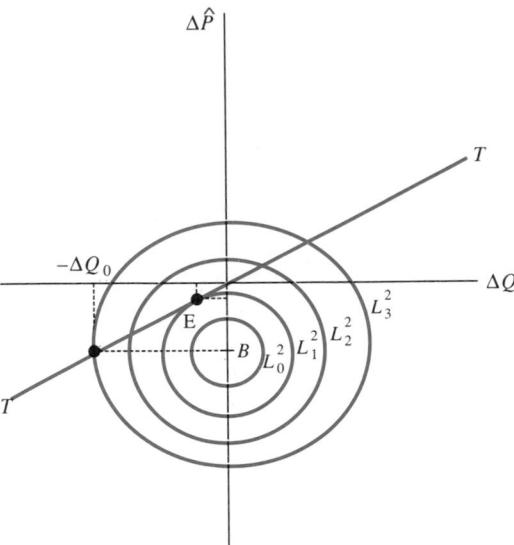

Figure 19-3
The Social Loss Indifference Curves and the
Policy Constraint: Equilibrium

This solution clarifies the nature of the policy trade-off. Inflation has not been eliminated because the output loss of doing so would have been too great. If full disinflation had been carried through, output would have dropped by the amount ΔQ_0, and society would have suffered a loss of L_3^2 in the graph. According to the loss function, the country is better off living with some of the inflation, and therefore a smaller loss of output.

19-2 THE LIMITATIONS OF ACTIVISM UNDER UNCERTAINTY

So far, we have been working in an idealized setting in which the only problem for policymakers is whether they have enough instruments with linearly independent effects to hit all of their targets. If so, they can reach the bliss point; if not, they must accept a trade-off, using the social loss function to minimize losses. Policymakers have problems that go far beyond this, however. In real life, conditions are uncertain, and the economic authorities can never know exactly how their actions will affect the target variables. This uncertainty profoundly affects the actions that are appropriate.

Kinds of Uncertainty

In fact, we can distinguish many different kinds of uncertainty. We have assumed that policymakers know exactly what the effects of their actions on the economy will be, that is, that they know the precise values of the coefficients of the model that represents the economy—the a's and b's of equations (19.1) to (19.5) in our framework. In practice, this is not the case. Policymakers have only an approximate idea of the true values of these coefficients.

A particular kind of coefficient uncertainty involves not the overall effects of an instrument on its targets, but the *timing* of those effects. It might be known with some confidence, for example, that a monetary contraction of a given magnitude tends, in the long run, to reduce nominal GNP by a given magnitude. The timing of that effect, however, is usually much more uncertain. One major complaint about policy activism, led by Nobel Laureate Milton Friedman, holds that policymakers should not move their policy instruments very often because of "long and variable" lags in the effects of the policies on the policy targets.[10]

Policymakers are bedeviled not only by coefficient uncertainty (or model uncertainty if they aren't even sure of the correct model linking the policy variables to the targets), but also by the fact that events totally outside their control affect the targets. If these "exogenous shocks"—and their effects—could be forecast accurately, then they could be taken into account by policymakers before they choose their instruments. Typically, however, even after good forecasts, exogenous events remain highly uncertain.

A Simple Model of Policymaking under Uncertainty

To add uncertainty to our framework in the simplest possible way, let us consider the case where the *only* target is output and the *only* instrument is monetary policy. We have one instrument and one target, but now we add uncertainty. Suppose that the economy is in a recession, so that the goal of policy is to raise output, $\Delta Q^* > 0$. The new "model" of the economy is specified as follows:

$$\Delta Q = \tilde{\alpha}\Delta M + \varepsilon, \qquad \text{with } \Delta Q^* > 0 \qquad \textbf{(19.10)}$$

The social loss function is, as before, quadratic:

$$L = (\Delta Q - \Delta Q^*)^2 \qquad \textbf{(19.11)}$$

In the new model in (19.10), the "error term" or "disturbance term," ε, reflects those factors, such as weather or labor strikes, for example, that affect output but are outside the policymakers' control. The variable ε is a random variable that fluctuates according to known probabilities but whose specific value is *not* known at the time that a choice must be made regarding ΔM. The variable can be either positive or negative, and has an average of zero. This kind of error is referred to as *additive uncertainty* because the effect of ε is *added on to* the effect of the policy instrument.

The second important point is that the coefficient α is now not known precisely, and it is therefore denoted with a "tilde" over it. The policymakers know what $\tilde{\alpha}$ is on average, but they do not know exactly what the coefficient will be when they undertake their monetary policy. Therefore, the effect of monetary policy on inflation cannot be determined exactly. Technically, the coefficient $\tilde{\alpha}$ represents *multiplicative uncertainty* because the effect of the uncertainty is multiplied by the policy instrument. (In Chapter 14, we illustrated the existence of multiplicative uncertainty when we said that several large-scale econometric models differ in their quantitative estimates of the multiplier effects of various policies.)

---

[10] See, for example, Milton Friedman, "The Lag in the Effect of Monetary Policy," *Journal of Political Economy*, October 1961.

What are the implications of uncertainty for policy? Without uncertainty, the policy choice is, of course, child's play. With one instrument and one target, the policymaker simply sets ΔM to hit ΔQ^*. But what should she do with uncertainty? One intuitive possibility—but not the right one (!)—would be for her to try to hit the optimal output target on average. We assume that policymakers know the average values of $\tilde{\alpha}$ and ε, which we take to be

$$\text{average } (\tilde{\alpha}) = \overline{\alpha}; \qquad \text{average } (\varepsilon) = 0$$

Then, the average change of output is equal to

$$\Delta Q = \overline{\alpha}\Delta M \qquad\qquad\text{(19.12)}$$

Thus, if ΔM is set equal to $(\Delta Q^*/\overline{\alpha})$, we know that we will hit the target of $\Delta Q = \Delta Q^*$, but only on average.

Of course there is no guarantee that the target will be hit in any given period. Consider, for example, the effect of multiplicative uncertainty. If ΔM is set based on the average of $\tilde{\alpha}$ ($\overline{\alpha}$), and the coefficient turns out to be *less* than expected, then ΔQ will be smaller than was expected and was desired. Monetary policy will have been too weak, and the raise in output will have been less than optimal. If, on the other hand, the coefficient $\tilde{\alpha}$ turns out to be above its average $\overline{\alpha}$, then output will boom above the target, with $\Delta Q > \Delta Q^*$. This will lead to overfull employment and an undesired welfare loss, with insufficient leisure time, bottlenecks in the economy, and shortages resulting from excess demand. ΔQ can also turn out to be greater than or less than ΔQ^* depending on whether ε (the additive uncertainty) turns out to be more or less than expected.

William Brainard of Yale University, in an important 1967 paper, showed that it is not good enough to aim on average for ΔQ^* when the social loss function is quadratic.[11] Brainard stressed that policymakers have to be *especially careful about the possibility that the random coefficients of the model turn out to be larger than average.* In the unforeseen case that $\tilde{\alpha}$ is above $\overline{\alpha}$, the target may well be missed by a large margin. And because the social loss function magnifies a miss by squaring it, the cost of a large miss is very, very great. The clear conclusion is that policymakers should be *cautious*—that is to say, less, rather than more, activist.

In our example, the policymaker should set ΔM at less than $\Delta Q^*/\overline{\alpha}$. Brainard showed in a formal proof that to minimize the expected social loss, the optimal choice for monetary policy is

$$\Delta M = \frac{\Delta Q^*}{(\overline{\alpha} + \sigma^2/\overline{\alpha})}$$

which is obviously less than $\Delta Q^*/\overline{\alpha}$.[12] On average, the economy should be run at less than full employment; otherwise, there is the danger of greatly overheating the economy if the coefficient on monetary policy turns out to be unexpectedly large.

---

[11] Brainard's now classical work on the subject is "Uncertainty and the Effectiveness of Policy," *American Economic Review*, May 1967.

[12] Where σ^2 is the variance of $\tilde{\alpha}$. This equation is for the case in which the multiplicative shock and the additive shock are uncorrelated.

Fluctuations in ε do not affect the choice of M in the same way as fluctuations of $\tilde{\alpha}$. This is because a large value of ε does not *magnify* the effect of ΔM in the same way a large value of $\tilde{\alpha}$ does. For this reason, policymakers can in fact pretend that ε will be at its average value when thinking about choosing a monetary policy. In other words, the presence of an additive error term does not affect the choice of monetary policy. This important result is known as *certainty equivalence*. With additive shocks, a linear economic model, and a quadratic (squared) loss function, then, policy instruments should be chosen as if there were no uncertainty.

In summary, the possibility of unanticipated multiplicative shocks means that policymakers should use restraint. On the other hand, unanticipated additive shocks have the property of certainty equivalence and thus do not affect the choice of optimal policies. The policymaker can simply assume that any additive shock will be at its average level.

19-3 CHOOSING AMONG POLICY INSTRUMENTS

So far the Tinbergen framework has provided us with a clear set of instruments and a clear set of targets. The goal is to pick the values of the instruments to minimize the (expected) value of the social loss function. Now we add yet another complication. In some cases, the policymaker has a choice of instruments. He can pick instrument A or instrument B, but not both. Which should he pick to minimize the expected social loss when deviations from targeted optimal values occur? This problem was first analyzed in a path-breaking study by William Poole of Brown University.[13]

Two familiar examples should make the problem clear. In an open economy with free capital mobility, the monetary policy authority can choose the exchange rate or the money supply as a policy instrument, *but not both*. In an open economy with fixed exchange rates but with capital controls, the monetary authority can choose the interest rate or the money supply, *but not both.* Supposing that the goal of the monetary authority is to stabilize output, which kind of monetary policy is best? Does it matter? These questions can be answered within a framework of minimizing the expected social losses that results when output deviates from the optimal level.

Consider an economy operating with fixed exchange rates and strict capital controls. Assume (for simplicity) that the strict Keynesian model holds. With prices thus fixed, we can use the *IS-LM* model to determine the levels of interest rates and output, as shown in Figure 19-4a. But as we did not do earlier, now we must allow for the possibility of *random shocks* to aggregate demand (shown as random shifts in the *IS* curve) or to money demand (shown as random shifts in the *LM* curve). Such shifts are illustrated in Figure 19-4b, where the *IS* curve fluctuates up or down depending on the direction of the aggregate demand shock, and in Figure 19-4c, where the *LM* curve may fluctuate up or down depending on the direction of the money demand shock.

---

[13] See Poole's "Optimal Choice of Monetary Policy Instruments in a Simple Stochastic Macro Model," *Quarterly Journal of Economics,* May 1970.

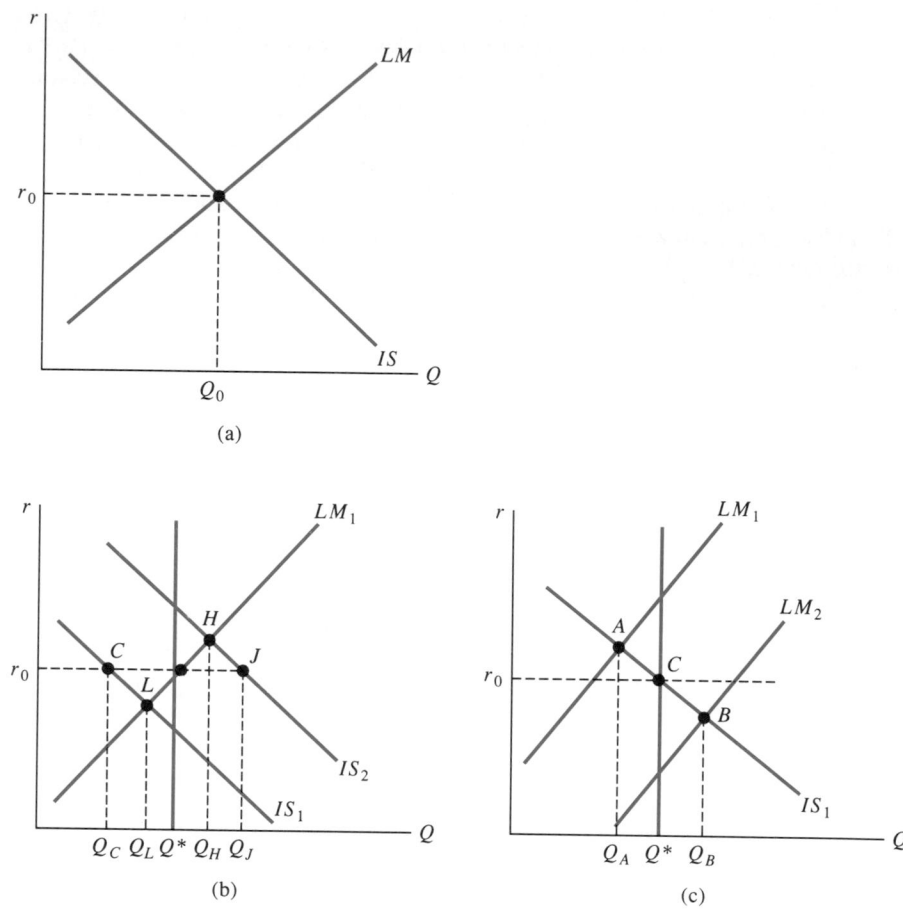

Figure 19-4
The Optimal Target for Monetary Policy in the Face of Economic Instability:
(a) Equilibrium in the *IS-LM* Framework; (b) Instability in Aggregate Demand; (c) Money Demand Instability

When the economy is buffeted by shifts in aggregate demand and money demand, output will tend to fluctuate as well. Suppose that $Q = Q^*$ is the optimum level of output, and that output is at this optimal level in the absence of the random shocks. When aggregate demand is unusually high (IS_2), output ends up at point $Q_H > Q^*$ as in Figure 19-4b, and when aggregate demand is unusually low (IS_1), output ends up at $Q_L < Q^*$. Similarly, when the demand for money is unusually high, the *LM* curve shifts to the *left* (LM_1),[14] causing a fall in output; a fall in the demand for money, on the other hand, is unexpectedly expansionary, with the *LM* curve shifting to the right (LM_2).

---

[14] Note that a rise in money demand, with no change in money supply, leads to an excess demand for money at the initial interest rate. Therefore, the money market will be in equilibrium again only if interest rates rise, or output falls, or some combination of the two takes place. For this reason, the rise in money demand leads to a leftward shift of the *LM* curve.

   The policymakers' goal now is to choose a policy that will stabilize output as much as possible. Specifically, the goal is to minimize $(Q - Q^*)^2$. Let us look at two kinds of monetary policies. In the first, the monetary authority chooses the money supply and holds it fixed. In the second, the monetary authority chooses the interest rate and holds it fixed. (It does the latter by announcing the interest rate at which it is ready to exchange money for government debt, as was described in Chapter 9.) In both cases, the policy is selected *before* the specific shock is known, that is, before the shifts in the *IS* and *LM* curves are evident.

   It is easy to show that the optimal type of monetary policy depends on the most likely *source* of economic shocks. Suppose, for example, that almost all shocks are *IS* shocks, as in Figure 19-4b. If the authorities maintain a constant money supply, the *LM* curve will remain at the position LM_1. In this case, output will move between points Q_H and Q_L in the graph. If, instead, the authorities choose the interest rate as the policy instrument and fix the rate at r_0 by moving the money supply appropriately, the economy would fluctuate more widely between points Q_C and Q_J. *Thus, if the economy is subject to IS shocks, then the money supply instrument is the better stabilizer.*

   What happens if most shocks are *LM* shocks and the *IS* curve is stationary? If the authorities fix the money supply, the *LM* curve will fluctuate in response to the shocks in money demand, and output will move between Q_A and Q_B. If the authorities fix the interest rate, however, then monetary policy will automatically offset the shifts in money demand, and the interest rate will remain stationary at r_0. The *LM* curve thus remains stationary and output does not fluctuate from Q^* (point C). If there is an unexpected rise in money demand, the monetary authorities would raise the money supply (by an open market purchase) rather than let interest rates rise; if there is an unexpected fall in money demand, the monetary authorities would reduce the money supply (by an open market sale). *Thus, if the economy is subject to LM shocks, then an interest-rate instrument is the better policy.*

   As Poole noted, the policymaker is likely to be operating in an economy in which both the *IS* and the *LM* curves shift unexpectedly, and policies are probably selected before any shifts are observed. Some judgment, then, must be made in advance as to what proportion of overall uncertainty can be attributed to *IS* shifts and what proportion to *LM* shifts. To the extent that *IS* shifts predominate, the money supply is the best policy; to the extent that *LM* shifts predominate, it is the interest rate.

   We finish with clarifications of two smaller points. First, in Tinbergen terminology, we speak of "instruments" (money, for example, or interest rates) and "targets" (output, say). In the monetary policy debate, however, we often speak of monetary instruments as "intermediate targets" and describe policy choices between money and interest rates as if they were choices between two intermediate targets. We speak of instruments as if they were targets because even if policymakers are choosing to fix M or r_0, they must generally first use even more basic instruments, such as open market operations. The open market operations are then used to hit the intermediate targets on the money supply or interest rate, which are, in turn, instruments in the service of the ultimate targets.

   Second, Poole identified a kind of "combination policy" as a compromise between a strict monetary policy or a strict interest-rate policy. The combination policy fixes an optimal linear relationship between M and r_0 in order to minimize an expected social loss. In describing the combination policy, however, Poole did indicate that it is hard to figure out and difficult to implement because it requires such a comprehensive knowledge of the underlying economic model.

19-4 THE LUCAS CRITIQUE OF THE THEORY OF ECONOMIC POLICY

By the early 1970s, it was clear from the work of several economists, including Friedman, Brainard and Poole, that the theory of economic policy as presented by Tinbergen had important limitations, especially with regard to uncertainty. An even more serious attack against the framework came in the mid-1970s, from Robert Lucas at the University of Chicago.[15] The so-called ''Lucas critique'' aggressively attacked the use of existing large-scale macroeconometric models in the formulation of macroeconomic policy. This critique, through its influence on economic thinking, cast a shadow over one of the most common tools used by policymakers.

The Tinbergen framework rests on the idea of a stable (unchanging) quantitative relationship linking policy instruments to targets. In applying the Tinbergen framework in practice, policymakers have used large-scale econometric models. In doing so, they have assumed that the policy multipliers calculated by their models are stable parameters linking policy instruments to targets. Lucas argued forcefully, and persuasively for many, that the parameters of large-scale models cannot be taken as stable. If the policies of the government were to change sharply, he said, the econometric coefficients of the large models would no longer be reliable, even though their failure might only be evident after reestimating the model in several years.

According to Lucas, large-scale models are poorly designed and estimated. He claims that the coefficients do not describe the real *structure* of the economy (and therefore are unstable); rather, they provide a statistical summary of how the economy worked on average in the past. If the policies stay the same, then the model will probably forecast the future reasonably correctly. But if the policy rules change, according to Lucas, then the model is not likely to predict how the economy will actually respond.

A major problem in Lucas's view is the treatment of expectations in standard large-scale models. Expectations of the future value of a variable are usually proxied econometrically by a function of lagged values of the variable being forecasted, under the implicit or explicit assumption that expectations formation is dominated by an adaptive expectations process. This simple method is seriously flawed in Lucas's view, since he doubts that expectations are really formed by mechanical extrapolations of past values of a variable. Lucas stresses that if the policy rules change, the formation of expectations are also likely to change, but in ways that will not be captured by standard large-scale econometric models.

---

[15] See Robert Lucas, ''Econometric Policy Evaluation: A Critique,'' *Carnegie Rochester Conference Series on Public Policy,* No. 1, 1976. Also see his *Studies in Business Cycle Theory* (Cambridge, Mass.: MIT Press, 1981).

To illustrate this point, suppose that a policymaker is trying to find the link between money supply changes and output. An econometrician might estimate a linear relationship between output and the change in the money supply as follows:

$$Q = b_0 + b_1(M - M_{-1}) \qquad (19.13)$$

The estimated coefficient b_1 might then be used to make a Tinbergen-type choice of optimal monetary policy, in this case, $M - M_{-1}$. Lucas would argue that (19.13) is a bad model on the grounds that while it is easy to estimate statistically, it is unlikely to offer an accurate picture of how future monetary policy changes would affect Q. A better model in Lucas's view, and one in line with rational expectations theory, would be

$$Q = a_0 + a_1(M - M^e) \qquad (19.14)$$

where M^e is the value of money that was expected for this period as of the previous period. Here, only *unexpected* changes in money affect output.[16]

Suppose that (19.14) is the true model, but the econometrician goes ahead and (mistakenly) estimates (19.13). The estimated coefficient b_1 would depend on the *average* relationship between money growth ($M - M_{-1}$) and unexpected money growth ($M - M^e$) during the period in the past when the statistics were gathered. If most of the money growth that occurred was unexpected, then one would see a correlation of money growth and output.[17] But this average relationship in the past might indicate nothing about the future. If all future money growth is perfectly forecast, then the future money growth would have *no* effect on output (because there would be no errors in expectations). The estimate of the coefficient b_1 would therefore give a very inaccurate guide to the "true" future relationship between money growth and output.

Lucas claimed that almost all econometric relations in large-scale models would prove to be unreliable, because econometricians had estimated models like (19.13) instead of models like (19.14). Major policy shifts, he believed, would lead to radically different empirical estimates of econometric relationships, once enough time had passed for a new econometric estimation of the models. Lucas's critique had a great effect because it accorded well with a major policy debacle that had occurred in the 1960s, the improper use of an estimated *short-run* Phillips curve as a guide to the *permanent* trade-off of unemployment and inflation.[18]

In the 1960s, many economists estimated equations of the form

$$\hat{P} = -\beta_0 U + \beta_1 \hat{P}_{-1} \qquad (19.15)$$

a relationship that they wrongly viewed as stable. A better specification would have been

$$\hat{P} = -\gamma_0 U + \gamma_1 \hat{P}^e \qquad (19.16)$$

---

[16] Remember that in Chapter 17 we described a model in which only unexpected changes in money affected output.

[17] It could have been the case that during the period, $(M - M^e)$ was equal to $(\frac{1}{2})(M - M_{-1})$; that is, one-half of the money growth was unexpected. In that case, the statistical estimate of b_1 would be equal to $(\frac{1}{2})a_1$, where a_1 is the coefficient in equation (19.14).

[18] See our discussion of the Phillips curve in Chapter 15.

where $\hat{P}^e$ is the inflation expectations for this period as of the previous period. In the early 1960s, the estimated coefficient of β_1 in (19.15) was on the order of 0.2. But the estimate was not reliable. During the 1960s, the relationship between lagged inflation $\hat{P}_{-1}$ and expected inflation $\hat{P}^e$ kept changing, and as a result, equations like (19.15) constantly underpredicted inflation in the 1960s. By the end of the 1960s, the statistical estimate of β_1 had risen to around 0.9. In this case, Lucas was right. The model had seriously misled policymakers by downplaying the role of expectations.

There are other clear cases where Lucas's point is well taken. We know, for example, that the effects of tax law changes depend heavily on whether they are perceived to be temporary or permanent. Yet many large-scale models have not allowed for this distinction, and therefore they are unreliable as policy tools.

More generally, how should we evaluate Lucas's critique? There is no doubt that many parts of large-scale models are not based on solid theory but rather on past average statistical relationships between variables. And the role of expectations had indeed been downplayed in many cases. For these reasons, the results of the large-scale models must be viewed with caution, particularly in cases where expectations are known to play an important role.

At the same time, however, the models continue to show their usefulness in interpreting major macroeconomic events, and they should not be dismissed out of hand. Considerable progress has in fact been made in adding expectational variables into the large-scale models, and this addresses some of Lucas's concerns.[19] At the same time, some *direct tests* of the Lucas proposition that policy changes lead to changes in the coefficients on behavioral equations have not turned up strong support for Lucas's theoretical point.[20]

19-5 RULES, DISCRETION, AND TIME CONSISTENCY

Up until now, we have described policy actions as occurring at one point in time, using a set of targets and instruments and a model of how the economy functions. The policymaker takes a single, discrete action in order to minimize the social loss function. While policymaking has traditionally been analyzed in this simple framework, economists have come to recognize that many of its most crucial issues arise from the fact that policymaking usually is a *sequence of actions*, taken over a long period of time. The question, then, is how to minimize social losses when policy actions have to be taken at *many* points in time.

One of the crucial issues is whether policymakers should act according

---

[19] Warwick McKibbin and Jeffrey Sachs, for example, in their study *Global Linkages: Macroeconomic Interdependence and Cooperation in the World Economy* (Washington, D.C.: The Brookings Institution, 1991), use a global model with a careful treatment of expectations, and show that such a large-scale model can track important developments in the world economy during the 1980s.

[20] Olivier Blanchard, for example, presented evidence showing that the behavioral coefficients were slow to adjust to the changes of monetary policy in the United States during the early 1980s. See his article "The Lucas Critique and the Volcker Deflation," *American Economic Review*, May 1984.

to *rules* which dictate the choices to be made at any moment of time, or whether they should act with *discretion*, in the sense of not being bound by any preset formula, but rather optimizing the choice of policy instruments at each point in time. Modern policy analysis has stressed the importance of rules—though flexible rules—for several reasons.

Time Consistency

Starting from some initial point, a policymaker must decide what is the best action to take over a certain time period. Perhaps several actions will have to be taken during the period in question. The policymaker can decide on the "right" set of policies by minimizing the expected social loss, using a given model of the economy and the instruments available. The right policy may involve a sequence of actions to be carried out today and at various future dates. When the future date arrives, however, it may seem better to pursue a different course of action than the one decided on at the outset. Should the policymaker recalculate and come up with a new optimal decision, or should she follow through with the initial plan? This issue of *time consistency* is usefully illustrated with an extended example.

Suppose that a policymaker must choose a monetary policy. He has two choices, a low money supply increase ($\hat{M}_L = 2\%$) or a high money supply increase ($\hat{M}_H = 6\%$). We suppose that the money supply increase determines the rate of inflation and that, indeed, the rate of money growth and the rate of inflation are equal. Thus, when $\hat{M}_L$ is chosen, $\hat{P} = 2\%$, and when $\hat{M}_H$ is chosen, $\hat{P} = 6\%$.

Each period, the union must negotiate a nominal wage contract, based on their *expectations* about the monetary policy (and consequently about the inflation) that will be chosen in the period. The goal of the union is simply to protect the real wage of the workers, by setting the nominal wage change equal to the expected inflation. If the union expects $\hat{M}_L$, then it will negotiate for $\hat{w}_L = 2\%$; if it expects $\hat{M}_H$, they will demand $\hat{w}_H = 6\%$. The sequence of actions is as follows:

1. The union settles on a nominal wage contract based on the expectation of monetary policy and hence inflation.
2. Policymakers choose the monetary policy.
3. The economy responds to the combination of monetary policy and wage setting.

There are four possible outcomes (the policy choice combined with wage change), and each one produces a given outcome in terms of inflation and unemployment. Some numbers here will help us be more specific. When $\hat{P} = \hat{w}$, unemployment stays at 5 percent. When inflation is *greater* than the nominal wage change, unemployment falls to 3 percent (because of the fall in the real wage). When inflation is *less* than the nominal wage change, unemployment rises to 7 percent.

Thus, if we summarize all the possible outcomes, we have

1. $\hat{M}_L$ and $\hat{w}_L$—inflation = 2%; unemployment = 5%
2. $\hat{M}_L$ and $\hat{w}_H$—inflation = 2%; unemployment = 7%
3. $\hat{M}_H$ and $\hat{w}_H$—inflation = 6%; unemployment = 5%
4. $\hat{M}_H$ and $\hat{w}_L$—inflation = 6%; unemployment = 3%

Now suppose that policymakers care a great deal about reducing unemployment, even at the cost of higher inflation. The workers, on the other hand, simply try to protect their real wage. Both the workers and the policymakers prefer less inflation to more inflation, but they give precedence to their other concerns.

Let us consider first the policymakers' choice. If the union has already chosen $\hat{w}_L$, then the policymakers will choose $\hat{M}_H$, because the policymakers prefer 3 percent unemployment to 5 percent unemployment. Similarly, if the union has chosen $\hat{w}_H$, then the policymakers will again choose $\hat{M}_H$, to make sure that unemployment stays at 5 percent (since the other choice of monetary policy would lead to 7 percent unemployment). Thus, no matter what the union does, the monetary authorities choose the inflationary monetary policy.

Now, let us consider the union's choice. Since the union *knows* in advance that the policymakers will choose the high inflation alternative, the union will protect the real wage by choosing $\hat{w}_H$. The policy outcome is therefore the third alternative listed, with $\hat{M} = \hat{M}_H$ and $\hat{w} = \hat{w}_H$. The macroeconomic outcome is inflation equal to 6 percent and unemployment equal to 5 percent.

This is a troubling outcome. For suppose instead that the money supply were set at $\hat{M}_L$ and that the wage were set at $\hat{w}_L$ (alternative 1). The result would be the same unemployment rate, the same real wage, but lower inflation. *Everybody would be better off.*

The problem is achieving the low-inflation solution. Suppose that policymakers *announce* at the very beginning that they are going to abide by a low-inflation monetary policy. They promise the union that $\hat{M}_L$ will be selected. Suppose, further, that on the basis of that promise, the union indeed selects $\hat{w}_L$. Once the wage is set, *the policymaker has an incentive to "cheat,"* that is, to reverse the initial decision and do something other than what was promised. By choosing $\hat{M}_H$ rather than $\hat{M}_L$ *after* the wage has been set, the unemployment rate can be reduced.

Let us summarize the argument up to this point. If wages are set first and monetary policy is set afterward, both the union and the policymaker are likely to pursue the inflationary option. The outcome is inefficient, in the sense that the same unemployment and real wage could be achieved with lower inflation, to everyone's benefit. The more efficient result could be achieved if the policymaker promises to follow the low-inflation solution, and thereby induces the workers to choose a low-inflation wage. If the policymaker then follows through on the promise, the economy ends up in a low-inflation equilibrium.

The problem is that the announcement of the low-inflation path is not very credible. The union knows (or should know) that the policymaker has an incentive to cheat on the promise once the wage has been set. Therefore, the low inflation equilibrium tends to be unachievable. The union, acting defensively, will not be convinced to set a low rate of wage change, since the policymaker cannot be compelled to follow through on a promise of low inflation. The attempt at low inflation unravels. The economy ends up in the high-inflation equilibrium.

Let us put this complex case into the "rules versus discretion" language. If the policymaker acts with *discretion* when monetary policy is made, it will pick the high-inflation monetary policy. Since the union knows this, it too will pick the high-inflation wage policy. If instead the policymaker could be made to act according to a low-inflation *rule*, then the better equilibrium could be achieved. The rule might simply say that the monetary authority is bound to choose $\hat{M}_L$ no matter what the circumstances. Milton Friedman has indeed suggested a so-called *X percent rule*, which would bind the policymaker to choose the same rate of money growth each period no matter what the circumstances.[21] Friedman has precisely been worried that the monetary authority has the temptation to inflate and that such a temptation can be controlled only by a formal rule. By setting a rule, and in effect "tying its own hands," the monetary authority limits its discretion and makes its announcement of a low-inflation policy credible.

Another set of terms from modern game theory is useful in describing this situation. The strategy $\hat{M}_H$ is the *time-consistent* strategy of the monetary authority in that it is the policy that would actually be followed by a rational policymaker free to choose the best monetary policy at the time that money growth is set. The strategy $\hat{M}_L$ is the optimal policy from the point of view of the initial announcement but it is *time inconsistent* in that there is a temptation to cheat on it once the actual choice of monetary policy is to be made.

We can state the issue of time consistency more formally. A *time-consistent policy* is one in which the policymaker optimizes each time that he selects a policy. As we have seen, the surprising conclusion is that such a period-by-period optimization can be very bad—there is simply too much discretion. The optimal policy (though time inconsistent) is to select a plan or rule that will accomplish the desired objectives at the beginning and then to adhere to it throughout time, without succumbing to the temptation to deviate from the rule. The temptation may be very great; cheating can often reduce social losses. The problem, though, is that other agents in the economy will quickly learn to anticipate the cheating, and any benefit from announcing optimal policies in the first place will be lost because they simply will not be believed.

Many economists have argued that for just these reasons policymakers are tempted to be overly inflationary. Robert Barro of Harvard University and David Gordon of the University of Rochester, for example, have argued for the importance of finding ways to make sure that policymakers adhere to optimal low-inflation plans and do not merely follow time-consistent plans.[22] A number of ways to get policymakers to do this have been suggested. One way is to reduce policymakers' discretion, forcing them—by law, for example—to pursue an explicit plan stated from the outset. This was the idea of the Gramm-Rudman-Hollings legislation in the United States, which tried to force the Congress and the president to follow a path of steadily falling budget deficits. As Box 19-1 shows, the attempt to commit the policymakers has been at best only partially successful, since even a law can be changed at a later date.

Another way to force the optimal policy choice is to "punish" politi-

---

[21] See Chapter 4 in Milton Friedman, *A Program for Monetary Stability* (New York: Fordham University Press, 1960).

[22] See their joint paper, "Rules, Discretion and Reputation in a Model of Monetary Policy," *Journal of Monetary Economics*, July 1983.

Box 19-1

The Gramm-Rudman-Hollings Budget Rule to Achieve a Zero Budget Deficit

The U.S. budget deficit steadily increased during the first half of the 1980s, a result of tax cuts coupled with higher defense spending by the Reagan administration. In 1985, the deficit reached $212 billion (or almost 6 percent of GDP), an all-time record at that time for the United States. Even as the deficit widened, Congress and the president were unable to agree on a policy package that would reduce the deficit to more desirable levels. In February 1985, President Reagan sent to Congress a deficit reduction proposal that centered on cutting only domestic expenditures (many of these in socially sensitive areas), and excluded any cut on defense spending. Furthermore, the president was sharply opposed to any tax increase. Majorities in both houses of Congress were dissatisfied with this proposal. However, the House of Representatives and the Senate were divided on the deficit reduction issue, and several coalitions existed within each chamber.[23]

Dissatisfaction mounted in Congress and among the general public with the inability to agree on a deficit reduction proposal that would be readily implemented. In this situation in late 1985, senators Phil Gramm (R., Tex.), Warren Rudman (R., N.H.), and Ernest Hollings (D., S.C.) introduced legislation to establish automatic spending cuts in case an agreement on a package that would reduce the deficit could not be reached. This proposal was quickly approved by Congress in October 1985 as the Balanced Budget and Emergency Control Act (Public Law 99–177). It is more commonly referred to as the Gramm-Rudman-Hollings (GRH) Act.

The GRH Act of 1985 established maximum deficit goals that started at $180 billion for fiscal year 1986 and were to be gradually reduced to zero by 1991. These goals were to be achieved by automatic, across-the-board cuts on spending programs in case the Congress and the president could not agree on a deficit reduction package. The act also established that the spending cuts were to be shared in equal proportions by domestic programs and defense spending. Later on, a series of social programs were exempted from the automatic cuts, as well as some of the defense outlays.

Rather quickly, the original target schedule was altered in 1987 (under the Balanced Budget and Emergency Deficit Control Reaffirmation Act) in light of the difficulty of meeting those targets. Table 19-1 shows the original deficit targets, the revised targets, the actual deficit, and official projections of the deficit for the period 1986–1995. The target schedule was altered again in late 1990 in another budget agreement between the White House and the Congress, after major increases in the

---

[23] For a discussion of the political background to the Gramm-Rudman-Hollings Act, see Darrel West, "Gramm-Rudman-Hollings and the Politics of Debt Reduction," *Annals of the American Academy of Political and Social Science*, September 1988.

projections for the budget deficit (to a large extent, a result of the economic recession that started in the third quarter of 1990 and the costs of the Gulf War). The so-called Omnibus Reconciliation Act of 1990 established spending cuts and tax increases for about $500 billion over the period 1991–1995, but not fixed deficit targets or "enforcement mechanisms" as Gramm-Rudman-Hollings. Still, according to the new projections, the budget deficit would reach over $300 billion in 1991, the year the deficit should have reached zero according to the original Gramm-Rudman-Hollings targets.

In spite of its tough language toward budget imbalances, the GRH Act made much less of a dent on the deficit than was called for on paper, as shown by the fact that actual deficits systematically exceeded targets throughout the period of operation of the act. How could this happen? Part of the reason lies behind the detailed workings of the GRH Act. The spending cuts are made according not to the actual deficit, but to a *forecast* of it made by the Congressional Budget Office (CBO) and the Office of Management and the Budget (OMB). Because projections have been based on highly optimistic assumptions about income growth and interest rates, the resulting budgetary actions have been insufficient to reduce the actual deficit to the GRH target. Moving some expenditures out of the budget has also helped to reduce the power of the GRH Act.

Another part of the reason was simply that whenever the law started to "bite," the GRH targets were changed through new legislation. It is probably the case that the GRH legislation played some role in limiting budget deficits, at least compared with what they otherwise would have been, but the outcomes fell far short of the ambitious targets. This experience shows the difficulties of establishing firm and operational rules to limit the discretion of policymakers at a later date.

cians who deviate from their announced policies. If a politician knows that he will lose an election, or not be believed in the future, he may take more care in backing away from policy commitments. Economists have begun to study the *credibility* of announcements by looking at the benefits and costs of cheating. Announced plans can be credible if the costs to one's reputation or electoral chances of deviating from them outweigh the short-run benefits that can be achieved by doing something else.

Once we recognize the problem of time consistency, we find that the issue arises in all aspects of economic policymaking. Consider, as another example, the case of tax rules. Governments are eager to collect taxes, which provide a noninflationary source of financing for their spending programs. To attain this objective, the law generally establishes stiff penalties for noncompliance. Nonetheless, many people evade their taxes either by underdeclaring their incomes or simply by failing to file a tax return. In the face of a budget squeeze, governments sometimes deviate from the established tax rules in order to collect additional revenue in the short run. One way they do this is by offering a *tax amnesty,* in which the government promises to abstain from any legal action against past tax evasion if taxes are paid up during the amnesty period.

TABLE   19-1

THE GRAMM-RUDMAN-HOLLINGS ACT AND THE BUDGET DEFICIT IN THE UNITED STATES, 1986–1995
(US$ BILLION)

Fiscal Year	GRH Act Deficit Target		Actual Deficit	Projection	
	Original	Revised		CBO ( )*	OMB
1986	172	172	221	—	—
1987	144	144	150	—	—
1988	108	144	155	—	—
1989	72	136	153	—	—
1990	36	100	220	159	122
1991	0	64	—	161 (309)	101
1992	0	28	—	124 (294)	73
1993	0	0	—	132 (221)	39
1994	—	—		(69)	
1995	—	—			(69)

Source: Robert Keith, "Sequestration Actiond for FY1991 Under the Gramm-Rudman-Hollings Act," Congressional Research Service Issue Brief, *May 1990.* Actual deficit from *Economic Report of the President*, February 1991.
* *Revised CBO projections, January 1991.*

A tax amnesty is a time-consistent policy, but not necessarily an optimal policy. The government agrees not to enforce a rule that it has pledged to enforce in the past in order to gain the benefit of additional *short-term* revenue. But there is a long-run cost to this action. The credibility of the government is damaged, and people may think that another tax amnesty will be granted some time in the future. Thus, more people may choose to evade taxes. Indeed, even the expectation that a tax amnesty would be allowed may have contributed to the shortfall in the first place. In formal terms, the tax amnesty might be the time-consistent policy but not necessarily the optimal policy when judged in long-run perspective.

Another example is patents. In order to reward creativity, those who discover a new technology are awarded a monopoly over their invention for a specified period of time. Once the breakthrough has been made, however, government authorities may be tempted to eliminate the patent protection in order to make the technology available to everybody. Thus, at times a medical breakthrough has led to a wonder drug, but its distribution has been hampered by the fact that it is controlled by a drug firm that has a temporary monopoly on production. The time-consistent policy might be to drop the patent protection to allow widespread distribution of the product. But dropping the patent protection would not be an optimal policy from the initial point of view because fear that the patent law will not be enforced may well reduce the incentive for creative people to develop new products and technologies. This is why most countries strictly enforce property rights over technological advances, even though this may lead to undesirable monopoly.

Rules Versus Discretion

As we have seen, the time-consistency problem is part of a more general issue, the debate between rules and discretion. Should policymakers have the freedom to make policy choices, or should they be bound to follow certain rules? The rules themselves, presumably, would be the result of an optimization process much like that described throughout the chapter. The shortcomings of period-by-period optimization are a major argument on the side of rules rather than discretion. But there are arguments that go the other way as well, in favor of discretion. When the economic model is not known with a high degree of reliability, and it is likely to learn about the structure of the economy in the course of time, strict rules are generally unwise. As information about the economy changes, the operating rules for policy are likely to change as well.

Advocates of rules stress that some flexibility can be built into the rules themselves. In particular, a distinction can be made between fixed rules and feedback rules. *Fixed rules* consist of specific policies that must be followed no matter what happens to the economy. By contrast, *feedback rules* allow policies to change as the state of the economy changes, but according to a predetermined formula. Perhaps the most famous proposal for a fixed rule is the monetarist suggestion, offered by Milton Friedman, that monetary policy should be limited to having a fixed growth rate of money, no matter what happens. Obviously, such a proposal is based on a deep distrust of any policy activism whatsoever. A typical feedback rule is one in which interest rates are raised or lowered in response to deviations of the unemployment rate from the natural rate.

Some actions simply cannot be bound by rules. When extremely unusual events occur, there will typically be no formal rules available for policymakers to use. A good example of a truly discretionary action was the monetary policy that came after the stock market collapse of Friday, October 13, 1987. After the Dow Jones Industrial Average (an index of stock prices on the New York Stock Exchange) had plummeted over 500 points in a single day, the Federal Reserve chairman loosened the reins on monetary policy and directly intervened with several securities houses to ensure them that they would have adequate liquidity the next day. This action is widely credited with having staved off a much deeper crisis after the stock market collapse.

19-6 SOME ASPECTS OF ACTUAL GOVERNMENT BEHAVIOR

We have been discussing the normative theory of economic policy, or how policymakers *should* behave. There is, however, another dimension to the theory of economic policy, that of positive theory, or how policymakers actually *do* behave. In this section, we look briefly at several different aspects of positive theory of government behavior. As you might guess, governments often deviate sharply from the policies suggested by the normative theory.

To start with, we must recognize that the public sector is not a single entity. Thus, any given government action is generally the result of several decisions taken at several different levels. Not only is the central government divided among branches (executive, legislative, and regulatory), but the central government is only one of the players. Others include local and regional governments, a central bank, semiautonomous agencies, public enterprises, and so on. These government institutions enjoy varying degrees of autonomy from the central administration.

An action that appears puzzling if we assume that it comes from a single policymaker can make eminent sense once we recognize how power is divided. For example, a recent study of Latin America has shown that expansionary government policies in the 1970s and early 1980s were often tied to state enterprises, regional governments, and quasi-fiscal expenditures of the central bank, rather than directly to the budget of the central government.[24] Thus, even when the finance minister was a fiscal conservative, very large and chronic budget deficits were often outside his control.

In general, a full positive theory of economic policymaking must focus on several dimensions of the political structure. What are the institutions that decide on economic policy? What are the incentives facing individuals within these institutions? Are there power centers that compete over a particular kind of policy, such as fiscal management? What are the electoral laws that govern political competition? Is the electorate economically literate enough to monitor the policy actions of politicians effectively? Is there a free press and free speech to allow for public oversight of economic policymaking? While we cannot explore these questions at length, they do suggest the complexity of formulating a positive theory of economic policymaking.

Rather than summarizing a general theory, let us take a single issue and see what the positive theory of policymaking adds to the normative theory. A general pattern that we have frequently mentioned is the tendency of governments to pursue overly expansionary fiscal policies. Several explanations have been put forward to explain this behavior. One, the inflationary bias of time-consistent policies, we have just discussed. But there are other explanations as well that rest on political as well as economic considerations.

First, there is the political business cycle, in which incumbent administrations attempt to influence election results by pursuing expansionary fiscal and monetary policies just before an election. Several analysts have carefully documented the existence of cyclical policy expansions timed to precede elections. Policy contractions—when they occur—generally follow the elections.[25]

Second, governments formed by a coalition of many parties may have difficulty agreeing on an unpopular austerity program when one is necessary. The empirical evidence shows that coalition governments had a hard time limiting the growth of government spending after the adverse supply shocks of the 1970s and therefore ended up with much larger budget deficits than did governments that were controlled by a single political party.[26] It has

---

[24] See Felipe Larrain and Marcelo Selowsky, eds., *The Public Sector and the Latin American Crisis* (San Francisco: ICS Press, International Center for Economic Growth, 1991).

[25] Two classic works on the political business cycle are Edward Tufte, *Political Control of the Economy* (Princeton, N.J.: Princeton University Press, 1978), and William Nordhaus, "The Political Business Cycle," *Review of Economic Studies*, April 1975.

[26] See Nouriel Roubini and Jeffrey Sachs, "Political and Economic Determinants of Budget Deficits in the Industrial Democracies," *European Economic Review*, May 1989.

also been suggested that in countries in which political power changes frequently between rival political parties, there may be a bias toward overly expansionary fiscal policies. The incumbent government knows that its successor will likely be the rival party, and thus the government in power is disposed to leave its rival with a burden of higher public debt.[27]

Third, politicians may care mainly about economic performance when they are in office, and not about the adjustments that will be needed later on. Thus, they may try to borrow whenever loanable funds are available, despite the fact that debt repayments will pose a heavy burden in the future. The issue here is whether the general public is well enough informed, and has sufficient influence, to temper the short-term biases of the politicians. In many countries in the 1970s, the answer was clearly no. In Chapter 22 we shall see how the development of the world capital markets in the early 1970s suddenly allowed many governments to borrow freely on world markets for the first time. Many governments went on spending sprees, either to finance grandiose investment programs or to finance the large budget deficits that followed from large domestic subsidies.

When we study hyperinflations in Chapter 23, we shall look at the concept of "weak" governments that do not have the political support or the institutional power necessary to control fiscal spending. By their nature, weak governments find it difficult to resist the pressures coming from different sectors of society and tend to increase spending in their attempt to satisfy these groups. At the same time, however, they have no ability to finance these expenses from tax collections, and this generates the huge fiscal deficits that set the stage for very high inflation.

Finally, in Chapter 23 we shall examine the puzzling issue of why governments postpone stabilization efforts. Waiting to attack a high inflation only aggravates the damage it does to the economy, yet governments may do just that if they become paralyzed by a struggle between different groups over how to distribute the costs of the stabilization program. Only with the emergence of a winner—by election, by coup, or more rarely, by a compromise between the competing groups—can the confrontation end and the stabilization begin.[28]

19-7 SUMMARY

The *normative theory of economic policy* analyzes how policymakers should act. Pioneering work on this subject was made by the Dutch economist Jan Tinbergen, who delineated the crucial steps of economic policymaking. First, the goals of economic policy are specified, usually in a *social welfare function* that the policymaker attempts to maximize. Based on it, the policymaker identifies the economic *targets*. Second, policy *instruments* available to reach the targets must be identified. Third, the policymaker must have a model of the economy linking the instruments to the targets, so as to choose the optimal value of the policy instruments.

---

[27] See Alberto Alesina and Guido Tabellini, "A Positive Theory of Fiscal Deficits and Government Debt in a Democracy," National Bureau of Economic Research Working Paper, No. 2308, 1987.

[28] See Alberto Alesina and Alan Drazen, "Why Are Stabilizations Delayed?" *American Economic Review,* forthcoming.

A widely accepted set of macroeconomic targets is full employment and zero inflation. Available instruments are, broadly speaking, monetary policy and fiscal policy. Tinbergen analyzed the theory of economic policy in a simple linear framework. When there are two targets and two instruments available, policymakers can achieve the desired level of both targets as long as the effects of the instruments on the targets are *linearly independent*. More generally, the policymaker will have many targets and many available instruments. If there are N targets, these targets may be satisfied as long as there are at least N linearly independent instruments.

The various policy instruments may in fact be under the control of different policymakers. Monetary policy, for example, may be controlled by the central bank and fiscal policy by the executive and legislative branches. If policymakers do not coordinate their policies as Tinbergen supposed, there may still be a way to arrive at the optimal policy mix in a decentralized manner. The solution is to assign each target to the instrument (and hence to the policymaker) that has the strongest relative effect on that particular target. This is known as the *effective market classification* approach, introduced by Robert Mundell.

When there are fewer instruments than targets, it will not be possible to attain all targets simultaneously. Society will face the familiar problem of a trade-off between the different goals. In this case, it is useful to define a social loss function that represents the costs to society of deviations of the targets from the optimum values. Policymakers should then chose the targets so as to minimize the social loss. An example of this problem is the goal of eliminating inflation when it can only be done at a cost in terms of lost output.

In reality, the problem of policymakers is much more complicated than an insufficient number of instruments relative to targets. Economic authorities, for example, have to work under conditions of *uncertainty*. Here, the crucial point is the type of uncertainty that policymakers face. If it comes from exogenous shocks outside the control of policymakers such as bad weather (*additive uncertainty*), then uncertainty may not greatly affect the optimal choice of policies. Under conditions of a linear model and a quadratic loss function, in fact, additive uncertainty may simply be ignored, by setting the uncertain variables at the expected levels. This result is known as *certainty equivalence*. If, on the other hand, uncertainty refers to the effects of instruments on targets (*multiplicative uncertainty*), then policymakers should in general be more cautious—less activist—in the use of instruments.

In some cases, policymakers have a choice of instruments in that they can choose instrument A or B, but not both. The monetary authority might have the choice of controlling interest rates or the stock of money, for example. As William Poole demonstrated, the choice of instrument depends on the source of shocks in the economy. When the money demand function is highly unstable, for example, then the interest rate should be preferred instrument; when the investment demand is highly unstable, however, then a money supply rule may be more appropriate.

The most forceful attack against the standard approach to economic policy came from Robert Lucas in the mid-1970s, in the so-called *Lucas critique*. Tinbergen's framework was based on the idea that there is a stable quantitative relationship linking policy instruments to targets, and the idea was implemented using large-scale econometric models. Lucas argued that the large-scale models are unreliable, in that when government policies change sharply, the policy coefficients of the econometric models are likely to prove unreliable. In essence, he argued that the large-scale models fail to treat expectations appropriately, and thus are unlikely to be effective in predicting the effects of changes in policy rules. The practical importance of the Lucas critique is still a subject of active debate.

Most crucial issues regarding policymaking relate to a sequence of actions taken over a period of time. Starting at some initial point, the policymaker must judge what are the best actions to take over a certain time period. Should the policymaker be bound by predetermined *rules*, or should he be free to act with *discretion* at each point in time? We have found that rules are useful in cases where the optimal policy is *time inconsistent*, in the sense that policymakers would be tempted to "cheat" on a preannounced optimal policy at a later stage. Put differently, the *time-consistent* policy, in which the policy choice is made at each point in time, can be distinctly inferior to setting a policy course at the beginning of a long period and then sticking to it.

An example of the time-consistency issue is anti-inflation policy. The optimal policy may be to promise monetary restraint and then stick to it. But such a course is also likely to be time inconsistent, since once the central bank makes the promise of low inflation—and the unions act on the promise by agreeing to low wage increases—there may be a big incentive of the central bank to renege on the promise in order to expand output in the short run. It is precisely this incentive to cheat that takes away credibility from the announced low-inflation policy.

There is also a *positive theory of economic policy*, which studies how policymakers actually behave. Quite frequently, governments deviate sharply from the policies suggested by the normative theory. A starting point for understanding this discrepancy is to recognize that policymaking is not usually performed by a single government entity. Government actions are the result of several decisions taken at many different and often competing levels (central, regional, and local governments; decentralized agencies; public enterprises; central bank).

The positive theory of economic policy has shed light on an apparent general tendency of governments to pursue overly expansionary fiscal policies. Several reasons for this tendency have been adduced, in addition to time-consistency problems. First, there may be a *political business cycle*, in which incumbent administrations pursue expansionary policies just before elections to influence the election results. Second, governments formed by *coalitions* of several parties may find it hard to agree on unpopular though necessary austerity measurers. Third, necessary stabilization may be postponed because of a struggle between different groups of society on how to distribute the costs of the stabilization program.

Key Concepts

normative theory of economic policy	certainty equivalence
targets	policy activism
linear independence	Lucas critique
effective market classification	credibility
	discretion

fixed rules
positive theory of economic
  policy
social welfare function
instruments
additive uncertainty
multiplicative uncertainty

mutually exclusive instruments
time consistency
time inconsistency
rules
feedback rules
political business cycle

Problems and Questions

1. Assume that policymakers want to achieve low inflation and full employment. Discuss the available instruments to attain those objectives in the following cases:

  a. A closed economy.
  b. A small open economy with full capital mobility.
  c. A small open economy with complete capital controls.
  d. A large open economy with full capital mobility.

2. Consider an economy in which policymakers want to increase the level of output without raising inflation. Assume that the effects of policy instruments on the targets can be represented, in deviations from the baseline, as:

$$\Delta Q = 1.3\Delta G + 0.3\Delta M$$
$$\Delta \hat{P} = 0.15\Delta G + 0.1\Delta M$$

where $\hat{P}$ represents the inflation rate and ΔQ, ΔG, and ΔM are expressed as percentages of Q.

  a. Are fiscal and monetary policy linearly independent instruments? What does the system of equations imply about the shape of the aggregate supply curve in this economy?
  b. What policy mix would achieve a rise of 2 percent in the level of output without raising inflation?
  c. Now assume that $\Delta \hat{P} = 2\Delta Q$. Is there any policy mix that would achieve the objectives in (b)? Why?

3. Discuss the benefits and disadvantages of having policymakers coordinate their policies rather than assigning one target to each policy instrument? Which of the two cases is better for achieving economic objectives? Why?

4. In some countries, the central bank is independent from the government. Consider a situation in which the government wants to reduce inflation without changing output, but the central bank would not change monetary policy.

  a. Can the government achieve its objectives by using only fiscal policy? Why?
  b. Assume that the effect of instruments on targets in this economy are represented by the following model (in deviations from the baseline):

$$\Delta Q = \Delta G + 0.2\Delta M$$
$$\Delta \hat{P} = 0.1\Delta G + 0.1\Delta M$$

and the loss function is

$$L = (\Delta Q - \Delta Q^*)^2 + (\Delta \hat{P} - \Delta \hat{P}^*)^2$$

What is the optimal fiscal policy that the government should pursue when its objectives are to reduce inflation by two points without changing the level of output, if the central bank does not change monetary policy? What is the value of the loss function?

   c. Assume now that the central bank decides to cooperate. What is the optimal policy mix? What is the value of the loss function?

5. How should policymakers respond to different types of uncertainties about the effects of their policies on the targets? How does your answer depend on the functional form of the loss function?

6. Consider a small open economy with full capital mobility in which policymakers want to stabilize the level of output. They have to decide between fixing the exchange rate (and they would lose control over the supply of money) or choosing the level of money supply (and they would not control the exchange rate). Which of the two policies would you recommend if the economy is subjected to shocks from the *IS* curve? Which would you recommend if the shocks come from the demand for money?

7. According to the Lucas critique, econometric models would predict better the consequences of small policy changes than of large ones. True or false? Explain.

8. Consider a government that wants to provide cheap housing to its population. In order to promote the construction of apartment buildings, the government promises not to impose rent control programs in the future.

   a. Once the apartment buildings are in place, would the government want to keep its promise not to impose rent controls?

   b. If the private sector knows that the government will not keep its promise, would they have the same incentive to construct apartment buildings?

   c. What is the optimal policy for the government to pursue? What is the time-consistent policy?

9. Discuss under what conditions it is better that policymakers' actions be limited by rules and when it is better for them to have discretion over policy choices.

10. What is the difference between positive and normative theories of economic policy? Consider an economy that is suffering from high inflation. Under which political conditions do you think that policymakers would be more willing to instrument a strong anti-inflationary program?

Financial Markets

We have so far assumed only three kinds of assets, money, domestic bonds, and foreign bonds. This simplification is useful for studying many problems in economics. Financial markets, however, are much more complex than this. In fact, there are many kinds of financial assets, including equity claims to the capital of corporations, bonds of different maturities, and more sophisticated securities, like options. There are also a wide variety of financial intermediaries, such as banks, money market funds, mutual funds, and insurance companies. These intermediaries take the savings of households and firms and reinvest them in other financial assets. Because of the variety of financial assets, there is no such a thing as a single interest rate or rate of return; rather there is a whole array of returns on alternative assets.

What purpose is served by having such a wide range of assets? When we first discussed the role of financial assets and the real interest rate, we showed how the existence of financial assets facilitates the intertemporal allocation of resources, and how the interest rate is a crucial factor in determining saving and investment. But just a few assets could serve to play this intertemporal role. The reason for the wide range of assets is quite different: it is to enable households and firms to reduce their risks as they manage their wealth. In general, economic agents dislike risk; that is, they are *risk averse*. As a result, they hold a wide *portfolio*—that is, a collection—of financial assets in order to spread their risks.

We start our study of financial markets with a discussion about various institutional aspects of financial markets in the United States and the rest of the world. We then go on to analyze how investors choose among the variety of financial assets available to them. First, we turn to the issue of how a risk-averse investor should choose an optimal portfolio of financial assets. This portfolio analysis sets the basis for the modern theory of financial market equilibrium, known as the "capital asset pricing model." Then we look at two particular choices, between domestic and foreign bonds and between short-term and long-term bonds.

20-1 SOME INSTITUTIONAL ASPECTS OF FINANCIAL MARKETS: THE U.S. CASE

What kinds of financial assets are available to investors in the United States? What markets are these assets traded in? And what about *financial intermediaries,* such as banks, which intermediate—that is, stand between—ultimate savers and ultimate borrowers of funds and facilitate their exchanges? While some characteristics of the U.S. market apply to financial markets in other countries as well, other characteristics are specific to the United States.

Financial Instruments and Markets

Individuals and institutions in the United States have many investment alternatives, including domestic financial instruments, real assets (real estate, land, precious metals, works of art, and so on), and foreign assets. The distinguishing feature of financial assets, or *securities,* is that they represent a contractual right to receive future payments if the conditions stated in the contract are met. Bonds, for example, represent a loan by the investor to another economic agent (a household, firm, or government) and promise repayments by the borrower to the bondholder. Bonds are a type of *fixed-income* security, in that the repayment stream on the bond is usually fixed at the time that the bond is issued. Stocks represent a claim on ownership on a corporation and entitle the holder to a stream of future dividends that vary with the profitability of the enterprise. Stocks are *variable-income* securities, since the future dividends are not fixed but rather depend on future profits.

Fixed-Income Assets: Bonds   There are many different types of bonds. Bonds are distinguished by their *terms to maturity,* that is, the time horizon of the loan. We thus find short-term, medium-term, and long-term bonds. For a given maturity, another important distinguishing factor is the *timing of payments. Coupon bonds* pay a fixed amount of interest periodically and the principal of the loan (or face value) at maturity. *Zero-coupon bonds* do not pay any interest, but just pay their face value at maturity. Investors obtain a positive return by purchasing these bonds at a discount. For example, an individual may pay $90.9 for a bond with a face value of $100 which is due in one year. The implicit rate of interest on such a bond is 10 percent, since $100/$90.9 = 1.10 = 1 + 10\%$.

Bonds are usually issued by various governmental bodies or by private corporations. Bonds issued by the U.S. Treasury Department have different names depending on their term to maturity. *Treasury bills* are short-term obligations, with maturity of up to 1 year; *Treasury notes* are government securities with maturities from 1 to 10 years; and *Treasury bonds* are longer-term assets, with maturities ranging from 10 years to 30 years. Local governments also issue their own long-term obligations, commonly called *municipal bonds.*

Bonds that do not have the backing of the federal government involve the risk of default if the issuing entity experiences heavy financial strains. Corporate and municipal bonds fall into this category. Several companies have specialized in rating bonds according to the probability of their repayment, the best known of which are Standard & Poor's Corporation and

Moody's Investors Service. Standard & Poor's ranking, for example, classifies bonds in a scale that goes from AAA to D, with many intermediate categories. AAA indicates the best bonds, judged to have a very high probability of full repayment; D is reserved for those obligations in default.

Private corporations have turned increasingly to financing their long-term investment projects through bond issues.[1] Only reputable firms in solid financial health can obtain financing in this way at market interest rates close to those paid by the U.S. Treasury. Companies considered less solid have to pay higher interest rates. Very risky businesses may have to issue very-high-yield bonds, the so-called *junk bonds*, to attract investors.

Other Fixed-Income Assets   Many types of fixed-income assets exist in addition to bonds. Perhaps the most common of these are deposits made at banking institutions. There are several kinds of bank accounts that allow the privilege of writing checks against them and which pay interest on the balance maintained. Among them are checking accounts, negotiable orders of withdrawal (NOW) accounts, and money market accounts. Savings deposits have somewhat less liquidity. In some cases, depositors are required to give notice 30 days before a withdrawal, although many savings accounts provide funds on demand. Savings accounts differ crucially from other demand deposits in that they normally do not involve checking privileges.

Variable-Income Assets   *Common stocks* of corporations are the quintessential variable-income assets. Every common share of a given company is a claim to the residual net income of that company, that is, the income after all expenses and taxes are paid. Every common share also represents a right of ownership over the firm. Shareholders vote for the directors of the corporation and can vote directly on many policies. Because shareholders are residual claimants, they are the "last in line" for payment in case the company must be liquidated. Creditors are paid before the shareholder receives any money. However, the liability of shareholders as owners of a corporation is limited. If the corporation ends up with negative net worth, the individual shareholders lose the value of their claim, but they cannot be required to put in more money to pay off the debts of the corporation.

Preferred stock is a cross between a bond and a common share of stock. This kind of asset establishes a given, fixed payment per year which is classified as a dividend (rather than as an interest payment). Unlike bonds, preferred stocks have an indefinite life. Such stocks are "preferred" in the sense that their (fixed) dividend must be paid before dividends are distributed to holders of common stocks. However, if the revenues of a corporation are not sufficient to pay contractual dividends to preferred stockholders in a given year, the corporation incurs no liability. In this case, nonpayment does not constitute a default as it does with a bond.

A more sophisticated type of variable-income asset is a *stock option*. Although options may be purchased on many different assets, the most

---

[1] The trend of companies toward higher reliance on debt financing—as opposed to equity financing—was a major characteristic of the 1980s. At the beginning of the 1990s, however, there were increasing signals of firms shifting their financing strategy away from debt and into equity. This has been attributed to an increasing awareness of the risks facing highly leveraged, that is, highly indebted, companies, in the wake of the difficulties experienced by the leveraged takeovers of the late 1980s.

common form of financial option is that on stock. A *call option* grants the option holder the right to purchase a given amount of shares of a corporation at a specific price within a given period of time. A *put option,* on the other hand, gives the right to *sell* a given number of shares of a corporation at a specific price within a given period of time.

Evidence on Asset Holdings   It is interesting to see how, faced with all these financial alternatives, investors actually hold their wealth. Table 20-1 shows a recent estimate of how household wealth in the United States is divided among different assets. The most important asset, with almost 35 percent of the total, is equities. This is followed by time and savings deposits, with some 19 percent, and then by U.S. government securities. It is perhaps surprising that corporate bonds account for only a tiny fraction of total household assets, as do foreign assets. In the latter case, the figure reported probably understates the true value of financial holdings of U.S. nationals abroad, since the foreign assets that households own are difficult for government agencies to monitor and track.

Markets   Many of the financial assets that we have talked about are traded in organized markets. *Primary markets* are those that conduct sales of newly issued securities to original buyers. When the General Motors Corporation wants to finance a project with long-term bonds, for example, it sells these bonds in a primary market. *Secondary markets*, on the other hand, trade

TABLE   20-1

FINANCIAL ASSETS HELD BY U.S. HOUSEHOLDS, 1988

	Value (US$ billion)	Proportion of the Total (percentage)
Checkable deposits and currency	505	4.2%
Time and savings deposits	2,236	18.4
Money market fund shares	298	2.5
Life insurance policies	313	2.6
Pension fund reserves	2,585	21.3
Mutual fund shares	417	3.4
Equity in business	4,222	34.8
Credit market instruments		
U.S. Treasury securities	569	4.7
Federal agency securities	222	1.8
Tax-exempt securities	268	2.2
Corporate and foreign bonds	72	0.6
Mortgages	111	0.9
Other	321	2.6
Total assets	12,139	100.0%

Source: Statistical Abstract of the United States, 1990 *(Washington, D.C.: U.S. Government Printing Office, 1990).*

previously owned securities. This distinction is important. When a newly issued share of IBM is sold, the proceeds of the sale accrue to IBM, but when a previously issued share is traded, the proceeds go to the owner of the shares. Secondary markets help corporations to sell their original issues of stocks or bonds by adding liquidity to those assets.

Secondary markets have a substantially higher volume of trading than do the primary markets, and they are much better known. Examples include the New York Stock Exchange (NYSE), by far the most important secondary market in the United States, and the American Stock Exchange (AMEX). Stocks, bonds, options, and other financial assets are traded on both exchanges. There are also some regional exchanges that function in cities like Boston, Cincinnati, and Philadelphia. In all these *exchange* markets, transactions of assets occur in a central location, in a single, physical place. The so-called *over-the-counter (OTC) market* represents another way to organize secondary market transactions. In the OTC market, dealers operating in geographically different places are connected through computer terminals where they place their bids or asking prices for securities.

Financial Intermediaries

Financial transactions may occur directly between borrowers and lenders, as when the Treasury sells government bonds to households, or they may occur through intermediaries, as when a bank invests its depositors funds in real estate loans. Financial intermediaries arise mainly because transactions costs are often too large for direct transactions between borrowers and lenders of funds. Individual savers normally do not have the resources, the time, or the information to evaluate prospective borrowers. Financial intermediaries specialize in evaluating potential borrowers, and thus are efficient institutions for channeling funds from savers to borrowers.

We can distinguish among several types of financial intermediaries according to the specific nature of their business: depository institutions, institutional investors, and investment intermediaries. Commercial banks are the best known, most traditional type of *depository institution*. Banks accept deposits from the public in various types of accounts—checking, NOW, money market, savings—and they also obtain funds through the sale of certificates of deposit. Banks pay an interest rate on these liabilities of theirs, and they seek to lend out these funds at a higher rate to various borrowers. The difference between the interest rate paid out to depositors and the lending rates paid in by borrowers, the "spread," is the traditional source of income in banking. (When there are widespread defaults on the loans that a bank has made, however, the spread in effect becomes negative.)

The United States has an extraordinarily high number of banks, almost 15,000 during the late 1980s. This is partly a result of state restrictions that prohibit banks from opening branches outside their home state, a policy derived from the McFadden Act of 1927. The five largest U.S. banks, measured by assets, are Citibank, N.A. (New York), Chase Manhattan Bank (New York), Bank of America (California), Chemical Bank (New York), and Morgan Guaranty Trust (New York).

Savings and loan associations (S&Ls) and mutual savings banks are similar types of depository institutions. For a long time, these entities could accept only savings deposits and could make loans only in the form of mortgages to finance housing. The wave of financial deregulation in the 1980s freed them to undertake many new kinds of business. But as the accompanying box shows, the results of this deregulation were disastrous. Because of special circumstances—a decline in S&L's net worth at the end of the 1970s, prior to deregulation—and because the government extended insurance on deposits in the S&Ls—these institutions were encouraged to borrow and lend recklessly, and sometimes fraudulently, in the 1980s. Credit unions are still another type of depository institutions. They receive deposits only from members of the credit union, who usually have a common employer, and they make loans, which tend to be short term, only to members.

A second category of financial intermediaries includes the so-called *"institutional investors,"* composed mainly of insurance companies, pension funds, and mutual funds. Insurance companies receive premiums from individuals and institutions who insure their property or lives (in the case of people) against unforeseen risks. Pension funds receive periodic contributions from employees and employers and provide retirement income to workers. They are, by their very nature, long-term investors who place their funds in both stocks and bonds. Private pension plans are managed by a financial institution, usually a bank or an insurance company, or by the employer company. Mutual funds and money market funds are *investment intermediaries*, that is, financial institutions that attract resources from many small investors and invest them in large portfolios of stocks and bonds. In this way, any investor with a small amount of assets can enjoy the benefits of diversification without the need to incur large transaction and information costs. Those who hold shares in these funds receive a share of the dividends, interest payments, and capital gains of the underlying assets.

The Regulation of Financial Intermediaries

Financial markets are not like markets for physical commodities where the goods being traded are delivered immediately. In a financial transaction, the purchaser receives an obligation of payments *at some future date*, and thus these transactions are based on the investor's confidence that the obligation will be fulfilled. Because financial instruments involve future commitments that may or may not be fulfilled, financial markets are susceptible to a wide variety of maladies, such as frauds and panics, that are not characteristic of other markets. For this reason, governments have recognized the need for firm regulation of financial markets. And when that need has been forgotten, as in the United States in the 1980s, the results have often been disastrous.

Financial regulations are drawn up to accomplish two primary objectives. One goal is to provide information to all potential investors so that they can make their decisions with adequate knowledge. In the service of this goal, the Securities and Exchange Commission (SEC) requires companies that issue securities to provide detailed information about their financial condition. This provision was first established in the Securities Act of 1933. All players who issue or trade securities are now asked for detailed information about their business situation and their activities.

The second goal of these regulations is to ensure the adequate health of all financial intermediaries so that investors' savings may be secure. Toward this end, banking institutions are required to maintain a minimum ratio of bank capital to total assets (now 6 percent). The higher the capital ratio, the stronger the position of a bank in the face of decreasing asset values. We shall see in Chapter 22 how the developing country debt crisis nearly bankrupted the major international commercial banks. Partly in response to that crisis, international bank regulators have been pressing the banks to increase their ratios of bank capital to assets.

If a bank fails in spite of all provisions to ensure its financial health, the government has set up an insurance scheme which guarantees the assets of depositors. The Federal Deposit Insurance Corporation (FDIC) has been insuring deposits in commercial banks since the aftermath of the Great Depression in the 1930s. Today, all bank deposits of $100,000 or less are guaranteed by the FDIC, and the banks have to pay an insurance premium for this service. A similar institution, the Federal Savings and Loan Insurance Corporation (FSLIC), was set up to insure deposits of up to $100,000 in savings and loan associations. The recent failure of many S&Ls put the FSLIC itself into insolvency, however, and the government has had to use taxpayer dollars to pay off depositors in the failed S&Ls, as we discuss in Box 20-1.

The existence of deposit insurance has been a crucial element in avoiding *bank runs* when rumors about problems in a financial institution circulate. A bank run occurs when depositors, hearing a rumor (which may well be false) that the bank is insolvent, all come to the bank at once to retrieve their funds. Even if the bank is fundamentally healthy, a bank run can cause the bank to collapse because generally it cannot liquidate its long-term investments rapidly enough to satisfy the depositors. The FDIC and the FSLIC have succeeded in reducing substantially the number of bank runs, but at the cost of other serious problems. With deposit insurance, potential depositors know that their money will be safe, so they never worry and usually do not ask about the quality of bank management in choosing their bank. But because the depositors do not monitor the bank management, the regulators must do so. This they manifestly failed to do with the S&Ls in the 1980s.

20-2 INSTITUTIONAL CHANGES IN GLOBAL FINANCIAL MARKETS

Since the early 1960s, financial markets around the world have become more and more integrated. Wealthholders have expanded their horizons, seeking diversification in foreign assets. In particular, institutional investors, such as insurance companies and pension funds, have turned increasingly to investments in foreign assets. Individual investors have followed this trend as well. Borrowers of funds have also looked abroad to satisfy their needs. Corporations, and even governments, have increasingly relied on external markets for financing by issuing securities that are sold to foreign investors. A case in point is the U.S. government. Out of its total debt at the end of 1990, about 20 percent was held by foreigners.

As part of this trend, financial institutions have abandoned their previous confinement to domestic capital markets and have turned increasingly to the international arena. Many banks have moved to establish a foothold in foreign markets through a network of offices abroad. In 1960, for example,

Box 20-1
The Savings and Loan Crisis: A Case of Lax Regulatory Control

In the late 1970s, interest rates rose to unprecedented levels in the United States. Savings and loans associations were badly hurt by this interest-rate increase because their assets were mostly long-term financial instruments in the form of fixed-interest mortgages, while their liabilities were primarily short-term deposits. Thus, higher interest rates forced them to pay more to depositors without receiving more from the existing portfolios of long-term loans. In present value terms, the high interest rates depressed the value of the S&Ls' assets relative to their liabilities and thereby threatened their solvency.

Depositors in S&Ls would have had good reason to worry about their funds were it not for the fact that their deposits were covered up to $100,000 in each account by insurance from the Federal Savings and Loan Insurance Corporation. In principle, the insurance fund was supposed to be financed out of charges to the S&Ls, which had to pay a certain proportion of their deposits into the fund. With so many S&Ls in trouble in the late 1980s, however, it became clear that the FSLIC lacked the funds to cover the depositors. Nonetheless, most people expected the U.S. government to make up for any losses incurred by the FSLIC, which is just what has happened.

With their funds insured, depositors had no incentive to take a closer look at the financial health of the S&Ls. They simply deposited their money with whoever paid the highest interest rate, a process that continued to drive interest rates up in the savings and loan market. Many S&Ls were essentially broke. The only chance their owners had to salvage something from the situation was to take big gambles using their depositors' money and hope that their long-shot ventures would succeed. But they also knew that if these projects failed, their capital was lost anyway, and that bill, that is, the cost of further gambling, would be paid by the FSLIC. In the end, the risky ventures mostly came crashing down, and the amount of S&L losses reached huge proportions.

But if depositors did not check the S&Ls behavior, what happened to the other parties that might have? The role of *government regulators* was especially lax during the 1980s. This was partly due to understaffing of the institutions that had the responsibility and the undertraining of their employees. An important part of the blame, however, must be placed on the financial deregulation of the early 1980s. In the philosophy of the Reagan administration, all economic regulation was considered bad, and efforts to supervise the banking industry were relaxed. The S&Ls were given more opportunities to gamble with—and ultimately lose—their depositors money, just a time when regulations should have been tightened.

The Bush administration has tackled this problem through the creation of a new institution, the Resolution Trust Corporation (RTC), that will take over the responsibilities of the FSLIC. This agency is in charge of liquidating or selling the insolvent S&Ls. The job facing the RTC is particularly tough, if only because the cost of cleaning up the S&L crisis has reached such vast proportions. As recently as 1987, some analysts estimated that the total cost of the bailout would be around $22 billion.[2] Failure to act promptly has only worsened the situation. Only two years later, by early 1989, the cost estimates had reached almost $190 billion.[3] In mid-1990, the estimated cost to taxpayers of the S&L crisis had soared further, with some estimates reaching $300 billion or higher. As of mid-1990, predictions were that the government would have to take over some 800 failed S&Ls.

only eight U.S. banks had branches in foreign countries, with assets of less than $4 billion. By 1988, more than 200 U.S. banks held branches abroad, with assets of almost $500 billion. A similar number of foreign banks operated over 600 offices in the United States.

When banks operate abroad, they typically take deposits and make loans in currencies other than that of the host country. U.S., European, and Japanese banks operating in London, for example, will take deposits and make loans not only in British pounds, but also in dollars, other European currencies, and yen. The market for bank deposits and bank loans in international currencies, typically called the *Eurocurrency market*, has boomed since the 1950s. The size of the market in terms of bank deposits in offshore currencies was estimated at over $3 trillion in 1987. Of these, some three quarters were Eurodollars (that is, dollar-denominated accounts).

Sources of Financial Globalization

The globalization of international financial markets is the result of many factors, among them, the increased volume of international trade, technological improvements, and the deregulation of cross-border transactions.

During the last three decades, international trade has increased at a faster pace than world output. Between 1964 and 1985, the dollar value of international trade grew at an average annual rate of 12.4 percent, while the dollar value of world output grew at an annual rate of 10.4 percent, as shown in Table 20-2. The greater openness in trade has required a growing trade in financial services and cross-border lending. However, the growth of international trade by itself cannot explain the spectacular expansion of international financial transactions since the 1960s. As shown in Table 20-2, international lending by banks has increased at an average annual rate of about 26 percent between 1964 and 1985, two-and-a-half times more than the increase in world output.

Technological progress in communications and data processing has also been an important factor in the expansion of international financial transactions. More powerful computers, improved computer software, and progress in the telecommunications sector have increased the speed and reduced the cost of information flows and transactions. Financial exchanges

---

[2] Dan Brumbaugh and Andrew Carron, "Thrift Industry Crisis: Causes and Solutions," *Brookings Papers on Economic Activity*, No. 2, 1987.

[3] Dan Brumbaugh, Andrew Carron, and Robert Litan, "Cleaning Up the Depository Institution Mess," *Brookings Papers on Economic Activity*, No. 1, 1989.

TABLE 20-2

WORLD OUTPUT, FOREIGN TRADE, AND INTERNATIONAL BANKING, 1964–1985

	Billions of US$ (current prices)				Annual Rate of Growth (percent)			
	1964	1972	1980	1985	1964–72	1972–80	1980–85	1964–85
World GDP*	1,605	3,336	10,172	12,885	9.6%	15.0%	4.7%	10.4%
Foreign trade*	188	463	2,150	2,190	12.0	21.2	0.4	12.4
Net international bank credit	12	122	810	1,485	33.6	26.7	12.9	25.8
Gross international bank credit	20	208	1,559	2,598	34.0	28.6	10.8	26.1

* Excluding Soviet bloc.

Source: Ralph Bryant, ''The Internationalization of Financial Intermediation: An Empirical Survey,'' Brookings Discussion Papers in International Economics, No. 51, September 1986, Table 3-1, p. 11.

in different parts of the world such as New York, Tokyo, London, and Singapore are now interconnected with the new technology, ushering in the continuous, 24-hour-per-day trading of securities.

Even with these technological changes, world financial markets could not have developed so extensively had it not been for the progressive opening and deregulation of domestic markets for international financial transactions. During the period between 1870 and 1914, the "golden age of the gold standard," capital could move freely among the major countries, relatively unhindered by capital controls. In the aftermath of World War I, and especially during the Great Depression, most countries introduced capital controls to help them cope with the great monetary instability in the world economy. These regulations were gradually eased in the period following World War II, but capital controls of one form or another remained in place in most of the major industrial countries well into the 1970s, and in some countries, until the end of the 1980s.

Starting in the mid-1970s, most of the major industrial countries began a process of eliminating controls on international capital flows, as well as controls on the international trade in financial services. For example, the United States moved in the mid-1970s to liberalize the access of foreign companies to the domestic financial market and to deregulate lending outside the country by U.S. financial institutions. In 1978, foreign banks were allowed to enter the U.S. market under similar conditions as those applied to domestic banks, a practice called *national treatment*. By 1988, there were more than 500 foreign bank offices operating in the United States, with more than 20 percent of the total assets of the banking system.

In Germany, capital controls existed until the mid-1970s. The rights of foreigners to invest in domestic bonds and in money market instruments were restricted, as were interest payments on bank deposits to nonresidents. During the 1970s, these financial restrictions were gradually lifted. Deregulation of international transactions in France gained force in the middle to late 1980s. Restrictions on repatriation of earnings were relaxed, exchange controls were phased out, and the Eurofranc market for bonds was reopened and exempted from the general 10 percent withholding tax.[4]

The United Kingdom moved toward international financial liberalization in 1979, when it removed exchange controls on foreign transactions. Domestic financial markets were also deregulated in the early to mid-1980s, in a process that reached its climax in October 1986. A sweeping liberalization of capital markets took place on that date, the so-called "Big Bang," implemented under the Financial Services Act. As part of all this, important changes occurred in the stock market, and foreign financial firms were allowed to expand their business activities in the London financial market.

Japan has undertaken two broad financial liberalizations, one in 1979–1980 and the other starting in 1984.[5] Until the late 1970s, Japan still had

---

[4] For more details on this liberalizing trend, see Maxwell Watson et al., *International Capital Markets: Development and Prospects* (Washington, D.C.: International Monetary Fund, January 1988).

[5] For a good analysis of the liberalization of Japanese capital markets vis-à-vis the rest of the world up to 1984, see Jeffrey Frankel, *The Yen/Dollar Agreement: Liberalizing Japanese Capital Markets,* Policy Analyses in International Economics (Washington, D.C.: Institute for International Economics, December 1984).

major barriers to international capital flows. Then, in 1979, a policy change allowed nonresidents to hold Japanese yen–denominated financial assets, including bonds, certificates of deposit, and short-term repurchase agreements (*gensaki*). A new round of liberalization started in Japan in 1984, this time aimed at liberalizing capital outflows rather than capital inflows. The new measures included a relaxation of restrictions on Japanese bank lending abroad, the easing of restrictions on foreign companies wishing to borrow in yens in the Japanese market, and the liberalization of foreign investments by Japanese institutional investors such as pension funds and insurance companies.

More recently, the free-trade agreement between the United States and Canada, which came into effect in January 1990, promoted financial liberalization between the two countries. In fact, the negotiations were set in an environment of rapid growth in financial activity between the two neighbors. As part of the agreement, Canada is committed to eliminate various ceilings on ownership, asset growth, and market share which apply to foreign firms, especially in the financial sector. For example, U.S. commercial banks will no longer be bound by an overall 16 percent limit set on the share of the total assets of the Canadian banking system that foreign banks can own.[6]

Developing countries have also been part of the push to capital market liberalization. Many countries have encouraged the inflow of foreign capital, partly by allowing foreign investors to invest in the local stock exchange. One popular way of investing in foreign stock markets of developing countries is through the use of mutual funds as investment instruments. Investments in developing country mutual funds has been booming. Following the successful introduction of the "Korea fund" in the mid-1980s, which offered a diversified share of Korean stocks, several funds were started in the late 1980s to invest in the stock markets of Indonesia, Malaysia, the Philippines, and Thailand.[7]

International Financial Integration and Europe 1992

Certainly the most important recent push to full capital market integration comes in the context of Europe's goal of creating a *single market by 1992*. A sweeping range of liberalizing measures has spanned trade in goods, services, and capital movements as part of the 1992 project.[8]

Project 1992 establishes the goal of removing capital controls among the members of the European Community and significantly scaling down the restrictions on financial activities within the EC. A specific provision, however, allows member countries the transitory imposition of capital controls if financial market or balance-of-payments problems arise. To meet the objectives set for international financial transactions, the EC has established three principles: (1) *mutual recognition*, whereby each country must accept what

---

[6] For a more detailed analysis of the financial aspects of the free trade agreement between the United States and Canada, see Mark Allen et al., *International Capital Markets: Development and Prospects* (Washington, D.C.: International Monetary Fund, April 1989).

[7] As reported in *The Economist*, February 17, 1990, p. 17.

[8] Two good references on this topic are Vittorio Grilli, "Financial Markets and 1992," *Brookings Papers on Economic Activity*, No. 2, 1989, and Mark Allen et al., *International Capital Markets*.

others do in their domestic markets, especially in the authorization, reorganization, and supervision of financial firms; (2) *home-country control*, according to which the main supervisory responsibility for financial firms is borne by their country of origin (as opposed to the host country); and (3) *minimum harmonization* of regulations, so that home-country control does not collide with regulations in the host country.

All restrictions on capital flows have been eliminated as of July 1990, including deposit accounts and trade in securities. As a consequence, an EC agent can establish a deposit in any country and buy or sell securities any place. Certain countries—Greece, Ireland, Portugal, and Spain—have been granted extensions up to the end of 1992 to attain full liberalization. One of the main concerns here is how to avoid an increase in tax evasion given the differences in the national tax systems, and several proposals are being discussed in this respect.

Regarding financial activities, banks from EC countries will be allowed to do business anywhere in the EC, as long as they have authorization to operate in their home country. Cross-border operations will be conducted under home-country rules even if these differ from those in the host country (minimum harmonization should help in this matter). Commercial banks will also be allowed to undertake securities transactions, a traditional investment banking activity in the United States. For banks outside the EC, Project 1992 establishes the principle of reciprocity: non-EC banks could be denied entry into the EC if their countries of origin do not grant national treatment to EC banks.

Further liberalization is also planned for the trading of securities. The goal is to construct a united European securities market through the linking of member countries' exchanges. When this is achieved, a corporation registered on the Paris stock exchange would have the right to be listed and traded on all other EC exchanges—Frankfurt, London, Milan, and so on. By the same token, mutual funds authorized by one country could be marketed throughout the Community.

20-3 OPTIMAL PORTFOLIO SELECTION UNDER RISK AVERSION

We have seen that there is a very wide array of financial assets and that, with increasing ease, investors may choose to hold financial assets from markets around the world. In this section, we turn to the theoretical basis for choosing a portfolio among the range of assets available to investors. Under what conditions will investors demand various kinds of assets? What is the relationship between the demand for a financial asset and its riskiness and expected rate of return? The modern theory of *portfolio selection* offers us some insights into these important questions.

We start from the assumption that most investors are *risk averse*; that is, they care about reducing risks as well as maximizing expected returns. When agents care only about the expected returns on their portfolios, but not about the risks, we say that they are *risk neutral*. But if most agents were truly risk neutral, individuals would buy no insurance, nor would investors make any effort to diversify their financial portfolios. They would be content to hold just one asset—the one that promised the highest expected return. On the contrary, since agents buy insurance and go to great length to diversify their portfolios, the assumption that investors are risk averse seems a good one.

When agents are risk averse, they tend to allocate their wealth among the many different assets available.[9] The essential adage of portfolio theory for risk-averse investors is "don't put all your eggs in one basket." In the world of international finance, this translates into "don't put all your wealth in the financial assets of one country, or even one currency."

In formal terms, a *portfolio* is a collection of assets, both financial (money, bonds, stocks, and so on) and real (land, gold, paintings, and so on). Portfolio theory begins with the proposition that wealthholders should care about the characteristics of their entire portfolio rather than those of some individual component of the portfolio or any single asset. An asset that is extremely risky on its own may prove to be quite safe in a portfolio with other assets that offset its risk. Thus, we will assume that investors care about two crucial features of a risky portfolio: its *expected rate of return* and its *risk*, represented by the *variance* of the portfolio.

The basic theory of portfolio selection was first developed by Nobel laureate Harry Markowitz in a seminal paper published in the early 1950s.[10] Its most important insight is that agents aim to attain some optimum combination of risk and return in their portfolios. To reach that combination, the optimal investment strategy involves *portfolio diversification*, that is, holding a portfolio that has small amounts of a large number of financial assets.

In order to find out what the optimal portfolio behavior is, we first must see how the risk and returns of a portfolio are determined by the risk and returns on the assets contained in the portfolio. Once we have established the link between the characteristics of the portfolio and those of its underlying assets, we can then derive the optimal composition of an investment portfolio.

Expected Returns of a Portfolio

To determine the expected return of a portfolio of assets, let us start with the notion of the expected return of an individual asset. Suppose that there is a long-term bond of the Maxum Company and that this bond has a 50 percent probability of giving a 10 percent return and a 50 percent chance of yielding a 20 percent return. The *expected return* is a weighted average of all the possible returns, where the weights correspond to the probabilities of occurrence of each outcome. In this example, the expected return is 15 percent: $= 0.5(10\%) + 0.5(20\%)$. In general, if an asset yields returns r_1 with probability p_1, r_2 with probability p_2, r_3 with probability p_3, and so on, up to r_n with probability p_n, then the expected return r^e on the asset is simply

$$r^e = p_1r_1 + p_2r_2 + p_3r_3 + \cdots + p_nr_n \qquad (20.1)$$

The probabilities in (20.1) must sum to one: $p_1 + p_2 + p_3 + \cdots + p_n = 1$.

Suppose now that an investor holds N different assets in his portfolio. We assume that the investor has a given amount of wealth, W_0, which he invests in the n assets. The share of the overall portfolio invested in asset j is

[9] For a thorough and detailed analysis of this problem, see Chapters 6 and 7 of William Sharpe and Gordon Alexander, *Investments* (Englewood Cliffs, N.J.: Prentice Hall, 1990).

[10] "Portfolio Selection," Journal of Finance, March 1952.

denoted by a_j. In absolute terms, $a_j W_0$ is invested in the jth asset. Since the shares of all the assets must sum to one, we have $a_1 + a_2 + a_3 + \cdots + a_n = 1$.

Let us now calculate the expected return of the overall portfolio, which we denote r_p^e. We first determine the expected return of each of the N assets, according to the formula just derived. We denote these expected returns as $r_1^e, r_2^e, \ldots, r_n^e$, for assets 1, 2, $\ldots$, n, respectively. The *expected return of the portfolio* (r_p^e) is then calculated as the weighted average of the expected return of the n assets that are part of the portfolio, where the weights correspond to the share of the portfolio invested in each of the assets. Specifically,

$$r_p^e = a_1 r_1^e + a_2 r_2^e + \cdots + a_n r_n^e \qquad \textbf{(20.2)}$$

Thus, the expected return of a portfolio depends both on the expected returns of each of the underlying assets in the portfolio and on the fraction of wealth allocated to each asset.

To take a simple example, suppose that there are two assets, 1 and 2. Asset 1 has an expected return of 10 percent; asset 2 has an expected return of 20 percent. If the portfolio is divided equally between the two assets, so that $a_1 = a_2 = 0.5$, then the expected return of the portfolio is simply 15 percent: $= 0.5(10\%) + 0.5(20\%)$. If 75 percent is invested in asset 1 and 25 percent is invested in asset 2, then the expected return is 12.5 percent: $= 0.75(10\%) + 0.25(20\%)$.

While investors base their decisions on the expected returns (r_p^e) of the portfolio, the final consequences for their wealth depend on the *actual* returns. Suppose that someone starts with a level of wealth W_0 and invests all of it in a portfolio, the actual return of which is r_p. The final level of wealth, then, will be $W_1 = W_0(1 + r_p)$. Obviously, given W_0, W_1 depends only on the actual return r_p. But investors do not know r_p, and they must base their decisions on the information they have: the expected return (r_p^e) and the risk, to which we now turn.

Risk of a Portfolio

We can conveniently measure the riskiness of a portfolio by looking at the variance of the returns it gives. But let us examine the concept of variance first at the level of an individual asset. Suppose that an investor is confronted with two different assets, a stock in the Bank of Prudence, which always has a return of 8 percent, and a stock in the Bank of Gamble, which in bad years does not make any money (return: 0 percent), but earns huge profits in good years (return: 16 percent). Both stocks have an expected return of 8 percent. However, the stock of the Bank of Prudence has no risk, while that of the Bank of Gamble is risky, in the sense that its return is variable.

A commonly used statistical measure of risk is called "variance" (σ^2). Technically, the *variance* of the return of an asset is defined as the squared sum of deviations from the average return, where each deviation is weighted by the probability of occurrence of that particular return. Using our earlier notation, suppose that the asset has returns $r_1, r_2, \ldots, r_n$, with probabilities $p_1, p_2, \ldots, p_n$. The expected return is r^e, as defined earlier in equation (20.1). Then, the variance is defined as

$$\sigma^2 = p_1(r_1 - r^e)^2 + p_2(r_2 - r^e)^2 + \cdots + p_n(r_n - r^e)^2 \qquad \textbf{(20.3)}$$

In our example of the two banks, the expected return is 8 percent in both cases, but the variances are different. For the Bank of Prudence, the variance is $(8\% - 8\%)^2 = 0\%$. This is an asset with zero variance, that is, it is riskless. For the Bank of Gamble, the variance is

$$\sigma^2 = 0.5(0.0 - 0.08)^2 + 0.5(0.16 - 0.08)^2 = 0.64$$

The *standard deviation* (σ), another common measure of risk in portfolio analysis, is simply the square root of the variance. This would be 0 for the first asset and 0.8 for the second asset.

Our next step is to calculate the variance of the portfolio, σ_p^2, based on the risk characteristics of the underlying assets. The portfolio variance is not simply the weighted average of the variances of the underlying assets (as was true with the expected return of the portfolio). To see why it is not, let us look at an example.

Suppose an investor has stock in two companies, with half his wealth invested in each. One of the firms, Raincoats Unlimited, is a designer and distributor of raincoats. When a year is very rainy, which we suppose happens half of the time, the stock of this company has a return of 25 percent; when a year turns out to be sunny (the other half of the time), its return is only 5 percent. The other company, Sunglasses Limited, makes a 25 percent return in sunny years and only 5 percent when the year is unusually rainy. The expected return for both companies is 15 percent per year, and the variance is 0.01 in each case.[11] Does this mean that the variance in the investor's portfolio is also 1 percent (which is the weighted average of the two)?

The answer is clearly no. In rainy years, the investor gets a 25 percent return on his stock of Raincoats Unlimited and a 5 percent return on Sunglasses Limited. Since he has half the stock invested in each of the assets, the portfolio returns 15 percent: $= 0.5(25\%) + 0.5(5\%)$. In sunny years, he obtains only 5 percent return on Raincoats Unlimited and 25 percent on his shares of Sunglasses Limited. The return of the portfolio is, once again, 15 percent. Note this remarkable result. By combining assets whose returns respond in *opposite* ways to the different possible circumstances (in this case, dry and wet years), an investor may obtain a portfolio with zero variance, that is, a riskless portfolio!

In the case we have just analyzed, we say that the returns are *negatively correlated*, because one stock tends to perform above average when the other stock tends to perform below average. Or, to put this another way, we can say that these returns have a *negative covariance*, a term that we define more precisely shortly.

Suppose, instead, that our investor combines Raincoats Unlimited with the stock of Umbrellas Limited, a company that also does well in rainy years, when it returns 25 percent, and poorly in sunny years, when it returns 5 percent. The raincoat company and the umbrella company thus have an identical structure of returns. If the investor holds half his wealth in each company, the expected return of his portfolio is 15 percent, but now the risk remains large as well because the risks of the two assets do not offset each

---

[11] The expected return for each asset is 15 percent [$= 0.5(25\%) + 0.5(5\%)$]. The variance is $0.01 = 0.5(0.25 - 0.15)^2 + 0.5(0.05 - 0.15)^2$.

other. The variance of a portfolio divided between the two stocks is 0.01, which is exactly the variance of the individual assets.[12] In this case, we say that the returns of the two assets are (perfectly) positively correlated or that they have a *positive covariance*.

We can now provide a formal derivation of the covariance of two assets. Using that definition, we can then calculate the variance of an entire portfolio as a function of the underlying variances and covariances of the assets that make up the portfolio. Consider two assets, 1 and 2, each with risky returns. Suppose that with probability p_1 these assets have returns r_{11} and r_{21}; with probability p_2, the assets have returns r_{12} and r_{22}; and so on. Suppose that there are n different possible combinations of outcomes, with n probabilities attached to these outcomes. The expected returns of the two assets are calculated in the usual way and are denoted r_1^e and r_2^e, respectively. The covariance of returns of the two assets is denoted $\text{cov}(r_1, r_2)$ and is calculated as follows:

$$\text{Cov}(r_1, r_2) = p_1(r_{11} - r_1^e)(r_{21} - r_2^e) + p_2(r_{12} - r_1^e)(r_{22} - r_2^e)$$
$$+ \cdots + p_n(r_{1n} - r_1^e)(r_{2n} - r_2^e) \qquad (20.4)$$

When the assets tend to have above-average returns at the same time, the covariance is *positive*; when the assets have returns that are independent of each other, then the covariance is *zero*; and when one asset has above-average returns when the other asset has below-average returns, then the covariance is *negative*.

We can now show how the variance of the overall portfolio depends on the underlying risk characteristics of the assets in the portfolio. Starting with a portfolio of just two assets, we can say that the variance of the portfolio obeys the following formula:[13]

$$\sigma_p^2 = a_1^2 \sigma_1^2 + a_2^2 \sigma_2^2 + 2a_1 a_2 \, \text{cov}(r_1, r_2) \qquad (20.5)$$

What does this expression tell us? *The variance of the portfolio is a weighted sum of the variances of the underlying assets plus a term that depends on the covariance of the two assets.* If the covariance is negative, this term reduces the overall variance of the portfolio. The risks of the two assets tend to offset each other, since one return tends to be high when the

---

[12] The formula for the variance of the return of a portfolio of two assets (1 and 2) is the following:

$$\text{Var}(r_p) = \text{var}(a_1 r_1 + a_2 r_2)$$

by definition of r_p from equation (20.2)

$$\text{Var}(r_p) = a_1^2 \, \text{var}(r_1) + a_2^2 \, \text{var}(r_2) + 2a_1 a_2 \, \text{cov}(r_1, r_2)$$

by definition of variance, where $\text{cov}(r_1 r_2) = \sigma_{12} = \sigma_1 \sigma_2 \rho_{12}$ and ρ_{12} is the correlation between the returns of asset 1 and 2.

[13] We can also measure the variance of the portfolio according to the definition of variance used earlier. If there are q possible outcomes for the returns of the portfolio (based on the possible outcomes of the underlying assets), we let $p_1, p_2, \ldots, p_q$ denote the probabilities of the q possible outcomes. We define the expected return of the portfolio as in (20.2). Then, the portfolio variance is defined as

$$\sigma_p^2 = p_1(r_{p1} - r_p^e)^2 + p_2(r_{p2} - r_p^e)^2$$
$$+ \cdots + p_q(r_{pq} - r_p^e)^2 \qquad (20.5a)$$

other return tends to be low. If the covariance is positive, the term raises the overall variance of the portfolio.

We can also state, without proof, a more general expression for the variance of a portfolio with n assets:

$$\sigma_p^2 = a_1^2\sigma_1^2 + a_2^2\sigma_2^2 + \cdots + a_n^2\sigma_n^2$$
$$+ 2a_1a_2 \operatorname{cov}(r_1, r_2) + 2a_1a_3 \operatorname{cov}(r_1, r_3) + \cdots + 2a_1a_n \operatorname{cov}(r_1, r_n)$$
$$+ 2a_2a_3 \operatorname{cov}(r_2, r_3) + 2a_2a_4 \operatorname{cov}(r_2, r_4) + \cdots + 2a_2a_n \operatorname{cov}(r_2, r_n)$$
$$+ \cdots + 2a_{n-1}a_n \operatorname{cov}(r_{n-1}, r_n) \tag{20.6}$$

Expected Utility as a Function of Risk and Return

The problem of wealthholders is how to allocate their wealth among the n assets so as to maximize *expected utility*, that is, how to choose portfolio shares $a_1, a_2, a_3, \ldots, a_n$. Portfolio theory assumes that wealthholders aim to maximize their expected utility (U^e), which in turn depends on the expected return of a portfolio of assets (r_p^e) and on its risk, which we measure by the standard deviation, σ_p (remember that the standard deviation of the portfolio is the square root of the variance of the portfolio). Thus we can write

$$U^e = U^e(\underset{+}{r_p^e}, \underset{-}{\sigma_p}) \tag{20.7}$$

Equation (20.7) says that the investors' expected utility goes up when the expected return of the portfolio increases and declines when the return becomes more variable, that is, when σ_p increases.

We can draw a map of *indifference curves* between return and standard deviation, as shown in Figure 20-1. As usual, an indifference curve connects

Figure 20-1
The Indifference Map of a Risk-Averse Investor

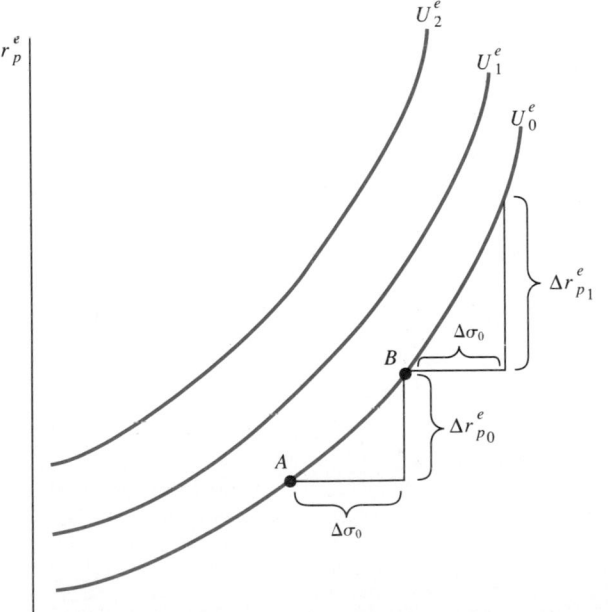

all the points that produce the same level of well-being, or utility. In this case, the indifference curves connect all the points with the same level of expected utility. Indifference curves have a positive slope because risk, represented by the standard deviation, produces disutility, while a higher expected return produces positive utility. In moving from point A to point B, an investor remains equally well off, simply trading off a higher expected return for a higher risk. The level of utility increases with a higher expected return for the same risk, or a lower risk for the same expected return. Therefore, the higher indifference curves in Figure 20-1 are associated with higher utility levels.

The Portfolio Set

But investor preferences are only one side of the portfolio problem. On the other side are the options that they have. In principle, they can choose among all existing assets and they can put together any possible portfolios made up of any number of shares of those assets. Thus, *each asset or each combination of assets in a specific portfolio can be represented by one point in the risk-return graph. To put this another way, we can characterize each portfolio by a given combination of expected return and standard deviation.*

Suppose that a portfolio can be made up of two assets, shown as points 1 and 2 in Figure 20-2a. Each point characterizes the risk and return of the particular asset. As we have drawn it, asset 1 has a higher expected return than asset 2, but both assets have the same standard deviation. By combining the two assets in a single portfolio, *more* possibilities of risk and return can be created. By taking all values of a_1 and a_2 (the shares of wealth held in assets 1 and 2, respectively) and using the formulas for portfolio return and portfolio risk, we can trace out *all* the combinations of risk and return that are achievable by combining the two assets in various proportions.[14] When the asset returns are independent of each other (that is, they have zero covariance), then portfolios composed of the two assets produce the possibilities shown by the curve in Figure 20-2b. When the assets are perfectly negatively correlated, it turns out that the resulting possibilities are shown by the two connected lines in Figure 20-2c. Note that at point 3 in this figure, half the portfolio is held in asset 1 and half the portfolio is held in asset 2, and all risk has been eliminated.

The set of all possible portfolios that can be constructed by various combinations of assets 1 and 2 has a fancy name, the *feasible portfolio set*. The feasible portfolio set shows the risk-return combinations that can be achieved by various portfolio choices. In real life, of course, investors want to restrict their attention to an important subset of the feasible set, the *efficient portfolio set*. In each of the two cases in Figure 20-2, we have darkened the line at the top most part of the portfolio curve. This indicates

---

[14] Technically, the possibilities are found as follows. Let r_1^e and r_2^e be the expected returns of the two assets. Let $\sigma_1 = \sigma_2$ be the standard deviations of the two assets. Let a_1 be the share invested in asset 1 and $a_2 = 1 - a_1$ be the share invested in asset 2. Then, the expected return of the portfolio and the risk are given as in equations (20.2) and (20.5). Specifically, $r_p^e = a_1 r_1^e + a_2 r_2^e$ and $\sigma_p^2 = a_1^2 \sigma_1^2 + a_2^2 \sigma_2^2 + 2a_1 a_2 \, \text{cov}(r_1, r_2)$. These values are then traced out for all possible values of a_1 between 0 and 1 to produce the curves in Figure 20-2.

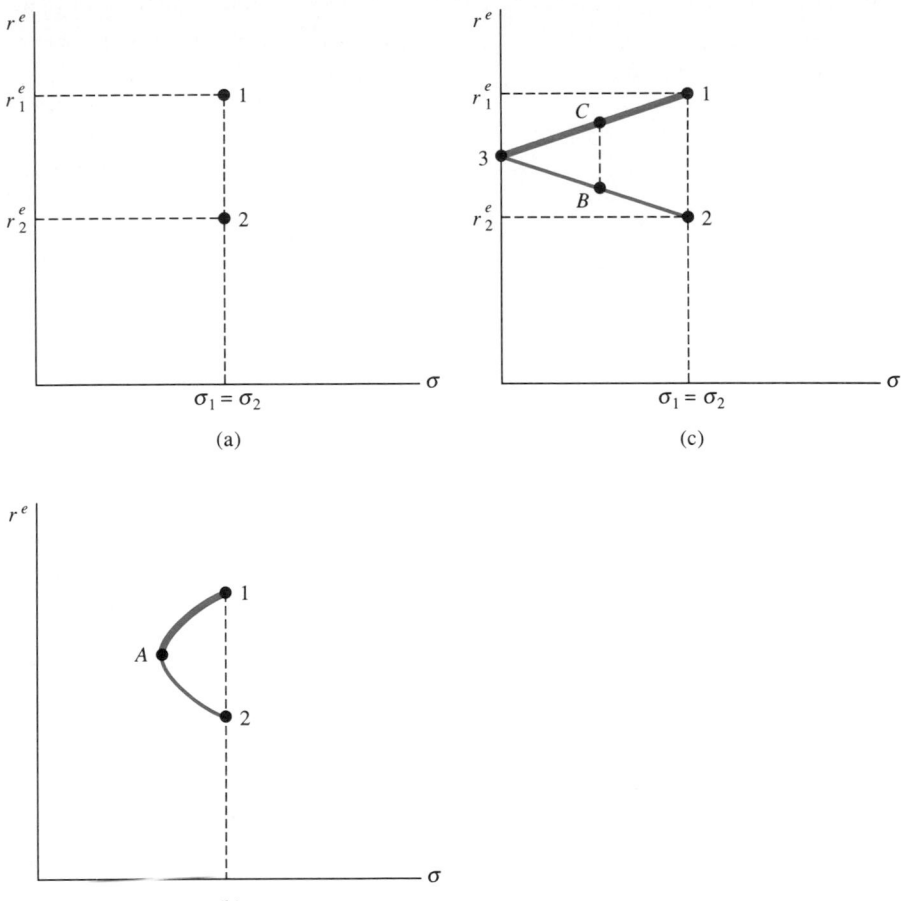

Figure 20-2
Possible Portfolio Sets Out of Two Assets

the possible portfolios that are efficient in that they produce *maximum return for a given risk* or *minimum risk for a given return*. Investors always look for efficient portfolios in order to maximize expected utility. For example, in Figure 20-2c, the investor would never consider portfolio B (with 25 percent of asset 1 and 75 percent of asset 2) because portfolio C is also available (with 75 percent of asset 1 and 25 percent of asset 2). Portfolio C has the same risk, but a higher expected return than B. Portfolio C is an efficient portfolio (there is no way to get higher expected returns without accepting more risk), while portfolio B is not. In Figure 20-2b the efficient portfolio set lies on the curve joining points *A* and 1. In Figure 20-2c, the set of efficient portfolios lies along the line segment that joins points 1 and 3.

Choosing the Optimal Portfolio

A rational investor will obviously choose a portfolio in the efficient set, but where in that set? To find the optimal point among all efficient portfolios, we need to reintroduce the indifference curves of Figure 20-1. Let us focus on the case in which the two assets are independent, as shown in Figure 20-2b.

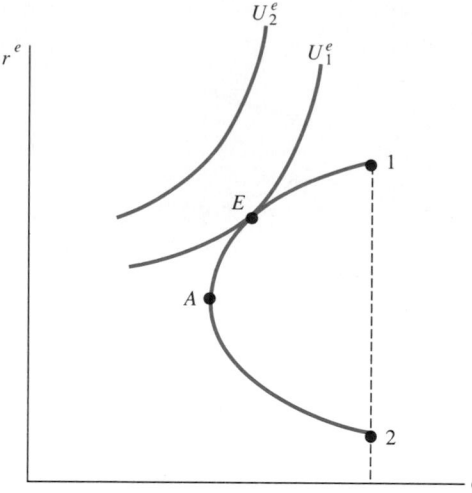

Figure 20-3
The Feasible Set, the Efficient Set, and Portfolio Equilibrium

This is reproduced on a larger scale in Figure 20-3, with the indifference curves added in.

As usual, the investor will want to select the portfolio that allows her to reach the highest indifference curve. Clearly, she will limit herself to the efficient portfolios. *Portfolio equilibrium is reached at the point of tangency between the efficient portfolio set (the curve that goes from A to 1) and the highest indifference curve that touches the efficient set.* This is shown as point E in Figure 20-3, where the indifference curve U_1^e is tangent to the efficient set. Notice that point E falls on a portfolio that contains both assets 1 and 2, and this will generally be the case. Of course, the investor would like to reach utility level U_2^e, but this is not possible because there is no portfolio that has such advantageous combination of risk and return.

With some trickier algebra, this analysis can be extended to the case of more than two assets. In Figure 20-4, there are five underlying assets, labeled by the points 1 through 5. By combining all these points, we find the feasible set of portfolios given by the darkened area in the figure. The efficient set of portfolios, as before, is the uppermost outer surface of this darkened area, connecting points A and C. Again, portfolio equilibrium is at

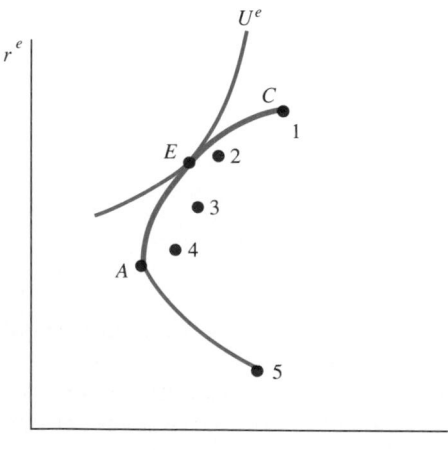

Figure 20-4
Portfolio Equilibrium with Many Assets

point *E,* where the indifference curve is tangent to the efficient portfolio set. In general, point *E* would be a portfolio that included most or all of the five underlying assets.

Some Characteristics of Optimal Portfolios

Consider again the equilibrium in Figure 20-3. The optimizing investor includes some of asset 2 in her portfolio even though asset 2 has a lower expected return than asset 1. In doing this, she is sacrificing some expected return in order to achieve a somewhat safer portfolio. If she were risk neutral, she would simply include only asset 1 in her portfolio and thereby achieve the maximum expected return. In general, the diversification motive leads people to include most or all available assets, if only in small amounts, in their portfolios. The two exceptions to this general principle occur (1) when one asset is perfectly correlated with another asset (or group of assets), so that including the asset does not reduce the portfolio risk, and (2) when transactions costs make it too expensive to hold very small amounts of a large number of assets in a portfolio.

How much return will an investor sacrifice in order to include a particular asset in his portfolio? That depends on two factors. The first, of course, is the extent of his risk aversion. If he is nearly risk neutral, then he will not choose to include many low-return assets in his portfolio, all other things being equal. The second factor is the extent to which a particular asset reduces the overall portfolio risk. This depends not only—indeed, not mainly—on the riskiness of the asset itself, but also on the covariance of the asset in question with the other assets in the portfolio. Efficient portfolios have one important characteristic: they include low-expected-return assets to the extent that such assets have a strong negative correlation with the rest of the portfolio.

20-4 CAPITAL MARKET EQUILIBRIUM: THE CAPITAL ASSET PRICING MODEL

The portfolio choice model can also be used to determine the demand-supply equilibrium for financial assets. In particular, the market equilibrium determines the price of the financial asset and its expected rate of return. Remember that with a financial asset, its price and expected return are inversely related. When a bond has a high price, for example, its rate of return in low; when the bond price is low, its rate of return is high.

The demand for an individual asset depends on its expected returns and on its risk in relation to all other possible assets that might go into a portfolio. If we take the risk characteristics of all assets as given, we can draw a demand curve for a particular asset. We could show this as a normal, downward-sloping demand curve relating the price of the asset to the amount demanded by all investors. Instead, since price and expected return are inversely related, we will depict the demand curve as an *upward-sloping* curve relating the expected return of the asset to the overall demand for that asset by investors, as in Figure 20-5. A higher expected return naturally leads to a higher total demand.

Suppose that the supply of the asset in question is fixed by the line *SS.* Then market supply and demand for the asset would be in equilibrium if the

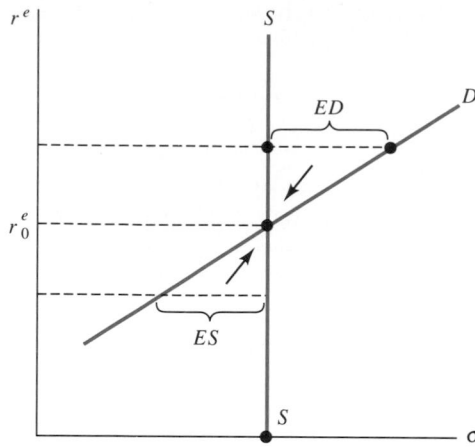

Figure 20-5
Demand, Supply, and the Equilibrium Expected Return of an Asset

expected return on the asset is at the level r^{e*}, as shown in the figure. Suppose that the asset in question is a bond with a market price P_b and a yield to maturity r. If demand for the bond exceeds the supply of the bond, then the price P_b would rise and the yield to maturity would fall. This would continue until the yield to maturity fell to the equilibrium level r^{e*}. Alternatively, if demand for the bond were to fall short of the supply at the initial price, the price of the bond would fall and its yield to maturity would rise until equilibrium is established at the rate of return r^{e*}.

In this way, we can use the portfolio theory we developed in the previous section, together with the market supply of assets (taken as given in the short run), to determine the expected returns of financial assets. This can be done with great analytical elegance and power using the so-called *capital asset pricing model* (CAPM), which was developed in the 1960s to study the market equilibrium for financial assets.[15]

Rather than describe the CAPM model in detail,[16] we report here on one of the fundamental results of the theory. The idea goes like this. Consider an asset that is negatively correlated with the other financial assets available for investment and thus highly attractive in that it helps to reduce the risk of investors' portfolios. The demand for such an asset will be very high, and that high demand will drive down the rate of return on the asset in market equilibrium.

This outcome appears in Figure 20-6. There we show the demand curve for two assets, one that is positively correlated with the other financial assets

---

[15] Nobel Laureate William Sharpe of Stanford University and the late John Lintner of Harvard University are generally considered the fathers of CAPM. The seminal early papers where the model was developed are Sharpe's "Capital Asset Prices: A Theory of Market Equilibrium Under Conditions of Risk," *Journal of Finance*, September 1964, and Lintner's "The Valuation of Risk Assets and the Selection of Risky Investments in Stock Portfolios and Capital Budgets," *Review of Economics and Statistics*, February 1965.

[16] Unfortunately, the CAPM model is largely beyond the scope of this text. A good, detailed presentation of this model may be found in a textbook on finance such as that by Sharpe and Alexander, *Investments*.

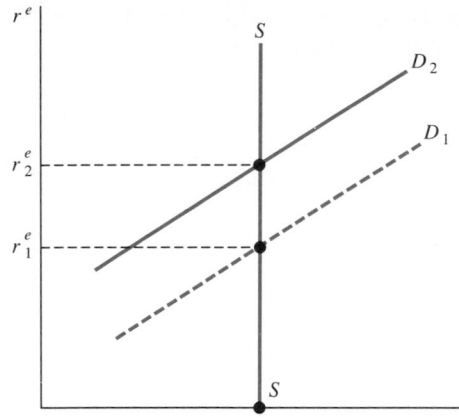

Figure 20-6
Equilibrium Rates of Return on Assets as Depending on Their Contribution to Portfolio Risk

and one that is negatively correlated.[17] The demand curve for the asset with the negative correlation (D_1) is farther to the right, which means that there is a higher demand for this asset at each expected rate of return. The supply of the two assets is the same, as given by the SS curve. Thus, even though the negatively correlated asset has a *lower* expected return in equilibrium than the other asset, investors will be happy to hold it because of its risk characteristics. The result is a relationship between the expected rate of return of an asset in market equilibrium and its correlation with the other assets in the financial markets. The asset that is negatively correlated with the market has an equilibrium rate of return that is lower than the asset that is positively correlated with the market.[18]

20-5 INTERNATIONAL INTEREST ARBITRAGE

One of the tricky aspects about international investing is that assets are expressed in different currencies. How does a 5 percent rate of return in Deutsche marks compare with a 10 percent rate of return in dollars? We have studied this issue briefly in other chapters. Here we will deepen our understanding of this important topic.

In Chapter 10, we introduced the concept of international interest arbitrage. We argued there that, under conditions of certainty, the return of one dollar invested in *foreign* bonds should be equal to the return of one dollar invested in *domestic* bonds when the returns are expressed in the same

---

[17] Technically, we are measuring the correlation of the asset with the overall market portfolio, that is, with a portfolio composed of all the financial assets available in the marketplace.

[18] In the CAPM theory, a general relationship is derived, known as the market equilibrium line, which links the equilibrium expected returns on an asset to the risk characteristics of the asset. When the asset is positively correlated with the overall portfolio of financial assets that are trading in the financial markets, its equilibrium rate of return is higher than the expected return of an asset with a negative correlation. The theory shows that what counts in determining an asset's expected rate of return is not the riskiness of the asset judged in isolation (say, by its variance), but rather its riskiness as related to the other assets, as measured by its covariance with the overall portfolio of assets trading in the financial markets.

currency. For the arbitrage condition to hold, we assumed no barriers to international trade in financial assets and complete certainty about the future. Here, we introduce the realistic complication of *exchange-rate uncertainty* to see how the interest arbitrage condition, equation (11.5), would change. For this discussion, we ignore other kinds of risks, such as default risk or the political risk that the property will be expropriated by the foreign government.

Suppose a U.S. Treasury bond pays interest of i per annum. That is, \$1 invested today yields \$$(1 + i)$ in one year. We call the *gross* return (in dollars) $1 + i$ and the *net* return i. Now, consider a German bond issued by the Bundesbank, denominated in Deutsche marks (DM), that pays i^*. We will take the United States to be the home country, and thus we want to compute the dollar return of the German bond in order to compare it with i. The crucial point is that the dollar return on the Bundesbank bond depends both on i^* and on movements in the exchange rate during the year. We define E as the exchange rate in dollars per Deutsche mark (\$/DM) in the current period and E_{+1} as the corresponding rate next period. For example, E was about 0.68 in early February 1991, implying that 1 Deutsche mark purchased about 0.68 U.S. dollars.

Now consider the purchase of the Deutsche mark bond in the current period. With \$1, one can buy $(1/E)$ bonds that each sell for 1 DM. At the end of the year, each bond pays $(1 + i^*)$ in *Deutsche marks,* so the total Deutsche mark yield is $(1 + i^*)/E$. The dollar value of this at the end of the year is $E_{+1}(1 + i^*)/E$. So, the gross returns in dollars of the home and foreign assets are

Home asset: $(1 + i)$

Foreign asset: $\dfrac{E_{+1}(1 + i^*)}{E}$

The problem is that E_{+1} is not known with certainty in the current period. If the exchange rate is floating, or is subject to a devaluation, then we can only estimate ("guess") what E will be at the end of next period.

In general then, we only have an expectation of E_{+1} in the current period, which we denote by E^e_{+1}, formed at the beginning of the investment period. The expected return on the foreign bond is thus $E^e_{+1}(1 + i^*)/E$. The actual yield, once the uncertainty is resolved, is $E_{+1}(1 + i^*)/E$. Since the expected (E^e_{+1}) and actual (E_{+1}) exchange rates usually differ, so will the expected and actual yields.

Uncovered Interest Arbitrage

If investors care only about expected yields but not risk, that is, if they are *risk neutral,* and if all investors have the same expectations, then all assets must have the same expected return. Otherwise, no one would choose to hold the assets with below-average expected returns. Market equilibrium therefore leads to the condition of *uncovered interest arbitrage* (uncovered because investors are not covered from the exchange-rate risk):

$$(1 + i) = \frac{E^e_{+1}(1 + i^*)}{E} \tag{20.8}$$

Notice that equation (20.8) is the same as expression (9.5). There, however, we neglected considerations of risk. To accommodate those here, we replace the actual value of the exchange rate in the next period (E_{+1}) by its expectation (E_{+1}^e).

Expression (20.8) can also be presented in a more familiar and intuitive form. Allowing for a small approximation, we can write (20.8) as follows:[19]

$$i = i^* + \frac{(E_{+1}^e - E)}{E} \qquad (20.9)$$

Equation (20.9) says that the domestic interest rate is equal to the foreign rate of interest plus the *expected* rate of currency depreciation. This highlights an important characteristic of foreign investments. The purchase of a foreign asset is not only an investment in a security that pays a given rate of interest (i^*), it is also an investment in foreign currency, the return on which depends on the depreciation (or appreciation) of the exchange rate. If, for example, the U.S. interest rate is 9 percent per year and the German rate is 6 percent, the German asset has a higher dollar return if the annual rate of dollar depreciation is more than 3 percent.

In general, though, investors also care about risk, in which case the uncovered interest arbitrage relationship has to be modified. In fact, because of the differing risks of holding the domestic asset compared with the foreign currency asset, there may be a risk premium, either positive or negative, on holding the domestic asset. In that case, the modified expression would be:

$$i = i^* + \frac{(E_{+1}^e - E)}{E} + Pr \qquad (20.10)$$

where Pr is a risk premium. When Pr is positive, equation (20.8) means that investors require a higher expected rate of return on the domestic asset than they do on the foreign asset.

What is the source of so-called "currency risk," Pr? As in the CAPM model, the size of Pr will depend not only on the size of currency fluctua-

---

[19] Equation (20.8) can be rewritten in the form

$$i = \frac{E_{+1}^e (1 + i^*)}{E} - \frac{E}{E}$$

or

$$i = i^* + \left[\frac{(E_{+1}^e - E)}{E} \right] i^* + \frac{(E_{+1}^e - E)}{E}$$

Since $(E_{+1}^e - E)/E$ and i^* are generally both small numbers, their product is generally very close to 0, and thus may be ignored. If we make that approximation, then equation (20.9) follows immediately.

How good an approximation is (20.9) of (20.8)? Suppose that $E = 0.60$ and that $E_{+1}^e = 0.63$ (that is, the dollar is expected to depreciate by 5 percent in the year). If $i^* = 0.06$, then $E_{+1}^e(1 + i^*)/E = 1.113$; on the other hand, $1 + i^* + (E_{+1}^e - E)/E = 1.110$. The approximation is quite good when both the foreign interest rate and the rate of expected depreciation are small. But one would surely not want to apply the approximation for countries undergoing high inflation (and consequently high rates of currency depreciation), because in that case $[(E_{+1}^e - E)/E]i^*$ would not be close to zero.

tions and how unexpected they are, but on the covariance of fluctuations in the exchange rate with the returns on other financial assets. Say, for example, that the U.S. dollar tends to appreciate unexpectedly when world oil prices rise unexpectedly. In that case, holding dollars rather than Deutsche marks would help to protect investors against the risk of oil price increases and the low returns on certain kinds of manufacturing stocks when oil prices rise. This kind of correlation would help to determine Pr. In fact, a stable relationship between exchange-rate changes with other kinds of risks is hard to identify, and as a result, economists have not yet been very successful in determining the magnitudes and sources of risk premia such as Pr.

Covered Interest Arbitrage

In the example we just discussed, the investor chooses between holding a domestic asset for one year and holding a foreign asset for one year and then converting the foreign exchange in which the asset is denominated at the exchange rate that prevails at that time. There is, in fact, another choice. When the investor buys the Deutsche mark bond today, she knows that she will have a certain amount of Deutsche marks to sell for dollars in the future (specifically, an amount $1 + i^*$). Rather than waiting a year to find out what the exchange rate will be, she can conclude a contract today, at a *preset price,* to sell the Deutsche marks in one year's time. Thus, the investor uses a *forward contract,* which is an agreement to buy or sell a commodity (or currency) at a specified date in the future, at a price that is set today.[20]

Using a forward contract, the investor can remove all the exchange-rate risk. Instead of buying the foreign bond and waiting to see what E_{+1} will be, the investor now sells the foreign exchange proceeds today at a fixed price known as the "forward price," denoted F. That is, the investor knows that she will have Deutsche mark $(1 + i^*)/E$ at the end of the year and that is what she agrees today to sell for a dollar amount $F(1 + i^*)/E$. The transaction does not occur until that future date, but the terms of the future exchange are set today.

Thus, a purchase of German bonds combined with a forward sale of the earnings from the bond yields a gross dollar return of $F(1 + i^*)/E$ with no exchange risk at all. Technically, we say that the investor *covers her position* in Deutsche marks, by selling the Deutsche marks forward, so that she is no longer exposed to risks of exchange-rate fluctuations. Because the purchase of Deutsche mark assets with a forward sale must have the same return as a direct purchase of dollar assets (since neither transaction has any exchange risk), we have a market equilibrium condition called *covered interest arbitrage:*

$$(1 + i) = \frac{F(1 + i^*)}{E} \tag{20.11}$$

---

[20] Technically, we should distinguish between two types of foreign exchange contracts: *futures contracts,* which are traded on public futures exchanges, and *forward contracts,* which are traded by commercial banks. Conceptually, they have the same purpose. In the text, we simply use one term, "forward contract," to refer to this type of transaction.

Expression (20.11) can be approximated as we did with (20.8), giving rise to:

$$i = i^* + \frac{(F - E)}{E} \qquad\qquad \textbf{(20.12)}$$

Equation (20.13) says that the local interest rate is equal to the foreign rate plus the *forward discount*, $(F - E)/E$. Note that the forward discount may be positive or negative. If $F > E$, we say that the dollar trades at a forward discount; in that case the dollar interest rate must be higher than the German interest rate. Conversely, if $F < E$, then the dollar trades at a forward premium; in that case, the dollar interest rate must be lower than the German interest rate.

If we combine equations (20.10) and (20.12), we now see a very important relationship:

$$F = E^e_{+1} + EPr \qquad\qquad \textbf{(20.13)}$$

This equation says that the forward rate equals the expected exchange rate in the next period, plus the exchange rate times the percentage risk premium on domestic assets relative to foreign assets. If all agents are risk neutral, so that Pr is equal to zero, then the forward rate records the market's expectation of the exchange rate in the next period. But, if investors are risk averse, so that there is a risk premium on holding domestic assets relative to foreign assets, then the forward rate will not equal the expected future exchange rate.

Information about forward exchange rates is reported daily in the financial press. Table 20-3 reports the three-month interest rates in dollars, yen, and deutsche marks, and the spot and forward exchange rates in dollars per Deutsche mark and dollars per yen. There you can see that the covered interest arbitrage relationship holds almost exactly. Minor differences, which run no higher than 0.0008 percent over a three-month period, can be attributed to transactions costs.

The forward exchange market is not only used by agents who invest in foreign assets. It is also used by companies and individuals involved in foreign trade of goods and services. Suppose that the IBM Corporation

TABLE 20-3

INTEREST RATES, SPOT EXCHANGE RATES AND FORWARD EXCHANGE RATES

	i	i*	E	F	i − i*	F − E/F
Dollar-Yen	1.178	1.467	0.00777	0.00774	−0.0031	−0.0038
Dollar-Deutsche mark	1.178	2.294	0.6293	0.6218	−0.0111	−0.0119

Notes: Interest rates refer to three-month eurocurrency market rates (percent).
    i = dollar interest rate.
    i* = foreign interest rate (yen, D-Mark).
    E = Spot exchange rate (dollars per yen and dollars per D-Mark).
    F = Three-month forward exchange rate (dollars per yen and dollars per D-Mark).
Source: *The Financial Times, December 6, 1991.*

obtains a steady flow of computer components from Japan. IBM can always wait to purchase yen in the spot market at the time of each shipment. But it also has the alternative of purchasing yen in the forward market and thereby avoiding the risk of exchange-rate fluctuations. If IBM takes this latter option, we say that it has *hedged* against the exchange risk.

20-6 THE TERM STRUCTURE OF INTEREST RATES

Bonds can differ not only by the currency of denomination, but also by the *maturity,* that is, the time until the bond is repaid by the borrower. Bonds of different maturities have different rates of return. In this section, we investigate the relationship between bond yields, or rates of return, and the maturity of the bonds.

To understand this relationship, we must first understand how to measure the rate of return on a multiyear bond. Consider the payout structure of the simplest kind of bond. Suppose that the bond is an N-year bond, with a face value (or par value) V and an interest rate i. As an example, we will let N be five years, V be $1,000, and i be 10 percent per annum. We will assume that the interest is paid annually, at the end of the year. The face value (or principal) $1,000 is repaid at the end of five years.

In this case, the bond has a payout stream as follows:

After year 1	100	(10% of $1,000)
After year 2	100	
After year 3	100	
After year 4	100	
After year 5	1,100	($1,000 plus 10% of $1,000)

After five years, the principal is repaid in one payment; during each of the years 1 to 5, interest is paid equal to the interest rate on the bond multiplied by the principal. Typically, to collect the interest on the bond, the bondholder must clip a coupon on the bond and offer it for redemption. In this case, the bond is called a *coupon bond,* with a coupon rate of 10 percent.

The yield to maturity (YTM) measures the rate of return that is earned by buying and holding a bond until maturity. Suppose the price of the bond is P. The YTM is found as the interest rate i_y at which the present value of the repayment stream is equal to the purchase price of the bond. Continuing with our numerical example, we would solve the following equation:

$$P = \frac{\$100}{(1 + i_y)} + \frac{\$100}{(1 + i_y)^2} + \frac{\$100}{(1 + i_y)^3}$$
$$+ \frac{\$100}{(1 + i_y)^4} + \frac{\$1,100}{(1 + i_y)^5} \qquad \textbf{(20.14)}$$

When the purchase price of the bond is equal to the principal, then the yield to maturity is equal to the coupon rate. Thus, if the five-year bond just described is purchased for $P = $1,000, then $i_y = 10$ percent.

If the purchase price of the bond is different from the principal, however, the yield to maturity is different from the coupon rate. Suppose, for example, that the five-year bond can be purchased for $900 rather than $1,000. It should be clear that the return to this bond would then exceed 10 percent, because the $900 purchase of the bond is going to be redeemed for $1,000 in five years, plus $100 in each of the intervening years. Setting $P = $900 in equation (20.14) we find $i_y = 12.83$ percent. Note that when the purchase price is above the face value, the YTM is below the coupon rate, and when the purchase price is below the face value, the YTM is above the coupon rate.

The Yield Curve

The yield to maturity may differ among assets for a variety of reasons, including different probabilities of default and different patterns in the fluctuations of expected returns. But it may also differ according to the maturity of the asset. Interest rates differ systematically on bonds of different maturities, even if all other attributes of the bond (such as default risk) are the same.

Consider someone who wants to invest $1,000 of savings in a Treasury bond. She will discover that the yield she receives depends on the time to maturity of the bond, with a structure of the following type:

Term to Maturity	Interest Rate
5-year bond	8.0%
8-year bond	8.5%
20-year bond	9.0%

Assuming that there is no default risk on any of these different assets, the interest rates differ only because of the length of time until the assets mature, or, to shorten the phrase, "maturity." We call the relationship between the maturity of the bond and the interest rate (yield to maturity) the term *structure of interest rates,* where "term" refers to the maturity of the asset.

The graphical presentation of the term structure of interest rates is called the *yield curve.* It is a plot of interest rates for a particular type of asset at different maturities. Consider the case of U.S. Treasury obligations, where one can find interest rates quoted on financial instruments with maturities that vary from a few days to 30 years. To compare the interest rates on these assets properly, we refer to the *annualized* yields to maturity for each type of bond. Figure 20-7 shows a yield curve for Treasury securities as published every day in the financial press.

Note that shorter-term rates are lower than longer-term ones, and thus the yield curve is upward sloping. For example, the rate on 3-month bills is 8.1 percent, while the interest rate on 10-year bonds is 8.6 percent. Although the yield curve is generally upward sloping, as shown in the graph, this is not always the case. At times, the yield curve is downward sloping, implying that short-term rates are higher than long-term rates; this is sometimes referred to as an "inverted yield curve."

Why is it that assets that are otherwise identical such as Treasury securities have different yields? And why does the yield curve change its shape in time? We can address these questions, if not conclusively answer them, with the help of different theories about the term structure of interest rates.

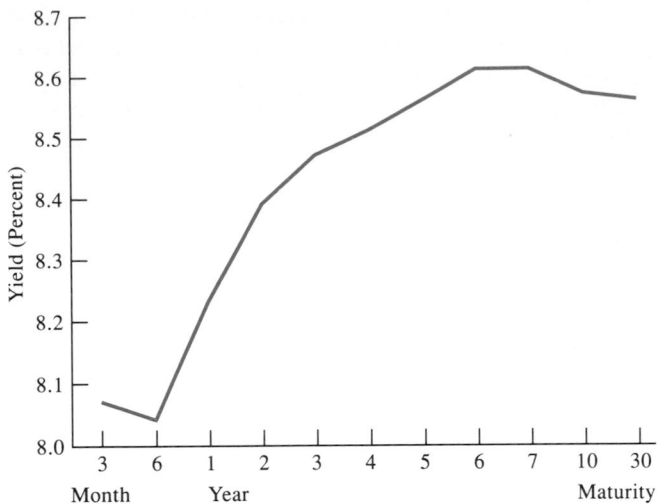

Figure 20-7
The Yield Curve of U.S. Treasury Securities

(Copyright © 1990 by The New York Times Company. Reprinted by permission.)

The Expectations Theory

The most important theory of the term structure of interest rates, known as the *expectations theory*,[21] builds on the observation that there are two ways to invest over a period of N years. The investor may hold an N-year bond, or the investor may buy a one-year bond and then, when the bond comes due, reinvest the proceeds to buy another one-year bond, and so on for all N years. If there is no uncertainty, then arbitrage in the financial markets will guarantee that the two methods should result in an identical return.

To illustrate this, consider a two-period investment. Suppose that the two-year bond has a yield to maturity of $i_{0,2}$ (the interest rate of a two-year bond in period 0).[22] Investing \$1 in this bond for two years yields $\$1(1 + i_{0,2})(1 + i_{0,2}) = \$1(1 + i_{0,2})^2$. The other option is to buy a one-year bond that pays $i_{0,1}$ and invest the proceeds at the end of the first year in another one-year bond whose yield is $i_{1,1}$ for a total return of $\$1(1 + i_{0,1})(1 + i_{1,1})$. The notation $i_{1,1}$ signifies the rate of return on a one-year bond starting in the next period and coming due one period after that (in the second period).

---

[21] The expectations theory has its origins in Irving Fisher, *The Theory of Interest as Determined by Impatience to Spend Income and Opportunity to Invest It* (New York: Macmillan, 1930). Friedrich Lutz contributed significantly to its analysis in the 1940s; see his article "The Structure of Interest Rates," *Quarterly Journal of Economics*, November 1940.

[22] We will use the following notation: $i_{t,z}$ denotes the annualized interest rate of a z-year bond, as of period t. One dollar invested in such a bond in period t results in an amount $(1 + i_{t,z})^z$ in period $t + z$. For example, if the five-year interest rate in 1991 is 11 percent, we would write

$$i_{1991,5} = 11\%$$

one dollar invested in 1991 would yield 1.69 ($= 1.11^5$) in 1996.

The only possible way for both one-year and two-year bonds to coexist in the market is to have the two strategies provide the *same* expected return. Only then will investors be willing to hold two-year and one-year bonds because they will be indifferent between the two strategies. Therefore, the market equilibrium condition is

$$(1 + i_{0,2})^2 = (1 + i_{0,1})(1 + i_{1,1}) \qquad \textbf{(20.15)}$$

What this equilibrium condition implies is that the two-year rate is a kind of average of today's and next period's one-year rate.[23] To show this, we multiply the terms in (20.15) to obtain

$$1 + 2i_{0,2} + i_{0,2}^2 = 1 + i_{0,1} + i_{1,1} + (i_{0,1})(i_{1,1})$$

Now, the terms $i_{0,2}^2$ and $(i_{0,1})(i_{1,1})$ are the products of two very small numbers, and thus may be approximated as being equal to zero. In this case, equation (20.15) may be approximated as[24]

$$i_{0,2} = \frac{(i_{0,1} + i_{1,1})}{2} \qquad \textbf{(20.16)}$$

Thus, the two-year interest rate is approximately the arithmetic average of today's and next period's one-year rate.

Equation (20.16) shows an arbitrage relationship. Since there are two ways to invest for two years, there must be a relationship between the two-year interest rate and the one-year interest rates today and in the next period. Specifically, the long-term (two-year) rate is an average of the short-term interest rates of this period and the next period. In fact, the short-term interest rates in future periods are not known in the present. That is, $i_{1,1}$ is not known at time zero. It can only be estimated, or guessed at. Let us denote the expected one-period yield starting next year as $i_{1,1}^e$.

The *expectations hypothesis of the term structure* holds that the arbitrage relationship in (20.16) still holds, but with next period's interest rate replaced by its expected value, that is, by the market's guess of $i_{1,1}$:

$$i_{0,2} = \frac{(i_{0,1} + i_{1,1}^e)}{2} \qquad \textbf{(20.17)}$$

The expectations hypothesis is exactly true if investors are risk neutral and have rational expectations.

By enlarging the time horizon, we can generalize this hypothesis to the long-term interest rate for any number of years (as long as securities exist with that maturity). Under the expectations hypothesis, the long-term inter-

---

[23] The precise expression for $i_{0,2}$ is as follows:

$$i_{0,2} = [(1 + i_{0,1})(1 + i_{1,1})]^{1/2} - 1$$

The expression developed in the text is more useful, however.

[24] How good an approximation is this? Suppose that $i_{0,2} = 0.08$ and $i_{1,1} = 0.11$. Then the terms that have been approximated as equal to zero are in fact equal to 0.0064 and 0.0088, respectively. The exact expression for $i_{0,2}$ would be 0.0949; our approximated value for $i_{0,2}$ would be 0.095. The difference is only 0.0001, or 0.1 percent, of the true interest rate.

est rate is approximately the arithmetic average of expected future short-term rates, as expressed here:[25]

$$i_{0,n} = \frac{(i_{0,1} + i_{1,1}^e + i_{2,1}^e + \cdots + i_{n-1,1}^e)}{n} \tag{20.18}$$

The expectations theory provides a clear hypothesis about the shape of the yield curve. According to the theory, *if the yield curve has a positive slope, as in Figure 20-7, then short-term interest rates in the future are expected to increase over today's level.* In the two-period example, if $i_{0,1}$ is less than $i_{0,2}$, it means that $i_{1,1}^e > i_{0,1}$.[26] In other words, the short-term interest rate would be expected to rise. A flat yield curve, where interest rates do not change depending on maturity, implies that future short-term interest rates are expected to remain at today's level.

The expectation theory of the yield curve neglects the fact that risk-averse investors may prefer to hold short-term assets rather than long-term assets simply to avoid risk, even if the result is a lower yield. Thus, the theory is sometimes modified by the *liquidity preference hypothesis,* which holds that because investors value liquidity (the lower risk of holding short-term assets), they must be compensated by a higher return for holding less liquid assets.[27] This amounts to a reformulation of the relationship between short- and long-term rates, as proposed by the expectations theory in equations (20.16) and (20.17):

$$i_{0,2} = \frac{(i_{0,1} + i_{1,1}^e)}{2} + L_2 \tag{20.19}$$

As before, the two-year interest rate is equal to the average of this year's and next year's interest rate, plus a liquidity premium (L_2). The liquidity premium is an extra return built into long-term bonds that compensates the bond holders for their greater risk of capital loss. Over a longer time horizon, the long-term interest rate is the average of expected future short-term rates plus a corresponding liquidity premium (L_n):[28]

$$i_{0,n} = \frac{(i_{0,1} + i_{1,1}^e + i_{2,1}^e + \cdots + i_{n-1,1}^e)}{n} + L_n \tag{20.20}$$

Economists are still debating the relative merits of the expectations theory of the term structure versus alternatives like the liquidity preference theory.[29]

---

[25] The exact condition is

$$i_{0,n} = [(1 + i_{0,1})(1 + i_{1,1}^e)(1 + i_{2,1}^e) \ldots (1 + i_{n-1,1}^e)]^{1/n} - 1$$

[26] Remember, according to equation (20.16), $i_{0,2} = (i_{0,1} + i_{1,1}^e)/2$. Thus, we have that $2(i_{0,2}) = i_{0,1} + i_{1,1}^e$. Now, if $i_{0,2} > i_{0,1}$, it is obviously the case that $2(i_{0,1}) < i_{0,1} + i_{1,1}^e$. Therefore, $i_{0,1} < i_{1,1}^e$.

[27] The liquidity preference theory was first presented by John Hicks in his book *Value and Capital* (London: Oxford University Press, 1939).

[28] Liquidity premiums are not necessarily the same across different maturities, and thus L_2 need not equal L_n. Empirical evidence tends to indicate that liquidity premiums for Treasury bonds increase up to about one year of maturity and are basically flat for longer terms.

[29] See, for example, Gregory Mankiw, "The Term Structure of Interest Rates Revisited," *Brookings Papers on Economic Activity,* No. 1, 1986.

20-7 SUMMARY

Financial markets include a wide range of assets (equities, bonds of different maturities, options, futures, and so on) that allow households and firms to reduce the risks they face in managing their wealth. Financial markets in the United States have a wide variety of assets. *Fixed-income assets* include corporate bonds; Treasury bills, Treasury notes, and Treasury bonds; municipal bonds; "junk" bonds, checking accounts; NOW accounts; money market accounts; and so on. *Variable-income securities* include common stocks, preferred stocks, and options. Most financial assets are traded in organized markets.

Primary markets conduct sales of newly issued securities to original buyers. *Secondary markets*—such as the New York Stock Exchange—trade previously owned securities. *Financial intermediaries* in the United States include depository institutions (commercial banks, savings and loan associations, and mutual savings banks), institutional investors (insurance companies and pension funds), and investment intermediaries (mutual funds). Financial markets are regulated to provide adequate information to investors and to ensure the adequate health of financial intermediaries. To protect investors, the U.S. government instituted a system of deposit insurance. This system has been severely tested since the late 1980s due to the savings and loan crisis and to several cases of bank failure.

One of the important trends since the early 1960s has been the growing integration of financial markets around the world. Factors leading to growing financial market integration include increased international trade, technological improvements, and deregulation. The *Eurocurrency market* (bank deposits in Europe denominated in a currency other than that of the country where the bank is located) has experienced a particularly rapid growth.

The extent of development of world financial markets has been facilitated by the progressive opening and deregulation of important domestic markets such as the United States, the United Kingdom, France, and Japan. The most important recent push to full financial integration is Europe's goal of creating a single market by 1992. Project 1992 seeks to remove all capital controls among the members of the European Community and significantly scale down restrictions on financial activities within the EC.

The formal theory of investment behavior is based on the assumption that individuals are *risk averse;* that is, they care about reducing risks as well as maximizing expected returns. Risk-averse agents tend to allocate their wealth in a portfolio of many different assets. *Portfolio theory* assumes that wealthholders care about the properties of their entire portfolio rather than the characteristics of individual components of the portfolio. In particular, they care about the portfolio's expected return and its risk, represented by its variance. To reach the optimum combination of risk and return, the optimal investment strategy involves *portfolio diversification,* that is, holding small amounts of a large number of financial assets.

Expected return of a portfolio of n assets is a weighted average of the expected return of each of the n assets that form the portfolio; the weights correspond to the share of the portfolio invested in each asset. *Variance* of a portfolio is a weighted average of the variances of the underlying assets plus a term depending on the covariance of the assets. Wealthholders seek to maximize their expected utility by allocating their wealth among the different assets available. *Expected utility* is a positive function of expected return and a negative function of the standard deviation (the squared root of the variance) of the portfolio.

Investors preferences are shown graphically by indifference curves between expected return and standard deviation. Their opportunities are represented by the *feasible portfolio set* of all the portfolios that can be constructed by combining available assets. The *efficient portfolio set* is a subset of portfolios that produce maximum return for a given risk or have minimum risk for a given return. *Portfolio equilibrium* is reached at the point of tangency between the efficient portfolio set and the highest indifference curve that touches the efficient set.

The *optimal portfolio* generally includes small amounts of most or all the assets available to the investor. This includes international diversification, which enlarges the set of opportunities to investors. Assets are more attractive to the extent that they are *negatively correlated* with the rest of the portfolio—even if they have low expected return—because they contribute more effectively to a reduction of portfolio risk.

Assets that are negatively correlated to other financial assets are highly attractive, as they help to reduce portfolio risk. Demand for these assets is very high, which tends to drive down their return. Conversely, assets which are positively correlated to other assets are relatively less attractive and have less demand; in equilibrium, they need to provide a higher return for investors to hold them. The equilibrium rate of return of a financial asset may be determined according to the *capital asset pricing model*.

A special case of portfolio choice is the choice between bonds denominated in different currencies. The *international interest arbitrage condition* holds that the return on foreign bonds should be equal to the return on domestic bonds, when expressed in the same currency. When exchange-rate uncertainty exists, however, the condition is more complicated. If investors care only about expected returns (but not risk), and if all investors share the same expectations, then all assets must have the same expected return. In this case, *uncovered interest arbitrage* holds that the domestic interest rate is equal to the foreign rate plus the expected rate of local currency depreciation. If agents are risk averse, then they will tend to demand a risk premium for holding the domestic currency or the foreign currency, and the uncovered interest arbitrage condition must be modified accordingly.

Investors can remove the exchange-rate risk of holding a foreign bond by using a *forward contract* (an agreement to buy or sell a currency at a specified date in the future, at a price that is set today). An investor in foreign bonds "covers" his position in foreign currency by selling that currency forward. *Covered interest arbitrage* holds that the domestic interest rate is equal to the foreign interest rate plus the *forward discount* (the premium of the forward exchange rate over the spot rate). This relationship holds true irrespective of risk.

Another special portfolio choice involves the choice between short-term bonds and long-term bonds. The rate of return of a multiyear asset is summarized by its *yield to maturity*. Assets of different maturities have different yields to maturity. The linkage between the maturity of the bond and its YTM is known as the *term structure of interest rates*. Under the expectations theory of the term structure (which assumes risk-neutral investors), the yield to maturity on a multiyear bond is an average of the expected yields on one-year bonds during the life of the bond. According to the *liquidity preference hypothesis,* however, there may be an extra risk premium added to the YTM of long-term assets to account for the extra riskiness of such assets.

Key Concepts

fixed-income assets	portfolio diversification
variable-income assets	expected return
yield to maturity (YTM)	variance of a portfolio
coupon bond	feasible portfolio set
coupon rate	efficient portfolio set
face value	mutual funds
term structure of interest rates	capital asset pricing model
probability of default	(CAPM)
yield curve	common stocks
pure expectations theory	preferred stocks
liquidity preference theory	primary market
international interest arbitrage	secondary market
uncovered interest arbitrage	institutional investors
covered interest arbitrage	investment intermediaries
forward exchange rate	financial regulation
forward contract	savings and loan crisis
forward premium	Eurocurrency market
risk aversion	Europe 1992

Problems and questions

1. What are the major empirical regularities that any theory of the term structure of interest rates should be consistent with? How do the pure expectations theory and the liquidity preference theory square with these empirical facts?

2. How does the degree of substitutability among short-term and long-term financial assets relate to the different hypotheses about the term structure of interest rates?

3. Suppose you read in the newspaper the following financial data:
The interest rate on government bills in the United Kingdom is 6 percent per annum, and in the United States it is 7 percent per annum. The spot exchange rate is $US1.60 = £1. What should be the one-year forward exchange rate $US/£? Is the dollar at a premium or a discount on the British pound? If the one-year forward exchange rate is different from the rate you calculated (say it is $US 1.70 = £1), could you make a riskless profit? Why?

4. A risk-averse investor is in equilibrium at a point such as E in Figure 20-4. Suddenly, a risk-free asset becomes available. Show graphically how this affects portfolio equilibrium. Discuss.

5. Suppose you select a portfolio of three assets (A, B, C) in which the expected returns are 0.08, 0.09, and 0.10, respectively; their standard deviations are 0.04, 0.06, and 0.08; the portfolio consists of 40 percent of asset A, 40 percent of asset B, and 20 percent of asset C; and the correlation coefficient between *A* and *B* is 0.6, between *A* and *C* is 0.4, and between *B* and *C* is 0.3.

    a. What is the expected return and risk of the portfolio? How does this compare with a portfolio that consists only of asset *C*?

    b. Suppose that you replace asset *A* with a risk-free asset having a 7 percent yield. How does this affect expected return and risk?

    c. Suppose, instead, that you replace asset A with a security having an expected return of 11 percent, a standard deviation of 0.10, and no correlation with assets *B* and *C*. How does this affect the portfolio's risk and expected return? Would you rather have this or asset *A* in our portfolio?

6. Explain the relationships between the portfolio choice model and the capital asset pricing model. Does acceptance of one imply acceptance of the other?

7. Although in theory investors should seek international diversification in their portfolios, the data indicate that U.S. investors have only a small fraction of their wealth allocated to international assets. How can you account for this fact? Do you expect the recent appearance of international mutual funds to affect this?

8. How does the growth of the Eurodollar market threaten the effectiveness of U.S. monetary policy?

9. Why do financial institutions tend to have problems if interest rates rise steadily for several years?

10. Financial markets need regulation in a way that other markets do not require. Why is this? What is financial regulation supposed to accomplish?

11. "Deposit insurance is a good thing because it avoids bank runs." Discuss.

chapter 21

Tradable and Nontradable Goods

So far, we have assumed that all commodities are subject to international trade. Now, in this chapter, we introduce a simple and important reality that has profound implications for the workings of an economy. The fact is that some goods are *nontradable*. Nontradable goods, of course, can only be consumed in the economy in which they are produced; they cannot be exported or imported. And their presence affects every important feature of an economy, from price determination, to the structure of output, to the effects of macroeconomic policy.

Consider the proverbial barber shop. The barber's clientele probably comes from the neighborhood, and it certainly comes from within the domestic economy. If the demand for the barber's services drops, he cannot conveniently export the excess capacity to give haircuts. If foreign barbers raise their prices for haircuts, the local barber will not experience a rush in international demand for his services. Haircuts in India are much cheaper than they are in the United States, perhaps $20 per haircut cheaper, but it does not make sense to buy a $2,000 air ticket from, say, New York to New Delhi to save $20 on a haircut.

This nontradable character of the barber's services has several direct implications. Without the possibility of net exports or imports, local demand and supply must balance. Without international trade, a drop in domestic demand cannot be met by an increase of net exports, and domestic prices can differ from foreign prices without setting in motion a shift of international demand.

There are many goods and services like haircuts that are not part of international trade. Housing rental markets are generally nontradable as well. Even if rents are cheaper in Santiago, Chile, than in Tokyo, it is hard for a Japanese household to take advantage of that fact. Thus, housing rentals differ widely, often by thousands of percent, among cities in different parts of the world. Various activities of service sectors, those of lawyers, doctors, teachers, housekeepers, and the like, also provide largely nontradable goods and services.

Although we recognized the existence of nontradable goods in earlier chapters (especially in Chapter 10, where we pointed out that nontradable goods undermine the case for purchasing power parity), we have based our formal models on the assumption that all goods enter into international trade. In Chapters 4 to 10, we assumed that only one good is produced and consumed in the world economy, and that that good is traded between the home country and the rest of the world. In Chapters 13 to 16, we made a distinction between imported and domestic goods, within the framework of the differentiated goods model. But in that model as well, all the goods that are produced are assumed to trade internationally.

Explicit consideration of the role of nontradable commodities was given early on by the classical economists such as John Stuart Mill and David Ricardo. Their analysis, however, generally considered all final goods to be tradable, and production inputs—capital, labor, and land—to be nontradable. Only in the late 1950s and early 1960s has the role of nontradable goods been considered in formal economic models.[1]

Perhaps the most important implication of the presence of nontradable goods is that the *internal structure of production* in an economy tends to change when the trade balance changes. In particular, as absorption rises or falls relative to income (so that the trade balance rises or falls), the mix of production in the economy between tradable goods and nontradable goods tends to change. And as we shall see, some of those production shifts, which involve the movement of workers and capital between the nontradable and tradable sectors of the economy, can be quite wrenching in their economic and even political impact.

Suppose, for example, that a government which has borrowed heavily in the past now needs to repay its foreign debt. In order to do this, it increases taxes. As a result, consumption declines. If all the goods in the economy are tradable, the effect of this fall in consumption will be a rise in output relative to absorption, and thus an increase in net exports. Steel manufacturers facing a fall in domestic demand for their product, for example, will simply export more steel abroad.

But this adjustment can take place only with tradable goods. If some goods are not tradable, the process cannot be so easy. Take the barber who faces the fall in domestic demand. He cannot simply sell more haircuts abroad when fewer local customers show up at his shop. And he may not be able to cut his prices much either, if his costs remain unchanged. Perhaps haircut prices will fall (relative to steel prices), but at the same time some barbers will go out of business, unable to cover costs at the lower prices. Unemployed barbers will have to look for other jobs, presumably in sectors of the economy in which production is being sustained (or increased) by exports.

Thus, the presence of nontradable goods in an economy makes the process of adjusting to downturns more complex and often more painful than

---

[1] Among the pioneers in the development of the tradable and nontradable goods model were James Meade, "The Price Adjustment and the Australian Balance of Payments," *Economic Record,* November 1956; W. E. Salter, "Internal and External Balance: The Role of Prices and Expenditure Effects," *Economic Record,* August 1959; T. Swan, "Economic Control in a Dependent Economy," *Economic Record,* March 1960; and W. Max Corden, "The Geometric Representation of Policies to Attain Internal and External Balance," *Review of Economic Studies,* October 1960.

it was in the economies we described in the previous chapters. In general, the prices of nontraded goods fall relative to the prices of traded goods, and at the same time, production of nontraded goods declines while production of traded goods rises. As workers shift out of the nontradable sector into the tradable sector, there is likely to be a period of at least temporary unemployment while they take time to match up with new job opportunities.

21-1 DETERMINANTS OF TRADABILITY AND A BROAD CLASSIFICATION OF GOODS

Now that we have described nontradable goods and offered some examples, let us see what kinds of goods tend to be nontradable or tradable. In principle, two main factors determine tradability or nontradability.

First, and most important, are transport costs, which create natural barriers to trade. The lower transport costs are as a proportion of the total cost of a good, the more likely it is that the good will be traded internationally. Goods with very high value per unit weight (and thus low transport costs as a proportion of value) tend to be highly tradable. The prime example is gold, which is nearly perfectly tradable, with almost identical prices on any given day in any of the major trading cities of the world. At the other extreme, remember the haircut that costs $25 in New York and $5 in New Delhi. It was the high transport costs that rendered this service nontradable. Many, but not all, services share this characteristic of high transport costs per unit of value. Technological progress in communications has recently allowed for the international trade of several kinds of financial services, including personal banking accounts, insurance, and so forth. Indeed, the developing world's exports of services have recently started to grow at a significant pace, especially in areas like data processing, engineering, computer software, and tourism. Workers in Jamaica, Manila, and South Korea, for example, feed basic information into computers for several multinational firms stationed in the United States.

The second factor that determines tradability or nontradability is the extent of trade protectionism. Tariffs and trade quotas can block the free flow of goods across national borders, even where transportation costs are low. The higher these artificial barriers to trade, the less likely it is that a good will be traded. Consider, for example, a 100 percent tariff on furniture. Suppose, for purposes of illustration, that a piece of furniture, say, a chair, costs $80 in the rest of the world, and it costs $20 to ship it to the domestic economy. The chair, then, would cost $100 at the port of entry in the domestic country. If the country imposes a 100 percent tariff, the domestic cost of the imported chair is now $200. Now suppose that the local industry sells this same chair at $150. Clearly, there will be no imports because the domestic industry can undersell the imports. But at the same time, there will be no exports because the domestic industry could not hope to compete in foreign markets with foreign producers whose costs are only $80. Thus, this chair will be neither imported nor exported: protectionism has rendered it a nontraded good.

The categories of what is tradable and what is nontradable are not immutable, of course. Technological improvements that reduce transport costs are likely to make more goods tradable. By contrast, increases in protectionism tend to increase the list of nontradable goods.

In practice, then, which goods belong to one category and which to the other? There are hundreds of thousands of goods and services, and we cannot hope to answer this question for each good. But we can try to classify goods into broad categories. One well-known classification used in most countries is the standard industrial classification (SIC) of the United Nations. According to the SIC, goods and services are divided into nine different categories by major industry:

1. Agriculture, hunting, forestry, and fishing
2. Mining and quarrying
3. Manufacturing
4. Electricity, gas, and water
5. Construction
6. Wholesale and retail trade, restaurants, and hotels
7. Transport, storage, and communications
8. Financing, insurance, real estate, and business services
9. Community, social, and personal services

Very roughly speaking, goods included in the first three categories, agriculture, mining and manufacturing, are typically the most tradable, while goods in the other categories are generally assumed to be nontradable. As a rule, construction (for example, homebuilding), services (categories 8 and 9), and domestic transportation (for example, bus and train services), are not easily tradable. But there are obvious and important exceptions. On the one hand, high transport costs render many kinds of agricultural products, such as garden vegetables, nontradable, while tariff barriers in agriculture and industry often impose formidable obstacles to trade. On the other hand, some construction activities are highly tradable, as shown by the work of huge South Korean construction firms on large building projects in the Middle East during the 1970s and 1980s. Some transportation services, such as international air travel and shipping, are obviously engaged in international trade. And, as we have noted, recent technological advances in communications have rendered many kinds of financial services internationally tradable.

21-2 Theoretical Framework

Let us now try to develop a simple theoretical model of tradable and nontradable goods, which we shall call the TNT model. We turn first to the supply conditions in the model.

Aggregate Supply in the TNT Model

Suppose that the home country produces and consumes two goods, tradables (T) and nontradables (N). At this stage of the discussion, we shall assume that the production processes for the two goods use only labor and that production in each sector is a linear function of the labor input:

$$Q_T = a_T L_T \quad \text{(tradable goods)} \qquad \textbf{(21.1a)}$$

$$Q_N = a_N L_N \quad \text{(nontradable goods)} \qquad \textbf{(21.1b)}$$

L_T and L_N are the amounts of labor used in the production of tradables and nontradables, respectively, and a_T and a_N are the coefficients representing the marginal productivities of labor in the production of the two kinds of goods. An additional unit of labor in sector T leads to a_T units more of output. Because the production functions are linear in L_T and L_N, the coefficients a_T and a_N represent the average productivities of labor as well as the marginal productivities.

It is useful to derive the production possibility frontier (PPF) of the economy in the TNT model. We assume that there is a given amount of labor (L) that may be employed in sector T or sector N. Therefore, assuming that labor is fully employed, we have

$$L = L_T + L_N \tag{21.2}$$

Using equations (21.1a) and (21.1b), we can write the expression in terms of output levels and the productivity coefficients. Because $L_T = Q_T/a_T$ and $L_N = Q_N/a_N$, we can rewrite (21.2) as follows:

$$L = \frac{Q_T}{a_T} + \frac{Q_N}{a_N} \tag{21.3}$$

This equation can, in turn, be rearranged to express Q_N as a function of Q_T (as well as L, a_T, and a_N, which are assumed to be fixed):

$$Q_N = a_N L - \left(\frac{a_N}{a_T}\right) Q_T \tag{21.4}$$

Expression (21.4), then, is the equation for the production possibility frontier (PPF). It expresses the maximal amount of Q_N that can be produced for each amount of Q_T produced in the economy. For example, if $Q_T = 0$ (all labor is working in the nontradable sector), then $Q_N = a_N L$. If Q_T is maximized instead, by allocating all labor to tradables production, then $Q_T = a_T L$ and $Q_N = 0$. In general, positive amounts of labor will be employed in both sectors.

The production possibility frontier is represented graphically in Figure 21-1. The X axis measures the production of tradable goods and the Y axis, the production of nontradables. If all labor is devoted to tradables, then production is at point A, with $Q_T = a_T L$ and $Q_N = 0$. If, instead, all labor is devoted to the nontradables sector, then production is at point B, with $Q_N = a_N N$ and $Q_T = 0$. The rest of the PPF consists simply of the line segment connecting points A and B, as shown in Figure 21-1. Any point on this line segment represents a possible combination of production of tradables and nontradables.

The slope of the PPF is equal to the relative price of tradables in terms of nontradables. Let us see why. For each type of good, the price of output is just equal to the cost of labor used in the production of a unit of the good (this results from the assumption of a production technology which is linear in labor input). Each unit of tradable output requires $1/a_T$ units of labor. With a wage level w, the labor cost of producing a unit of T is simply w/a_T. The labor cost of producing a unit of N is simply w/a_N. Thus,

$$P_T = \frac{w}{a_T}$$

$$P_N = \frac{w}{a_N} \tag{21.5}$$

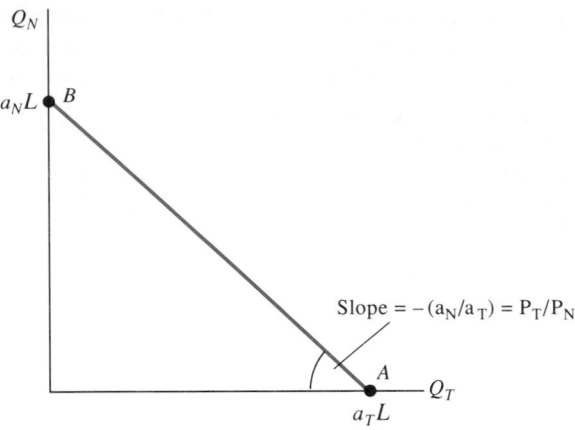

Figure 21-1
The Production Possibility Frontier with Labor
as the Only Input

Note that the equation can also be interpreted as the profit-maximizing condition that the marginal product of labor should be equated to the product wage, where the product wage is measured as the ratio of the wage to the output price. That is, $a_T = w/P_T$ and $a_N = w/P_N$.

From (21.5) we see that $P_T/P_N = a_N/a_T$. We also know from (21.4) that $-(a_N/a_T)$ is equal to the slope of the PPF. Thus, the steeper the PPF, the higher the relative price of tradable goods to nontradable goods in the economy. This simple fact has important implications later on.

In the TNT model, it is usual to label the relative price of tradable goods in terms of nontradable goods as "the real exchange rate." Letting e be the real exchange rate in this model, we have

$$e = \frac{P_T}{P_N} = \frac{a_N}{a_T} \tag{21.6}$$

Obviously, the slope of the PPF is also equal to (the negative value of) the real exchange rate $(-e)$. (Note here an important semantical confusion in standard economics terminology. In models with differentiated products, like those in Chapters 13 and 14, the term "real exchange rate" is used to measure EP^*/P. In the TNT model, the *same* term is used to measure P_T/P_N.)

Aggregate Demand in the TNT Model

Now that we have talked about the supply side of the economy, it is time to introduce aggregate demand. We shall concentrate on *consumption* decisions and neglect investment spending,[2] a simplification that allows us to focus on the most important novelties of the TNT model.

Total absorption is equal to spending on tradable goods and nontradable goods. More formally, $A = P_T C_T + P_N C_N$, where A is total absorption

---

[2] In this basic scenario, we do not distinguish between the private sector and the government; thus, C should be interpreted as total consumption.

and C_T and C_N are the levels of consumption (in real terms) of tradable and nontradable goods. Absorption is divided between the two goods, and we would expect that consumption of each type of good would depend on the overall level of absorption and the relative price of the two kinds of goods. For our purposes, we can simplify this further and suppose (unless otherwise noted) that households consume C_T and C_N in fixed proportions, regardless of relative prices—that is, we assume that the ratio C_T/C_N is fixed. When total spending rises, both C_T and C_N rise in the same proportion; when total spending falls, both C_T and C_N fall in the same proportion.

With this assumption in mind, we can graph the spending choices of households, as shown in Figure 21-2. Household consumption choices lie on the line $0C$. When absorption is low, spending is at a point like B, where both C_T and C_N are low. When absorption is high, spending is at a point like D, where both C_T and C_N are high. Notice, however, that the ratio C_T/C_N is fixed as absorption rises and falls along the $0C$ line.

The $0C$ line will play a key role in the determination of market equilibrium, which is the subject of the next section.

Market Equilibrium in the TNT Model

The central assumption of the TNT model is that because there can be no exports or imports of N, the domestic consumption of N must equal domestic production of N. By contrast, tradable goods can be imported or exported, and thus domestic consumption of T can differ from domestic production. Specifically, we have the following key relationships:

$$Q_N = C_N$$
$$TB = Q_T - C_T \tag{21.7}$$

Note that the trade balance (in units of the tradable good) is equal to the excess of production of tradables over consumption of tradables. We know from Chapter 6 that $Q_T - C_T$ can also be written as $X_T - IM_T$, where X_T is the level of exports of T and IM_T is the level of imports of T.

Let us consider the nature of market equilibrium in the TNT model by superimposing the $0C$ schedule on the PPF, as we do in Figure 21-3. Suppose that household consumption is at point A on the $0C$ curve. At that point, consumption of nontradables is given by C_N^A, and consumption of tradables

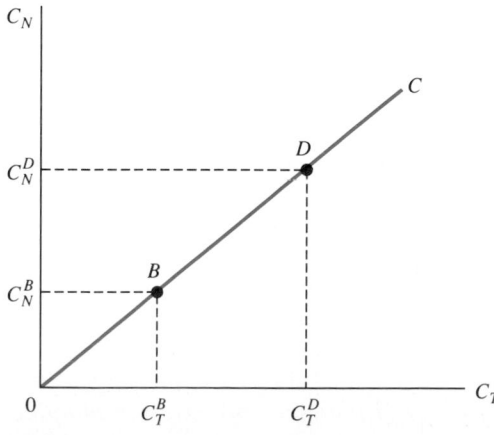

Figure 21-2
A Graphical Representation of the Consumption Path in the TNT Model

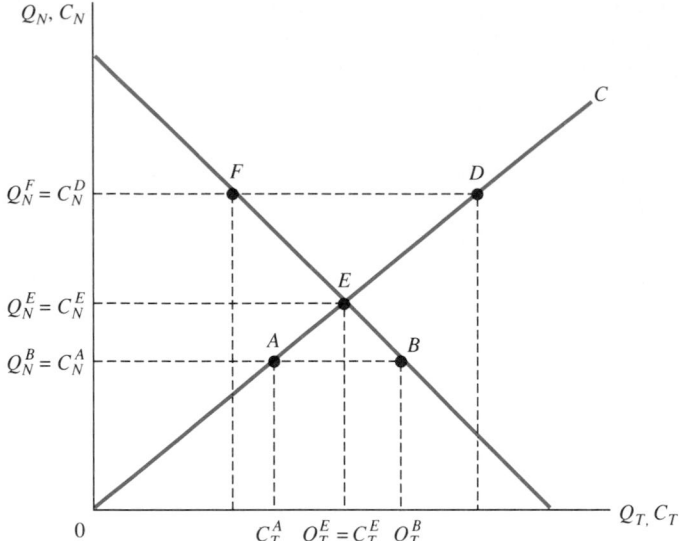

Figure 21-3
The PPF, the Consumption Path, and Equilibrium.

is given by C_T^A. With consumption of nontradables equal to C_N^A, the production of nontradables must also be C_N^A. That is, $Q_N^B = C_N^A$, as we said earlier. Thus, the production point must lie on the PPF at exactly the point where Q_N is equal to C_N. To be precise, the production point corresponding to absorption A must be at point B, which lies on the same horizontal line as point A.

Notice that at point B the production of tradables is at the level Q_T^B, which is greater than the absorption of tradables, given by C_T^A. Thus, when absorption is at A, and production is therefore at point B, the economy has a trade surplus, since $Q_T^B > C_T^A$. Consumption and production of nontradables are equal (as they must be). Now consider the situation if absorption is at point D. In this case, production must be at point F, which lies on the same horizontal line as point D. (Production must be at point F when absorption is at point D, of course, so that the nontradable goods market is in balance.)

Comparing the two absorption points, A and D, we can draw an important lesson. When overall absorption is high, there is more spending on both tradable and nontradable goods. The higher demand for nontradable goods requires greater production of nontradable goods in order that demand and supply for nontradable goods be in balance. But higher production of nontradables can occur only by shifting resources out of the tradable sector and into the nontradable sector. Higher overall demand therefore leads to a rise in the production of nontradable goods, but a *fall* in the production of tradable goods. This asymmetry reflects a simple fact. An increase in demand for nontradables can only be satisfied by greater domestic production; by contrast, an increase in demand for tradables can be satisfied by imports.

Point E at the intersection of the PPF and the $0C$ curves, is the point at which consumption and production are equal for both tradable and nontradable goods. At this point, the trade account is exactly balanced; that is, the consumption of tradables, C_T, equals the production of tradables, Q_T. Point E is sometimes called the point of *internal balance* and *external balance*.

"Internal balance" refers to the fact that the demand for nontradables equals the supply of nontradables (which is always satisfied); "external balance" refers to the fact that the trade account is zero.

Borrowing and Repayment in the TNT Model

We can now use the apparatus just developed to enrich our analysis of international borrowing and lending. In earlier chapters, we noted that borrowing in one period requires repayment in later periods. Specifically, trade deficits must be balanced later on (in present value terms) by future trade surpluses. Now we can show a crucial point, that *a shift from a situation of borrowing to repayment also requires a corresponding shift in the patterns of domestic production.*

Suppose, for example, that an economy has been consuming more than its income and that domestic residents have been borrowing abroad to maintain this expensive life-style. In Figure 21-4, this pattern is depicted by consumption at point D and production at point F. The country's net debt (not shown in the diagram) builds up over time as the economy's firms, households, and government, in the aggregate, borrow from the rest of the world. But the country's intertemporal budget constraint dictates that the situation must eventually change. At some point, the economy must shift back to trade surplus so that domestic residents can service the international debts they have accumulated.

We want to examine very closely the economic effects of the shift back to trade surplus. The shift from trade deficit to surplus, of course, requires a drop in consumption relative to output. Say that consumption falls from point D to point B on the $0C$ curve. When that happens, the demand for nontradable goods in the economy declines (as does the demand for tradables). Workers in the nontradable sector—the barber from our initial example, together with fellow workers in construction and other services—begin to lose their jobs because domestic demand for their goods is declining. These workers now must find jobs in the tradable sector of the economy where, indeed, there is still growth. Despite the fall in domestic demand,

Figure 21-4
The Case of Foreign Borrowing and Repayment

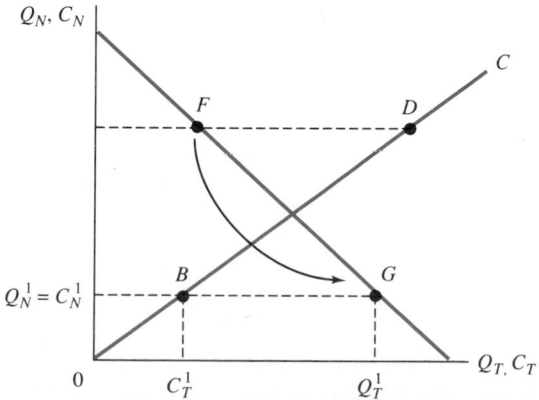

firms in the tradable sector have expanded production because they can sell their output abroad on the world market.

Thus, the shift from trade deficit to trade surplus involves a shift in domestic production from point F to point G (which is on the same horizontal line as point B). Note that in the process of generating a trade surplus, the production of tradables has increased, while the production of nontradables has declined. To put this another way, the trade surplus comes about not merely because of a fall in demand, but also because of a shift in supply from nontradables production to tradables production.

A clear example of resources shifting from nontradables to tradables occurred in Chile after 1982. In the late 1970s, Chileans borrowed heavily, indeed too heavily, on the international capital markets. As happened in much of the developing world, international credits for Chile dried up in the early 1980s, after the period of heavy borrowing. Creditors became fearful of the ability of Chileans to service their debts, especially after the rise in world interest rates in the early 1980s.[3] Chileans had to stop running large trade deficits and start running trade surpluses, as seen in Table 21-1. Domestic demand in Chile plummeted. In effect, absorption fell from a point like D to a point like B in Figure 21-4.

TABLE 21-1

CHILE'S ADJUSTMENT PROCESS, 1979–1985

| Year | National Unemployment Rate by Economic Activity* | | | | Building Permits and Starts (area, thousands of squared meters) | Trade Balance/GDP (%) |
	Total	Agriculture and Fishing	Construction	Industry		
1979	13.6	7.3	28.9	12.5	3,591	−1.7
1980	10.4	5.0	18.7	11.2	4,643	−2.8
1981	11.3	6.2	25.8	11.8	5,638	−8.2
1982	19.6	9.4	50.8	26.6	2,365	0.3
1983	14.6	5.8	38.2	17.9	2,771	5.0
1984	13.9	5.5	30.7	14.2	3,209	1.9
1985	12.0	4.9	23.8	5.4	3,831	5.3

* *Figures correspond to the* National Employment Survey, *compiled every year by the National Bureau of Statistics in the period October–December.*
Source: *Central Bank of Chile.*

The economy had to undergo a major reallocation of resources of the sort we have just described. As we see in Table 21-1, the shift from trade deficit to trade surplus was accompanied by the shift out of nontradables production, especially construction, and into tradables production, led by the agricultural sector. There was a large increase in unemployment among

---

[3] We discuss the origins of the international debt crisis in Chapter 22.

Box 21-1
Structural Adjustment Programs

The movement of resources from nontradable goods production to tradable goods production requires a significant economic restructuring of the economy. Many complications can arise during such structural transitions, especially high unemployment if workers are laid off jobs in nontradables production more rapidly than they can find new jobs in tradables production. The delay in finding new jobs may result from the costs of moving to where the new jobs are, wage rigidities in the tradables sector, problems in disseminating information about what the new work is and where it is, and so on. To minimize these social costs, governments may implement a package of policies, sometimes called *structural adjustment programs,* in order to facilitate the transfer of resources and to remove barriers that restrict factor mobility. These policy actions support the shift in resources to the tradables sector and reduce the economic rigidities that can hamper adjustment.

On the microeconomic side, structural adjustment programs often include the following kinds of measures: (1) policies that improve efficiency in the use of resources by the public sector, including the rationalization of public investment, the restructuring of state-owned companies, and the privatization of some public enterprises; (2) measures that improve the structure of economic incentives, such as trade liberalization (to develop the export sector and reduce the distortions caused by tariffs, quotas, and other trade restrictions) and reforms of the price system, especially in agriculture and public enterprises; and (3) measures that strengthen the economic institutions that are crucial for the success of the adjustment program, like the customs service and tax administration. These microeconomic measures, designed to enhance the flow of resources in the economy and the shift of labor and capital to the tradables sector, are typically supplemented by macroeconomic measures, which include fiscal austerity, a tight monetary policy, and often a currency devaluation (for reasons described shortly).

During the 1980s, the World Bank played a visible role in helping countries to design structural adjustment policies and in lending money to countries to help them reduce the costs of restructuring. At the same time, the International Monetary Fund (IMF) supervised the introduction of accompanying macroeconomic measures, including cuts in budget deficits and exchange-rate devaluations. The policy packages implemented jointly by the World Bank and the IMF generated considerable controversy, both as to their effectiveness and as to the adequacy of the money they were willing to lend to support the policy measures. Several criticisms have been aimed at the role of the World Bank in its support of adjustment programs. Among them, it has been said that (1) the amount of resources devoted to adjustment loans by the Bank has been insufficient in relation to the countries' needs; that (2) the conditions on which the loans were based have occasionally been unrealistic, being too optimistic either about the response of private agents to price incentives, or about the political sustainability of the programs; and that (3) the World Bank may pay too little attention to equity issues, some critics having suggested

> that the overriding concern behind some of these programs has been economic efficiency at the cost of equity.[4] Of course, these views are very different from the way the Bank evaluates its own role in supporting adjustment.[5]
>
> However well designed the policy packages, it is clear that the costs of transition from trade deficits to trade surpluses among the debtor developing countries during the 1980s have been extremely high. Such countries have seen large increases in unemployment, and sharp declines in production and employment of nontradables have not been promptly matched by large increases in tradables production and employment.

construction workers, and many of these workers shifted to work in the fruit export business or in agroindustry.

In reality, the adjustment process is far from painless, as the Chilean experience attests. As we see in Table 21-1, unemployment soared at the time that workers were laid off from construction. Workers need time for retraining in order to adjust their skills to the newly available jobs. Also, as is frequently true, the economic restructuring in Chile required a geographical reallocation of labor, which took more time and occasioned significant economic and social costs. These factors, among others, explain why the unemployment rate increased so substantially when Chile underwent the fundamental economic restructuring that was necessary to bring about the shift from trade deficit to trade surplus.

The Dutch Disease

The shift of production between tradables and nontradables tends to occur whenever there are large shifts in the level of domestic spending. This can happen when an economy starts to repay its debts, but it can occur for other reasons as well. One common case that has received considerable attention from economists is that of a country which experiences a large change in wealth because of *shifts in the value of natural resources held by the residents of the country.* A nation can find itself dramatically enriched after major discoveries of natural resources in its territory (as when Norway discovered the magnitude of its North Sea oil deposits in the 1970s) or when the world price of its natural resources changes dramatically (as when the oil-exporting countries enjoyed a large jump in income at the end of the 1970s).

The effects of large changes in wealth resulting from resource discoveries or resource price changes can be very dramatic, indeed so dramatic that they have been given a special name, *the Dutch disease.*[6] The name

---

[4] For a critical analysis of the role of the World Bank in structural adjustment programs see, for example, Edmar Bacha and Richard Feinberg, ''The World Bank and Structural Adjustment in Latin America,'' *World Development,* March 1986.

[5] See, for example, a recent report prepared by the World Bank's staff on adjustment lending: Vittorio Corbo et al., *Report on Adjustment Lending: Policies for the Recovery of Growth* (Washington, D.C.: The World Bank, 1990).

[6] For a good survey of the Dutch disease problem, see W. Max Corden, ''Booming Sector and Dutch Disease Economics: Survey and Consolidation,'' *Oxford Economic Papers,* November 1984.

comes from the fact that the Netherlands, a large holder of natural gas deposits, experienced major shifts in domestic production following the discovery of substantial gas deposits in the 1960s. As the exports of this natural resource boomed, the guilder appreciated in real terms, thereby squeezing the profitability of other exports, especially manufactures. We shall see, however, that the "disease" part of the term is something of a misnomer. The shifts in production occasioned by changes in resource wealth are not really a "disease" of the economy.

Let us consider the effects of a discovery of oil in a country which, say, had a tradables sector that consisted solely of non-oil industries, such as manufacturing, before the discovery. Suppose that the new oil reserves increase tradable output by the amount Q_0. Before the oil discovery, the production possibility frontier is given by the PPF line (PF) in Figure 21-5. After the oil discovery, the country can now produce Q_0 *more* units of tradable goods than it could before the oil discovery, so that the PPF shifts horizontally to the right by the amount Q_0, as shown in the figure.

Suppose, now, that before and after the oil discovery, the country's trade is balanced; that is, given world interest rates and household preferences, there is no desire for borrowing or lending. Thus, before the oil discovery, economic equilibrium is at the point A in Figure 21-5, at the intersection of the PPF and the OC curve. After the oil discovery, economic equilibrium shifts to point B. Note that the oil discovery has, naturally, led to an expansion of demand (reflecting the increased wealth of the nation) and that this expansion of demand has caused an increase in consumption of both tradable and nontradable goods.

Now let us look closely at the effects of this spending increase on the *production patterns* in the economy. The shifts in production patterns are somewhat subtle. As we can see in Figure 21-5, production of nontradables increases as a result of the spending boom, from point Q_N^A to Q_N^B. Production

Figure 21-5
Effects of Oil Discovery in a Hypothetical Country: A Case of Dutch Disease

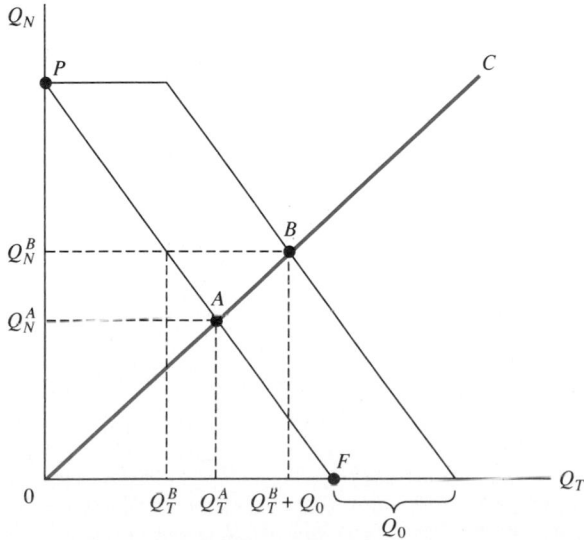

of tradables also increases, but in a more complicated way. At point B, production of "traditional" non-oil tradables is at the level Q_T^B and production of oil is at the level Q_0. Total tradable production is therefore at the level $Q_T^B + Q_0$. Thus, when we compare tradable production before and after the oil discovery, we find three things. First, non-oil production has *fallen*, from Q_T^A down to Q_T^B. Second, oil production has *risen*, from zero to Q_0. And, third, total tradable production, that is, the sum of the two subsectors, has gone up, from Q_T^A to $Q_T^B + Q_0$.

The *Dutch disease*, then, is the term applied to the fact that non-oil tradable production declines as a result of the oil discovery. In concrete terms, an important discovery of oil—or gas, or diamonds, or other natural resource—is likely to lead to a shrinkage in traditional manufacturing. The reason should be clear. The positive wealth effect of the natural resource boom draws resources away from the traditional tradables sector and into the nontradables sector. And, as we have said, the higher demand for nontradables can only be met by greater domestic production of nontradables, while the higher demand for tradables can be satisfied by an increase in imports (with an actual drop of domestic production).

Note that the "disease"—the shrinkage of the manufacturing sector— may *seem* like a disease, especially to workers and owners in that sector, but in fact the production shift is the optimal response to an increase in wealth. It is only through the decline in tradables production that domestic households can enjoy the benefits of increased consumption of nontradables.

The Dutch disease phenomenon was evident in the major oil-exporting countries in the late 1970s when world oil prices soared.[7] In these countries, the higher oil wealth prompted a shift toward nontradables, especially construction, and put a squeeze on traditional tradable sectors, including agriculture and industry exposed to international trade. When world oil prices collapsed in the mid-1980s, the Dutch disease was reversed. Domestic demand in the oil-rich countries plummeted, causing significant unemployment in the construction industry and a shift of employment back to agriculture and other tradable goods sectors.

A prime example of Dutch disease in Latin America (and one unrelated to oil) appeared in Colombia in the second half of the 1970s.[8] Traditionally, Colombia has been heavily dependent on coffee, which accounted for almost two-thirds of its exports in the late 1960s and about 45 percent of its exports in 1974. Weather problems in Brazil and an earthquake in Guatemala contributed in 1975 to a significant scarcity of coffee in world markets. Thus, coffee prices boomed, increasing almost five times over the next two years.

---

[7] For an analysis of the Dutch disease in the case of Indonesia, a large oil producer, see Wing Woo and Anwar Nasution, "Indonesian Economic Policies and Their Relation to External Debt Management," in J. Sachs and S. Collins, eds., *Developing Country Debt and Economic Performance,* Vol. 3 (Chicago: National Bureau of Economic Research, University of Chicago Press, 1989).

[8] Two interesting analysis of the Dutch disease in Colombia are Sebastian Edwards, "Commodity Export Prices and the Real Exchange Rate," in S. Edwards and L. Ahamed, eds., *Economic Adjustment and Exchange Rates in Developing Countries* (Chicago: National Bureau of Economic Research, University of Chicago Press, 1986), and Linda Kamas, "Dutch Disease Economics and the Colombian Export Boom," *World Development,* September 1986.

Coffee production in Colombia was quick to respond, and it increased by 76 percent between 1974 and 1981. As a consequence of this boom, Colombia enjoyed a surge in export revenues of almost 300 percent over the next five years. But, as the theory predicts, the country's real exchange rate appreciated considerably —about 20 percent between 1975 and 1980—and this hurt the competitiveness of the noncoffee tradables sector. The evolution of the real price of coffee and the real exchange rate is shown on Figure 21-6 for the period 1974–1980 (as usual, a fall in the real exchange rate in the graph signifies a real appreciation).

Thus, Colombia experienced a boom in the coffee sector and a substantial expansion of nontradable activities, especially in construction and government services. However, the growth rate of output among other tradable goods was reduced substantially, principally among manufactures, as shown in Table 21-2.

The general symptoms of the Dutch disease, although most widely associated with a natural resource boom, can also arise when other forces cause a large shift in domestic demand. For example, countries that receive vast increases in foreign aid are likely to experience a consumption boom. Recipients of foreign aid often find that the financial assistance from the outside world inadvertently squeezes the tradable sectors within its economy. When this happens, aid can actually damage precisely those economic sectors most in need of development.

Note that a domestic fiscal expansion is likely to have the same effects on production as a resource boom. Higher fiscal spending that is not offset by a decline in private spending can lead to an overall shift in demand toward nontradable goods and thus to a shift of production from tradables to nontradables. When Stephen Marris examined the sectoral effects of the large fiscal expansion during the first half of the 1980s in the United States, he

Figure 21-6

The Real Exchange Rate and the Real Price of Coffee in Colombia, 1975–1980

(From Linda Kamas, "Dutch Disease Economics and the Colombian Export Boom," World Development, *September 1986.)*

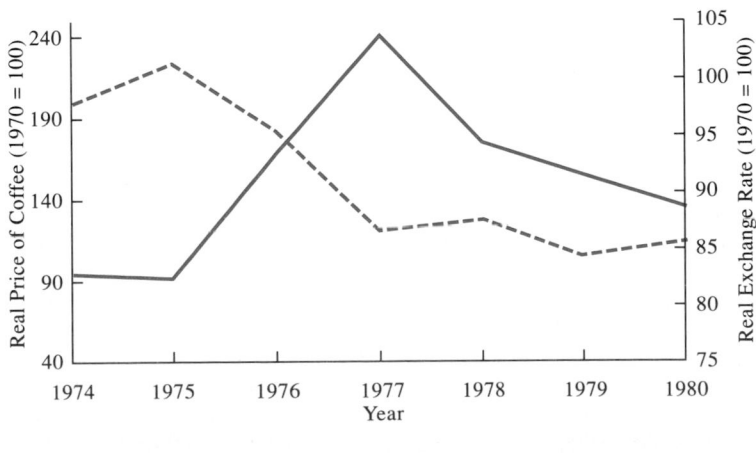

Real price of coffee   Real exchange rate

TABLE 21-2

THE RECOMPOSITION OF PRODUCTION IN COLOMBIA DURING DUCTH DISEASE, 1970–1981
(ANNUAL AVERAGE PERCENT GROWTH OF PRODUCTION IN SELECTED SECTORS)

	Growth		% Change
	1970–1975	**1976–1981**	
Nontradables			
Construction and public works	3.3	5.8	+2.5
Residential rent	3.7	4.3	+0.6
Government services	4.1	8.6	+4.5
Personal services	2.8	2.8	+0.0
Tradables (noncoffee)			
Textiles, clothing, and leather	5.1	−0.6	−5.7
Paper and printing	9.3	5.3	−4.0
Refined petroleum products	8.0	0.3	−7.7
Chemicals and rubber	10.2	3.7	−6.5
Manufactures of metals	6.1	3.6	−2.5
Other manufactures	4.8	1.9	−2.9
Transport materials	12.6	4.6	−8.0
Machinery and equipment	10.5	4.8	−5.7
Coffee	4.1	10.8	+6.7

Source: Linda Kamas, "*Dutch Disease Economics and the Colombian Export Boom*,"
World Development, *September 1986.*

found that significant parts of the tradables sector were squeezed, while the nontradable goods sector boomed.[9] Historically, episodes of economic populism as well as sharp increases in military expenditures have also provided vivid examples of large increases in fiscal spending which constricted production in the tradables sector.

21-3 TRADABLES, NONTRADABLES, AND THE PRICE LEVEL

One of the striking regularities in the world economy is that rich countries are "more expensive" than poor countries. Tourists and international businessmen find that it is more expensive to visit Europe and Japan than it is to visit Latin America or Africa. Careful studies have confirmed what most of us believe, that the cost of living, represented by a basket of commodities

---

[9] Stephen Marris, of the Institute for International Economics, has documented the pattern of response to the policies of the early 1980s among tradables and nontradables. See *Deficits and the Dollar: The World Economy at Risk,* Policy Analyses in International Economics 14, Institute for International Economics, updated edition, 1987.

that includes food, housing, and consumer goods, is indeed higher in the richer countries than in the poorer countries.

The reasons for this discrepancy are not obvious. Tradable goods should cost approximately the same throughout the world, aside from transport costs and tariffs which generally do not add a lot to the price of goods. Therefore, if most goods in the world were tradables, differences in price levels across countries would be small. The most pronounced differences lie in the prices of nontraded goods.

But why should nontraded goods be more expensive in richer countries? One obvious thought is that "wages are higher." This is true, but labor productivity is also higher in the richer countries, and this can offset the higher wage costs. As it turns out, the TNT model gives a clear explanation of these differences in prices across countries.

Prices, Wages, and Productivity

To put the matter clearly, we need to compare the price levels of two countries in a common currency. Let P be the price level of the home economy, then, and P^* be the price level of the foreign country in the foreign currency. Then, the price level of the foreign country in the domestic currency is EP^*, where E is the domestic exchange rate (units of domestic currency per unit of foreign currency). We want to compare P and EP^*.

The price levels P and EP^* are weighted averages of the prices of tradable goods and nontradable goods. Let σ be the weight in the price index attached to the tradable good, and $1 - \sigma$ be the weight attached to the nontradable good. For simplicity, let us assume that this weighting is the same in the two countries:

$$P = \sigma P_T + (1 - \sigma)P_N$$
$$EP^* = (EP_T^*) + (1 - \sigma)(EP_N^*) \tag{21.8}$$

Now, let us assume that purchasing power parity holds for the tradable goods. This means that the prices of tradables—cars, consumer durables, grains, oil, gold, and so on—are the same in the two countries:

$$P_T = EP_T^* \tag{21.9}$$

Since the prices of tradables are the same in both countries, P will be higher than EP^* if and only if P_N is greater than EP_N^*.[10] In other words, assuming that purchasing power parity holds for tradable goods, the difference in price levels in the two countries depends only on the difference in the prices of nontradable goods.

But what determines the prices P_N and EP_N^*? We can find these prices in the following way. The wage level in the economy is linked to the prices of tradable goods. We know from equation (21.5) that $P_T = w/a_T$, or, rearrang-

---

[10] This can be established by simple algebra. By subtracting the expression for EP^* from the expression for P in equation (19.8), and using the purchasing power parity relation, we get

$$P - EP^* = (1 - \sigma)(P_N - EP_N^*)$$

Thus, $P > EP^*$ if and only if $P_N > EP_N^*$.

ing terms, $w = P_T a_T$. This equation determines the wage level in terms of the price of tradable goods (P_T), and the productivity coefficient in the production of tradable goods (a_T).

In turn, the cost of nontradable goods is given by the cost of labor used in producing a unit of N. Because each unit of production of N requires $1/a_N$ units of labor, the cost of labor is w/a_N. Therefore the price of nontradable output is given by $P_N = w/a_N$. And since $w = P_T a_T$ and $P_N = w/a_N$, we can combine these two expressions to find

$$P_N = P_T \left(\frac{a_T}{a_N} \right) \qquad (21.10)$$

Notice that the nontradable price is simply a multiple of the tradable price, where the multiple depends on the productivity of labor in the two sectors.

In the foreign country, the comparable expression is[11]

$$EP_N^* = P_T \left(\frac{a_T^*}{a_N^*} \right) \qquad (21.11)$$

Notice that the foreign nontradables price is similarly a multiple of the tradables price, where the multiple in this case depends on the productivity of labor in the two sectors in the *foreign* economy.

Let us look more carefully at what these expressions mean now. Nontradable prices are *high* when labor is highly productive in the tradables sector, that is, when a_T is large. Here is why. Highly productive labor commands a high wage, and when labor productivity in tradables is large, the wage is high in terms of tradable goods. A high wage, in turn, means high labor costs in nontradable production as well. Thus, a high value of a_T means a high-price P_N. At the same time, nontradable prices will be *low* if labor is highly productive in the nontradables sector, that is, when a_N is large. When labor productivity in nontradables is large, the amount of labor used per unit of production in nontradables is small. Thus, a high value of a_N means a low price P_N.

For this reason, the price of nontradables (P_N) depends on the *relative* productivity of labor in the two sectors (a_T/a_N). High productivity in tradables means high wages in terms of tradable goods, but high productivity in nontradables means *low* labor input per unit of nontradables production. Thus, the price of nontradables P_N depends on the *ratio* a_T/a_N rather than on the productivity in either sector individually.

It is now possible to compare the prices of nontradables in the two countries. From equations (21.10) and (21.11), we see immediately that the domestic economy is "more expensive" than abroad when $(a_T/a_N) > (a_T^*/a_N^*)$. The domestic economy is "less expensive" than abroad when $(a_T/a_N) < (a_T^*/a_N^*)$. In simpler language, *one country will be expensive as compared to the other if the relative productivity in its tradable sector (a_T/a_N) is higher than abroad. What matters here is the difference in relative productivity, and not in absolute productivity between the two countries.*

Let us consider the implications of this finding. Suppose that the home

---

[11] The derivation is as follows. $P_N^* = (P_T^*)(a_T^*/a_N^*)$, just as in the home country. Now, multiply both sides of this equation by the exchange rate, to get the following equality: $(EP_N^*) = (EP_T^*)(a_T^*/a_N^*)$. Now, note that EP_T^* equals P_T, by the assumption of purchasing power parity. Thus, we find $EP_N^* = P_T(a_T^*/a_N^*)$, as in equation (21.11) in the text.

country is twice as productive as the foreign country in *both* sectors of the economy ($a_T = 2a_T^*$, $a_N = 2a_N^*$). The home wage (expressed in a common currency) will be twice as high as abroad. But the price of nontradable goods will be *identical* in the two countries. Even though the domestic wage is twice as high as abroad, the labor productivity in nontradable production is also twice as high, so the costs of labor per unit of output are the same in the two countries!

Now suppose that the home economy is twice as productive in the tradable goods sector, but exactly as productive in the nontradable goods sector ($a_T = 2a_T^*$, $a_N = a_N^*$). The home country might be better at producing automobiles than the foreign country, but no better at producing haircuts, let us say. Then, the wage at home will be twice as high as the wage abroad, as before, when expressed in a common currency. But now, the labor cost of producing the nontradable good will be twice as high than abroad because productivity is no higher in the nontradable sector. Haircuts at home will be twice as expensive as abroad. The overall domestic price level will be higher at home.

Suppose now that the home economy has the same productivity in tradables production, but twice the productivity in nontradables production ($a_T = a_T^*$, $a_N = 2a_N^*$). In this case, the wage will be exactly the same in the two countries when expressed in a common currency. But the cost of nontradables will be *less* at home than abroad, since less labor is used per unit of output in the nontradable sector. In this situation, the home economy will be cheaper than abroad.

We can now see the answer to the original question more clearly. Does a rich country tend to be more expensive than a poor country, and if so, why? On the one hand, labor costs are higher in the rich country, while on the other hand, productivity is also higher. We now know that what counts is the balance of productivity between the tradables and nontradables sectors. High productivity in tradables raises wage costs in the production of nontradables, while high productivity in nontradables lowers wage costs in the production of nontradables. A country is relatively expensive in the prices of its nontradables, then, if productivity is relatively high in the production of its tradables, which drives up labor costs in the production of its nontradables.

Can we say more than this? On the empirical level, the answer is yes. History has shown a particular pattern in the growth of productivity, one that is illustrated in Figure 21-7. When countries become richer through higher labor productivity, the rate of increase in productivity *tends to be fastest in the tradable sector*. Higher productivity means a shifting up and to the right of the production possibility frontier, as shown in the figure. But since productivity growth is fastest in tradables, the production possibility frontier shifts out faster along the X axis than it shifts up along the Y axis. In other words, the increase in production is biased toward the tradables sector.[12]

---

[12] Bela Balassa, in a classic 1964 paper, was one of the first to point out this systematic trend: ". . . in present-day industrial economies, productivity increases in the tertiary [services] sector appear to be smaller than the rise of productivity in agriculture and manufacturing. Data derived for the nineteen-fifties indicate, for example, that in the seven major industrial countries examined, productivity increases in the service sector were in all cases lower than the

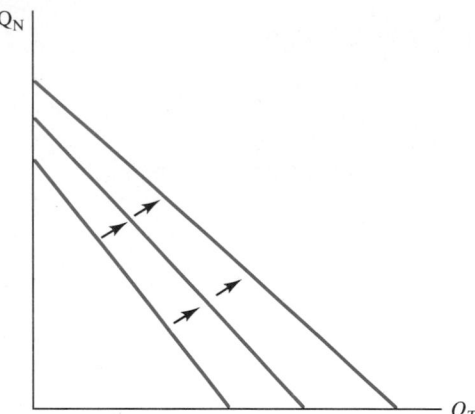

Figure 21-7
Productivity Growth with a Bias Toward Tradables

This bias toward rapid growth of productivity in the tradables sector means that as countries develop, the ratio a_T/a_N tends to grow. In fact, both a_T and a_N rise in the course of economic development, but a_T tends to grow more rapidly than a_N. Thus, rich countries tend to have higher values of a_T/a_N than do poorer countries. We can therefore conclude that *rich countries do tend to be more expensive than poor countries,* not because they are richer in general, but because they are richer in an unbalanced manner, with relatively higher productivity in the tradables sector than in the nontradables sector.

There is yet another noteworthy consequence of a faster productivity increase in the tradable goods sector. When a_T/a_N rises in a country, the price of nontradables rises relative to the price of tradables. If a_T/a_N rises more rapidly than a_T^*/a_N^*, then the home country will tend to have an appreciation of its real exchange rate relative to the foreign country, in the sense that P will rise relative to EP^*. In this case, *even if the two countries are linked by a fixed exchange rate, their inflation rates will differ* because the home country will experience a faster rise in the prices of nontradables.

This is why inflation rates tend to vary even among countries within a fixed-exchange-rate regime. Even though countries linked by a fixed exchange rate will tend to have the same inflation rate for tradable goods, the faster-growing countries tend to have higher inflation because they tend to have higher inflation rates for nontradable goods. This tendency was clearly evident during the 1960s, when the fastest-growing economy in the industrial world, Japan, also had one of the highest inflation rates. In Europe, the more rapidly growing countries also tended to have higher inflation rates than the more slowly growing economies. This pattern is documented clearly in Table 21-3.

---

rise of productivity for the national economy as a whole as well as for agriculture and industry taken separately." See Bela Balassa, "The Purchasing-Power Parity Doctrine: A Reappraisal," *Journal of Political Economy*, December 1964.

TABLE 21-3

INFLATION AND GROWTH IN THE 1960S: THE
CASE OF THE INDUSTRIALIZED COUNTRIES
(AVERAGE RATES, 1960–1969)

Country	Inflation Rate	Growth Rate
Japan	5.37%	11.59%
Spain	5.73	7.37
Italy	3.67	6.33
France	3.84	5.72
Finland	5.01	5.4
Denmark	5.3	5.2
Norway	3.48	5.02
Austria	3.34	4.87
Belgium	2.65	4.85
Switzerland	3.13	4.78
Ireland	3.98	4.47
Sweden	3.74	4.31
United States	2.31	4.19
New Zealand	3.23	4.07
United Kingdom	3.45	3.12

Source: International Monetary Fund, International Financial
Statistics, *various issues.*

Comparing Real Income Levels in Different Countries

One of the most important and interesting kinds of international comparison
is that made among living standards in various countries. Which country is
the richest, or poorest? How large is the gap between standards of living in
rich and poor countries? These questions are trickier than they seem at first
glance because of differences in relative prices in different countries. We
have, for example, good reasons to suppose that the price of nontradables is
lower in poorer countries than in richer countries. These differences in
relative prices cause important distortions in the basic measurements of real
income and real living standards.

Consider this illustration. According to official data, per capita income
in India in 1989 was $340 (in U.S. dollars), compared with per capita income
in the United States of $20,910. Thus, the data said, the gap in real income
was $20,570, and the U.S. per capita income was over 61 times that of India.
But these data neglect a crucial point. The cost of living, that is, the price
level, is much lower in India than in the United States. Thus, a per capita
income of $340 can buy a lot more in goods in India, at Indian prices, than it
could in the United States at U.S. prices. It is not very surprising, then, that
the same dollar income goes farther in India.

Any international comparison of living standards must take this difference into account. To do this we need to measure India's income, not in actual dollars but in dollars corrected for purchasing power. The correct comparison of purchasing power is found by answering the following question: How many dollars *at U.S. prices* would be needed to reach India's level of real per capita income? To arrive at a dollars-per-capita figure that can be used for a comparison we let Y_{US} be the per capita income of the United States and let Y_I be the per capita income of India, with each expressed in its respective domestic currency. Let P be the U.S. price index in dollars, and let P_I be the Indian price index in rupees, *where the two price indices cover a common basket of commodities.*

The standard way of comparing incomes is to compare Y_{US} with Y_I/E, where E is the exchange rate in dollars per rupee. The correct comparison, however, would be $(Y_I/P_I)P_{US}$, because this expression tells us the number of dollars needed, at U.S. prices (P_{US}), to achieve India's real per capita income level. The ratio P_I/P_{US} is sometimes called the PPP exchange rate, which we denote as $E^{PPP}_{(I/US)}$. It answers the question, How many rupees are needed to purchase the same basket of consumer goods that one U.S. dollar purchases in the United States?

Alan Heston, Irving Kravis, and Robert Summers, of the International Comparisons Unit at the University of Pennsylvania, have used this method in a series of important articles and books over the past several years.[13] The basic procedure is to take a broad basket of goods and services and value it both at domestic currency prices and at international dollar prices. The ratio of the domestic cost to the dollar cost of the basket is the PPP exchange rate, which then may be used to convert value of GDP in the domestic currency to a more meaningful dollar measure. This latter measure indicates more accurately the gaps between countries in the purchasing power of per capita income.

Table 21-4 helps to visualize the differences between the results achieved with both methods. Column (1) shows per capita GDP calculated using market exchange rates, column (2) shows the corresponding measure using PPP exchange rates, and column (3) shows the ratio between the two: (2)/(1). The differences between the two measures show an interesting systematic pattern. Market exchange rates tend to overstate the differences between rich and poor countries. Even after corrections for PPP, however, the gaps are still huge. In 1980, for example, per capita income at market exchange rates was $140 in Ethiopia, and $16,440 in Switzerland, a ratio of 117 to 1! The PPP measure of income for that year shows Ethiopia with $325 and Switzerland with $10,013, a much smaller ratio—although still sizable—of 30 to 1.

In summary, then, here are several "rules of thumb" that have some practical significance in making international country comparisons:

[13] Two recent pieces are R. Summers and A. Heston, "A New Set of International Comparisons of Real Product and Price Level Estimates for 130 Countries, 1950–85," *Review of Income and Wealth,* March 1988, and A. Heston and R. Summers, "What We Have Learned about Prices and Quantities from International Comparisons: 1987," *American Economic Review,* May 1988.

TABLE   21-4

PER CAPITA INCOME: MARKET VERSUS PPP EXCHANGE RATES,
SELECTED COUNTRIES (US$, 1980)

	Market Exchange Rate (1)	PPP Exchange Rate (2)	Ratio (2)/(1)
Low income			
Bangladesh	130	540	4.2
Ethiopia	140	325	2.3
India	240	614	2.6
Pakistan	300	989	3.3
Middle Income			
Bolivia	570	1,529	2.7
Egypt	580	995	1.7
El Salvador	660	1,410	2.1
Thailand	670	1,694	2.5
Philippines	690	1,551	2.2
Peru	930	2,456	2.6
Colombia	1,180	2,552	2.2
Turkey	1,470	2,319	1.6
Korea	1,520	2,369	1.6
Brazil	2,050	3,356	1.6
Mexico	2,090	4,333	2.1
Chile	2,150	4,271	2.0
Argentina	2,390	4,342	1.8
Venezuela	3,630	4,422	1.2
Singapore	4,430	5,817	1.3
Israel	4,500	6,145	1.4
High Income			
Spain	5,400	6,131	1.1
Italy	6,480	7,164	1.1
United Kingdom	7,920	7,975	1.0
Australia	9,820	8,349	0.9
Japan	9,890	8,117	0.8
Austria	10,230	8,230	0.8
United States	11,360	11,404	1.0
Netherlands	11,470	9,036	0.8
France	11,730	9,688	0.8
Belgium	12,180	9,228	0.8
Sweden	13,520	8,863	0.7
West Germany	13,590	9,795	0.7
Switzerland	16,440	10,013	0.6

Source: World Bank, World Development Report 1982 *(Oxford: Oxford University Press, 1982), and R. Summers and A. Heston, "A New Set of International Comparisons of Real Product and Price Level Estimates for 130 Countries, 1950–85,"* Review of Income and Wealth, *(New York: International Association for Research in Income and Wealth March 1988).*

1. Richer countries tend to have higher price levels in dollars; that is, they tend to be more expensive. This is because richer economies tend to have a higher ratio of (a_T/a_N).

2. Faster-growing countries tend to experience real appreciations in their currencies, in the sense that P/EP^* tends to increase.

3. For two countries linked by fixed exchange rates, the faster-growing country tends to experience higher inflation.

4. Dollar comparisons of per capita income tend to overstate the differences in real purchasing power between rich and poor countries, because of the fact that rich countries are systematically more expensive than poor countries.

21-4 DEMAND SHOCKS AND THE REAL EXCHANGE RATE

To introduce the TNT model in the simplest possible framework, we have assumed that production in each sector is a linear function of labor. Because of that assumption, relative prices between nontradables and tradables are determined by the technology of production, with $P_N/P_T = a_T/a_N$. Demand factors have played no role in the determination of relative prices. Now, we want to investigate a more realistic setting in which both labor and capital are used in the production of both goods. In this case, the relative price of tradables and nontradables is determined both by technology and aggregate demand.

The production functions now take the usual form:

$$Q_T = Q_T(L_T, \bar{K}_T) \tag{21.12a}$$

$$Q_N = Q_N(L_N, \bar{K}_N \tag{21.12b}$$

We assume that the level of capital is fixed in each sector and that these production functions are subject to the usual condition of a *decreasing marginal productivity of labor*. These more realistic technological assumptions lead to an important change in the shape of the production possibility frontier (PPF) of the economy. When production was linear, the PPF was a straight line, as in Figure 21-1. Now, the PPF is "bowed out," as in Figure 21-8.

What accounts for the new form of the PPF? As we go from point A to point B, the tradable sector is releasing units of labor which get reallocated to the production of nontradables. But every new worker added to nontradable production results in a lesser and lesser increase in the output of N, because the stock of capital in the N sector is fixed. At the bottom of the PPF, near point A, a small shift in labor from tradables to nontradables produces a large gain in nontradables production. At the top of the PPF, however, near point B, a small shift of labor from tradables to nontradables produces almost no increase in nontradables production.

The slope of the PPF at any point measures the decrease in nontradable production that must occur for a given increase in tradable production in the economy. That is, the slope measures the *cost* of producing an additional unit of tradable goods in terms of nontradable goods. In a competitive economy, this cost will be equal to the relative price of tradables in terms of nontradables, P_T/P_N. Therefore, the slope of the PPF at any point will be

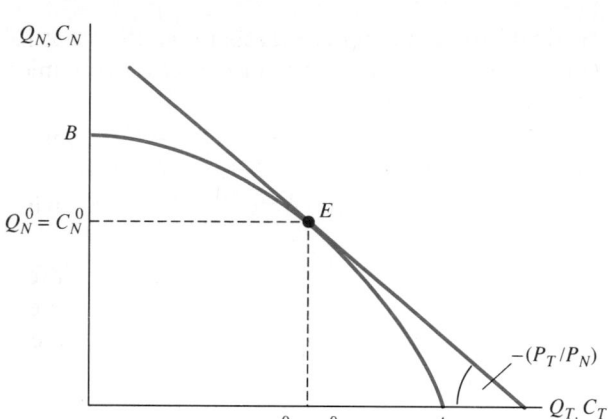

Figure 21-8
The PPF with Variable Labor and Fixed Capital

equal to the relative price P_T/P_N. When the relative price P_T/P_N is high, firms will choose to produce mostly tradable goods, at a point close to A. When P_T/P_N is low, firms will shift their production heavily toward nontradable goods, and away from the less lucrative tradable goods. They will tend to produce at a point closer to B. The linkage of production to the relative price P_T/P_N is shown in Figure 21-9.

We can use Figure 21-9 to measure the value of total GDP in the economy. Let us measure GDP, which we denote Q, in terms of nontradable goods prices:

$$Q = Q_N + \left(\frac{P_T}{P_N}\right) Q_T \qquad \textbf{(21.13)}$$

Figure 21-9
Relative Prices and the Production Structure

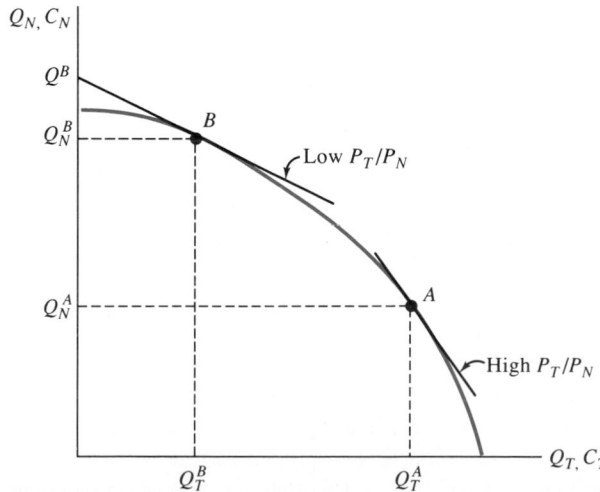

Clearly, GDP is the sum of nontradable goods production *plus* the value of tradable goods production (expressed in units of nontradable goods). Suppose that production takes place at point B in Figure 21-9. Output of tradables is Q_T^B, and output of nontradables is Q_N^B. The slope at point B is equal to the (low) relative price P_T/P_N. Note that the *value* of tradable goods production, $(P_T/P_N)Q_T^B$, is shown by the line segment from Q_N^B to Q_B on the Y axis. You can see this by noting that the line segment from Q_N^B to Q_B has a length that is equal to Q_T^B multiplied by the slope of the PPF at point B. In summary, the value Q_B measures total domestic output in units of the nontradable good.

As we now turn to the demand side, we shall continue to assume that households divide their consumption between nontradables and tradables in a fixed proportion. And, to keep things as simple as possible, we also continue to assume that this proportion is not a function of the relative price P_T/P_N.

Now let us look at the interaction of relative prices and the production structure of the economy as illustrated in Figure 21-10. Suppose that consumption is at point B. Production must therefore be at point A, on the same horizontal line as point B. There is a trade deficit, equal to the amount $C_T^B - Q_T^A$. The relative price of tradables to nontradables, (P_T/P_N), is simply the slope of the PPF at point A. In this situation, the economy would be borrowing from abroad. Eventually, the economy must shift from trade deficit to surplus to service its accumulated debts, and this adjustment, as we have seen earlier, will involve a fall in the consumption of nontradables and tradables, combined with an increase in the production of tradable goods and a fall in the production of tradables.

As this adjustment takes place, consumption shifts from point B to point D. At the new consumption point, production would have to shift from point A to point E, on the same horizontal line as the new consumption point. Note that the relative price of tradables increases (or, what is the same

Figure 21-10

Overconsumption and Adjustment: From Trade Deficit to Trade Surplus

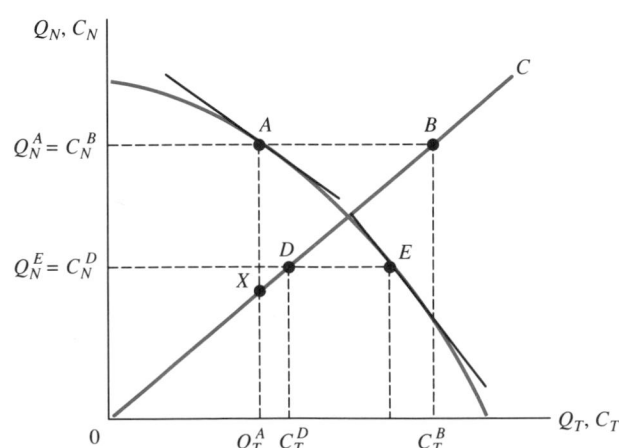

thing, the relative price of nontradables falls) as a result of the decline in consumption spending. The slope of the PPF at the new production point E is steeper than it was at the original point A, showing that P_T/P_N increases in the adjustment process.

What are the economics of this adjustment process? When aggregate demand falls, the decrease in demand for nontradable goods causes unemployment in the nontradable sector. Prices for nontradable goods fall relative to tradable goods. The decline in the relative price of nontradable goods (and the rise in the relative price of tradable goods) causes tradable goods firms to hire the labor that has become unemployed in the nontradable goods sector. Thus, the increase in P_T/P_N, (or, equivalently, the decline in P_N/P_T) is the signal to firms to lay off workers in the nontradable sector and to hire them in the tradable sector.

The structural adjustment of the economy, then, requires a shift not only in production, but also in relative prices. Specifically, the shift from trade deficit to trade surplus requires three things: (1) a decline in consumption relative to income; (2) a real exchange-rate depreciation, meaning, in this context, a rise in P_T/P_N; and (3) a shift in production from nontradable production to tradable production.

A Keynesian Version of the Tradable/Nontradable Model

So far, we have assumed that the economy is always at full employment, and therefore always on the production possibility frontier. Some shocks may require a fall in absolute prices and wages, however, and that may be hard to achieve under conditions of full employment. A transitory period of unemployment may prove necessary in order to restore a new full-employment equilibrium.

Consider the case in which the exchange rate and foreign prices are fixed, so that P_T is given. Suppose also the economy must shift from a trade deficit to a trade surplus through a cutback in domestic consumption. We have just seen that this adjustment typically involves an increase in P_T/P_N. With the price of tradables itself fixed in nominal terms, the adjustment would require an actual fall in the nominal price level of nontradables. With this problem in mind, let us return to Figure 21-10. If consumption falls but P_N is sticky downward, production will not shift to point E. Nontradable production will fall as the demand for N falls, but output in the tradable sector will not increase. The result will be production at point X, which is inside the production possibility frontier. There will be unemployment, and no rise in the production of tradable goods. Eventually, the unemployment will result in downward pressure on wages and nontraded goods prices. In the end, P_N will fall, and tradable production will eventually increase to the point E.

Is this hopeless situation inevitable? Does a negative demand shock have to produce unemployment until the price of nontradables (and the wage rate) falls enough to restore equilibrium? Not necessarily. Suppose that the authorities respond to the negative demand shock with a nominal *devaluation* of the domestic currency. If P_N is sticky, a devaluation can result in the necessary increase in P_T/P_N, not by cutting P_N but by raising P_T. In this way, production could remain on the PPF, at point E in the graph. This is a key argument for devaluing the currency in response to a contraction in demand.[14]

Devaluation and the Structuralist Critique

The arguments we have just given suggest that a devaluation may be an important policy instrument when it is necessary to correct an external imbalance through an increase of net exports when nominal prices (or wages) are rigid. But not all economists share this view. Instead, some argue, devaluations are unnecessarily *contractionary*. The main argument of the "structuralist" economists is that the production structure of the economy might be rigid in the short run, *even if relative prices do change*. In that case, an increase in the relative price of tradable goods would not bring about a quick enough rise in the production of tradables.

   The structuralists stress that there are important lags in an economy's ability to increase exports. Production capacity in the tradable sector may be close to its upper limit, making it difficult to expand output in the short term. When this happens, the production possibility frontier is kinked, as in Figure 21-11. The capacity limits might take a long time to change, and lags may arise from the specific technological characteristics of the production process.

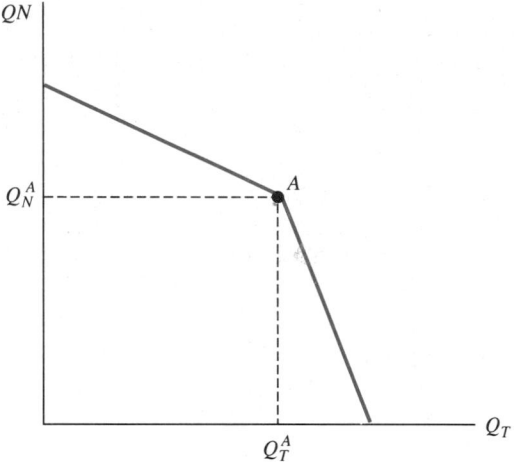

Figure 21-11
The Production Possibility Frontier under
Structuralist Conditions

   Consider, for example, the production of fruit for export. Even after farmers have made the necessary investment decisions, trees need several years of development to produce fruit. In Chile, where fresh fruits had become in the late 1980s the third most important item among exports, the investment decisions responsible for this expansion had been mostly taken

----

[14] A situation such as this one is analyzed at length by Rudiger Dornbusch, "Real and Monetary Aspects of the Effects of Exchange Rate Changes," in Robert Z. Aliber, ed., *National Monetary Policies and the International Financial System* (Chicago: The University of Chicago Press, 1974).

during the 1970s. Or it may be that factors of production, including labor, may be specific to each sector, at least in the short run, and that is why they show little response to relative prices.

Lack of supply responsiveness to devaluation is not enough to make a devaluation contractionary, however. In addition, the structuralists point to the contractionary demand-side effects of devaluation.[15] A first channel of demand contraction is the effect of devaluation on real money balances. A devaluation of the exchange rate provokes a rise in prices, which in turn reduces nominal money balances. In terms of the *IS-LM* model, the *IS* curve shifts back, and aggregate demand falls.

A second important channel is through redistribution effects. Suppose that the population is composed of two groups, those that primarily derive their income from wages and those that own the capital and receive profits. When nominal wages are sticky, a devaluation will redistribute income from workers to capitalists. If the former group has a higher propensity to consume than the latter, as evidence suggests, then aggregate demand will decline. The classic example of such a redistribution of income is the case of Argentina, which was studied by the late Latin American economist Carlos Díaz Alejandro. He showed that the Argentinian devaluation of 1958 redistributed income from wage earners to landowners, and thereby led to a fall in aggregate demand and output.[16]

Empirical evidence tends to support the view that devaluations are contractionary in the short run, but not over the longer run. The reason is clear. While contractionary demand-side effects act quickly in the economy, the beneficial supply-side effects take time to operate. Thorvaldur Gylfasson and Michael Schmid have studied the effects of devaluation for 10 countries, 5 developing and 5 industrialized, using data for the 1970s. They concentrated in the medium to long-run effects of this policy action and have reported contractionary effects in only two countries, India and the United Kingdom.[17] More recently, Sebastian Edwards has studied the output effects of devaluation for 12 developing countries in the period 1965–1980. His results indicate that devaluations tend to provoke contractionary effects during the first year after the exchange-rate change, but that these contractionary effects are totally reversed in the second year.[18]

The importance of devaluations as a tool of economic policy has been highlighted during the 1980s, as developing countries have attempted to cope

[15] See Paul Krugman and Lance Taylor, "Contractionary Effects of Devaluation," *Journal of International Economics*, August 1978. However, an extension of their framework to allow for some response of exports and nominal wages through time shows that the Krugman-Taylor result can be reversed and that a devaluation can give rise to a business cycle; see Felipe Larrain and Jeffrey Sachs, "Contractionary Devaluation and Dynamic Adjustment of Exports and Wages," National Bureau of Economic Research Working Paper, No. 2078, November 1986.

[16] Two of Díaz Alejandro's seminal works on this subject are "A Note on the Impact of Devaluation and the Redistributive Effect," *Journal of Political Economy*, December 1963, and *Exchange Rate Devaluation in a Semi-Industrialized Economy: The Experience of Argentina, 1955–61* (Cambridge, Mass.: MIT Press, 1964).

[17] See their joint paper, "Does Devaluation Cause Stagflation?" *Canadian Journal of Economics and Political Science*, November 1983.

[18] S. Edwards, "Are Devaluations Contractionary?" *Review of Economics and Statistics*, August 1986.

with the foreign debt crisis in part through significant devaluations of the exchange rate, an issue that we discuss in much greater detail in Chapter 22.

21-5 SUMMARY

Not all commodities are *tradable,* that is, subject to international trade. *Nontradable* goods and services—such as haircuts, housing rentals, and lawyers' services—can be consumed only in the economy in which they are produced. The existence of nontraded goods has several important economic implications. For such goods, local demand and supply must balance; a drop in domestic demand cannot be met by an increase in net exports; and domestic prices can differ from foreign prices without provoking a shift of international demand. As absorption rises or falls relative to income, the mix of production in the economy will tend to change. These production shifts involve the movement of workers and capital between the nontradable and tradable sectors of the economy and can take a significant amount of time.

There are two main *determinants of tradability.* First, and most important, are *transport costs,* which create natural barriers to trade. The lower they are (as a proportion of the total cost of the good), the more likely that the good will be traded internationally. Second, is the extent of *trade protectionism,* represented by tariff and nontariff barriers. These can block international trade even when transportation costs are low.

Goods can be classified between tradables and nontradables. The standard industrial classification of the United Nations distinguishes nine different economic sectors. Roughly speaking, agriculture, mining, and manufacturing are the most tradable types of goods. Construction, transportation, and the various services categories are not as easily tradable, though there are important exceptions. High transport costs and artificial barriers render several agricultural and industrial products into nontradables. On the other hand, recent technological advances in communications have allowed many kinds of financial services to be traded internationally.

The theoretical framework of the tradable-nontradable model assumes that the home country produces and consumes both tradables and nontradables. Specifying the production function of the two goods and the available amount of inputs allows us to derive the *production possibility frontier* between tradables and nontradables. The PPF represents the maximal amount of one type of good that can be produced for each amount of production of the other type. The slope of the PPF at a given point is the relative price between the two types of goods. In this model, the relative price of tradable goods in terms of nontradable goods is called the *real exchange rate.*

Total absorption in the TNT model is equal to spending on tradable goods and nontradable goods. The central assumption of the model is that domestic consumption of nontradables must equal their production because there are no exports or imports of such goods. The trade balance is equal to the excess of production of tradables over the domestic absorption of tradables. Equilibrium is found by superimposing the preferences of the economy on the PPF.

The TNT model is useful for analyzing some macroeconomic aspects of international borrowing and lending. If the economy has been borrowing abroad to consume more than its income (that is, running a trade deficit), the country's net debt builds up over time. Due to the intertemporal budget constraint, at some point the economy must shift back to trade surplus in order to service its international debt. This requires a drop in absorption relative to output, which reduces the demand for nontradable goods. Firms in the tradable sector will expand their production despite the fall in domestic demand, because they can sell their output in the world market. Thus, a shift from a situation of borrowing to repayment also requires a corresponding shift in the pattern of domestic production.

This *adjustment process* may involve short-run declines in output and employment. To minimize these social costs, governments sometimes implement a package of policies aimed at facilitating the transfer of resources, under the rubric of *structural adjustment programs*. Such programs typically include public sector reforms, trade liberalization, strengthening of economic institutions, and tight macroeconomic policies. During the 1980s, international institutions assisted countries in designing structural adjustment policies and supported them through lending, and in some cases through a negotiated reduction of debt servicing.

The shift of production between tradables to nontradables may also result from large changes in a country's wealth due to shifts in the value of an economy's natural resources. There are cases of dramatic enrichment, such as Norway's discovery of huge oil deposits in the North Sea in the 1970s, or oil-exporting countries' large gain from the surge in oil prices at the end of the 1970s. In these cases, nontradables typically experience a boom (due to wealth-induced increases in spending), while tradables other than the natural resource may experience a significant production decline, as resources shift into nontradables production. This phenomenon is known as the *Dutch disease*. Not all cases of resource shifts due to commodity booms have been related to oil. Colombia experienced a "Dutch disease" as a result of the coffee boom in the second half of the 1970s.

The *cost of living* in rich countries is higher than that in poor ones, and the difference in prices is most pronounced in nontradable goods. The TNT model helps to explain this phenomenon. One country will be more expensive than another if the price of its nontradable goods is higher than abroad. This will be the case if the productivity of its tradable sector *relative* to its nontradable sector is higher than abroad. As countries become richer, it has been observed that the rate of increase in productivity tends to be faster in the tradable sector than in the nontradable sector. This explains why rich countries tend to be more expensive than poor ones.

International comparisons of living standards should take the phenomenon of differing prices of nontradables into account. The way to make correct comparisons is to measure the income of the different countries in a common currency, but corrected for differences in the price levels in the countries. When this correction is made, it becomes clear that simple comparisons of per capita income levels (in which each country's income is stated in dollars at the official exchange rate) tend to overstate the differences in real incomes among rich and poor countries. This is because the overall price levels tend to be lower in poorer countries than richer countries.

If both capital and labor are used in the production of goods, the PPF no longer is a straight line (as when labor is the only input in production), but rather has a "bowed-out" shape. In this case, a shift of resources between tradable and nontradable goods production must be accompanied by a shift in the relative prices of the two sectors. In particular, the shift from trade deficit to trade surplus, which requires a decline in absorption relative to income, and a shift in production from nontradables to tradables, also requires a real exchange-rate depreciation (that is, a rise in the price of tradables relative to nontradables).

Under conditions of price and wage stickiness, unemployment may result when resources must be shifted between the tradables and nontradables sectors. If the nominal exchange rate is fixed and nontradables prices are sticky, then both P_T and P_N will be fixed. Now, if domestic absorption falls, the relative price of tradables to nontradables (P_T/P_N) will not increase as would be necessary to move resources from the nontradable sector to the tradable sector. The result will be a fall in nontradable goods production and absorption, but no compensating rise in tradable goods production. The economy will therefore suffer an increase in unemployment, and production will occur inside the PPF. In this case, a *devaluation* might produce the necessary increase in P_T/P_N, not by cutting P_N but by raising P_T. This is an argument in favor of devaluation when resources must be shifted from the nontradable sector to the tradable sector.

Structuralist economists, however, consider devaluations unnecessarily contractionary because they think that the production structure of the economy might be rigid in the short run even if relative prices change. In support of their view, they argue that productive capacity in the tradable sector may be close to its upper limit and that technological lags may exist, so that tradable production cannot be increased quickly. At the same time, structuralists stress several contractionary demand-side effects of devaluation, such as its effect on reducing real money balances and its induced income redistribution from workers to capitalists. Empirical evidence tends to support the view that devaluations are contractionary in the short run, but not in the longer run.

Key Concepts

tradable goods
production possibility frontier
  (PPF)
structural adjustment programs
purchasing power parity
  exchange rate
redistributive effect of
  devaluation
artificial barriers to trade
Dutch disease
contractionary devaluation

natural barriers to trade
relative price of tradable goods
  in terms of nontradable goods
relative productivity differential
structuralist critique to
  devaluation
nontradable goods
real exchange rate
absolute productivity differential
real balance effect of devaluation

Problems and Questions

1. Explain whether the following goods and services are tradable or nontradable. Are there special circumstances in which your answer does not hold?

   a. Cement.
   b. Cars.
   c. Bread.

   d. Data processing services for a bank.

   e. Copper.

2. Suppose that $a_T = 3$ and $a_N = 2$ and that the total amount of labor available is 120,000 man hours per year. Only labor is used in production, and the wage rate is $10 per hour.

   a. Write the equation of the production possibility frontier between tradables and nontradables.

   b. Draw the PPF in a graph.

   c. Determine the relative price (P_T/P_N).

   d. Determine the slope of the PPF.

   e. What is the price of tradables and that of nontradables?

3. Are absorption and aggregate demand the same thing in the model of Section 21-2? Why or why not?

4. Why is the TNT model essential to understand the equilibrium of a country that shifts from borrowing to repayment? What part of the story would the differentiated products model of Chapters 13 and 14 lose?

5. "International comparisons of living standards based on per capita income are problematic because protectionism creates important differences in the prices of tradable goods across countries." Discuss.

6. "Richer countries are more expensive than poor countries because their wages are higher," says economist X. "No, the reason is that richer countries have a more rapid growth in productivity," says economist Z. Who is right? Why?

7. Why do faster-growing countries tend to experience higher inflation rates than economies with slower economic growth?

8. Suppose a poor country, well described by the model of Section 19-4, receives a massive amount of foreign aid, much larger than before. What will likely happen to the following variables?

   a. The relative price P_T/P_N.

   b. The point of production in the PPF.

   c. The point of consumption.

   d. The trade balance.

9. Discuss the effects on GDP measured in terms of nontradable goods of the following shocks (use a graph):

   a. A sharp drop in the international price of coffee, the major export commodity of the country.

   b. An announcement that huge oil reserves have just been discovered in the country.

   c. A sharp contraction of fiscal policy.

10. "The argument of structuralist economists that devaluations are contractionary is based on the rigidity of relative prices P_T/P_N." Discuss.

The Developing Country Debt Crisis

The developing world experienced an economic crisis during the 1980s that was without precedent since the Great Depression in the 1930s. So extensive was the crisis that many analysts refer to the 1980s as the lost decade of economic development in the Third World. Dozens of countries, especially in Africa and Latin America, suffered sharp declines in per capita income in the early 1980s which in many cases were not reversed during the entire decade. Thus, on a per capita basis, many countries were poorer at the end of the 1980s than at the beginning.

Almost all the developing countries that experienced severe economic strains in the past decade had at least one thing in common—a very large foreign debt and, thus, a heavy burden of debt service. The ratio of foreign debt to GDP, a measure of the burden of the debt, is shown in Table 22-1 for different regions of the world. This ratio increased in all regions in the 1980s, but as the table reveals, the heaviest debt burdens were found in Africa and Latin America, which experienced the worst crises.

The debt crisis of the developing world is usually dated to August 1982, when the government of Mexico shocked the financial world by announcing that it would be unable to honor its debt commitments according to schedule. Several countries, such as Jamaica, Peru, Poland, and Turkey, had fallen into debt crisis before that date, but now dozens of other countries quickly followed Mexico in acknowledging their profound debt difficulties. Almost a decade after the shocking announcement by the Mexican government, few of these countries have yet recovered.

The debt crisis remains the single most important obstacle to economic progress in the developing world. In this chapter, we use some of the tools developed earlier in this book to explain the debt crisis—its origins, its effects on the developing countries, its effects on the commercial banks that lent much of the money, and its possible solutions.

22-1 AN OVERVIEW OF THE DEBT CRISIS

A remarkable aspect of the debt crisis is the force with which it hit the middle-income developing economies of Latin America, while at the same

TABLE 22-1

EVOLUTION OF THE DEBT BURDEN IN THE DEVELOPING WORLD, 1973–1989 (ACCORDING TO THE DEBT-GDP RATIO)

	1973	1974	1975	1976	1977	1978	1979	1980	1981	1982	1983	1984	1985	1986	1987	1988	1989
Developing countries*	22.4%	21.8%	23.8%	25.7%	24.9%	25.6%	24.7%	24.4%	27.8%	31.0%	32.9%	33.9%	35.6%	37.8%	37.5%	34.7%	31.8%
By region																	
Africa	19.4	19.6	21.6	25.8	31.4	32.4	30.6	28.3	31.4	34.9	37.6	41.3	45.6	48.6	48.3	47.6	49.7
Asia	19.7	18.9	20.4	22.4	17.2	15.9	16.7	17.2	18.6	21.9	23.1	24.0	26.4	29.5	28.3	26.1	22.3
Europe	24.5	23.1	22.8	24.6	21.6	23.7	30.9	29.1	34.2	32.8	34.3	36.3	40.3	41.0	44.8	42.4	40.4
Latin America	23.0	22.8	25.5	26.4	29.0	31.8	32.2	34.5	39.8	43.0	46.8	46.4	45.4	44.1	43.7	38.7	36.7

* From 1973 to 1976 refers to non-oil developing countries. 1977 refers to indebted developing countries. 1978 refers to capital importing developing countries. From 1979 to 1989 refers to all developing countries.
Source: International Monetary Fund, World Economic Outlook, Washington, D.C. various issues.

TABLE 22-2

MACROECONOMIC PERFORMANCE IN LATIN AMERICA AND EAST ASIA, 1970–1988

Country	GDP Growth (%)		Inflation (%)		Per capita GDP in 1988 (dollars)
	1970–81	1981–88	1970–81	1981–88	
Latin America					
Argentina	1.6	−0.8	130.8	340.1	2,520
Brazil	7.6	2.4	40.5	254.2	2,160
Chile	2.8	2.1	42.7	19.7	1,510
Mexico	6.7	0.7	17.5	70.1	1,760
Peru	3.4	0.7	33.8	213.9	1,300
Venezuela	3.7	1.2	9.1	21.5	3,250
Colombia	5.2	3.3	21.7	23.1	1,180
Average	4.4	1.4	42.3	134.7	1,954
East Asia					
Indonesia	8.0	4.9	17.0	8.7	440
Korea	8.1	9.4	16.7	6.0	2,690
Malaysia	7.8	5.0	6.2	3.3	3,600
Singapore	8.7	6.5	6.1	2.1	9,070
Thailand	7.1	6.1	10.0	4.2	1,000
Philippines	5.9	1.1	13.5	13.8	630
Average	7.6	5.5	11.6	6.4	2,905

Sources: Gross domestic product is from Data Resources, International Monetary Fund, Inc. (DRI), International Data Base, based on country sources, and International Financial Statistics. Inflation is the annual average rate between the dates shown based on the consumer price index from IFS. Per capita GDP is from World Development Report, 1989.

time almost bypassing the middle-income economies in East Asia. Compare, for example, the developments of real GDP and inflation in the two regions, as shown in Table 22-2. Latin America fell into deep crisis, while East Asia largely escaped the crisis. One of our goals will be to explain why some economies succumbed to these problems while others did not.

The debt crisis threatened ruin not only for the debtor countries but also for the creditor financial institutions, mainly large, international commercial banks, that had lent to them. As Keynes once remarked, "If you owe your bank $100, then you're in trouble; if you owe your bank $1 million, then your bank's in trouble." But this time it wasn't just $1 million at stake. Rather, it was hundreds of billions of dollars, more than the entire capital of the world's largest banks. The prospects of default by the large debtor nations raised the specter of mass insolvencies of the world's most important commercial banks.

In fact, as we shall see, the debtor countries did not, in general, default on their loans, at least not during the first few years of the crisis. Rather, for many years they continued to service their debts, even at great sacrifice to internal economic stability. As a result, bank creditors recovered much of their financial health during the 1980s, and are now in a stronger position to accept negotiated reductions in the debt burdens of the developing countries. Some of the major banks, however, remain in financial difficulty as a result of bad domestic loans in addition to troubled less developed country (LDC) debts.

But the saddest sequel of the debt crisis has been its effects on the most needy in the developing world, the poor in general, and children in particular. The greatest absolute suffering caused by the crisis has occurred in the low-income countries in Africa. Many citizens in these countries were already living at the edge of subsistence before the crisis hit, and in the poorer countries, the collapse of economic development in the 1980s caused a sharp worsening of the trends in infant mortality, child malnutrition, and related calamities, as described in Box 22-1.

22-2 THE ORIGINS OF THE DEBT CRISIS

Explaining why the debt crisis occurred is no simple task. As it normally happens with complicated phenomena, there is no single factor that can explain the debt crisis. The extent of the crisis provides a crucial clue, however. The fact that dozens of countries succumbed *simultaneously* suggests international factors (such as higher world interest rates) played a key role in the onset of the crisis. On the other hand, the fact that some countries were hard hit while others were not suggests that domestic factors, that is, factors internal to the debtor countries, also played a role. How else can we explain the fact that Latin America fell into a deep crisis while East Asia did not?

We shall see that the crisis indeed resulted from a complex combination of elements, some of which were external to the individual debtor countries, and thus beyond their control, while others were the direct result of economic policies pursued within particular indebted nations. Our objective is now to understand the interaction of these external and internal factors.

Box 22-1
Social Development and the Debt Crisis

The United Nations Children's Fund (UNICEF) warned in 1989 that social development was being thrown into reverse in many countries by the debt crisis.[1] In particular, an increasing number of children are lacking adequate satisfaction of their most basic human needs. This is especially tragic because inadequacies of this kind at a young age provoke *permanent* damage. The matter is urgent from a moral point of view, of course. But from the perspective of future growth, it is of grave concern as well inasmuch as the human capital of a population—its health and its educational accomplishments—is one of the key factors in economic development. The social setbacks of the 1980s will cast a long shadow ahead over the future economic health of the developing world.

As economic conditions have worsened, governments have found themselves with fewer resources and fiscal spending has been hurt. The part of this expenditure destined for social programs has been hard hit, partly because, unlike other sectors of society, the poor have no effective lobby protecting them against spending cuts. Thus, during the 1980s, the share of fiscal spending going to health and education has fallen in most developing countries of Africa and Latin America. During the same period, the share of total government spending going to defense tended to increase, as shown in Table 22-3.

Even modest cuts in income and in social programs have severe effects on the very poor, who spend 75 percent or more of their disposable income just on food. But program cuts and income reductions for the poor have been severe, not modest. Throughout Africa and Latin America many health clinics have been closed or rendered ineffective by a lack of trained personnel and of basic health supplies. Even in Latin American countries that are not among the very poorest in the world, the situation has been so bad that their health services have not had the money to buy vaccines. This is what actually happened in Ecuador, Panama, Paraguay, and Peru early in 1989. Expenditures in education infrastructure and materials (school buildings, books, and so on) have also dropped significantly, and fiscal austerity has led to large cutbacks in teachers.

With economic growth halted or even reversed by the crisis in most of Africa and Latin America, social expenditures have suffered and social indicators have started worsen. In the words of UNICEF,

> The average weight-for-age of young children, a vital indicator
> of normal growth, is falling in many of the countries for which
> figures are available. In the 37 poorest nations, spending per
> head on health has been reduced by 50 percent, and on educa-
> tion by 25 percent, over the last few years. And in almost half

---

[1] UNICEF, *The State of the World's Children*, 1989 (Oxford: Oxford University Press, 1989).

of the 103 developing countries from which recent information is available, the proportion of 6-to-11 year-olds enrolled in primary school is now falling.

In other words, it is children who are bearing the heaviest burden of debt and recession in the 1980s. And in tragic summary, it can be estimated that at least half a million young children have died in the last twelve months as a result of the slowing down or the reversal of progress in the developing world.[2]

TABLE 22-3

GOVERNMENT SPENDING ON EDUCATION, HEALTH, AND DEFENSE IN DEVELOPING COUNTRIES, 1972 VERSUS 1988
(PERCENTAGE OF TOTAL GOVERNMENT SPENDING)

	Education		Health		Defense	
	1972	1988	1972	1988	1972	1988
Low Income						
Bangladesh*	14.8	10.6	5.0	5.0	5.1	10.0
Burkina Faso	20.6	14.0	8.2	5.2	11.5	17.9
Kenya	21.9	21.5	7.9	6.1	6.0	9.2
Malawi	15.8	10.0	5.5	5.9	3.1	5.6
Pakistan	1.2	2.6	1.1	0.9	39.9	29.5
Sri Lanka	13.0	7.8	6.4	5.4	3.1	9.6
Tanzania*	17.3	8.3	7.2	5.7	11.9	15.8
Uganda	15.3	15.0	5.3	2.4	23.1	26.3
Lower Middle Income						
Bolivia	31.3	18.4	6.3	1.9	18.8	14.5
Chile	14.3	12.0	8.2	6.3	6.1	10.4
Mexico	16.4	7.4	4.5	1.1	4.5	1.4
Morocco	19.2	17.0	4.8	3.0	12.3	15.1
Peru	23.6	15.3	5.5	5.8	14.5	20.0
El Salvador	21.4	17.1	10.9	7.1	6.6	25.7
Tunisia	30.5	14.6	7.4	5.9	4.9	5.7
Turkey	18.1	12.7	3.2	2.4	15.5	10.4
Upper Middle Income						
Argentina	20.0	6.9	—	2.1	10.0	6.9
Korea	15.8	19.0	1.2	2.2	25.8	27.1
Oman	3.7	10.7	5.9	4.8	39.3	38.2
Uruguay	9.5	7.1	1.6	4.8	5.6	10.2
Venezuela	18.6	19.6	11.7	10.0	10.3	5.8

The 1988 column refers to 1987.
Source: *The World Bank,* World Development Report, 1989 *and* World Development Report, 1990 *(Oxford: Oxford University Press, 1989 and 1990).*

---

[2] Ibid., p. 1.

External Factors

The worldwide oil price increases of 1973–1974 contributed to a rapid expansion of the Eurodollar market, the offshore banking network based in Europe that borrowed and lent international funds.[3] The oil-exporting countries of the Middle East deposited their huge increases in earnings in the international banks operating in Europe. These banks in turn lent this new inflow of deposits to borrowers in the developing world. The oil shock therefore contributed to a tremendous increase in the availability of international credits for developing countries. The governments in the developing world, many of which had been unable to atract bank loans before 1973, suddenly found that the commercial banks were eager to lend.[4]

What's more, the loans were available at very low interest rates, indeed interest rates that were negative in real terms. For many of the largest borrowing countries, such as Argentina, Brazil, and Mexico, it seemed that the combination of low interest rates and rapid growth of export earnings (partly based on high international prices for the raw material exports of these countries) assured that servicing loans in the future would be no problem.

It is interesting to focus for a moment on the behavior of commercial banks at that time. Many of them followed the lead of a most prominent banker, Citicorp's Chairman Walter Wriston, who stated that "countries never go bankrupt." Thus, for a while it seemed that bankers disregarded the risks of international loans, as they had done periodically in the past.[5] Rather, the leading banks systematically increased their lending to developing countries by remarkable amounts. Some major banks lent more than 100 percent of their capital to a few developing countries.[6] And, based on the earnings of the banks in the late 1970s, the lending strategy seemed to be working well. The combination of low interest rates and high export growth among the borrowing countries suggested to the banks that the borrowers

---

[3] Chapter 20 analyzes the growth of cross-border lending by international banks and the evolution of the Eurodollar market since its start in the early 1950s.

[4] It is sometimes thought that the oil shock played a more direct role, by forcing oil-importing developing countries to borrow from abroad in order to pay the higher oil bills. In fact, both oil-exporting countries and oil-importing countries took part in the rapid increase in borrowing, and the debt crisis hit both kinds of countries.

[5] Peter Lindert and Peter Morton have made this point, saying that "the international financial community has often preferred to repeat the past rather than study it." See their joint article "How Sovereign Debt Has Worked," in Jeffrey Sachs, ed., *Developing Country Debt and Economic Performance*, National Bureau of Economic Research (Chicago: The University of Chicago Press, 1989).

[6] The combined loans to just four Latin American countries—Argentina, Brazil, Mexico, and Venezuela—represented well over 100 percent of the primary capital for several large U.S. money center banks at the outbreak of the debt crisis. The ratios of loans to capital in December 1982 were: Bank of America, 137 percent; Chase Manhattan, 165 percent; Chemical, 164 percent; Citicorp, 197 percent; Manufacturers Hanover, 206 percent; Morgan Guaranty, 123 percent. Washington, DC: Federal Financial Institutions Examination Council, *Country Exposure Lending Survey*, April 1983.

would be able to service their debts. But, of course, nothing could ensure that the rosy conditions would continue.

The big increase in bank lending accounted for much of the increase in indebtedness of the developing countries. We should note, however, that other kinds of lenders also increased their lending in the same period. Creditor governments, operating through export credit agencies, lent money to the developing countries so that they could purchase the products of exporters in those same creditor countries. These government-to-government loans represented a higher proportion of the debt in the poorer countries (particularly in Africa), and a lower proportion of the debt in the middle-income developing countries (particularly in Latin America and East Asia).

The structure of developing country debt as of the early 1980s can be seen in Table 22-4. Notice that in both Latin America and Africa, most of the debt was owed by governments rather than by private firms and households. In Latin America, most of the debt was borrowed from commercial banks, while in Africa, most of the debt was borrowed from official, that is, govern-

TABLE 22-4a

THE STRUCTURE OF DEVELOPING COUNTRY DEBT BY CREDITOR, 1982 (IN US$ BILLION AND % IN BRACKETS)

All developing countries	836.1
	(100)
Official	249.9
	(29.9)
Commercial banks	427.9
	(51.2)
Other private	158.3
	(18.9)
Africa	122.4
	(100)
Official	58.7
	(48.0)
Commercial banks	39.7
	(32.4)
Other private	24.0
	(19.6)
Latin America and the Caribbean	331.2
	(100)
Official	40.5
	(12.2)
Commercial banks	224.4
	(67.8)
Other private	66.2
	(20.0)

Source: International Monetary Fund, World Economic Outlook, *May 1990.*

TABLE 22-4b

THE STRUCTURE OF DEVELOPING COUNTRY DEBT BY DEBTOR, 1982* (IN US$ BILLION AND % IN BRACKETS)

All developing countries	562.5 (100)
Public and publicly guaranteed	460.2 (81.8)
Private nonguaranteed	102.3 (18.2)
Africa and the Middle East	113.3 (100)
Public and publicly guaranteed	108.6 (95.8)
Private nonguaranteed	4.7 (4.2)
Latin America and the Caribbean	238.4 (100)
Public and publicly guaranteed	176.1 (73.9)
Private nonguaranteed	62.3 (26.1)

* Long-term debt only.
Source: World Bank, World Debt Tables, 1989.

mental, sources. In Latin America, the debt crisis was therefore a crisis of governments that owed too much to private commercial banks. In Africa, the debt crisis was a crisis of governments that owed too much to other governments and to international financial institutions, such as the World Bank.

At the end of the 1970s, few analysts were worried about the developing country debt. A happy ending to the debt scenario, however, was extremely dependent on interest rates remaining low and on export growth of the developing countries remaining high. Then, in the early 1980s, the economic situation changed dramatically. World interest rates increased sharply as a consequence of anti-inflationary programs in the industrialized countries, led by the policies of Federal Reserve Chairman Paul A. Volcker. At the same time, the terms of trade deteriorated for the debtor world as raw materials prices fell. Thus, the export earnings of the developing countries stopped growing rapidly and in some cases started to decline.

The combined effect of higher interest rates and falling export prices meant that debtors ended up paying very high *real* interest rates on their foreign credits, with devastating effects. Table 22-5 shows the evolution of interest rates and export prices for Latin American borrowers. In the 1970s, real interest rates were highly negative for the borrowing countries; that is, nominal interest rates were below the inflation rate (as measured by the annual change in export prices). In the early 1980s, however, real interest

TABLE   22-5

INTEREST RATES AND FINANCIAL VULNERABILITY IN LATIN AMERICA (A) INTEREST RATES, 1972–1986 (%)

Year	Nominal LIBOR	Rate of Change in Export Unit Prices	Real LIBOR
1972	5.4	9.2	−3.5
1973	9.3	33.0	−17.5
1974	11.2	57.5	−29.4
1975	7.6	−5.7	14.1
1976	6.1	8.1	−1.8
1977	6.4	10.6	−3.8
1978	8.3	−3.7	12.5
1979	12.0	21.0	−7.4
1980	14.2	21.2	−5.8
1981	16.5	−2.8	19.9
1982	13.3	−11.2	27.5
1983	9.8	−6.5	17.4
1984	11.2	2.6	8.4
1985	8.6	0.6	9.3
1986	6.7	−12.7	22.2

(B) FINANCIAL VULNERABILITY, 1980–1981 (%)

Country	Debt at Floating Rates	Interest Payments/Exports
Argentina	58.3	15.1
Brazil	64.3	28.3
Colombia	39.2	16.3
Chile	58.2	28.2
Mexico	73.0	19.0
Peru	28.0	19.8
Venezuela	81.4	10.4
All Latin America	64.5	28.0

Source: *Andres Bianchi et al., "Adjustment in Latin America, 1981–86," in Vittorio Corbo, Morris Goldstein, and Mohsin Khan, ed.,* Growth Oriented Adjustment Programs *(Washington, D.C.: International Monetary Fund and The World Bank, 1987).*

rates turned sharply positive. Indeed, they shot up to an average of well over 20 percent per year in 1981–1983.

The debtor countries were highly vulnerable to the rise in interest rates because much of their borrowing had been contracted at variable rates. This means that at the time they borrowed on long-term loans, they did not know—and could not know—the interest rates at which the loans would

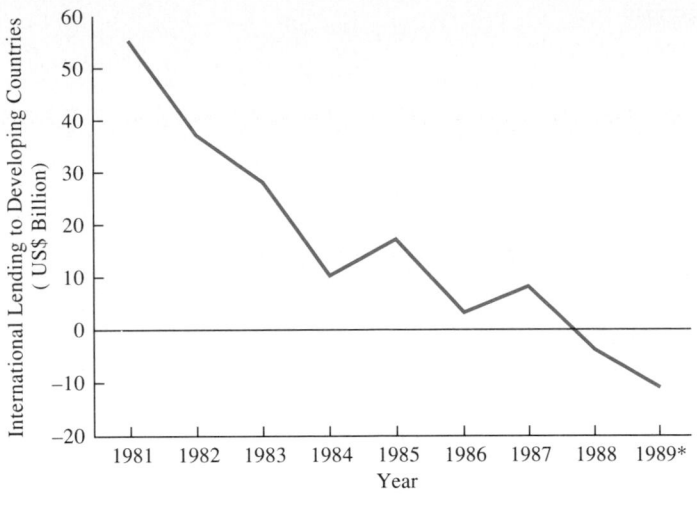

* First three quarters

Figure 22-1

The Collapse of International Lending to Developing Countries in the 1980s

(From International Monetary Fund, International Capital Markets, *April 1990.)*

have to be repaid. Instead, most loan contracts between the debtor governments and the commercial banks stated that the interest rates due on the loans in the future would depend on the world market interest rates *at the time that the repayments were due*.[7] For Latin America as a whole, about 65 percent of the debt had this feature of variable interest rates. Thus, when interest rates rose sharply in the early 1980s, the bill owed by Latin America for debt service increased sharply and unexpectedly. Interest payments quickly rose to around 30 percent of export earnings by the region in 1980–1981, as shown in Table 22-5.

In the face of this sharp increase in interest rates and the simultaneous fall in export earnings, external lending to the debtor nations and inflows of foreign investment abruptly declined. Total net capital flows into Latin America, that is, new loans minus repayments of old loans, declined from a peak of $38 billion in 1981, to $20 billion in 1982 and a mere $3.2 billion in 1983. This was a generalized pattern around the developing world. Figure 22-1 shows the evolution of net international lending through commercial banks and bond markets in the period 1981–1989 for the developing world as

---

[7] In technical language, interest rates were typically quoted as a "spread over LIBOR." LIBOR stands for London Interbank Offered Rate, and it is the short-term interest rate that the international banks charge each other for loans in the London money market. A developing country would have to pay a fixed amount ("spread") over the LIBOR rate. In a typical contract, the government of Mexico might borrow $100 million at "LIBOR plus 1" on a five-year loan. This means that in the future, when Mexico is paying interest on its loan, it would have to pay the LIBOR interest rate at the future date plus one percentage point. The extra one percentage point is included to account for the risk that Mexico might default on the loan at some point in the future. When the loans were undertaken at the end of the 1970s, LIBOR was about 10 percent per year. When the loans were being serviced in the early 1980s, LIBOR had jumped, unexpectedly, to around 15 percent per year.

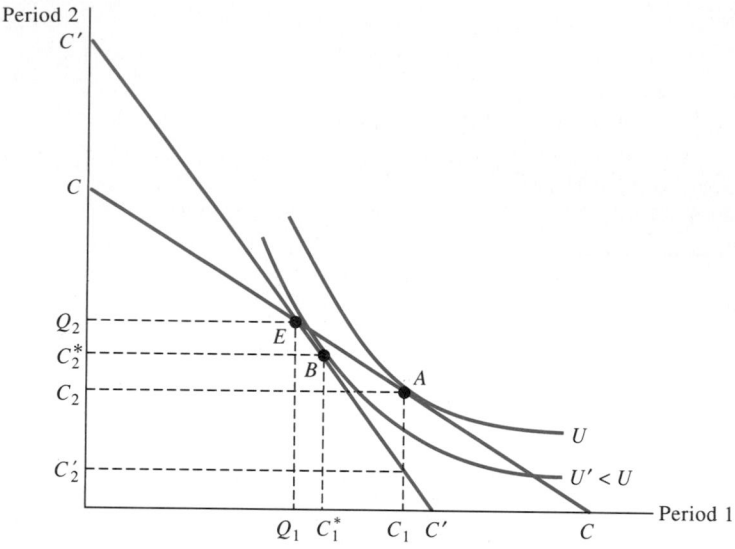

Figure 22-2
The Interest Rate Shock on a Debtor Country

a whole. The graph shows the astonishing collapse of net lending. Indeed, in 1988 and 1989 net lending was at negative levels. In other words, new loans were less than repayments of principal on old loans.

We can use the analytical apparatus of our two-period model (from Chapters 4 to 6) to study the problem of the rise in interest rates. Let us start by supposing for simplicity that a country has a given endowment of present and future output, shown by point E in Figure 22-2. At the low interest rate r_0, consumption possibilities are represented by the line CC, and the economy chooses to consume at point A. There, the country is borrowing from the rest of the world to finance the current account deficit of the magnitude $(C_1 - Q_1)$.

Suppose now that the borrower has a variable interest rate contract, and thus the borrowing takes place *before* the interest rate is known. The borrowers behave *as if* the interest rate were known to be, say, r_0, but in fact the actual interest rate can turn out to be quite different. What happens, then, if real interest rates shoot up above r_0?

In terms of our figure, the new consumption possibilities lie along the line $C'C'$, determined by the higher interest rate r_1. If the borrowers had known that the interest rate would be r_1, they would have consumed differently, at C_1^* and C_2^*, and would have borrowed much less.[8] But when the interest rate becomes known as of the second period, it is too late. The economy has already consumed C_1 in the first period (based on the wrong interest-rate expectation), and consumption in period 2 must fall all the way to C_2'. Thus, second-period consumption turns out to be much lower than expected.

_____

[8] Note that the rise in interest rates might have been so big that at r_1 the borrowers would actually have preferred to be lenders instead.

_____

Domestic Policies

Domestic policies also had an important responsibility in generating the crisis. In the easy lending period of the 1970s, few people—among neither the bankers nor the borrowers—paid enough attention to how the debtor countries were using their borrowed resources. Were the loans financing investments that would generate resources with which to repay the debt? Were they simply used to finance a consumption boom? Or were the borrowed funds taken out of the country as capital flight? In fact, how they were used depended greatly on domestic economic policies.

In general, the debt crisis struck with the greatest vengeance in countries that had overly expansionary fiscal policies and highly distorted trade policies, especially policies that created a heavy bias against exports. As we shall see, big differences emerged between Latin American and the East Asian debtor countries in the management of these two policy areas.

Fiscal Policies The availability of external credits allowed many governments to increase their expenditure enormously without raising any additional taxes or suffering the costs of inflationary finance. Of course, the heavy foreign borrowing could only be maintained for a limited period of time. When foreign capital abruptly stopped flowing in at the beginning of the 1980s, the governments of debtor countries were unable to cut spending and raise tax revenues enough to cover the fiscal gap. This led to a shift from foreign financing to domestic financing of the deficit, and that is the subject of the next section.

In the most heavily indebted countries, Argentina, Brazil, and Mexico, public-sector deficits lay at the core of the debt problem. After the 1973 oil shock, Brazil pursued a deliberate development strategy based on a major public investment program and large energy subsidies to the economy. The investment projects required substantial financing from abroad. Mexico's fiscal expansion is partially explained by heavy investments in the oil sector that were based on overly optimistic expectations about future oil prices. The Mexican government dismissed preliminary signs in the early 1980s of a weakening in the world economy and in the world oil markets, and public-sector expansion continued unabated. In 1982, the Mexican fiscal deficit approached a record 18 percent of GDP.

Argentina also undertook large fiscal deficits. In this case, the deficits resulted from political instability in the 1970s, heavy defense spending at the end of the 1970s and early 1980s for the Falklands/Malvinas war, inefficient state enterprises and local governments that ran chronic deficits, and a persistent failure to collect tax revenues. Heavy foreign borrowing allowed the government to avoid inflationary finance in the short run, but eventually the international lending dried up, and Argentina was pushed into a hyperinflation.

It is tempting to label expansionary fiscal policies simply as mistakes. Although policy errors were, no doubt, an important part of the problem, wanton fiscal expenditures such as these were more than mere mistakes. Latin American countries have been characterized by a tendency toward *populist policies*; that is, governments try to build popular support by undertaking large spending programs even if the costs of those programs run beyond the capacity of the governments to pay for them.

One of the pressures that leads to populist policies seems to arise from the large income inequalities in Latin America. On the one side are the very rich, who command a large share of national income and whose economic power translates into enough political power to avoid heavy taxation. On the other side are the lower classes, who command only a small share of the national income but whose huge numbers as percent of the population translate into heavy demands for public spending. The combination produces high demands for spending, matched by a low ability of the government to raise tax revenues. This was not and is not the case in East Asia, where income distribution has been much more equitable.

Trade Policies Another big difference between the countries that fell into crisis and those that escaped crisis lay in their orientation to international trade. Countries that escaped the crisis had freer international trade (less hindered by tariffs and other protectionist barriers), realistic exchange rates that made exporting profitable, and in general, policies that encouraged the international competitiveness of the export sector.

Table 22-6 provides some illustrative measures of trade policy and export performance. Along with data on exports, the table shows an "index of foreign trade" that the World Bank constructs to categorize countries along a scale from 1 to 4 according to their trade policies. The higher the rating, the more open and freer the trading system. As we can see from the table, the East Asian economies tended to have freer trade regimes. At the same time, the East Asian countries had both high and rising shares of exports in GDP, demonstrating the importance of export growth in the overall economy. In Latin America, by contrast, the trade regimes were more closed, and the share of exports in GDP was both lower than in the Asian countries and not rising as rapidly.

Because of these Latin American antiexport policies, the foreign borrowing of the 1970s did not contribute to any significant increase in the region's export capacity in the 1980s. When the lending to Latin America slowed down in the early 1980s, then, the debts could not be serviced out of a large increase in export earnings. Instead, the Latin American countries found that they had to cut imports in order to pay the debt service, and the result was a major contraction of living standards. In East Asia, by contrast, export earnings soared in the 1980s and provided the means to service the debts that were falling due.

Most of the countries that experienced payments problems had another thing in common: they allowed their currencies to become highly overvalued, and thereby created further sharp disincentives to exports. The countries of the Southern Cone of Latin America were prime examples. In Argentina, Chile, and Uruguay, the local currencies were pegged to the dollar, despite high rates of domestic inflation. The result in each country was a significant real appreciation, in the sense that P_N/P_T rose sharply. The incentives to export—and to invest in the export sector—were thus reduced and that contributed to the future debt-servicing problems.

The countries of East Asia fared much better in their exchange-rate management. South Korea reacted early to the oil shock of 1979–1980 and significantly devalued its currency, while at the same time implementing belt tightening in its budget. Indonesia devalued sharply in 1978, which helped the country tremendously in its subsequent adjustment effort. Only the Phil-

TABLE   22-6

CHARACTERISTICS OF THE TRADE REGIME AND
OPENNESS TO TRADE

	Trade Regime*	Exports of Goods and Services/GDP (%)
Latin America		
Argentina	1	15
Peru	1	22
Colombia	2	15
Costa Rica	2	32
Mexico	2	16
Brazil	3	14
Chile	3	29
Uruguay	3	25
Average	2.1	21.0
East Asia		
Indonesia	2	23
Philippines	2	22
Korea	4	36
Malaysia	3	55
Thailand	3	27
Hong Kong	4	106
Singapore	4	129
Average	3.1	56.9

* The World Bank reports estimates of the trade regime over 1973–1985
based on the effective rate of protection, direct trade controls, exports
incentives, and exchange-rate overvaluation. The countries are classified
into four groups, from "inward oriented" (to which we assign a value of
1) to "outward oriented" to which we assign a 4.
Source: The World Bank, World Development Report, Washington,
D.C. 1987.

ippines in East Asia allowed the real exchange rate to appreciate significantly, and not surprisingly, its economic performance turned out to be closer to that of Latin America than to that of its geographical neighbors.

Capital Flight

A side effect of large fiscal deficits and overvalued exchange rates in Latin America was extensive *capital flight*. Capital flight occurs when domestic residents convert their domestic wealth into foreign exchange, in order to hold their wealth outside the country.[9] In economies with fixed exchange

---

[9] When domestic wealth is invested abroad in the developed countries, the polite term "portfolio diversification" is used. When the same process occurs in the developing countries, the term "capital flight" is used instead. In more traditional usage, the term "capital flight" was

rates and open capital markets, this can be done legally, simply by converting domestic currency holdings into foreign exchange. In countries with capital controls, illegal means (such as underinvoicing of exports) are required. During the 1970s and early 1980s, there was substantial capital flight in Latin America. As governments became increasingly indebted to foreign banks, domestic residents in Latin America substantially increased their wealthholdings abroad.

The link between capital flight and fiscal deficits is often quite direct.[10] We know that under fixed exchange rates, attempts of the government to finance a deficit by borrowing from the central bank lead to an excess supply of the national currency in the hands of households. In turn, households take this money and convert it into foreign exchange at the official exchange rate. The foreign-exchange reserves of the central bank decrease, while the foreign-exchange holdings of the public (capital flight, if held offshore) go up.

Capital flight is also exacerbated by expectations of a future currency devaluation. After it became clear in the late 1970s that local currencies were grossly overvalued in many Latin American countries, private agents started moving their assets abroad in order to avoid the impact of the coming devaluations. Empirical studies have indeed detected a strong relationship between exchange-rate overvaluation and capital flight.[11]

It is impossible to know exactly how much capital flight there is because people do not keep records about it and they try hard to maintain the secrecy of their transactions. Thus, all available figures are only estimates.

One popular way to calculate capital flight is to equate it with the unexplained portion of the balance of payments. The idea is this. In a given year, the sources of external funds for the country are foreign credits, which increase the level of external debt (ΔD), and foreign direct investment (FDI). The known uses of these funds are financing a current account deficit (CAD) and accumulating official reserves (ΔR). Any "unexplained" uses of funds are then considered capital flight (KF), which is then defined as

$$KF = (\Delta D + FDI) - (CAD + \Delta R) \qquad \textbf{(22.1)}$$

Equation (22.1) is the simplest way to estimate capital flight. But, as with most indirect means of measurement, it is not perfect. For example, it does not capture some popular methods of moving money out of the country, such as the underinvoicing of exports or the overinvoicing of imports. It does provide a good starting point for the analysis, however. This equation was used to calculate the data for capital flight in the most highly indebted countries of Latin America during the period 1976–1985 that appear in Table 22-7.

---

restricted to the case in which money was moved abroad in response to political instability. During the 1980s debate over the international debt crisis, however, this term was generalized to include any situation in which domestic residents in the debtor countries held their wealth offshore.

[10] There are other reasons for capital flight as well, although we do not go into them here. Political instability itself can cause wealthholders to take their money offshore. Tax evasion is another powerful impetus to capital flight.

[11] See John Cuddington, "Capital Flight: Estimates, Issues and Explanations," *Princeton Studies in International Finance,* No. 58 (Princeton University), December 1986.

TABLE 22-7

CAPITAL FLIGHT OUT OF LATIN AMERICA

Country	Capital Flight (US$ billions)		Total 1976–85	Capital Flight/Change in External Debt (%)
	1976–82	1983–85		
Argentina	27	−1	26	62.7%
Brazil	3	7	10	12.0
Chile	0	1	1	6.4
Mexico	36	17	53	64.8
Peru	−1	1	0	0.0
Venezuela	25	6	31	101.3

Source: Sebastian Edwards and Felipe Larrain, "Debt, Adjustment and Recovery in Latin America: An Introduction," in S. Edwards and F. Larrain, eds., Debt, Adjustment and Recovery: Latin America's Prospects for Growth and Development *(Oxford and Cambridge: Basil Blackwell, 1989).*

As the table shows, the case of Venezuela is indeed remarkable. The country's debt is more than fully explained by capital flight! In Argentina and Mexico, capital flight accounts for over 60 percent of the increase in debt. Brazil and Chile, in contrast, show a modest incidence of capital flight.

22-3 ADJUSTMENT PROBLEMS AND PROSPECTS IN DEBTOR COUNTRIES

Loans to the developing world, which had started on a large scale in 1973, suddenly dried up in 1982. To measure the shift from lending to repayment, we can use the concept of *net resource transfer* (NRT) that was analyzed in Chapter 6. Remember that the NRT measures the net resources flowing from the world capital markets to an economy. As we said in equation (6.22), the NRT is measured as the net capital inflows to an economy (new loans minus repayments) minus the interest payments made on the existing debt. Table 22-8 shows that the turning point in net resource transfers to Latin America came in 1982. While in 1981 the region experienced a net resource *inflow* of over $11 billion, in 1982 it suffered a net *outflow* of almost $19 billion. After 1982, there was a sustained period of net resource outflows that has lasted until the beginning of the next decade.

These negative net resource transfers happened because of sharp reductions in net capital inflows combined with higher interest payments to foreign creditors. The data in Table 22-8 tell that the drying up of new loans was the most dramatic component. Between 1981 and 1983, net new lending declined from almost $40 billion to only less than $3 billion, a drop of over 90 percent.

In cumulative terms, Latin America received a net resource transfer of $91 billion between 1974 and 1981, while it made a staggering net resource transfer abroad of almost $224 billion between 1982 and 1990. This massive

TABLE   22-8

THE NET TRANSFER OF RESOURCES TO LATIN AMERICA, 1974–1990 (US$ BILLIONS)

Year	Net Capital Inflows	Net Payments of Profits and Interest	Net Transfer of Resources
1974	11.4	5.0	6.4
1975	14.3	5.6	8.7
1976	17.9	6.8	11.1
1977	17.2	8.2	9.0
1978	26.2	10.2	16.0
1979	29.1	13.6	15.5
1980	32.0	18.9	13.1
1981	39.8	28.5	11.3
1982	20.1	38.8	−18.7
1983	2.9	34.5	−31.6
1984	10.4	37.3	−26.9
1985	3.0	35.3	−32.3
1986	9.9	32.7	−22.8
1987	15.1	31.4	−16.3
1988	5.5	34.3	−28.8
1989	10.1	37.4	−27.3
1990	17.9	36.8	−18.9
Total 1974–1981	187.9	96.8	91.1
Total 1982–1990	94.9	318.5	−223.6

Source: *Economic Commission for Latin America and the Caribbean (ECLAC),* Preliminary Overview of the Economy of Latin America and the Caribbean, 1990 *(Santiago, Chile, December 1990).*

outflow of resources invites a comparison with the experience of Germany after World War I. Germany, as the vanquished country after World War I, had to pay major war reparations to the victors, which amounted to an average 2.5 percent of GDP per year between 1925 and 1932. This was such a major drain on the German economy that after a few years the country fell into hyperinflation, soon followed by an eventual suspension of all reparations payments. Yet Latin America did pay out net annual transfers of an average 4.2 percent of GDP in the period 1982–1985, almost double what Germany paid to the Allies after World War I.

The Debt Crisis, Trade, and Domestic Economic Activity

The sudden collapse of foreign financing and the worsening in the terms of trade of the debtor countries led to a sharp drop in aggregate demand. We

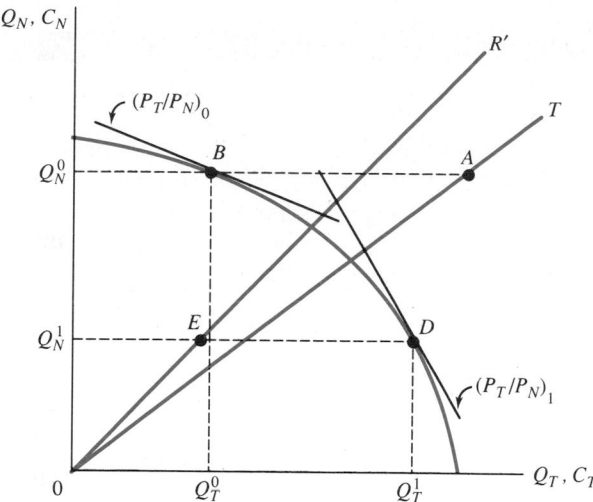

Figure 22-3
A Debtor Country's Adjustment to the
Debt Crisis

can represent this situation using the graphic apparatus developed in Chapter 21. Figure 22-3 shows a typical Latin American economy living beyond its means in the precrisis period. Consumption is initially at point A, production at B, and the trade deficit is AB. After 1982, this situation had to change because foreign lenders were no longer willing to finance the excess of spending over income. Faced with that reality, countries had no choice but to cut back sharply on consumption.

The sharp drop in consumption led to an unprecedented adjustment of trade balances. In Latin America, for example, the trade balance went from a deficit of \$2 billion in 1981 to a surplus of about \$32 billion in 1983. Adjustments of these magnitudes in such a short period of time provoked considerable trauma in the affected countries. Since it was impossible to expand exports very rapidly, the adjustment in the trade balance came from a compression of imports. The region's imports collapsed by almost \$42 billion between 1981 and 1984, a drop of 43 percent, while the nominal dollar value of exports *declined* over the same period.[12]

Faced with the need to cut back on consumption, the ideal economic adjustment would have been a production shift from point B to D, while consumption would go to a point like E. The distance DE, then, would be the trade surplus necessary to service the foreign obligations. With this, the relative price of tradable goods would increase significantly, from $(P_T/P_N)_0$ to

---

[12] The export slump was mainly due to a sharp decline of almost 30 percent in the international dollar prices of export goods from the region. Indeed, the worsening of export prices was so profound that the *value* of exports went down despite an increase of about 25 percent in their volume. The fall of dollar prices for exports resulted from several factors, including the appreciation of the dollar vis-à-vis other currencies in the first half of the 1980s, a recession in the industrial world in the early 1980s, and the fact that an increase in export volumes of some Latin American goods, mainly raw materials, caused a fall in the relative price of these exported goods in world markets.

$(P_T/P_N)_1$ in the graph. In practice, however, the adjustment in production was far from smooth, and considerable unemployment emerged in many countries. In the previous chapter, we identified reasons why the adjustment might involve an intervening period of unemployment: lack of factor mobility, long lags in investment in the tradable goods sector, and rigidity of nominal prices. For these reasons, the Latin American countries did not traverse smoothly along the PPF from B to D. Instead, the typical economy produced below capacity for several years, somewhere between points E and D (but probably closer to E in the short term).

Characteristically, the hardest hit industry in the adjustment process was the construction sector. In some countries, unemployment rates in this sector reached more than 50 percent after 1982; such was the case of Chile, previously shown in Table 21-1. Part of the reason for this major setback was that construction was typically the sector that had seen the biggest expansion during the boom that took place between the late 1970s and 1981. The services sector saw a similar pattern of contraction, although not as marked.

Changes in the Debt Burden After 1980

A summary indicator of the external debt burden is the debt-to-GNP ratio, as presented in Table 22-9 for some of the highly indebted countries in the developing world. Note that there has been a tremendous *increase* in this

TABLE   22-9

EVOLUTION OF THE DEBT/GNP RATIO AMONG HIGHLY INDEBTED COUNTRIES, SELECTED YEARS, 1980–1989 (PERCENT)

	1980	1982	1985	1989
Latin America				
Argentina	48.4%	83.8%	84.2%	119.7%
Brazil	30.6	36.1	48.7	24.1
Chile	45.2	76.7	143.3	78.3
Colombia	20.9	26.9	42.0	45.8
Mexico	30.3	52.5	55.2	51.2
Peru	51.0	49.7	89.4	70.8
Venezuela	42.1	41.4	59.1	79.9
Asia				
Indonesia	28.0	29.2	44.4	59.8
Korea	48.7	52.3	52.5	15.8
Malaysia	28.0	52.4	70.3	51.6
Philippines	49.5	62.5	83.5	65.7
Thailand	25.9	34.8	47.8	34.1
Eastern Europe				
Hungary	44.8	45.4	70.2	75.8
Poland	—	—	48.7	68.3
Yugoslavia	25.6	31.5	48.2	33.5

Source: World Bank, World Debt Tables, 1990–1991 *(Washington, D.C.: The Bank, December 1990).*

ratio since 1980, even though new lending to these countries slowed markedly after the onset of the debt crisis. For most countries, the rise in the debt-GNP ratio did result from a rise in the debt but also a fall in the dollar value of GDP.

The reduction of the dollar value of GDP is due partly to the widespread economic depression of the region after 1981. But it is also the result of a less obvious factor, the major real depreciation of domestic currencies in the area. To illustrate this point, let us borrow the diagram from the previous graph for Figure 22-4. Here, the total GDP *measured in units of tradable goods* is given by Q_A.[13] Now suppose that there is a real depreciation, so that production moves from point A to point B. Note that GDP measured in units of tradable goods shifts from Q_A to Q_B. Even though the economy remains on the production possibility frontier, the value of production in units of tradable goods declines. The reason should be clear. When P_N/P_T falls, the value of nontradable production measured in units of tradable goods also falls. In other words, each unit of nontradable goods that is produced becomes worth less when measured in units of tradable goods.

The implications of real devaluation for the debt crisis are striking. Suppose that the debt is at the level D^*, as shown in Figure 22-4. At the initial production point A, the debt is well below the level of national income (Q_A, measured in terms of tradables). As shown here, the debt is some 70 percent of GDP. But now suppose that a real devaluation occurs when lending is cut off from abroad and that production shifts from point A to point B. Now, the same debt is more than *100 percent* of national income.

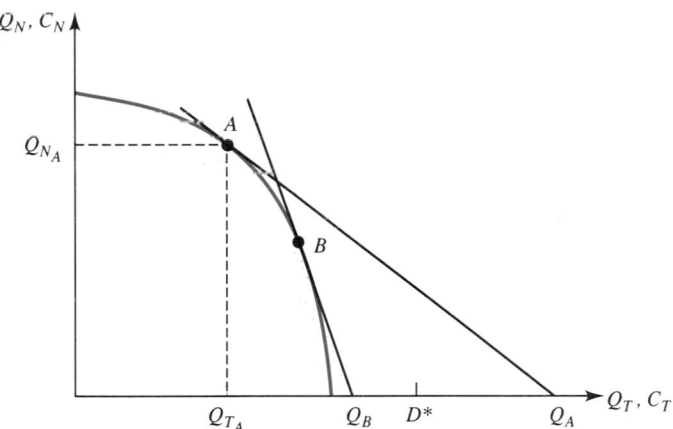

Figure 22-4
A Graphical Representation of GDP and Foreign Debt

---

[13] Remember why GDP (in tradable units) is given by the point Q_A in the figure. Note that $Q_A = Q_{TA} + (P_N/P_T)Q_{NA}$. The line segment from the origin to Q_{TA} measures the production of tradables. The line segment from Q_{TA} to Q_A measures the value $(P_N/P_T)Q_{NA}$. This latter point can be verified by observing that the slope of the PPF at point A is equal to the relative price P_N/P_T. Then, the segment from Q_{TA} to Q_A is equal to the slope at point A multiplied by the value Q_{NA}.

When production was at point A, the debt seemed small relative to income, but this was because nontradable goods production at point A had a high value. Once the economy shifts resources to tradables, the value of GDP measured in tradables goes down. All of a sudden, the debt looms as a much larger burden.

In retrospect, part of the debt-servicing capacity of the developing countries, at least as it was perceived in the late 1970s, turned out to be an illusion. During the high-borrowing period, the relative price of nontradable goods was very high. The economies seemed rich and the debt burden seemed small. But much of the value of domestic production was in the form of barbershops and construction firms, neither of which added much to the potential to produce tradable goods. Thus, once the economies were called upon to service their loans, the value of their production *in tradable goods units* fell sharply, thereby raising the ratio of debt to GDP.

The Adjustment Process From the Saving-Investment Perspective

During the period of heavy borrowing, world real interest rates were low, and the countries could borrow to keep domestic investment above domestic saving. When the cutoff in new loans came, domestic interest rates in the debtor countries rose to the level at which domestic investment and domestic saving were equalized once again. This process is shown in Figure 22-5. In the 1970s, interest rates were at r_0, leading to investment in excess of saving. In the 1980s, interest rates rose to r_1, that is, to the point where domestic saving and investment balanced once again.

From the diagram, we see clearly that the cutoff of foreign lending has the effect of squeezing domestic investment spending, and perhaps of raising domestic saving as well (depending on the responsiveness of domestic saving to the change in the interest rate). The collapse of investment spending not only depressed current aggregate demand, but also lowered the growth rate of the economy. This is one important avenue through which the debt crisis of the 1980s will continue to reverberate for years to come. In Latin America, investment spending fell from 25 percent of GDP or so in the 1970s

Figure 22-5
Debtor Adjustment in the Saving-Investment Framework

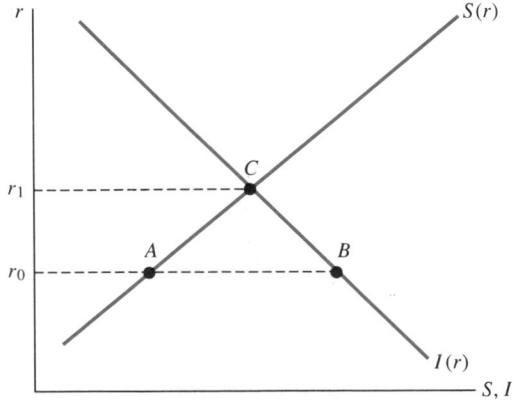

to around 17 percent of GDP by 1987. In some cases, the collapse of investment was even more pronounced. In the late-1980s, Argentina was investing less than 10 percent of GDP, an amount that was insufficient to cover the depreciation of the capital stock, much less to promote growth. This will lead to significantly lower living standards in Argentina in the 1990s than would have been the case without the crisis.

The Foreign Debt Problem and the Budget Crisis

Because most of the foreign borrowing by the developing countries was undertaken by governments, the debt crisis had serious implications for public-sector budgets. During the 1970s, access to foreign loans allowed debtor governments to run large budget deficits without the need of an inflation tax. This luxury ended in the early 1980s, when the lending dried up. In addition, the rise in world interest rates in the early 1980s greatly magnified the burden on the budget of the debt that had been contracted in the 1970s.

Thus, governments were caught between two pincers: on the one hand, the interest costs of their foreign debt shot up sharply and unexpectedly; on the other, they were no longer able to borrow abroad to cover their budget deficits. Either they had to close the budget deficit or they had to use *domestic* means of financing the deficit. Many governments were thus pushed into relying on the inflation tax to pay the bills in the 1980s, and Latin America experienced the highest inflation rates in its history.

In fact, several other events also worsened the budgetary problems in the early 1980s. Many countries suffered sharp deterioration in their terms of trade, thereby lowering the earnings of state enterprises engaged in exports, and thus reducing tax receipts from exports. Many private-sector firms also fell into financial crisis at the time, and in several countries the governments took over their debts, partially or totally, thereby raising the overall level of public-sector indebtedness. Additionally, as the debt crisis hit, real exchange rates depreciated sharply (that is, the price of tradables in terms of nontradables rose). Because the debt-servicing burden was set in dollars, while the government's tax revenues depended mostly on the nontradable sector, the real depreciation of the exchange rate greatly magnified the debt-service burden as a proportion of domestic taxes.

The options available to governments facing the intense fiscal crisis were politically, economically, and socially unattractive. Public-sector expenditures were cut significantly throughout the developing world.[14] In particular, public wages and investment were sharply curtailed, creating considerable political and social tension. Even social spending was significantly cut back, with very adverse consequences for public health, nutrition, and education, especially among the poor.

Faced with growing budget deficits despite their efforts, governments were forced to search for alternative sources of finance. Wherever domestic

---

[14] For an analysis of the public-sector response to the shocks of the 1970s and early 1980s in Latin America, see Felipe Larrain and Marcelo Selowsky, eds., *The Public Sector and the Latin American Crisis* (San Francisco: ICS Press, International Center for Economic Growth, 1991).

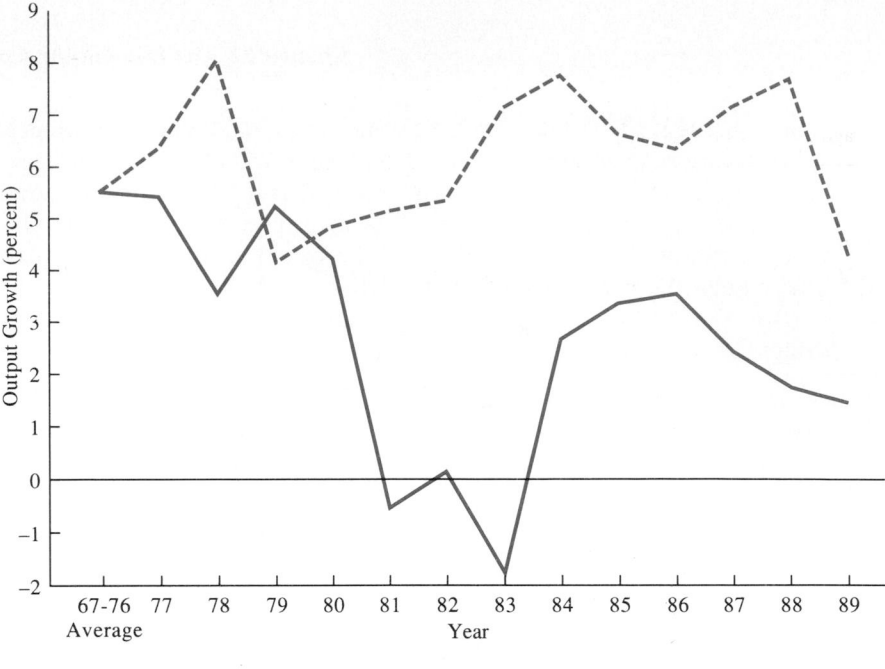

Figure 22-6

Output Growth in Developing Countries: A Comparison of Countries with and Without Debt-Servicing Difficulties

(From International Monetary Fund, World Economic Outlook, *May 1990.)*

financial markets were not able to handle significant amounts of public borrowing, governments had to resort to printing money. As we saw in Chapter 9, printing money is indeed one way to finance the deficit. We called this the *monetization of the budget deficit.*[15] In 1982, Bolivia, for example, had relied increasingly on the inflation tax until a true hyperinflation was under way in 1984–1985. The governments of other countries maintained some access to domestic saving through the local capital markets, thus postponing the inflation tax for a while. But even in these other countries, the amounts that could be borrowed in these local markets were limited, and most governments eventually had to increase their use of inflationary financing.

Money-financed budget deficits fuel inflation. One result of the debt crisis, therefore, was an explosion of inflation around the world. The inflationary trends were pronounced in many countries with debt problems, but the most remarkable inflations were concentrated in the heavily indebted countries in Latin America and Eastern Europe. As we shall see in Chapter 23, these two regions saw so many outbreaks of hyperinflation that the 1980s had more hyperinflationary episodes than any other decade in world history.

The Adjustment Problem: A Summary

The adjustment process of the economy had tremendous costs in the debtor countries. To appreciate the impact of the debt problem, we can compare the performance of developing countries that have experienced debt problems with those that have not. Figure 22-6 plots the output growth rates of both

[15] See Section 9-4, ''The Money Supply and the Government Budget Constraint.''

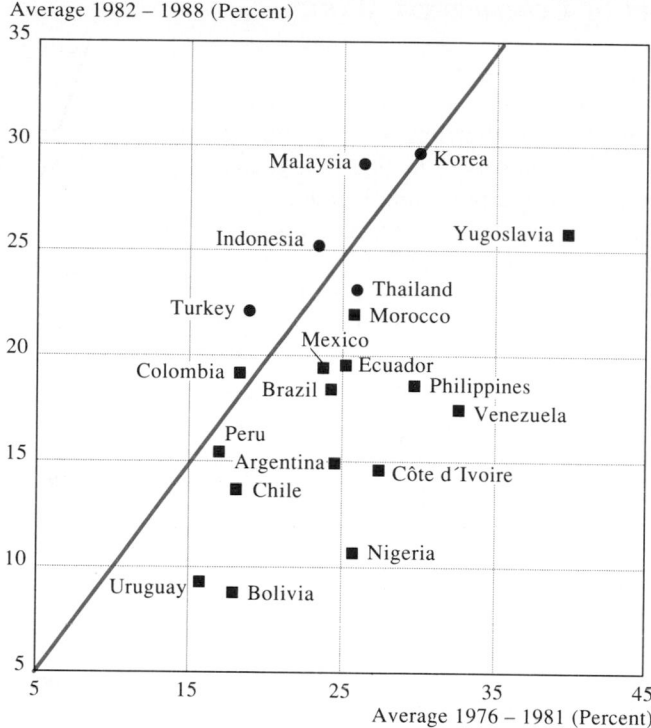

Average 1982 – 1988 (Percent)

Figure 22-7

The Investment/GDP Rate in Selected Countries: 1976–1981 Versus 1982–1988 (in percent)

(From International Monetary Fund, World Financial Outlook, *April 1989.)*

groups for the period 1977–1989. The result is striking. Up until the late 1970s, the performance of the two groups was not too different. With the onset of the debt crisis, the situation changed dramatically after 1980. Within one year, a huge gap in growth rates developed between the two groups that continued through the decade. While the problem debtors underwent declines in real output and then sluggish growth, developing countries without debt-servicing problems continued their growth unabated.

A similar picture emerges when we look at investment across countries. Figure 22-7 compares average investment-to-GDP rates in 1982–1988 (measured on the *Y* axis) with their counterpart in 1976–1981 (on the *X* axis) for each country in the graph. Points below the 45-degree line indicate higher investment rates in 1976–1981 than during 1982–1988. The square points in the graph correspond to 15 heavily indebted problem countries; the round points are used for debtor countries without recent debt-servicing problems. The result is, once again, very revealing. The countries with debt-servicing problems have tended to show a sharp fall in investment rates, while the countries without debt-service problems have not.

22-4 THE PROBLEMS OF COMMERCIAL BANK CREDITORS

The debt crisis proved to be not only a disaster for the debtor countries, but also for the creditor institutions that had loaned the money. Commercial banks, in particular, found themselves in deep trouble in the early 1980s, after their extensive lending in the previous decade. The sudden realization in 1982 that a large portion of commercial bank loans might never be repaid sent shock waves through the world capital markets. All of a sudden, it appeared that the world's leading financial institutions might fall into bankruptcy because of their unwise and excessive lending to the developing world.

To understand the fragility of the banking system as of 1982, it is important to recall how a commercial bank operates. The regular activity of such a bank is to obtain deposits from the public and then make loans to different customers with those funds. The bank's shareholders also contribute their own money in this process, but the shareholders' money, called bank capital, is only a tiny fraction of the money that the banks lend out of depositors' funds. A typical financial structure of a bank is shown in Table 22-10a. The bank's loanable funds come from two sources, the deposits and the shareholder's capital. Typically, the shareholder's capital represents only 5 to 10 percent of the total loans, while the depositors' money represents between 90 and 95 percent of the loans.[16] In Table 22-10a, we say that deposits are $90 million, capital is $10 million, and loans are $100 million.

The bank's net worth, or shareholder capital, is equal to the value of its loans minus the value of its debts to depositors. In our illustration, the shareholder capital is $10 million (= $100 million in loans − $90 million in deposits), a small fraction of the value of the bank's loans. Because the bank uses mostly borrowed funds to make loans, even a small change in the value of the loans can cause an enormous change in the value of the shareholder capital. Consider, in Table 22-10b, what happens when only 10 percent of the loans go bad. The market value of the loans drops from $100 million to $90 million, and the market value of shareholder capital drops from $10 million to 0. In other words, a mere 10 percent drop in the value of the outstanding loans leads to a complete (100 percent) wipeout of shareholder equity.

[16] We are working with this simplified balance sheet only for illustrative purposes. In fact, the bank's balance sheet is far more complicated. A bank's assets include not only the loans that it has made, but its investments in other kinds of securities (Treasury bills, for example), real estate (the bank's headquarter building, for example), and equities. The bank's liabilities include not only its depositors' funds but other kinds of borrowed funds, such as the funds generated by floating short-term fixed interest obligations (certificates of deposit, for example) and long-term bonds.

Table 22-10

The Simplified Financial Structure of a Typical Bank

(A)

Assets	Liabilities	
Loans 100	Deposits	90
	Capital	10

(B)

Assets	Liabilities	
Loans 90	Deposits	90
	Capital	0

(C)

Assets	Liabilities	
Loans 85	Deposits	90
	Capital	−5

We should note one tricky point about accounting here. Bank regulators are often lax in how they oversee banks, and particularly in how they allow the banks to report their net worth. They often allow banks to pretend that nothing is wrong, even when the market value of a bank's loans has declined markedly. The regulators often allow banks to pretend that their loans are worth the full face value of the original loan, even when the prospects of repayment are quite low. Thus, a bank can pretend on its books that its $1 million loan to Brazil is worth $1 million, despite the fact that most analysts think that Brazil will pay back only one-third of the loan. Even when the bank's loans decline in market value, the bank might still pretend that its loans are worth the full value of the original loan.[17]

Now although the *real* situation is like that in the (b) part of Table 22-10, the bank might continue to report its condition as in the (a) part, as if nothing bad had happened to shareholder equity. Even though the *market value* of the bank's capital has disappeared, the *book capital* (as stated in the official reports of the bank) would continue to show a value of $10 million. In essence, the bank is pretending that it can pay back its depositors out of the value of its loans, and continue to pay dividends to its shareholders even though the loans will not provide enough money to do both.

---

[17] The market value of the loan is determined by the price that a third party would be willing to pay the bank to take over ownership of the loan. This price, of course, can be far below the face value of the loan.

In Table 22-10c, the situation is even more dramatic. Now, the loans have dropped by 15 percent, to a value of $85 million. The bank's net worth is now negative (= $85 million in loans − $90 million in deposits). In this case, the bank does not have enough money to pay back its depositors, and it may have to shut down. If it does close down, in most countries the government will use official funds to pay the depositors, according to its program of deposit insurance.

With this background, it is easy to understand why the creditor world faced the potential collapse of its financial system when the debt crisis exploded in the early 1980s. Many major international commercial banks were threatened with insolvency. The financial institutions most affected by the crisis were the big nine so-called money center banks in the United States. Their loans to developing countries represented almost 290 percent of the book value of their capital by the end of 1982, with loans to Latin America alone amounting to about 180 percent of the same base. This exposure to Latin America was substantially higher than that of the smaller U.S. banks, as Table 22-11 shows.

With the situation of the banks so precarious in 1982, the U.S. Treasury centered its efforts on bolstering the banks. Pressure was put on debtor countries to continue servicing their debts in order to fend off any bankruptcy of a major bank. Under official pressure from the governments of the United States and the other major industrial countries, the debtor countries did indeed continue to service their debts (at least they paid the interest),

TABLE   22-11

EXPOSURE OF U.S. BANKS IN THE DEBTOR COUNTRIES AS A PERCENTAGE OF BANK CAPITAL, VARIOUS PERIODS, 1982–1988

Region	End 1982	End 1986	End 1988
	All U.S. Banks		
All LDCs	186.5	94.8	63.4
Latin America	118.8	68.0	47.3
	Nine Major Banks		
All LDCs	287.7	153.9	108.0
Latin America	176.5	110.2	83.6
	All Other Banks		
All LDCs	116.0	55.0	32.2
Latin America	78.6	39.7	21.8
Addendum			
Total bank capital ($ billions)			
All U.S. banks	70.6	116.1	135.6
Nine Major banks	29.0	46.7	55.8
All other banks	41.6	69.4	79.8

Source: *Federal Financial Institutions Examination Council, "Country Exposure Lending Survey," April 25, 1983, April 24, 1987, and April 12, 1989.*

though at the enormous cost that we examined in the previous section. By the end of 1980s, the situation of the banks regarding LDC debt was much improved, though several of the key U.S. banks continued to suffer from bad domestic loans. As regards LDC debts, the biggest nine U.S. banks had reduced their exposure to all developing countries from 288 percent of book capital in 1982 to only 108 percent of book capital in 1988. For the remaining U.S. banks, total loans to developing countries represented less than one-third of their net worth.

The improvement in the situation of the banks had a clear explanation. After 1982, the U.S. banks embarked on a successful plan to increase shareholder capital, while at the same time sharply restricting their loans to the less developed countries (or LDCs, in short). In every year, the banks have received substantially more interest payments from the developing world than they have granted loans. Some banks further reduced their exposure by selling LDC debt at a discount to other banks, to foreign investors, or to speculators.[18]

The sale of LDC loans by banks eager to rid themselves of these risky assets soon led to the development of an active *secondary market* for LDC debt. Banks found that there were buyers who would purchase the banks' claims on Mexico, Brazil, and other debtor countries, as long as the price was low enough. For example, a debt of the Mexican government worth $100 in face value, could be sold for about $50, reflecting the market's perception that Mexico would only repay about one-half of the debt in the long term.

Between 1987 and 1989, volume of trading on the secondary market grew considerably, and the prices of LDC debt fell sharply. The fall in price reflected two trends. First, many countries simply stopped servicing their debts, either partially or totally, including Argentina, Bolivia, Brazil, Costa Rica, Cuba, Ecuador, Honduras, Nicaragua, and Peru. Second, commercial banks became more willing to acknowledge losses on their balance sheets as soon as their own risks of insolvency had passed. Table 22-12 shows the persistent downward trend in secondary market prices for the debts of most Latin American countries throughout the 1986–1989 period, with the biggest drop occurring in 1987. Something very similar happened with the debt of other Third World countries. In 1990, however, prices showed an important recovery in the cases of Chile, Mexico, and Venezuela, which had benefited from a combination of economic recovery and a reduction in the debt burden through a renegotiation of the loans and a trade of debts for other kinds of financial assets.

Even though the banks dodged insolvency in the 1980s, they did not escape from the decade unscathed. Their share values have been hit hard by the excessive lending of the 1970s. Indeed, the stock market prices of U.S.

---

[18] Several countries—including Argentina, Brazil, Chile, and Mexico—implemented mechanisms to reduce their foreign debt by using the secondary market discounts. These were the so-called "debt swaps," an exchange of foreign debt for domestic debt or equity at a discount. Chile's program was the largest of all. For an assessment of the macroeconomic implications of debt swaps based on the Chilean case, see Felipe Larrain and Andres Velasco, "Can Swaps Solve the Debt Crisis? Lessons from the Chilean Experience," *Princeton Studies in International Finance,* No. 69 (Princeton University), November 1990.

TABLE 22-12

SECONDARY MARKET PRICES FOR LATIN AMERICAN DEBT, 1986–1989
(AS A % OF PAR VALUE)

	1986			1987			1988			1989		
	Jan	June	Dec	Jan	June	Dec	Jan	June	Dec	Jan	June	Dec
Argentina	62	65	66	64	52	35	32	25	21	20	13	13
Bolivia	—	6	7	8	9	11	11	11	10	10	11	11
Brazil	75	74	74	72	62	46	46	51	41	37	31	21
Colombia	82	81	86	86	85	65	65	65	57	56	57	64
Costa Rica	48	35	35	36	15	15	11	12	13	14	17	—
Chile	67	67	68	70	61	61	60	56	60	61	59	65
Ecuador	68	64	65	65	50	37	35	27	13	13	12	15
Mexico	69	59	56	57	57	51	50	51	43	40	40	35
Nicaragua	—	4	4	4	5	4	4	2	2	2	1	1
Peru	25	20	18	18	14	7	7	6	5	5	3	6
Uruguay	—	63	66	68	74	60	59	60	60	60	56	50
Venezuela	80	76	74	75	71	58	55	55	41	38	37	35
Average*	—	64.9	64.2	63.7	58.5	46.5	45.1	45.4	37.7	35.2	31.9	27.5

* *Weighted average for all Latin America according to bank debt.*
Source: *Economic Commission for Latin America and the Caribbean (ECLAC),* Preliminary Overview of the Economy of Latin America and the Caribbean, 1989 *(Santiago, Chile: December 1989).*

banks came to reflect a substantial anticipated loss on their developing country loans, a loss of about the same order of magnitude as the secondary market discounts on these assets.[19]

22-5 TOWARD A SOLUTION OF THE DEBT CRISIS

Historically, countries facing a debt crisis have surmounted their problem using a combination of actions. On the one hand, they have reduced domestic spending enough to service part of the debt, while on the other hand they have renegotiated the terms of the debt contracts with their creditors in order to reduce the debt burden to a reasonable level. This combination, domestic austerity together with a negotiated reduction of the debt burden, appears to be the mix of actions that will end the current debt crisis as well.

Nonetheless, it has taken a long time to arrive at this compromise solution to the current debt crisis. By the end of 1990, when the crisis had

[19] See Jeffrey Sachs and Harry Huizinga, "The U.S. Commercial Banks and the Developing Country Debt Crisis," *Brookings Papers on Economic Activity,* No. 2, 1987, for an analysis of bank stock prices and the secondary market for LDC debt.

entered into its ninth year, most of the problem debtor countries were still caught in the crisis, and little negotiated reduction of the debt had occurred. Some countries had unilaterally stopped paying debts, but had not yet succeeded in renegotiating their debt contracts with the commercial banks.

Difficulties in Reaching a Solution

It is not hard to understand why the compromise solution was not reached quickly. The creditor governments were most worried about the health of the commercial banks. Thus, they pressured the debtor countries into making large debt-service payments each year, even if that resulted in very serious internal economic crises in the debtor countries. This simple strategy did indeed result in large trade surpluses in the debtor countries—enough to make large payments to the commercial banks—but at a fearful cost. The economies in many debtor countries collapsed under the sudden shift from borrowing to repayments, economic growth came to a halt, and many countries were thrown into hyperinflation by the heavy burden of their debts on their domestic budgets.

The creditor governments introduced a less severe policy, known as the Baker Plan, by the end of 1985.[20] Under the new plan, the creditor governments continued to oppose any negotiated reduction of the debt burden, still fearing for the financial health of the banks, but they did support short-term relief of the debt burden by allowing the debtor country and the banks to renegotiate and stretch out the repayment schedule. The debtor countries were also to receive more financial support from the International Monetary Fund (IMF) and the World Bank. In return for this increased financing, the debtor governments committed themselves to pursue long-term reforms under the watchful eye of the IMF and World Bank.

The creditor governments also eased the terms on repayment of debts owed directly to them rather than to the banks. While the commercial banks and the debtor countries renegotiated their contracts within the context of the "London Club," the government-to-government debts were renegotiated within the context of the "Paris Club."[21] Both the banks and the government creditors in the Paris Club made the renegotiation of the debt contingent on the debtor country reaching an agreement on its reform program with the IMF.

Notwithstanding the efforts of the Baker Plan, the debt crisis continued unsolved through much of the developing world. Simply postponing some debt payments was not enough; real debt reduction was needed, as had proven to be the case in earlier debt crisis in history. The next phase of the debt crisis therefore took the step to actual debt reduction.

---

[20] The Baker Plan was named after then U.S. Secretary of the Treasury James Baker III, who initiated the policy.

[21] The "Paris Club" refers to meetings held under the auspices of the French Ministry of Finance, at which creditor governments agree to postpone or otherwise ease the terms of repayments on loans owed by debtor governments to them. The "London Club" refers to negotiations between the banks and the debtor country, and reflects the fact that the early negotiations often took place in London. More recently, the name has become a misnomer, since an increasing number of negotiations have taken place in New York.

The Brady Plan

As it became clear that the Baker Plan did not provide a solution to the debt problem, several analysts started to suggest new alternatives. Although the new proposals were very numerous,[22] most of them shared three basic principles. First, debtor countries needed a permanent reduction of the debt burden. Second, the magnitude of debt reduction should be decided on a case-by-case basis which recognizes, for example, that Bolivia can pay a smaller proportion of its debt than Argentina, which in turn can pay less than Brazil and Mexico. Third, debt relief should be given only to those economies that are willing to pursue significant policy reform programs under international supervision. A fourth principle was somewhat more controversial, but finally found acceptance. It held that the commercial banks should receive protection against future losses in return for accepting a negotiated reduction of the debt. This protection should take the form of guarantees, given by official creditors and by the debtor country itself, on the new debt that remains after debt reduction.

The controversy over new approaches to solve the debt crisis was becoming increasingly heated when the newly inaugurated Bush administration surprised most analysts with the announcement of the Brady Plan.[23] This new proposal marked a fundamental departure from the Baker Plan in that it recognized that a reduction of commercial bank debt was an important part of the solution to the problem. At the same time, it singled out the International Monetary Fund and the World Bank for playing a key role in supporting debt reduction through their lending policies.

The Brady Plan was an explicit recognition that for most debtor countries, the repayment of their external debts in full was out of reach, even with additional loans in the short to medium term. The Brady plan was short on specifics and left details to be worked out between each country and its foreign creditors. However, it outlined the general mechanism to achieve debt reduction: countries had to negotiate with their bank creditors to reduce their liabilities, either through a reduction in the interest rate or a cut in the principal.[24]

Under the new scheme, the banks were to be presented with a "menu" of debt-reduction options by the debtor country, and the banks would voluntarily choose among them. At the same time, some banks could choose to lend new credits to the debtor country instead of accepting a reduction of the debt. Why would the banks agree to negotiate a reduction of the debt of a particular country? The main argument was that the banks should recognize that the country's debt is so large that it can never be repaid in full. *By trying to collect the debt in full, the banks could so destabilize the debtor country that they would end up with less repayment than if they agreed to an orderly reduction of the debt through negotiation.*

---

[22] The July/August 1988 issue of *International Economy* counted 24 major proposals to solve the debt crisis. For an analysis of the most important proposals, see Jeffrey Sachs, "New Approaches to the Latin American Debt Crisis," *Essays in International Finance*, No. 174 (Princeton University), July 1989.

[23] This plan is named after U.S. Secretary of the Treasury Nicholas Brady, who announced it in March 1989.

[24] For a detailed analysis of the Brady Plan, see Jeffrey Sachs, "Making the Brady Plan Work," *Foreign Affairs* (Council on Foreign Relations), Summer 1989.

This argument became known as the "debt overhang" motivation for debt reduction.[25] The overhang of bad debt actually reduced the long-term capacity of the debtor to make debt payments. By cutting the overhang of bad debt through negotiations, both the creditors and the debtor would actually be made better off.

By 1991, several countries had reached agreements with the commercial banks in the framework of the Brady Plan. After lengthy negotiations, Mexico's bank creditors agreed to reduce Mexico's commercial bank debt by about 35 percent. Costa Rica attained a much deeper debt reduction of about 65 percent. Venezuela also negotiated a package that included debt reduction. Less consequential agreements were reached with some other countries. Many other countries, including Ecuador and Poland, were negotiating debt-reduction packages with their bank creditors by the end of 1990.

One flaw continued to hamper the application of the Brady Plan, the so-called "free-rider" problem. Even when the banks as a group could agree to reduce a country's debt, each individual bank was interested in minimizing its own losses. Thus, each bank hoped that the *other* banks would forgive enough debt so that it would not have to. In other words, each bank tried to "ride for free" on the concessions of the other banks. In a bankruptcy court, the bankruptcy judge makes sure that each creditor shares equally in a reduction of debt. But in the global debt crisis, there is no bankruptcy judge, so that each bank continued to try to minimize its own contribution to the overall reduction of the debt. Until the free-rider problem is more effectively overcome, it is likely that the amount of debt relief under the Brady Plan will be too little and too late to solve the debt crisis in many countries.

In addition to the Brady Plan, which addressed the problem of commercial bank debt, the creditor governments also undertook new initiatives to reduce the burden of government-to-government debt. In 1987, they agreed to a policy of debt reduction on government-to-government debt for the poorest countries of Sub-Saharan Africa, and in 1991, they intensified this effort for the poorest countries. By 1991, relief on official debts was also put on the agenda for some other countries. Egypt and Poland became the first recipients of this expanded policy in 1991, when the Paris Club of official creditors reduced the government-to-government debts of these two countries by half. At the same time, the U.S. government launched a new policy called the Enterprise of the Americas Initiative in which the United States said that it would reduce some government-to-government debts of countries undertaking fundamental economic reforms. Since the debt crisis continues for dozens of countries, it is likely that these initiatives will be further extended in coming years.

Reducing the burden of debt, however, is not enough for debtor countries to resume growth. At the same time it is necessary to implement major policy measures to restructure the economy. These measures fall under two

[25] This argument was first developed by Jeffrey Sachs, "The Debt Overhang of Developing Countries," in R. Findlay, G. Calvo, P. Kouri, and J. Braga de Macedo, eds., *Debt, Stabilization and Development: Essays in the Honor of Carlos Díaz Alejandro* (Oxford: Basil Blackwell, 1989). It was elaborated by Paul Krugman, "Market-Based Debt-Reduction Schemes," in Jacob Frenkel, ed., *Analytical Issues in Debt* (Washington, D.C.: International Monetary Fund, 1988).

broad categories, reform of the public sector and the liberalization of markets. Public-sector reform aims at reducing the size and involvement of the government in the economy, and often includes an aggressive privatization program for public enterprises.[26] In many countries, a reform of the tax system to improve its efficiency and equity is also necessary. Liberalization amounts mainly to opening the economy to trade with the rest of the world, with measures to liberalize both the current account and the capital account of the balance of payments.

The process of economic reform is, however, often a painful one and results take some time to show. At the beginning of the 1990s in Latin America, Chile and Mexico were at the forefront of economic reform, with most of the structural changes already consolidated or in the process of consolidation. Other countries, like Argentina and Brazil, were only starting to implement the necessary reforms.[27]

22-6 SUMMARY

Developing countries experienced a profound economic crisis in the 1980s that was without precedent since the 1930s, and as a result many of these countries were poorer at the end of the 1980s than at the beginning. Almost all nations that experienced severe economic strains were burdened by a very large foreign debt and an onerous schedule of debt servicing. The crisis hit economies in Africa and Latin America especially hard, while it almost bypassed the middle-income countries of East Asia. In the poorer countries—especially in Africa, but also in Latin America—the collapse of economic development in the 1980s sharply worsened the trends in infant mortality, child malnutrition, and other social indicators.

The *debt crisis* resulted from some common *external factors* and also from domestic economic policies pursued in individual debtor countries. The oil shock contributed to a large increase in the availability of low-interest-rate loans for developing countries. Most of the debt in both Latin America and Africa was borrowed by governments rather than by the private sector. Africa mostly borrowed from official sources (other governments and international institutions) and Latin America from commercial banks. Economic conditions changed markedly from the second half of the 1970s to the early 1980s, when world interest rates rose sharply and the terms of trade deteriorated for the debtor world. Debtors were highly vulnerable to an increase in interest rates since a large portion of the loans had been contracted at variable rates. As a result of these shocks, external lending and foreign investment flows abruptly declined.

Domestic policies also had an important responsibility in generating the crisis. Countries pursued overly expansionary fiscal policies as long as they could count on foreign finance. Bad policies regarding trade and exchange rates also were important factors. Latin American countries had

---

[26] See the concluding chapter in F. Larrain and M. Selowsky, *The Public Sector and the Latin American Crisis* (San Francisco: ICS Press, 1991).

[27] For an assessment of the progress of reform in Latin America in the early 1990s, see John Williamson, *Latin American Adjustment: How Much Has Happened?* (Washington, D.C.: Institute for International Economics, 1990).

closed trade regimes and allowed exchange rates to become highly overvalued. By contrast, the East Asian countries that escaped the crisis had freer international trade and more realistic exchange rates that made exporting profitable. In Latin America, the combination of large fiscal deficits and overvalued exchange rates also resulted in extensive *capital flight*.

The collapse of foreign financing and the worsening in the terms of trade at the beginning of the 1980s led to a sharp drop of aggregate demand. Trade balances quickly adjusted, from large deficits to massive surpluses, principally through a compression of imports. The adjustment was very costly and involved major increases in unemployment. The combination of economic depression and real devaluation of debtor countries' currencies increased the *debt burden,* however measured, to very high levels. Debt/GDP ratios climbed in many cases over 100 percent. Another way to interpret this adjustment process is from the saving-investment perspective. When external loans were cut off, domestic interest rates in debtor countries had to increase significantly, thereby squeezing domestic investment.

The foreign debt crisis is generally the mirror image of a *fiscal crisis*, as most of the external borrowing was undertaken by governments. Foreign loans had financed large budget deficits up to the early 1980s. With external financing gone, governments could not cut the deficits so quickly, and had to rely on domestic sources of finance such as domestic borrowing or monetary emission. This process tended to fuel very high inflations.

Commercial bank creditors—especially big money center banks in the United States—were also hardly hit by the debt crisis, as loans to developing countries represented a large fraction of their capital base. Since bank capital is a small fraction of total loans, a small reduction in the value of loans can cause a major decline in shareholder capital. By the end of the 1980s, the *exposure of banks* to developing country debt had decreased significantly. This was a consequence of a successful plan by banks to increase their capital base, and of reducing their stock of developing country debt, for example, through the sale of debt in the secondary market. Some debtor countries encouraged *debt swaps* through the secondary market both to reduce their external debt and to promote foreign investment.

Historically, countries facing a debt crisis have gone out of it through a combination of domestic austerity and a negotiated reduction of the debt burden. In the current crisis, it has taken a long time to arrive at a compromise solution. Initially, creditor governments put pressure on debtor countries to keep their payments on schedule. In late 1985, the *Baker Plan* supported short-term relief of debtors through voluntary renegotiations with their creditors and loans for debtors from multilateral institutions. Negotiations for a permanent reduction in the debt burden, however, were still opposed.

In early 1989, the *Brady Plan* was a major change in the debt scenario, in that it recognized that a negotiated reduction of commercial bank debt was an important part of the solution to the problem. Banks would agree to this if they recognized that trying to collect the debt in full could so destabilize the debtor country that they would end up with less repayment than if they agreed to an orderly reduction of debt (the so-called "debt overhang" argument). Under the Brady Plan, *debt reduction* was to be granted only to countries that agreed to undertake major domestic reforms to reduce the size of the state and open their economies. As of late 1990, Mexico, Costa Rica, and Venezuela had reached agreements with commercial banks under the Brady Plan scheme.

Key Concepts

debt crisis	debt-GDP ratio
variable interest rates	populist policies
capital flight	bank exposure
secondary market for LDC debt	Paris Club
Baker Plan	debt overhang
debt burden	debt-service ratio
LIBOR	overvalued exchange rate
net resource transfer	money-center banks
debt swaps	London Club
Brady Plan	debt reduction

Problems and Questions

1. Many analysts think that bank loans to developing countries in the 1970s were not evaluated with enough care. Which are the appropriate macroeconomic variables to look at before lending money to a foreign government?

2. Define three different indicators of debt burden. Which of these is a better indicator of a country's liquidity problem? And which one indicates better a country's solvency problems? Why?

3. Comment on the following statement: "As a result of the debt crisis of the early 1980s, government throughout Latin America are rejecting inward-looking policies and extensive state ownership, for a market-based approach that emphasizes openness and private enterprise."

4. To what extent can exchange-rate management and trade policies account for the different performances of Latin America and East Asia during the debt crisis? Are there other important factors as well to account for this difference?

5. It has been said that the debt crisis will hinder economic development in developing countries well after the crisis itself is over. Analyze at least two different reasons to justify this statement.

6. A country has a debt-to-GDP ratio of 100 percent. Suddenly, the price of its major export, coffee, shoots up 50 percent in world markets. Analysts believe that this price rise will last at least five years. Suppose analysts are right. Use a graph like Figure 22-4 to analyze the changes that this price increase implies for the country's relative prices and its foreign debt burden.

7. Bank XYZ has $1 billion in deposits and a capital base of $100 million. The bank has lent $250 million (in equal proportions) to three Latin American countries whose debt is trading at an average of 50 percent of par value in the secondary market. What is the financial situation of this bank? Can the bank continue in operations?

8. Discuss the main reasons that led the international financial community to reevaluate the debt strategy in 1989. What are the main points of the new strategy announced then? How does it depart from the previous strategy?

9. Should developing countries be treated similarly in the context of a debt-relief proposal? What should be the criteria to differentiate them, if any?

10. Under which circumstances does it make sense for a commercial bank to lend more to a developing country with significant debt-servicing problems? Under which circumstances will it make sense for the bank to agree to debt reduction?

chapter 23

Stopping High Inflation

In Chapter 11 we described how persistent inflation can originate from expansionary monetary and fiscal policies. We showed how the inflation tax can be used by governments to finance public-sector deficits when, for one reason or another, public spending is persistently above government revenues. In Chapter 15, we discussed many aspects of ending inflation, and we examined the short-run trade-offs between unemployment and inflation.

In this chapter, we return to these two themes, but in a special context. Here we focus on countries that have reached extraordinarily high rates of inflation, limiting our attention to cases of *very high inflation,* which we define as an annual inflation rate of 100 percent or more, and cases of *hyperinflation,* which we define, following the classic definition given by Columbia University economist Phillip Cagan, as an inflation of more than 50 percent per month.[1] (While 50 percent per month might not seem spectacular, note that 50 percent per month compounded for a mere 12 months leads to an annual inflation rate of almost 13,000 percent!)

The cases of very high inflation and hyperinflation might seem like theoretical oddities—like freak shows, perhaps, at an economic circus. Indeed, through 1990, there had only been 15 cases of hyperinflation in all known world history. Unfortunately, in recent years, these economic scourges have been anything but rare. While there were no hyperinflations in the world for the 34 years between 1949 and 1983, there were seven hyperinflations during the second half of the 1980s! And during the 1980s, many other countries have experienced high inflations in which the rate exceeded 100 percent over a 12-month period.[2]

---

[1] Cagan defined hyperinflations "as beginning in the month the rise in prices exceeds 50 percent and as ending in the month before the monthly rise in prices drops below that amount and stays below for at least a year." See P. Cagan, "The Monetary Dynamics of Hyperinflation," in Milton Friedman, ed., *Studies in the Quantity Theory of Money* (Chicago: University of Chicago Press, 1956).

[2] About 50 cases have originated in 15 countries. Thus, many of these economies have experienced several years of very high inflation, as Table 23-2 shows.

There are few economic phenomena that are more socially destructive than a hyperinflation. The painful memories of the 1923 German hyperinflation, for example, still linger, and those memories are widely regarded as one reason that the German central bank, the Bundesbank, remains so zealously on guard against inflationary excesses. One important reason for economists to study hyperinflations closely is to learn how to prevent their outbreak and their very damaging effects. There are other reasons as well. Because they are such extreme cases, hyperinflations help us to see certain economic phenomena more clearly than we can see them in more "normal" cases. In the first half of this chapter, then, we examine the circumstances which lead to very high inflations and hyperinflations. In the second part, we consider the possible policy approaches to ending them.

23-1 A HISTORICAL PERSPECTIVE ON VERY HIGH INFLATIONS AND HYPERINFLATIONS

It is indeed interesting that all true hyperinflations known in world history have occurred in this century. History has recorded earlier episodes of high inflations, but none turns out to have reached nearly the extraordinary rates achieved during the twentieth century.

Early Cases of High Inflation

The best known report of high inflation in the ancient world was the case of the Roman Empire in the third century A.D. At the time, the more traditional methods of regular tax collection—and sometimes wealth confiscation—became less important as a means to finance government spending. Instead, the Roman emperors became fond of "debasing" the currency, that is, reducing the metallic content of coins that circulated at a given face value. Thus, the *silver denarius*, which had over a 90 percent silver content in the first century A.D., was already debased to a 28 percent silver content under emperor Gordian in 238 A.D. and a content of only 0.02 percent under Claudius Victorinus in 268 A.D. This led to the famous edict of Diocletian (301 A.D.), the first elaborate scheme of price and wage controls known in history, which set price ceilings for over 900 goods and established wage limits for some 130 different types of labor. Some historians have felt that monetary instability and high inflation actually contributed to the downfall of the empire. As damaging as the inflation may have been, the best evidence shows that the inflation during this period averaged only 3 to 4 percent per year.[3]

Another famous early inflation is that of Spain in the sixteenth century, following the discovery of great deposits of precious metals in America, especially in Mexico and Peru. Following the Mercantilist tradition, the Spanish kings encouraged the flow to Spain of as much specie as possible, and tried to block its flow out of the country. The inflow of gold and silver increased the money supply and indeed raised prices significantly, but again, the annual rates of inflation were quite low by present standards. At the height of the inflationary trend in the second half of the 1500s, the inflation

---

[3] See, for example, H. Michell, "The Edict of Diocletian: A Study of Price Fixing in the Roman Empire," *Canadian Journal of Economics and Political Science*, February 1947.

rate in Andalusia, the region hardest hit, reached around 20 percent per year for 1561 and 1562. However, the average inflation rate for the period 1551–1600 was probably less than 2 percent per year.[4]

There are only three known truly high inflations before this century, but none reached the hyperinflationary threshold defined by Cagan. The three episodes were related to civil wars and revolutions, which, as we shall see, are prone to cause high inflations. The first case is the U.S. War of Independence (1775–1783). The newly independent American colonies relied little on taxation and foreign borrowing to finance their war effort. Instead, they printed paper money, the so-called "Continentals," to cover about 80 percent or so of total expenditures. Prices rose by about 1,000 percent during the most inflationary two-year period 1779–1780. This inflation rate, while impressively high, amounted to a monthly rate of roughly 10 percent.

The next high inflation came with the French Revolution. The post-Revolutionary government established in France in 1789 was immediately strapped for cash, and it resorted to the easiest means of financing available, printing new money. The new paper currency, called *assignats,* flooded into circulation, and prices naturally started to rise as well. In 1794, inflation reached 100 percent, but the worst was to come the next year, when prices increased by more than 3,000 percent. Although high, this inflation still fell short of the hyperinflationary threshold.

The third case of very high inflation before the twentieth century came at the time of the U.S. Civil War (1861–1965). Both the North and the South resorted to money printing, but the Confederate government in the South proved to be more inflationary, as it relied less on taxes and sales of public bonds and more on money emission. Between October 1861 and February 1864, inflation in the Confederacy was fairly stable at about 10 percent per month. The highest monthly inflation rate, 40 percent, occurred in March 1864. Price increases in the North were much less dramatic: during 1863 and 1864 inflation rates averaged some 20 percent per year. This discrepancy between the North and the South was not only due to a larger monetization of the deficit. As the armies of the North occupied Southern territory, the region where Confederate money was accepted started to shrink. Thus, people living in that area sent Southern money where it still was accepted. But in those remaining regions, this process had the same effect as a large government deficit, that is, a sharp increase in the money supply which fueled inflation.[5]

---

[4] The late Earl Hamilton of Duke University provided a highly documented account of Spanish inflation in the sixteenth and seventeenth centuries, based on many years of research in old Spanish archives. See his book *American Treasure and the Price Revolution in Spain, 1501–1650* (Cambridge, Mass.: Harvard University Press, 1934).

[5] An interesting account of this experience is provided by Eugene Lerner in two articles: "The Monetary and Fiscal Programs of the Confederate Government, 1861–65," *Journal of Political Economy,* December 1954, and "Money, Prices and Wages in the Confederacy, 1861–65," *Journal of Political Economy,* February 1955.

The Emergence of Hyperinflations in the Twentieth Century

The fact that hyperinflations have occurred only in this century should not come as a big surprise in view of the history of money (see Box 8-1 in Chapter 8). High inflations must always be preceded by major increases in the supply of money, and such huge increases in the money supply can occur only in systems with fiat money. Under metallic currency systems, the supply of metals does not increase at rates necessary to produce high inflations or hyperinflations. It is only when governments abandon a metal standard that such high inflations are possible. Before the twentieth century, paper currency systems were rare, and indeed were often introduced for just such extraordinary circumstances as revolutions or civil wars. In normal periods, the inflation rate was held down by the link between money and the supply of precious metals.

In the twentieth century, of course, fiat money became the rule and not the exception. One side effect has been the onset of hyperinflations, and the even more common occurrence of high inflations. Interestingly, the 15 hyperinflations in this century did not occur as isolated events, but rather came in bursts linked to global economic and political events. It is clear that external dislocations have played a fundamental role in all the world's hyperinflations.

There are three clearly identifiable time periods when groups of countries succumbed to hyperinflation: the aftermath of World War I, the aftermath of World War II, and the debt crisis of the 1980s. Table 23-1 shows some summary data characterizing each of the 15 hyperinflations, defined according to Cagan. These data describe chronology (the first month of the hyperinflation, the last month, and duration) and prices (total increase in prices during the episode, average monthly inflation, and maximum inflation per month). One interesting characteristic stands out in all hyperinflations: the increase in prices is always greater than the rise in the money supply, and therefore *real* money balances decrease to very low levels. (Later in the chapter we show how our simple analytical model of money supply and demand accounts for this important observation.)

In the aftermath of World War I, five countries in Central Europe and Asia fell into the grips of hyperinflation, Austria, Germany, Hungary, Poland and the Soviet Union.[6] All these hyperinflations occurred in a relatively short period of time, from 1921 to 1924, and all emerged in the chaotic conditions that followed the end of World War I.

Austria and Hungary were carved out of the collapsed Hapsburg Empire at the end of World War I. Both countries lost much of their traditional land, while at the same time they were required to absorb the large bureaucracy of the former Empire. As losers of World War I, they also faced the grim prospects of reparation payments to the victorious allied powers. In addition, the Austrian government was burdened by the need to make large transfer payments to the unemployed. The Hungarian authorities extended

---

[6] For a good description and analysis of the Austrian, German, Hungarian, and Polish experiences, see Thomas Sargent, "The Ends of Four Big Inflations," in Robert Hall, ed., *Inflation: Causes and Effects* (Chicago: National Bureau of Economic Research, University of Chicago Press, 1982).

TABLE 23-1

A HISTORICAL LOOK AT HYPERINFLATIONS

	Post–World War I					Post–World War II			Decade of the 1980s						
	Austria	Germany	Hungary	Poland	Russia	China*	Greece	Hungary	Argentina	Bolivia	Brazil	Nicaragua§	Peru‖	Poland	Yugoslavia
Beginning month of hyperinflation	Oct. 1921	Aug. 1922	Mar. 1923	Jan. 1923	Dec. 1921	Feb. 1947	Nov. 1943	Aug. 1945	May 1989	Apr. 1984	Dec. 1989	Apr. 1987	Sept. 1988	Oct. 1989	Sept. 1989
Final month of hyperinflation	Aug. 1922	Nov. 1923	Feb. 1924	Jan. 1924	Jan. 1924	Mar. 1949	Nov. 1944	Jul. 1946	Mar. 1990	Sept. 1985	Mar. 1990	Mar. 1991	Apr. 1989	Jan. 1990	Dec. 1989
Duration (no. of months)	11	16	12	13	26	26	13	12	11	18	4	48	8	4	4
Ratio of prices of end to prices at start	69.9	$1.02(10^{10})$	44	699	$1.24(10^5)$	$4.15(10^6)$	$4.7(10^8)$	$3.81(10^{27})$	664.5	1,028.5	8.0	$5.53(10^5)$	23.54	3.96	5.18
Average monthly inflation rate	47.1	322	46	81.4	57	79.7	365	19,800	65.95	48.1	68.6	46.45	48.4	41.2	50.9
Maximum monthly inflation rate	134	32,400	98	275	213	919.9	$85.5(10^6)$	$41.9(10^{15})$	196.6	182.8	81.3	261.15	114.1	77.3	59.7

* China: Cost of living in Shanghai.
§ Nicaragua: We consider Hyperinflation starts in April 1987, despite an inflation rate over 50% in June 1986. At the moment of writing this book, Nicaragua had not had 12 consecutive months of inflation below 50%.
‖ Peru: Only in September 1988 the inflation rate is higher than 50%. In the remaining months it is slightly below that level. We consider April 1989 the last month of Peru's first hyperinflation when inflation was 48.6 percent.

Sources: Data for Austria, Germany, and Hungary are from Phillip Cagan, "The Monetary Dynamics of Hyperinflation," in Milton Friedman, ed., Studies in the Quantity Theory of Money (Chicago: University of Chicago Press, 1956), p. 26; data for China are from Shun-Hsin Chou, The Chinese Inflation, 1937–1949 (New York: Columbia University Press, 1963); and data for the decade of the 1980s are from the International Monetary Fund, International Financial Statistics, various issues, and country data sources.

great amounts of highly subsidized credits to the private sector. Thus public budgets were under very heavy strains in both countries. Eventually, these strains erupted as hyperinflations.

Poland was also a new state. After the partitions of Poland at the end of the eighteenth century, its pieces had been absorbed in the Hapsburg, Russian, and German empires, and Poland was re-created out of these pieces at the end of World War I. Poland suffered not only the birth pains of a new and fragile country patched together at the end of the war, it also bore the heavy costs of a war with the Soviet Union that lasted until late in 1920. The Soviet Union was created in the most chaotic circumstances of all the new states. This country was established through a violent revolution and civil war that followed upon Russia's costly participation in World War I. The hyperinflation erupted in the wake of both economic devastation and the civil war.

Germany was not a new state, although the prewar regime was crushed. A new and fragile democracy, known as the Weimar Republic, was established, and the new regime was immediately buried under the burdens resulting from the war. With the huge reparations imposed by the Treaty of Versailles, the new state began with a crushing fiscal burden. The situation worsened enormously in 1923 when the French occupied the area of the Ruhr, the industrial heartland of the country. The Germans responded to the occupation with passive resistance and widespread labor strikes. The government paid the strikers by taking loans from the Reichsbank (as the German central bank was called at the time). Finally, a hyperinflation exploded. In a period of 15 months, prices rose by about *1 trillion percent*. At its highest, the *monthly* inflation rate topped 30,000 percent!

The next round of hyperinflations occurred in the wake of World War II, when three widely separated countries, China, Greece, and Hungary, slid into monetary chaos. After nearly a decade of war with the Japanese, in 1945 China fell into a civil war between the Nationalist faction under Chiang Kai-shek and the Communists under Mao Tse-Tung. The heavy strain on the budget during the war became even more intense under the internal confrontation, and hyperinflation ensued.

An interesting aspect of China at that time was the proliferation of currencies. The Japanese-occupied territory had three different monies circulating in parallel: the Nationalist government established a basic currency, the *fapi* (later on replaced by the gold *yuan,* which in turn gave way to the silver *yuan*) and separate regional currencies for Manchuria and Taiwan, and the communists had several regional currencies circulating in the areas they controlled. Between 1947 and early 1949, there were several separate hyperinflations in different currencies going on in parallel in China. After the Nationalist faction retreated to Taiwan in 1949, inflation came down from its astronomical levels, but still remained high for some time (although it was milder in Taiwan than on the mainland).[7]

A civil war also followed World War II in Greece. The Germans occupied the country from 1940 to 1944 and placed severe demands on the government, which were met increasingly by printing money. When the Germans were driven out by the British in 1944, a civil war exploded between

---

[7] See Shun-Hsin Chou, *The Chinese Inflation, 1937–1949* (New York: Columbia University Press, 1963).

the two main resistance groups: the monarchists and the communists, while noncommunists controlled the civil administration. Hyperinflation erupted in the midst of the civil war.

Hungary's hyperinflation in 1946 is remarkable in two ways. First, it is the only country to have experienced *two* hyperinflations in the short period of 20 years. Second, it is the highest hyperinflation in world history. Prices rose an astonishing 3.8 *octillion* times (3.8 × 10²⁷) in a mere one year, and the average monthly inflation rate was 19,800 percent. Hungary, which in the early 1940s allied itself with the Axis powers, had been an important battleground, and it lost an estimated 40 percent of its physical capital. As a loser of the war, it had to pay staggering reparations to the Allies, especially to the Soviets. It is calculated that reparation and occupation costs (that is, payments to the occupying Soviet army) represented 25 to 50 percent of government spending in 1945–1946. One further explanation of Hungary's extraordinary inflation rate was its widespread use of indexed deposits and later of indexed currency (the *tax pengo*). This practice shrank the demand for nonindexed money, which was the base of the inflation tax, and thus collecting a given amount of revenue required increasing inflation rates.[8]

The third round of hyperinflations occurred in the 1980s, when Argentina, Bolivia, Brazil, Nicaragua, Peru, Poland, and Yugoslavia joined this no-longer-so-exclusive club. War was not a factor in these hyperinflations, with the partial exception of that in Nicaragua. In all these countries, the foreign debt crisis contributed to their financial chaos, the burdens of their debt payments representing a large portion of their budgetary expenditures. At the same time, populist policies also contributed significantly to the onset of hyperinflation in the Latin American countries. Finally, the hyperinflations in both Poland and Yugoslavia reflected in part the strains of reforming an economy from a planned to a market system.

Recent Cases of High Inflation

In addition to the 15 cases of hyperinflation, there are many more experiences of very high inflations that did not turn into hyperinflations. If we define "very high inflations" as those experiences where prices increase by 100 percent or more per year, the group of cases that qualify increases significantly.

Table 23-2 shows a list of these countries for the 1952–1989 period, along with their average inflation rates. At this count, there have been 20 countries which have experienced high inflations in the last four decades, of which seven actually fell into hyperinflation.

23-2 KEY CONDITIONS TRIGGERING HYPERINFLATION

The hyperinflations in this century have had many common elements. Of course, each has some unique characteristics that depend on the country in which it occurred, the time period, and the external circumstances. But *all* hyperinflations share significant elements, and this has allowed economists

---

[8] An interesting analysis of this experience is provided by William Bomberger and Gail Makinen, "The Hungarian Hyperinflation and Stabilization of 1945–46," *Journal of Political Economy*, October 1983.

TABLE   23-2

EXPERIENCES OF VERY HIGH INFLATION, 1952–1989

Country	Period	Inflation (annual average rate)
Africa		
Ghana	1977	116.5
	1978	103.2
	1981	116.5
	1983	122.9
Sierra Leone	1987	178.7
Uganda	1981	108.7
	1984	132.4
	1986–1988	195.3
Zaire	1983	100.8
	1987–1989	113.1
Asia		
Korea	1952	144.7
Indonesia	1962–1965	162.2
	1967–1968	115.4
Eastern Europe		
Poland	1982	100.8
Turkey	1980	110.2
Yugoslavia	1987–1988	154.8
Middle East		
Israel	1980–1985	183.5
Latin America		
Argentina	1975–1985	244.8
	1987–1988	220.1
Bolivia	1982–1983	193.4
	1986	276.3
Brazil	1981	105.6
	1983–1988	237.8
Chile	1973–1976	348.9
Mexico	1983	101.8
	1986	104.3
	1987–1988	122.8
Nicaragua	1985–1986	399.7
Paraguay	1952	119.0
Peru	1983–1985	127.0
	1987	127.0
Uruguay	1968	125.3

Source: International Monetary Fund, International Financial Statistics. *Washington, D.C., various issues.*

to formulate a general theory of the phenomenon. In the next section we shall look at the process of how large budget deficits are transformed into major price explosions. First, however, we want to determine what conditions in the environment make these huge budgetary imbalances possible.

Remember, of course, that hyperinflations have occurred only in regimes with fiat money. Under a metallic money or a gold standard, the stock of precious metal simply cannot rise at a rate sufficient to support the price increases. The act of printing paper currency of ever-higher denominations, on the other hand, is technologically feasible, and all too easy. The existence of fiat money, then, is only the basic condition for hyperinflation. Other events usually trigger the inflationary takeoff.

War, Civil War, and Revolution

One traditional view links hyperinflations with war. According to this view, the strain on the public budget brought about by the financing of a war effort leads to major public deficits that eventually become monetized.[9] Forrest Capie of the City University, London, has recently refined this view. He has pointed out that hyperinflations have not been closely linked with wars of aggression between two countries, but rather with civil wars, revolutions, or states of deep social unrest.[10] It is not war itself that is a critical condition triggering hyperinflation, Capie hypothesizes, because a war raises patriotism and thus makes it easier to finance the budget through tax collections and borrowing from the public. But if the hostility occurs between different groups within a country, collecting taxes becomes extremely difficult because important parts of the population evade taxes as part of their struggle. In the absence of other alternatives, the difficulties of internal confrontation thus make the government turn to its printing presses to finance its budget.

There is considerable support for Capie's skepticism about the role of war per se. All the hyperinflations in the 1920s, for example, occurred several years after World War I had ended. As shown in Table 23-1, they started between October 1921 and March 1923, at least three years after the end of the war. In Germany, the wartime inflation had been checked by 1920, and the price explosion occurred two years later. Poland and Russia continued fighting against each other after World War I had ended, but their conflict ended in 1920, one to three years before hyperinflation developed in these countries (see Table 23-1). It is even clearer that war itself had no part in any of the hyperinflations of the 1980s, with the possible exception of Nicaragua.[11]

The role of civil war, revolution, or deep social unrest is, on the other hand, clearly a factor in many of the hyperinflations, especially those before the 1980s. In the Soviet Union, revolution and civil war clearly were the factors underlying the monetary chaos. Hungary experienced major internal

---

[9] Such a view is expressed, among others, by Earl Hamilton, "The Role of War in Modern Inflation," *The Journal of Economic History,* March 1977.

[10] See his article, "Conditions in Which Hyperinflation Has Appeared," *Carnegie-Rochester Conference Series in Public Policy,* Vol. 24, 1986.

[11] Technically, Nicaragua was not at war at the time of the hyperinflation, but it was certainly facing a severe internal struggle that was partially financed from abroad.

confrontations, and succeeding governments, ranging from monarchy to Bolshevik dictatorship and to repressive right-wing dictatorship, violently and rapidly overthrew each other after World War I. Poland suffered substantial social and political turmoil when the end of World War I brought not peace but a continuing confrontation with Russia that only ended in 1920. Germany experienced several armed uprisings in 1922 and 1923 and important breakdowns of public order. The same internally unstable conditions may be found in two of the three countries undergoing hyperinflation in the late 1940s. China and Greece were experiencing civil war, although this was not the case in Hungary.

In the 1980s, civil war may have been an important element only in Nicaragua. Peru faced deep social unrest from the strong guerrilla activity of the Shining Path insurgency, but the violence did not reach the dimensions of a civil war or a revolution. No significant form of violence existed in the other economies, however. In 1984, Bolivia was the first country to experience a hyperinflation totally unrelated to any armed struggle, internal or external. This was also the case in Argentina, Brazil, Poland, and Yugoslavia.

Weak Governments

We have argued that hyperinflations have many times occurred in countries undergoing some type of important internal dissension. Not all revolutions and civil wars have provoked hyperinflations, however, and not all hyperinflations have emerged under these conditions. The existence of weak governments has been pointed out as another important condition that triggers hyperinflations.

There are, however, some important practical problems in specifying the hypothesis concerning weak governments. First, it is often difficult to separate a government's weakness from the presence of social unrest or civil war. A weak government can lead to internal unrest, which, in turn, feeds back and further weakens the government. Second, weakness is hard to measure. Third, the argument may become merely tautological: whenever a hyperinflation exists people will label the government as weak.

In spite of these problems, some prominent analysts have attempted to identify this condition in the various hyperinflationary episodes we have named.[12] The most conspicuously weak governments came after World War I. Austria and Hungary were both new states created from pieces of the Austro-Hungarian empire, and significant doubts existed inside and outside these countries about their future viability. Germany was ruled by an inexperienced socialist government that could not pass a much needed tax reform. The new state of Poland after World War I was left with an inexperienced civil administration after many of its prewar civil authorities left the country. Hungary also fits the model of a weak government. Although the ruling party, the Smallholders, was elected with 60 percent of the vote in 1945, the country's sovereignty was severely compromised by the Allied Control Commission, led by the Soviet Union. When the central bank attempted to

---

[12] Among those who argue forcefully for the weak government condition is Forrest Capie, "Conditions in Which Hyperinflation Has Appeared."

put the brakes on monetary emission, for example, the Commission refused to allow it.[13]

In general, weak or inexperienced governments lack the ability to enforce tax collections and to implement necessary budgetary reforms. In addition, they are easily tempted to placate different groups of the population with transfers and subsidies in order to build up a political base. Under these situations, then, they are likely to turn to inflationary finance, and this sets the stage for high inflation.

External Shocks with Budgetary Implications

An interesting parallel between the experiences of hyperinflation in the 1920s and those in the 1980s lies in the role played by external shocks that had major adverse effects on the budget. In the 1920s, the problem centered on the war reparations that Austria, Hungary, and especially Germany owed to the Allies, as set in the treaties of Trianon and Versailles. In the case of Germany, the staggering value of the reparation payments that the country sent abroad was the central element of public finance from 1919 to 1923. (This is the issue that prompted the first writings to become famous of the greatest twentieth-century political economist, John Maynard Keynes, who argued passionately against setting an unpayable reparations burden upon Germany.[14])

In Austria and Hungary, the reparation obligations were feared to be large, even though the Reparation Commission of the Allied powers arrived at no fixed schedule of payments. Nonetheless, the mere fact that the Reparation Commission had a major, albeit unknown, claim on the assets of both governments cast a significant shadow over public finances in the two countries. Under a fiat regime, the value of the currency ultimately rests on the ability of the government to keep its budget under control not only in the present but also in the future. If economic agents feel that public finances may collapse (say, for example, because of future reparation payments), they may provoke a speculative attack on the currency. (Recall our analysis of a speculative attack on the currency in Chapter 11.) After World War II, Hungary was another case of large effective reparations and occupation payments contributing to a fiscal crisis.

During the 1980s, the external shock that dented the budget was not war reparations but the debt crisis (analyzed in the previous chapter). The debt problem was certainly not the only factor behind the price explosion, but in several countries it was an important ingredient. All the countries in question had very high levels of public debt (as a proportion of GDP) that was mostly, or exclusively, held by the government. In most cases, those governments serviced most or all the interest due on this debt until the

---

[13] Bomberger and Makinen, "The Hungarian Hyperinflation and Stabilization of 1945–46."

[14] See John M. Keynes, "The Economic Consequences of the Peace," published originally in December 1919. A recent edition is found on *The Collected Writings of John Maynard Keynes* (London: Macmillan, 1971).

macroeconomic consequences became unbearable. Several countries, among them Argentina, Bolivia, Brazil, and Poland, largely serviced their interest payments until the onset of hyperinflation, after which they partly or fully suspended payments.

23-3 THE ECONOMIC DYNAMICS OF HYPERINFLATION

As we have seen, a common feature of all hyperinflations is a colossal increase in the money supply, which has come about because a government needs to finance a huge budget deficit. Once started, inflation feeds on itself in a very dramatic way. Higher inflation causes a sharp drop in the real value of tax collections. This, in turn, increases the budget deficit, or requires further cuts in public spending just to stay at the same level of deficit. If the government is too weak or fragmented, it will be unable to respond both to the initial budget deficit and to the growth of the budget deficit caused by the weakening of tax collections. In this section, we want to study this process in greater detail, along the way developing a simple model of hyperinflation that follows the classic work of Phillip Cagan.

The seed of hyperinflation is a major increase in the monetary financing of the budget deficit. Typically, an external or internal shock arises which pushes the government into a large fiscal deficit. Once the deficit rises, the government usually scrambles to find nonmonetary means to finance it, through foreign credits if possible, or if that is not possible, it might try to borrow domestically in the bond market or from private banks. If the deficit turns out to be temporary, then indeed the government can avoid starting a high inflation as long as monetary policy remains under control.

After a while, the stock of debt builds up, and creditors become extremely reluctant to continue to finance the government's deficit. They become aware of default risk (in the event of foreign financing) or of inflationary risk (in the event of domestic financing). Typically, the government turns to monetary financing when its other sources of financing dry up. If it attempts to delay the onset of inflation as long as possible, it will maintain a fixed exchange rate even after the money financing starts. As we learned in Chapter 11, the result now is a fall in foreign-exchange reserves which continues until a speculative attack on the currency occurs and brings on the end of the fixed exchange-rate regime.

If the deficit that must be covered by monetary means is sufficiently high, then the ensuing inflation can develop into a hyperinflation. Based on available evidence from historical cases, it seems that a persistent money-financed deficit must be about 10 to 12 percent of GNP to generate a hyperinflation. Even with such a deficit, the hyperinflation does not start immediately upon the shift to money financing. As we shall see, there are many important events that typically ensue as a high inflation develops.

The Case of Bolivia

To illustrate this dynamic process, it is useful to examine a concrete historical case in some detail. We have chosen the case of Bolivia largely because it was the first country to develop a full-blown hyperinflation in the 1980s and

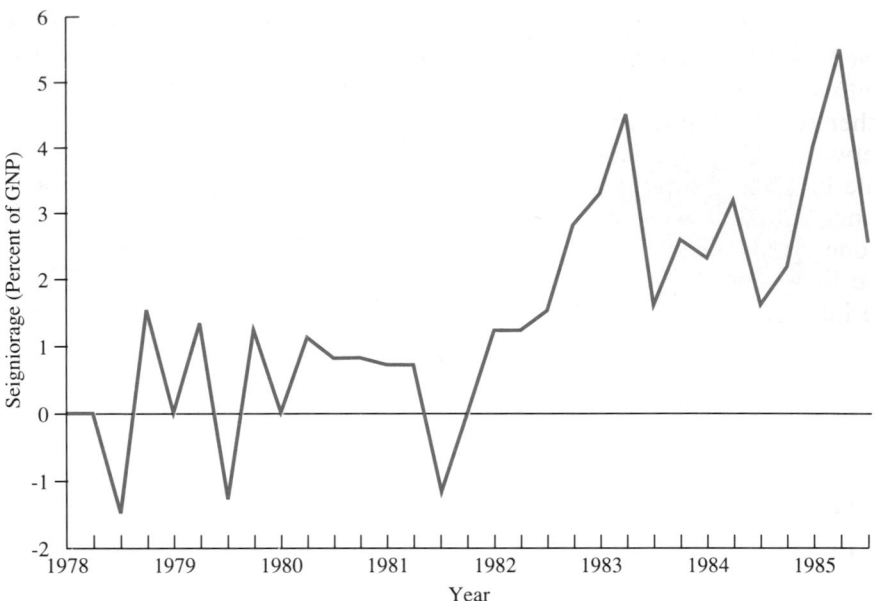

Figure 23-1

Seigniorage Collection as a Percentage of GNP in Bolivia, 1978–1985

(From Jeffrey Sachs, "The Bolivian Hyperinflation and Stabilization," NBER Working Paper No. 2073, November 1986.)

the only case of successful stabilization of a hyperinflation in the 1980s.[15] It was also, incidentally, the first hyperinflation in history to that date without a clear link to a war, civil war or revolution, although other such cases have since occurred in the 1980s.

Figure 23-1 shows the government revenue from seigniorage as a proportion of GNP on a quarterly basis for the period 1978–1985 in Bolivia. One noticeable pattern is the seasonal increase in seigniorage in the fourth quarters of most years, which is associated with end-of-year expenses of the government. However, the most important pattern in the figure is the significant increase in seigniorage after mid-1982, which continues until the third quarter of 1985. During the period shown, seigniorage collection averaged around 12 percent of GNP per year (or 3 percent of annual GNP per quarter).

Part of the explanation for this rise in seigniorage was a rise in the budget deficit which was caused importantly by the rising cost of servicing foreign debt. But the truth is that Bolivia had already been running a large deficit even before 1982. The key factor in starting the money printing was a *shift* in financing the deficit, from nonmonetary means, mainly foreign borrowing, to monetary means.

---

[15] Another reason is that we, the authors of this book, have a firsthand knowledge of this case, from our experience as economic advisors to the government of President Victor Paz Estenssoro, which ended the hyperinflation. For a detailed analysis of the Bolivian situation, see Jeffrey Sachs and Juan Antonio Morales, "Bolivia's Economic Crisis," in J. Sachs, ed., *Developing Country Debt and Economic Performance*, Vol. 2 (Chicago: University of Chicago Press, 1990).

As with other developing countries, Bolivia's access to foreign loans dried up in the early 1980s (for reasons we described in Chapter 22). Indeed, Bolivia led the way, falling into a foreign debt crisis a year earlier than the other countries did, in part because of extraordinary internal political chaos between 1979 and 1982, the period when Bolivia was emerging from military rule into democratic governance. Having run out of foreign sources of finance, the Bolivian government turned to its central bank. The shift to money financing led to a rise in inflation rates, but not all of a sudden. As we see in Figure 23-2, inflation started to rise after 1981, but it reached hyperinflationary rates only in 1984. During this period of rising inflation, how-

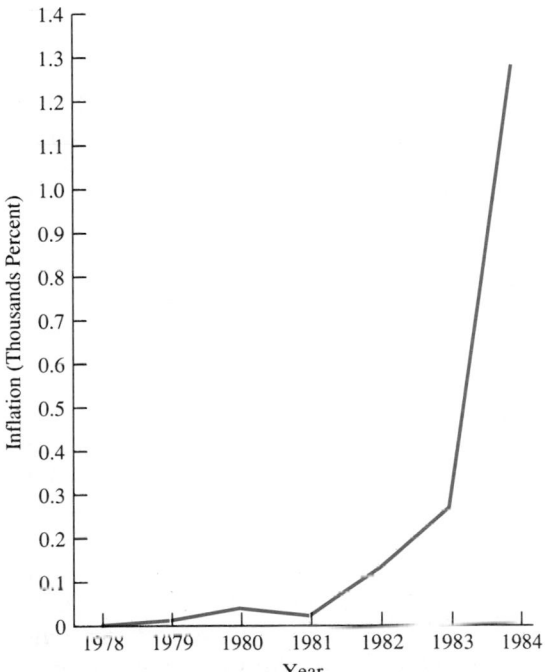

Figure 23-2
Bolivia's Inflation Rate, 1978–1985

(From International Monetary Fund, International Financial
Statistics, *various issues.)*

ever, the seigniorage itself remained fairly stable, at the new high level of about 12 percent per year.

A Monetary Model of Hyperinflation

We can formalize our discussion of monetary events following a rise in seigniorage financing using the classic model of hyperinflation developed by Phillip Cagan.[16] He was the first to observe that at times of hyperinflation,

---

[16] Cagan, "The Monetary Dynamics of Hyperinflation."

the level of demand for real money balances depends almost entirely on the level of *expected inflation*. In Chapter 9, we said that money demand depends on the nominal interest rate (i), which is approximately equal to the real rate (r) plus expected inflation ($\hat{P}^e$). Thus, we can write the money demand function as follows:

$$\frac{M}{P} = m(i) = m(r + \hat{P}^e) \tag{23.1}$$

At times of very high inflation, almost all the shifts in i are due to shifts in $\hat{P}^e$ rather than to changes in r. The annual real interest rate may vary by a few percentage points, while the nominal interest rate may vary by hundreds or thousands of points. Thus, Cagan rewrote (23.1) in a simplified form:

$$\frac{M}{P} = m(\hat{P}^e) \tag{23.2}$$

This strategic simplification allowed him to focus on the dynamics of expected inflation. Note that when expected inflation is high, households will want to hold very low real money balances (M/P), since the opportunity cost of holding money (instead of interest-bearing assets or durable goods) is very high. When $\hat{P}^e$ is low, the M/P they hold will be high.

If the economy reaches a steady-state rate of inflation, then eventually expected inflation and actual inflation are equal. In that case, (23.2) would be rewritten to show that real money balances are a function of actual inflation:

$$\frac{M}{P} = m(\hat{P}) \tag{23.2'}$$

Now, let us turn to the supply of money. The money supply rises over time because the government is borrowing from the central bank (that is, it is "printing money") in order to pay its bills. Let SE be the amount of real spending that must be covered by printing money. Then,

$$SE = \frac{\Delta M}{P} \tag{23.3}$$

where ΔM is the increase in the money stock, P is the price level, and SE, or seigniorage, is the real value of goods that can be purchased using the newly issued money. Note that $\Delta M/P$ can be rewritten as $(\Delta M/M)(M/P)$. In words, the level of seigniorage is equal to the percentage rate of growth of money ($\Delta M/M$) multiplied by the level of *real* money balances (M/P). Equation (23.3) can therefore be rewritten as

$$SE = \left(\frac{\Delta M}{M}\right)\left(\frac{M}{P}\right) \tag{23.4}$$

The concept of seigniorage is closely related to, but not exactly the same as, the concept of the inflation tax. *Seigniorage* measures the amount of real resources the government is able to capture by printing money. The *inflation tax* measures the decline in the value of real money balances caused by inflation, and is given by the expression:[17]

$$IT = \left(\frac{\Delta P}{P}\right)\left(\frac{M}{P}\right) \tag{23.5}$$

---

[17] Recall our discussion of seigniorage and the inflation tax in Chapter 11.

When inflation is present, money is constantly losing its real value. House-holds have to increase their nominal money holdings merely to keep real money balances constant.

When inflation is constant, and real money balances M/P are constant, households will be increasing their nominal money holdings at exactly the same rate that the government is collecting seigniorage revenue. That is, $\Delta M/M = \Delta P/P$, so that according to (23.4), we see that $SE = (\Delta P/P)(M/P)$. That is, *in the steady state, $SE = IT$.*

Thus, in the steady state, we can link the amount of seigniorage that the government needs with the inflation tax. Suppose that the government must raise an amount of seigniorage SE. Since, in the steady state we have that $SE = \hat{P}m(\hat{P})$, we can calculate the inflation rate that corresponds with each level of seigniorage. When we do that, we find a relationship as follows:

$$SE = f(\hat{P}), \qquad \text{for } \hat{P} < \hat{P}_{MAX}$$
$$\overset{+}{SE} = f(\hat{P}), \qquad \text{for } \hat{P} > \hat{P}_{MAX} \qquad \textbf{(23.6)}$$

where $f(\hat{P})$ signifies that SE is a function of the inflation rate.

This relationship is graphed in Figure 23-3. The inflation rate rises with the amount of seigniorage, up to a certain maximal level of seigniorage, SE_{MAX}. The inflation rate $\hat{P}_{MAX}$ produces the maximal amount of seigniorage possible with a *stable rate of inflation*. It is possible to collect more seignior-age than SE_{MAX}, but only if the inflation rate is constantly increasing, and by enough to fool the population (a point we explain in a minute).

At inflation rates higher than $\hat{P}_{MAX}$, seigniorage would actually be lower, not higher than SE_{MAX} (as shown by the dashed lines in the figure). The reason is that at very high inflation rates, real money balances $m(\hat{P})$ are so low that the inflation tax $\hat{P}m(\hat{P})$ generates very little revenue for the government. A government trying to finance a given amount of seigniorage

Figure 23-3
The Steady-State Relationship Between Sei-gniorage and Inflation

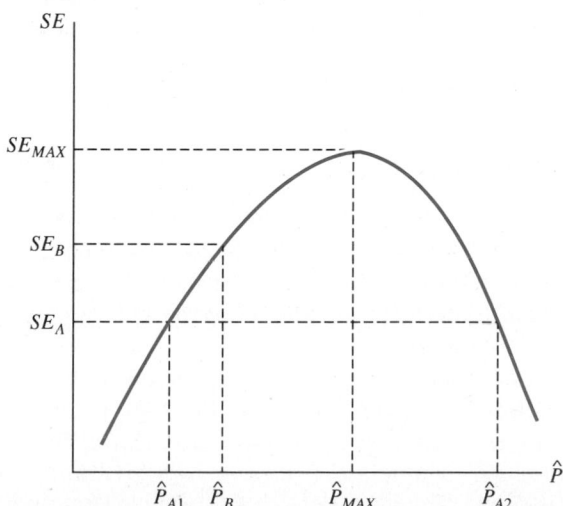

with the inflation tax would always try to operate to the left of the $\hat{P}_{\text{MAX}}$ point in the graph. In other words, if a level of seigniorage SE_A is desired, the government would always aim for the inflation rate $\hat{P}_{A1}$ rather than $\hat{P}_{A2}$.

One interpretation of high inflation is simply that the seigniorage needs of the government go up, so that steady-state inflation also rises. Equation (23.6) and Figure 23-3 show how much the inflation rate must rise in the steady state when there is a permanent change in the amount of seigniorage the government needs. If it rises from SE_A to SE_B, then inflation (in the steady state) would have to rise from $\hat{P}_{A1}$ to $\hat{P}_B$.

Consider, also, a simple numerical example. Suppose that a country starts from a steady state where seigniorage needs are 2 percent of GNP per year and money balances are stable at 10 percent of GNP (that is, $\Delta m = 0$). From equation (23.6) we can see that the resulting inflation rate is 0.2, or 20 percent per annum. ($IT/\text{GNP} = SE/\text{GNP} = 0.02$, $M/\text{GNP} = 0.10$, $\Delta P/P = 0.2$). Now, if seigniorage needs rise to 6 percent of GNP and money balances fall to 5 percent of GNP, the annual inflation rate goes up to 120 percent ($IT/\text{GNP} = SE/\text{GNP} = 0.06$, $M/\text{GNP} = 0.05$; $\Delta P/P = 1.2$).

Unfortunately, this model is too simple. Hyperinflations are generally not events in which the inflation rate settles into a new permanent high level after a budgetary shock. Hyperinflations tend to be explosive phenomena in which the inflation rate increases wildly until stabilization comes. The big difference between the steady state and the actual dynamics of the situation lies in the fact that in real life, households generally do not expect the high inflation rates that occur.

Cagan showed how we can best interpret the dynamics of the hyperinflation by extending the analysis beyond the case of a stable long-run inflation rate. Hyperinflations are rare, unexpected phenomena. It is reasonable to suppose, as Cagan did, that during a hyperinflation, in which the inflation rate is rising sharply, inflationary expectations tend to lag behind actual price increases. Specifically, $\hat{P}^e < \hat{P}$. For this reason, households will tend to have *higher* real money balances than they would if their inflationary expectations were more accurate. And since money balances are higher than they would be in the steady state, it is possible for the government to raise more inflation tax revenues at any given inflation rate than it can in the steady state. Remember that the inflation tax is $\hat{P}m(\hat{P}^e)$. If $m(\hat{P}^e)$ is greater than it would be in the steady state, because $\hat{P}^e < \hat{P}$, then it is clear that the inflation tax is also higher than in the steady state.

Suppose, for example, that there is zero inflation in the economy and that the government starts at zero seigniorage. But then there is a jump in the seigniorage the government needs (because of an unexpected increase in fiscal spending, say). What happens to inflation? Initially, it jumps as the government starts to print money to pay its bills but not all the way up to what would be the new steady-state level. Households do not yet expect the high inflation, so they continue to hold high real money balances. It is possible, therefore, for the government to collect a high level of the inflation tax even when there is a relatively low inflation.

In the course of time, as households come to expect higher levels of inflation, they revise their inflation estimate $\hat{P}^e$ upward, and they begin to economize on real money balances. Thus, $m(\hat{P}^e)$ begins to fall, *and there must be a higher rate of inflation just to collect the same amount of inflation tax that was being collected before.* Thus, as households realize that the inflation rate is rising, and cut back on the real money balances they want to hold, the inflation rate rises as well, so that the government can continue to collect the inflation tax that it needs to pay for government expenditures.

In extreme cases, the government's seigniorage needs exceed the maximum amount of seigniorage that can be obtained by printing money at any constant inflation rate, no matter how high. In that case, there is no *stable* inflation rate at which the government can collect the seigniorage it needs. Rather, as it prints the money necessary to pay its bills, the inflation rate rises without bound. The eventual result is a hyperinflation.

During the period of rising inflation, households are constantly fooled by the inflation rate (that is, $\hat{P}^e$ is constantly below $\hat{P}$), and therefore they are constantly holding higher real money balances than they would if they could correctly anticipate the inflation. Thus, the government can collect an inflation tax that is persistently above SE_{MAX}. In other words, during a hyperinflation, the government collects more in seigniorage than it could at any stable inflation rate. Because the sharply escalating inflation fools people and they hold more money than they would otherwise, they are therefore subject to being heavily taxed by the government.

The monetary dynamics of hyperinflation, as Cagan first described them, are shown in Figure 23-4. Before time zero (the start of the hyperinflationary process), we suppose that the inflation rate is zero, the expected inflation rate is zero, and seigniorage needs are also zero. A shock occurs, and SE rises, in fact, to a level above SE_{MAX}. Inflation starts to rise as the government prints money to pay its bills. Initially, it takes time for the public to realize that the inflation rate is rising. Inflationary expectations lag behind actual inflation, as shown in Figure 23-4. Therefore, demand for real money balances falls gradually, not abruptly. As $\hat{P}^e$ rises, $m(\hat{P}^e)$ falls, and the inflation rate needed to produce any given inflation tax also rises. Over time, the inflation rate increases, and without bound (assuming that SE remains above SE_{MAX}). Only with a constantly rising inflation rate can the government collect the revenues that it needs.

The dynamics of inflation and real money balances are well illustrated by the case of Bolivia. After the budgetary shock in 1982, the Bolivian government started to print money at a fairly constant rate of 12 percent of

Figure 23-4
The Monetary Dynamics of Hyperinflation

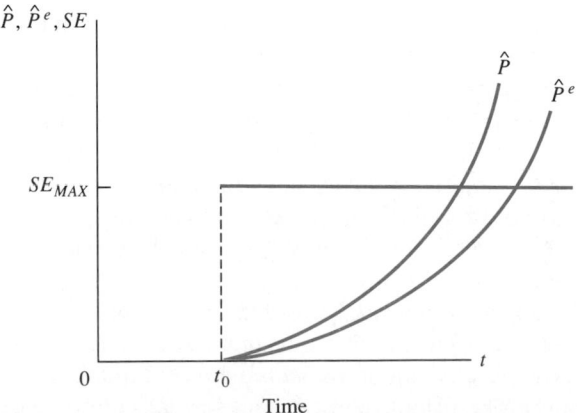

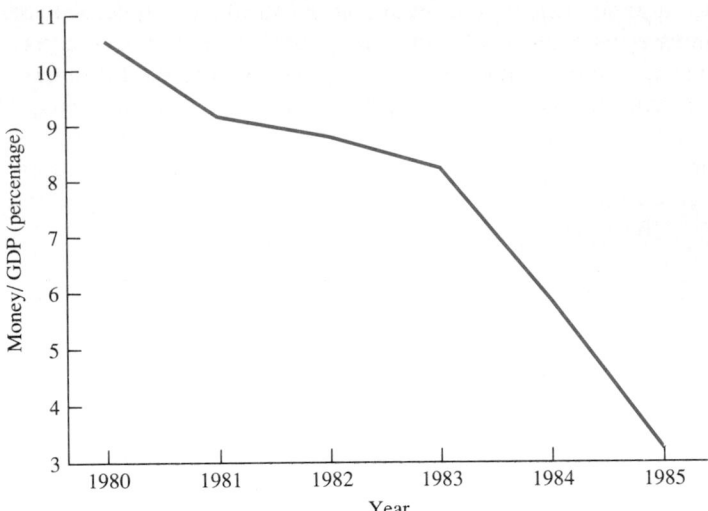

Figure 23-5

The Collapse of Real Money Balances During High Inflation: Bolivia, 1980–1985

(From International Monetary Fund, International Financial Statistics, *various issues.)*

GNP per year. Initially, the inflationary effects were "modest" (at several hundred percent per year). But, as shown in Figure 23-5, real money balances dropped steadily after 1982, presumably as households' inflationary expectations rose in line with the soaring inflation. The drop in money demand is quite spectacular. In 1980–1983, money represented an average of about 9 percent of GDP; in 1985, money went down to a mere 3.2 percent of GDP.

This pattern of collapsing real money balances is typical of all hyperinflations. People discover that holding the domestic currency is very costly, because it loses value by the day. At the worst of the German hyperinflation, for example, prices were doubling every three days; in Hungary, prices were actually tripling in a single day. When this happens, the velocity of circulation increases significantly because everybody wants to get rid of the local money as rapidly as possible, though in the aggregate this is impossible. Indeed, Keynes once quipped that during hyperinflation, it was characteristic to order *two* beers at a time (to get rid of the currency and to avoid a future price increase) and to take taxis rather than buses, since you pay for taxis at the end of the ride (with money that is worth less than when you got into the cab).

The dynamics of ever-faster-increasing prices leads to currency substitution. People do not want to hold the local currency, and they desperately search for some other stable unit of value, inevitably a trusted foreign currency. During recent hyperinflations in Latin America and in Poland, local residents turned to the U.S. dollar in their flight from the domestic currency (in Yugoslavia, the Deutsche mark became the preferred alternative currency). In this process, the economy becomes increasingly *dollarized* (or whatever the foreign currency). The prices of goods and services come to be quoted in dollars, and the role of the local money all but collapses. Of the three uses of money, as a store of value, as a unit of account, and as a medium of exchange, only the third persists, and even there we find important currency substitution in that dollars are used for large transactions.

Fiscal Dynamics

Even if the seigniorage needs of a country change very little over the course of a hyperinflation (as we saw in Figure 23-1 to be true of Bolivia), there is likely to be extreme turbulence in fiscal policy. The hyperinflation typically causes a devastation of the tax system, which undermines all fiscal policy. In Chapter 11, we described the so-called "Olivera–Tanzi effect," which holds that the real tax collections tend to fall as inflation accelerates, and Figure 11-6 illustrated that effect in Bolivia during the period 1980–1986. In 1980, tax revenues were on the order of 10 percent of GNP; by mid-1985, just before the end of the hyperinflation, they had declined to less than 1.5 percent per year.

As tax revenues collapsed in Bolivia, the government had to cut back on spending *just to keep its seigniorage needs from expanding further,* a pattern that is common in hyperinflations. The government cut sharply into public spending and virtually stopped all public investment spending, but its best efforts did little more than keep the budget deficit from rising more. Indeed, the government deficit was 22 percent of GNP in 1982, 18 percent in 1983, and 30 percent in 1984. Tax collections simply fell so rapidly that it was nearly impossible to close the budget deficit by cutting spending. Only when, in 1985, a new government in Bolivia made a Herculean effort to raise tax collections was the deficit spending brought under control.

23-4 STABILIZATION POLICIES FOR ENDING HYPERINFLATIONS

Stopping high inflations requires a special combination of economic polices affecting the exchange rate, the public budget, the supply of money, and, in some cases, direct measures aimed at wages and prices. A key element for the success of any stabilization program is how positively the people respond to it. The critical role of expectations highlights the importance of polices that can build confidence in the program.

Hyperinflations often do not end on the first try, but only after several stabilization attempts have failed. A case in point is Bolivia, where six stabilization efforts collapsed before the successful one was tried by a new government in August 1985. In two early tries, November 1982 and April 1985, many of the right measures were put in place, but the government was too weak politically to resist the pressures from different interest groups. On several occasions during 1982–1985, the government succumbed to the pressures of trade unions and granted large wage increases to compensate for cutbacks in budget subsidies. The government was also defeated in its attempts to increase tax collections by opposition in the Bolivian Congress.

It is particularly interesting that when stabilization programs succeed, hyperinflations tend to end almost overnight. Figure 23-6 shows the *weekly* inflation rates in Bolivia before and after the stabilization program was launched during the week of August 26 to September 1, 1985 (week 0).

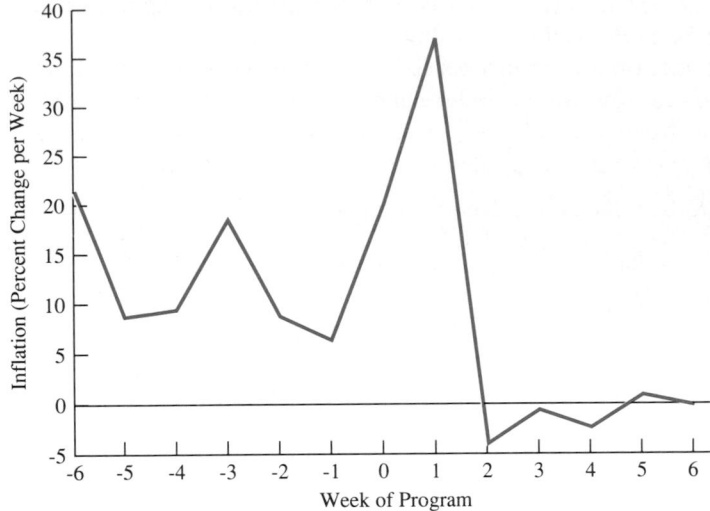

Figure 23-6

Weekly Inflation Rates in Bolivia Around the Launching of
Stabilization (Week 0: August 26–September 1)

*(From Jeffrey Sachs, "The Bolivian Hyperinflation and Stabilization," NBER
Working Paper No. 2073, November 1986.)*

Notice how inflation was totally under control by the second week of the
program, when prices actually *declined*, and subsequently stabilized.[18]

A similar pattern is found in the other stabilization episodes. In Germany, for example, inflation stopped in a matter of days in November 1923.
Similar things happened in Poland in January 1924 and in Hungary in February 1924. All hyperinflations, without exception, have ended abruptly,
though often after several previous attempts at stabilization have failed. In
the rest of this section, we shall examine the different elements of an antihy-
perinflation program and consider some reasons why inflation stops almost
overnight.

Exchange-Rate Stabilization

We have discussed the dollarization process that occurs during hyperinflations. In a dollarized economy, purchasing power parity is likely to hold
remarkably well. Most prices are actually quoted in dollar terms, P^*, and
then converted into domestic currency prices by multiplying by the prevailing exchange rate. Thus, almost by virtue of the fact that prices are quoted in
dollars but paid for in the domestic currency, we find the relationship $P = EP^*$. The *exchange rate* is therefore the crucial link between dollar prices
and local currency prices for most goods and services. During the hy-
perinflation, the exchange rate depreciates at approximately the same rate

---

[18] A few months later, in January 1986, the hyperinflation almost returned, because of
some bad luck (falling export prices) and some policy mistakes. After a close call, the government was able to maintain control of the situation.

that domestic prices increase. If the exchange rate can be stabilized, domestic prices can also be stabilized.

In most hyperinflations there are at least two exchange rates, an official rate and a free market rate which is substantially above the official rate. Indeed, the gap between the two can often be hundreds or thousands of percent. Purchasing power parity generally applies to the free market rate or to a weighted average of the official rate and the free market rate. A successful stabilization usually requires first a major devaluation of the official exchange rate so that it aligns with the free market rate and then a stabilized value for the newly unified exchange rate. The typical stabilization program aims to fix the exchange rate at a sustainable level, that is, a level that can be defended by the central bank without a speculative attack that depletes the foreign-exchange reserves. We know from our analysis in earlier chapters, especially Chapter 11, that a stable exchange rate requires a tight fiscal policy. If the government tries to print money and maintain a fixed exchange rate at the same time, it will end up losing foreign-exchange reserves and ultimately suffering a speculative attack against the currency and a balance-of-payments crisis.

For this reason, a devaluation alone is usually not enough to stabilize the exchange rate. Fiscal policy must also be tightened, though perhaps not tight enough to balance the budget right at the beginning of a stabilization program. If the central bank has some foreign-exchange reserves with which to defend the currency, or if the government is able to negotiate a loan from abroad to increase its reserve holdings, this will strengthen the government's ability to stabilize the exchange rate in the short run. But in the long run, there is only one way to keep the exchange rate stable, through tight fiscal policy that relieves the government of the necessity to rely on seigniorage financing.

Because most domestic prices are linked to the dollar via purchasing power parity, once the exchange rate is stabilized, the inflation can stop almost overnight. As we shall see shortly, the key distinction between a hyperinflation and a merely "very high" inflation is that in a hyperinflation, almost all vestiges of inflationary inertia are eliminated, since firms and workers stop relying on long-term contracts and backward-looking indexation. Rather, prices are dollarized and, therefore, linked to the exchange rate. Stabilizing the exchange rate, then, ends the high inflation.

Comprehensive Budget Policies

No exchange rate can remain stable unless the underlying budget deficit—and need for seigniorage—is brought under control. This is why the most *fundamental* step in ending hyperinflations is to eliminate the underlying budgetary problems that led to the hyperinflation in the first place. In a seminal contribution to monetary economics, Thomas Sargent stressed that hyperinflations end when a fundamental change is made in budgetary policy, both in the size of deficits and how they are financed. This conclusion is based on his analysis of four out of five hyperinflations in the 1920s (omitting Russia). In Sargent's words,

> . . . the changes that ended the hyperinflations were not isolated restrictive actions within a given set of rules of the game or general policy. Earlier attempts to stabilize the exchanges in Hun-

gary under Hegedus, and also in Germany, failed precisely because they did not change the rules of the game under which fiscal policy had to be conducted.[19]

An element in this process is often an increase in the political independence of the central bank, so that it can resist pressures to finance the government's budget deficit through money printing. In Germany, for example, the new and independent Rentenbank took over the functions of the old Reichsbank. An important early test of the Rentenbank's independence came in December 1923, one month after stabilization had been achieved, when the government asked the Rentenbank to exceed the limits that had been set on new government borrowing. The Rentenbank simply refused, thereby establishing its independence and requiring the government either to find new, nonmonetary means of finance or to cut spending and raise revenues.

Of course, it is not enough to stop central bank financing of government deficits. It is also necessary to improve the underlying budget situation. Fiscal austerity usually entails several measures. First, the prices of goods and services provided by public enterprises typically fall to very low levels in real terms during the hyperinflation, and usually these must be raised significantly. The goal is to eliminate the deficits of state firms, which are ultimately borne by the central government and they thus constitute a primary source of money creation. In Bolivia, for example, the single change that most greatly improved the budget at the start of the stabilization program was a sharp rise in the price of fuels, which raised the profits of the state oil company by several percent of GNP.

Second, tax revenues must be raised. In part, this will happen automatically when prices stop rising (after the exchange rate is stabilized). In other words, the Olivera—Tanzi effect also works in reverse: just as high inflation lowers real tax collections, the end of high inflation almost surely raises real tax collections. Figure 23-7 shows the plummeting of tax revenues in Bolivia during the period of rapidly accelerating inflation and their swift recovery following stabilization. After tax revenues had declined to a mere 1.3 percent of GNP in the first half of 1985—inflation had reached almost 40,000 percent on an annualized basis during that period—they recovered to over 10 percent of GNP in the second half of the year, once stabilization was accomplished. Tax revenues have remained well over 10 percent of GNP since 1986. Of course, the decline in inflation was not the only element explaining the increase of government revenues, deliberate policies increasing public-sector prices were even more important, but the end of the high inflation was important in collecting some of the taxes.

The damage done to the tax system is not fully reversible, however, in the very short run. The decline in real tax collections during the hyperinflation generally weakens the system of tax administration. Therefore, a *comprehensive tax reform* is often necessary soon after the start of stabilization. It takes time, however, to put a tax reform plan in place because it normally needs legislative approval. While it waits, the government can often provide incentives for the prepayment of taxes and can apply stiffer penalties for noncompliance.

---

[19] Sargent, "The Ends of Four Big Inflations," p. 90.

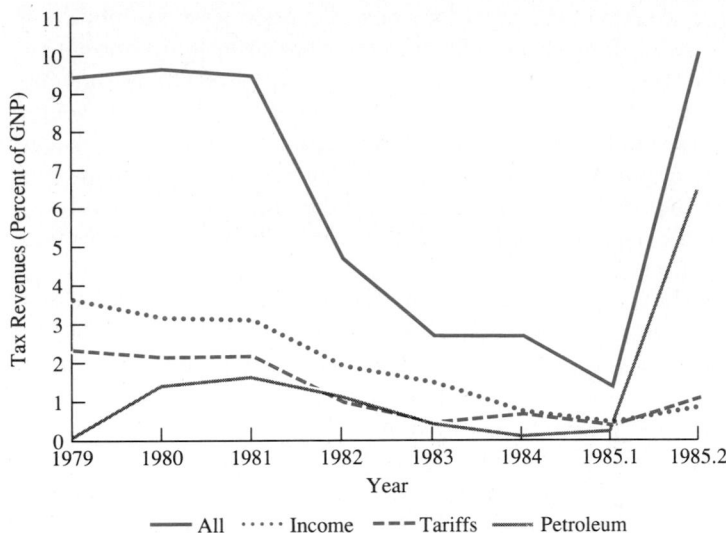

Figure 23-7

The Evolution of Tax Revenues in Bolivia by Category of Tax, 1979–1985

(From Jeffrey Sachs, "The Bolivian Hyperinflation and Stabilization," NBER Working Paper No. 2073, November 1986.)

Other measures to improve the fiscal situation in the short run include the elimination of direct subsidies and tax exemptions. One popular form of government subsidy is the granting of credits to the private sector at highly negative real interest rates. The subsidies implicit in these loans are considered a kind of "quasi-fiscal" expenditure. In Peru's high inflation, for example, subsidized credits to agriculture, mining, and industry in general, provoked a quasi-fiscal loss of almost 1.5 percent of GDP in 1987.[20] Successful stabilization programs have generally moved quickly to eliminate this drain on resources.

It is a notable irony that many of the measures used to cut the budget—ends to subsidies, currency devaluations, higher public-sector prices, and higher consumption taxes—are likely to result in a burst of "corrective" inflation in the short term. Therefore, a hyperinflation can even accelerate in the first month of the stabilization program, just as the corrective measures are being put in place. If the adjustments close the fiscal gap, however, the chances are very good that inflation will come to a halt after the initial burst.

Monetary and Credit Policies

The stabilization of the exchange rate and prices brings about an increase in the real money balances that the public wants to hold. A key policy issue is how to accommodate this increase in the demand for money. Recall from

---

[20] For an analysis of Peru's hyperinflation, including all the fiscal data, see Carlos Paredes and Jeffrey Sachs, eds., *Stabilization and Growth in Peru* (Washington, D.C.: The Brookings Institution, 1991).

Chapter 9 that the change in the monetary base (or high-powered money) is equal to the change in domestic credit plus the change in international reserves.[21] To satisfy this higher demand for money, the government thus has three options open to it: it can increase domestic credit to the public sector (that is, the central bank can purchase bonds from the Treasury), it can increase domestic credit to the private sector (that is, the central bank can grant more credit to private banks), or it can validate foreign reserve inflows through the balance of payments (that is, the central bank can buy foreign exchange at a fixed rate).

In Bolivia, for example, the government chose the third option, which is clearly the safest strategy for keeping an inflation under control. After the end of the hyperinflation, Bolivian households wanted to increase their holdings of money balances. To the extent that they held foreign assets (as many wealthy Bolivians did), the Bolivians cashed in their foreign assets and sold the foreign exchange to the central bank in return for domestic currency. The domestic money supply rose as the central bank accumulated foreign-exchange reserves. Confidence in the local currency increased as people saw that there were foreign reserves backing the increase in the domestic monetary base. Had the government taken the road of aggressive credit creation to remonetize the economy without a significant increase in its foreign reserves, the public may have doubted the ultimate success of its stabilization program.

Monetary Reform: The Introduction of a New Currency

The introduction of a new currency often accompanies successful stabilizations. The most popular way to do this is to "cut the zeros" of a very depreciated currency. In Germany in 1924, for example, a new rentenmark was equivalent to *one trillion* (10^{12}) old paper marks. However popular this new currency policy may be, however, it is not a fundamental part of a stabilization package. Neither it is the only type of monetary reform, as we shall see.

In the simplest type of monetary reform, a new currency is introduced in order to cut the number of zeroes applied to all prices, wages, and financial assets throughout the economy. This is mainly a *cosmetic* change that does no harm, and it may accomplish some savings in costs (of ink, paper, time, calculator space, and so on). Bolivia undertook this move in 1986, several months after the start of the stabilization program, in a change from *pesos* to *bolivianos,* at a conversion of 1 million old pesos for one new boliviano.

In a more complex type of monetary reform, a new currency is introduced not only to cut the zeros, but also to create a special scheme for repayments of long-term contracts that exist in the old currency. Here is the problem. Suppose that in Argentina in 1985, people expected inflation to continue unabated at a rate of 50 percent per month. A borrower might be willing to take out a loan at 110 percent interest for the two months. The nominal interest rate is high, but the real interest rate (after inflation) is quite low. Suppose, however, that just after such a loan is signed, the government surprises everyone and actually ends the high inflation. The borrower would

---

[21] See equation (9.1) in Chapter 9.

go bankrupt if he had to repay the loan at the original interest rate, which would now be a *real* interest rate of 110 percent. To cover situations like this, a more complex kind of monetary reform has been designed in some countries (including Argentina in 1985 and Brazil in 1986), in which long-term loans can be repaid in the new currency, but with the interest rate adjusted according to a preset formula.[22]

Finally, there is the option of a *confiscatory* reform that exchanges old currency for new without adjusting the monetary conversion in line with the changes in wages and prices. For example, with no change in wage and price levels, the old money may be converted to the new money at a ratio of 10 to 1. This will put a major squeeze on real money balances which will surely lead to a significant economic contraction. This is the kind of monetary reform that took place in Germany in 1948. It is generally most helpful in a situation of *repressed* inflation, in which the money supply has gone up sharply but price controls have prevented a rise in prices alongside the money supply increase. The monetary reform then brings the money supply back down in line with prices, rather than allowing prices to rise sharply in line with the money supply.

Alleviating the External Constraint

All countries undergoing hyperinflation reach an extremely low level of international reserves that makes it difficult to defend the exchange rate and thus to stabilize prices. More generally, countries have often fallen into hyperinflation *because* of the heavy burden of international obligations on the budget. It is therefore highly desirable for a government undertaking a stabilization program to obtain a balance-of-payments support loan with which to raise international reserves, and more generally, to negotiate a package of international support to relieve the external financial burden on the budget. This long-term support might involve a combination of new loans and relief on existing debt.

In the 1920s, the League of Nations provided important balance-of-payments support for the stabilization programs in Austria and Hungary. Germany had part of its reparations burden alleviated and received new international loans, though the overall relief was not sufficient in the long term. In the 1980s, Bolivia benefited substantially by a combination of new loans (from the IMF, the World Bank, and other international agencies) and debt relief from commercial banks and foreign governments. Other countries that were in hyperinflation in the 1980s have not yet received adequate international support, and that is one reason why various stabilization attempts in these countries have failed.

The Problem of Confidence

In all hyperinflation experiences, real interest rates remain quite high, and much higher than world levels, even after stabilization has been achieved. Why is this? The main reason is that people are still skeptical about the

---

[22] The special kind of monetary reform introduced a "tablita" or schedule for repayments of long-term contracts, converting the amount due in the old currency into a lesser amount due in the new currency.

continued success of the program. Therefore, agents incorporate the possibility of a currency devaluation into the local currency interest rate, making the nominal interest rate high—and in fact, much higher than the inflation rate. As credibility in the stabilization program builds up among the public, interest rates will fall.

High real interest rates in the short run are likely to generate loud cries for an expansion of domestic credit. The temptation to force these rates down through a credit expansion is extremely dangerous, however. A return to easy money at the beginning of a stabilization program can prompt a loss of international reserves and a subsequent speculative attack on the domestic currency, followed by a significant devaluation and a resurgence of high inflation.

An extreme example of high real interest rates in the aftermath of stabilization was provided by Germany in late 1923. After stabilization had been achieved in mid-November, nominal interest rates were still at between 0.5 percent and 6.5 percent *per day,* as shown in Table 23-3. But with stable prices, these were also the levels of *real* interest rates. And a 0.5 percent daily rate is equivalent to an annualized 500 percent, while 3 percent per day is about 150 percent per *month.* Interest rates quickly declined from those astronomical levels, but they remained quite high for six months after stabilization.[23] Table 23-3 also shows the evolution of interest rates in Bolivia, which show a qualitative pattern similar to that in Germany. Nominal rates in local currency remained at around 20 percent per month from October 1985 to March 1986, that is, after prices had stabilized (except for brief outbursts of inflation in December 1985 and January 1986).

It is important to restore confidence as rapidly as possible, and thereby reduce the domestic interest rates. Otherwise, the high interest rates can themselves undermine the stabilization program. This can happen in three ways. First, the high interest rates can lead to pressures for a rapid expansion of the money supply, thereby jeopardizing the newly stable exchange rate. Second, the high interest rates can worsen the budgetary situation if the government has a high level of internal debt. Third, the high interest rates can lead to financial distress for enterprises, causing bankruptcies, unemployment, and political tensions.

Why Do Governments Postpone Stabilization?

In several high-inflation experiences, stabilizations were delayed for some time before a coherent program was launched to stop inflation. Yet there is widespread evidence that the longer the wait to attack the problem, the more the damage to the economy, and the more costly the policy reforms eventually needed to stabilize the economy. So then, why are stabilizations delayed?

It is always awkward to blame this behavior solely on the irrational actions of policymakers, though this surely has played a role in many countries. But there are other explanations as well. Alberto Alesina of Harvard

---

[23] For an analysis of this issue, see Rudiger Dornbusch, "Lessons from the German Inflation Experience of the 1920s," in R. Dornbusch, S. Fischer, and J. Bossons, eds., *Macroeconomics and Finance, Essays in the Honor of Franco Modigliani* (Cambridge, Mass.: MIT Press, 1989).

TABLE 23-3

INTEREST RATES FOLLOWING STABILIZATION: GERMANY, 1923, AND BOLIVIA, 1985–1986 (PERCENT)

(a) Germany

1923 Interest Rates per Day			1924 Interest Rates at Annual Rate	
December	3	1–3.5	January	87.6
	4	2.25	February	34.9
	5	1.5–2	March	33.1
	7	2	April	45.9
	8	1.5	May	27.8
	10	0.25–1.5		
	11	0.5		
	12	0.5		
	13	0.17		
	17	0.5		
	18	0.25–0.5		
	19	0.25–0.75		
	20	1.2		
	21	6.5		
	22	2.5		

(b) Bolivia

1985	Monthly Rates	1986	Monthly Rates
September	45	January	19
October	31	February	20
November	22	March	20
December	21	April	19
		May	13
		June	8
		July	8
		August	8
		September	7
		October	7
		November	3

Source: Data for Germany are from Rudiger Dornbusch, "Lessons from the German Inflation Experience of the 1920s," in R. Dornbusch, S. Fischer, and J. Bossons, eds., Macroeconomics and Finance, Essays in the Honor of Franco Modigliani *(Cambridge, MA: MIT Press) Reprinted by permission). Data for Bolivia are from Jeffrey Sachs, "The Bolivian Hyperinflation and Stabilization," NBER Working Paper No. 2073, August 1986.*

University and Allan Drazen of Tel-Aviv University have provided one such answer that focuses on governments to weak to implement a stabilization program contrary to the wishes of organized interest groups.[24] For Alesina and Drazen, the problem of achieving a successful stabilization is basically distributional.

The starting point is a recognition that different groups in the population are not indifferent to the way stabilization is attained. If the government balances the budget by cutting public-sector wages and employment, for example, this will affect workers most directly. If it raises income taxes and export levies on companies, the burden will fall most heavily on capitalists.

How, then, are the costs of stabilization distributed? Each group will fight to shift the burden to the others. As Alesina and Drazen put it, there is a "war of attrition" between different groups that have conflicting distributional objectives. If the government is "weak," it cannot impose a solution that is strongly opposed by powerful organized forces in the society. The war of attrition therefore continues, and no stabilization efforts can be attempted. Eventually the confrontation ends, and winners emerge through political elections, through legislative negotiations, through a cession of power of decree to policymakers, or by some other means. The winners can then decide how the burden will be allocated among the different groups, and begin their stabilization program.

Historical experience gives some support to this hypothesis. For example, it was widely recognized in France, Germany, and Italy after World War I that their big budget deficits had to be slashed. There was much conflict, however, over how to distribute the higher taxes that were required. Parties on the right of the political spectrum advocated proportional income taxes and indirect levies, while parties on the left favored taxes on capital and more progressive income taxes.[25] Finally, the political stalemate was broken as one side or another was able to muster power.

In a remarkable number of cases, stabilization ensues only after a new government takes power, with the authority to "clean up the mess" left by the earlier government. Thus, one of the key mechanisms for breaking a stalemate is a new election and a new constellation of political forces.

23-5 HETERODOX STABILIZATION PROGRAMS

"Heterodox" stabilization programs are those that use direct intervention into wage and price setting in addition to the more standard monetary and fiscal measures. Heterodox programs are based on the idea that inflation has a large component of inertia which leads it to perpetuate itself. As we saw in Chapters 14 and 15, inflation inertia comes about because of long-term labor contracts, backward-looking wage indexation, and other mechanisms that introduce automatic wage and price adjustments based on *past inflation*.

The heterodox approach argues that budget adjustments and tight monetary policy alone are insufficient to stop high inflations. Under circum-

---

[24] See their joint work "Why Are Stabilizations Delayed?" National Bureau of Economic Research Working Paper, No. 3053, August 1989.

[25] This point is stressed by Harvard University historian Charles Maier in his book *Recasting Bourgeois Europe: Stabilization in France, Germany and Italy in the Decade After World War I* (Princeton, N.J.: Princeton University Press, 1975).

stances of inertial inflation, the argument goes, using only orthodox measures can lead to an unnecessarily deep recession. Even after the exchange rate is fixed, domestic prices can continue to rise, ultimately producing a profit squeeze in the tradeable sector of the economy. Advocates of heterodox stabilization programs argue that *incomes policies*—that is, some form of wage and price controls—should be crucial elements in a stabilization program. In the extreme, some advocates of heterodoxy go as far as to suggest that wage and price controls alone are sufficient to stop inflation, and that orthodox fiscal and monetary restraints have no role.

To break the inflationary inertia, proponents of a heterodox shock program argue for coordinated ceilings on wages and prices at the start of the stabilization process. The benefits of this policy, if it succeeds, are easy to see. It can break up both the inertia and people's inflationary expectations, and this promotes confidence in the program. Furthermore, it can cut inflation very quickly to low levels.

Nevertheless, heterodox programs have a number of noteworthy potential shortcomings. First, wage and price controls may be superfluous. If inflation inertia is very low, the inflation will soon stop on its own. Second, price controls may be difficult to enforce beyond a very small group of commodities and this lack of administrative feasibility can make many of the controls ineffective. Third, controls might be anticipated. Enterprises may jack up their prices, even by several hundred percent, when they know the controls are coming. Fourth, controls may be addictive, giving policymakers the idea that inflation can be stopped without the pain of making important underlying changes in monetary and fiscal policy. Fifth, controls can introduce a great deal of rigidity in the relative price structure of the economy, and this may cause shortages. Finally, controls may prove hard to phase out. Should the phasing out be a gradual or one-shot process? And if gradual, what is the correct timing?

Recent experience in Latin America and in Israel provides some lessons on the use of heterodox methods. In Argentina, Brazil, and Peru, three heterodox programs have all failed, the Austral Plan of Argentina in 1985, the Cruzado Plan of Brazil in 1986, and the Inti Plan of Peru in 1985. In these cases, inflation stayed down only a few months, and then returned with renewed strength. In Israel and Mexico, by contrast, heterodox methods were used, apparently with much more success. Both countries succeeded in achieving lasting stabilization after inflation had reached triple-digit (though not hyperinflationary) rates.[26]

Note that in Bolivia, a much higher inflation was eliminated without any heterodox elements being employed. Rather than fixing prices, the Bolivian government actually decontrolled almost all prices at the start of the stabilization program. The most important difference between the cases where stabilization worked—Bolivia, Israel, and Mexico—and the three heterodox experiments that failed was the control of the budget. In the failed stabilization attempts, the persistence of significant budget deficits prevented exchange-rate stabilization beyond a few months.

---

[26] For an analysis of the heterodox programs, see Michael Bruno, Guido Di Tella, Rudiger Dornbusch, and Stanley Fischer, eds., *Inflation Stabilization: the Experiences of Israel, Argentina, Brazil, Bolivia, and Mexico* (Cambridge, Mass.: MIT Press, 1988).

We can draw some important lessons from these experiences. First, strong budgetary adjustment is absolutely essential for successful stabilization. Second, wage and price controls alone are insufficient to stop inflation. Third, there are no clear conclusions regarding wage and price controls when applied *in addition to* the orthodox package. We do not really know whether the costs of stabilization in Israel and Mexico were lowered by the use of wage and price controls or whether the costs in Bolivia were raised by the more orthodox methods used. One strong possibility is that for a country in true hyperinflation, as in Bolivia, inflation inertia is eliminated, so that heterodox wage and price measures are irrelevant. When inflation rates are lower, as they were in Israel and Mexico, there might be enough inflation inertia left to make additional wage and price controls useful.

23-6 STABILIZATION IN EASTERN EUROPE

In 1989 and 1990, two economies in Eastern Europe—Poland and Yugoslavia—experienced hyperinflation, as shown in Table 23-1. Many other countries in the region, including Bulgaria, Hungary, and the Soviet Union, also experienced significant increases in inflation in the early 1990s. Is there a reason to consider stabilization in Eastern Europe a distinct phenomenon requiring special measures? The answer is yes. Conditions in the region are sufficiently special as to merit a specific analysis, though many of the features of a standard stabilization program are applicable there as well.

Stabilization in Eastern Europe is special in that the macroeconomic instability occurs in a socialist economy (that is, an economy dominated by state ownership), and stabilization should be viewed as part of an overall process of transformation. In all the countries of Eastern Europe, governments of the region have proclaimed their intention to replace the one-party rule of the Communist party, state ownership of industry, and central planning, with a Western European–style system of multiparty democracy, private ownership, and a market system.

The strategy for fundamental economic reform involves three main elements: macroeconomic stabilization, economic liberalization, and privatization of state enterprises.[27] Economic liberalization is a broad term including steps to open the economy to international trade, to create competition on domestic markets, and to institute a legal system to protect private property rights. Our central concern here is with the first of the issues, macroeconomic stabilization. We will touch upon the others as they affect this process. As it turns out, stabilization programs cannot be analyzed in complete isolation from the other parts of reform.

At the heart of high inflations in Eastern Europe and the Soviet Union are large budget deficits that lead to rapid money growth. This is no different from other places. There are, however, important special features of socialist economies which need to be considered in the design and imple-

---

[27] See David Lipton and Jeffrey Sachs, "Creating a Market Economy in Eastern Europe: The Case of Poland," *Brookings Papers on Economic Activity*, No. 1, 1990.

mentation of stabilization programs: (1) the soft budget constraint of public firms, (2) the lack of wage discipline in state companies, (3) the existence of large subsidies to the household sector, and (4) the presence—in general—of a monetary overhang. We analyze each of these issues in the paragraphs that follow.

State enterprises in the socialist economies have traditionally been subject to a *soft budget constraint,* that is, to a host of privileges such as low-cost credit, direct subsidies, and tax exemptions. This special treatment has cushioned state firms from the realities of market competition. State managers are thus prone to overexpand investment, and to be quite generous regarding wage increases. If investments turn sour, or if profits are squeezed on account of large wage hikes, the effect on the manager is minimum or nil. Moreover, state managers in the communist period knew that the government stood ready to bail out loss-making firms. A proof of this is that bankruptcies have been extremely rare or nil, despite massive losses. In Poland, for example, only 11 state firms went bust after the passage of a bankruptcy law in 1983.

Wage discipline has been traditionally very weak in state enterprises, since the state managers do not care much about profits. Moreover, the state managers are often appointed by the workers themselves, and thus are ready to give in to worker's demands! For these reasons, managers have not had the incentives to limit wage increases, which could always be financed with cheap credit from the central bank. This situation has led to wage increases that have often exceeded productivity improvements by a wide margin. Examples of this were the Soviet Union in 1988–1991 and Poland in 1987–1989.

Also, the communist regimes often extended *large subsidies* to the household sector, which contributed to large budget deficits. Since the communist governments were so unpopular, they were afraid to pass along cost increases to the consumers, and instead used budgetary subsidies to try to keep consumer prices low. The result, however, was simply a huge budget deficit, which created the macroeconomic conditions for high inflation. In Poland, for example, subsidies to food, agricultural inputs, and coal were over 8 percent of GDP in 1989.

Eastern Europe's economies often suffer from a *monetary overhang,* that is, large amounts of purchasing power that have been accumulated as a result of money creation in the past (used to finance previous budget deficits) combined with a system of controlled prices. In effect, the inflation that would normally result from the money printing is "bottled up" by price controls. The results are shortages and *repressed inflation* rather than open inflation. Once prices are liberalized, however, the inflationary pressures are let loose, and the price level tends to rise sharply. This is obviously a complicating factor at the start of a stabilization program.

Most economists judging the situation believe that the keys to macroeconomic stabilization involve the following steps: imposing hard budget constraints for the state enterprises; establishing a realistic price structure in the economy, partly based on open trade and currency convertibility; eliminating—or at least significantly reducing—budgetary subsidies, in order to get the budget deficit under control; imposing wage controls on the workers in state enterprises, as a substitute for market discipline on wages; and ending the monetary overhang, usually by allowing controlled prices to rise to market-clearing levels.[28]

Setting *hard budget constraints* on state enterprises amounts to imposing very tight limits on credit to these companies and ending the provision of subsidies from the budget. In essence, state firms must be forced to become financially independent of the budget and the central bank, with profitability becoming the key criterion to assess the performance of the enterprise. Privatization of public firms—although not something that can be accomplished in the very short run—is, without question, the key way to impose a hard budget constraint on the enterprises in the medium term.[29]

Another particular feature of Eastern European stabilization is the need to *liberalize prices* that have been fixed by controls at the same time that overall macroeconomic stabilization is attempted. This means that stabilization programs typically start with a one-time burst of inflation, as controlled prices are set free. In order to avoid destabilizing speculation and uncertainties, it is best to carry out price liberalization rapidly, rather than over a period of months or years as the Soviet Union attempted during 1991. Gradual price liberalization episodes have almost all left the situation more destabilized than without the partial steps. Since price liberalization is aimed at establishing a realistic price structure in the economy, and since international prices provide the best indicators for domestic prices, the ending of price controls should be combined with actions to open the economy to trade with the rest of the world. Thus, price liberalization should be combined with a move to a convertible currency and to a major reduction in artificial trade barriers such as quotas, tariffs, and licenses.[30]

Wage discipline must be imposed to avoid the occurrence of a wage-price spiral after price liberalization takes place. The imposition of a hard budget constraint and a profit motive at state firms help to maintain wage discipline, but usually direct wage controls are also needed, to take into account that managers have little incentive to resist the wage demands of the workers. In Poland, for example, a system of so-called "excess wage taxes" was put in place, according to which enterprises had to pay punitive taxes on wage payments that exceeded certain centrally dictated norms. While this is far from an ideal wage system, it is perhaps an adequate temporary measure until state enterprises are privatized.

As part of the effort to cut the budget deficit, the *cuts in government subsidies* should be large. In Poland's stabilization, for example, the cut in subsidies amounted to about 8 percent of GDP. Spending cuts on subsidies may not produce a similar reduction on the budget deficit, because there are strong pressures to increase other components of government spending. The

[28] Some economists also advocated a *monetary reform*, usually involving a confiscation of some of the excess money, as an alternative to price liberalization. Another possible option that has been mentioned is the large-scale sale of government assets to the public in return for the excess currency. In practice, the notion of absorbing the monetary overhang through asset sales has not proved to be practicable.

[29] For a detailed discussion of privatization, see Olivier Blanchard et. al., *Reform in Eastern Europe* (Cambridge, Mass.: MIT Press, 1991), and David Lipton and Jeffrey Sachs, "Privatization in Eastern Europe: The Case of Poland," *Brookings Papers on Economic Activity*, No. 2, 1990.

[30] For a discussion of currency convertibility, see Box 10-1 in Chapter 10.

cuts in subsidies have been coupled with targeted assistance efforts to help the most needy who are most vulnerable to the subsidy cuts. Spending on social programs—including unemployment insurance—tend to rise during massive economic restructuring.

The countries of Eastern Europe have shown that it is possible to stabilize and liberalize a formerly centrally planned, socialist economy very rapidly. But they have not yet succeeded in privatizing the state-owned industries. Until that occurs successfully, the reforming countries will be at risk of a further outbreak of macroeconomic instability. Even with the best of intentions by the governments, the pressures of wage increases in the state enterprises, and the political pressures that lead to soft budget constraints of the state enterprises can probably be resolved only by transferring the ownership of the enterprises back to the private sector.

23-7 SUMMARY

Several countries in the course of this century have reached extraordinarily high levels of inflation. We define *very high inflation* as an annual rate of inflation of 100 percent or more and *hyperinflation* as an inflation of 50 percent per month (equivalent to almost 13,000 percent per year). There have been only 15 cases of hyperinflation, all of them in the present century.

There are some key conditions which have triggered hyperinflation. First, these phenomena have occurred only in regimes of *fiat money*. Second, many hyperinflations have tended to occur during or in the aftermaths of war, civil war, or revolution, as a consequence of strains on the budget. In the 1980s, external shocks and high foreign indebtedness of governments have played a key role.

The common feature of all hyperinflations is a colossal increase in the money supply, which generally results from the need to finance huge budget deficits. Moreover, once a high inflation gets started, the budgetary situation may become unstable: high inflation causes a sharp drop in tax collections, which in turn increases the budget deficit and leads to more inflation. Based on historical evidence, it seems that a persistent money-financed budget deficit on the order of 10-12 percent of GNP leads to a hyperinflation.

Stopping high inflations requires a special combination of policies regarding the exchange rate, the public budget, the money supply and, in some cases, direct measures aimed at wages and prices. Successful stabilization is also helped by public confidence in the package of measures. Hyperinflations, when they stop, tend to end almost overnight, though the policy reforms needed even after the end of hyperinflation in order to sustain the low inflation rate may take months or years to put into effect.

During hyperinflations, *inflationary inertia* is virtually eliminated as economies become increasingly *dollarized*. Thus, purchasing power parity is likely to hold remarkably well. Exchange-rate stabilization is therefore a key to halt inflation because the exchange rate is the crucial link between dollar prices and domestic currency prices. But no exchange rate can be stabilized unless the underlying budget deficit—and the need for seigniorage—is brought under control. Some measures used to cut the budget deficit (the end of subsidies, currency devaluation, higher public-sector prices) are likely to result in a burst of *corrective inflation* in the short term. Thus, the inflation rate can sometimes jump up at the start of a stabilization program, just before the inflation ends.

International reserves usually reach very low levels during hyperinflation. Thus, it is highly desirable for a government undertaking stabilization to obtain a balance-of-payments support loan or to attain debt relief at the start of a stabilization program. These kinds of support help the central bank to defend the exchange rate and also to boost the public confidence in the program.

Heterodox stabilization programs are those that rely on direct intervention into wage and price setting in addition to the more standard monetary and fiscal measures. They are based on the idea that inflation has a large inertial component, the result of long-term labor contracts, backward-looking wage indexation and other mechanisms. Under these conditions, their advocates argue, orthodox measures can lead to an unnecessarily deep recession. Heterodox programs, however, have a number of shortcomings, among them wage and price controls may be superfluous and difficult to enforce, they can introduce substantial rigidity in relative prices, and they may prove hard to phase out. Empirical evidence is mixed with regard to these programs. What is clear, though, is that wage and price controls alone are insufficient to stop inflation.

Stabilization in Eastern Europe in the early 1990s is special in that it is part of an overall effort to create capitalist economies out of the formerly centrally planned socialist economies. Two countries in the region, Poland and Yugoslavia, experienced hyperinflation starting in 1989. At the heart of these hyperinflations, and high inflations elsewhere in Eastern Europe, lie large budget deficits, as was the case in other places. There are, however, some important special features of these economies which need to be considered in the design of stabilization programs: (1) the *soft budget constraint* of public firms, (2) the lack of *wage discipline* in state companies, (3) the existence of large subsidies to the household sector, and (4) the general presence of a *monetary overhang*.

The stabilization programs of the region should take special care in addressing these economic characteristics. Nonetheless, it must be recognized that short-term macroeconomic stabilization programs are unlikely to succeed unless they are combined with programs of privatization of state industry, since only privately owned firms are likely to respond effectively to market forces in the intermediate run.

Key Concepts

very high inflation	inflationary inertia
hyperinflation	backward-looking indexation
debasing the currency	monetary reform
metallic standard	confiscatory reform
fiat money	balance-of-payments support
seigniorage collection	loan
expected inflation	remonetization
inflation tax	orthodox programs
price stabilization	heterodox programs
dollarization	corrective inflation
purchasing power parity	repressed inflation
exchange-rate stabilization	incomes policies

wage and price controls   hard budget constraint
soft budget constraint   monetary overhang

Problems and Questions

1. ''The hyperinflations after World War I and those of the 1980s had a common origin in external shocks.'' Comment.

2. Does an increase in the growth rate of money raise or lower the government's real revenue from money creation?

3. ''In Germany in 1923, the depreciation of tax revenues reached a point at which taxes cost more to collect than they brought in, so that the budgetary deficit and rate of inflation would have been less had the ordinary machinery of taxation been discarded and the government relied on inflation alone'' (D. H. Aldcroft, *From Versailles to Wall Street 1919–1929*, 1981). Comment on this statement.

4. What is the difference between seigniorage and the inflation tax? Under which conditions are these two concepts equivalent?

5. How can you explain the fact that succesful stabilization programs are always followed by a period of very high money growth rates? What does this imply for the conduction of monetary policy in a stabilization program?

6. Some analysts have concluded that the German hyperinflation after World War I, although very costly at the time, provoked an important long-term benefit for the country. Do you agree? Explain.

7. During high-inflation experiences, governments can collect more seigniorage than it is possible in steady state for fairly long periods. Is this correct? Why?

8. Analyze the conditions under which heterodox stabilization programs may be more effective in stopping hyperinflation than orthodox programs.

9. ''Because hyperinflations everywhere are ultimately caused by a major fiscal deficit, there is no good reason to have a special stabilization policy for the East European economies.'' Comment.

10. The cure for a monetary overhang is a confiscatory currency reform, some economists argue. Analyze the pros and cons of this policy. Is there any other way to cure the overhang?

Index